Literature
Across Cultures

Literature
Across Cultures

SECOND EDITION

Sheena Gillespie

Terezinha Fonseca

Carol A. Sanger

QUEENSBOROUGH COMMUNITY COLLEGE
CITY UNIVERSITY OF NEW YORK

ALLYN and BACON
Boston   London   Toronto   Sydney   Tokyo   Singapore

Vice President, Humanities: Joseph Opiela
Marketing Manager: Lisa Kimball
Editorial-Production Administrator: Donna Simons
Editorial-Production Service: Omegatype Typography, Inc.
Composition and Prepress Buyer: Linda Cox
Manufacturing Buyer: Suzanne Lareau
Art Director: Linda Knowles

Copyright © 1998, 1994 by Allyn & Bacon
A Viacom Company
160 Gould Street
Needham Heights, MA 02194

Internet: www.abacon.com
America Online: keyword: College Online

Library of Congress Cataloging-in-Publication Data
Literature across cultures / [compiled by] Sheena Gillespie, Terezinha
   Fonseca, Carol Sanger. — 2nd ed.
       p.   cm.
   Includes indexes.
   ISBN 0-205-27205-3 (pbk. : alk. paper)
   1. Literature—Collections.   I. Gillespie, Sheena.
II. Fonseca, Terezinha.   III. Sanger, Carol.
PN6014.G43   1998
808.8—dc21   97-11641
                                                 CIP

Credits begin on page 1028, which constitutes an extension of the copyright page.

Printed in the United States of America
10 9 8 7 6 5 4 3 2   RRDV   02 01 00 99 98

To Flo, Gabriel, and Amanda, best of friends.

In memory of Alair de Oliviera Gomes, a Brazilian with a vocation for deep thought, beauty, and friendship.

To Jerry Zukor, whose encouragement and support have been a source of strength.

Contents

Part One: *Origins and Insights*   *33*

Fiction

Essays

Poetry

Part Two: *Gender and Identity*   *327*

Macbeth

Drama

Part Three: *War and Violence*   469 The Things they Carried

Fiction

Essays

Poetry

Drama

Part Four: *Race and Difference* 587   the Color Purple

Fiction

Essays

Poetry

Preface for Instructors

"Perhaps we should try to think of American culture as a conversation among different voices—even if it's a conversation that some of us weren't able to join until recently," Henry Louis Gates, Jr., has said. This anthology invites students to become acquainted with these new voices in their study of literature.

Our reading selections attempt to expose students to texts from diverse cultures and, through their study of and conversations with these traditional and modernist voices, to provide them with broader contexts in which to discuss vital issues such as origins and insights, gender and identity, war and violence, race and difference, and individualism and community. The readings in these five thematic sections, grouped according to genre, suggest different ways of understanding and responding to traditional genres by exploring both their literary and cultural contexts.

The second edition of *Literature Across Cultures* incorporates the many excellent suggestions and critiques by our reviewers and colleagues at Queensborough Community College. We have added two essays to each section, a second novella, and several traditional short stories and poems, and we focus on a particular poet in each part by presenting four of his or her texts. We have also expanded the appendix on researching literary sources, as well as the glossary of literary and cultural terms. Many questions following the selections, as well as the writing topics for each part, have been revised. The research topics at the end of each part now include a collaborative project. Many of the added texts are available on video through the publisher.

In Part One, on origins and insights, students will find a diversity of literary texts from both familiar and new writers who speculate on topics such as the influence of tradition and culture, the degree to which the past informs the present, and the interaction of personal and cultural memories.

The gender and identity texts in Part Two provide a starting point for a more open debate between men and women on gender differences. They explore the relations between women and men, and they probe the crucial links between gender and identity.

The war and violence selections in Part Three pose questions about war as a cause and as an effect of the daily violence that erupts in homes and on the streets in communities around the world. They suggest ways by which students may reevaluate heroic myths of war. They also examine new sensibilities that promote the merits of political negotiation and cite the misuses of power in a global, pluralistic society.

The race and difference texts in Part Four invite students to understand better the historical realities of personal indignities and social injustices resulting from individual and institutional attitudes toward sexual preference, ethnicity, gender, and class. Some writers in this part express anger and disillusionment about their sense of entrapment and exclusion from the North American mainstream. This chapter also includes texts from the literature of AIDS, as this condition finds emotional correlatives in the fiction, poetry, and drama of our time.

The individualism and community texts in Part Five explore the dialectic of self and society, examining the degree to which our ability to say "I" is predicated on our need and willingness to say "we." Students will be asked to seek answers to questions such as these: What constitutes a community? How do the features of a community relate to individuals, some of whom submit and some of whom rebel? To what extent does the community promote the individual? What are an individual's responsibilities to the larger community?

Discussion questions follow each short story, cluster of poems, and play to assist students in making informed responses to the text. Their aim is to enrich the student's view of literary texts by suggesting multiple possibilities for the production of meaning. Specifically, the rationale we devised here links the expression of personal meanings in journal writing with meanings produced on textual, cultural, and collaborative levels. Writing assignments and research topics conclude each part.

The editorial apparatus includes a section on reading and writing about literature that addresses typical student reservations about the value of literature by approaching reading as a social act, in which students interact not only with the writers of the text but also, through discussion, with their peers.

A guided critical analysis of Kate Chopin's "The Story of an Hour" emphasizes the importance of close textual reading and includes a discussion of the story's cultural contexts. This section also includes samples of student journal responses and summaries of their peer discussions of the text.

Using a sample student critical analysis of Sherwood Anderson's "Hands," another section takes students step by step through the process of writing a critical essay, beginning with interpreting a literary text, generating ideas for a critical paper, writing a first draft, learning from peer critiques, and revising the final draft.

The editorial apparatus also includes an appendix on interacting with the literary genres; it includes strategies for discussing the texts as cultural productions.

This apparatus is intended to help students develop the analytical and critical skills they need to read and write about literature.

The appendix "Researching Literary Sources" includes information on using the library and locating critical sources, as well as a discussion of the research paper, MLA documentation, and two documented student essays.

The appendix "Critical Approaches: A Case Study of *Hamlet*" includes a discussion of several critical approaches to the play, including psychoanalytic, psychosocial, New Critical, feminist, reader-response, and New Historical.

"A Note about Film" discusses such elements within film as film and literature, psychology and character, and imagery and technique.

The apparatus also includes biographical endnotes that introduce the writers and a glossary of literary and cultural terms.

The text is accompanied by an instructor's manual, which includes strategies for discussing literature in an interactive classroom, selected critical bibliographies, a filmography for each unit, and selected audio and visual resources.

ACKNOWLEDGMENTS

We are grateful to Joe Opiela, our editor, who has guided us through the second edition of our textbook, and to his assistant, Kate Tolini, who worked patiently with us throughout the process. Our special thanks also go to Tony Pipolo for his appendix on film and his suggestions and filmographies in the instructor's manual.

Sonia Lysingier, Evelyn J. Kirstein, Ruth Kirstein, Ellen Higgins, and Duane Crumb served as consultants. Our students offered invaluable criticism, and Devon McCabe and J. P. Lydon Fonseca made insightful suggestions for the instructor's manual.

Patricia D'Angeli and Isabel Pipolo contributed excellent research papers.

We acknowledge our gratitude to Margaret Cavanaugh, Patty Gorton, and Kathy Howard for their generous assistance in the preparation of the manuscript, to Marge Caronna, Dr. Kyu Kim, Prof. Maxine Genn, and the library staff of Queensborough Community College for their research assistance, and to Isabel Pipolo for typing the instructor's manual.

We acknowledge the valuable contributions of Rebecca Bell-Metereau, Southwest Texas State University; Arlene Cleft-Pillow, North Carolina Central University; Joan Gordon, Nassau Community College; and Sybil Schlesinger, Babson College; who reviewed the manuscript for Allyn and Bacon. We continue to be grateful to our first edition reviewers, whose advice is still reflected in these pages: Lucien Agosta, California State University—Sacramento; Vivian R. Brown, Laredo Junior College; Mary Ellen Bryne, Ocean County College; Douglas E. Crowell, Texas Technical University; Robert Dees, Orange Coast College; James Egan, University of Akron; Ann O. Gebhard, SUNY—Cortland; Stephen Hahn, William Paterson College; Corrinne Hales, California State University—Fresno; John Iorio, University of South Florida; James O'Neil, Edison Community College; Melissa Pennell, University of Lowell; and Kathleen Tichnor, Brevard Community College.

Preface for Students

People and their cultures perish in isolation, but they are born or reborn in contact with other men and women, with men and women of another culture, another creed, another race. If we do not recognize our humanity in others, we will not recognize it in ourselves.

Carlos Fuentes

As teachers and students of literature, we believe that one of the most effective ways to understand people of other cultures, creeds, or races is through language; a person's words are the windows through which we gain access to his or her world. In this anthology, we invite you to travel with us to worlds beyond your own, to engage in a conversation among cultures, to explore unfamiliar traditions, and to evaluate human relationships in an attempt to understand better the meanings of community in our own pluralistic society and the multicultural society of the approaching twenty-first century.

We hope that as you listen to these voices, past and present, you will feel compelled to enter the conversation, to add your own voice and your own words. As you engage in dialogue with the selections, both in writing and in discussion with your fellow students, you will experiment with new ways of looking at yourself, enlarging the windows from which you view the world. The journey we invite you to share will be challenging—many of the voices, both classical and contemporary, expect you to respond.

In Part One, "Origins and Insights," you will encounter many cultural variations: the oral traditions and affinity with the worlds of nature and spirit of Native Americans, the love of language and pride in their history of Hispanics, the emphasis on kinship and music in the literature of African Americans, the cultural complexity and generational conflicts of Asian Americans, and the poignancy of family loyalty among Italian Americans.

In Part Two, "Gender and Identity," you will be invited to examine traditional cross-cultural concepts of masculinity and femininity and to evaluate the degree to which they have affected both men and women in their individual quests for identity. Some of the voices in this part will ask you to decide whether gender conflicts should be confronted or avoided. Other voices will pose possibilities for freeing both sexes from the confines of traditional roles so that both men and women may become more dynamic and fulfilled.

In Part Three, "War and Violence," you will evaluate older heroic myths of war from other cultures, as well as newer sensibilities advocating compromise as the desirable outcome of political conflict. You may also speculate on the misuses of power in a global, pluralistic society. Most of all, you will be asked to consider whether the recognition of our shared humanity will enable us to look beyond violence to peace.

In Part Four, "Race and Difference," you will be asked to reexamine many of the racial stereotypes with which we all have grown up. Some of these voices from diverse ethnic groups will invite you to share the anguish and anger of exclusion; others will challenge your preconceptions about race, class, and sexual preference; and still others will ask whether differences should be silenced or articulated, respected or shunned.

In Part Five, "Individualism and Community," you will confront the conflict experienced in every culture between the needs and desires of our individual selves and the needs and desires of the community. Many voices in this part debate the issue of individual freedom versus social responsibility; others advocate that solo voices join in the discord and harmony of the human chorus.

As you converse with the voices, both old and new, in this anthology, you will travel into uncharted territories, to real and imagined worlds where many of the familiar guideposts will no longer apply. But this is as it should be. Preparation for the global village of the twenty-first century requires your generation to sharpen its definition of an educated person. By adding your voice to the cultural conversations in this anthology, you will begin that process, perhaps leaving the familiar in favor of the unfamiliar.

Literature
Across Cultures

Reading and Writing as a Social Act

Why read literature? is the question many instructors pose during the first class session of Introduction to Literature.

Writer and critic Robert Scholes suggests that since students like writers who have stories to tell, "learning to read books—or pictures, or films—is not just a matter of learning to read, it is a matter of learning to read and write the texts of our lives."

Why do writers write? They write to be read; they write for you, their audience. Most writers value their relationship with their readers. For example, the well-known Russian writer Anton Chekov (1860–1904) has stated that "when I write, I reckon entirely upon the reader to add for himself the subjective elements that are lacking in the story." Similarly, the writer Grace Paley (b. 1922) reinforces the significance of the reader's role when she writes, "Maybe the reader of a particular story knows better than the writer what it means." Writers also write to communicate their insights to you in the hope that you will recognize aspects of your own thoughts and experiences in their stories.

Although many students express skepticism about finding meanings in the literature of the past, most acknowledge readily that human beings throughout history have had experiences in common. According to the novelist Albert Camus (1913–1960), "Every great work of art makes the human face more admirable and richer." His suggestion is that as we share in reading of the sufferings and joys of others, we better understand our own. The novelist James Baldwin (1924–1987) also reminds us of the continuity of human experiences in his short story "Sonny's Blues":

For while the tale of how we suffer, and how we are delighted, and how we may triumph is never new, it always must be heard. There isn't any other tale to tell. It's the only light we've got in all this darkness.

We invite you to approach the reading of the texts in this anthology from the vantage points suggested by Camus and Baldwin. Perhaps thinking about fiction, poetry, and drama as expressions of human suffering, delight, and triumph will make it possible for you to understand Medea's anger at being abandoned by her husband in favor of a younger woman; to empathize with Hamlet's attempt to find his real identity; and to share in the triumph of a nineteenth-century New England housewife's revolt. You might even discover something about yourself. As the novelist Toni Morrison reminds us, interacting with literature is a dynamic process engaging both reader and writer: "The imagination that produces work which bears and invites rereading, which points to future readings as well as contemporary ones, implies a shareable world and an especially flexible language. Readers and writers both struggle to interpret and perform within a common language shareable imaginative worlds."

THE MEANING OF LITERATURE

What is literature? Traditionally set apart from other kinds of discourse, literature has been defined by the *Webster's Universal Unabridged Dictionary* as "all writings in prose or verse, especially those of an imaginative or critical character." Although this definition, like many others, has proved to be incomplete, it does highlight the presence of two major features of literature: its language and its imaginative character. When combined, these two elements produce a fictional world that reflects and evokes reality.

One story in this anthology can be used to illustrate this power of literature. The introduction to "The Sniper" transports us, not to the real world of urban guerrillas in Dublin, but to the fictional atmosphere of a Dublin that Liam O'Flaherty especially re-created as a unique literary experience:

> The long June twilight faded into night, Dublin lay enveloped in darkness but for the dim light of the moon that shone through fleecy clouds, casting a pale light as of approaching dawn over the streets and the dark waters of the Liffey. Around the beleaguered Four Courts the heavy guns roared. Here and there through the city, machine-guns and rifles broke the silence of the night, spasmodically, like dogs barking on lone farms. Republicans and Free Staters were waging civil war.
>
> "The Sniper"

Although O'Flaherty might have modeled his portrayal of Dublin on a factual description of this Irish city caught in the civil war between the Republicans and Free Staters, his city, in strictly literary terms, is fictional. His text articulates imaginatively and creatively the significance of an actual historical event.

In O'Flaherty's text, atmosphere and imagery provide insights into events that we have not experienced directly. Characterization is another way literature can broaden our experience. You will observe, in other texts in this volume, how characters such as Antigone, Hamlet, Miss Julie and Roselily have dramatized across the centuries some of the most terrifying and stimulating possibilities of human experience. In this sense, literature can be defined as the enactment of human possibilities, or as a vehicle that will help us to discover more about ourselves and the meaning we can make of life. For the French philosopher Jean-Paul Sartre (1905–1980), the function of literature is to search for the meaning of life and to speculate about the role of human beings in the world.

Perhaps the best way to define literature is in practice, encountering the literary experience face-to-face through the readings in this anthology. In the process, you may notice that a literary work leads you to encounter not one precise, correct reading but a range of meanings evoked by the interaction of the text with your own experience as a reader. For instance, *Hamlet,* a work that is widely discussed from different critical perspectives, illustrates the variety of meanings that Shakespeare's readers have produced in the process of interpreting this play. In fact, one appendix in this anthology is devoted to exploring some of these various critical approaches and responses, known as psychoanalytic, formalist, reader-response, feminist, and New Historical (see the appendix "Critical Approaches").

THE FUNCTION OF LITERATURE

Following the literary tradition that the Latin poet Horace (65–8 B.C.) established for poetry, some scholars emphasize "to instruct" or "to delight," or both, as the major functions of literature. Recent scholarly opinion indicates that another function of literature is to actively shape our culture. For example, some literary historians believe that human beings learned how to cultivate a romantic idea of love only after reading works of literature that portrayed love in this light rather than as a social or sexual arrangement between a man and a woman. Both ancient and modern approaches emphasize two of literature's major functions: to construct and articulate sociocultural realities and to involve you as the reader in an invigorating interaction with these realities.

When you address the questions we formulate under "Cultural Contexts" in this anthology, you will be asked to interact with your classmates, to take sides, to make decisions, and to add your voice to various cultural and political issues related to class, race, gender, war, and violence. Consider, for instance, Wilfred Owen's poem "Disabled," in which his portrait of a disabled veteran stimulates our involvement in the violence perpetuated by World War I. By presenting such a viewpoint, literature can empower us—it can promote our active engagement with the world through our encounter with the poem's disclosure of the reality of violence caused by war. Thus, literature can fulfill a major cultural function in society.

STRATEGIES FOR READING LITERATURE: A STEP-BY-STEP GUIDELINE

Reading literature is a process in which you, as a reader, should engage actively. To respond well to literature, you must take a critical approach that involves three major procedures: previewing, highlighting, and annotating.

Previewing

Even before you read a text, preview it by asking yourself some questions about the title, the writer, and the type of writing you are encountering:

- ◆ What does the title suggest?
- ◆ Have I heard of this author before?
- ◆ Does my anthology provide any information about this text?
- ◆ What type of text is this—a poem, a story, or a play?
- ◆ What kind of structure does it possess?
- ◆ How is the text organized? By paragraphs, stanzas, acts, scenes?

Highlighting

Read the text closely, and highlight—by underlining words or coloring them with a highlighting pen—the sections that particularly strike you from the point of view of style, structure, ideas, characterization, or any other key features you have observed as a reader. Notice, for example, in the passage below taken from James Joyce's short story "Eveline," the repetition of the verb form "used to" and some of its variants that indicate repeated action in the past. Identifying such a pattern enables you to discern the strong emotional links that Eveline has with the past. From this you may infer her psychological inability to accept change as a possibility for the future.

> One time there ***used to*** be a field there in which they ***used to*** play every evening with other people's children. Then a man from Belfast bought the field and built houses in it—not like the little brown houses but bright brick houses with shining roofs. The children of the avenue ***used to*** play together in that field— the Devines, the Waters, the Dunns, little Keogh the cripple, she and her brothers and sisters. Ernest, however, never played: he was too grown up. Her father ***used*** often ***to*** hunt them in out of the field with his blackthorn stick; but ***usually*** little Keogh ***used to*** keep ***nix*** and call out when he saw her father coming. Still they seemed to have been rather happy then…

Annotating

Annotating means making marginal notes on the book's pages, or using a pad or note cards. Once you reach this phase, you are involved in the critical process of selecting, summarizing, and annotating ideas. After a second and third reading, your notes will eventually lead you to respond to the literary and cultural impact of the text by identifying its words, imagery, and themes. Responding actively to the text therefore becomes a challenge for you as a reader, because you will interact with it and define its meanings on the basis of both the factual evidence that you find there and your own insights and experiences.

The following guided reading of Kate Chopin's "The Story of an Hour" should help you to understand what we mean by interaction between the reader and the text. After previewing, highlighting, and annotating the text, you might consider approaching your analysis of the "Textual Considerations" of "The Story of an Hour" as a detective trying to solve a crime. Arm yourself with a dictionary and thesaurus, and be on the alert for the many textual hints and clues that the writer has supplied for you. Pay close attention to the text by examining how the author uses nouns, adjectives, images, and symbols to construct plot and to build characterization.

Kate Chopin (1851–1904)

The Story of an Hour

"The Story of an Hour"

Textual Considerations

1. Knowing that **Mrs. Mallard** was afflicted with a heart trouble, great care was taken to break to her as gently as possible the news of her husband's death.

What kinds of expectations does the opening paragraph raise in the reader about the protagonist and the plot of the story? Have you noticed that the protagonist is addressed as Mrs. Mallard and that the starting point of the story is "the news of her husband's death"?

2. It was her sister Josephine who told her, in broken sentences, veiled hints that revealed in half concealing. Her husband's friend Richards was there, too, near her. It was he who had been in the newspaper office when intelligence of the railroad disaster was received, with Brently Mallard's name leading the list of "killed." He had only taken the time to assure himself of its truth by a second telegram, and

Respond to Josephine's and Richards's attitude about breaking the news to Mrs. Mallard.

had hastened to forestall any less careful, less tender friend in bearing the sad message.

3. She did not hear the story as many women have heard the same, with a paralyzed inability to accept its significance. She wept at once, with sudden, **wild abandonment,** in her sister's arms. When the storm of grief had spent itself she went to her room alone. She would have no one follow her.

Focus on paragraph 3. What does the phrase "wild abandonment" suggest? Are you surprised by Mrs. Mallard's insistence on being left alone after hearing such bad news? Explain.

4. There stood, facing the open window, a comfortable, roomy armchair. Into this she sank, pressed down by a physical exhaustion that haunted her body and seemed to reach into her soul.

What examples do you find of images of freedom and repression in paragraphs 4 and 5? Comment on these examples.

5. She could see in the open square before her house the **tops of trees that were all aquiver with the new spring life. The delicious breath of rain was in the air.** In the street below a peddler was crying his wares. The notes of a distant song which some one was singing reached her faintly, and countless sparrows were twittering in the eaves.

Writers frequently use nature to open a symbolic level for the text. What is unusual about the text's emphasis on spring, given the events of the story thus far? What other aspects of nature emerge in paragraphs 5 and 6? What do they suggest about Mrs. Mallard's state of mind? What kind of expectations do they raise in the reader?

6. There were patches of blue sky showing here and there through the clouds that had met and piled above the other in the west facing her window.

7. She sat with her head thrown back upon the cushion of the chair quite motionless, except when a sob came up into her throat and shook her, as a child who has cried itself to sleep continues to sob in its dreams.

Characterize your response to paragraphs 7 and 8.

8. She was **young,** with a **fair,** calm face, whose **lines bespoke repression** and even a certain strength. But now there was a dull stare in her eyes, whose gaze was fixed away off yonder

What new aspects of Mrs. Mallard's personality occur in paragraph 8? To what might "the lines of repression" be attributable? Consider the difference between a "glance of reflection" and a "suspen-

on one of those patches of blue sky. It was not a **glance of reflection,** but rather indicated a **suspension of intelligent thought.**

sion of intelligent thought."

9. There was **something coming to her** and she was waiting for it, fearfully. What was it? She did not know; it was too subtle and elusive to name. But she felt it, creeping out of the sky, reaching toward her through the sounds, the scents, the color that filled the air.

What dramatic pattern is the text shaping in terms of plot (events, to rising action), characterization (Mrs. Mallard's reaction), and your own response as a reader? Focus on paragraphs 9 and 10.

10. Now her bosom rose and fell tumultuously. She was beginning to recognize this thing that was approaching to possess her, and she was striving to beat it back with her will— as powerless as her two white slender hands would have been.

11. When she abandoned herself a little word escaped her **slightly parted lips.** She said it over and over under her breath: **"Free,** free, free!" **The vacant stare** and the look of terror that had followed it went from her eyes. They stayed keen and bright. Her **pulses beat fast,** and the coursing **blood warmed** and relaxed every inch of her body.

What does "the vacant stare" suggest? What does "the look of terror" convey? Contrast the descriptions of Mrs. Mallard's bodily responses in paragraphs 4 and 11. To what extent are these physical and psychological reversals gender based (characteristic of women more than men)?

12. She did not stop to ask if it were not a **monstrous** joy that held her. A clear and exalted perception enabled her to dismiss the suggestion as trivial.

Check your thesaurus for various connotations of "monstrous." Speculate about Chopin's description of Mrs. Mallard's joy as "monstrous" in paragraph 12.

13. She knew that she would weep again when she saw the kind tender hands folded in death; the face that had never looked save with love upon her, fixed and gray and dead. But she saw beyond that **bitter moment a long procession of years to come** that would belong to her absolutely. And she opened and spread her arms out to them in welcome.

Notice how Mrs. Mallard contrasts the "bitter moment" of the present with "a long procession of years to come." To what extent does this contrast suggest her desire to rewrite her personal history? To what extent does the world of closed windows and fixed gender identities versus the evocations of freedom and self-discovery create narrative suspense?

14. There would be no one to live for during those coming years: **she would live for herself. There would be no powerful will bending her in** that blind persistence with which men and women believe they have a right to impose a private will upon a fellow-creature. A kind intention or a cruel intention made the act seem no less a crime as she looked upon it in that brief moment of illumination.

Does Mrs. Mallard surprise you with her realistic portrait of male and female relations? What does this moment of illumination amount to?

15. And yet she had loved him—sometimes. Often she had not. What did it matter! What could love, the unsolved mystery, count for in face of this possession of self-assertion which she suddenly recognized as the strongest impulse of her being!

To what extent do you empathize with Mrs. Mallard's desire for autonomy and psychological space?

16. "Free! Body and soul free!" she kept whispering.

How do you characterize Mrs. Mallard's emotional outburst?

Explain why Chopin withholds the protagonist's first name until paragraph 17.

17. Josephine was kneeling before the closed door with her lips to the keyhole, imploring for admission. "**Louise,** open the door! I beg; open the door—you will make yourself ill. What are you doing, Louise? For heaven's sake open the door."

18. "Go away. I am not making myself ill." No; she was drinking in the very elixir of life through that open window.

Identify the two voices that interact in this paragraph.

19. Her fancy was running riot along **those days ahead of her.** Spring days, and summer days, and all sorts of days that would be her own. She breathed a quick prayer that life might be long. It was only **yesterday she** had thought with a shudder that life might be long.

React to the way the text juxtaposes the repression of the past and the possibilities of the future. Such a pattern culminates in paragraph 20 in the image that Mrs. Mallard "carries herself unwittingly like a goddess of Victory." To what extent does Chopin suggest that Mrs. Mallard's triumph will be transitory?

20. She arose at length and opened the door to her sister's importunities. There was a feverish triumph in her eyes, and she carried herself unwit-

tingly like a goddess of Victory. She clasped her sister's waist, and together they descended the stairs. Richards stood waiting for them at the bottom.

21. Some one was opening the front door with a **latchkey.** It was Brently Mallard who entered, a little travel-stained, composedly carrying his **grip-sack** and **umbrella.** He had been far from the scene of the accident, and did not even know there had been one. He stood amazed at Josephine's piercing cry: at Richards's quick motion to screen him from the view of his **wife.** But Richards was too late.

Read this paragraph carefully. Comment on the images of "latchkey," "gripsack," and "umbrella." What significance do you attach to Louise being referred to as "his wife"? To what extent does Richards's inability to protect Mrs. Mallard destabilize the action of the story? What kind of suspense or expectation does this paragraph create in the reader?

22. When the doctors came they said that she had died of heart disease—**of joy that kills.**

How do you account for the ironic turn of the last sentence? Is it appropriate that the doctors misread the true cause of Mrs. Mallard's death? Explain.

Read "The Story of an Hour" again at least twice. More ideas will no doubt surface at each new reading, and you will react to more details concerning the arrangement of the events, Mrs. Mallard's reactions and expectations, and your own ability as a reader to produce more meanings in response to the text. As you deepen your understanding of the story, you will also become more aware of its cultural implications. To assist your interaction with the cultural possibilities of Chopin's text, you may discuss gender-related questions such as the ones listed in "Cultural Contexts" below.

Cultural Contexts

1. To what extent does "The Story of an Hour" reflect a feminist outlook on the roles of women? What evidence is there that the story is told from the perspective of a female narrator?
2. Consider what the text reveals about marriage as an institution. Is the concept of marriage that Chopin's text explores still applicable to contemporary gender relations?
3. Are men and women today more liberated than they were a century ago? Discuss the differences you see between then and now in the socially defined roles and "fixed gender identities" (identities determined by gender and social roles).

Following are some literature students' responses to the two literary and cultural topics listed below.

1. Respond to Kate Chopin's use of nature imagery in "The Story of an Hour."

2. React to the new meanings "The Story of an Hour" evokes as you think about the issues of gender and identity. Does this text reaffirm traditional ideas about gender relations, or does it provoke readers to discover different truths about gender relations?

In their responses to topic one, Chopin's use of nature imagery, the students previewed, highlighted, and annotated the text before they outlined how Chopin's suggestive use of imagery communicates Mrs. Mallard's new expectations about her future:

> Kate Chopin uses a great deal of imagery in "The Story of an Hour." Her description of "the tops of trees that were all aquiver with the new spring life" in paragraph 5 is a good example of her use of a nature image to communicate Mrs. Mallard's new feeling toward life, blooming, and rebirth.
>
> In paragraph 8, the image of "those patches of blue sky," showing that even though the dominant color of the sky might be gray it possesses "patches of blue," suggests that the color blue is also an indicator of new spring life. In spring the color of the sky is blue. However, it is important to realize that Chopin's reference to the clouds can function as a foreshadowing, indicating that the blue sky is as far off as Mrs. Mallard's expectations of freedom.
>
> Danielle Lucas

> Kate Chopin's reference to "the new spring life," "the notes of a distant song," "the delicious breath of rain," and "sparrows twittering" obviously suggests how Mrs. Mallard begins to respond to life. She is born again like new spring life, and she is ready to take in a new clean breath like "the delicious breath of rain." Her aspiration is to live her own life like the sparrow who is free to fly. Chopin uses the "patches of blue sky...through the clouds" as an image of a clearing in Mrs. Mallard's life. Gone is the husband with his "powerful will bending her in." There is a clearing of "blue sky" for her.
>
> Chopin says that Mrs. Mallard drinks in the very "elixir of life through the open window." Such an image supports the idea that Chopin uses nature imagery to show the freedom that Mrs. Mallard has now acquired.
>
> Mary Ellen Hogan

Two other students, Mike Lonergan and Robert Longstreet, also covered the preliminary reading strategies before they analyzed the issue of gender and identity as part of the larger cultural network Chopin's text evokes:

> "The Story of an Hour" by Kate Chopin reaffirms traditional ideas about gender relations with a riptide that illuminates the reader.
>
> Mr. and Mrs. Mallard portray a typical married couple of the late 1800s. Brently Mallard, the husband, is the head of the household, while Louise

Mallard, his wife, is his possession. To quote Emily Dickinson, Louise "rose to his requirement…to take the honorable work of women, and of wife" (Poem 172).

Like a typical wife of this era, Mrs. Mallard was supposed to obey her husband without any rebukes. Knowing nothing different, Mrs. Mallard accepted these social norms of her time.

However, Chopin's "The Story of an Hour" reveals the aged wrinkle in this status quo arrangement by showing how, subconsciously, Mrs. Mallard's inner self and soul were being repressed and sentenced to death by lack of use.

Mike Lonergan

"The Story of an Hour" is not a story that reaffirms traditional ideas about gender relations. In fact, Kate Chopin's text does just the opposite. It shows that no matter what your gender is, you should never lose your identity. The story suggests that instead of ignoring the restrictions of gender relations or hiding from them, you should try to eliminate them.

Robert Longstreet

WRITING AS A SOCIAL ACT

Even the best writers feel challenged and intimidated by public exposure of their texts. Geoffrey Chaucer (1343–1400), for instance, sent one of his books away with a plea for its favorable reception. Yet, although writing is in many ways a private activity, most of the writing you will do in your introductory course to literature will come out of a public context, in which your texts will be read, shared, critiqued, and evaluated by your peers and instructor. Often, too, you will have the chance to engage in group discussion and to record in written form the conclusions your group reaches about the interpretation of a text. On such occasions, your instructor will divide your class into small groups and ask you to compare your own interpretation of a text with those of your classmates. Finally, after the secretary of your group records the group's conclusions, your group will then proceed to revise and edit your writing. In such a collaborative context, writing becomes a social act.

The texts below show the results of some peer groups' invigorating discussions of Chopin's "The Story of an Hour." Notice that the discussion conducted by group one led the students to equate marriage with the loss of self:

The Mallards' marriage is the marriage of two to make up one. In fact, their marriage can be represented as A + B = C. As in the chemical reaction necessary to human survival, wherein a molecule of glucose must give up a portion of itself to become a part of a larger molecule (dehydration synthesis), so it is in marriage. One part of the self must be given up to form the sacred union of marriage. It is an unfortunate circumstance of marriage that identity and the self must be its sacrificial lamb.

Our group concluded that it is not possible to have a "successful" marriage without some loss of self. Mr. and Mrs. Mallard have just such a marriage: a "successful" one.

Recorded by Karen Digirolano

Unlike group one, whose overall observations about the loss of self in marriage offer insight into the Mallards' marriage, group two analyzes the evidence that the text provides about the Mallards as husband and wife:

Mr. Mallard was a typical husband, who never thought twice about his wife's thoughts or wishes. Neither did he think about the imposition of his own will over hers. Their marriage seemed a typical one. Mrs. Mallard, in fact, even "loved him—sometimes." For all intents and purposes, Mrs. Mallard seemed to have been a dutiful wife.

When informed of the news that her husband was dead, she acted as any woman would at her loss. However, when alone in her room, Mrs. Mallard came to know a feeling foreign to her: "There would be no one to live for during those coming years: she would live for herself. There would be no powerful will bending her in." She found herself looking forward to "those days ahead of her" which would truly be hers and no one else's. She even "spread her arms out to them in welcome."

The doctors were wrong when they said that Mrs. Mallard died of "the joy that kills." The shock to her weak heart was of sadness. When she saw her husband, she realized that her freedom was lost—once again.

Recorded by Rina Russo

Group three's analysis of Mrs. Mallard's life in the past, present, and future shows a sense of historical development:

When Mrs. Mallard moves away from the past and the present to think of the days ahead in the future, she is obviously elated. She prays to live a long life, whereas before her husband died she had prayed for a short one. Mrs. Mallard's first reactions show us that when her husband was alive, she had no optimistic outlook on the future. She only wanted to die.

After his death, she drinks from the elixir of the open window, or from all the freedom (the birds, the trees, and the blue sky) that she witnesses outside. Through all these revelations, we can see how Mrs. Mallard evaluates her life in the past, present, and future.

Recorded by Mary Ellen Hogan

Group four saw "The Story of an Hour" as a text that explores Mrs. Mallard's loss of freedom and her imprisonment in a marriage from which she could be set free only by death:

Mrs. Mallard is sketched as a young, good-looking woman with a heart condition whose husband "never looked save with love upon her." However, the fact that Mr. Mallard was a loving and kind husband had not been enough to keep his wife from dreading the thought of living a long life.

The enormity of Mrs. Mallard's "monstrous joy" on digesting the implications of Brently Mallard's death paints the picture of a woman feeling so imprisoned in her marriage that she cries out, "Free! Body and soul free!"

Mrs. Mallard dies when she sees her husband returning home. If, on one hand, the shock of her newly gained freedom, now lost again, destroys her, on the other hand her death sets her free from the imprisonment of her marriage.

Recorded by Doris Fleischer

After exploring the text and conducting a heated discussion about the Mallards and their marriage, group five concluded that Mr. and Mrs. Mallard were victims of their historical time:

We got the impression that even though Mrs. Mallard had an identity of her own, she was above all Mr. Mallard's wife. Thus, it was their nineteenth-century marriage that held Mrs. Mallard back from being the individual she really was: "She was young with a calm face whose lines bespoke repression."

Our group concluded that Mr. Mallard, like most husbands of his time, did not know how his wife felt. He probably thought he was a good husband to his wife. In fact, she sometimes loved him and "she knew that she would weep again when she saw the kind, tender hands folded in death." Our conclusion is that Mr. and Mrs. Mallard both were victims of the time they lived in.

Recorded by Damien Donohue

WRITING THE LITERARY ESSAY: A STEP-BY-STEP GUIDELINE

To help you achieve your goal of becoming an able writer, we provide six guidelines that student writer Yasuko Osahi followed as she completed an essay on a literary work. Yasuko's instructor asked her students to write about one of several short stories, using the theme "Individualism and the Community."

Yasuko chose to write her two-page essay on "Hands," by Sherwood Anderson, because she wanted to learn more about American life through reading the work of writers like Anderson. Besides providing her with the source of information she needed, Anderson's text (see pages 882–885) also stimulated her imagination because of the similarities it evoked between the communities portrayed in "Hands" and her mother's community in a small village in Japan.

Yasuko also knew that her *audience* (made up of her classmates and her instructor) and the *purpose* of her essay (to communicate to her audience her critical observations about "Hands") would control the development of her essay. And because she would be writing for a college audience, Yasuko knew also that she must organize her paper by presenting evidence from Anderson's text and following the conventions used to write a literary essay.

Guideline One: Techniques for Generating Ideas

Because writing is an act of discovery, Yasuko initially used some warm-up techniques to discover and generate ideas about her topic.

Brainstorming. First, Yasuko *brainstormed* her topic by jotting down on a piece of paper all the ideas that occurred to her from her reading of Anderson's story.

Biddlebaum: lived in two places

Pennsylvania and Winesburg, Ohio

Biddlebaum changes his real name.

New profession: berry picker

Carries the past with him

Afraid of people, but feels good with George Willard

How does the town react to him?

Do they see him as a threat to them?

They don't fear Biddlebaum, just make fun of him.

Pennsylvania and his past life

A victim of violence

The townspeople: ruthless, no pity for individuals

Almost killed him

Why?

Did they see Biddlebaum as a threat to them?

Why did they fear him? Who is to be blamed?

Journal Entry. Yasuko used her journal for *focused freewriting*—nonstop writing that flows freely, without concern for organization or editing of any kind. Freewriting should not be confused with disorganized writing, however. Freewriting is a focused kind of writing that helps you to get started by recalling any ideas or experiences as they occur to you. To keep her writing flowing, Yasuko asked questions related to *what, why, when, how, where,* and *who.* This technique helped her to relax and to establish a firm relationship with her topic. Occasionally, she got stuck. However, she persisted, continuing to write some of the key words related to her topic until her writing gained its own momentum. She did not use all the ideas she wrote down in her journal, but the entry below shows that through writing she learned how to associate ideas, to communicate her reactions about her topic, and to explore feelings and emotions.

I like "Hands," but can't relate the story to "Individualism-Community."
What does community really mean? The townspeople? Biddlebaum lived in
two places. I'll start with the first one. Violent people, like in my mother's
village. You can't be different. A teacher. His real name was Adolph Myers.
Myers, Myers, then Biddlebaum. A dreamer. Anderson says that his characters
are "grotesque." Look up this word. Individualism. Biddlebaum gives us an
example of individualism. I like the story, and I sympathize with Biddlebaum.
The town's people see him as a threat. They fear him. Town's people and community. Community. Biddlebaum's community. Now I see the point. Biddlebaum's first community. Relationship: Biddlebaum-community. His second
community. Somebody in class said that if you don't understand the end of
the story, you'll miss the point. Bread. At the end he is just eating bread
crumbs. Why?

Clustering.　Since Yasuko responds well to visual texts and likes to relate them to
writing, she used *clustering* to develop and connect ideas about her topic. She
wrote down her topic in the middle of a page and circled it. Then she drew con-
necting lines that radiated from the main topic to subtopics—ideas or words that
occurred to her. Next she circled the subtopics and continued to draw other con-
necting lines to expose further ideas and relationships among them.

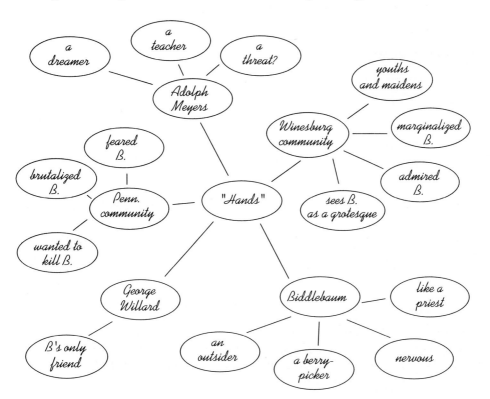

A Rough Outline. Yasuko continued to explore her topic by associating ideas and classifying them in a *rough outline*.

*Biddlebaum: a teacher. Uses his hands
to communicate. Dreams of ideal times.
Pennsylvania community: people liars, brutes. Use
violence. Biddlebaum as a threat? Do they fear him? Why?
Winesburg community: isolated, new name, lonely,
a grotesque, berry picker who sets a record.
People don't fear him; just laugh at him;
George Willard his only friend.
The real Biddlebaum is like a priest: above the laugh of
the community.
Communities in "Hands" and Japanese communities.
Similar in many ways. They hate people who
threaten them because they are different.
Why can't we accept individuals who are different?*

Guideline Two: Finding a Thesis

After examining the ideas in her brainstorming, journal entry, clustering, and rough outline, Yasuko noticed that her overall response to "Hands" was moving in the direction of one specific thesis statement or central idea. Gradually, as the pattern she was pursuing emerged, she was able to reinforce her sense of purpose and audience and to write a thesis statement. To formulate her thesis statement, Yasuko wrote down her topic and then expressed her opinion or commented on the topic.

`Topic:`

The conflict between individualism and community in "Hands."

+

`Student's comment, opinion, or attitude about the topic:`

Communities use violence only when they are under threat.

=

`Thesis statement:`

The conflict between individualism and community in "Hands" shows that communities, like Biddlebaum's Pennsylvania community, use violence only against individuals who pose a threat to their stability.

Yasuko's thesis statement shows how she narrowed her topic and phrased it using language that is clear, precise, and specific. It is important to remember, however, that even though your thesis statement functions as a contract that you sign with your readers, you might have to change or revise it as you move from draft to essay.

Guideline Three: Organizing the Paper

As the outline below shows, at this point Yasuko was ready to support her thesis statement on the basis of various ideas that she organized to build the body of her essay.

A Formal Outline

Thesis Statement
The conflict between individualism and community in "Hands" shows that communities, like Biddlebaum's Pennsylvania community, use violence only against individuals who pose a threat to their stability.

Supporting Ideas
I.   The Pennsylvania Community

    A. Biddlebaum as a threat to the community

        1. Biddlebaum: a real threat?

        2. The conflict of Biddlebaum-Pennsylvania community

    B. The community's reaction to Biddlebaum

        1. The community's disregard for individual rights

        2. The community's use of violence

II. The Winesburg Community

    A. Biddlebaum as a member of the community

        1. Biddlebaum: a real member?

        2. Biddlebaum as an outsider

        3. Biddlebaum as a grotesque

    B. The community's reaction to Biddlebaum

        1. The community's view of Biddlebaum as a grotesque

        2. The community's acceptance of Biddlebaum

III. The Real Biddlebaum

    A. Neither a threat nor a grotesque

    B. A holy man above his community

A formal outline like Yasuko's may be used as a preliminary form of planning before you write your first draft, or during revision to check the organization of the draft. Either way, such an outline should serve as a guide, never a hindrance to making changes that improve your essay. Notice that in her outline Yasuko arranged the information in an order (Pennsylvania community, Winesburg community) that contrasts with the order (Winesburg, Pennsylvania) presented by Anderson in his short story. In her approach, Yasuko used a cause-and-effect pattern to show how the violent behavior of the Pennsylvania community accounts for the grotesque position that Biddlebaum occupies in Winesburg.

Yasuko's essay might be classified as an "analysis essay," or an essay that focuses on the study of one single element in relation to the whole. Her instructor might have considered other kinds of essays as well, such as the following examples:

1. A comparison-and-contrast essay discusses similarities and differences between elements in the same work or in different works.

    EXAMPLE: Compare and contrast the roles of the two communities in "Hands."

    or

    Compare and contrast the conflict between the individual and society in "Hands" and "Eveline."

2. A debate essay presents one or the other side of an argument.

    EXAMPLE: Take a position and explain whether individual rights should ever overshadow the claims of society. Support your arguments with examples from the texts discussed in class.

3. A reaction essay presents the reader's feelings and reactions about a work of literature or a literary issue.

    EXAMPLE: React to the statement that cities and places that are full of dislocated, grotesque people provide ideal settings for short stories. Use at least three of the texts discussed in class to support your arguments.

4. A combination essay combines several approaches. To write her analytical essay studying individualism and community in "Hands" (exploring one specific element in relation to the whole), Yasuko also used cause-and-effect (examination of the causes and the effects that are likely to result from them) as well as comparison and contrast (focus on the similarities and differences of two elements).

Guideline Four: Rough Draft with Peers' Comments

At this point, Yasuko wrote and revised several versions of her essay until she decided on a rough draft that she shared with some of her classmates. Here is Yasuko's essay, followed by an evaluation form supplied by her instructor and filled out by her peer editors.

Essay on Individualism and the Community

The conflict between individualism and community in "Hands" shows Biddlebaum's struggle against the two communities in which he lived: the Pennsylvania community and the Winesburg community. When viewed from this perspective, this conflict also shows that communities like Biddlebaum's Pennsylvania community use violence only against individuals who pose a threat to their stability. But what really happened in Pennsylvania was that one day one of Biddlebaum's students acted in a romantic way toward him, spreading rumors about his potential homosexuality. Then the boys' parents got together, and after making some inquiries about Biddlebaum's habits, hastily concluded that he was a threat to their youth. In my opinion, what happens to Biddlebaum in Pennsylvania throws some light on how communities respond to a potential threat against themselves.

It is a dissatisfied member of the community who leads his community in a hate-chase against Adolph Myers. No one in the Pennsylvania community dared to raise a voice in Biddlebaum's defense. Parents, in fact, disregarded Biddlebaum's individual rights. Ironically, even though Biddlebaum's hands become the focal point of his downfall, it's through them that Biddlebaum manages to communicate his love of humanity. Led by its violent rage against Biddlebaum, the community beat, kicked, and almost killed him.

After leaving Pennsylvania, twenty years later we find Biddlebaum settled in another community, the community of Winesburg in Ohio. He decided to go to Winesburg because he had an aunt who lived there. That is when he changed his original name of Adolph Myers to Biddlebaum, and made a living as a berry picker. After his aunt's death he lives completely alone. Biddlebaum was a berry picker who made only one friend, George Willard. In spite of their close relationship, there are times in which

Biddlebaum and George do not feel comfortable with each other.

On one hand, the Winesburg community was proud of his ability to pick berries, but on the other hand, he was seen as weird and grotesque. However, the Winesburg community learns to accept Biddlebaum as a grotesque. This was shown in the opening paragraph of the story where Anderson presents Biddlebaum pacing up and down the veranda of his house.

Biddlebaum's mannerisms were made fun of by the youths and maidens, who managed to have a good laugh at his expense. At first the Winesburg community seems to react in a cruel way, but its reaction shows how Biddlebaum and his community unsettle each other.

From the point of view of the reader, who can see both communities, abusing and making fun of grotesque individuals like Biddlebaum made the Winesburg community feel confident and secure. However, unlike Biddlebaum's Winesburg community, his Pennsylvania community doesn't act in the same way. It is not violent. It is neither more sensitive nor enlightened than his Pennsylvania community. It would probably unleash the same kind of violence that his Pennsylvania community unleashed against him. The reason it didn't do so was that Biddlebaum never became a threat to that community. He isolated himself and was very careful not to mingle with anyone except George Willard.

My mother had also told me some stories about her small village in the Far East--horror tales about sons and daughters who were severely punished until they learned that individuals don't belong to themselves but to their communities. Such stories showed that what was at stake was not only the preservation of values and traditions, but also the community's defense of themselves against any kind of threat posed by their members.

Peer Editing Evaluation Form

WRITER: Yasuko Osahi

PEER EDITORS: Mary Anne Saboya, Gaby Jackson, Michael Hughes, Tony Spindola

1. *What does the writer want to say about the literary text in this paper? What aspects of the text does he or she focus on?*

    The writer wants to explore the conflict of individualism and community in "Hands." She focuses on how Biddlebaum relates to the two communities: the Winesburg and the Pennsylvania community.

2. *What kind of audience does the writer seem to be addressing? Which aspects of the paper might especially strike the audience? Why? Consider the writer's choice of subject, depth of information, point of view, tone, and voice.*

    Yasuko seems to be addressing her classmates and her instructors. Her thesis statement, "Communities use violence only against individuals who pose a threat to their stability," is powerful enough to strike her audience. Her choice of subject is good, but she needs to use more quotes to prove she is working close to the text. She also needs to soften the tone she uses in her essay.

3. *What are the strengths of the paper? How might the paper be revised to better fulfill the writer's purpose and meaning?*

    The strengths of the paper are Yasuko's choice of subject and her analysis of the two communities. Paragraphs 1, 3, and 4 need revision because at times she summarizes rather than interprets the story. Paragraphs 2 and 5 seem to go off track. Yasuko should rewrite them.

4. *Have you noticed any words and sentences that do not work? How would you rephrase them?*

    We noticed that in paragraph 5 she uses passive structures that are very vague. We would rephrase these sentences like this:
    - In the opening of the story, Anderson shows Biddlebaum pacing up and down the veranda of his house.
    - The youths and maidens made fun of him and managed to laugh at his expense.

5. *Other comments*

    Select a title that appeals to your readers.

Guideline Five: Revising

After reading her peers' comments on her rough draft, Yasuko knew that she would have to revise her paper and rewrite most of its paragraphs.

Yasuko revised her paper and handed it in to her instructor. A few days later, her instructor returned it with some marginal comments and an overall evaluation.

The Conflict of Individualism
and Community in "Hands"

Be more specific. See "Strategies for Revision" #5.

The conflict between individualism and community in ("Hands") shows Biddlebaum's struggle against
two of the communities in which he lived: the Pennsylvania community and Winesburg community. When
viewed from this perspective, this conflict also

A powerful thesis statement. It shows psychological depth.

shows that communities like Biddlebaum's Pennsylvania community {use violence only against individ- *tend to*
uals who pose a threat to their stability. But
did Biddlebaum really pose a threat to the youth
of the Pennsylvania community? Does Anderson's
text present Biddlebaum as a homosexual who was
corrupting the Pennsylvania youth? Why is it that
Myers's Pennsylvania community reacted so violently
against him, while his second community, the one
in Winesburg, manages to establish a truce with

Isn't your opinion implied in the text? Have you considered the role of the narrator?

him? In my opinion, what happens to Biddlebaum in   *a new*
Pennsylvania throws some light on how a community   *¶?*
responds to a potential threat against itself.

It is a dissatisfied member of the community
who leads his community in a hate-chase against
Adolph Myers. No one in the Pennsylvania
community dared to raise a voice in Biddlebaum's
defense. Parents, in fact, disregarded

Is this community afraid of B.? What does the text suggest about that?

Biddlebaum's individual rights. Led by its
violent rage against Biddlebaum, the community
beat, kicked, and almost killed him.

Anderson's text also suggests that it may be
fear or the spirit of preservation that controls
the action that the Pennsylvania townspeople take
against Biddlebaum. The community wanted to
defend itself against the schoolteacher. The
amount of violence it uses by "swearing and
throwing sticks and great balls of soft mud" at

him suggests that it feared Biddlebaum. If it got rid of him, it would also be able to eliminate the fear that he inspired. Once again the community would be able to restore its emotional balance.

Isn't this out of place? Either delete or rewrite it.

Ironically, even though Biddlebaum's hands become the focal point of his tragedy, and Biddlebaum himself "felt that the hands must be to blame" (292), it is through them that Biddlebaum manages to inspire his students to dream.

To consider Biddlebaum's position in Winesburg, Ohio, we have to ask whether Biddlebaum has really become a member of his community. The fact that he is a berry picker who contributes to the Winesburg economy does not seem to count because Biddlebaum "did not think of himself as in any way a part of the life of the town where he had lived for twenty years" (289). He was still an outsider who contrasted with the other berry pickers. However, unlike his Pennsylvania community, Biddlebaum's Winesburg community learns to accept him as "grotesque." In fact, Anderson's text opens with a description of how Adolph Myers, now Biddlebaum, an old and eccentric individual who nervously paces up and down the veranda of his shabby house, contrasts with the "youths and maidens" of Winesburg, Ohio.

This argument merits development. What about a quote?

Is there any thing in text that suggests that? Use quotes.

The fact that Biddlebaum and the "youths and maidens" unsettle each other seems to suggest that Biddlebaum will never become a real member of the Winesburg community. From the point of view of the reader, who can see both communities, abusing and making fun of grotesque individuals like Biddlebaum made the Winesburg community feel confident and secure. However, unlike Biddlebaum's Winesburg community, his Pennsylvania community doesn't seem to act the same way. They are not violent. They are neither more sensitive nor more enlightened than his Pennsylvania community. They would probably unleash the same kind of violence that his Pennsylvania community unleashed against him. The reason they don't do so is that Biddlebaum never became a threat to the community. He isolated himself and was very careful not to mingle with anyone, except George Willard.

What about the I on whom the real B. is? Check your outline. ←

My mother had also told me some stories about her small village in the Far East—horror tales about sons and daughters severely punished until they learned that individuals don't belong to themselves, but to their communities. Such

How does your conclusion tie in with "Hands?"

stories showed that what was at stake was not only the preservation of values and traditions, but also the community's defense of itself against any kind of threat posed by its members.

Yasuko,
Even though you've made some good points in your rough draft, your essay still needs a lot of work. Put it aside for a day or two, but during that time continue to read "Hands" to clarify your ideas.
Start your revision by reading your text aloud. Then develop your I/s more fully, use quotes to support your arguments, and follow the guidelines above.

After reading her instructor's comments, Yasuko rewrote and reorganized her paper. During this process, she consulted the strategies for revision described below.

Strategies for Revising the Literary Essay

1. **Select and Chose a Title Carefully**
   Select a title that describes or announces the topic without restating the thesis statement. Make sure that your title appeals to the reader.

2. **Replace Plot Summary with Analysis and Interpretation**
   Remember that all literary interpretations begin with critical observations. Thus, to avoid laying out a plot summary—or retelling the story—strive to use verbs that will assist you in achieving and maintaining the critical focus you need to write a literary essay.

explore	portray	include
analyze	argue	highlight
mention	refer	discuss
demonstrate	suggest	examine
show	illustrate	explain
reveal	emphasize	express
present	use	chronicle
write	indicate	outline

   EXAMPLE: In "Hands," Sherwood Anderson reveals how an individual becomes a potential threat to his community.

   "Hands" explores the conflict between individualism and society on several levels.

   Remember, however, that *purpose* and *audience* should always control your writing. Thus, if your presumed audience has not read the text, some plot summary would be necessary.

3. **Favor the Active Voice**
   The overuse of passive constructions—constructions with a subject that does not do the action or is acted upon—may weaken your sentences. Whenever possible, try to infuse energy and conviction into your sentences by using the active voice.

   PASSIVE: Biddlebaum's mannerisms are made fun of by the "youths and maidens" of Winesburg.

   ACTIVE: The "youths and maidens" of Winesburg make fun of Biddlebaum.

   PASSIVE: The conflict between the individual and society is explored in the opening of the story.

   ACTIVE: The opening of "Hands" explores the conflict between individual and society.

4. **Use the Present Tense to Analyze Literary Texts**

Like other works of art, such as paintings, literary texts possess a time of their own. In a sense, they live forever, because they live outside time. Consequently, you should use the present tense to analyze texts and to describe the underlying action of their plots.

EXAMPLE: **The Pennsylvania community in "Hands" feels more** confident and secure if it can eliminate individuals like Biddlebaum.

"Hands" presents George Willard as Biddlebaum's only friend.

5. **Establish a Clear Context in Your First Paragraph**

Identify the title, author, and characters in the work you are analyzing as if you were writing not only for your classmates and instructor but for a broader audience. This is especially important when you write the first paragraph of your essay.

VAGUE: "Hands" portrays the tension that may arise between an individual and his community.

REVISED: "Hands," one of Sherwood Anderson's stories in *Winesburg, Ohio*, portrays the tension that arises between an individual, Biddlebaum, and his community.

6. **Revise for Content and Organization**

Your focus here should be the overall development of the essay. Concentrate on the title, thesis statement, supporting ideas, and organization.

◆ Is the title of your essay suggestive?
◆ Is the thesis clear and persuasive?
◆ Is your essay logically organized?

Consider whether the opening paragraph introduces the topic and whether the conclusion summarizes the main ideas or offers an overall evaluation of the thesis. If necessary, rewrite your thesis statement and rearrange the major sections of your essay by adding, deleting, condensing, or changing the order of its various elements.

7. **Paragraph Organization**

◆ Relate each paragraph to the thesis of the essay.
◆ Make the main idea of each paragraph clear.
◆ See that the parts of the paragraph relate to each other.
◆ Make your paragraph more interesting by using rhetorical questions, quotations, examples, and illustrations that will keep the reader's attention.

8. **Revise for Purpose and Audience**

Ask yourself whether your essay fulfills its purpose to inform, entertain, persuade, or call its readers to action.

◆ Who are your readers?
◆ Is your essay appropriate for your readers?

Put yourself in the intended reader's place, and check your paper for clarity and precision of meaning from the reader's point of view.

9. **Revise for Tone**

◆ What kind of attitude have you expressed in presenting your topic to your reader?
◆ Are you writing as an authority on your subject?
◆ Is your writing too formal or too informal? Is it ironic, direct?
◆ What kind of language are you using to express this tone?

Put yourself in the place of your intended reader, and listen to the sound of the speaking voice of your text.

Guideline Six: Editing and Preparing Your Manuscript

After revision, you may start to focus on the presentation of your essay. In this phase of the writing process, you should consider wordiness, redundancy, grammatical errors, mechanical problems (spelling, punctuation, capital letters, abbreviations), and the format required for preparing your manuscript. Bear in mind that the ear can detect flaws that the eye misses. Therefore, try reading your text aloud to catch mistakes that emerge not so much on the broader level of paragraph organization but on the more local level of the sentence or phrase.

See guidelines for title, margins, paging, source citations, in the section "Researching Literary Sources" (pages 942–967). If your school has a tutoring program, your instructor may ask you to work with a writing tutor to revise your text for clarity.

Writing the Final Draft

The final draft of Yasuko's essay on "Hands" follows. Do you consider her essay strong and effective enough? Would you suggest any further revision?

Osahi 1

Yasuko Osahi

Professor Jackson

English Composition II

May 27, 1994

The Conflict of Individualism

and Community in "Hands"

The conflict between individualism and community in Sherwood Anderson's short story "Hands" shows the struggle of one individual-- the protagonist, Wing Biddlebaum, or Adolph Myers--against two main communities: the Pennsylvania community and the Winesburg community. When viewed from this perspective, this conflict also shows that communities like Biddlebaum's Pennsylvania community tend to use violence against individuals who pose a threat to their stability. But did Biddlebaum really pose a threat to the youth of the Pennsylvania community? Does Anderson's text present Biddlebaum as a homosexual who was corrupting the Pennsylvania youth? Why is it that Myers's Pennsylvania community reacted so violently against him, while his second community, the one in Winesburg, manages to establish a truce with him?

The narrator's description of what happened in Biddlebaum's Pennsylvania community throws much light on how a community responds to a potential threat against itself:

Osahi 2

> With lanterns in their hands a dozen
> men came to the door of the house
> where he lived alone and commanded
> that he dress and come forth. It was
> raining and one of the men had a rope
> in his hands. They had intended to
> hang the schoolmaster, but something
> in his figure, so small, white, and
> pitiful, touched their hearts and
> they let him escape. (292)

It is through the narrator's eyes that we see
how any dissatisfied member of a community,
like one of Biddlebaum's students, can lead his
community in a hate-chase if he is clever
enough to unleash some of the community's
covert fears:

> A half-witted boy of the school
> became enamored of the young master.
> . . . Strange, hideous accusations
> fell from his loose-hung lips.
> Through the Pennsylvania town went a
> shiver. Hidden, shadowy doubts that
> had been in men's minds concerning
> Adolph Myers were galvanized into
> beliefs. (291)

Anderson's text also suggests that it may be
fear or the spirit of preservation that controls the action that the Pennsylvania townspeople take against Biddlebaum. The community
wanted to defend itself against the school-

Osahi 3

teacher. The amount of violence it uses by "swearing and throwing sticks and great balls of soft mud" at him suggests that it feared Biddlebaum. If it got rid of him, it would also be able to eliminate the fear that his hands inspired. Once again the community would be able to restore its emotional balance. Ironically, even though Biddlebaum's "hands" became the focal point of his tragedy, and Biddlebaum himself "felt that the hands must be to blame" (292), it is through them that Biddlebaum manages to inspire his students to dream: "under the caress of his hands doubt and disbelief went out of the minds of the boys and they began also to dream" (291).

To consider Biddlebaum's position in Winesburg, Ohio, we have to ask whether Biddlebaum has really become a member of his community. The fact that he is a berry picker who contributes to the Winesburg economy does not seem to count because Biddlebaum "did not think of himself as in any way a part of the life of the town where he had lived for twenty years" (289). He was still an outsider who contrasted with the other berry pickers. However, unlike his Pennsylvania community, Biddlebaum's Winesburg community learns to accept him as a "grotesque." In fact, Anderson's text opens with a description of how Adolph Myers, now Biddlebaum, an old and eccentric individual who ner-

Osahi 4

vously paces up and down the veranda of his
shabby house, contrasts with the "youths and
maidens" of Winesburg, Ohio. The fact that Biddlebaum and the "youths and maidens" unsettle
each other seems to suggest that Biddlebaum
will never become a real member of the Winesburg community.

From the point of view of the reader, who
can see the reality of both communities, the
Winesburg "youths and maidens" also seem to
react in a cruel way, by making fun of Biddlebaum's mannerisms and by having a good laugh at
his expense. However, they don't seem to act
out of fear. Their critique of Biddlebaum
seems to give them just the sense of power they
need to feel confident and secure about themselves: "'Oh, you Wing Biddlebaum, comb your
hair, it's falling into your eyes,' commanded
the voice to the man, who was bald and whose
nervous little hands fiddled about the bare
white forehead as though arranging a mass of
tangled locks" (289). Biddlebaum, the weird and
eccentric outsider, seems to reaffirm the feelings that they belong in their own community.
In some ways, the Winesburg community is neither better nor more civilized than Biddlebaum's Pennsylvania community. If driven by
the fear of a potential threat to its stability, it might probably unleash the same kind of
violence against people.

Osahi 5

Neither community ever learns who Biddlebaum really is. Through Anderson's narrator,
however, the reader gets a good glimpse of his
real personality. The narrator stresses Biddlebaum's childlike innocence and his love of
humanity. Last, but not least, the narrator
also casts Biddlebaum in the figure of a holy
man. The religious images at the end of the
text presenting Biddlebaum "like a priest
engaged in some service of his church" (292)
suggest that Biddlebaum possesses the sensibil-
ity of a religious man--one that neither community would be able to appreciate.

"Hands" brought to my mind some of my
mother's stories about her small village in
Japan. Those horror tales portrayed sons and
daughters who were severely punished when they
refused to conform. For me, such tales also
show that what was at stake, as much in my
mother's village as in the communities in
"Hands," was not only the preservation of traditional values but the communities' defense of
themselves against individuals who are different and who pose a threat to their stability.

Work Cited

Anderson, Sherwood. "Hands." <u>Literature Across
    Cultures.</u> Eds. Sheena Gillespie, Terezinha
    Fonseca, and Carol Sanger. Boston: Allyn
    and Bacon, 1994: 882-887.

PART ONE
Origins and Insights

Fiction

The Death of Ivan Ilych, Leo Tolstoy ◆ *Roman Fever*, Edith
Wharton ◆ *First Confession*, Frank O'Connor ◆ *A Power Struggle*,
Bessie Head ◆ *The Watch*, Elie Wiesel ◆ *The Sky Is Gray*, Ernest J.
Gaines ◆ *Young Goodman Brown*, Nathaniel Hawthorne ◆ *Araby*,
James Joyce

Essays

My People, Chief Seattle ◆ *Knoxville: Summer 1915*, James Agee

Poetry

The Father Poem Two, Sue Doro ◆ *The Hatmaker*, Keith Gilyard ◆
Going Home, Maurice Kenny ◆ *During a Son's Dangerous Illness*,
Denise Levertov ◆ *Lost Sister*, Cathy Song ◆ *Song for My Name*,
Linda Hogan ◆ *Moving Away* (1), Gary Soto ◆ *Moving Away* (2),
Gary Soto ◆ *The Jewish Cemetery at Newport*, Henry Wadsworth
Longfellow ◆ *Fern Hill*, Dylan Thomas ◆ *It's Something Our
Family Has Always Done*, Wing Tek Lum ◆ *warm heart contains
life*, Evangelina Vigil-Piñón ◆ *My Grandmother's Hands*, Maria
Mazziotti Gillan ◆ *Gentle Communion*, Pat Mora ◆ *A Breeze Swept
Through*, Luci Tapahonso ◆ *Fishermen*, James A. Emanuel ◆ *What
My Child Learns of the Sea*, Audre Lorde ◆ *Frederick Douglass*,
Robert Hayden ◆ *Tour 5*, Robert Hayden ◆ *Those Winter Sundays*,
Robert Hayden ◆ *Runagate Runagate*, Robert Hayden

Drama

Oedipus Rex, Sophocles ◆ *The Tragedy of Hamlet, Prince of
Denmark*, William Shakespeare

The artist's imagination has always been captivated by the idea of the past and its relationship to the present. Stories from the oral traditions of ancient cultures as well as our own evoke the powers and mysteries of the past by portraying a time in which myths, fables, legends, and archetypes dictated the values of human actions within the community. The ritual of storytelling was an integral part of communal life, as tribe members from the oldest to the youngest listened to, recalled, or retold stories about creation, good and evil, war and peace, life and death.

How can we reach and understand the past? What can we learn from it? Why are memories an important part of our private and communal selves? Some writers in Part One begin with what the author Toni Morrison calls "sites of memory"—places that have affected these writers' lives because of emotional or sensory associations with them. The speaker in "Fern Hill," for example, takes us back to the Welsh landscapes and summer experiences that framed his childhood, and the speaker in "Moving Away" reminds his brother and sister of their first home and the family events there that shaped their present lives.

Historical places such as colonial Williamsburg, Ellis Island, and Martin Luther King's Memorial, or even photographs of a grandparent's birthplace, are also important sites of memory. They often motivate us to listen to the voices of the past or to search for our roots in an attempt to establish a dialogue with our past selves as we explore further our own terrain.

The past has been variously defined as a "foreign country," a "bucket of ashes," a "field of errors and ignorance," or a temporal continuum with the power "to delight and instruct." As you examine various aspects of the past in Part One texts, remember that we can try to understand our personal and historical pasts only with the aid of our memory and our imagination. As the writer Lynne Sharon Schwartz reminds us, "Memory is something we reconstruct, something we create. Memory is a story we make up from snatches of the past."

People who have influenced our lives are often important catalysts in reconstructing and understanding our stories. The protagonist in "First Confession," for instance, remembers with gratitude the Irish priest who offered him forgiveness instead of punishment, while the young son in "The Sky Is Gray" reflects on his mother's comment "You not a bum…You a Man."

To what extent is it important also to try to understand our collective pasts? Is it plausible to say that our identity and our individual lives are sometimes shaped by a fixed historical reality? Some of the writers in Part One speculate about these questions by examining the conditions under which people become particularly aware of historical identities. Robert Hayden's poem "Runagate Runagate," for example, reconstructs what it means to be a renegade caught in the grim historical reality that shaped the destiny of African slaves in the United States.

In "The Watch," Holocaust survivor Elie Wiesel explores his protagonist's attempt to retrieve a watch that symbolizes his past, "the soul and memory of that time" of war and holocaust. "Once more," says the protagonist as he attempts to defy time and to retrieve the past, "I am the bar mitzvah child.... I get ready to re-enact the scene my memory recalls."

The drama *Hamlet* offers another example of how men and women can identify themselves with the past. One major question you will explore is why the Danish prince wavers between remembering and forgetting the past that seems to link him and the political future of Denmark. What do people do when they realize that they carry the burden of the past with them or that the past can become an obstacle to their growth and to a redefinition of themselves?

In texts such as "A Power Struggle" and "Song for My Name," we encounter yet another aspect of the past in myths that attempt to voice the collective and private truths of humanity. Bessie Head's story of the Tlabina clan presents the origin of the power struggle between two brothers as a cosmological myth based on the primeval conflict between the principles of good and evil, and in Hogan's poem the speaker constructs a private myth to help her understand the terms of her existence—from her birth to the mystery of her death.

As you explore these and other selections from the sites of memory, consider them as catalysts for your own recollections and discoveries of your personal and communal past, for as writer Oscar Wilde reminds us, "Memory is the diary we carry about with us."

Leo Tolstoy
1886

The Death of Ivan Ilych

I

During an interval in the Melvinski trial in the large building of the Law Courts, the members and public prosecutor met in Ivan Egorovich Shebek's private room, where the conversation turned on the celebrated Krasovski case. Fëdor Vasilievich warmly maintained that it was not subject to their jurisdiction, Ivan Egorovich maintained the contrary, while Peter Ivanovich, not having entered into the discussion as the start, took no part in it but looked through the *Gazette* which had just been handed in.

"Gentlemen," he said, "Ivan Ilych has died!"

"You don't say so!"

"Here, read it yourself," replied Peter Ivanovich, handing Fëdor Vasilievich the paper still damp from the press. Surrounded by a black border were the words: "Praskovya Fëdorovna Goloviná, with profound sorrow, informs relatives and friends of the demise of her beloved husband Ivan Ilych Golovin, Member of the Court of Justice, which occurred on February the 4th of this year 1882. The funeral will take place on Friday at one o'clock in the afternoon."

Ivan Ilych had been a colleague of the gentlemen present and was liked by them all. He had been ill for some weeks with an illness said to be incurable. His post had been kept open for him, but there had been conjectures that in case of his death Alexeev might receive his appointment, and that either Vinnikov or Shtabel would succeed Alexeev. So on receiving the news of Ivan Ilych's death the first thought of each of the gentlemen in that private room was of the changes and promotions it might occasion among themselves or their acquaintances.

"I shall be sure to get Shtabel's place or Vinnikov's," thought Fedor Vasilievich. "I was promised that long ago, and the promotion means an extra eight hundred rubles a year for me besides the allowance."

"Now I must apply for my brother-in-law's transfer from Kaluga," thought Peter Ivanovich. "My wife will be very glad, and then she won't be able to say that I never do anything for her relations."

"I thought he would never leave his bed again," said Peter Ivanovich aloud. "It's very sad."

"But what really was the matter with him?"

"The doctors couldn't say—at least they could, but each of them said something different. When last I saw him I thought he was getting better."

"And I haven't been to see him since the holidays. I always meant to go."

"Had he any property?"

"I think his wife had a little—but something quite trifling."

"We shall have to go to see her, but they live so terribly far away."

"Far away from you, you mean. Everything's far away from your place."

"You see, he never can forgive my living on the other side of the river," said Peter Ivanovich, smiling at Shebek. Then, still talking of the distances between different parts of the city, they returned to the Court.

Besides considerations as to the possible transfers and promotions likely to result from Ivan Ilych's death, the mere fact of the death of a near acquaintance aroused, as usual, in all who heard of it the complacent feeling that, "it is he who is dead and not I."

Each one thought or felt, "Well, he's dead but I'm alive!" But the more intimate of Ivan Ilych's acquaintances, his so-called friends, could not help thinking also that they would now have to fulfil the very tiresome demands of propriety by attending the funeral service and paying a visit of condolence to the widow.

Fëdor Vasilievich and Peter Ivanovich had been his nearest acquaintances. Peter Ivanovich had studied law with Ivan Ilych and had considered himself to be under obligations to him.

Having told his wife at dinner-time of Ivan Ilych's death and of his conjecture that it might be possible to get her brother transferred to their circuit, Peter Ivanovich sacrificed his usual nap, put on his evening clothes, and drove to Ivan Ilych's house.

At the entrance stood a carriage and two cabs. Leaning against the wall in the hall downstairs near the cloak-stand was a coffin-lid covered with cloth of gold, ornamented with gold cord and tassels, that had been polished up with metal powder. Two ladies in black were taking off their fur cloaks. Peter Ivanovich recognized one of them as Ivan Ilych's sister, but the other was a stranger to him. His colleague Schwartz was just coming downstairs, but on seeing Peter Ivanovich enter he stopped and winked at him, as if to say: "Ivan Ilych has made a mess of things—not like you and me."

Schwartz's face with his Piccadilly whiskers and his slim figure in evening dress had as usual an air of elegant solemnity which contrasted with the playfulness of his character and had a special piquancy here, or so it seemed to Peter Ivanovich.

Peter Ivanovich allowed the ladies to precede him and slowly followed them upstairs. Schwartz did not come down but remained where he was, and Peter Ivanovich understood that he wanted to arrange where they should play bridge that evening. The ladies went upstairs to the widow's room, and Schwartz with seriously compressed lips but a playful look in his eyes, indicated by a twist of his eyebrows the room to the right where the body lay.

Peter Ivanovich, like everyone else on such occasions, entered feeling uncertain what he would have to do. All he knew was that at such times it is always safe to cross oneself. But he was not quite sure whether one should make obeisances while doing so. He therefore adopted a middle course. On entering the room he began crossing himself and made a slight movement resembling a bow. At the same time, as far as the motion of his head and arm allowed, he surveyed the room. Two young men—apparently nephews, one of whom was a high-school pupil—were leaving the room, crossing themselves as they did so. An old woman was standing motionless, and a lady with strangely arched eyebrows was saying something to her in a whisper. A vigorous, resolute Church Reader, in a frock coat, was reading something in a loud voice with an expression that precluded any contradiction. The butler's assistant, Gerasim, stepping lightly in front of Peter Ivanovich, was strewing something on the floor. Noticing this, Peter Ivanovich was immediately aware of a faint odour of a decomposing body.

The last time he had called on Ivan Ilych, Peter Ivanovich had seen Gerasim in the study. Ivan Ilych had been particularly fond of him and he was performing the duty of a sick nurse.

Peter Ivanovich continued to make the sign of the cross, slightly inclining his head in an intermediate direction between the coffin, the Reader, and the icons on the table in a corner of the room. Afterwards, when it seemed to him that this movement of his arm in crossing himself had gone on too long, he stopped and began to look at the corpse.

The dead man lay, as dead men always lie, in a specially heavy way, his rigid limbs sunk in the soft cushions of the coffin, with the head forever bowed on the pillow. His yellow waxen brow with bald patches over his sunken temples was thrust up in the way peculiar to the dead, the protruding nose seeming to press on the upper lip. He was much changed and had grown even thinner since Peter Ivanovich had last seen him, but, as is always the case with the dead, his face was handsomer and above all more dignified than when he was alive. The expression on the face said that what was necessary had been accomplished, and accomplished rightly. Besides this there was in that expression a reproach and a warning to the living. This warning seemed to Peter Ivanovich out of place, or at least not applicable to him. He felt a certain discomfort and so he hurriedly crossed himself once more and turned and went out of the door—too hurriedly and too regardless of propriety, as he himself was aware.

Schwartz was waiting for him in the adjoining room with legs spread wide apart and both hands toying with his top hat behind his back. The mere sight of that playful, well-groomed, and elegant figure refreshed Peter Ivanovich. He felt that Schwartz was above all these happenings and would not surrender to any depressing influences. His very look said that this incident of a church service for Ivan Ilych could not be a sufficient reason for infringing the order of the session—in other words, that it would certainly not prevent his unwrapping a new pack of cards and shuffling them that evening while a footman placed four fresh candles on the table: in fact, that there was no reason for supposing that this incident would hinder their spending the evening agreeably. Indeed he said this in a whisper as Peter Ivanovich passed him, proposing that they should meet for a game at Fëdor Vasilievich's. But apparently Peter Ivanovich was not destined to play bridge that evening. Praskovya Fëdorovna (a short, fat woman who despite all efforts to the contrary had continued to broaden steadily from her shoulders downwards and who had the same extraordinarily arched eyebrows as the lady who had been standing by the coffin), dressed all in black, her head covered with lace, came out of her own room with some other ladies, conducted them to the room where the dead body lay, and said: "The service will begin immediately. Please go in."

Schwartz, making an indefinite bow, stood still, evidently neither accepting nor declining this invitation. Praskovya Fëdorovna, recognizing Peter Ivanovich, sighed, went close up to him, took his hand, and said: "I know you were a true friend of Ivan Ilych…" and looked at him awaiting some suitable response. And Peter Ivanovich knew that, just as it had been the right thing to cross himself in that room, so what he had to do here was to press her hand, sigh, and say, "Believe me…." So he did all this and as he did it felt that the desired result had been achieved: that both he and she were touched.

"Come with me. I want to speak to you before it begins," said the widow. "Give me your arm."

Peter Ivanovich gave her his arm and they went to the inner rooms, passing Schwartz, who winked at Peter Ivanovich compassionately.

"That does for our bridge! Don't object if we find another player. Perhaps you can cut in when you do escape," said his playful look.

Peter Ivanovich sighed still more deeply and despondently, and Praskovya Fëdorovna pressed his arm gratefully. When they reached the drawing-room, upholstered in pink cretonne and lighted by a dim lamp, they sat down at the table—she on a sofa and Peter Ivanovich on a low pouffe, the springs of which yielded spasmodically under his weight. Praskovya Fëdorovna had been on the point of warning him to take another seat, but felt that such a warning was out of keeping with her present condition and so changed her mind. As he sat down on the pouffe Peter Ivanovich recalled how Ivan Ilych had arranged this room and had consulted him regarding this pink cretonne with green leaves. The whole room was full of furniture and knick-knacks, and on her way to the sofa the lace of the widow's black shawl caught on the carved edge of the table. Peter Ivanovich rose to detach it, and the springs of the pouffe, relieved of his weight, rose also and gave him a push. The widow began detaching her shawl herself, and Peter Ivanovich again sat down, suppressing the rebellious springs of the pouffe under him. But the widow had not quite freed herself and Peter Ivanovich got up again, and again the pouffe rebelled and even creaked. When this was all over she took out a clean cambric handkerchief and began to weep. The episode with the shawl and the struggle with the pouffe had cooled Peter Ivanovich's emotions and he sat there with a sullen look on his face. This awkward situation was interrupted by Sokolov, Ivan Ilych's butler, who came to report that the plot in the cemetery that Praskovya Fëdorovna had chosen would cost two hundred rubles. She stopped weeping and, looking at Peter Ivanovich with the air of a victim, remarked in French that it was very hard for her. Peter Ivanovich made a silent gesture signifying his full conviction that it must indeed be so.

"Please smoke," she said in a magnanimous yet crushed voice, and turned to discuss with Sokolov the price of the plot for the grave.

Peter Ivanovich while lighting his cigarette heard her inquiring very circumstantially into the prices of different plots in the cemetery and finally decide which, she would take. When that was done she gave instructions about engaging the choir. Sokolov then left the room.

"I look after everything myself," she told Peter Ivanovich, shifting the albums that lay on the table; and noticing that the table was endangered by his cigarette-ash, she immediately passed him an ashtray, saying as she did so: "I consider it an affectation to say that my grief prevents my attending to practical affairs. On the contrary, if anything can—I won't say console me, but—distract me, it is seeing to everything concerning him." She again took out her handkerchief as if preparing to cry, but suddenly, as if mastering her feeling, she shook herself and began to speak calmly. "But there is something I want to talk to you about."

Peter Ivanovich bowed, keeping control of the springs of the pouffe, which immediately began quivering under him.

"He suffered terribly the last few days."

"Did he?" said Peter Ivanovich.

"Oh, terribly! He screamed unceasingly, not for minutes but for hours. For the last three days he screamed incessantly. It was unendurable. I cannot understand how I bore it; you could hear him three rooms off. Oh, what I have suffered!"

"Is it possible that he was conscious all that time?" asked Peter Ivanovich.

"Yes," she whispered. "To the last moment. He took leave of us a quarter of an hour before he died, and asked us to take Volodya away."

The thought of the sufferings of this man he had known so intimately, first as a merry little boy, then as a school-mate, and later as a grown-up colleague, suddenly struck Peter Ivanovich with horror, despite an unpleasant consciousness of his own and this woman's dissimulation. He again saw that brow, and that nose pressing down on the lip, and felt afraid for himself.

"Three days of frightful suffering and then death! Why, that might suddenly, at any time, happen to me," he thought, and for a moment felt terrified. But—he did not himself know how—the customary reflection at once occurred to him that this had happened to Ivan Ilych and not to him, and that it should not and could not happen to him, and that to think that it could would be yielding to depression which he ought not to do, as Schwartz's expression plainly showed. After which reflection Peter Ivanovich felt reassured, and began to ask with interest about the details of Ivan Ilych's death, as though death was an accident natural to Ivan Ilych but certainly not to himself.

After many details of the really dreadful physical sufferings Ivan Ilych had endured (which details he learnt only from the effect those sufferings had produced on Praskovya Fëdorovna's nerves) the widow apparently found it necessary to get to business.

"Oh, Peter Ivanovich, how hard it is! How terribly, terribly, hard!" and she again began to weep.

Peter Ivanovich sighed and waited for her to finish blowing her nose. When she had done so he said, "Believe me…" and she again began talking and brought out what was evidently her chief concern with him—namely, to question him as to how she could obtain a grant of money from the government on the occasion of her husband's death. She made it appear that she was asking Peter Ivanovich's advice about her pension, but he soon saw that she already knew about that to the minutest detail, more even than he did himself. She knew how much could be got out of the government in consequence of her husband's death, but wanted to find out whether she could not possibly extract something more. Peter Ivanovich tried to think of some means of doing so, but after reflecting for a while and, out of propriety, condemning the government for its niggardliness, he said he thought that nothing more could be got. Then she sighed and evidently began to devise means of getting rid of her visitor. Noticing this, he put out his cigarette, rose, pressed her hand, and went out into the anteroom.

In the dining-room where the clock stood that Ivan Ilych had liked so much and had bought at an antique shop, Peter Ivanovich met a priest and a few acquaintances who had come to attend the service, and he recognized Ivan Ilych's daughter, a handsome young woman. She was in black and her slim figure appeared slimmer than ever. She had a gloomy, determined, almost angry expression, and bowed to Peter Ivanovich as though he were in some way to blame. Behind her, with the same offended look, stood a wealthy young man, an examining magistrate, whom Peter Ivanovich also knew and who was her fiancé, as he had heard. He bowed mournfully to them and was about to pass into the death-chamber, when from under the stairs appeared the figure of Ivan Ilych's schoolboy son, who was extremely like his father. He seemed a little Ivan Ilych, such as Peter Ivanovich remembered when they studied law together. His tear-stained eyes had in them the look that is seen in the eyes of boys of thirteen or fourteen who are not pureminded. When he saw Peter Ivanovich he scowled morosely and shamefacedly. Peter Ivanovich nodded to him and entered the death-chamber. The service began: candles, groans, incense, tears, and sobs. Peter Ivanovich stood looking gloomily down at his feet. He did not look once at the dead man, did not yield to any depressing influence, and was one of the first to leave the room. There was no one in the anteroom, but Gerasim darted out of the dead man's room, rummaged with his strong hands among the fur coats to find Peter Ivanovich's, and helped him on with it.

"Well, friend Gerasim," said Peter Ivanovich, so as to say something. "It's a sad affair, isn't it?"

"It's God's will. We shall all come to it some day," said Gerasim, displaying his teeth—the even, white teeth of a healthy peasant—and, like a man in the thick of urgent work, he briskly opened the front door, called the coachman, helped Peter Ivanovich into the sledge, and sprang back to the porch as if in readiness for what he had to do next.

Peter Ivanovich found the fresh air particularly pleasant after the smell of incense, the dead body, and carbolic acid.

"Where to, sir?" asked the coachman.

"It's not too late even now.... I'll call round on Fëdor Vasilievich."

He accordingly drove there and found them just finishing the first rubber, so that it was quite convenient for him to cut in.

II

Ivan Ilych's life had been most simple and most ordinary and therefore most terrible.

He had been a member of the Court of Justice, and died at the age of forty-five. His father had been an official who after serving in various ministries and departments in Petersburg had made the sort of career which brings men to positions from which by reason of their long service they cannot be dismissed, though they are obviously unfit to hold any responsible position, and for whom therefore posts are specially created, which though fictitious carry salaries of from six to ten thousand rubles that are not fictitious, and in receipt of which they live on to a great age.

Such was the Privy Councillor and superfluous member of various superfluous institutions, Ilya Epimovich Golovin.

He had three sons, of whom Ivan Ilych was the second. The eldest son was following in his father's footsteps only in another department, and was already approaching that stage in the service at which a similar sinecure would be reached. The third son was a failure. He had ruined his prospects in a number of positions and was now serving in the railway department. His father and brothers, and still more their wives, not merely disliked meeting him, but avoided remembering his existence unless compelled to do so. His sister had married Baron Greff, a Petersburg official of her father's type. Ivan Ilych was *le phénix de la famille* as people said. He was neither as cold and formal as his elder brother nor as wild as the younger, but was a happy mean between them—an intelligent, polished, lively, and agreeable man. He had studied with his younger brother at the School of Law, but the latter had failed to complete the course and was expelled when he was in the fifth class. Ivan Ilych finished the course well. Even when he was at the School of Law he was just what he remained for the rest of his life: a capable, cheerful, good-natured, and sociable man, though strict in the fulfilment of what he considered to be his duty: and he considered his duty to be what was so considered by those in authority. Neither as a boy nor as a man was he a toady, but from early youth was by nature attracted to people of high station as a fly is drawn to the light, assimilating their ways and views of life and establishing friendly relations with them. All the enthusiasms of childhood and youth passed without leaving much trace on him; he succumbed to sensuality, to vanity, and latterly among the highest classes to liberalism, but always within limits which his instinct unfailingly indicated to him as correct.

At school he had done things which had formerly seemed to him very horrid and made him feel disgusted with himself when he did them; but when later on he saw that such actions were done by people of good position and that they did not regard them as wrong, he was able not exactly to regard them as right, but to forget about them entirely or not be at all troubled at remembering them.

Having graduated from the School of Law and qualified for the tenth rank of the civil service, and having received money from his father for his equipment, Ivan Ilych ordered himself clothes at Scharmer's, the fashionable tailor, hung a medallion inscribed *respice finem*[1] on his watch-chain, took leave of his professor and the prince who was patron of the school, had a farewell dinner with his comrades at Donon's first-class restaurant, and with his new and fashionable portmanteau, linen, clothes, shaving and other toilet appliances, and a travelling rug all purchased at the best shops, he set off for one of the provinces where, through his father's influence, he had been attached to the Governor as an official for special service.

---

[1] "Reflect on your end."

In the province Ivan Ilych soon arranged as easy and agreeable a position for himself as he had had at the School of Law. He performed his official tasks, made his career, and at the same time amused himself pleasantly and decorously. Occasionally he paid official visits to country districts, where he behaved with dignity both to his superiors and inferiors, and performed the duties entrusted to him, which related chiefly to the sectarians,[2] with an exactness and incorruptible honesty of which he could not but feel proud.

In official matters, despite his youth and taste for frivolous gaiety, he was exceedingly reserved, punctilious, and even severe; but in society he was often amusing and witty, and always good-natured, correct in his manner, and *bon enfant,* as the Governor and his wife—with whom he was like one of the family—used to say of him.

In the province he had an affair with a lady who made advances to the elegant young lawyer, and there was also a milliner; and there were carousals with aides-de-camp who visited the district, and after-supper visits to a certain outlying street of doubtful reputation; and there was too some obsequiousness to his chief and even to his chief's wife, but all this was done with such a tone of good breeding that no hard names could be applied to it. It all came under the heading of the French saying: "*Il faut que jeunesse se passe.*"[3] It was all done with clean hands, in clean linen, with French phrases, and above all among people of the best society and consequently with the approval of people of rank.

So Ivan Ilych served for five years and then came a change in his official life. The new and reformed judicial institutions were introduced, and new men were needed. Ivan Ilych became such a new man. He was offered the post of examining magistrate, and he accepted it though the post was in another province and obliged him to give up the connexions he had formed and to make new ones. His friends met to give him a send-off; they had a group-photograph taken and presented him with a silver cigarette-case, and he set off to his new post.

As examining magistrate Ivan Ilych was just as *comme il faut* and decorous a man, inspiring general respect and capable of separating his official duties from his private life, as he had been when acting as an official on special service. His duties now as examining magistrate were far more interesting and attractive than before. In his former position it had been pleasant to wear an undress uniform made by Scharmer, and to pass through the crowd of petitioners and officials who were timorously awaiting an audience with the Governor, and who envied him as with free and easy gait he went straight into his chief's private room to have a cup of tea and a cigarette with him. But not many people had been directly dependent on him—only police officials and the sectarians when he went on special missions—and he liked to treat them politely, almost as comrades, as if he were letting them feel that he who had the power to crush them was treating them in this simple, friendly way. There were then but few such people. But now, as an examining magistrate, Ivan Ilych felt that everyone without exception, even the most important and self-

---

[2] Dissident Christian sects that had broken off from the Russian Orthodox Church.   [3] "Youth must have its fling."

satisfied, was in his power, and that he need only write a few words on a sheet of paper with a certain heading, and this or that important, self-satisfied person would be brought before him in the role of an accused person or a witness, and if he did not choose to allow him to sit down, would have to stand before him and answer his questions. Ivan Ilych never abused his power; he tried on the contrary to soften its expression, but the consciousness of it and of the possibility of softening its effect, supplied the chief interest and attraction of his office. In his work itself, especially in his examinations, he very soon acquired a method of eliminating all considerations irrelevant to the legal aspect of the case, and reducing even the most complicated case to a form in which it would be presented on paper only in its externals, completely excluding his personal opinion of the matter, while above all observing every prescribed formality. The work was new and Ivan Ilych was one of the first men to apply the new Code of 1864.[4]

On taking up the post of examining magistrate in a new town, he made new acquaintances and connexions, placed himself on a new footing, and assumed a somewhat different tone. He took up an attitude of rather dignified aloofness towards the provincial authorities, but picked out the best circle of legal gentlemen and wealthy gentry living in the town and assumed a tone of slight dissatisfaction with the government, of moderate liberalism, and of enlightened citizenship. At the same time, without at all altering the elegance of his toilet, he ceased shaving his chin and allowed his beard to grow as it pleased.

Ivan Ilych settled down very pleasantly in this new town. The society there, which inclined towards opposition to the Governor, was friendly, his salary was larger, and he began to play *vint*,[5] which he found added not a little to the pleasure of life, for he had a capacity for cards, played good-humouredly, and calculated rapidly and astutely, so that he usually won.

After living there for two years he met his future wife, Praskovya Fёdorovna Mikhel, who was the most attractive, clever, and brilliant girl of the set in which he moved, and among other amusements and relaxations from his labours as examining magistrate, Ivan Ilych established light and playful relations with her.

While he had been an official on special service he had been accustomed to dance, but now as an examining magistrate it was exceptional for him to do so. If he danced now, he did it as if to show that though he served under the reformed order of things, and had reached the fifth official rank, yet when it came to dancing he could do it better than most people. So at the end of an evening he sometimes danced with Praskovya Fёdorovna, and it was chiefly during these dances that he captivated her. She fell in love with him. Ivan Ilych had at first no definite intention of marrying, but when the girl fell in love with him he said to himself: "Really, why shouldn't I marry?"

Praskovya Fёdorovna came of a good family, was not bad-looking, and had some little property. Ivan Ilych might have aspired to a more brilliant match, but

---

[4] The emancipation of the serfs in 1861 was followed by a thorough all-around reform of judicial proceedings. [TRANS.]   [5] A form of bridge. [TRANS.]

even this was good. He had his salary, and she, he hoped, would have an equal income. She was well connected, and was a sweet, pretty, and thoroughly correct young woman. To say that Ivan Ilych married because he fell in love with Praskovya Fëdorovna and found that she sympathized with his views of life would be as incorrect as to say that he married because his social circle approved of the match. He was swayed by both these considerations: the marriage gave him personal satisfaction, and at the same time it was considered the right thing by the most highly placed of his associates.

So Ivan Ilych got married.

The preparations for marriage and the beginning of married life, with its conjugal caresses, the new furniture, new crockery, and new linen, were very pleasant until his wife became pregnant—so that Ivan Ilych had begun to think that marriage would not impair the easy, agreeable, gay, and always decorous character of his life, approved of by society and regarded by himself as natural, but would even improve it. But from the first months of his wife's pregnancy, something new, unpleasant, depressing, and unseemly, and from which there was no way of escape, unexpectedly showed itself.

His wife, without any reason—*de gaieté de cœur* as Ivan Ilych expressed it to himself—began to disturb the pleasure and propriety of their life. She began to be jealous without any cause, expected him to devote his whole attention to her, found fault with everything, and made coarse and ill-mannered scenes.

At first Ivan Ilych hoped to escape from the unpleasantness of this state of affairs by the same easy and decorous relation to life that had served him heretofore: he tried to ignore his wife's disagreeable moods, continued to live in his usual easy and pleasant way, invited friends to his house for a game of cards, and also tried going out to his club or spending his evenings with friends. But one day his wife began upbraiding him so vigorously, using such coarse words, and continued to abuse him every time he did not fulfil her demands, so resolutely and with such evident determination not to give way till he submitted—that is, till he stayed at home and was bored just as she was—that he became alarmed. He now realized that matrimony—at any rate with Praskovya Fëdorovna—was not always conducive to the pleasures and amenities of life, but on the contrary often infringed both comfort and propriety, and that he must therefore entrench himself against such infringement. And Ivan Ilych began to seek for means of doing so. His official duties were the one thing that imposed upon Praskovya Fëdorovna, and by means of his official work and the duties attached to it he began struggling with his wife to secure his own independence.

With the birth of their child, the attempts to feed it and the various failures in doing so, and with the real and imaginary illnesses of mother and child, in which Ivan Ilych's sympathy was demanded but about which he understood nothing, the need of securing for himself an existence outside his family life became still more imperative.

As his wife grew more irritable and exacting and Ivan Ilych transferred the centre of gravity of his life more and more to his official work, so did he grow to like his work better and become more ambitious than before.

Very soon, within a year of his wedding, Ivan Ilych had realized that marriage, though it may add some comforts to life, is in fact a very intricate and difficult affair towards which in order to perform one's duty, that is, to lead a decorous life approved of by society, one must adopt a definite attitude just as towards one's official duties.

And Ivan Ilych evolved such an attitude towards married life. He only required of it those conveniences—dinner at home, housewife, and bed—which it could give him, and above all that propriety of external forms required by public opinion. For the rest he looked for light-hearted pleasure and propriety, and was very thankful when he found them, but if he met with antagonism and querulousness he at once retired into his separate fenced-off world of official duties, where he found satisfaction.

Ivan Ilych was esteemed a good official, and after three years was made Assistant Public Prosecutor. His new duties, their importance, the possibility of indicting and imprisoning anyone he chose, the publicity his speeches received, and the success he had in all these things, made his work still more attractive.

More children came. His wife became more and more querulous and ill-tempered, but the attitude Ivan Ilych had adopted towards his home life rendered him almost impervious to her grumbling.

After seven years' service in that town he was transferred to another province as Public Prosecutor. They moved, but were short of money and his wife did not like the place they moved to. Though the salary was higher the cost of living was greater, besides which two of their children died and family life became still more unpleasant for him.

Praskovya Fëdorovna blamed her husband for every inconvenience they encountered in their new home. Most of the conversations between husband and wife, especially as to the children's education, led to topics which recalled former disputes, and those disputes were apt to flare up again at any moment. There remained only those rare periods of amorousness which still came to them at times but did not last long. These were islets at which they anchored for a while and then again set out upon that ocean of veiled hostility which showed itself in their aloofness from one another. This aloofness might have grieved Ivan Ilych had he considered that it ought not to exist, but he now regarded the position as normal, and even made it the goal at which he aimed in family life. His aim was to free himself more and more from those unpleasantnesses and to give them a semblance of harmlessness and propriety. He attained this by spending less and less time with his family, and when obliged to be at home he tried to safeguard his position by the presence of outsiders. The chief thing however was that he had his official duties. The whole interest of his life now centered in the official world and that interest absorbed him. The consciousness of his power, being able to ruin anybody he wished to ruin, the importance, even the external dignity of his entry into court, or meetings with his subordinates, his success with superiors and inferiors, and above all his masterly handling of cases, of which he was conscious—all this gave him pleasure and filled his life, together with chats with his colleagues, dinners, and bridge. So that on the whole Ivan Ilych's life continued to flow as he considered it should do—pleasantly and properly.

So things continued for another seven years. His eldest daughter was already sixteen, another child had died, and only one son was left, a schoolboy and a subject of dissension. Ivan Ilych wanted to put him in the School of Law, but to spite him Praskovya Fëdorovna entered him at the High School. The daughter had been educated at home and had turned out well: the boy did not learn badly either.

III

So Ivan Ilych lived for seventeen years after his marriage. He was already a Public Prosecutor of long standing, and had declined several proposed transfers while awaiting a more desirable post, when an unanticipated and unpleasant occurrence quite upset the peaceful course of his life. He was expecting to be offered the post of presiding judge in a University town, but Happe somehow came to the front and obtained the appointment instead. Ivan Ilych became irritable, reproached Happe, and quarrelled both with him and with his immediate superiors—who became colder to him and again passed him over when other appointments were made.

This was in 1880, the hardest year of Ivan Ilych's life. It was then that it became evident on the one hand that his salary was insufficient for them to live on, and on the other that he had been forgotten, and not only this, but that what was for him the greatest and most cruel injustice appeared to others a quite ordinary occurrence. Even his father did not consider it his duty to help him. Ivan Ilych felt himself abandoned by everyone, and that they regarded his position with a salary of 3,500 rubles as quite normal and even fortunate. He alone knew that with the consciousness of the injustices done him, with his wife's incessant nagging, and with the debts he had contracted by living beyond his means, his position was far from normal.

In order to save money that summer he obtained leave of absence and went with his wife to live in the country at her brother's place.

In the country, without his work, he experienced *ennui* for the first time in his life, and not only *ennui* but intolerable depression, and he decided that it was impossible to go on living like that, and that it was necessary to take energetic measures.

Having passed a sleepless night pacing up and down the veranda, he decided to go to Petersburg and bestir himself, in order to punish those who had failed to appreciate him and to get transferred to another ministry.

Next day, despite many protests from his wife and her brother, he started for Petersburg with the sole object of obtaining a post with a salary of five thousand rubles a year. He was no longer bent on any particular department, or tendency, or kind of activity. All he now wanted was an appointment to another post with a salary of five thousand rubles, either in the administration, in the banks, with the railways, in one of the Empress Marya's Institutions, or even in the customs—but it had to carry with it a salary of five thousand rubles and be in a ministry other than that in which they had failed to appreciate him.

And this quest of Ivan Ilych's was crowned with remarkable and unexpected success. At Kursk an acquaintance of his, F.I. Ilyin, got into the first-class carriage, sat down beside Ivan Ilych, and told him of a telegram just received by the Governor of Kursk announcing that a change was about to take place in the ministry: Peter Ivanovich was to be superseded by Ivan Semënovich.

The proposed change, apart from its significance for Russia, had a special significance for Ivan Ilych, because by bringing forward a new man, Peter Petrovich, and consequently his friend Zachar Ivanovich, it was highly favourable for Ivan Ilych, since Zachar Ivanovich was a friend and colleague of his.

In Moscow this news was confirmed, and on reaching Petersburg Ivan Ilych found Zachar Ivanovich and received a definite promise of an appointment in his former department of justice.

A week later he telegraphed to his wife: "Zachar in Miller's place. I shall receive appointment on presentation of report."

Thanks to this change of personnel, Ivan Ilych had unexpectedly obtained an appointment in his former ministry which placed him two stages above his former colleagues besides giving him five thousand rubles salary and three thousand five hundred rubles for expenses connected with his removal. All his ill humour towards his former enemies and the whole department vanished, and Ivan Ilych was completely happy.

He returned to the country more cheerful and contented than he had been for a long time. Praskovya Fëdorovna also cheered up and a truce was arranged between them. Ivan Ilych told of how he had been fêted by everybody in Petersburg, how all those who had been his enemies were put to shame and now fawned on him; how envious they were of his appointment, and how much everybody in Petersburg had liked him.

Praskovya Fëdorovna listened to all this and appeared to believe it. She did not contradict anything, but only made plans for their life in the town to which they were going. Ivan Ilych saw with delight that these plans were his plans, that he and his wife agreed, and that, after a stumble, his life was regaining its due and natural character of pleasant lightheartedness and decorum.

Ivan Ilych had come back for a short time only, for he had to take up his new duties on the 10th of September. Moreover, he needed time to settle into the new place, to move all his belongings from the province, and to buy and order many additional things: in a word, to make such arrangements as he had resolved on, which were almost exactly what Praskovya Fëdorovna too had decided on.

Now that everything had happened so fortunately, and that he and his wife were at one in their aims and moreover saw so little of one another, they got on together better than they had done since the first years of marriage. Ivan Ilych had thought of taking his family away with him at once, but the insistence of his wife's brother and her sister-in-law, who had suddenly become particularly amiable and friendly to him and his family, induced him to depart alone.

So he departed, and the cheerful state of mind induced by his success and by the harmony between his wife and himself, the one intensifying the other, did not leave him. He found a delightful house, just the thing both he and his wife had dreamt of. Spacious, lofty reception rooms in the old style, a convenient and dignified study, rooms for his wife and daughter, a study for his son—it might have been specially built for them. Ivan Ilych himself superintended the arrangements, chose the wall-papers, supplemented the furniture (preferably with antiques which he considered particularly *comme il faut*), and supervised the upholstering. Everything progressed and progressed and approached the ideal he had set himself: even when things were only half completed they exceeded his expectations. He saw what a refined and elegant character, free from vulgarity, it would all have when it was ready. On falling asleep he pictured to himself how the reception-room would look. Looking at the yet unfinished drawing-room he could see the fireplace, the screen, the what-not, the little chairs dotted here and there, the dishes and plates on the walls, and the bronzes, as they would be when everything was in place. He was pleased by the thought of how his wife and daughter, who shared his taste in this matter, would be impressed by it. They were certainly not expecting as much. He had been particularly successful in finding, and buying cheaply, antiques which gave a particularly aristocratic character to the whole place. But in his letters he intentionally understated everything in order to be able to surprise them. All this so absorbed him that his new duties—though he liked his official work—interested him less than he had expected. Sometimes he even had moments of absentmindedness during the Court Sessions, and would consider whether he should have straight or curved cornices for his curtains. He was so interested in it all that he often did things himself, rearranging the furniture, or rehanging the curtains. Once when mounting a stepladder to show the upholsterer, who did not understand, how he wanted the hangings draped, he made a false step and slipped, but being a strong and agile man he clung on and only knocked his side against the knob of the window frame. The bruised place was painful but the pain soon passed, and he felt particularly bright and well just then. He wrote: "I feel fifteen years younger." He thought he would have everything ready by September, but it dragged on till mid-October. But the result was charming not only in his eyes but to everyone who saw it.

In reality it was just what is usually seen in the houses of people of moderate means who want to appear rich, and therefore succeed only in resembling others like themselves: there were damasks, dark wood, plants, rugs, and dull and polished bronzes—all the things people of a certain class have in order to resemble other people of that class. His house was so like the others that it would never have been noticed, but to him it all seemed to be quite exceptional. He was very happy when he met his family at the station and brought them to the newly furnished house all lit up, where a footman in a white tie opened the door into the ball decorated with plants, and when they went on into the drawing-room and the study uttering exclamations of delight. He conducted them everywhere, drank in their praises eagerly, and beamed with pleasure. At tea that evening, when Praskovya Fëdorovna among other things asked him about his fall, he laughed and showed them how he had gone flying and had frightened the upholsterer.

"It's a good thing I'm a bit of an athlete. Another man might have been killed, but I merely knocked myself, just here; it hurts when it's touched, but it's passing off already—it's only a bruise."

So they began living in their new home—in which, as always happens, when they got thoroughly settled in they found they were just one room short—and with the increased income, which as always was just a little (some five hundred rubles) too little, but it was all very nice.

Things went particularly well at first, before everything was finally arranged and while something had still to be done: this thing bought, that thing ordered, another thing moved, and something else adjusted. Though there were some disputes between husband and wife, they were both so well satisfied and had so much to do that it all passed off without any serious quarrels. When nothing was left to arrange it became rather dull and something seemed to be lacking, but then, they were then making acquaintances, forming habits, and life was growing fuller.

Ivan Ilych spent his mornings at the law courts and came home to dinner, and at first he was generally in a good humour, though he occasionally became irritable just on account of his house. (Every spot on the tablecloth or the upholster, and every broken window blind string, irritated him. He had devoted so much trouble to arranging it all that every disturbance of it distressed him.) But on the whole his life ran its course as he believed life should do: easily, pleasantly, and decorously.

He got up at nine, drank his coffee, read the paper, and then put on his undress uniform and went to the law courts. There the harness in which he worked had already been stretched to fit him and be donned it without a hitch: petitioners, inquiries at the chancery, the chancery itself, and the sittings public and administrative. In all this the thing was to exclude everything fresh and vital, which always disturbs the regular course of official business, and to admit only official relations with people, and then only on official grounds. A man would come, for instance, wanting some information. Ivan Ilych, as one in whose sphere the matter did not lie, would have nothing to do with him: but if the man had some business with him in his official capacity, something that could be expressed on officially stamped paper, he would do everything, positively everything he could within the limits of such relations, and in doing so would maintain the semblance of friendly human relations, that is, would observe the courtesies of life. As soon as the official relations ended, so did everything else. Ivan Ilych possessed this capacity to separate his real life from the official side of affairs and not mix the two, in the highest degree, and by long practice and natural aptitude had brought it to such a pitch that sometimes, in the manner of a virtuoso, he would even allow himself to let the human and official relations mingle. He let himself do this just because he felt that he could at any time he chose resume the strictly official attitude again and drop the human relation. And he did it all easily, pleasantly, correctly and even artistically. In the intervals between the sessions he smoked, drank tea, chatted a little about politics, a little about general topics, a little about cards, but most of all about official appointments. Tired, but with the feelings of a virtuoso—one of the first violins who has played his part in an orchestra with precision—he would return home to find that his wife and daughter had been out paying calls, or had a visitor, and that his son had been to school, had done his homework with his tutor, and was duly learning what is taught at High Schools. Everything was as it should be. After dinner, if they had no visitors, Ivan Ilych sometimes read a book that was being much discussed at the time, and in the evening settled down to work, that is, read official papers, compared the depositions of witnesses, and noted paragraphs of the Code applying to them. This was neither dull nor amusing. It was dull when he might have been playing bridge, but if no bridge was available it was at any rate better than doing nothing or sitting with his wife. Ivan Ilych's chief pleasure was giving little dinners to which he invited men and women of good social position, and just as his drawing room resembled all other drawing rooms so did his enjoyable little parties resemble all other such parties.

Once they even gave a dance. Ivan Ilych enjoyed it and everything went off well, except that it led to a violent quarrel with his wife about the cakes and sweets. Praskovya Fëdorovna had made her own plans, but Ivan Ilych insisted on getting everything from an expensive confectioner and ordered too many cakes, and the quarrel occurred because some of those cakes were left over and the confectioner's bill came to forty-five rubles. It was a great and disagreeable quarrel. Praskovya Fëdorovna called him "a fool and an imbecile," and he clutched at his head and made angry allusions to divorce.

But the dance itself had been enjoyable. The best people were there, and Ivan Ilych had danced with Princess Trufonova, a sister of the distinguished founder of the Society "Bear my Burden."

The pleasures connected with his work were pleasures of ambition; his social pleasures were those of vanity; but Ivan Ilych's greatest pleasure was playing bridge. He acknowledged that whatever disagreeable incident happened in his life, the pleasure that beamed like a ray of light above everything else was to sit down to bridge with good players, not noisy partners, and of course to four-handed bridge (with five players it was annoying to have to stand out, though one pretended not to mind), to play a clever and serious game (when the cards allowed it), and then to have supper and drink a glass of wine. After a game of bridge, especially if he had won a little (to win a large sum was unpleasant), Ivan Ilych went to bed in specially good humour.

So they lived. They formed a circle of acquaintances among the best people and were visited by people of importance and by young folk. In their views as to their acquaintances, husband, wife, and daughter were entirely agreed, and tacitly and unanimously kept at arm's length and shook off the various shabby friends and relations who, with much show of affection, gushed into the drawing room with its Japanese plates on the walls. Soon these shabby friends ceased to obtrude themselves and only the best people remained in the Golovins' set.

Young men made up to Lisa, and Petrishchev, an examining magistrate and Dmitri Ivanovich Petrishchev's son and sole heir, began to be so attentive to her that Ivan Ilych had already spoken to Praskovya Fëdorovna about it, and considered whether they should not arrange a party for them, or get up some private theatricals.

So they lived, and all went well, without change, and life flowed pleasantly.

IV

They were all in good health. It could not be called ill health if Ivan Ilych sometimes said that he had a queer taste in his mouth and felt some discomfort in his left side.

But this discomfort increased and, though not exactly painful, grew into a sense of pressure in his side accompanied by ill humour. And his irritability became worse and worse and began to mar the agreeable, easy, and correct life that had established itself in the Golovin family. Quarrels between husband and wife became more and more frequent, and soon the ease and amenity disappeared and even the decorum was barely maintained. Scenes again became frequent, and very few of those islets remained on which husband and wife could meet without an explosion. Praskovya Fëdorovna now had good reason to say that her husband's temper was trying. With characteristic exaggeration she said he had always had a dreadful temper, and that it had needed all her good nature to put up with it for twenty years. It was true that now the quarrels were started by him. His bursts of temper always came just before dinner, often just as he began to eat his soup. Sometimes he noticed that a plate or dish was chipped, or the food was not right, or his son put his elbow on the table, or his daughter's hair was not done as he liked it, and for all this he blamed Praskovya Fëdorovna. At first she retorted and said disagreeable things to him, but once or twice he fell into such a rage at the beginning of dinner that she realized it was due to some physical derangement brought on by taking food, and so she restrained herself and did not answer, but only hurried to get the dinner over. She regarded this self-restraint as highly praiseworthy. Having come to the conclusion that her husband had a dreadful temper and made her life miserable, she began to feel sorry for herself, and the more she pitied herself the more she hated her husband. She began to wish he would die; yet she did not want him to die because then his salary would cease. And this irritated her against him still more. She considered herself dreadfully unhappy just because not even his death could save her, and though she concealed her exasperation, that hidden exasperation of hers increased his irritation also.

After one scene in which Ivan Ilych had been particularly unfair and after which he had said in explanation that he certainly was irritable but that it was due to his not being well, she said that if he was ill it should be attended to, and insisted on his going to see a celebrated doctor.

He went. Everything took place as he had expected and as it always does. There was the usual waiting and the important air assumed by the doctor, with which he was so familiar (resembling that which he himself assumed in court), and the sounding and listening, and the questions which called for answers that were foregone conclusions and were evidently unnecessary, and the look of importance which implied that "if only you put yourself in our hands we will arrange everything—we know indubitably, how it has to be done, always in the same way for everybody alike." It was all just as it was in the law courts. The doctor put on just the same air towards him as he himself put on towards an accused person.

The doctor said that so-and-so indicated that there was so-and-so inside the patient, but if the investigation of so-and-so did not confirm this, then he must assume that and that. If he assumed that and that, then…and so on. To Ivan Ilych only one question was important: was his case serious or not? But the doctor ignored that inappropriate question. From his point of view it was not the one under consideration, the real question was to decide between a floating kidney, chronic catarrh, or appendicitis. It was not a question of Ivan Ilych's life or death, but one between a floating kidney and appendicitis. And that question the doctor solved brilliantly, as it seemed to Ivan Ilych, in favour of the appendix, with the reservation that should an examination of the urine give fresh indications the matter would be reconsidered. All this was just what Ivan Ilych had himself brilliantly accomplished a thousand times in dealing with men on trial. The doctor summed up just as brilliantly, looking over his spectacles triumphantly and even gaily at the accused. From the doctor's summing up Ivan Ilych concluded that things were bad, but that for the doctor, and perhaps for everybody else, it was a matter of indifference, though for him it was bad. And this conclusion struck him painfully, arousing in him a great feeling of pity for himself and of bitterness towards the doctor's indifference to a matter of such importance.

He said nothing of this, but rose, placed the doctor's fee on the table, and remarked with a sigh: "We sick people probably often put inappropriate questions. But tell me, in general, is this complaint dangerous, or not?..."

The doctor looked at him sternly over his spectacles with one eye, as if to say: "Prisoner, if you will not keep to the questions put to you, I shall be obliged to have you removed from the court."

"I have already told you what I consider necessary and proper. The analysis may show something more." And the doctor bowed.

Ivan Ilych went out slowly, seated himself disconsolately in his sledge, and drove home. All the way home he was going over what the doctor had said, trying to translate those complicated, obscure, scientific phrases into plain language and find in them an answer to the question: "Is my condition bad? Is it very bad? Or is there as yet nothing much wrong?" And it seemed to him that the meaning of what the doctor had said was that it was very bad. Everything in the streets seemed depressing. The cabmen, the houses, the passers-by, and the shops, were dismal. His ache, this dull gnawing ache that never ceased for a moment, seemed to have acquired a new and more serious significance from the doctor's dubious remarks. Ivan Ilych now watched it with a new and oppressive feeling.

He reached home and began to tell his wife about it. She listened, but in the middle of his account his daughter came in with her hat on, ready to go out with her mother. She sat down reluctantly to listen to this tedious story, but could not stand it long, and her mother too did not bear him to the end.

"Well, I am very glad," she said. "Mind now to take your medicine regularly. Give me the prescription and I'll send Gerasim to the chemist's." And she went to get ready to go out.

While she was in the room Ivan Ilych had hardly taken time to breathe, but he sighed deeply when she left it.

"Well," he thought, "perhaps it isn't so bad after all."

He began taking his medicine and following the doctor's directions, which had been altered after the examination of the urine. But then it happened that there was a contradiction between the indications drawn from the examination of the urine and the symptoms that showed themselves. It turned out that what was happening differed from what the doctor had told him, and that he had either forgotten, or blundered, or hidden something from him. He could not, however, be blamed for that, and Ivan Ilych still obeyed his orders implicitly and at first derived some comfort from doing so.

From the time of his visit to the doctor, Ivan Ilych's chief occupation was the exact fulfilment of the doctor's instructions regarding hygiene and the taking of medicine, and the observation of his pain and his excretions. His chief interests came to be people's ailments and people's health. When sickness, deaths, or recoveries were mentioned in his presence, especially when the illness resembled his own, he listened with agitation which he tried to hide, asked questions, and applied what he heard to his own case.

The pain did not grow less, but Ivan Ilych made efforts to force himself to think that he was better. And he could do this so long as nothing agitated him. But as soon as he had any unpleasantness with his wife, any lack of success in his official work, or held bad cards at bridge, he was at once acutely sensible of his disease. He had formerly borne such mischances, hoping soon to adjust what was wrong, to master it and attain success, or make a grand slam. But now every mischance upset him and plunged him into despair. He would say to himself: "There now, just as I was beginning to get better and the medicine had begun to take effect, comes this accursed misfortune, or unpleasantness...." And he was furious with the mishap, or with the people who were causing the unpleasantness and killing him, for he felt that this fury was killing him but could not restrain it. One would have thought that it should have been clear to him that this exasperation with circumstances and people aggravated his illness, and that he ought therefore to ignore unpleasant occurrences. But he drew the very opposite conclusion: he said that he needed peace, and he watched for everything that might disturb it and became irritable at the slightest infringement of it. His condition was rendered worse by the fact that he read medical books and consulted doctors. The progress of his disease was so gradual that he could deceive himself when comparing one day with another—the difference was so slight. But when he consulted the doctors it seemed to him that he was getting worse, and even very rapidly. Yet despite this he was continually consulting them.

That month he went to see another celebrity, who told him almost the same as the first had done but put his questions rather differently, and the interview with this celebrity only increased Ivan Ilych's doubts and fears. A friend of a friend of his, a very good doctor, diagnosed his illness again quite differently from the others, and though he predicted recovery, his questions and suppositions bewildered Ivan Ilych still more and increased his doubts. A homœopathist diagnosed the disease in yet another way, and prescribed medicine which Ivan Ilych took secretly for a week. But after a week, not feeling any improvement and having lost confidence both in the former doctor's treatment and in this one's, he became still more despondent. One day a lady acquaintance mentioned a cure effected by a wonder-working icon. Ivan Ilych caught himself listening attentively and beginning to believe that it had occurred. This incident alarmed him. "Has my mind really weakened to such an extent?" he asked himself. "Nonsense! It's all rubbish. I mustn't give way to nervous fears but having chosen a doctor must keep strictly to his treatment. That is what I will do. Now it's all settled. I won't think about it, but will follow the treatment seriously till summer, and then we shall see. From now there must be no more of this wavering!" This was easy to say but impossible to carry out. The pain in his side oppressed him and seemed to grow worse and more incessant, while the taste in his mouth grew stranger and stranger. It seemed to him that his breath had a disgusting smell, and he was conscious of a loss of appetite and strength. There was no deceiving himself: something terrible, new, and more important than anything before in his life, was taking place within him of which he alone was aware. Those about him did not understand or would not understand it, but thought everything in the world was going on as usual. That tormented Ivan Ilych more than anything. He saw that his household, especially his wife and daughter who were in a perfect whirl of visiting, did not understand anything of it and were annoyed that he was so depressed and so exacting, as if he were to blame for it. Though they tried to disguise it he saw that he was an obstacle in their path, and that his wife had adopted a definite line in regard to his illness and kept to it regardless of anything he said or did. Her attitude was this: "You know," she would say to her friends, "Ivan Ilych can't do as other people do, and keep to the treatment prescribed for him. One day he'll take his drops and keep strictly to his diet and go to bed in good time, but the next day unless I watch him he'll suddenly forget his medicine, eat sturgeon—which is forbidden—and sit up playing cards till one o'clock in the morning."

"Oh, come, when was that?" Ivan Ilych would ask in vexation. "Only once at Peter Ivanovich's."

"And yesterday with Shebek."

"Well, even if I hadn't stayed up, this pain would have kept me awake."

"Be that as it may you'll never get well like that, but will always make us wretched."

Praskovya Fëdorovna's attitude to Ivan Ilych's illness, as she expressed it both to others and to him, was that it was his own fault and was another of the annoyances he caused her. Ivan Ilych felt that this opinion escaped her involuntarily—but that did not make it easier for him.

At the law courts too, Ivan Ilych noticed, or thought he noticed, a strange attitude towards himself. It sometimes seemed to him that people were watching him inquisitively as a man whose place might soon be vacant. Then again, his friends would suddenly begin to chaff him in a friendly way about his low spirits, as if the awful, horrible, and unheard-of thing that was going on within him, incessantly gnawing at him and irresistibly drawing him away, was a very agreeable subject for jests. Schwartz in particular irritated him by his jocularity, vivacity, and *savoir-faire,* which reminded him of what he himself had been ten years ago.

Friends came to make up a set and they sat down to cards. They dealt, bending the new cards to soften them, and he sorted the diamonds in his hand and found he had seven. His partner said "No trumps" and supported him with two diamonds. What more could be wished for? It ought to be jolly and lively. They would make a grand slam. But suddenly Ivan Ilych was conscious of that gnawing pain, that taste in his mouth, and it seemed ridiculous that in such circumstances he should be pleased to make a grand slam.

He looked at his partner Mikhail Mikhaylovich, who rapped the table with his strong hand and instead of snatching up the tricks pushed the cards courteously and indulgently towards Ivan Ilych that he might have the pleasure of gathering them up without the trouble of stretching out his hand for them. "Does he think I am too weak to stretch out my arm?" thought Ivan Ilych, and forgetting what he was doing he over-trumped his partner, missing the grand slam by three tricks. And what was most awful of all was that he saw how upset Mikhail Mikhaylovich was about it but did not himself care. And it was dreadful to realize why he did not care.

They all saw that he was suffering, and said: "We can stop if you are tired. Take a rest." Lie down? No, he was not at all tired, and he finished the rubber. All were gloomy and silent. Ivan Ilych felt that he had diffused this gloom over them and could not dispel it. They had supper and went away, and Ivan Ilych was left alone with the consciousness that his life was poisoned and was poisoning the lives of others, and that this poison did not weaken but penetrated more and more deeply into his whole being.

With this consciousness, and with physical pain besides the terror, he must go to bed, often to lie awake the greater part of the night. Next morning he had to get up again, dress, go to the law courts, speak, and write; or if he did not go out, spend at home those twenty-four hours a day each of which was a torture. And he had to live thus all alone on the brink of an abyss, with no one who understood or pitied him.

V

So one month passed and then another. Just before the New Year his brother-in-law came to town and stayed at their house. Ivan Ilych was at the law courts and Praskovya Fëdorovna had gone shopping. When Ivan Ilych came home and entered his study he found his brother-in-law there—a healthy, florid man—unpacking his portmanteau himself. He raised his head on hearing Ivan Ilych's footsteps and looked up at him for a moment without a word. That stare told Ivan Ilych everything. His brother-in-law opened his mouth to utter an exclamation of surprise but checked himself, and that action confirmed it all.

"I have changed, eh?"

"Yes, there is a change."

And after that, try as he would to get his brother-in-law to return to the subject of his looks, the latter would say nothing about it. Praskovya Fëdorovna came home and her brother went out to her. Ivan Ilych locked the door and began to examine himself in the glass, first full face, then in profile. He took up a portrait of himself taken with his wife, and compared it with what he saw in the glass. The change in him was immense. Then he bared his arms to the elbow, looked at them, drew the sleeves down again, sat down on an ottoman, and grew blacker than night.

"No, no, this won't do!" he said to himself, and jumped up, went to the table, took up some law papers, and began to read them, but could not continue. He unlocked the door and went into the reception-room. The door leading to the drawing-room was shut. He approached it on tiptoe and listened.

"No, you are exaggerating!" Praskovya Fëdorovna was saying.

"Exaggerating! Don't you see it? Why, he's a dead man! Look at his eyes—there's no light in them. But what is it that is wrong with him?"

"No one knows. Nikolaevich said something, but I don't know what. And Leshchetitsky[6] said quite the contrary...."

Ivan Ilych walked away, went to his own room, lay down, and began musing: "The kidney, a floating kidney." He recalled all the doctors had told him of how it detached itself and swayed about. And by an effort of imagination he tried to catch that kidney and arrest it and support it. So little was needed for this, it seemed to him. "No, I'll go to see Peter Ivanovich again."[7] He rang, ordered the carriage, and got ready to go.

"Where are you going, Jean?" asked his wife, with a specially sad and exceptionally kind look.

This exceptionally kind look irritated him. He looked morosely at her.

"I must go to see Peter Ivanovich."

He went to see Peter Ivanovich, and together they went to see his friend, the doctor. He was in, and Ivan Ilych had a long talk with him.

Reviewing the anatomical and physiological details of what in the doctor's opinion was going on inside him, he understood it all.

There was something, a small thing, in the vermiform appendix. It might all come right. Only stimulate the energy of one organ and check the activity of another, then absorption would take place and everything would come right. He got home rather late for dinner, ate his dinner, and conversed cheerfuly, but could not for a long time bring himself to go back to work in his room. At last, however, he went to his study and did what was necessary, but the consciousness that he had put something aside—an important, intimate matter which he would revert to when his work was done—never left him. When he had finished his work he remembered that this intimate matter was the thought of his vermiform appendix. But he did not give himself up to it, and went to the drawing room for tea. There were callers there, including the examining magistrate who was a desirable match for his daughter, and they were conversing, playing the piano, and singing. Ivan Ilych, as Praskovya Fëdorovna remarked, spent that evening more cheerfully than usual, but he never for a moment forgot that he had postponed the important matter of the appendix. At eleven o'clock he said good-night and went to his bedroom. Since his illness he had slept alone in a small room next to his study. He undressed and took up a novel by Zola, but instead of reading it he fell into thought, and in his imagination that desired improvement in the vermiform appendix occurred. There was the absorption and evacuation and the re-establishment of normal activity. "Yes, that's it!" he said to himself. "One need only assist nature, that's all." He remembered his medicine, rose, took it, and lay down on his back watching for the beneficent action of the medicine and for it to lessen the pain. "I need only take it regularly and avoid all injurious influences. I am already feeling better, much better." He began touching his side: it was not painful to the touch. "There, I really

---

[6] Nikolaevich, Leshchetitsky, two doctors, the latter a celebrated specialist. [TRANS.]   [7] That was the friend whose friend was a doctor. [TRANS.]

don't feel it. It's much better already." He put out the light and turned on his side…. "The appendix is getting better, absorption is occurring." Suddenly he felt the old, familiar, dull, gnawing pain, stubborn and serious. There was the same familiar loathsome taste in his mouth. His heart sank and he felt dazed. "My God! My God!" he muttered. "Again, again! and it will never cease." And suddenly the matter presented itself in a quite different aspect. "Vermiform appendix! Kidney!" he said to himself. "It's not a question of appendix or kidney, but of life and…death. Yes, life was there and now it is going, going and I cannot stop it. Yes. Why deceive myself? Isn't it obvious to everyone but me that I'm dying, and that it's only a question of weeks, days…it may happen this moment. There was light and now there is darkness. I was here and now I'm going there! Where?" A chill came over him, his breathing ceased, and he felt only the throbbing of his heart.

"When I am not, what will there be? There will he nothing. Then where shall I be when I am no more? Can this be dying? No, I don't want to!" He jumped up and tried to light the candle, felt for it with trembling hands, dropped candle and candlestick on the floor, and fell back on his pillow.

"What's the use? It makes no difference," he said to himself, staring with wide-open eyes into the darkness. "Death. Yes, death. And none of them know or wish to know it, and they have no pity for me. Now they are playing." (He heard through the door the distant sound of a song and its accompaniment.) "It's all the same to them, but they will die too! Fools! I first, and they later, but it will be the same for them. And now they are merry…the beasts!"

Anger choked him and he was agonizingly, unbearably miserable. "It is impossible that all men have been doomed to suffer this awful horror!" He raised himself.

"Something must be wrong. I must calm myself—must think it all over from the beginning." And he again began thinking. "Yes, the beginning of my illness: I knocked my side, but I was still quite well that day and the next. It hurt a little, then rather more. I saw the doctors, then followed despondency and anguish, more doctors, and I drew nearer to the abyss. My strength grew less and I kept coming nearer and nearer, and now I have wasted away and there is no light in my eyes. I think of the appendix—but this is death! I think of mending the appendix, and all the while here is death! Can it really be death?" Again terror seized him and he gasped for breath. He leant down and began feeling for the matches, pressing with his elbow on the stand beside the bed. It was in his way and hurt him, he grew furious with it, pressed on it still harder, and upset it. Breathless and in despair he fell on his back, expecting death to come immediately.

Meanwhile the visitors were leaving. Praskovya Fëdorovna was seeing them off. She heard something fall and came in.

"What has happened?"

"Nothing. I knocked it over accidentally."

She went out and returned with a candle. He lay there panting heavily, like a man who has run a thousand yards, and stared upwards at her with a fixed look.

"What is it Jean?"

"No…o…thing. I upset it." ("Why speak of it? She won't understand," he thought.)

And in truth she did not understand. She picked up the stand, lit his candle, and hurried away to see another visitor off. When she came back he still lay on his back, looking upwards.

"What is it? Do you feel worse?"

"Yes."

She shook her head and sat down.

"Do you know, Jean, I think we must ask Leshchetitsky to come and see you here."

This meant calling in the famous specialist, regardless of expense. He smiled malignantly and said "No." She remained a little longer and then went up to him and kissed his forehead.

While she was kissing him he hated her from the bottom of his soul and with difficulty refrained from pushing her away.

"Good-night. Please God you'll sleep."

"Yes."

VI

Ivan Ilych saw that he was dying and he was in continual despair.

In the depth of his heart he knew he was dying, but not only was he not accustomed to the thought, he simply did not and could not grasp it.

The syllogism he had learnt from Kiezewetter's Logic: "Caius is a man, men are mortal, therefore Caius is mortal," had always seemed to him correct as applied to Caius, but certainly not as applied to himself. That Caius—man in the abstract—was mortal, was perfectly correct, but he was not Caius, not an abstract man, but a creature quite, quite separate from all others. He had been little Vanya, with a mamma and a papa, with Mitya and Volodya, with the toys, a coachman and a nurse, afterwards with Katenka and with all the joys, griefs, and delights of childhood, boyhood, and youth. What did Caius know of the smell of that striped leather ball Vanya had been so fond of? Had Caius kissed his mother's hand like that, and did the silk of her dress rustle so for Caius? Had he rioted like that at school when the pastry was bad? Had Caius been in love like that? Could Caius preside at a session as he did? "Caius really was mortal, and it was right for him to die; but for me, little Vanya, Ivan Ilych, with all my thoughts and emotions, it's altogether a different matter. It cannot be that I ought to die. That would be too terrible."

Such was his feeling.

"If I had to die like Caius I should have known it was so. An inner voice would have told me so, but there was nothing of the sort in me and I and all my friends felt that our case was quite different from that of Caius. And now here it is!" he said to himself. "It can't be. It's impossible But here it is. How is this? How is one to understand it?"

He could not understand it, and tried to drive this false, incorrect, morbid thought away and to replace it by other proper and healthy thoughts. But that thought, and not the thought only but the reality itself, seemed to come and confront him.

And to replace that thought he called up a succession of others, hoping to find in them some support. He tried to get back into the former current of thoughts that had once screened the thought of death from him. But strange to say, all that had formerly shut off, hidden, and destroyed his consciousness of death, no longer had that effect. Ivan Ilych now spent most of his time in attempting to reestablish that old current. He would say to himself: "I will take up my duties again—after all I used to live by them." And banishing all doubts he would go to the law courts, enter into conversation with his colleagues, and sit carelessly as was his wont, scanning the crowd with a thoughtful look and leaning both his emaciated arms on the arms of his oak chair; bending over as usual to a colleague and drawing his papers nearer he would interchange whispers with him, and then suddenly raising his eyes and sitting erect would pronounce certain words and open the proceedings. But suddenly in the midst of those proceedings the pain in his side, regardless of the stage the proceedings had reached, would begin its own gnawing work. Ivan Ilych would turn his attention to it and try to drive the thought of it away, but without success. *It* would come and stand before him and look at him, and he would be petrified and the light would die out of his eyes, and he would again begin asking himself whether *It* alone was true. And his colleagues and subordinates would see with surprise and distress that he, the brilliant and subtle judge, was becoming confused and making mistakes. He would shake himself, try to pull himself together, manage somehow to bring the sitting to a close, and return home with the sorrowful consciousness that his judicial labours could not as formerly hide from him what he wanted them to hide, and could not deliver him from *It*. And what was worst of all was that *It* drew his attention to itself not in order to make him take some action but only that he should look at *It*, look it straight in the face: look at it and, without doing anything, suffer inexpressibly.

And to save himself from this condition Ivan Ilych looked for consolations—new screens—and new screens were found and for a while seemed to save him, but then they immediately fell to pieces or rather became transparent, as if *It* penetrated them and nothing could veil *It*.

In these latter days he would go into the drawing room he had arranged—that drawing room where he had fallen and for the sake of which (how bitterly ridiculous it seemed) he had sacrificed his life—for he knew that his illness originated with that knock. He would enter and see that something had scratched the polished table. He would look for the cause of this and find that it was the bronze ornamentation of an album, that had got bent. He would take up the expensive album which he had lovingly arranged, and feel vexed with his daughter and her friends for their untidiness—for the album was torn here and there and some of the photographs turned upside down. He would put it carefully in order and bend the ornamentation back into position. Then it would occur to him to place all those things in another corner of the room, near the plants. He would call the footman, but his daughter or wife would come to help him. They would not agree, and his wife would contradict him, and he would dispute and grow angry. But that was all right, for then he did not think about *It*. *It* was invisible.

But then, when he was moving something himself, his wife would say: "Let the servants do it. You will hurt yourself again." And suddenly *It* would flash through the screen and he would see it. It was just a flash, and he hoped it would disappear, but he would involuntarily pay attention to his side. "It sits there as before, gnawing just the same!" And he could no longer forget *It,* but could distinctly see it looking at him from behind the flowers. "What is it all for?"

"It really is so! I lost my life over that curtain as I might have done when storming a fort. Is that possible? How terrible and how stupid. It can't be true! It can't, but it is."

He would go to his study, lie down, and again be alone with *It:* face to face with *It*. And nothing could be done with *It* except to look at it and shudder.

VII

How it happened it is impossible to say because it came about step by step, unnoticed, but in the third month of Ivan Ilych's illness, his wife, his daughter, his son, his acquaintances, the doctors, the servants, and above all he himself, were aware that the whole interest he had for other people was whether he would soon vacate his place, and at last release the living from the discomfort caused by his presence and he himself released from his sufferings.

He slept less and less. He was given opium and hypodermic injections of morphine, but this did not relieve him. The dull depression he experienced in a somnolent condition at first gave him a little relief, but only as something new, afterwards it became as distressing as the pain itself or even more so.

Special foods were prepared for him by the doctors' orders, but all those foods became increasingly distasteful and disgusting to him.

For his excretions also special arrangements had to be made, and this was a torment to him every time—a torment from the uncleanliness, the unseemliness, and the smell, and from knowing that another person had to take part in it.

But just through this most unpleasant matter, Ivan Ilych obtained comfort. Gerasim, the butler's young assistant, always came in to carry the things out. Gerasim was a clean, fresh peasant lad, grown stout on town food and always cheerful and bright. At first the sight of him, in his clean Russian peasant costume, engaged on that disgusting task embarrassed Ivan Ilych.

Once when he got up from the commode too weak to draw up his trousers, he dropped into a soft armchair and looked with horror at his bare, enfeebled thighs with the muscles so sharply marked on them.

Gerasim with a firm light tread, his heavy boots emitting a pleasant smell of tar and fresh winter air, came in wearing a clean Hessian apron, the sleeves of his print shirt tucked up over his strong, bare young arms; and refraining from looking at his sick master out of consideration for his feelings, and restraining the joy of life that beamed from his face, he went up to the commode.

"Gerasim!" said Ivan Ilych in a weak voice.

Gerasim started, evidently afraid he might have committed some blunder, and with a rapid movement turned his fresh, kind, simple young face which just showed the first downy signs of a beard.

"Yes, sir?"

"That must be very unpleasant for you. You must forgive me. I am helpless."

"Oh, why, sir," and Gerasim's eyes beamed and he showed his glistening white teeth, "what's a little trouble? It's a case of illness with you, sir."

And his deft strong hands did their accustomed task, and he went out of the room stepping lightly. Five minutes later he as lightly returned.

Ivan Ilych was still sitting in the same position in the armchair.

"Gerasim," he said when the latter had replaced the freshly-washed utensil. "Please come here and help me." Gerasim went up to him. "Lift me up. It is hard for me to get up, and I have sent Dmitri away."

Gerasim went up to him, grasped his master with his strong arms deftly but gently, in the same way that he stepped—lifted him, supported him with one hand, and with the other drew up his trousers and would have set him down again, but Ivan Ilych asked to be led to the sofa. Gerasim, without an effort and without apparent pressure, led him, almost lifting him, to the sofa and placed him on it.

"Thank you. How easily and well you do it all!"

Gerasim smiled again and turned to leave the room. But Ivan Ilych felt his presence such a comfort that he did not want to let him go.

"One thing more, please move up that chair. No, the other one—under my feet. It is easier for me when my feet are raised."

Gerasim brought the chair, set it down gently in place, and raised Ivan Ilych's legs on to it. It seemed to Ivan Ilych that he felt better while Gerasim was holding up his legs.

"It's better when my legs are higher," he said. "Place that cushion under them."

Gerasim did so. He again lifted the legs and placed them, and again Ivan Ilych felt better while Gerasim held his legs. When he set them down Ivan Ilych fancied he felt worse.

"Gerasim," he said. "Are you busy now?"

"Not at all, sir," said Gerasim, who had learnt from the townsfolk how to speak to gentlefolk.

"What have you still to do?"

"What have I to do? I've done everything except chopping the logs for tomorrow."

"Then hold my legs up a bit higher, can you?"

"Of course I can. Why not?" And Gerasim raised his master's legs higher and Ivan Ilych thought that in that position he did not feel any pain at all.

"And how about the logs?"

"Don't trouble about that, sir. There's plenty of time."

Ivan Ilych told Gerasim to sit down and hold his legs, and began to talk to him. And strange to say it seemed to him that he felt better while Gerasim held his legs up.

After that Ivan Ilych would sometimes call Gerasim and get him to hold his legs on his shoulders, and he liked talking to him. Gerasim did it all easily, willingly, simply, and with a good nature that touched Ivan Ilych. Health, strength, and vitality in other people were offensive to him, but Gerasim's strength and vitality did not mortify but soothed him.

What tormented Ivan Ilych most was the deception, the lie, which for some reason they all accepted, that he was not dying but was simply ill, and that he only need keep quiet and undergo a treatment and then something very good would result. He however knew that do what they would nothing would come of it, only still more agonizing suffering and death. This deception tortured him—their not wishing to admit what they all knew and what he knew, but wanting to lie to him concerning his terrible condition, and wishing and forcing him to participate in that lie. Those lies—lies enacted over him on the eve of his death and destined to degrade this awful, solemn act to the level of their visitings, their curtains, their sturgeon for dinner—were a terrible agony for Ivan Ilych. And strangely enough, many times when they were going through their antics over him he had been within a hairbreadth of calling out to them: "Stop lying! You know and I know that I am dying. Then at least stop lying about it!" But he had never had the spirit to do it. The awful, terrible act of his dying was, he could see, reduced by those about him to the level of a casual, unpleasant, and almost indecorous incident (as if someone entered a drawing room diffusing an unpleasant odour) and this was done by that very decorum which he had served all his life long. He saw that no one felt for him, because no one even wished to grasp his position. Only Gerasim recognized it and pitied him. And so Ivan Ilych felt at ease only with him. He felt comforted when Gerasim supported his legs (sometimes all night long) and refused to go to bed, saying: "Don't you worry, Ivan Ilych. I'll get sleep enough later on," or when he suddenly became familiar and exclaimed: "If you weren't sick it would be another matter, but as it is, why should I grudge a little trouble?" Gerasim alone did not lie; everything showed that he alone understood the facts of the case and did not consider it necessary to disguise them, but simply felt sorry for his emaciated and enfeebled master. Once when Ivan Ilych was sending him away he even said straight out: "We shall all of us die, so why should I grudge a little trouble?"— expressing the fact that he did not think his work burdensome, because he was doing it for a dying man and hoped someone would do the same for him when his time came.

Apart from this lying, or because of it, what most tormented Ivan Ilych was that no one pitied him as he wished to be pitied. At certain moments after prolonged suffering he wished most of all (though he would have been ashamed to confess it) for someone to pity him as a sick child is pitied. He longed to be petted and comforted. He knew he was an important functionary, that he had a beard turning grey, and that therefore what he longed for was impossible, but still he longed for it. And in Gerasim's attitude towards him there was something akin to what he wished for, and so that attitude comforted him. Ivan Ilych wanted to weep, wanted to be petted and cried over, and then his colleague Shebek would come, and instead of weeping and being petted, Ivan Ilych would assume a serious, severe, and profound air, and by force of habit would express his opinion on a decision of the Court of Cassation and would stubbornly insist on that view. This falsity around him and within him did more than anything else to poison his last days.

VIII

It was morning. He knew it was morning because Gerasim had gone, and Peter the footman had come and put out the candles, drawn back one of the curtains, and begun quietly to tidy up. Whether it was morning or evening, Friday or Sunday, made no difference, it was all just the same: the gnawing, unmitigated, agonizing pain, never ceasing for an instant, the consciousness of life inexorably waning but not yet extinguished, the approach of that ever dreaded and hateful Death which was the only reality, and always the same falsity. What were days, weeks, hours, in such a case?

"Will you have some tea, sir?"

"He wants things to be regular, and wishes the gentlefolk to drink tea in the morning," thought Ivan Ilych, and only said "No."

"Wouldn't you like to move onto the sofa, sir?"

"He wants to tidy up the room, and I'm in the way. I am uncleanliness and disorder," he thought, and said only:

"No, leave me alone."

The man went on bustling about. Ivan Ilych stretched out his hand. Peter came up, ready to help.

"What is it, sir?"

"My watch."

Peter took the watch which was close at hand and gave it to his master.

"Half-past eight. Are they up?"

"No, sir, except Vladimir Ivanovich" (the son) "who has gone to school. Praskovya Fëdorovna ordered me to wake her if you asked for her. Shall I do so?"

"No, there's no need to." "Perhaps I'd better have some tea," he thought, and added aloud: "Yes, bring me some tea."

Peter went to the door, but Ivan Ilych dreaded being left alone. "How can I keep him here? Oh yes, my medicine." "Peter, give me my medicine." "Why not? Perhaps it may still do me some good." He took a spoonful and swallowed it. "No, it won't help. It's all tomfoolery, all deception," he decided as soon as he became aware of the familiar, sickly hopeless taste. "No, I can't believe in it any longer. But the pain, why this pain? If it would only cease just for a moment!" And he moaned. Peter turned towards him. "It's all right. Go and fetch me some tea."

Peter went out. Left alone Ivan Ilych groaned not so much with pain, terrible though that was, as from mental anguish. Always and for ever the same, always these endless days and nights. If only it would come quicker! If only what would come quicker? Death darkness?... No, no! Anything rather than death!

When Peter returned with the tea on a tray, Ivan Ilych stared at him for a time in perplexity, not realizing who and what he was. Peter was disconcerted by that look and his embarrassment brought Ivan Ilych to himself.

"Oh, tea! All right, put it down. Only help me to wash and put on a clean shirt."

And Ivan Ilych began to wash. With pauses for rest, he washed his hands and then his face, cleaned his teeth, brushed his hair, and looked in the glass. He was terrified by what he saw, especially by the limp way in which his hair clung to his pallid forehead.

While his shirt was being changed he knew that he would be still more frightened at the sight of his body, so he avoided looking at it. Finally he was ready. He drew on a dressing-gown, wrapped himself in a plaid, and sat down in the armchair to take his tea. For a moment he felt refreshed, but as soon as he began to drink the tea he was again aware of the same taste, and the pain also returned. He finished it with an effort, and then lay down stretching out his legs, and dismissed Peter.

Always the same. Now a spark of hope flashes up, then a sea of despair rages, and always pain; always pain, always despair, and always the same. When alone he had a dreadful and distressing desire to call someone, but he knew beforehand that with others present it would be still worse. "Another dose of morphine—to lose consciousness. I will tell him, the doctor, that he must think of something else. It's impossible, impossible, to go on like this."

An hour and another pass like that. But now there is a ring at the door bell. Perhaps it's the doctor? It is. He comes in fresh, hearty, plump, and cheerful, with that look on his face that seems to say: "There now, you're in a panic about something, but we'll arrange it all for you directly!" The doctor knows this expression is out of place here, but he has put it on once for all and can't take it off—like a man who has put on a frock-coat in the morning to pay a round of calls.

The doctor rubs his hands vigorously and reassuringly.

"Brr! How cold it is! There's such a sharp frost; just let me warm myself!" he says, as if it were only a matter of waiting till he was warm, and then he would put everything right.

"Well now, how are you?"

Ivan Ilych feels that the doctor would like to say: "Well, how are our affairs?" but that even he feels that this would not do, and says instead: "What sort of a night have you had?"

Ivan Ilych looks at him as much as to say: "Are you really never ashamed of lying?" But the doctor does not wish to understand this question, and Ivan Ilych says: "Just as terrible as ever. The pain never leaves me and never subsides. If only something…"

"Yes, you sick people are always like that…. There, now I think I am warm enough. Even Praskovya Fëdorovna, who is so particular, could find no fault with my temperature. Well, now I can say good morning," and the doctor presses his patient's hand.

Then, dropping his former playfulness, he begins with a most serious face to examine the patient, feeling his pulse and taking his temperature, and then begins the sounding and auscultation.

Ivan Ilych knows quite well and definitely that all this is nonsense and pure deception, but when the doctor, getting down on his knee, leans over him, putting his ear first higher then lower, and performs various gymnastic movements over him with a significant expression on his face, Ivan Ilych submits to it all as he used to submit to the speeches of the lawyers, though he knew very well that they were all lying and why they were lying.

The doctor, kneeling on the sofa, is still sounding him when Praskovya Fëdorovna's silk dress rustles at the door and she is heard scolding Peter for not having let her know of the doctor's arrival.

She comes in, kisses her husband, and at once proceeds to prove that she has been up a long time already, and only owing to a misunderstanding failed to be there when the doctor arrived.

Ivan Ilych looks at her, scans her all over, sets against her the whiteness and plumpness and cleanness of her hands and neck, the gloss of her hair, and the sparkle of her vivacious eyes. He hates her with his whole soul. And the thrill of hatred he feels for her makes him suffer from her touch.

Her attitude towards him and his disease is still the same. Just as the doctor had adopted a certain relation to his patient which he could not abandon, so had she formed one towards him—that he was not doing something he ought to do and was himself to blame, and that she reproached him lovingly for this—and she could not now change that attitude.

"You see he doesn't listen to me and doesn't take his medicine at the proper time. And above all he lies in a position that is no doubt bad for him—with his legs up."

She described how he made Gerasim hold his legs up.

The doctor smiled with a contemptuous affability that said: "What's to be done? These sick people do have foolish fancies of that kind, but we must forgive them."

When the examination was over the doctor looked at his watch, and then Praskovya Fëdorovna announced to Ivan Ilych that it was of course as he pleased, but she had sent today for a celebrated specialist who would examine him and have a consultation with Michael Danilovich (their regular doctor).

"Please don't raise any objections. I am doing this for my own sake," she said ironically, letting it be felt that she was doing it all for his sake and only said this to leave him no right to refuse. He remained silent, knitting his brows. He felt that he was so surrounded and involved in a mesh of falsity that it was hard to unravel anything.

Everything she did for him was entirely for her own sake, and she told him she was doing for herself what she actually was doing for herself, as if that was so incredible that he must understand the opposite.

At half-past eleven the celebrated specialist arrived. Again the sounding began and the significant conversations in his presence and in another room, about the kidneys and the appendix, and the questions and answers, with such an air of importance that again, instead of the real question of life and death which now alone confronted him, the question arose of the kidney and appendix which were not behaving as they ought to and would now he attacked by Michael Danilovich and the specialist and forced to amend their ways.

The celebrated specialist took leave of him with a serious though not hopeless look, and in reply to the timid question Ivan Ilych, with eyes glistening with fear and hope, put to him as to whether there was a chance of recovery, said that he could not vouch for it but there was a possibility. The look of hope with which Ivan Ilych watched the doctor out was so pathetic that Praskovya Fëdorovna, seeing it, even wept as she left the room to hand the doctor his fee.

The gleam of hope kindled by the doctor's encouragement did not last long. The same room, the same pictures, curtains, wallpaper, medicine bottles, were all there, and the same aching suffering body, and Ivan Ilych began to moan. They gave him a subcutaneous injection and he sank into oblivion.

It was twilight when he came to. They brought him his dinner and he swallowed some beef tea with difficulty, and then everything was the same again and night was coming on.

After dinner, at seven o'clock, Praskovya Fëdorovna came into the room in evening dress, her full bosom pushed up by her corset, and with traces of powder on her face. She had reminded him in the morning that they were going to the theatre. Sarah Bernhardt was visiting the town and they had a box, which he had insisted on their taking. Now he had forgotten about it and her toilet offended him, but he concealed his vexation when he remembered that he had himself insisted on their securing a box and going because it would be an instructive and aesthetic pleasure for the children.

Praskovya Fëdorovna came in, self-satisfied but yet with a rather guilty air. She sat down and asked how he was, but, as he saw, only for the sake of asking and not in order to learn about it, knowing that there was nothing to learn—and then went on to what she really wanted to say: that she would not on any account have gone but that the box had been taken and Helen and their daughter were going as well as Petrishchev (the examining magistrate, their daughter's fiancé), and that it was out of the question to let them go alone; but that she would have much preferred to sit with him for a while; and he must be sure to follow the doctor's orders while she was away.

"Oh, and Fëdor Petrovich" (the fiancé) "would like to come in. May he? And Lisa?"

"All right."

Their daughter came in in full evening dress, her fresh young flesh exposed (making a show of that very flesh which in his own case caused so much suffering), strong, healthy, evidently in love, and impatient with illness, suffering, and death, because they interfered with her happiness.

Fëdor Petrovich came in too, in evening dress, his hair curled *à la Capoul*, a tight stiff collar round his long sinewy neck, an enormous white shirt-front, and narrow black trousers tightly stretched over his strong thighs. He had one white glove tightly drawn on, and was holding his opera hat in his hand.

Following him the schoolboy crept in unnoticed, in a new uniform, poor little fellow, and wearing gloves. Terribly dark shadows showed under his eyes, the meaning of which Ivan Ilych knew well.

His son had always seemed pathetic to him, and now it was dreadful to see the boy's frightened look of pity. It seemed to Ivan Ilych that Vasya was the only one besides Gerasim who understood and pitied him.

They all sat down and again asked how he was. A silence followed. Lisa asked her mother about the opera-glasses, and there was an altercation between mother and daughter as to who had taken them and where they had been put. This occasioned some unpleasantness.

Fëdor Petrovich inquired of Ivan Ilych whether he had ever seen Sarah Bernhardt. Ivan ilych did not at first catch the question, but then replied: "No, have you seen her before?"

"Yes, in *Adrienne Lecouvreur*."

Praskovya Fëdorovna mentioned some rôles in which Sarah Bernhardt was particularly good. Her daughter disagreed. Conversation sprang up as to the elegance and realism of her acting—the sort of conversation that is always repeated and is always the same.

In the midst of the conversation Fëdor Petrovich glanced at Ivan Ilych and became silent. The others also looked at him and grew silent. Ivan Ilych was staring with glittering eyes straight before him, evidently indignant with them. This had to be rectified, but it was impossible to do so. The silence had to be broken, but for a time no one dared to break it and they all became afraid that the conventional deception would suddenly become obvious and the truth become plain to all. Lisa was the first to pluck up courage and break that silence, but by trying to hide what everybody was feeling, she betrayed it.

"Well, if we are going it's time to start," she said, looking at her watch, a present from her father, and with a faint and significant smile at Fëdor Petrovich relating to something known only to them. She got up with a rustle of her dress.

They all rose, said good-night, and went away.

When they had gone it seemed to Ivan Ilych that he felt better; the falsity had gone with them. But the pain remained—that same pain and that same fear that made everything monotonously alike, nothing harder and nothing easier. Everything was worse.

Again minute followed minute and hour followed hour. Everything remained the same and there was no cessation. And the inevitable end of it all became more and more terrible.

"Yes, send Gerasim here," he replied to a question Peter asked.

IX

His wife returned late at night. She came in on tiptoe, but he heard her, opened his eyes, and made haste to close them again. She wished to send Gerasim away and to sit with him herself, but he opened his eyes and said: "No, go away."

"Are you in great pain?"

"Always the same."

"Take some opium."

He agreed and took some. She went away.

Till about three in the morning he was in a state of stupefied misery. It seemed to him that he and his pain were being thrust into a narrow, deep black sack, but though they were pushed further and further in they could not be pushed to the bottom. And this, terrible enough in itself, was accompanied by suffering. He was frightened yet wanted to fall through the sack, he struggled but yet cooperated. And suddenly he broke through, fell, and regained consciousness. Gerasim was sitting at the foot of the bed dozing quietly and patiently, while he himself lay with his emaciated stockinged legs resting on Gerasim's shoulders; the same shaded candle was there and the same unceasing pain.

"Go away, Gerasim," he whispered.

"It's all right, sir. I'll stay a while."

"No. Go away."

He removed his legs from Gerasim's shoulders, turned sideways onto his arm, and felt sorry for himself. He only waited till Gerasim had gone into the next room and then restrained himself no longer but wept like a child. He wept on account of his helplessness, his terrible loneliness, the cruelty of man, the cruelty of God, and the absence of God.

"Why hast Thou done all this? Why hast Thou brought me here? Why, why dost Thou torment me so terribly?"

He did not expect an answer and yet wept because there was no answer and could be none. The pain again grew more acute, but he did not stir and did not call. He said to himself: "Go on! Strike me! But what is it for? What have I done to Thee? What is it for?"

Then he grew quiet and not only ceased weeping but even held his breath and became all attention. It was as though he were listening not to an audible voice but to the voice of his soul, to the current of thoughts arising within him.

"What is it you want?" was the first clear conception capable of expression in words, that he heard.

"What do you want? What do you want?" he repeated to himself.

"What do I want? To live and not to suffer," he answered.

And again he listened with such concentrated attention that even his pain did not distract him.

"To live? How?" asked his inner voice.

"Why, to live as I used to—well and pleasantly."

"As you lived before, well and pleasantly?" the voice repeated.

And in imagination he began to recall the best moments of his pleasant life. But strange to say none of those best moments of his pleasant life now seemed at all what they had then seemed—none of them except the first recollections of childhood. There, in childhood, there had been something really pleasant with which it would be possible to live if it could return. But the child who had experienced that happiness existed no longer, it was like a reminiscence of somebody else.

As soon as the period began which had produced the present Ivan Ilych, all that had then seemed joys now melted before his sight and turned into something trivial and often nasty.

And the further he departed from childhood and the nearer he came to the present the more worthless and doubtful were the joys. This began with the School of Law. A little that was really good was still found there—there was lightheartedness, friendship, and hope. But in the upper classes there had already been fewer of such good moments. Then during the first years of his official career, when he was in the service of the Governor, some pleasant moments again occurred; they were the memories of love for a woman. Then all became confused and there was still less of what was good; later on again there was still less that was good, and the further he went the less there was. His marriage, a mere accident, then the disenchantment that followed it, his wife's bad breath and the sensuality and hypocrisy: then that deadly official life and those preoccupations about money, a year of it, and two, and ten, and twenty, and always the same thing. And the longer it lasted the more deadly it became. "It is as if I had been going downhill while I imagined I was going up. And that is really what it was. I was going up in public opinion, but to the same extent life was ebbing away from me. And now it is all done and there is only death."

"Then what does it mean? Why? It can't be that life is so senseless and horrible. But if it really has been so horrible and senseless, why must I die and die in agony? There is something wrong!"

"Maybe I did not live as I ought to have done," it suddenly occurred to him. "But how could that be, when I did everything properly?" he replied, and immediately dismissed from his mind this, the sole solution of all the riddles of life and death, as something quite impossible.

"Then what do you want now? To live? Live how? Live as you lived in the law courts when the usher proclaimed 'The judge is coming!' The judge is coming, the judge!" he repeated to himself. "Here he is, the judge. But I am not guilty!" he exclaimed angrily. "What is it for?" And he ceased crying, but turning his face to the wall continued to ponder on the same question: Why, and for what purpose, is there all this horror? But however much he pondered he found no answer. And whenever the thought occurred to him, as it often did, that it all resulted from his not having lived as he ought to have done, he at once recalled the correctness of his whole life and dismissed so strange an idea.

X

Another fortnight passed. Ivan Ilych now no longer left his sofa. He would not lie in bed but lay on the sofa, facing the wall nearly all the time. He suffered ever the same unceasing agonies and in his loneliness pondered always on the same insoluble question: "What is this? Can it be that it is Death?" And the inner voice answered: "Yes, it is Death."

"Why these sufferings?" And the voice answered, "For no reason—they just are so." Beyond and besides this there was nothing.

From the very beginning of his illness, ever since he had first been to see the doctor, Ivan Ilych's life had been divided between two contrary and alternating moods: now it was despair and the expectation of this uncomprehended and terrible death, and now hope and an intently interested observation of the functioning of his organs. Now before his eyes there was only a kidney or an intestine that temporarily evaded its duty, and now only that incomprehensible and dreadful death from which it was impossible to escape.

These two states of mind had alternated from the very beginning of his illness, but the further it progressed the more doubtful and fantastic became the conception of the kidney, and the more real the sense of impending death.

He had but to call to mind what he had been three months before and what he was now, to call to mind with what regularity he had been going downhill, for every possibility of hope to be shattered.

Latterly during that loneliness in which he found himself as he lay facing the back of the sofa, a loneliness in the midst of a populous town and surrounded by numerous acquaintances and relations but that yet could not have been more complete anywhere—either at the bottom of the sea or under the earth—during that terrible loneliness Ivan Ilych had lived only in memories of the past. Pictures of his past rose before him one after another. They always began with what was nearest in time and then went back to what was most remote—to his childhood—and rested there. If he thought of the stewed prunes that had been offered him that day, his mind went back to the raw shrivelled French plums of his childhood, their peculiar flavour and the flow of saliva when he sucked their stones and along with the memory of that taste came a whole series of memories of those days: his nurse, his brother, and their toys. "No, I mustn't think of that.... It is too painful," Ivan Ilych said to himself, and brought himself back to the present—to the button on the back of the sofa and the creases in its morocco. "Morocco is expensive, but it does not wear well: there had been a quarrel about it. It was a different kind of quarrel and a different kind of morocco that time when we tore father's portfolio and were punished, and mamma brought us some tarts...." And again his thoughts dwelt on his childhood, and again it was painful and he tried to banish them and fix his mind on something else.

Then again together with that chain of memories another series passed through his mind—of how his illness had progressed and grown worse. There also the further back he looked the more life there had been. There had been more of what was good in life and more of life itself. The two merged together. "Just as the pain went on getting worse and worse, so my life grew worse and worse," he thought. "There is one bright spot there at the back, at the beginning of life, and afterwards all becomes blacker and blacker and proceeds more and more rapidly—in inverse ratio to the square of the distance from death," thought Ivan Ilych. And the example of a stone falling downwards with increasing velocity entered his mind. Life, a series of increasing sufferings, flies further and further towards its end—the most terrible suffering. "I am flying...." He shuddered, shifted himself, and tried to resist, but was already aware that resistance was impossible, and again, with eyes weary of gazing but unable to cease seeing what was before them, he stared at the back of the sofa and waited—awaiting that dreadful fall and shock and destruction.

"Resistance is impossible!" he said to himself. "If I could only understand what it is all for! But that too is impossible. An explanation would be possible if it could be said that I have not lived as I ought to. But it is impossible to say that," and he remembered all the legality, correctitude, and propriety of his life. "That at any rate can certainly not be admitted," he thought, and his lips smiled ironically as if someone could see that smile and be taken in by it. "There is no explanation! Agony, death...What for?"

XI

Another two weeks went by in this way and during that fortnight an event occurred that Ivan Ilych and his wife had desired. Petrishchev formally proposed. It happened in the evening. The next day Praskovya Fëdorovna came into her husband's room considering how best to inform him of it, but that very night there had been a fresh change for the worse in his condition. She found him still lying on the sofa but in a different position. He lay on his back, groaning and staring fixedly straight in front of him.

She began to remind him of his medicines, but he turned his eyes towards her with such a look that she did not finish what she was saying; so great an animosity, to her in particular, did that look express.

"For Christ's sake let me die in peace!" he said.

She would have gone away, but just then their daughter came in and went up to say good morning. He looked at her as he had done at his wife, and in reply to her inquiry about his health said dryly that he would soon free them all of himself. They were both silent and after sitting with him for a while went away.

"Is it our fault?" Lisa said to her mother. "It's as if we were to blame! I am sorry for papa, but why should we be tortured?"

The doctor came at his usual time. Ivan Ilych answered "Yes" and "No," never taking his angry eyes from him, and at last said: "You know you can do nothing for me, so leave me alone."

"We can ease your sufferings."

"You can't even do that. Let me be."

The doctor went into the drawing-room and told Praskovya Fëdorovna that the case was very serious and that the only resource left was opium to allay her husband's sufferings, which must be terrible.

It was true, as the doctor said, that Ivan Ilych's physical sufferings were terrible, but worse than the physical sufferings were his mental sufferings, which were his chief torture.

His mental sufferings were due to the fact that that night, as he looked at Gerasim's sleepy, good-natured face with its prominent cheekbones, the question suddenly occurred to him: "What if my whole life has really been wrong?"

It occurred to him that what had appeared perfectly impossible before, namely that he had not spent his life as he should have done, might after all be true. It occurred to him that his scarcely perceptible attempts to struggle against what was considered good by the most highly placed people, those scarcely noticeable impulses which he had immediately suppressed, might have been the real thing, and all the rest false. And his professional duties and the whole arrangement of his life and of his family, and all his social and official interests, might all have been false. He tried to defend all those things to himself and suddenly felt the weakness of what he was defending. There was nothing to defend.

"But if that is so," he said to himself, "and I am leaving this life with the consciousness that I have lost all that was given me and it is impossible to rectify it— what then?"

He lay on his back and began to pass his life in review in quite a new way. In the morning when he saw first his footman, then his wife, then his daughter, and then the doctor, their every word and movement confirmed to him the awful truth that had been revealed to him during the night. In them he saw himself—all that for which he had lived—and saw clearly that it was not real at all, but a terrible and huge deception which had hidden both life and death. This consciousness intensified his physical suffering tenfold. He groaned and tossed about, and pulled at his clothing which choked and stifled him. And he hated them on that account.

He was given a large dose of opium and became unconscious, but at noon his sufferings began again. He drove everybody away and tossed from side to side.

His wife came to him and said:

"Jean, my dear, do this for me. It can't do any harm and often helps. Healthy people often do it."

He opened his eyes wide.

"What? Take communion? Why? It's unnecessary! However…"

She began to cry.

"Yes, do, my dear. I'll send for our priest. He is such a nice man."

"All right. Very well," he muttered.

When the priest came and heard his confession, Ivan Ilych was softened and seemed to feel a relief from his doubts and consequently from his sufferings, and for a moment there came a ray of hope. He again began to think of the vermiform appendix and the possibility of correcting it. He received the sacrament with tears in his eyes.

When they laid him down again afterwards he felt a moment's ease, and the hope that he might live awoke in him again. He began to think of the operation that had been suggested to him. "To live! I want to live!" he said to himself.

His wife came in to congratulate him after his communion, and when uttering the usual conventional words she added:

"You feel better, don't you?"

Without looking at her he said "Yes."

Her dress, her figure, the expression of her face, the tone of her voice, all revealed the same thing. "This is wrong, it is not as it should be. All you have lived for and still live for is falsehood and deception, hiding life and death from you." And as soon as he admitted that thought, his hatred and his agonizing physical suffering again sprang up, and with that suffering a consciousness of the unavoidable, approaching end. And to this was added a new sensation of grinding shooting pain and a feeling of suffocation.

The expression of his face when he uttered that "yes" was dreadful. Having uttered it, he looked her straight in the eyes, turned on his face with a rapidity extraordinary in his weak state and shouted:

"Go away! Go away and leave me alone!"

XII

From that moment the screaming began that continued for three days, and was so terrible that one could not hear it through two closed doors without horror. At the moment he answered his wife he realized that he was lost, that there was no return, that the end had come, the very end, and his doubts were still unsolved and remained doubts.

"Oh! Oh! Oh!" he cried in various intonations. He had begun by screaming "I won't!" and continued screaming on the letter *O*.

For three whole days, during which time did not exist for him, he struggled in that black sack into which he was being thrust by an invisible, resistless force. He struggled as a man condemned to death struggles in the hands of the executioner, knowing that he cannot save himself. And every moment he felt that despite all his efforts he was drawing nearer and nearer to what terrified him. He felt that his agony was due to his being thrust into that black hole and still more to his not being able to get right into it. He was hindered from getting into it by his conviction that his life had been a good one. That very justification of his life held him fast and prevented his moving forward, and it caused him most torment of all.

Suddenly some force struck him in the chest and side, making it still harder to breathe, and he fell through the hole and there at the bottom was a light. What had happened to him was like the sensation one sometimes experiences in a railway carriage when one thinks one is going backwards while one is really going forwards and suddenly becomes aware of the real direction.

"Yes, it was all not the right thing," he said to himself, "but that's no matter. It can be done. But what *is* the right thing?" he asked himself, and suddenly grew quiet.

This occurred at the end of the third day, two hours before his death. Just then his schoolboy son had crept softly in and gone up to the bedside. The dying man was still screaming desperately and waving his arms. His hand fell on the boy's head, and the boy caught it, pressed it to his lips, and began to cry.

At that very moment Ivan Ilych fell through and caught sight of the light, and it was revealed to him that though his life had not been what it should have been, this could still be rectified. He asked himself, "What *is* the right thing?" and grew still, listening. Then he felt that someone was kissing his hand. He opened his eyes, looked at his son, and felt sorry for him. His wife came up to him and he glanced at her. She was gazing at him open-mouthed, with undried tears on her nose and cheek and a despairing look on her face. He felt sorry for her too.

"Yes, I am making them wretched," he thought. "They are sorry, but it will be better for them when I die." He wished to say this but had not the strength to utter it. "Besides, why speak? I must act," he thought. With a look at his wife he indicated his son and said: "Take him away...sorry for him...sorry for you too..." He tried to add, "Forgive me," but said "forgo" and waved his hand, knowing that He whose understanding mattered would understand.

And suddenly it grew clear to him that what had been oppressing him and would not leave him was all dropping away at once from two sides, from ten sides, and from all sides. He was sorry for them, he must act so as not to hurt them: release them and free himself from these sufferings. "How good and how simple!" he thought. "And the pain?" he asked himself. "What has become of it? Where are you, pain?"

He turned his attention to it.

"Yes, here it is. Well, what of it? Let the pain be."

"And death...where is it?"

He sought his former accustomed fear of death and did not find it. "Where is it? What death?" There was no fear because there was no death.

In place of death there was light.

"So that's what it is!" he suddenly exclaimed aloud. "What joy!"

To him all this happened in a single instant, and the meaning of that instant did not change. For those present his agony continued for another two hours. Something rattled in his throat, his emaciated body twitched, then the gasping and rattle became less and less frequent.

"It is finished!" said someone near him.

He heard these words and repeated them in his soul.

"Death is finished," he said to himself. "It is no more!"

He drew in a breath, stopped in the midst of a sigh, stretched out, and died.

Translated by Louise and Maude Aylmer

Journal Entry

Apply this Zen proverb to "The Death of Ivan Ilych": "No day comes back again; an inch of time is worth a foot of jade."

Textual Considerations

1. Why does Tolstoy begin with Ivan's death as a prelude to the story of his life? What are the effects of narrating Part I from the point of view of a minor character?
2. What is your reaction to the way in which Ivan's family and friends respond to his death? Are their attitudes toward death in general similar to or different from those of society today? Explain.
3. What evidence does Tolstoy cite to support the first sentence in Part II? Consider, for example, the description of Ivan's childhood, education, and career, as well as his attitudes towards marriage and success. Is there anything wrong with his ambitions? To what extent do you disagree or agree with Tolstoy's assessment?
4. As Ivan confronts his powerlessness in the face of the indignities of disease and his impending death, he becomes increasingly alienated from his family and friends. Why? Cite evidence.
5. What is Gerasim's role in the story? How is his philosophy about sickness and death different from that of the others? Why does Ivan derive comfort from his presence? How do you explain his kindness to Ivan?
6. Why does Ivan think increasingly of his childhood in his dying days? What insights does he gain?
7. How do you interpret the dream about the black sack?

Cultural Contexts

1. Discuss with your group Ivan's own assessment of his life as he confronts death.

> His marriage, a mere accident, then the disenchantment that followed it, his wife's bad breath and the sensuality and hypocrisy: then that deadly official life and those preoccupations about money, a year of it, and two, and ten, and twenty, and always the same thing. And the longer it lasted the more deadly it became.

Does the story support his assessment? Do you agree with it? Why or why not? Is it possible to avoid boredom and monotony? Do most people settle for satisfaction instead of joy? How do these emotional states differ? What might we learn from Ivan's experiences?

Edith Wharton
1936

Roman Fever

I

From the table at which they had been lunching two American ladies of ripe but well-cared-for middle age moved across the lofty terrace of the Roman restaurant and, leaning on its parapet, looked first at each other, and then down on the outspread glories of the Palatine and the Forum, with the same expression of vague but benevolent approval.

As they leaned there a girlish voice echoed up gaily from the stairs leading to the court below. "Well, come along, then," it cried, not to them but to an invisible companion, "and let's leave the young things to their knitting"; and a voice as fresh laughed back: "Oh, look here, Babs, not actually *knitting*—" "Well, I mean figuratively," rejoined the first. "After all, we haven't left our poor parents much else to do...." and at that point the turn of the stairs engulfed the dialogue.

The two ladies looked at each other again, this time with a tinge of smiling embarrassment, and the smaller and paler one shook her head and colored slightly.

"Barbara!" she murmured, sending an unheard rebuke after the mocking voice in the stairway.

The other lady, who was fuller, and higher in color, with a small determined nose supported by vigorous black eyebrows, gave a good-humored laugh. "That's what our daughters think of us!"

Her companion replied by a deprecating gesture. "Not of us individually. We must remember that. It's just the collective modern idea of Mothers. And you see—" Half-guiltily she drew from her handsomely mounted black handbag a twist of crimson silk run through by two fine knitting needles. "One never knows," she murmured. "The new system has certainly given us a good deal of time to kill; and sometimes I get tired just looking—even at this." Her gesture was now addressed to the stupendous scene at their feet.

The dark lady laughed again, and they both relapsed upon the view, contemplating it in silence, with a sort of diffused serenity which might have been borrowed from the spring effulgence of the Roman skies. The luncheon hour was long past, and the two had their end of the vast terrace to themselves. At its opposite extremity a few groups, detained by a lingering look at the outspread city, were gathering up guidebooks and fumbling for tips. The last of them scattered, and the two ladies were alone on the air-washed height.

"Well, I don't see why we shouldn't just stay here," said Mrs. Slade, the lady of the high color and energetic brows. Two derelict basket chairs stood near and she pushed them into the angle of the parapet, and settled herself in one, her gaze upon the Palatine. "After all, it's still the most beautiful view in the world."

"It always will be, to me," assented her friend Mrs. Ansley, with so slight a stress on the "me" that Mrs. Slade, though she noticed it, wondered if it were not merely accidental, like the random underlinings of old-fashioned letter writers.

"Grace Ansley was always old-fashioned," she thought; and added aloud, with a retrospective smile: "It's a view we've both been familiar with for a good many years. When we first met here we were younger than our girls are now. You remember?"

"Oh, yes, I remember," murmured Mrs. Ansley, with the same undefinable stress. "There's that headwaiter wondering," she interpolated. She was evidently far less sure than her companion of herself and of her rights in the world.

"I'll cure him of wondering," said Mrs. Slade, stretching her hand toward a bag as discreetly opulent-looking as Mrs. Ansley's. Signing to the headwaiter, she explained that she and her friend were old lovers of Rome, and would like to spend the end of the afternoon looking down on the view—that is, if it did not disturb the service? The headwaiter, bowing over her gratuity, assured her that the ladies were most welcome, and would be still more so if they would condescend to remain for dinner. A full-moon night, they would remember....

Mrs. Slade's black brows drew together, as though references to the moon were out of place and even unwelcome. But she smiled away her frown as the headwaiter retreated. "Well, why not? We might do worse. There's no knowing, I suppose, when the girls will be back. Do you even know back from *where*? I don't!"

Mrs. Ansley again colored slightly. "I think those young Italian aviators we met at the Embassy invited them to fly to Tarquinia for tea. I suppose they'll want to wait and fly back by moonlight."

"Moonlight—moonlight! What a part it still plays. Do you suppose they're as sentimental as we were?"

"I've come to the conclusion that I don't in the least know what they are," said Mrs. Ansley. "And perhaps we didn't know much more about each other."

"No; perhaps we didn't."

Her friend gave her a shy glance. "I never should have supposed you were sentimental, Alida."

"Well, perhaps I wasn't." Mrs. Slade drew her lids together in retrospect; and for a few moments the two ladies, who had been intimate since childhood, reflected how little they knew each other. Each one, of course, had a label ready to attach to the other's name; Mrs. Delphin Slade, for instance, would have told herself, or anyone who asked her, that Mrs. Horace Ansley, twenty-five years ago, had been exquisitely lovely—no, you wouldn't believe it, would you?...though, of course, still charming, distinguished.... Well, as a girl she had been exquisite; far more beautiful than her daughter Barbara, though certainly Babs, according to the new standards at any rate, was more effective—had more *edge*, as they say. Funny where she got it, with those two nullities as parents. Yes; Horace Ansley was—well, just the duplicate of his wife. Museum specimens of old New York. Good-looking, irreproachable, exemplary. Mrs. Slade and Mrs. Ansley had lived opposite each other—actually as well as figuratively—for years. When the drawing-room curtains in No. 20 East 73rd Street were renewed, No. 23, across the way, was always aware of it. And of all the movings, buyings, travels, anniversaries, illnesses—the tame chronicle of an estimable pair. Little of it escaped Mrs. Slade. But she had grown bored with it by the time her husband made his big *coup* in Wall Street, and when they bought in upper Park Avenue had already begun to think: "I'd rather live opposite a speakeasy for a change; at least one might see it raided." The idea of seeing Grace raided was so amusing that (before the move) she launched it at a woman's lunch. It made a hit, and went the rounds—she sometimes wondered if it had crossed the street, and reached Mrs. Ansley. She hoped not, but didn't much mind. Those were the days when respectability was at a discount, and it did the irreproachable no harm to laugh at them a little.

A few years later, and not many months apart, both ladies lost their husbands. There was an appropriate exchange of wreaths and condolences, and a brief renewal of intimacy in the half-shadow of their mourning; and now, after another interval, they had run across each other in Rome, at the same hotel, each of them the modest appendage of a salient daughter. The similarity of their lot had again drawn them together, lending itself to mild jokes, and the mutual confession that, if in old days it must have been tiring to "keep up" with daughters, it was now, at times, a little dull not to.

No doubt, Mrs. Slade reflected, she felt her unemployment more than poor Grace ever would. It was a big drop from being the wife of Delphin Slade to being his widow. She had always regarded herself (with a certain conjugal pride) as his equal in social gifts, as contributing her full share to the making of the exceptional couple they were: but the difference after his death was irremediable. As the wife of the famous corporation lawyer, always with an international case or two on hand, every day brought its exciting and unexpected obligation: the impromptu entertaining of eminent colleagues from abroad, the hurried dashes on legal business to London, Paris or Rome, where the entertaining was so handsomely reciprocated; the amusement of hearing in her wake: "What, that handsome woman with the good clothes and the eyes is Mrs. Slade—*the* Slade's wife? Really? Generally the wives of celebrities are such frumps."

Yes; being *the* Slade's widow was a dullish business after that. In living up to such a husband all her faculties had been engaged; now she had only her daughter to live up to, for the son who seemed to have inherited his father's gifts had died suddenly in boyhood. She had fought through that agony because her husband was there, to be helped and to help; now, after the father's death, the thought of the boy had become unbearable. There was nothing left but to mother her daughter; and dear Jenny was such a perfect daughter that she needed no excessive mothering. "Now with Babs Ansley I don't know that I *should* be so quiet," Mrs. Slade sometimes half-enviously reflected; but Jenny, who was younger than her brilliant friend, was that rare accident, an extremely pretty girl who somehow made youth and prettiness seem as safe as their absence. It was all perplexing—and to Mrs. Slade a little boring. She wished that Jenny would fall in love—with the wrong man, even; that she might have to be watched, out-maneuvered, rescued. And instead, it was Jenny who watched her mother, kept her out of drafts, made sure that she had taken her tonic....

Mrs. Ansley was much less articulate than her friend, and her mental portrait of Mrs. Slade was slighter, and drawn with fainter touches. "Alida Slade's awfully brilliant; but not as brilliant as she thinks," would have summed it up; though she would have added, for the enlightenment of strangers, that Mrs. Slade had been an extremely dashing girl; much more so than her daughter, who was pretty, of course, and clever in a way, but had none of her mother's—well, "vividness," someone had once called it. Mrs. Ansley would take up current words like this, and cite them in quotation marks, as unheard-of audacities. No; Jenny was not like her mother. Sometimes Mrs. Ansley thought Alida Slade was disappointed; on the whole she had had a sad life. Full of failures and mistakes; Mrs. Ansley had always been rather sorry for her....

So these two ladies visualized each other, each through the wrong end of her little telescope.

II

For a long time they continued to sit side by side without speaking. It seemed as though, to both, there was a relief in laying down their somewhat futile activities in the presence of the vast Memento Mori which faced them. Mrs. Slade sat quite still, her eyes fixed on the golden slope of the Palace of the Caesars, and after a while Mrs. Ansley ceased to fidget with her bag, and she too sank into meditation. Like many intimate friends, the two ladies had never before had occasion to be silent together, and Mrs. Ansley was slightly embarrassed by what seemed, after so many years, a new stage in their intimacy, and one with which she did not yet know how to deal.

Suddenly the air was full of that deep clangor of bells which periodically covers Rome with a roof of silver. Mrs. Slade glanced at her wristwatch. "Five o'clock already," she said, as though surprised.

Mrs. Ansley suggested interrogatively: "There's bridge at the Embassy at five." For a long time Mrs. Slade did not answer. She appeared to be lost in contemplation, and Mrs. Ansley thought the remark had escaped her. But after a while she said, as if speaking out of a dream: "Bridge, did you say? Not unless you want to.... But I don't think I will, you know."

"Oh, no," Mrs. Ansley hastened to assure her. "I don't care to at all. It's so lovely here; and so full of old memories, as you say." She settled herself in her chair, and almost furtively drew forth her knitting. Mrs. Slade took sideway note of this activity, but her own beautifully cared-for hands remained motionless on her knee.

"I was just thinking," she said slowly, "what different things Rome stands for to each generation of travelers. To our grandmothers, Roman fever; to our mothers, sentimental dangers—how we used to be guarded!—to our daughters, no more dangers than the middle of Main Street. They don't know it—but how much they're missing!"

The long golden light was beginning to pale, and Mrs. Ansley lifted her knitting a little closer to her eyes. "Yes; how we were guarded!"

"I always used to think," Mrs. Slade continued, "that our mothers had a much more difficult job than our grandmothers. When Roman fever stalked the streets it must have been comparatively easy to gather in the girls at the danger hour; but when you and I were young, with such beauty calling us, and the spice of disobedience thrown in, and no worse risk than catching cold during the cool hour after sunset, the mothers used to be put to it to keep us in—didn't they?"

She turned again toward Mrs. Ansley, but the latter had reached a delicate point in her knitting. "One, two, three—slip two; yes, they must have been," she assented, without looking up.

Mrs. Slade's eyes rested on her with a deepened attention. "She can knit—in the face of *this!* How like her...."

Mrs. Slade leaned back, brooding, her eyes ranging from the ruins which faced her to the long green hollow of the Forum, the fading glow of the church fronts beyond it, and the outlying immensity of the Colosseum. Suddenly she thought: "It's all very well to say that our girls have done away with sentiment and moonlight. But if Babs Ansley isn't out to catch that young aviator—the one who's a Marchese—then I don't know anything. And Jenny has no chance beside her. I know that too. I wonder if that's why Grace Ansley likes the two girls to go everywhere together? My poor Jenny as a foil—!" Mrs. Slade gave a hardly audible laugh, and at the sound Mrs. Ansley dropped her knitting.

"Yes—?"

"I—oh, nothing. I was only thinking how your Babs carries everything before her. That Campolieri boy is one of the best matches in Rome. Don't look so innocent, my dear—you know he is. And I was wondering, ever so respectfully, you understand...wondering how two such exemplary characters as you and Horace had managed to produce anything quite so dynamic." Mrs. Slade laughed again, with a touch of asperity.

Mrs. Ansley's hands lay inert across her needles. She looked straight out at the great accumulated wreckage of passion and splendor at her feet. But her small profile was almost expressionless. At length she said: "I think you overrate Babs, my dear."

Mrs. Slade's tone grew easier. "No; I don't. I appreciate her. And perhaps envy you. Oh, my girl's perfect; if I were a chronic invalid I'd—well, I think I'd rather be in Jenny's hands. There must be times...but there! I always wanted a brilliant daughter...and never quite understood why I got an angel instead."

Mrs. Ansley echoed her laugh in a faint murmur. "Babs is an angel too."

"Of course—of course! But she's got rainbow wings. Well, they're wandering by the sea with their young men; and here we sit...and it all brings back the past a little too acutely."

Mrs. Ansley had resumed her knitting. One might almost have imagined (if one had known her less well, Mrs. Slade reflected) that, for her also, too many memories rose from the lengthening shadows of those august ruins. But no; she was simply absorbed in her work. What was there for her to worry about? She knew that Babs would almost certainly come back engaged to the extremely eligible Campolieri. "And she'll sell the New York house, and settle down near them in Rome, and never be in their way…she's much too tactful. But she'll have an excellent cook, and just the right people in for bridge and cocktails…and a perfectly peaceful old age among her grandchildren."

Mrs. Slade broke off this prophetic flight with a recoil of self-disgust. There was no one of whom she had less right to think unkindly than of Grace Ansley. Would she never cure herself of envying her? Perhaps she had begun too long ago.

She stood up and leaned against the parapet, filling her troubled eyes with the tranquilizing magic of the hour. But instead of tranquilizing her the sight seemed to increase her exasperation. Her gaze turned toward the Colosseum. Already its golden flank was drowned in purple shadow, and above it the sky curved crystal clear, without light or color. It was the moment when afternoon and evening hang balanced in mid-heaven.

Mrs. Slade turned back and laid her hand on her friend's arm. The gesture was so abrupt that Mrs. Ansley looked up, startled.

"The sun's set. You're not afraid, my dear?"

"Afraid—?"

"Of Roman fever or pneumonia? I remember how ill you were that winter. As a girl you had a very delicate throat, hadn't you?"

"Oh, we're all right up here. Down below, in the Forum, it does get deathly cold, all of a sudden…but not here."

"Ah, of course you know because you had to be so careful." Mrs. Slade turned back to the parapet. She thought: "I must make one more effort not to hate her." Aloud she said: "Whenever I look at the Forum from up here, I remember that story about a great-aunt of yours, wasn't she? A dreadfully wicked great-aunt?"

"Oh, yes; great-aunt Harriet. The one who was supposed to have sent her young sister out to the Forum after sunset to gather a night-blooming flower for her album. All our great-aunts and grandmothers used to have albums of dried flowers."

Mrs. Slade nodded. "But she really sent her because they were in love with the same man—"

"Well, that was the family tradition. They said Aunt Harriet confessed it years afterward. At any rate, the poor little sister caught the fever and died. Mother used to frighten us with the story when we were children."

"And you frightened *me* with it, that winter when you and I were here as girls. The winter I was engaged to Delphin."

Mrs. Ansley gave a faint laugh. "Oh, did I? Really frightened you? I don't believe you're easily frightened."

"Not often; but I was then. I was easily frightened because I was too happy. I wonder if you know what that means?"

"I—yes…" Mrs. Ansley faltered.

"Well, I suppose that was why the story of your wicked aunt made such an impression on me. And I thought: 'There's no more Roman fever, but the Forum is deathly cold after sunset—especially after a hot day. And the Colosseum's even colder and damper'."

"The Colosseum—?"

"Yes. It wasn't easy to get in, after the gates were locked for the night. Far from easy. Still, in those days it could be managed; it *was* managed, often. Lovers met there who couldn't meet elsewhere. You knew that?"

"I—I dare say. I don't remember."

"You don't remember? You don't remember going to visit some ruins or other one evening, just after dark, and catching a bad chill? You were supposed to have gone to see the moon rise. People always said that expedition was what caused your illness."

There was a moment's silence; then Mrs. Ansley rejoined: "Did they? It was all so long ago."

"Yes. And you got well again—so it didn't matter. But I suppose it struck your friends—the reason given for your illness, I mean—because everybody knew you were so prudent on account of your throat, and your mother took such care of you.... You *had* been out late sight-seeing, hadn't you, that night?"

"Perhaps I had. The most prudent girls aren't always prudent. What made you think of it now?"

Mrs. Slade seemed to have no answer ready. But after a moment she broke out: "Because I simply can't bear it any longer—!"

Mrs. Ansley lifted her head quickly. Her eyes were wide and very pale. "Can't bear what?"

"Why—your not knowing that I've always known why you went."

"Why I went—?"

"Yes. You think I'm bluffing, don't you? Well, you went to meet the man I was engaged to—and I can repeat every word of the letter that took you there."

While Mrs. Slade spoke Mrs. Ansley had risen unsteadily to her feet. Her bag, her knitting and gloves, slid in a panic-stricken heap to the ground. She looked at Mrs. Slade as though she were looking at a ghost.

"No, no—don't," she faltered out.

"Why not? Listen, if you don't believe me. 'My one darling, things can't go on like this. I must see you alone. Come to the Colosseum immediately after dark tomorrow. There will be somebody to let you in. No one whom you need fear will suspect'—but perhaps you've forgotten what the letter said?"

Mrs. Ansley met the challenge with an unexpected composure. Steadying herself against the chair she looked at her friend, and replied: "No; I know it by heart too."

"And the signature? 'Only *your* D.S.' Was that it? I'm right, am I? That was the letter that took you out that evening after dark?"

Mrs. Ansley was still looking at her. It seemed to Mrs. Slade that a slow struggle was going on behind the voluntarily controlled mask of her small quiet face. "I shouldn't have thought she had herself so well in hand," Mrs. Slade reflected, almost resentfully. But at this moment Mrs. Ansley spoke. "I don't know how you knew. I burnt that letter at once."

"Yes; you would, naturally—you're so prudent!" The sneer was open now. "And if you burnt the letter you're wondering how on earth I know what was in it. That's it, isn't it?"

Mrs. Slade waited, but Mrs. Ansley did not speak.

"Well, my dear, I know what was in that letter because I wrote it!"

"You wrote it?"

"Yes."

The two women stood for a minute staring at each other in the last golden light. Then Mrs. Ansley dropped back into her chair. "Oh," she murmured, and covered her face with her hands.

Mrs. Slade waited nervously for another word or movement. None came, and at length she broke out: "I horrify you."

Mrs. Ansley's hands dropped to her knee. The face they uncovered was streaked with tears. "I wasn't thinking of you. I was thinking—it was the only letter I ever had from him!"

"And I wrote it. Yes; I wrote it! But I was the girl he was engaged to. Did you happen to remember that?"

Mrs. Ansley's head drooped again. "I'm not trying to excuse myself...I remembered...."

"And still you went?"

"Still I went."

Mrs. Slade stood looking down on the small bowed figure at her side. The flame of her wrath had already sunk, and she wondered why she had ever thought there would be any satisfaction in inflicting so purposeless a wound on her friend. But she had to justify herself.

"You do understand? I found out—and I hated you, hated you. I knew you were in love with Delphin—and I was afraid; afraid of you, of your quiet ways, your sweetness...your...well, I wanted you out of the way, that's all. Just for a few weeks; just till I was sure of him. So in a blind fury I wrote that letter...I don't know why I'm telling you now."

"I suppose," said Mrs. Ansley slowly, "it's because you've always gone on hating me."

"Perhaps. Or because I wanted to get the whole thing off my mind." She paused. "I'm glad you destroyed the letter. Of course I never thought you'd die."

Mrs. Ansley relapsed into silence, and Mrs. Slade, leaning above her, was conscious of a strange sense of isolation, of being cut off from the warm current of human communion. "You think me a monster!"

"I don't know.... It was the only letter I had, and you say he didn't write it?"

"Ah, how you care for him still!"

"I cared for that memory," said Mrs. Ansley.

Mrs. Slade continued to look down on her. She seemed physically reduced by the blow—as if, when she got up, the wind might scatter her like a puff of dust. Mrs. Slade's jealousy suddenly leapt up again at the sight. All these years the woman had been living on that letter. How she must have loved him, to treasure the mere memory of its ashes! The letter of the man her friend was engaged to. Wasn't it she who was the monster?

"You tried your best to get him away from me, didn't you? But you failed; and I kept him. That's all."

"Yes. That's all."

"I wish now I hadn't told you. I'd no idea you'd feel about it as you do; I thought you'd be amused. It all happened so long ago, as you say; and you must do me the justice to remember that I had no reason to think you'd ever taken it seriously. How could I, when you were married to Horace Ansley two months afterward? As soon as you could get out of bed your mother rushed you off to Florence and married you. People were rather surprised—they wondered at its being done so quickly; but I thought I knew. I had an idea you did it out of *pique*—to be able to say you'd got ahead of Delphin and me. Girls have such silly reasons for doing the most serious things. And your marrying so soon convinced me that you'd never really cared."

"Yes. I suppose it would," Mrs. Ansley assented.

The clear heaven overhead was emptied of all its gold. Dusk spread over it, abruptly darkening the Seven Hills. Here and there lights began to twinkle through the foliage at their feet. Steps were coming and going on the deserted terrace—waiters looking out of the doorway at the head of the stairs, then reappearing with trays and napkins and flasks of wine. Tables were moved, chairs straightened. A feeble string of electric lights flickered out. Some vases of faded flowers were carried away, and brought back replenished. A stout lady in a dust coat suddenly appeared, asking in broken Italian if anyone had seen the elastic band which held together her tattered Baedeker. She poked with her stick under the table at which she had lunched, the waiters assisting.

The corner where Mrs. Slade and Mrs. Ansley sat was still shadowy and deserted. For a long time neither of them spoke. At length Mrs. Slade began again: "I suppose I did it as a sort of joke—"

"A joke?"

"Well, girls are ferocious sometimes, you know. Girls in love especially. And I remember laughing to myself all that evening at the idea that you were waiting around there in the dark, dodging out of sight, listening for every sound, trying to get in— Of course I was upset when I heard you were so ill afterward."

Mrs. Ansley had not moved for a long time. But now she turned slowly toward her companion. "But I didn't wait. He'd arranged everything. He was there. We were let in at once," she said.

Mrs. Slade sprang up from her leaning position. "Delphin there? They let you in?—Ah, now you're lying!" she burst out with violence.

Mrs. Ansley's voice grew clearer, and full of surprise. "But of course he was there. Naturally he came—"

"Came? How did he know he'd find you there? You must be raving!"

Mrs. Ansley hesitated, as though reflecting. "But I answered the letter. I told him I'd be there. So he came."

Mrs. Slade flung her hands up to her face. "Oh, God—you answered! I never thought of your answering...."

"It's odd you never thought of it, if you wrote the letter."

"Yes. I was blind with rage."

Mrs. Ansley rose, and drew her fur scarf about her. "It is cold here. We'd better go...I'm sorry for you," she said, as she clasped the fur about her throat.

The unexpected words sent a pang through Mrs. Slade. "Yes; we'd better go." She gathered up her bag and cloak. "I don't know why you should be sorry for me," she muttered.

Mrs. Ansley stood looking away from her toward the dusky secret mass of the Colosseum. "Well—because I didn't have to wait that night."

Mrs. Slade gave an unquiet laugh. "Yes; I was beaten there. But I oughtn't to begrudge it to you, I suppose. At the end of all these years. After all, I had everything; I had him for twenty-five years. And you had nothing but that one letter that he didn't write."

Mrs. Ansley was again silent. At length she turned toward the door of the terrace. She took a step, and turned back, facing her companion.

"I had Barbara," she said, and began to move ahead of Mrs. Slade toward the stairway.

Journal Entry

React to the idea that "when people talk about their pasts, tell their own stories, they are culling anecdotes from their stacks of memories, tapping certain of the past days on the shoulder."

Textual Considerations

1. Analyze the implications of Wharton's choice of Rome as the "site of memory." Consider, for example, whether the events that occur could have taken place elsewhere.
2. What are the literal and figurative meanings of the story's title?
3. Find as many examples as you can of foreshadowing, and show how Wharton uses this technique to prepare the reader for the ending.
4. Contrast the attitudes of the protagonists toward aging and widowhood. To what extent are they reconciled to their present? How have their historical pasts affected their attitudes toward the present?

Cultural Contexts

1. "Roman Fever" explores the urge that human beings sometimes feel to return to the past in an attempt to reconcile its contradictions with the present. Working with your group, make a list of the features and traits that Mrs. Slade uses to unravel the mysteries and enigmas of the past.
2. To what extent have the lives of both protagonists been shaped by social pressures such as gender roles and social class? How are their daughters' expectations for their lives similar to or different from those of their mothers?

Frank O'Connor
1951

First Confession

All the trouble began when my grandfather died and my grandmother— my father's mother—came to live with us. Relations in the one house are a strain at the best of times, but, to make matters worse, my grandmother was a real old countrywoman and quite unsuited to the life in town. She had a fat, wrinkled face, and, to Mother's great indignation, went round the house in bare feet—the boots had her crippled, she said. For dinner she had a jug of porter and a pot of potatoes with—sometimes—a bit of salt fish, and she poured out the potatoes on the table and ate them slowly, with great relish, using her fingers by way of a fork.

Now, girls are supposed to be fastidious, but I was the one who suffered most from this. Nora, my sister, just sucked up to the old woman for the penny she got every Friday out of the old-age pension, a thing I could not do. I was too honest, that was my trouble; and when I was playing with Bill Connell, the sergeant-major's son, and saw my grandmother steering up the path with the jug of porter sticking out from beneath her shawl I was mortified. I made excuses not to let him come into the house, because I could never be sure what she would be up to when we went in.

When Mother was at work and my grandmother made the dinner I wouldn't touch it. Nora once tried to make me, but I hid under the table from her and took the bread-knife with me for protection. Nora let on to be very indignant (she wasn't, of course, but she knew Mother saw through her, so she sided with Gran) and came after me. I lashed out at her with the bread-knife, and after that she left me alone. I stayed there till Mother came in from work and made my dinner, but when Father came in later Nora said in a shocked voice: "Oh, Dadda, do you know what Jackie did at dinnertime?" Then, of course, it all came out; Father gave me a flaking; Mother interfered, and for days after that he didn't speak to me and Mother barely spoke to Nora. And all because of that old woman! God knows, I was heart-scalded.

Then, to crown my misfortunes, I had to make my first confession and communion. It was an old woman called Ryan who prepared us for these. She was about the one age with Gran; she was well-to-do, lived in a big house on Montenotte, wore a black cloak and bonnet, and came every day to school at three o'clock when we should have been going home, and talked to us of hell. She may have mentioned the other place as well, but that could only have been by accident, for hell had the first place in her heart.

She lit a candle, took out a new half-crown, and offered it to the first boy who would hold one finger—only one finger!—in the flame for five minutes by the school clock. Being always very ambitious I was tempted to volunteer, but I thought it might look greedy. Then she asked were we afraid of holding one

finger—only one finger!—in a little candle flame for five minutes and not afraid of burning all over in roasting hot furnaces for all eternity. "All eternity! Just think of that! A whole lifetime goes by and it's nothing, not even a drop in the ocean of your sufferings." The woman was really interesting about hell, but my attention was all fixed on the half-crown. At the end of the lesson she put it back in her purse. It was a great disappointment; a religious woman like that, you wouldn't think she'd bother about a thing like a half-crown.

Another day she said she knew a priest who woke one night to find a fellow he didn't recognize leaning over the end of his bed. The priest was a bit frightened—naturally enough—but he asked the fellow what he wanted, and the fellow said in a deep, husky voice that he wanted to go to confession. The priest said it was an awkward time and wouldn't it do in the morning, but the fellow said that last time he went to confession, there was one sin he kept back, being ashamed to mention it, and now it was always on his mind. Then the priest knew it was a bad case, because the fellow was after making a bad confession and committing a mortal sin. He got up to dress, and just then the cock crew in the yard outside, and—lo and behold!—when the priest looked round there was no sign of the fellow, only a smell of burning timber, and when the priest looked at his bed didn't he see the print of two hands burned in it? That was because the fellow had made a bad confession. This story made a shocking impression on me.

But the worst of all was when she showed us how to examine our conscience. Did we take the name of the Lord, our God, in vain? Did we honor our father and our mother? (I asked her did this include grandmothers and she said it did.) Did we love our neighbors as ourselves? Did we covet our neighbor's goods? (I thought of the way I felt about the penny that Nora got every Friday.) I decided that, between one thing and another, I must have broken the whole ten commandments, all on account of that old woman, and so far as I could see, so long as she remained in the house I had no hope of ever doing anything else.

I was scared to death of confession. The day the whole class went I let on to have a toothache, hoping my absence wouldn't be noticed; but at three o'clock, just as I was feeling safe, along comes a chap with a message from Mrs. Ryan that I was to go to confession myself on Saturday and be at the chapel for communion with the rest. To make it worse, Mother couldn't come with me and sent Nora instead.

Now, that girl had ways of tormenting me that Mother never knew of. She held my hand as we went down the hill, smiling sadly and saying how sorry she was for me, as if she were bringing me to the hospital for an operation.

"Oh, God help us!" she moaned. "Isn't it a terrible pity you weren't a good boy? Oh, Jackie, my heart bleeds for you! How will you ever think of all your sins? Don't forget you have to tell him about the time you kicked Gran on the shin."

"Lemme go!" I said, trying to drag myself free of her. "I don't want to go to confession at all."

"But sure, you'll have to go to confession, Jackie," she replied in the same regretful tone. "Sure, if you didn't, the parish priest would be up to the house, looking for you. 'Tisn't, God knows, that I'm not sorry for you. Do you remember the time you tried to kill me with the bread-knife under the table? And the language you used to me? I don't know what he'll do with you at all, Jackie. He might have to send you up to the bishop."

I remember thinking bitterly that she didn't know the half of what I had to tell—if I told it. I knew I couldn't tell it, and understood perfectly why the fellow in Mrs. Ryan's story made a bad confession; it seemed to me a great shame that people wouldn't stop criticizing him. I remember that steep hill down to the church, and the sunlit hillsides beyond the valley of the river, which I saw in the gaps between the houses like Adam's last glimpse of Paradise.

Then, when she had maneuvered me down the long flight of steps to the chapel yard, Nora suddenly changed her tone. She became the raging malicious devil she really was.

"There you are!" she said with a yelp of triumph, hurling me through the church door. "And I hope he'll give you the penitential psalms, you dirty little caffler."

I knew then I was lost, given up to eternal justice. The door with the colored-glass panels swung shut behind me, the sunlight went out and gave place to deep shadow, and the wind whistled outside so that the silence within seemed to crackle like ice under my feet. Nora sat in front of me by the confession box. There were a couple of old women ahead of her, and then a miserable-looking poor devil came and wedged me in at the other side, so that I couldn't escape even if I had the courage. He joined his hands and rolled his eyes in the direction of the roof, muttering aspirations in an anguished tone, and I wondered had he a grandmother too. Only a grandmother could account for a fellow behaving in that heartbroken way, but he was better off than I, for he at least could go and confess his sins; while I would make a bad confession and then die in the night and be continually coming back and burning people's furniture.

Nora's turn came, and I heard the sound of something slamming and then her voice as if butter wouldn't melt in her mouth, and then another slam, and out she came. God, the hypocrisy of women! Her eyes were lowered, her head was bowed, and her hands were joined very low down on her stomach, and she walked up the aisle to the side altar looking like a saint. You never saw such an exhibition of devotion; and I remembered the devilish malice with which she had tormented me all the way from our door, and wondered were all religious people like that, really. It was my turn now. With the fear of damnation in my soul I went in, and the confessional door closed of itself behind me.

It was pitch-dark and I couldn't see priest or anything else. Then I really began to be frightened. In the darkness it was a matter between God and me, and He had all the odds. He knew what my intentions were before I even started; I had no chance. All I had ever been told about confession got mixed up in my mind, and I knelt to one wall and said: "Bless me, father, for I have sinned; this is my first confession." I waited for a few minutes, but nothing happened, so I tried it on the other wall. Nothing happened there either. He had me spotted all right.

It must have been then that I noticed the shelf at about one height with my head. It was really a place for grown-up people to rest their elbows, but in my distracted state I thought it was probably the place you were supposed to kneel. Of course, it was on the high side and not very deep, but I was always good at climbing and managed to get up all right. Staying up was the trouble. There was room only for my knees, and nothing you could get a grip on but a sort of wooden moulding a bit above it. I held on to the moulding and repeated the words a little louder, and this time something happened all right. A slide was slammed back; a little light entered the box, and a man's voice said: "Who's there?"

"'Tis me, father," I said for fear he mightn't see me and go away again. I couldn't see him at all. The place the voice came from was under the moulding, about level with my knees, so I took a good grip of the moulding and swung myself down till I saw the astonished face of a young priest looking up at me. He had to put his head on one side to see me, and I had to put mine on one side to see him, so we were more or less talking to one another upside-down. It struck me as a queer way of hearing confessions, but I didn't feel it my place to criticize.

"Bless me, father, for I have sinned; this is my first confession," I rattled off all in one breath, and swung myself down the least shade more to make it easier for him.

"What are you doing up there?" he shouted in an angry voice, and the strain the politeness was putting on my hold of the moulding, and the shock of being addressed in such an uncivil tone, were too much for me. I lost my grip, tumbled, and hit the door an unmerciful wallop before I found myself flat on my back in the middle of the aisle. The people who had been waiting stood up with their mouths open. The priest opened the door of the middle box and came out, pushing his biretta back from his forehead; he looked something terrible. Then Nora came scampering down the aisle.

"Oh, you dirty little caffler!" she cried. "I might have known you'd do it. I might have known you'd disgrace me. I can't leave you out of my sight for one minute."

Before I could even get to my feet to defend myself she bent down and gave me a clip across the ear. This reminded me that I was so stunned I had even forgotten to cry, so that people might think I wasn't hurt at all, when in fact I was probably maimed for life. I gave a roar out of me.

"What's all this about?" the priest hissed, getting angrier than ever and pushing Nora off me. "How dare you hit the child like that, you little vixen?"

"But I can't do my penance with him, father," Nora cried, cocking an outraged eye up at him.

"Well, go and do it, or I'll give you some more to do," he said, giving me a hand up. "Was it coming to confession you were, my poor man?" he asked me.

"'Twas, father," said I with a sob.

"Oh," he said respectfully, "a big hefty fellow like you must have terrible sins. Is this your first?"

"'Tis, father," said I.

"Worse and worse," he said gloomily. "The crimes of a lifetime. I don't know will I get rid of you at all today. You'd better wait now till I'm finished with these old ones. You can see by the looks of them they haven't much to tell."

"I will, father," I said with something approaching joy.

The relief of it was really enormous. Nora stuck out her tongue at me from behind his back, but I couldn't even be bothered retorting. I knew from the very moment that man opened his mouth that he was intelligent above the ordinary. When I had time to think, I saw how right I was. It only stood to reason that a fellow confessing after seven years would have more to tell than people that went every week. The crimes of a lifetime, exactly as he said. It was only what he expected, and the rest was the cackle of old women and girls with their talk of hell, the bishop, and the penitential psalms. That was all they knew. I started to make my examination of conscience, and barring the one bad business of my grandmother it didn't seem so bad.

The next time, the priest steered me into the confession box himself and left the shutter back the way I could see him get in and sit down at the further side of the grille from me.

"Well, now," he said, "what do they call you?"

"Jackie, father," said I.

"And what's a-trouble to you, Jackie?"

"Father" I said, feeling I might as well get it over while I had him in good humor, "I had it all arranged to kill my grandmother."

He seemed a bit shaken by that, all right, because he said nothing for quite a while.

"My goodness," he said at last, "that'd be a shocking thing to do. What put that into your head?"

"Father," I said, feeling very sorry for myself, "she's an awful woman."

"Is she?" he asked. "What way is she awful?"

"She takes porter, father," I said, knowing well from the way Mother talked of it that this was a mortal sin, and hoping it would make the priest take a more favorable view of my case.

"Oh, my!" he said, and I could see he was impressed.

"And snuff, father," said I.

"That's a bad case, sure enough, Jackie," he said.

"And she goes round in her bare feet, father," I went on in a rush of self-pity, "and she knows I don't like her, and she gives pennies to Nora and none to me, and my da sides with her and flakes me, and one night I was so heart-scalded I made up my mind I'd have to kill her."

"And what would you do with the body?" he asked with great interest.

"I was thinking I could chop that up and carry it away in a barrow I have," I said.

"Begor, Jackie," he said, "do you know you're a terrible child?"

"I know, father," I said, for I was just thinking the same thing myself. "I tried to kill Nora too with a bread-knife under the table, only I missed her."

"Is that the little girl that was beating you just now?" he asked.

"Tis, father."

"Someone will go for her with a bread-knife one day, and he won't miss her," he said rather cryptically. "You must have great courage. Between ourselves, there's a lot of people I'd like to do the same to but I'd never have the nerve. Hanging is an awful death."

"Is it, father?" I said with the deepest interest—I was always very keen on hanging. "Did you ever see a fellow hanged?"

"Dozens of them," he said solemnly. "And they all died roaring."

"Jay!" I said.

"Oh, a horrible death!" he said with great satisfaction. "Lots of the fellows I saw killed their grandmothers too, but they all said 'twas never worth it."

He had me there for a full ten minutes talking, and then walked out the chapel yard with me. I was genuinely sorry to part with him, because he was the most entertaining character I'd ever met in the religious line. Outside, after the shadow of the church, the sunlight was like the roaring of waves on a beach; it dazzled me; and when the frozen silence melted and I heard the screech of trams on the road my heart soared. I knew now I wouldn't die in the night and come back, leaving marks on my mother's furniture. It would be a great worry to her, and the poor soul had enough.

Nora was sitting on the railing, waiting for me, and she put on a very sour puss when she saw the priest with me. She was mad jealous because a priest had never come out of the church with her.

"Well," she asked coldly, after he left me, "what did he give you?"

"Three Hail Marys," I said.

"Three Hail Marys," she repeated incredulously. "You mustn't have told him anything."

"I told him everything," I said confidently.

"About Gran and all?"

"About Gran and all."

(All she wanted was to be able to go home and say I'd made a bad confession.)

"Did you tell him you went for me with the bread-knife?" she asked with a frown.

"I did to be sure."

"And he only gave you three Hail Marys?"

"That's all."

She slowly got down from the railing with a baffled air. Clearly, this was beyond her. As we mounted the steps back to the main road she looked at me suspiciously.

"What are you sucking?" she asked.

"Bullseyes."

"Was it the priest gave them to you?"

"'Twas."

"Lord God," she wailed bitterly, "some people have all the luck! 'Tis no advantage to anybody trying to be good. I might just as well be a sinner like you."

Journal Entry

Discuss the conflict between punishment and forgiveness in "First Confession."

Textual Considerations

1. The story, a recollection of a childhood experience, is told in the past tense from a first-person point of view. What are the advantages of this narrative technique? How might the story differ if Nora were to tell it? Explain.

2. Focus on O'Connor's use of humor. How does it affect the story's meaning? Cite two passages, and explain how the humor is achieved.
3. Characterize Jackie and speculate as to why he is obsessed with making a bad confession. How does this first experience affect his attitude toward the church?

Cultural Contexts

1. Evaluate the role of religion in the life of this community. Can your group relate to Jackie's fear of the confessional? Why or why not? To what extent have personal and communal attitudes toward religion changed since this story was written?
2. Discuss with your group the role of the extended family in the story. To what extent are your childhood memories of family members similar to or different from Jackie's? How have they shaped your present?

Bessie Head
1989

A Power Struggle

The universe had a more beautiful dream. It was not the law of the jungle or the survival of the fittest but a dream that had often been the priority of saints—the power to make evil irrelevant. All the people of Southern Africa had lived out this dream before the dawn of the colonial era. Time and again it shed its beam of light on their affairs although the same patterns of horror would arise like dark engulfing waves.

It was as though once people had lived in settled communities for any length of time, hostilities of an intolerable nature developed due to power struggles, rivalries and jealousies. Not all the stories were attractive or coherent; they were often so direct and brutal that it was almost like darkness destroying darkness and no rule was untainted by it. It was before these fierce passions for power that people often gave way and it formed the base of the tangled story of tribal movement and migration. When it was all over only a tree, a river bank, a hill or a mountain lingered in the memory as the dwelling place of a tribe.

There were two brothers of the Tlabina clan, Davhana and Baeli. In more ways than one Davhana was destined to rule. He was the born heir to the throne and in acknowledgement of this, the old chief, their father, had, once his health began to fail him, handed to Davhana the sacred rain-making apparatus—a symbol of his destiny. But Davhana was also a fearfully rich personality with glowing black eyes. There was about him the restless beauty of the earth in motion and he could laugh for so long and so loudly that his laughter was like the sound of the wind rushing across the open plains. He was tall and strongly-built with lithe, agile movements. People humorously accorded to him the formal and often meaningless titles a king held as his due such as "Beautiful One" or "Great Lion" but unlike other kings, Davhana earned them with his living personality. In spite of this his succession was not assured and his destiny took an unpredictable turn.

They were at the burial ceremony for their father when his brother, Baeli, abruptly threw down the first challenge to his succession. It was Davhana's right as his father's successor to turn the first sod in his grave. It was also a confirmation before the assembled people that he would rule. Davhana had his digging implement raised but his younger brother, Baeli, stepped in ahead of him and turned the first sod. The older brother stepped back instantly, his digging implement relaxed at his side. He flung his head back with an impatient gesture and stared at the horizon, his mouth curled down in contempt. The younger brother straightened up quietly. He too looked into the distance, a smile on his lips and menace in his eyes. The gestures were so unexpected that the assembled people stirred instinctively and stifled gasps of surprise swept through the crowd. There was not anyone present who did not know that the succession was open to dispute.

Immediately, the dispute did not concern the people. The real power struggle would take place in the inner circle of relatives and councillors. It was often an impersonal process as far as the mass of the people were concerned—what they respected was not so much a chief in person as the position he occupied. And yet, there seemed a contradiction in this. It was real men of passion who fought for that position and should an evil man gain the throne, people would suffer. People had a number of cynical attitudes to cover such events. One of their attitudes was: "We pay homage to all the chief's sons, since which one of them will finally become chief is uncertain...." If things became too disruptive a large number of men would suddenly remember that they had not branded their cattle or attended to their everyday affairs.

The two young men of passion turned away from the funeral ceremony and walked side by side for some distance; Davhana purposefully keeping pace with his brother.

"Baeli," he asked in his direct way. "Why did you turn the first sod on father's grave? It was my duty by right! You have shamed me in front of all the people! Why did you do it?"

He listened with his whole body for his brother's reply but no reply was forthcoming—only the pacing of their feet walking in unison filled the silence. Davhana looked sideways at his brother's face. Baeli stared straight ahead; the smile still lingered around his mouth and there was an aloofness in his eyes. Had they in such an abrupt manner suddenly recognized that they were total strangers to each other? A day ago they had shared a youth together, hunted together and appeared to laugh at the same jokes. Only Davhana felt the pain. His personality radiated outwards, always reaching towards love and friendship. His brother's personality turned inwards into a whirlpool of darkness. He felt himself being dragged down into that whirlpool and instinctively he turned and walked off in his own direction.

Davhana walked until he reached a clearing outside the village. Evening was approaching. The night was warm. A full yellow moon arose behind a small hill in the distance. The atmosphere was deeply silent and still. The subdued murmurs of insects in the grass were peaceful and sweet. The young man settled himself on the earth and was soon lost in his own thoughts. Now and then he sighed deeply as though he were reaching a crossroad with himself, as though he were drawing to himself the scattered fragments of his youthful life. He had lived with the reckless generosity of his personality and nothing in his past seemed a high peak. He had lived, danced, eaten and sung in the full enjoyment of the pleasures of the moment. The events of the day cast their dark shadows over him.

Softly approaching footsteps stirred him out of his reverie. The moonlight outlined the form of one of the elders of the tribe. Davhana turned his head with his glowing look, inviting the old man to seat himself. The old man squatted low beside his reclining form and stared for some time in a detached way at the small hill behind which the moon had arisen.

"Do your thoughts trouble you, Beautiful One?" the old man asked at last. "I have stood here for some time and heard you sigh and sigh."

"Oh no, Uncle," the young man said, with a vigorous shake of his head. "Nothing troubles me. If I sigh it may be only for a carefree youth which I am about to lose."

The elder plucked at a few strands of grass and continued to stare at the distant hill.

"Everyone took note today of the awful deed your brother committed," he said. "It was the most awful breach of good manners and some of us are questioning its motive."

The young man curled his mouth in contempt again as though it were beneath him to recognize avarice and ambition.

"Baeli has always had strange tendencies," he said. "Though I have liked him as my brother."

The old man kept silent a while. When he spoke his voice was as sweet and peaceful as the subdued murmurs of the insects in the grass.

"I have come to teach you a few things about life," he said. "People have never been given a gift like you before, Beautiful One, and they look eagerly forward to your rule because they think that a time of prosperity and happiness lies before them. All these years you have lived with the people and your ways were good to them. When a man built his yard you stopped to tie a knot in the rafters and the hunting spoils you shared generously with all your men, never demanding an abundant share for yourself. You spread happiness and laughter wherever you travelled. People understand these qualities. They are the natural gifts of a good man. But these very gifts can be a calamity in a ruler. A ruler has to examine the dark side of human life and understand that men belong to that darkness. There are many men born with inadequate gifts and this disturbs them. They have no peace within themselves and once their jealousy is aroused they do terrible things...."

The old man hesitated, uncertain of how to communicate his alarms and fears. A ruler could only reach the day of installation without bloodshed provided no other member of his family had declared his ambition publicly. Baeli had publicly declared his ambition and it needed only a little of that poison for all sorts of perverse things to happen. They had some horrible things in their history. They had been ruled by all sorts of lunatics and mental defectives who had mutually poisoned or assassinated each other. His grandfather had been poisoned by a brother who had in turn been assassinated by another brother. Not even Davhana's father's rule was untainted by it—there were several assassinations behind his father's peaceful and lengthy reign.

"You will soon find out the rules of life, Beautiful One," the old man murmured. "You will have to kill or be killed."

The young man said nothing in reply. The old man sat bathed in moonlight and the subdued murmurs of insects in the grass were peaceful and sweet.

The struggle that unfolded between Davhana and his brother was so subtle that it was difficult to deal with. It took place when men sat deep in council debating the issues of the day. There was always a point at which Baeli could command all the attention to himself and in doing so make his brother, Davhana, irrelevant. Baeli would catch a debate just at the point at which his brother had spoken and while a question or statement trembled in the air awaiting a reply, Baeli would step in and deflect men's thoughts in a completely new direction, thus making the previous point completely invalid. Some men began to enjoy this game and daily, Davhana rapidly lost ground with them. He refused at crucial points to assert his power and allowed dialogues to drift away from him. He indulged in no counter-intrigue when it became evident from the laughter of the men that his brother had begun to intrigue with them.

When they moved into the dark side of the moon, the most fearful massacre took place. Davhana alone escaped with his life and fled into the dark night. He had a wound in his right shoulder where a spear had pierced him as he lay asleep in his hut. He did not know who had stabbed him but in the confusion of the struggle in the dark he broke free of the hands that lunged at him and escaped.

Once, during his flight in the dark, Davhana paused again and took stock of his destiny. It was still scattered and fragmentary but the freshness and beauty of his youth lay on him like a protective mantle. If power was the unfocused demoniacal stare of his brother then he would have none of that world. Nothing had paralysed, frustrated and enraged him more than that stare.

"He can take all that he desires," Davhana thought. "I shall not go back there. I want to live."

He chose for himself that night the life of one who would take refuge where he could find it and so he continued his flight into the night.

The people of the Tlabina clan awoke the following morning to a new order. They had a murderer as their ruler. Baeli had slain whatever opposition he was likely to encounter and no one was immediately inclined to oppose him. The ritual of installation proceeded along its formal course. When Baeli appeared a chorus of adulation greeted him and everyone present made humble obeisance. The usual speeches were made to the impersonal office of kingship.

After three moons had waxed and waned word travelled back to the people that their ruler, Davhana, was alive and well and had sought refuge with a powerful Pedi clan. The people of the Tlabina clan began to vanish from their true home, sometimes in large groupings, sometimes in small trickles until they had abandoned Baeli. If the wild dogs ate him, who knows?

A power struggle was the great dialogue of those times and many aspects of the dialogue were touched by the grandeur of kings like Davhana. It was hardly impersonal as living men always set the dialogue in motion. They forced people under duress to make elaborate choices between good and evil. This thread of strange philosophical beauty was deeply woven into the history of the land and the story was repeated many times over so that it became the only history people ever knew.

With the dawn of the colonial era this history was subdued. A new order was imposed on life. People's kings rapidly faded from memory and became myths of the past. No choices were left between what was good and what was evil. There was only slavery and exploitation.

Journal Entry

Respond to the theme of sibling rivalry by comparing your family's experiences and those of the Tlabina clan brothers.

Textual Considerations

1. Analyze how the movement of the narrative voice throughout the text attempts to capture the interaction of dialogue and the sense of physical action.
2. Discuss the old man's premises about the conditions that make a good ruler.
3. Focus on Head's description of the Tlabina brothers on a realistic level. To what extent do they function also on the **symbolic** or **mythical** level? (See the glossary.)

Cultural Contexts

1. From classical works like *Oedipus Rex* to contemporary tales like "A Power Struggle," writers have wrestled with the idea that "should an evil man gain the throne, people would suffer." Analyze the political implications of this hypothesis in relation not only to "A Power Struggle" but to contemporary political events as well.
2. Bessie Head says: "A ruler has to examine the dark side of human life and understand that men belong to that darkness. There are many men born with inadequate gifts and this disturbs them. They have no peace within themselves and once their jealousy is aroused they do terrible things." Analyze the larger implication of Head's thesis, and apply it to power struggles in our own time.

Elie Wiesel
1964

The Watch

For my bar mitzvah, I remember, I had received a magnificent gold watch. It was the customary gift for the occasion, and was meant to remind each boy that henceforth he would be held responsible for his acts before the Torah and its timeless laws.

But I could not keep my gift. I had to part with it the very day my native town became the pride of the Hungarian nation by chasing from its confines every single one of its Jews. The glorious masters of our municipality were jubilant: they were rid of us, there would be no more kaftans on the streets. The local newspaper was brief and to the point: from now on, it would be possible to state one's place of residence without feeling shame.

The time was late April, 1944.

In the early morning hours of that particular day, after a sleepless night, the ghetto was changed into a cemetery and its residents into gravediggers. We were digging feverishly in the courtyard, the garden, the cellar, consigning to the earth, temporarily we thought, whatever remained of the belongings accumulated by several generations, the sorrow and reward of long years of toil.

My father took charge of the jewelry and valuable papers. His head bowed, he was silently digging near the barn. Not far away, my mother, crouched on the damp ground, was burying the silver candelabra she used only on Shabbat eve; she was moaning softly, and I avoided her eyes. My sisters burrowed near the cellar. The youngest, Tziporah, had chosen the garden, like myself. Solemnly shoveling, she declined my help. What did she have to hide? Her toys? Her school notebooks? As for me, my only possession was my watch. It meant a lot to me. And so I decided to bury it in a dark, deep hole, three paces away from the fence, under a poplar tree whose thick, strong foliage seemed to provide a reasonably secure shelter.

All of us expected to recover our treasures. On our return, the earth would give them back to us. Until then, until the end of the storm, they would be safe.

Yes, we were naïve. We could not foresee that the very same evening, before the last train had time to leave the station, an excited mob of well-informed friendly neighbors would be rushing through the ghetto's wide-open houses and courtyards, leaving not a stone or beam unturned, throwing themselves upon the loot.

Twenty years later, standing in our garden, in the middle of the night, I remember the first gift, also the last, I ever received from my parents. I am seized by an irrational, irresistible desire to see it, to see if it is still there in the same spot, and if defying all laws of probability, it has survived—like me—by accident, not knowing how or why. My curiosity becomes obsession. I think neither of my father's money nor of my mother's candlesticks. All that matters in this town is my gold watch and the sound of its ticking.

Despite the darkness, I easily find my way in the garden. Once more I am the bar mitzvah child; here is the barn, the fence, the tree. Nothing has changed. To my left, the path leading to the Slotvino Rebbe's house. The Rebbe, though, had changed: the burning bush burned itself out and there is nothing left, not even smoke. What could he possibly have hidden the day we went away? His phylacteries? His prayer shawl? The holy scrolls inherited from his famous ancestor Rebbe Meirl of Premishlan? No, probably not even that kind of treasure. He had taken everything along, convinced that he was thus protecting not only himself but his disciples as well. He was proved wrong, the wonder rabbi.

But I mustn't think of him, not now. The watch, I must think of the watch. Maybe it was spared. Let's see, three steps to the right. Stop. Two forward. I recognize the place. Instinctively, I get ready to re-enact the scene my memory recalls. I fall on my knees. What can I use to dig? There is a shovel in the barn; its door is never locked. But by groping around in the dark I risk stumbling and waking the people sleeping in the house. They would take me for a marauder, a thief, and hand me over to the police. They might even kill me. Never mind, I'll have to manage without a shovel. Or any other tool. I'll use my hands, my nails. But it is difficult; the soil is hard, frozen, it resists as if determined to keep its secret. Too bad, I'll punish it by being the stronger.

Feverishly, furiously, my hands claw the earth, impervious to cold, fatigue and pain. One scratch, then another. No matter. Continue. My nails inch ahead, my fingers dig in, I bear down, my every fiber participates in the task. Little by little the hole deepens. I must hurry. My forehead touches the ground. Almost. I break out in a cold sweat, I am drenched, delirious. Faster, faster. I shall rip the earth from end to end, but I must know. Nothing can stop or frighten me. I'll go to the bottom of my fear, to the bottom of night, but I will know.

What time is it? How long have I been here? Five minutes, five hours? Twenty years. This night was defying time. I was laboring to exhume not an object but time itself, the soul and memory of that time. Nothing could be more urgent, more vital.

Suddenly a shiver goes through me. A sharp sensation, like a bite. My fingers touch something hard, metallic, rectangular. So I have not been digging in vain. The garden is spinning around me, over me. I stand up to catch my breath. A moment later, I'm on my knees again. Cautiously, gently I take the box from its tomb. Here it is, in the palm of my hand: the last relic, the only remaining symbol of everything I had loved, of everything I had been. A voice inside me warns: Don't open it, it contains nothing but emptiness, throw it away and run. I cannot heed the warning; it is too late to turn back. I need to know, either way. A slight pressure of my thumb and the box opens. I stifle the cry rising in my throat: the watch is there. Quick, a match. And another. Fleetingly, I catch a glimpse of it. The pain is blinding: could this thing, this object, be my gift, my pride? My past? Covered with dirt and rust, crawling with worms, it is unrecognizable, revolting. Unable to move, wondering what to do, I remain staring at it with the disgust one feels for love betrayed or a body debased. I am angry with myself for having yielded to curiosity. But disappointment gives way to profound pity: the watch too lived through war and holocaust, the kind reserved for watches perhaps. In its way, it too is a survivor, a ghost infested with humiliating sores and obsolete memories. Suddenly I feel the urge to carry it to my lips, dirty as it is, to kiss and console it with my tears, as one might console a living being, a sick friend returning from far away and requiring much kindness and rest, especially rest.

I touch it, I caress it. What I feel, besides compassion, is a strange kind of gratitude. You see, the men I had believed to be immortal had vanished into fiery clouds. My teachers, my friends, my guides had all deserted me. While this thing, this nameless, lifeless thing had survived for the sole purpose of welcoming me on my return and providing an epilogue to my childhood. And there awakens in me a desire to confide in it, to tell it my adventures, and in exchange, listen to its own.

What had happened in my absence: who had first taken possession of my house, my bed? Or rather, no; our confidences could wait for another time, another place: Paris, New York, Jerusalem. But first I would entrust it to the best jeweler in the world, so that the watch might recover its luster, its memory of the past.

It is growing late. The horizon is turning a deep red. I must go. The tenants will soon be waking, they will come down to the well for water. No time to lose. I stuff the watch into my pocket and cross the garden. I enter the courtyard. From under the porch a dog barks. And stops at once: he knows I am not a thief, anything but a thief. I open the gate. Halfway down the street I am overcome by violent remorse: I have just committed my first theft.

I turn around, retrace my steps through courtyard and garden. Again I find myself kneeling, as at Yom Kippur services, beneath the poplar. Holding my breath, my eyes refusing to cry, I place the watch back into its box, close the cover, and my first gift once more takes refuge deep inside the hole. Using both hands, I smoothly fill in the earth to remove all traces.

Breathless and with pounding heart, I reach the still deserted street. I stop and question the meaning of what I have just done. And find it inexplicable.

In retrospect, I tell myself that probably I simply wanted to leave behind me, underneath the silent soil, a reflection of my presence. Or that somehow I wanted to transform my watch into an instrument of delayed vengeance: one day, a child would play in the garden, dig near the tree and stumble upon a metal box. He would thus learn that his parents were usurpers, and that among the inhabitants of his town, once upon a time, there had been Jews and Jewish children, children robbed of their future.

The sun was rising and I was still walking through the empty streets and alleys. For a moment I thought I heard the chanting of schoolboys studying Talmud; I also thought I heard the invocations of Hasidim reciting morning prayers in thirty-three places at once. Yet above all these incantations, I heard distinctly, but as though coming from far away, the tick-tock of the watch I had just buried in accordance with Jewish custom. It was, after all, the very first gift that a Jewish child had once been given for his very first celebration.

Since that day, the town of my childhood has ceased being just another town. It has become the face of a watch.

Journal Entry

Respond to the protagonist's comment that both he and his family were naive. In what ways does he indicate that he is less naive twenty years later?

Textual Considerations

1. What prompts Wiesel to dig up the watch twenty years later? What does he mean when he says that he was laboring to exhume "time itself, the soul and memory of that time"?

2. Discuss Wiesel's use of such literary devices as repetition, symbolism, and fragmented sentences to convey the narrator's attachment to his watch. Identify the climactic scene in the text, and speculate on the meaning that this scene indicates his watch has for the narrator.
3. Except for the opening section of the essay, most of the narrative is written in the present tense. Where in the account of his return to his native town does Wiesel revert to the past tense? Why does he do so? What effect does he achieve?

Cultural Contexts

1. Consider how "The Watch" explores the concept that human beings may personally be entrapped by a historical event. To what extent has the narrator in Wiesel's story come to terms with his historical past?
2. Discuss with your group the degree to which our personal past contributes to our present selves, and debate whether understanding our pasts is necessary for self-realization.

Ernest J. Gaines
1963

The Sky Is Gray

1

Go'n be coming in a few minutes. Coming round that bend down there full speed. And I'm go'n get out my handkerchief and wave it down, and we go'n get on it and go.

I keep on looking for it, but Mama don't look that way no more. She's looking down the road where we just come from. It's a long old road, and far's you can don't see nothing but gravel. You got dry weeds on both sides, too, and you got trees on both sides, and fences on both sides, too. And you got cows in the pastures and they standing close together. And when we was coming out here to catch the bus I seen the smoke coming out of the cows's noses.

I look at my mama and I know what she's thinking. I been with Mama so much, just me and her, I know what she's thinking all the time. Right now it's home—Auntie and them. She's thinking if they got enough wood—if she left enough there to keep them warm till we get back. She's thinking if it go'n rain and if any of them have to go out in the rain. She's thinking 'bout the hog—if he go'n get out, and if Ty and Val be able to get him back in. She always worry like that when she leaves the house. She don't worry too much if she leave me there with the smaller ones, 'cause she know I'm go'n look after them and look after Auntie and everything else. I'm the oldest and she say I'm the man.

I look at my mama and I love my mama. She's wearing that black coat and that black hat and she's looking sad. I love my mama and I want to put my arm round her and tell her. But I'm not supposed to do that. She say that's weakness and that's crybaby stuff, and she don't want no crybaby round her. She don't want you to be scared, either. 'Cause Ty's scared of ghosts and she's always whipping him. I'm scared of the dark, too, but I make 'tend I ain't. I make 'tend I ain't 'cause I'm the oldest, and I got to set a good sample for the rest. I can't ever be scared and I can't ever cry. And that's why I never said nothing 'bout my teeth. It's been hurting me and hurting me close to a month now, but I never said it. I didn't say it 'cause I didn't want act like a crybaby, and 'cause I know we didn't have enough money to go have it pulled. But, Lord, it been hurting me. And look like it wouldn't start till at night when you was trying to get yourself little sleep. Then soon's you shut your eyes—ummm-ummm, Lord, look like it go right down to your heartstring.

"Hurting, hanh?" Ty'd say.

I'd shake my head, but I wouldn't open my mouth for nothing. You open your mouth and let that wind in, and it almost kill you.

I'd just lay there and listen to them snore. Ty there, right 'side me, and Auntie and Val over by the fireplace. Val younger than me and Ty, and he sleeps with Auntie. Mama sleeps round the other side with Louis and Walker.

I'd just lay there and listen to them, and listen to that wind out there, and listen to that fire in the fireplace. Sometimes it'd stop long enough to let me get little rest. Sometimes it just hurt, hurt, hurt. Lord, have mercy.

2

Auntie knowed it was hurting me. I didn't tell nobody but Ty, 'cause we buddies and he ain't go'n tell anybody. But some kind of way Auntie found out. When she asked me, I told her no, nothing was wrong. But she knowed it all the time. She told me to mash up a piece of aspirin and wrap it in some cotton and jugg it down in that hole. I did it, but it didn't do no good. It stopped for a little while, and started right back again. Auntie wanted to tell Mama, but I told her, "Uh-uh." 'Cause I knowed we didn't have any money, and it just was go'n make her mad again. So Auntie told Monsieur Bayonne, and Monsieur Bayonne came over to the house and told me to kneel down 'side him on the fireplace. He put his finger in his mouth and made the Sign of the Cross on my jaw. The tip of Monsieur Bayonne's finger is some hard, cause he's always playing on that guitar. If we sit outside at night we can always hear Monsieur Bayonne playing on his guitar. Sometimes we leave him out there playing on the guitar.

Monsieur Bayonne made the Sign of the Cross over and over on my jaw, but that didn't do no good. Even when he prayed and told me to pray some, too, that tooth still hurt me.

"How you feeling?" he say.

"Same," I say.

He kept on praying and making the Sign of the Cross and I kept on praying, too.

"Still hurting?" he say.

"Yes, sir."

Monsieur Bayonne mashed harder and harder on my jaw. He mashed so hard he almost pushed me over on Ty. But then he stopped.

"What kind of prayers you praying, boy?" he say.

"Baptist," I say.

"Well, I'll be—no wonder that tooth still killing him. I'm going one way and he pulling the other. Boy, don't you know any Catholic prayers?"

"I know 'Hail Mary,'" I say.

"Then you better start saying it."

"Yes, sir."

He started mashing on my jaw again, and I could hear him praying at the same time. And, sure enough, after awhile it stopped hurting me.

Me and Ty went outside where Monsieur Bayonne's two hounds was and we started playing with them. "Let's go hunting," Ty say. "All right," I say; and we went on back in the pasture. Soon the hounds got on a trail, and me and and Ty followed them all 'cross the pasture and then back in the woods, too. And then they cornered this little old rabbit and killed him, and me and Ty made them get back, and we picked up the rabbit and started on back home. But my tooth had started hurting me again. It was hurting me plenty now, but I wouldn't tell Monsieur Bayonne. That night I didn't sleep a bit, and first thing in the morning Auntie told me to go back and let Monsieur Bayonne pray over me some more. Monsieur Bayonne was in his kitchen making coffee when I got there. Soon's he seen me he knowed what was wrong.

"All right, kneel down there 'side that stove," he say. "And this time make sure you pray Catholic. I don't know nothing 'bout that Baptist, and I don't want know nothing 'bout him."

3

Last night Mama say, "Tomorrow we going to town."

"It ain't hurting me no more," I say. "I can eat anything on it."

"Tomorrow we going to town," she say.

And after she finished eating, she got up and went to bed. She always go to bed early now. 'Fore Daddy went in the Army, she used to stay up late. All of us sitting out on the gallery or round the fire. But now, look like soon's she finish eating she go to bed.

This morning when I woke up, her and Auntie was standing 'fore the fireplace. She say: "Enough to get there and get back. Dollar and a half to have it pulled. Twenty-five for me to go, twenty-five for him. Twenty-five for me to come back, twenty-five for him. Fifty cents left. Guess I get little piece of salt meat with that."

"Sure can use it," Auntie say. "White beans and no salt meat ain't white beans."

"I do the best I can," Mama say.

They was quiet after that, and I made 'tend I was still asleep.

"James, hit the floor," Auntie say.

I still made 'tend I was asleep. I didn't want them to know I was listening.

"All right," Auntie say, shaking me by the shoulder. "Come on. Today's the day."

I pushed the cover down to get out, and Ty grabbed it and pulled it back.

"You, too, Ty," Auntie said.

"I ain't getting no teef pulled," Ty say.

"Don't mean it ain't time to get up," Auntie say. "Hit it, Ty."

Ty got up grumbling.

"James, you hurry up and get in your clothes and eat your food," Auntie say. "What time y'all coming back?" she say to Mama.

"That 'leven o'clock bus," Mama say. "Got to get back in that field this evening."

"Get a move on you, James," Auntie say.

I went in the kitchen and washed my face, then I ate my breakfast. I was having bread and syrup. The bread was warm and hard and tasted good. And I tried to make it last a long time.

Ty came back there grumbling and mad at me.

"Got to get up," he say. "I ain't having no teefs pulled. What I got to be getting up for?"

Ty poured some syrup in his pan and got a piece of bread. He didn't wash his hands, neither his face, and I could see that white stuff in his eyes.

"You the one getting your teef pulled," he say. "What I got to get up for. I bet if I was getting a teef pulled, you wouldn't be getting up. Shucks; syrup again. I'm getting tired of this old syrup. Syrup, syrup, syrup. I'm go'n take with the sugar diabetes. I want me some bacon sometime."

"Go out in the field and work and you can have your bacon," Auntie say. She stood in the middle door looking at Ty. "You better be glad you got syrup. Some people ain't got that—hard's time is."

"Shucks," Ty say. "How can I be strong."

"I don't know too much 'bout your strength," Auntie say; "but I know where you go'n be hot at, you keep that grumbling up. James, get a move on you; your mama waiting."

I ate my last piece of bread and went in the front room. Mama was standing 'fore the fireplace warming her hands. I put on my coat and cap, and we left the house.

4

I look down there again, but it still ain't coming. I almost say, "It ain't coming yet," but I keep my mouth shut. 'Cause that's something else she don't like. She don't like for you to say something just for nothing. She can see it ain't coming. I can see it ain't coming, so why say it ain't coming. I don't say it, I turn and look at the river that's back of us. It's so cold the smoke's just raising up from the water. I see a bunch of pool-doos not too far out—just on the other side the lilies. I'm wondering if you can eat pool-doos. I ain't too sure, 'cause I ain't never ate none. But I done ate owls and blackbirds, and I done ate redbirds, too. I didn't want to kill the redbirds, but she made me kill them. They had two of them back there. One in my trap, one in Ty's trap. Me and Ty was go'n play with them and let them go, but she made me kill them 'cause we needed the food.

"I can't," I say. "I can't."

"Here," she say. "Take it."

"I can't," I say. "I can't. I can't kill him, Mama, please."

"Here," she say. "Take this fork, James."

"Please, Mama, I can't kill him," I say.

I could tell she was go'n hit me. I jerked back, but I didn't jerk back soon enough.

"Take it," she say.

I took it and reached in for him, but he kept on hopping to the back.

"I can't, Mama," I say. The water just kept on running down my face. "I can't," I say.

"Get him out of there," she say.

I reached in for him and he kept on hopping to the back. Then I reached in farther, and he pecked me on the hand.

"I can't, Mama," I say.

She slapped me again.

I reached in again, but he kept on hopping out my way. Then he hopped to one side and I reached there. The fork got him on the leg and I heard his leg pop. I pulled my hand out 'cause I had hurt him.

"Give it here," she say, and jerked the fork out of my hand.

She reached in and got the little bird right in the neck. I heard the fork go in his neck, and I heard it go in the ground. She brought him out and helt him right in front of me.

"That's one," she say. She shook him off and gived me the fork. "Get the other one."

"I can't, Mama," I say. "I'll do anything, but don't make me do that."

She went to the corner of the fence and broke the biggest switch over there she could find. I knelt 'side the trap, crying.

"Get him out of there," she say.

"I can't, Mama."

She started hitting me 'cross the back. I went down on the ground, crying.

"Get him," she say.

"Octavia?" Auntie say.

'Cause she had come out of the house and she was standing by the tree looking at us.

"Get him out of there," Mama say.

"Octavia," Auntie say, "explain to him. Explain to him. Just don't beat him. Explain to him."

But she hit me and hit me and hit me.

I'm still young—ain't no more than eight; but I know now; I know why I had to do it. (They was so little, though. They was so little. I 'member how I picked the feathers off them and cleaned them and helt them over the fire. Then we all ate them. Ain't had but a little bitty piece each, but we all had a little bitty piece, and everybody just looked at me 'cause they was so proud.) Suppose she had to go away? That's why I had to do it. Suppose she had to go away like Daddy went away? Then who was go'n look after us? They had to be somebody left to carry on. I didn't know it then, but I know it now. Auntie and Monsieur Bayonne talked to me and made me see.

5

Time I see it I get out my handkerchief and start waving. It's still 'way down there, but I keep waving anyhow. Then it come up and stop and me and Mama get on. Mama tell me go sit in the back while she pay. I do like she say, and the people look at me. When I pass the little sign that say "White" and "Colored," I start looking for a seat. I just see one of them back there, but I don't take it, 'cause I want my mama to sit down herself. She comes in the back and sit down, and I lean on the seat. They got seats in the front, but I know I can't sit there, 'cause I have to sit back of the sign. Anyhow, I don't want to sit there if my mama go'n sit back here.

They got a lady sitting 'side my mama and she looks at me and smiles little bit. I smile back, but I don't open my mouth, 'cause the wind'll get in and make that tooth ache. The lady take out a pack of gum and reach me a slice, but I shake my head. The lady just can't understand why a little boy'll turn down gum, and she reach me a slice again. This time I point to my jaw. The lady understands and smiles little bit, and I smile little bit, but I don't open my mouth, though.

They got a girl sitting 'cross from me. She got on a red overcoat and her hair's plaited in one big plait. First, I make 'tend I don't see her over there but then I start looking at her little bit. She make 'tend she don't see me, either, but I catch her looking that way. She got a cold, and every now and then she h'ist that little handkerchief to her nose. She ought to blow it, but she don't. Must think she's too much a lady or something.

Every time she h'ist that little handkerchief, the lady 'side her say something in her ear. She shakes her head and lays her hands in her lap again. Then I catch her kind of looking where I'm at. I smile at her little bit. But think she'll smile back? Uh-uh. She just turn up her little old nose and turn her head. Well, I show her both of us can turn us head. I turn mine too and look out at the river.

The river is gray. The sky is gray. They have pool-doos on the water. The water is wavy, and the pool-doos go up and down. The bus go round a turn, and you got plenty trees hiding the river. Then the bus go round another turn, and I can see the river again.

I look toward the front where all the white people sitting. Then I look at that little old gal again. I don't look right at her, 'cause I don't want all them people to know I love her. I just look at her little bit, like I'm looking out that window over there. But she knows I'm looking that way, and she kind of look at me, too. The lady sitting 'side her catch her this time, and she leans over and says something in her ear.

"I don't love him nothing," that little old gal says out loud.

Everybody back there hear her mouth, and all of them look at us and laugh.

"I don't love you, either," I say. "So you don't have to turn up your nose, Miss."

"You the one looking," she say.

"I wasn't looking at you," I say. "I was looking out that window, there."

"Out that window, my foot," she say. "I seen you. Everytime I turned round you was looking at me."

"You must of been looking yourself if you seen me all them times," I say.

"Shucks," she say, "I got me all kind of boyfriends."

"I got girlfriends, too," I say.

"Well, I just don't want you getting your hopes up," she say.

I don't say no more to that little old gal cause I don't want have to bust her in the mouth. I lean on the seat where Mama sitting, and I don't even look that way no more. When we get to Bayonne, she jugg her little old tongue out at me. I make 'tend I'm go'n hit her, and she duck down 'side her mama. And all the people laugh at us again.

6

Me and Mama get off and start walking in town. Bayonne is a little bitty town. Baton Rouge is a hundred times bigger than Bayonne. I went to Baton Rouge once—me, Ty, Mama, and Daddy. But that was 'way back yonder, 'fore Daddy went in the Army. I wonder when we go'n see him again. I wonder when. Look like he ain't ever coming back home.... Even the pavement all cracked in Bayonne. Got grass shooting right out the sidewalk. Got weeds in the ditch, too; just like they got at home.

It's some cold in Bayonne. Look like it's colder than it is home. The wind blows in my face, and I feel that stuff running down my nose. I sniff. Mama says use that handkerchief. I blow my nose and put it back.

We pass a school and I see them white children playing in the yard. Big old red school, and them children just running and playing. Then we pass a café, and I see a bunch of people in there eating. I wish I was in there 'cause I'm cold. Mama tells me keep my eyes in front where they belong.

We pass stores that's got dummies, and we pass another café, and then we pass a shoe shop, and that bald-head man in there fixing on a shoe. I look at him and I butt into that white lady, and Mama jerks me in front and tells me stay there.

We come up to the courthouse, and I see the flag waving there. This flag ain't like the one we got at school. This one here ain't got but a handful of stars. One at school got a big pile of stars—one for every state. We pass it and we turn and there it is—the dentist office. Me and Mama go in, and they got people sitting every-where you look. They even got a little boy in there younger than me.

Me and Mama sit on that bench, and a white lady come in there and ask me what my name is. Mama tells her and the white lady goes on back. Then I hear somebody hollering in there. Soon's that little boy hear him hollering, he starts hollering too. His mama pats him and pats him, trying to make him hush up, but he ain't thinkin 'bout his mama.

The man that was hollering in there comes out holding his jaw. He is a big old man and he's wearing overalls and a jumper.

"Got it, hanh?" another man asks him.

The man shakes his head—don't want open his mouth.

"Man, I thought they was killing you in there," the other man says. "Hollering like a pig under a gate."

The man don't say nothing. He just heads for the door, and the other man follows him.

"John Lee," the white lady says. "John Lee Williams."

The little boy juggs his head down in his mama's lap and holler more now. His mama tells him go with the nurse, but he ain't thinking 'bout his mama. His mama tells him again, but he don't even hear her. His mama picks him up and takes him in there, and even when the white lady shuts the door I can still hear little old John Lee.

"I often wonder why the Lord let a child like that suffer," a lady says to my mama. The lady's sitting right in front of us on another bench. She's got on a white dress and a black sweater. She must be a nurse or something herself, I reckon.

"Not us to question," a man says.

"Sometimes I don't know if we shouldn't," the lady says.

"I know definitely we shouldn't," the man says. The man looks like a preacher. He's big and fat and he's got on a black suit. He's got a gold chain, too.

"Why?" the lady says.

"Why anything?" the preacher says.

"Yes," the lady says. "Why anything?"

"Not us to question," the preacher says.

The lady looks at the preacher a little while and looks at Mama again.

"And look like it's the poor who suffers the most," she says. "I don't understand it."

"Best not to even try," the preacher says. "He works in mysterious ways—wonders to perform."

Right then little John Lee bust out hollering, and everybody turn they head to listen.

"He's not a good dentist," the lady says. "Dr. Robillard is much better. But more expensive. That's why most of the colored people come here. The white people go to Dr. Robillard. Y'all from Bayonne?"

"Down the river," my mama says. And that's all she go'n say, 'cause she don't talk much. But the lady keeps on looking at her, and so she says, "Near Morgan."

"I see," the lady says.

7

"That's the trouble with the black people in this country today," somebody else says. This one here's sitting on the same side me and Mama's sitting, and he is kind of sitting in front of that preacher. He looks like a teacher or somebody that goes to college. He's got on a suit, and he's got a book that he's been reading. "We don't question is exactly our problem," he says. "We should question and question and question—question everything."

The preacher just looks at him a long time. He done put a toothpick or something in his mouth, and he just keeps on turning it and turning it. You can see he don't like that boy with that book.

"Maybe you can explain what you mean," he says.

"I said what I meant," the boy says. "Question everything. Every stripe, every star, every word spoken. Everything."

"It 'pears to me that this young lady and I was talking 'bout God, young man," the preacher says.

"Question Him, too," the boy says.

"Wait," the preacher says, "Wait now."

"You heard me right," the boy says. "His existence as well as everything else. Everything."

The preacher just looks across the room at the boy. You can see he's getting madder and madder. But mad or no mad, the boy ain't thinking 'bout him. He looks at that preacher just's hard's the preacher looks at him.

"Is this what they coming to?" the preacher says. "Is that what we educating them for?"

"You're not educating me," the boy says. "I wash dishes at night so that I can go to school in the day. So even the words you spoke need questioning."

The preacher just looks at him and shakes his head.

"When I come in this room and seen you there with your book, I said to myself, 'here's an intelligent man.' How wrong a person can be."

"Show me one reason to believe in the existence of a God," the boy says.

"My heart tells me," the preacher says.

"'My heart tells me,'" the boy says. "'My heart tells me.' Sure, 'My heart tells me.' And as long as you listen to what your heart tells you, you will have only what the white man gives you and nothing more. Me, I don't listen to my heart. The purpose of the heart is to pump blood throughout the body, and nothing else."

"Who's your paw, boy?" the preacher says.

"Why?"

"Who is he?"

"He's dead."

"And your mom?"

"She's in Charity Hospital with pneumonia. Half killed herself, working for nothing."

"And 'cause he's dead and she's sick, you mad at the world?"

"I'm not mad at the world. I'm questioning the world. I'm questioning it with cold logic sir. What do words like Freedom, Liberty, God, White, Colored mean? I want to know. That's why *you* are sending us to school, to read and to ask questions. And because we ask these questions, you call us mad. No sir, it is not us who are mad."

"You keep saying 'us'?"

"'Us.' Yes—us. I'm not alone."

The preacher just shakes his head. Then he looks at everybody in the room—everybody. Some of the people look down at the floor, keep from looking at him. I kind of look 'way myself, but soon's I know he done turn his head, I look that way again.

"I'm sorry for you," he says to the boy.

"Why?" the boy says. "Why not be sorry for yourself? Why are you so much better off than I am? Why aren't you sorry for these other people in here? Why not be sorry for the lady who had to drag her child into the dentist office? Why not be sorry for the lady sitting on that bench over there? Be sorry for them. Not for me. Some way or the other I'm going to make it."

"No, I'm sorry for you," the preacher says.

"Of course, of course," the boy says, nodding his head. "You're sorry for me because I rock that pillar you're leaning on."

"You can't ever rock the pillar I'm leaning on, young man. It's stronger than anything man can ever do."

"You believe in God because a man told you to believe in God," the boy says. "A white man told you to believe in God. And why? To keep you ignorant so he can keep his feet on your neck."

"So now we the ignorant?" the preacher says.

"Yes," the boy says. "Yes." And he opens his book again.

The preacher just looks at him sitting there. The boy done forgot all about him. Everybody else make 'tend they done forgot the squabble, too.

Then I see that preacher getting up real slow. Preacher's great big old man and be got to brace himself to get up. He comes over where the boy is sitting. He just stands there a little while looking down at him, but the boy don't raise his head.

"Get up, boy," preacher says.

The boy looks up at him, then he shuts his book real slow and stands up. Preacher just hauls back and hit him in the face. The boy falls back 'gainst the wall, but be straightens himself up and looks right back at that preacher.

"You forgot the other cheek," he says.

The preacher hauls back and hit him again on the other side. But this time the boy braces himself and don't fall.

"That hasn't changed a thing," he says.

The preacher just looks at the boy. The preacher's breathing real hard like he just run up a big hill. The boy sits down and opens his book again.

"I feel sorry for you," the preacher says. "I never felt so sorry for a man before."

The boy makes 'tend he don't even hear that preacher. He keeps on reading his book. The preacher goes back and gets his hat off the chair.

"Excuse me," he says to us. "I'll come back some other time. Y'all, please excuse me."

And he looks at the boy and goes out the room. The boy h'ist his hand up to his mouth one time to wipe 'way some blood. All the rest of the time he keeps on reading. And nobody else in there say a word.

8

Little John Lee and his mama come out the dentist office, and the nurse calls somebody else in. Then little bit later they come out, and the nurse calls another name. But fast's she calls somebody in there, somebody else comes in the place where we sitting, and the room stays full.

The people coming in now, all of them wearing big coats. One of them says something 'bout sleeting, another one says he hope not. Another one says he think it ain't nothing but rain. 'Cause, he says, rain can get awful cold this time of year.

All round the room they talking. Some of them talking to people right by them, some of them talking to people clear 'cross the room, some of them talking to anybody'll listen. It's a little bitty room, no bigger than us kitchen, and I can see everybody in there. The little old room's full of smoke, 'cause you got two old men smoking pipes over by that side door. I think I feel my tooth thumping me some, and I hold my breath and wait. I wait and wait, but it don't thump me no more. Thank God for that.

I feel like going to sleep, and I lean back 'gainst the wall. But I'm scared to go to sleep. Scared 'cause the nurse might call my name and I won't hear her. And Mama might go to sleep, too, and she'll be mad if neither one of us heard the nurse.

I look up at Mama. I love my mama. I love my mama. And when cotton come I'm go'n get her a new coat. And I ain't go'n get a black coat, either. I think I'm go'n get her a red one.

"They got some books over there," I say. "Want read one of them?"

Mama looks at the books, but she don't answer me.

"You got yourself a little man there," the lady says.

Mama don't say nothing to the lady, but she must've smiled, 'cause I seen the lady smiling back. The lady looks at me a little while, like she's feeling sorry for me.

"You sure got that preacher out here in a hurry," she says to that boy.

The boy looks up at her and looks in his book again. When I grow up I want be just like him. I want clothes like that and I want to keep a book with me, too.

"You really don't believe in God?" the lady says.

"No," he says.

"But why?" the lady says.

"Because the wind is pink," he says.

"What?" the lady says.

The boy don't answer her no more. He just reads in his book.

"Talking 'bout the wind is pink," that old lady says. She's sitting on the same bench with the boy and she's trying to look in his face. The boy makes 'tend the old lady ain't even there. He just keeps on reading. "Wind is pink," she says again. "Eh, Lord, what children go'n be saying next?"

The lady 'cross from us bust out laughing.

"That's a good one," she says. "The wind is pink. Yes sir, that's a good one."

"Don't you believe the wind is pink?" the boy says. He keeps his head down in the book.

"Course I believe it, honey," the lady says. "Course I do." She looks at us and winks her eye. "And what color is grass, honey?"

"Grass? Grass is black."

She bust out laughing again. The boy looks at her.

"Don't you believe grass is black?" he says.

The lady quits her laughing and looks at him. Everybody else looking at him, too. The place quiet, quiet.

"Grass is green, honey," the lady says. "It was green yesterday, it's green today, and it's go'n be green tomorrow."

"How do you know it's green?"

"I know because I know."

"You don't know it's green," the boy says. "You believe it's green because someone told you it was green. If someone had told you it was black you'd believe it was black."

"It's green," the lady says. "I know green when I see green."

"Prove it's green," the boy says.

"Sure, now," the lady says. "Don't tell me it's coming to that."

"It's coming to just that," the boy says. "Words mean nothing. One means no more than the other."

"That's what it all coming to?" the old lady says. That old lady got on a turban and she got on two sweaters. She got a green sweater under a black sweater. I can see the green sweater 'cause some of the buttons on the other sweater's missing.

"Yes ma'am," the boy says. "Words mean nothing. Action is the only thing. Doing. That's the only thing."

"Other words, you want the Lord to come down here and show Hisself to you?" she says.

"Exactly, ma'am," he says.

"You don't mean that, I'm sure?" she says.

"I do, ma'am," he says.

"Done, Jesus," the old lady says, shaking her head.

"I didn't go 'long with that preacher at first," the other lady says; "but now— I don't know. When a person say the grass is black, he's either a lunatic or something's wrong."

"Prove to me that it's green," the boy says.

"It's green because the people say it's green."

"Those same people say we're citizens of these United States," the boy says.

"I think I'm a citizen," the lady says.

"Citizens have certain rights," the boy says. "Name me one right that you have. One right, granted by the Constitution, that you can exercise in Bayonne."

The lady don't answer him. She just looks at him like she don't know what he's talking 'bout. I know I don't.

"Things changing," she says.

"Things are changing because some black men have begun to think with their brains and not their hearts," the boy says.

"You trying to say these people don't believe in God?"

"I'm sure some of them do. Maybe most of them do. But they don't believe that God is going to touch these white people's hearts and change things tomorrow. Things change through action. By no other way."

Everybody sit quiet and look at the boy. Nobody says a thing. Then the lady 'cross the room from me and Mama just shakes her head.

"Let's hope that not all your generation feel the same way you do," she says.

"Think what you please, it doesn't matter," the boy says. "But it will be men who listen to their heads and not their hearts who will see that your children have a better chance than you had."

"Let's hope they ain't all like you, though," the old lady says. "Done forgot the heart absolutely."

"Yes ma'am, I hope they aren't all like me," the boy says. "Unfortunately, I was born too late to believe in your God. Let's hope that the ones who come after will have your faith—if not in your God, then in something else, something definitely that they can lean on. I haven't anything. For me, the wind is pink, the grass is black."

9

The nurse comes in the room where we all sitting and waiting and says the doctor won't take no more patients till one o'clock this evening. My mama jumps up off the bench and goes up to the white lady.

"Nurse, I have to go back in the field this evening," she says.

"The doctor is treating his last patient now," the nurse says. "One o'clock this evening."

"Can I at least speak to the doctor?" my mama asks.

"I'm his nurse," the lady says.

"My little boy's sick," my mama says. "Right now his tooth almost killing him."

The nurse looks at me. She's trying to make up her mind if to let me come in. I look at her real pitiful. The tooth ain't hurting me at all, but Mama says it is, so I make 'tend for her sake.

"This evening," the nurse says, and goes on back in the office.

"Don't feel 'jected, honey," the lady says to Mama. "I been round them a long time—they take you when they want to. If you was white, that's something else; but we the wrong color."

Mama don't say nothing to the lady, and me and her go outside and stand 'gainst the wall. It's cold out there. I can feel that wind going through my coat. Some of the other people come out of the room and go up the street. Me and Mama stand there a little while and we start walking. I don't know where we going. When we come to the other street we just stand there.

"You don't have to make water, do you?" Mama says.

"No, ma'am," I say.

We go on up the street. Walking real slow. I can tell Mama don't know where she's going. When we come to a store we stand there and look at the dummies. I look at a little boy wearing a brown overcoat. He's got on brown shoes, too. I look at my old shoes and look at his'n again. You wait till summer, I say.

Me and Mama walk away. We come up to another store and we stop and look at them dummies, too. Then we go on again. We pass a café where the white people in there eating. Mama tells me keep my eyes in front where they belong, but I can't help from seeing them people eat. My stomach starts to growling 'cause I'm hungry. When I see people eating, I get hungry; when I see a coat, I get cold.

A man whistles at my mama when we go by a filling station. She makes 'tend she don't even see him. I look back and I feel like hitting him in the mouth. If I was bigger, I say; if I was bigger, you'd see.

We keep on going. I'm getting colder and colder, but I don't say nothing. I feel that stuff running down my nose and I sniff.

"That rag," Mama says.

I get it out and wipe my nose. I'm getting cold all over now—my face, my hands, my feet, everything. We pass another little café, but this'n for white people, too, and we can't go in there, either. So we just walk. I'm so cold now I'm 'bout ready to say it. If I knowed where we was going I wouldn't be so cold, but I don't know where we going. We go, we go, we go. We walk clean out of Bayonne. Then we cross the street and we come back. Same thing I seen when I got off the bus this morning. Same old trees, same old walk, same old weeds, same old cracked pave— same old everything.

I sniff again.

"That rag," Mama says.

I wipe my nose real fast and jugg that handkerchief back in my pocket 'fore my hand gets too cold. I raise my head and I can see David's hardware store. When we come up to it, we go in I don't know why, but I'm glad.

It's warm in there. It's so warm in there you don't ever want to leave. I look for the heater, and I see it over by them barrels. Three white men standing round the heater talking in Creole. One of them comes over to see what my mama want.

"Got any axe handles?" she says.

Me, Mama and the white man start to the back, but Mama stops me when we come up to the heater. She and the white man go on. I hold my hands over the heater and look at them. They go all the way to the back, and I see the white man pointing to the axe handles 'gainst the wall. Mama takes one of them and shakes it like she's trying to figure how much it weighs. Then she rubs her hand over it from one end to the other end. She turns it over and looks at the other side, then she shakes it again, and shakes her head and puts it back. She gets another one and she does it just like she did the first one, then she shakes her head. Then she gets a brown one and do it that, too. But she don't like this one, either. Then she gets another one, but 'fore she shakes it or anything, she looks at me. Look like she's trying to say something to me, but I don't know what it is. All I know is I done got warm now and I'm feeling right smart better. Mama shakes this axe handle just like she did the others, and shakes her head and says something to the white man. The white man just looks at his pile of axe handles, and when Mama pass him to come to the front, the white man just scratch his head and follows her. She tells me come on and we go on and start walking again.

We walk and walk, and no time at all I'm cold again. Look like I'm colder now 'cause I can still remember how good it was back there. My stomach growls and I suck it in to keep Mama from hearing it. She's walking right 'side me, and it growls so loud you can hear it a mile. But Mama don't say a word.

10

When we come up to the courthouse, I look at the clock. It's got quarter to twelve. Mean we got another hour and a quarter to be out here in the cold. We go and stand 'side a building. Something hits my cap and I look up at the sky. Sleet's falling.

I look at Mama standing there. I want stand close 'side her, but she don't like that. She say that's crybaby stuff. She say you got to stand for yourself, by yourself.

"Let's go back to that office," she says.

We cross the street. When we get to the dentist office I try to open the door, but I can't. I twist and twist, but I can't. Mama pushes me to the side and she twist the knob, but she can't open the door, either. She turns 'way from the door. I look at her, but I don't move and I don't say nothing. I done seen her like this before and I'm scared of her.

"You hungry?" she says. She says it like she's mad at me, like I'm the cause of everything.

"No, ma'am," I say.

"You want eat and walk back, or you rather don't eat and ride?"

"I ain't hungry," I say.

I ain't just hungry, but I'm cold, too. I'm so hungry and cold I want to cry. And look like I'm getting colder and colder. My feet done got numb. I try to work my toes, but I don't even feel them. Look like I'm go'n die. Look like I'm go'n stand right here and freeze to death. I think 'bout home. I think 'bout Val and Auntie and Ty and Louis and Walker. It's 'bout twelve o'clock and I know they eating dinner now. I can hear Ty making jokes. He done forgot 'bout getting up early this morning and right now he's probably making jokes. Always trying to make somebody laugh. I wish I was right there listening to him. Give anything in the world if I was home round the fire.

"Come on," Mama says.

We start walking again. My feet so numb I can't hardly feel them. We turn the corner and go on back up the street. The clock on the courthouse starts hitting for twelve.

The sleet's coming down plenty now. They hit the pave and bounce like rice. Oh, Lord; oh, Lord, I pray. Don't let me die, don't let me die, don't let me die, Lord.

11

Now I know where we going. We going back of town where the colored people eat. I don't care if I don't eat. I been hungry before. I can stand it. But I can't stand the cold.

I can see we go'n have a long walk. It's 'bout a mile down there. But I don't mind. I know when I get there I'm go'n warm myself. I think I can hold out. My hands numb in my pockets and my feet numb, too, but if I keep moving I can hold out. Just don't stop no more, that's all.

The sky's gray. The sleet keeps on falling. Falling like rain now—plenty, plenty. You can hear it hitting the pave. You can see it bouncing. Sometimes it bounces two times 'fore it settles.

We keep on going. We don't say nothing. We just keep on going, keep on going.

I wonder what Mama's thinking. I hope she ain't mad at me. When summer come I'm go'n pick plenty cotton and get her a coat. I'm go'n get her a red one.

I hope they'd make it summer all the time. I'd be glad if it was summer all the time—but it ain't. We got to have winter, too. Lord, I hate the winter. I guess everybody hate the winter.

I don't sniff this time. I get out my handkerchief and wipe my nose. My hands's so cold I can hardly hold the handkerchief.

I think we getting close, but we ain't there yet. I wonder where everybody is. Can't see a soul but us. Look like we the only two people moving round today. Must be too cold for the rest of the people to move round in.

I can hear my teeth. I hope they don't knock together too hard and make that bad one hurt. Lord, that's all I need, for that bad one to start off.

I hear a church bell somewhere. But today ain't Sunday. They must be ringing for a funeral or something.

I wonder what they doing at home. They must be eating. Monsieur Bayonne might be there with his guitar. One day Ty played with Monsieur Bayonne's guitar and broke one of the strings. Monsieur Bayonne was some mad with Ty. He say Ty wasn't go'n ever 'mount to nothing. Ty can go just like Monsieur Bayonne when he ain't there. Ty can make everybody laugh when he starts to mocking Monsieur Bayonne.

I used to like to be with Mama and Daddy. We used to be happy. But they took him in the Army. Now, nobody happy no more.... I be glad when Daddy comes home.

Monsieur Bayonne say it wasn't fair for them to take Daddy and give Mama nothing and give us nothing. Auntie say, "Shhh, Etienne. Don't let them hear you talk like that." Monsieur Bayonne say, "It's God truth. What they giving his children? They have to walk three and half miles to school hot or cold. That's anything to give for a paw? She's got to work in the field rain or shine just to make ends meet. That's anything to give for a husband?" Auntie say, "Shhh, Etienne, shhh." "Yes, you right," Monsieur Bayonne say. "Best don't say it in front of them now. But one day they go'n find out. One day." "Yes, I suppose so," Auntie say. "Then what, Rose Mary?" Monsieur Bayonne say. "I don't know, Etienne," Auntie say. "All we can do is us job, and leave everything else in His hand..."

We getting closer, now. We getting closer. I can even see the railroad tracks.

We cross the tracks, and now I see the café. Just to get in there, I say. Just to get in there. Already I'm starting to feel little better.

12

We go in. Ahh, it's good. I look for the heater; there 'gainst the wall. One of them little brown ones. I just stand there and hold my hands over it. I can't open my hands too wide 'cause they almost froze.

Mama's standing right 'side me. She done unbuttoned her coat. Smoke rises out of the coat, and the coat smells like a wet dog.

I move to the side so Mama can have more room. She opens out her hands and rubs them together. I rub mine together, too, 'cause this keep them from hurting. If you let them warm too fast, they hurt you sure. But if you let them warm just little bit at a time, and you keep rubbing them, they be all right every time.

They got just two more people in the café. A lady back of the counter, and a man on this side the counter. They been watching us ever since we come in.

Mama gets out the handkerchief and count up the money. Both of us know how much money she's got there. Three dollars. No, she ain't got three dollars 'cause she had to pay us way up here. She ain't got but two dollars and a half left. Dollar and a half to get my tooth pulled, and fifty cents for us to go back on, and fifty cents worth of salt meat.

She stirs the money round with her finger. Most of the money is change 'cause I can hear it rubbing together. She stirs it and stirs it. Then she looks at the door. It's still sleeting. I can hear it hitting 'gainst the wall like rice.

"I ain't hungry, Mama," I say.

"Got to pay them something for they heat," she says.

She takes a quarter out the handkerchief and ties the handkerchief up again. She looks over her shoulder at the people, but she still don't move. I hope she don't spend the money. I don't want her spending it on me. I'm hungry, I'm almost starving I'm so hungry, but I don't want her spending the money on me.

She flips the quarter over like she's thinking. She's must be thinking 'bout us walking back home. Lord, I sure don't want walk home. If I thought it'd do any good to say something, I'd say it. But Mama makes up her own mind 'bout things.

She turns 'way from the heater right fast, like she better hurry up and spend the quarter 'fore she change her mind. I watch her go toward the counter. The man and the lady look at her. She tells the lady something and the lady walks away. The man keeps on looking at her. Her back's turned to the man, and she don't even know he's standing there.

The lady puts some cakes and a glass of milk on the counter. Then she pours up a cup of coffee and sets it 'side the other stuff. Mama pays her for the things and comes on back where I'm standing. She tells me sit down at the table 'gainst the wall.

The milk and the cakes's for me; the coffee's for Mama. I eat slow and I look at her. She's looking outside at the sleet. She's looking real sad. I say to myself, I'm go'n make all this up one day. You see, one day, I'm go'n make all this up. I want say it now; I want tell her how I feel right now; but Mama don't like for us to talk like that.

"I can't eat all this," I say.

They ain't got but just three little old cakes there. I'm so hungry right now, the Lord knows I can eat a hundred times three. But I want my mama to have one.

Mama don't even look my way. She knows I'm hungry, she knows I want it. I let it stay there a little while, then I get it and eat it. I eat just on my front teeth, though, 'cause if cake touch that back tooth I know what'll happen. Thank God it ain't hurt me at all today.

After I finish eating I see the man go to the juke box. He drops a nickel in it, then he just stand there a little while looking at the record. Mama tells me keep my eyes in front where they belong. I turn my head like she say, but then I hear the man coming toward us.

"Dance, pretty?" he says.

Mama gets up to dance with him. But 'fore you know it, she done grabbed the little man in the collar and done heaved him 'side the wall.

He hit the wall so hard he stop the juke box from playing.

"Some pimp," the lady back of the counter says. "Some pimp."

The little man jumps up off the floor and starts toward my mama. 'Fore you know it, Mama done sprung open her knife and she's waiting for him.

"Come on," she says. "Come on. I'll gut you from your neighbo to your throat. Come on."

I go up to the little man to hit him, but Mama makes me come and stand 'side her. The little man looks at me and Mama and goes on back to the counter.

"Some pimp," the lady back of the counter says. "Some pimp." She starts laughing and pointing at the little man. "Yes sir, you a pimp, all right. Yes sir-ree."

13

"Fasten that coat, let's go," Mama says.

"You don't have to leave," the lady says. Mama don't answer the lady, and we right out in the cold again. I'm warm right now—my hands, my ears, my feet—but I know this ain't go'n last too long. It done sleet so much now you got ice everywhere you look.

We cross the railroad tracks, and soon's we do, I get cold. That wind goes through this little old coat like it ain't even there. I got on a shirt and a sweater under the coat, but that wind don't pay them no mind. I look up and I can see we got a long way to go. I wonder if we go'n make it 'fore I get too cold.

We cross over to walk on the sidewalk. They got just one sidewalk back here, and it's over there.

After we go just a little piece, I smell bread cooking. I look, then I see a baker shop. When we get closer, I can smell it more better. I shut my eyes and make 'tend I'm eating. But I keep them shut too long and I butt up 'gainst a telephone post. Mama grabs me and see if I'm hurt. I ain't bleeding or nothing and she turns me loose.

I can feel I'm getting colder and colder, and I look up to see how far we still got to go. Uptown is 'way up yonder. A half mile more, I reckon. I try to think of something. They say think and you won't get cold. I think of that poem, "Annabel Lee." I ain't been to school in so long—this bad weather—I reckon they done passed "Annabel Lee" by now. But passed it or not, I'm sure Miss Walker go'n make me recite it when I get there. That woman don't never forget nothing. I ain't never seen nobody like that in my life.

I'm still getting cold. "Annabel Lee" or no "Annabel Lee," I'm still getting cold. But I can see we getting closer. We getting there gradually.

Soon's we turn the corner, I seen a little old white lady up in front of us. She's the only lady on the street. She's all in black and she's got a long black rag over her head.

"Stop," she says.

Me and Mama stop and look at her. She must be crazy to be out in all this bad weather. Ain't got but a few other people out there, and all of them's men.

"Y'all done ate?" she says.

"Just finish," Mama says.

"Y'all must be cold then?" she says.

"We headed for the dentist," Mama says. "We'll warm up when we get there."

"What dentist?" the old lady says. "Mr. Bassett?"

"Yes, ma'am," Mama says.

"Come on in," the old lady says. "I'll telephone him and tell him y'all coming."

Me and Mama follow the old lady in the store. It's a little bitty store, and it don't have much in there. The old lady takes off her head rag and folds it up.

"Helena?" somebody calls from the back.

"Yes, Alnest?" the old lady says.

"Did you see them?"

"They're here. Standing beside me."

"Good. Now you can stay inside."

The old lady looks at Mama. Mama's waiting to hear what she brought us in here for. I'm waiting for that, too.

"I saw y'all each time you went by," she says. "I came out to catch you, but you were gone."

"We went back of town," Mama says.

"Did you eat?"

"Yes, ma'am."

The old lady looks at Mama a long time, like she's thinking Mama might just be saying that. Mama looks right back at her. The old lady looks at me to see what I have to say. I don't say nothing. I sure ain't going 'gainst my mama.

"There's food in the kitchen," she says to Mama. "I've been keeping it warm."

Mama turns right around and starts for the door.

"Just a minute," the old lady says. Mama stops. "The boy'll have to work for it. It isn't free."

"We don't take no handout," Mama says.

"I'm not handing out anything," the old lady says. "I need my garbage moved to the front. Ernest has a bad cold and can't go out there."

"James'll move it for you," Mama says.

"Not unless you eat," the old lady says. "I'm old, but I have my pride, too, you know."

Mama can see she ain't go'n beat this old lady down, so she just shakes her head.

"All right," the old lady says. "Come into the kitchen."

She leads the way with that rag in her hand. The kitchen is a little bitty little old thing, too. The table and the stove just 'bout fill it up. They got a little room to the side. Somebody in there layin 'cross the bed cause I can see one of his feet. Must be the person she was talking to: Ernest or Alnest—something like that.

"Sit down," the old lady says to Mama. "Not you," she says to me. "You have to move the cans."

"Helena?" the man says in the other room.

"Yes, Alnest?" the old lady says.

"Are you going out there again?"

"I must show the boy where the garbage is, Alnest," the old lady says.

"Keep your shawl over your head," the old man says.

"You don't have to remind me, Alnest. Come, Boy," the old lady says.

We go out in the yard. Little old back yard ain't no bigger than the store or the kitchen. But it can sleet here just like it can sleet in any big back yard. And 'fore you know it, I'm trembling.

"There," the old lady says, pointing to the cans. I pick up one of the cans and set it right back down. The can's so light. I'm go'n see what's inside of it.

"Here," the old lady says. "Leave that can alone."

I look back at her standing there in the door. She's got that black rag wrapped round her shoulders, and she's pointing one of her little old fingers at me.

"Pick it up and carry it to the front," she says. I go by her with the can, and she's looking at me all the time. I'm sure the can's empty. I'm sure she could've carried it herself—maybe both of them at the same time. "Set it on the sidewalk by the door and come back for the other one," she says.

I go and come back, and Mama looks at me when I pass her. I get the other can and take it to the front. It don't feel a bit heavier than that first one. I tell myself I ain't go'n be nobody's fool, and I'm go'n look inside this can to see just what I been hauling. First, I look up the street, then down the street. Nobody coming. Then I look over my shoulder toward the door. That little old lady done slipped up there quiet's a mouse, watching me again. Look like she knowed what I was go'n do.

"Ehh, Lord," she says. "Children, children. Come in here, boy, and go wash your hands."

I follow her in the kitchen. She points toward the bathroom, and I go in there and wash up. Little bitty old bathroom, but it's clean, clean. I don't use any of her towels; I wipe my hands on my pants legs.

When I come back in the kitchen, the old lady done dished up the food. Rice, gravy, meat—and she even got some lettuce and tomato in a saucer. She even got a glass of milk and a piece of cake there, too. It looks so good, I almost start eating 'fore I say my blessing.

"Helena?" the old man says.

"Yes, Alnest?"

"Are they eating?"

"Yes," she says.

"Good," he says. "Now you'll stay inside."

The old lady goes in there where he is and I can hear them talking. I look at Mama. She's eating slow like she's thinking. I wonder what's the matter now. I reckon she's thinking 'bout home.

The old lady comes back in the kitchen.

"I talked to Dr. Bassett's nurse," she says. "Dr. Bassett will take you as soon as you get there."

"Thank you, ma'am," Mama says.

"Perfectly all right," the old lady says. "Which one is it?"

Mama nods toward me. The old lady looks at me real sad. I look sad, too.

"You're not afraid, are you?" she says.

"No, ma'am," I say.

"That's a good boy," the old lady says. "Nothing to be afraid of. Dr. Bassett will not hurt you."

When me and Mama get through eating, we thank the old lady again.

"Helena, are they leaving?" the old man says.

"Yes, Alnest."

"Tell them I say good-bye."

"They can hear you, Alnest."

"Good-bye both mother and son," the old man says. "And may God be with you."

Me and Mama tell the old man good-bye, and we follow the old lady in the front room. Mama opens the door to go out, but she stops and comes back in the store.

"You sell salt meat?" she says.

"Yes."

"Give me two bits worth."

"That isn't very much salt meat," the old lady says.

"That's all I have," Mama says.

The old lady goes back of the counter and cuts a big piece off the chunk. Then she wraps it up and puts it in a paper bag.

"Two bits," she says.

"That looks like awful lot of meat for a quarter," Mama says.

"Two bits," the old lady says. "I've been selling salt meat behind this counter twenty-five years. I think I know what I'm doing."

"You got a scale there," Mama says.

"What?" the old lady says.

"Weigh it," Mama says.

"What?" the old lady says. "Are you telling me how to run my business?"

"Thanks very much for the food," Mama says.

"Just a minute," the old lady says.

"James," Mama says to me. I move toward the door.

"Just one minute, I said," the old lady says.

Me and Mama stop again and look at her. The old lady takes the meat out of the bag and unwraps it and cuts 'bout half of it off. Then she wraps it up again and juggs it back in the bag and gives the bag to Mama. Mama lays the quarter on the counter.

"Your kindness will never be forgotten," she says. "James," she says to me.

We go out, and the old lady comes to the door to look at us. After we go a little piece I look back, and she's still there watching us.

The sleet's coming down heavy, heavy now, and I turn up my coat collar to keep my neck warm. My mama tells me turn it right back down.

"You not a bum," she says. "You a man."

Journal Entry

What forces have formed the mother's character? Why does she raise her children as she does? Consider the incident with the redbirds as well as the last line of the story.

Textual Considerations

1. How does the author's choice of an eight-year-old child as narrator contribute to your understanding of the story's events? What, if any, are the limitations placed on the author by his use of a young boy to recreate the story?
2. The title "The Sky Is Gray" obviously describes the weather. What does the title refer to on a symbolic level? What other symbols are there, and how does the author use them to enhance the theme?
3. How does racial prejudice operate in the story? Why does the author include the old woman and her husband? How do you respond to their presence?

Cultural Contexts

1. The story takes place in the American South during the 1940s. How does the author's use of the settings (the bus trip, the dentist's office, and the café) contribute to our understanding of historical conditions before the Civil Rights movement in the United States?
2. Working with your group, analyze the meaning of the discussion between the young man and the preacher in the dentist's office. Consider also how their argument affects James.

Nathaniel Hawthorne
1835

Young Goodman Brown

Young Goodman[1] Brown came forth, at sunset, into the street at Salem village; but put his head back, after crossing the threshold, to exchange a parting kiss with his young wife. And Faith, as the wife was aptly named, thrust her pretty head into the street, letting the wind play with the pink ribbons of her cap while she called to Goodman Brown.

"Dearest heart," whispered she, softly and rather sadly, when her lips were close to his ear, "prithee put off your journey until sunrise and sleep in your own bed to-night. A lone woman is troubled with such dreams and such thoughts that she's afeared of herself sometimes. Pray tarry with me this night, dear husband, of all nights in the year."

---

[1]*Goodman:* Polite term of address for a man who ranks below gentleman.

"My love and my Faith," replied young Goodman Brown, "of all nights in the year, this one night must I tarry away from thee. My journey, as thou callest it, forth and back again, must needs be done 'twixt now and sunrise. What, my sweet, pretty wife, dost thou doubt me already, and we but three months married?"

"Then God bless you!" said Faith, with the pink ribbons; "and may you find all well when you come back."

"Amen!" cried Goodman Brown. "Say thy prayers, dear Faith, and go to bed at dusk, and no harm will come to thee."

So they parted; and the young man pursued his way until, being about to turn the corner by the meeting-house, he looked back and saw the head of Faith still peeping after him with a melancholy air, in spite of her pink ribbons.

"Poor little Faith!" thought he, for his heart smote him. "What a wretch am I to leave her on such an errand! She talks of dreams, too. Me-thought as she spoke there was trouble in her face, as if a dream had warned her what work is to be done to-night. But no, no; 'twould kill her to think it. Well, she's a blessed angel on earth; and after this one night, I'll cling to her skirts and follow her to heaven."

With this excellent resolve for the future, Goodman Brown felt himself justified in making more haste on his present evil purpose. He had taken a dreary road, darkened by all the gloomiest trees of the forest, which barely stood aside to let the narrow path creep through, and closed immediately behind. It was all as lonely as could be; and there is this peculiarity in such a solitude, that the traveller knows not who may be concealed by the innumerable trunks and the thick boughs overhead; so that with lonely footsteps he may yet be passing through an unseen multitude.

"There may be a devilish Indian behind every tree," said Goodman Brown, to himself and he glanced fearfully behind him as he added, "What if the devil himself should be at my very elbow!"

His head being turned back, he passed a crook of the road, and, looking forward again, beheld the figure of a man, in grave and decent attire, seated at the foot of an old tree. He arose at Goodman Brown's approach and walked onward side by side with him.

"You are late, Goodman Brown," said he. "The clock of the Old South was striking as I came through Boston, and that is full fifteen minutes agone."

"Faith kept me back a while," replied the young man, with a tremor in his voice, caused by the sudden appearance of his companion, though not wholly unexpected.

It was now deep dusk in the forest, and deepest in that part of it where these two were journeying. As nearly as could be discerned, the second traveller was about fifty years old, apparently in the same rank of life as Goodman Brown, and bearing a considerable resemblance to him, though perhaps more in expression than features. Still they might have been taken for father and son. And yet, though the elder person was as simply clad as the younger, and as simple in manner too, he had an indescribable air of one who knew the world, and who would not have felt abashed at the governor's dinner table, or in King William's[2] court, were it possible

---

[2] *King William:* William III, king of England from 1689 to 1702.

that his affairs should call him thither. But the only thing about him that could be fixed upon as remarkable was his staff, which bore the likeness of a great black snake, so curiously wrought that it might almost be seen to twist and wriggle itself like a living serpent. This, of course, must have been an ocular deception, assisted by the uncertain light.

"Come, Goodman Brown," cried his fellow-traveller, "this is a dull pace for the beginning of a journey. Take my staff, if you are so soon weary."

"Friend," said the other, exchanging his slow pace for a full stop, "having kept covenant by meeting thee here, it is my purpose now to return whence I came. I have scruples touching the matter thou wot'st[3] of."

"Sayest thou so?" replied he of the serpent, smiling apart. "Let us walk on, nevertheless, reasoning as we go; and if I convince thee not thou shalt turn back. We are but a little way in the forest yet."

"Too far! too far!" exclaimed the goodman, unconsciously resuming his walk. "My father never went into the woods on such an errand, nor his father before him. We have been a race of honest men and good Christians since the days of the martyrs; and shall I be the first of the name of Brown that ever took this path and kept—"

"Such company, thou wouldst say," observed the elder person, interpreting his pause. "Well said, Goodman Brown! I have been as well acquainted with your family as with ever a one among the Puritans; and that's no trifle to say. I helped your grandfather, the constable, when he lashed the Quaker woman so smartly through the streets of Salem; and it was I that brought your father a pitch-pine knot, kindled at my own hearth, to set fire to an Indian village, in King Philip's war.[4] They were my good friends, both; and many a pleasant walk have we had along this path, and returned merrily after midnight. I would fain be friends with you for their sake."

"If it be as thou sayest," replied Goodman Brown, "I marvel they never spoke of these matters, or, verily, I marvel not, seeing that the least rumor of the sort would have driven them from New England. We are a people of prayer, and good works to boot, and abide no such wickedness."

"Wickedness or not," said the traveller with the twisted staff, "I have a very general acquaintance here in New England. The deacons of many a church have drunk the communion wine with me; the selectmen of divers towns make me their chairman; and a majority of the Great and General Court are firm supporters of my interest. The governor and I, too—But these are state secrets."

"Can this be so!" cried Goodman Brown, with a stare of amazement at his undisturbed companion. "Howbeit, I have nothing to do with the governor and council; they have their own ways, and are no rule for a simple husbandman[5] like me. But, were I to go on with thee, how should I meet the eye of that good old man, our minister, at Salem village? Oh, his voice would make me tremble both Sabbath day and lecture day!"

---

[3]*wot'st:* knowest. [4]*King Philip's war:* War waged between the Colonists (1675–1676) and the Wampanoag Indians, led by Metacomet, known as "King Philip." [5]*husbandman:* A common man; sometimes used specifically to denote a farmer.

Thus far the elder traveller had listened with due gravity; but now burst into a fit of irrepressible mirth, shaking himself so violently that his snake-life staff actually seemed to wriggle in sympathy.

"Ha! ha! ha!" shouted he again and again; then composing himself, "Well, go on, Goodman Brown, go on; but, prithee, don't kill me with laughing."

"Well, then, to end the matter at once," said Goodman Brown, considerably nettled, "there is my wife, Faith. It would break her dear little heart; and I'd rather break my own."

"Nay, if that be the case," answered the other, "e'en go thy ways, Goodman Brown. I would not for twenty old women like the one hobbling before us that Faith should come to any harm."

As he spoke he pointed his staff at a female figure on the path, in whom Goodman Brown recognized a very pious and exemplary dame, who had taught him his catechism in youth, and was still his moral and spiritual adviser, jointly with the minister and Deacon Gookin.

"A marvel, truly, that Goody[6] Cloyse should be so far in the wilderness at night fall," said he. "But with your leave, friend, I shall take a cut through the woods until we have left this Christian woman behind. Being a stranger to you, she might ask whom I was consorting with and whither I was going."

"Be it so," said his fellow-traveller. "Betake you the woods, and let me keep the path."

Accordingly the young man turned aside, but took care to watch his companion, who advanced softly along the road until he had come within a staff's length of the old dame. She, meanwhile, was making the best of her way, with singular speed for so aged a woman, and mumbling some indistinct words—a prayer, doubtless—as she went. The traveller put forth his staff and touched her withered neck with what seemed the serpent's tail.

"The devil!" screamed the pious old lady.

"Then Goody Cloyse knows her old friend?" observed the traveller, confronting her and leaning on his writhing stick.

"Ah, forsooth, and is it your worship indeed?" cried the good dame. "Yea, truly is it, and in the very image of my old gossip, Goodman Brown, the grandfather of the silly fellow that now is. But—would your worship believe it?—my broomstick hath strangely disappeared, stolen, as I suspect, by that unhanged witch, Goody Cory, and that, too, when I was all anointed with the juice of small-age and cinquefoil and wolf's bane—"

"Mingled with fine wheat and the fat of a new-born babe," said the shape of old Goodman Brown.

"Ah, your worship knows the recipe," cried the old lady, cackling aloud. "So, as I was saying, being all ready for the meeting, and no horse to ride on, I made up my mind to foot it; for they tell me there is a nice young man to be taken into communion to-night. But now your good worship will lend me your arm, and we shall be there in a twinkling."

---

[6]*Goody:* Contraction of "Goodwife," a polite title for a married woman of humble rank.

"That can hardly be," answered her friend. "I may not spare you my arm, Goody Cloyse; but here is my staff, if you will."

So saying, he threw it down at her feet, where, perhaps, it assumed life, being one of the rods which its owner had formerly lent to the Egyptian magi. Of this fact, however, Goodman Brown could not take cognizance. He had cast up his eyes in astonishment, and, looking down again, beheld neither Goody Cloyse nor the serpentine staff but his fellow-traveller alone, who waited for him as calmly as if nothing had happened.

"That old woman taught me my catechism," said the young man; and there was a world of meaning in this simple comment.

They continued to walk onward, while the elder traveller exhorted his companion to make good speed and persevere in the path, discoursing so aptly that his arguments seemed rather to spring up in the bosom of his auditor than to be suggested by himself. As they went, he plucked a branch of maple to serve for a walking-stick, and began to strip it of the twigs and little boughs, which were wet with evening dew. The moment his fingers touched them they became strangely withered and dried up as with a week's sunshine. Thus the pair proceeded, at a good free pace, until suddenly, in a gloomy hollow of the road, Goodman Brown sat himself down on the stump of a tree and refused to go any farther.

"Friend," said he, stubbornly, "my mind is made up. Not another step will I budge on this errand. What if a wretched old woman do choose to go to the devil when I thought she was going to heaven: is that any reason why I should quit my dear Faith and go after her?"

"You will think better of this by and by," said his acquaintance, composedly. "Sit here and rest yourself a while; and when you feel like moving again, there is my staff to help you along."

Without more words, he threw his companion the maple stick, and was as speedily out of sight as if he had vanished into the deepening gloom. The young man sat a few moments by the roadside, applauding himself greatly, and thinking with how clear a conscience he should meet the minister in his morning walk, nor shrink from the eye of good old Deacon Gookin. And what calm sleep would be his that very night, which was to have been spent so wickedly, but so purely and sweetly now, in the arms of Faith! Amidst these pleasant and praiseworthy meditations, Goodman Brown heard the tramp of horses along the road, and deemed it advisable to conceal himself within the verge of the forest, conscious of the guilty purpose that had brought him thither, though now so happily turned from it.

On came the hoof-tramps and the voices of the riders, two grave old voices, conversing soberly as they drew near. These mingled sounds appeared to pass along the road, within a few yards of the young man's hiding-place; but, owing doubtless to the depth of the gloom at that particular spot, neither the travellers nor their steeds, were visible. Though their figures brushed the small boughs by the wayside, it could not be seen that they intercepted, even for a moment, the faint gleam from the strip of bright sky athwart which they must have passed. Goodman Brown alternately crouched and stood on tiptoe, pulling aside the branches and thrusting forth his head as far as he durst without discerning so much as a shadow. It vexed him the more, because he could have sworn, were such a thing possible, that he recognized the voices of the minister and Deacon Gookin, jogging along quietly as they were wont to do, when bound to some ordination or ecclesiastical council. While yet within hearing, one of the riders stopped to pluck a switch.

"Of the two, reverend sir," said the voice like the deacon's, "I had rather miss an ordination dinner than to-night's meeting. They tell me that some of our community are to be here from Falmouth and beyond, and others from Connecticut and Rhode Island, besides several of the Indian powwows, who, after their fashion, know almost as much deviltry as the best of us. Moreover, there is a goodly young woman to be taken into communion."

"Mighty well, Deacon Gookin!" replied the solemn old tones of the minister. "Spur up, or we shall be late. Nothing can be done, you know until I get on the ground."

The hoofs clattered again; and the voices, talking so strangely in the empty air, passed on through the forest, where no church had ever been gathered or solitary Christian prayed. Whither, then, could these holy men be journeying so deep into the heathen wilderness? Young Goodman Brown caught hold of a tree for support, being ready to sink down on the ground, faint and overburdened with the heavy sickness of his heart. He looked up to the sky, doubting whether there really was a heaven above him. Yet, there was the blue arch, and the stars brightening in it.

"With heaven above, and Faith below, I will yet stand firm against the devil!" cried Goodman Brown.

While he still gazed upward into the deep arch of the firmament and had lifted his hands to pray, a cloud, though no wind was stirring, hurried across the zenith and hid the brightening stars. The blue sky was still visible, except directly overhead, where this black mass of cloud was sweeping swiftly northward. Aloft in the air, as if from the depths of the cloud, came a confused and doubtful sound of voices. Once the listener fancied that he could distinguish the accents of townspeople of his own, men and women, both pious and ungodly, many of whom he had met at the communion table, and had seen others rioting at the tavern. The next moment, so indistinct were the sounds, he doubted whether he had heard aught but the murmur of the old forest, whispering without a wind. Then came a stronger swell of those familiar tones, heard daily in the sunshine at Salem village, but never until now from a cloud of night. There was one voice, of a young woman, uttering lamentations, yet with an uncertain sorrow, and entreating for some favor, which, perhaps, it would grieve her to obtain; and all the unseen multitude, both saints and sinners, seemed to encourage her onward.

"Faith!" shouted Goodman Brown, in a voice of agony and desperation; and the echoes of the forest mocked him, crying, "Faith! Faith!" as if bewildered wretches were seeking her all through the wilderness.

The cry of grief, rage, and terror was yet piercing the night, when the unhappy husband held his breath for a response. There was a scream, drowned immediately in a louder murmur of voices, fading into far-off laughter, as the dark cloud swept away, leaving the clear and silent sky above Goodman Brown. But something fluttered lightly down through the air and caught on the branch of a tree. The young man seized it, and beheld a pink ribbon.

"My Faith is gone!" cried he, after one stupefied moment. "There is no good on earth; and sin is but a name. Come, devil; for to thee is this world given."

And, maddened with despair, so that he laughed loud and long, did Goodman Brown grasp his staff and set forth again, at such a rate that he seemed to fly along the forest path, rather than to walk or run. The road grew wilder and drearier and more faintly traced, and vanished at length, leaving him in the heart of the dark wilderness, still rushing onward with the instinct that guides mortal man to evil. The whole forest was peopled with frightful sounds—the creaking of the trees, the howling of wild beasts, and the yell of Indians; while sometimes the wind tolled like a distant church bell, and sometimes gave a broad roar around the traveller, as if all Nature were laughing him to scorn. But he was himself the chief horror of the scene, and shrank not from its other horrors.

"Ha! ha! ha!" roared Goodman Brown when the wind laughed at him. "Let us hear which will laugh loudest! Think not to frighten me with your deviltry! Come witch, come wizard, come Indian powwow, come devil himself, and here comes Goodman Brown. You may as well fear him as he fears you!"

In truth, all through the haunted forest there could be nothing more frightful than the figure of Goodman Brown. On he flew among the black pines, brandishing his staff with frenzied gestures, now giving vent to an inspiration of horrid blasphemy, and now shouting forth such laughter as set all the echoes of the forest laughing like demons around him. The fiend in his own shape is less hideous than when he rages in the breast of man. Thus sped the demoniac on his course, until, quivering among the trees, he saw a red light before him, as when the felled trunks and branches of a clearing have been set on fire, and throw up their lurid blaze against the sky, at the hour of midnight. He paused, in a lull of the tempest that had driven him onward, and heard the swell of what seemed a hymn, rolling solemnly from a distance with the weight of many voices. He knew the tune; it was a familiar one in the choir of the village meeting-house. The verse died heavily away, and was lengthened by a chorus, not of human voices, but of all the sounds of the benighted wilderness pealing in awful harmony together. Goodman Brown cried out; and his cry was lost to his own ear by its unison with the cry of the desert.

In the interval of silence he stole forward until the light glared full upon his eyes. At one extremity of an open space, hemmed in, by the dark wall of the forest, arose a rock, bearing some rude, natural resemblance either to an altar or a pulpit, and surrounded by four blazing pines, their tops aflame, their stems untouched, like candles at an evening meeting. The mass of foliage that had overgrown the summit of the rock was all on fire, blazing high into the night and fitfully illuminating the whole field. Each pendent twig and leafy festoon was in a blaze. As the red light arose and fell, a numerous congregation alternately shone forth, then disappeared in shadow, and again grew, as it were, out of the darkness, peopling the heart of the solitary woods at once.

"A grave and dark-clad company," quoth Goodman Brown.

In truth, they were such. Among them, quivering to-and-fro between gloom and splendor, appeared faces that would be seen next day at the council board of the province, and others which, Sabbath after Sabbath, looked devoutly heavenward, and benignantly over the crowded pews, from the holiest pulpits in the land. Some affirm that the lady of the governor was there. At least there were high dames well known to her, and wives of honored husbands, and widows, a great multitude, and ancient maidens, of excellent repute, and fair young girls, who trembled lest their mothers should espy them. Either the sudden gleams of light flashing over the obscure field bedazzled Goodman Brown, or he recognized a score of the church-members of Salem village famous for their especial sanctity. Good old Deacon Gookin had arrived, and waited at the skirts of that venerable saint, his revered pastor. But, irreverently consorting, with these grave, reputable, and pious people, these elders of the church, these chaste dames and dewy virgins, there were men of dissolute lives and women of spotted fame, wretches given over to all mean and filthy vice, and suspected even of horrid crimes. It was strange to see, that the good shrank not from the wicked, nor were the sinners abashed by the saints. Scattered also among their pale-faced enemies were the Indian priests, or powwows, who had often scared their native forest with more hideous incantations than any known to English witchcraft.

"But, where is Faith?" thought Goodman Brown; and, as hope came into his heart, he trembled

Another verse of the hymn arose, a slow and mournful strain, such as the pious love, but joined to words which expressed all that our nature can conceive of sin, and darkly hinted at far more. Unfathomable to mere mortals is the lore of fiends. Verse after verse was sung; and still the chorus of the desert swelled between, like the deepest tone of a mighty organ; and, with the final peal of that dreadful anthem there came a sound, as if the roaring wind, the rushing streams, the howling beasts, and every other voice of the unconcerted wilderness were mingling and according with the voice of guilty man in homage to the prince of all. The four blazing pines threw up a loftier flame, and obscurely discovered shapes and visages of horror on the smoke wreaths above the impious assembly. At the same moment the fire on the rock shot redly forth and formed a glowing arch above its base, where now appeared a figure. With reverence be it spoken, the figure bore no slight similitude, both in garb and manner, to some grave divine of the New England churches.

"Bring forth the converts!" cried a voice that echoed through the field and rolled into the forest.

At the word, Goodman Brown stepped forth from the shadow of the trees and approached the congregation, with whom he felt a loathful brotherhood by the sympathy of all that was wicked in heart. He could have well nigh sworn that the shape of his own dead father beckoned him to advance, looking downward from a smoke wreath, while a woman, with dim features of despair, threw out her hand to warn him back. Was it his mother? But he had no power to retreat one step, nor to resist, even in thought, when the minister and good old Deacon Gookin seized his arms and led him to the blazing rock. Thither came also the slender form of a veiled female, led between Goody Cloyse, that pious teacher of the catechism, and

Martha Carrier,[7] who had received the devil's promise to be queen of hell. A rampant hag was she. And there stood the proselytes beneath the canopy of fire.

"Welcome, my children," said the dark figure, "to the communion of your race. Ye have found thus young your nature and your destiny. My children, look behind you!"

They turned; and flashing forth, as it were, in a sheet of flame, the fiend worshippers were seen; the smile of welcome gleamed darkly on every visage.

"There," resumed the sable form, "are all whom ye have reverenced from youth. Ye deemed them holier than yourselves, and shrank from your own sin, contrasting it with their lives of righteousness and prayerful aspirations heavenward. Yet here are they all in my worshipping assembly. This night it shall be granted you to know their secret deeds: how hoary-bearded elders of the church have whispered wanton words to the young maids of their households; how many a woman, eager for widow's weeds, has given her husband a drink at bedtime, and let him sleep his last sleep in her bosom; how beardless youths have made haste to inherit their fathers' wealth; and how fair damsels—blush not, sweet ones—have dug little graves in the garden, and bidden me, the sole guest, to an infant's funeral. By the sympathy of your human hearts for sin ye shall scent out all the places—whether in church, bed-chamber, street, field, or forest—where crime has been committed, and shall exult to behold the whole earth one stain of guilt, one mighty blood spot. Far more than this. It shall be yours to penetrate, in every bosom, the deep mystery of sin, the fountain of all wicked arts, and which inexhaustibly supplies more evil impulses than human power—than my power at its utmost—can make manifest in deeds. And now, my children, look upon each other."

They did so; and, by the blaze of the hell-kindled torches, the wretched man beheld his Faith, and the wife her husband, trembling before that unhallowed altar.

"Lo, there ye stand, my children," said the figure, in a deep and solemn tone, almost sad with its despairing awfulness, as if his once angelic nature could yet mourn for our miserable race. "Depending upon one another's hearts, ye had still hoped that virtue were not all a dream. Now are ye undeceived. Evil is the nature of mankind. Evil must be your only happiness. Welcome, again, my children, to the communion of your race."

"Welcome," repeated the fiend worshippers, in one cry of despair and triumph.

And there they stood, the only pair, as it seemed, who were yet hesitating on the verge of wickedness in this dark world. A basin was hollowed, naturally, in the rock. Did it contain water, reddened by the lurid light? or was it blood? or, perchance, a liquid flame? Herein did the shape of evil dip his hand and prepare to lay the mark of baptism upon their foreheads, that they might be partakers of the mystery of sin, more conscious of the secret guilt of others, both in deed and thought, than they could now be of their own. The husband cast one look at his pale wife, and Faith at him. What polluted wretches would the next glance show them to each other, shuddering alike at what they disclosed and what they saw!

"Faith! Faith!" cried the husband, "look up to heaven, and resist the wicked one."

---

[7] *Martha Carrier:* One of the women hanged for witchcraft in Salem in 1697.

Whether Faith obeyed he knew not. Hardly had he spoken when he found himself amid calm night and solitude, listening to a roar of the wind which died heavily away through the forest. He staggered against the rock, and felt it chill and damp; while a hanging twig, that had been all on fire, besprinkled his cheek with the coldest dew.

The next morning young Goodman Brown came slowly into the street of Salem village, staring around him like a bewildered man. The good old minister was taking a walk along the graveyard to get an appetite for breakfast and meditate his sermon, and bestowed a blessing, as he passed, on Goodman Brown. He shrank from the venerable saint as if to avoid an anathema. Old Deacon Gookin was at domestic worship, and the holy words of his prayer were heard through the open window. "What God doth the wizard pray to?" quoth Goodman Brown. Goody Cloyse, that excellent old Christian, stood in the early sunshine at her own lattice, catechizing a little girl who had brought her a pint of morning's milk. Goodman Brown snatched away the child as from the grasp of the fiend himself. Turning the corner by the meeting-house, he spied the head of Faith, with the pink ribbons, gazing anxiously forth, and bursting into such joy at sight of him that she skipped along the street and almost kissed her husband before the whole village. But Goodman Brown looked sternly and sadly into her face, and passed on without a greeting.

Had Goodman Brown fallen asleep in the forest and only dreamed a wild dream of a witch-meeting?

Be it so, if you will; but, alas! it was a dream of evil omen for young Goodman Brown. A stern, a sad, a darkly meditative, a distrustful, if not a desperate man did he become from the night of that fearful dream. On the Sabbath day, when the congregation were singing a holy psalm, he could not listen because an anthem of sin rushed loudly upon his ear and drowned all the blessed strain. When the minister spoke from the pulpit with power and fervid eloquence, and, with his hand on the open Bible, of the sacred truths of our religion, and of saint-like lives and triumphant deaths, and of future bliss or misery unutterable, then did Goodman Brown turn pale, dreading lest the roof should thunder down upon the gray blasphemer and his hearers.

Journal Entry

How does the end of the story affect your understanding of what happened to Brown?

Textual Considerations

1. Why is it important that the story begins and ends in Salem village?
2. Why does Young Goodman Brown go into the forest at night?
3. Why is it significant that the stranger Brown meets in the forest looks like Brown's father and also like Brown? Explain.
4. Discuss the symbolic meaning of Young Goodman Brown's name. What function does it serve in the story?
5. Using evidence from the text, explain where Hawthorne casts doubts on the supernatural nature of the story.

Cultural Contexts

1. Consult the glossary for a definition of allegory. At what point in the story does the reader realize that "Young Goodman Brown" may be read as a moral allegory? Contrast the village of Salem with the forest from an allegorical point of view.
2. Explain how Hawthorne explores the negative counterparts of the theological virtues of faith, hope, and charity. In your opinion, does "Young Goodman Brown" support the view that "evil is the nature of Mankind"?

James Joyce
1905

Araby

North Richmond Street, being blind, was a quiet street except at the hour when the Christian Brothers' School set the boys free. An uninhabited house of two stories stood at the blind end, detached from its neighbors in a square ground. The other houses of the street, conscious of decent lives within them, gazed at one another with brown imperturbable faces.

The former tenant of our house, a priest, had died in the back drawing-room. Air, musty from having been long enclosed, hung in all the rooms, and the waste room behind the kitchen was littered with old useless paper. Among these I found a few paper-covered books, the pages of which were curled and damp: *The Abbot,* by Walter Scott, *The Devout Communicant* and *The Memoirs of Vidoca.* I liked the last best because its leaves were yellow. The wild garden behind the house contained a central apple-tree and a few straggling bushes under one of which I found the late tenant's rusty bicycle-pump. He had been a very charitable priest: in his will he had left all his money to institutions and the furniture of his house to his sister.

When the short days of winter came dusk fell before we had well eaten our dinners. When we met in the street the houses had grown somber. The space of sky above us was the color of ever-changing violet and towards it the lamps of the street lifted their feeble lanterns. The cold air stung us and we played till our bodies glowed. Our shouts echoed in the silent street. The career of our play brought us through the dark muddy lanes behind the houses where we ran the gantlet of the rough tribes from the cottages, to the back doors of the dark dripping gardens where odors arose from the ashpits, to the dark odorous stables where a coachman smoothed and combed the horse or shook music from the buckled harness. When we returned to the street light from the kitchen windows had filled the areas. If my uncle was seen turning the corner we hid in the shadow until we had seen him safely housed. Or if Mangan's sister came out on the doorstep to call her brother in to his tea we watched her from our shadow peer up and down the street. We waited to see whether she would remain or go in and, if she remained, we left our shadow and walked up to Mangan's steps resignedly. She was waiting for us, her figure defined by the light from the half-opened door. Her brother always teased her before he obeyed and I stood by the railings looking at her. Her dress swung as she moved her body and the soft rope of her hair tossed from side to side.

Every morning I lay on the floor in the front parlor watching her door. The blind was pulled down to within an inch of the sash so that I could not be seen. When she came out on the doorstep my heart leaped. I ran to the hall, seized my books and followed her. I kept her brown figure always in my eye and, when we came near the point at which our ways diverged, I quickened my pace and passed her. This happened morning after morning. I had never spoken to her, except for a few casual words, and yet her name was like a summons to all my foolish blood.

Her image accompanied me even in places the most hostile to romance. On Saturday evenings when my aunt went marketing I had to go to carry some of the parcels. We walked through the flaring streets, jostled by drunken men and bargaining women, amid the curses of laborers, the shrill litanies of shop-boys who stood on guard by the barrels of pigs' cheeks, the nasal chanting of street-singers, who sang a *come-all-you* about O'Donovan Rossa, or a ballad about the troubles in our native land. These noises converged in a single sensation of life for me: I imagined that I bore my chalice safely through a throng of foes. Her name sprang to my lips at moments in strange prayers and praises which I myself did not understand. My eyes were often full of tears (I could not tell why) and at times a flood from my heart seemed to pour itself out into my bosom. I thought little of the future. I did not know whether I would ever speak to her or not or, if I spoke to her, how I could tell her of my confused adoration. But my body was like a harp and her words and gestures were like fingers running upon the wires.

One evening I went into the back drawing-room in which the priest had died. It was a dark rainy evening and there was no sound in the house. Through one of the broken panes I heard the rain impinge upon the earth, the fine incessant needles of water playing in the sodden beds. Some distant lamp or lighted window gleamed below me. I was thankful that I could see so little. All my senses seemed to desire to veil themselves and, feeling that I was about to slip from them, I pressed the palms of my hands together until they trembled, murmuring: *O love! O love!* many times.

At last she spoke to me. When she addressed the first words to me I was so confused that I did not know what to answer. She asked me was I going to *Araby*. I forget whether I answered yes or no. It would be a splendid bazaar, she said; she would love to go.

—And why can't you? I asked.

While she spoke she turned a silver bracelet round and round her wrist. She could not go, she said, because there would be a retreat that week in her convent. Her brother and two other boys were fighting for their caps and I was alone at the railings. She held one of the spikes, bowing her head towards me. The light from the lamp opposite our door caught the white curve of a neck, lit up her hair that rested there and, falling, lit up the hand upon the railing. It fell over one side of her dress and caught the white border of a petticoat, just visible as she stood at ease.

—It's well for you, she said.

—If I go, I said, I will bring you something.

What innumerable follies laid waste my waking and sleeping thoughts after that evening! I wished to annihilate the tedious intervening days. I chafed against the work of school. At night in my bedroom and by day in the classroom her image came between me and the page I strove to read. The syllables of the word *Araby* were called to me through the silence in which my soul luxuriated and cast an Eastern enchantment over me. I asked for leave to go to the bazaar on Saturday night. My aunt was surprised and hoped it was not some Freemason affair. I answered few questions in class, I watched my master's face pass from amiability to sternness; he hoped I was not beginning to idle. I could not call my wandering thoughts together. I had hardly any patience with the serious work of life which, now that it stood between me and my desire, seemed to me child's play, ugly monotonous child's play.

On Saturday morning I reminded my uncle that I wished to go to the bazaar in the evening. He was fussing at the hall-stand, looking for the hatbrush, and answered me curtly:

—Yes, boy, I know.

As he was in the hall I could not go into the front parlor and lie at the window. I left the house in bad humor and walked slowly towards the school. The air was pitilessly raw and already my heart misgave me.

When I came home to dinner my uncle had not yet been home. Still it was early. I sat staring at the clock for some time and, when its ticking began to irritate me, I left the room. I mounted the staircase and gained the upper part of the house. The high cold empty gloomy rooms liberated me and I went from room to room singing. From the front window I saw my companions playing below in the street. Their cries reached me weakened and indistinct and, leaning my forehead against the cool glass, I looked over at the dark house where she lived. I may have stood there for an hour, seeing nothing but the brown-clad figure cast by my imagination, touched discreetly by the lamplight at the curved neck, at the hand upon the railings and at the border below the dress.

When I came downstairs again I found Mrs. Mercer sitting at the fire. She was an old garrulous woman, a pawnbroker's widow, who collected used stamps for some pious purpose. I had to endure the gossip of the tea-table. The meal was prolonged beyond an hour and still my uncle did not come. Mrs. Mercer stood up to go: she was sorry she couldn't wait any longer, but it was after eight o'clock and she did not like to be out late, as the night air was bad for her. When she had gone I began to walk up and down the room, clenching my fists. My aunt said:

—I'm afraid you may put off your bazaar for this night of Our Lord.

At nine o'clock I heard my uncle's latchkey in the halldoor. I heard him talking to himself and heard the hall-stand rocking when it had received the weight of his overcoat. I could interpret these signs. When he was midway through his dinner I asked him to give me the money to go to the bazaar. He had forgotten.

—The people are in bed and after their first sleep now, he said.

I did not smile. My aunt said to him energetically:

—Can't you give him the money and let him go? You've kept him late enough as it is.

My uncle said he was very sorry he had forgotten. He said he believed in the old saying: *All work and no play makes Jack a dull boy.* He asked me where I was going and, when I had told him a second time he asked me did I know *The Arab's Farewell to His Steed.* When I left the kitchen he was about to recite the opening lines of the piece to my aunt.

I held a florin tightly in my hand as I strode down Buckingham Street towards the station. The sight of the streets thronged with buyers and glaring with gas recalled to me the purpose of my journey. I took my seat in a third-class carriage of a deserted train. After an intolerable delay the train moved out of the station slowly. It crept onward among ruinous houses and over the twinkling river. At Westland Row Station a crowd of people pressed to the carriage doors; but the porters moved them back, saying that it was a special train for the bazaar. I remained alone in the bare carriage. In a few minutes the train drew up beside an improvised wooden platform. I passed out on to the road and saw by the lighted dial of a clock that it was ten minutes to ten. In front of me was a large building which displayed a magical name.

I could not find any sixpenny entrance and, fearing that the bazaar would be closed, I passed in quickly through a turnstile, handing a shilling to a weary-looking man. I found myself in a big hall girdled at half its height by a gallery. Nearly all the stalls were closed and the greater part of the hall was in darkness. I recognized a silence like that which pervades a church after a service. I walked into the center of the bazaar timidly. A few people were gathered about the stalls which were still open. Before a curtain, over which the words *Café Chantant* were written in colored lamps, two men were counting money on a salver. I listened to the fall of the coins.

Remembering with difficulty why I had come I went over to one of the stalls and examined porcelain vases and flowered tea-sets. At the door of the stall a young lady was talking and laughing with two young gentlemen. I remarked their English accents and listened vaguely to their conversation.

—O, I never said such a thing!

—O, but you did!

—O, but I didn't!

—Didn't she say that?

—Yes. I heard her.

—O, there's a...fib!

Observing me the young lady came over and asked me did I wish to buy anything. The tone of her voice was not encouraging; she seemed to have spoken to me out of a sense of duty. I looked humbly at the great jars that stood like eastern guards at either side of the dark entrance to the stall and murmered:

—No, thank you.

The young lady changed the position of one of the vases and went back to the two young men. They began to talk of the same subject. Once or twice the young lady glanced at me over her shoulder.

I lingered before her stall, though I knew my stay was useless, to make my interest in her wares seem the more real. Then I turned away slowly and walked down the middle of the bazaar. I allowed the two pennies to fall against the sixpence in my pocket. I heard a voice call from one end of the gallery that the light was out. The upper part of the hall was now completely dark.

Gazing up into the darkness I saw myself as a creature driven and derided by vanity; and my eyes burned with anguish and anger.

Journal Entry

What self-insights does the narrator show during the course of the story?

Textual Considerations

1. How does Joyce use setting in "Araby" to reflect the narrator's experience? Cite examples.
2. How does the boy feel about Mangan's sister? Why are both characters unnamed?
3. Where does the narrator's quest for Araby take on the semblance of a religious mission? Cite examples of religious symbolism.
4. Many critics see "Araby" as a quest story. What is the narrator seeking? What difficulties does he encounter? To what extent is his quest successful?

Cultural Contexts

1. According to Joyce, his intention in *Dubliners*—the collection of short stories in which "Araby" and "Eveline" (see Part Five) were published—was "to write a chapter of the moral history of my country and I chose Dublin for the scene because that city seemed to me the centre of paralysis." How does Joyce's comment apply to "Araby"? Cite examples.

Chief Seattle
c. 1855

My People

Yonder sky that has wept tears upon my people for centuries untold, and which to us appears changeless and eternal, may change. Today is fair. Tomorrow may be overcast with clouds. My words are like the stars that never change. Whatever Seattle says the great chief at Washington can rely upon with as much certainty as he can upon the return of the sun or the seasons. The White Chief says that Big Chief at Washington sends us greetings of friendship and goodwill. That is kind of him for we know he has little need of our friendship in return. His people are many. They are like the grass that covers vast prairies. My people are few. They resemble the scattering trees of a storm-swept plain. The great, and—I presume—good, White Chief sends us word that he wishes to buy our lands but is willing to allow us enough to live comfortably. This indeed appears just, even generous, for the Red Man no longer has rights that he need respect, and the offer may be wise also, as we are no longer in need of an extensive country.... I will not dwell on, nor mourn over, our untimely decay, nor reproach our paleface brothers with hastening it, as we too may have been somewhat to blame.

Youth is impulsive. When our young men grow angry at some real or imaginary wrong, and disfigure their face with black paint, it denotes that their hearts are black, and then they are often cruel and relentless, and our old men and old women are unable to restrain them. Thus it has ever been. Thus it was when the white men first began to push our forefathers further westward. But let us hope that the hostilities between us may never return. We would have everything to lose and nothing to gain. Revenge by young men is considered gain, even at the cost of their own lives, but old men who stay at home in times of war, and mothers who have sons to lose, know better.

Our good father at Washington—for I presume he is now our father as well as yours, since King George has moved his boundaries further north—our great good father, I say, sends us word that if we do as he desires he will protect us. His brave warriors will be to us a bristling wall of strength, and his wonderful ships of war will fill our harbors so that our ancient enemies far to the northward—the Hydas and Tsimpsians—will cease to frighten our women, children, and old men. Then in reality will he be our father and we his his children. But can that ever be? Your God is not our God! Your God loves your people and hates mine. He folds his strong and protecting arms lovingly about the paleface and leads him by the hand as a father leads his infant son—but He has forsaken His red children—if they really are his. Our God, the Great Spirit, seems also to have forsaken us. Your God makes your people wax strong every day. Soon they will fill the land. Our people are ebbing away like a rapidly receding tide that will never return. The white man's God cannot love our people or He would protect them. They seem to be orphans who can look nowhere for help. How then can we be brothers? How can your God become our God and renew our prosperity and awaken in us dreams of returning greatness? If we have a common heavenly father He must be partial—for He came to his paleface children. We never saw Him. He gave you laws but He had no word for His red children whose teeming multitudes once filled this vast continent as stars fill the firmament. No; we are two distinct races with separate origins and separate destinies. There is little in common between us.

To us the ashes of our ancestors are sacred and their resting place is hallowed ground. You wander far from the graves of your ancestors and seemingly without regret. Your religion was written upon tables of stone by the iron finger of your God so that you could not forget. The Red Man could never comprehend nor remember it. Our religion is the traditions of our ancestors—the dreams of our old men, given them in solemn hours of night by the Great Spirit; and the visions of our sachems[1]; and it is written in the hearts of our people.

Your dead cease to love you and the land of their nativity as soon as they pass the portals of the tomb and wander way beyond the stars. They are soon forgotten and never return. Our dead never forget the beautiful world that gave them being.

Day and night cannot dwell together. The Red Man has ever fled the approach of the White Man, as the morning mist flees before the morning sun. However, your proposition seems fair and I think that my people will accept it and will retire to the reservation you offer them. Then we will dwell apart in peace, for the words of the Great White Chief seem to be the words of nature speaking to my people out of dense darkness.

It matters little where we pass the remnant of our days. They will not be many. A few more moons; a few more winters—and not one of the descendants of the mighty hosts that once moved over this broad land or lived in happy homes, protected by the Great Spirit, will remain to mourn over the graves of a people once more powerful and hopeful than yours. But why should I mourn at the untimely fate of my people? Tribe follows tribe, and nation follows nation, like the waves of the sea. It is the order of nature, and regret is useless. Your time of decay may be distant, but it will surely come, for even the White Man whose God walked and talked with him as friend with friend, cannot be exempt from the common destiny. We may be brothers after all. We will see.

We will ponder your proposition, and when we decide we will let you know. But should we accept it, I here and now make this condition that we will not be denied the privilege without molestation of visiting at any time the tombs of our ancestors, friends and children. Every part of this soil is sacred in the estimation of my people. Every hillside, every valley, every plain and grove, has been hallowed by some sad or happy event in days long vanished.... The very dust upon which you now stand responds more lovingly to their footsteps than to yours, because it is rich with the blood of our ancestors and our bare feet are conscious of the sympathetic

---

[1]*sachems:* Tribal chiefs.

touch.... Even the little children who lived here and rejoiced here for a brief season will love these somber solitudes and at eventide they greet shadowy returning spirits. And when the last Red Man shall have perished, and the memory of my tribe shall have become a myth among the White Men, these shores will swarm with the invisible dead of my tribe, and when your children's children think themselves alone in the field, the store, the shop, upon the highway, or in the silence of the pathless woods, they will not be alone.... At night when the streets of your cities and villages are silent and you think them deserted, they will throng with the returning hosts that once filled and still love this beautiful land. The White Man will never be alone.

Let him be just and deal kindly with my people, for the dead are not powerless. Dead, did I say? There is not death, only a change of worlds.

Journal Entry

Review the second paragraph, and write a journal entry responding to Chief Seattle's comparisons of youth and age.

Textual Considerations

1. Chief Seattle's speech contains many examples of figurative language including "my words are like the stars that never change." What other metaphors and similes can you cite? How effective are they?
2. Is Chief Seattle seeking to inform or persuade his audience? Who is his intended audience?
3. Chief Seattle uses contrast and comparison at several points in his speech. What differences between the traditions of his people and "the White Man" are highlighted by this technique?
4. "There is not death, only a change of worlds." How does Chief Seattle's attitude toward death compare to yours?

Cultural Contexts

1. Chief Seattle uses compromise rather than confrontation in his dealings with the U.S. Government. Which aspects of his traditional beliefs might account for his choice? To what extent do you agree with his choice?

James Agee
1957

Knoxville: Summer 1915

We are talking now of summer evenings in Knoxville, Tennessee in the time that I lived there so successfully disguised to myself as a child. It was a little bit mixed sort of block, fairly solidly lower middle class, with one or two juts apiece on either side of that. The houses corresponded: middle-sized gracefully fretted wood houses built in the late nineties and early nineteen hundreds, with small front and side and more spacious back yards, and trees in the yards, and porches. These were softwooded trees, poplars, tulip trees, cottonwoods. There were fences around one or two of the houses, but mainly the yards ran into each other with only now and then a low hedge that wasn't doing very well. There were few good friends among the grown people, and they were not poor enough for the other sort of intimate acquaintance, but everyone nodded and spoke, and even might talk short times, trivially, and at the two extremes of the general or the particular, and ordinarily next-door neighbors talked quite a bit when they happened to run into each other, and never paid calls. The men were mostly small businessmen, one or two very modestly executives, one or two worked with their hands, most of them clerical, and most of them between thirty and forty-five.

But it is of these evenings, I speak.

Supper was at six and was over by half past. There was still daylight, shining softly and with a tarnish, like the lining of a shell; and the carbon lamps lifted at the corners were on in the light, and the locusts were started, and the fire flies were out, and a few frogs were flopping in the dewy grass, by the time the fathers and the children came out. The children ran out first hell bent and yelling those names by which they were known; then the fathers sank out leisurely in crossed suspenders, their collars removed and their necks looking tall and shy. The mothers stayed back in the kitchen washing and drying, putting things away, recrossing their traceless footsteps like the lifetime journeys of bees, measuring out the dry cocoa for breakfast. When they came out they had taken off their aprons and their skirts were dampened and they sat in rockers on their porches quietly.

It is not of the games children play in the evening that I want to speak now, it is of a contemporaneous atmosphere that has little to do with them: that of the fathers of families, each in his space of lawn, his shirt fishlike pale in the unnatural light and his face nearly anonymous, hosing their lawns. The hoses were attached at spiggots that stood out of the brick foundations of the houses. The nozzles were variously set but usually so there was a long sweet stream of spray, the nozzle wet in the hand, the water trickling the right forearm and the peeled-back cuff, and the water whishing out a long loose and low-curved cone, and so gentle a sound. First an insane noise of violence in the nozzle, then the still irregular sound of adjustment, then the smoothing into steadiness and a pitch as accurately tuned to the size and style of stream as any violin. So many qualities of sound out of one hose: so many choral differences out of those several hoses that were in earshot. Out of any one hose, the almost dead silence of the release, and the short still arch of the separate big drops, silent as a held breath, and the only noise the flattering noise on leaves and the slapped grass at the fall of each big drop. That, and the intense hiss with the intense stream; that, and that same intensity not growing less but growing more quiet and delicate with the turn of the nozzle, up to that extreme tender whisper when the water was just a wide bell of film. Chiefly, though, the hoses were set much alike, in a compromise between distance and tenderness of spray (and quite surely a sense of art behind this compromise, and a quiet deep joy, too real to recognize itself), and the sounds therefore were pitched much alike; pointed by the snorting start of a new hose; decorated by some man playful with the nozzle; left empty, like God by the sparrow's fall, when any single one of them desists: and all, though near alike, of various pitch; and in this unison. These sweet pale streamings in the light lift out their pallors and their voices all together, mothers hushing their children, the hushing unnaturally prolonged, the men gentle and silent and each snail-like withdrawn into the quietude of what he singly is doing, the urination of huge children stood loosely military against an invisible wall, and gentle happy and peaceful, tasting the mean goodness of their living like the last of their suppers in their mouths; while the locusts carry on this noise of hoses on their much higher and sharper key. The noise of the locust is dry, and it seems not to be rasped or vibrated but urged from him as if through a small orifice by a breath that can never give out. Also there is never one locust but an illusion of at least a thousand. The noise of each locust is pitched in some classic locust range out of which none of them varies more than two full tones: and yet you seem to hear each locust discrete from all the rest, and there is a long, slow, pulse in their noise, like the scarcely defined arch of a long and high set bridge. They are all around in every tree, so that the noise seems to come from nowhere and everywhere at once, from the whole shell heaven, shivering in your flesh and teasing your eardrums, the boldest of all the sounds of night. And yet it is habitual to summer nights, and is of the great order of noises, like the noises of the sea and of the blood her precocious grandchild, which you realize you are hearing only when you catch yourself listening. Meantime from low in the dark, just outside the swaying horizons of the hoses, conveying always grass in the damp of dew and its strong green-black smear of smell, the regular yet spaced noises of the crickets, each a sweet cold silver noise threenoted, like the slipping each time of three matched links of a small chain.

But the men by now, one by one, have silenced their hoses and drained and coiled them. Now only two, and now only one, is left, and you see only ghostlike shirt with the sleeve garters, and sober mystery of his mild face like the lifted face of large cattle enquiring of your presence in a pitchdark pool of meadow; and now he too is gone; and it has become that time of evening when people sit on their porches, rocking gently and talking gently and watching the street and the standing up into their sphere of possession of the trees, of birds hung havens, hangars. People go by; things go by. A horse, drawing a buggy, breaking his hollow iron music on the asphalt; a loud auto; a quiet auto; people in pairs, not in a hurry, scuffling, switching their weight of aestival body, talking casually, the taste hovering over them of vanilla, strawberry, pasteboard and starched milk, the image upon them of lovers and horsemen, squared with clowns in hueless amber. A street car raising its iron moan; stopping, belling and starting; stertorous; rousing and raising again its iron increasing moan and swimming its gold windows and straw seats on past and past and past, the bleak spark crackling and cursing above it like a small malignant spirit set to dog its tracks; the iron whine rises on rising speed; still risen, faints; halts; the faint stinging bell; rises again, still fainter; fainter, lifting, lifts, faints foregone: forgotten. Now is the night one blue dew.

> Now is the night one blue dew, my father has drained, he has coiled the hose.
> Low on the length of lawns, a frailing of fire who breathes.
> Content, silver, like peeps of light, each cricket makes his comment over and
> over in the drowned grass.
> A cold toad thumpily flounders.
> Within the edges of damp shadows of side yards are hovering children nearly
> sick with joy of fear, who watch the unguarding of a telephone pole.
> Around white carbon corner lamps bugs of all sizes are lifted elliptic, solar systems. Big hardshells bruise themselves, assailant: he is fallen on his back,
> legs squiggling.
> Parents on porches: rock and rock: From damp strings morning glories: hang
> their ancient faces.
> The dry and exalted noise of the locusts from all the air at once enchants my
> eardrums.

On the rough wet grass of the back yard my father and mother have spread quilts. We all lie there, my mother, my father, my uncle, my aunt, and I too am lying there. First we were sitting up, then one of us lay down, and then we all lay down, on our stomachs, or on our sides, or on our backs, and they have kept on talking. They are not talking much, and the talk is quiet, of nothing in particular, of nothing at all in particular, of nothing at all. The stars are wide and alive, they seem each like a smile of great sweetness, and they seem very near. All my people are larger bodies than mine, quiet, with voices gentle and meaningless like the voices of sleeping birds. One is an artist, he is living at home. One is a musician, she is living at home. One is my mother who is good to me. One is my father who is good to me. By some chance, here they are, all on this earth; and who shall ever tell the sorrow of being on this earth, lying, on quilts, on the grass, in a summer evening, among the sounds of the night. May God bless my people, my uncle, my aunt, my mother, my good father, oh, remember them kindly in their time of trouble; and in the hour of their taking away.

After a little I am taken in and put to bed. Sleep, soft smiling, draws me unto her: and those receive me, who quietly treat me, as one familiar and well-beloved in that home: but will not, oh, will not, not now, not ever, but will not ever tell me who I am.

Journal Entry

Why is Agee concerned at the end of the essay with his identity? Respond to the last paragraph of his essay.

Textual Considerations

1. What sounds does Agee describe in the essay? What feelings does he seem to associate with the sounds of a summer evening in Knoxville in 1915?
2. What significance does the image of the men who are watering their lawns hold?
3. Agee uses many examples of figurative language to create the mood of his essay. Find one example each of simile, metaphor, alliteration, and personification that reinforces the tranquility of the scene.
4. The language of the first paragraph is fairly straightforward and declarative. How does it change after that? What is the effect of the verses toward the end?

Cultural Contexts

1. What does Agee mean when he describes his neighborhood as "solidly lower middle class"? What is the overall impression that Agee offers of Knoxville in the summer of 1915? To what extent does he identify with this place? Explain.

Sue Doro
1992

The Father Poem Two

my father,
dark gray,
dusty factory father,
left with one lung
from filthy air,   5
aching with rheumatism,
from winter cold air
blowing on sweaty shoulders.

my father,
cursing your job, through us,   10
your family,
mean to my mother
my brother, my sister,
me.

yelling, coughing.   15
spitting angry yellow,
green and red.

my father, swallowing pills
to keep on your feet.
swallowing pills   20
to get to sleep.

my father,
two months into retirement,
an uncashed check
on the kitchen table,   25
found dead,
by the lady who ran
the downstairs tavern.

my father, dead,
your body melting   30
into the floor boards
near a shoe box
of assorted pills,
an empty brandy bottle,
and a bucket of spit   35
lined with newspaper.
your pain is finished now.

my father, dead but not gone,
alive but not living,
I remember you,   40
coming home
from a ten hour work day,
taking off your glasses
to reveal white circles
of sunken eyes   45
surrounded by soot,
because sometimes
you were too tired
to clean up at work,
in the washroom   50
your union fought for.

on those nights,
I remember
when the white circles
were around your eyes,   55
and your clothes
smelled like Johnnie's Bar,
you'd spit on the floor
and at mamma,
swearing, as you flung what was left   60
of your pay check,
and she would pick up the scattered bills,
the rolling coins,
and tuck them in her apron pocket,
while you kept on   65
cursing her for being there,
and I hid
behind the doorway,
not wanting to leave her
alone with you,   70
but too afraid
to stand next to her
and fight.

my father dead but not gone,
alive but not living,   75
were you always mean?
or were there days
I never knew?
lost years on a farm,
when you were a little boy,   80
summers gone loving
in the sun with the woman
who would become my mother.

days of slow drives to Milwaukee
in a truck full of fresh farm eggs   85
and sand stuffed chickens,
to make them weigh more when you got there.
old days when you were the man
my mother loved,
before you worked   90
in a rich man's factory,
and taverns became your second home.

potatoes-in-the-cellar days,
when both of you were young and new
and lived in Berlin, Wisconsin,   95
and went to band concerts in the park,
gathered hickory nuts,
and knew everyone in town.

what did you feel
when the depression   100
robbed you of your business?

how scared were you
to come to a big city
with a wife and 2 babies?
how guilty did you feel   105
for leaving your oldest child behind?

and how crazy did it make you
to be a family provider
who could not provide
in a system that demands it   110
as part of manhood?

my father,
a good welder,
proud to be
one of the best   115
in your department.
sealing seams
of World War II bombs,
from inside their smoky guts.
welding slabs of blue metal,   120
to create corn silos,
for farms you would only dream of,
frames for trucks
you could never afford.

how did it feel   125
when a time came,
and your shaky hands
and watering eyes
couldn't keep the torch steady?

on the day you collapsed at work,   130
the shop doctor gave you
a prescription for pain pills,
and a week of sick leave.
when you returned,
you found you'd been transferred   135
to the tool crib.

your use as a profit machine,
was over.
a welding career finished,
your new assignment: 140
to hand others their tools.

you were sick, and old at fifty-five,
and I feared and hated
and did not understand you.
did you feel bad   145
after swearing at me
for not emptying your bucket
fast enough?
did you feel ashamed
when you cursed and blamed me   150
for mamma's dying,
and your only son's death?
and for not being able

to breathe   hear   see
or walk without a cane?   155

after mamma died, you wanted me
to take her place.
I stayed late at school each night,
until the janitor made me leave.

you'd come home to sit in your red rocker   160
by the window,
looking out on Lisbon Avenue,
and you'd rock and talk
to yourself
about corn silos,   165
and dead relatives.

did you ever think
of the man you used to be?
did you ever question
the choices that you made?   170

were you sorry
for the pain
you put your family through,
the misery no child should endure?

did you wonder, as I do,   175
how much was from the rich man?
how much,
from you?

my father,
dark gray dusty factory father,   180
dead but not gone,
alive but not living,

for thirty years
you had a clock number.
a.o. smith company   185
knew you by it.

as for me,

I knew you
by your anger,
your choices,   190

and our communal pain.

Keith Gilyard
1993

The Hatmaker
(for Mary Lewis Gilyard)

i
cold metal snake down
A snake
E snake
F snake
cold metal subway down   5
to the district
to make hats

fingers flipping through felt
rifling through ribbon
paste   sequins   mesh   feathers   10
hard tight straw
didn't matter what style

hats since 1947

dark eyed dark faced momma
swept north of georgia on new hope   15
swept up to new york
new york, harbor of hope
swept to this big puzzle town
this half lit skyscraper town
this dazzle & dark mixed town   20
this dazzle & dull mixed town
this big rubik's cube town

swept north
brown georgia girl
fingers molding material   25
into hats to sit atop
empty heads of ladies who could never
have her grace

hats since 1947
hats since 1947   30

didn't matter what style
she didn't wear em much nohow

machines sucking hats from her fingers
sucked hats of pain from her fingers

didn't matter   35

sew on saturday

didn't matter

do overtime

didn't matter what style

she had youth to pour into hats in '47   40
youth into hats 38 years ago
just a new mover making this move
trying to beat this big puzzle town
beat this big 1947 jackie robinson town

hats since jackie was rookie of the year   45
hats to go see the black comet lose his
but not his head
big fun loving nerve wracked georgia boy
with flashy feet

fun loving georgia girl fan   50
with working fingers

hats since 1947
machines spilling hats since 1947

didn't matter what style
she didn't much wear em nohow   55

hustle bustle out hats
sewing machine foot stomp dance
hats for ladies in all styles

bosses doing finger tap dance
on the cash register   60
machine hum register jingle dance

great worker mary you are
good hatmaking girl you are
never sick
foot pedal machine stomp dance   65
since '47

tried to keep an eye on this big puzzle town
tried to get it rooted in this
slippery as a seal's back
big puzzle town   70

metal snake down
struggling & sewing & struggling
wiggling out hats since '47
fingers shedding hats since '47
didn't matter what style   75

hats don't keep off much chill nohow
in this cold metal big puzzle town

ii
as long as too many women of thick fingered greed
or thin fingered vanity
scooped them up   80
and kept retailers happy
hats dripped from her brow

motherhood wore a hat
her children wore hats on their backs
hats on their backs in this cold metal town   85
hats on their backs and knew
a brown georgia hatmaking girl would never
let them down

hats had her up at six
in bed by ten   90
then nine
then eight
even seven

hats in some pleasant dreams
hats in her greatest nightmares   95

hats since 1947
hats since 1947

hats get heavy since '47
hundreds of thousands of hats get
real heavy since '47   100
keeping four children in hats
gets real heavy

children get heavy

especially that son on the run
hardheaded boy   105
that do it his way boy
that in one ear out the other pants leg ripping

too hard on shoes boy
that disrupt class street running drug seeking
jail peeping sense leaking   110
boy

iii
maybe worked on a million hats since 1947
maybe a million heads wearing her fingers since '47
heads bobbing to the rhythm
of sewing machine madness   115

hats since 1947
hats since 1947

never mattered what style
she never wore em much nohow

fingers as wheels on limousines   120
a hard driving answer for this town
a hard driven answer for this town
a hard children in hats answer
for this big puzzle town
a can't cover all bases but   125
i'm doing the best i can answer
for this cold metal big puzzle town

hats since 1947
hats since 1947

didn't matter what style   130
never really for her nohow

and the boy could not go hatless
wore her pride as his main skimmer in this town
wore his mother as answer
in this big puzzle town   135
wears her even now on this
cold bitter night in this
cold metal town
this big puzzle
cold metal   140
snake metal
machine mad
son of a hatmaker's town

this son of a hatmaker's town

Journal Entry

Compare and contrast parental legacies in both poems.

Textual Considerations

1. How does repeating the lines "my father, dead but not gone, / alive but not living" throughout "The Father Poem Two" affect the tone, mood, and theme of the poem?
2. Summarize what the speaker in Doro's poem has learned about herself through her attempts to analyze her father's history.
3. Gilyard refers several times in "The Hatmaker" to his mother's daily journey to work by subway. How does this technique contribute to the rhythm and meaning of the poem?
4. Gilyard, like Doro, uses repetition to affect tone, mood, and theme. Find at least three examples and analyze their effectiveness.

Cultural Contexts

1. To what extent have the lives of the protagonists in both poems been shaped by economic necessity and class differences?
2. Discuss with your group whether both texts may be viewed as protest poems. Consider what each implies about the theme of entrapment. To what extent do the texts suggest that we can overcome our personal and cultural histories?

Kenny, Levertov, and Song

Maurice Kenny
1987

Going Home

The book lay unread in my lap
snow gathered at the window
from Brooklyn it was a long ride
the Greyhound followed the plow
from Syracuse to Watertown   5
to country cheese and maples
tired rivers and closed paper mills
home to gossipy aunts...
their dandelions and pregnant cats...
home to cedars and fields of boulders   10
cold graves under willow and pine

home from Brooklyn to the reservation
that was not home
to songs I could not sing
to dances I could not dance   15
from Brooklyn bars and ghetto rats
to steaming horses stomping frozen earth
barns and privies lost in blizzards
home to a Nation, Mohawk
to faces, I did not know   20
and hands which did not recognize me
to names and doors
my father shut

Denise Levertov
1987

During a Son's Dangerous Illness

You could die before me—
I've known it
always, the
dreaded worst, "unnatural" but
possible   5
in the play
of matter, matter and
growth and
fate.

My sister Philippa died   10
twelve years before I was born—
the perfect, laughing firstborn,
a gift to be cherished as my orphaned mother
had not been cherished. Suddenly:
death, a baby   15

cold and still.

Parent, child—death ignores
protocol, a sweep of its cape brushes
this one or that one at random

into the dust, it was   20
not even looking.
                    What becomes
of the past if the future
snaps off, brittle,
the present left as a jagged edge   25
opening on nothing?

Grief for the menaced world—lost rivers,
poisoned lakes—all creatures, perhaps
to be fireblasted
                    off the   30
whirling cinder we
love but not enough…
The grief I'd know if I
lived into
your unthinkable death   35
is a splinter
of that selfsame grief,
infinitely smaller but
the same in kind:
one   40
stretching the mind's fibers to touch
eternal nothingness,
the other
tasting in fear, the
desolation of   45
survival.

Cathy Song
1983

Lost Sister

1
In China,
even the peasants
named their first daughters
Jade—
the stone that in the far fields   5

could moisten the dry season,
could make men move mountains
for the healing green of the inner hills
glistening like slices of winter melon.

And the daughters were grateful: 10
they never left home.
To move freely was a luxury
stolen from them at birth.
Instead, they gathered patience,
learning to walk in shoes   15
the size of teacups,[1]
without breaking—
the arc of their movements
as dormant as the rooted willow,
as redundant as the farmyard hens.   20
But they traveled far
in surviving,
learning to stretch the family rice,
to quiet the demons,
the noisy stomachs.   25

2
There is a sister
across the ocean,
who relinquished her name,
diluting jade green
with the blue of the Pacific.   30
Rising with a tide of locusts,
she swarmed with others
to inundate another shore.
In America,
there are many roads   35
and women can stride along with men.

But in another wilderness,
the possibilities,
the loneliness,
can strangulate like jungle vines.   40
The meager provisions and sentiments
of once belonging—
fermented roots, Mah-Jongg[2] tiles and firecrackers—
set but a flimsy household
in a forest of nightless cities.   45
A giant snake rattles above,
spewing black clouds into your kitchen.

Dough-faced landlords
slip in and out of your keyholes,
making claims you don't understand,   50
tapping into your communication systems
of laundry lines and restaurant chains.

You find you need China:
your one fragile identification,
a jade link   55
handcuffed to your wrist.

You remember your mother
who walked for centuries,
footless—
and like her,   60
you have left no footprints,
but only because
there is an ocean in between,
the unremitting space of your rebellion.

[1] A reference to the practice of binding young girls' feet so that they remain small. This practice was
common in China until the Communist revolution.

[2] Or mahjong, an ancient Chinese game played with dice and tiles.

◆

Journal Entry

Record your associations with the phrase "going home."

Textual Considerations

1. Contrast Kenny's associations with Brooklyn and the reservation. What images did
   you find most effective?
2. In Levertov's poem, how does the "son's dangerous illness" serve as a catalyst for
   the speaker's memories of her mother and her older sister's death? Explain the
   meaning of "death ignores protocol."
3. In "Lost Sister," contrast the description of a woman's life in China with a woman's
   life in the United States.
4. Explain why the lost sister and her mother have "left no footprints."

Cultural Contexts

1. Discuss with your group the portraits of family members that emerge through personal and ancestral memories in the three poems.
2. Analyze the meaning of lines 21–26 of Levertov's poem, and discuss the meaning's
   relevance to "Lost Sister" and "Going Home."

Linda Hogan
1979

Song for My Name

Before sunrise
think of brushing out an old woman's
dark braids.
Think of your hands,
fingertips on the soft hair.   5

If you have this name,
your grandfather's dark hands
lead horses toward the wagon
and a cloud of dust follows,
ghost of silence.   10

That name is full of women
with black hair
and men with eyes like night.
It means no money
tomorrow.   15

Such a name my mother loves
while she works gently
in the small house.
She is a white dove
and in her own land   20
the mornings are pale,
birds sing into the white curtains
and show off their soft breasts.

If you have a name like this,
there's never enough water.   25
There is too much heat.
When lightning strikes, rain
refuses to follow.
It's my name,
that of a woman living   30
between the white moon
and the red sun, waiting to leave.
It's the name that goes with me
back to earth
no one else can touch.   35

Gary Soto
1977

Moving Away [1]

Remember that we are moving away   brother
From those years
In the same house with a white stepfather
What troubled him has been forgotten

But what troubled us has settled   5
Like dirt
In the nests of our knuckles
And cannot be washed away

All those times you woke shivering
In the night   10
From a coldness I
Could not understand
And cupped a crucifix beneath the covers

All those summers we hoed our yard
In the afternoon sun   15
The heat waving across our faces
And we waved back wasps
While the one we hated
Watched us from under a tree and said nothing

We will remember those moments   brother   20

And now that we are far
From one another
What I want to speak of
Is the quiet of a room just before daybreak
And you next to me   sleeping   25

Gary Soto
1977

Moving Away [2]

Remember that you are moving away   sister
From what was a summer
Of hunger
And of thorns deep in your feet
Prayers that unraveled   5
Like mama's stockings
At the day's end
When she came back from candling eggs

Those small things you knew on the old street
Have vanished   a holly bush   10
And its bright jays
The rocks you scratched
From the yard
And were your dolls   blond dolls
Given heartbeats   names   legs   15
The sighs of those
About to cry
                    Remember that you have left
Grandpa nodding like a tall weed
Over his patch of chilies and tomatoes   20
Left a jar of secrets
Buried in the vacant lot
On a hot day
And our family some distance
From your life   25
Remember

Journal Entry

React to this statement: "The past that constitutes our identity cannot be erased."

Textual Considerations

1. Speculate on the meanings of Hogan's title, "Song for My Name." What significance do you attach to the speaker's not revealing her name?
2. How does Hogan explore the effects of color, sound, and rhythm to evoke recollections from the past?

3. What images most effectively convey the bonds of love between the brothers in Soto's poem? How does Soto use repetition to reinforce meaning?
4. Contrast the tones of Soto's poems. Of what significance is the speaker's use of the second-person pronoun throughout most of the poem about his sister? Analyze what the last stanza conveys about the sister's relation to the family.

Cultural Contexts

1. The speakers of these poems search for their origins in different ways. Explain how their memories of the past authenticate their narrative voices and contribute to their individual histories.
2. Speculate with your group about the implications of Gary Soto's gender-split poems. In how many ways can we read Soto's poems? How do these poems mirror each other? What kinds of effects do they create for you as reader?

Longfellow and Thomas ◆

Henry Wadsworth Longfellow
1854

The Jewish Cemetery at Newport[1]

How strange it seems! These Hebrews in their graves,
    Close by the street of this fair seaport town,
Silent beside the never-silent waves,
    At rest in all this moving up and down!

The trees are white with dust, that o'er their sleep   5
    Wave their broad curtains in the south-wind's breath.
While underneath these leafy tents they keep
    The long, mysterious Exodus of Death[2]

And these sepulchral stones, so old and brown,
    That pave with level flags their burial-place,   10
Seem like the tablets of the Law, thrown down
    And broken by Moses at the mountain's base.[3]

The very names recorded here are strange,
    Of foreign accent, and of different climes;
Alvares and Rivera interchange   15
    With Abraham and Jacob of old times.[4]

"Blessed be God, for he created Death!"
    The mourners said, "and Death is rest and peace;"
Then added, in the certainty of faith,
    "And giveth Life that nevermore shall cease."   20

Closed are the portals of their Synagogue,
    No Psalms of David now the silence break,
No Rabbi reads the ancient Decalogue[5]
    In the grand dialect the Prophets spake.

Gone are the living, but the dead remain,   25
    And not neglected; for a hand unseen,
Scattering its bounty, like a summer rain,
    Still keeps their graves and their remembrance green.

How came they here? What burst of Christian hate,
    What persecution, merciless and blind,   30
Drove o'er the sea—that desert desolate—
    These Ishmaels and Hagars of mankind?[6]

They lived in narrow streets and lanes obscure,
    Ghetto and Judenstrass,[7] in mirk and mire;
Taught in the school of patience to endure   35
    The life of anguish and the death of fire.

All their lives long, with the unleavened bread
    And bitter herbs of exile and its fears,
The wasting famine of the heart they fed,
    And slaked its thirst with marah of their tears.   40

Anathema maranatha![8] was the cry
    That rang from town to town, from street to street;
At every gate the accursed Mordecai[9]
    Was mocked and jeered, and spurned by Christian feet.

Pride and humiliation hand in hand   45
    Walked with them through the world where'er they went;
Trampled and beaten were they as the sand,
    And yet unshaken as the continent.

For in the background figures vague and vast
    Of patriarchs and of prophets rose sublime,   50
And all the great traditions of the Past
    They saw reflected in the coming time.

And thus forever with reverted look
    The mystic volume of the world they read,
Spelling it backward, like a Hebrew book,   55
    Till life became a Legend of the Dead.

But ah! what once has been shall be no more!
   The groaning earth in travail and in pain
Brings forth its races, but does not restore,
   And the dead nations never rise again.   60

[1] The oldest synagogue in the United States is in Newport, Rhode Island.

[2] A reference to the second book of the Old Testament, which recounts the expulsion of the Jews from Egypt.

[3] See Exodus 32:19.

[4] The Jewish population in Newport was mostly of Spanish and Portuguese heritage.

[5] The Ten Commandments.

[6] Two exiles whose stories are recorded in Genesis.

[7] Literally, "Jew Street" (German). Jews lived in restricted areas, or ghettos.

[8] "Anathema" is an accursed person, or a formal curse; "Maranatha" means "O Lord, come." The combination is a powerful curse, calling on God to destroy the Jews. See 1 Corinthians 16:22.

[9] In the Book of Esther, Mordecai, Esther's uncle, sat at the king's gate, angering the chief minister, Haman, by refusing to bow before him. Haman plotted to kill Mordecai and all the Jews, but was executed.

Dylan Thomas
1946

Fern Hill

Now as I was young and easy under the apple boughs
About the lilting house and happy as the grass was green,
   The night above the dingle[1] starry,
     Time let me hail and climb
   Golden in the heydays of his eyes,   5
And honored among wagons I was prince of the apple towns
And once below a time I lordly had the trees and leaves
   Trail with daisies and barley
   Down the rivers of the windfall light.

And as I was green and carefree, famous among the barns 10
About the happy yard and singing as the farm was home,
    In the sun that is young once only,
        Time let me play and be
    Golden in the mercy of his means,
And green and golden I was huntsman and herdsman, the calves 15
Sang to my horn, the foxes on the hills barked clear and cold,
    And the sabbath rang slowly
    In the pebbles of the holy streams.

All the sun long it was running, it was lovely, the hay
Fields high as the house, the tunes from the chimneys, it was air 20
    And playing, lovely and watery
        And fire green as grass.
    And nightly under the simple stars
As I rode to sleep the owls were bearing the farm away,
All the moon long I heard, blessed among stables, the nightjars 25
    Flying with the ricks, and the horses
        Flashing into the dark.

And then to awake, and the farm, like a wanderer white
With the dew, come back, the cock on his shoulder: it was all
    Shining, it was Adam and maiden, 30
        The sky gathered again
    And the sun grew round that very day.
So it must have been after the birth of the simple light
In the first, spinning place, the spellbound horses walking warm
    Out of the whinnying green stable 35
        On to the fields of praise.

And honored among foxes and pheasants by the gay house
Under the new made clouds and happy as the heart was long,
    In the sun born over and over,
        I ran my heedless ways, 40
    My wishes raced through the house high hay
And nothing I cared, at my sky blue trades, that time allows
In all his tuneful turning so few and such morning songs
    Before the children green and golden
        Follow him out of grace, 45

> Nothing I cared, in the lamb white days, that time would take me
> Up to the swallow thronged loft by the shadow of my hand,
>   In the moon that is always rising,
>   Nor that riding to sleep
>   I should hear him fly with the high fields   50
> And wake to the farm forever fled from the childless land.
> Oh as I was young and easy in the mercy of his means,
>   Time held me green and dying
>   Though I sang in my chains like the sea.
>
> ¹ Wooded valley.

Journal Entry

Explain the paradox in the last two lines of "Fern Hill."

Textual Considerations

1. Compare and contrast the speakers' attitudes toward time in these poems. To what extent do the speakers view time as benevolent, malevolent, or indifferent?
2. Discuss the effects of Longfellow's historical analysis of anti-Semitism in "The Jewish Cemetery at Newport." What can this poem teach new generations about the past?
3. Analyze how Dylan Thomas's use of color reinforces his theme in "Fern Hill." How do his references to music also contribute to the poem's meaning?
4. In stanza 4 in "Fern Hill," the speaker compares his own childhood to what other experience of newness and innocence?
5. That speaker sounds an ominous note for the first time in stanza 5. What foreshadowings of this danger can you find in earlier stanzas?

Cultural Contexts

1. What attitudes about the past do these poems elicit? Use evidence from the texts to describe Thomas's evocation of childhood and Longfellow's historical exploration of Judaism.
2. Is there a "site of memory" that has shaped your own historical past? Describe it to your group, and discuss the extent to which we are influenced by landscapes from the past.

Lum and Vigil-Piñón

Wing Tek Lum
1987

It's Something Our Family Has Always Done

On every trip away from these islands
on the day of departure and on the day of return
we go to the graves, all seven of them,
but for one the sum total of all of our ancestors
who died in this place we call home.   5

The drive to the cemetery is only five minutes long.
Stopping by a florist adds maybe ten minutes more.
Yet my wife and I on the day of our flight
are so rushed with packing and last minute chores.
Why do we still make the time to go?   10

The concrete road is one lane wide.
We turn around at the circle up at the top,
always to park just to the side of the large banyan tree
as the road begins its slope back down.
I turn the wheels; we now lock our car.   15

As if by rote, we bring anthuriums,
at least two flowers for each of our dead.
On our way we stop to pay our respects to the "Old Man"
—that first one lain here, all wind and water before him—
who watches over this graveyard, and our island home.   20

Approaching my grandparents, we divide up our offering,
placing their long stems into the holes filled with sand.
Squatting in front of each marble tablet,
I make it a point to read off their names in Chinese.
My hands pull out crabgrass running over stone.   25

I stand erect, clutching palm around fist,
swinging the air three times up and down.
My wife from the waist bows once, arms at her sides.
I manage to whisper a few phrases out loud,
conversing like my father would, as if all could hear.   30

We do Grandfather, Grandmother, and my parents below them.
Following the same path we always take,
we make our way through the tombstones and mounds,
skirting their concrete borders, to the other two Lums
and to our Granduncle on the Chang side.   35

Back up the hill, we spend a few moments by the curb
picking off black, thin burrs from our cuffs and socks.
We talk about what errands we must do next.
I glance around us at these man-made gardens,
thrust upon a slope of earth, spirit houses rising to the sky.   40

As I get into our car, and look out at the sea,
I am struck with the same thought as always.
We spend so little time in front of these graves
asking each in turn to protect us when we are far away.
I question them all: what good does it really do?   45

I have read ancient poets who parted with sorrow
from family and friends, fearing never to return.
Our oral histories celebrate brave peasants
daring oceans and the lonely beds: they looked even more
to blessings at long distance from their spirit dead.   50

My father superstitious, even to the jet age,
still averred: but every little bit helps.
These sentiments I know, but I confess I do not feel.
Maybe it's for this loss that I still come here.
They are family, and I respect them so.   55

Evangelina Vigil-Piñón
1982

warm heart contains life
to our amás

warm heart contains life
heart's warmth
which penetrates through pen
lifeblood that reveals inner thoughts
subtly   5
like rustling leaves would secrets
to the winter wind

secrets collected
pressed between pages
to be kissed by lips red   10
protruding with warmth, desire
sometimes hurt, pain:

recuerdos
like that autumn leaf you singled out
and saved   15
pressed in-between the memories of your mind
diary never written
but always remembered, felt
scripted en tu mente—
your daughters will never read it   20
but they'll inherit it
and they'll know it
when they look into your eyes
shining luz de amor, corazón
unspoken, untold   25
keepsake for our treasure chests
que cargamos aquí adentro
radiant with jewels
sculpted by sentimientos y penas
y bastante amor: 30

      intuition tells us
      better having lived through pain
      than never having felt
      life's full intensity

Journal Entry

Respond to the concept of heritage in "It's Something Our Family Has Always Done" and in "warm heart contains life."

Textual Considerations

1. Characterize the speaker's emotions in Lum's poem as he visits the family burial grounds.
2. To what extent does the speaker answer his question, "What good does it really do?" (l. 45)?
3. Characterize the relation between the past and the future in Vigil-Piñón's poem. To what extent does the speaker's bilingual text contribute to the poem's meaning? Explain.
4. Speculate on the implications of the title of Vigil-Piñón's poem.

Cultural Contexts

1. In a text she edited in 1983 entitled *Woman of Her Word: Hispanic Women Write,* Vigil-Piñón describes the Latina writer: "As a person in the literature, the Latina is a woman of her word—*mujer de su palabra*. In this role, the Latina is self-sacrificing to her family as a mother and wife. She conveys values to her family members by way of example, and through the oral tradition, and, as such, she represents a tie to the cultural past." Discuss with your group how the oral tradition functions in Vigil-Piñón's poem. Then review stanza 10 of Lum's poem. How has his oral tradition also contributed to his cultural heritage?

Gillan and Mora

Maria Mazziotti Gillan
1980

My Grandmother's Hands

I never saw them.
Once she sent a picture of herself,
skinny as a hook, her backdrop
a cobbled street and a house
of stones, an arched doorway.   5
In a black dress and black stockings,
she smiles over toothless gums,
old—years before she should have been,
buttoned neck to shin in heavy black.
Her eyes express an emotion   10
it is difficult to read.

I think of my mother's mother
and her mother's mother, traced
back from us on the thin thread of memory.
In that little mountain village,   15
the beds where the children
were born and the old ones died
were passed from one generation
to the next, but when my mother married,
she left her family behind. The ribbon   20
between herself and the past
ended with her,
though she tried to pass it on.

And my own children cannot understand
a word of the old language,   25
the past of the village so far
removed that they cannot find
the connection between it
and themselves, will not pass it on.
They cannot possess it,   30
not in the way that we possessed it
in the 17th street kitchen
where the Italian stories and the words
fell over us like confetti.

All the years of our growing,   35
my mother's arms held us
secure in that tenement kitchen,
the old stories weaving connections
between ourselves and the past,
teaching us so much about love   40
and the gift of self
and I wonder: Did I fail
my own children? Where
is the past I gave to them
like a gift? I have tried   45
to love them so that always,
they will imagine that love
wrapping them, like a cashmere sweater
warm and soothing on their skin.
The skein of the past spun from that love,   50
stretches back from them to me to my mother,
the old country, the old language lost,
but in this new world, saved and cherished:
the tablecloth my grandmother made,
the dresser scarves she crocheted,   55
and the love she taught us to weave
a thread of woven silk
to lead us home.

Pat Mora
1991

Gentle Communion

Even the long-dead are willing to move.
Without a word, she came with me from the desert.
Mornings she wanders through my rooms
making beds, folding socks.

Since she can't hear me anymore,   5
Mamande ignores the questions I never knew
to ask, about her younger days, her red
hair, the time she fell and broke her nose
in the snow. I will never know.

When I cry to make her laugh,   10
to disprove her sad album face, she leaves
the room, resists me as she resisted
grinning for cameras, make-up, English.

While I write, she sits and prays,
feet apart, legs never crossed,   15
the blue housecoat buttoned high
as her hair dries white, girlish
around her head and shoulders.

She closes her eyes, bows her head,
and like a child presses her hands together,   20
her patient flesh steeple, the skin
worn, like the pages of her prayer book.

Sometimes I sit in her wide-armed
chair as I once sat in her lap.
Alone, we played a quiet I Spy.   25
She peeled grapes I still taste.

She removes the thin skin, places
the luminous coolness on my tongue.
I know not to bite or chew. I wait
for the thick melt,   30
our private green honey.

Journal Entry

Contrast the title of each poem with its first line. What is the effect on meaning?

Textual Considerations

1. What metaphors does Gillan use to connect her grandmother's and mother's past and present? Why does she ask if she has failed her own children? How would you answer her question?
2. What portrait of the speaker's mother emerges in "Gentle Communion"? Cite the images you found most effective.
3. How would you describe the relationship between mother and daughter in each poem? On what is it based?

Cultural Contexts

1. Discuss with your group the importance of language in each poem. For example, consider that both speakers are poets, the children do not speak Italian, and the mother does not speak English in "Gentle Communion". Discuss the role of stories in "My Grandmother's Hands."

Tapahonso, Emanuel, and Lorde ◆

Luci Tapahonso
1984

A Breeze Swept Through
For my daughters, Lori Tazbah and Misty Dawn

The first born of dawn woman
slid out amid crimson fluid streaked with stratus clouds
    her body glistening August sunset pink
    light steam rising from her like rain on warm rocks
      (A sudden cool breeze swept through   5
      the kitchen and grandpa smiled then sang
      quietly knowing the moment.)
She came when the desert day cooled
and dusk began to move in
in that intricate changing of time   10
    she gasped and it flows from her now
    with every breath   with every breath
    she travels now
        sharing scarlet sunsets
        named for wild desert flowers   15
        her smile a blessing song.

And in mid-November
early morning darkness
after days of waiting pain
the second one cried   wailing   20
sucking first earth breath
separating the heavy fog
she cried and kicked   tiny brown limbs
fierce movements as outside
the mist lifted as   25
the sun is born again.
    (East of Acoma, a sandstone boulder
    split in two—a sharp, clean crack.)
She is born of damp mist and early sun.
She is born again   woman of dawn.   30
She is born knowing the warm smoothness of rock.
She is born knowing her own morning strength.

James A. Emanuel
1968

Fishermen

When three, he fished these lakes,
Curled sleeping on a lip of rock,
Crib blankets tucked from ants and fishbone flies,
Twitching as the strike of bass and snarling reel
Uncoiled my shouts not quit   5
Till he jerked blinking up on all-fours,
Swaying with the winking leaves.
Strong awake, he shook his cane pole like a spoon
And dipped among the wagging perch
Till, tired, he drew his silver rubber blade   10
And poked the winding fins that tugged our string,
Or sprayed the dimpling minnows with his plastic gun,
Or, rainstruck, squirmed to my armpit in the poncho.

Ten years uncurled him, thinned him hard.
Now, far he casts his line into the wrinkled blue   15
And easy toes a rock, reel on his thigh
Till bone and crank cry out the strike
He takes with manchild chuckles, cunning
In his play of zigzag line and plunging silver.

Now fishing far from me, he strides through rain, shoulders   20
A spiny ridge of pines, and disappears
Near lakes that cannot be, while I must choose
To go or stay: bring blanket, blade, and gun,
Or stand a fisherman.

Audre Lorde
1992

What My Child Learns of the Sea

What my child learns of the sea
Of the summer thunder
Of the bewildering riddle that hides at the vortex of spring
She will learn in my twilight
And childlike   5
Revise every autumn.

What my child learns
As her winters fall out of time
Ripened in my own body
To enter her eyes with first light.   10

This is why
More than blood,
Or the milk I have given
One day a strange girl will step
To the back of a mirror   15
Cutting my ropes
Of sea and thunder and sun.
Of the way she will taste her autumns
Toast-brittle, or warmer than sleep
And the words she will use for winter   20
I stand already condemned.

◆

Journal Entry

Discuss the significance of the title of each poem.

Textual Considerations

1. Create a profile of both daughters in Tapahonso's poem.
2. Tapahonso makes extensive use of visual and sensory imagery. Choose two or three examples, and discuss their effectiveness in communicating the poem's theme.

3. Compare and contrast the three fishing trips in Emanuel's poem.
4. Explain the significance of the last line of the text.
5. What will the child in Lorde's poem "revise every autumn"?
6. Discuss the significance of nature imagery in Lorde's poem.

Cultural Contexts

1. Discuss what the three poems imply about the role of the parents. Is the process described by Emanuel and Lorde inevitable? What did you learn about the role of parents from these poems?

Hayden

Robert Hayden
1947

*Frederick Douglass**

When it is finally ours, this freedom, this liberty, this beautiful
and terrible thing, needful to man as air,
usable as earth; when it belongs at last to all,
when it is truly instinct, brain matter, diastole, systole,
reflex action; when it is finally won; when it is more   5
than the gaudy mumbo jumbo of politicians:
this man, this Douglass, this former slave, this Negro
beaten to his knees, exiled, visioning a world
where none is lonely, none hunted, alien,
this man, superb in love and logic, this man   10
shall be remembered. Oh, not with statues' rhetoric,
not with legends and poems and wreaths of bronze alone,
but with the lives grown out of his life, the lives
fleshing his dream of the beautiful, needful thing.

*****Frederick Douglass** Born a slave, Douglass (1817–95) escaped and became an important spokesman for the abolitionist movement and later for civil rights for African Americans.

Robert Hayden
1962

Tour 5

The road winds down through autumn hills
in blazonry of farewell scarlet
and recessional gold,
past cedar groves, through static villages
whose names are all that's left   5
of Choctaw, Chickasaw.[1]

We stop a moment in a town
watched over by Confederate sentinels,
buy gas and ask directions of a rawboned man
whose eyes revile us as the enemy.   10

Shrill gorgon silence breathes behind
his taut civility
and in the ever-tautening air,
dark for us despite its Indian summer glow.
We drive on, following the route   15
of highwaymen and phantoms,

Of slaves and armies.
Children, wordless and remote,
wave at us from kindling porches.
And now the land is flat for miles,   20
the landscape lush, metallic, flayed,
its brightness harsh as bloodstained swords.

---

[1] American Indian tribes, originally of Mississippi.

Robert Hayden
1962

Those Winter Sundays

Sundays too my father got up early
and put his clothes on in the blueblack cold,
then with cracked hands that ached
from labor in the weekday weather made
banked fires blaze. No one ever thanked him.   5

I'd wake and hear the cold splintering, breaking.
When the rooms were warm, he'd call,
and slowly I would rise and dress,
fearing the chronic angers of that house,

Speaking indifferently to him,   10
who had driven out the cold
and polished my good shoes as well.
What did I know, what did I know
of love's austere and lonely offices?

Robert Hayden
1985

Runagate Runagate

I.

Runs falls rises stumbles on from darkness into darkness
and the darkness thicketed with shapes of terror
and the hunters pursuing and the hounds pursuing
and the night cold and the night long and the river
to cross and the jack-muh-lanterns beckoning beckoning   5
and blackness ahead and when shall I reach that somewhere
morning and keep on going and never turn back and keep on going

    Runagate
          Runagate
                    Runagate   10

Many thousands rise and go
many thousands crossing over

                    O mythic North
             O star-shaped yonder Bible city

Some go weeping and some rejoicing   15
some in coffins and some in carriages
some in silks and some in shackles

    Rise and go or fare you well

No more auction block for me
no more driver's lash for me   20

    If you see my Pompey, 30 yrs of age,
    new breeches, plain stockings, negro shoes;
    if you see my Anna, likely young mulatto
    branded E on the right cheek, R on the left,
    catch them if you can and notify subscriber,   25
    Catch them if you can, but it won't be easy.
    They'll dart underground when you try to catch them,
    plunge into quicksand, whirlpools, mazes,
    turn into scorpions when you try to catch them.

And before I'll be a slave   30
I'll be buried in my grave

    North star and bonanza gold
    I'm bound for the freedom, freedom-bound
    and oh Susyanna don't you cry for me

      Runagate   35

          Runagate

II.
Rises from their anguish and their power,

          Harriet Tubman,

          woman of earth, whipscarred,
          a summoning, a shining   40

          Mean to be free

And this was the way of it, brethren brethren,
way we journeyed from Can't to Can.

    Moon so bright and no place to hide,
    the cry up and the paterollers riding,   45
    hound dogs belling in bladed air.
    And fear starts a-murbling, Never make it,
    we'll never make it. *Hush that now,*
    and she's turned upon us, levelled pistol
    glinting in the moonlight: 50

Dead folks can't jaybird-talk she says:
you keep on going now or die, she says.

Wanted   Harriet Tubman   alias The General
alias Moses   Stealer of Slaves

In league with Garrison   Alcott   Emerson   55
Garrett   Douglass   Thoreau   John Brown

Armed and known to be Dangerous

Wanted   Reward   Dead or Alive

Tell me, Ezekiel, oh tell me do you see
mailed Jehovah coming to deliver me?   60

Hoot-owl calling in the ghosted air,
five times calling to the hants in the air.
Shadow of a face in the scary leaves,
shadow of a voice in the talking leaves:

Come ride-a my train   65

Oh that train, ghost-story train
through swamp and savanna movering movering,
over trestles of dew, through caves of the wish,
Midnight Special on a sabre track movering movering,
first stop Mercy and the last Hallelujah.   70

Come ride-a my train

Mean mean mean to be free.

Journal Entry

How does Frederick Douglass's idea that "we have to do with the past only as it is useful for the present and the future" apply to the poems by Hayden?

Textual Considerations

1. According to Hayden, when and how will Douglass be remembered?
2. Research the origins of "mumbo jumbo" in line 6. How does Hayden's use affect the poem's meaning?
3. What is the effect of delaying the subject of the first sentence until line 7 and the verb until line 11?

4. Does Hayden imply that there will come a time when freedom will belong to all? Do you agree? Why or why not?

5. Describe the effects of stopping for gas in "Tour 5."

6. Contrast the language of the first and last stanzas. What is the effect on the poem's mood and meaning?

7. Characterize the father in "Those Winter Sundays." What is the effect of using *too* in the first line?

8. How does the son attempt to subdue the "chronic angers" of the house? How does use of repetition in line 13 reinforce the meaning?

9. What kind of relationship do father and son share? Explain the meaning of "offices" in the last line.

10. In "Runagate Runagate," Hayden uses the interaction of several voices to orchestrate the phonic meanings of the poem. Identify some of these voices, and extend your study of sound to explore how devices such as alliteration, onomatopoeia, rhyme, and meter contribute to the phonic pattern of the poem.

11. Consult a dictionary for various definitions of *runagate*. How does a better understanding of the meaning of the title affect your response to the powerful epic voice of the speaker in lines such as "and before I'll be a slave / I'll be buried in my grave"?

12. To portray how "voiceless" people succeeded in constructing the history of the past, Hayden presents Harriet Tubman, Frederick Douglass, and others as models of individual heroism and courage. Identify each of these figures, and investigate how these "voiceless voices" from the past contributed to the collective history of the United States.

Cultural Contexts

1. Read over the following statement from an interview with Robert Hayden published in 1973.

> There's a tendency today—more than a tendency, it's almost a conspiracy—to delimit poets, to restrict them to the political and the socially or racially conscious. To me, this indicates gross ignorance of the poet's true function as well as of the function and value of poetry as an art. With a few notable exceptions, poets have generally been on the side of justice and humanity. I can't imagine any poet worth his salt today not being aware of social evils, human needs. But I feel I have the right to deal with these matters in my own way, in terms of my own understanding of what a poet is. I resist whatever would force me into a role as politician, sociologist, or yea-sayer to current ideologies. I know who I am, and pretty much what I want to say.

To what extent does the statement apply to his poems in the anthology?

DRAMA

Sophocles
430 B.C.

Oedipus Rex

CHARACTERS

OEDIPUS, *King of Thebes, supposed son of Polybos and Merope,*
  King and Queen of Corinth
IOKASTE, *wife of Oedipus and widow of the late King Laios*
KREON, *brother of Iokaste, a prince of Thebes*
TEIRESIAS, *a blind seer who serves Apollo*
PRIEST
MESSENGER, *from Corinth*
SHEPHERD, *former Servant of Laios*
SECOND MESSENGER, *from the palace*
CHORUS OF THEBAN ELDERS
CHORAGOS, *leader of the Chorus*
ANTIGONE *and* ISMENE, *young daughters of Oedipus and Iokaste.*
  They appear in the Exodos but do not speak.
Suppliants, Guards, Servants

SCENE.   *Before the palace of* OEDIPUS, *King of Thebes. A central door
and two lateral doors open onto a platform which runs the length of the facade.
On the platform, right and left, are altars; and three steps lead down into
the orchestra, or chorus-ground. At the beginning of the action these steps
are crowded by suppliants who have brought branches and chaplets of olive leaves
and who sit in various attitudes of despair.* OEDIPUS *enters.*

PROLOGUE

OEDIPUS.   My children, generations of the living
  In the line of Kadmos,° nursed at his ancient hearth:
  Why have you strewn yourselves before these altars
  In supplication, with your boughs and garlands?
  The breath of incense rises from the city   5
  With a sound of prayer and lamentation.
                                        Children,
  I would not have you speak through messengers,
  And therefore I have come myself to hear you—
  I, Oedipus, who bear the famous name.

2 *Kadmos:* Founder of Thebes, according to legend.

(*To a* PRIEST.) You, there, since you are eldest in the company,   10
Speak for them all, tell me what preys upon you,
Whether you come in dread, or crave some blessing:
Tell me, and never doubt that I will help you
In every way I can; I should be heartless
Were I not moved to find you suppliant here.   15
PRIEST.   Great Oedipus, O powerful king of Thebes!
You see how all the ages of our people
Cling to your altar steps: here are boys
Who can barely stand alone, and here are priests
By weight of age, as I am a priest of God,   20
And young men chosen from those yet unmarried;
As for the others, all that multitude,
They wait with olive chaplets in the squares,
At the two shrines of Pallas,° and where Apollo°
Speaks in the glowing embers.
                                        Your own eyes   25
Must tell you: Thebes is tossed on a murdering sea
And can not lift her head from the death surge.
A rust consumes the buds and fruits of the earth;
The herds are sick; children die unborn,
And labor is vain. The god of plague and pyre   30
Raids like detestable lightning through the city,
And all the house of Kadmos is laid waste,
All emptied, and all darkened: Death alone
Battens upon the misery of Thebes.

You are not one of the immortal gods, we know;   35
Yet we have come to you to make our prayer
As to the man surest in mortal ways
And wisest in the ways of God. You saved us
From the Sphinx,° that flinty singer, and the tribute
We paid to her so long; yet you were never   40
Better informed than we, nor could we teach you:
A god's touch, it seems, enabled you to help us.

Therefore, O mighty power, we turn to you:
Find us our safety, find us a remedy,
Whether by counsel of the gods or of men.   45
A kin of wisdom tested in the past
Can act in a time of troubles, and act well.

---

24 *Pallas:* Pallas Athena, Zeus's daughter; goddess of wisdom; *Apollo:* Zeus's son, god of the sun, truth, and poetry.   **39** *Sphinx:* A monster with the body of a lion, the wings of a bird, and the face of a woman. The Sphinx had challenged Thebes with a riddle, killing those who failed to solve it. When Oedipus answered correctly, the Sphinx killed herself.

Noblest of men, restore
Life to your city! Think how all men call you
Liberator for your boldness long ago;   50
Ah, when your years of kingship are remembered,
Let them not say *We rose, but later fell*—
Keep the State from going down in the storm!
Once, years ago, with happy augury,
You brought us fortune; be the same again!   55
No man questions your power to rule the land:
But rule over men, not over a dead city!
Ships are only hulls, high walls are nothing,
When no life moves in the empty passageways.
OEDIPUS.   Poor children! You may be sure I know   60
All that you longed for in your coming here.
I know that you are deathly sick; and yet,
Sick as you are, not one is as sick as I.
Each of you suffers in himself alone
His anguish, not another's; but my spirit   65
Groans for the city, for myself, for you.

I was not sleeping, you are not waking me.
No, I have been in tears for a long while
And in my restless thought walked many ways.
In all my search I found one remedy,   70
And I have adopted it: I have sent Kreon,
Son of Menoikeus, brother of the queen,
To Delphi,° Apollo's place of revelation,
To learn there, if he can,
What act or pledge of mine may save the city.   75
I have counted the days, and now, this very day,
I am troubled, for he has overstayed his time.
What is he doing? He has been gone too long.
Yet whenever he comes back, I should do ill
Not to take any action the god orders.   80
PRIEST.   It is a timely promise. At this instant
They tell me Kreon is here.
OEDIPUS.   O Lord Apollo!
May his news be fair as his face is radiant!
PRIEST.   Good news, I gather! he is crowned with bay,
The chaplet is thick with berries.
OEDIPUS.   We shall soon know;   85
He is near enough to hear us now. (*Enter* KREON.) O prince:

---

73 *Delphi:* Location of the prophetic oracle, regarded as the keeper of religious truth.

Brother: son of Menoikeus:
What answer do you bring us from the god?
KREON.   A strong one. I can tell you, great afflictions
Will turn out well, if they are taken well.   90
OEDIPUS.   What was the oracle? These vague words
Leave me still hanging between hope and fear.
KREON.   Is it your pleasure to hear me with all these
Gathered around us? I am prepared to speak,
But should we not go in?
OEDIPUS.   Speak to them all,   95
It is for them I suffer, more than for myself.
KREON.   Then I will tell you what I heard at Delphi.
In plain words
The god commands us to expel from the land of Thebes
An old defilement we are sheltering.   100
It is a deathly thing, beyond cure;
We must not let it feed upon us longer.
OEDIPUS.   What defilement? How shall we rid ourselves of it?
KREON.   By exile or death, blood for blood. It was
Murder that brought the plague-wind on the city.   105
OEDIPUS.   Murder of whom? Surely the god has named him?
KREON.   My Lord: Laios once ruled this land,
Before you came to govern us.
OEDIPUS.   I know;
I learned of him from others; I never saw him.
KREON.   He was murdered; and Apollo commands us now   110
To take revenge upon whoever killed him.
OEDIPUS.   Upon whom? Where are they? Where shall we find a clue
To solve that crime, after so many years?
KREON.   Here in this land, he said. Search reveals
Things that escape an inattentive man.   115
OEDIPUS.   Tell me: Was Laios murdered in his house,
Or in the fields, or in some foreign country?
KREON.   He said he planned to make a pilgrimage.
He did not come home again.
OEDIPUS.   And was there no one,
No witness, no companion, to tell what happened?   120
KREON.   They were all killed but one, and he got away
So frightened that he could remember one thing only.
OEDIPUS.   What was that one thing? One may be the key
To everything, if we resolve to use it.
KREON.   He said that a band of highwaymen attacked them,   125
Outnumbered them, and overwhelmed the king.
OEDIPUS.   Strange, that a highwayman should be so daring—
Unless some faction here bribed him to do it.

KREON.   We thought of that. But after Laios' death
New troubles arose and we had no avenger.   130
OEDIPUS.   What troubles could prevent your hunting down the killers?
KREON.   The riddling Sphinx's song
Made us deaf to all mysteries but her own.
OEDIPUS.   Then once more I must bring what is dark to light.
It is most fitting that Apollo shows,   135
As you do, this compunction for the dead.
You shall see how I stand by you, as I should,
Avenging this country and the god as well,
And not as though it were for some distant friend,
But for my own sake, to be rid of evil.   140
Whoever killed King Laios might—who knows?—
Lay violent hands even on me—and soon.
I act for the murdered king in my own interest.

Come, then, my children: leave the altar steps,
Lift up your olive boughs!
　　　　　　　　　　　　　One of you go   145
And summon the people of Kadmos to gather here.
I will do all that I can; you may tell them that.   (*Exit a* PAGE.)
So, with the help of God,
We shall be saved—or else indeed we are lost.
PRIEST.   Let us rise, children. It was for this we came,   150
And now the king has promised it.
Phoibos° has sent us an oracle; may he descend
Himself to save us and drive out the plague.

(*Exeunt*° OEDIPUS *and* KREON *into the palace by the central door. The* PRIEST
and the SUPPLIANTS *disperse right and left. After a short pause
the* CHORUS *enters the orchestra.*)

PARODOS

Strophe 1

CHORUS.   What is God singing in his profound
Delphi of gold and shadow?
What oracle for Thebes, the Sunwhipped city?
Fear unjoints me, the roots of my heart tremble.
Now I remember, O Healer, your power, and wonder: 5
Will you send doom like a sudden cloud, or weave it
Like nightfall of the past?
Speak to me, tell me, O
Child of golden Hope, immortal Voice.

152 *Phoibos:* Apollo.　*s.d. Exeunt:* Latin term meaning "they exit."

Antistrophe 1

Let me pray to Athene, the immortal daughter of Zeus,   10
And to Artemis° her sister
Who keeps her famous throne in the market ring,
And to Apollo, archer from distant heaven—
O gods, descend! Like three streams leap against
The fires of our grief, the fires of darkness;   15
Be swift to bring us rest!
As in the old time from the brilliant house
Of air you stepped to save us, come again!

Strophe 2

Now our afflictions have no end,
Now all our stricken host lies down   20
And no man fights off death with his mind;
The noble plowland bears no grain,
And groaning mothers can not bear—
See, how our lives like birds take wing,
Like sparks that fly when a fire soars,   25
To the shore of the god of evening.

Antistrophe 2

The plague burns on, it is pitiless,
Though pallid children laden with death
Lie unwept in the stony ways,
And old gray women by every path   30
Flock to the strand about the altars
There to strike their breasts and cry
Worship of Phoibos in wailing prayers:
Be kind, God's golden child!

Strophe 3

There are no swords in this attack by fire,   35
No shields, but we are ringed with cries.
Send the besieger plunging from our homes
Into the vast sea-room of the Atlantic
Or into the waves that foam eastward of Thrace—
For the day ravages what the night spares—   40
Destroy our enemy, lord of the thunder!
Let him be riven by lightning from heaven!

11 *Artemis:* Goddess of the hunt.

Antistrophe 3

Phoibos Apollo, stretch the sun's bowstring,
That golden cord, until it sing for us,
Flashing arrows in heaven!

Artemis, Huntress,

Race with flaring lights upon our mountains!   45
O scarlet god,° O golden-banded brow,
O Theban Bacchos in a storm of Maenads,°

(*Enter* OEDIPUS, *center.*)

Whirl upon Death, that all the Undying hate!
Come with blinding torches, come in joy!   50

SCENE 1

OEDIPUS. Is this your prayer? It may be answered. Come,
Listen to me, act as the crisis demands,
And you shall have relief from all these evils.

Until now I was a stranger to this tale,
As I had been a stranger to the crime.   5
Could I track down the murderer without a clue?
But now, friends,
As one who became a citizen after the murder,
I make this proclamation to all Thebans:
If any man knows by whose hand Laios, son of Labdakos, 10
Met his death, I direct that man to tell me everything,
No matter what he fears for having so long withheld it.
Let it stand as promised that no further trouble
Will come to him, but he may leave the land in safety.
Moreover: If anyone knows the murderer to be foreign, 15
Let him not keep silent: he shall have his reward from me.
However, if he does conceal it; if any man
Fearing for his friend or for himself disobeys this edict,
Hear what I propose to do:

I solemnly forbid the people of this country,   20
Where power and throne are mine, ever to receive that man
Or speak to him, no matter who he is, or let him
Join in sacrifice, lustration, or in prayer.
I decree that he be driven from every house,
Being, as he is, corruption itself to us: the Delphic   25
Voice of Apollo has pronounced this revelation.

---

47 *scarlet god:* Bacchos, god of wine and revelry. 48 *Maenads:* Female attendants of Bacchos.

Thus I associate myself with the oracle
And take the side of the murdered king.

As for the criminal, I pray to God—
Whether it be a lurking thief, or one of a number—   30
I pray that that man's life be consumed in evil and wretchedness.
And as for me, this curse applies no less
If it should turn out that the culprit is my guest here,
Sharing my hearth.
                         You have heard the penalty.
I lay it on you now to attend to this   35
For my sake, for Apollo's, for the sick
Sterile city that heaven has abandoned.
Suppose the oracle had given you no command:
Should this defilement go uncleansed for ever?
You should have found the murderer: your king,   40
A noble king, had been destroyed!
                                    Now I,
Having the power that he held before me,
Having his bed, begetting children there
Upon his wife, as he would have, had he lived—
Their son would have been my children's brother,   45
If Laios had had luck in fatherhood!
(And now his bad fortune has struck him down)—
I say I take the son's part, just as though
I were his son, to press the fight for him
And see it won! I'll find the hand that brought   50
Death to Labdakos' and Polydoros' child,
Heir of Kadmos' and Agenor's line.°
And as for those who fail me,
May the gods deny them the fruit of the earth,
Fruit of the womb, and may they rot utterly!   55
Let them be wretched as we are wretched, and worse!

For you, for loyal Thebans, and for all
Who find my actions right, I pray the favor
Of justice, and of all the immortal gods.
CHORAGOS.   Since I am under oath, my lord, I swear   60
    I did not do the murder, I can not name
    The murderer. Phoibos ordained the search;
    Why did he not say who the culprit was?
OEDIPUS.   An honest question. But no man in the world
    Can make the gods do more than the gods will.   65

51–52 *Labdakos, Polydoros, Kadmos,* and *Agenor:* Ancestors of Laios.

CHORAGOS.   There is an alternative, I think—
OEDIPUS.   Tell me.
  Any or all, you must not fail to tell me.
CHORAGOS.   A lord clairvoyant to the lord Apollo,
  As we all know, is the skilled Teiresias.
  One might learn much about this from him, Oedipus.   70
OEDIPUS.   I am not wasting time:
  Kreon spoke of this, and I have sent for him—
  Twice, in fact; it is strange that he is not here.
CHORAGOS.   The other matter—that old report—seems useless.
OEDIPUS.   What was that? I am interested in all reports.   75
CHORAGOS.   The king was said to have been killed by highwaymen.
OEDIPUS.   I know. But we have no witnesses to that.
CHORAGOS.   If the killer can feel a particle of dread,
  Your curse will bring him out of hiding!
OEDIPUS.   No.
  The man who dared that act will fear no curse.   80

           (*Enter the blind seer* TEIRESIAS, *led by a* PAGE.)

CHORAGOS.   But there is one man who may detect the criminal.
  This is Teiresias, this is the holy prophet
  In whom, alone of all men, truth was born.
OEDIPUS.   Teiresias: seer: student of mysteries,
  Of all that's taught and all that no man tells,   85
  Secrets of Heaven and secrets of the earth:
  Blind though you are, you know the city lies
  Sick with plague; and from this plague, my lord,
  We find that you alone can guard or save us.

  Possibly you did not hear the messengers?   90
  Apollo, when we sent to him,
  Sent us back word that this great pestilence
  Would lift, but only if we established clearly
  The identity of those who murdered Laios.
  They must be killed or exiled.
                    Can you use   95
  Birdflight° or any art of divination
  To purify yourself, and Thebes, and me
  From this contagion? We are in your hands.
  There is no fairer duty
  Than that of helping others in distress.   100
TEIRESIAS.   How dreadful knowledge of the truth can be
  When there's no help in truth! I knew this well,
  But did not act on it; else I should not have come.

---

96 *Birdflight:* The flight of birds was one sign used to predict the future.

OEDIPUS. What is troubling you? Why are your eyes so cold?

TEIRESIAS. Let me go home. Bear your own fate, and I'll   105
   Bear mine. It is better so: trust what I say.

OEDIPUS. What you say is ungracious and unhelpful
   To your native country. Do not refuse to speak.

TEIRESIAS. When it comes to speech, your own is neither temperate
   Nor opportune. I wish to be more prudent.   110

OEDIPUS. In God's name, we all beg you—

TEIRESIAS.   You are all ignorant.
   No; I will never tell you what I know.
   Now it is my misery; then, it would be yours.

OEDIPUS. What! You do know something, and will not tell us?
   You would betray us all and wreck the State?   115

TEIRESIAS. I do not intend to torture myself, for you.
   Why persist in asking? You will not persuade me.

OEDIPUS. What a wicked old man you are! You'd try a stone's
   Patience! Out with it! Have you no feeling at all?

TEIRESIAS. You call me unfeeling. If you could only see   120
   The nature of your own feelings…

OEDIPUS.   Why,
   Who would not feel as I do? Who could endure
   Your arrogance toward the city?

TEIRESIAS.   What does it matter?
   Whether I speak or not, it is bound to come.

OEDIPUS. Then, if "it" is bound to come, you are bound to tell me.   125

TEIRESIAS. No, I will not go on. Rage as you please.

OEDIPUS. Rage? Why not!
                And I'll tell you what I think:
   You planned it, you had it done, you all but
   Killed him with your own hands: if you had eyes,
   I'd say the crime was yours, and yours alone.   130

TEIRESIAS. So? I charge you, then,
   Abide by the proclamation you have made:
   From this day forth
   Never speak again to these men or to me;
   You yourself are the pollution of this country.   135

OEDIPUS. You dare say that! Can you possibly think you have
   Some way of going free, after such insolence?

TEIRESIAS. I have gone free. It is the truth sustains me.

OEDIPUS. Who taught you shamelessness? It was not your craft.

TEIRESIAS. You did. You made me speak. I did not want to.   140

OEDIPUS. Speak what? Let me hear it again more clearly.

TEIRESIAS. Was it not clear before? Are you tempting me?

OEDIPUS. I did not understand it. Say it again.

TEIRESIAS. I say that you are the murderer whom you seek.

OEDIPUS. Now twice you have spat out infamy. You'll pay for it!   145

TEIRESIAS.   Would you care for more? Do you wish to be really angry?
OEDIPUS.   Say what you will. Whatever you say is worthless.
TEIRESIAS.   I say you live in hideous shame with those
   Most dear to you. You can not see the evil.
OEDIPUS.   Can you go on babbling like this for ever?   150
TEIRESIAS.   I can, if there is power in truth.
OEDIPUS.   There is:
   But not for you, not for you,
   You sightless, witless, senseless, mad old man!
TEIRESIAS.   You are the madman. There is no one here
   Who will not curse you soon, as you curse me.   155
OEDIPUS.   You child of total night! I would not touch you;
   Neither would any man who sees the sun.
TEIRESIAS.   True: it is not from you my fate will come.
   That lies within Apollo's competence,
   As it is his concern.
OEDIPUS.   Tell me, who made   160
   These fine discoveries? Kreon? or someone else?
TEIRESIAS.   Kreon is no threat. You weave your own doom.
OEDIPUS.   Wealth, power, craft of statemanship!
   Kingly position, everywhere admired!
   What savage envy is stored up against these,   165
   If Kreon, whom I trusted, Kreon my friend,
   For this great office which the city once
   Put in my hands unsought—if for this power
   Kreon desires in secret to destroy me!

   He has bought this decrepit fortune-teller, this   170
   Collector of dirty pennies, this prophet fraud—
   Why, he is no more clairvoyant than I am!
                                      Tell us:
   Has your mystic mummery ever approached the truth?
   When that hellcat the Sphinx was performing here,
   What help were you to these people?   175
   Her magic was not for the first man who came along:
   It demanded a real exorcist. Your birds—
   What good were they? or the gods, for the matter of that?
   But I came by,
   Oedipus, the simple man, who knows nothing—   180
   I thought it out for myself, no birds helped me!
   And this is the man you think you can destroy,
   That you may be close to Kreon when he's king!
   Well, you and your friend Kreon, it seems to me,
   Will suffer most. If you were not an old man,   185
   You would have paid already for your plot.

CHORAGOS.   We can not see that his words or yours
   Have been spoken except in anger, Oedipus,
   And of anger we have no need. How to accomplish
   The god's will best: that is what most concerns us.   190
TEIRESIAS.   You are a king. But where argument's concerned
   I am your man, as much a king as you.
   I am not your servant, but Apollo's.
   I have no need of Kreon or Kreon's name.

   Listen to me. You mock my blindness, do you?   195
   But I say that you, with both your eyes, are blind:
   You can not see the wretchedness of your life,
   Nor in whose house you live, no, nor with whom.
   Who are your father and mother? Can you tell me?
   You do not even know the blind wrongs   200
   That you have done them, on earth and in the world below.
   But the double lash of your parents' curse will whip you
   Out of this land some day, with only night
   Upon your precious eyes.
   Your cries then—where will they not be heard?   205
   What fastness of Kithairon° will not echo them?
   And that bridal-descant of yours—you'll know it then,
   The song they sang when you came here to Thebes
   And found your misguided berthing.
   All this, and more, that you can not guess at now,   210
   Will bring you to yourself among your children.

   Be angry, then. Curse Kreon. Curse my words.
   I tell you, no man that walks upon the earth
   Shall be rooted out more horribly than you.
OEDIPUS.   Am I to bear this from him?—Damnation   215
   Take you! Out of this place! Out of my sight!
TEIRESIAS.   I would not have come at all if you had not asked me.
OEDIPUS.   Could I have told that you'd talk nonsense, that
   You'd come here to make a fool of yourself, and of me?
TEIRESIAS.   A fool? Your parents thought me sane enough.   220
OEDIPUS.   My parents again!—Wait: who were my parents?
TEIRESIAS.   This day will give you a father and break your heart.
OEDIPUS.   Your infantile riddles! Your damned abracadabra!
TEIRESIAS.   You were a great man once at solving riddles.
OEDIPUS.   Mock me with that if you like; you will find it true.   225
TEIRESIAS.   It was true enough. It brought about your ruin.
OEDIPUS.   But if it saved this town?

---

206 *Kithairon:* Mountain where the infant Oedipus was left for dead.

TEIRESIAS (*to the* PAGE).   Boy, give me your hand.
OEDIPUS.   Yes, boy; lead him away.
                    —While you are here
  We can do nothing. Go; leave us in peace.
TEIRESIAS.   I will go when I have said what I have to say.   230
  How can you hurt me? And I tell you again:
  The man you have been looking for all this time,
  The damned man, the murderer of Laios,
  That man is in Thebes. To your mind he is foreign-born,
  But it will soon be shown that he is a Theban,   235
  A revelation that will fail to please.
                  A blind man,
  Who has his eyes now; a penniless man, who is rich now;
  And he will go tapping the strange earth with his staff.
  To the children with whom he lives now he will be
  Brother and father—the very same; to her   240
  Who bore him, son and husband—the very same
  Who came to his father's bed, wet with his father's blood.
  Enough. Go think that over.
  If later you find error in what I have said,
  You may say that I have no skill in prophecy.   245

        (*Exit* TEIRESIAS, *led by his* PAGE. OEDIPUS *goes into the palace.*)

ODE 1

Strophe 1

CHORUS.   The Delphic stone of prophecies
  Remembers ancient regicide
  And a still bloody hand.
  That killer's hour of flight has come.
  He must be stronger than riderless   5
  Coursers of untiring wind,
  For the son of Zeus° armed with his father's thunder
  Leaps in lightning after him;
  And the Furies° hold his track, the sad Furies.

Antistrophe 1

Holy Parnassos° peak of snow   10
Flashes and blinds that secret man,
That all shall hunt him down:
Though he may roam the forest shade
Like a bull gone wild from pasture

---

7 *son of Zeus:* Apollo.   9 *Furies:* Female spirits who avenged evil deeds.   10 *Parnassos:* Holy mountain, dwelling place of Zeus, king of the gods.

To rage through grooms of stone. 15
Doom comes down on him; flight will not avail him;
For the world's heart calls him desolate,
And the immortal voices follow, for ever follow.

Strophe 2

But now a wilder thing is heard
From the old man skilled at hearing Fate in the wing-beat of a bird. 20
Bewildered as a blown bird, my soul hovers and can not find
Foothold in this debate, or any reason or rest of mind.
But no man ever brought—none can bring
Proof of strife between Thebes' royal house,
Labdakos' line, and the son of Polybos;° 25
And never until now has any man brought word
Of Laios' dark death staining Oedipus the King.

Antistrophe 2

Divine Zeus and Apollo hold
Perfect intelligence alone of all tales ever told;
And well though this diviner works, he works in his own night; 30
No man can judge that rough unknown or trust in second sight,
For wisdom changes hands among the wise.
Shall I believe my great lord criminal
At a raging word that a blind old man let fall?
I saw him, when the carrion woman° faced him of old, 35
Prove his heroic mind. These evil words are lies.

SCENE 2

KREON.   Men of Thebes:
   I am told that heavy accusations
   Have been brought against me by King Oedipus.

   I am not the kind of man to bear this tamely.

   If in these present difficulties 5
   He holds me accountable for any harm to him
   Through anything I have said or done—why, then,
   I do not value life in this dishonor.
   It is not as though this rumor touched upon
   Some private indiscretion. The matter is grave. 10
   The fact is that I am being called disloyal
   To the State, to my fellow citizens, to my friends.
CHORAGOS.   He may have spoken in anger, not from his mind.

25 *Polybos:* Oedipus' adoptive father, king of Corinth.   35 *woman:* The Sphinx.

KREON.   But did you not hear him say I was the one
  Who seduced the old prophet into lying?   15
CHORAGOS.   The thing was said; I do not know how seriously.
KREON.   But you were watching him! Were his eyes steady?
  Did he look like a man in his right mind?
CHORAGOS.   I do not know.
  I can not judge the behavior of great men.
  But here is the king himself.

(*Enter* OEDIPUS.)

OEDIPUS.   So you dared come back.   20
  Why? How brazen of you to come to my house,
  You murderer!
            Do you think I do not know
  That you plotted to kill me, plotted to steal my throne?
  Tell me, in God's name: am I coward, a fool,
  That you should dream you could accomplish this?   25
  A fool who could not see your slippery game?
  A coward, not to fight back when I saw it?
  You are the fool, Kreon, are you not? hoping
  Without support or friends to get a throne?
  Thrones may be won or bought: you could do neither.   30
KREON.   Now listen to me. You have talked; let me talk, too.
  You can not judge unless you know the facts.
OEDIPUS.   You speak well: there is one fact; but I find it hard
  To learn from the deadliest enemy I have.
KREON.   That above all I must dispute with you.   35
OEDIPUS.   That above all I will not hear you deny.
KREON.   If you think there is anything good in being stubborn
  Against all reason, then I say you are wrong.
OEDIPUS.   If you think a man can sin against his own kind
  And not be punished for it, I say you are mad.   40
KREON.   I agree. But tell me: what have I done to you?
OEDIPUS.   You advised me to send for that wizard, did you not?
KREON.   I did. I should do it again.
OEDIPUS.   Very well. Now tell me:
  How long has it been since Laios—
KREON.   What of Laios?
OEDIPUS.   Since he vanished in that onset by the road?   45
KREON.   It was long ago, a long time.
OEDIPUS.   And this prophet,
  Was he practicing here then?
KREON.   He was; and with honor, as now.
OEDIPUS.   Did he speak of me at that time?
KREON.   He never did,
  At least, not when I was present.

OEDIPUS.   But…the enquiry?
   I suppose you held one?
KREON.   We did, but we learned nothing.   50
OEDIPUS.   Why did the prophet not speak against me then?
KREON.   I do not know; and I am the kind of man
   Who holds his tongue when he has no facts to go on.
OEDIPUS.   There's one fact that you know, and you could tell it.
KREON.   What fact is that? If I know it, you shall have it.   55
OEDIPUS.   If he were not involved with you, he could not say
   That it was I who murdered Laios.
KREON.   If he says that, you are the one that knows it!—
   But now it is my turn to question you.
OEDIPUS.   Put your questions. I am no murderer.   60
KREON.   First, then: You married my sister?
OEDIPUS.   I married your sister.
KREON.   And you rule the kingdom equally with her?
OEDIPUS.   Everything that she wants she has from me.
KREON.   And I am the third, equal to both of you?
OEDIPUS.   That is why I call you a bad friend.   65
KREON.   No. Reason it out, as I have done.
   Think of this first: would any sane man prefer
   Power, with all a king's anxieties,
   To that same power and the grace of sleep?
   Certainly not I.   70
   I have never longed for the king's power—only his rights.
   Would any wise man differ from me in this?
   As matters stand, I have my way in everything
   With your consent, and no responsibilities.
   If I were king, I should be a slave to policy.   75
   How could I desire a scepter more
   Than what is now mine—untroubled influence?
   No, I have not gone mad; I need no honors,
   Except those with the perquisites I have now.
   I am welcome everywhere; every man salutes me,   80
   And those who want your favor seek my ear,
   Since I know how to manage what they ask.
   Should I exchange this ease for that anxiety?
   Besides, no sober mind is treasonable.
   I hate anarchy   85
   And never would deal with any man who likes it.
   Test what I have said. Go to the priestess
   At Delphi, ask if I quoted her correctly.
   And as for this other thing: if I am found
   Guilty of treason with Teiresias,   90
   Then sentence me to death. You have my word
   It is a sentence I should cast my vote for—

But not without evidence!

                  You do wrong

When you take good men for bad, bad men for good.

A true friend thrown aside—why, life itself   95

Is not more precious!

                      In time you will know this well:

For time, and time alone, will show the just man,

Though scoundrels are discovered in a day.

CHORAGOS.   This is well, said, and a prudent man would ponder it.

  Judgments too quickly formed are dangerous.   100

OEDIPUS.   But is he not quick in his duplicity?

  And shall I not be quick to parry him?

  Would you have me stand still, hold my peace, and let

  This man win everything, through my inaction?

KREON.   And you want—what is it, then? To banish me?   105

OEDIPUS.   No, not exile. It is your death I want,

  So that all the world may see what treason means.

KREON.   You will persist, then? You will not believe me?

OEDIPUS.   How can I believe you?

KREON.   Then you are a fool.

OEDIPUS.   To save myself?

KREON.   In justice, think of me.   110

OEDIPUS.   You are evil incarnate.

KREON.   But suppose that you are wrong?

OEDIPUS.   Still I must rule.

KREON.   But not if you rule badly.

OEDIPUS.   O city, city!

KREON.   It is my city, too!

CHORAGOS.   Now, my lords, be still. I see the queen,

  Iokaste, coming from her palace chambers;   115

  And it is time she came, for the sake of you both.

  This dreadful quarrel can be resolved through her.

(*Enter* IOKASTE.)

IOKASTE.   Poor foolish men, what wicked din is this?

  With Thebes sick to death, is it not shameful

  That you should rake some private quarrel up?   120

  (*To* OEDIPUS.) Come into the house.

                   —And you, Kreon, go now:

  Let us have no more of this tumult over nothing.

KREON.   Nothing? No, sister: what your husband plans for me

  Is one of two great evils: exile or death.

OEDIPUS.   He is right.

               Why, woman I have caught him squarely   125

  Plotting against my life.

KREON.   No! Let me die
   Accurst if ever I have wished you harm!
IOKASTE.   Ah, believe it, Oedipus!
   In the name of the gods, respect this oath of his
   For my sake, for the sake of these people here!   130

Strophe 1

CHORAGOS.   Open your mind to her, my lord. Be ruled by her, I beg you!
OEDIPUS.   What would you have me do?
CHORAGOS.   Respect Kreon's word. He has never spoken like a fool,
   And now he has sworn an oath.
OEDIPUS.   You know what you ask?
CHORAGOS.   I do.
OEDIPUS.   Speak on, then.
CHORAGOS.   A friend so sworn should not be baited so,   135
   In blind malice, and without proof.
OEDIPUS.   You are aware, I hope, that what you say
   Means death for me, or exile at the least.

Strophe 2

CHORAGOS.   No, I swear by Helios, first in heaven!
   May I die friendless and accurst,   140
   The worst of deaths, if ever I meant that!
   It is the withering fields
      That hurt my sick heart:
   Must we bear all these ills,
   And now your bad blood as well?   145
OEDIPUS.   Then let him go. And let me die, if I must,
   Or be driven by him in shame from the land of Thebes.
   It is your unhappiness, and not his talk,
   That touches me.
              As for him—
   Wherever he goes, hatred will follow him.   150
KREON.   Ugly in yielding, as you were ugly in rage!
   Natures like yours chiefly torment themselves.
OEDIPUS.   Can you not go? Can you not leave me?
KREON.   I can.
   You do not know me; but the city knows me,
   And in its eyes I am just, if not in yours.   (*Exit* KREON.) 155

Antistrophe 1

CHORAGOS.   Lady Iokaste, did you not ask the King to go to his chambers?
IOKASTE.   First tell me what has happened.
CHORAGOS.   There was suspicion without evidence; yet it rankled.
   As even false charges will.

IOKASTE.   On both sides?
CHORAGOS.   On both.
IOKASTE.   But what was said?   160
CHORAGOS.   Oh let it rest, let it be done with!
   Have we not suffered enough?
OEDIPUS.   You see to what your decency has brought you:
   You have made difficulties where my heart saw none.

Antistrophe 2

CHORAGOS.   Oedipus, it is not once only I have told you—   165
   You must know I should count myself unwise
   To the point of madness, should I now forsake you—
        You, under whose hand,
            In the storm of another time,
          Our dear land sailed out free.   170
     But now stand fast at the helm!
IOKASTE.   In God's name, Oedipus, inform your wife as well:
   Why are you so set in this hard anger?
OEDIPUS.   I will tell you, for none of these men deserves
   My confidence as you do. It is Kreon's work,   175
   His treachery, his plotting against me.
IOKASTE.   Go on, if you can make this clear to me.
OEDIPUS.   He charges me with the murder of Laios.
IOKASTE.   Has he some knowledge? Or does he speak from hearsay?
OEDIPUS.   He would not commit himself to such a charge,   180
   But he has brought in that damnable soothsayer
   To tell his story.
IOKASTE.   Set your mind at rest.
   If it is a question of soothsayers, I tell you
   That you will find no man whose craft gives knowledge
   Of the unknowable.
                     Here is my proof: 185
   An oracle was reported to Laios once
   (I will not say from Phoibos himself, but from
   His appointed ministers, at any rate)
   That his doom would be death at the hands of his own son—
   His son, born of his flesh and of mine!   190

   Now, you remember the story: Laios was killed
   By marauding strangers where three highways meet;
   But his child had not been three days in this world
   Before the king had pierced the baby's ankles
   And left him to die on a lonely mountainside.   195

   Thus, Apollo never caused that child
   To kill his father, and it was not Laios' fate

To die at the hands of his son, as he had feared.
This is what prophets and prophecies are worth!
Have no dread of them.
                     It is God himself 200
Who can show us what he wills, in his own way.

OEDIPUS. How strange a shadowy memory crossed my mind,
  Just now while you were speaking; it chilled my heart.

IOKASTE. What do you mean? What memory do you speak of?

OEDIPUS. If I understand you, Laios was killed 205
  At a place where three roads meet.

IOKASTE.   So it was said;
  We have no later story.

OEDIPUS.   Where did it happen?

IOKASTE. Phokis, it is called: at a place where the Theban Way
  Divides into the roads toward Delphi and Daulia.

OEDIPUS: When?

IOKASTE.   We had the news not long before you came 210
  And proved the right to your succession here.

OEDIPUS. Ah, what net has God been weaving for me?

IOKASTE. Oedipus! Why does this trouble you?

OEDIPUS.   Do not ask me yet.
  First, tell me how Laios looked, and tell me
  How old he was.

IOKASTE.   He was tall, his hair just touched 215
  With white; his form was not unlike your own.

OEDIPUS. I think that I myself may be accurst
  By my own ignorant edict.

IOKASTE.   You speak strangely.
  It makes me tremble to look at you, my king.

OEDIPUS. I am not sure that the blind man can not see. 220
  But I should know better if you were to tell me—

IOKASTE. Anything—though I dread to hear you ask it.

OEDIPUS. Was the king lightly escorted, or did he ride
  With a large company, as a ruler should?

IOKASTE. There were five men with him in all: one was a herald; 225
  And a single chariot, which he was driving.

OEDIPUS. Alas, that makes it plain enough!
                     But who—
  Who told you how it happened?

IOKASTE.   A household servant,
  The only one to escape.

OEDIPUS.   And is he still
  A servant of ours?

IOKASTE.   No; for when he came back at last 230
  And found you enthroned in the place of the dead king,
  He came to me, touched my hand with his, and begged

That I would send him away to the frontier district
Where only the shepherds go—
As far away from the city as I could send him.   235
I granted his prayer; for although the man was a slave,
He had earned more than this favor at my hands.
OEDIPUS.   Can he be called back quickly?
IOKASTE.   Easily.
   But why?
OEDIPUS.   I have taken too much upon myself
   Without enquiry; therefore I wish to consult him.   240
IOKASTE.   Then he shall come.
                                          But am I not one also
   To whom you might confide these fears of yours?
OEDIPUS.   That is your right; it will not be denied you,
   Now least of all; for I have reached a pitch
   Of wild foreboding. Is there anyone
   To whom I should sooner speak?   245

   Polybos of Corinth is my father.
   My mother is a Dorian: Merope.
   I grew up chief among the men of Corinth
   Until a strange thing happened—   250
   Not worth my passion, it may be, but strange.
   At a feast, a drunken man maundering in his cups
   Cries out that I am not my father's son!
   I contained myself that night, though I felt anger
   And a sinking heart. The next day I visited   255
   My father and mother, and questioned them. They stormed,
   Calling it all the slanderous rant of a fool;
   And this relieved me. Yet the suspicion
   Remained always aching in my mind;
   I knew there was talk; I could not rest;   260
   And finally, saying nothing to my parents,
   I went to the shrine at Delphi.

   The god dismissed my question without reply;
   He spoke of other things.
                                 Some were clear,
   Full of wretchedness, dreadful, unbearable: 265
   As, that I should lie with my own mother, breed
   Children from whom all men would turn their eyes;
   And that I should be my father's murderer.

   I heard all this, and fled. And from that day
   Corinth to me was only in the stars   270

Descending in that quarter of the sky,
As I wandered farther and farther on my way
To a land where I should never see the evil
Sung by the oracle. And I came to this country
Where, so you say, King Laios was killed.   275

I will tell you all that happened there, my lady.
There were three highways
Coming together at a place I passed;
And there a herald came towards me, and a chariot
Drawn by horses, with a man such as you describe   280
Seated in it. The groom leading the horses
Forced me off the road at his lord's command;
But as this charioteer lurched over towards me
I struck him in my rage. The old man saw me
And brought his double goad down upon my head   285
As I came abreast.
                        He was paid back, and more!
Swinging my club in this right hand I knocked him
Out of his car, and he rolled on the ground.
                                                        I killed him.

I killed them all.
Now if that stranger and Laios were—kin,   290
Where is a man more miserable than I?
More hated by the gods? Citizen and alien alike
Must never shelter me or speak to me—
I must be shunned by all.
                                And I myself
Pronounced this malediction upon myself!   295

Think of it: I have touched you with these hands,
These hands that killed your husband. What defilement!

Am I all evil, then? It must be so,
Since I must flee from Thebes, yet never again
See my own countrymen, my own country,   300
For fear of joining my mother in marriage
And killing Polybos, my father.
                                        Ah,
If I was created so, born to this fate,
Who could deny the savagery of God?

O holy majesty of heavenly powers!   305
May I never see that day! Never!

Rather let me vanish from the race of men
Than know the abomination destined me!
CHORAGOS.   We too, my lord, have felt dismay at this.
　But there is hope: you have yet to hear the shepherd.   310
OEDIPUS.   Indeed, I fear no other hope is left me.
IOKASTE.   What do you hope from him when he comes?
OEDIPUS.   This much:
　If his account of the murder tallies with yours,
　Then I am cleared.
IOKASTE.   What was it that I said
　Of such importance?
OEDIPUS.   Why, "marauders," you said,   315
　Killed the king, according to this man's story.
　If he maintains that still, if there were several,
　Clearly the guilt is not mine: I was alone.
　But if he says one man, singlehanded, did it,
　Then the evidence all points to me.   320
IOKASTE.   You may be sure that he said there were several;
　And can he call back that story now? He can not.
　The whole city heard it as plainly as I.
　But suppose he alters some detail of it:
　He can not ever show that Laios' death   325
　Fulfilled the oracle: for Apollo said
　My child was doomed to kill him; and my child—
　Poor baby!—it was my child that died first.

　No. From now on, where oracles are concerned,
　I would not waste a second thought on any.   330
OEDIPUS.   You may be right.
　　　　　　　　　　　　　　　But come: let someone go
　For the shepherd at once. This matter must be settled.
IOKASTE: I will send for him.
　I would not wish to cross you in anything,
　And surely not in this.—Let us go in.   (*Exeunt into the palace.*) 335

ODE 2

Strophe 1

CHORUS.   Let me be reverent in the ways of right,
　Lowly the paths I journey on;
　Let all my words and actions keep
　The laws of the pure universe
　From highest Heaven handed down.   5
　For Heaven is their bright nurse,
　Those generations of the realms of light;

Ah, never of mortal kind were they begot,
Nor are they slaves of memory, lost in sleep:
Their Father is greater than Time, and ages not.   10

Antistrophe 1

The tyrant is a child of Pride
Who drinks from his great sickening cup
Recklessness and vanity,
Until from his high crest headlong
He plummets to the dust of hope.   15
That strong man is not strong.
But let no fair ambition be denied;
May God protect the wrestler for the State
In government, in comely policy,
Who will fear God, and on his ordinance wait.   20

Strophe 2

Haughtiness and the high hand of disdain
Tempt and outrage God's holy law;
And any mortal who dares hold
No immortal Power in awe
Will be caught up in a net of pain: 25
The price for which his levity is sold.
Let each man take due earnings, then,
And keep his hands from holy things,
And from blasphemy stand apart—
Else the crackling blast of heaven   30
Blows on his head, and on his desperate heart.
Though fools will honor impious men,
In their cities no tragic poet sings.

Antistrophe 2

Shall we lose faith in Delphi's obscurities,
We who have heard the world's core   35
Discredited, and the sacred wood
Of Zeus at Elis praised no more?
The deeds and the strange prophecies
Must make a pattern yet to be understood.
Zeus, if indeed you are lord of all,   40
Throned in light over night and day,
Mirror this in your endless mind:
Our masters call the oracle
Words on the wind, and the Delphic vision blind!
Their hearts no longer know Apollo,   45
And reverence for the gods has died away.

SCENE 3.

(*Enter* IOKASTE.)

IOKASTE.   Princes of Thebes, it has occurred to me
  To visit the altars of the gods, bearing
  These branches as a suppliant, and this incense.
  Our king is not himself: his noble soul
  Is overwrought with fantasies of dread,   5
  Else he would consider
  The new prophecies in the light of the old.
  He will listen to any voice that speaks disaster,
  And my advice goes for nothing. (*She approaches the altar, right.*)
                    To you, then, Apollo,
  Lycean lord, since you are nearest, I turn in prayer   10
  Receive these offerings, and grant us deliverance
  From defilement. Our hearts are heavy with fear
  When we see our leader distracted, as helpless sailors
  Are terrified by the confusion of their helmsman.

(*Enter* MESSENGER.)

MESSENGER.   Friends, no doubt you can direct me: 15
  Where shall I find the house of Oedipus,
  Or, better still, where is the king himself?
CHORAGOS.   It is this very place, stranger; he is inside.
  This is his wife and mother of his children.
MESSENGER.   I wish her happiness in a happy house,   20
  Blest in all the fulfillment of her marriage.
IOKASTE.   I wish as much for you: your courtesy
  Deserves a like good fortune. But now, tell me:
  Why have you come? What have you to say to us?
MESSENGER.   Good news, my lady, for your house and your husband.   25
IOKASTE.   What news? Who sent you here?
MESSENGER.   I am from Corinth.
  The news I bring ought to mean joy for you,
  Though it may be you will find some grief in it.
IOKASTE.   What is it? How can it touch us in both ways?
MESSENGER.   The word is that the people of the Isthmus   30
  Intend to call Oedipus to be their king.
IOKASTE.   But old King Polybos—is he not reigning still?
MESSENGER.   No. Death holds him in his sepulchre.
IOKASTE.   What are you saying? Polybos is dead?
MESSENGER.   If I am not telling the truth, may I die myself.   35
IOKASTE (*to a* MAIDSERVANT).   Go in, go quickly; tell this to your master.
  O riddlers of God's will, where are you now!
  This was the man whom Oedipus, long ago,

Feared so, fled so, in dread of destroying him—
But it was another fate by which he died.   40

(*Enter* OEDIPUS *center*)

OEDIPUS.   Dearest Iokaste, why have you sent for me?
IOKASTE.   Listen to what this man says, and then tell me
   What has become of the solemn prophecies.
OEDIPUS.   Who is this man? What is his news for me?
IOKASTE.   He has come from Corinth to announce your father's death!   45
OEDIPUS.   Is it true, stranger? Tell me in your own words.
MESSENGER.   I can not say it more clearly: the king is dead.
OEDIPUS.   Was it by treason? Or by an attack of illness?
MESSENGER.   A little thing brings old men to their rest.
OEDIPUS.   It was sickness, then?
MESSENGER.   Yes, and his many years.   50
OEDIPUS.   Ah!
   Why should a man respect the Pythian hearth,° or
   Give heed to the birds that jangle above his head?
   They prophesied that I should kill Polybos,
   Kill my own father; but he is dead and buried,   55
   And I am here—I never touched him, never,
   Unless he died of grief for my departure,
   And thus, in a sense, through me. No. Polybos
   Has packed the oracles off with him underground.
   They are empty words.
IOKASTE.   Had I not told you so?   60
OEDIPUS.   You had; it was my faint heart that betrayed me.
IOKASTE.   From now on never think of those things again.
OEDIPUS.   And yet—must I not fear my mother's bed?
IOKASTE.   Why should anyone in this world be afraid,
   Since Fate rules us and nothing can be foreseen?   65
   A man should live only for the present day.

   Have no more fear of sleeping with your mother:
   How many men, in dreams, have lain with their mothers!
   No reasonable man is troubled by such things.
OEDIPUS.   That is true; only—   70
   If only my mother were not still alive!
   But she is alive. I can not help my dread.
IOKASTE.   Yet this news of your father's death is wonderful.
OEDIPUS.   Wonderful. But I fear the living woman.
MESSENGER.   Tell me, who is this woman that you fear?   75

---

52 *Pythian hearth:* Delphi; the alternative name came from the dragon Python, which once guarded
Delphi until Apollo vanquished it.

OEDIPUS. It is Merope, man; the wife of King Polybos.

MESSENGER. Merope? Why should you be afraid of her?

OEDIPUS. An oracle of the gods, a dreadful saying.

MESSENGER. Can you tell me about it or are you sworn to silence?

OEDIPUS. I can tell you, and I will.   80
    Apollo said through his prophet that I was the man
    Who should marry his own mother, shed his father's blood
    With his own hands. And so, for all these years
    I have kept clear of Corinth, and no harm has come—
    Though it would have been sweet to see my parents again.   85

MESSENGER. And is this the fear that drove you out of Corinth?

OEDIPUS. Would you have me kill my father?

MESSENGER.   As for that
    You must be reassured by the news I gave you.

OEDIPUS. If you could reassure me, I would reward you.

MESSENGER. I had that in mind, I will confess: I thought   90
    I could count on you when you returned to Corinth.

OEDIPUS. No: I will never go near my parents again.

MESSENGER. Ah, son, you still do not know what you are doing—

OEDIPUS. What do you mean? In the name of God tell me!

MESSENGER. —If these are your reasons for not going home.   95

OEDIPUS. I tell you, I fear the oracle may come true.

MESSENGER. And guilt may come upon you through your parents?

OEDIPUS. That is the dread that is always in my heart.

MESSENGER. Can you not see that all your fears are groundless?

OEDIPUS. Groundless? Am I not my parents' son?   100

MESSENGER. Polybos was not your father.

OEDIPUS.   Not my father?

MESSENGER. No more your father than the man speaking to you.

OEDIPUS. But you are nothing to me!

MESSENGER.   Neither was he.

OEDIPUS. Then why did he call me son?

MESSENGER.   I will tell you:
    Long ago he had you from my hands, as a gift.   105

OEDIPUS. Then how could he love me so, if I was not his?

MESSENGER. He had no children, and his heart turned to you.

OEDIPUS. What of you? Did you buy me? Did you find me by chance?

MESSENGER. I came upon you in the woody vales of Kithairon.

OEDIPUS. And what were you doing there?

MESSENGER.   Tending my flocks.   110

OEDIPUS. A wandering shepherd?

MESSENGER.   But your savior, son, that day.

OEDIPUS. From what did you save me?

MESSENGER.   Your ankles should tell you that.

OEDIPUS. Ah, stranger, why do you speak of that childhood pain?

MESSENGER. I pulled the skewer that pinned your feet together.

OEDIPUS. I have had the mark as long as I can remember.   115

MESSENGER. That was why you were given the name you bear.°

OEDIPUS. God! Was it my father or my mother who did it?
Tell me!

MESSENGER.   I do not know. The man who gave you to me
Can tell you better than I.

OEDIPUS. It was not you that found me, but another?   120

MESSENGER. It was another shepherd gave you to me.

OEDIPUS. Who was he? Can you tell me who he was?

MESSENGER. I think he was said to be one of Laios' people.

OEDIPUS. You mean the Laios who was king here years ago?

MESSENGER. Yes; King Laios; and the man was one of his herdsmen.   125

OEDIPUS. Is he still alive? Can I see him?

MESSENGER.   These men here
Know best about such things.

OEDIPUS.   Does anyone here
Know this shepherd that he is talking about?
Have you seen him in the fields, or in the town?
If you have, tell me. It is time things were made plain.   130

CHORAGOS. I think the man he means is that same shepherd
You have already asked to see. Iokaste perhaps
Could tell you something.

OEDIPUS.   Do you know anything
About him, Lady? Is he the man we have summoned?
Is that the man this shepherd means?

IOKASTE.   Why think of him?   135
Forget this herdsman. Forget it all.
This talk is a waste of time.

OEDIPUS.   How can you say that,
When the clues to my true birth are in my hands?

IOKASTE. For God's love, let us have no more questioning!
Is your life nothing to you?   140
My own is pain enough for me to bear.

OEDIPUS. You need not worry. Suppose my mother a slave,
And born of slaves: no baseness can touch you.

IOKASTE. Listen to me, I beg you: do not do this thing!

OEDIPUS: I will not listen; the truth must be made known.   145

IOKASTE. Everything that I say is for your own good!

OEDIPUS.   My own good
Snaps my patience, then; I want none of it.

IOKASTE. You are fatally wrong! May you never learn who you are!

---

116 *the name you bear:* "Oedipus" translates as "the one with a swollen foot."

OEDIPUS.   Go, one of you, and bring the shepherd here.
  Let us leave this woman to brag of her royal name.   150
IOKASTE.   Ah, miserable!
  That is the only word I have for you now.
  That is the only word I can ever have.   (*Exit into the palace.*)
CHORAGOS.   Why has she left us, Oedipus? Why has she gone
  In such a passion of sorrow? I fear this silence: 155
  Something dreadful may come of it.
OEDIPUS.   Let it come!
  However base my birth, I must know about it.
  The Queen, like a woman, is perhaps ashamed
  To think of my low origin. But I
  Am a child of Luck; I can not be dishonored.   160
  Luck is my mother; the passing months, my brothers,
  Have seen me rich and poor.
                    If this is so,
  How could I wish that I were someone else?
  How could I not be glad to know my birth?

ODE 3

Strophe

CHORUS.   If ever the coming time were known
  To my heart's pondering,
  Kithairon, now by Heaven I see the torches
  At the festival of the next full moon,
  And see the dance, and hear the choir sing   5
  A grace to your gentle shade:
  Mountain where Oedipus was found,
  O mountain guard of a noble race!
  May the god° who heals us lend his aid,
  And let that glory come to pass   10
  For our king's cradling-ground.

Antistrophe

Of the nymphs that flower beyond the years,
  Who bore you,° royal child,
  To Pan° of the hills or the timberline Apollo,
  Cold in delight where the upland clears,   15
  Or Hermes° for whom Kyllene's° heights are piled?
  Or flushed as evening cloud,

9 *god:* Apollo.   13 *Who bore you:* The Chorus wonders whether Oedipus might be the son of a nymph and a god: Pan, Apollo, Hermes, or Dionysus.   14 *Pan:* God of nature; from the waist up, he is human, from the waist down, a goat.   16 *Hermes:* Zeus's son, messenger of the gods; *Kyllene;* Sacred mountain, the birthplace of Hermes.

Great Dionysos,° roamer of mountains,
He—was it he who found you there,
And caught you up in his own proud   20
Arms from the sweet god-ravisher
Who laughed by the Muses'° fountains?

SCENE 4

OEDIPUS.   Sirs: though I do not know the man,
I think I see him coming, this shepherd we want:
He is old, like our friend here, and the men
Bringing him seem to be servants of my house.
But you can tell, if you have ever seen him.   5

(*Enter* SHEPHERD *escorted by* SERVANTS.)

CHORAGOS.   I know him, he was Laios' man. You can trust him.
OEDIPUS.   Tell me first, you from Corinth: is this the shepherd
We were discussing?
MESSENGER.   This is the very man.
OEDIPUS (*to* SHEPHERD).   Come here. No, look at me. You must answer
Everything I ask.—You belonged to Laios?   10
SHEPHERD.   Yes: born his slave, brought up in his house.
OEDIPUS.   Tell me: what kind of work did you do for him?
SHEPHERD.   I was a shepherd of his, most of my life.
OEDIPUS.   Where mainly did you go for pasturage?
SHEPHERD.   Sometimes Kithairon, sometimes the hills near-by.   15
OEDIPUS.   Do you remember ever seeing this man out there?
SHEPHERD.   What would he be doing there? This man?
OEDIPUS.   This man standing here. Have you ever seen him before?
SHEPHERD.   No. At least, not to my recollection.
MESSENGER.   And that is not strange, my lord. But I'll refresh   20
His memory. he must remember when we two
Spent three whole seasons together, March to September,
On Kithairon or thereabouts. He had two flocks;
I had one. Each autumn I'd drive mine home
And he would go back with his to Laios' sheepfold.—   25
Is this not true, just as I have described it?
SHEPHERD.   True, yes; but it was all so long ago.
MESSENGER.   Well, then: do you remember back in those days,
That you gave me a baby boy to bring up as my own?
SHEPHERD.   What if I did? What are you trying to say?   30
MESSENGER.   King Oedipus was once that little child.
SHEPHERD.   Damn you, hold your tongue!

---

18 *Dionysos:* (Dionysus) God of wine, sometimes called Bacchos.   22 *Muses:* Nine goddesses, sisters,
who are the patronesses of poetry, music, art, and the sciences.

OEDIPUS.   No more of that!
   It is your tongue needs watching, not this man's.
SHEPHERD.   My king, my master, what is it I have done wrong?
OEDIPUS.   You have not answered his question about the boy.   35
SHEPHERD.   He does not know...He is only making trouble...
OEDIPUS.   Come, speak plainly, or it will go hard with you.
SHEPHERD.   In God's name, do not torture an old man!
OEDIPUS.   Come here, one of you; bind his arms behind him.
SHEPHERD.   Unhappy king! What more do you wish to learn?   40
OEDIPUS.   Did you give this man the child he speaks of?
SHEPHERD.   I did.
   And I would to God I had died that very day.
OEDIPUS.   You will die now unless you speak the truth.
SHEPHERD.   Yet if I speak the truth, I am worse than dead.
OEDIPUS (*to* ATTENDANT).   He intends to draw it out, apparently—   45
SHEPHERD.   No! I have told you already that I gave him the boy.
OEDIPUS.   Where did you get him? From your house? From somewhere else?
SHEPHERD.   Not from mine, no. A man gave him to me.
OEDIPUS.   Is that man here? Whose house did he belong to?
SHEPHERD.   For God's love, my king, do not ask me any more!   50
OEDIPUS.   You are a dead man if I have to ask you again.
SHEPHERD.   Then...Then the child was from the palace of Laios.
OEDIPUS.   A slave child? or a child of his own line?
SHEPHERD.   Ali, I am on the brink of dreadful speech!
OEDIPUS.   And I of dreadful hearing. Yet I must hear.   55
SHEPHERD.   If you must be told, then...
                                    They said it was Laios' child;
   But it is your wife who can tell you about that.
OEDIPUS.   My wife—Did she give it to you?
SHEPHERD.   My lord she did.
OEDIPUS.   Do you know why?
SHEPHERD.   I was told to get rid of it.
OEDIPUS.   Oh heartless mother!
SHEPHERD.   But in dread of prophecies...   60
OEDIPUS.   Tell me.
SHEPHERD.   It was said that the boy would kill his own father.
OEDIPUS.   Then why did you give him over to this old man?
SHEPHERD.   I pitied the baby, my king,
   And I thought that this man would take him far away
   To his own country.
                        He saved him—but for what a fate!   65
   For if you are what this man says you are,
   No man living is more wretched than Oedipus.
OEDIPUS.   Ah God!
   It was true!

All the prophecies!
—Now,
O Light, may I look on you for the last time!   70
I, Oedipus,
Oedipus, damned in his birth, in his marriage damned,
Damned in the blood he shed with his own hand!

(*He rushes into the palace.*)

ODE 4

Strophe 1

CHORUS.   Alas for the seed of men.
What measure shall I give these generations
That breathe on the void and are void
And exist and do not exist?
Who bears more weight of joy   5
Than mass of sunlight shifting in images,
Or who shall make his thought stay on
That down time drifts away?
Your splendor is all fallen.
O naked brow of wrath and tears,   10
O change of Oedipus!
I who saw your days call no man blest—
Your great days like ghosts gone.

Antistrophe 1

That mind was a strong bow.
Deep, how deep you drew it then, hard archer,   15
At a dim fearful range,
And brought dear glory down!
You overcame the stranger°—
The virgin with her hooking lion claws—
And though death sang, stood like a tower   20
To make pale Thebes take heart.
Fortress against our sorrow!
True king, giver of laws,
Majestic Oedipus!
No prince in Thebes had ever such renown,   25
No prince won such grace of power.

Strophe 2

And now of all men ever known
Most pitiful is this man's story:

18 *stranger:* The Sphinx.

His fortunes are most changed; his state
Fallen to a low slave's
Ground under bitter fate.
O Oedipus, most royal one!
The great door° that expelled you to the light
Gave at night—ah, gave night to your glory:
As to the father, to the fathering son.
All understood too late.
How could that queen whom Laios won,
The garden that he harrowed at his height,
Be silent when that act was done?

30

35

Antistrophe 2

But all eyes fail before time's eye,
All actions come to justice there.
Though never willed, though far down the deep past,
Your bed, your dread sirings,
Are brought to book at last.
Child by Laios doomed to die,
Then doomed to lose that fortunate little death,
Would God you never took breath in this air
That with my wailing lips I take to cry:
For I weep the world's outcast.
I was blind, and now I can tell why:
Asleep, for you had given ease of breath
To Thebes, while the false years went by.

40

45

50

EXODOS°

(*Enter, from the palace,* SECOND MESSENGER.)

SECOND MESSENGER.   Elders of Thebes, most honored in this land,
What horrors are yours to see and hear, what weight
Of sorrow to be endured, if, true to your birth,
You venerate the line of Labdakos!
I think neither Istros nor Phasis, those great rivers,
Could purify this place of all the evil
It shelters now, or soon must bring to light—
Evil not done unconsciously, but willed.
The greatest griefs are those we cause ourselves.

5

CHORAGOS.   Surely, friend, we have grief enough already;
What new sorrow do you mean?
SECOND MESSENGER.   The queen is dead.

10

---

33 *door:* Refers to the birth process.   *Exodos:* Final scene.

CHORAGOS.   O miserable queen! But at whose hand?
SECOND MESSENGER.   Her own.
    The full horror of what happened you can not know,
    For you did not see it; but I, who did, will tell you
    As clearly as I can how she met her death.   15

    When she had left us,
    In passionate silence, passing through the court,
    She ran to her apartment in the house,
    Her hair clutched by the fingers of both hands.
    She closed the doors behind her; then, by that bed   20
    Where long ago the fatal son was conceived—
    That son who should bring about his father's death—
    We heard her call upon Laios, dead so many years,
    And heard her wail for the double fruit of her marriage,
    A husband by her husband, children by her child.   25
    Exactly how she died I do not know:
    For Oedipus burst in moaning and would not let us
    Keep vigil to the end: it was by him
    As he stormed about the room that our eyes were caught.
    From one to another of us he went, begging a sword,   30
    Hunting the wife who was not his wife, the mother
    Whose womb had carried his own children and himself.
    I do not know: it was none of us aided him,
    But surely one of the gods was in control!
    For with a dreadful cry   35
    He hurled his weight, as though wrenched out of himself,
    At the twin doors: the bolts gave, and he rushed in.
    And there we saw her hanging, her body swaying
    From the cruel cord she had noosed about her neck.
    A great sob broke from him, heartbreaking to hear,   40
    As he loosed the rope and lowered her to the ground.

    I would blot out from my mind what happened next!
    For the king ripped from her gown the golden brooches
    That were her ornament, and raised them, and plunged them down
    Straight into his own eyeballs, crying, "No more,   45
    No more shall you look on the misery about me,
    The horrors of my own doing! Too long you have known
    The faces of those whom I should never have seen,
    Too long been blind to those for whom I was searching!
    From this hour, go in darkness!" And as he spoke,   50
    He struck at his eyes—not once, but many times;
    And the blood spattered his beard,
    Bursting from his ruined sockets like red hail.

So from the unhappiness of two this evil has sprung,
A curse on the man and woman alike. The old   55
Happiness of the house of Labdakos
Was happiness enough: where is it today?
It is all wailing and ruin, disgrace, death—all
The misery of mankind that has a name—
And it is wholly and for ever theirs.   60

CHORAGOS.   Is he in agony still? Is there no rest for him?

SECOND MESSENGER.   He is calling for someone to open the doors wide
   So that all the children of Kadmos may look upon
   His father's murderer, his mother's—no,
   I can not say it!
                    And then he will leave Thebes,   65
   Self-exiled, in order that the curse
   Which he himself pronounced may depart from the house.
   He is weak, and there is none to lead him,
   So terrible is his suffering.
                    But you will see:
   Look, the doors are opening; in a moment   70
   You will see a thing that would crush a heart of stone.

(*The central door is opened,* OEDIPUS, *blinded, is led in.*)

CHORAGOS.   Dreadful indeed for men to see.
   Never have my own eyes
   Looked on a sight so full of fear.

   Oedipus!   75
   What madness came upon you, what demon
   Leaped on your life with heavier
   Punishment than a mortal man can bear?
   No: I can not even
   Look at you, poor ruined one.   80
   And I would speak, question, ponder,
   If I were able. No.
   You make me shudder.

OEDIPUS.   God. God.
   Is there a sorrow greater?   85
   Where shall I find harbor in this world?
   My voice is hurled far on a dark wind.
   What has God done to me?—

CHORAGOS.   Too terrible to think of, or to see.

Strophe 1

OEDIPUS.   O cloud of night,   90
   Never to be turned away: night coming on,

I can not tell how: night like a shroud!
My fair winds brought me here.

                          O God. Again
The pain of the spikes where I had sight,
The flooding pain   95
Of memory, never to be gouged out.
CHORAGOS.   This is not strange.
   You suffer it all twice over, remorse in pain,
   Pain in remorse.

Antistrophe 1

OEDIPUS.   Ah dear friend   100
   Are you faithful even yet, you alone?
   Are you still standing near me, will you stay here,
   Patient, to care for the blind?

                          The blind man!
   Yet even blind I know who it is attends me,
   By the voice's tone—   105
   Though my new darkness hide the comforter.
CHORAGOS.   Oh fearful act!
   What god was it drove you to rake black
   Night across your eyes?

Strophe 2

OEDIPUS.   Apollo. Apollo. Dear   110
   Children, the god was Apollo.
   He brought my sick, sick fate upon me.
   But the blinding hand was my own!
   How could I bear to see
   When all my sight was horror everywhere?   115
CHORAGOS.   Everywhere; that is true.
OEDIPUS.   And now what is left?
   Images? Love? A greeting even,
   Sweet to the senses? Is there anything?
   Ah, no, friends: lead me away.   120
   Lead me away from Thebes.

                    Lead the great wreck
   And hell of Oedipus, whom the gods hate.
CHORAGOS.   Your misery, you are not blind to that.
   Would God you had never found it out!

Antistrophe 2

OEDIPUS.   Death take the man who unbound   125
   My feet on that hillside
   And delivered me from death to life! What life?

If only I had died,
 This weight of monstrous doom
 Could not have dragged me and my darlings down.   130
CHORAGOS.   I would have wished the same.
OEDIPUS.   Oh never to have come here
 With my father's blood upon me! Never
 To have been the man they call his mother's husband!
 Oh accurst! Oh child of evil,   135
 To have entered that wretched bed—
                                          the selfsame one!
 More primal than sin itself, this fell to me.
CHORAGOS.   I do not know what words to offer you.
 You were better dead than alive and blind.
OEDIPUS.   Do not counsel me any more. This punishment   140
 That I have laid upon myself is just.
 If I had eyes,
 I do not know how I could bear the sight
 Of my father, when I came to the house of Death,
 Or my mother: for I have sinned against them both   145
 So vilely that I could not make my peace
 By strangling my own life.
                          Or do you think my children,
 Born as they were born, would be sweet to my eyes?
 Ah never, never! Nor this town with its high walls,
 Nor the holy images of the gods.
                          For I,   150
 Thrice miserable!—Oedipus, noblest of all the line
 Of Kadmos, have condemned myself to enjoy
 These things no more, by my own malediction
 Expelling that man whom the gods declared
 To be a defilement in the house of Laios.   155
 After exposing the rankness of my own guilt,
 How could I look men frankly in the eyes?
 No, I swear it,
 If I could have stifled my hearing at its source,
 I would have done it and made all this body
 A tight cell of misery, blank to light and sound: 160
 So I should have been safe in my dark mind
 Beyond external evil.
                          Ah Kithairon!
 Why did you shelter me? When I was cast upon you,
 Why did I not die? Then I should never   165
 Have shown the world my execrable birth.

 Ah Polybos! Corinth, city that I believed
 The ancient seat of my ancestors: how fair

I seemed, your child! And all the while this evil
Was cancerous within me!
                   For I am sick   170
In my own being, sick in my origin.
O three roads, dark ravine, woodland and way
Where three roads met; you, drinking my father's blood,
My own blood, spilled by my own hand: can you remember
The unspeakable things I did there, and the things   175
I went on from there to do?
                   O marriage, marriage!
The act that engendered me, and again the act
Performed by the son in the same bed—
                         Ah, the net
Of incest, mingling fathers, brothers, sons,
With brides, wives, mothers: the last evil   180
That can be known by men: no tongue can say
How evil!
        No. For the love of God, conceal me
Somewhere far from Thebes; or kill me; or hurl me
Into the sea, away from men's eyes for ever.

Come, lead me. You need not fear to touch me.   185
Of all men, I alone can bear this guilt.

(*Enter* KREON.)

CHORAGOS.   Kreon is here now. As to what you ask,
    He may decide the course to take. He only
    Is left to protect the city in your place.
OEDIPUS.   Alas, how can I speak to him? What right have I   190
    To beg his courtesy whom I have deeply wronged?
KREON.   I have not come to mock you, Oedipus,
    Or to reproach you, either.
    (*To* ATTENDANTS.)   —You, standing there:
    If you have lost all respect for man's dignity,
    At least respect the flame of Lord Helios: 195
    Do not allow this pollution to show itself
    Openly here, an affront to the earth
    And Heaven's rain and the light of day. No, take him
    Into the house as quickly as you can.
    For it is proper   200
    That only the close kindred see his grief.
OEDIPUS.   I pray you in God's name, since your courtesy
    Ignores my dark expectation, visiting
    With mercy this man of all men most execrable:
    Give me what I ask—for your good, not for mine.   205
KREON.   And what is it that you turn to me begging for?

OEDIPUS.   Drive me out of this country as quickly as may be
  To a place where no human voice can ever greet me.
KREON.   I should have done that before now—only,
  God's will had not been wholly revealed to me.   210
OEDIPUS.   But his command is plain: the parricide
  Must be destroyed. I am that evil man.
KREON.   That is the sense of it, yes; but as things are,
  We had best discover clearly what is to be done.
OEDIPUS.   You would learn more about a man like me?   215
KREON.   You are ready now to listen to the god.
OEDIPUS.   I will listen. But it is to you
  That I must turn for help. I beg you, hear me.

The woman is there—
Give her whatever funeral you think proper:
She is your sister.   220
                —But let me go, Kreon!
Let me purge my father's Thebes of the pollution
Of my living here, and go out to the wild hills,
To Kithairon, that has won such fame with me,
The tomb my mother and father appointed for me,   225
And let me die there, as they willed I should.
And yet I know
Death will not ever come to me through sickness
Or in any natural way: I have been preserved
For some unthinkable fate. But let that be.   230

As for my sons, you need not care for them.
They are men, they will find some way to live.
But my poor daughters, who have shared my table,
Who never before have been parted from their father—
Take care of them, Kreon; do this for me.   235

And will you let me touch them with my hands
A last time, and let us weep together?
Be kind, my lord,
Great prince, be kind!
                Could I but touch them,
They would be mine again, as when I had my eyes.   240

(*Enter* ANTIGONE *and* ISMENE, *attended.*)

Ah, God!
Is it my dearest children I hear weeping?
Has Kreon pitied me and sent my daughters?

KREON.   Yes, Oedipus: I knew that they were dear to you
  In the old days, and know you must love them still.   245
OEDIPUS.   May God bless you for this—and be a friendlier
  Guardian to you than he has been to me!

Children, where are you?
Come quickly to my hands: they are your brother's—
Hands that have brought your father's once clear eyes   250
To this way of seeing—
                                    Ah dearest ones,
I had neither sight nor knowledge then, your father
By the woman who was the source of his own life!
And I weep for you—having no strength to see you—,
I weep for you when I think of the bitterness   255
That men will visit upon you all your lives.
What homes, what festivals can you attend
Without being forced to depart again in tears?
And when you come to marriageable age,
Where is the man, my daughters, who would dare   260
Risk the bane that lies on all my children?
Is there any evil wanting? Your father killed
His father; sowed the womb of her who bore him;
Engendered you at the fount of his own existence!
That is what they will say of you.

                                    Then, whom   265
Can you ever marry? There are no bridegrooms for you,
And your lives must wither away in sterile dreaming.

O Kreon, son of Menoikeus!
You are the only father my daughters have,
Since we, their parents, are both of us gone for ever.   270
They are your own blood: you will not let them
Fall into beggary and loneliness;
You will keep them from the miseries that are mine!
Take pity on them; see, they are only children,
Friendless except for you. Promise me this,   275
Great prince, and give me your hand in token of it.

          (KREON *clasps his right hand.*)

Children.
I could say much, if you could understand me,
But as it is, I have only this prayer for you:
Live where you can, be as happy as you can—   280
Happier, please God, than God has made your father.

KREON.   Enough. You have wept enough. Now go within.
OEDIPUS.   I must; but it is hard.
KREON.   Time eases all things.
OEDIPUS.   You know my mind, then?
KREON.   Say what you desire.
OEDIPUS.   Send me from Thebes!
KREON.   God grant that I may!   285
OEDIPUS.   But since God hates me...
KREON.   No, he will grant your wish.
OEDIPUS.   You promise?
KREON.   I can not speak beyond my knowledge.
OEDIPUS.   Then lead me in.
KREON.   Come now, and leave your children.
OEDIPUS.   No! Do not take them from me!
KREON.   Think no longer
    That you are in command here, but rather think   290
    How, when you were, you served your own destruction.

(*Exeunt into the house all but the* CHORUS;
the CHORAGOS *chants directly to the audience.*)

CHORAGOS.   Men of Thebes: look upon Oedipus.

    This is the king who solved the famous riddle
    And towered up, most powerful of men.
    No mortal eyes but looked on him with envy,   295
    Yet in the end ruin swept over him.

    Let every man in mankind's frailty
    Consider his last day; and let none
    Presume on his good fortune until he find
    Life, at his death, a memory without pain.   300

Journal Entry

What insights does Oedipus discover about himself as he explores his origins?

Textual Considerations

1. Cite specific examples of Sophocles' use of dramatic irony throughout the play, and discuss their thematic significance.
2. What are the functions of the chorus? How is their view of the gods similar to or different from that of Iokaste?
3. What is the thematic significance of the plague as the background of the drama?
4. Discuss the thematic relevance of the metaphor of blindness versus sight in relation to Oedipus and Teiresias.

5. What role does Iokaste play in *Oedipus the King*? What position does she assume in relation to the Oracle?
6. To what extent can we explain Oedipus's character in terms of *hubris,* or human pride? Do you emphathize with him? Why or why not?

Cultural Contexts

1. Is Oedipus a victim of fate or a victim of his own unconscious? Explain.
2. Sophocles' play culminates with the revelation that Oedipus has committed parricide and incest. Working with your group, attack or defend the thesis that Sophocles presents Oedipus' story as a movement toward morality, social order, and civilization.

William Shakespeare
c 1600

The Tragedy of Hamlet Prince of Denmark

DRAMATIS PERSONAE

CLAUDIUS, *King of Denmark*
HAMLET, *son to the late, and nephew to the present, King*
POLONIUS, *Lord Chamberlain*
HORATIO, *friend to* HAMLET
LAERTES, *son to* POLONIUS
VOLTEMAND
CORNELIUS
ROSENCRANTZ ⎱— *courtiers*
GUILDENSTERN
OSRIC
A GENTLEMAN
A PRIEST
MARCELLUS
BARNARDO ⎱— *officers*
FRANCISCO
REYNALDO, *servant to* POLONIUS
Players
Two clowns, *gravediggers*
FORTINBRAS, *Prince of Norway*
A Norwegian captain
English ambassadors

GERTRUDE, *Queen of Denmark, mother to* HAMLET
OPHELIA, *daughter to* POLONIUS
GHOST *of* HAMLET*'s father*
Lords, Ladies, Officers, Soldiers, Sailors, Messengers, Attendants

SCENE. Elsinore

ACT I

SCENE I. A guard platform of the castle.

Enter BARNARDO and FRANCISCO, two sentinels.

BARNARDO.	Who's there?
FRANCISCO.	Nay, answer me. Stand and unfold° yourself.
BARNARDO.	Long live the King!°
FRANCISCO.	Barnardo?
BARNARDO.	He.

5

FRANCISCO.	You come most carefully upon your hour.
BARNARDO.	'Tis now struck twelve. Get thee to bed, Francisco.
FRANCISCO.	For this relief much thanks. 'Tis bitter cold, And I am sick at heart.
BARNARDO.	Have you had quiet guard?
FRANCISCO.	Not a mouse stirring.

/10

BARNARDO.   Well, good night.
   If you do meet Horatio and Marcellus,
   The rivals° of my watch, bid them make haste.

Enter HORATIO and MARCELLUS.

FRANCISCO.   I think I hear them. Stand, ho! Who is there?
HORATIO.   Friends to this ground.
MARCELLUS.   And liegemen to the Dane.°

15

FRANCISCO.   Give you° good night.
MARCELLUS.   O, farewell, honest soldier.
   Who hath relieved you?
FRANCISCO.   Barnardo hath my place.
   Give you good night.   *Exit* FRANCISCO.
MARCELLUS.   Holla, Barnardo!
BARNARDO.   Say——
   What, is Horatio there?
HORATIO.   A piece of him.
BARNARDO.   Welcome, Horatio. Welcome, good Marcellus.

20

MARCELLUS.   What, has this thing appeared again tonight?
BARNARDO.   I have seen nothing.
MARCELLUS.   Horatio says 'tis but our fantasy,
   And will not let belief take hold of him

SCENE I. 2. *unfold:* disclose.   3. *Long live the King:* (perhaps a password, perhaps a greeting).
13. *rivals:* partners.   15. *liegemen to the Dane:* loyal subjects to the King of Denmark.
16. *Give you:* God give you.

Touching this dreaded sight twice seen of us; 25
Therefore I have entreated him along
With us to watch the minutes of this night,
That, if again this apparition come,
He may approve° our eyes and speak to it.

HORATIO. Tush, tush, 'twill not appear.

BARNARDO. Sit down awhile, 30
And let us once again assail your ears,
That are so fortified against our story,
What we have two nights seen.

HORATIO. Well, sit we down,
And let us hear Barnardo speak of this.

BARNARDO. Last night of all, 35
When yond same star that's westward from the pole°
Had made his course t' illume that part of heaven
Where now it burns, Marcellus and myself,
The bell then beating one——

Enter GHOST.

MARCELLUS. Peace, break thee off. Look where it comes again. 40

BARNARDO. In the same figure like the king that's dead.

MARCELLUS. Thou art a scholar; speak to it, Horatio.

BARNARDO. Looks it not like the king? Mark it, Horatio.

HORATIO. Most like: it harrows me with fear and wonder.

BARNARDO. It would be spoke to.

MARCELLUS. Speak to it, Horatio. 45

HORATIO. What art thou that usurp'st this time of night,
Together with that fair and warlike form
In which the majesty of buried Denmark°
Did sometimes march? By heaven I charge thee, speak.

MARCELLUS. It is offended.

BARNARDO. See, it stalks away. 50

HORATIO. Stay! Speak, speak, I charge thee, speak. *Exit* GHOST.

MARCELLUS. 'Tis gone and will not answer.

BARNARDO. How now, Horatio? You tremble and look pale.
Is not this something more than fantasy?
What think you on't? 55

HORATIO. Before my God, I might not this believe
Without the sensible and true avouch°
Of mine own eyes.

MARCELLUS. Is it not like the King?

29. *approve:* confirm.   36. *pole:* polestar.   48. *buried Denmark:* the buried King of Denmark.
57. *sensible and true avouch:* sensory and true proof.

HORATIO.   As thou art to thyself.
Such was the very armor he had on   60
When he the ambitious Norway° combated:
So frowned he once, when, in an angry parle,°
He smote the sledded Polacks° on the ice.
'Tis strange.

MARCELLUS.   Thus twice before, and jump° at this dead hour,   65
With martial stalk hath he gone by our watch.

HORATIO.   In what particular thought to work I know not;
But, in the gross and scope° of my opinion,
This bodes some strange eruption to our state.

MARCELLUS.   Good now, sit down, and tell me he that knows,   70
Why this same strict and most observant watch
So nightly toils the subject° of the land,
And why such daily cast of brazen cannon
And foreign mart° for implements of war,
Why such impress° of shipwrights, whose sore task   75
Does not divide the Sunday from the week,
What might be toward° that this sweaty haste
Doth make the night joint-laborer with the day?
Who is't that can inform me?

HORATIO.   That can I.
At least the whisper goes so: our last king,   80
Whose image even but now appeared to us,
Was, as you know, by Fortinbras of Norway,
Thereto pricked on by a most emulate pride,
Dared to the combat; in which our valiant Hamlet
(For so this side of our known world esteemed him)   85
Did slay this Fortinbras, who, by a sealed compact
Well ratified by law and heraldry,°
Did forfeit, with his life, all those his lands
Which he stood seized° of, to the conqueror;
Against the which a moiety competent°   90
Was gagèd° by our King, which had returned
To the inheritance of Fortinbras,
Had he been vanquisher, as, by the same comart°
And carriage of the article designed,°
His fell to Hamlet. Now, sir, young Fortinbras,   95
Of unimprovèd° mettle hot and full,

61. *Norway:* King of Norway.   62. *parle:* parley.   63. *sledded Polacks:* Poles in sledges.
65. *jump:* just.   68. *gross and scope:* general drift.   72. *toils the subject:* makes the subjects toil.
74. *mart:* trading.   75. *impress:* forced service.   77. *toward:* in preparation.   87. *law and heraldry:*
heraldic law (governing the combat).   89. *seized:* possessed.   90. *moiety competent:* equal portion.
91. *gagèd:* engaged, pledged.   93. *comart:* agreement.   94. *carriage of the article designed:* import of
the agreement drawn up.   96. *unimprovèd:* untried.

Hath in the skirts° of Norway here and there
Sharked up° a list of lawless resolutes,°
For food and diet, to some enterprise
That hath a stomach in't;° which is no other,   100
As it doth well appear unto our state,
But to recover of us by strong hand
And terms compulsatory, those foresaid lands
So by his father lost; and this, I take it,
Is the main motive of our preparations,   105
The source of this our watch, and the chief head°
Of this posthaste and romage° in the land.
BARNARDO.   I think it be no other but e'en so;
    Well may it sort° that this portentous figure
    Comes armèd through our watch so like the King   110
    That was and is the question of these wars.
HORATIO.   A mote it is to trouble the mind's eye:
    In the most high and palmy state of Rome,
    A little ere the mightiest Julius fell,
    The graves stood tenantless, and the sheeted dead   115
    Did squeak and gibber in the Roman streets;°
    As stars with trains of fire and dews of blood,
    Disasters° in the sun; and the moist star,°
    Upon whose influence Neptune's empire stands,
    Was sick almost to doomsday with eclipse.   120
    And even the like precurse° of feared events,
    As harbingers° preceding still° the fates
    And prologue to the omen° coming on,
    Have heaven and earth together demonstrated
    Unto our climatures° and countrymen.   125

Enter GHOST.

But soft, behold, lo where it comes again!
I'll cross it,° though it blast me.—Stay, illusion.   *It spreads his° arms.*
If thou hast any sound or use of voice,
Speak to me.
If there be any good thing to be done   130

---

97. *skirts:* borders.   98. *Sharked up:* collected indiscriminately (as a shark gulps its prey).
98. *resolutes:* desperadoes.   100. *hath a stomach in't:* i.e., requires courage.   106. *head:* fountain-
head, origin.   107. *romage:* bustle.   109. *sort:* befit.   116. *Did squeak...Roman streets:* (the break
in the sense which follows this line suggests that a line has dropped out).   118. *Disasters:* threatening
signs.   118. *moist star:* moon.   121. *precurse:* precursor, foreshadowing.   122. *harbingers:*
forerunners.   122. *still:* always.   123. *omen:* calamity.   125. *climatures:* regions.   127. *cross it:*
(1) cross its path, confront it (2) make the sign of the cross in front of it.   127. s.d. *his:* i.e., its,
the ghost's (though possibly what is meant is that Horatio spreads his own arms, making a cross of
himself).

That may to thee do ease and grace to me,
Speak to me.
If thou art privy to thy country's fate,
Which happily° foreknowing may avoid,
O, speak!   135
Or if thou hast uphoarded in thy life
Extorted° treasure in the womb of earth,
For which, they say, you spirits oft walk in death,   *The cock crows.*
Speak of it. Stay and speak. Stop it, Marcellus.
MARCELLUS.   Shall I strike at it with my partisan°?   140
HORATIO.   Do, if it will not stand.
BARNARDO.   'Tis here.
HORATIO.   'Tis here.
MARCELLUS.   'Tis gone.   *Exit* GHOST.
We do it wrong, being so majestical,
To offer it the show of violence,
For it is as the air, invulnerable,   145
And our vain blows malicious mockery.
BARNARDO.   It was about to speak when the cock crew.
HORATIO.   And then it started, like a guilty thing
Upon a fearful summons. I have heard,
The cock, that is the trumpet to the morn,
Doth with his lofty and shrill-sounding throat   150
Awake the god of day, and at his warning,
Whether in sea or fire, in earth or air,
Th' extravagant and erring° spirit hies
To his confine; and of the truth herein   155
This present object made probation.°
MARCELLUS.   It faded on the crowing of the cock.
Some say that ever 'gainst° that season comes
Wherein our Savior's birth is celebrated,
This bird of dawning singeth all night long,   160
And then, they say, no spirit dare stir abroad,
The nights are wholesome, then no planets strike,°
No fairy takes,° nor witch hath power to charm:
So hallowed and so gracious is that time.
HORATIO.   So have I heard and do in part believe it.   165
But look, the morn in russet mantle clad
Walks o'er the dew of yon high eastward hill.
Break we our watch up, and by my advice
Let us impart what we have seen tonight

---

134. *happily:* haply, perhaps.   137. *Extorted:* ill-won.   140. *partisan:* pike (a long-handled weapon).
154. *extravagant and erring:* out of bounds and wandering.   156. *probation:* proof.
158. *'gainst:* just before.   162. *strike:* exert an evil influence.   163. *takes:* bewitches.

Unto young Hamlet, for upon my life 170
This spirit, dumb to us, will speak to him.
Do you consent we shall acquaint him with it,
As needful in our loves, fitting our duty?
MARCELLUS.   Let's do't, I pray, and I this morning know
Where we shall find him most convenient.   *Exeunt.* 175

SCENE II.   *The castle.*

Flourish.° Enter CLAUDIUS, *King of Denmark,* GERTRUDE *the Queen,*
COUNCILORS, POLONIUS *and his son* LAERTES, HAMLET, *cum aliis°*
[*including* VOLTEMAND *and* CORNELIUS].

KING.   Though yet of Hamlet our dear brother's death
The memory be green, and that it us befitted
To bear our hearts in grief, and our whole kingdom
To be contracted in one brow of woe,
Yet so far hath discretion fought with nature 5
That we with wisest sorrow think on him
Together with remembrance of ourselves.
Therefore our sometime sister,° now our Queen,
Th' imperial jointress° to this warlike state,
Have we, as 'twere, with a defeated joy, 10
With an auspicious° and a dropping eye,
With mirth in funeral, and with dirge in marriage,
In equal scale weighing delight and dole,
Taken to wife. Nor have we herein barred
Your better wisdoms, which have freely gone 15
With this affair along. For all, our thanks.
Now follows that you know young Fortinbras,
Holding a weak supposal of our worth,
Or thinking by our late dear brother's death
Our state to be disjoint and out of frame,° 20
Colleaguèd with this dream of his advantage,°
He hath not failed to pester us with message,
Importing the surrender of those lands
Lost by his father, with all bands of law,
To our most valiant brother. So much for him. 25
Now for ourself and for this time of meeting.
Thus much the business is: we have here writ
To Norway, uncle of young Fortinbras—
Who, impotent and bedrid, scarcely hears

SCENE II. s.d. *Flourish:* fanfare of trumpets.   s.d. *cum aliis:* with others (Latin).   8. *our sometime sister:* my (the royal "we") former sister-in-law.   9. *jointress:* joint tenant, partner.   11. *auspicious:* joyful.   20. *frame:* order.   21. *advantage:* superiority.

Of this his nephew's purpose—to suppress   30
His further gait° herein, in that the levies,
The lists, and full proportions° are all made
Out of his subject;° and we here dispatch
You, good Cornelius, and you, Voltemand,
For bearers of this greeting to old Norway,   35
Giving to you no further personal power
To business with the King, more than the scope
Of these delated articles° allow.
Farewell, and let your haste commend your duty.
CORNELIUS, VOLTEMAND.   In that, and all things, will we show our duty.   40
KING.   We doubt it nothing. Heartily farewell.   *Exit* VOLTEMAND *and* CORNELIUS.
And now, Laertes, what's the news with you?
You told us of some suit. What is't, Laertes?
You cannot speak of reason to the Dane
And lose your voice.° What wouldst thou beg, Laertes,   45
That shall not be my offer, not thy asking?
The head is not more native° to the heart,
The hand more instrumental to the mouth,
Than is the throne of Denmark to thy father.
What wouldst thou have, Laertes?
LAERTES.   My dread lord,   50
Your leave and favor to return to France,
From whence, though willingly I came to Denmark
To show my duty in your coronation,
Yet now I must confess, that duty done,
My thoughts and wishes bend again toward France   55
And bow them to your gracious leave and pardon.
KING.   Have you your father's leave? What says Polonius?
POLONIUS.   He hath, my lord, wrung from me my slow leave
By laborsome petition, and at last
Upon his will I sealed my hard consent.°   60
I do beseech you give him leave to go.
KING.   Take thy fair hour, Laertes. Time be thine,
And thy best graces spend it at thy will.
But now, my cousin° Hamlet, and my son——
HAMLET.   [*Aside*]   A little more than kin, and less than kind!°   65
KING.   How is it that the clouds still hang on you?
HAMLET.   No so, my lord. I am too much in the sun.°

31. *gait:* proceeding.   32. *proportions:* supplies for war.   33. *Out of his subject:* i.e., out of old Norway's subjects and realm.   38. *delated articles:* detailed documents.   45. *lose your voice:* waste your breath.   47. *native:* related.   60. *Upon his...hard consent:* to his desire I gave my reluctant consent.   64. *cousin:* kinsman.   65. *kind:* (pun on the meanings "kindly" and "natural"; though doubly related—*more than kin*—Hamlet asserts that he neither resembles Claudius in nature nor feels kindly toward him).   67. *sun:* sunshine of royal favor (with a pun on "son").

QUEEN. Good Hamlet, cast thy nighted color off,
  And let thine eye look like a friend on Denmark.
  Do not forever with thy vailèd° lids   70
  Seek for thy noble father in the dust.
  Thou know'st 'tis common; all that lives must die,
  Passing through nature to eternity.
HAMLET. Ay, madam, it is common.°
QUEEN.   If it be,
  Why seems it so particular with thee?   75
HAMLET. Seems, madam? Nay, it is. I know not "seems."
  'Tis not alone my inky cloak, good mother,
  Nor customary suits of solemn black,
  Nor windy suspiration° of forced breath,
  No, nor the fruitful river in the eye,   80
  Nor the dejected havior of the visage,
  Together with all forms, moods, shapes of grief,
  That can denote me truly. These indeed seem,
  For they are actions that a man might play,
  But I have that within which passes show;   85
  These but the trappings and the suits of woe.
KING. 'Tis sweet and commendable in your nature, Hamlet,
  To give these mourning duties to your father,
  But you must know your father lost a father,
  That father lost, lost his, and the survivor bound   90
  In filial obligation for some term
  To do obsequious° sorrow. But to persever
  In obstinate condolement° is a course
  Of impious stubbornness. 'Tis unmanly grief.
  It shows a will most incorrect to heaven,   95
  A heart unfortified, a mind impatient,
  An understanding simple and unschooled.
  For what we know must be and is as common
  As any the most vulgar° thing to sense,
  Why should we in our peevish opposition   100
  Take it to heart? Fie, 'tis a fault to heaven,
  A fault against the dead, a fault to nature,
  To reason most absurd, whose common theme
  Is death of fathers, and who still hath cried,
  From the first corse° till he that died today,   105
  "This must be so." We pray you throw to earth
  This unprevailing° woe, and think of us

70. *vailèd:* lowered.   74. *common:* (1) universal, (2) vulgar.   79. *windy suspiration:* heavy sighing.
92. *obsequious:* suitable to obsequies (funerals).   93. *condolement:* mourning.   99. *vulgar:* common.
105. *corse:* corpse.   107. *unprevailing:* unavailing.

As of a father, for let the world take note
You are the most immediate to our throne,
And with no less nobility of love   110
Than that which dearest father bears his son
Do I impart toward you. For your intent
In going back to school in Wittenberg,
It is most retrograde° to our desire,
And we beseech you, bend you° to remain   115
Here in the cheer and comfort of our eye,
Our chiefest courtier, cousin, and our son.
QUEEN.   Let not thy mother lose her prayers, Hamlet.
    I pray thee stay with us, go not to Wittenberg.
HAMLET.   I shall in all my best obey you, madam.   120
KING.   Why, 'tis a loving and a fair reply.
    Be as ourself in Denmark. Madam, come.
    This gentle and unforced accord of Hamlet
    Sits smiling to my heart, in grace whereof
    No jocund health that Denmark drinks today,   125
    But the great cannon to the clouds shall tell,
    And the King's rouse° the heaven shall bruit° again,
    Respeaking earthly thunder. Come away.   *Flourish. Exeunt all but* HAMLET.
HAMLET.   O that this too too sullied° flesh would melt,
    Thaw, and resolve itself into a dew,   130
    Or that the Everlasting had not fixed
    His canon° 'gainst self-slaughter. O God, God,
    How weary, stale, flat, and unprofitable
    Seem to me all the uses of this world!
    Fie on't, ah, fie, 'tis an unweeded garden   135
    That grows to seed. Things rank and gross in nature
    Possess it merely.° That it should come to this:
    But two months dead, nay, not so much, not two,
    So excellent a king, that was to this
    Hyperion° to a satyr, so loving to my mother   140
    That he might not beteem° the winds of heaven
    Visit her face too roughly. Heaven and earth,
    Must I remember? Why, she would hang on him
    As if increase of appetite had grown
    by what it fed on; and yet within a month—   145
    Let me not think on't; frailty, thy name is woman—
    A little month, or ere those shoes were old

114. *retrograde:* contrary.   115. *bend you:* incline.   127. *rouse:* deep drink.   127. *bruit:*
announce noisily.   129. *sullied:* (Q2 has *sallied,* here modernized to *sullied,* which makes sense
and is therefore given; but the Folio reading, *solid,* which fits better with *melt,* is quite possibly
correct).   132. *canon:* law.   137. *merely:* entirely.   140. *Hyperion:* the sun god, a model of
beauty.   141. *beteem:* allow.

With which she followed my poor father's body
Like Niobe,° all tears, why she, even she—
O God, a beast that wants discourse of reason°   150
Would have mourned longer—married with my uncle,
My father's brother, but no more like my father
Than I to Hercules. Within a month,
Ere yet the salt of most unrighteous tears
Had left the flushing° in her gallèd eyes,   155
She married. O, most wicked speed, to post°
With such dexterity to incestuous° sheets!
It is not, nor it cannot come to good.
But break my heart, for I must hold my tongue.

Enter HORATIO, MARCELLUS, *and* BARNARDO.

HORATIO.   Hail to your lordship!
HAMLET.   I am glad to see you well.   160
   Horatio—or I do forget myself.
HORATIO.   The same, my lord, and your poor servant ever.
HAMLET.   Sir, my good friend, I'll change° that name with you.
   And what make you from Wittenberg, Horatio?
   Marcellus.   165
MARCELLUS.   My good lord!
HAMLET.   I am very glad to see you.   [*To* BARNARDO.]   Good even, sir.
   But what, in faith, make you from Wittenberg?
HORATIO.   A truant disposition, good my lord.
HAMLET.   I would not hear your enemy say so,   170
   Nor shall you do my ear that violence
   To make it truster° of your own report
   Against yourself. I know you are no truant.
   But what is your affair in Elsinore?
   We'll teach you to drink deep ere you depart.   175
HORATIO.   My lord, I came to see your father's funeral.
HAMLET.   I prithee do not mock me, fellow student.
   I think it was to see my mother's wedding.
HORATIO.   Indeed, my lord, it followed hard upon.
HAMLET.   Thrift, thrift, Horatio. The funeral baked meats   180
   Did coldly furnish forth the marriage tables.
   Would I had met my dearest° foe in heaven
   Or ever I had seen that day, Horatio!
   My father, methinks I see my father.

---

149. *Niobe:* (a mother who wept profusely at the death of her children).   150. *wants discourse of reason:* lacks reasoning power.   155. *left the flushing:* stopped reddening.   156. *post:* hasten.
157. *incestuous:* (canon law considered marriage with a deceased brother's widow to be incestuous).
163. *change:* exchange.   172. *truster:* believer.   182. *dearest:* most intensely felt.

HORATIO.   Where, my lord?

HAMLET.   In my mind's eye, Horatio.   185

HORATIO.   I saw him once. 'A° was a goodly king.

HAMLET.   'A was a man, take him for all in all,
   I shall not look upon his like again.

HORATIO.   My lord, I think I saw him yesternight.

HAMLET.   Saw? Who?   190

HORATIO.   My lord, the King your father.

HAMLET.   The King my father?

HORATIO.   Season your admiration° for a while
   With an attent ear till I may deliver
   Upon the witness of these gentlemen
   This marvel to you.

HAMLET.   For God's love let me hear!   195

HORATIO.   Two nights together had these gentlemen,
   Marcellus and Barnardo, on their watch
   In the dead waste and middle of the night
   Been thus encountered. A figure like your father,
   Armèd at point exactly, cap-a-pe,°   200
   Appears before them, and with solemn march
   Goes slow and stately by them. Thrice he walked
   By their oppressed and fear-surprisèd eyes,
   Within his truncheon's length,° whilst they, distilled°
   Almost to jelly with the act° of fear,   205
   Stand dumb and speak not to him. This to me
   In dreadful° secrecy impart they did,
   And I with them the third night kept the watch,
   Where, as they had delivered, both in time,
   Form of the thing, each word made true and good,   210
   The apparition comes. I knew your father.
   These hands are not more like.

HAMLET.   But where was this?

MARCELLUS.   My lord, upon the platform where we watched.

HAMLET.   Did you not speak to it?

HORATIO.   My lord, I did;
   But answer made it none. Yet once methought   215
   It lifted up it° head and did address
   Itself to motion like as it would speak:
   But even then the morning cock crew loud,
   And at the sound it shrunk in haste away
   And vanished from our sight.

---

186. *'A:* he.   192. *Season your admiration:* control your wonder.   200. *cap-a-pe:* head to foot.
204. *truncheon's length:* space of a short staff.   204. *distilled:* reduced.   205. *act:* action.
207. *dreadful:* terrified.   216. *it:* its.

HAMLET.   'Tis very strange.   220

HORATIO.   As I do live, my honored lord, 'tis true,
  And we did think it writ down in our duty
  To let you know of it.

HAMLET.   Indeed, indeed, sirs, but this troubles me.
  Hold you the watch tonight?

ALL.   We do, my lord.   225

HAMLET.   Armed, say you?

ALL.   Armed, my lord.

HAMLET.   From top to toe?

ALL.   My lord, from head to foot.

HAMLET.   Then saw you not his face.

HORATIO.   O, yes, my lord. He wore his beaver° up.   230

HAMLET.   What, looked he frowningly?

HORATIO.   A countenance more in sorrow than in anger.

HAMLET.   Pale or red?

HORATIO.   Nay, very pale.

HAMLET.   And fixed his eyes upon you?

HORATIO.   Most constantly.

HAMLET.   I would I had been there.   235

HORATIO.   It would have much amazed you.

HAMLET.   Very like, very like. Stayed it long?

HORATIO.   While one with moderate haste might tell° a hundred.

BOTH.   Longer, longer.

HORATIO.   Not when I saw't.

HAMLET.   His beard was grizzled,° no?   240

HORATIO.   It was as I have seen it in his life,
  A sable silvered.°

HAMLET.   I will watch tonight.
  Perchance 'twill walk again.

HORATIO.   I warr'nt it will.

HAMLET.   If it assume my noble father's person,
  I'll speak to it though hell itself should gape   245
  And bid me hold my peace. I pray you all,
  If you have hitherto concealed this sight,
  Let it be tenable° in your silence still,
  And whatsoever else shall hap tonight,
  Give it an understanding but no tongue;   250
  I will requite your loves. So fare you well.
  Upon the platform 'twixt eleven and twelve
  I'll visit you.

ALL.   Our duty to your honor.

---

230. *beaver:* visor, face guard.   238. *tell:* count.   240. *grizzled:* gray.   242. *sable silvered:* black mingled with white.   248. *tenable:* held.

HAMLET.   Your loves, as mine to you. Farewell.   *Exeunt* [*all but* HAMLET].
  My father's spirit—in arms? All is not well.   255
  I doubt° some foul play. Would the night were come!
  Till then sit still, my soul. Foul deeds will rise,
  Though all the earth o'erwhelm them, to men's eyes.   *Exit.*

SCENE III.   *A room.*

Enter LAERTES *and* OPHELIA, *his sister.*

LAERTES.   My necessaries are embarked. Farewell.
  And, sister, as the winds give benefit
  And convoy° is assistant, do not sleep,
  But let me hear from you.
OPHELIA.   Do you doubt that?
LAERTES.   For Hamlet, and the trifling of his favor,   5
  Hold it a fashion and a toy° in blood,
  A violet in the youth of primy° nature,
  Forward,° not permanent, sweet, not lasting,
  The perfume and suppliance° of a minute,
  No more.
OPHELIA.   No more but so?
LAERTES.   Think it no more.   10
  For nature crescent° does not grow alone
  In thews° and bulk, but as this temple° waxes,
  The inward service of the mind and soul
  Grows wide withal. Perhaps he loves you now,
  And now no soil nor cautel° doth besmirch   15
  The virtue of his will; but you must fear,
  His greatness weighed,° his will is not his own.
  For he himself is subject to his birth.
  He may not, as unvalued° persons do,
  Carve for himself; for on his choice depends   20
  The safety and health of this whole state;
  And therefore must his choice be circumscribed
  Unto the voice and yielding of that body
  Whereof he is the head. Then if he says he loves you,
  It fits your wisdom so far to believe it   25
  As he in his particular act and place
  May give his saying deed, which is no further
  Than the main voice of Denmark goes withal.
  Then weigh what loss your honor may sustain

---

256. *doubt:* suspect.   SCENE III.   3. *convoy:* conveyance.   6. *toy:* idle fancy.
7. *primy:* springlike.   8. *Forward:* premature.   9. *suppliance:* diversion.   11. *crescent:* growing.
12. *thews:* muscles and sinews.   12. *temple:* i.e., the body.   15. *cautel:* deceit.   17. *greatness
weighed:* high rank considered.   19. *unvalued:* of low rank.

If with too credent° ear you list his songs,   30
Or lose your heart, or your chaste treasure open
To his unmastered importunity.
Fear it, Ophelia, fear it, my dear sister,
And keep you in the rear of your affection,
Out of the shot and danger of desire.   35
The chariest maid is prodigal enough
If she unmask her beauty to the moon.
Virtue itself scapes not calumnious strokes.
The canker° galls the infants of the spring
Too oft before their buttons° be disclosed,   40
And in the morn and liquid dew of youth
Contagious blastments are most imminent.
Be wary then; best safety lies in fear;
Youth to itself rebels, though none else near.
OPHELIA.   I shall the effect of this good lesson keep   45
As watchman to my heart, but, good my brother,
Do not, as some ungracious° pastors do,
Show me the steep and thorny way to heaven,
Whiles, like a puffed and reckless libertine,
Himself the primrose path of dalliance treads   50
And recks not his own rede.°

Enter POLONIUS.

LAERTES.   O, fear me not.
I stay too long. But here my father comes.
A double blessing is a double grace;
Occasion smiles upon a second leave.
POLONIUS.   Yet here, Laertes? Aboard, aboard, for shame!   55
The wind sits in the shoulder of your sail,
And you are stayed for. There—my blessing with thee,
And these few precepts in thy memory
Look thou character.° Give thy thoughts no tongue,
Nor any unproportioned° thought his act.   60
Be thou familiar, but by no means vulgar.
Those friends thou hast, and their adoption tried,
Grapple them unto thy soul with hoops of steel,
But do not dull thy palm with entertainment
Of each new-hatched, unfledged courage.° Beware   65
Of entrance to a quarrel; but being in,
Bear't that th' opposèd may beware of thee.

---

30. *credent:* credulous.   39, *canker:* cankerworm.   40. *buttons:* buds.   47. *ungracious:* lacking
grace.   51. *recks not his own rede:* does not heed his own advice.   59. *character:* inscribe.
60. *unproportioned:* unbalanced.   65. *courage:* gallant youth.

Give every man thine ear, but few thy voice;
Take each man's censure,° but reserve thy judgment.
Costly thy habit as thy purse can buy,   70
But not expressed in fancy; rich, not gaudy,
For the apparel oft proclaims the man,
And they in France of the best rank and station
Are of a most select and generous, chief in that.°
Neither a borrower nor a lender be,   75
For loan oft loses both itself and friend,
And borrowing dulls the edge of husbandry.°
This above all, to thine own self be true,
And it must follow, as the night the day,
Thou canst not then be false to any man.   80
Farewell. My blessing season this° in thee!
LAERTES.   Most humbly do I take my leave, my lord.
POLONIUS.   The time invites you. Go, your servants tend.°
LAERTES.   Farewell, Ophelia, and remember well
What I have said to you.
OPHELIA.   'Tis in my memory locked,   85
And you yourself shall keep the key of it.
LAERTES.   Farewell.   *Exit* LAERTES.
POLONIUS.   What is't, Ophelia, he hath said to you?
OPHELIA.   So please you, something touching the Lord Hamlet.
POLONIUS.   Marry,° well bethought.   90
'Tis told me he hath very oft of late
Given private time to you, and you yourself
Have of your audience been most free and bounteous.
If it be so—as so 'tis put on me,
And that in way of caution—I must tell you   95
You do not understand yourself so clearly
As it behooves my daughter and your honor.
What is between you? Give me up the truth.
OPHELIA.   He hath, my lord, of late made many tenders°
Of his affection to me.   100
POLONIUS.   Affection pooh! You speak like a green girl,
Unsifted° in such perilous circumstance.
Do you believe his tenders, as you call them?
OPHELIA.   I do not know, my lord, what I should think.

---

69. *censure:* opinion.   74. *Are of…in that:* show their fine taste and their gentlemanly instincts more in that than in any other point of manners (Kittredge).   77. *husbandry:* thrift.   81. *season this:* make fruitful this (advice).   83. *tend:* attend.   90. *Marry:* (a light oath, from "By the Virgin Mary").
99. *tenders:* offers (in line 103 it has the same meaning, but in line 106 Polonius speaks of *tenders* in the sense of counters or chips; in line 109 *Tend'ring* means "holding," and *tender* means "give," "present").   102. *Unsifted:* untried.

POLONIUS.   Marry, I will teach you. Think yourself a baby.   105
    That you have ta'en these tenders for true pay
    Which are not sterling. Tender yourself more dearly,
    Or (not to crack the wind of the poor phrase)
    Tend'ring it thus you'll tender me a fool.°
OPHELIA.   My lord, he hath importuned me with love   110
    In honorable fashion.
POLONIUS.   Ay, fashion you may call it. Go to, go to.
OPHELIA.   And hath given countenance to his speech, my lord,
    With almost all the holy vows of heaven.
POLONIUS.   Ay, springes to catch woodcocks.° I do know,   115
    When the blood burns, how prodigal the soul
    Lends the tongue vows. These blazes, daughter,
    Giving more light than heat, extinct in both,
    Even in their promise, as it is a-making,
    You must not take for fire. From this time   120
    Be something scanter of your maiden presence.
    Set your entreatments° at a higher rate
    Than a command to parley. For Lord Hamlet,
    Believe so much in him that he is young,
    And with a larger tether may he walk   125
    Than may be given you. In few, Ophelia,
    Do not believe his vows, for they are brokers,°
    Not of that dye° which their investments° show,
    But mere implorators° of unholy suits,
    Breathing like sanctified and pious bonds,°   130
    The better to beguile. This is for all:
    I would not, in plain terms, from this time forth
    Have you so slander° any moment leisure
    As to give words or talk with the Lord Hamlet.
    Look to't, I charge you. Come you ways.   135
OPHELIA.   I shall obey, my lord.   *Exeunt.*

SCENE IV.   *A guard platform.*

Enter HAMLET, HORATIO, *and* MARCELLUS.

HAMLET.   The air bites shrewdly;° it is very cold.
HORATIO.   It is a nipping and an eager° air.
HAMLET.   What hour now?
HORATIO.   I think it lacks of twelve.
MARCELLUS.   No, it is struck.

---

109. *tender me a fool:* (1) present me with a fool, (2) present me with a baby.   115. *springes to catch*
woodcocks: snares to catch stupid birds.   122. *entreatments:* interviews.   127. *brokers:* procurers.
128. *dye:* i.e., kind.   128. *investments:* garments.   129. *implorators:* solicitors.   130. *bonds:* pledges.
133. *slander:* disgrace.   SCENE IV. 1. *shrewdly:* bitterly.   2. *eager:* sharp.

HORATIO.   Indeed? I heard it not. It then draws near the season   5
Wherein the spirit held his wont to walk.

A flourish of trumpets, and two pieces go off.

What does this mean, my lord?
HAMLET.   The King doth wake° tonight and takes his rouse,°
Keeps wassail, and the swagg'ring upspring° reels,
And as he drains his draughts of Rhenish° down   10
The kettledrum and trumpet thus bray out
The triumph of his pledge.°
HORATIO.   Is it a custom?
HAMLET.   Ay, marry, is't,
But to my mind, though I am native here
And to the manner born, it is a custom   15
More honored in the breach than the observance.
This heavy-headed revel east and west
Makes us traduced and taxed of° other nations.
They clepe° us drunkards and with swinish phrase
Soil our addition,° and indeed it takes   20
From our achievements, though performed at height,
The pith and marrow of our attribute.°
So oft it chances in particular men
That for some vicious mole° of nature in them,
As in their birth, wherein they are not guilty,   25
(Since nature cannot choose his origin)
By the o'ergrowth of some complexion,°
Oft breaking down the pales° and forts of reason,
Or by some habit that too much o'erleavens°
The form of plausive° manners, that (these men,   30
Carrying, I say, the stamp of one defect,
Being nature's livery, or fortune's star°)
Their virtues else, be they as pure as grace,
As infinite as man may undergo,
Shall in the general censure° take corruption   35
From that particular fault. The dram of evil
Doth all the noble substance of a doubt,
To his own scandal.°

---

8. *wake:* hold a revel by night.   8. *takes his rouse:* carouses.   9. *upspring:* (a dance).
10. *Rhenish:* Rhine wine.   12. *The triumph of his pledge:* the achievement (of drinking a wine cup in one draught) of his toast.   18. *taxed of:* blamed by.   19. *clepe:* call.   20. *addition:* reputation (literally, "title of honor").   22. *attribute:* reputation.   24. *mole:* blemish.   27. *complexion:* natural disposition.   28. *pales:* enclosures.   29. *o'erleavens:* mixes with, corrupts.   30. *plausive:* pleasing.
32. *nature's livery, or fortune's star:* nature's equipment (i.e., "innate"), or a person's destiny determined by the stars.   35. *general censure:* popular judgment.   36–38. *The dram...own scandal:* (though the drift is clear, there is no agreement as to the exact meaning of these lines).

Enter GHOST.

HORATIO.	Look, my lord, it comes.

HAMLET.   Angels and ministers of grace defend us!
Be thou a spirit of health° or goblin damned,   40
Bring with thee airs from heaven or blasts from hell,
Be thy intents wicked or charitable,
Thou com'st in such a questionable° shape
That I will speak to thee. I'll call thee Hamlet,
King, father, royal Dane. O, answer me!   45
Let me not burst in ignorance, but tell
Why thy canonized° bones, hearsèd in death,
Have burst their cerements,° why the sepulcher
Wherein we saw thee quietly interred
Hath oped his ponderous and marble jaws   50
To cast thee up again. What may this mean
That thou, dead corse, again in complete steel,
Revisits thus the glimpses of the moon,
Making night hideous, and we fools of nature
So horridly to shake our disposition°   55
With thoughts beyond the reaches of our souls?
Say, why is this? Wherefore? What should we do?

GHOST *beckons* HAMLET.

HORATIO.   It beckons you to go away with it,
As if it some impartment° did desire
To you alone.

MARCELLUS.   Look with what courteous action   60
It waves you to a more removèd ground.
But do not go with it.

HORATIO.   No, by no means.

HAMLET.   It will not speak. Then I will follow it.

HORATIO.   Do not, my lord.

HAMLET.   Why, what should be the fear?
I do not set my life at a pin's fee,   65
And for my soul, what can it do to that,
Being a thing immortal as itself?
It waves me forth again. I'll follow it.

HORATIO.   What if it tempt you toward the flood, my lord,
Or to the dreadful summit of the cliff   70
That beetles° o'er his base into the sea,

---

40. *spirit of health:* good spirit.   43. *questionable:* (1) capable of discourse, (2) dubious.
47. *canonized:* buried according to the canon or ordinance of the church.   48. *cerements:* waxed linen
shroud.   55. *shake our disposition:* disturb us.   59. *impartment:* communication.   71. *beetles:* juts
out.

And there assume some other horrible form
Which might deprive your sovereignty of reason°
And draw you into madness? Think of it.
The very place puts toys° of desperation, 75
Without more motive, into every brain
That looks so many fathoms to the sea
And hears it roar beneath.
HAMLET.   It waves me still.
  Go on; I'll follow thee.
MARCELLUS.   You shall not go, my lord.
HAMLET.   Hold off your hands. 80
HORATIO.   Be ruled. You shall not go.
HAMLET.   My fate cries out
  And makes each petty artere° in this body
  As hardy as the Nemean lion's nerve.°
  Still am I called! Unhand me, gentlemen.
  By heaven, I'll make a ghost of him that lets° me! 85
  I say, away! Go on. I'll follow thee.   *Exit* GHOST *and* HAMLET.
HORATIO.   He waxes desperate with imagination.
MARCELLUS.   Let's follow. 'Tis not fit thus to obey him.
HORATIO.   Have after! To what issue will this come?
MARCELLUS.   Something is rotten in the state of Denmark. 90
HORATIO.   Heaven will direct it.
MARCELLUS.   Nay, let's follow him.   *Exeunt.*

SCENE V.   *The battlements.*

Enter GHOST *and* HAMLET.

HAMLET.   Whither wilt thou lead me? Speak; I'll go no further.
GHOST.   Mark me.
HAMLET.   I will.
GHOST.   My hour is almost come,
  When I to sulf'rous and tormenting flames
  Must render up myself.
HAMLET.   Alas, poor ghost.
GHOST.   Pity me not, but lend thy serious hearing 5
  To what I shall unfold.
HAMLET.   Speak. I am bound to hear.
GHOST.   So art thou to revenge, when thou shalt hear.
HAMLET.   What?
GHOST.   I am thy father's spirit,
  Doomed for a certain term to walk the night, 10

73. *deprive your sovereignty of reason:* destroy the sovereignty of your reason.   75. *toys:* whims, fancies.
82. *artere:* artery.   83. *Nemean lion's nerve:* sinews of the mythical lion slain by Hercules.
85. *lets:* hinders.

And for the day confined to fast in fires,
Till the foul crimes° done in my days of nature
Are burnt and purged away. But that I am forbid
To tell the secrets of my prison house,
I could a tale unfold whose lightest word   15
Would harrow up thy soul, freeze thy young blood,
Make thy two eyes like stars start from their spheres,°
Thy knotted and combinèd locks to part,
And each particular hair to stand an end
Like quills upon the fearful porpentine.°   20
But this eternal blazon° must not be
To ears of flesh and blood. List, list, O, list!
If thou didst ever thy dear father love——
HAMLET.   O God!
GHOST.   Revenge his foul and most unnatural murder.   25
HAMLET.   Murder?
GHOST.   Murder most foul, as in the best it is,
  But this most foul, strange, and unnatural.
HAMLET.   Haste me to know't, that I, with wings as swift
  As meditation° or the thoughts of love,   30
  May sweep to my revenge.
GHOST.   I find thee apt,
  And duller shouldst thou be than the fat weed
  That roots itself in ease on Lethe wharf,°
  Wouldst thou not stir in this. Now, Hamlet, hear.
  'Tis given out that, sleeping in my orchard,   35
  A serpent stung me. So the whole ear of Denmark
  Is by a forgèd process° of my death
  Rankly abused. But know, thou noble youth,
  The serpent that did sting thy father's life
  Now wears his crown.
HAMLET.   O my prophetic soul!   40
  My uncle?
GHOST.   Ay, that incestuous, that adulterate° beast,
  With witchcraft of his wits, with traitorous gifts—
  O wicked wit and gifts, that have the power
  So to seduce!—won to his shameful lust   45
  The will of my most seeming-virtuous queen.
  O Hamlet, what a falling-off was there,
  From me, whose love was of that dignity
  That it went hand in hand even with the vow

SCENE V. 12. *crimes:* sins.   17. *spheres:* (in Ptolemaic astronomy, each planet was fixed in a hollow transparent shell concentric with the earth).   20. *fearful porpentine:* timid porcupine.   21. *eternal blazon:* revelation of eternity.   30. *meditation:* thought.   33. *Lethe wharf:* bank of the river of forgetfulness in Hades.   37. *forgèd process:* false account.   42. *adulterate:* adulterous.

I made to her in marriage, and to decline   50
Upon a wretch whose natural gifts were poor
To those of mine.
But virtue, as it never will be moved,
Though lewdness° court it in a shape of heaven,
So lust, though to a radiant angel linked,   55
Will sate itself in a celestial bed
And prey on garbage.
But soft, methinks I scent the morning air;
Brief let me be. Sleeping within my orchard,
My custom always of the afternoon,   60
Upon my secure° hour thy uncle stole
With juice of cursed hebona° in a vial,
And in the porches of my ears did pour
The leperous distillment, whose effect
Holds such an enmity with blood of man   65
That swift as quicksilver it courses through
The natural gates and alleys of the body,
And with a sudden vigor it doth posset°
And curd, like eager° droppings into milk,
The thin and wholesome blood. So did it mine,   70
And a most instant tetter° barked about
Most lazarlike° with vile and loathsome crust
All my smooth body.
Thus was I, sleeping, by a brother's hand
Of life, of crown, of queen at once dispatched,   75
Cut off even in the blossoms of my sin,
Unhouseled, disappointed, unaneled,°
No reck'ning made, but sent to my account
With all my imperfections on my head.
O, horrible! O, horrible! Most horrible!   80
If thou hast nature in thee, bear it not.
Let not the royal bed of Denmark be
A couch for luxury° and damnèd incest.
But howsomever thou pursues this act,
Taint not thy mind, nor let thy soul contrive   85
Against thy mother aught. Leave her to heaven
And to those thorns that in her bosom lodge
To prick and sting her. Fare thee well at once.
The glowworm shows the matin° to be near

54. *lewdness:* lust.   61. *secure:* unsuspecting.   62. *hebona:* a poisonous plant.   68. *posset:* curdle.
69. *eager:* acid.   71. *tetter:* scab.   72. *lazarlike:* leperlike.   77. ***Unhouseled, disappointed, unaneled:***
without the sacrament of communion, unabsolved, without extreme unction.   83. *luxury:* lust.
89. *matin:* morning.

And 'gins to pale his uneffectual fire.   90
Adieu, adieu, adieu. Remember me.   *Exit.*
HAMLET.   O all you host of heaven! O earth! What else?
And shall I couple hell? O fie! Hold, hold, my heart,
And you, my sinews, grow now instant old,
But bear me stiffly up. Remember thee?   95
Ay, thou poor ghost, whiles memory holds a seat
In this distracted globe.° Remember thee?
Yea, from the table° of my memory
I'll wipe away all trivial fond° records,
All saws° of books, all forms, all pressures° past   100
That youth and observation copied there,
And thy commandment all alone shall live
Within the book and volume of my brain,
Unmixed with baser matter. Yes, by heaven!
O most pernicious woman!   105
O villain, villain, smiling, damnèd villain!
My tables—meet it is I set it down
That one may smile, and smile, and be a villain.
At least I am sure it may be so in Denmark.   [*Writes.*]
So, uncle, there you are. Now to my word: 110
It is "Adieu, adieu, remember me."
I have sworn't.
HORATIO AND MARCELLUS.   [*Within*]   My lord, my lord!

Enter HORATIO *and* MARCELLUS.

MARCELLUS.   Lord Hamlet!
HORATIO.   Heavens secure him!
HAMLET.   So be it!
MARCELLUS.   Illo, ho, ho,° my lord!   115
HAMLET.   Hillo, ho, ho, boy! Come, bird, come.
MARCELLUS.   How is't, my noble lord?
HORATIO.   What news, my lord?
HAMLET.   O, wonderful!
HORATIO.   Good my lord, tell it.
HAMLET.   No, you will reveal it.
HORATIO.   Not I, my lord, by heaven.
MARCELLUS.   Nor I, my lord.   120
HAMLET.   How say you then? Would heart of man once think it?
  But you'll be secret?
BOTH.   Ay, by heaven, my lord.

---

97. *globe:* i.e., his head.   98. *table:* tablet, notebook.   99. *fond:* foolish.   100. *saws:* maxims.
100. *pressures:* impressions.   115. *Illo, ho, ho:* (falconer's call to his hawk).

HAMLET.   There's never a villain dwelling in all Denmark
   But he's an arrant knave.
HORATIO.   There needs no ghost, my lord, come from the grave   125
   To tell us this.
HAMLET.   Why, right, you are in the right;
  And so, without more circumstance° at all,
  I hold it fit that we shake hands and part:
  You, as your business and desire shall point you,
  For every man hath business and desire   130
  Such as it is, and for my own poor part,
  Look you, I'll go pray.
HORATIO.   These are but wild and whirling words, my lord.
HAMLET.   I am sorry they offend you, heartily;
  Yes, faith, heartily.
HORATIO.   There's no offense, my lord.   135
HAMLET.   Yes, by Saint Patrick, but there is, Horatio,
  And much offense too. Touching this vision here,
  It is an honest ghost,° that let me tell you.
  For your desire to know what is between us,
  O'ermaster't as you may. And now, good friends,   140
  As you are friends, scholars, and soldiers,
  Give me one poor request.
HORATIO.   What is't, my lord? We will.
HAMLET.   Never make known what you have seen tonight.
BOTH.   My lord, we will not.
HAMLET.   Nay, but swear't.
HORATIO.   In faith,   145
  My lord, not I.
MARCELLUS.   Nor I, my lord—in faith.
HAMLET.   Upon my sword.
MARCELLUS.   We have sworn, my lord, already.
HAMLET.   Indeed, upon my sword, indeed.

            GHOST *cries under the stage.*

GHOST.   Swear.
HAMLET.   Ha, ha, boy, say'st thou so? Art thou there, truepenny?°   150
  Come on. You hear this fellow in the cellarage.
  Consent to swear.
HORATIO.   Propose the oath, my lord.
HAMLET.   Never to speak of this that you have seen.
  Swear by my sword.
GHOST.   [*Beneath*] Swear.   155

---

127. *circumstance:* details.   138. *honest ghost:* i.e., not a demon in his father's shape.
150. *truepenny:* honest fellow.

HAMLET.   *Hic et ubique?*° Then we'll shift our ground;
   Come hither, gentlemen,
   And lay your hands again upon my sword.
   Swear by my sword
   Never to speak of this that you have heard.   160
GHOST.   [*Beneath*]   Swear by his sword.
HAMLET.   Well said, old mole! Canst work i' th' earth so fast?
   A worthy pioner!° Once more remove, good friends.
HORATIO.   O day and night, but this is wondrous strange!
HAMLET.   And therefore as a stranger give it welcome.   165
   There are more things in heaven and earth, Horatio,
   Than are dreamt of in your philosophy.
   But come:
   Here as before, never, so help you mercy,
   How strange or odd some'er I bear myself   170
   (As I perchance hereafter shall think meet
   To put an antic disposition° on),
   That you, at such times seeing me, never shall
   With arms encumb'red° thus, or this headshake,
   Or by pronouncing of some doubtful phrase,   175
   As "Well, well, we know," or "We could, an if we would,"
   Or "If we list to speak," or "There be, an if they might,"
   Or such ambiguous giving out, to note
   That you know aught of me—this do swear,
   So grace and mercy at your most need help you.   180
GHOST.   [*Beneath*]   Swear.   [*They swear.*]
HAMLET.   Rest, rest, perturbèd spirit. So, gentlemen,
   With all my love I do commend me° to you,
   And what so poor a man as Hamlet is
   May do t' express his love and friending to you,   185
   God willing, shall not lack. Let us go in together,
   And still your fingers on your lips, I pray.
   The time is out of joint. O cursèd spite,
   That ever I was born to set it right!
   Nay, come, let's go together.   *Exeunt.*   190

ACT II

Scene I.   *A room.*

Enter old POLONIUS, *with his man* REYNALDO.

POLONIUS.   Give him this money and these notes, Reynaldo.
REYNALDO.   I will, my lord.

---

156. *Hic et ubique:* here and everywhere (Latin).   163. *pioner:* digger of mines.   172. *antic disposition:* fantastic behavior.   174. *encumb'red:* folded.   183. *commend me:* entrust myself.

POLONIUS.   You shall do marvell's° wisely, good Reynaldo,
    Before you visit him, to make inquire
    Of his behavior.
REYNALDO.   My lord, I did intend it.   5
POLONIUS.   Marry, well said, very well said. Look you sir,
    Inquire me first what Danskers° are in Paris,
    And how, and who, what means, and where they keep,°
    What company, at what expense; and finding
    By this encompassment° and drift of question   10
    That they do know my son, come you more nearer
    Than your particular demands° will touch it.
    Take you as 'twere some distant knowledge of him,
    As thus, "I know his father and his friends,
    And in part him." Do you mark this, Reynaldo?   15
REYNALDO.   Ay, very well, my lord.
POLONIUS.   "And in part him, but," you may say, "not well,
    But if't be he I mean, he's very wild,
    Addicted so and so," And there put on him
    What forgeries° you please; marry, none so rank   20
    As may dishonor him—take heed of that—
    But, sir, such wanton, wild, and usual slips
    As are companions noted and most known
    To youth and liberty.
REYNALDO.   As gaming, my lord.
POLONIUS.   Ay, or drinking, fencing, swearing, quarrelling,   25
    Drabbing.° You may go so far.
REYNALDO.   My lord, that would dishonor him.
POLONIUS.   Faith, no, as you may season it in the charge.
    You must not put another scandal on him,
    That he is open to incontinency.°   30
    That's not my meaning. But breathe his faults so quaintly°
    That they may seem the taints of liberty,
    The flash and outbreak of a fiery mind,
    A savageness in unreclaimèd blood,
    Of general assault.°
REYNALDO.   But, my good lord——   35
POLONIUS.   Wherefore should you do this?
REYNALDO.   Ay, my lord,
    I would know that.
POLONIUS.   Marry, sir, here's my drift,
    And I believe it is a fetch of warrant.°

SCENE I. 3. *marvell's:* marvelous(ly).   7. *Danskers:* Danes.   8. *keep:* dwell.   10. *encompassment:*
circling.   12. *demands:* questions.   20. *forgeries:* inventions.   26. *Drabbing:* wenching.
30. *incontinency:* habitual licentiousness.   31. *quaintly:* ingeniously, delicately.   35. *Of general
assault:* common to all men.   38. *fetch of warrant:* justifiable device.

You laying these slight sullies on my son
As 'twere a thing a little soiled i' th' working, 40
Mark you,
Your party in converse, him you would sound,
Having ever seen in the prenominate crimes°
The youth you breathe of guilty, be assured
He closes with you in this consequence:° 45
"Good sir," or so, or "friend," or "gentleman"—
According to the phrase or the addition°
Of man and country—

REYNALDO.   Very good, my lord.

POLONIUS.   And then, sir, does 'a° this—'a does—
What was I about to say? By the mass, I was about 50
to say something! Where did I leave?

REYNALDO.   At "closes in the consequence," at "friend
or so," and "gentleman."

POLONIUS.   At "closes in the consequence"—Ay, marry!
He closes thus: "I know the gentleman; 55
I saw him yesterday, or t'other day,
Or then, or then, with such or such, and, as you say,
There was 'a gaming, there o'ertook in's rouse,
There falling out at tennis"; or perchance,
"I saw him enter such a house of sale," 60
Videlicet,° a brothel, or so forth.
See you now—
Your bait of falsehood take this carp of truth,
And thus do we of wisdom and of reach,°
With windlasses° and with assays of bias,° 65
By indirections find directions out.
So, by my former lecture and advice,
Shall you my son. You have me, have you not?

REYNALDO.   My lord, I have.

POLONIUS.   God bye ye, fare ye well.

REYNALDO.   Good my lord. 70

POLONIUS.   Observe his inclination in yourself.°

REYNALDO.   I shall, my lord.

POLONIUS.   And let him ply his music.

REYNALDO.   Well, my lord.

POLONIUS.   Farewell.   *Exit* REYNALDO.

---

43. *Having...crimes:* if he has ever seen in the aforementioned crimes.   5. *He closes...this consequence:* he falls in with you in this conclusion.   47. *addition:* title.   49. *'a:* he. 61. *Videlicet:* namely.   64. *reach:* far-reaching awareness(?).   65. *windlasses:* circuitous courses.   65. *assays of bias:* indirect attempts (metaphor from bowling; *bias* = curved course).   71. *in yourself:* for yourself.

Enter OPHELIA.

How now, Ophelia, what's the matter?

OPHELIA.   O my lord, my lord, I have been so affrighted!   75

POLONIUS.   With what, i' th' name of God?

OPHELIA.   My lord, as I was sewing in my closet,°
  Lord Hamlet, with his doublet all unbraced,°
  No hat upon his head, his stockings fouled,
  Ungartered, and down-gyvèd° to his ankle,   80
  Pale as his shirt, his knees knocking each other,
  And with a look so piteous in purport,°
  As if he had been loosèd out of hell
  To speak of horror—he comes before me.

POLONIUS.   Mad for thy love?

OPHELIA.   My lord, I do not know,   85
  But truly I do fear it.

POLONIUS.   What said he?

OPHELIA.   He took me by the wrist and held me hard;
  Then goes he to the length of all his arm,
  And with his other hand thus o'er his brow
  He falls to such perusal of my face   90
  As 'a would draw it. Long stayed he so.
  At last, a little shaking of mine arm,
  And thrice his head thus waving up and down,
  He raised a sigh so piteous and profound
  As it did seem to shatter all his bulk   95
  And end his being. That done, he lets me go,
  And, with his head over his shoulder turned,
  He seemed to find his way without his eyes,
  For out o' doors he went without their helps,
  And to the last bended their light on me.   100

POLONIUS.   Come, go with me. I will go seek the King.
  This is the very ecstasy° of love,
  Whose violent property fordoes° itself
  And leads the will to desperate undertakings
  As oft as any passions under heaven   105
  That does afflict our natures. I am sorry.
  What, have you given him any hard words of late?

OPHELIA.   No, my good lord; but as you did command,
  I did repel his letters and denied
  His access to me.

---

77. *closet:* private room. 78. *doublet all unbraced:* jacket entirely unlaced. 80. *down-gyvèd:* hanging
down like fetters. 82. *purport:* expression. 102. *ecstasy:* madness. 103. *property fordoes:* quality
destroys.

POLONIUS.   That hath made him mad.   110
  I am sorry that with better heed and judgment
  I had not quoted° him. I feared he did but trifle
  And meant to wrack thee; but beshrew my jealousy.°
  By heaven, it is as proper° to our age
  To cast beyond ourselves° in our opinions   115
  As it is common for the younger sort
  To lack discretion. Come, go we to the King.
  This must be known, which, being kept close, might move
  More grief to hide than hate to utter love.°
  Come. *Exeunt.*   120

SCENE II. *The castle.*

Flourish. Enter KING *and* QUEEN, ROSENCRANTZ, *and* GUILDENSTERN [*with others*].

KING. Welcome, dear Rosencrantz and Guildenstern.
  Moreover that° we much did long to see you,
  The need we have to use you did provoke
  Our hasty sending. Something have you heard
  Of Hamlet's transformation: so call it,   5
  Sith° nor th' exterior nor the inward man
  Resembles that it was. What it should be,
  More than his father's death, that thus hath put him
  So much from th' understanding of himself,
  I cannot dream of. I entreat you both   10
  That, being of so° young days brought up with him,
  And sith so neighbored to his youth and havior,°
  That you vouchsafe your rest° here in our court
  Some little time, so by your companies
  To draw him on to pleasures, and to gather   15
  So much as from occasion you may glean,
  Whether aught to us unknown afflicts him thus,
  That opened° lies within our remedy.
QUEEN. Good gentlemen, he hath much talked of you,
  And sure I am, two men there is not living   20
  To whom he more adheres. If it will please you
  To show us so much gentry° and good will
  As to expend your time with us awhile
  For the supply and profit of our hope,
  Your visitation shall receive such thanks   25
  As fits a king's remembrance.

---

112. *quoted:* noted.   113. *beshrew my jealousy:* curse on my suspicions.   114. *proper:* natural.
115. *To cast beyond ourselves:* to be over-calculating.   117–119. *Come, go…utter love:* (the general meaning is that while telling the King of Hamlet's love may anger the King, more grief would come from keeping it secret).   SCENE II. 2. *Moreover that:* beside the fact that.   6. *Sith:* since.
11. *of so:* from such.   12. *youth and havior:* behavior in his youth.   13. *vouchsafe your rest:* consent to remain.   18. *opened:* revealed.   22. *gentry:* courtesy.

ROSENCRANTZ.   Both your Majesties
  Might, by sovereign power you have of us,
  Put your dread pleasure more into command
  Than to entreaty.
GUILDENSTERN.   But we both obey,
  And here give up ourselves in the full bent°   30
  To lay our service freely at your feet,
  To be commanded.
KING.   Thanks, Rosencrantz and gentle Guildenstern.
QUEEN.   Thanks, Guildenstern and gentle Rosencrantz.
  And I beseech you instantly to visit   35
  My too much changèd son. Go, some of you,
  And bring these gentlemen where Hamlet is.
GUILDENSTERN.   Heavens make our presence and our practices
  Pleasant and helpful to him!
QUEEN.   Ay, amen!

Exeunt ROSENCRANTZ *and* GUILDENSTERN [*with some* ATTENDANTS]. *Enter* POLONIUS.

POLONIUS.   Th' ambassadors from Norway, my good lord,   40
  Are joyfully returned.
KING.   Thou still° hast been the father of good news.
POLONIUS.   Have I, my lord? Assure you, my good liege,
  I hold my duty, as I hold my soul,
  Both to my God and to my gracious king;   45
  And I do think or else this brain of mine
  Hunts not the trail of policy so sure°
  As it hath used to do, that I have found
  The very cause of Hamlet's lunacy.
KING.   O, speak of that! That do I long to hear.   50
POLONIUS.   Give first admittance to th' ambassadors.
  My news shall be the fruit to that great feast.
KING.   Thyself do grace to them and bring them in.   *Exit* POLONIUS.
  He tells me, my dear Gertrude, he hath found
  The head and source of all your son's distemper.   55
QUEEN.   I doubt° it is no other but the main,°
  His father's death and our o'erhasty marriage.
KING.   Well, we shall sift him.

Enter POLONIUS, VOLTEMAND, *and* CORNELIUS.

                    Welcome, my good friends.
  Say, Voltemand, what from our brother Norway?
VOLTEMAND.   Most fair return of greetings and desires.   60
  Upon our first,° he sent out to suppress

---

30. *in the full bent:* entirely (the figure is of a bow bent to its capacity).   42. *still:* always.
47. *Hunts not…so sure:* does not follow clues of political doings with such sureness.
56. *doubt:* suspect.   56. *main:* principal point.   61. *first:* first audience.

His nephew's levies, which to him appeared
To be a preparation 'gainst the Polack;
But better looked into, he truly found
It was against your Highness, whereat grieved,   65
That so his sickness, age, and impotence
Was falsely borne in hand,° sends out arrests
On Fortinbras; which he, in brief, obeys,
Receives rebuke from Norway, and in fine,°
Makes vow before his uncle never more   70
To give th' assay° of arms against your Majesty.
Whereon old Norway, overcome with joy,
Gives him threescore thousand crowns in annual fee
And his commission to employ those soldiers,
So levied as before, against the Polack,   75
With an entreaty, herein further shown,   *Gives a paper.*
That it might please you to give quiet pass
Through your dominions for this enterprise,
On such regards of safety and allowance°
As therein are set down.

KING.   It likes us well;   80
  And at our more considered time° we'll read,
  Answer, and think upon this business.
  Meantime, we thank you for your well-took labor.
  Go to your rest; at night we'll feast together.
  Most welcome home!   *Exeunt* AMBASSADORS.

POLONIUS.   This business is well ended.   85
  My liege and madam, to expostulate°
  What majesty should be, what duty is,
  Why day is day, night night, and time is time.
  Were nothing but to waste night, day, and time.
  Therefore, since brevity is the soul of wit,°   90
  And tediousness the limbs and outward flourishes,
  I will be brief. Your noble son is mad.
  Mad call I it, for, to define true madness,
  What is't but to be nothing else but mad?
  But let that go.

QUEEN.   More matter, with less art.   95

POLONIUS.   Madam, I swear I use no art at all.
  That he's mad, 'tis true: 'tis true 'tis pity,
  And pity 'tis 'tis true—a foolish figure.°
  But farewell it, for I will use no art.

---

67. *borne in hand:* deceived.   69. *in fine:* finally.   71. *assay:* trial.   79. *regards of safety and allowance:* i.e., conditions.   81. *considered time:* time proper for considering.
86. *expostulate:* discuss.   90. *wit:* wisdom, understanding.   98. *figure:* figure of rhetoric.

Mad let us grant him then; and now remains   100
That we find out the cause of this effect,
Or rather say, the cause of this defect,
For this effect defective comes by cause.
Thus it remains, and the remainder thus.
Perpend.°   105
I have a daughter: have, while she is mine,
Who in her duty and obedience, mark,
Hath given me this. Now gather, and surmise.   [*Reads*] *the letter.*
"To the celestial, and my soul's idol, the most
beautified Ophelia"—   110
That's an ill phrase, a vile phrase; "beautified" is a
vile phrase. But you shall hear. Thus:
"In her excellent white bosom, these, &c."
QUEEN.   Came this from Hamlet to her?
POLONIUS.   Good madam, stay awhile. I will be faithful.   115
        "Doubt thou the stars are fire,
            Doubt that the sun doth move;
        Doubt° truth to be a liar,
            But never doubt I love.
O dear Ophelia, I am ill at these numbers.° I have   120
not art to reckon my groans; but that I love thee
best, O most best, believe it. Adieu.
    Thine evermore, most dear lady, whilst this
        machine° is to him, Hamlet."
This in obedience hath my daughter shown me,   125
And more above° hath his solicitings,
As they fell out by time, by means, and place,
All given to mine ear.
KING.   But how hath she
    Received his love?
POLONIUS.   What do you think of me?
KING.   As of man faithful and honorable.   130
POLONIUS.   I would fain prove so. But what might you think,
    When I had seen this hot love on the wing
    (As I perceived it, I must tell you that,
    Before my daughter told me), what might you,
    Or my dear Majesty your Queen here, think,   135
    If I had played the desk or table book,°
    Or given my heart a winking,° mute and dumb,
    Or looked upon this love with idle sight?

---

105. *Perpend:* consider carefully.   118. *Doubt:* suspect.   120. *ill at these numbers:* unskilled in verses.
124. *machine:* complex device (here, his body).   126. *more above:* in addition.   136. *played the desk or table book:* i.e., been a passive recipient of secrets.   137. *winking:* closing of the eyes.

What might you think? No, I went round to work
And my young mistress thus I did bespeak: 140
"Lord Hamlet is a prince, out of thy star.°
This must not be." And then I prescripts gave her,
That she should lock herself from his resort,
Admit no messengers, receive no tokens.
Which done, she took the fruits of my advice,   145
And he, repellèd, a short tale to make,
Fell into a sadness, then into a fast,
Thence to a watch,° thence into a weakness,
Thence to a lightness,° and, by this declension,
Into the madness wherein now he raves,   150
And all we mourn for.
KING.   Do you think 'tis this?
QUEEN.   It may be, very like.
POLONIUS.   Hath there been such a time, I would fain know that,
   That I have positively said "'Tis so,"
   When it proved otherwise?
KING.   Not that I know.   155
POLONIUS.   [*Pointing to his head and shoulder*]   Take this from this, if this be
   otherwise.
   If circumstances lead me, I will find
   Where truth is hid, though it were hid indeed
   Within the center.°
KING.   How may we try it further?
POLONIUS.   You know sometimes he walks four hours together   160
   Here in the lobby.
QUEEN.   So he does indeed.
POLONIUS.   At such a time I'll loose my daughter to him.
   Be you and I behind an arras° then.
   Mark the encounter. If he love her not,
   And be not from his reason fall'n thereon,   165
   Let me be no assistant for a state
   But keep a farm and carters.
KING.   We will try it.

Enter HAMLET *reading on a book.*

QUEEN.   But look where sadly the poor wretch comes reading.
POLONIUS.   Away, I do beseech you both, away.   *Exit* KING *and* QUEEN.
   I'll board him presently.° O, give me leave.   170
   How does my good Lord Hamlet?

141. *star:* sphere.   148. *watch:* wakefulness.   149. *lightness:* mental derangement.
159. *center:* center of the earth.   163. *arras:* tapestry hanging in front of a wall.
170. *board him presently:* accost him at once.

HAMLET.   Well, God-a-mercy.

POLONIUS.   Do you know me, my lord?

HAMLET.   Excellent well. You are a fishmonger.°

POLONIUS.   Not I, my lord.   175

HAMLET.   Then I would you were so honest a man.

POLONIUS.   Honest, my lord?

HAMLET.   Ay, sir. To be honest, as this world goes, is to be one man picked out of ten thousand.

POLONIUS.   That's very true, my lord.   180

HAMLET.   For if the sun breed maggots in a dead dog, being a good kissing carrion°——Have you a daughter?

POLONIUS.   I have, my lord.

HAMLET.   Let her not walk i' th' sun. Conception° is a blessing, but as your daughter may conceive, friend, look to't.   185

POLONIUS.   [*Aside*]   How say you by that? Still harping on my daughter. Yet he knew me not at first. 'A said I was a fishmonger. 'A is far gone, far gone. And truly in my youth I suffered much extremity for love, very near this. I'll speak to him again.—What do you read, my lord?

HAMLET.   Words, words, words.   190

POLONIUS.   What is the matter, my lord?

HAMLET.   Between who?

POLONIUS.   I mean that matter° that you read, my lord.

HAMLET.   Slanders, sir; for the satirical rogue says here that old men have gray beards, that their faces are wrinkled, their eyes purging thick amber and plum-   195
tree gum, and that they have a plentiful lack of wit, together with most weak hams. All which, sir, though I most powerfully and potently believe, yet I hold it not honestly° to have it thus set down; for you yourself, sir, should be old as I am if, like a crab, you could go backward.

POLONIUS.   [*Aside*]   Though this be madness, yet there is method in't. Will you   200
walk out of the air, my lord?

HAMLET.   Into my grave.

POLONIUS.   Indeed, that's out of the air.   [*Aside*]   How pregnant° sometimes his replies are! A happiness° that often madness hits on, which reason and san-
ity could not so prosperously be delivered of. I will leave him and suddenly   205
contrive the means of meeting between him and my daughter.—My lord, I will take my leave of you.

HAMLET.   You cannot take from me anything that I will more willingly part withal—except my life, except my life, except my life.

Enter GUILDENSTERN *and* ROSENCRANTZ.

---

174. *fishmonger:* dealer in fish (slang for a procurer).   181–182. *a good kissing carrion:* (perhaps the meaning is "a good piece of flesh to kiss," but many editors emend *good* to *god,* taking the word to refer to the sun).   184. *Conception:* (1) understanding, (2) becoming pregnant.   193. *matter:* (Polonius means "subject matter," but Hamlet pretends to take the word in the sense of "quarrel").
198. *honesty:* decency.   203. *pregnant:* meaningful.   204. *happiness:* apt turn of phrase.

POLONIUS.　Fare you well, my lord.　　　　　　　　　　　　　　210

HAMLET.　These tedious old fools!

POLONIUS.　You go to seek the Lord Hamlet? There he is.

ROSENCRANTZ.　[*To* POLONIUS]　God save you, sir!　*Exit* POLONIUS.

GUILDENSTERN.　My honored lord!

ROSENCRANTZ.　My most dear lord!　　　　　　　　　　　　　215

HAMLET.　My excellent good friends! How dost thou, Guildenstern? Ah, Rosencrantz! Good lads, how do you both?

ROSENCRANTZ.　As the indifferent° children of the earth.

GUILDENSTERN.　Happy in that we are not overhappy.
On Fortune's cap we are not the very button.　　　　　　　　220

HAMLET.　Nor the soles of her shoe?

ROSENCRANTZ.　Neither, my lord.

HAMLET.　Then you live about her waist, or in the middle of her favors?

GUILDENSTERN.　Faith, her privates° we.

HAMLET.　In the secret parts of Fortune? O, most true! She is a strumpet. What　225
news?

ROSENCRANTZ.　None, my lord, but that the world's grown honest.

HAMLET.　Then is doomsday near. But your news is not true. Let me question
more in particular. What have you, my good friends, deserved at the hands of
Fortune that she sends you to prison hither?　　　　　　　　230

GUILDENSTERN.　Prison, my lord?

HAMLET.　Denmark's a prison.

ROSENCRANTZ.　Then is the world one.

HAMLET.　A goodly one, in which there are many confines, wards,° and dungeons,
Denmark being one o' th' worst.　　　　　　　　　　　　235

ROSENCRANTZ.　We think not so, my lord.

HAMLET.　Why, then 'tis none to you, for there is nothing either good or bad but
thinking makes it so. To me it is a prison.

ROSENCRANTZ.　Why then your ambition makes it one. 'Tis too narrow for your
mind.　　　　　　　　　　　　　　　　　　　　240

HAMLET.　O God, I could be bounded in a nutshell and count myself a king of
infinite space, were it not that I have bad dreams.

GUILDENSTERN.　Which dreams indeed are ambition, for the very substance of the
ambitious is merely the shadow of a dream.

HAMLET.　A dream itself is but a shadow.　　　　　　　　　　245

ROSENCRANTZ.　Truly, and I hold ambition of so airy and light a quality that it is
but a shadow's shadow.

HAMLET.　Then are our beggars bodies, and our monarchs and outstretched heroes
the beggars' shadows.° Shall we to th' court? For, by my fay,° I cannot reason.

BOTH.　We'll wait upon you.　　　　　　　　　　　　　　250

---

218. *indifferent:* ordinary.　224. *privates:* ordinary men (with a pun on "private parts").
234. *wards:* cells.　248–249. *Then are…beggars' shadows:* i.e., by your logic, beggars (lacking ambition) are substantial, and great men are elongated shadows.　249. *fay:* faith.

HAMLET.   No such matter. I will not sort you with the rest of my servants, for, to speak to you like an honest man, I am most dreadfully attended. But in the beaten way of friendship, what make you at Elsinore?

ROSENCRANTZ.   To visit you, my lord; no other occasion.

HAMLET.   Beggar that I am, I am even poor in thanks, but I thank you; and sure, 255 dear friends, my thanks are too dear a halfpenny.° Were you not sent for? Is it your own inclining? Is it a free visitation? Come, come, deal justly with me. Come, come; nay, speak.

GUILDENSTERN.   What should we say, my lord?

HAMLET.   Why anything—but to th' purpose. You were sent for, and there is a 260 kind of confession in your looks, which your modesties have not craft enough to color. I know the good King and Queen have sent for you.

ROSENCRANTZ.   To what end, my lord?

HAMLET.   That you must teach me. But let me conjure you by the rights of our fellowship, by the consonancy of our youth, by the obligation of our ever- 265 preserved love, and by what more dear a better proposer can charge you withal, be even and direct with me, whether you were sent for or no.

ROSENCRANTZ.   [*Aside to* GUILDENSTERN]   What say you?

HAMLET.   [*Aside*]   Nay then, I have an eye of you.—If you love me, hold not off.

GUILDENSTERN.   My lord, we were sent for. 270

HAMLET.   I will tell you why; so shall my anticipation prevent your discovery,° and your secrecy to the King and Queen molt no feather. I have of late, but wherefore I know not, lost all my mirth, forgone all custom of exercises; and indeed, it goes so heavily with my disposition that this goodly frame, the earth, seems to me a sterile promontory; this most excellent canopy, the air, 275 look you, this brave o'erhanging firmament, this majestical roof fretted° with golden fire: why, it appeareth nothing to me but a foul and pestilent con- gregation of vapors. What a piece of work is a man, how noble in reason, how infinite in faculties, in form and moving how express° and admirable, in action how like an angel, in apprehension how like a god: the beauty of the world, 280 the paragon of animals; and yet to me, what is this quintessence of dust? Man delights not me; nor woman neither, though by your smiling you seem to say so.

ROSENCRANTZ.   My lord, there was no such stuff in my thoughts.

HAMLET.   Why did ye laugh then, when I said "Man delights not me"? 285

ROSENCRANTZ.   To think my lord, if you delight not in man, what lenten° enter- tainment the players shall receive from you. We coted° them on the way, and hither are they coming to offer you service.

HAMLET.   He that plays the king shall be welcome; his Majesty shall have tribute of me; the adventurous knight shall use his foil and target;° the lover shall not 290 sigh gratis; the humorous man° shall end his part in peace; the clown shall

---

256. *too dear a halfpenny:* i.e., nor worth a halfpenny.   271. *prevent your discovery:* forestall your disclosure.   276. *fretted:* adorned.   279. *express:* exact.   286. *lenten:* meager.   287. *coted:* overtook.   290. *target:* shield.   291. *humorous man:* i.e., eccentric man (among stock characters in dramas were men dominated by a "humor" or odd trait).

make those laugh whose lungs are tickle o' th' sere;° and the lady shall say her mind freely, or° the blank verse shall halt° for't. What players are they?

ROSENCRANTZ.   Even those you were wont to take such delight in, the tragedians of the city. 295

HAMLET.   How chances it they travel? Their residence, both in reputation and profit, was better both ways.

ROSENCRANTZ.   I think their inhibition° comes by the means of the late innovation.°

HAMLET.   Do they hold the same estimation they did when I was in the city? Are they so followed? 300

ROSENCRANTZ.   No indeed, are they not.

HAMLET.   How comes it? Do they grow rusty?

ROSENCRANTZ.   Nay, their endeavor keeps in the wonted pace, but there is, sir, an eyrie° of children, little eyases, that cry out on the top of question° and are most tyrannically° clapped for't. These are now the fashion, and so berattle the 305 common stages° (so they call them) that many wearing rapiers are afraid of goosequills° and dare scarce come thither.

HAMLET.   What, are they children? Who maintains 'em? How are they escoted?° Will they pursue the quality° no longer than they can sing? Will they not say afterwards, if they should grow themselves to common players (as it is most 310 like, if their means are no better), their writers do them wrong to make them exclaim against their own succession?°

ROSENCRANTZ.   Faith, there has been much to-do on both sides, and the nation holds it no sin to tarre° them to controversy. There was, for a while, no money bid for argument° unless the poet and the player went to cuffs in the question. 315

HAMLET.   Is't possible?

GUILDENSTERN.   O, there has been much throwing about of brains.

HAMLET.   Do the boys carry it away?

ROSENCRANTZ.   Ay, that they do, my lord—Hercules and his load° too.

HAMLET.   It is not very strange, for my uncle is King of Denmark, and those that 320 would make mouths at him while my father lived give twenty, forty, fifty, a hundred ducats apiece for his picture in little. 'Sblood,° there is something in this more than natural, if philosophy could find it out.   *A flourish.*

GUILDENSTERN.   There are the players.

HAMLET.   Gentlemen, you are welcome to Elsinore. Your hands, come then. Th' 325 appurtenance of welcome is fashion and ceremony. Let me comply° with you

---

292. *tickle o' th' sere:* on hair trigger (*sere* = part of the gunlock).   293. *or:* else.   293. *halt:* limp. 298. *inhibition:* hindrance.   298. *innovation:* (probably an allusion to the companies of child actors that had become popular and were offering serious competition to the adult actors).   304. *eyrie:* nest. 304. *eyases, that...of question:* unfledged hawks that cry shrilly above others in matters of debate. 305. *tyrannically:* violently.   305–306. *berattle the common stages:* cry down the public theaters (with the adult acting companies).   307. *goosequills:* pens (of satirists who ridicule the public theaters and their audiences).   308. *escoted:* financially supported.   309. *quality:* profession of acting. 312. *succession:* future.   314. *tarre:* incite.   315. *argument:* plot of a play.   319. *Hercules and his load:* i.e., the whole world (with a reference to the Globe Theatre, which had a sign that represented Hercules bearing the globe).   322. *'Sblood:* by God's blood.   326. *comply:* be courteous.

in this garb,° lest my extent° to the players (which I tell you must show fairly
outwards) should more appear like entertainment than yours. You are welcome. But my uncle-father and aunt-mother are deceived.

GUILDENSTERN.   In what, my dear lord?   330

HAMLET.   I am but mad north-northwest:° when the wind is southerly I know a
hawk from a handsaw.°

     Enter POLONIUS.

POLONIUS.   Well be with you, gentlemen.

HAMLET.   Hark you, Guildenstern, and you too; at each ear a hearer. That great
baby you see there is not yet out of his swaddling clouts.   335

ROSENCRANTZ.   Happily° he is the second time come to them, for they say an old
man is twice a child.

HAMLET.   I will prophesy he comes to tell me of the players. Mark it.—You say
right, sir; a Monday morning, 'twas then indeed.

POLONIUS.   My lord, I have news to tell you.   340

HAMLET.   My lord, I have news to tell you. When Roscius° was an actor in Rome——

POLONIUS.   The actors are come hither, my lord.

HAMLET.   Buzz, buzz.°

POLONIUS.   Upon my honor——

HAMLET.   Then came each actor on his ass——   345

POLONIUS.   The best actors in the world, either for tragedy, comedy, history, pastoral, pastoral-comical, historical-pastoral, tragical-historical, tragical-comical-
historical-pastoral; scene individable,° or poem unlimited.° Seneca° cannot be
too heavy, nor Plautus° too light. For the law of writ and the liberty,° these are   350
the only men.

HAMLET.   O Jeptha, judge of Israel,° what a treasure hadst thou!

POLONIUS.   What a treasure had he, my lord?

HAMLET.   Why,

     "One fair daughter, and no more,
       The which he lovèd passing well."   355

POLONIUS.   [*Aside*]   Still on my daughter.

HAMLET.   Am I not i' th' right, old Jeptha?

POLONIUS.   If you call me Jeptha, my lord, I have a daughter that I love passing well.

---

327. *garb:* outward show.   327. *extent:* behavior.   331. *north-northwest:* i.e., on one point of
the compass only.   332. *hawk from a handsaw (hawk* can refer not only to a bird but to a kind of
pickax; *handsaw*—a carpenter's tool—may involve a similar pun on "hernshaw," a heron).
336. *Happily:* perhaps.   341. *Roscius:* (a famous Roman comic actor).   343. *Buzz, buzz:* (an interjection, perhaps indicating that the news is old).   348. *scene individable:* plays observing the unities of
time, place, and action.   348. *poem unlimited:* plays not restricted by the tenets of criticism.
348. *Seneca:* (Roman tragic dramatist).   349. *Plautus:* (Roman comic dramatist).   349. *For the law
of writ and liberty:* (perhaps "for sticking to the text and for improvising"; perhaps "for classical plays
and for modern loosely written plays").   351. *Jeptha, judge of Israel:* (the title of a ballad on the
Hebrew judge who sacrificed his daughter; see Judges 11).

HAMLET.   Nay, that follows not.

POLONIUS.   What follows, then, my lord?   360

HAMLET.   Why,

"As by lot, God wot,"

and then, you know,

"It came to pass, as most like it was."

The first row of the pious chanson° will show you   365

more, for look where my abridgment° comes.

Enter the PLAYERS.

You are welcome, masters, welcome, all. I am glad to see thee well. Welcome,
good friend. O, old friend, why, they face is valanced° since I saw thee last.
Com'st thou to beard me in Denmark? What, my young lady° and mistress?
By'r Lady, your ladyship is nearer to heaven than when I saw you last by the   370
altitude of a chopine.° Pray God your voice, like a piece of uncurrent gold, be
not cracked within the ring.°—Masters, you are all welcome. We'll e'en to't
like French falconers, fly at anything we see. We'll have a speech straight.
Come, give us a taste of your quality. Come, a passionate speech.

PLAYER.   What speech, my good lord?   375

HAMLET.   I heard thee speak me a speech once, but it was never acted, or if it was,
not above once, for the play, I remember, pleased not the million; 'twas caviary
to the general,° but it was (as I received it, and others, whose judgments in such
matters cried in the top of° mine) an excellent play, well digested in the scenes,
set down with as much modesty as cunning.° I remember one said there were   380
no sallets° in the lines to make the matter savory; nor no matter in the phrase
that might indict the author of affectation, but called it an honest method, as
wholesome as sweet, and by very much more handsome than fine.° One speech
in't I chiefly loved. 'Twas Aeneas' tale to Dido, and thereabout of it especially
when he speaks of Priam's slaughter. If it live in your memory, begin at this   385
line—let me see, let me see:

"The rugged Pyrrhus, like th' Hyrcanian
    beast°——"

'Tis not so; it begins with Pyrrhus:

"The rugged Pyrrhus, he whose sable° arms,
Black as his purpose, did the night resemble   390
When he lay couchèd in th' ominous horse,°
Hath now this dread and black complexion smeared

365. *row of the pious chanson:* stanza of the scriptural song.   366. *abridgment:* (1) i.e., entertainers,
who abridge the time, (2) interrupters.   368. *valanced:* fringed (with a beard).   369. *young lady:* i.e.,
boy for female roles.   371. *chopine:* thick-soled shoe.   371–372. *like a piece…the ring:* (a coin was
unfit for legal tender if a crack extended from the edge through the ring enclosing the monarch's head.
Hamlet, punning on *ring,* refers to the change of voice that the boy actor will undergo).
377–378. *caviary to the general:* i.e., too choice for the multitude.   379. *in the top of:* overtopping.
380. *modesty as cunning:* restraint as art.   381. *sallets:* salads, spicy jests.   383. *more handsome than
fine:* well-proportioned rather than ornamented.   387. *Hyrcanian beast:* i.e., tiger (Hyrcania was in
Asia).   389. *sable:* black.   391. *ominous horse:* i.e., wooden horse at the siege of Troy.

With heraldry more dismal.° Head to foot
Now is he total gules, horridly tricked°
With blood of father, mothers, daughters, sons,   395
Baked and impasted° with the parching streets,
Than lend a tyrannous and a damnèd light
To their lord's murder. Roasted in wrath and fire,
And thus o'ersizèd° with coagulate gore,
With eyes like carbuncles, the hellish Pyrrhus   400
Old grandsire Priam seeks."
So, proceed you.

POLONIUS.   Fore God, my lord, well spoken, with good accent and good discretion.

PLAYER.   "Anon he finds him,
Striking too short at Greeks. His antique sword,   405
Rebellious to his arm, lies where it falls,
Repugnant to command.° Unequal matched,
Pyrrhus at Priam drives, in rage strikes wide,
But with the whiff and wind of his fell sword
Th' unnervèd father falls. Then senseless Ilium,°   410
Seeming to feel this blow, with flaming top
Stoops to his base,° and with a hideous crash
Takes prisoner Pyrrhus' ear. For lo, his sword,
Which was declining on the milky head
Of reverend Priam, seemed i' th' air to stick.   415
So as a painted tyrant° Pyrrhus stood,
And like a neutral to his will and matter°
Did nothing.
But as we often see, against° some storm,
A silence in the heavens, the rack° stand still,   420
The bold winds speechless, and the orb below
As hush as death, anon the dreadful thunder
Doth rend the region, so after Pyrrhus' pause,
A rousèd vengeance sets him new awork,
And never did the Cyclops' hammers fall   425
On Mars's armor, forged for proof eterne,°
With less remorse than Pyrrhus' bleeding sword
Now falls on Priam.
Out, out, thou strumpet Fortune! All you gods,
In general synod° take away her power,   430
Break all the spokes and fellies° from her wheel,

---

393. *dismal:* ill-omened.   394. *total gules, horridly tricked:* all red, horridly adorned.
396. *impasted:* encrusted.   399. *o'ersizèd:* smeared over.   407. *Repugnant to command:* disobedient.
410. *senseless Ilium:* insensate Troy.   412. *Stoops to his base:* collapses (*his* = its).
416. *painted tyrant:* tyrant in a picture.   417. *matter:* task.   419. *against:* just before.
420. *rack:* clouds.   426. *proof eterne:* eternal endurance.   430. *synod:* council.   431. *fellies:* rims.

And bowl the round nave° down the hill of heaven,
　As low as to the fiends."
POLONIUS.　This is too long.
HAMLET.　It shall to the barber's, with your beard.— Prithee say on. He's for a jig 435
　or a tale of bawdry, or he sleeps. Say on; come to Hecuba.
PLAYER.　"But who (ah woe!) had seen the mobled° queen——"
HAMLET.　"The mobled queen"?
POLONIUS.　That's good. "Mobled queen" is good.
PLAYER.　"Run barefoot up and down, threat'ning the flames 440
　With bisson rheum;° a clout° upon that head
　Where late the diadem stood, and for a robe,
　About her lank and all o'erteemèd° loins,
　A blanket in the alarm of fear caught up—
　Who this had seen, with tongue in venom steeped 445
　'Gainst Fortune's state would treason have pronounced.
　But if the gods themselves did see her then,
　When she saw Pyrrhus make malicious sport
　In mincing with his sword her husband's limbs,
　The instant burst of clamor that she made 450
　(Unless things mortal move then not at all)
　Would have made milch° the burning eyes of heaven
　And passion in the gods."
POLONIUS.　Look, whe'r° he has not turned his color, and has tears in's eyes.
　Prithee no more. 455
HAMLET.　'Tis well, I'll have thee speak out the rest of this soon. Good my lord, will
　you see the players well bestowed?° Do you hear? Let them be well used, for
　they are the abstract and brief chronicles of the time. After your death you were
　better have a bad epitaph than their ill report while you live.
POLONIUS.　My lord, I will use them according to their desert. 460
HAMLET.　God's bodkin,° man, much better! Use every man after his desert, and
　who shall scape whipping? Use them after your own honor and dignity. The
　less they deserve, the more merit is in your bounty. Take them in.
POLONIUS.　Come, sirs.
HAMLET.　Follow him, friends. We'll hear a play tomorrow. [*Aside to* PLAYER] 465
　Dost thou hear me, old friend? Can you play *The Murder of Gonzago*?
PLAYER.　Ay, my lord.
HAMLET.　We'll ha't tomorrow night. You could for a need study a speech of some
　dozen or sixteen lines which I would set down and insert in't, could you not?
PLAYER.　Ay, my lord. 470

---

432. *nave:* hub.　437. *mobled:* muffled.　441. *bisson rheum:* blinding tears.　441. *clout:* rag.
443. *o'erteemèd:* exhausted with childbearing.　452. *milch:* moist (literally, "milk-giving").
454. *whe'r:* whether.　457. *bestowed:* housed.　461. *God's bodkin:* by God's little body.

HAMLET.   Very well. Follow that lord, and look you mock him not. My good friends,
I'll leave you till night. You are welcome to Elsinore.   *Exeunt* POLONIUS *and*
PLAYERS.
ROSENCRANTZ.   Good my lord.   *Exeunt* ROSENCRANTZ *and* GUILDENSTERN.
HAMLET.   Ay, so, God bye to you.—Now I am alone.

O, what a rogue and peasant slave am I!   475
Is it not monstrous that this player here,
But in a fiction, in a dream of passion,°
Could force his soul so to his own conceit°
That from her working all his visage wanned,
Tears in his eyes, distraction in his aspect,   480
A broken voice, and his whole function° suiting
With forms° to his conceit? And all for nothing!
For Hecuba!
What's Hecuba to him, or he to Hecuba,
That he should weep for her? What would he do   485
Had he the motive and the cue for passion
That I have? He would drown the stage with tears
And cleave the general ear with horrid speech,
Make mad the guilty and appall the free,°
Confound the ignorant, and amaze indeed   490
The very faculties of eyes and ears.
Yet I,
A dull and muddy-mettled° rascal, peak
Like John-a-dreams,° unpregnant of° my cause,
And can say nothing. No, not for a king,   495
Upon whose property and most dear life
A damned defeat was made. Am I a coward?
Who calls me villain? Breaks my pate across?
Plucks off my beard and blows it in my face?
Tweaks me by the nose? Gives me the lie i' th' throat   500
As deep as to the lungs? Who does me this?
Ha, 'swounds,° I should take it, for it cannot be
But I am pigeon-livered° and lack gall
To make oppression bitter, or ere this
I should ha' fatted all the region kites°   505
With this slave's offal. Bloody, bawdy villain!
Remorseless, treacherous, lecherous, kindless° villain!
O, vengeance!
Why, what an ass am I! This is most brave,°

---

477. *dream of passion:* imaginary emotion.   478. *conceit:* imagination.   481. *function:* action.
482. *forms:* bodily expressions.   489. *appall the free:* terrify (make pale?) the guiltless.   493. *muddy-mettled:* weak-spirited.   493–494. *peak/Like John-a-dreams:* mope like a dreamer.   495. *unpregnant of:* unquickened by.   502. *'swounds:* by God's wounds.   503. *pigeon-livered:* gentle as a dove.
505. *region kites:* kites (scavenger birds) of the sky.   507. *kindless:* unnatural.   509. *brave:* fine.

That I, the son of a dear father murdered,   510
Prompted to my revenge by heaven and hell,
Must, like a whore, unpack my heart with words
And fall a-cursing like a very drab,°
A stallion!° Fie upon 't, foh! About,° my brains.
Hum——   515
I have heard that guilty creatures sitting at a play
Have by the very cunning of the scene
Been struck so to the soul that presently°
They have proclaimed their malefactions.
For murder, though it have no tongue, will speak   520
With most miraculous organ. I'll have these players
Play something like the murder of my father
Before mine uncle. I'll observe his looks,
I'll tent° him to the quick. If 'a do blench,°
I know my course. The spirit that I have seen   525
May be a devil, and the devil hath power
T' assume a pleasing shape, yea, and perhaps
Out of my weakness and my melancholy,
As he is very potent with such spirits,
Abuses me to damn me. I'll have grounds   530
More relative° than this. The play's the thing
Wherein I'll catch the conscience of the King.   *Exit.*

ACT III

SCENE I.   *The castle.*

Enter KING, QUEEN, POLONIUS, OPHELIA, ROSENCRANTZ, GUILDENSTERN, LORDS.

KING.   And can you by no drift of conference°
  Get from him why he puts on this confusion,
  Grating so harshly all his days of quiet
  With turbulent and dangerous lunacy?
ROSENCRANTZ.   He does confess he feels himself distracted,   5
  But from what cause 'a will by no means speak.
GUILDENSTERN.   Nor do we find him forward to be sounded,°
  But with a crafty madness keeps aloof
  When we would bring him on to some confession
  Of his true state.
QUEEN.   Did he receive you well?   10

---

513. *drab:* prostitute.   514. *stallion:* male prostitute (perhaps one should adopt the Folio reading,
scullion = kitchen wrench).   514. *About:* to work.   518. *presently:* immediately.   524. *tent:* probe.
524. *blench:* flinch.   531. *relative:* (probably "pertinent," but possibly "able to be related plausibly").
SCENE I. 1. *drift of conference:* management of conversation.   7. *forward to be sounded:* willing to be
questioned.

ROSENCRANTZ.   Most like a gentleman.

GUILDENSTERN.   But with much forcing of his disposition.°

ROSENCRANTZ.   Niggard of question,° but of our demands
    Most free in his reply.

QUEEN.   Did you assay° him
    To any pastime?   15

ROSENCRANTZ.   Madam, it so fell out that certain players
    We o'erraught° on the way; of these we told him,
    And there did seem in him a kind of joy
    To hear of it. They are here about the court,
    And, as I think, they have already order   20
    This night to play before him.

POLONIUS.   'Tis most true,
    And he beseeched me to entreat your Majesties
    To hear and see the matter.

KING.   With all my heart, and it doth much content me
    To hear him so inclined.   25
    Good gentlemen, give him a further edge
    And drive his purpose into these delights.

ROSENCRANTZ.   We shall, my lord.   *Exeunt* ROSENCRANTZ *and* GUILDENSTERN.

KING.   Sweet Gertrude, leave us too,
    For we have closely° sent for Hamlet hither,
    That he, as 'twere by accident, may here   30
    Affront° Ophelia.
    Her father and myself (lawful espials°)
    Will so bestow ourselves that, seeing unseen,
    We may of their encounter frankly judge
    And gather by him, as he is behaved,   35
    If't be th' affliction of his love or no
    That thus he suffers for.

QUEEN.   I shall obey you.
    And for your part, Ophelia, I do wish
    That your good beauties be the happy cause
    Of Hamlet's wildness. So shall I hope your virtues   40
    Will bring him to his wonted way again,
    To both your honors.

OPHELIA.   Madam, I wish it may.   *Exit* QUEEN.

POLONIUS.   Ophelia, walk you here.—Gracious, so please you,
    We will bestow ourselves.   [*To* OPHELIA]   Read on this book,
    That show of such an exercise may color°   45
    Your loneliness. We are oft to blame in this,

---

12. *forcing of his disposition:* effort.   13. *Niggard of question:* uninclined to talk.   14. *assay:* tempt.
17. *o'erraught:* overtook.   29. *closely:* secretly.   31. *Affront:* meet face to face.   32. *espials:* spies.
45. *exercise may color:* act of devotion may give a plausible hue to (the book is one of devotion).

'Tis too much proved, that with devotion's visage
And pious action we do sugar o'er
The devil himself.
KING.   [*Aside*]   O, 'tis too true.
How smart a lash that speech doth give my conscience!   50
The harlot's cheek, beautied with plast'ring art,
Is not more ugly to the thing that helps it
Than is my deed to my most painted word.
O heavy burden!
POLONIUS.   I hear him coming. Let's withdraw, my lord.   *Exeunt* KING *and*   55
POLONIUS.

Enter HAMLET.

HAMLET.   To be, or not to be: that is the question:
Whether 'tis nobler in the mind to suffer
The slings and arrows of outrageous fortune,
Or to take arms against a sea of troubles,
And by opposing end them. To die, to sleep—   60
No more—and by a sleep to say we end
The heartache, and the thousand natural shocks
That flesh is heir to! 'Tis a consummation
Devoutly to be wished. To die, to sleep—
To sleep—perchance to dream: ay, there's the rub,°   65
For in that sleep of death what dreams may come
When we have shuffled off this mortal coil,°
Must give us pause. There's the respect°
That makes calamity of so long life:°
For who would bear the whips and scorns of time,   70
Th' oppressor's wrong, the proud man's contumely,
The pangs of despised love, the law's delay,
The insolence of office, and the spurns
That patient merit of th' unworthy takes,
When he himself might his quietus° make   75
With a bare bodkin?° Who would fardels° bear,
To grunt and swear under a weary life,
But that the dread of something after death,
The undiscovered country, from whose bourn°
No traveler returns, puzzles the will,   80
And makes us rather bear those ills we have,
Than fly to others that we know not of?

---

65. *rub:* impediment (obstruction to a bowler's ball).   67. *coil:* (1) turmoil, (2) a ring of rope (here the flesh encircling the soul).   68. *respect:* consideration.   69. *makes calamity of so long life:* (1) makes calamity so long-lived, (2) makes living so long a calamity.   75. *quietus:* full discharge (a legal term). 76. *bodkin:* dagger.   76. *fardels:* burdens.   79. *bourn:* region.

Thus conscience° does make cowards of us all,
And thus the native hue of resolution
Is sickled o'er with the pale cast° of thought,   85
And enterprises of great pitch° and moment,
With this regard° their current turn awry,
And lose the name of action.—Soft you now,
The fair Ophelia!—Nymph, in thy orisons°
Be all my sins remembered.

OPHELIA.   Good my lord,   90
How does your honor for this many a day?

HAMLET. I humbly thank you; well, well, well.

OPHELIA. My lord, I have remembrances of yours
That I have longèd long to redeliver.
I pray you now, receive them.

HAMLET.   No, not I.   95
I never gave you aught.

OPHELIA. My honored lord, you know right well you did,
And with them words of so sweet breath composed
As made these things more rich. Their perfume lost,
Take these again, for to the noble mind   100
Rich gifts wax poor when givers prove unkind.
There, my lord.

HAMLET. Ha, ha! Are you honest?°

OPHELIA. My lord?

HAMLET. Are you fair?   105

OPHELIA. What means your lordship?

HAMLET. That if you be honest and fair, your honesty should admit no discourse
to your beauty.°

OPHELIA. Could beauty, my lord, have better commerce than with honesty?

HAMLET. Ay, truly; for the power of beauty will sooner transform honesty from what 110
it is to a bawd° than the force of honesty can translate beauty into his likeness.
This was sometime a paradox, but now the time gives it proof. I did love you
once.

OPHELIA. Indeed, my lord, you made me believe so.

HAMLET. You should not have believed me, for virtue cannot so inoculate° our 115
old stock but we shall relish of it.° I loved you not.

OPHELIA. I was the more deceived.

HAMLET. Get thee to a nunnery. Why wouldst thou be a breeder of sinners? I am
myself indifferent honest,° but yet I could accuse me of such things that it were
better my mother had not borne me: I am very proud, revengeful, ambitious, 120

---

83. *conscience:* self-consciousness, introspection. 85. *cast:* color. 86. *pitch:* height (a term from
falconry). 87. *regard:* consideration. 89. *orisons:* prayers. 103. *Are you honest:* (1) are you modest, (2) are you chaste, (3) have you integrity. 107–108. *your honesty…to your beauty:* your modesty
should permit no approach to your beauty. 111. *bawd:* procurer. 115. *inoculate:* graft.
116. *relish of it:* smack of it (our old sinful nature). 119. *indifferent honest:* moderately virtuous.

with more offenses at my beck° than I have thoughts to put them in, imagination to give them shape, or time to act them in. What should such fellows as I do crawling between earth and heaven? We are arrant knaves all; believe none of us. Go thy ways to a nunnery. Where's your father?

OPHELIA. At home, my lord. 125

HAMLET. Let the doors be shut upon him, that he may play the fool nowhere but in's own house. Farewell.

OPHELIA. O help him, you sweet heavens!

HAMLET. If thou dost marry, I'll give thee this plague for thy dowry: be thou as chaste as ice, as pure as snow, thou shalt not escape calumny. Get thee to a 130 nunnery. Go, farewell. Or if thou wilt needs marry, marry a fool, for wise men know well enough what monsters° you make of them. To a nunnery, go, and quickly too. Farewell.

OPHELIA. Heavenly powers, restore him!

HAMLET. I have heard of your paintings, well enough. God hath given you one 135 face, and you make yourselves another. You jig and amble, and you lisp; you nickname God's creatures and make your wantonness your ignorance.° Go to, I'll no more on't; it hath made me mad. I say we will have no moe° marriage. Those that are married already—all but one—shall live. The rest shall keep as they are. To a nunnery, go. *Exit.* 140

OPHELIA. O what a noble mind is here o'erthrown!
The courtier's, soldier's, scholar's, eye, tongue, sword,
Th' expectancy and rose° of the fair state,
The glass of fashion, and the mold of form,°
Th' observed of all observers, quite, quite down! 145
And I, of ladies most deject and wretched,
That sucked the honey of his musicked vows,
Now see that noble and most sovereign reason
Like sweet bells jangled, out of time and harsh,
That unmatched form and feature of blown° youth 150
Blasted with ecstasy.° O, woe is me
T' have seen what I have seen, see what I see!

Enter KING *and* POLONIUS.

KING. Love? His affections° do not that way tend,
Nor what he spake, though it lacked form a little,
Was not like madness. There's something in his soul 155
O'er which his melancholy sits on brood,
And I do doubt° the hatch and the disclose
Will be some danger; which for to prevent,

---

121. *beck:* call. 132. *monsters:* horned beasts, cuckolds. 137. *make your wantonness your ignorance:* excuse your wanton speech by pretending ignorance. 138. *moe:* more. 143. *expectancy and rose:* i.e., fair hope. 144. *The glass...of form:* the mirror of fashion, and the pattern of excellent behavior. 150. *blown:* blooming. 151. *ecstasy:* madness. 153. *affections:* inclinations. 157. *doubt:* fear.

I have in quick determination
Thus set it down: he shall with speed to England   160
For the demand of our neglected tribute.
Haply the seas, and countries different,
With variable objects, shall expel
This something-settled° matter in his heart,
Whereon his brains still beating puts him thus   165
From fashion of himself. What think you on't?
POLONIUS.   It shall do well. But yet do I believe
  The origin and commencement of his grief
  Sprung from neglected love. How now, Ophelia?
  You need not tell us what Lord Hamlet said;   170
  We heard it all. My lord, do as you please,
  But if you hold it fit, after the play,
  Let his queen mother all alone entreat him
  To show his grief. Let her be round° with him,
  And I'll be placed, so please you, in the ear   175
  Of all their conference. If she find him not,°
  To England send him, or confine him where
  Your wisdom best shall think.
KING.   It shall be so.
  Madness in great ones must not unwatched go.   *Exeunt.*

SCENE II.   *The castle.*

Enter HAMLET *and three of the* PLAYERS.

HAMLET.   Speak the speech, I pray you, as I pronounced it to you, trippingly on the
  tongue. But if you mouth it, as many of our players do, I had as lief the town
  crier spoke my lines. Nor do not saw the air too much with your hand, thus, but
  use all gently, for in the very torrent, tempest, and (as I may say) whirlwind of   5
  your passion, you must acquire and beget a temperance that may give it
  smoothness. O, it offends me to the soul to hear a robustious periwig-pated°
  fellow tear a passion to tatters, to very rags, to split the ears of the groundlings,°
  who for the most part are capable of° nothing but inexplicable dumb shows°
  and noise. I would have such a fellow whipped for o'erdoing Termagant. It
  out-herods Herod.° Pray you avoid it.   10
PLAYER.   I warrant your honor.
HAMLET.   Be not too tame neither, but let your own discretion be your tutor. Suit
  the action to the word, the word to the action, with this special observance,

164. *something-settled:* somewhat settled.   174. *round:* blunt.   176. *find him not:* does not find him
out.   SCENE II. 6. *robustious periwig-pated:* boisterous wig-headed.   7. *groundlings:* those who
stood in the pit of the theater (the poorest and presumably most ignorant of the audience).
8. *are capable of:* are able to understand.   8. *dumb shows:* (it had been the fashion for actors to preface
plays or parts of plays with silent mime).   9–10. *Termagant…Herod:* (boisterous characters in the old
mystery plays).

that you o'erstep not the modesty of nature. For anything so o'erdone is from°
the purpose of playing, whose end, both at the first and now, was and is, to 15
hold, as 'twere, the mirror up to nature; to show virtue her own feature, scorn
her own image, and the very age and body of the time his form and pressure.°
Now, this overdone, or come tardy off, though it makes the unskillful laugh,
cannot but make the judicious grieve, the censure of the which one must in
your allowance o'erweigh a whole theater of others. O, there be players that I 20
have seen play, and heard others praise, and that highly (not to speak it pro-
fanely), that neither having th' accent of Christians, nor the gait of Christian,
pagan, nor man, have so strutted and bellowed that I have thought some of
Nature's journeymen° had made men, and not made them well, they imitated
humanity so abominably. 25

PLAYER. I hope we have reformed that indifferently° with us, sir.

HAMLET. O, reform it altogether! And let those that play your clowns speak no more
than is set down for them, for there be of them that will themselves laugh, to
set on some quantity of barren spectators to laugh too, though in the meantime
some necessary question of the play be then to be considered. That's villainous 30
and shows a most pitiful ambition in the fool that uses it. Go make you ready.
Exit Players.

Enter POLONIUS, GUILDENSTERN, *and* ROSENCRANTZ.

How now, my lord? Will the King hear this piece of work?

POLONIUS. And the Queen too, and that presently.

HAMLET. Bid the players make haste. *Exit* POLONIUS.

Will you two help to hasten them? 35

ROSENCRANTZ.
GUILDENSTERN. } Ay, my lord. *Exeunt they two.*

HAMLET. What, ho, Horatio!

Enter HORATIO.

HORATIO. Here, sweet lord, at your service.

HAMLET. Horatio, thou art e'en as just a man
As e'er my conversation coped withal.° 40

HORATIO. O, my dear lord——

HAMLET.   Nay, do you think I flatter.
For what advancement° may I hope from thee,
That no revenue hast but thy good spirits
To feed and clothe thee? Why should the poor be flattered?
No, let the candied° tongue lick absurd pomp, 45
And crook the pregnant° hinges of the knee
Where thrift° may follow fawning. Dost thou hear?

14. *from:* contrary to.   17. *pressure:* image, impress.   24. *journeymen:* workers not yet masters of
their craft.   26. *indifferently:* tolerably.   40. *coped withal:* met with.   42. *advancement:* promotion.
45. *candied:* sugared, flattering.   46. *pregnant:* (1) pliant, (2) full of promise of good fortune.
47. *thrift:* profit.

Since my dear soul was mistress of her choice
And could of men distinguish her election,
S' hath sealed thee° for herself, for thou hast been   50
As one, in suff'ring all, that suffers nothing,
A man that Fortune's buffets and rewards
Hast ta'en with equal thanks; and blest are those
Whose blood° and judgment are so well commeddled°
That they are not a pipe for Fortune's finger   55
To sound what stop she please. Give me that man
That is not passions' slave, and I will wear him
In my heart's core, ay, in my heart of heart,
As I do thee. Something too much of this—
There is a play tonight before the King.   60
One scene of it comes near the circumstance
Which I have told thee, of my father's death.
I prithee, when thou seest that act afoot,
Even with the very comment° of thy soul
Observe my uncle. If his occulted° guilt   65
Do not itself unkennel in one speech,
It is a damnèd ghost that we have seen,
And my imaginations are as foul
As Vulcan's stithy.° Give him heedful note,
For I mine eyes will rivet to his face,   70
And after we will both our judgments join
In censure of his seeming.°
HORATIO.   Well, my lord.
  If 'a steal aught the whilst this play is playing,
  And scape detecting, I will pay the theft.

Enter Trumpets and Kettledrums, KING, QUEEN, POLONIUS, OPHELIA, ROSENCRANTZ,
     GUILDENSTERN, *and other* LORDS *attendant with his Guard carrying torches.*
                     Danish March. Sound a Flourish.

HAMLET.   They are coming to the play: I must be idle;° Get you a place.   75
KING.   How fares our cousin Hamlet?
HAMLET.   Excellent, i' faith, of the chameleon's dish;° I eat the air, promise-
     crammed; you cannot feed capons so.
KING.   I have nothing with this answer, Hamlet; these words are not mine.
HAMLET.   No, nor mine now.   [*To* POLONIUS]   My lord, you played once i' th' 80
     university, you say?
POLONIUS.   That did I, my lord, and was accounted a good actor.

---

50. *S'hath sealed thee:* she (the soul) has set a mark on you.   54. *blood:* passion.   54. *commeddled:*
blended.   64. *very comment:* deepest wisdom.   65. *occulted:* hidden.   69. *stithy:* forge, smithy.
72. *censure of his seeming:* judgment on his looks.   75. *be idle:* play the fool.
77. *the chameleon's dish:* air (on which chameleons were thought to live).

HAMLET.   What did you enact?
POLONIUS.   I did enact Julius Caesar. I was killed i' th' Capitol; Brutus killed me.
HAMLET.   It was a brute part of him to kill so capital a calf there. Be the players ready?   85
ROSENCRANTZ.   Ay, my lord they stay upon your patience.
QUEEN.   Come hither, my dear Hamlet, sit by me.
HAMLET.   No, good mother. Here's metal more attractive.°
POLONIUS.   [*To the* KING]   O ho! Do you mark that?
HAMLET.   Lady, shall I lie in your lap?   90

He lies at OPHELIA*'s feet.*

OPHELIA.   No, my lord.
HAMLET.   I mean, my head upon your lap?
OPHELIA.   Ay, my lord.
HAMLET.   Do you think I meant country matters?°
OPHELIA.   I think nothing, my lord.   95
HAMLET.   That's a fair thought to lie between maids' legs.
OPHELIA.   What is, my lord?
HAMLET.   Nothing.
OPHELIA.   You are merry, my lord.
HAMLET.   Who, I?   100
OPHELIA.   Ay, my lord.
HAMLET.   O God, your only jig-maker!° What should a man do but be merry? For
   look you how cheerfully my mother looks, and my father died within's two
   hours.
OPHELIA.   Nay, 'tis twice two months, my lord.   105
HAMLET.   So long? Nay then, let the devil wear black, for I'll have a suit of sables.°
   O heavens! Die two months ago, and not forgotten yet? Then there's hope a
   great man's memory may outlive his life half a year. But, by'r Lady, 'a must
   build churches then, or else shall 'a suffer not thinking on, with the hobby-
   horse,° whose epitaph is "For O, for O, the hobby-horse is forgot!"   110

The trumpets sound. Dumb show follows:

*Enter a King and a Queen very lovingly, the Queen embracing him, and
he her. She kneels; and makes show of protestation unto him. He takes her
up, and declines his head upon her neck. He lies him down upon a bank of
flowers. She, seeing him asleep, leaves him. Anon comes in another man:
takes off his crown, kisses it, pours poison in the sleeper's ears, and leaves
him. The Queen returns, finds the King dead, makes passionate action.
The poisoner, with some three or four, come in again, seem to condole with*

---

88. *attractive:* magnetic.   94. *country matters:* rustic doings (with a pun on the vulgar word for the
pudendum).   102. *jig-maker:* composer of songs and dances (often a Fool, who performed them).
106. *sables:* (pun on "black" and "luxurious furs").   109–110. *hobby-horse:* mock horse worn by a performer in the morris dance.

> *her. The dead body is carried away. The poisoner woos the Queen with gifts;*
> *she seems harsh awhile, but in the end accepts love.* [*Exeunt.*]

OPHELIA. What means this, my lord?
HAMLET. Marry, this is miching mallecho;° it means mischief.
OPHELIA. Belike this show imports the argument° of the play.

Enter PROLOGUE.

HAMLET. We shall know by this fellow. The players cannot keep counsel; they'll
    tell all.   115
OPHELIA. Will 'a tell us what this show meant?
HAMLET. Ay, or any show that you will show him. Be not you ashamed to show,
    he'll not shame to tell you what it means.
OPHELIA. You are naught,° you are naught; I'll mark the
    play.   120
PROLOGUE. For us, and for our tragedy,
    Here stooping to your clemency,
    We beg your hearing patiently. [*Exit.*]
HAMLET. Is this a prologue, or the posy of a ring?°
OPHELIA. 'Tis brief, my lord.   125
HAMLET. As a woman's love.

Enter [*two* PLAYERS *as*] KING *and* QUEEN.

PLAYER KING. Full thirty times hath Phoebus' cart° gone round
    Neptune's salt wash° and Tellus'° orbèd ground,
    And thirty dozen moons with borrowed sheen
    About the world have times twelve thirties been,   130
    Since love our hearts, and Hymen did our hands,
    Unite commutual in most sacred bands.
PLAYER QUEEN. So many journeys may the sun and moon
    Make us again count o'er ere love be done!
    But woe is me, you are so sick of late,   135
    So far from cheer and from your former state,
    That I distrust° you. Yet, though I distrust,
    Discomfort you, my lord, it nothing must.
    For women fear too much, even as they love,
    And women's fear and love hold quantity,   140
    In neither aught, or in extremity.°
    Now what my love is, proof° hath made you know,

---

112. *miching mallecho:* sneaking mischief.   113. *argument:* plot.   119. *naught:* wicked, improper.
124. *posy of a ring:* motto inscribed in a ring.   127. *Phoebus' cart:* the sun's chariot.   128. *Neptune's salt wash:* the sea.   128. *Tellus:* Roman goddess of the earth.   137. *distrust:* am anxious about.
140–141. *And women's...in extremity:* (perhaps the idea is that women's anxiety is great or little in proportion to their love. The previous line, unrhymed, may be a false start that Shakespeare neglected to delete).   142. *proof:* experience.

And as my love is sized, my fear is so.
Where love is great, the littlest doubts are fear;
Where little fears grow great, great love grows there. 145
PLAYER KING.   Faith, I must leave thee, love, and shortly too;
My operant° powers their functions leave to do:
And thou shalt live in this fair world behind,
Honored, beloved, and haply one as kind
For husband shalt thou—— 150
PLAYER QUEEN.   O, confound the rest!
Such love must needs be treason in my breast.
In second husband let me be accurst!
None wed the second but who killed the first.
HAMLET.   [*Aside*]   That's wormwood.°
PLAYER QUEEN.   The instances° that second marriage move° 155
Are base respects of thrift,° but none of love.
A second time I kill my husband dead
When second husband kisses me in bed.
PLAYER KING.   I do believe you think what now you speak,
But what we do determine oft we break. 160
Purpose is but the slave to memory,
Of violent birth, but poor validity,°
Which now like fruit unripe sticks on the tree,
But fall unshaken when they mellow be.
Most necessary 'tis that we forget 165
To pay ourselves what to ourselves is debt.
What to ourselves in passion we propose,
The passion ending, doth the purpose lose.
The violence of either grief or joy
Their own enactures° with themselves destroy; 170
Where joy most revels, grief doth most lament;
Grief joys, joy grieves, on slender accident.
This world is not for aye, nor 'tis not strange
That even our loves should with our fortunes change,
For tis a question left us yet to prove, 175
Whether love lead fortune, or else fortune love.
The great man down, you mark his favorite flies;
The poor advanced makes friends of enemies;
And hitherto doth love on fortune tend,
For who not needs shall never lack a friend; 180
And who in want a hollow friend doth try,
Directly seasons him° his enemy.

---

147. *operant:* active.   154. *wormwood:* a bitter herb.   155. *instances:* motives.   155. *move:* induce.
156. *respects of thrift:* considerations of profit.   162. *validity:* strength.   170. *enactures:* acts.
182. *season him:* ripens him into.

But, orderly to end where I begun,
Our wills and fates do so contrary run
That our devices still are overthrown;   185
Our thoughts are ours, their ends none of our own.
So think thou wilt no second husband wed,
But die thy thoughts when thy first lord is dead.
PLAYER QUEEN.   Nor earth to me give food, nor heaven light,
Sport and repose lock from me day and night,   190
To desperation turn my trust and hope,
An anchor's° cheer in prison be my scope,
Each opposite that blanks° the face of joy
Meet what I would have well, and it destroy:
Both here and hence pursue me lasting strife,   195
If, once a widow, ever I be wife!
HAMLET.   If she should break it now!
PLAYER KING.   'Tis deeply sworn. Sweet, leave me here awhile;
My spirits grow dull, and fain I would beguile
The tedious day with sleep.
PLAYER QUEEN.   Sleep rock thy brain,   [*He*] *sleeps.*   200
And never come mischance between us twain!   *Exit.*
HAMLET.   Madam, how like you this play?
QUEEN.   The lady doth protest too much, methinks.
HAMLET.   O, but she'll keep her word.
KING.   Have you heard the argument?° Is there no offense in't?   205
HAMLET.   No, no, they do but jest, poison in jest; no offense i' th' world.
KING.   What do you call the play?
HAMLET.   *The Mousetrap.* Marry, how? Tropically.° This play is the image of a murder
done in Vienna: Gonzago is the Duke's name; his wife, Baptista. You shall see
anon. 'Tis a knavish piece of work, but what of that? Your Majesty, and we that 210
have free° souls, it touches us not. Let the galled jade winch;° our withers are
unwrung.

Enter LUCIANUS.

This is one Lucianus, nephew to the King.
OPHELIA.   You are as good as a chorus, my lord.
HAMLET.   I could interpret° between you and your love, if I could see the puppets 215
dallying.
OPHELIA.   You are keen,° my lord, you are keen.
HAMLET.   It would cost you a groaning to take off mine edge.
OPHELIA.   Still better, and worse.

---

192. *anchor's:* anchorite's, hermit's.   193. *opposite that blanks:* adverse thing that blanches.
205. *argument:* plot.   208. *Tropically:* figuratively (with a pun on "trap").   211. *free:* innocent.
211. *galled jade winch:* chafed horse wince.   215. *interpret:* (like a showman explaining the action of
puppets).   217. *keen:* (1) sharp, (2) sexually aroused.

HAMLET.   So you mistake° your husbands.—Begin, murderer. Leave thy damnable   220
    faces and begin. Come, the croaking raven doth bellow for revenge.

LUCIANUS.   Thoughts black, hands apt, drugs fit, and
    time agreeing,
    Confederate season,° else no creature seeing,
    Thou mixture rank, of midnight weeds collected,   225
    With Hecate's ban° thrice blasted, thrice infected,
    Thy natural magic and dire property°
    On wholesome life usurps immediately.

Pours the poison in his ears.

HAMLET.   'A poisons him i' th' garden for his estate. His name's Gonzago. The story
    is extant, and written in very choice Italian. You shall see anon how the murderer   230
    gets the love of Gonzago's wife.

OPHELIA.   The King rises.

HAMLET.   What, frighted with false fire?°

QUEEN.   How fares my lord?

POLONIUS.   Give o'er the play.   235

KING.   Give me some light. Away!

POLONIUS.   Lights, lights, lights!   *Exeunt all but* HAMLET *and* HORATIO.

HAMLET.   Why, let the strucken deer go weep,
      The hart ungallèd play:
    For some must watch, while some must sleep;   240
      Thus runs the world away.
    Would not this, sir, and a forest of feathers°—if the rest of my fortunes turn
    Turk° with me—with two Provincial roses° on my razed° shoes, get me a fel-
    lowship in a cry° of players?

HORATIO.   Half a share.   245

HAMLET.   A whole one, I.
    For thou dost know, O Damon dear,
      This realm dismantled was
    Of Jove himself; and now reigns here
      A very, very—pajock.°   250

HORATIO.   You might have rhymed.°

HAMLET.   O good Horatio, I'll take the ghost's word for a thousand pound. Didst
    perceive.

HORATIO.   Very well, my lord.

HAMLET.   Upon the talk of poisoning?   255

---

220. *mistake:* err in taking.   224. *Confederate season:* the opportunity allied with me.
226. *Hecate's ban:* the curse of the goddess of sorcery.   227. *property:* nature.   233. *false fire:* blank
discharge of firearms.   242. *feathers:* (plumes were sometimes part of a costume).   242–243. *turn
Turk:* i.e., go bad, treat me badly.   243. *Provincial roses:* rosettes like the roses of Provence (?).
243. *razed:* ornamented with slashes.   244. *cry:* pack, company.   250. *pajock:* peacock.   251. *You
might have rhymed:* i.e., rhymed "was" with "ass."

HORATIO.   I did very well note him.

HAMLET.   Ah ha! Come, some music! Come, the recorders!°

    For if the King like not the comedy,

    Why then, belike he likes it not, perdy.°

  Come, some music!   260

Enter ROSENCRANTZ *and* GUILDENSTERN.

GUILDENSTERN.   Good my lord, vouchsafe me a word with you.

HAMLET.   Sir, a whole history.

GUILDENSTERN.   The King, sir——

HAMLET.   Ay, sir, what of him?

GUILDENSTERN.   Is in his retirement marvelous distemp'red.   265

HAMLET.   With drink, sir?

GUILDENSTERN.   No, my lord, with choler.°

HAMLET.   Your wisdom should show itself more richer to signify this to the doc-
    tor, for, for me to put him to his purgation would perhaps plunge him into
    more choler.   270

GUILDENSTERN.   Good my lord, put your discourse into some frame,° and start
    not so wildly from my affair.

HAMLET.   I am tame, sir; pronounce.

GUILDENSTERN.   The Queen, your mother, in most great affliction of spirit hath sent   275
    me to you.

HAMLET.   You are welcome.

GUILDENSTERN.   Nay, good my lord, this courtesy is not of the right breed. If it
    shall please you to make me a wholesome answer, I will do your mother's com-
    mandment: if not, your pardon and my return shall be the end of my business.

HAMLET.   Sir, I cannot.   280

ROSENCRANTZ.   What, my lord?

HAMLET.   Make you a wholesome° answer; my wit's diseased. But, sir, such answer
    as I can make, you shall command, or rather, as you say, my mother. Therefore
    no more, but to the matter. My mother, you say——

ROSENCRANTZ.   Then thus she says: your behavior hath struck her into amazement   285
    and admiration.°

HAMLET.   O wonderful son, that can so stonish a mother! But is there no sequel
    at the heels of this mother's admiration? Impart.

ROSENCRANTZ.   She desires to speak with you in her closet ere you go to bed.

HAMLET.   We shall obey, were she ten times our mother. Have you any further   290
    trade with us?

ROSENCRANTZ.   My lord, you once did love me.

HAMLET.   And do still, by these pickers and stealers.°

---

257. *recorders:* flutelike instruments.   259. *perdy:* by God (French: *par dieu*).   267. *choler:* anger
(but Hamlet pretends to take the word in its sense of "bilousness").   271. *frame:* order, control.
282. *wholesome:* sane.   286. *admiration:* wonder.   293. *pickers and stealers:* i.e., hands (with reference to the prayer; "Keep my hands from picking and stealing").

ROSENCRANTZ.   Good my lord, what is your cause of distemper? You do surely bar
the door upon your own liberty, if you deny your griefs to your friend.   295
HAMLET.   Sir, I lack advancement.°
ROSENCRANTZ.   How can that be, when you have the voice of the King himself for
your succession in Denmark?

Enter the PLAYERS *with recorders.*

HAMLET.   Ay, sir, but "while the grass grows"—the proverb° is something musty.
O, the recorders. Let me see one. To withdraw° with you—why do you go   300
about to recover the wind° of me as if you would drive me into a toil?°
GUILDENSTERN.   O my lord, if my duty be too bold, my love is too unmannerly.°
HAMLET.   I do not well understand that. Will you play upon this pipe?
GUILDENSTERN.   My lord, I cannot.
HAMLET.   I pray you.   305
GUILDENSTERN.   Believe me, I cannot.
HAMLET.   I pray you.
GUILDENSTERN.   Believe me, I cannot.
HAMLET.   I do beseech you.
GUILDENSTERN.   I know no touch of it, my lord.   310
HAMLET.   It is as easy as lying. Govern these ventages° with your fingers and
thumb, give it breath with your mouth, and it will discourse most eloquent
music. Look you, these are the stops.
GUILDENSTERN.   But these cannot I command to any utt'rance of harmony; I have
not the skill.   315
HAMLET.   Why, look you now, how unworthy a thing you make of me! You would
play upon me; you would seem to know my stops; you would pluck out the
heart of my mystery; you would sound me from my lowest note to the top of
my compass;° and there is much music, excellent voice, in this little organ,° yet
cannot you make it speak. 'Sblood, do you think I am easier to be played on   320
than a pipe? Call me what instrument you will, though you can fret° me, you
cannot play upon me.

Enter POLONIUS.

God bless you, sir!
POLONIUS.   My lord, the Queen would speak with you, and presently.
HAMLET.   Do you see yonder cloud that's almost in shape of a camel?   325
POLONIUS.   By th' mass and 'tis, like a camel indeed.
HAMLET.   Methinks it is like a weasel.
POLONIUS.   It is backed like a weasel.

296. *advancement:* promotion.   299. *proverb:* ("While the grass groweth, the horse starveth").
300. *withdraw:* speak in private.   301. *recover the wind:* get the windward side (as in hunting).
301. *toil:* snare.   302. *if my duty...too unmannerly:* i.e., if these questions seem rude, it is because my
love for you leads me beyond good manners.   311. *ventages:* vents, stops on a recorder.
319. *compass:* range of voice.   319. *organ:* i.e., the recorder.   321. *fret:* vex (with a pun alluding to
the frets, or ridges, that guide the fingering on some instruments).

HAMLET.   Or like a whale.

POLONIUS.   Very like a whale.   330

HAMLET.   Then I will come to my mother by and by.   [*Aside*]   They fool me to
the top of my bent.°—I will come by and by.°

POLONIUS.   I will say so.   *Exit.*

HAMLET.   "By and by" is easily said. Leave me, friends.   *Exeunt all but* HAMLET.
'Tis now the very witching time of night,   335
When churchyards yawn, and hell itself breathes out
Contagion to this world. Now could I drink hot blood
And do such bitter business as the day
Would quake to look on. Soft, now to my mother.
O heart, lose not thy nature; let not ever   340
The soul of Nero° enter this firm bosom.
Let me be cruel, not unnatural;
I will speak daggers to her, but use none.
My tongue and soul in this be hypocrites:
How in my words somever she be shent,°   345
To give them seals° never, my soul, consent!   *Exit.*

SCENE III.   The castle.

Enter KING, ROSENCRANTZ, and GUILDENSTERN.

KING.   I like him not, nor stands it safe with us
To let his madness range. Therefore prepare you.
I your commission will forthwith dispatch,
And he to England shall along with you.
The terms° of our estate may not endure   5
Hazard so near's° as doth hourly grow
Out of his brows.

GUILDENSTERN.   We will ourselves provide.
Most holy and religious fear it is
To keep those many many bodies safe
That live and feed upon your Majesty.   10

ROSENCRANTZ.   The single and peculiar° life is bound
With all the strength and armor of the mind
To keep itself from noyance,° but much more
That spirit upon whose weal depends and rests
The lives of many. The cess of majesty°   15
Dies not alone, but with a gulf° doth draw
What's near it with it; or it is a massy wheel

331–332. *They fool…my bent:* they compel me to play the fool to the limit of my capacity.   332. *by and by:* very soon.   341. *Nero:* (Roman emperor who had his mother murdered).   345. *shent:* rebuked.   346. *give them seals:* confirm them with deeds.   SCENE III. 5. *terms:* conditions.
6. *near's:* near us.   11. *peculiar:* individual, private.   13. *noyance:* injury.   15. *cess of majesty:* cessation (death) of a king.   16. *gulf:* whirlpool.

Fixed on the summit of the highest mount,
To whose huge spokes ten thousand lesser things
Are mortised and adjoined, which when it falls,   20
Each small annexment, petty consequence,
Attends° the boist'rous ruin. Never alone
Did the King sigh, but with a general groan.
KING.   Arm° you, I pray you, to this speedy voyage,
For we will fetters put about this fear,   25
Which now goes too free-footed.
ROSENCRANTZ.   We will haste us.   *Exeunt* GENTLEMEN.

                    Enter POLONIUS.

POLONIUS.   My lord, he's going to his mother's closet.°
Behind the arras I'll convey myself
To hear the process.° I'll warrant she'll tax him home,°
And, as you said, and wisely was it said,   30
'Tis meet that some more audience than a mother,
Since nature makes them partial, should o'erhear
The speech of vantage.° Fare you well, my liege.
I'll call upon you ere you go to bed
And tell you what I know.
KING.   Thanks, dear my lord.   *Exit* [POLONIUS].   35
O, my offense is rank, it smells to heaven;
It hath the primal eldest curse° upon't,
A brother's murder. Pray can I not,
Though inclination be as sharp as will.
My stronger guilt defeats my strong intent,   40
And like a man to double business bound
I stand in pause where I shall first begin,
And both neglect. What if this cursèd hand
Were thicker than itself with brother's blood,
Is there not rain enough in the sweet heavens   45
To wash it white as snow? Whereto serves mercy
But to confront° the visage of offense?
And what's in prayer but this twofold force,
To be forestallèd ere we come to fall,
Or pardoned being down? Then I'll look up.   50
My fault is past. But, O, what form of prayer
Can serve my turn? "Forgive me my foul murder"?
That cannot be, since I am still possessed
Of those effects° for which I did the murder,

---

22. *Attends:* waits on, participates in.   24. *Arm:* prepare.   27. *closet:* private room.
29. *process:* proceedings.   29. *tax him home:* censure him sharply.   33. *of vantage:* from an
advantageous place.   37. *primal eldest curse:* (curse of Cain, who killed Abel).   47. *confront:* oppose.
54. *effects:* things gained.

My crown, mine own ambition, and my queen.   55
May one be pardoned and retain th' offense?
In the corrupted currents of this world
Offense's gilded hand may shove my justice,
And oft 'tis seen the wicked prize itself
Buys out the law. But 'tis not so above.   60
There is no shuffling;° there the action lies
In his true nature, and we ourselves compelled,
Even to the teeth and forehead of our faults,
To give in evidence. What then? What rests?°
Try what repentance can. What can it not?   65
Yet what can it when one cannot repent?
O wretched state! O bosom black as death!
O limèd° soul, that struggling to be free
Art more engaged!° Help, angels! Make assay.°
Bow, stubborn knees, and, heart with strings of steel,   70
Be soft as sinews of the newborn babe.
All may be well.   [*He kneels.*]

Enter HAMLET.

HAMLET.   Now might I do it pat, now 'a is a-praying,
And now I'll do't. And so 'a goes to heaven,
And so am I revenged. That would be scanned.°   75
A villain kills my father, and for that
I, his sole son, do this same villain send
To heaven.
Why, this is hire and salary, not revenge.
'A took my father grossly, full of bread,°   80
With all his crimes broad blown,° as flush° as May;
And how his audit° stands, who knows save heaven?
But in our circumstance and course of thought,
'Tis heavy with him; and am I then revenged,
To take him in the purging of his soul,   85
When he is fit and seasoned for his passage?
No.
Up, sword, and know thou a more horrid hent.°
When he is drunk asleep, or in his rage,
Or in th' incestuous pleasure of his bed,   90
At game a-swearing, or about some act
That has no relish° of salvation in't—

61. *shuffling:* trickery.   64. *rests:* remains.   68. *limèd:* caught (as with birdlime, a sticky substance
spread on boughs to snare birds).   69. *engaged:* ensnared.   69. *assay:* an attempt.   75. *would be
scanned:* ought to be looked into.   80. *bread:* i.e., worldly gratification.   81. *crimes broad blown:* sins
in full bloom.   81. *flush:* vigorous.   82. *audit:* account.   88. *hent:* grasp (here, occasion for
seizing).   92. *relish:* flavor.

Then trip him, that his heels may kick at heaven,
And that his soul may be as damned and black
As hell, whereto it goes. My mother stays.   95
This physic° but prolongs thy sickly days.   *Exit.*

KING.   [*Rises*]   My words fly up, my thoughts remain below.
Words without thoughts never to heaven go.   *Exit.*

SCENE IV.   *The Queen's closet.*

Enter [*Queen*] GERTRUDE *and* POLONIUS.

POLONIUS.   'A will come straight. Look you lay home° to him.
Tell him his pranks have been too broad° to bear with,
And that your Grace hath screened and stood between
Much heat and him. I'll silence me even here.
Pray you be round with him.   5

HAMLET.   [*Within*]   Mother, Mother, Mother!

QUEEN.   I'll warrant you; fear me not. Withdraw; I hear him coming.   [POLONIUS
hides behind the arras.]

Enter HAMLET.

HAMLET.   Now, Mother, what's the matter?

QUEEN.   Hamlet, thou hast thy father much offended.

HAMLET.   Mother, you have my father much offended.   10

QUEEN.   Come, come, you answer with an idle° tongue.

HAMLET.   Go, go, you question with a wicked tongue.

QUEEN.   Why, how now, Hamlet?

HAMLET.   What's the matter now?

QUEEN.   Have you forgot me?

HAMLET.   No, by the rood,° not so!   15
You are the Queen, your husband's brother's wife,
And, would it were not so, you are my mother.

QUEEN.   Nay, then I'll set those to you that can speak.

HAMLET.   Come, come, and sit you down. You shall not budge.
You go not till I set you up a glass°
Where you may see the inmost part of you!   20

QUEEN.   What wilt thou do? Thou wilt not murder me?
Help, ho!

POLONIUS.   [*Behind*]   What, ho! Help!

HAMLET.   [*Draws*]   How now? A rat? Dead for a ducat, dead!

[*Makes a pass through the arras and*] *kills* POLONIUS.

POLONIUS.   [*Behind*]   O, I am slain!

---

96. *physic:* (Claudius' purgation by prayer, as Hamlet thinks in line 85).
SCENE IV. 1. *lay home:* thrust (rebuke) him sharply.   2. *broad:* unrestrained.   11. *idle:* foolish.
14. *rood:* cross.   19. *glass:* mirror.

QUEEN.   O me, what hast thou done?   25
HAMLET.   Nay, I know not. Is it the King?
QUEEN.   O, what a rash and bloody deed is this!
HAMLET.   A bloody deed—almost as bad, good Mother,
  As kill a king, and marry with his brother.
QUEEN.   As kill a king?
HAMLET.   Ay, lady, it was my word.   30

Lifts up the arras and sees POLONIUS.

  Thou wretched, rash, intruding fool, farewell!
  I took thee for thy better. Take thy fortune.
  Thou find'st to be too busy is some danger.—
  Leave wringing of your hands. Peace, sit you down
  And let me wring your heart, for so I shall   35
  If it be made of penetrable stuff,
  If damnèd custom have not brazed° it so
  That it be proof° and bulwark against sense.°
QUEEN.   What have I done that thou dar'st wag thy tongue
  In noise so rude against me?
HAMLET.   Such an act   40
  That blurs the grace and blush of modesty,
  Calls virtue hypocrite, takes off the rose
  From the fair forehead of an innocent love,
  And sets a blister° there, makes marriage vows
  As false as dicers' oaths. O, such a deed   45
  As from the body of contraction° plucks
  The very soul, and sweet religion makes
  A rhapsody° of words! Heaven's face does glow
  O'er this solidity and compound mass
  With heated visage, as against the doom   50
  Is thoughtsick at the act.°
QUEEN.   Ay me, what act,
  That roars so loud and thunders in the index?°
HAMLET.   Look here upon this picture, and on this,
  The counterfeit presentment° of two brothers.
  See what a grace was seated on this brow: 55
  Hyperion's curls, the front° of Jove himself,
  An eye like Mars, to threaten and command,
  A station° like the herald Mercury
  New lighted on a heaven-kissing hill—

37. *brazed:* hardened like brass.   38. *proof:* armor.   38. *sense:* feeling.   44. *sets a blister:* brands (as a harlot).   46. *contraction:* marriage contract.   48. *rhapsody:* senseless string.   48–51. *Heaven's face...the act:* i.e., the face of heaven blushes over this earth (compounded of four elements), the face hot, as if Judgment Day were near, and it is thoughtsick at the act.   52. *index:* prologue.
54. *counterfeit presentment:* represented image.   56. *front:* forehead.   58. *station:* bearing.

A combination and a form indeed   60
Where every god did seem to set his seal
To give the world assurance of a man.
This was your husband. Look you now what follows.
Here is your husband, like a mildewed ear
Blasting his wholesome brother. Have you eyes?   65
Could you on this fair mountain leave to feed,
And batten° on this moor? Ha! Have you eyes?
You cannot call it love, for at your age
The heyday° in the blood is tame, it's humble,
And waits upon the judgment, and what judgment   70
Would step from this to this? Sense° sure you have,
Else could you not have motion, but sure that sense
Is apoplexed,° for madness would not err,
Nor sense to ecstasy° was ne'er so thralled
But it reserved some quantity of choice   75
To serve in such a difference. What devil was't
That thus hath cozened you at hoodman-blind?°
Eyes without feeling, feeling without sight,
Ears without hands or eyes, smelling sans° all,
Or but a sickly part of one true sense   80
Could not so mope.°
O shame, where is thy blush? Rebellious hell,
If thou canst mutine in a matron's bones,
To flaming youth let virtue be as wax
And melt in her own fire. Proclaim no shame   85
When the compulsive ardor° gives the charge,
Since frost itself as actively doth burn,
And reason panders will.°
QUEEN.   O Hamlet, speak no more.
Thou turn'st mine eyes into my very soul,
And there I see such black and grainèd° spots   90
As will not leave their tinct.°
HAMLET.   Nay, but to live
In the rank sweat of an enseamèd° bed,
Stewed in corruption, honeying and making love
Over the nasty sty——
QUEEN.   O, speak to me no more.
These words like daggers enter in my ears.   95
No more, sweet Hamlet.

---

67. *batten:* feed gluttonously.   69. *heyday:* excitement.   71. *Sense:* feeling.   73. *apoplexed:*
paralyzed.   74. *ecstasy:* madness.   77. *cozened you at hoodman-blind:* cheated you at blindman's
buff.   79. *sans:* without.   81. *mope:* be stupid.   86. *compulsive ardor:* compelling passion.
88. *reason panders will:* reason acts as a procurer for desire.   90. *grainèd:* dye in grain (fast dyed).
91. *tinct:* color.   92. *enseamèd:* (perhaps "soaked in grease," i.e., sweaty; perhaps "much wrinkled").

HAMLET. A murderer and a villain,
  A slave that is not twentieth part the tithe°
  Of your precedent lord, a vice° of kings,
  A cutpurse of the empire and the rule,
  That from a shelf the precious diadem stole   100
  And put it in his pocket——
QUEEN. No more.

Enter GHOST.

HAMLET. A king of shreds and patches—
  Save me and hover o'er me with your wings,
  You heavenly guards! What would your gracious figure?
QUEEN. Alas, he's mad.   105
HAMLET. Do you not come your tardy son to chide,
  That, lapsed in time and passion, lets go by
  Th' important acting of your dread command?
  O, say!
GHOST. Do not forget. This visitation   110
  Is but to whet thy almost blunted purpose.
  But look, amazement on thy mother sits.
  O, step between her and her fighting soul!
  Conceit° in weakest bodies strongest works.
  Speak to her, Hamlet.
HAMLET. How is it with you, lady?   115
QUEEN. Alas, how is't with you,
  That you do bend your eye on vacancy,
  And with th' incorporal° air do hold discourse?
  Forth at your eyes your spirits wildly peep,
  And as the sleeping soldiers in th' alarm   120
  Your bedded hair° like life in excrements°
  Start up and stand an end.° O gentle son,
  Upon the heat and flame of thy distemper
  Sprinkle cool patience. Whereon do you look?
HAMLET. On him, on him! Look you, how pale he glares!   125
  His form and cause conjoined, preaching to stones,
  Would make them capable.°—Do not look upon me,
  Lest with this piteous action you convert
  My stern effects.° Then what I have to do
  Will want true color; tears perchance for blood.   130
QUEEN. To whom do you speak this?

---

97. *tithe:* tenth part. 98. *vice:* (like the Vice, a fool and mischief-maker in the old morality plays).
114. *Conceit:* imagination. 118. *incorporal:* bodiless. 121. *bedded hair:* hairs laid flat.
121. *excrements:* outgrowths (here, the hair). 122. *an end:* on end. 127. *capable:* receptive.
128–129. *convert/My stern effects:* divert my stern deeds.

HAMLET.   Do you see nothing there?
QUEEN.   Nothing at all; yet all that is I see.
HAMLET.   Nor did you nothing hear?
QUEEN.   No, nothing but ourselves.
HAMLET.   Why, look you there! Look how it steals away!
   My father, in his habit° as he lived!   135
   Look where he goes even now out at the portal!   *Exit* GHOST.
QUEEN.   This is the very coinage of your brain.
   This bodiless creation ecstacy
   Is very cunning in.
HAMLET.   Ecstacy?
   My pulse as yours doth temperately keep time   140
   And makes as healthful music. It is not madness
   That I have uttered. Bring me to the test,
   And I the matter will reword, which madness
   Would gambol° from. Mother, for love of grace,
   Lay not that flattering unction° to your soul,   145
   That not your trespass but my madness speaks.
   It will but skin and film the ulcerous place
   Whiles rank corruption, mining° all within,
   Infects unseen. Confess yourself to heaven,
   Repent what's past, avoid what is to come,   150
   And do not spread the compost° on the weeds
   To make them ranker. Forgive me this my virtue.
   For in the fatness of these pursy° times
   Virtue itself of vice must pardon beg,
   Yea, curb° and woo for leave to do him good.   155
QUEEN.   O Hamlet, thou hast cleft my heart in twain.
HAMLET.   O, throw away the worser part of it,
   And live the purer with the other half.
   Good night—but go not to my uncle's bed.
   Assume a virtue, if you have it not.   160
   That monster custom, who all sense doth eat,
   Of habits devil, is angel yet in this,
   That to the use° of actions fair and good
   He likewise gives a frock or livery°
   That aptly is put on. Refrain tonight,   165
   And that shall lend a kind of easiness
   To the next abstinence; the next more easy;

135. *habit:* garment (Q1, though a "bad" quarto, is probably correct in saying that at line 101 the ghost enters "in his nightgown," i.e., dressing gown).   144. *gambol:* start away.   145. *unction:* ointment.   148. *mining:* undermining.   151. *compost:* fertilizing substance.   153. *pursy:* bloated. 155. *curb:* bow low.   163. *use:* practice.   164. *livery:* characteristic garment (punning on "habits" in line 162).

For use almost can change the stamp of nature,
And either° the devil, or throw him out
With wondrous potency. Once more, good night,   170
And when you are desirous to be blest,
I'll blessing beg of you.—For this same lord,
I do repent; but heaven hath pleased it so,
To punish me with this, and this with me,
That I must be their° scourge and minister.   175
I will bestow° him and will answer well
The death I gave him. So again, good night.
I must be cruel only to be kind.
Thus bad begins, and worse remains behind.
One word more, good lady.
QUEEN.   What shall I do?   180
HAMLET.   Not this, by no means, that I bid you do:
Let the bloat King tempt you again to bed,
Pinch wanton on your cheek, call you his mouse,
And let him, for a pair of reechy° kisses,
Or paddling in your neck with his damned fingers,   185
Make you to ravel° all this matter out,
That I essentially am not in madness,
But mad in craft. 'Twere good you let him know,
For who that's but a queen, fair, sober, wise,
Would from a paddock,° from a bat, a gib,°   190
Such dear concernings hide? Who would do so?
No, in despite of sense and secrecy,
Unpeg the basket on the house's top,
Let the birds fly, and like the famous ape,
To try conclusions,° in the basket creep   195
And break your own neck down.
QUEEN.   Be thou assured, if words be made of breath,
And breath of life, I have no life to breathe
What thou hast said to me.
HAMLET.   I must to England; you know that?
QUEEN.   Alack,   200
I had forgot. 'Tis so concluded on.
HAMLET.   There's letters sealed, and my two school fellows,
Whom I will trust as I will adders fanged,
They bear the mandate;° they must sweep my way
And marshall me to knavery. Let it work;   205

169. *either*: (probably a word is missing after *either*; among suggestions are "master," "curb," and "house"; but possibly *either* is a verb meaning "make easier").   175. *their*: i.e., the heavens'.
176. *bestow*: stow, lodge.   184. *reechy*: foul (literally "smoky").   186. *ravel*: unravel, reveal.
190. *paddock*: toad.   190. *gib*: tomcat.   195. *To try conclusions*: to make experiments.
204. *mandate*: command.

For 'tis the sport to have the enginer
Hoist with his own petar,° and 't shall go hard
But I will delve one yard below their mines
And blow them at the moon. O, 'tis most sweet
When in one line two crafts° directly meet.   210
This man shall set me packing:
I'll lug the guts into the neighbor room.
Mother, good night. Indeed, this counselor
Is now most still, most secret, and most grave,
Who was in life a foolish prating knave.   215
Come, sir, to draw toward an end with you.
Good night, Mother.

> [*Exit the* QUEEN. *Then*] *exit* HAMLET, *tugging in* POLONIUS.

ACT IV

SCENE I.   *The castle.*

> *Enter* KING *and* QUEEN, *with* ROSENCRANTZ *and* GUILDENSTERN.

KING.   There's a matter in these sighs. These profound heaves
  You must translate; 'tis fit we understand them.
  Where is your son?
QUEEN.   Bestow this place on us a little while.

> *Exeunt* ROSENCRANTZ *and* GUILDENSTERN.

  Ah, mine own lord, what have I seen tonight!   5
KING.   What, Gertrude? How does Hamlet?
QUEEN.   Mad as the sea and wind when both contend
  Which is the mightier. In his lawless fit,
  Behind the arras hearing something stir,
  Whips out his rapier, cries, "A rat, a rat!"   10
  And in this brainish apprehension° kills
  The unseen good old man.
KING.   O heavy deed!
  It had been so with us, had we been there.
  His liberty is full of threats to all,
  To you yourself, to us, to every one.   15
  Alas, how shall this bloody deed be answered?
  It will be laid to us, whose providence°
  Should have kept short, restrained, and out of haunt°
  This mad young man. But so much was our love

---

207. *petar:* bomb.   210. *crafts:* (1) boats, (2) acts of guile, crafty schemes.
SCENE I. 11. *brainish apprehension:* mad imagination.   17. *providence:* foresight.
18. *out of haunt:* away from association with others.

We would not understand what was most fit,   20
But, like the owner of a foul disease,
To keep it from divulging, let it feed
Even on the pith of life. Where is he gone?
QUEEN.   To draw apart the body he hath killed;
O'er whom his very madness, like some ore   25
Among a mineral° of metals base,
Shows itself pure. 'A weeps for what is done.
KING.   O Gertrude, come away!
The sun no sooner shall the mountains touch
But we will ship him hence, and this vile deed   30
We must will all our majesty and skill
Both countenance and excuse. Ho, Guildenstern!

Enter ROSENCRANTZ *and* GUILDENSTERN.

Friends both, go join you with some further aid:
Hamlet in madness hath Polonius slain,
And from his mother's closet hath he dragged him.   35
Go seek him out; speak fair, and bring the body
Into the chapel. I pray you haste in this.   *Exeunt* ROSENCRANTZ
    and GUILDENSTERN.
Come, Gertrude, we'll call up our wisest friends
And let them know both what we mean to do
And what's untimely done…°   40
Whose whisper o'er the world's diameter,
As level as the cannon to his blank°
Transport his poisoned shot, may miss our name
And hit the woundless° air, O, come away!
My soul is full of discord and dismay.   *Exeunt.*   45

SCENE II.   *The castle.*

Enter HAMLET.

HAMLET.   Safely stowed.
GENTLEMEN.   [*Within*] Hamlet! Lord Hamlet!
HAMLET.   But soft, what noise? Who calls on Hamlet?
O, here they come.

Enter ROSENCRANTZ *and* GUILDENSTERN.

ROSENCRANTZ.   What have you done, my lord, with the dead body?   5
HAMLET.   Compounded it with dust, whereto 'tis kin.

25–26. *ore / Among a mineral:* vein of gold in a mine.   40. *Done…:* (evidently something has
dropped out of the text. Capell's conjecture, "So, haply slander," is usually printed).   42. *Blank:* white
center of a target.   44. *woundless:* invulnerable.

ROSENCRANTZ.   Tell us where 'tis, that we may take it thence
  And bear it to the chapel.
HAMLET.   Do not believe it.
ROSENCRANTZ.   Believe what?   10
HAMLET.   That I can keep your counsel and not mine own. Besides, to be demanded
    of° a sponge, what replication° should be made by the son of a king?
ROSENCRANTZ.   Take you me for a sponge, my lord?
HAMLET.   Ay, sir, that soaks up the King's countenance,° his rewards, his authorities.
    But such officers do the King best service in the end. He keeps them, like an   15
    ape, in the corner of his jaw, first mouthed, to be last swallowed. When he needs
    what you have gleaned, it is but squeezing you and, sponge, you shall be dry
    again.
ROSENCRANTZ.   I understand you not, my lord.
HAMLET.   I am glad of it: a knavish speech sleeps in a foolish ear.   20
ROSENCRANTZ.   My lord, you must tell us where the body is and go with us to the
    King.
HAMLET.   The body is with the King, but the King is not with the body. The King
    is a thing——
GUILDENSTERN.   A thing, my lord?   25
HAMLET.   Of nothing. Bring me to him. Hide fox, and all after.°   *Exeunt.*

SCENE III.   The castle.

Enter KING, and two or three.

KING.   I have sent to seek him and to find the body:
  How dangerous is it that this man goes loose!
  Yet must not we put the strong law on him:
  He's loved of the distracted° multitude,
  Who like not in their judgment, but their eyes,   5
  And where 'tis so, th' offender's scourge is weighed,
  But never the offense. To bear° all smooth and even,
  This sudden sending him away must seem
  Deliberate pause.° Diseases desperate grown
  By desperate appliance are relieved,   10
  Or not at all.

Enter ROSENCRANTZ, GUILDENSTERN, and all the rest.

  How now? What hath befall'n?
ROSENCRANTZ.   Where the dead body is bestowed, my lord,
  We cannot get from him.
KING.   But where is he?

SCENE II. 11–12. *demanded of:* questioned by.   12. *replication:* reply.   14. *countenance:* favor.
26. *Hide fox, and all after:* (a cry in a game such as hide-and-seek; Hamlet runs from the stage).
SCENE III. 4. *distracted:* bewildered, senseless.   7. *bear:* carry out.   9. *pause:* planning.

ROSENCRANTZ.   Without, my lord; guarded, to know your pleasure.

KING.   Bring him before us.

ROSENCRANTZ.   Ho! Bring in the lord.   15

They enter.

KING.   Now, Hamlet, where's Polonius?

HAMLET.   At supper.

KING.   At supper? Where?

HAMLET.   Not where he eats, but where 'a is eaten. A certain convocation of politic°
worms are e'en at him. Your worm is your only emperor for diet. We fat all   20
creatures else to fat us, and we fat ourselves for maggots. Your fat king and your
lean beggar is but variable service° —two dishes, but to one table. That's the
end.

KING.   Alas, alas!

HAMLET.   A man may fish with the worm that hath eat of a king, and eat of the fish   25
that hath fed of that worm.

KING.   What dost thou mean by this?

HAMLET.   Nothing but to show you how a king may go a progress° through the
guts of a beggar.

KING.   Where is Polonius?   30

HAMLET.   In heaven. Send thither to see. If your messenger find him not there, seek
him i' th' other place yourself. But if indeed you find him not within this
month, you shall nose him as you go up the stairs into the lobby.

KING.   [*To* ATTENDANTS]   Go seek him there.

HAMLET.   'A will stay till you come.   *Exeunt* ATTENDANTS.   35

KING.   Hamlet, this deed, for thine especial safety,
Which we do tender° as we dearly grieve
For that which thou hast done, must send thee hence
With fiery quickness. Therefore prepare thyself.
The bark is ready and the wind at help,   40
Th' associates tend,° and everything is bent
For England.

HAMLET.   For England?

KING.   Ay, Hamlet.

HAMLET.   Good.

KING.   So is it, if thou knew'st our purposes.

HAMLET.   I see a cherub° that sees them. But come, for England! Farewell, dear
Mother.

KING.   Thy loving father, Hamlet.   45

HAMLET.   My mother—father and mother is man and wife, man and wife is one
flesh, and so, my mother. Come, for England!   *Exit.*

---

19. *politic:* statesmanlike, shrewd.   22. *variable service:* different courses.   28. *progress:* royal
journey.   37. *tender:* hold dear.   41. *tend:* wait.   44. *cherub:* angel of knowledge.

KING.   Follow him at foot;° tempt him with speed aboard.
  Delay it not; I'll have him hence tonight.
  Away! For everything is sealed and done   50
  That else leans° on th' affair. Pray you make haste.   *Exeunt all but the* KING.
  And, England, if my love thou hold'st at aught—
  As my great power thereof may give thee sense,
  Since yet thy cicatrice° looks raw and red
  After the Danish sword, and thy free awe°   55
  Pays homage to us—thou mayst not coldly set
  Our sovereign process,° which imports at full
  By letters congruing to that effect
  The present° death of Hamlet. Do it, England,
  For like the hectic° in my blood he rages,   60
  And thou must cure me. Till I know 'tis done,
  Howe'er my haps,° my joys were ne'er begun.   *Exit.*

SCENE IV.   *A plain in Denmark.*

Enter FORTINBRAS *with his Army over the stage.*

FORTINBRAS.   Go, Captain, from me greet the Danish king.
  Tell him that by his license Fortinbras
  Craves the conveyance of° a promised march
  Over his kingdom. You know the rendezvous.
  If that his Majesty would aught with us,   5
  We shall express our duty in his eye;°
  And let him know so.
CAPTAIN.   I will do't, my lord.
FORTINBRAS.   Go softly° on.   *Exeunt all but the* CAPTAIN.

Enter HAMLET, ROSENCRANTZ, &c.

HAMLET.   Good sir, whose powers° are these?
CAPTAIN.   They are of Norway, sir.   10
HAMLET.   How purposed, sir, I pray you?
CAPTAIN.   Against some part of Poland.
HAMLET.   Who commands them, sir?
CAPTAIN.   The nephew to old Norway, Fortinbras.
HAMLET.   Goes it against the main° of Poland, sir,   15
  Or for some frontier?
CAPTAIN.   Truly to speak, and with no addition,°
  We go to gain a little patch of ground

48. *at foot:* closely.   51. *leans:* depends.   54. *cicatrice:* scar.   55. *free awe:* uncompelled submission.
56–57. *coldly set / Our sovereign process:* regard slightly our royal command.   59. *present:* instant.
60. *hectic:* fever.   62. *haps:* chances, fortunes.   SCENE IV. 3. *conveyance of:* escort for.
6. *in his eye:* before his eyes (i.e., in his presence).   8. *softly:* slowly.   9. *powers:* forces.
15. *main:* main part.   17. *with no addition:* plainly.

That hath in it no profit but the name.
To pay five ducats, five, I would not farm it,   20
Nor will it yield to Norway or the Pole
A ranker° rate, should it be sold in fee.°
HAMLET.   Why, then the Polack never will defend it.
CAPTAIN.   Yes, it is already garrisoned.
HAMLET.   Two thousand souls and twenty thousand ducats   25
Will not debate° the question of this straw.
This is th' imposthume° of much wealth and peace,
That inward breaks, and shows no cause without
Why the man dies. I humbly thank you, sir.
CAPTAIN.   God bye you, sir.   [*Exit.*]
ROSENCRANTZ.   Will't please you go, my lord?   30
HAMLET.   I'll be with you straight. Go a little before.   *Exeunt all but* HAMLET.
How all occasions do inform against me
And spur my dull revenge! What is a man,
If his chief good and market° of his time
Be but to sleep and feed? A beast, no more.   35
Sure he that made us with such large discourse,°
Looking before and after, gave us not
That capability and godlike reason
To fust° in us unused. Now, whether it be
Bestial oblivion,° or some craven scruple   40
Of thinking too precisely on th' event°—
A thought which, quartered, hath but one part wisdom
And ever three parts coward—I do not know
Why yet I live to say, "This thing's to do,"
Sith I have cause, and will, and strength, and means   45
To do't. Examples gross° as earth exhort me.
Witness this army of such mass and charge,°
Led by a delicate and tender prince,
Whose spirit, with divine ambition puffed,
Makes mouths at the invisible event,°   50
Exposing what is mortal and unsure
To all that fortune, death, and danger dare,
Even for an eggshell. Rightly to be great
Is not° to stir without great argument,°
But greatly° to find quarrel in a straw   55
When honor's at the stake. How stand I then,

---

22. *ranker:* higher.   22. *in fee:* outright.   26. *debate:* settle.   27. *imposthume:* abscess,
ulcer.   34. *market:* profits.   36. *discourse:* understanding.   39. *fust:* grow moldy.
40. *oblivion:* forgetfulness.   41. *event:* outcome.   46. *gross:* large, obvious.   47. *charge:* expense.
50. *Makes mouths at the invisible event:* makes scornful faces (is contemptuous of) the unseen outcome.
54. *not:* (the sense seems to require "not not").   54. *argument:* reason.   55. *greatly:* i.e., nobly.

That have a father killed, a mother stained,
Excitements° of my reason and my blood,
And let all sleep, while to my shame I see
The imminent death of twenty thousand men   60
That for a fantasy and trick of fame°
Go to their graves like beds, fight for a plot
Whereon the numbers cannot try the cause,
Which is not tomb enough and continent°
To hide the slain? O, from this time forth,   65
My thoughts be bloody, or be nothing worth!   *Exit.*

SCENE V.   *The castle.*

Enter HORATIO, [*Queen*] GERTRUDE, *and a* GENTLEMAN.

QUEEN.   I will not speak with her.
GENTLEMAN.   She is importunate, indeed distract.
   Her mood will needs be pitied.
QUEEN.   What would she have?
GENTLEMAN.   She speaks much of her father, says she hears
   There's tricks i' th' world, and hems, and beats her heart,   5
   Spurns enviously at straws,° speaks things in doubt°
   That carry but half sense. Her speech is nothing,
   Yet the unshapèd use of it doth move
   The hearers to collection;° they yawn° at it,
   And botch the words up fit to their own thoughts,   10
   Which, as her winks and nods and gestures yield them,
   Indeed would make one think there might be thought,
   Though nothing sure, yet much unhappily.
HORATIO.   'Twere good she were spoken with, for she may strew
   Dangerous conjectures in ill-breeding minds.   15
QUEEN.   Let her come in.   [*Exit* GENTLEMAN.]
   [*Aside*]   To my sick soul (as sin's true nature is)
   Each toy seems prologue to some great amiss;°
   So full of artless jealousy° is guilt
   It spills° itself in fearing to be spilt.   20

Enter OPHELIA [*distracted.*]

OPHELIA.   Where is the beauteous majesty of Denmark?
QUEEN.   How now, Ophelia?

---

58. *Excitement:* incentives.   61. *fantasy and trick of fame:* illusion and trifle of reputation.
64. *continent:* receptacle, container.   SCENE V. 6. *Spurns enviously at straws:* objects spitefully to
insignificant matters.   6. *in doubt:* uncertainly.   8–9. *Yet the...to collection:* i.e., yet the formless manner of it moves her listeners to gather up some sort of meaning.   9. *yawn:* gape (?).   18. *amiss:*
misfortune.   19. *artless jealousy:* crude suspicion.   20. *spills:* destroys.

OPHELIA. [*She sings.*]   How should I your truelove know
     From another one?
       By his cockle hat° and staff   25
       And his sandal shoon.°
QUEEN. Alas, sweet lady, what imports this song?
OPHELIA. Say you? Nay, pray you mark.
       He is dead and gone, lady,   [*Song*]
         He is dead and gone;   30
     At his head a grass-green turf,
       At his heels a stone,
  O, ho!
QUEEN. Nay, but Ophelia——
OPHELIA. Pray you mark.   35
  [*Sings.*]   White his shroud as the mountain snow——

Enter KING.

QUEEN. Alas, look here, my lord.
OPHELIA.   Larded° all with sweet flowers   [*Song*]
     Which bewept to the grave did not go
       With truelove showers.   40
KING. How do you, pretty lady?
OPHELIA. Well, God dild° you! They say the owl was a baker's daughter.° Lord,
  we know what we are, but know not what we may be. God be at your table!
KING. Conceit° upon her father.
OPHELIA. Pray let's have not words of this, but when they ask you what it means, 45
  say you this:
     Tomorrow is Saint Valentine's day.°   [*Song*]
       All in the morning betime,
    And I a maid at your window,
       To be your Valentine.   50

    Then up he rose and donned his clothes
       And dupped° the chamber door,
    Let in the maid, that out a maid
       Never departed more.
KING. Pretty Ophelia.   55
OPHELIA. Indeed, la, without an oath, I'll make an end on't:

---

25. *cockle hat:* (a cockleshell on the hat was the sign of a pilgrim who had journeyed to shrines overseas. The association of lovers and pilgrims was a common one).   26. *shoon:* shoes.
38. *Larded:* decorated.   42. *dild:* yield, i.e., reward.   42. *baker's daughter:* (an allusion to a tale of a baker's daughter who begrudged bread to Christ and was turned into an owl).   44. *Conceit:* brooding.
47. *Saint Valentine's day:* Feb. 14 (the notion was that a bachelor would become the truelove of the first girl he saw on this day).   52. *dupped:* opened (did up).

[*Sings.*]   By Gis° and by Saint Charity,
              Alack, and fie for shame!
          Young men will do't if they come to't,   60
              By Cock,° they are to blame.
          Quoth she, "Before you tumbled me,
              You promised me to wed."
     He answers:
              "So would I 'a' done, by yonder sun,   65
                  An thou hadst not come to my bed."
KING.   How long hath she been thus?
OPHELIA.   I hope all will be well. We must be patient, but I cannot choose but weep
   to think they would lay him i' th' cold ground. My brother shall know of it; and
   so I thank you for your good counsel. Come, my coach! Good night, ladies, 70
   good night. Sweet ladies, good night, good night.   *Exit.*
KING.   Follow her close; give her a good watch, I pray you.   [*Exit* HORATIO.]
     O, this is the poison of deep grief; it springs
     All from her father's death—and now behold!
     O Gertrude, Gertrude,   75
     When sorrows come, they come not single spies,
     But in battalions: first, her father slain;
     Next, your son gone, and he most violent author
     Of his own just remove; the people muddied,°
     Thick and unwholesome in their thoughts and whispers   80
     For good Polonius' death, and we have done but greenly°
     In huggermugger° to inter him; poor Ophelia
     Divided from herself and her fair judgment,
     Without the which we are pictures or mere beasts;
     Last, and as much containing as all these,   85
     Her brother is in secret come from France,
     Feeds on his wonder,° keeps himself in clouds,
     And wants not buzzers° to infect his ear
     With pestilent speeches of his father's death,
     Wherein necessity, of matter beggared,°   90
     Will nothing stick° our person to arraign
     In ear and ear. O my dear Gertrude, this,
     Like to a murd'ring piece,° in many places
     Gives me a superfluous death.   *A noise within.*

                    Enter a MESSENGER.

---

57. *Gis:* (contraction of "Jesus").   60. *Cock:* (1) God, (2) phallus.   79. *muddied:* muddled.
81. *greenly:* foolishly.   82. *huggermugger:* secret haste.   87. *wonder:* suspicion.   88. *wants not buzzers:* does not lack talebearers.   90. *of matter beggared:* unprovided with facts.   91. *Will nothing stick:* will not hesitate.   93. *murd'ring piece:* (a cannon that shot a kind of shrapnel).

QUEEN.   Alack, what noise is this?
KING.   Attend, where are my Switzers?° Let them guard the door.   95
  What is the matter?
MESSENGER.   Save yourself, my lord.
  The ocean, overpeering of his list,°
  Eats not the flats with more impiteous haste
  Than your Laertes, in a riotous head,°
  O'erbears your officers. The rabble call him lord,   100
  And, as the world were now but to begin,
  Antiquity forgot, custom not known,
  The ratifiers and props of every word,
  They cry, "Choose we! Laertes shall be king!"
  Caps, hands, and tongues applaud it to the clouds,   105
  "Laertes shall be king! Laertes King!"   *A noise within*.
QUEEN.   How cheerfully on the false trail they cry!
  O, this is counter,° you false Danish dogs!

Enter LAERTES *with others*.

KING.   The doors are broke.
LAERTES.   Where is this king?—Sirs, stand you all without.   110
ALL.   No, let's come in.
LAERTES.   I pray you give me leave.
ALL.   We will, we will.
LAERTES.   I thank you. Keep the door.   [*Exeunt his* FOLLOWERS.]   O thou vile
  King,
Give me my father.
QUEEN.   Calmly, good Laertes.
LAERTES.   That drop of blood that's calm proclaims me bastard,   115
  Cries cuckold° to my father, brands the harlot
  Even here between the chaste unsmirchèd brow
  Of my true mother.
KING.   What is the cause, Laertes,
  That thy rebellion looks so giantlike?
  Let him go, Gertrude. Do not fear° our person.   120
  There's such divinity doth hedge a king
  That treason can but peep to° what it would,
  Acts little of his will. Tell me, Laertes,
  Why thou art thus incensed. Let him go, Gertrude.
  Speak, man.   125
LAERTES.   Where is my father?
KING.   Dead.

95. *Switzers:* Swiss guards.   97. *list:* shore.   99. *in a riotous head:* with a rebellious force.
109. *counter:* (a hound runs counter when he follows the scent backward from the prey).
116. *cuckold:* man whose wife is unfaithful.   120. *fear:* fear for.   122. *peep to:* i.e., look at from
a distance.

QUEEN.   But not by him.

KING.   Let him demand his fill.

LAERTES.   How came he dead? I'll not be juggled with.
   To hell allegiance, vows to the blackest devil,
   Conscience and grace to the profoundest pit!   130
   I dare damnation. To this point I stand,
   That both the worlds I give to negligence,°
   Let come what comes, only I'll be revenged
   Most throughly for my father.

KING.   Who shall stay you?

LAERTES.   My will, not all the world's.   135
   And for my means, I'll husband them° so well
   They shall go far with little.

KING.   Good Laertes,
   If you desire to know the certainty
   Of your dear father, is't writ in your revenge
   That swoopstake° you will draw both friend and foe,   140
   Winner and loser?

LAERTES.   None but his enemies.

KING.   Will you know them then?

LAERTES.   To his good friends thus wide I'll ope my arms
   And like the kind life-rend'ring pelican°
   Repast° them with my blood.

KING.   Why, now you speak   145
   Like a good child and a true gentleman.
   That I am guiltless of your father's death,
   And am most sensibly° in grief for it,
   It shall as level to your judgment 'pear
   As day does to your eye.   150

A noise within: "Let her come in."

LAERTES.   How now? What noise is that?

Enter3 OPHELIA.

   O heat, dry up my brains; tears seven times salt
   Burn out the sense and virtue° of mine eye!
   By heaven, thy madness shall be paid with weight
   Till our scale turn the beam.° O Rose of May,   155
   Dear maid, kind sister, sweet Ophelia!
   O heavens, is't possible a young maid's wits
   Should be as mortal as an old man's life?

---

132. *That both...to negligence:* i.e., I care not what may happen (to me) in this world or the next.
136. *husband them:* use them economically.   140. *swoopstake:* in a clean sweep.
144. *pelican:* (thought to feed its young with its own blood).   145. *Repast:* feed.
148. *sensibly:* acutely.   153. *virtue:* power.   155. *turn the beam:* weigh down the bar (of the balance).

Nature is fine° in love, and where 'tis fine,
It sends some precious instance° of itself 160
After the thing it loves.
OPHELIA.   They bore him barefaced on the bier   [*Song*]
   Hey non nony, nony, hey nony
   And in his grave rained many a tear——
Fare you well, my dove! 165
LAERTES.   Hadst thou thy wits, and didst persuade revenge,
It could not move thus.
OPHELIA.   You must sing "A-down a-down, and you call him a-down-a." O, how
the wheel° becomes it! It is the false steward, that stole his master's daughter.
LAERTES.   This nothing's more than matter.° 170
OPHELIA.   There's rosemary, that's for remembrance. Pray you, love, remember.
And there is pansies, that's for thoughts.
LAERTES.   A document° in madness, thoughts and remembrance fitted.
OPHELIA.   There's fennel° for you, and columbines. There's rue for you, and
here's some for me. We may call it herb of grace o' Sundays. O, you must wear 175
your rue with a difference. There's a daisy. I would give you some violets, but
they withered all when my father died. They say 'a made a good end.
[*Sings*]   For bonny sweet Robin is all my joy.
LAERTES.   Thought and affliction, passion, hell itself,
She turns to favor° and to prettiness. 180
OPHELIA.   And will' a not come again?   [*Song*]
  And will 'a not come again?
   No, no, he is dead,
   Go to thy deathbed,
   He never will come again. 185
   His beard was as white as snow,
   All flaxen was his poll.°
   He is gone, he is gone,
   And we cast away moan.
  God 'a' mercy on his soul! 190
And of all Christian souls, I pray God. God bye you.   *Exit.*
LAERTES.   Do you see this, O God?
KING.   Laertes, I must commune with your grief,
Or you deny me right. Go but apart,
Make choice of whom your wisest friends you will, 195

---

159. *fine:* refined, delicate.   160. *instance:* sample.   169. *wheel:* (of uncertain meaning, but probably
a turn or dance of Ophelia's, rather than Fortune's wheel).   170. *This nothing's more than matter:* this
nonsense has more meaning than matters of consequence.   173. *document:* lesson.   174. *fennel:* (the
distribution of flowers in the ensuing lines has symbolic meaning, but the meaning is disputed. Perhaps
fennel, flattery; *columbines,* cuckoldry; *rue,* sorrow for Ophelia and repentance for the Queen; *daisy,* dis-
sembling; *violets,* faithfulness. For other interpretations, see J. W. Lever in *Review of English Studies,*
New Series 3 [1952], pp. 123–129).   180. *favor:* charm, beauty.   187. *All flaxen was his poll:* white
as flax was his head.

And they shall hear and judge 'twixt you and me.
If by direct or by collateral° hand
They find us touched,° we will our kingdom give,
Our crown, or life, and all that we call ours,
To you in satisfaction; but if not,   200
Be you content to lend your patience to us,
And we shall jointly labor with your soul
To give it due content.
LAERTES.   Let this be so.
His means of death, his obscure funeral—
No trophy, sword, nor hatchment° o'er his bones,   205
No noble rite nor formal ostentation°—
Cry to be heard, as 'twere from heaven to earth,
That I must call't in question.
KING.   So you shall;
And where th' offense is, let the great ax fall.
I pray you go with me.   *Exeunt.*   210

SCENE VI.   *The castle.*

Enter HORATIO *and others.*

HORATIO.   What are they that would speak with me?
GENTLEMAN.   Seafaring men, sir. They say they have
letters for you.
HORATIO.   Let them come in.   [*Exit* ATTENDANT.]
I do not know from what part of the world   5
I should be greeted, if not from Lord Hamlet.

Enter SAILORS.

SAILOR.   God bless you, sir.
HORATIO.   Let Him bless thee too.
SAILOR.   'A shall, sir, an't please Him. There's a letter for you, sir—it came from
th' ambassador that was bound for England—if your name be Horatio, as I am   10
let to know it is.
HORATIO.   [*Reads the letter.*]   "Horatio, when thou shalt have overlooked° this, give
these fellows some means to the King. They have letters for him. Ere we were
two days old at sea, a pirate of very warlike appointment° gave us chase. Finding
ourselves too slow of sail, we put on a compelled valor, and in the grapple I   15
boarded them. On the instant they got clear of our ship; so I alone became their
prisoner. They have dealt with me like thieves of mercy, but they knew what
they did: I am to do a good turn for them. Let the King have the letters I have
sent, and repair thou to me with as much speed as thou wouldest fly death. I

197. *collateral:* indirect.   198. *touched:* implicated.   205. *hatchment:* tablet bearing the coat of arms
of the dead.   206. *ostentation:* ceremony.   SCENE VI. 12. *overlooked:* surveyed.
14. *appointment:* equipment.

have words to speak in thine ear will make thee dumb; yet are they much too 20
light for the bore° of the matter. These good fellows will bring thee where I am.
Rosencrantz and Guildenstern hold their course for England. Of them I have
much to tell thee. Farewell.

> He that thou knowest thine, Hamlet."

Come, I will give you way for these your letters, 25
And do't the speedier that you may direct me
To him from whom you brought them.   *Exeunt.*

SCENE VII.   *The castle.*

Enter KING *and* LAERTES.

KING.   Now must your conscience my acquittance seal,
And you must put me in your heart for friend,
Sith you have heard, and with a knowing ear,
That he which hath your noble father slain
Pursued my life.

LAERTES.   It well appears. But tell me 5
Why you proceeded not against these feats
So criminal and so capital° in nature,
As by your safety, greatness, wisdom, all things else,
You mainly° were stirred up.

KING.   O, for two special reasons,
Which may to you perhaps seem much unsinewed,° 10
But yet to me they're strong. The Queen his mother
Lives almost by his looks, and for myself—
My virtue or my plague, be it either which—
She is so conjunctive° to my life and soul,
That, as the star moves not but in his sphere, 15
I could not but by her. The other motive
Why to a public count° I might not go
Is the great love the general gender° bear him,
Who, dipping all his faults in their affection,
Would, like the spring that turneth wood to stone,° 20
Convert his gyves° to graces; so that my arrows,
Too slightly timbered° for so loud a wind,
Would have reverted to my bow again,
And not where I had aimed them.

LAERTES.   And so have I a noble father lost, 25
A sister driven into desp'rate terms,°

21. *bore:* caliber (here, "importance").   SCENE VII. 7. *capital:* deserving death.
9. *mainly:* powerfully.   10. *unsinewed:* weak.   14. *conjunctive:* closely united.
17. *count:* reckoning.   18. *general gender:* common people.   20. *spring that turneth wood to stone:* (a
spring in Shakespeare's county was so charged with lime that it would petrify wood placed in it).
21. *gyves:* fetters.   22. *timbered:* shafted.   26. *terms:* conditions.

Whose worth, if praises may go back again,°
Stood challenger on mount of all the age
For her perfections. But my revenge will come.
KING.   Break not your sleeps for that. You must not think   30
That we are made of stuff so flat and dull
That we can let our beard be shook with danger,
And think it pastime. You shortly shall hear more.
I loved your father, and we love ourself,
And that, I hope, will teach you to imagine——   35

Enter a MESSENGER *with letters.*

How now? What news?
MESSENGER.   Letters, my lord, from Hamlet:
These to your Majesty; this to the Queen.
KING.   From Hamlet? Who brought them?
MESSENGER.   Sailors, my lord, they say; I saw them not.
They were given me by Claudio; he received them   40
Of him that brought them.
KING.   Laertes, you shall hear them.—
Leave us.   *Exit* MESSENGER.
    [*Reads.*]   "High and mighty, you shall know I am set naked° on your kingdom.
Tomorrow shall I beg leave to see your kingly eyes; even when I shall (first
asking your pardon thereunto) recount the occasion of my sudden and more   45
strange return.
                                        Hamlet."
What should this mean? Are all the rest come back?
Or is it some abuse,° and no such thing?
LAERTES.   Know you the hand?
KING.   'Tis Hamlet's character.° "Naked"!   50
And in a postscript here, he says "alone."
Can you devise° me?
LAERTES.   I am lost in it, my lord. But let him come.
It warms the very sickness in my heart
That I shall live and tell him to his teeth,   55
"Thus did'st thou."
KING.   If it be so, Laertes
(As how should it be so? How otherwise?),
Will you be ruled by me?
LAERTES.   Ay, my lord,
So you will not o'errule me to a peace.
KING.   To thine own peace. If he be now returned,   60
As checking at° his voyage, and that he means

_____

27. *go back again:* revert to what is past.   43. *naked:* destitute.   49. *abuse:* deception.
50. *character:* handwriting.   52. *devise:* advise.   61. *checking at:* turning away from (a term
in falconry).

No more to undertake it, I will work him
To an exploit now ripe in my device,
Under the which he shall not choose but fall;
And for his death no wind of blame shall breathe,   65
But even his mother shall uncharge the practice°
And call it accident.

LAERTES.   My lord, I will be ruled;
The rather if you could devise it so
That I might be the organ.

KING.   It falls right.
You have been talked of since your travel much,   70
And that in Hamlet's hearing, for a quality
Wherein they say you shine. Your sum of parts
Did not together pluck such envy from him
As did that one, and that, in my regard,
Of the unworthiest siege.°

LAERTES.   What part is that, my lord?   75

KING.   A very riband in the cap of youth,
Yet needful too, for youth no less becomes
The light and careless livery that it wears
Than settled age his sables and his weeds,°
Importing health and graveness. Two months since   80
Here was a gentlemen of Normandy.
I have seen myself, and served against, the French,
And they can° well on horseback, but this gallant
Had witchcraft in't. He grew unto his seat,
And to such wondrous doing brought his horse   85
As had he been incorpsed and deminatured
With the brave beast. So far he topped my thought
That I, in forgery° of shapes and tricks,
Come short of what he did.

LAERTES.   A Norman was't?

KING.   A Norman.   90

LAERTES.   Upon my life, Lamord.

KING.   The very same.

LAERTES.   I know him well. He is the brooch° indeed
And gem of all the nation.

KING.   He made confession° of you,
And gave you such a masterly report,   95
For art and exercise in your defense,
And for your rapier most especial,

---

66. *uncharge the practice:* not charge the device with treachery.   75. *siege:* rank.   79. *sables and his weeds:* i.e., sober attire.   83. *can:* do   88. *forgery:* invention.   92. *brooch:* ornament.
94. *confession:* report.

That he cried out 'twould be a sight indeed
If one could match you. The scrimers° of their nation 100
He swore that neither motion, guard, nor eye,
If you opposed them. Sir, this report of his
Did Hamlet so envenom with his envy
That he could nothing do but wish and beg
Your sudden coming o'er to play with you.
Now, out of this——
LAERTES.   What out of this, my lord? 105
KING.   Laertes, was your father dear to you?
Or are you like the painting of a sorrow,
A face without a heart?
LAERTES.   Why ask you this?
KING.   Not that I think you did not love your father,
But that I know love is begun by time, 110
And that I see, in passages of proof,°
Time qualifies° the spark and fire of it.
There lives within the very flame of love
A kind of wick or snuff° that will abate it,
And nothing is at a like goodness still,° 115
For goodness, growing to a plurisy,°
Dies in his own too-much. That we would do
We would do when we would, for this "would" changes,
And hath abatements and delays as many
As there are tongues, are hands, are accidents, 120
And then this "should" is like a spendthrift sigh,°
That hurts by easing. But to the quick° of th' ulcer—
Hamlet comes back; what would you undertake
To show yourself in deed your father's son
More than in words?
LAERTES.   To cut his throat i' th' church! 125
KING.   No place indeed should murder sanctuarize;°
Revenge should have no bounds. But, good Laertes,
Will you do this? Keep close within your chamber.
Hamlet returned shall know you are come home.
We'll put on those° shall praise your excellence 130
And set a double varnish on the fame
The Frenchman gave you, bring you in fine° together
And wager on your heads. He, being remiss,
Most generous, and free from all contriving,

99. *scrimers:* fencers.   111. *passages of proof:* proved cases.   112. *qualifies:* diminishes.
114. *snuff:* residue of burnt wick (which dims the light).   115. *still:* always.   116. *plurisy:* fullness,
excess.   121. *spendthrift sigh:* (sighing provides ease, but because it was thought to thin the blood and
so shorten life it was spendthrift).   122. *quick:* sensitive flesh.   126. *sanctuarize:* protect.
130. *We'll put on those:* we'll incite persons who.   132. *in fine:* finally.

Will not peruse the foils, so that with ease,   135
Or with a little shuffling, you may choose
A sword unbated,° and, in a pass of practice,°
Requite him for your father.
LAERTES.   I will do't,
And for that purpose I'll anoint my sword.
I bought an unction of a mountebank,°   140
So mortal that, but dip a knife in it,
Where it draws blood, no cataplasm° so rare,
Collected from all simples° that have virtue°
Under the moon, can save the thing from death
That is but scratched withal, I'll touch my point   145
With this contagion, that, if I gall him slightly,
It may be death.
KING.   Let's further think of this,
Weigh what convenience both of time and means
May fit us to our shape.° If this should fail,
And that our drift look through° our bad performance.   150
'Twere better not assayed. Therefore this project
Should have a back or second, that might hold
If this did blast in proof.° Soft, let me see.
We'll make a solemn wager on our cunnings—
I ha't!   155
When in your motion you are hot and dry—
As make your bouts more violent to that end—
And that he calls for drink, I'll have prepared him
A chalice for the nonce,° whereon but sipping,
If he by chance escape your venomed stuck,°   160
Our purpose may hold there.—But stay, what noise?

Enter QUEEN.

QUEEN.   One woe doth tread upon another's heel.
So fast they follow. Your sister's drowned, Laertes.
LAERTES.   Drowned! O, where?
QUEEN.   There is a willow grows askant° the brook,   165
That shows his hoar° leaves in the glassy stream:
Therewith° fantastic garlands did she make
Of crowflowers, nettles, daisies, and long purples,

---

137. *unbated:* not blunted.   137. *pass of practice:* treacherous thrust.   140. *mountebank:* quack.
142. *cataplasm:* poultice.   143. *simples:* medicinal herbs.   143. *virtue:* (power to heal).
149. *shape:* role.   150. *drift look through:* purpose show through.   153. *blast in proof:* burst (fail) in
performance   159. *nonce:* occasion.   160. *stuck:* thrust.   165. *askant:* aslant.
166. *hoar:* silver-gray.   167. *Therewith:* i.e., with willow twigs.

That liberal° shepherds give a grosser name, 169

But our cold maids do dead men's fingers call them. 170

There on the pendent boughs her crownet° weeds

Clamb'ring to hang, an envious sliver° broke,

When down her weedy trophies and herself

Fell in the weeping brook. Her clothes spread wide,

And mermaidlike awhile they bore her up, 175

Which time she chanted snatches of old lauds,°

As one incapable° of her own distress,

Or like a creature native and indued°

Unto that element. But long it could not be

Till that her garments, heavy with their drink, 180

Pulled the poor wretch from her melodious lay

To muddy death.

LAERTES.   Alas, then she is drowned?

QUEEN.   Drowned, drowned.

LAERTES.   Too much of water hast thou, poor Ophelia,

And therefore I forbid my tears; but yet 185

It is our trick;° nature her custom holds,

Let shame say what it will: when these are gone,

The woman° will be out. Adieu, my lord.

I have a speech o'fire, that fain would blaze,

But that this folly drowns it.   *Exit.*

KING.   Let's follow, Gertrude. 190

How much I had to do to calm his rage!

Now fear I this will give it start again;

Therefore let's follow.   *Exeunt.*

ACT V

SCENE I.   *A churchyard.*

Enter two CLOWNS.°

CLOWN.   Is she to be buried in Christian burial when she willfully seeks her own

    salvation?

OTHER.   I tell thee she is. Therefore make her grave straight.° The crowner° hath

    sate on her, and finds it Christian burial.

CLOWN.   How can that be, unless she drowned herself in her own defense? 5

OTHER.   Why, 'tis found so.

---

169. *liberal:* free-spoken, coarse-mouthed.   171. *crownet:* coronet.   172. *envious sliver:* malicious branch.   176. *lauds:* hymns.   177. *incapable:* unaware.   178. *indued:* in harmony with. 186. *trick:* trait, way.   188. *woman:* i.e., womanly part of me.   SCENE I. s.d. *Clowns:* rustics. 3. *straight:* straightway.   3. *crowner:* coroner.

CLOWN. It must be *se offendendo;°* it cannot be else. For here lies the point: if I
    drown myself wittingly, it argues an act, and an act hath three branches— it is
    to act, to do, to perform. Argal,° she drowned herself wittingly.

OTHER. Nay, but hear you, Goodman Delver. 10

CLOWN. Give me leave. Here lies the water—good. Here stands the man—good.
    If the man go to this water and drown himself, it is, will he nill he,° he goes;
    mark you that. But if the water come to him and drown him, he drowns not
    himself. Argal, he that is not guilty of his own death, shortens not his own life.

OTHER. But is this law? 15

CLOWN. Ay marry, is't—crowner's quest° law.

OTHER. Will you ha' the truth on't? If this had not been a gentlewoman, she
    should have been buried out o' Christian burial.

CLOWN. Why, there, thou say'st. And the more pity that great folk should have
    count'nance° in this world to drown or hang themselves more than their even- 20
    Christen.° Come, my spade. There is no ancient gentlemen but gard'ners,
    ditchers, and gravemakers. They hold up° Adam's profession.

OTHER. Was he a gentleman?

CLOWN. 'A was the first ever bore arms.°

OTHER. Why, he had none. 25

CLOWN. What, art a heathen? How dost thou understand the Scripture? The
    Scripture says Adam digged. Could he dig without arms? I'll put another
    question to thee. If thou answerest me not to the purpose, confess thyself——

OTHER. Go to.

CLOWN. What is he that builds stronger than either the mason, the shipwright, or 30
    the carpenter?

OTHER. The gallowsmaker, for that frame outlives a thousand tenants.

CLOWN. I like thy wit well, in good faith. The gallows does well. But how does it
    well? It does well to those that do ill. Now thou dost ill to say the gallows is
    built stronger than the church. Argal, the gallows may do well to thee. To't 35
    again, come.

OTHER. Who builds stronger than a mason, a shipwright, or a carpenter?

CLOWN. Ay, tell me that, and unyoke.°

OTHER. Marry, now I can tell.

CLOWN. To't. 40

OTHER. Mass,° I cannot tell.

Enter HAMLET *and* HORATIO *afar off.*

CLOWN. Cudgel thy brains no more about it, for your dull ass will not mend his
    pace with beating. And when you are asked this question next, say "grave-
    maker." The houses he makes lasts till doomsday. Go, get thee in, and fetch

---

7. *se offendendo:* (blunder for *se defendendo,* a legal term meaning "in self-defense").
9. *Argal:* (blunder for Latin *ergo,* "therefore"). 12. *will he nill he:* will he or will he not (whether he
will or will not). 16. *quest:* inquest. 20. *count'nance:* privilege. 21. *even-Christen:* fellow
Christian. 22. *hold up:* keep up. 24. *bore arms:* had a coat of arms (the sign of a gentleman).
38. *unyoke:* i.e., stop work for the day. 41. *Mass:* by the mass.

me a stoup° of liquor.   *Exit Other* CLOWN.   45

In youth when I did love, did love,   [*Song*]
    Methought it was very sweet
To contract—O—the time for—a—my behove,°
    O, methought there—a—was nothing—a—meet.

HAMLET.   Has this fellow no feeling of his business? 'A sings in gravemaking.   50
HORATIO.   Custom hath made it in him a property of easiness.°
HAMLET.   'Tis e'en so. The hand of little employment hath the daintier sense.°
CLOWN.   But age with his stealing steps   [*Song*]
    Hath clawed me in his clutch,
And hath shipped me into the land,   55
    As if I had never been such.   *Throws up a skull.*

HAMLET.   That skull had a tongue in it, and could sing once. How the knave jowls°
it to the ground, as if 'twere Cain's jawbone, that did the first murder! This
might be the pate of a politician, which this ass now o'erreaches,° one that
would circumvent God, might it not?   60
HORATIO.   It might, my lord.
HAMLET.   Or, of a courtier, which could say "Good morrow, sweet lord! How dost
thou, sweet lord?" This might be my Lord Such-a-one, that praised my Lord
Such-a-one's horse when 'a went to beg it, might it not?
HORATIO.   Ay, my lord.   65
HAMLET.   Why, e'en so, and now my Lady Worm's, chapless,° and knocked about
the mazzard° with a sexton's spade. Here's fine revolution, and we had the trick
to see't. Did these bones cost no more the breeding but to play at loggets° with
them? Mine ache to think on't.
CLOWN.   A pickax and a spade, a spade,   [*Song*]   70
    For and a shrouding sheet;
    O, a pit of clay for to be made
    For such a quest is meet.   *Throws up another skull.*
HAMLET.   There's another. Why may not that be the skull of a lawyer? Where be his
quiddities° now, his quillities,° his cases, his tenures,° and his tricks? Why does   75
he suffer this mad knave now to knock him about the sconce° with a dirty
shovel, and will not tell him of his action of battery? Hum! This fellow might
be in's time a great buyer of land, with his statutes, his recognizances, his fines,°
his double vouchers, his recoveries. Is this the fine° of his fines, and the recovery
of his recoveries, to have his fine pate full of fine dirt? Will his vouchers vouch   80
him no more of his purchases, and double ones too, than the length and

---

45. *stoup:* tankard.   48. *behove:* advantage.   51. *in him a property of easiness:* easy for him.   52. *hath the daintier sense:* is more sensitive (because it is not calloused).   57. *jowls:* hurls.
59. *o'erreaches:* (1) reaches over, (2) has the advantage over.   66. *chapless:* lacking the lower jaw.
67. *mazzard:* head.   68. *loggets:* (a game in which small pieces of wood were thrown at an object).
75. *quiddities:* subtle arguments (from Latin *quidditas,* "whatness").   75. *quillities:* fine distinctions.
75. *tenures:* legal means of holding land.   76. *sconce:* head.   78. *his statutes, his recognizances, his fines:* his documents giving a creditor control of a debtor's land, his bonds of surety, his documents changing an entailed estate into fee simple (unrestricted ownership).   79. *fine:* end.

breadth of a pair of indentures?° The very conveyances° of his lands will scarcely lie in this box, and must th' inheritor himself have no more, ha?

HORATIO.   Not a jot more, my lord.

HAMLET.   Is not parchment made of sheepskins?   85

HORATIO.   Ay, my lord, and of calveskins too.

HAMLET.   They are sheep and calves which seek out assurance° in that. I will speak to this fellow. Whose grave's this, sirrah?

CLOWN.   Mine, sir.

    [*Sings.*]   O, a pit of clay for to be made   90
                For such a guest is meet.

HAMLET.   I think it be thine indeed, for thou liest in't.

CLOWN.   You lie out on't, sir, and therefore 'tis not yours. For my part, I do not lie in't, yet it is mine.

HAMLET.   Thou dost lie in't, to be in't and say it is thine. 'Tis for the dead, not for   95
the quick;° therefore thou liest.

CLOWN.   'Tis a quick lie, sir; 'twill away again from me to you.

HAMLET.   What man dost thou dig it for?

CLOWN.   For no man, sir.

HAMLET.   What woman then?   100

CLOWN.   For none neither.

HAMLET.   Who is to be buried in't?

CLOWN.   One that was a woman, sir: but, rest her soul, she's dead.

HAMLET.   How absolute° the knave is! We must speak by the card,° or equivocation° will undo us. By the Lord, Horatio, this three years I have took note of it, the   105
age is grown so picked° that the toe of the peasant comes so near the heel of the courtier he galls his kibe.° How long hast thou been a grave-maker?

CLOWN.   Of all the days i' th' year, I came to't that day that our last king Hamlet overcame Fortinbras.

HAMLET.   How long is that since?   110

CLOWN.   Cannot you tell that? Every fool can tell that. It was that very day that young Hamlet was born—he that is mad, and sent into England.

HAMLET.   Ay, marry, why was he sent into England?

CLOWN.   Why, because 'a was mad. 'A shall recover his wits there; or, if 'a do not, 'tis no great matter there.   115

HAMLET.   Why?

CLOWN.   'Twill not be seen in him there. There the men are as mad as he.

HAMLET.   How came he mad?

CLOWN.   Very strangely, they say.

HAMLET.   How strangely?   120

CLOWN.   Faith, e'en with losing his wits.

---

82. *indentures:* contracts.   82. *conveyances:* legal documents for the transference of land.
87. *assurance:* safety.   96. *quick:* living.   104. *absolute:* positive, decided.   104. *by the card:* by the compass card, i.e., exactly.   104. *equivocation:* ambiguity.   106. *picked:* refined.   107. *kibe:* sore on the back of the heel.

HAMLET. Upon what ground?

CLOWN. Why, here in Denmark. I have been sexton here, man and boy, thirty years.

HAMLET. How long will a man lie i' th' earth ere he rot?

CLOWN. Faith, if 'a be not rotten before 'a die (as we have many pocky corses°   125
nowadays that will scarce hold the laying in), 'a will last you some eight year
or nine year. A tanner will last you nine year.

HAMLET. Why he, more than another?

CLOWN. Why, sir, his hide is so tanned with his trade that 'a will keep out water a
great while, and your water is a sore decayer of your whoreson dead body.   130
Here's a skull now hath lien you i' th' earth three and twenty years.

HAMLET. Whose was it?

CLOWN. A whoreson mad fellow's it was. Whose do you think it was?

HAMLET. Nay, I know not.

CLOWN. A pestilence on him for a mad rogue! 'A poured a flagon of Rhenish on   135
my head once. This same skull, sir, was, sir, Yorick's skull, the King's jester.

HAMLET. This?

CLOWN. E'en that.

HAMLET. Let me see. [*Takes the skull.*]   Alas, poor Yorick! I knew him, Horatio, a
fellow of infinite jest, of most excellent fancy. He hath borne me on his back a   140
thousand times. And now how abhorred in my imagination it is! My gorge rises
at it. Here hung those lips that I have kissed I know not how oft. Where be
your gibes now? Your gambols, your songs, your flashes of merriment that were
wont to set the table on a roar? Not one now to mock your own grinning?
Quite chapfall'n°? Now get you to my lady's chamber, and tell her, let her paint   145
an inch thick, to this favor° she must come. Make her laugh at that. Prithee,
Horatio, tell me one thing.

HORATIO. What's that, my lord?

HAMLET. Dost thou think Alexander looked o' this fashion i' th' earth?

HORATIO. E'en so.   150

HAMLET. And smelt so? Pah!   [*Puts down the skull.*]

HORATIO. E'en so, my lord.

HAMLET. To what base use we may return, Horatio! Why may not imagination
trace the noble dust of Alexander till 'a find it stopping a bunghole?

HORATIO. 'Twere to consider too curiously,° to consider so.   155

HAMLET. No, faith, not a jot, but to follow him thither with modesty enough,°
and likelihood to lead it; as thus: Alexander died, Alexander was buried, Alexander returneth to dust; the dust is earth; of earth we make loam; and why of
that loam whereto he was converted might they not stop a beer barrel?

Imperious Caesar, dead and turned to clay,   160
Might stop a hole to keep the wind away.

---

125. *pocky corses:* bodies of persons who had been infected with the pox (syphilis).
145. *chapfall'n:* (1) down in the mouth, (2) jawless.   146. *favor:* facial appearance.
155. *curiously:* minutely.   156. *with modesty enough:* without exaggeration.

O, that that earth which kept the world in awe
Should patch a wall t' expel th winter's flaw!°
But soft, but soft awhile! Here comes the King.

      Enter KING, QUEEN, LAERTES, *and a coffin, with* LORDS *attendant*
      [*and a* DOCTOR OF DIVINITY].

The Queen, the courtiers. Who is this they follow?   165
And with such maimèd° rites? This doth betoken
The corse they follow did with desp'rate hand
Fordo it° own life. 'Twas of some estate.°
Couch° we awhile, and mark.   [*Retires with* HORATIO.]
LAERTES.   What ceremony else?
HAMLET.   That is Laertes,   170
  A very noble youth. Mark.
LAERTES.   What ceremony else?
DOCTOR.   Her obsequies have been as far enlarged
  As we have warranty. Her death was doubtful,°
  And, but that great command o'ersways the order,   175
  She should in ground unsanctified been lodged
  Till the last trumpet. For charitable prayers,
  Shards,° flints, and pebbles should be thrown on her.
  Yet here she is allowed her virgin crants,°
  Her maiden strewments,° and the bringing home   180
  Of bell and burial.
LAERTES.   Must there no more be done?
DOCTOR.   No more be done.
  We should profane the service of the dead
  To sing a requiem and such rest to her
  As to peace-parted souls.
LAERTES.   Lay her i' th' earth,   185
  And from her fair and unpolluted flesh
  May violets spring! I tell thee, churlish priest,
  A minist'ring angel shall my sister be
  When thou liest howling!
HAMLET.   What, the fair Ophelia?
QUEEN.   Sweets to the sweet! Farewell.   *Scatters flowers.*   190
  I hoped thou shouldst have been my Hamlet's wife.
  I thought thy bride bed to have decked, sweet maid,
  And not have strewed thy grave.
LAERTES.   O, treble woe
  Fall ten times treble on that cursèd head

163. *flaw:* gust.   166. *maimèd:* incomplete.   168. *Fordo it:* destroy its.   168. *estate:* high rank.
169. *Couch:* hide.   174. *doubtful:* suspicious.   178. *Shards:* broken pieces of pottery.   179. *crants:*
garlands.   180. *strewments:* i.e., of flowers.

Whose wicked deed thy most ingenious sense°   195
Deprived thee of! Hold off the earth awhile,
Till I have caught her once more in mine arms.   *Leaps in the grave.*
Now pile your dust upon the quick and dead
Till of this flat a mountain you have made
T'o'ertop old Pelion° or the skyish head   200
Of blue Olympus.

HAMLET.   [*Coming forward*]   What is he whose grief
  Bears such an emphasis, whose phrase of sorrow
  Conjures the wand'ring stars,° and makes them stand
  Like wonder-wounded hearers? This is I,
  Hamlet the Dane.

LAERTES.   The devil take thy soul!   *Grapples with him.*°   205

HAMLET.   Thou pray'st not well.
  I prithee take thy fingers from my throat,
  For, though I am not splenitive° and rash,
  Yet have I in me something dangerous,
  Which let they wisdom fear. Hold off thy hand.   210

KING.   Pluck them asunder.

QUEEN.   Hamlet, Hamlet!

ALL.   Gentlemen!

HORATIO.   Good my lord, be quiet.   ATTENDANTS *part them.*

HAMLET.   Why, I will fight with them upon this theme
  Until my eyelids will no longer wag.

QUEEN.   O my son, what theme?   215

HAMLET.   I loved Ophelia. Forty thousand brothers
  Could not with all their quantity of love
  Make up my sum. What wilt thou do for her?

KING.   O, he is mad, Laertes.

QUEEN.   For love of God forbear him.   220

HAMLET.   'Swounds, show me what thou't do.
  Woo't weep? Woo't fight? Woo't fast? Woo't tear thyself?
  Woo't drink up eisel?° Eat a crocodile?
  I'll do't. Dost thou come here to whine?
  To outface me with leaping in her grave?   225
  Be buried quick with her, and so will I.
  And if thou prate of mountains, let them throw

---

195. *most ingenious sense:* finely endowed mind.   200. *Pelion:* (according to classical legend, giants in
their fight with the gods sought to reach heaven by piling Mount Pelion and Mount Ossa on Mount
Olympus).   203. *wand'ring stars:* planets.   205. s.d. *Grapples with him:* (Q1, a bad quarto, presumably reporting a version that toured, has a previous direction saying "Hamlet leaps in after Laertes."
Possibly he does so, somewhat hysterically. But such a direction—absent from the two good texts, Q2
and F—makes Hamlet the aggressor, somewhat contradicting his next speech. Perhaps Laertes leaps out
of the grave to attack Hamlet).   208. *splenitive:* fiery (the spleen was thought to be the seat of anger).
223. *eisel:* vinegar.

Millions of acres on us, till our ground,
Singeing his pate against the burning zone,°
Make Ossa like a wart! Nay, an thou'lt mouth, 230
I'll rant as well as thou.
QUEEN.   This is mere madness;
And thus a while the fit will work on him.
Anon, as patient as the female dove
When that her golden couplets are disclosed,°
His silence will sit drooping.
HAMLET.   Hear you, sir. 235
What is the reason that you use me thus?
I loved you ever. But it is no matter.
Let Hercules himself do what he may,
The cat will mew, and the dog will have his day.
KING.   I pray thee, good Horatio, wait upon him.   *Exit* HAMLET *and* HORATIO. 240
[*To* LAERTES]   Strengthen your patience in our last night's speech.
We'll put the matter to the present push.°
Good Gertrude, set some watch over your son.
This grave shall have a living° monument.
An hour of quiet shortly shall we see; 245
Till then in patience our proceeding be.   *Exeunt.*

SCENE II.   The castle.

Enter HAMLET and HORATIO.

HAMLET.   So much for this, sir; now shall you see the other.
You do remember all the circumstance?
HORATIO.   Remember it, my lord!
HAMLET.   Sir, in my heart there was a kind of fighting
That would not let me sleep. Methought I lay 5
Worse than the mutines in the bilboes.° Rashly
(And praised be rashness for it) let us know,
Our indiscretion sometime serves us well
When our deep plots do pall,° and that should learn us
There's a divinity that shapes our ends, 10
Rough-hew them how we will.
HORATIO.   That is most certain.
HAMLET.   Up from my cabin,
My sea gown scarfed about me, in the dark
Groped I to find out them, had my desire,
Fingered° their packet, and in fine° withdrew 15

---

229. *burning zone:* sun's orbit.   234. *golden couplets are disclosed:* (the dove lays two eggs, and the
newly hatched [disclosed] young are covered with golden down).   242. *present push:* immediate test.
244. *living:* lasting (with perhaps also a reference to the plot against Hamlet's life).
SCENE II 6. *mutines in the bilboes:* mutineers in fetters.   9. *pall:* fail.   15. *Fingered:* stole.
15. *in fine:* finally.

To mine own room again, making so bold,
My fears forgetting manners, to unseal
Their grand commission; where I found, Horatio—
Ah, royal knavery!—an exact command,
Larded° with many several sorts of reasons,   20
Importing Denmark's health, and England's too,
With, ho, such bugs and goblins in my life,°
That on the supervise,° no leisure bated,°
No, not to stay the grinding of the ax,
My head should be struck off.
HORATIO.   Is't possible?   25
HAMLET.   Here's the commission; read it at more leisure,
But wilt thou hear now how I did proceed?
HORATIO.   I beseech you.
HAMLET.   Being thus benetted round with villains,
Or° I could make a prologue to my brains,   30
They had begun the play. I sat me down,
Devised a new commission, wrote it fair.
I once did hold it, as our statists° do,
A baseness to write fair,° and labored much
How to forget that learning, but, sir, now   35
It did me yeoman's service. Wilt thou know
Th' effect° of what I wrote?
HORATIO.   Ay, good my lord.
HAMLET.   An earnest conjuration from the King,
As England was his faithful tributary,
As love between them like the palm might flourish,   40
As peace should still her wheaten garland wear
And stand a comma° 'tween their amities,
And many suchlike as's of great charge,°
That on the view and knowing of these contents,
Without debatement further, more or less,   45
He should those bearers put to sudden death,
Not shriving° time allowed.
HORATIO.   How was this sealed?
HAMLET.   Why, even in that was heaven ordinant.°
I had my father's signet in my purse,
Which was the model° of that Danish seal,   50
Folded the writ up in the form of th' other,
Subscribed it, gave't th' impression, placed it safely,
The changeling never known. Now, the next day

---

20. *Larded:* enriched.   22. *such bugs and goblins in my life:* such bugbears and imagined terrors if I
were allowed to live.   23. *supervise:* reading.   23. *leisure bated:* delay allowed.   30. *Or:* ere.
33. *statists:* statesmen.   34. *fair:* clearly.   37. *effect:* purport.   42. *comma:* link.
43. *great charge:* (1) serious exhortation, (2) heavy burden (punning on *as's* and "asses").
47. *shriving:* absolution.   48. *ordinant:* ruling.   50. *model:* counterpart.

Was our sea fight, and what to this was sequent
Thou knowest already. 55
HORATIO.　So Guildenstern and Rosencrantz go to't.
HAMLET.　Why, man, they did make love to this employment.
They are not near my conscience; their defeat
Does by their own insinuation° grow.
'Tis dangerous when the baser nature comes 60
Between the pass° and fell° incensèd points
Of might opposites.
HORATIO.　　　　　　Why, what a king is this!
HAMLET.　Does it not, think thee, stand me now upon°—
He that hath killed my king, and whored my mother,
Popped in between th' election° and my hopes, 65
Thrown out his angle° for my proper life,°
And with such coz'nage°—is't not perfect conscience
To quit° him with this arm? And is't not to be damned
To let this canker of our nature come
In further evil? 70
HORATIO.　It must be shortly known to him from England
What is the issue of the business there.
HAMLET.　It will be short; the interim's mine,
And a man's life's no more than to say "one."
But I am very sorry, good Horatio, 75
That to Laertes I forgot myself,
For by the image of my cause I see
The portraiture of his. I'll court his favors.
But sure the bravery° of his grief did put me
Into a tow'ring passion.
HORATIO.　　　　　Peace, who comes here? 80

Enter young OSRIC, *a courtier.*

OSRIC.　Your lordship is right welcome back to Denmark.
HAMLET.　I humbly thank you, sir.　[*Aside to* HORATIO]　Dost know this waterfly?
HORATIO.　[*Aside to* HAMLET]　No, my good lord.
HAMLET.　[*Aside to* HORATIO]　Thy state is the more gracious, for 'tis a vice to
know him. He hath much land, and fertile. Let a beast be lord of beasts, and 85
his crib shall stand at the king's mess.° 'Tis a chough,° but, as I say, spacious° in
the possession of dirt.
OSRIC.　Sweet lord, if your lordship were at leisure, I should impart a thing to you
from his Majesty.
HAMLET.　I will receive it, sir, with all diligence of spirit. Put your bonnet to his right 90
use. 'Tis for the head.

---

59. *insinuation:* meddling.　61. *pass:* thrust.　61. *fell:* cruel.　63. *stand me now upon:* become
incumbent upon me.　65. *election:* (the Danish monarchy was elective).　66. *angle:* fishing line.
66. *my proper life:* my own life.　67. *coz'nage:* trickery.　68. *quit:* pay back.　79. *bravery:* bravado.
86. *mess:* table.　86. *chough:* jackdaw (here, chatterer).　86. *spacious:* well off.

OSRIC.   I thank your lordship, it is very hot.

HAMLET.   No, believe me, 'tis very cold; the wind is northerly.

OSRIC.   It is indifferent cold, my lord, indeed.

HAMLET.   But yet methinks it is very sultry and hot for my complexion.°   95

OSRIC.   Exceedingly, my lord; it is very sultry, as 'twere —I cannot tell how. But, my lord, his Majesty bade me signify to you that 'a has laid a great wager on your head. Sir, this is the matter——

HAMLET.   I beseech you remember.

HAMLET *moves him to put on his hat.*

OSRIC.   Nay, good my lord; for ease, in good faith. Sir, here is newly come to court   100
Laertes—believe me, an absolute gentleman, full of most excellent differences,° of very soft society and great showing. Indeed, to speak feelingly°of him, he is the card° or calendar of gentry; for you shall find in him the continent° of what part of a gentleman would see.

HAMLET.   Sir, his definement° suffers no perdition° in you, though, I know, to divide   105
him inventorially would dozy° th' arithmetic of memory, and yet but yaw neither in respect of his quick sail.° But, in the verity of extolment, I take him to be a soul of great article,° and his infusion° of such dearth and rareness as, to make true diction° of him, his semblable° is his mirror, and who else would trace him, his umbrage,° nothing more.   110

OSRIC.   Your lordship speaks most infallibly of him.

HAMLET.   The concernancy,° sir? Why do we wrap the gentleman in our more rawer breath?

OSRIC.   Sir?

HORATIO.   Is't not possible to understand in another tongue? You will to't,° sir,   115
really.

HAMLET.   What imports the nomination of this gentleman?

OSRIC.   Of Laertes?

HORATIO.   [*Aside to* HAMLET]   His purse is empty already. All's golden words are spent.   120

HAMLET.   Of him, sir.

OSRIC.   I know you are not ignorant——

HAMLET.   I would you did, sir; yet, in faith, if you did, it would not much approve° me. Well, sir?

OSRIC.   You are not ignorant of what excellence Laertes is——   125

HAMLET.   I dare not confess that, lest I should compare with him in excellence; but to know a man well were to know himself.

---

95. *complexion:* temperament.   101. *differences:* distinguishing characteristics.   102. *feelingly:* justly.
103. *card:* chart.   103. *continent:* summary.   105. *definement:* description.   105. *perdition:* loss.
106. *dozy:* dizzy.   106–107. *and yet...quick sail:* i.e., and yet only stagger despite all (*yaw neither*) in trying to overtake his virtues.   108. *article:* (literally, "item," but here perhaps "traits" or "importance").   108. *infusion:* essential quality.   109. *diction:* description.   109. *semblable:* likeness.   110. *umbrage:* shadow.   112. *concernancy:* meaning.   115. *will to't:* will get there.
123. *approve:* commend.

OSRIC.   I mean, sir, for his weapon; but in the imputation° laid on him by them, in his meed° he's unfellowed.

HAMLET.   What's his weapon?   130

OSRIC.   Rapier and dagger.

HAMLET.   That's two of his weapons—but well.

OSRIC.   The King, sir, hath wagered with him six Barbary horses, against the which he has impawned,° as I take it, six French rapiers and poniards, with their assigns,° as girdle, hangers,° and so. Three of the carriages,° in faith, are very   135 dear to fancy, very responsive° to the hilts, most delicate carriages, and of very liberal conceit.°

HAMLET.   What call you the carriages?

HORATIO.   [*Aside to* HAMLET]   I knew you must be edified by the margent° ere you had done.   140

OSRIC.   The carriages, sir, are the hangers.

HORATIO.   The phrase would be more germane to the matter if we could carry a cannon by our sides. I would it might be hangers till then. But on! Six Barbary horses against six French swords, their assigns, and three liberal-conceited carriages—that's the French bet against the Danish. Why is this all impawned,   145 as you call it?

OSRIC.   The King, sir, hath laid, sir, that in a dozen passes between yourself and him he shall not exceed you three hits; he hath laid on twelve for nine, and it would come to immediate trial if your lordship would vouchsafe the answer.

HAMLET.   How if I answer no?   150

OSRIC.   I mean, my lord, the opposition of your person in trial.

HAMLET.   Sir, I will walk here in the hall. If it please his Majesty, it is the breathing time of day with me.° Let the foils be brought, the gentleman willing, and the King hold his purpose. I will win for him an I can; if not, I will gain nothing but my shame and the odd hits.   155

OSRIC.   Shall I deliver you e'en so?

HAMLET.   To this effect, sir, after what flourish your nature will.

OSRIC.   I commend my duty to your lordship.

HAMLET.   Yours, yours. [*Exit* OSRIC.]   He does well to commend it himself; there are no tongues else for's turn.   160

HORATIO.   This lapwing° runs away with the shell on his head.

HAMLET.   'A did comply, sir, with his dug° before 'a sucked it. Thus has he, and many more of the same breed that I know the drossy age dotes on, only got the tune of the time and, out of an habit of encounter,° a kind of yeasty°

---

128. *imputation:* reputation.   129. *meed:* merit.   134. *impawned:* wagered.   135. *assigns:* accompaniments.   135. *hangers:* straps hanging the sword to the belt.   135. *carriages:* (an affected word for hangers).   136. *responsive:* corresponding.   137. *liberal conceit:* elaborate design.
139. *margent:* i.e., marginal (explanatory) comment.   152–153. *breathing time of day with me:* time when I take exercise.   161 *lapwing:* (the new-hatched lapwing was thought to run around with half its shell on its head).   162. *'A did comply, sir, with his dug:* he was ceremoniously polite to his mother's breast.   164. *out of an habit of encounter:* out of his own superficial way of meeting and conversing with people.   164. *yeasty:* frothy.

collection, which carries them through and through the most fanned and 165
winnowed opinions; and do but blow them to their trial, the bubbles are out.°

    Enter a LORD.

LORD.   My lord, his Majesty commended him to you by young Osric, who brings
back to him that you attend him in the hall. He sends to know if your pleasure
hold to play with Laertes, or that you will take longer time.

HAMLET.   I am constant to my purposes; they follow the King's pleasure. If his 170
fitness speaks, mine is ready; now or whensoever, provided I be so able as now.

LORD.   The King and Queen and all are coming down.

HAMLET.   In happy time.

LORD.   The Queen desires you to use some gentle entertainment° to Laertes before
you fall to play. 175

HAMLET.   She well instructs me. [*Exit* LORD.]

HORATIO.   You will lose this wager, my lord.

HAMLET.   I do not think so. Since he went into France I have been in continual
practice. I shall win at the odds. But thou wouldst not think how ill all's here
about my heart. But it is no matter. 180

HORATIO.   Nay, good my lord——

HAMLET.   It is but foolery, but it is such a kind of gaingiving° as would perhaps
trouble a woman.

HORATIO.   If your mind dislike anything, obey it. I will forestall their repair hither
and say you are not fit. 185

HAMLET.   Not a whit, we defy augury. There is a special providence in the fall of a
sparrow.° If it be now, 'tis not to come; if it be not to come, it will be now; if
it be not now, yet it will come. The readiness is all. Since no man of aught he
leaves knows, what is't to leave betimes?° Let be.

    A table prepared. [*Enter*] *Trumpets, Drums, and* OFFICERS *with cushions;*
    KING, QUEEN, [OSRIC,] *and all the State, with foils, daggers,* [*and stoups of wine
borne in*]; *and* LAERTES.

KING.   Come, Hamlet, come, and take this hand from me. 190

    The KING *puts* LAERTES*'s hand into* HAMLET*'s.*

HAMLET.   Give me your pardon, sir. I have done you wrong,
But pardon't, as you are a gentleman.
This presence° knows, and you must needs have heard,
How I am punished with a sore distraction.
What I have done 195
That might your nature, honor, and exception°

---

166. *the bubbles are out:* i.e., they are blown away (the reference is to the "yeasty collection").   174. *to use some gentle entertainment:* to be courteous.   182. *gaingiving:* misgiving.   186–187. *the fall of a sparrow:* (cf. Matthew 10:29 "Are not two sparrows sold for a farthing? and one of them shall not fall on the ground without your Father").   189. *betimes:* early.   193. *presence:* royal assembly.   196. *exception:* disapproval.

Roughly awake, I here proclaim was madness.
Was't Hamlet wronged Laertes? Never Hamlet.
If Hamlet from himself be ta'en away,
And when he's not himself does wrong Laertes,   200
Then Hamlet does it not, Hamlet denies it.
Who does it then? His madness. If't be so,
Hamlet is of the faction° that is wronged;
His madness is poor Hamlet's enemy.
Sir, in this audience,   205
Let my disclaiming from a purposed evil
Free me so far in your most generous thoughts
That I have shot my arrow o'er the house
And hurt my brother.
LAERTES.   I am satisfied in nature,
Whose motive in this case should stir me most   210
To my revenge. But in my terms of honor
I stand aloof, and will no reconcilement
Till by some elder master of known honor
I have a voice and precedent° of peace
To keep my name ungored. But till that time   215
I do receive your offered love like love,
And will not wrong it.
HAMLET.   I embrace it freely,
And will this brother's wager frankly play,
Give us the foils. Come on.
LAERTES.   Come, one for me.
HAMLET.   I'll be your foil,° Laertes. In mine ignorance   220
Your skill shall, like a star i' th' darkest night,
Stick fiery off° indeed.
LAERTES.   You mock me, sir.
HAMLET.   No, by this hand.
KING.   Give me the foils, young Osric. Cousin Hamlet,
You know the wager?
HAMLET.   Very well, my lord.   225
Your grace has laid the odds o' th' weaker side.
KING.   I do not fear it, I have seen you both;
But since he is bettered,° we have therefore odds.
LAERTES.   This is too heavy; let me see another.
HAMLET.   This likes me well. These foils have all a length?   *Prepare to play.*   230
OSRIC.   Ay, my good lord.
KING.   Set me the stoups of wine upon that table.
If Hamlet give the first or second hit,

203. *faction:* party, side.   214. *voice and precedent:* authoritative opinion justified by precedent.
220. *foil:* (1) blunt sword, (2) background (of metallic leaf) for a jewel.   222. *Stick fiery off:* stand out
brilliantly.   228. *bettered:* has improved (in France).

Or quit° in answer of the third exchange,
Let all the battlements their ordnance fire.   235
The King shall drink to Hamlet's better breath,
And in the cup an union° shall he throw
Richer than that which four successive kings
In Denmark's crown have worn. Give me the cups,
And let the kettle° to the trumpet speak,   240
The trumpet to the cannoneer without,
The cannons to the heavens, the heaven to earth,
"Now the King drinks to Hamlet." Come, begin.   *Trumpets the while.*
And you, the judges, bear a wary eye.

HAMLET.   Come on, sir.
LAERTES.   Come, my lord.   *They play.*
HAMLET.   One.
LAERTES.   No.
HAMLET.   Judgment?   245
OSRIC.   A hit, a very palpable hit.

Drum, trumpets, and shot. Flourish; a piece goes off.

LAERTES.   Well, again.
KING.   Stay, give me drink. Hamlet, this pearl is thine.
Here's to thy health. Give him the cup.
HAMLET.   I'll play this bout first; set it by awhile.
Come. [*They play.*] Another hit. What say you?   250
LAERTES.   A touch, a touch; I do confess't.
KING.   Our son shall win.
QUEEN.   He's fat,° and scant of breath.
Here, Hamlet, take my napkin, rub thy brows.
The Queen carouses to thy fortune, Hamlet.
HAMLET.   Good madam!
KING.   Gertrude, do not drink.   255
QUEEN.   I will, my lord; I pray you pardon me. [*Drinks.*]
KING.   [*Aside*] It is the poisoned cup; it is too late.
HAMLET.   I dare not drink yet, madam—by and by.
QUEEN.   Come, let me wipe thy face.
LAERTES.   My lord, I'll hit him now.
KING.   I do not think't.   260
LAERTES.   [*Aside*] And yet it is almost against my conscience.
HAMLET.   Come for the third, Laertes. You do but dally.
I pray you pass with your best violence;
I am sure you make a wanton° of me.
LAERTES.   Say you so? Come on. [*They*] *play.*   265
OSRIC.   Nothing neither way.

---

234. *quit:* repay, hit back. 237. *union:* pearl. 240. *kettle:* kettledrum. 252. *fat:* (1) sweaty,
(2) out of training. 264. *wanton:* spoiled child.

LAERTES.   Have at you now!

In scuffling they change rapiers [and both are wounded].

KING.   Part them. They are incensed.
HAMLET.   Nay, come—again!   [*The* QUEEN *falls.*]
OSRIC.   Look to the Queen there, ho!
HORATIO.   They bleed on both sides. How is it, my lord?
OSRIC.   How is't, Laertes?   270
LAERTES.   Why, as a woodcock to mine own springe,° Osric.
    I am justly killed with mine own treachery.
HAMLET.   How does the Queen?
KING.   She sounds° to see them bleed.
QUEEN.   No, no, the drink, the drink! O my dear Hamlet!
    The drink, the drink! I am poisoned.   [*Dies.*]   275
HAMLET.   O villainy! Ho! Let the door be locked.
    Treachery! Seek it out.   [LAERTES *falls.*]
LAERTES.   It is here, Hamlet. Hamlet, thou art slain;
    No med'cine in the world can do thee good.
    In thee there is not half an hour's life.   280
    The treacherous instrument is in thy hand,
    Unbated and envenomed. The foul practice°
    Hath turned itself on me, Lo, here I lie,
    Never to rise again. Thy mother's poisoned.
    I can no more. The King, the King's to blame.   285
HAMLET.   The point envenomed too?
    Then, venom, to thy work.   *Hurts the* KING.
ALL.   Treason! Treason!
KING.   O, yet defend me, friends, I am but hurt.
HAMLET.   Here, thou incestuous, murd'rous, damnèd Dane,   290
    Drink off his potion. Is thy union here?
    Follow my mother,   KING *dies.*
LAERTES.   He is justly served.
    It is a poison tempered° by himself,
    Exchange forgiveness with me, noble Hamlet.
    Mine and my father's death come not upon thee,   295
    Nor thine on me!   *Dies.*
HAMLET.   Heaven made thee free of it! I follow thee.
    I am dead, Horatio. Wretched Queen, adieu!
    You that look pale and tremble at this chance,
    That are but mutes° or audience to this act,   300
    Had I but time (as this fell sergeant,° Death,
    Is strict in his arrest) O, I could tell you—
    But let it be. Horatio, I am dead;

271. *springe:* snare.   273. *sounds:* swoons.   282. *practice:* deception.   293. *tempered:* mixed.
300. *mutes:* performers who have no words to speak.   301. *fell sergeant:* dread sheriff's officer.

Thou livest; report me and my cause aright
To the unsatisfied.°
HORATIO.   Never believe it.   305
  I am more an antique Roman° than a Dane.
  Here's yet some liquor left.
HAMLET.   As th' art a man,
  Give me the cup. Let go. By heaven, I'll ha't!
  O God, Horatio, what a wounded name,
  Things standing thus unknown, shall live behind me!   310
  If thou didst ever hold me in thy heart,
  Absent thee from felicity° awhile,
  And in this harsh world draw thy breath in pain,
  To tell my story.   *A march afar off.* [*Exit* OSRIC.]
                    What warlike noise is this?

                    Enter OSRIC.

OSRIC.   Young Fortinbras, with conquest come from Poland,   315
  To th' ambassadors of England gives
  This warlike volley.
HAMLET.   O, I die, Horatio!
  The potent poison quite o'ercrows° my spirit.
  I cannot live to hear the news from England,
  But I do prophesy th' election lights   320
  On Fortinbras. He has my dying voice.
  So tell him, with th' occurrents,° more and less,
  Which have solicited°—the rest is silence.   *Dies.*
HORATIO.   Now cracks a noble heart. Good night, sweet Prince,
  And flights of angels sing thee to thy rest.   *March within.*   325
  Why does the drum come hither?

Enter FORTINBRAS, *with the* AMBASSADORS *with Drum, Colors, and* ATTENDANTS.

FORTINBRAS.   Where is this sight?
HORATIO.   What is it you would see?
  If aught of woe or wonder, cease your search.
FORTINBRAS.   This quarry° cries on havoc.° O proud Death,
  What feast is toward° in thine eternal cell   330
  That thou so many princes at a shot
  So bloodily has struck?
AMBASSADOR.   The sight is dismal;
  And our affairs from England come too late.
  The ears are senseless that should give us hearing

305. *unsatisfied:* uninformed.   306. *antique Roman:* (with reference to the old Roman fashion of suicide).   312. *felicity:* i.e., the felicity of death.   318. *o'ercrows:* overpowers (as a triumphant cock crows over its weak opponent).   322. *occurrents:* occurrences.   323. *solicited:* incited.   329. *quarry:* heap of slain bodies.   329. *cries on havoc:* proclaims general slaughter.   330. *toward:* in preparation.

To tell him his commandment is fulfilled,   335
That Rosencrantz and Guildenstern are dead.
Where should we have our thanks?
HORATIO.   Not from his° mouth,
  Had it th' ability of life to thank you.
  He never gave commandment for their death.
  But since, so jump° upon this bloody question,   340
  You from the Polack wars, and you from England,
  Are here arrived, give order that these bodies
  High on a stage° be placèd to the view,
  And let me speak to th' yet unknowing world
  How these things came about. So shall you hear   345
  Of carnal, bloody, and unnatural acts,
  Of accidental judgments, casual° slaughters,
  Of deaths put on by cunning and forced cause,
  And, in this upshot, purposes mistook
  Fall'n on th' inventors' heads. All this can I   350
  Truly deliver.
FORTINBRAS.   Let us haste to hear it,
  And call the noblest to the audience.
  For me, with sorrow I embrace my fortune.
  I have some rights of memory° in this kingdom,
  Which now to claim my vantage doth invite me.   355
HORATIO.   Of that I shall have also cause to speak,
  And from his mouth whose voice will draw on° more.
  But let this same be presently performed,
  Even while men's minds are wild, lest more mischance
  On° plots and errors happen.
FORTINBRAS.   Let four captains   360
  Bear Hamlet like a soldier to the stage,
  For he was likely, had he been put on,°
  To have proved most royal; and for his passage°
  The soldiers' music and the rite of war
  Speak loudly for him.   365
  Take up the bodies. Such a sight as this
  Becomes the field,° but here shows much amiss.
  Go, bid the soldiers shoot.

   Exeunt marching; after the which a peal of ordnance are shot off.

                              FINIS

                                          Edited by Edward Hubler

---

337. *his:* (Claudius's).   340. *jump:* precisely.   343. *stage:* platform.   347. *casual:* not humanly
planned, chance.   354. *rights of memory:* remembered claims.   357. *voice will draw on:* vote will
influence.   359. *On:* on top of.   362. *put on:* advanced (to the throne).   363. *passage:* death.
367. *field:* battlefield.

Journal Entry

Discuss the difference between Ophelia's and Hamlet's madness.

Textual Considerations

1. In act 2, Hamlet tries to discover the facts about Claudius' guilt while the king attempts to uncover the truth about Hamlet's madness. Explain what their plans have in common.
2. Discuss the degree to which Hamlet's bitterness and sorrow are attributable to his mother's remarrying rather than to his father's death.
3. To what extent is Laertes a **foil** to Hamlet? (See the glossary.) Compare, for example, their responses to their fathers' murders.
4. Investigate the dramatic development of the play from its two extremes—the ghost's urge to disclose his story to Hamlet in act 1, scene 5, and Hamlet's urge to reveal his story to Horatio in act 5, scene 2. What do these scenes reveal about Old Hamlet's and Hamlet's attitudes toward their origins? How effectively do these scenes enhance the dramatic action of the play?
5. Review Hamlet's interview with Ophelia in act 3, scene 1. Consider what his comments reveal about the motives and attitudes that prompt him to cast Ophelia, rather than Claudius, as his antagonist.
6. Discuss how Hamlet's act of remembering and forgetting the ghost—or his ambivalence toward the ghost's narrative—informs his own private identity and his public responsibility to Denmark.

Cultural Contexts

1. What can we infer about Ophelia's and Gertrude's roles in *Hamlet?* Do these feminine characters merely fulfill the gender roles in the play, or do they also add to our understanding of Hamlet's character? Investigate also how Ophelia and Gertrude narrate the past, and how they establish a dramatic dialogue with the present and the future. How do Hamlet's attacks on these characters and on women in general affect your response to the drama?
2. Explore the father–son relationship in *Hamlet.* In your discussion, debate with your group whether Hamlet, by inheriting the past and his father's designs, is also forced to inherit his father's moral law.
3. Attempt a dramatic production of one of the scenes of *Hamlet.* To enlarge your understanding of the play, research some portrayals of Hamlet such as Laurence Olivier's and Mel Gibson's. Then discuss with your group how you would handle scenery, costumes, casting, theme, and characters.

WRITING TOPICS

1. The understanding of parent by child or child by parent in this universally significant relationship is the focus of several relationships in Part One. Select two authors, and compare and contrast the portrayal of parents in the texts by Doro, Gilyard, and Gillan, or the role of parents in the poems by Levertov, Emanuel, Lorde, or Tapahonso. What insights did the speakers gain through their recollections of family? To what extent are their relationships characterized by conflicting emotions?

2. A particular place evokes significant insights for the characters in "Araby," "The Watch," and "Roman Fever." Analyze the interaction between people and places that make these insights possible.

3. Several short stories in Part One focus on the passage of time and the changes that occur in the lives of the characters. Using "Araby," "The Death of Ivan Ilych," "First Confession," "The Watch," or "Young Goodman Brown," compare and contrast the attitudes that any two characters in two of the stories take toward the passage of time.

4. Ernest Gaines and Robert Hayden focus on the heritage of African Americans. Analyze the interaction of past and present in "The Sky Is Gray" and "Tour 5." Include the role of setting in your analysis.

5. Rewrite Hamlet's dilemma from Horatio's point of view, and discuss the degree to which his view corresponds with your own.

6. Explore the mother/son relationship in "The Sky Is Gray" and "The Hatmaker." How are the mothers similar or different? To what extent do they conform to traditional roles? How have their character traits influenced the behavior and values of their sons? What emotional ties were you aware of in both texts?

7. The protagonists in "Araby," "The Sky Is Gray," "The Watch," and "Roman Fever" are involved in literal and symbolic journeys. Trace these journeys in any two texts, and analyze their emotional, physical, and/or psychological significance for the characters' lives.

8. In "Knoxville: Summer 1915," James Agee captures the complexity of our relationship to places, particularly to the places where we grew up, while in "My People," Chief Seattle explains why kinship with nature is an indispensible part of Native-American heritage. Compare and contrast the role of Nature in each essay. How have their responses to Nature affected both speakers' lives?

9. At the outset of the play *Oedipus Rex*, Oedipus as King is attempting to answer an objective question: Who murdered King Laios? As the drama progresses, however, Oedipus as an individual is confronted with the *subjective* question: Who am I? Explain what he learns about himself as he seeks to answer both questions.

10. Compare and contrast the journey from innocence to experience as portrayed in "Araby," "The Sky Is Gray," and/or "Young Goodman Brown." Focus on what each protagonist has gained as well as lost.

RESEARCH TOPICS

1. Carry out a research project on your family's history: tape interviews with family members, and collect old family photos, letters, diaries, memoirs, or any other family records that you might use as supporting evidence. Then check library sources, such as newspapers and magazines, to identify the major sociohistorical events that were part of your family's history. In writing the paper, consider assuming the personal voice of a family member and narrating your family history from his or her point of view.

2. Some novelists and intellectuals have shown a strong preference for "the pastness of the past"; others believe that only through a commitment to the present can a country re-create itself. Carry out research to demonstrate the advantages and/or disadvantages of both positions. You might explore, for instance, how African Americans or Native Americans had to come to terms with the burdens of the past, such as slavery and exploitation, in order to define their present and re-create themselves. Consult as your primary sources works by African Americans (Margaret Walker, Gwendolyn Brooks, and Robert Hayden); Native Americans (Linda Hogan, Maurice Kenny, Duane Niatum); and Asian Americans (Janice Mirikitani, Maxine Hong Kingston, Amy Tan).

3. Many critics have argued that *Hamlet* belongs to the literary tradition of the revenge tragedy—a type of drama whose literary conventions demand suspense, violence, and revenge for a murder. Research the conventions of the revenge play, and demonstrate the extent to which you would or would not apply such conventions to *Hamlet*.

4. Write a research topic in which you explore your understanding of "Young Goodman Brown" in relation to the story of Adam and Eve (*Genesis*) and Young Goodman Brown's view of his own Puritan ancestors.

GROUP RESEARCH TOPIC

Several popular films of recent years including *Hook, Back to the Future, Big, The Terminator,* and *Terminator 2,* have, in varied ways, tied the theme of time travel to the possibility of changing the course of an individual's life, either at its origins or in the future. Analyze one or more of these films with your group, and in a documented essay consulting at least three sources, discuss how such fantasies express genuine human desires and aspirations.

PART TWO
Gender and Identity

Fiction

The Revolt of "Mother," Mary E. Wilkins Freeman ◆ *A Respectable Woman,* Kate Chopin ◆ *The Storm,* Kate Chopin ◆ *Roselily,* Alice Walker ◆ *Name Games,* Michael Dorris ◆ *The Yellow Wallpaper,* Charlotte Perkins Gilman ◆ *Another Evening at the Club,* Alifa Rifaat

Essays

Professions for Women, Virginia Woolf ◆ *One Man's Kids,* Daniel Meier

Poetry

The Faithful Wife, Barbara L. Greenberg ◆ *Genesis,* Mahwash Shoaib ◆ *Afterbirth,* Mahwash Shoaib ◆ *The Silk Carpet,* Mahwash Shoaib ◆ *Ragazza,* Maryfrances Wagner ◆ *Petals of Silence,* Maria Mazziotti Gillan ◆ *Borders,* Pat Mora ◆ *Elena,* Pat Mora ◆ *Home Burial,* Robert Frost ◆ *The Harlem Dancer,* Claude McKay ◆ *What Lips My Lips Have Kissed,* Edna St. Vincent Millay ◆ *My Last Duchess,* Robert Browning ◆ *Porphyria's Lover,* Robert Browning ◆ *To His Coy Mistress,* Andrew Marvell ◆ *The Willing Mistress,* Aphra Behn ◆ *The Young Warrior,* Gayle Two Eagles ◆ *For My Lover, Returning to His Wife,* Anne Sexton ◆ *Bright Star,* John Keats ◆ *She Proves the Inconsistency of the Desires and Criticism of Men Who Accuse Women of What They Themselves Cause,* Sor Juana Inés de la Cruz ◆ *30 ("When to the Sessions of Sweet Silent Thought"),* William Shakespeare ◆ *116 ("Let Me Not to the Marriage of True Minds"),* William Shakespeare ◆ *129 ("Th' Expense of Spirit in a Waste of Shame"),* William Shakespeare ◆ *130 ("My Mistress' Eyes Are Nothing Like the Sun"),* William Shakespeare

Drama

Medea, Euripides ◆ *From Preface to Miss Julie,* August Strindberg ◆ *Miss Julie,* August Strindberg

The culturally diverse texts in Part Two present a number of points of view on the relationships between men and women and their perceptions of each other. The writers ask, among other things, why various cultures have constructed different images of women at different points in their history, images as wide-ranging as goddess, rebel, warrior, sex object, mother, wife, and "other." Since most cultures have been dominated by men, the choice of female image no doubt projects a powerful representation of the male's own image. Many male and female writers included here invite you to evaluate the merit of sexual politics that promotes a male-dominated model of gender relationships.

Looking back, we discover several traditions that have created images of women to represent specific models of male–female relations. Major among these is the idealizing tradition, which portrays women as different and superior beings. For example, the Greek story of Pygmalion—the legendary sculptor who fell in love with the female statue he carved according to his own inspired view of beauty—illustrates an extreme idealization of the notion of woman. Such an idealization often transforms a woman into a love object that men can use to escape immediate reality. Other idealizing traditions, such as platonic love and courtly love, also explore the Pygmalion model of gender relations. Keats's sonnet "Bright Star" (1819), for example, evokes a romantic concept of women in the poet's transforming his mistress into an image of permanence essential to his orderly view of the world. Shakespeare's sonnet "My Mistress' Eyes Are Nothing Like the Sun" playfully rejects the idealizing tradition of his poetic predecessors; he views his lover more realistically, in keeping with his Renaissance tradition.

Sor Juana Inés de la Cruz, in "She Proves the Inconsistency…," addresses the mystique of gender relations through the Christian focus that polarizes the image of a woman into an "angel" or "demon." The poet protests against the tradition that debased women in seventeenth-century Mexico, reflecting the cultural oppression of "raw erotic play," or the game of male power and dominance in which, if a woman says no, "she has no heart," and if she says yes, "she's a whore." To keep pace with the social evolution of "the modern woman," we should perhaps ask what has happened to the polar image of "virgin–whore" in our own day. To what extent have women and men been able to overcome the "raw erotic play" that has tended to shape male–female relations in terms of male power and dominance?

Other texts focus on various aspects of marriage. Frost's poem "Home Burial" and Mora's "Elena" examine the difficulties men and women often encounter in trying to communicate their emotions to each other. Two short stories, "The Revolt of 'Mother'," set in nineteenth-century New England, and "Another Evening at the Club," which takes place in present-day Egypt, explore the extent to which the cult of feminine domesticity and financial dependence has perpetuated the power of the patriarchal system. The selections by Chopin, Millay, Sexton, and Greenberg, explore the question of women's sexuality, while Native American Gayle Two Eagles's poem raises the possibility that great warrior deeds can be successfully appropriated by women.

The dramas *Medea* and *Miss Julie* focus on the destructive effects of dominance in gender relationships. *Medea,* Euripides' classical Greek play, reinforces the myth of woman as *femme fatale* by dramatizing the story of a forsaken woman who resorts to an extreme revenge to re-establish her sense of justice. In Strindberg's nineteenth-century play *Miss Julie,* the protagonist is unable to liberate herself from her obsession to dominate her lover and servant Jean, a reversal of the usual gender role pattern.

As you join the debate here between feminists and patriarchs in these and other texts from various cultures and traditions, you will be invited to speculate on questions such as the following: Are men rightly in charge of the family and tribe? Should women be accorded the same personal, political, and economic rights as men? How have men and women used traditional concepts of sexuality, femininity and masculinity to manipulate each other? To what extent has the ancient ideal of male supremacy been detrimental to men as well as women? How have traditional societal roles influenced gender identity? What new possibilities are there for healthier gender relationships and more fulfilled individual selves? For despite the difficulties involved in forming relationships, one theme in all these texts remains constant: We are social beings whose personal and cultural identities are rooted in our need for relatedness.

Mary E. Wilkins Freeman
1891

The Revolt of "Mother"

"Father!"

"What is it?"

"What are them men diggin' over there in the field for?"

There was a sudden dropping and enlarging of the lower part of the old man's face, as if some heavy weight had settled therein; he shut his mouth tight, and went on harnessing the great bay mare. He hustled the collar on to her neck with a jerk.

"Father!"

The old man slapped the saddle upon the mare's back.

"Look here, father, I want to know what them men are diggin' over in the field for, an' I'm goin' to know."

"I wish you'd go into the house, mother, an' 'tend to your own affairs," the old man said then. He ran his words together, and his speech was almost as inarticulate as a growl.

But the woman understood; it was her most native tongue. "I ain't goin' into the house till you tell me what them men are doin' over there in the field," said she.

Then she stood waiting. She was a small woman, short and straight-waisted like a child in her brown cotton gown. Her forehead was mild and benevolent between the smooth curves of gray hair; there were meek downward lines about her nose and mouth; but her eyes, fixed upon the old man, looked as if the meekness had been the result of her own will, never of the will of another.

They were in the barn, standing before the wide open doors. The spring air, full of the smell of growing grass and unseen blossoms, came in their faces. The deep yard in front was littered with farm wagons and piles of wood; on the edges, close to the fence and the house, the grass was a vivid green, and there were some dandelions.

The old man glanced doggedly at his wife as he tightened the last buckles on the harness. She looked as immovable to him as one of the rocks in his pasture-land, bound to the earth with generations of blackberry vines. He slapped the reins over the horse, and started forth from the barn.

"*Father!*" said she.

The old man pulled up. "What is it?"

"I want to know what them men are diggin' over there in the field for."

"They're diggin' a cellar, I s'pose, if you've got to know."

"A cellar for what?"

"A barn."

"A barn? You ain't goin' to build a barn over there where we was goin' to have a house, father?"

The old man said not another word. He hurried the horse into the farm wagon, and clattered out of the yard, jouncing as sturdily on his seat as a boy.

The woman stood a moment looking after him, then she went out of the barn across a corner of the yard to the house. The house, standing at right angles with the great barn and a long reach of sheds and out-buildings, was infinitesimal compared with them. It was scarcely as commodious for people as the little boxes under the barn eaves were for doves.

A pretty girl's face, pink and delicate as a flower, was looking out of one of the house windows. She was watching three men who were digging over in the field which bounded the yard near the road line. She turned quietly when the woman entered.

"What are they digging for, mother?" said she. "Did he tell you?"

"They're diggin' for—a cellar for a new barn."

"Oh, mother, he ain't going to build another barn?"

"That's what he says."

A boy stood before the kitchen glass combing his hair. He combed slowly and painstakingly, arranging his brown hair in a smooth hillock over his forehead. He did not seem to pay any attention to the conversation.

"Sammy, did you know father was going to build a new barn?" asked the girl.

The boy combed assiduously.

"Sammy!"

He turned, and showed a face like his father's under his smooth crest of hair. "Yes, I s'pose I did," he said, reluctantly.

"How long have you known it?" asked his mother.

"'Bout three months, I guess."

"Why didn't you tell of it?"

"Didn't think 'twould do no good."

"I don't see what father wants another barn for," said the girl, in her sweet, slow voice. She turned again to the window, and stared out at the digging men in the field. Her tender, sweet face was full of a gentle distress. Her forehead was as bald and innocent as a baby's with the light hair strained back from it in a row of curl-papers. She was quite large, but her soft curls did not look as if they covered muscles.

Her mother looked sternly at the boy. "Is he goin' to buy more cows?" said she.

The boy did not reply; he was tying his shoes.

"Sammy, I want you to tell me if he's goin' to buy more cows."

"I s'pose he is."

"How many?"

"Four, I guess."

His mother said nothing more. She went into the pantry, and there was a clatter of dishes. The boy got his cap from a nail behind the door, took an old arithmetic from the shelf, and started for school. He was lightly built, but clumsy. He went out of the yard with a curious spring in the hips, that made his loose home-made jacket tilt up in the rear.

The girl went to the sink, and began to wash the dishes that were piled up there. Her mother came promptly out of the pantry, and shoved her aside. "You wipe 'em," said she; "I'll wash. There's a good many this mornin'."

The mother plunged her hands vigorously into the water, the girl wiped the plates slowly and dreamily. "Mother," said she, "don't you think it's too bad father's going to build that new barn, much as we need a decent house to live in?"

Her mother scrubbed a dish fiercely. "You ain't found out yet we're women-folks, Nanny Penn," said she. "You ain't seen enough of men-folks yet to. One of these days you'll find it out, an' then you'll know that we know only what men-folks think we do, so far as any use of it goes, an' how we'd ought to reckon men-folks in with Providence, an' not complain of what they do any more than we do of the weather."

"I don't care; I don't believe George is anything like that, anyhow," said Nanny. Her delicate face flushed pink, her lips pouted softly, is if she were going to cry.

"You wait an' see. I guess George Eastman ain't no better than other men. You hadn't ought to judge father, though. He can't help it, 'cause he don't look at things jest the way we do. An' we've been pretty comfortable here, after all. The roof don't leak—ain't never but once—that's one thing. Father's kept it shingled right up."

"I do wish we had a parlor."

"I guess it won't hurt George Eastman any to come to see you in a nice clean kitchen. I guess a good many girls don't have as good a place as this. Nobody's ever heard me complain."

"I ain't complained either, mother."

"Well, I don't think you'd better, a good father an' a good home as you've got. S'pose your father made you go out an' work for your livin'? Lots of girls have to that ain't no stronger an' better able to than you be."

Sarah Penn washed the frying-pan with a conclusive air. She scrubbed the out-side of it as faithfully as the inside. She was a masterly keeper of her box of a house. Her one living-room never seemed to have in it any of the dust which the friction of life with inanimate matter produces. She swept, and there seemed to be no dirt to go before the broom; she cleaned, and one could see no difference. She was like an artist so perfect that he has apparently no art. To-day she got out a mixing bowl and a board, and rolled some pies, and there was no more flour upon her than upon her daughter who was doing finer work. Nanny was to be married in the fall, and she was sewing on some white cambric and embroidery. She sewed industri-ously while her mother cooked, her soft milk-white hands and wrists showed whiter than her delicate work.

"We must have the stove moved out in the shed before long," said Mrs. Penn. "Talk about not havin' things, it's been a real blessin' to be able to put a stove up in that shed in hot weather. Father did one good thing when he fixed that stove-pipe out there."

Sarah Penn's face as she rolled her pies had that expression of meek vigor which might have characterized one of the New Testament saints. She was making mince pies. Her husband, Adoniram Penn, liked them better than any other kind. She baked twice a week. Adoniram often liked a piece of pie between meals. She hurried this morning. It had been later than usual when she began, and she wanted to have a pie baked for dinner. However deep a resentment she might be forced to hold against her husband, she would never fail in sedulous attention to his wants.

Nobility of character manifests itself at loop-holes when it is not provided with large doors. Sarah Penn's showed itself to-day in flaky dishes of pastry. So she made the pies faithfully, while across the table she could see, when she glanced up from her work, the sight that rankled in her patient and steadfast soul—the digging of the cellar of the new barn in the place where Adoniram forty years ago had promised her their new house should stand.

The pies were done for dinner. Adoniram and Sammy were home a few minutes after twelve o'clock. The dinner was eaten with serious haste. There was never much conversation at the table in the Penn family. Adoniram asked a blessing, and they ate promptly, then rose up and went about their work.

Sammy went back to school, taking soft sly lopes out of the yard like a rabbit. He wanted a game of marbles before school, and feared his father would give him some chores to do. Adoniram hastened to the door and called after him, but he was out of sight.

"I don't see what you let him go for, Mother," said he. "I wanted him to help me unload that wood."

Adoniram went to work out in the yard unloading wood from the wagon. Sarah put away the dinner dishes, while Nanny took down her curl-papers and changed her dress. She was going down to the store to buy some more embroidery and thread.

When Nanny was gone, Mrs. Penn went to the door. "Father!" she called.

"Well, what is it!"

"I want to see you jest a minute."

"I can't leave this wood nohow. I've got to git it unloaded an' go for a load of gravel afore two o'clock. Sammy had ought to helped me. You hadn't ought to let him go to school so early."

"I want to see you jest a minute."

"I tell ye I can't, nohow, mother."

"Father, you come here." Sarah Penn stood in the door like a queen; she held her head as if it bore a crown; there was that patience which makes authority royal in her voice. Adoniram went.

Mrs. Penn led the way into the kitchen, and pointed to a chair. "Sit down, father," said she; "I've got somethin' I want to say to you."

He sat down heavily; his face was quite stolid, but he looked at her with restive eyes. "Well, what is it, mother?"

"I want to know what you're buildin' that new barn for, father?"

"I ain't got nothin' to say about it."

"It can't be you think you need another barn?"

"I tell ye I ain't got nothin' to say about it, mother, an' I ain't goin' to say nothin'."

"Be you goin' to buy more cows?"

Adoniram did not reply; he shut his mouth tight.

"I know you be, as well as I want to. Now, father, look here"—Sarah Penn had not sat down; she stood before her husband in the humble fashion of a Scripture woman—"I'm goin' to talk real plain to you; I never have sence I married you, but I'm goin' to now. I ain't never complained, an' I ain't goin' to complain now, but I'm goin' to talk plain. You see this room here, father; you look at it well. You see there ain't no carpet on the floor, an' you see the paper is all dirty, an' droppin' off the walls. We ain't had no new paper on it for ten year, an' then I put it on myself, an' it didn't cost but ninepence a roll. You see this room, father; it's all the one I've had to work in an' eat in an' sit in sence we was married. There ain't another woman in the whole town whose husband ain't got half the means you have but what's got better. It's all the room Nanny's got to have her company in; an' there ain't one of her mates but what's got better, an' their fathers not so able as hers is. It's all the room she'll have to be married in. What would you have thought, father, if we had had our weddin' in a room no better than this? I was married in my mother's parlor, with a carpet on the floor, an' stuffed furniture, an' a mahogany card-table. An' this is all the room my daughter will have to be married in. Look here, father!"

Sarah Penn went across the room as though it were a tragic stage. She flung open a door and disclosed a tiny bedroom, only large enough for a bed and bureau, with a path between. "There, father," said she—"there's all the room I've had to sleep in forty year. All my children were born there—the two that died, an' the two that's livin'. I was sick with a fever there."

She stepped into another door and opened it. It led into the small, ill-lighted pantry. "Here," said she, "is all the buttery I've got—every place I've got for my dishes, to set away my victuals in, an' to keep my milk-pans in. Father, I've been takin' care of the milk of six cows in this place, an' now you're goin' to build a new barn, an' keep more cows, an' give me more to do in it."

She threw open another door. A narrow crooked flight of stairs wound upward from it. "There, father," said she. "I want you to look at the stairs that go up to them two unfinished chambers that are all the places our son an' daughter have had to sleep in all their lives. There ain't a prettier girl in town nor a more ladylike one than Nanny, an' that's the place she has to sleep in. It ain't so good as your horse's stall; it ain't so warm an' tight."

Sarah Penn went back and stood before her husband. "Now, father," said she, "I want to know if you think you're doin' right an' accordin' to what you profess. Here, when we was married, forty year ago, you promised me faithful that we should have a new house built in that lot over in the field before the year was out. You said you had money enough, an' you wouldn't ask me to live in no such place as this. It is forty year now, an' you've been makin' more money, an' I've been savin' of it for you ever since, an' you ain't built no house yet. You've built sheds an' cow-houses an' one new barn, an' now you're goin' to build another. Father, I want to know if you think it's right. You're lodgin' your dumb beasts better than you are your own flesh an' blood. I want to know if you think it's right."

"I ain't got nothin' to say."

"You can't say nothin' without ownin' it ain't right, father. An' there's another thing—I ain't complained; I've got along forty year, an' I s'pose I should forty more, if it wa'n't for that—if we don't have another house. Nanny she can't live with us after she's married. She'll have to go somewheres else to live away from us, an' it don't seem as if I could have it so, noways, father. She wa'n't ever strong. She's got considerable color, but there wa'n't never any backbone to her. I've always took the heft of everything off her, an' she ain't fit to keep house an' do everything herself. She'll be all worn out inside of a year. Think of her doin' all the washin' an' ironin' an' bakin' with them soft white hands an' arms, an' sweepin'! I can't have it so, noways, father."

Mrs. Penn's face was burning; her mild eyes gleamed. She had pleaded her little cause like a Webster;[1] she had ranged from severity to pathos; but her opponent employed that obstinate silence which makes eloquence futile with mocking echoes. Adoniram arose clumsily.

"Father, ain't you got nothin' to say?" said Mrs. Penn.

"I've got to go off after that load of gravel. I can't stan' here talkin' all day."

"Father, won't you think it over, an' have a house built there instead of a barn?"

"I ain't got nothin' to say."

Adoniram shuffled out. Mrs. Penn went into her bedroom. When she came out, her eyes were red. She had a roll of unbleached cotton cloth. She spread it out on the kitchen table, and began cutting out some shirts for her husband. The men over in the field had a team to help them this afternoon; she could hear their halloos. She had a scanty pattern for the shirts; she had to plan and piece the sleeves.

Nanny came home with her embroidery, and sat down with her needlework. She had taken down her curl-papers, and there was a soft roll of fair hair like an aureole over her forehead; her face was as delicately fine and clear as porcelain. Suddenly she looked up, and the tender red flamed all over her face and neck. "Mother," said she.

"What say?"

"I've been thinking—I don't see how we're goin' to have any—wedding in this room. I'd be ashamed to have his folks come if we didn't have anybody else."

"Mebbe we can have some new paper before then; I can put it on. I guess you won't have no call to be ashamed of your belongin's."

"We might have the wedding in the new barn," said Nanny, with gentle pettishness. "Why, mother, what makes you look so?"

Mrs. Penn had started, and was staring at her with a curious expression. She turned again to her work, and spread out a pattern carefully on the cloth. "Nothin'," said she.

Presently Adoniram clattered out of the yard in his two-wheeled dump cart, standing as proudly upright as a Roman charioteer. Mrs. Penn opened the door and stood there a minute looking out; the halloos of the men sounded louder.

[1] Daniel Webster (1782–1852) was an American orator, lawyer, and statesman.

It seemed to her all through the spring months that she heard nothing but the halloos and the noises of saws and hammers. The new barn grew fast. It was a fine edifice for this little village. Men came on pleasant Sundays, in their meeting suits and clean shirt bosoms, and stood around it admiringly. Mrs. Penn did not speak of it, and Adoniram did not mention it to her, although sometimes, upon a return from inspecting it, he bore himself with injured dignity.

"It's a strange thing how your mother feels about the new barn," he said, confidentially, to Sammy one day.

Sammy only grunted after an odd fashion for a boy; he had learned it from his father.

The barn was all completed ready for use by the third week in July. Adoniram had planned to move his stock in on Wednesday; on Tuesday he received a letter which changed his plans. He came in with it early in the morning. "Sammy's been to the post-office," said he, "an' I've got a letter from Hiram." Hiram was Mrs. Penn's brother, who lived in Vermont.

"Well," said Mrs. Penn, "what does he say about the folks?"

"I guess they're all right. He says he thinks if I come up country right off there's a chance to buy jest the kind of a horse I want." He stared reflectively out of the window at the new barn.

Mrs. Penn was making pies. She went on clapping the rolling-pin into the crust, although she was very pale, and her heart beat loudly.

"I dun' know but what I'd better go," said Adoniram. "I hate to go off jest now, right in the midst of hayin', but the ten-acre lot's cut, an' I guess Rufus an' the others can git along without me three or four days. I can't get a horse round here to suit me, nohow, an' I've got to have another for all that wood-haulin' in the fall. I told Hiram to watch out, an if he got wind of a good horse to let me know. I guess I'd better go."

"I'll get your clean shirt an' collar," said Mrs. Penn calmly.

She laid out Adoniram's Sunday suit and his clean clothes on the bed in the little bedroom. She got his shaving-water and razor ready. At last she buttoned on his collar and fastened his black cravat.

Adoniram never wore his collar and cravat except on extra occasions. He held his head high, with a rasped dignity. When he was all ready, with his coat and hat brushed, and a lunch of pie and cheese in a paper bag, he hesitated on the threshold of the door. He looked at his wife, and his manner was defiantly apologetic. "*If* them cows come to-day, Sammy can drive 'em into the new barn," said he, "an' when they bring the hay up, they can pitch it in there."

"Well," replied Mrs. Penn.

Adoniram set his shaven face ahead and started. When he had cleared the door-step, he turned and looked back with a kind of nervous solemnity. "I shall be back by Saturday if nothin' happens," said he.

"Do be careful, father," returned his wife.

She stood at the door with Nanny at her elbow and watched him out of sight. Her eyes had a strange, doubtful expression in them; her peaceful forehead was contracted. She went in, and about her baking again. Nanny sat sewing. Her wedding-day was drawing nearer, and she was getting pale and thin with her steady sewing. Her mother kept glancing at her.

"Have you got that pain in your side this mornin'?" she asked.

"A little."

Mrs. Penn's face, as she worked, changed, her perplexed forehead smoothed, her eyes were steady, her lips firmly set. She formed a maxim for herself, although incoherently with her unlettered thoughts. "Unsolicited opportunities are the guide-posts of the Lord to the new roads of life," she repeated in effect, and she made up her mind to her course of action.

"S'posin' I *had* wrote to Hiram," she muttered once, when she was in the pantry—"s'posin' I had wrote, an' asked him if he knew of any horse? But I didn't, an' father's goin' wa'n't none of my doin'. It looks like a providence." Her voice rang out quite loud at the last.

"What are you talkin' about, mother?" called Nanny.

"Nothin'."

Mrs. Penn hurried her baking; at eleven o'clock it was all done. The load of hay from the west field came slowly down the cart track, and drew up at the new barn. Mrs. Penn ran out. "Stop!" she screamed—"stop!"

The men stopped and looked; Sammy upreared from the top of the load, and stared at his mother.

"Stop!" she cried out again. "Don't you put the hay in that barn; put it in the old one."

"Why, he said to put it in here," returned one of the haymakers, wonderingly. He was a young man, a neighbor's son, whom Adoniram hired by the year to help on the farm.

"Don't you put the hay in the new barn; there's room enough in the old one, ain't there?" said Mrs. Penn.

"Room enough," returned the hired man, in his thick, rustic tones. "Didn't need the new barn, nohow far as room's concerned. Well, I s'pose he changed his mind." He took hold of the horses' bridles.

Mrs. Penn went back to the house. Soon the kitchen windows were darkened, and a fragrance like warm honey came into the room.

Nanny laid down her work. "I thought father wanted them to put the hay into the new barn?" she said wonderingly.

"It's all right," replied her mother.

Sammy slid down from the load of hay, and came in to see if dinner was ready.

"I ain't goin' to get a regular dinner to-day, as long as father's gone," said his mother. "I've let the fire go out. You can have some bread an' milk an' pie. I thought we could get along." She set out some bowls of milk, some bread, and a pie on the kitchen table. "You'd better eat your dinner now," said she. "You might jest as well get through with it. I want you to help me afterward."

Nanny and Sammy stared at each other. There was something strange in their mother's manner. Mrs. Penn did not eat anything herself. She went into the pantry, and they heard her moving dishes while they ate. Presently she came out with a pile of plates. She got the clothes-basket out of the shed, and packed them in it. Nanny and Sammy watched. She brought out cups and saucers, and put them in with the plates.

"What you goin' to do, mother?" inquired Nanny, in a timid voice. A sense of something unusual made her tremble, as if it were a ghost. Sammy rolled his eyes over his pie.

"You'll see what I'm goin' to do," replied Mrs. Penn. "If you're through, Nanny, I want you to go upstairs an' pack up your things; an' I want you, Sammy, to help me take down the bed in the bedroom."

"Oh, mother, what for?" gasped Nanny.

"You'll see."

During the next few hours a feat was performed by this simple, pious New England mother which was equal in its way to Wolfe's storming of the Heights of Abraham.[2] It took no more genius and audacity of bravery for Wolfe to cheer his wondering soldiers up those steep precipices, under the sleeping eyes of the enemy, than for Sarah Penn, at the head of her children, to move all their little household goods into the new barn while her husband was away.

Nanny and Sammy followed their mother's instructions without a murmur; indeed, they were overawed. There is a certain uncanny and superhuman quality about all such purely original undertakings as their mother's was to them. Nanny went back and forth with her light loads, and Sammy tugged with sober energy.

At five o'clock in the afternoon the little house in which the Penns had lived for forty years had emptied itself into the new barn.

Every builder builds somewhat for unknown purposes, and is in a measure a prophet. The architect of Adoniram Penn's barn, while he designed it for the comfort of four-footed animals, had planned better than he knew for the comfort of humans. Sarah Penn saw at a glance its possibilities. Those great box-stalls, with quilts hung before them, would make better bedrooms than the one she had occupied for forty years, and there was a tight carriage-room. The harness-room, with its chimney and shelves, would make a kitchen of her dreams. The great middle space would make a parlor, by-and-by, fit for a palace. Upstairs there was as much room as down. With partitions and windows, what a house would there be! Sarah looked at the row of stanchions before the allotted space for cows, and reflected that she would have her front entry there.

At six o'clock the stove was up in the harness-room, the kettle was boiling, and the table set for tea. It looked almost as home-like as the abandoned house across the yard had ever done. The young hired man milked, and Sarah directed him calmly to bring the milk to the new barn. He came gaping, dropping little blots of foam from the brimming pails on the grass. Before the next morning he had spread the story of Adoniram Penn's wife moving into the new barn all over the little village. Men assembled in the store and talked it over, women with shawls over their heads scuttled into each other's houses before their work was done. Any deviation from the ordinary course of life in this quiet town was enough to stop all progress

---

[2] James Wolfe (1727–1759) was a British general whose troops stormed the French army on the Plains of Abraham above Quebec.

in it. Everybody paused to look at the staid, independent figure on the side track. There was a difference of opinion with regard to her. Some held her to be insane; some, of a lawless and rebellious spirit.

Friday the minister went to see her. It was in the forenoon, and she was at the barn door shelling pease[3] for dinner. She looked up and returned his salutation with dignity, then she went on with her work. She did not invite him in. The saintly expression of her face remained fixed, but there was an angry flush over it.

The minister stood awkwardly before her, and talked. She handled the pease as if they were bullets. At last she looked up, and her eyes showed the spirit that her meek front had covered for a lifetime.

"There ain't no use talkin', Mr. Hersey," she said. "I've thought it all over an' over, an' I believe I'm doin' what's right. I've made it the subject of prayer, an' it's betwixt me an' the Lord an' Adoniram. There ain't no call for anybody else to worry about it."

"Well, of course, if you have brought it to the Lord in prayer, and feel satisfied that you are doing right, Mrs. Penn," said the minister, helplessly. His thin gray-bearded face was pathetic. He was a sickly man; his youthful confidence had cooled; he had to scourge himself up to some of his pastoral duties as relentlessly as a Catholic ascetic, and then he was prostrated by the smart.

"I think it's right jest as much as I think it was right for our forefathers to come over from the old country 'cause they didn't have what belonged to 'em," said Mrs. Penn. She arose. The barn threshold might have been Plymouth Rock from her bearing. "I don't doubt you mean well, Mr. Hersey," said she, "but there are things people hadn't ought to interfere with. I've been a member of the church for over forty year. I've got my own mind an' my own feet, an' I'm goin' to think my own thoughts an' go my own ways, an' nobody but the Lord is goin' to dictate to me unless I've a mind to have him. Won't you come in an' set down? How is Mis' Hersey?"

"She is well, I thank you," replied the minister. He added some more perplexed apologetic remarks; then he retreated.

He could expound the intricacies of every character study in the Scriptures, he was competent to grasp the Pilgrim Fathers and all historical innovators, but Sarah Penn was beyond him. He could deal with primal causes, but parallel ones worsted him. But, after all, although it was aside from his province, he wondered more how Adoniram Penn would deal with his wife than how the Lord would. Everybody shared the wonder. When Adoniram's four new cows arrived, Sarah ordered three to be put in the old barn, the other in the house shed where the cooking-stove had stood. That added to the excitement. It was whispered that all four cows were domiciled in the house.

Towards sunset on Saturday, when Adoniram was expected home, there was a knot of men in the road near the new barn. The hired man had milked, but he still hung around the premises. Sarah Penn had supper all ready. There were brown bread and baked beans and a custard pie; it was the supper that Adoniram loved on a Saturday night. She had on a clean calico, and she bore herself imperturbably.

---

[3] Old or variant spelling of "peas."

Nanny and Sammy kept close at her heels. Their eyes were large, and Nanny was full of nervous tremors. Still there was to them more pleasant excitement than anything else. An inborn confidence in their mother over their father asserted itself.

Sammy looked out of the harness-room window. "There he is," he announced, in an awed whisper. He and Nanny peeped around the casing. Mrs. Penn kept on about her work. The children watched Adoniram leave the new horse standing in the drive while he went to the house door. It was fastened. Then he went around to the shed. That door was seldom locked, even when the family was away. The thought how her father would be confronted by the cow flashed upon Nanny. There was a hysterical sob in her throat. Adoniram emerged from the shed and stood looking about in a dazed fashion. His lips moved; he was saying something, but they could not hear what it was. The hired man was peeping around a corner of the old barn, but nobody saw him.

Adoniram took the new horse by the bridle and led him across the yard to the new barn. Nanny and Sammy slunk close to their mother. The barn doors rolled back, and there stood Adoniram, with the long mild face of the great Canadian farm horse looking over his shoulder.

Nanny kept behind her mother, but Sammy stepped suddenly forward, and stood in front of her.

Adoniram stared at the group. "What on airth you all down here for?" said he. "What's the matter over to the house?"

"We've come here to live, father," said Sammy. His shrill voice quavered out bravely.

"What"—Adoniram sniffled—"what is it smells like cooking?" said he. He stepped forward and looked in the open door of the harness-room. Then he turned to his wife. His old bristling face was pale and frightened. "What on airth does this mean, mother?" he gasped.

"You come in here, father," said Sarah. She led the way, into the harness-room and shut the door. "Now, father," said she, "you needn't be scared. I ain't crazy. There ain't nothin' to be upset over. But we've come here to live, an' we're goin' to live here. We've got jest as good a right here as new horses an' cows. The house wa'n't fit for us to live in any longer, an' I made up my mind I wa'n't goin' to stay there. I've done my duty by you forty year, an' I'm goin' to do it now; but I'm goin' to live here. You've got to put in some windows and partitions; an' you'll have to buy some furniture."

"Why, mother!" the old man gasped.

"You'd better take your coat off an' get washed—there's the wash-basin—an' then we'll have supper."

"Why, mother!"

Sammy went past the window, leading the new horse to the old barn. The old man saw him, and shook his head speechlessly. He tried to take off his coat, but his arms seemed to lack the power. His wife helped him. She poured some water into the tin basin, and put in a piece of soap. She got the comb and brush, and smoothed his thin gray hair after he had washed. Then she put the beans, hot bread, and tea on the table. Sammy came in, and the family drew up. Adoniram sat looking dazedly at his plate, and they waited.

"Ain't you goin' to ask a blessin', father?" said Sarah.

And the old man bent his head and mumbled.

All through the meal he stopped eating at intervals, and stared furtively at his wife; but he ate well. The home food tasted good to him, and his old frame was too sturdily healthy to be affected by his mind. But after supper he went out, and sat down on the step of the smaller door at the right of the barn, through which he had meant his Jerseys to pass in stately file, but which Sarah designed for her front house door, and he leaned his head on his hands.

After the supper dishes were cleared away and the milk-pans washed, Sarah went out to him. The twilight was deepening. There was a clear green glow in the sky. Before them stretched the smooth level of field; in the distance was a cluster of hay-stacks like the huts of a village; the air was very cool and calm and sweet. The landscape might have been an ideal one of peace.

Sarah bent over and touched her husband on one of his thin, sinewy shoulders. "Father!"

The old man's shoulders heaved: he was weeping.

"Why, don't do so, father," said Sarah.

"I'll—put up the—partitions, an'—everything you—want, mother."

Sarah put her apron up to her face; she was overcome by her own triumph.

Adoniram was like a fortress whose walls had no active resistance, and went down the instant the right besieging tools were used. "Why, mother," he said, hoarsely, "I hadn't no idee you was so set on't as all this comes to."

Journal Entry

Record your responses to Mother's revolt.

Textual Considerations

1. How does Freeman use the setting to contribute to the story's conflict?
2. How would you describe the relationship between the Penns? Does Freeman portray them by their works or actions or both? Explain.
3. To what extent are Sammy and Nanny essential to the story? What is their function?
4. Freeman uses expressions like "immovable as one of the works" or "meek vigor which might have characterized one of the New Testament Saints" to describe Mrs. Penn. Identify other expressions that sketch her physical and psychological portrait.

Cultural Contexts

1. Analyze the relation between revolt and identity in the story. Explore the causes that motivate Mrs. Penn to break out of her socially defined role as obedient wife.
2. Although Adoniram Penn reflects the patriarchal tradition, how does he change during the course of the story? How is he different from other males in the story, including the minister? What does the story suggest about individuality versus societal expectations for men as well as women?

Kate Chopin
1894

A Respectable Woman

Mrs. Baroda was a little provoked to learn that her husband expected his friend, Gouvernail, up to spend a week or two on the plantation.

They had entertained a good deal during the winter; much of the time had also been passed in New Orleans in various forms of mild dissipation. She was looking forward to a period of unbroken rest, now, and undisturbed tête-à-tête with her husband, when he informed her that Gouvernail was coming up to stay a week or two.

This was a man she had heard much of but never seen. He had been her husband's college friend; was now a journalist, and in no sense a society man or "a man about town," which were, perhaps, some of the reasons she had never met him. But she had unconsciously formed an image of him in her mind. She pictured him tall, slim, cynical; with eye-glasses, and his hands in his pockets; and she did not like him. Gouvernail was slim enough, but he wasn't very tall nor very cynical; neither did he wear eye-glasses nor carry his hands in his pockets. And she rather liked him when he first presented himself.

But why she liked him she could not explain satisfactorily to herself when she partly attempted to do so. She could discover in him none of those brilliant and promising traits which Gaston, her husband, had often assured her that he possessed. On the contrary, he sat rather mute and receptive before her chatty eagerness to make him feel at home and in face of Gaston's frank and wordy hospitality. His manner was as courteous toward her as the most exacting woman could require; but he made no direct appeal to her approval or even esteem.

Once settled at the plantation he seemed to like to sit upon the wide portico in the shade of one of the big Corinthian pillars, smoking his cigar lazily and listening attentively to Gaston's experience as a sugar planter.

"This is what I call living," he would utter with deep satisfaction, as the air that swept across the sugar field caressed him with its warm and scented velvety touch. It pleased him also to get on familiar terms with the big dogs that came about him, rubbing themselves sociably against his legs. He did not care to fish, and displayed no eagerness to go out and kill grosbecs when Gaston proposed doing so.

Gouvernail's personality puzzled Mrs. Baroda, but she liked him. Indeed, he was a lovable, inoffensive fellow. After a few days, when she could understand him no better than at first, she gave over being puzzled and remained piqued. In this mood she left her husband and her guest, for the most part, alone together. Then finding that Gouvernail took no manner of exception to her action, she imposed her society upon him, accompanying him in his idle strolls to the mill and walks along the batture. She persistently sought to penetrate the reserve in which he had unconsciously enveloped himself.

"When is he going—your friend?" she one day asked her husband. "For my part, he tires me frightfully."

"Not for a week yet, dear. I can't understand; he gives you no trouble."

"No. I should like him better if he did: if he were more like others, and I had to plan somewhat for his comfort and enjoyment."

Gaston took his wife's pretty face between his hands and looked tenderly and laughingly into her troubled eyes. They were making a bit of toilet sociably together in Mrs. Baroda's dressing-room.

"You are full of surprises, ma belle," he said to her. "Even I can never count upon how you are going to act under given conditions." He kissed her and turned to fasten his cravat before the mirror.

"Here you are," he went on, "taking poor Gouvernail seriously and making a commotion over him, the last thing he would desire or expect."

"Commotion!" she hotly resented. "Nonsense! How can you say such a thing? Commotion, indeed! But, you know, you said he was clever."

"So he is. But the poor fellow is run down by overwork now. That's why I asked him here to take a rest."

"You used to say he was a man of ideas." she retorted, unconciliated. "I expected him to be interesting, at least. I'm going to the city in the morning to have my spring gowns fitted. Let me know when Mr. Gouvernail is gone; I shall be at my Aunt Octavie's."

That night she went and sat alone upon a bench that stood beneath a live oak tree at the edge of the gravel walk.

She had never known her thoughts or her intentions to be so confused. She could gather nothing from them but the feeling of a distinct necessity to quit her home in the morning.

Mrs. Baroda heard footsteps crunching the gravel; but could discern in the darkness only the approaching red point of a lighted cigar. She knew it was Gouvernail, for her husband did not smoke. She hoped to remain unnoticed, but her white gown revealed her to him. He threw away his cigar and seated himself upon the bench beside her; without a suspicion that she might object to his presence.

"Your husband told me to bring this to you, Mrs. Baroda," he said, handing her a filmy, white scarf with which she sometimes enveloped her head and shoulders. She accepted the scarf from him with a murmur of thanks, and let it lie in her lap.

He made some commonplace observation upon the baneful effect of the night air at that season. Then as his gaze reached out into the darkness, he murmured, half to himself:

"'Night of south winds—night of the large few stars!
Still nodding night—'"

She made no reply to this apostrophe to the night, which indeed, was not addressed to her.

Gouvernail was in no sense a diffident man, for he was not a self-conscious one. His periods of reserve were not constitutional, but the result of moods. Sitting there beside Mrs. Baroda, his silence melted for the time.

He talked freely and intimately in a low, hesitating drawl that was not unpleasant to hear. He talked of the old college days when he and Gaston had been a good deal to each other; of the days of keen and blind ambitions and large intentions. Now there was left with him, at least, a philosophic acquiescence to the existing order—only a desire to be permitted to exist, with now and then a little whiff of genuine life, such as he was breathing now.

Her mind only vaguely grasped what he was saying. Her physical being was for the moment predominant. She was not thinking of his words, only drinking in the tones of his voice. She wanted to reach out her hand in the darkness and touch him with the sensitive tips of her fingers upon the face or the lips. She wanted to draw close to him and whisper against his cheek—she did not care what—as she might have done if she had not been a respectable woman.

The stronger the impulse grew to bring herself near him, the further, in fact, did she draw away from him. As soon as she could so do without an appearance of too great rudeness, she rose and left him there alone.

Before she reached the house, Gouvernail had lighted a fresh cigar and ended his apostrophe to the night.

Mrs. Baroda was greatly tempted that night to tell her husband—who was also her friend—of this folly that had seized her. But she did not yield to the temptation. Beside being a respectable woman she was a very sensible one; and she knew there are some battles in life which a human being must fight alone.

When Gaston arose in the morning, his wife had already departed. She had taken an early morning train to the city. She did not return till Gouvernail was gone from under her roof.

There was some talk of having him back during the summer that followed. That is, Gaston greatly desired it; but this desire yielded to his wife's strenuous opposition.

However, before the year ended, she proposed, wholly from herself, to have Gouvernail visit them again. Her husband was surprised and delighted with the suggestion coming from her.

"I am glad, chère amie, to know that you have finally overcome your dislike for him; truly he did not deserve it."

"Oh," she told him, laughingly, after pressing a long, tender kiss upon his lips, "I have overcome everything! you will see. This time I shall be very nice to him."

Kate Chopin
1899

The Storm

I

The leaves were so still that even Bibi thought it was going to rain. Bobinôt, who was accustomed to converse on terms of perfect equality with his little son, called the child's attention to certain sombre clouds that were rolling with sinister intention from the west, accompanied by a sullen, threatening roar. They were at Friedheimer's store and decided to remain there till the storm had passed. They sat within the door on two empty kegs. Bibi was four years old and looked very wise.

"Mama'll be 'fraid, yes," he suggested with blinking eyes.

"She'll shut the house. Maybe she got Sylvie helpin' her this evenin'," Bobinôt responded reassuringly.

"No; she ent got Sylvie. Sylvie was helpin' her yistiday," piped Bibi.

Bobinôt arose and going across to the counter purchased a can of shrimps, of which Calixta was very fond. Then he returned to his perch on the keg and sat stolidly holding the can of shrimps while the storm burst. It shook the wooden store and seemed to be ripping great furrows in the distant field. Bibi laid his little hand on his father's knee and was not afraid.

II

Calixta, at home, felt no uneasiness for their safety. She sat at a side window sewing furiously on a sewing machine. She was greatly occupied and did not notice the approaching storm. But she felt very warm and often stopped to mop her face on which the perspiration gathered in beads. She unfastened her white sacque at the throat. It began to grow dark, and suddenly realizing the situation she got up hurriedly and went about closing windows and doors.

Out on the small front gallery she had hung Bobinôt's Sunday clothes to air and she hastened out to gather them before the rain fell. As she stepped outside, Alcée Laballière rode in at the gate. She had not seen him very often since her marriage, and never alone. She stood there with Bobinôt's coat in her hands, and the big rain drops began to fall. Alcée rode his horse under the shelter of a side projection where the chickens had huddled and there were plows and a harrow piled up in the corner.

"May I come and wait on your gallery till the storm is over, Calixta?" he asked.

"Come 'long in, M'sieur Alcée."

His voice and her own startled her as if from a trance, and she seized Bobinôt's—vest. Alcée, mounting to the porch, grabbed the trousers and snatched Bibi's braided jacket that was about to be carried away by a sudden gust of wind. He expressed an intention to remain outside, but it was soon apparent that he might as well have been out in the open: the water beat in upon the boards in driving sheets, and he went inside, closing the door after him. It was even necessary to put something beneath the door to keep the water out.

"My! what a rain! It's good two years sence it rain' like that," exclaimed Calixta as she rolled up a piece of bagging and Alcée helped her to thrust it beneath the crack.

She was a little fuller of figure than five years before when she married; but she had lost nothing of her vivacity. Her blue eyes still retained their melting quality; and her yellow hair, dishevelled by the wind and rain, kinked more stubbornly than ever about her ears and temples.

The rain beat upon the low, shingled roof with a force and clatter that threatened to break an entrance and deluge them there. They were in the dining room—the sitting room—the general utility room. Adjoining was her bed room, with Bibi's couch along side her own. The door stood open, and the room with its white, monumental bed, its closed shutters, looked dim and mysterious.

Alcée flung himself into a rocker and Calixta nervously began to gather up from the floor the lengths of a cotton sheet which she had been sewing.

"If this keeps up, *Dieu sait*[1] if the levees goin' to stan' it!" she exclaimed.

"What have you got to do with the levees?"

"I got enough to do! An' there's Bobinôt with Bibi out in that storm—if he only didn't left Friedheimer's!"

"Let us hope, Calixta, that Bobinôt's got sense enough to come in out of a cyclone."

She went and stood at the window with a greatly disturbed look on her face. She wiped the frame that was clouded with moisture. It was stiflingly hot. Alcée got up and joined her at the window, looking over her shoulder. The rain was coming down in sheets obscuring the view of far-off cabins and enveloping the distant wood in a gray mist. The playing of the lightning was incessant. A bolt struck a tall chinaberry tree at the edge of the field. It filled all visible space with a blinding glare and the crash seemed to invade the very boards they stood upon.

Calixta put her hands to her eyes, and with a cry, staggered backward. Alcée's arm encircled her, and for an instant he drew her close and spasmodically to him.

"*Bonté!*"[2] she cried, releasing herself from his encircling arm and retreating from the window, "the house'll go next! If I only knew w'ere Bibi was!" She would not compose herself; she would not be seated. Alcée clasped her shoulders and looked into her face. The contact of her warm palpitating body when he had unthinkingly drawn her into his arms, had aroused all the old-time infatuation and desire for her flesh.

"Calixta," he said, "don't be frightened. Nothing can happen. The house is too low to be struck, with so many tall trees standing about. There! aren't you going to be quiet? say, aren't you?" He pushed her hair back from her face that was warm and steaming. Her lips were as red and moist as pomegranate seed. Her white neck and a glimpse of her full, firm bosom disturbed him powerfully. As she

---

[1] God knows. [2] "Goodness!"

glanced up at him the fear in her liquid blue eyes had given place to a drowsy gleam that unconsciously betrayed a sensuous desire. He looked down into her eyes and there was nothing for him to do but to gather her lips in a kiss. It reminded him of Assumption.

"Do you remember—in Assumption, Calixta?" he asked in a low voice broken by passion. Oh! she remembered; for in Assumption he had kissed her and kissed and kissed her; until his senses would well nigh fail, and to save her he would resort to a desperate flight. If she was not an immaculate dove in those days, she was still inviolate; a passionate creature whose very defenselessness had made her defense, against which his honor forbade him to prevail. Now—well, now—her lips seemed in a manner free to be tasted, as well as her round, white throat and her whiter breasts.

They did not heed the crashing torrents, and the roar of the elements made her laugh as she lay in his arms. She was a revelation in that dim, mysterious chamber; as white as the couch she lay upon. Her firm, elastic flesh that was knowing for the first time its birthright, was like a creamy lily that the sun invites to contribute its breath and perfume to the undying life of the world.

The generous abundance of her passion, without guile or trickery, was like a white flame which penetrated and found response in depths of his own sensuous nature that had never yet been reached.

When he touched her breasts they gave themselves up in quivering ecstasy, inviting his lips. Her mouth was a fountain of delight. And when he possessed her, they seemed to swoon together at the very borderland of life's mystery.

He stayed cushioned upon her, breathless, dazed, enervated, with his heart beating like a hammer upon her. With one hand she clasped his head, her lips lightly touching his forehead. The other hand stroked with a soothing rhythm his muscular shoulders.

The growl of the thunder was distant and passing away. The rain beat softly upon the shingles, inviting them to drowsiness and sleep. But they dared not yield.

The rain was over; and the sun was turning the glistening green world into a palace of gems. Calixta, on the gallery, watched Alcée ride away. He turned and smiled at her with a beaming face; and she lifted her pretty chin in the air and laughed aloud.

III

Bobinôt and Bibi, trudging home, stopped without at the cistern to make themselves presentable.

"My! Bibi, w'at will yo' mama say! You ought to be ashame'. You oughtn' put on those good pants, Look at 'em! An' that mud on yo' collar! How you got that mud on yo' collar, Bibi? I never saw such a boy!" Bibi was the picture of pathetic resignation. Bobinôt was the embodiment of serious solicitude as he strove to remove from his own person and his son's the signs of their tramp over heavy roads and through wet fields. He scraped the mud off Bibi's bare legs and feet with a stick and carefully removed all traces from his heavy brogans. Then, prepared for the worst—the meeting with an over-scrupulous housewife, they entered cautiously at the back door.

Calixta was preparing supper. She had set the table and was dripping coffee at the hearth. She sprang up as they came in.

"Oh, Bobinôt! You back! My! but I was uneasy. W'ere you been during the rain? An' Bibi? he ain't wet? he ain't hurt?" She had clasped Bibi and was kissing him effusively. Bobinôt's explanations and apologies which he had been composing all along the way, died on his lips as Calixta felt him to see if he were dry, and seemed to express nothing but satisfaction at their safe return.

"I brought you some shrimps, Calixta," offered Bobinôt, hauling the can from his ample side pocket and laying it on the table.

"Shrimps! Oh, Bobinôt! you too good fo' anything!" and she gave him a smacking kiss on the cheek that resounded. "*J'vous réponds*,[3] we'll have a feas' tonight! umph-umph!"

Bobinôt and Bibi began to relax and enjoy themselves, and when the three seated themselves at table they laughed much and so loud that anyone might have heard them as far away as Laballière's.

IV

Alcée Laballière wrote to his wife, Clarisse, that night. It was a loving letter, full of tender solicitude. He told her not to hurry back, but if she and the babies liked it at Biloxi, to stay a month longer. He was getting on nicely; and though he missed them, he was willing to bear the separation a while longer—realizing that their health and pleasure were the first things to be considered.

V

As for Clarisse, she was charmed upon receiving her husband's letter. She and the babies were doing well. The society was agreeable; many of her old friends and acquaintances were at the bay. And the first free breath since her marriage seemed to restore the pleasant liberty of her maiden days. Devoted as she was to her husband, their intimate conjugal life was something which she was more than willing to forego for a while.

So the storm passed and everyone was happy.

Journal Entry

What do "A Respectable Woman" and "The Storm" suggest about sexuality and fidelity in marriage?

Textual Considerations

1. Create a profile of Mrs. Baroda in "A Respectable Woman." Is she a respectable woman? Why or why not? What is the husband's role in the story? What kind of marriage do they have?
2. What is your response to Gouvernail in "A Respectable Woman?" What evidence is there that he is attracted to Mrs. Baroda?

---

[3] "I tell you"

3. What evidence does "The Storm" offer about the past relationship of Calixta and Alcée?
4. How does Chopin use point of view to develop characterization in the first two sections of "The Storm"?
5. What is the symbolic significance of the storm? What chain of events does the storm set in motion? Pay particular attention to Chopin's use of language in "The Storm." Do her images reflect her attitude toward her characters? How? Does her choice of words imply empathy or judgment? Select evidence from the text to justify your point of view.
6. In "The Storm," what is your response to the last sentence: "So the storm passed and everyone was happy"?

Cultural Contexts

1. Chopin chose not to publish "The Storm" during her lifetime. How might readers in the 1890s have responded to her lack of condemnation of adultery or to the fact that both Calixta and Alcée enjoy their sexual encounter as equals? Working with your group, argue whether you accept or reject Calixta's and Alcée's attitude towards marriage.

Alice Walker
1973

Roselily

Dearly Beloved

She dreams; dragging herself across the world. A small girl in her mother's white robe and veil, knee raised waist high through a bowl of quicksand soup. The man who stands beside her is against this standing on the front porch of her house, being married to the sound of cars whizzing by on highway 61.

we are gathered here

Like cotton to be weighed. Her fingers at the last minute busily removing dry leaves and twigs. Aware it is a superficial sweep. She knows he blames Mississippi for the respectful way the men turn their heads up in the yard, the women stand waiting and knowledgeable, their children held from mischief by teachings from the wrong God. He glares beyond them to the occupants of the cars, white faces glued to promises beyond a country wedding, noses thrust forward like dogs on a track. For him they usurp the wedding.

in the sight of God

Yes, open house. That is what country black folks like. She dreams she does not already have three children. A squeeze around the flowers in her hands chokes off three and four and five years of breath. Instantly she is ashamed and frightened in her superstition. She looks for the first time at the preacher, forces humility into her eyes, as if she believes he is, in fact, a man of God. She can imagine God, a small black boy, timidly pulling the preacher's coattail.

to join this man and this women

She thinks of ropes, chains, handcuffs, his religion. His place of worship. Where she will be required to sit apart with covered head. In Chicago, a word she hears when thinking of smoke, from his description of what a cinder was, which they never had in Panther Burn. She sees hovering over the heads of the clean neighbors in her front yard black specks falling, clinging, from the sky. But in Chicago. Respect, a chance to build. Her children at last from underneath the detrimental wheel. A chance to be on top. What a relief, she thinks. What a vision, a view, from up so high.

in holy matrimony.

Her fourth child she gave away to the child's father who had some money. Certainly a good job. Had gone to Harvard. Was a good man but weak because good language meant so much to him he could not live with Roselily. Could not abide TV in the living room, five beds in three rooms, no Bach except from four to six on Sunday afternoons. No chess at all. She does not forget to worry about her son among his father's people. She wonders if the New England climate will agree with him. If he will ever come down to Mississippi, as his father did, to try to right the country's wrongs. She wonders if he will be stronger than his father. His father cried off and on throughout her pregnancy. Went to skin and bones. Suffered nightmares, retching and falling out of bed. Tried to kill himself. Later told his wife he found the right baby through friends. Vouched for, the sterling qualities that would make up his character.

   It is not her nature to blame. Still, she is not entirely thankful. She supposes New England, the North, to be quite different from what she knows. It seems right somehow to her that people who move there to live return home completely changed. She thinks of the air, the smoke, the cinders. Imagines cinders big as hailstones; heavy, weighing on the people. Wonders how pressure finds it way into the veins, roping the springs of laughter.

If there's anybody here that knows a reason why

But of course they know no reason why beyond what they daily have come to know. She thinks of the man who will be her husband, feels shut away from him because of the stiff severity of his plain black suit. His religion. A lifetime of black and white. Of veils. Covered head. It is as if her children are already gone from her. Not dead, but exalted on a pedestal, a stalk that has no roots. She wonders how to make new roots. It is beyond her. She wonders what one does with memories in a brand-new life. This had seemed easy, until she thought of it. "The reasons why…the people who"…she thinks, and does not wonder where the thought is from.

these two should not be joined

She thinks of her mother, who is dead. Dead, but still her mother. Joined. This is confusing. Of her father. A gray old man who sold wild mink, rabbit, fox skins to Sears, Roebuck. He stands in the yard, like a man waiting for a train. Her young sisters stand behind her in smooth green dresses, with flowers in their hands and hair. They giggle, she feels, at the absurdity of the wedding. They are ready for something new. She thinks the man beside her should marry one of them. She feels old. Yoked. An arm seems to reach out from behind her and snatch her backward. She thinks of cemeteries and the long sleep of grandparents mingling in the dirt. She believes that she believes in ghosts. In the soil giving back what it takes.

together

In the city. He sees her in a new way. This she knows, and is grateful. But is it new enough? She cannot always be a bride and virgin, wearing robes and veil. Even now her body itches to be free of satin and voile, organdy and lily of the valley. Memories crash against her. Memories of being bare to the sun. She wonders what it will be like. Not to have to go to a job. Not to work in a sewing plant. Not to worry about learning to sew straight seams in workingmen's overalls, jeans, and dress pants. Her place will be in the home, he has said, repeatedly, promising her rest she had prayed for. But now she wonders. When she is rested, what will she do? They will make babies—she thinks practically about her fine brown body, his strong black one. They will be inevitable. Her hands will be full. Full of what? Babies. She is not comforted.

let him speak

She wishes she had asked him to explain more of what he meant. But she was impatient. Impatient to be done with sewing. With doing everything for three children, alone. Impatient to leave the girls she had known since childhood, their children growing up, their husbands hanging around her, already old, seedy. Nothing about them that she wanted, or needed. The fathers of her children driving by, waving, not waving; reminders of times she would just as soon forget. Impatient to see the South Side, where they would live and build and be respectable and respected and free. Her husband would free her. A romantic hush. Proposal. Promises. A new life! Respectable, reclaimed, renewed. Free! In robe and veil.

or forever hold

She does not even know if she loves him. She loves his sobriety. His refusal to sing just because he knows the tune. She loves his pride. His blackness and his gray car. She loves his understanding of her *condition*. She thinks she loves the effort he will make to redo her into what he truly wants. His love of her makes her completely conscious of how unloved she was before. This is something; though it makes her unbearably sad. Melancholy. She blinks her eyes. Remembers she is finally being married, like other girls. Like other girls, women? Something strains upward behind her eyes. She thinks of the something as a rat trapped, concerned, scurrying to and fro in her head, peering through the windows of her eyes. She wants to live for once. But doesn't know quite what that means. Wonders if she has ever done it. If she ever will. The preacher is odious to her. She wants to strike him out of the way, out of her light, with the back of her hand. It seems to her he has always been standing in front of her, barring her way.

his peace.

The rest she does not hear. She feels a kiss, passionate, rousing, within the general pandemonium. Cars drive up blowing their horns. Firecrackers go off. Dogs come from under the house and begin to yelp and bark. Her husband's hand is like the clasp of an iron gate. People congratulate. Her children press against her. They look with awe and distaste mixed with hope at their new father. He stands curiously apart, in spite of the people crowding about to grasp his free hand. He smiles at them all but his eyes are as if turned inward. He knows they cannot understand that he is not a Christian. He will not explain himself. He feels different, he looks it. The old women thought he was like one of their sons except that he had somehow got away from them. Still a son, not a son. Changed.

    She thinks how it will be later in the night in the silvery gray car. How they will spin through the darkness of Mississippi and in the morning be in Chicago, Illinois. She thinks of Lincoln, the president. That is all she knows about the place. She feels ignorant, *wrong*, backward. She presses her worried fingers into his palm. He is standing in front of her. In the crush of well-wishing people, he does not look back.

Journal Entry

Explain the paradox implicit in the name "Roselily." Why is it appropriate?

Textual Considerations

1. What effects does Walker achieve by using the text of the marriage service to interrupt Roselily's thoughts? What do we learn about her past and her ambivalence about the future?
2. Characterize her husband by listing his faults and his virtues. What is his attitude toward marriage? How does he envision Roselily's role? What is her response?

3. Religion plays an important role in the story. Why does Roselily think of the preacher as someone who is always "barring her way"? What is her husband's attitude toward *his* religion?
4. Roselily wants freedom, yet at the end of the ceremony "her husband's hand is like the clasp of an iron gate." Cite and explain other images of entrapment.

Cultural Contexts

1. Roselily reflects upon the father of her fourth child who is white and who met her during the Civil Rights Movement in the 1960s. Why does Walker focus on him? What do we know about him? How does Roselily feel about having given him the child? What is your response to her action?
2. Contrasts form the basis of this story. How does Walker use differences in setting, characterization, religion, family, and community to heighten potential conflicts in the relationship? To what extent are Roselily's needs for freedom and respectability resolved?

Michael Dorris
1993

Name Games

"*Shirley-Shirley bo-berley* banana-fana, fe-ferley, fee-fi mo merley: *Shirley!*"

"Yes," I answered as I awoke, which is strange because my name is Alex. I thought perhaps I had received a message from a former life and tried to concentrate hard on nothing so that I could recapture my Shirley existence, but I was not receiving. It was very early in the morning, so there was probably too much psychic static, the way sometimes you can't tune in even a nearby AM radio station because signals from Wheeling, West Virginia, or Chicago, Illinois, keep flickering off and on. You have to wait until the sun comes up. Somehow that quiets all the interference, but I don't know how. I tried to focus on that question, to visualize it. Noel believes that's the solution to problems of unclear conceptualization.

I shut my eyes and saw a horizon with little zigzagging lightning bolts, like from the RKO tower in old news cavalcades, trying to sneak around the sides. When the sun appeared, they fell as black streams of acid rain on the brightly lit fields of growing corn just shy of the earth's tilt.

I put on my terrycloth robe and went into the living room, where Noel was sleeping on the divan because last night he had been too annoyed with me to share a bed. The evening had started out fine, though I should have sensed hostility when he used his key instead of knocking. His flight from Dallas had been half empty, and those passengers who demanded refills of coffee or Bloody Marys had, for the most part, been seated on the aisle. Noel had not aggravated the sensitive muscles in his lumbar region by having to bend too often or too extensively from the waist, and as a result, he didn't need to lie on the floor for an hour, as he usually did after a long day, with the special Oriental wooden dowel braced beneath the small of his back.

"What's for dinner I'm starved," he said in one breath. He refused to eat airline food, even the fruit plate.

"You have a selection: soy burger patties, eggs, trail mix, tofu, cheese corn puffs, mushrooms, Triscuits. Take your pick." I did not mention the single Le Menu Veal Parmigiana dinner, my personal favorite, which I had wrapped in aluminum foil and labeled "Bones for stock" before putting it in the rear of the freezer.

"It's cold here after Texas," Noel complained. "Do we have any ramen noodles?"

He opened the cabinet and began to move cans, dry pasta, bottles of herbs, then he froze.

"What, may I ask, is *this?*" He turned toward where I was seated in front of the TV. He held out, as though it were red dye #2, an unopened economy box of Duz detergent.

"You get a free tumbler inside," I explained.

"Well, I hope you *enjoy* it." He slammed the box on the counter in disgust, went into the bathroom and locked the door. We'd had this argument before but I had eliminated it from my mind during a recent purge of negative thoughts. Now it came back: Noel prides himself on product loyalty. He came from an All-Temperature Cheer–using family, and reasoned that if a soap had done a good job on clothes, year after year, it deserved continued support.

When Noel finally came out of the bathroom, his face was grim. He answered my questions in monosyllabic words as he stood browsing the refrigerator and picked at a handful of trail mix. No, he didn't have an early call tomorrow. Yes, his co-worker Sandra had broken up with her husband. No, he didn't want me to run down to the store and get him his noodles.

All the chairs in the living room pointed toward the television, so he couldn't sit without seeming to join me for the end of *Starman,* but he did close his eyes. Eventually he put his fists over his ears as well and began to breathe deeply through his mouth, so I surrendered and turned off the videotape before its conclusion.

The instant I left the room to brush my teeth he made up the couch with the single one-hundred percent goosedown bed pillow and the afghan from his mother, and by the time I had gargled, he was pretending to be asleep without saying good night.

I'm no stranger to Noel's moods, so I let him be, which I knew drove him crazy. I hummed to myself too, but not so loud that he could claim I did it to annoy him. I left the bedroom door slightly ajar, let the light spill out, and took a long time with my stretching exercises. I even wrote a nice newsy letter to my sister Bets, chuckling aloud at some of the more amusing lines, before setting the alarm and switching off the lamp. Then I called, in a pleasant voice, "Night, Noel." From the other room I heard him punch the pillow and roll over, but of course he didn't respond.

I hoped that Noel was ready to make peace this morning because I was anxious to ask his opinion about the emergence of "The Name Game" from my subconscious. I tiptoed to the refrigerator, took the half-filled bag of Colombian-blend beans out of the freezer, and shook a scoopful into the electric grinder. Every noise magnified in the quiet apartment, and at the sound of the whir, Noel opened his eyes. We stared at each other, our expressions carefully neutral, while he decided on his attitude. I put a whole-wheat croissant into the toaster oven, poured the ground coffee into a Melitta filter, and added hot water up to the brim.

One of us had to take the risk. I carried two glasses of grapefruit juice to the couch and was relieved when, after a pause, Noel shifted his legs to make room for me. That was definitely a good sign, so I put his glass on the end table and told him about my Name Game dream. He swirled the juice around in his mouth, swallowed, wiped the ring moisture from the table with the end of his afghan.

"Former life?" I suggested.

"You've got Shirley MacLaine on the brain," he said. That was a cheap shot, a remark not worthy of a person who was open to reaching for new possibilities.

"Your concern is deeply appreciated."

"Wasn't 'Shirley' the name in the original song?" Noel punched at my legs with his feet in apology. "Maybe it's as simple as you're just remembering the words the way they were written down."

"Even so…" He could be right about the lyrics, but I was reluctant to abandon what might be a rare subconscious clue to my psychic identity. Noel knew I was fascinated to think of history unfurling backwards in an interlocking chain of yins and yangs, males and females, with us along for the ride. The disappointment must have shown on my face.

"On the other hand," he said, "maybe it's more than that." He drew up his legs further, and I leaned against his hip. He reached to brush the hair away from my forehead. "You think we knew each other when you were a Shirley?"

"Without a doubt." Noel and I are cosmic twins, which is what has kept us together through all our arguments and crises. Our adviser, a gray-haired woman named Alicia whom we swear by, uncovered this amazing kinship the first time we visited her, when we were trying to decide if Noel should move in. Alicia immediately noticed that our left palms each had islands in Venus, which is very unusual, and that was only the first indication of our bond. A few months later, Noel had cashed in his accumulated mileage to get me a pass on an international flight he was working, and we spent a weekend layover in Amsterdam. On the Sunday, walking hand in hand along a canal, we suddenly stopped and looked out at the water in silence. It was a heavy, overcast day, somewhat chilly. A wind from the North Sea made waves against the stone embankment, and I thought how depressing it was that our getaway couldn't last forever. I looked at Noel and his eyes were bright and troubled.

"I just experienced this positive tsunami of sadness," he said, echoing my emotion.

Later we recounted our thoughts to Alicia and she explained that Noel and I may once have been Dutch and lived together—as brother and sister, father and son, lovers, who knew?—in a house on that exact street, which was why those feelings of being where we belonged had washed over us.

"Who was the brother and who was the sister?" I wondered aloud, but Alicia, after studying our auras could not tell.

"What did we do for a living?" Noel wanted know. He was always thinking about quitting his flight attendant's job, despite its travel advantages and insurance benefits.

"I see one of you as a merchant," Alicia decided. Because she was from Ireland, she often used words that sounded old fashioned: "cobblers" fixed shoes and "tinkers" sold Avon door-to-door.

I leaned against Noel, resting my cheek on the rough wool of the afghan.

We both started to say something, almost in synch, and I laughed. More and more often it happened that our minds simultaneously hit on the same idea. I'd be thinking of Noel and he'd telephone from wherever he was, or I would have prepared precisely what he wanted for dinner. Alicia called this our "harmonizing."

"You first," I invited, feeling forgiven about the Duz and therefore generous.

Noel took a deep breath, let it out, and swung his feet to the floor. He drew the cover around his body and rested his elbows on his knees. I sensed conflict, and put my hand on his back to show support.

"You know Sandra?" he asked the floor.

I nodded. Noel became emotionally involved with the personal problems of his fellow attendants, took their worries to heart.

"Well, she left him, her husband."

"I'm sure it's for the best," I said. "You said she wasn't happy."

"Alex, she left him for me."

There are moments in life when time freezes, or at least into slow motion. My hand was glued to Noel's back and nothing would make it move. The cooling element in the refrigerator clattered and when it stopped the silence was so absolute that from the bedroom I could hear a click as the numbers changed on my clock radio.

"I'm going to try it," he went on at last. "I have to know."

I heard him, understood the spoken words, but all I could think of was my hand. How heavy it had become, how useless. If I managed to lift it from the rise and fall of Noel's breath, where would I find to set it down?

Journal Entry

Explain the significance of the title.

Textual Considerations

1. Create a character profile of Noel and Alex listing their good and bad points.
2. What is Alicia's role in the story? What does she add to our knowledge of their relationship?

3. "Alex, she left him for me." Describe your response to this statement. Did you anticipate it at any prior point in the story? If so, where?

Cultural Contexts

1. Discuss with your group your responses to Alex's reactions to Noel's decision. How effective are the physical descriptions of her hand to suggest her emotional state? Does "Name Games" portray contemporary attitudes toward gender relationships? Why or why not?

Charlotte Perkins Gilman
1899

The Yellow Wallpaper

It is very seldom that mere ordinary people like John and myself secure ancestral halls for the summer.

A colonial mansion, a hereditary estate, I would say a haunted house, and reach the height of romantic felicity—but that would be asking too much of fate!

Still I will proudly declare that there is something queer about it.

Else, why should it be let so cheaply? And why have stood so long untenanted?

John laughs at me, of course, but one expects that in marriage.

John is practical in the extreme. He has not patience with faith, an intense horror of superstition, and he scoffs openly at any talk of things not to be felt and seen and put down in figures.

John is a physician, and *perhaps*—(I would not say it to a living soul, of course, but this is dead paper and a great relief to my mind)—*perhaps* that is one reason I do not get well faster.

You see he does not believe I am sick!

And what can one do?

If a physician of high standing, and one's own husband, assures friends and relatives that there is really nothing the matter with one but temporary nervous depression—a slight hysterical tendency—what is one to do?

My brother is also a physician, and also of high standing, and he says the same thing.

So I take phosphates or phosphites—whichever it is, and tonics, and journeys, and air, and exercise, and am absolutely forbidden to "work" until I am well again.

Personally, I disagree with their ideas.

Personally, I believe that congenial work, with excitement and change, would do me good.

But what is one to do?

I did write for a while in spite of them, but it *does* exhaust me a good deal—having to be so sly about it, or else meet with heavy opposition.

I sometimes fancy that in my condition if I had less opposition and more society and stimulus—but John says the very worst thing I can do is to think about my condition, and I confess it always makes me feel bad.

So I will let it alone and talk about the house.

The most beautiful place! It is quite alone, standing well back from the road, quite three miles from the village. It makes me think of English places that you read about, for there are hedges and walls and gates that lock, and lots of separate little houses for the gardeners and people.

There is a *delicious* garden! I never saw such a garden—large and shady, full of box-bordered paths, and lined with long grape-covered arbors with seats under them.

There were greenhouses, too, but they are all broken now.

There was some legal trouble, I believe, something about the heirs and coheirs; anyhow, the place has been empty for years.

That spoils my ghostliness, I am afraid, but I don't care—there is something strange about the house—I can feel it.

I even said so to John one moonlight evening, but he said what I felt was a *draught,* and shut the window.

I get unreasonably angry with John sometimes. I'm sure I never used to be so sensitive. I think it is due to this nervous condition.

But John says if I feel so, I shall neglect proper self-control; so I take pains to control myself—before him, at least, and that makes me very tired.

I don't like our room a bit. I wanted one downstairs that opened on the piazza and had roses all over the window, and such pretty old-fashioned chintz hangings! but John would not hear of it.

He said there was only one window and not room for two beds, and no near room for him if he took another.

He is very careful and loving, and hardly lets me stir without special direction.

I have a schedule prescription for each hour in the day; he takes all care from me, and so I feel basely ungrateful not to value it more.

He said we came here solely on my account, that I was to have perfect rest and all the air I could get. "Your exercise depends on your strength, my dear," said he, "and your food somewhat on your appetite, but air you can absorb all the time." So we took the nursery at the top of the house.

It is a big, airy room, the whole floor nearly, with windows that look all ways, and air and sunshine galore. It was nursery first and then playroom and gymnasium, I should judge; for the windows are barred for little children, and there are rings and things in the walls.

The paint and paper look as if a boys' school had used it. It is stripped off—the paper—in great patches all around the head of my bed, about as far as I can reach, and in a great place on the other side of the room low down. I never saw a worse paper in my life.

One of those sprawling flamboyant patterns committing every artistic sin.

It is dull enough to confuse the eye in following, pronounced enough to constantly irritate and provoke study, and when you follow the lame uncertain curves for a little distance they suddenly commit suicide—plunge off at outrageous angles, destroy themselves in unheard of contradictions.

The color is repellent, almost revolting; a smoldering unclean yellow, strangely faded by the slow-turning sunlight.

It is a dull yet lurid orange in some places, a sickly sulphur tint in others.

No wonder the children hated it! I should hate it myself if I had to live in this room long.

There comes John, and I must put this away,—he hates to have me write a word.

We have been here two weeks, and I haven't felt like writing before, since that first day.

I am sitting by the window now, up in this atrocious nursery, and there is nothing to hinder my writing as much as I please, save lack of strength.

John is away all day, and even some nights when his cases are serious.

I am glad my case is not serious!

But these nervous troubles are dreadfully depressing.

John does not know how much I really suffer. He knows there is no *reason* to suffer, and that satisfies him.

Of course it is only nervousness. It does weigh on me so not to do my duty in any way!

I meant to be such a help to John, such a real rest and comfort, and here I am a comparative burden already!

Nobody would believe what an effort it is to do what little I am able,—to dress and entertain, and order things.

It is fortunate Mary is so good with the baby. Such a dear baby!

And yet I *cannot* be with him, it makes me so nervous.

I suppose John never was nervous in his life. He laughs at me so about this wall-paper!

At first he meant to repaper the room, but afterwards he said that I was letting it get the better of me, and that nothing was worse for a nervous patient than to give way to such fancies.

He said that after the wall-paper was changed it would be the heavy bedstead, and then the barred windows, and then that gate at the head of the stairs, and so on.

"You know the place is doing you good," he said, "and really, dear, I don't care to renovate the house just for a three months' rental."

"Then do let us go downstairs," I said, "there are such pretty rooms there."

Then he took me in his arms and called me a blessed little goose, and said he would go down to the cellar, if I wished, and have it whitewashed into the bargain.

But he is right enough about the beds and windows and things.

It is an airy and comfortable room as any one need wish, and, of course, I would not be so silly as to make him uncomfortable just for a whim.

I'm really getting quite fond of the big room, all but that horrid paper.

Out of one window I can see the garden, those mysterious deepshaded arbors, the riotous old-fashioned flowers, and bushes and gnarly trees.

Out of another I get a lovely view of the bay and a little private wharf belonging to the estate. There is a beautiful shaded lane that runs down there from the house. I always fancy I see people walking in these numerous paths and arbors, but John has cautioned me not to give way to fancy in the least. He says that with my imaginative power and habit of story-making, a nervous weakness like mine is sure to lead to all manner of excited fancies, and that I ought to use my will and good sense to check the tendency. So I try.

I think sometimes that if I were only well enough to write a little it would relieve the press of ideas and rest me.

But I find I get pretty tired when I try.

It is so discouraging not to have any advice and companionship about my work. When I get really well, John says we will ask Cousin Henry and Julia down for a long visit; but he says he would as soon put fireworks in my pillow-case as to let me have those stimulating people about now.

I wish I could get well faster.

But I must not think about that. This paper looks to me as if it *knew* what a vicious influence it had!

There is a recurrent spot where the pattern lolls like a broken neck and two bulbous eyes stare at you upside down.

I get positively angry with the impertinence of it and the everlastingness. Up and down and sideways they crawl, and those absurd, unblinking eyes are everywhere. There is one place where two breadths didn't match, and the eyes go all up and down the line, one a little higher than the other.

I never saw so much expression in an inanimate thing before, and we all know how much expression they have! I used to lie awake as a child and get more entertainment and terror out of blank walls and plain furniture than most children could find in a toy-store.

I remember what a kindly wink the knobs of our big, old bureau used to have, and there was one chair that always seemed like a strong friend.

I used to feel that if any of the other things looked too fierce I could always hop into that chair and be safe.

The furniture in this room is no worse than inharmonious, however, for we had to bring it all from downstairs. I suppose when this was used as a playroom they had to take the nursery things out, and no wonder! I never saw such ravages as the children have made here.

The wall-paper, as I said before, is torn off in spots, and it sticketh closer than a brother—they must have had perseverance as well as hatred.

Then the floor is scratched and gouged and splintered, the plaster itself is dug out here and there, and this great heavy bed which is all we found in the room, looks as if it had been through the wars.

But I don't mind it a bit—only the paper.

There comes John's sister. Such a dear girl as she is, and so careful of me! I must not let her find me writing.

She is a perfect and enthusiastic housekeeper, and hopes for no better profession. I verily believe she thinks it is the writing which made me sick!

But I can write when she is out, and see her a long way off from these windows.

There is one that commands the road, a lovely shaded winding road, and one that just looks off over the country. A lovely country, too, full of great elms and velvet meadows.

This wall-paper has a kind of sub-pattern in a different shade, a particularly irritating one, for you can only see it in certain lights, and not clearly then.

But in the places where it isn't faded and where the sun is just so—I can see a strange, provoking, formless sort of figure, that seems to skulk about behind that silly and conspicuous front design.

There's sister on the stairs!

Well, the Fourth of July is over! The people are all gone and I am tired out. John thought it might do me good to see a little company, so we just had mother and Nellie and the children down for a week.

Of course I didn't do a thing. Jennie sees to everything now.

But it tired me all the same.

John says if I don't pick up faster he shall send me to Weir Mitchell in the fall.

But I don't want to go there at all. I had a friend who was in his hands once, and she says he is just like John and my brother, only more so!

Besides, it is such an undertaking to go so far.

I don't feel as if it was worth while to turn my hand over for anything, and I'm getting dreadfully fretful and querulous.

I cry at nothing, and cry most of the time.

Of course I don't when John is here, or anybody else, but when I am alone.

And I am alone a good deal just now. John is kept in town very often by serious cases, and Jennie is good and lets me alone when I want her to.

So I walk a little in the garden or down that lovely lane, sit on the porch under the roses, and lie down up here a good deal.

I'm getting really fond of the room in spite of the wall-paper. Perhaps *because* of the wall-paper.

It dwells in my mind so!

I lie here on this great immovable bed—it is nailed down, I believe—and follow that pattern about by the hour. It is as good as gymnastics, I assure you. I start, we'll say, at the bottom, down in the corner over there where it has not been touched, and I determine for the thousandth time that I *will* follow that pointless pattern to some sort of a conclusion.

I know a little of the principle of design, and I know this thing was not arranged on any laws of radiation, or alternation, or repetition, or symmetry, or anything else that I ever heard of.

It is repeated, of course, by the breadths, but not otherwise.

Looked at in one way each breadth stands alone, the bloated curves and flourishes—a kind of "debased Romanesque" with *delirium tremens*—go waddling up and down in isolated columns of fatuity.

But, on the other hand, they connect diagonally, and the sprawling outlines run off in great slanting waves of optic horror, like a lot of wallowing seaweeds in full chase.

The whole thing goes horizontally, too, at least it seems so, and I exhaust myself in trying to distinguish the order of its going in that direction.

They have used a horizontal breadth for a frieze, and that adds wonderfully to the confusion.

There is one end of the room where it is almost intact, and there, when the crosslights fade and the low sun shines directly upon it, I can almost fancy radiation after all—the interminable grotesques seem to form around a common centre and rush off in headlong plunges of equal distraction.

It makes me tired to follow it. I will take a nap I guess.

I don't know why I should write this.

I don't want to.

I don't feel able.

And I know John would think it absurd. But I *must* say what I feel and think in some way—it is such a relief!

But the effort is getting to be greater than the relief.

Half the time now I am awfully lazy, and lie down ever so much.

John says I mustn't lose my strength, and has me take cod liver oil and lots of tonics and things, to say nothing of ale and wine and rare meat.

Dear John! He loves me very dearly, and hates to have me sick. I tried to have a real earnest reasonable talk with him the other day, and tell him how I wish he would let me go and make a visit to Cousin Henry and Julia.

But he said I wasn't able to go, nor able to stand it after I got there; and I did not make out a very good case for myself, for I was crying before I had finished.

It is getting to be a great effort for me to think straight. Just this nervous weakness I suppose.

And dear John gathered me up in his arms, and just carried me upstairs and laid me on the bed, and sat by me and read to me till it tired my head.

He said I was his darling and his comfort and all he had, and that I must take care of myself for his sake, and keep well.

He says no one but myself can help me out of it, that I must use my will and self-control and not let any silly fancies run away with me.

There's one comfort, the baby is well and happy, and does not have to occupy this nursery with the horrid wall-paper.

If we had not used it, that blessed child would have! What a fortunate escape! Why, I wouldn't have a child of mine, an impressionable little thing, live in such a room for worlds.

I never thought of it before, but it is lucky that John kept me here after all, I can stand it so much easier than a baby, you see.

Of course I never mention it to them any more—I am too wise,—but I keep watch of it all the same.

There are things in that paper that nobody knows but me, or ever will.

Behind that outside pattern the dim shapes get clearer every day.

It is always the same shape, only very numerous.

And it is like a woman stooping down and creeping about behind that pattern. I don't like it a bit. I wonder—I begin to think—I wish John would take me away from here!

It is so hard to talk with John about my case, because he is so wise, and because he loves me so.

But I tried it last night.

It was moonlight. The moon shines in all around just as the sun does.

I hate to see it sometimes, it creeps so slowly, and always comes in by one window or another.

John was asleep and I hated to waken him, so I kept still and watched the moonlight on that undulating wall-paper till I felt creepy.

The faint figure behind seemed to shake the pattern, just as if she wanted to get out.

I got up softly and went to feel and see if the paper *did* move, and when I came back John was awake.

"What is it, little girl?" he said. "Don't go walking about like that—you'll get cold."

I thought it was a good time to talk, so I told him that I really was not gaining here, and that I wished he would take me away.

"Why darling!" said he, "our lease will be up in three weeks, and I can't see how to leave before.

"The repairs are not done at home, and I cannot possibly leave town just now. Of course if you were in any danger, I could and would, but you really are better, dear, whether you can see it or not. I am a doctor, dear, and I know. You are gaining flesh and color, your appetite is better, I feel really much easier about you."

"I don't weigh a bit more," said I, "nor as much; and my appetite may be better in the evening when you are here, but it is worse in the morning when you are away!"

"Bless her little heart!" said he with a big hug, "she shall be as sick as she pleases! But now let's improve the shining hours by going to sleep, and talk about it in the morning!"

"And you won't go away?" I asked gloomily.

"Why, how can I, dear? It is only three weeks more and then we will take a nice little trip of a few days while Jennie is getting the house ready. Really dear you are better!"

"Better in body perhaps—" I began, and stopped short, for he sat up straight and looked at me with such a stern, reproachful look that I could not say another word.

"My darling," said he, "I beg of you, for my sake and for our child's sake, as well as for your own, that you will never for one instant let that idea enter your mind! There is nothing so dangerous, so fascinating, to a temperament like yours. It is a false and foolish fancy. Can you not trust me as a physician when I tell you so?"

So of course I said no more on that score, and we went to sleep before long. He thought I was asleep first, but I wasn't, and lay there for hours trying to decide whether that front pattern and the back pattern really did move together or separately.

On a pattern like this, by daylight, there is a lack of sequence, a defiance of law, that is a constant irritant to a normal mind.

The color is hideous enough, and unreliable enough, and infuriating enough, but the pattern is torturing.

You think you have mastered it, but just as you get well underway in following, it turns a back-somersault and there you are. It slaps you in the face, knocks you down, and tramples upon you. It is like a bad dream.

The outside pattern is a florid arabesque, reminding one of a fungus. If you can imagine a toadstool in joints, an interminable string of toadstools, budding and sprouting in endless convolutions—why, that is something like it.

That is, sometimes!

There is one marked peculiarity about this paper, a thing nobody seems to notice but myself, and that is that it changes as the light changes.

When the sun shoots in through the east window—I always watch for that first long, straight ray—it changes so quickly that I never can quite believe it.

That is why I watch it always.

By moonlight—the moon shines in all night when there is a moon—I wouldn't know it was the same paper.

At night in any kind of light, in twilight, candle light, lamplight, and worst of all by moonlight, it becomes bars! The outside pattern I mean, and the woman behind it is as plain as can be.

I didn't realize for a long time what the thing was that showed behind, that dim sub-pattern, but now I am quite sure it is a woman.

By daylight she is subdued, quiet. I fancy, it is the pattern that keeps her so still. It is so puzzling. It keeps me quiet by the hour.

I lie down ever so much now. John says it is good for me, and to sleep all I can.

Indeed he started the habit by making me lie down for an hour after each meal.

It is a very bad habit I am convinced, for you see I don't sleep.

And that cultivates deceit, for I don't tell them I'm awake—O no!

The fact is I am getting a little afraid of John.

He seems very queer sometimes, and even Jennie has an inexplicable look.

It strikes me occasionally, just as a scientific hypothesis,—that perhaps it is the paper!

I have watched John when he did not know I was looking, and come into the room suddenly on the most innocent excuses, and I've caught him several times *looking at the paper!* And Jennie too. I caught Jennie with her hand on it once.

She didn't know I was in the room, and when I asked her in a quiet, a very quiet voice, with the most restrained manner possible, what she was doing with the paper—she turned around as if she had been caught stealing, and looked quite angry—asked me why I should frighten her so!

Then she said that the paper stained everything it touched, that she had found yellow smooches on all my clothes and John's, and she wished we would be more careful!

Did not that sound innocent? But I know she was studying that pattern, and I am determined that nobody shall find it out but myself!

Life is very much more exciting now than it used to be. You see I have something more to expect, to look forward to, to watch. I really do eat better, and am more quiet than I was.

John is so pleased to see me improve! He laughed a little the other day, and said I seemed to be flourishing in spite of my wall-paper.

I turned it off with a laugh. I had no intention of telling him it was *because* of the wall-paper—he would make fun of me. He might even want to take me away.

I don't want to leave now until I have found it out. There is a week more, and I think that will be enough.

I'm feeling ever so much better! I don't sleep much at night, for it is so interesting to watch developments; but I sleep a good deal in the daytime.

In the daytime it is tiresome and perplexing.

There are always new shoots on the fungus, and new shades of yellow all over it. I cannot keep count of them, though I have tried conscientiously.

It is the strangest yellow, that wall-paper! It makes me think of all the yellow things I ever saw—not beautiful ones like buttercups, but old foul, bad yellow things.

But there is something else about that paper—the smell! I noticed it the moment we came into the room, but with so much air and sun it was not bad. Now we have had a week of fog and rain, and whether the windows are open or not, the smell is here.

It creeps all over the house.

I find it hovering in the dining-room, skulking in the parlor, hiding in the hall, lying in wait for me on the stairs.

It gets into my hair.

Even when I go to ride, if I turn my head suddenly and surprise it—there is that smell!

Such a peculiar odor, too! I have spent hours in trying to analyze it, to find what it smelled like.

It is not bad—at first, and very gentle, but quite the subtlest, most enduring odor I ever met.

In this damp weather it is awful, I wake up in the night and find it hanging over me.

It used to disturb me at first. I thought seriously of burning the house—to reach the smell.

But now I am used to it. The only thing I can think of that it is like is the *color* of the paper! A yellow smell.

There is a very funny mark on this wall, low down, near the mopboard. A streak that runs round the room. It goes behind every piece of furniture, except the bed, a long, straight, even *smooch,* as if it had been rubbed over and over.

I wonder how it was done and who did it, and what they did it for. Round and round and round—round and round and round—it makes me dizzy!

I really have discovered something at last.

Through watching so much at night, when it changes so, I have finally found out.

The front pattern *does* move—and no wonder! The woman behind shakes it!

Sometimes I think there are a great many women behind, and sometimes only one, and she crawls around fast, and her crawling shakes it all over.

Then in the very bright spots she keeps still, and in the very shady spots she just takes hold of the bars and shakes them hard.

And she is all the time trying to climb through. But nobody could climb through that pattern—it strangles so; I think that is why it has so many heads.

They get through, and then the pattern strangles them off and turns them upside down, and makes their eyes white!

If those heads were covered or taken off it would not be half so bad.

I think that woman gets out in the daytime!

And I'll tell you why—privately—I've seen her!

I can see her out of every one of my windows!

It is the same woman, I know, for she is always creeping, and most women do not creep by daylight.

I see her on that long road under the trees, creeping along, and when a carriage comes she hides under the blackberry vines.

I don't blame her a bit. It must be very humiliating to be caught creeping by daylight!

I always lock the door when I creep by daylight. I can't do it at night, for I know John would suspect something at once.

And John is so queer now, that I don't want to irritate him. I wish he would take another room! Besides, I don't want anybody to get that woman out at night but myself.

I often wonder if I could see her out of all the windows at once.

But, turn as fast as I can, I can only see out of one at one time.

And though I always see her, she *may* be able to creep faster than I can turn!

I have watched her sometimes away off in the open country, creeping as fast as a cloud shadow in a high wind.

If only that top pattern could be gotten off from the under one! I mean to try it, little by little.

I have found out another funny thing, but I shan't tell it this time! It does not do to trust people too much.

There are only two more days to get this paper off, and I believe John is beginning to notice. I don't like the look in his eyes.

And I heard him ask Jennie a lot of professional questions about me. She had a very good report to give.

She said I slept a good deal in the daytime.

John knows I don't sleep very well at night, for all I'm so quiet!

He asked me all sorts of questions, too, and pretended to be very loving and kind.

As if I couldn't see through him!

Still, I don't wonder he acts so, sleeping under this paper for three months.

It only interests me, but I feel sure John and Jennie are secretly affected by it.

Hurrah! This is the last day, but it is enough. John to stay in town over night, and won't be out until this evening.

Jennie wanted to sleep with me—the sly thing! but I told her I should undoubtedly rest better for a night all alone.

That was clever, for really I wasn't alone a bit! As soon as it was moonlight and that poor thing began to crawl and shake the pattern, I got up and ran to help her.

I pulled and she shook, I shook and she pulled, and before morning we had peeled off yards of that paper.

A strip about as high as my head and half around the room.

And then when the sun came and that awful pattern began to laugh at me, I declared I would finish it to-day!

We go away to-morrow, and they are moving all my furniture down again to leave things as they were before.

Jennie looked at the wall in amazement, but I told her merrily that I did it out of pure spite at the vicious thing.

She laughed and said she wouldn't mind doing it herself, but I must not get tired.

How she betrayed herself that time!

But I am here, and no person touches this paper but me—not *alive!*

She tried to get me out of the room—it was too patent! But I said it was so quiet and empty and clean now that I believed I would lie down again and sleep all I could; and not to wake me even for dinner—I would call when I woke.

So now she is gone, and the servants are gone, and the things are gone, and there is nothing left but that great bedstead nailed down, with the canvas mattress we found on it.

We shall sleep downstairs to-night, and take the boat home to-morrow.

I quite enjoy the room, now it is bare again.

How those children did tear about here!

This bedstead is fairly gnawed!

But I must get to work.

I have locked the door and thrown the key down into the front path.

I don't want to go out, and I don't want to have anybody come in, till John comes.

I want to astonish him.

I've got a rope up here that even Jennie did not find. If that woman does get out, and tries to get away, I can tie her!

But I forgot I could not reach far without anything to stand on!

This bed will *not* move!

I tried to lift and push it until I was lame, and then I got so angry I bit off a little piece at one corner—but it hurt my teeth.

Then I peeled off all the paper I could reach standing on the floor. It sticks horribly and the pattern just enjoys it! All those strangled heads and bulbous eyes and waddling fungus growths just shriek with derision!

I am getting angry enough to do something desperate. To jump out of the window would be admirable exercise, but the bars are too strong even to try.

Besides I wouldn't do it. Of course not. I know well enough that a step like that is improper and might be misconstrued.

I don't like to *look* out of the windows even—there are so many of those creeping women, and they creep so fast.

I wonder if they all come out of that wall-paper as I did?

But I am securely fastened now by my well-hidden rope—you don't get *me* out in the road there!

I suppose I shall have to get back behind the pattern when it comes night, and that is hard!

It is so pleasant to be out in this great room and creep around as I please!

I don't want to go outside. I won't, even if Jennie asks me to.

For outside you have to creep on the ground, and everything is green instead of yellow.

But here I can creep smoothly on the floor, and my shoulder just fits in that long smooch around the wall, so I cannot lose my way.

Why there's John at the door!

It is no use, young man, you can't open it!

How he does call and pound!

Now he's crying for an axe.

It would be a shame to break down that beautiful door!

"John dear!" said I in the gentlest voice, "the key is down by the front steps, under a plantain leaf!"

That silenced him for a few moments.

Then he said—very quietly indeed, "Open the door, my darling!"

"I can't," said I. "The key is down by the front door under a plantain leaf!"

And then I said it again, several times, very gently and slowly, and said it so often that he had to go and see, and he got it of course, and came in. He stopped short by the door.

"What is the matter?" he cried. "For God's sake, what are you doing?"

I kept on creeping just the same, but I looked at him over my shoulder.

"I've got out at last," said I, "in spite of you and Jane. And I've pulled off most of the paper, so you can't put me back!"

Now why should that man have fainted? But he did, and right across my path by the wall, so that I had to creep over him every time!

Journal Entry

Analyze the role of the speaker's journal in "The Yellow Wallpaper."

Textual Considerations

1. Prepare a profile of John listing his good and bad points. Is he responsible for his wife's emotional state? Why or why not? To what extent do you agree with him that she should not write?
2. Analyze the connection between meaning and symbolism in the story. Consider, for example, the physical description of the bedroom, particularly the wallpaper. How do the narrator's description of and feelings toward it change? Why is the color appropriate? What pattern does she discover and what does it represent?
3. How does the author use stylistic changes to mirror the narrator's mental disintegration? Cite examples from the text.
4. Explain the narrator's statement "I've got out at last" in the next-to-last paragraph. To what extent is this true? Is there any sense in which madness can be liberating? Explain.

Cultural Contexts

1. Discuss with your group the reasons for the current popularity of "The Yellow Wallpaper."
2. The rest cure prescribed by the narrator's doctor and physician-husband was standard in Victorian medical theory for what is now known as postpartum depression. Discuss with your group how this "cure" might affect emotional depression and sense of identity.

Alifa Rifaat
1983

Another Evening at the Club

In a state of tension, she awaited the return of her husband. At a loss to predict what would happen between them, she moved herself back and forth in the rocking chair on the wide wooden veranda that ran along the bank and occupied part of the river itself, its supports being fixed in the river bed, while around it grew grasses and reeds. As though to banish her apprehension, she passed her fingers across her hair. The specters of the eucalyptus trees ranged along the garden fence rocked before her gaze, with white egrets slumbering on their high branches like huge white flowers among the thin leaves.

The crescent moon rose from behind the eastern mountains and the peaks of the gently stirring waves glistened in its feeble rays, intermingled with threads of light leaking from the houses of Manfalout scattered along the opposite bank. The colored bulbs fixed to the trees in the garden of the club at the far end of the town stood out against the surrounding darkness. Somewhere over there her husband now sat, most likely engrossed in a game of chess.

It was only a few years ago that she had first laid eyes on him at her father's house, meeting his gaze that weighed up her beauty and priced it before offering the dowry. She had noted his eyes ranging over her as she presented him with the coffee in the Japanese cups that were kept safely locked away in the cupboard for important guests. Her mother had herself laid them out on the silver-plated tray with its elaborately embroidered spread. When the two men had taken their coffee, her father had looked up at her with a smile and had told her to sit down, and she had seated herself on the sofa facing them, drawing the end of her dress over her knees and looking through lowered lids at the man who might choose her as his wife. She had been glad to see that he was tall, well-built and clean-shaven except for a thin greying moustache. In particular she noticed the well-cut coat of English tweed and the silk shirt with gold links. She had felt herself blushing as she saw him returning her gaze. Then the man turned to her father and took out a gold case and offered him a cigarette.

"You really shouldn't, my dear sir," said her father, patting his chest with his left hand and extracting a cigarette with trembling fingers. Before he could bring out his box of matches Abboud Bey had produced his lighter.

"No, after you, my dear sir," said her father in embarrassment. Mingled with her sense of excitement at this man who gave out such an air of worldly self-confidence was a guilty shame at her father's inadequacy.

After lighting her father's cigarette Abboud Bey sat back, crossing his legs, and took out a cigarette for himself. He tapped it against the case before putting it in the corner of his mouth and lighting it, then blew out circles of smoke that followed each other across the room.

"It's a great honor for us, my son," said her father, smiling first at Abboud Bey, then at his daughter, at which Abboud Bey looked across at her and asked:

"And the beautiful little girl's still at secondary school?"

She lowered her head modestly and her father had answered:

"As from today she'll be staying at home in readiness for your happy life together. Allah permitting," and at a glance from her father she had hurried off to join her mother in the kitchen.

"You're a lucky girl," her mother had told her. "He's a real find. Any girl would be happy to have him. He's an Inspector of Irrigation though he's not yet forty. He earns a big salary and gets a fully furnished government house wherever he's posted, which will save us the expense of setting up a house—and I don't have to tell you what our situation is—and that's beside the house he owns in Alexandria where you'll be spending your holidays."

Samia had wondered to herself how such a splendid suitor had found his way to her door. Who had told him that Mr. Mahmoud Barakat, a mere clerk at the Court of Appeal, had a beautiful daughter of good reputation?

The days were then taken up with going the rounds of Cairo's shops and choosing clothes for the new grand life she would be living. This was made possible by her father borrowing on the security of his government pension. Abboud Bey, on his part, never visited her without bringing a present. For her birthday, just before they were married, he bought her an emerald ring that came in a plush box bearing the name of a well-known jeweler in Kasr el-Nil Street. On her wedding night, as he put a diamond bracelet round her wrist, he had reminded her that she was marrying someone with a brilliant career in front of him and that one of the most important things in life was the opinion of others, particularly one's equals and seniors. Though she was still only a young girl she must try to act with suitable dignity.

"Tell people you're from the well-known Barakat family and that your father was a judge," and he went up to her and gently patted her cheeks in a fatherly, reassuring gesture that he was often to repeat during their times together.

Then, yesterday evening, she had returned from the club somewhat light-headed from the bottle of beer she had been required to drink on the occasion of someone's birthday. Her husband, noting the state she was in, hurriedly took her back home. She had undressed and put on her nightgown, leaving her jewelry on the dressing table, and was fast asleep seconds after getting into bed. The following morning, fully recovered, she slept late, then rang the bell as usual and had breakfast brought to her. It was only as she was putting her jewelry away in the wooden and mother-of-pearl box that she realized that her emerald ring was missing.

Could it have dropped from her finger at the club? In the car on the way back? No, she distinctly remembered it last thing at night, remembered the usual difficulty she had in getting it off her finger. She stripped the bed of its sheets, turned over the mattress, looked inside the pillow cases, crawled on hands and knees under the bed. The tray of breakfast lying on the small bedside table caught her eye and she remembered the young servant coming in that morning with it, remembered the noise of the tray being put down, the curtain being drawn, the tray then being lifted up again and placed on the bedside table. No one but the servant had entered the room. Should she call her and question her?

Eventually, having taken two aspirins, she decided to do nothing and await the return of her husband from work.

Directly he arrived she told him what had happened and he took her by the arm and seated her down beside him:

"Let's calm down and go over what happened."

She repeated, this time with further details, the whole story.

"And you've looked for it?"

"Everywhere. Every possible and impossible place in the bedroom and the bathroom. You see, I remember distinctly taking it off last night."

He grimaced at the thought of last night, then said:

"Anybody been in the room since Gazia when she brought in the breakfast?"

"Not a soul. I've even told Gazia not to do the room today."

"And you've not mentioned anything to her?"

"I thought I'd better leave it to you."

"Fine, go and tell her I want to speak to her. There's no point in your saying anything but I think it would be as well if you were present when I talk to her."

Five minutes later Gazia, the young servant girl they had recently employed, entered behind her mistress. Samia took herself to a far corner of the room while Gazia stood in front of Abboud Bey, her hands folded across her chest, her eyes lowered.

"Yes, sir?"

"Where's the ring?"

"What ring are you talking about, sir?"

"Now don't make out you don't know. The one with the green stone. It would be better for you if you hand it over and then nothing more need be said."

"May Allah blind me if I've set eyes on it."

He stood up and gave her a sudden slap on the face. The girl reeled back, put one hand to her cheek, then lowered it again to her chest and made no answer to any of Abboud's questions. Finally he said to her:

"You've got just fifteen seconds to say where you've hidden the ring or else, I swear to you, you're not going to have a good time of it."

As he lifted up his arm to look at his watch the girl flinched slightly but continued in her silence. When he went to the telephone Samia raised her head and saw that the girl's cheeks were wet with tears. Abboud Bey got through to the Superintendent of Police and told him briefly what had occurred.

"Of course I haven't got any actual proof but seeing that no one else entered the room, it's obvious she's pinched it. Anyway I'll leave the matter in your capable hands—I know your people have their ways and means."

He gave a short laugh, then listened for a while and said: "I'm really most grateful to you."

He put down the receiver and turned to Samia:

"That's it, my dear. There's nothing more to worry about. The Superintendent has promised me we'll get it back. The patrol car's on the way."

The following day, in the late afternoon, she'd been sitting in front of her dressing-table rearranging her jewelry in its box when an earring slipped from her grasp and fell to the floor. As she bent to pick it up she saw the emerald ring stuck between the leg of the table and the wall. Since that moment she had sat in a state of panic awaiting her husband's return from the club. She even felt tempted to walk down to the water's edge and throw it into the river so as to be rid of the unpleasantness that lay ahead.

At the sound of the screech of tires rounding the house to the garage, she slipped the ring onto her finger. As he entered she stood up and raised her hand to show him the ring. Quickly, trying to choose her words but knowing that she was expressing herself clumsily, explained what an extraordinary thing it was that it should have lodged itself between the dressing-table and the wall, what an extraordinary coincidence she should have dropped the earring and so seen it, how she'd thought of ringing him at the club to tell him the good news but...

She stopped in mid-sentence when she saw his frown and added weakly: "I'm sorry. I can't think how it could have happened. What do we do now?"

He shrugged his shoulders as though in surprise.

"Are you asking me, my dear lady? Nothing of course."

"But they've been beating up the girl—you yourself said they'd not let her be till she confessed."

Unhurriedly, he sat himself down as though to consider this new aspect of the matter. Taking out his case, he tapped a cigarette against it in his accustomed manner, then moistened his lips, put the cigarette in place and lit it. The smoke rings hovered in the still air as he looked at his watch and said:

"In any case she's not got all that long before they let her go. They can't keep her for more than forty-eight hours without getting any evidence or a confession. It won't kill her to put up with things for a while longer. By now the whole town knows the servant stole the ring—or would you like me to tell everyone: 'Look, folks, the fact is that the wife got a bit tiddly on a couple sips of beer and the ring took off on its own and hid itself behind the dressing-table'? What do you think?"

"I know the situation's a bit awkward…"

"Awkward? It's downright ludicrous. Listen, there's nothing to be done but to give it to me and the next time I go down to Cairo I'll sell it and get something else in its place. We'd be the laughing-stock of the town."

He stretched out his hand and she found herself taking off the ring and placing it in the outstretched palm. She was careful that their eyes should not meet. For a moment she was on the point of protesting and in fact uttered a few words:

"I'd just like to say we could…"

Putting the ring away in his pocket, he bent over her and with both hands gently patted her on the cheeks. It was gesture she had long become used to, a gesture that promised her that this man who was her husband and the father of her child had also taken the place of her father who, as though assured that he had found her a suitable substitute, had followed up her marriage with his own funeral. The gesture told her more eloquently than any words that he was the man, she the woman, he the one who carried the responsibilities, made the decisions, she the one whose role it was to be beautiful, happy, carefree. Now, though, for the first time in their life together the gesture came like a slap in the face.

Directly he removed his hands her whole body was seized with an uncontrollable trembling. Frightened he would notice, she rose to her feet and walked with deliberate steps towards the large window. She leaned her forehead against the comforting cold surface and closed her eyes tightly for several seconds. When she opened them she noticed that the café lights strung between the trees on the opposite shore had been turned on and that there were men seated under them and a waiter moving among the tables. The dark shape of a boat momentarily blocked out the café scene; in the light from the hurricane lamp hanging from its bow she saw it cutting through several of those floating islands of Nile waterlillies that, rootless, are swept along with the current.

Suddenly she became aware of his presence alongside her.

"Why don't you go and change quickly while I take the car out? It's hot and it would be nice to have supper at the club."

"As you like. Why not?"

By the time she had turned round from the window she was smiling.

Journal Entry

Imagine yourself as the wife of the Inspector of Irrigation. How would your responses to your husband be similar to or different from Samia's?

Textual Considerations

1. Rifaat uses flashbacks at several points in the story. Cite two or three examples and discuss their relation to the story's meaning.
2. Analyze Rifaat's use of nonverbal language such as gazes, glances, slaps, and gestures to reinforce the story's theme. What examples do you find most effective?
3. Comment on the role of the servant girl. To what extent is she Samia's victim as well as Abboud's?
4. What is the significance of the story's title? How does it relate to the concluding paragraph of the text?

Cultural Contexts

1. Discuss with your group the significance of the dowry in the story. How does it affect Samia's relationship with her husband? How does his wife's presence as an object affect the husband's identity?
2. Analyze the roles of the various communities in the story—parents, police, and friends. How does the husband's role in the community affect his identity and his actions?

Virginia Woolf
1931

Professions for Women

When your secretary invited me to come here, she told me that your Society is concerned with the employment of women and she suggested that I might tell you something about my own professional experiences. It is true I am a woman; it is true I am employed, but what professional experiences have I had? It is difficult to say. My profession is literature; and in that profession there are fewer experiences for women than in any other, with the exception of the stage—fewer, I mean, that are peculiar to women. For the road was cut many years ago—by Fanny Burney, by Aphra Behn, by Harriet Martineau, by Jane Austen, by George Eliot— many famous women, and many more unknown and forgotten, have been before me, making the path smooth, and regulating my steps. Thus, when I came to write, there were very few material obstacles in my way. Writing was a reputable and harmless occupation. The family peace was not broken by the scratching of a pen. No demand was made upon the family purse. For ten and sixpence one can buy paper enough to write all the plays of Shakespeare—if one has a mind that way. Pianos and models, Paris, Vienna and Berlin, masters and mistresses, are not needed by a writer. The cheapness of writing paper is, of course, the reason why women have succeeded as writers before they have succeeded in the other professions.

But to tell you my story—it is a simple one. You have only got to figure to yourselves a girl in a bedroom with a pen in her hand. She had only to move that pen from left to right—from ten o'clock to one. Then it occurred to her to do what is simple and cheap enough after all—to slip a few of those pages into an envelope, fix a penny stamp in the corner, and drop the envelope in the red box at the corner. It was thus that I became a journalist; and my effort was rewarded on the first day of the following month—a very glorious day it was for me—by a letter from an editor containing a check for one pound ten shillings and sixpence. But to show you how little I deserve to be called a professional woman, how little I know of the struggles and difficulties of such lives, I have to admit that instead of spending that sum upon bread and butter, rent, shoes and stockings, or butcher's bills, I went out and bought a cat—a beautiful cat, a Persian cat, which very soon involved me in bitter disputes with my neighbors.

What could be easier than to write articles and to buy Persian cats with the profits? But wait a moment. Articles have to be about something. Mine, I seem to remember, was about a novel by a famous man. And while I was writing this review, I discovered that if I were going to review books I should need to do battle with a certain phantom. And the phantom was a woman, and when I came to know her better I called her after the heroine of a famous poem, The Angel in the House. It was she who used to come between me and my paper when I was writing reviews. It was she who bothered me and wasted my time and so tormented me that at last I killed her. You who come of a younger and happier generation may not have heard of her—you may not know what I mean by the Angel in the House. I will describe her as shortly as I can. She was intensely sympathetic. She was immensely charming. She was utterly unselfish. She excelled in the difficult arts of family life. She sacrificed herself daily. If there was chicken, she took the leg; if there was a draught she sat in it—in short she was so constituted that she never had a mind or a wish of her own but preferred to sympathize always with the minds and wishes of others. Above all—I need not say it—she was pure. Her purity was supposed to be her chief beauty—her blushes, her great grace. In those days—the last of Queen Victoria—every house had its Angel. And when I came to write I encountered her with the very first words. The shadow of her wings fell on my page; I heard the rustling of her skirts in the room. Directly, that is to say, I took my pen in hand to review that novel by a famous man, she slipped behind me and whispered: "My dear, you are a young woman. You are writing about a book that has been written by a man. Be sympathetic; be tender; flatter; deceive; use all the arts and wiles of our sex. Never let anybody guess that you have a mind of your own. Above all, be pure." And she made as if to guide my pen. I now record the one act for which I take some credit to myself, though the credit rightly belongs to some excellent ancestor of mine who left me a certain sum of money—shall we say five hundred pounds a year?—so that it was not necessary for me to depend solely on charm for my living. I turned upon her and caught her by the throat. I did my best to kill her. My excuse, if I were to be had up in a court of law, would be that I acted in self-defense. Had I not killed her she would have killed me. She would have plucked the heart out of my writing. For, as I found, directly I put pen to paper, you cannot review even a novel without having a mind of your own, without expressing what you think to be the truth about human relations, morality, sex. And all these questions, according to the Angel in the House, cannot be dealt with freely and openly by women; they must charm, they must conciliate, they must—to put it bluntly—tell lies if they are to succeed. Thus, whenever I felt the shadow of her wing or the radiance of her halo upon my page, I took up the inkpot and flung it at her. She died hard. Her fictitious nature was of great assistance to her. It is far harder to kill a phantom than a reality. She was always creeping back when I thought I had despatched her. Though I flatter myself that I killed her in the end, the struggle was severe; it took much time that had better have been spent upon learning Greek grammar; or in roaming the world in search of adventures. But it was a real experience; it was an experience that was bound to befall all women writers at that time. Killing the Angel in the House was part of the occupation of a woman writer.

But to continue my story. The Angel was dead; what then remained? You may say that what remained was a simple and common object—a young woman in a bedroom with an inkpot. In other words, now that she had rid herself of falsehood, that young woman had only to be herself. Ah, but what is "herself"? I mean, what is a woman? I assure you, I do not know. I do not believe that you know. I do not believe that anybody can know until she has expressed herself in all the arts and professions open to human skill. That indeed is one of the reasons why I have come here—out of respect for you, who are in process of showing us by your experiments what a woman is, who are in process of providing us, by your failures and successes, with that extremely important piece of information.

But to continue the story of my professional experiences. I made one pound ten and six by my first review; and I bought a Persian cat with the proceeds. Then I grew ambitious. A Persian cat is all very well, I said; but a Persian cat is not enough. I must have a motor car. And it was thus that I became a novelist—for it is a very strange thing that people will give you a motor car if you will tell them a story. It is a still stranger thing that there is nothing so delightful in the world as telling stories. It is far pleasanter than writing reviews of famous novels. And yet, if I am to obey your secretary and tell you my professional experiences as a novelist, I must tell you about a very strange experience that befell me as a novelist. And to understand it you must try first to imagine a novelist's state of mind. I hope I am not giving away professional secrets if I say that a novelist's chief desire is to be as unconscious as possible. He has to induce in himself a state of perpetual lethargy. He wants life to proceed with the utmost quiet and regularity. He wants to see the same faces, to read the same books, to do the same things day after day, month after month, while he is writing, so that nothing may break the illusion in which he is living—so that nothing may disturb or disquiet the mysterious nosings about, feelings round, darts, dashes and sudden discoveries of that very shy and illusive spirit, the imagination. I suspect that this state is the same both for men and women. Be that as it may, I want you to imagine me writing a novel in a state of trance. I want you to figure to yourselves a girl sitting with a pen in her hand, which for minutes, and indeed for hours, she never dips into the inkpot. The image that comes to my mind when I think of this girl is the image of a fisherman lying sunk in dreams on the verge of a deep lake with a rod held out over the water. She was letting her imagination sweep unchecked round every rock and cranny of the world that lies submerged in the depths of our unconscious being. Now came the experience, the experience that I believe to be far commoner with women writers than with men. The line raced through the girl's fingers. Her imagination had rushed away. It had sought the pools, the depths, the dark places where the largest fish slumber. And then there was a smash. There was an explosion. There was foam and confusion. The imagination had dashed itself against something hard. The girl was roused from her dream. She was indeed in a state of the most acute and difficult distress. To speak without figure she had thought of something, something about the body, about the passions which it was unfitting for her as a woman to say. Men, her reason told her, would be shocked. The consciousness of what men will say of a woman who speaks the truth about her passions had roused her from her artist's state of unconsciousness. She could write no more. The trance was over. Her imagination could work no longer. This I believe to be a very common experience with women writers—they are impeded by the extreme conventionality of the other sex. For though men sensibly allow themselves great freedom in these respects, I doubt that they realize or can control the extreme severity with which they condemn such freedom in women.

These then were two very genuine experiences of my own. These were two of the adventures of my professional life. The first—killing the Angel in the House—

I think I solved. She died. But the second, telling the truth about my own experiences as a body, I do not think I solved. I doubt that any woman has solved it yet. The obstacles against her are still immensely powerful—and yet they are very difficult to define. Outwardly, what is simpler than to write books? Outwardly, what obstacles are there for a woman rather than for a man? Inwardly, I think the case is very different; she has still many ghosts to fight, many prejudices to overcome. Indeed it will be a long time still, I think, before a woman can sit down to write a book without finding a phantom to be slain, a rock to be dashed against. And if this is so in literature, the freest of all professions for women, how is it in the new professions which you are now for the first time entering?

Those are the questions that I should like, had I time, to ask you. And indeed, if I have laid stress upon these professional experiences of mine, it is because I believe that they are, though in different forms, yours also. Even when the path is nominally open—when there is nothing to prevent a woman from being a doctor, a lawyer, a civil servant—there are many phantoms and obstacles, as I believe, looming in her way. To discuss and define them is I think of great value and importance; for thus only can the labor be shared, the difficulties be solved. But besides this, it is necessary also to discuss the ends and the aims for which we are fighting, for which we are doing battle with these formidable obstacles. Those aims cannot be taken for granted; they must be perpetually questioned and examined. The whole position, as I see it—here in this hall surrounded by women practising for the first time in history I know not how many different professions—is one of extraordinary interest and importance. You have won rooms of your own in the house hitherto exclusively owned by men. You are able, though not without great labor and effort, to pay the rent. You are earning your five hundred pounds a year. But this freedom is only a beginning; the room is your own, but it is still bare. It has to be furnished; it has to be decorated; it has to be shared. How are you going to furnish it, how are you going to decorate it? With whom are you going to share it, and upon what terms? These, I think, are questions of the utmost importance and interest. For the first time in history you are able to ask them; for the first time you are able to decide for yourselves what the answers should be. Willingly would I stay and discuss those questions and answers—but not tonight. My time is up; and I must cease.

Journal Entry

Imagine yourself furnishing a room of your life. Write a journal entry on your aspirations using this metaphor.

Textual Considerations

1. What reasons does Woolf provide to support her thesis that "writing was a reputable and harmless occupation" for women? What do they suggest about a woman's place in Woolf's society?
2. What does the Angel in the House encourage Woolf to do? Is *angel* an appropriate term? Why or why not?

3. Consider Woolf's statement concerning the angel: "Had I not killed her she would have killed me." Is the angel still present today? Do you agree that a woman must kill her to survive, both personally and professionally?
4. Explain Woolf's statement that the woman writer still has "many ghosts to fight." How does she relate this concept to women in other professions?

Cultural Contexts

1. Discuss with your group Woolf's concept that "it is far harder to kill a phantom than a reality." Why is this so? What forms do these phantoms take in contemporary culture?

Daniel Meier
1987

One Man's Kids

I teach first graders. I live in a world of skinned knees, double-knotted shoelaces, riddles that I've heard a dozen times, stale birthday cakes, hurt feelings, wandering stories, and one lost shoe ("and if you don't find it my mother'll kill me"). My work is dominated by 6-year-olds.

It's 10:45, the middle of snack, and I'm helping Emily open her milk carton. She has already tried the other end without success, and now there's so much paint and ink on the carton from her fingers that I'm not sure she should drink it at all. But I open it. Then I turn to help Scott clean up some milk he has just spilled onto Rebecca's whale crossword puzzle.

While I wipe my milk- and paint-covered hands, Jenny wants to know if I've seen that funny book about penguins that I read in class. As I hunt for it in a messy pile of books, Jason wants to know if there is a new seating arrangement for lunch tables. I find the book, turn to answer Jason, then face Maya, who is fast approaching with a new knock-knock joke. After what seems like the 10th "Who's there?" I laugh and Maya is pleased.

Then Andrew wants to know how to spell "flukes" for his crossword. As I get to "u," I give a hand signal for Sarah to take away the snack. But just as Sarah is almost out the door, two children complain that "we haven't even had ours yet." I stop the snack mid-flight, complying with their request for graham crackers. I then return to Andrew, noticing that he has put "flu" for 9 Down, rather than 9 Across. It's now 10:50.

My work is not traditional male work. It's not a singular pursuit. There is not a large pile of paper to get through or one deal to transact. I don't have one area of expertise or knowledge. I don't have the singular power over language of a lawyer, the physical force of a construction worker, the command over fellow workers of a surgeon, the wheeling and dealing transitions of a businessman. My energy is not spent in pursuing, climbing, achieving, conquering, or cornering some goal or object.

My energy is spent in encouraging, supporting, consoling, and praising my children. In teaching, the inner rewards come from without. On any given day, quite apart from teaching reading and spelling, I bandage a cut, dry a tear, erase a frown, tape a torn doll, and locate a long-lost boot. The day is really won through matters of the heart. As my students groan, laugh, shudder, cry, exult, and wonder, I do too. I have to be soft around the edges.

A few years ago, when I was interviewing for an elementary-school teaching position, every principal told me with confidence that, as a male, I had an advantage over female applicants because of the lack of male teachers. But in the next breath, they asked with a hint of suspicion why I chose to work with young children. I told them that I wanted to observe and contribute to the intellectual growth of a maturing mind. What I really felt like saying, but didn't, was that I loved helping a child learn to write his name for the first time, finding someone a new friend, or sharing in the hilarity of reading about Winnie the Pooh getting so stuck in a hole that only his head and rear show.

I gave that answer to those principals, who were mostly male, because I thought they wanted a "male" response. This meant talking about intellectual matters. If I had taken a different course and talked about my interest in helping children in their emotional development, it would have been seen as closer to a "female" answer. I even altered my language, not once mentioning the word "love" to describe what I do indeed love about teaching. My answer worked; every principal nodded approvingly.

Some of the principals also asked what I saw myself doing later in my career. They wanted to know if I eventually wanted to go into educational administration. Becoming a dean of students or a principal has never been one of my goals, but they seemed to expect me, as a male, to want to climb higher on the career stepladder. So I mentioned that, at some point, I would be interested in working with teachers as a curriculum coordinator. Again, they nodded approvingly.

If those principals had been female instead of male, I wonder whether their questions, and my answers, would have been different. My guess is that they would have been.

At other times, when I'm at a party or a dinner and tell someone that I teach young children, I've found that men and women respond differently. Most men ask about the subjects I teach and the courses I took in my training. Then, unless they bring up an issue such as merit pay, the conversation stops. Most women, on the other hand, begin the conversation on a more immediate and personal level. They say things like "those kids must love having a male teacher" or "that age is just wonderful, you must love it." Then, more often than not, they'll talk about their own kids or ask me specific questions about what I do. We're then off and talking shop.

Possibly, men would have more to say to me, and I to them, if my job had more of the trappings and benefits of more traditional male jobs. But my job has no bonuses or promotions. No complimentary box seats at the ball park. No cab fare home. No drinking buddies after work. No briefcase. No suit. (Ties get stuck in paint jars.) No power lunches. (I eat peanut butter and jelly, chips, milk, and cookies with the kids.) No taking clients out for cocktails. The only place I take my kids is to the playground.

Although I could have pursued a career in law or business, as several of my friends did, I chose teaching instead. My job has benefits all its own. I'm able to bake cookies without getting them stuck together as they cool, buy cheap sewing materials, take out splinters, and search just the right trash cans for useful odds and ends. I'm sometimes called "Daddy" and even "Mommy" by my students, and if there's ever a lull in the conversation at a dinner party, I can always ask those assembled if they've heard the latest riddle about why the turkey crossed the road. (He thought he was a chicken.)

Journal Entry

Discuss the significance of the essay's title.

Textual Considerations

1. What is the effect of Meier's introducing his pupils with incidents from his classroom experience?
2. Meier's essay was originally published in "About Men," in the *New York Times Magazine*. How might his intended audience respond to his essay? What is your response?
3. Clarify Meier's purpose. Is he seeking only to inform his readers, or does he also wish to persuade? Cite evidence for your point of view.

Cultural Contexts

1. "My work is not traditional male work." How does the author define male work? How is it different from female work? What do these distinctions suggest about gender stereotypes in the workplace? What does Meier's essay imply about society's attitude toward teaching children as a professional choice for a male?

Barbara L. Greenberg
1979

The Faithful Wife

But if I *were* to have a lover, it would be someone
who could take nothing from you. I would, in conscience,
not dishonor you. He and I would eat at Howard Johnson's

which you and I do not enjoy. With him I would go
fishing because it is not your sport. He would wear blue   5
which is your worst color; he would have none of your virtues.

Not strong, not proud, not just, not provident, my lover
would blame me for his heart's distress, which you would never
think to do. He and I would drink too much and weep together

and I would bruise his face as I would not bruise your face   10
even in my dreams. Yes I would dance with him, but to a music
you and I would never choose to hear, and in a place

where you and I would never wish to be. He and I would speak
Spanish, which is not your tongue, and we would take
long walks in fields of burdock, to which you are allergic.   15

We would make love only in the morning. It would be
altogether different. I would know him with my other body,
the one that you have never asked to see.

Mahwash Shoaib
1994

Genesis

I.

The child of the sultan was born on a most
auspicious night. Nine months the nation had waited
with bated breath and when the time came, the
sultan ordered the chastest women of the land
to care for his wife. *She* didn't have to scream   5
that much, the harem would've made a fuss anyway.
Silks swirled and incandescent jewels shone

around her room, as the maids scurried past
sterner guards carrying items of need. Steam rising
from boiling water drew saffron hues from   10
the flickering torches and in the haze,
the panting, heaving women enacted the story of
centuries, spewing mild oaths. Her closest maids held her
clenched hands, and the midwife told her to push and
push, more, just a little while longer. And   15
she did, good woman that she was.

Prayers resounded outside the room and
the treasurer counted tinkling coins to be
dispatched at the happy news. With a final push, the
child was born and the maids quickly put him in   20
skeins of wool; he was bathed in rose water
and swathed in clothes of gold. A tray of coins
was passed over his head, blessed money to be given
to the poor. The men shouted from one turret to
another, "Sultana has borne a son!" The   25

sultan granted amnesty to many prisoners and
promised a pearl the size of an egg to the mother
of his son. Gifts of sonnets and gold piled up for
the new heir. The people of the moated city danced
for days, the royal feasts were remembered   30
for decades. And the royal historian wrote in his
private diary: "The wild oat is sown."

Mahwash Shoaib
1994

Afterbirth

II.
I
wife, mother,
feel
as if
I am   5
on the
verge
of becoming
a cipher.
He   10
that is
born,
like he
that is
celebrating   15
in his
harem,
will
become
the scourge   20
of my
life.
I am kin
to the
moon,   25
for
silence
is our
life;
but,   30
her
step-sister,
I am
denied
all   35
the charms.

Milk,
blood,
and tears
flow   40
freely
freely
from my
body,
and   45
still,
I am
empty
as a
dry   50
boarded-up
well.

Mahwash Shoaib
1995

The Silk Carpet

He asks if she had her period this month
she says yes.
He rants
she slides from the sofa to the floor
to squat on the carpet.   5
Her cheek resting on her arm on the table, she
passes her hand over the silk carpet as if brushing a dog,
the pile returning caress for caress.

He speaks
she smiles at the carpet the size of a rug   10
the Baghdad boy flew on to his beloved Yasmin.
She gazes at the middle border with oval rounded forms
shaped like praying hands,
the outer and inner borders
containing darker, lighter red   15
chevrons edged by blue,
and marvels at the intricate arabesques.
She runs her finger on the convoluted flowers
climbing green-brown vines,
arriving at the jeweled medallion in the center: 20

there a netting of buds crystallizes into a small lotus.
Planting her hand on the lotus,
she wishes to plunge through
the flower and raises her head an instant to look at him
but the colors of the carpet radiate.   25
They become a tapestry of leaf-greens, change
from rose-brown to rust to copper,
but mostly remain a warm, khaki gold.
She will only take it out for special people and
it will last at least until she or her children die.   30

He lashes
each drop of blood from her body
seeps into the carpet as the blood
from the knots and scabs of the children's hands
mingled with their sweat   35
to enrich each timeworn Persian knot.
They squatted on low stools,
their eyes riveted on the threads
in their fingers, oblivious to the undulant heat.
The looms moved clack clack in long arcs.   40
Tying deft knots around the warp strings,
weaving the weft between them,
they beat the fiber tight with metal combs in hushed swishes
fearing the break of the silken thread in the shuttle
the danger of missing a row,   45
trying to remember the pattern sung to them
wondering what lessons are being learnt at school,
the pattern must be achieved, must be created,
maintained.

He talks   50
of commitment, of order, of honor, of generation.
He leaves
she sweeps her hand up from the acrylic carpet in an arc,
the rayon fibers bristling under her hand
like day-old stubble   55
nothing like silk
but the colors still speak
the hands of the children resonate:
the pattern must be maintained.
And opening her fist convulsively,   60
loose rayon threads sticking to her hollow palm,
she looks at her fingers trembling with tension
and asks
is this all the world is

Journal Entry

Respond to the portrayals of marriage by Greenberg and Shoaib.

Textual Considerations

1. Prepare a profile of the husband in "The Faithful Wife." How is he different from the lover she fantasies about?
2. Comment on the effectiveness of Greenberg's use of humor in "The Faithful Wife."
3. Discuss how the differences in line lengths in "Genesis" and "Afterbirth" work stylistically and thematically.
4. Investigate the inferences of the last line of "Genesis" and the origin of the proverb. What do you think it contributes to the tone of the poem?
5. What is the symbolic significance of the titles of Shoaib's poems? To what extent do they reflect the themes of the poems?

Cultural Contexts

1. Imagine that you are the speaker's husband in "The Faithful Wife." Write a letter responding to your wife's criticisms.
2. Postpartum depression is the clinical depression some mothers experience after childbirth. Debate whether the speaker in "Afterbirth" is going through postpartum depression because of the situation in "Genesis."

Wagner and Gillan ◆

Maryfrances Wagner
1983

Ragazza

A good Italian woman
will cover her dust-free house
with crocheted doilies,
bear dark-eyed sons,
know what to do   5
with artichokes and chick peas.
Her floors will shine.
She will serve tender brucaluni
in her perfect sauce,
make her own cannoli shells,   10
bake biscottas for every wedding.
Supper will be hot at six o'clock.
She will always wear dresses.

She will not balance the checkbook.
He can doze behind the paper 15
when she washes dishes.
Because she will never leave him,
he will forgive her bulging thighs.
Because he will never leave her,
she won't notice unfamiliar stains. 20

Italian men always know *ragazze*
who work the fields in Bivona.
For airfare one will come.
In time she will learn English.
In time they may learn to love. 25

Maria Mazziotti Gillan
1981

Petals of Silence

The softness which comes to me at dawn
has petals made of silence
Upstairs, my husband, my children sleep,
dreaming their own shadows.

In these moments, stolen from the night, 5
no one needs me. I have my own quiet joys.
My notebook page is clean and white,
My pen moves across it almost by itself.
Even the cat sleeps content in the corner.

I collect the edges of myself around me, 10
curl in the flowers of my stillness
where I find the strength to emerge
into the world of this house,
your bubbling lives.

It is not that I love you less 15
or would wish you gone;
it is only this need
to gather my forces,
to drink from my own fountain
that causes these retreats from you, my loves. 20

Someday, perhaps my daughter will read this poem,
see her reflection in its glass,
as she sits alone, in the clarity of each morning,
with the sound of the crickets and her ghosts
and the place inside herself   25
that nothing, nothing can shatter.

Journal Entry

Contrast the images of marriage in "Ragazza" and "Petals of Silence," both by Italian-American poets.

Textual Considerations

1. Identify images that express the speaker's concepts of personal identity in "Petals of Silence."
2. State the accomplishments of the "good Italian woman" in "Ragazza," and contrast them with what she will not do (ll. 14, 17, and 20).
3. Consider the implications of the titles of both poems. How do they contribute to the meaning of the texts?

Cultural Contexts

1. Discuss with your group the cultural and gender implications of the conclusion of both poems.

Pat Mora
1986

Borders

My research suggests that men and women may
speak different languages that they assume
are the same. —Carol Gilligan

If we're so bright,
why didn't we notice?

I
The side-by-side translations
were the easy ones.
Our tongues tasted *luna*   5
chanting, chanting to the words
it touched; our lips circled
moon sighing its longing.
We knew: similar but different.

II
And we knew of grown-up talk,   10
how even in our own home
like became unlike,
how the child's singsong
                               I want, I want
burned our mouth   15
when we whispered in the dark.

III
But us? You and I
who've talked for years
tossing words back and forth
                           success, happiness   20
back and forth
over coffee, over wine
at parties, in bed
and I was sure you heard,
  understood,   25
though now I think of it
I can remember screaming
to be sure.

So who can hear
the words we speak   30
you and I, like but unlike,
and translate us to us
side by side?

Pat Mora
1986

Elena

My Spanish isn't enough.
I remember how I'd smile
listening to my little ones,
understanding every word they'd say,
their jokes, their songs, their plots.   5
    Vamos a pedirle dulces a mamá. Vamos.
But that was in Mexico.
Now my children go to American high schools.
They speak English. At night they sit around
the kitchen table, laugh with one another.   10
I stand by the stove and feel dumb, alone.
I bought a book to learn English.
My husband frowned, drank more beer.
My oldest said, "*Mamá,* he doesn't want you
to be smarter than he is." I'm forty,   15
embarrassed at mispronouncing words,
embarrassed at the laughter of my children,
the grocer, the mailman. Sometimes I take
my English book and lock myself in the bathroom,
say the thick words softly,   20
for if I stop trying, I will be deaf
when my children need my help.

Robert Frost
1930

Home Burial

He saw her from the bottom of the stairs
Before she saw him. She was starting down,
Looking back over her shoulder at some fear.
She took a doubtful step and then undid it
To raise herself and look again. He spoke   5
Advancing toward her: "What is it you see
From up there always?—for I want to know."
She turned and sank upon her skirts at that,
And her face changed from terrified to dull.
He said to gain time: "What is it you see?"   10
Mounting until she cowered under him.
"I will find out now—you must tell me, dear."
She, in her place, refused him any help,
With the least stiffening of her neck and silence.
She let him look, sure that he wouldn't see,   15
Blind creature; and awhile he didn't see.
But at last he murmured, "Oh," and again, "Oh."

"What is it—what?" she said.

              "Just that I see."

"You don't," she challenged. "Tell me what it is."

"The wonder is I didn't see at once.   20
I never noticed it from here before.
I must be wonted to it—that's the reason.
The little graveyard where my people are!
So small the window frames the whole of it.
Not so much larger than a bedroom, is it?   25
There are three stones of slate and one of marble,
Broad-shouldered little slabs there in the sunlight
On the sidehill. We haven't to mind *those*.
But I understand: it is not the stones,
But the child's mound ——"

           "Don't, don't, don't, don't," she cried.   30

She withdrew, shrinking from beneath his arm
That rested on the banister, and slid downstairs;
And turned on him with such a daunting look,
He said twice over before he knew himself:
"Can't a man speak of his own child he's lost?"   35

"Not you!—Oh, where's my hat? Oh, I don't need it!
I must get out of here. I must get air.—
I don't know rightly whether any man can."

"Amy! Don't go to someone else this time.
Listen to me. I won't come down the stairs."   40
He sat and fixed his chin between his fists.
"There's something I should like to ask you, dear."

"You don't know how to ask it."

                              "Help me, then."

Her fingers moved the latch for all reply.

"My words are nearly always an offense.   45
I don't know how to speak of anything
So as to please you. But I might be taught,
I should suppose. I can't say I see how.
A man must partly give up being a man
With womenfolk. We could have some arrangement   50
By which I'd bind myself to keep hands off
Anything special you're a-mind to name.
Though I don't like such things 'twixt those that love.
Two that don't love can't live together without them.
But two that do can't live together with them."   55
Don't carry it to someone else this time.
Tell me about it if it's something human.
Let me into your grief. I'm not so much
Unlike other folks as your standing there   60
Apart would make me out. Give me my chance.
I do think, though, you overdo it a little.
What was it brought you up to think it the thing
To take your mother-loss of a first child
So inconsolably—in the face of love.   65
You'd think his memory might be satisfied—"

"There you go sneering now!"

                        "I'm not, I'm not!
You make me angry. I'll come down to you.
God, what a woman! And it's come to this,
A man can't speak of his own child that's dead."   70

"You can't because you don't know how to speak.
If you had any feelings, you that dug
With your own hand—how could you?—his little grave;
I saw you from that very window there,
Making the gravel leap and leap in air,   75
Leap up, like that, like that, and land so lightly
And roll back down the mound beside the hole.
I thought, Who is that man? I didn't know you.
And I crept down the stairs and up the stairs
To look again, and still your spade kept lifting.   80
Then you came in. I heard your rumbling voice
Out in the kitchen, and I don't know why,
But I went near to see with my own eyes.
You could sit there with the stains on your shoes
Of the fresh earth from your own baby's grave   85
And talk about your everyday concerns.
You had stood the spade up against the wall
Outside there in the entry, for I saw it."

"I shall laugh the worst laugh I ever laughed.
I'm cursed. God, if I don't believe I'm cursed."   90

"I can repeat the very words you were saying:
'Three foggy mornings and one rainy day
Will rot the best birch fence a man can build.'
Think of it, talk like that at such a time!
What had how long it takes a birch to rot   95
To do with what was in the darkened parlor?
You *couldn't* care! The nearest friends can go
With anyone to death, comes so far short
They might as well not try to go at all.
No, from the time when one is sick to death,   100
One is alone, and he dies more alone.
Friends make pretense of following to the grave,
But before one is in it, their minds are turned
And making the best of their way back to life
And living people, and things they understand.   105
But the world's evil. I won't have grief so
If I can change it. Oh, I won't, I won't!"

"There, you have said it all and you feel better.
You won't go now. You're crying. Close the door.
The heart's gone out of it: why keep it up?   110
Amy! There's someone coming down the road!"

"You—oh, you think the talk is all. I must go—
Somewhere out of this house. How can I make you—"

"If—you—do!" She was opening the door wider.
"Where do you mean to go? First tell me that.   115
I'll follow and bring you back by force. I *will!*—"

◆

Journal Entry

Analyze the causes of the lack of communication between the men and women in "Borders," "Elena," and "Home Burial."

Textual Considerations

1. Explain the significance of the title "Borders." Why is the speaker's frequent use of "we," "our," and "us" ironic?
2. How does Mora use changes in setting to portray the importance of language in Elena's identity as wife and mother?
3. Explain the dramatic situation of "Home Burial," citing in detail the events that lead to the confrontation on the stairs.
4. According to Amy, why does her husband merit her anger? To what extent do you agree that the father feels the loss of the child less than the mother does? Explain.
5. Review the last five lines of the poem. What is your response? With whom do you empathize and why?

Textual Considerations

1. Apply Carol Gilligan's thesis (see p. 390) to "Borders." What does she mean by "different languages"? Review lines 50–55 of "Home Burial." What do they suggest about the husband's attitude toward his wife, toward communication within their relationship, and toward love. How is Gilligan's thesis relevant also to "Home Burial"?

Claude McKay
1917

The Harlem Dancer

Applauding youths laughed with young prostitutes
And watched her perfect, half-clothed body sway;
Her voice was like the sound of blended flutes
Blown by black players upon a picnic day.
She sang and danced on gracefully and calm,   5
The light gauze hanging loose about her form;
To me she seemed a proudly-swaying palm
Grown lovelier for passing through a storm.
Upon her swarthy neck black shiny curls
Luxuriant fell; and tossing coins in praise,   10
The wine-flushed, bold-eyed boys, and even the girls,
Devoured her shape with eager, passionate gaze;
But looking at her falsely-smiling face,
I knew her self was not in that strange place.

Edna St. Vincent Millay
1923

What Lips My Lips Have Kissed

What lips my lips have kissed, and where, and why,
I have forgotten, and what arms have lain
Under my head till morning; but the rain
Is full of ghosts tonight, that tap and sigh
Upon the glass and listen for reply,   5
And in my heart there stirs a quiet pain
For unremembered lads that not again
Will turn to me at midnight with a cry.
Thus in the winter stands the lonely tree,
Nor knows what birds have vanished one by one,   10
Yet knows its boughs more silent than before:
I cannot say what loves have come and gone,
I only know that summer sang in me
A little while, that in me sings no more.

Journal Entry

Describe the moods evoked by the speakers in "The Harlem Dancer" and "What Lips My Lips Have Kissed."

Textual Considerations

1. Contrast the speaker's perceptions of the dancer with those of her audience in McKay's poem.
2. What evidence does he cite to justify his conclusion in the last line of the poem? Do you agree with his judgment? Why or why not?
3. State the theme of the first eight lines of Millay's poem. Does the speaker's gender affect your response? How?
4. How effective is Millay's use of nature imagery to communicate meaning in the sonnet's sextet? Cite examples to justify your point of view.

Cultural Contexts

1. Discuss with your group what both poems suggest about the relation between sexuality and identity, and between sexuality and youth.

Robert Browning ◆

Robert Browning
1842

My Last Duchess

Ferrara
That's my last Duchess painted on the wall,
Looking as if she were alive; I call
That piece a wonder, now: Frà Pandolf's[1] hands
Worked busily a day, and there she stands.
Will't please you sit and look at her? I said   5
"Frà Pandolf" by design, for never read
Strangers like you that pictured countenance,
The depth and passion of its earnest glance,
But to myself they turned (since none puts by
The curtain I have drawn for you, but I)   10
And seemed as they would ask me, if they durst,
How such a glance came there; so, not the first
Are you to turn and ask thus. Sir, 'twas not
Her husband's presence only, called that spot

Of joy into the Duchess' cheek: perhaps   15
Frà Pandolf chanced to say "Her mantle laps
Over my Lady's wrist too much," or "Paint
Must never hope to reproduce the faint
Half-flush that dies along her throat": such stuff
Was courtesy, she thought, and cause enough   20
For calling up that spot of joy. She had
A heart—how shall I say?—too soon made glad,
Too easily impressed; she liked whate'er
She looked on, and her looks went everywhere.
Sir, 'twas all one! My favor at her breast,   25
The dropping of the daylight in the West,
The bough of cherries some officious fool
Broke in the orchard for her, the white mule
She rode with round the terrace—all and each
Would draw from her alike the approving speech,   30
Or blush, at least. She thanked men,—good; but thanked
Somehow—I know not how—as if she ranked
My gift of a nine-hundred-years-old name
With anybody's gift. Who'd stoop to blame
This sort of trifling? Even had you skill   35
In speech—(which I have not)—to make your will
Quite clear to such an one, and say, "Just this
Or that in you disgusts me; here you miss,
Or there exceed the mark"—and if she let
Herself be lessoned so, nor plainly set   40
Her wits to yours, forsooth, and made excuse,
—E'en then would be some stooping, and I choose
Never to stoop. Oh, Sir, she smiled, no doubt,
Whene'er I passed her; but who passed without
Much the same smile? This grew; I gave commands;   45
Then all smiles stopped together. There she stands
As if alive. Will't please you rise? We'll meet
The company below, then. I repeat,
The Count your Master's known munificence
Is ample warrant that no just pretense   50
Of mine for dowry will be disallowed;
Though his fair daughter's self, as I avowed
At starting, is my object. Nay, we'll go
Together down, Sir! Notice Neptune, though,
Taming a sea-horse, thought a rarity,   55
Which Claus of Innsbruck[2] cast in bronze for me.

---

[1] *Frà Pandolf's:* A fictitious artist.

[2] *Claus of Innsbruck:* Also a fictitious artist.

Robert Browning
1834

Porphyria's Lover

The rain set early in to-night,
  The sullen wind was soon awake,
It tore the elm-tops down for spite,
  And did its worst to vex the lake:
  I listened with heart fit to break.   5
When glided in Porphyria; straight
  She shut the cold out and the storm,
And kneeled and made the cheerless grate
  Blaze up, and all the cottage warm;
  Which done, she rose, and from her form   10
Withdrew the dripping cloak and shawl,
  And laid her soiled gloves by, untied
Her hat and let the damp hair fall,
  And, last, she sat down by my side
  And called me. When no voice replied,   15
She put my arm about her waist,
  And made her smooth white shoulder bare,
And all her yellow hair displaced,
  And, stooping, made my cheek lie there,
  And spread, o'er all, her yellow hair,   20
Murmuring how she loved me—she
  Too weak, for all her heart's endeavour,
To set its struggling passion free
  From pride, and vainer ties dissever,
  And give herself to me for ever.   25
But passion sometimes would prevail,
  Nor could to-night's gay feast restrain
A sudden thought of one so pale
  For love of her, and all in vain:
  So, she was come through wind and rain.   30
Be sure I looked up at her eyes
  Happy and proud; at last I knew
Porphyria worshipped me; surprise
  Made my heart swell, and still it grew
  While I debated what to do.   35
That moment she was mine, mine, fair,
  Perfectly pure and good: I found

A thing to do, and all her hair
    In one long yellow string I wound
        Three times her little throat around,   40
And strangled her. No pain felt she;
    I am quite sure she felt no pain.
As a shut bud that holds a bee,
    I warily oped her lids: again
        Laughed the blue eyes without a stain.   45
And I untightened next the tress
    About her neck; her cheek once more
Blushed bright beneath my burning kiss:
    I propped her head up as before,
        Only, this time my shoulder bore   50
Her head, which droops upon it still:
    The smiling rosy little head,
So glad it has its utmost will,
    That all it scorned at once is fled,
        And I, its love, am gained instead!   55
Porphyria's love: she guessed not how
    Her darling one wish would be heard.
And thus we sit together now,
    And all night long we have not stirred,
        And yet God has not said a word!   60

◆

Journal Entry

Record your response to the fate of the women in both poems.

Textual Considerations

1. What crime has the Duke's last Duchess committed?
2. Characterize the dramatic situation in "My Last Duchess." Consider the setting and the purpose of the visit (ll. 47–53), and speculate why Browning concludes the poem with the statement of Neptune taming a sea-horse.
3. Discuss how Browning's use of dramatic irony results in our learning more about the Duke than he understands about himself. Consider, for example, his motivation for ordering the Duchess's death. Cite evidence to show how the Duchess became a projection of the Duke's fears and insecurities.
4. Who tells the story in "Porphyria's Lover"? Is the speaker addressing his lover, his reader, or is he engaging in a dialogue with himself? Cite evidence to support your point of view.
5. Compare and contrast the mental state of the speakers in both poems.

Cultural Contexts

1. Discuss with your group the causes of the violence against women that Browning presents in both poems.
2. Discuss with your group the thematic role of social class in each poem. Consider, for example, the extent to which the Duchess was aware of class distinctions, and how her attitude toward people from lower classes affected the Duke. In "Porphyria's Lover," focus on the role that the setting plays in identifying the lovers' social class.

Marvell and Behn

Andrew Marvell
1681

To His Coy Mistress

Had we but world enough, and time,
This coyness, lady, were no crime.
We would sit down, and think which way
To walk, and pass our long love's day.
Thou by the Indian Ganges'[1] side   5
Shoudst rubies find; I by the tide
Of Humber[2] would complain. I would
Love you ten years before the flood,
And you should, if you please, refuse
Till the conversion of the Jews.   10
My vegetable love should grow
Vaster than empires and more slow;
An hundred years should go to praise
Thine eyes, and on thy forehead gaze;
Two hundred to adore each breast,   15
But thirty thousand to the rest;
An age at least to every part,
And the last age should show your heart.
For, lady, you deserve this state,
Nor would I love at lower rate.   20
    But at my back I always hear
Time's wingèd chariot hurrying near;
And yonder all before us lie
Deserts of vast eternity.

Thy beauty shall no more be found;   25
Nor, in thy marble vault, shall sound
My echoing song; then worms shall try
That long-preserved virginity,
And your quaint honor turn to dust,
And into ashes all my lust: 30
The grave's a fine and private place,
But none, I think, do there embrace.
    Now therefore, while the youthful hue
Sits on thy skin like morning dew
And while thy willing soul transpires   35
At every pore with instant fires,
Now let us sport us while we may,
And now, like amorous birds of prey,
Rather at once our time devour
Than languish in his slow-chapped power.   40
Let us roll all our strength and all
Our sweetness up into one ball,
And tear our pleasures with rough strife
Through the iron gates of life:
Thus, though we cannot make our sun   45
Stand still, yet we will make him run.

---

¹ *Ganges:* River in northern India.

² *Humber:* Estuary in northern England formed by the Ouse and Trent rivers.

Aphra Behn
1673

The Willing Mistress

Amyntas led me to a grove,
    Where all the trees did shade us;
The sun itself, though it had strove,
    It could not have betrayed us.
The place secured from human eyes   5
    No other fear allows
But when the winds that gently rise
    Do kiss the yielding boughs.

Down there we sat upon the moss,
  And did begin to play   10
A thousand amorous tricks, to pass
  The heat of all the day.
A many kisses did he give
  And I returned the same,
Which made me willing to receive   15
  That which I dare not name.

His charming eyes no aid required
  To tell their softening tale;
On her that was already fired
  'Twas easy to prevail.   20
He did but kiss and clasp me round,
  Whilst those his thoughts expressed:

And laid me gently on the ground;
  Ah who can guess the rest?

Journal Entry

Discuss the thematic significance of the title of each poem.

Textual Considerations

1. Explain what the image "I would love you ten years before the flood" in the first section of Marvell's poem suggests about the speaker's attitude toward time.
2. How do the images Marvell uses in the second and third sections of "To His Coy Mistress" mirror or contradict those in the first section?
3. How does the speaker in "To His Coy Mistress" characterize himself as a lover?
4. To what extent would you define "The Willing Mistress" as a seduction poem?
5. Discuss female–male attitude towards love in "The Willing Mistress."

Cultural Considerations

1. "To His Coy Mistress" is known as one of the most celebrated erotic poems in English literature. Cite examples of erotic elements in the poem.
2. Describe the relationship between the world of love and the outside world in "The Willing Mistress."

Gayle Two Eagles
1984

The Young Warrior

The young warrior,
Seeing the world through brand-new eyes,
Brought up thinking she was special and good.

Lakota people can be proud again.

When an injustice is done to one of "the people,"   5
The warriors gather.

The woman warrior is among them,
Proud and strong,
Because she is a fighter.

The words flow off the tongues of the new orators,   10
Telling of the old ways,
And why being Indian is worth fighting for,
Mesmerized by the sense of strength and duty,
To become a warrior and keep the Lakota ways alive.

Tradition as told by men,   15
Written in history books by white men,
Religion didn't escape their influence.

Despite being told the women's squad is assigned the kitchen,
She guards the rooms and buildings from passing racists.

While the Lakota people make their stand,   20
Quiet defiance to the men who say, "respect your brother's vision,"
She mutters, "respect your sister's vision too."

She supported you in Wounded Knee,
She was with you at Sioux Falls,
Custer,   25
And Sturgis,
And has always remembered you,
Her Indian people,
In her prayers.

She has listened to women who were beaten by the men they love,   30
Or their husbands,
And gave strength to women who were raped,
As has the Sacred Mother Earth.

At some point asking where Tradition for women was being decided.

As a Traditional Lakota woman you are asked to approach a relative 35
or your spouse to speak your thoughts and feelings at a public meeting,
Not to touch a feather, or not to handle food at what the white culture
once referred to as the "sick time."

Woman warrior once told to break the stereotype of the white people,
She is also told to walk ten steps behind a man. 40

The new eyes that once were in awe at what the world had to offer,
Looks down at this new girl child,
The Lakota woman warrior knows her daughter also has a vision.

Anne Sexton
1967

For My Lover, Returning to His Wife

She is all there.
She was melted carefully down for you
and cast up from your childhood,
cast up from your one hundred favorite aggies.

She has always been there, my darling. 5
She is, in fact, exquisite.
Fireworks in the dull middle of February
and as real as a cast-iron pot.

Let's face it, I have been momentary.
A luxury. A bright red sloop in the harbor. 10
My hair rising like smoke from the car window.
Littleneck clams out of season.

She is more than that. She is your have to have,
has grown you your practical your tropical growth.
This is not an experiment. She is all harmony. 15
She sees to oars and oarlocks for the dinghy,

has placed wild flowers at the window at breakfast,
sat by the potter's wheel at midday,
set forth three children under the moon,
three cherubs drawn by Michelangelo, 20

done this with her legs spread out
in the terrible months in the chapel.
If you glance up, the children are there
like delicate balloons resting on the ceiling.

She has also carried each one down the hall   25
after supper, their heads privately bent,
two legs protesting, person to person,
her face flushed with a song and their little sleep.

I give you back your heart.
I give you permission—   30

for the fuse inside her, throbbing
angrily in the dirt, for the bitch in her
and the burying of her wound—
for the burying of her small red wound alive—

for the pale flickering flare under her ribs,   35
for the drunken sailor who waits in her left pulse,
for the mother's knee, for the stockings,
for the garter belt, for the call—

the curious call
when you will burrow in arms and breasts   40
and tug at the orange ribbon in her hair
and answer the call, the curious call.

She is so naked and singular.
She is the sum of yourself and your dream.
Climb her like a monument, step after step.   45
She is solid.

As for me, I am a watercolor.
I wash off.

Journal Entry

Respond to the significance of the title of each poem.

Textual Considerations

1. How effective is the speaker's connection to the past and present in explaining the evolving identity of the young warrior? Cite examples.
2. How would you characterize the young warrior's "vision." On what factors is it based?

3. Discuss how Sexton's use of contrasting images of the wife and mistress contribute to your sense of the transience of the love affair described in the poem. With whom do you empathize—the mistress or the wife? Explain.
4. What does the poem reveal about the husband? Consider, for example, his dual roles as husband and lover. What is your attitude toward him?

Cultural Contexts

1. Discuss with your group what the two poems imply about the complexity of reconciling personal and gender identity.

Keats and de la Cruz

John Keats
1819

Bright Star

Bright star, would I were steadfast as thou art—
    Not in lone splendor hung aloft the night
And watching, with eternal lids apart,
    Like nature's patient, sleepless Eremite,[1]
The moving waters at their priestlike task   5
    Of pure ablution round earth's human shores,
Or gazing on the new soft fallen mask
    Of snow upon the mountains and the moors—
No—yet still steadfast, still unchangeable,
    Pillowed upon my fair love's ripening breast,   10
To feel forever its soft fall and swell,
    Awake forever in a sweet unrest,
Still, still to hear her tender-taken breath,
And so live ever—or else swoon to death.

[1] *Eremite:* hermit, devotee

Sor Juana Inés de la Cruz
1680

She Proves the Inconsistency of the Desires and Criticism of Men Who Accuse Women of What They Themselves Cause

Foolish men who accuse
women unreasonably,
you blame yet never see
you cause what you abuse.

You crawl before her, sad,   5
begging for a quick cure;
why ask her to be pure
when you have made her bad?

You combat her resistance
and then with gravity,   10
you call frivolity
the fruit of your intents.

In one heroic breath
your reason fails, like a wild
bogeyman made up by a child   15
who then is scared to death.

With idiotic pride
you hope to find your prize:
a regal whore like Thaïs
and Lucretia for a bride.   20

Has anyone ever seen
a stranger moral fervor:
you who dirty the mirror
regret it is not clean?

You treat favor and disdain   25
with the same shallow mock-
ing voice: love you and you squawk,
demur and you complain.

No answer at her door
will be a proper part: 30
say no—she has no heart,
say yes—and she's a whore.

Two levels to your game
in which *you* are the fool:
one you blame as cruel,   35
one who yields, you shame.

How can one not be bad
the way your love pretends
to be? Say no and she offends.
Consent and you are mad.   40

With all the fury and pain
your whims cause her, it's good
for her who has withstood
you. Now go and complain!

You let her grief take flight   45
and free her with new wings.
Then after sordid things
you say she's not upright.

Who is at fault in all
this errant passion? She   50
who falls for his pleas, or he
who pleads for her to fall?

Whose guilt is greater in
this raw erotic play?
The girl who sins for pay   55
or man who pays for sin?

So why be shocked or taunt
her for the steps you take?
Care for her as you make
her, or shape her as you want,   60

but do not come with pleas
and later throw them in
her face, screaming of sin
when you were at her knees.

You fight us from birth   65
with weapons of arrogance.
Between promise and pleading stance,
you are devil, flesh, and earth.

Journal Entry

Consider how the romantic concept of the female as goddess or idealized being might affect the sense of identity of both male and female.

Textual Considerations

1. Select three examples of similes and metaphors in "Bright Star," and discuss their appeal to the senses, the meanings they suggest, and the emotions they arouse in the reader. Comment also on Keats's use of comparison and contrast in relation to theme.
2. Summarize the key points of de la Cruz's arguments. To what extent do you agree or disagree with her logic and point of view?
3. Describe the tone of de la Cruz's poem. Is the speaker sarcastic, angry, bitter, or objective? Cite examples to support your answer.

Cultural Contexts

1. Discuss the degree to which the portrayals of the women in both poems are relevant to women's position in society today.
2. Discuss the effects of stereotypes such as goddess, madonna, or whore on gender relationships.

Shakespeare

William Shakespeare
c. 1609

30

When to the sessions of sweet silent thought
I summon up remembrance of things past,
I sigh the lack of many a thing I sought,
And with old woes new wail my dear time's waste.
Then can I drown an eye, unused to flow,   5
For precious friends hid in death's dateless night,
And weep afresh love's long since cancelled woe,
And moan th'expense of many a vanished sight.
Then can I grieve at grievances foregone,
And heavily from woe to woe tell o'er   10
Then sad account of fore-bemoanèd moan,
Which I new pay as if not paid before.
    But if the while I think on thee, dear friend,
    All losses are restored, and sorrows end.

William Shakespeare
c. 1609

116
Let me not to the marriage of true minds
Admit impediments. Love is not love
Which alters when it alterations find,
Or bends with the remover to remove.
O no, it is an ever-fixèd mark   5
That looks on tempests and is never shaken;
It is the star to every wand'ring bark,
Whose worth's unknown, although his height be taken.
Love's not time's fool, though rosy lips and cheeks
Within his bending sickle's compass come.   10
Love alters not with his brief hours and weeks,
But bears it out ev'n to the edge of doom.
    If this be error and upon me proved,
    I never writ, nor no man ever loved.

William Shakespeare
c. 1609

129
Th'expense of spirit in a waste of shame
Is lust in action, and till action, lust
Is perjur'd, murd'rous, bloody, full of blame,
Savage, extreme, rude, cruel, not to trust,
Enjoy'd no sooner but despisèd straight,   5
Past reason hunted, and no sooner had,
Past reason hated as a swallowed bait
On purpose laid to make the taker mad:
[Mad] in pursuit and in possession so,
Had, having, and in quest to have, extreme,   10
A bliss in proof, and prov'd, [a] very woe,
Before, a joy propos'd, behind, a dream.
    All this the world well knows, yet none knows well
    To shun the heaven that leads men to this hell.

William Shakespeare
c. 1609

130

My mistress' eyes are nothing like the sun;
Coral is far more red than her lips' red;
If snow be white, why then her breasts are dun;
If hairs be wires, black wires grow on her head.
I have seen roses damasked,[1] red and white,   5
But no such roses see I in her cheeks;
And in some perfumes is there more delight
Than in the breath that from my mistress reeks.
I love to hear her speak, yet well I know
That music hath a far more pleasing sound;   10
I grant I never saw a goddess go;[2]
My mistress, when she walks, treads on the ground.
And yet, by heaven, I think my love as rare
As any she belied with false compare.

[1] *damasked:* variegated

[2] *a goddess go:* walk

◆

Journal Entry

Compare and contrast the treatment of love in the four sonnets.

Textual Considerations

1. Discuss Shakespeare's use of comparison of "old" versus "new" in sonnet 30. How do these relate to the overall meaning of the sonnet?
2. How does Shakespeare's use of negative statements in sonnet 116 enhance the theme? Cite examples.
3. How does Shakespeare's use of repetition and reversal in sonnet 129 convey the speaker's feelings about lust? To what extent do you agree or disagree with the speaker's point of view?
4. Make a list of similes Shakespeare uses to characterize his mistress in sonnet 130. What portrait of her emerges in the sonnet?

Cultural Contexts

1. What does the sonnet 130 reveal about Shakespeare's use of the convention of the idealized mistress?
2. Discuss how Shakespeare explores the theme of time in its relation to love, beauty, and poetry in the four sonnets.

Euripides
431 B.C.

Medea

CHARACTERS

NURSE
CREON, *King of Corinth*
CHILDREN OF MEDEA
MEDEA
TUTOR
JASON
CHORUS, *Corinthian Women*
AEGEUS, *King of Athens*
MESSENGER

The scene represents the home of Medea at Corinth.

(*Enter* NURSE.)

NURSE.   How I wish that the ship Argo had never winged its way through the gray Clashing Rocks to the land of the Colchians! How I wish the pines had never been hewn down in the glens of Pelion, to put oars into the hands of the Heroes who went to fetch for Pelias the Golden Fleece! Then Medea my mistress would not have sailed to the towers of Iolcus, her heart pierced through and through with love for Jason, would not have prevailed on the daughters of Pelias to murder their father, would not now be dwelling here in Corinth with her husband and children. When she fled here she found favor with the citizens to whose land she had come and was herself a perfect partner in all things for Jason. (And therein lies a woman's best security, to avoid conflict with her husband.) But now there is nothing but enmity, a blight has come over their great love.

Jason has betrayed his own children and my mistress to sleep beside a royal bride, the daughter of Creon who rules this land, while Medea, luckless Medea, in her desolation invokes the promises he made, appeals to the pledges in which she put her deepest trust, and calls Heaven to witness the sorry recompense she has from Jason. Ever since she realized her husband's perfidy, she has been lying there prostrated, eating no food, her whole frame subdued to sorrow, wasting away with incessant weeping. She has not lifted an eye nor ever turned her face from the floor. The admonitions of her friends she receives with unhearing ears, like a rock or a wave of the sea. Only now and then she turns her white neck and talks to herself, in sorrow, of her dear father and her country and the home which she betrayed to come here with a husband who now holds her in contempt. Now she knows, from bitter experience, how sad a thing it is to lose one's fatherland. She hates her own children and has no pleasure at the sight of them. I fear she may form some new and horrible resolve. For hers is a dangerous mind, and she will not lie down to injury. I know her and she frightens me [lest she make her way stealthily into the palace where his couch is spread and drive a sharp sword into his vitals or even kill both the King and the bridegroom and then incur some greater misfortune.] She is cunning. Whoever crosses swords with her will not find victory easy, I tell you.

But here come the children, their playtime over. Little thought have they of their mother's troubles. Children do not like sad thoughts.

(*Enter* TUTOR, *with boys.*)

TUTOR. Ancient household chattel of my mistress, why are you standing here all alone at the gates, muttering darkly to yourself? What makes Medea want you to leave her alone?

NURSE. Aged escort of Jason's children, when their master's affairs go ill, good slaves find not only their misfortune but also their heart's grief. My sorrow has now become so great that a longing came over me to come out here and tell to earth and sky the story of my mistress's woes.

TUTOR. What? Is the poor lady not yet through with weeping?

NURSE. I wish I had your optimism. Why, her sorrow is only beginning, it's not yet at the turning point.

TUTOR. Poor foolish woman!—if one may speak thus of one's masters. Little she knows of the latest ills!

NURSE. What's that, old man? Don't grudge me your news.

TUTOR. It's nothing at all. I'm sorry I even said what I said.

NURSE. Please, I beg of you, don't keep it from a fellow slave. I'll keep it dark, if need be.

TUTOR. I had drawn near the checkerboards where the old men sit, beside the sacred water of Pirene, and there, when nobody thought I was listening, I heard somebody say that Creon the ruler of this land was planning to expel these children *and* their mother from Corinth. Whether the tale is true or not I do not know. I would wish it were not so.

NURSE. But will Jason ever allow his children to be so treated, even if he *is* at variance with their mother?

TUTOR. Old loves are weaker than new loves, and that man is no friend to this household.

NURSE. That's the end of us then, if we are to ship a second wave of trouble before we are rid of the first.

TUTOR. Meanwhile you keep quiet and don't say a word. This is no time for the mistress to be told.

NURSE. O children, do you hear what love your father bears you? Since he is my master, I do not wish him dead, but he is certainly proving enemy of those he should love.

TUTOR. Like the rest of the world. Are you only now learning that every man loves himself more than his neighbor? [Some justly, others for profit, as] now for a new bride their father hates these children.

NURSE. Inside, children, inside. It will be all right. (*To the* TUTOR.) And you keep them alone as much as you can, and don't let them near their mother when she's melancholy. I have already noticed her casting a baleful eye at them as if she would gladly do them mischief. She'll not recover from her rage, I know well, till the lightning of her fury has struck somebody to the ground. May it be enemies, not loved ones, that suffer!

MEDEA. (within) Oh! my grief! the misery of it all! Why can I not die?

NURSE. What did I tell you, dear children? Your mother's heart is troubled, her anger is roused. Hurry indoors, quick. Keep out of her sight, don't go near her. Beware of her fierce manner, her implacable temper. Hers is a selfwilled nature. Go now, get you inside, be quick. Soon, it is clear, her sorrow like a gathering cloud will burst in a tempest of fury. What deed will she do then, that impetuous, indomitable heart, poisoned by injustice?

(*Exeunt children with* TUTOR.)

MEDEA. (within) O misery! the things I have suffered, cause enough for deep lamentations! O you cursed sons of a hateful mother, a plague on you! And on your father! Ruin seize the whole household!

NURSE. Ah me, unhappy me! Why will you have your sons partake of their father's guilt? Why hate them? Ah children, your danger overwhelms me with anxiety. The souls of royalty are vindictive; they do not easily forget their resentment, possibly because being used to command they are seldom checked. It is better to be used to living among equals. For myself, at any rate, I ask not greatness but a safe old age. Moderation! Firstly, the very name of it is excellent; to practise it is easily the best thing for mortals. Excess avails to no good purpose for men, and if the gods are provoked, brings greater ruin on a house.

(*Enter* CHORUS.)

CHORUS. *I heard a voice, I heard a cry. It was the unhappy Colchian woman's. She is not yet calm. Pray tell us, old woman. From the court outside I heard her cries within. I do not rejoice, woman, in the griefs of this house. Dear, dear it is to me.*

NURSE. It is a home no more; the life has gone out of it. Its master a princess' bed enthralls, while the mistress in her chamber is pining to death, and her friends have no words to comfort her heart.

MEDEA. (within) Oh! Would that a flaming bolt from Heaven might pierce my brain! What is the good of living any longer? O Misery! Let me give up this life I find so hateful. Let me seek lodging in the house of death.

CHORUS. *O Zeus, O Earth, O Light, hear what a sad lament the hapless wife intones. What is this yearning, rash woman, after that fearful bed? Will you hasten to the end that is Death? Pray not for that. If your husband worships a new bride, it is a common event; be not exasperated. Zeus will support your cause. Do not let grief for a lost husband waste away your life.*

MEDEA. (within)   Great Zeus and Lady Themis, see you how I am treated, for all the strong oaths with which I bound my cursed husband? May I live to see him and his bride, palace and all, in one common destruction, for the wrongs that they inflict, unprovoked, on me! O father, O country, that I forsook so shamefully, killing my brother, my own!

NURSE.   Hear what she says, how she cries out to Themis of Prayers and to Zeus whom mortals regard as the steward of oaths. With no small revenge will my mistress bate her rage.

CHORUS.   *I wish she would come into our presence and hear the sound of the words we would speak. Then she might forget the resentment in her heart and change her purpose. May my zeal be ever at the service of my friends. But bring her here, make her come forth from the palace. Tell her that here too are friends. Make haste before she does any harm to those within. Furious is the surge of such a sorrow.*

NURSE.   I shall do so, though I am not hopeful of persuading the mistress. But I freely present you with the gift of my labor. Yet she throws a baleful glare, like a lioness with cubs, at any servant who approaches her as if to speak. Blunderers and fools! that is the only proper name for the men of old who invented songs to bring the joy of life to feasts and banquets and festive boards, but never discovered a music of song or sounding lyre to dispel the weary sorrows of humanity, that bring death and fell havoc and destruction of homes. Yet what a boon to man, could these ills be cured by some! At sumptuous banquets why raise a useless strain? The food that is served and the satisfaction that comes to full men, that in itself is pleasure enough.

(*Exit* NURSE.)

CHORUS.   *I hear a cry of grief and deep sorrow. In piercing accents of misery she proclaims her woes, her ill-starred marriage and her love betrayed. The victim of grievous wrongs, she calls on the daughter of Zeus, even Themis, Lady of Vows, who led her through the night by difficult straits across the briny sea to Hellas.*

(*Enter* MEDEA.)

MEDEA.   Women of Corinth, do not criticize me, I come forth from the palace. Well I know that snobbery is a common charge, that may be levelled against recluse and busy man alike. And the former, by their choice of a quiet life, acquire an extra stigma: they are deficient in energy and spirit. There is no justice in the eyes of men; a man who has never harmed them they may hate at sight, without ever knowing anything about his essential nature. An alien, to be sure, should adapt himself to the citizens with whom he lives. Even the citizen is to be condemned if he is too selfwilled or too uncouth to avoid offending his fellows. So I…but this unexpected blow which has befallen me has broken my heart.

It's all over, my friends; I would gladly die. Life has lost its savor. The man who was everything to me, well he knows it, has turned out to be the basest of men. Of all creatures that feel and think, we women are the unhappiest species. In the first place, we must pay a great dowry to a husband who will be the tyrant of our bodies (that's a further aggravation of the evil); and there is another fearful hazard: whether we shall get a good man or a bad. For separations bring disgrace on the woman and it is not possible to renounce one's husband. Then, landed among strange habits and regulations unheard of in her own home, a woman needs second sight to know how best to handle her bedmate. And if we manage this well and have a husband who does not find the yoke of intercourse too galling, ours is a life to be envied. Otherwise, one is better dead. When the man wearies of the company of his wife, he goes outdoors and relieves the disgust of his heart [having recourse to some friend or the companions of his own age], but we women have only one person to turn to.

They say that we have a safe life at home, whereas men must go to war. Nonsense! I had rather fight three battles than bear one child. But be that as it may, you and I are not in the same case. You have your city here, your paternal homes; you know the delights of life and association with your loved ones. But I, homeless and forsaken, carried off from a foreign land, am being wronged by a husband, with neither mother nor brother nor kinsman with whom I might find refuge from the storms of misfortune. One little boon I crave of you, if I discover any ways and means of punishing my husband for these wrongs: your silence. Woman in most respects is a timid creature, with no heart for strife and aghast at the sight of steel; but wronged in love, there is no heart more murderous than hers.

LEADER.   Do as you say, Medea, for just will be your vengeance. I do not wonder that you bemoan your fate. But I see Creon coming, the ruler of this land, bringing tidings of new plans.

(*Enter* CREON.)

CREON.   You there, Medea, looking black with rage against your husband; I have proclaimed that you are to be driven forth in exile from this land, you and your two sons. Immediately. I am the absolute judge of the case, and I shall not go back to my palace till I have cast you over the frontier of the land.

MEDEA.   Ah! Destruction, double destruction is my unhappy lot. My enemies are letting out every sail and there is no harbor into which I may flee from the menace of their attack. But ill-treated and all, Creon, still I shall put the question to you: Why are you sending me out of the country?

CREON.   I am afraid of you—there's no need to hide behind a cloak of words— afraid you will do my child some irreparable injury. There's plenty logic in that fear. You are a wizard possessed of evil knowledge. You are stung by the loss of your husband's love. And I have heard of your threats—they told me of them—to injure bridegroom and bride and father of the bride. Therefore before anything happens to me, I shall take precautions. Better for me now to be hateful in your eyes than to relent and rue it greatly later.

MEDEA.   Alas! Alas! Often ere now—this is not the first time—my reputation has hurt me and done me grievous wrong. If a man's really shrewd, he ought never to have his children taught too much. For over and above a name for uselessness that it will earn them, they incur the hostility and envy of their fellow men. Offer clever reforms to dullards, and you will be thought a useless fool yourself. And the reputed wiseacres, feeling your superiority, will dislike you intensely. I myself have met this fate. Because I have skill, some are jealous of me, others think me unsociable. But my wisdom does not go very far. However, you are afraid you may suffer something unpleasant at my hands, aren't you? Fear not, Creon; it is not my way to commit my crimes against kings. What wrong have you done me? You have only bestowed your daughter on the suitor of your choice. No, it is my husband I hate. You, I dare say, knew what you were doing in the matter. And now I don't grudge success to your scheme. Make your match, and good luck to you. But allow me to stay in this country. Though foully used, I shall keep my peace, submitting to my masters.

CREON. Your words are comforting to hear, but inside my heart there is a horrible fear that you are plotting some mischief, which makes me trust you even less than before. The hot-tempered woman, like the hot-tempered man, is easier to guard against than the cunning and silent. But off with you at once, make no speeches. My resolve is fixed; for all your skill you will not stay amongst us to hate me.

MEDEA. Please no, I beseech you, by your knees, by the young bride...

CREON. You are wasting your words; you will never convince me.

MEDEA. Will you drive me out and have no respect for my prayers?

CREON. Yes, for I love you less than I love my own family.

MEDEA. O fatherland, how strongly do I now remember you!

CREON. Yes, apart from my children, that is *my* dearest love.

MEDEA. Alas! the loves of men are a mighty evil.

CREON. In my opinion, that depends on the circumstances.

MEDEA. O Zeus, do not forget the author of this wickedness.

CREON. On your way, vain woman, and end my troubles.

MEDEA. The troubles are mine, I have no lack of troubles.

CREON. In a moment you will be thrust out by the hands of servants.

MEDEA. No, no, not that. But Creon I entreat you...

CREON. You seem to be bent on causing trouble, woman.

MEDEA. I shall go into exile. It is not *that* I beg you to grant me.

CREON. Why then are you clinging so violently to my hand?

MEDEA. Allow me to stay for this one day to complete my plans for departure and get together provision for my children, since their father prefers not to bother about his own sons. Have pity on them. You too are the father of children. It is natural that you should feel kindly. Stay or go, I care nothing for myself. It's them I weep for in their misfortune.

CREON. My mind is not tyrannical enough; mercy has often been my undoing. So now, though I know that it is a mistake, woman, you will have your request. But I give you warning: if tomorrow's divine sun sees you and your children inside the borders of this country, you die. True is the word I have spoken. [Stay, if you must, this one day. You'll not have time to do what I dread.]

(*Exit* CREON.)

CHORUS. *Hapless woman! overwhelmed by sorrow! Where will you turn? What stranger will afford you hospitality? God has steered you, Medea, into an unmanageable surge of troubles.*

MEDEA.   Ill fortune's everywhere, who can gainsay it? But it is not yet as bad as that, never think so. There is still heavy weather ahead for the new bride and groom, and no little trouble for the maker of the match. Do you think I would ever have wheedled the king just now except to further my own plans? I would not even have spoken to him, nor touched him either. But he is such a fool that though he might have thwarted my plans by expelling me from the country he has allowed me to stay over for this one day, in which I shall make corpses of three of my enemies, father and daughter and my own husband.

My friends, I know several ways of causing their death, and I cannot decide which I should turn my hand to first. Shall I set fire to the bridal chamber or make my way in stealthily to where their bed is laid and drive a sword through their vitals? But there is one little difficulty. If I am caught entering the palace or devising my bonfire I shall be slain and my enemies shall laugh. Better take the direct way and the one for which I have the natural gift. Poison. Destroy them with poison. So be it.

But suppose them slain. What city will receive me? Whose hospitality will rescue me and afford me a land where I shall be safe from punishment, a home where I can live in security? It cannot be. I shall wait, therefore, a little longer and if any tower of safety shows up I shall carry out the murders in stealth and secrecy. However, if circumstances drive me to my wits' end, I shall take a sword in my own hands and face certain death to slay them. I shall not shirk the difficult adventure. No! by Queen Hecate who has her abode in the recesses of my hearth—her I revere above all gods and have chosen to assist me—never shall any one of them torture my heart with impunity. I shall make their marriage a torment and grief to them. Bitterly shall they rue the match they have made and the exile they inflict on me.

But enough! Medea, use all your wiles; plot and devise. Onward to the dreadful moment. Now is the test of courage. Do you see how you are being treated? It is not right that the seed of Sisyphus and Aeson should gloat over you, the daughter of a noble sire and descendant of the Sun. But you realize that. Moreover by our mere nature we women are helpless for good, but adept at contriving all manner of wickedness.

CHORUS.   *Back to their sources flow the sacred rivers. The world and morality are turned upside-down. The hearts of men are treacherous; the sanctions of Heaven are undermined. The voice of time will change, and our glory will ring down the ages. Womankind will be honored. No longer will ill-sounding report attach to our sex.*

The strains of ancient minstrelsy will cease, that hymned our faithlessness. Would that Phoebus, Lord of Song, had put into woman's heart the inspired song of the lyre. Then I would have sung a song in answer to the tribe of males. History has much to tell of the relations of men with women.

You, Medea, in the mad passion of your heart sailed away from your father's home, threading your way through the twin rocks of the Euxine, to settle in a foreign land. Now, your bed empty, your lover lost, unhappy woman, you are being driven forth in dishonor into exile.

> *Gone is respect for oaths. Nowhere in all the breadth of Hellas is honor any more to be found; it has vanished into the clouds. Hapless one, you have no father's house to which you might fly for shelter from the gales of misfortune; and another woman, a princess, has charmed your husband away and stepped into your place.*

(*Enter* JASON.)

JASON.   Often and often ere now I have observed that an intractable nature is a curse almost impossible to deal with. So with you. When you might have stayed on in this land and in this house by submitting quietly to the wishes of your superiors, your forward tongue has got you expelled from the country. Not that your abuse troubles *me* at all. Keep on saying that Jason is a villain of the deepest dye. But for your insolence to royalty consider yourself more than fortunate that you are only being punished by exile. I was constantly mollifying the angry monarch and expressing the wish that you be allowed to stay. But in unabated folly you keep on reviling the king. That is why you are to be expelled.

But still, despite everything, I come here now with unwearied goodwill, to contrive on your behalf, Madam, that you and the children will not leave this country lacking money or anything else. Exile brings many hardships in its wake. And even if you do hate me, I could never think cruelly of you.

MEDEA.   Rotten, heart-rotten, that is the word for you. Words, words, magnificent words. In reality a craven. You come to me, you come, my worst enemy! This isn't bravery, you know, this isn't valor, to come and face your victims. No! it's the ugliest sore on the face of humanity, Shamelessness. But I thank you for coming. It will lighten the weight on my heart to tell your wickedness, and it will hurt you to hear it. I shall begin my tale at the very beginning.

I saved your life, as all know who embarked with you on the Argo, when you were sent to master with the yoke the fire-breathing bulls and to sow with dragon's teeth that acre of death. The dragon, too, with wreathed coils, that kept safe watch over the Golden Fleece and never slept—I slew it and raised for you the light of life again. Then, forsaking my father and my own dear ones, I came to Iolcus where Pelias reigned, came with you, more than fond and less than wise. On Pelias too I brought death, the most painful death there is, at the hands of his own children. Thus I have removed every danger from your path.

And after all those benefits at my hands, you basest of men, you have betrayed me and made a new marriage, though I have borne you children. If you were still childless, I could have understood this love of yours for a new wife. Gone now is all reliance on pledges. You puzzle me. Do you believe that the gods of the old days are no longer in office? Do you think that men are now living under a new dispensation? For surely you know that you have broken all your oaths to me. Ah my hand, which you so often grasped, and oh my knees, how all for nothing have we been defiled by this false man, who has disappointed all our hopes.

But come, I shall confide in you as though you were my friend, not that I expect to receive any benefit from you. But let that go. My questions will serve to underline your infamy. As things are now, where am I to turn? Home to my father? But when I came here with you, I betrayed my home and my country. To the wretched daughters of Pelias? They would surely give me a royal welcome to their home; I only murdered their father. For it is how it is. My loved ones at home have learned to hate me; the others, whom I need not have harmed, I have made enemies to oblige you. And so in return for these services you have made me envied among the women of Hellas! A wonderful, faithful husband I have in you, if I must be expelled from the country into exile, deserted by my friends, alone with my friendless children! A fine story to tell of the new bridegroom, that his children and the woman who saved his life are wandering about in aimless beggary! O Zeus, why O why have you given to mortals sure means of knowing gold from tinsel, yet men's exteriors show no mark by which to descry the rotten heart?

LEADER.   Horrible and hard to heal is the anger of friend at strife with friend.

JASON.   It looks as if I need no small skill in speech if, like a skilful steersman riding the storm with close-reefed sheets, I am to escape the howling gale of your verbosity, woman. Well, since you are making a mountain out of the favors you have done me, I'll tell *you* what *I* think. It was the goddess of Love and none other, mortal or immortal, who delivered me from the dangers of my quest. You have indeed much subtlety of wit, but it would be an invidious story to go into, how the inescapable shafts of Love compelled you to save my life. Still, I shall not put too fine a point on it. If you helped me in some way or other, good and well. But as I shall demonstrate, in the matter of my rescue you got more than you gave.

    In the first place, you have your home in Greece, instead of in a barbarian land. You have learned the blessings of Law and Justice, instead of the Caprice of the Strong. And all the Greeks have realized your wisdom, and you have won great fame. If you had been living on the edges of the earth, nobody would ever have heard of you. May I have neither gold in my house nor skill to sing a sweeter song than Orpheus if my fortune is to be hid from the eyes of men. That, then, is my position in the matter of the fetching of the Fleece. (It was you who proposed the debate.)

    There remains my wedding with the Princess, which you have cast in my teeth. In this connection I shall demonstrate, one, my wisdom; two, my rightness; three, my great service of love to you and my children. (Be quiet please.) When I emigrated here from the land of Iolcus, dragging behind me an unmanageable chain of troubles, what greater windfall could I have hit upon, I an exile, than a marriage with the king's daughter? Not that I was weary of your charms (that's the thought that galls you) or that I was smitten with longing for a fresh bride; still less that I wanted to outdo my neighbors in begetting numerous children. Those I have are enough, there I have no criticism to make. No! what I wanted, first and foremost, was a good home where we would lack for nothing (well I knew that the poor man is shunned and avoided by all his friends); and secondly, I wanted to bring up the children in a style worthy of my house, and, begetting other children to be brothers to the children born of you, to bring them all together and unite the families. Then my happiness would be complete. What do *you* want with more children? As for me, it will pay me to advance the children I have by means of those I intend to beget. Surely that is no bad plan? You yourself would admit it, if jealousy were not pricking you.

     You women have actually come to believe that, lucky in love, you are lucky in all things, but let some mischance befall that love, and you will think the best of all possible worlds a most loathsome place. There ought to have been some other way for men to beget their children, dispensing with the assistance of women. Then there would be no trouble in the world.

LEADER.   Jason, you arrange your arguments very skillfully. And yet in my opinion, like it or not, you have acted unjustly in betraying your wife.

MEDEA.   Yes! I do hold many opinions that are not shared by the majority of people. In my opinion, for example, the plausible scoundrel is the worst type of scoundrel. Confident in his ability to trick out his wickedness with fair phrases he shrinks from no depth of villainy. But there is a limit to his cleverness. As there is also to yours. You may well drop that fine front with me, and all that rhetoric. One word will floor you. If you had been an honorable man, you would have sought my consent to the new match and not kept your plans secret from your own family.

JASON.   And if I had announced to you my intention to marry, I am sure I would have found you a most enthusiastic accomplice. Why! even now you cannot bring yourself to master your heart's deep resentment.

MEDEA.   That's not what griped you. No! your foreign wife was passing into an old age that did you little credit.

JASON.   Accept my assurance, it was not for the sake of a woman that I made the match I have made. As I told you once already, I wanted to save you and to beget princes to be brothers to my own sons, thereby establishing our family.

MEDEA.   May it never be mine…a happiness that hurts, a blessedness that frets my soul.

JASON.   Do you know how to change your prayer to show better sense? "May I regard nothing useful as grievous, no good fortune as ill."

MEDEA.   Insult me. *You* have a refuge, but I am helpless, faced with exile.

JASON.   It was your own choice. Don't blame anyone else.

MEDEA.   What did I do? Did I betray you and marry somebody else?

JASON.   You heaped foul curses on the king.

MEDEA.   And to your house also I shall prove a curse.

JASON.   Look here, I do not intend to continue this discussion any further. If you want anything of mine to assist you or the children in your exile, just tell me. I am ready to give it with an ungrudging hand and to send letters of introduction to my foreign friends who will treat you well. If you reject this offer, woman, you will be a great fool. Forget your anger, and you will find it greatly to your advantage.

MEDEA.   I would not use your friends on any terms or accept anything of yours. Do not offer it. The gifts of the wicked bring no profit.

JASON.   At any rate, heaven be my witness that I am willing to render every assistance to you and the children. But you do not like what is good for you. Your obstinacy repulses your friends; it will only aggravate your suffering.

MEDEA.   Be off with you. As you loiter outside here, you are burning with longing for the girl who has just been made your wife. Make the most of the union. Perhaps, god willing, you are making the kind of marriage you will some day wish unmade.

(*Exit* JASON.)

CHORUS.   *Love may go too far and involve men in dishonor and disgrace. But if the goddess comes in just measure, there is none so rich in blessing. May you never launch at me, O Lady of Cyprus, your golden bow's passion-poisoned arrows, which no man can avoid.*

May Moderation content me, the fairest gift of Heaven. Never may the Cyprian pierce my heart with longing for another's love and bring on me angry quarrelings and never-ending recriminations. May she have respect for harmonious unions and with discernment assort the matings of women.

O Home and Fatherland, never, never, I pray, may I be cityless. It is an intolerable existence, hopeless, piteous, grievous. Let me die first, die and bring this life to a close. There is no sorrow that surpasses the loss of country.

My eyes have seen it; not from hearsay do I speak. You have neither city nor friend to pity you in your most terrible trials. Perish, abhorred, the man who never brings himself to unbolt his heart in frankness to some honored friends! Never shall such a man be a friend of mine.

(*Enter* AEGEUS, *in traveler's dress.*)

AEGEUS.   Medea, good health to you. A better prelude than that in addressing one's friends, no man knows.

MEDEA.   Good health be yours also, wise Pandion's son, Aegeus. Where do you come from to visit this land?

AEGEUS.   I have just left the ancient oracle of Phoebus.

MEDEA.   What sent you to the earth's oracular hub?

AEGEUS.   I was enquiring how I might get children.

MEDEA.   In the name of Heaven, have you come thus far in life still childless?

AEGEUS.   By some supernatural influence I am still without children.

MEDEA.   Have you a wife or are you still unmarried?

AEGEUS.   I have a wedded wife to share my bed.

MEDEA.   Tell me, what did Phoebus tell you about offspring?

AEGEUS.   His words were too cunning for a mere man to interpret.

MEDEA.   Is it lawful to tell me the answer of the god?

AEGEUS.   Surely. For, believe me, it requires a cunning mind to understand.

MEDEA.   What then was the oracle? Tell me, if I may hear it.

AEGEUS.   I am not to open the cock that projects from the skin...

MEDEA.   Till you do what? Till you reach what land?

AEGEUS.   Till I return to my ancestral hearth.

MEDEA.   Then what errand brings your ship to this land?

AEGEUS.   There is one Pittheus, king of Troezen…

MEDEA.   The child of Pelops, as they say, and a most pious man.

AEGEUS.   To him I will communicate the oracle of the god.

MEDEA.   Yes, he is a cunning man and well-versed in such matters.

AEGEUS.   Yes, and of all my comrades in arms the one I love most.

MEDEA.   Well, good luck to you, and may you win your heart's desire.

AEGEUS.   Why, what's the reason for those sad eyes, that wasted complexion?

MEDEA.   Aegeus, I've got the basest husband in all the world.

AEGEUS.   What do you mean? Tell me the reason of your despondency, tell me plainly.

MEDEA.   Jason is wronging me; I never did him wrong.

AEGEUS.   What has he done? Speak more bluntly.

MEDEA.   He has another wife, to lord it over me in our home.

AEGEUS.   You don't mean that he has done so callous, so shameful a deed!

MEDEA.   Indeed he did. Me that used to be his darling he now despises.

AEGEUS.   Has he fallen in love? Does he hate your embraces?

MEDEA.   Yes, it's a grand passion! He was born to betray his loved ones.

AEGEUS.   Let him go, then, since he is so base, as you say.

MEDEA.   He became enamored of getting a king for a father-in-law.

AEGEUS.   Who gave him the bride? Please finish your story.

MEDEA.   Creon, the ruler of this Corinth.

AEGEUS.   In that case, Madam, I can sympathize with your resentment.

MEDEA.   My life is ruined. What is more, I am being expelled from the land.

AEGEUS.   By whom? This new trouble is hard.

MEDEA.   Creon is driving me out of Corinth into exile.

AEGEUS.   And does Jason allow this? I don't like that either.

MEDEA.   He says he does not, but he'll stand it. Oh! I beseech you by this beard, by these knees, a suppliant I entreat you, show pity, show pity for my misery. Do not stand by and see me driven forth to a lonely exile. Receive me into your land, into your home and the shelter of your hearth. So may the gods grant you the children you desire, to throw joy round your deathbed. You do not know what a lucky path you have taken to me. I shall put an end to your childlessness. I shall make you beget heirs of your blood. I know the magic potions that will do it.

AEGEUS.   Many things make me eager to do this favor for you, Madam. Firstly, the gods, and secondly, the children that you promise will be born to me. In that matter I am quite at my wits' end. But here is how I stand. If you yourself come to Athens, I shall try to be your champion, as in duty bound. This warning, however, I must give you! I shall not consent to take you with me out of Corinth. If you yourself come to my palace, you will find a home and a sanctuary. Never will I surrender you to anybody. But your own efforts must get you away from this place. I wish to be free from blame in the eyes of my hosts also.

MEDEA.   And so you shall. But just let me have a pledge for these services, and I shall have all I could desire of you.

AEGEUS.   Do you not trust me? What is your difficulty?

MEDEA.   I do trust you. But both the house of Pelias and Creon are my enemies. Bound by oaths, you would never hand me over to them if they tried to extradite me. But with an agreement of mere words, unfettered by any sacred pledge, you might be won over by their diplomatic advances to become *their* friend. For I have no influence or power, whereas they have the wealth of a royal palace.

AEGEUS.   You take great precautions, Madam. Still, if you wish, I will not refuse to do your bidding. For me too it will be safer that way, if I have some excuse to offer to your enemies, and *you* will have more security. Dictate the oath.

MEDEA.   Swear by the Floor of Earth, by the Sun my father's father, by the whole family of the gods, one and all——

AEGEUS.   To do or not do what? Say on.

MEDEA.   Never yourself to cast me out of your country and never, willingly, during your lifetime, to surrender me to any of my foes that desire to seize me.

AEGEUS.   I swear by the Earth, by the holy majesty of the Sun, and by all the gods, to abide by the terms you propose.

MEDEA.   Enough! And if you abide not by your oath, what punishment do you pray to receive?

AEGEUS.   The doom of sacrilegious mortals.

MEDEA.   Go and fare well. All is well. I shall arrive at your city as soon as possible, when I have done what I intend to do, and obtained my desire.

LEADER.   (*as* AEGEUS *departs*)   May Maia's son, the Lord of Journeys, bring you safe to Athens, and may you achieve the desire that hurries you homeward; for you are a generous man in my esteem.

MEDEA.   O Zeus and his Justice, O Light of the Sun! The time has come, my friends, when I shall sing songs of triumph over my enemies. I am on my way. Now I can hope that my foes will pay the penalty. Just as my plans were most storm-tossed at sea, this man has appeared, a veritable harbor, where I shall fix my moorings, when I get to the town and citadel of Pallas.

Now I shall tell you all my plans; what you hear will not be said in fun. I shall send one of my servants to ask Jason to come and see me. When he comes, I shall make my language submissive, tell him I approve of everything else and am quite contented [with his royal marriage and his betrayal of me, that I agree it is all for the best]; I shall only ask him to allow my children to remain. Not that I wish to leave them in a hostile land [for my enemies to insult]. No! I have a cunning plan to kill the princess. I shall send them with gifts to offer to the bride, to allow them to stay in the land—a dainty robe and a headdress of beaten gold. If she takes the finery and puts it on her, she will die in agony. She and anyone who touches her. So deadly are the poisons in which I shall steep my gifts.

But now I change my tone. It grieves me sorely, the horrible deed I must do next. I shall murder my children, these children of mine. No man shall take them away from me. Then when I have accomplished the utter overthrow of the house of Jason, I shall flee from the land, to escape the consequences of my own dear children's murder and my other accursed crimes. My friends, I cannot bear being laughed at by my enemies.

So be it. Tell me, what has life to offer them. They have no father, no home, no refuge from danger.

My mistake was in leaving my father's house, won over by the words of a Greek. But, as god is my ally, he shall pay for his crime. Never, if I can help it, shall he behold his sons again in this life. Never shall he beget children by his new bride. She must die by my poisons, die the death she deserves. Nobody shall despise *me* or think me weak or passive. Quite the contrary. I am a good friend, but a dangerous enemy. For that is the type the world delights to honor.

LEADER.   You have confided your plan in me, and I should like to help you, but since I also would support the laws of mankind, I entreat you not to do this deed.

MEDEA.   It is the only way. But I can sympathize with your sentiments. You have not been wronged like me.

LEADER.   Surely you will not have the heart to destroy your own flesh and blood?

MEDEA.   I shall. It will hurt my husband most that way.

LEADER.   But it will make you the unhappiest woman in the world.

MEDEA.   Let it. From now on all words are superfluous. (*To the* NURSE.)   Go now, please, and fetch Jason. Whenever loyalty is wanted, I turn to you. Tell him nothing of my intentions, as you are a woman and a loyal servant of your mistress.

(*Exit* NURSE.)

CHORUS.   *The people of Erechtheus have been favored of Heaven from the beginning. Children of the blessed gods are they, sprung from a hallowed land that no foeman's foot has trodden. Their food is glorious Wisdom. There the skies are always clear, and lightly do they walk in that land where once on a time blonde Harmony bore nine chaste daughters, the Muses of Pieria.*

Such is the tale, which tells also how Aphrodite sprinkled the land with water from the fair steams of Cephissus and breathed over it breezes soft and fragrant. Ever on her hair she wears a garland of sweet-smelling roses, and ever she sends the Loves to assist in the court of Wisdom. No good thing is wrought without their help.

How then shall that land of sacred rivers, that hospitable land receive you the slayer of your children? It would be sacrilege for you to live with them. Think. You are stabbing your children. Think. You are earning the name of murderess. By your knees we entreat you, by all the world holds sacred, do not murder your children.

Whence got you the hardihood to conceive such a plan? And in the horrible act, as you bring death on your own children, how will you steel your heart and hand? When you cast your eyes on them, your own children, will you not weep that you should be their murderess? When your own children fall at your feet and beg for mercy, you will never be able to dye your hands with their blood. Your heart will not stand it.

(*Enter* JASON, *followed by the* NURSE.)

JASON.   I come at your bidding. Though you hate me, I shall not refuse you an audience. What new favor have you to ask of me, woman?

MEDEA.   Jason, please forgive me for all I said. After all the services of love you have rendered me before, I can count on you to put up with my fits of temper. I have been arguing the matter out with myself. Wretched woman (thus I scolded myself), why am I so mad as to hate those that mean me well, to treat as enemies the rulers of this land and my husband who, in marrying a princess and getting brothers for my children, is only doing what is best for us all? What is the matter with me? Why am I still furious, when the gods are showering their blessings on me? Have I not children of my own? Am I forgetting that I am an exile from my native land, in sore need of friends? These reflections let me see how very foolish I have been and how groundless is my resentment. Now, I want to thank you. I think you are only doing the right thing in making this new match. I have been the fool. I ought to have entered into your designs, helped you to accomplish them, even stood by your nuptial couch and been glad to be of service to the new bride. But I am what I am… to say no worse, a woman. You ought not therefore to imitate me in my error or to compete with me in childishness. I beg your pardon, and confess that I was wrong then. But now I have taken better counsel, as you see.

Children, children, come here, leave the house, come out and greet your father as I do. Speak to him. Join your mother in making friends with him, forgetting our former hate. It's a truce; the quarrel is over. Take his right hand. Alas! my imagination sickens strangely. My children, will you stretch out loving arms like that in the long hereafter? My grief! How quick my tears are! My fears brim over. It is that long quarrel with your father, now done with, that fills my tender eyes with tears.

LEADER.   From my eyes, too, the burning tears gush forth. May Sorrow's advance proceed no further.

JASON.   That is the talk I like to hear, woman. The past I can forgive. It is only natural for your sex to show resentment when their husbands contract another marriage. But your heart has now changed for the better. It took time, to be sure, but you have now seen the light of reason. That's the action of a wise woman. As for you, my children, your father has not forgotten you. God willing, he has secured your perfect safety. I feel sure that you will yet occupy the first place here in Corinth, with your brothers. Merely grow up. Your father, and any friends he has in heaven, will see to the rest. May I see you, sturdy and strong, in the flower of your youth, triumphant over my enemies.

You there, why wet your eyes with hot tears, and avert your pale cheek? Why are you not happy to hear me speak thus?

MEDEA.   It's nothing. Just a thought about the children here.

JASON.   Why all this weeping over the children? It's too much.

MEDEA.   I am their mother. Just now when you were wishing them long life, a pang of sorrow came over me, in case things would not work out that way.

JASON.   Cheer up, then. I shall see that they are all right.

MEDEA.   Very well, I shall not doubt your word. Women are frail things and naturally apt to cry. But to return to the object of this conference, something has
been said, something remains to be mentioned. Since it is their royal pleasure
to expel me from the country—oh yes! it's the best thing for me too, I know
well, not to stay on here in the way of you and the king; I am supposed to be
their bitter enemy—*I* then shall go off into exile. But see that the children are
reared by your own hand, ask Creon to let *them* stay.

JASON.   I don't know if he will listen to me, but I shall try, as I ought.

MEDEA.   At least you can get your wife to intercede with her father on their behalf.

JASON.   Certainly, and I imagine I shall persuade her.

MEDEA.   If she is a woman like the rest of us. In this task, I too shall play my part. I
shall send the children with gifts for her, gifts far surpassing the things men
make to-day [a fine robe, and a head-dress of beaten gold]. Be quick there. Let
one of my maids bring the finery here. What joy will be hers, joys rather, joys
innumerable, getting not only a hero like you for a husband, but also raiment
which the Sun, my father's father, gave to his children.   (MEDEA *takes the casket
from a maid who has brought it, and hands it to the children.*)   Here, my children, take these wedding gifts in your hands. Carry them to the princess, the
happy bride, and give them to her. They are not the kind of gifts she will despise.

JASON.   Impetuous woman! Why leave yourself thus empty-handed? Do you think
a royal palace lacks for raiment and gold? Keep these things for yourself, don't
give them away. If my wife has any regard for me at all, she will prefer me to
wealth, I'm sure.

MEDEA.   Please let me. They say that gifts persuade even the gods, and gold is
stronger than ten thousand words. Hers is the fortune of the hour; her now is
god exalting. She has youth, and a king for a father. And to save my children
from exile, I would give my very life, let alone gold.

Away, my children, enter the rich palace and entreat your father's young
wife, my mistress, to let you stay in Corinth. Give her the finery. That is most
important. She must take these gifts in her hands. Go as fast as you can. Success attend your mission, and may you bring back to your mother the tidings
she longs to hear.

(*Exeunt Children with* TUTOR *and* JASON.)

CHORUS.   *Now are my hopes dead. The children are doomed. Already they are on the
road to death. She will take it, the bride will take the golden diadem, and with it
will take her ruin, luckless girl. With her own hands she will put the precious cir-
clet of death on her blonde hair.*

*The beauty of it, the heavenly sheen, will persuade her to put on the robe and
the golden crown. It is in the halls of death that she will put on her bridal dress
forthwith. Into that fearful trap she will fall. Death will be her portion, hapless
girl. She cannot overleap her doom.*

*And you, poor man. Little luck your royal father-in-law is bringing you.
Unwittingly, you are bringing death on your children, and on your wife an awful
end. Ill-starred man, what a way you are from happiness.*

And now I weep for your sorrow, hapless mother of these children. You will slaughter them to avenge the dishonor of your bed betrayed, criminally betrayed by your husband who now sleeps beside another bride.

(*Enter Children with their* TUTOR.)

TUTOR. Mistress, here are your children, reprieved from exile. Your gifts the royal bride took gladly in her hands. The children have made their peace with *her*. What's the matter? Why stand in such confusion, when fortune is smiling? [Why do you turn away your cheek? Why are you not glad to hear my message?]

MEDEA. Misery!

TUTOR. That note does not harmonize with the news I have brought.

MEDEA. Misery, and again Misery!

TUTOR. Have I unwittingly brought you bad news? I thought it was good. Was I mistaken?

MEDEA. Your message was…your message. It is not you I blame.

TUTOR. Why then are your eyes downcast and your tears flowing?

MEDEA. Of necessity, old man, of strong necessity. This is the gods' doing, and mine, in my folly.

TUTOR. Have courage. Some day your children will bring you too back home.

MEDEA. Ah me! Before that day I shall bring others to another home.

TUTOR. You are not the first woman to be separated from her children. We are mortals and must endure calamity with patience.

MEDEA. That I shall do. Now go inside and prepare their usual food for the children.

(*Exit* TUTOR.)

O my children, my children. For you indeed a city is assured, and a home in which, leaving me to my misery, you will dwell for ever, motherless. But I must go forth to exile in a strange land, before I have ever tasted the joy of seeing *your* happiness, before I have got you brides and bedecked your marriage beds and held aloft the bridal torches. Alas! my own self-will has brought me to misery. Was it all for nothing, my children, the rearing of you, and all the agonizing labor, all the fierce pangs I endured at your birth? Ah me, there was a time when I had strong hopes, fool as I was, that you would tend my old age and with your own hands dress my body for the grave, a fate that the world might envy. Now the sweet dream is gone. Deprived of you, I shall live a life of pain and sorrow. And you, in another world altogether will never again see your mother with your dear, dear eyes.

O the pain of it! Why do your eyes look at me, my children? Why smile at me that last smile? Ah! What can I do? My heart is water, women, at the sight of my children's bright faces. I could never do it. Goodbye to my former plans. I shall take my children away with me. Why should I hurt their father by *their* misfortunes, only to reap a double harvest of sorrow myself? No! I cannot do it. Goodbye to my plans.

And yet…what is the matter with me? Do I want to make myself a laughing-stock by letting my enemies off scot-free? I must go through with it. What a coward heart is mine, to admit those soft pleas. Come, my children, into the palace. Those that may not attend my sacrifices can see to it that they are absent. I shall not let my hand be unnerved.

Ah! Ah! Stop, my heart. Do not you commit this crime. Leave them alone, unhappy one, spare the children. Even if they live far from us, they will bring you joy. No! by the unforgetting dead in hell, it cannot be! I shall not leave my children for my enemies to insult. [In any case they must die. And if die they must, *I* shall slay them, who gave them birth.] My schemes are crowned with success. She shall not escape. Already the diadem is on her head; wrapped in the robe the royal bride is dying, I know it well. And now I am setting out on a most sorrowful road [and shall send these on one still more sorrowful]. I wish to speak to my children. Give your mother your hands, my children, give her your hands to kiss.

O dear, dear hand. O dear, dear mouth, dear shapes, dear noble faces, happiness be yours, but not here. Your father has stolen this world from you. How sweet to touch! The softness of their skin, the sweetness of their breath, my babies! Away, away, I cannot bear to see you any longer. (*Children retire within.*) My misery overwhelms me. O I *do* realize how terrible is the crime I am about, but passion overrules my resolutions, passion that causes most of the misery in the world.

CHORUS.   *Often ere now I have grappled with subtle subjects and sounded depths of argument deeper than woman may plumb. But, you see, we also have a Muse who teaches us philosophy. It is a small class—perhaps you might find one in a thousand—the women that love the Muse.*

And I declare that in this world those who have had no experience of paternity are happier than the fathers of children. Without children a man does not know whether they are a blessing or a curse, and so he does not miss a joy he has never had and he escapes a multitude of sorrows. But them that have in their home young, growing children that they love, I see them consumed with anxiety, day in day out, how they are to rear them properly, how they are to get a livelihood to leave to them. And, after all that, whether the children for whom they toil are worth it or not, who can tell?

And now I shall tell you the last and crowning sorrow for all mortals. Suppose they have found livelihood enough, their children have grown up, and turned out honest. Then, if it is fated that way, death carries their bodies away beneath the earth. What then is the use, when the love of children brings from the gods this crowning sorrow to top the rest?

MEDEA.   My friends, all this time I have been waiting for something to happen, watching to see what they will do in the royal palace. Now I see one of Jason's attendants coming this way. His excited breathing shows that he has a tale of strange evils to tell.

(*Enter* MESSENGER.)

MESSENGER. What a horrible deed of crime you have done, Medea. Flee, flee. Take anything you can find, sea vessel or land carriage.

MEDEA. Tell me, what has happened that I should flee.

MESSENGER. The princess has just died. Her father Creon, too, killed by your poisons.

MEDEA. Best of news! From this moment and for ever you are one of my friends and benefactors.

MESSENGER. What's that? Are you sane and of sound mind, woman? You have inflicted a foul outrage on a king's home, yet you rejoice at the word of it and are not afraid.

MEDEA. I too have a reply that I might make to you. But take your time, my friend. Speak on. How did they die? You would double my delight, if they died in agony.

MESSENGER. When your children, both your offspring, arrived with their father and entered the bride's house, we rejoiced, we servants who had been grieved by your troubles. Immediately a whisper ran from ear to ear that you and your husband had patched up your earlier quarrel. And one kisses your children's hands, another their yellow hair. I myself, in my delight, accompanied the children to the women's rooms. The mistress, whom we now respect in your place, did not see the two boys at first, but cast a longing look at Jason. Then, however, resenting the entrance of the children, she covered her eyes with a veil and averted her white cheek.

Your husband tried to allay the maiden's angry resentment, saying, "You must not hate your friends. Won't you calm your temper, and turn your head this way? You must consider your husband's friends your own. Won't you accept the gifts and ask your father to recall their sentence of exile, for my sake?" Well, when she saw the finery, she could not refrain, but promised her husband everything, and before Jason and your children were far away from the house she took the elaborate robes and put them on her. She placed the golden diadem on her clustering locks and began to arrange her coiffure before a shining mirror, smiling at her body's lifeless reflection. Then she arose from her seat and walked through the rooms, stepping delicately with her fair white feet, overjoyed with the gifts. Time and time again, standing erect, she gazes with all her eyes at her ankles.

But then ensued a fearful sight to see. Her color changed, she staggered, and ran back, her limbs all atremble, and only escaped falling by sinking upon her chair. An old attendant, thinking, I suppose, it was a panic fit, or something else of divine sending, raised a cry of prayer, until she sees a white froth drooling from her mouth, sees her rolling up the pupils of her eyes, and all the blood leaving her skin. Then, instead of a cry of prayer, she let out a scream of lamentation. Immediately one maid rushed to Creon's palace, another to the new bridegroom, to tell of the bride's misfortune. From end to end, the house echoed to hurrying steps. A quick walker, stepping out well, would have reached the end of the two hundred yard track, when the poor girl, lying there quiet, with closed eyes, gave a fearful groan and began to come to. A double plague assailed her. The golden diadem on her head emitted a strange flow of devouring fire, while the fine robes, the gifts of your children, were eating up the poor girl's white flesh. All aflame, she jumps from her seat and flees, shaking her head and hair this way and that, trying to throw off the crown. But the golden band held firmly, and after she had shaken her hair more violently, the fire began to blaze twice as fiercely. Overcome by the agony she falls on the ground, and none but her father could have recognized her. The position of her eyes could not be distinguished, nor the beauty of her face. The blood, clotted with fire, dripped from the crown of her head, and the flesh melted from her bones, like resin from a pinetree, as the poisons ate their unseen way. It was a fearful sight. All were afraid to touch the corpse, taught by what had happened to her.

But her father, unlucky man, rushed suddenly into the room, not knowing what had happened, and threw himself on the body. At once he groaned, and embracing his daughter's form he kissed it and cried, "My poor, poor child, what god has destroyed you so shamefully? Who is it deprives this aged tomb of his only child? Ah! let me join you in death, my child." Then, when he ceased his weeping and lamentation and sought to lift his aged frame upright, he stuck to the fine robes, like ivy to a laurel bush. His struggles were horrible. He would try to free a leg, but the girl's body stuck to his. And if he pulled violently, he tore his shrunken flesh off his bones. At last his life went out; doomed, he gave up the ghost. Side by side lie the two bodies, daughter and old father. Who would not weep at such a calamity?

It seems to me...I need not speak of what's in store for you; you yourself will see how well the punishment fits the crime...it's not the first time the thought has come, that the life of a man is a shadow. [I might assert with confidence that the mortals who pass for philosophers and subtle reasoners are most to be condemned.] No mortal man has lasting happiness. When the tide of fortune flows his way, one man may have more prosperity than another, but happiness never.

(*Exit* MESSENGER.)

LEADER.   It seems that this day Fate is visiting his sins on Jason. Unfortunate daughter of Creon, we pity your calamity. The love of Jason has carried you through the gates of death.

MEDEA.   My friends, I am resolved to act, and act quickly [to slay the children and depart from the land]. I can delay no longer, or my children will fall into the murderous hands of those that love them less than I do. In any case they must die. And if they must, I shall slay them, who gave them birth. Now, my heart, steel yourself. Why do we still hold back? The deed is terrible, but necessary. Come, my unhappy hand, seize the sword, seize it. Before you is a course of misery, life-long misery; on now to the starting post. No flinching now, no thinking of the children, the darling children, that call you mother. This day, this one short day, forget your children. You have all the future to mourn for them. Aye, to mourn. Though you mean to kill them, at least you loved them. Oh! I am a most unhappy woman.

(*Exit* MEDEA.)

CHORUS.　*O Earth, O glorious radiance of the Sun, look and behold the accursed woman. Stop her before she lays her bloody, murderous hands on her children. Sprung are they from your golden race, O Sun, and it is a fearful thing that the blood of a god should be spilt by mortals. Nay, stop her, skyborn light, prevent her. Deliver the house from the misery of slaughter, and the curse of the unforgetting dead.*

　　Gone, gone for nothing, are your maternal pangs. For nothing did you bear these lovely boys, O woman, who made the inhospitable passage through the gray Clashing Rocks! Why let your spleen poison your heart? Why this murderlust, where love was? On the man that spills the blood of kinsmen the curse of heaven descends. Go where he may, it rings ever in his ears, bringing sorrows and tribulations on his house.

　　(*The Children are heard within.*)

　　Listen, listen. It is the cry of the children. O cruel, ill-starred woman.

ONE OF THE CHILDREN.　(*within*)　Ah me! What am I to do? Where can I escape my mother's murderous hands?

THE OTHER.　(*within*)　I know not, my dear, dear brother. She is killing us.

CHORUS.　*Should we break in? Yes! I will save them from death.*

ONE OF THE CHILDREN.　(*within*)　Do, for god's sake. Save us. We need your help.

THE OTHER.　(*within*)　Yes, we are already in the toils of the sword.

CHORUS.　*Heartless woman! Are you made of stone or steel? Will you slaughter the children, your own seed, slaughter them with your own hands?*

　　Only one woman, only one in the history of the world, laid murderous hands on her children, Ino whom the gods made mad, driven from home to a life of wandering by the wife of Zeus. Hapless girl, bent on that foul slaughter, she stepped over a precipice by the shore and fell headlong into the sea, killing herself and her two children together. What crime, more horrible still, may yet come to pass? O the loves of women, fraught with sorrow, how many ills ere now have you brought on mortals!

　　(*Enter* JASON, *attended.*)

JASON.　You women there, standing in front of this house, is Medea still within, who wrought these dreadful deeds? Or has she made her escape? I tell you, she had better hide under the earth or take herself off on wings to the recesses of the sky, unless she wishes to give satisfaction to the family of the king. Does she think she can slay the rulers of the land and get safely away from this house? But I am not so anxious about her as I am about the children. The victims of her crimes will attend to her. It's my own children I am here to save, in case the relatives of the king do them some injury, in revenge for the foul murders their mother has committed.

LEADER.　Jason, poor Jason, you do not know the sum of your sorrows, or you would not have said these words.

JASON.　What is it? She does not want to kill me too, does she?

LEADER.　Your children are dead, slain by their mother's hand.

JASON.　For pity's sake, what do you mean? You have slain me, woman.

LEADER.　Your children are dead, make no mistake.

JASON. Why, where did she slay them? Indoors or out here?

LEADER. Open the doors and you will see their bodies.

JASON. Quick, servants, loosen the bolts, undo the fastenings. Let me see the double horror, the dead bodies of my children, and the woman who…oh! let me punish her.

> MEDEA *appears aloft in a chariot drawn by winged dragons. She has the bodies of the children.*

MEDEA. What's all this talk of battering and unbarring? Are you searching for the bodies and me who did the deed? Spare yourself the trouble. If you have anything to ask of me, speak if you will, but never shall you lay a hand on me. I have a magic chariot, given me by the Sun, my father's father, to protect me against my enemies.

JASON. You abominable thing! You most loathsomest woman, to the gods and me and all mankind. You had the heart to take the sword to your children, you their mother, leaving me childless. And you still behold the earth and the sun, you who have done this deed, you who have perpetrated this abominable outrage. My curses on you! At last I have come to my senses, the senses I lost when I brought you from your barbarian home and country to a home in Greece, an evil plague, treacherous alike to your father and the land that reared you. There is a fiend in you, whom the gods have launched against me. In your own home you had already slain your brother when you came aboard the Argo, that lovely ship. Such was your beginning. Then you married me and bore me children, whom you have now destroyed because I left your bed. No Greek woman would ever have done such a deed. Yet I saw fit to marry you, rather than any woman of Greece, a wife to hate me and destroy me, not a woman at all, but a tigress, with a disposition more savage than Tuscan Scylla. But why all this? Ten thousand reproaches could not sting you; your impudence is too engrained. The devil take you, shameless, abominable murderess of your children. I must bemoan my fate; no joy shall I have of my new marriage, and I shall never see alive the children I begot and reared and lost.

MEDEA. I might have made an elaborate rebuttal of the speech you have made, but Zeus the Father knows what you received at my hands and what you have done. You could not hope, nor your princess either, to scorn my love, make a fool of me, and live happily ever after. Nor was Creon, the matchmaker, to drive me out of the country with impunity. Go ahead, then. Call me tigress if you like, or Scylla that haunts the Tuscan coast. I don't mind, now I have got properly under your skin.

JASON. You too are suffering. You have your share of the sorrow.

MEDEA. True, but it's worth the grief, since you cannot scoff.

JASON. O children, what a wicked mother you got!

MEDEA. O children, your father's sins have caused your death.

JASON. Yet it was not *my* hand that slew them.

MEDEA. No, it was your lust, and your new marriage.

JASON. Because your love was scorned you actually thought it right to murder.

MEDEA. Do you think a woman considers that a small injury?

JASON.   Good women do. But you are wholly vicious.

MEDEA.   The children here are dead. That will sting you.

JASON.   No! they live to bring fierce curses on your head.

MEDEA.   The gods know who began it all.

JASON.   They know, indeed, they know the abominable wickedness of your heart.

MEDEA.   Hate me then. I despise your bitter words.

JASON.   And I yours. But it is easy for us to be quit of each other.

MEDEA.   How, pray? Certainly I am willing.

JASON.   Allow me to bury these bodies and lament them.

MEDEA.   Certainly not. I shall bury them with my own hands, taking them to the sanctuary of Hera of the Cape, where no enemy may violate their tombs and do them insult. Here in the land of Sisyphus we shall establish a solemn festival, and appoint rites for the future to expiate their impious murder. I myself shall go to the land of Erechtheus, to live with Aegeus, the son of Pandion. You, as is proper, will die the death you deserve, [struck on the head by a fragment of the Argo,] now you have seen the bitter fruits of your new marriage.

JASON.   May you be slain by the Curse of your children, and Justice that avenges murder!

MEDEA.   What god or power above will listen to you, the breaker of oaths, the treacherous guest?

JASON.   Oh! abominable slayer of children.

MEDEA.   Get along to the palace and bury your wife.

JASON.   I go, bereft of my two sons.

MEDEA.   You have nothing yet to bemoan. Wait till you are old.

JASON.   My dear, dear children!

MEDEA.   Yes, dear to their mother, not to you.

JASON.   And yet you slew them.

MEDEA.   I did, to hurt you.

JASON.   Alas! my grief! I long to kiss their dear mouths.

MEDEA.   Now you speak to them, now you greet them, but in the past you spurned them.

JASON.   For god's sake, let me touch my children's soft skin.

MEDEA.   No! You have gambled and lost.

JASON.   O Zeus, do you hear how I am repelled, how I am wronged by this foul tigress, that slew her own children? But such lament as I may and can make, I hereby make. I call upon the gods. I invoke the powers above to bear me witness that you slew my children and now prevent me from embracing their bodies and giving them burial. Would that I had never begotten them, to live to see them slain at your hands.

CHORUS.   *Zeus on Olympus hath a wide stewardship. Many things beyond expectation do the gods fulfil. That which was expected has not been accomplished; for that which was unexpected has god found the way. Such was the end of this story.*

(*Exeunt.*)

Translated by Moses Hadas and John McLean

Journal Entry

Prepare a character profile of Medea based on the nurse's first speech.

Textual Considerations

1. Characterize Jason. To what extent do you consider his decision to abandon Medea justifiable? Are his arguments convincing? Why or why not?
2. How do Medea's encounters with Creon and Aegeus reinforce her decision to kill her children?
3. The chorus of Corinthian women plays an important role in the drama. What is their view of gender relationships? To what extent do they empathize with Medea? What is their attitude toward Jason?
4. What does the play reveal about the conflict between reason and passion? To what extent are both Jason and Medea responsible for the fate of their children?

Cultural Contexts

1. Debate with your group the degree to which the identities of women in Greek culture were derived solely from their societal roles as daughters, wives, and mothers. To what extent did they view themselves as powerless in the objective world? How does that affect individual identity and gender relationships?
2. The concept of preserving communal values was an important aspect of Greek culture. To what extent does Euripides present Jason and Medea as tearing apart the social fabric of the family and community? Do you hold them accountable for their actions? Why or why not?

August Strindberg
1888

From the Preface to Miss Julie

Strindberg's Preface sets out his intentions in writing Miss Julie, *a play concerned with the problem of "social climbing or falling, of higher or lower, better or worse, man or woman." He discusses the struggle for dominance between Miss Julie and Jean, and characterizes Miss Julie as a woman forced to "wreak vengeance" upon herself.*

Miss Julie is a modern character. Not that the man-hating half-woman has not existed in all ages but because now that she has been discovered, she has come out in the open to make herself heard. The half-woman is a type who pushes her way ahead, selling herself nowadays for power, decorations, honors, and diplomas, as formerly she used to do for money. The type implies a retrogressive step in evolution, an inferior species who cannot endure. Unfortunately, they are able to pass on their wretchedness; degenerate men seem unconsciously to choose their mates from among them. And so they breed, producing an indeterminate sex for whom life is a torture. Fortunately, the offspring go under either because they are out of harmony with reality or because their repressed instincts break out uncontrollably or because their hopes of achieving equality with men are crushed. The type is tragic, revealing the drama of a desperate struggle against Nature, tragic as the romantic heritage now being dissipated by naturalism, which has a contrary aim: happiness, and happiness belongs only to the strong and skillful species.

But Miss Julie is also a relic of the old warrior nobility now giving way to a new nobility of nerve and intellect, a victim of her own flawed constitution, a victim of the discord caused in a family by a mother's "crime," a victim of the delusions and conditions of her age—and together these are the equivalent of the concept of Destiny, or Universal Law, of antiquity. Guilt has been abolished by the naturalist, along with God, but the consequences of an action—punishment, imprisonment or the fear of it—that he cannot erase, for the simple reason that they remain, whether he pronounces acquittal or not. Those who have been injured are not as kind and understanding as an unscathed outsider can afford to be. Even if her father felt constrained not to seek revenge, his daughter would wreak vengeance upon herself, as she does here, out of an innate or acquired sense of honor, which the upper classes inherit—from where? From barbarism, from the ancient Aryan home of the race, from medieval chivalry. It is a beautiful thing, but nowadays a hindrance to the survival of the race. It is the nobleman's harikari, which compels him to slit open his own stomach when someone insults him and which survives in a modified form in the duel, that privilege the nobility. That is why Jean, the servant, lives, while Miss Julie cannot live without honor. The slave's advantage over the nobleman is that he lacks this fatal preoccupation with honor. But in all of us Aryans there is something of the nobleman, or a Don Quixote. And so we sympathize with the suicide, whose act means a loss of honor. We are noblemen enough to be pained when we see the mighty fallen and as superfluous as a corpse, yes, even if the fallen should rise again and make amends through an honorable act. The servant Jean is a race-founder, someone in whom the process of differentiation can be detected. Born the son of a tenant farmer, he has educated himself in the things a gentleman should know. He has been quick to learn, has finely developed senses (smell, taste, sight) and a feeling for what is beautiful. He is already moving up in the world and is not embarrassed about using other people's help. He is alienated from his fellow servants, despising them as parts of a past he has already put behind him. He fears and flees them because they know his secrets, pry into his intentions, envy his rise, and look forward eagerly to his fall. Hence his dual, indecisive nature, vacillating between sympathy for people in high social positions and hatred for those who currently occupy those positions. He is an aristocrat, as he himself says, has learned the secrets of good society, is polished on the surface but coarse beneath, wears a frock coat tastefully but without any guarantee that his body is clean.

He has respect for Miss Julie, but is afraid of Kristine because she knows his dangerous secrets. He is sufficiently callous not to let the night's events disturb his plans for the future. With both a slave's brutality and a master's lack of squeamishness, he can see blood without fainting; and shake off misfortune easily. Consequently, he comes through the struggle unscathed and will probably end up an innkeeper. And even if *he* does not become a Rumanian count, his son will become a university student and possibly a county police commissioner....

Apart from the fact that Jean is rising in the world, he is superior to Miss Julie because he is a man. Sexually, he is an aristocrat because of his masculine strength, his more keenly developed senses, and his capacity for taking the initiative. His sense of inferiority is mostly due to the social circumstances in which he happens to be living, and he can probably shed it along with his valet's jacket.

His slave mentality expresses itself in the fearful respect he has for the Count (the boots) and his religious superstition; but he respects the Count mainly as the occupant of the kind of high position to which he himself aspires; and the respect remains even after he has conquered the daughter of the house and seen how empty the lovely shell was.

I do not believe that love in any "higher" sense can exist between two people of such different natures, and so I have Miss Julie's love as something she fabricates in order to protect and excuse herself; and I have Jean suppose himself capable of loving her under other social circumstances. I think it is the same with love as with the hyacinth, which must take root in darkness *before* it can produce a sturdy flower. Here a flower shoots up, blooms, and goes to seed all at once, and that is why it dies so quickly.

Translated by Harry G. Carlson

August Strindberg
1888

Miss Julie

CHARACTERS

MISS JULIE, twenty-five years old
JEAN, her father's valet, thirty years old
KRISTINE, her father's cook, thirty-five years old

(*The action takes place in the count's kitchen on midsummer eve.*)

Scene: *A large kitchen, the ceiling and side walls of which are hidden by draperies. The rear wall runs diagonally from down left to up right. On the wall down left are two shelves with copper, iron, and pewter utensils; the shelves are lined with scalloped paper. Visible to the right is most of a set of large, arched glass doors, through which can be seen a fountain with a statue of Cupid, lilac bushes in bloom, and the tops of some Lombardy poplars. At down left is the corner of a large tiled stove; a portion of its hood is showing. At right, one end of the servants' white pine dining table juts out; several chairs stand around it. The stove is decorated with birch branches; juniper twigs are strewn on the floor. On the end of the table stands a large Japanese spice jar, filled with lilac blossoms. An ice box, a sink, and a washstand. Above the door is an old-fashioned bell on a spring; to the left of the door, the mouthpiece of a speaking tube is visible.)*

*(*KRISTINE *is frying something on the stove. She is wearing a light-colored cotton dress and an apron.* JEAN *enters. He is wearing livery and carries a pair of high riding boots with spurs, which he puts down on the floor where they can be seen by the audience.)*

JEAN.   Miss Julie's crazy again tonight; absolutely crazy!

KRISTINE.   So you finally came back?

JEAN.   I took the Count to the station and when I returned past the barn I stopped in for a dance. Who do I see but Miss Julie leading off the dance with the gamekeeper! But as soon as she saw me she rushed over to ask me for the next waltz. And she's been waltzing ever since—I've never seen anything like it. She's crazy!

KRISTINE.   She always has been, but never as bad as the last two weeks since her engagement was broken off.

JEAN.   Yes, I wonder what the real story was there. He was a gentleman, even if he wasn't rich. Ah! These people have such romantic ideas.   (*Sits at the end of the table.*)   Still, it's strange, isn't it? I mean that she'd rather stay home with the servants on midsummer eve instead of going with her father to visit relatives?

KRISTINE.   She's probably embarrassed after that row with her fiancé.

JEAN.   Probably! He gave a good account of himself, though. Do you know how it happened, Kristine? I saw it, you know, though I didn't let on I had.

KRISTINE.   No! You saw it?

JEAN.   Yes, I did.—That evening they were out near the stable, and she was "training" him—as she called it. Do you know what she did? She made him jump over her riding crop, the way you'd teach a dog to jump. He jumped twice and she hit him each time. But the third time he grabbed the crop out of her hand, hit her with it across the cheek, and broke it in pieces. Then he left.

KRISTINE.   So, that's what happened! I can't believe it!

JEAN.   Yes, that's the way it went!—What have you got for me that's tasty Kristine?

KRISTINE   (*serving him from the pan*).   Oh, it's only a piece of kidney I cut from the veal roast.

JEAN   (*smelling the food*).   Beautiful! That's my favorite *délice.*[1]   (*Feeling the plate.*)   But you could have warmed the plate!

---

[1] *délice:* Delight.

KRISTINE. You're fussier than the Count himself, once you start! (*She pulls his hair affectionately.*)

JEAN (*angry*). Stop it, leave my hair alone! You know I'm touchy about that.

KRISTINE. Now, now, it's only love, you know that. (JEAN *eats.* KRISTINE *opens a bottle of beer.*)

JEAN. Beer? On midsummer eve? No thank you! I can do better than that. (*Opens a drawer in the table and takes out a bottle of red wine with yellow sealing wax.*) See that? Yellow seal! Give me a glass! A wine glass! I'm drinking this *pur.*[2]

KRISTINE (*returns to the stove and puts on a small saucepan*). God help the woman who gets you for a husband! What a fussbudget.

JEAN. Nonsense! You'd be damned lucky to get a man like me. It certainly hasn't done you any harm to have people call me your sweetheart. (*Tastes the wine.*) Good! Very good! Just needs a little warming. (*Warms the glass between his hands.*) We bought this in Dijon. Four francs a liter, not counting the cost of the bottle, or the customs duty.—What are you cooking now? It stinks like hell!

KRISTINE. Oh, some slop Miss Julie wants to give Diana.

JEAN. Watch your language, Kristine. But why should you have to cook for that damn mutt on midsummer eve? Is she sick?

KRISTINE. Yes, she's sick! She sneaked out with the gatekeeper's dog—and now there's hell to pay. Miss Julie won't have it!

JEAN. Miss Julie has too much pride about some things and not enough about others, just like her mother was. The Countess was most at home in the kitchen and the cowsheds, but a *one*-horse carriage wasn't elegant enough for her. The cuffs of her blouse were dirty, but she had to have her coat of arms on her cufflinks.—And Miss Julie won't take proper care of herself either. If you ask me, she just isn't refined. Just now when she was dancing in the barn, she pulled the gamekeeper away from Anna and made him dance with her. *We* wouldn't behave like that, but that's what happens when aristocrats pretend they're common people—they get *common!*—But she is quite a woman! Magnificent! What shoulders, and what—et cetera!

KRISTINE. Oh, don't overdo it! I've heard what Clara says, and she dresses her.

JEAN. Ha, Clara! You're all jealous of each other! I've been out riding with her.... And the way she dances!

KRISTINE. Listen, Jean! You're going to dance with me, when I'm finished here, aren't you?

JEAN. Of course I will.

KRISTINE. Promise?

JEAN. Promise? When I say I'll do something, I do it! By the way, the kidney was very good. (*Corks the bottle.*)

JULIE (*in the doorway to someone outside*). I'll be right back! You go ahead for now! (JEAN *sneaks the bottle back into the table drawer and gets up respectfully.*

---

[2] *pur:* Pure; the first drink from the bottle.

Miss Julie *enters and crosses to* Kristine *by the stove.*) Well? Is it ready? (Kristine *indicates that* Jean *is present.*)

JEAN (*gallantly*).   Are you ladies up to something secret?

JULIE (*flicking her handkerchief in his face*).   None of your business!

JEAN.   Hmm! I like the smell of violets!

JULIE (*coquettishly*).   Shame on you! So you know about perfumes, too? You certainly know how to dance. Ah, ah! No peeking! Go away.

JEAN (*boldly but respectfully*).   Are you brewing up a magic potion for midsummer eve? Something to prophesy by under a lucky star, so you'll catch a glimpse of your future husband!

JULIE (*caustically*).   You'd need sharp eyes to see him! (*To* Kristine.) Pour out half a bottle and cork it well.—Come and dance a schottische[3] with me, Jean…

JEAN (*hesitating*).   I don't want to be impolite to anyone, and I've already promised this dance to Kristine…

JULIE.   Oh, she can have another one—can't you, Kristine? Won't you lend me Jean?

KRISTINE.   It's not up to me, ma'am. (*To* Jean.) If the mistress is so generous, it wouldn't do for you to say no. Go on, Jean, and thank her for the honor.

JEAN.   To be honest, and no offense intended, I wonder whether it's wise for you to dance twice running with the same partner, especially since these people are quick to jump to conclusions…

JULIE (*flaring up*).   What's that? What sort of conclusions? What do you mean?

JEAN (*submissively*).   If you don't understand, ma'am, I must speak more plainly. It doesn't look good to play favorites with your servants.…

JULIE.   Play favorites! What an idea! I'm astonished! As mistress of the house, I honor your dance with my presence. And when I dance, I want to dance with someone who can lead, so I won't look ridiculous.

JEAN.   As you order, ma'am! I'm at your service!

JULIE (*gently*).   Don't take it as an order! On a night like this we're all just ordinary people having fun, so we'll forget about rank. Now, take my arm!—Don't worry, Kristine! I won't steal your sweetheart! (Jean *offers his arm and leads* Miss Julie *out.*)

> ***Mime:*** (*The following should be played as if the actress playing* Kristine *were really alone. When she has to, she turns her back to the audience. She does not look toward them, nor does she hurry as if she were afraid they would grow impatient. Schottische music played on a fiddle sounds in the distance.* Kristine *hums along with the music. She clears the table, washes the dishes, dries them, and puts them away. She takes off her apron. From a table drawer she removes a small mirror and leans it against the bowl of lilacs on the table. She lights a candle, heats a hairpin over the flame, and uses it to set a curl on her forehead. She crosses to the door and listens, then returns to the table. She finds the handkerchief* Miss Julie *left behind, picks*

---

3 *schottische:* A Scottish round dance resembling a polka.

it up, and smells it. Then, preoccupied, she spreads it out, stretches it, smoothes out the wrinkles, and folds it into quarters, and so forth.)

JEAN (*enters alone*). God, she really *is* crazy! What a way to dance! Everybody's laughing at her behind her back. What do you make of it, Kristine?

KRISTINE. Ah! It's that time of the month for her, and she always gets peculiar like that. Are you going to dance with me now?

JEAN. You're not mad at me, are you, for leaving....?

KRISTINE. Of course not!—Why should I be, for a little thing like that? Besides, I know my place...

JEAN (*puts his arm around her waist*). You're a sensible girl, Kristine, and you'd make a good wife...

JULIE (*entering; uncomfortably surprised; with forced good humor*). What a charming escort—running away from his partner.

JEAN. On the contrary, Miss Julie. Don't you see how I rushed back to the partner I abandoned!

JULIE (*changing her tone*). You know, you're a superb dancer!—But why are you wearing livery on a holiday? Take it off at once!

JEAN. Then I must ask you to go outside for a moment. You see, my black coat is hanging over here...(*Gestures and crosses right.*)

JULIE. Are you embarrassed about changing your coat in front of me? Well, go in your room then. Either that or stay and I'll turn my back.

JEAN. With your permission, ma'am! (*He crosses right. His arm is visible as he changes his jacket.*)

JULIE (*to* KRISTINE). Tell me, Kristine—you two are so close—. Is Jean your fiancé?

KRISTINE. Fiancé? Yes, if you wish. We can call him that.

JULIE. What do you mean?

KRISTINE. You had a fiancé yourself, didn't you? So...

JULIE. Well, we were properly engaged...

KRISTINE. But nothing came of it, did it? (JEAN *returns dressed in a frock coat and bowler hat.*)

JULIE. *Très gentil, monsieur Jean! Très gentil!*

JEAN. *Vous voulez plaisanter, madame!*

JULIE. *Et vous voulez parler français!*[4] Where did you learn that?

JEAN. In Switzerland, when I was wine steward in one of the biggest hotels in Lucerne!

JULIE. You look like a real gentleman in that coat! *Charmant!*[5] (*Sits at the table.*)

JEAN. Oh, you're flattering me!

JULIE (*offended*). Flattering you?

---

[4] *Très gentil...français!:* Very pleasing, Mr. Jean! Very pleasing. You would trifle with me, madam! And you want to speak French! [5] *Charmant:* Charming.

JEAN. My natural modesty forbids me to believe that you would really compliment someone like me, and so I took the liberty of assuming that you were exaggerating, which polite people call flattering.

JULIE. Where did you learn to talk like that? You must have been to the theater often.

JEAN. Of course. And I've done a lot of traveling.

JULIE. But you come from here, don't you?

JEAN. My father was a farmhand on the district attorney's estate nearby. I used to see you when you were little, but you never noticed me.

JULIE. No! Really?

JEAN. Sure. I remember one time especially…but I can't talk about that.

JULIE. Oh, come now! Why not? Just this once!

JEAN. No, I really couldn't, not now. Some other time, perhaps.

JULIE. Why some other time? What's so dangerous about now?

JEAN. It's not dangerous, but there are obstacles.—Her, for example. (*Indicating* KRISTINE, *who has fallen asleep in a chair by the stove.*)

JULIE. What a pleasant wife she'll make! She probably snores, too.

JEAN. No, she doesn't, but she talks in her sleep.

JULIE (*cynically*). How do *you* know?

JEAN (*audaciously*). I've heard her! (*Pause, during which they stare at each other.*)

JULIE. Why don't you sit down?

JEAN. I couldn't do that in your presence.

JULIE. But if I order you to?

JEAN. Then I'd obey.

JULIE. Sit down then.—No, wait. Can you get me something to drink first?

JEAN. I don't know what we have in the ice box. I think there's only beer.

JULIE. Why do you say "only"? My tastes are so simple I prefer beer to wine. (JEAN *takes a bottle of beer from the ice box and opens it. He looks for a glass and a plate in the cupboard and serves her.*)

JEAN. Here you are, ma'am.

JULIE. Thank you. Won't you have something yourself?

JEAN. I'm not partial to beer, but if it's an order…

JULIE. An order?—Surely a gentleman can keep his lady company.

JEAN. You're right, of course. (*Opens a bottle and gets a glass.*)

JULIE. Now, drink to my health! (*He hesitates.*) What? A man of the world—and shy?

JEAN (*in mock romantic fashion, he kneels and raises his glass*). Skål to my mistress!

JULIE. Bravo!—Now kiss my shoe, to finish it properly. (*Jean hesitates, then boldly seizes her foot and kisses it lightly.*) Perfect! You should have been an actor.

JEAN (*rising*). That's enough now, Miss Julie! Someone might come in and see us.

JULIE. What of it?

JEAN. People talk, that's what! If you knew how their tongues were wagging just now at the dance, you'd…

JULIE. What were they saying? Tell me!—Sit down!

JEAN (*sits*). I don't want to hurt you, but they were saying things—suggestive things, that, that…well, you can figure it out for yourself! You're not a child. If a woman is seen drinking alone with a man—let alone a servant—at night—then…

JULIE. Then what? Besides, we're not alone. Kristine is here.

JEAN. Asleep!

JULIE. Then I'll wake her up. (*Rising.*) Kristine! Are you asleep? (KRISTINE *mumbles in her sleep.*)

JULIE. Kristine!—She certainly can sleep!

KRISTINE (*in her sleep*). The Count's boots are brushed—put the coffee on—right away, right away—uh, huh—oh!

JULIE (*grabbing* KRISTINE*'s nose*). Will you wake up!

JEAN (*severely*). Leave her alone—let her sleep!

JULIE (*sharply*). What?

JEAN. Someone who's been standing over a stove all day has a right to be tired by now. Sleep should be respected…

JULIE (*changing her tone*). What a considerate thought—it does you credit—thank you! (*Offering her hand.*) Come outside and pick some lilacs for me!

> (*During the following,* KRISTINE *awakens and shambles sleepily off right to bed.*)

JEAN. Go with you?

JULIE. With me!

JEAN. We couldn't do that! Absolutely not!

JULIE. I don't understand. Surely you don't imagine…

JEAN. No, I don't, but the others might.

JULIE. What? That I've fallen in love with a servant?

JEAN. I'm not a conceited man, but such things happen—and for these people, nothing is sacred.

JULIE. I do believe you're an aristocrat!

JEAN. Yes, I am.

JULIE. And I'm stepping down…

JEAN. Don't step down, Miss Julie, take my advice. No one'll believe you stepped down voluntarily. People will always say you fell.

JULIE. I have a higher opinion of people than you. Come and see!—Come! (*She stares at him broodingly.*)

JEAN. You're very strange, do you know that?

JULIE. Perhaps! But so are you!—For that matter, everything is strange. Life, people, everything. Like floating scum, drifting on and on across the water, until it sinks down and down! That reminds me of a dream I have now and then. I've climbed up on top of a pillar. I sit there and see no way of getting down. I get dizzy when I look down, and I must get down, but I don't have the courage to jump. I can't hold on firmly, and I long to be able to fall, but I don't fall. And yet I'll have no peace until I get down, no rest unless I get down, down on the ground! And if I did get down to the ground, I'd want to be under the earth…Have you ever felt anything like that?

JEAN.   No. I dream that I'm lying under a high tree in a dark forest. I want to get up, up on top, and look out over the bright landscape, where the sun is shining, and plunder the bird's nest up there, where the golden eggs lie. And I climb and climb, but the trunk's so thick and smooth, and it's so far to the first branch. But I know if I just reached that first branch, I'd go right to the top, like up a ladder. I haven't reached it yet, but I will, even if it's only in a dream!

JULIE.   Here I am chattering with you about dreams. Come, let's go out! Just into the park!   (*She offers him her arm, and they start to leave.*)

JEAN.   We'll have to sleep on nine midsummer flowers, Miss Julie, to make our dreams come true!   (*They turn at the door.* JEAN *puts his hand to his eye.*)

JULIE.   Did you get something in your eye?

JEAN.   It's nothing—just a speck—it'll be gone in a minute.

JULIE.   My sleeve must have brushed against you. Sit down and let me help you. (*She takes him by the arm and seats him. She tilts his head back and with the tip of a handkerchief tries to remove the speck.*)   Sit still, absolutely still!   (*She slaps his hand.*)   Didn't you hear me?—Why, you're trembling; the big, strong man is trembling!   (*Feels his biceps.*)   What muscles you have!

JEAN   (*warning*).   Miss Julie!

JULIE.   Yes, *monsieur* Jean.

JEAN.   *Attention! Je ne suis qu'un homme!*[6]

JULIE.   Will you sit still!—There! Now it's gone! Kiss my hand and thank me.

JEAN   (*rising*).   Miss Julie, listen to me!—Kristine has gone to bed!—Will you listen to me!

JULIE.   Kiss my hand first!

JEAN.   Listen to me!

JULIE.   Kiss my hand first!

JEAN.   All right, but you've only yourself to blame!

JULIE.   For what?

JEAN.   For what? Are you still a child at twenty-five? Don't you know that it's dangerous to play with fire?

JULIE.   Not for me. I'm insured.

JEAN   (*boldly*).   No, you're not! But even if you were, there's combustible material close by.

JULIE.   Meaning you?

JEAN.   Yes! Not because it's me, but because I'm young—

JULIE.   And handsome—what incredible conceit! A Don Juan perhaps! Or a Joseph![7] Yes, that's it, I do believe you're a Joseph!

JEAN.   Do you?

JULIE.   I'm almost afraid so.   (JEAN *boldly tries to put his arm around her waist and kiss her. She slaps his face.*)   How dare you?

---

[6] *Attention! Je ne suis qu'un homme!:* Watch out! I am only a man!   [7] *Don Juan…Joseph:* Don Juan in Spanish legend is a seducer of women; in Genesis, Joseph resists the advances of Potiphar's wife.

JEAN.   Are you serious or joking?

JULIE.   Serious.

JEAN.   Then so was what just happened. You play games too seriously, and that's dangerous. Well, I'm tired of games. You'll excuse me if I get back to work. I haven't done the Count's boots yet and it's long past midnight.

JULIE.   Put the boots down!

JEAN.   No! It's the work I have to do. I never agreed to be your playmate, and never will. It's beneath me.

JULIE.   You're proud.

JEAN.   In certain ways, but not in others.

JULIE.   Have you ever been in love?

JEAN.   We don't use that word, but I've been fond of many girls, and once I was sick because I couldn't have the one I wanted. That's right, sick like those princes in the Arabian Nights—who couldn't eat or drink because of love.

JULIE.   Who was she?   (JEAN *is silent.*)   Who was she?

JEAN.   You can't force me to tell you that.

JULIE.   But if I ask you as an equal, as a—friend! Who was she?

JEAN.   You!

JULIE   (*sits*).   How amusing…

JEAN.   Yes, if you like! It was ridiculous!—You see, that was the story I didn't want to tell you earlier. Maybe I will now. Do you know how the world looks from down below?—Of course you don't. Neither do hawks and falcons, whose backs we can't see because they're usually soaring up there above us. I grew up in a shack with seven brothers and sisters and a pig, in the middle of a wasteland, where there wasn't a single tree. But from our window I could see the tops of apple trees above the wall of your father's garden. That was the Garden of Eden, guarded by angry angels with flaming swords. All the same, the other boys and I managed to find our way to the Tree of Life.—Now you think I'm contemptible, I suppose.

JULIE.   Oh, all boys steal apples.

JEAN.   You say that, but you think I'm contemptible anyway. Oh well! One day I went into the Garden of Eden with my mother, to weed the onion beds. Near the vegetable garden was a small Turkish pavilion in the shadow of jasmine bushes and overgrown with honeysuckle. I had no idea what it was used for, but I'd never seen such a beautiful building. People went in and came out again, and one day the door was left open. I sneaked close and saw walls covered with pictures of kings and emperors, and red curtains with fringes at the windows—now you know the place I mean. I—(*Breaks off a sprig of lilac and holds it in front of* MISS JULIE's *nose.*)—I'd never been inside the manor house, never seen anything except the church—but this was more beautiful. From then on, no matter where my thoughts wandered, they returned—there. And gradually I got a longing to experience, just once, the full pleasure of—*enfin,*[8] I sneaked in, saw, and marveled! But then I heard someone coming! There

---

[8] *enfin:* Finally.

was only one exit for ladies and gentlemen, but for me there was another, and I had no choice but to take it! (MISS JULIE, *who has taken the lilac sprig, lets it fall on the table.*) Afterwards, I started running. I crashed through a raspberry bush, flew over a strawberry patch, and came up onto the rose terrace. There I caught sight of a pink dress and a pair of white stockings—it was you. I crawled under a pile of weeds, and I mean under—under thistles that pricked me and wet dirt that stank. And I looked at you as you walked among the roses, and I thought: if it's true that a thief can enter heaven and be with the angels, then why can't a farmhand's son here on God's earth enter the manor house garden and play with the Count's daughter?

JULIE (*romantically*). Do you think all poor children would have thought the way you did?

JEAN (*at first hesitant, then with conviction*). If *all* poor—yes—of course. Of course!

JULIE. It must be terrible to be poor!

JEAN (*with exaggerated suffering*). Oh, Miss Julie! Oh!—A dog can lie on the Countess's sofa, a horse can have his nose patted by a young lady's hand, but a servant—(*Changing his tone.*)—oh, I know—now and then you find one with enough stuff in him to get ahead in the world, but how often?—Anyhow, do you know what I did then?—I jumped in the millstream with my clothes on, was pulled out, and got a beating. But the following Sunday, when my father and all the others went to my grandmother's, I arranged to stay home. I scrubbed myself with soap and water, put on my best clothes, and went to church so that I could see you! I saw you and returned home, determined to die. But I wanted to die beautifully and pleasantly, without pain. And then I remembered that it was dangerous to sleep under an elder bush. We had a big one, and it was in full flower. I plundered its treasures and bedded down under them in the oat bin. Have you ever noticed how smooth oats are?—and soft to the touch, like human skin…! Well, I shut the lid and closed my eyes. I fell asleep and woke up feeling very sick. But I didn't die, as you can see. What was I after?—I don't know. There was no hope of winning you, of course.—You were a symbol of the hopelessness of ever rising out of the class in which I was born.

JULIE. You're a charming storyteller. Did you ever go to school?

JEAN. A bit, but I've read lots of novels and been to the theater often. And then I've listened to people like you talk—that's where I learn most.

JULIE. Do you listen to what we say?

JEAN. Naturally! And I've heard plenty, too, driving the carriage or rowing the boat. Once I heard you and a friend…

JULIE. Oh?—What did you hear?

JEAN. I'd better not say. But I was surprised a little. I couldn't imagine where you learned such words. Maybe at bottom there isn't such a great difference between people as we think.

JULIE. Shame on you! We don't act like you when we're engaged.

JEAN (*staring at her*). Is that true?—You don't have to play innocent with me, Miss…

JULIE.   The man I gave my love to was a swine.

JEAN.   That's what you all say—afterwards.

JULIE.   All?

JEAN.   I think so. I know I've heard that phrase before, on similar occasions.

JULIE.   What occasions?

JEAN.   Like the one I'm talking about. The last time...

JULIE   (*rising*).   Quiet! I don't want to hear any more!

JEAN.   That's interesting—that's what *she* said, too. Well, if you'll excuse me, I'm going to bed.

JULIE   (*gently*).   To bed? On midsummer eve?

JEAN.   Yes! Dancing with the rabble out there doesn't amuse me much.

JULIE.   Get the key to the boat and row me out on the lake. I want to see the sun come up.

JEAN.   Is that wise?

JULIE.   Are you worried about your reputation?

JEAN.   Why not? Why should I risk looking ridiculous and getting fired without a reference, just when I'm trying to establish myself. Besides, I think I owe something to Kristine.

JULIE.   So, now it's Kristine...

JEAN.   Yes, but you, too.—Take my advice, go up and go to bed!

JULIE.   Am I to obey you?

JEAN.   Just this once—for your own good! Please! It's very late. Drowsiness makes people giddy and liable to lose their heads! Go to bed! Besides—unless I'm mistaken—I hear the others coming to look for me. And if they find us together, you'll be lost!

(*The* CHORUS *approaches, singing.*)

CHORUS.

> The swineherd found his true love
> a pretty girl so fair,
> The swineherd found his true love
> but let the girl beware.

> For then he saw the princess
> the princess on the golden hill,
> but then saw the princess,
> so much fairer still.

> So the swineherd and the princess
> they danced the whole night through,
> and he forgot his first love,
> to her he was untrue.

> And when the long night ended,
> and in the light of day, of day,
> the dancing too was ended,
> and the princess could not stay.

> Then the swineherd lost his true love,
> and the princess grieves him still,
> and never more she'll wander
> from atop the golden hill.

JULIE.   I know all these people and I love them, just as they love me. Let them come in and you'll see.

JEAN.   No, Miss Julie, they don't love you. They take your food, but they spit on it! Believe me! Listen to them, listen to what they're singing!—No, don't listen to them!

JULIE   (*listening*).   What are they singing?

JEAN.   It's a dirty song! About you and me!

JULIE.   Disgusting! Oh! How deceitful!—

JEAN.   The rabble is always cowardly! And in a battle like this, you don't fight; you can only run away!

JULIE.   Run away? But where? We can't go out—or into Kristine's room.

JEAN.   True. But there's my room. Necessity knows no rules. Besides, you can trust me. I'm your friend and I respect you.

JULIE.   But suppose—suppose they look for you in there?

JEAN.   I'll bolt the door, and if anyone tries to break in, I'll shoot!—Come!   (*On his knees.*)   Come!

JULIE   (*urgently*).   Promise me…?

JEAN.   I swear!   (MISS JULIE *runs off right. Jean hastens after her.*)

> **Ballet:**   (*Led by a fiddler, the servants and farm people enter, dressed festively, with flowers in their hats. On the table they place a small barrel of beer and a keg of schnapps both garlanded. Glasses are brought out, and the drinking starts. A dance circle is formed and "The Swineherd and the Princess" is sung. When the dance is finished, everyone leaves, singing.*)
>
> (MISS JULIE *enters alone. She notices the mess in the kitchen, wrings her hands, then takes out her powder puff and powders her nose.*)

JEAN   (*enters, agitated*).   There, you see? And you heard them. We can't possibly stay here now, you know that.

JULIE.   Yes, I know. But what can we do?

JEAN.   Leave, travel, far away from here.

JULIE.   Travel? Yes, but where?

JEAN.   To Switzerland, to the Italian lakes. Have you ever been there?

JULIE.   No. Is it beautiful?

JEAN.   Oh, an eternal summer—oranges growing everywhere, laurel trees, always green…

JULIE.   But what'll we do there?

JEAN.   I'll open a hotel—with first-class service for first-class people.

JULIE.   Hotel?

JEAN.   That's the life, you know. Always new faces, new languages. No time to worry or be nervous. No hunting for something to do—there's always work

to be done: bells ringing night and day, train whistles blowing, carriages coming and going, and all the while gold rolling into the till! That's the life!

JULIE.   Yes, it sounds wonderful. But what'll I do?

JEAN.   You'll be mistress of the house: the jewel in our crown! With your looks…
and your manner—oh—success is guaranteed! It'll be wonderful! You'll sit in
your office like a queen and push an electric button to set your slaves in
motion. The guests will file past your throne and timidly lay their treasures
before you.—You have no idea how people tremble when they get their bill.—
I'll salt the bills⁹ and you'll sweeten them with your prettiest smile.—Let's get
away from here—(*Takes a timetable out of his pocket.*)—Right away, on the
next train!—We'll be in Malmö six-thirty tomorrow morning, Hamburg at
eight-forty; from Frankfort to Basel will take a day, then on to Como by way
of the St. Gotthard Tunnel, in, let's see, three days. Three days!

JULIE.   That's all very well! But Jean—you must give me courage!—Tell me you
love me! Put your arms around me!

JEAN   (*hesitating*).   I want to—but I don't dare. Not in this house, not again. I
love you—never doubt that—you don't doubt it, do you, Miss Julie?

JULIE   (*shy; very feminine*).   "Miss!"—Call me Julie! There are no barriers
between us anymore. Call me Julie!

JEAN   (*tormented*).   I can't! There'll always be barriers between us as long as we
stay in this house.—There's the past and there's the Count. I've never met
anyone I had such respect for.—When I see his gloves lying on a chair, I feel
small.—When I hear that bell up there ring, I jump like a skittish horse.—And
when I look at his boots standing there so stiff and proud, I feel like
bowing! (*Kicking the boots.*)   Superstitions and prejudices we learned as
children—but they can easily be forgotten. If I can just get to another country,
a republic, people will bow and scrape when they see my livery—*they'll* bow
and scrape, you hear, not me! I wasn't born to cringe. I've got stuff in me, I've
got character, and if I can only grab onto that first branch, you watch me
climb! I'm a servant today, but next year I'll own my own hotel. In ten years
I'll have enough to retire. Then I'll go to Rumania and be decorated. I
could—mind you I said *could*—end up a count!

JULIE.   Wonderful, wonderful!

JEAN.   Ah, in Rumania you just buy your title, and so you'll be a countess after all.
My countess!

JULIE.   But I don't care about that—that's what I'm putting behind me! Show me
you love me, otherwise—otherwise, what am I?

JEAN.   I'll show you a thousand times—afterwards! Not here! And whatever you
do, no emotional outbursts, or we'll both be lost! We must think this through
coolly, like sensible people. (*He takes out a cigar, snips the end, and lights
it.*)   You sit there, and I'll sit here. We'll talk as if nothing happened.

JULIE   (*desperately*).   Oh, my God! Have you no feelings?

JEAN.   Me? No one has more feelings than I do, but I know how to control them.

---

⁹ *salt the bills:* Inflate or pad the bills.

JULIE.   A little while ago you could kiss my shoe—and now!

JEAN.   (*harshly*).   Yes, but that was before. Now we have other things to think about.

JULIE.   Don't speak harshly to me!

JEAN.   I'm not—just sensibly! We've already done one foolish thing, let's not have any more. The Count could return any minute, and by then we've got to decide what to do with our lives. What do you think of my plans for the future? Do you approve?

JULIE.   They sound reasonable enough. I have only one question. for such a big undertaking you need capital—do you have it?

JEAN   (*chewing on the cigar*).   Me?: Certainly! I have my professional expertise, my wide experience, and my knowledge of languages. That's capital enough, I should think!

JULIE.   But all that won't even buy a train ticket.

JEAN.   That's true. That's why I'm looking for a partner to advance me the money.

JULIE.   Where will you find one quickly enough?

JEAN.   That's up to you, if you want to come with me.

JULIE.   But I can't; I have no money of my own.   (*Pause.*)

JEAN.   Then it's all off…

JULIE.   And…

JEAN.   Things stay as they are.

JULIE.   Do you think I'm going to stay in this house as your lover? With all the servants pointing their fingers at me? Do you imagine I can face my father after this? No! Take me away from here, away from shame and dishonor—Oh, what have I done! My God, my God!   (*She cries.*)

JEAN.   Now, don't start that old song!—What have you done? The same as many others before you.

JULIE   (*screaming convulsively*).   And now you think I'm contemptible!—I'm falling, I'm falling!

JEAN.   Fall down to my level and I'll lift you up again.

JULIE.   What terrible power drew me to you? The attraction of the weak to the strong? The falling to the rising? Or was it love? Was this love? Do you know what love is?

JEAN.   Me? What do you take me for? You don't think this was my first time, do you?

JULIE.   The things you say, the thoughts you think!

JEAN.   That's the way I was taught, and that's the way I am! Now don't get excited and don't play the grand lady, because we're in the same boat now!—Come on, Julie, I'll pour you a glass of something special!   (*He opens a drawer in the table, takes out a wine bottle, and fills two glasses already used.*)

JULIE.   Where did you get that wine?

JEAN.   From the cellar.

JULIE.   My father's burgundy!

JEAN.   That'll do for his son-in-law, won't it?

JULIE.   And I drink beer! Beer!

JEAN.   That only shows I have better taste.

JULIE.   Thief!

JEAN.   Planning to tell?

JULIE.   Oh, oh! Accomplice of a common thief! Was I drunk? Have I been walking in a dream the whole evening? Midsummer eve! A time of innocent fun!

JEAN.   Innocent, eh?

JULIE   (*pacing back and forth*).   Is there anyone on earth more miserable than I am at this moment?

JEAN.   Why should you be? After such a conquest? Think of Kristine in there. Don't you think she has feelings, too?

JULIE.   I thought so awhile ago, but not anymore. No, a servant is a servant...

JEAN.   And a whore is a whore!

JULIE   (*on her knees, her hands clasped*).   Oh, God in heaven, end my wretched life! Take me away from this filth I'm sinking into! Save me! Save me!

JEAN.   I can't deny I feel sorry for you. When I lay in that onion bed and saw you in the rose garden, well...I'll be frank...I had the same thoughts all boys have.

JULIE.   And you wanted to die for me!

JEAN.   In the oat bin? That was just talk.

JULIE.   A lie, in other words.

JEAN   (*beginning to feel sleepy*).   More or less! I got the idea from a newspaper story about a chimney sweep who curled up in a firewood bin full of lilacs because he got a summons for not supporting his illegitimate child...

JULIE.   So, that's what you're like...

JEAN.   I had to think of something. And that's the kind of story women always go for.

JULIE.   Swine!

JEAN.   *Merde!*[10]

JULIE.   And now you've seen the hawk's back...

JEAN.   Not exactly its *back*...

JULIE.   And I was to be the first branch...

JEAN.   But the branch was rotten...

JULIE.   I was to be the sign on the hotel...

JEAN.   And I the hotel...

JULIE.   Sit at your desk, entice your customers, pad their bills...

JEAN.   That I'd do myself.

JULIE.   How can anyone be so thoroughly filthy?

JEAN.   Better clean up then!

JULIE.   You lackey, you menial, stand up, when I speak to you!

JEAN.   Menial's strumpet, lackey's whore, shut up and get out of here! Who are you to lecture me on coarseness? None of my kind is ever as coarse as you were tonight. Do you think one of your maids would throw herself at a man the way you did? Have you ever seen any girl of my class offer herself like that? I've only seen it among animals and streetwalkers.

---

[10] *Merde!*: Excrement!

JULIE (*crushed*).   You're right. Hit me, trample on me. I don't deserve any better. I'm worthless. But help me! If you see any way out of this, help me, Jean, please!

JEAN (*more gently*).   I'd be lying if I didn't admit to a sense of triumph in all this, but do you think that a person like me would have dared even to look at someone like you if you hadn't invited it? I'm still amazed...

JULIE.   And proud...

JEAN.   Why not? Though I must say it was too easy to be really exciting.

JULIE.   Go on, hit me, hit me harder!

JEAN (*rising*).   No! Forgive me for what I've said! I don't hit a man when he's down, let alone a woman. I can't deny though, that I'm pleased to find out that what looked so dazzling to us from below was only tinsel, that the hawk's back was only gray, after all, that the lovely complexion was only powder, that those polished fingernails had black edges, and that a dirty handkerchief is still dirty, even if it smells of perfume...! On the other hand, it hurts me to find out that what I was striving for wasn't finer, more substantial. It hurts me to see you sunk so low that you're inferior to your own cook. It hurts like watching flowers beaten down by autumn rains and turned into mud.

JULIE.   You talk as if you were already above me.

JEAN.   I am. You see, I could make you a countess, but you could never make me a count.

JULIE.   But I'm the child of a count—something you could never be!

JEAN.   That's true. But I could be the father of counts—if...

JULIE.   But you're a thief. I'm not.

JEAN.   There are worse things than being a thief! Besides, when I'm working in a house, I consider myself sort of a member of the family, like one of the children. And you don't call it stealing when a child snatches a berry off a full bush. (*His passion is aroused again.*)   Miss Julie, you're a glorious woman, much too good for someone like me! You were drinking and you lost your head. Now you want to cover up your mistake by telling yourself that you love me! You don't. Maybe there was a physical attraction—but then your love is no better than mine.—I could never be satisfied to be no more than an animal to you, and I could never arouse real love in you.

JULIE.   Are you sure of that?

JEAN.   You're suggesting it's possible—Oh, I could fall in love with you, no doubt about it. You're beautiful; you're refined—(*Approaching and taking her hand.*)—cultured, lovable when you want to be, and once you start a fire in a man, it never goes out. (*Putting his arm around her waist.*)   You're like hot, spicy wine, and one kiss from you...(*He tries to lead her out, but she slowly frees herself.*)

JULIE.   Let me go!?—You'll never win me like that.

JEAN.   *How* then?—Not like that? Not with caresses and pretty speeches. Not with plans about the future or rescue from disgrace! *How* then?

JULIE.   How? How? I don't know!—I have no idea!—I detest you as I detest rats, but I can't escape from you.

JEAN. Escape with me!

JULIE (*pulling herself together*).   Escape? Yes, we must escape!—But I'm so tired. Give me a glass of wine?   (JEAN *pours the wine. She looks at her watch.*)   But we must talk first. We still have a little time.   (*She drains the glass, then holds it out for more.*)

JEAN. Don't drink so fast. It'll go to your head.

JULIE.   What does it matter?

JEAN.   What does it matter? It's vulgar to get drunk! What did you want to tell me?

JULIE.   We must escape! But first we must talk, I mean I must talk. You've done all the talking up to now. You told about your life, now I want to tell about mine, so we'll know all about each other before we go off together.

JEAN.   Just a minute! Forgive me! If you don't want to regret it afterwards, you'd better think twice before revealing any secrets about yourself.

JULIE.   Aren't you my friend?

JEAN.   Yes, sometimes! But don't rely on me.

JULIE.   You're only saying that.—Besides, everyone already knows my secrets.— You see, my mother was a commoner—very humble background. She was brought up believing in social equality, women's rights, and all that. The idea of marriage repelled her. So, when my father proposed, she replied that she would never become his wife, but he could be her lover. He insisted that he didn't want the woman he loved to be less respected than he. But his passion ruled him, and when she explained that the world's respect meant nothing to her, he accepted her conditions.

But now his friends avoided him and his life was restricted to taking care of the estate, which couldn't satisfy him. I came into the world—against my mother's wishes, as far as I can understand. She wanted to bring me up as a child of nature, and, what's more, to learn everything a boy had to learn, so that I might be an example of how a woman can be as good as a man. I had to wear boy's clothes and learn to take care of horses, but I was never allowed in the cowshed. I had to groom and harness the horses and go hunting—and even had to watch them slaughter animals—that was disgusting! On the estate men were put on women's jobs and women on men's jobs—with the result that the property became run down and we became the laughingstock of the district. Finally, my father must have awakened from his trance because he rebelled and changed everything his way. My parents were then married quietly. Mother became ill—I don't know what illness it was—but she often had convulsions, hid in the attic and in the garden, and sometimes stayed out all night. Then came the great fire, which you've heard about. The house, the stables, and the cowshed all burned down, under very curious circumstances, suggesting arson, because the accident happened the day after the insurance had expired. The quarterly premium my father sent in was delayed because of a messenger's carelessness and didn't arrive in time.   (*She fills her glass and drinks.*)

JEAN.   Don't drink any more!

JULIE.   Oh, what does it matter.—We were left penniless and had to sleep in the carriages. My father had no idea where to find money to rebuild the house because he had so slighted his old friends that they had forgotten him. Then my mother suggested that he borrow from a childhood friend of hers, a brick manufacturer who lived nearby. Father got the loan without having to pay interest, which surprised him. And that's how the estate was rebuilt.—(*Drinks again.*) Do you know who started the fire?

JEAN. The Countess, your mother.

JULIE. Do you know who the brick manufacturer was?

JEAN. Your mother's lover?

JULIE. Do you know whose money it was?

JEAN. Wait a moment—no, I don't.

JULIE. It was my mother's.

JEAN. You mean the Count's, unless they didn't sign an agreement when they were married.

JULIE. They didn't.—My mother had a small inheritance which she didn't want under my father's control, so she entrusted it to her—friend.

JEAN. Who stole it!

JULIE. Exactly! He kept it.—All this my father found out, but he couldn't bring it to court, couldn't repay his wife's lover, couldn't prove it was his wife's money! It was my mother's revenge for being forced into marriage against her will. It nearly drove him to suicide—there was a rumor that he tried with a pistol, but failed. So, he managed to live through it and my mother had to suffer for what she'd done. You can imagine that those were a terrible five years for me. I loved my father, but I sided with my mother because I didn't know the circumstances. I learned from her to hate men—you've heard how she hated the whole male sex—and I swore to her I'd never be a slave to any man.

JEAN. But you got engaged to that lawyer.

JULIE. In order to make him my slave.

JEAN. And he wasn't willing?

JULIE. He was willing, all right, but I wouldn't let him. I got tired of him.

JEAN. I saw it—out near the stable.

JULIE. What did you see?

JEAN. I saw—how he broke off the engagement.

JULIE. That's a lie! I was the one who broke it off. Has he said that he did? That swine...

JEAN. He was no swine, I'm sure. So, you hate men, Miss Julie?

JULIE. Yes!—Most of the time! But sometimes—when the weakness comes, when passion burns! Oh, God, will the fire never die out?

JEAN. Do you hate me, too?

JULIE. Immeasurably! I'd like to have you put to death, like an animal...

JEAN. I see—the penalty for bestiality—the woman gets two years at hard labor and the animal is put to death. Right?

JULIE. Exactly!

JEAN. But there's no prosecutor here—and no animal. So, what'll we do?

JULIE. Go away!

JEAN. To torment each other to death?

JULIE.   No! To be happy for—two days, a week, as long as we can be happy, and then—die...

JEAN.   Die? That's stupid! It's better to open a hotel!

JULIE   (*without listening*).   —on the shore of Lake Como, where the sun always shines, where the laurels are green at Christmas and the oranges glow.

JEAN.   Lake Como is a rainy hole, and I never saw any oranges outside the stores. But tourists are attracted there because there are plenty of villas to be rented out to lovers, and that's a profitable business.—Do you know why? Because they sign a lease for six months—and then leave after three weeks!

JULIE   (*naively*).   Why after three weeks?

JEAN.   They quarrel, of course! But they still have to pay the rent in full! And so you rent the villas out again. And that's the way it goes, time after time. There's never a shortage of love—even if it doesn't last long!

JULIE.   You don't want to die with me?

JEAN.   I don't want to die at all! For one thing, I like living, and for another, I think suicide is a crime against the Providence which gave us life.

JULIE.   You believe in God? *You?*

JEAN.   Of course I do. And I go to church every other Sunday.—To be honest, I'm tired of all this, and I'm going to bed.

JULIE.   Are you? And do you think I can let it go at that. A man owes something to the woman he's shamed.

JEAN   (*taking out his purse and throwing a silver coin on the table*).   Here! I don't like owing anything to anybody.

JULIE   (*pretending not to notice the insult*).   Do you know what the law states...

JEAN.   Unfortunately the law doesn't state any punishment for the woman who seduces a man!

JULIE   (*as before*).   Do you see any way out but to leave, get married, and then separate?

JEAN.   Suppose I refuse such a *mésalliance?*[11]

JULIE.   *Mésalliance...*

JEAN.   Yes, for me! You see, I come from better stock than you. There's no arsonist in my family.

JULIE.   How do you know?

JEAN.   You can't prove otherwise. We don't keep charts on our ancestors—there's just the police records! But I've read about your family. Do you know who the founder was? He was a miller who let the king sleep with his wife one night during the Danish War. I don't have any noble ancestors like that. I don't have any noble ancestors at all, but I could become one myself.

JULIE.   This is what I get for opening my heart to someone unworthy, for giving my family's honor...

JEAN.   Dishonor!—Well, I told you so: when people drink, they talk, and talk is dangerous!

JULIE.   Oh, how I regret it!—How I regret it!—If you at least loved me.

---

[11] *mésalliance:* Misalliance or mismatch, especially regarding relative social status.

JEAN.   For the last time—what do you want? Shall I cry; shall I jump over your riding crop? Shall I kiss you and lure you off to Lake Como for three weeks, and then God knows what...? What shall I do? What do you want? This is getting painfully embarrassing! But that's what happens when you stick your nose in women's business. Miss Julie! I see that you're unhappy. I know you're suffering, but I can't understand you. We don't have such romantic ideas; there's not this kind of hate between us. Love is a game we play when we get time off from work, but we don't have all day and night, like you. I think you're sick, really sick. Your mother was crazy, and her ideas have poisoned your life.

JULIE.   Be kind to me. At least now you're talking like a human being.

JEAN.   Be human yourself, then. You spit on me, and you won't let me wipe myself off—

JULIE.   Help me! Help me! Just tell me what to do, where to go!

JEAN.   In God's name, if I only knew myself.

JULIE.   I've been crazy, out of my mind, but isn't there any way out?

JEAN.   Stay here and keep calm! No one knows anything!

JULIE.   Impossible! The others know and Kristine knows.

JEAN.   No they don't, and they'd never believe a thing like that!

JULIE   (*hesitantly*).   But—it could happen again!

JEAN.   That's true!

JULIE.   And then?

JEAN   (*frightened*).   Then?—Why didn't I think about that? Yes, there is only one thing to do—get away from here! Right away! I can't come with you, then we'd be finished, so you'll have to go alone—away—anywhere!

JULIE.   Alone?—Where?—I can't do that!

JEAN.   You must! And before the Count gets back! If you stay, you know what'll happen. Once you make a mistake like this, you want to continue because the damage has already been done.... Then you get bolder and bolder—until finally you're caught! So leave! Later you can write to the Count and confess everything—except that it was me! He'll never guess who it was, and he's not going to be eager to find out, anyway.

JULIE.   I'll go if you come with me.

JEAN.   Are you out of your head? Miss Julie runs away with her servant! In two days it would be in the newspapers, and that's something your father would never live through.

JULIE.   I can't go and I can't stay! Help me! I'm so tired, so terribly tired.—Order me! Set me in motion—I can't think or act on my own...

JEAN.   What miserable creatures you people are! You strut around with your noses in the air as if you were the lords of creation! All right, I'll order you. Go upstairs and get dressed! Get some money for the trip, and then come back down!

JULIE   (*in a half-whisper*).   Come up with me!

JEAN.   To your room?—Now you're crazy again!   (*Hesitates for a moment.*)   No! Go, at once!   (*Takes her hand to lead her out.*)

JULIE   (*as she leaves*).   Speak kindly to me, Jean!

JEAN.   An order always sounds unkind—now you know how it feels.   (JEAN, *alone, sighs with relief. He sits at the table, takes out a notebook and pencil, and begins adding up figures, counting aloud as he works. He continues in dumb show until Kristine enters, dressed for church. She is carrying a white tie and shirt front.*)

KRISTINE.   Lord Jesus, what a mess! What have you been up to?

JEAN.   Oh, Miss Julie dragged everybody in here. You mean you didn't hear anything? You must have been sleeping soundly.

KRISTINE.   Like a log.

JEAN.   And dressed for church already?

KRISTINE.   Of course! You remember you promised to come with me to communion today!

JEAN.   Oh, yes, that's right.—And you brought my things. Come on, then!   (*He sits down.* KRISTINE *starts to put on his shirt front and tie. Pause.* JEAN *begins sleepily.*)   What's the gospel text for today?

KRISTINE.   On St. John's Day?—the beheading of John the Baptist, I should think!

JEAN.   Ah, that'll be a long one, for sure.—Hey, you're choking me!—Oh, I'm sleepy, so sleepy!

KRISTINE.   Yes, what have you been doing, up all night? Your face is absolutely green.

JEAN.   I've been sitting here gabbing with Miss Julie.

KRISTINE.   She has no idea what's proper, that one!   (*Pause.*)

JEAN.   You know, Kristine…

KRISTINE.   What?

JEAN.   It's really strange when you think about it.—Her!

KRISTINE.   What's so strange?

JEAN.   Everything!   (*Pause.*)

KRISTINE   (*looking at the half-empty glasses standing on the table*).   Have you been drinking together, too?

JEAN.   Yes.

KRISTINE.   Shame on you!—Look me in the eye!

JEAN.   Well?

KRISTINE.   Is it possible? Is it possible?

JEAN   (*thinking it over for a moment*).   Yes, it is.

KRISTINE.   Ugh! I never would have believed it! No, shame on you, shame!

JEAN.   You're not jealous of her, are you?

KRISTINE.   No, not of her! If it had been Clara or Sofie I'd have scratched your eyes out!—I don't know why, but that's the way I feel.—Oh, its disgusting!

JEAN.   Are you angry at her, then?

KRISTINE.   No, at you! That was an awful thing to do, awful! Poor girl!—No, I don't care who knows it—I won't stay in a house where we can't respect the people we work for.

JEAN.   Why should we respect them?

KRISTINE.   You're so clever, you tell me! Do you want to wait on people who can't behave decently? Do you? You disgrace yourself that way, if you ask me.

JEAN.   But it's a comfort to know they aren't any better than us.

KRISTINE. Not for me. If they're no better, what do we have to strive for to better ourselves.—And think of the Count! Think of him! As if he hasn't had enough misery in his life! Lord Jesus! No, I won't stay in this house any longer!—And it had to be with someone like you! If it had been that lawyer, if it had been a real gentleman…

JEAN. What do you mean?

KRISTINE. Oh, you're all right for what you are, but there are men and gentlemen, after all!—No, this business with Miss Julie I can never forget. She was so proud, so arrogant with men, you wouldn't have believed she could just go and give herself—and to someone like you! And she was going to have poor Diana shot for running after the gatekeepers' mutt!—Yes, I'm giving my notice, I mean it—I won't stay here any longer. On the twenty-fourth of October, I leave!

JEAN. And then?

KRISTINE. Well, since the subject has come up, it's about time you looked around for something since we're going to get married, in any case.

JEAN. Where am I going to look? I couldn't find a job like this if I was married.

KRISTINE. No, that's true. But you can find work as a porter or as a caretaker in some government office. The state doesn't pay much, I know, but it's secure, and there's a pension for the wife and children…

JEAN (*grimacing*). That's all very well, but it's a bit early for me to think about dying for a wife and children. My ambitions are a little higher than that.

KRISTINE. Your ambitions, yes! Well, you have obligations, too! Think about them!

JEAN. Don't start nagging me about obligations. I know what I have to do! (*Listening for something outside.*) Besides, this is something we have plenty of time to think over. Go and get ready for church.

KRISTINE. Who's that walking around up there?

JEAN. I don't know, unless it's Clara.

KRISTINE (*going*). You don't suppose it's the Count, who came home without us hearing him?

JEAN (*frightened*). The Count? No, I don't think so. He'd have rung.

KRISTINE (*going*). Well, God help us! I've never seen anything like this before. (*The sun has risen and shines through the treetops in the park. The light shifts gradually until it slants in through the windows.* JEAN *goes to the door and signals.* MISS JULIE *enters, dressed in travel clothes and carrying a small bird cage, covered with a cloth, which she places on a chair.*)

JULIE. I'm ready now.

JEAN. Shh! Kristine is awake.

JULIE (*very nervous during the following*). Does she suspect something?

JEAN. She doesn't know anything. But my God, you look awful!

JULIE. Why? How do I look?

JEAN. You're pale as a ghost and—excuse me, but your face is dirty.

JULIE. Let me wash up then.—(*She goes to the basin and washes her hands and face.*) Give me a towel!—Oh—the sun's coming up.

JEAN. Then the goblins will disappear.

JULIE. Yes, there must have been goblins out last night!—Jean, listen, come with me! I have some money now.

JEAN (*hesitantly*). Enough?

JULIE. Enough to start with. Come with me! I just can't travel alone on a day like this—midsummer day on a stuffy train—jammed in among crowds of people staring at me. Eternal delays at every station, while I'd wish I had wings. No, I can't, I can't! And then there'll be memories, memories of midsummer days when I was little. The church—decorated with birch leaves and lilacs; dinner at the big table with relatives and friends; the afternoons in the park, dancing, music, flowers, and games. Oh, no matter how far we travel, the memories will follow in the baggage car, with remorse and guilt!

JEAN. I'll go with you—but right away, before it's too late. Right this minute!

JULIE. Get dressed, then! (*Picking up the bird cage.*)

JEAN. But no baggage! It would give us away!

JULIE. No, nothing! Only what we can have in the compartment with us.

JEAN (*has taken his hat*). What've you got there? What is it?

JULIE. It's only my greenfinch. I couldn't leave her behind.

JEAN. What? Bring a bird cage with us? You're out of your head! Put it down!

JULIE. It's the only thing I'm taking from my home—the only living being that loves me, since Diana was unfaithful. Don't be cruel! Let me take her!

JEAN. Put the cage down, I said!—And don't talk so loudly—Kristine will hear us!

JULIE. No, I won't leave her in the hands of strangers! I'd rather you killed her.

JEAN. Bring the thing here, then, I'll cut its head off!

JULIE. Oh! But don't hurt her! Don't…no, I can't.

JEAN. Bring it here! I can!

JULIE (*taking the bird out of the cage and kissing it*). Oh, my little Serena, must you die and leave your mistress?

JEAN. Please don't make a scene! Your whole future is at stake! Hurry up! (*He snatches the bird from her, carries it over to the chopping block, and picks up a meat cleaver. MISS JULIE turns away.*) You should have learned how to slaughter chickens instead of how to fire pistols. (*He chops off the bird's head.*) Then you wouldn't feel faint at the sight of blood.

JULIE (*screaming*). Kill me, too! Kill me! You, who can slaughter an innocent animal without blinking an eye! Oh, how I hate, how I detest you! There's blood between us now! I curse the moment I set eyes on you! I curse the moment I was conceived in my mother's womb!

JEAN. What good does cursing do? Let's go!

JULIE (*approaching the chopping block, as if drawn against her will*). No, I don't want to go yet. I can't…until I see…Shh! I hear a carriage—(*She listens, but her eyes never leave the cleaver and the chopping block.*)…Oh—I'd like to see your blood and your brains on a chopping block!—I'd like to see your whole sex swimming in a sea of blood, like my little bird…I think I could drink from your skull! I'd like to bathe my feet in your open chest and eat your heart roasted whole!—You think I'm weak. You think I love you because my womb craved your seed. You think I want to carry your spawn under my heart and nourish it with my blood—bear your child and take your name! By the way, what is your family name? I've never heard it.—Do you have one? I was to be Mrs. Bootblack—or Madame Pigsty.—You dog, who wears my collar, you lackey, who bears my coat of arms on your buttons—do I have to share you with my cook, compete with my own servant? Oh! Oh! Oh!—You think I'm a coward who wants to run away! No, now I'm staying—and let the storm break! My father will come home…to find his desk broken open…and his money gone! Then he'll ring—that bell…twice for his valet—and then he'll send for the police…and then I'll tell everything! Everything! Oh, what a relief it'll be to have it all end—if only it will end!—And then he'll have a stroke and die…That'll be the end of all of us—and there'll be peace… quiet…eternal rest!—And then our coat of arms will be broken against his coffin—the family title extinct—but the valet's line will go on in an orphanage…win laurels in the gutter, and end in jail!

JEAN. There's the blue blood talking! Very good, Miss Julie! Just don't let that miller out of the closet! (KRISTINE *enters, dressed for church, with a psalm-book in her hand.*)

JULIE (*rushing to* KRISTINE *and falling into her arms, as if seeking protection*). Help, me Kristine! Help me against this man!

KRISTINE (*unmoved and cold*). What a fine way to behave on a Sunday morning! (*Sees the chopping block.*) And look at this mess!—What does all this mean? Why all this screaming and carrying on?

JULIE. Kristine! You're a woman and my friend! Beware of this swine!

JEAN (*uncomfortable*). While you ladies discuss this, I'll go in and shave. (*Slips off right.*)

JULIE. You must listen to me so you'll understand!

KRISTINE. No, I could never understand such disgusting behavior! Where are you off to in your traveling clothes?—And he had his hat on.—Well?—Well?—

JULIE. Listen to me, Kristine! Listen, and I'll tell you everything—

KRISTINE. I don't want to hear it…

JULIE. But you must listen to me…

KRISTINE. What about? If it's about this silliness with Jean, I'm not interested, because it's none of my business. But if you're thinking of tricking him into running out, we'll soon put a stop to that!

JULIE (*extremely nervous*). Try to be calm now, Kristine, and listen to me! I can't stay here, and neither can Jean—so we must go away…

KRISTINE. Hm, hm!

JULIE (*brightening*). You see, I just had an idea—What if all three of us go— abroad—to Switzerland and start a hotel together?—I have money, you see— and Jean and I could run it—and I thought you, you could take care of the kitchen…Wouldn't that be wonderful?—Say yes! And come with us, and then everything will be settled!—Oh, do say yes! (*Embracing* KRISTINE *and patting her warmly.*)

KRISTINE (*coolly, thoughtfully*). Hm, hm!

JULIE (*presto tempo*).[12] You've never traveled, Kristine.—You must get out and see the world. You can't imagine how much fun it is to travel by train—always new faces—new countries.—And when we get to Hamburg, we'll stop off at the zoo—you'll like that.—and then we'll go to the theater and the opera—and when we get to Munich, dear, there we have museums, with Rubens and Raphael, the great painters, as you know.—You've heard of Munich, where King Ludwig lived—the king who went mad.—And then we'll see his castles—they're still there and they're like castles in fairy tales.—And from there it isn't far to Switzerland—and the Alps.—Imagine—the Alps have snow on them even in the middle of summer!—And oranges grow there and laurel trees that are green all year round—

> (JEAN *can be seen in the wings right, sharpening his razor on a strop which he holds with his teeth and his left hand. He listens to the conversation with satisfaction, nodding now and then in approval.* MISS JULIE *continues tempo prestissimo.*)[13]

And then we'll start a hotel—and I'll be at the desk, while Jean greets the guests…does the shopping…writes letters.—You have no idea what a life it'll be—the train whistles blowing and the carriages arriving and the bells ringing in the rooms and down in the restaurant.—And I'll make out the bills—and I know how to salt them!…You'll never believe how timid travelers are when they have to pay their bills!—And you—you'll be in charge of the kitchen.—Naturally, you won't have to stand over the stove yourself.—And since you're going to be seen by people, you'll have to wear beautiful clothes.—And you, with your looks—no, I'm not flattering you—one fine day you'll grab yourself a husband!—You'll see!—A rich Englishman—they're so easy to—(*Slowing down.*)—catch—and then we'll get rich—and build ourselves a villa on Lake Como.—It's true it rains there a little now and then, but—(*Dully.*)—the sun has to shine sometimes—although it looks dark—and then…of course we could always come back home again—(*Pause.*)—here—or somewhere else—

KRISTINE. Listen, Miss Julie, do you believe all this?

JULIE (*crushed*). Do I believe it?

KRISTINE. Yes!

JULIE (*wearily*). I don't know. I don't believe in anything anymore. (*She sinks down on the bench and cradles her head in her arms on the table.*) Nothing! Nothing at all!

KRISTINE (*turning right to where* JEAN *is standing*). So, you thought you'd run out!

JEAN (*embarrassed; puts the razor on the table*). Run out? That's no way to put it. You hear Miss Julie's plan, and even if she is tired after being up all night, it's still a practical plan.

---

[12] *presto tempo:* At a rapid pace. [13] *tempo prestissimo:* At a very rapid pace.

KRISTINE.   Now you listen to me! Did you think I'd work as a cook for that…

JEAN   (*sharply*).   You watch what you say in front of your mistress! Do you understand?

KRISTINE.   Mistress!

JEAN.   Yes!

KRISTINE.   Listen to him! Listen to him!

JEAN.   Yes, you listen! It'd do you good to listen more and talk less! Miss Julie is your mistress. If you despise her, you have to despise yourself for the same reason!

KRISTINE.   I've always had enough self-respect—

JEAN.   —to be able to despise other people!

KRISTINE.   —to stop me from doing anything that's beneath me. You can't say that the Count's cook has been up to something with the groom or the swineherd! Can you?

JEAN.   No, you were lucky enough to get hold of a gentleman!

KRISTINE.   Yes, a gentleman who sells the Count's oats from the stable.

JEAN.   You should talk—taking a commission from the grocer and bribes from the butcher.

KRISTINE.   What?

JEAN.   And you say you can't respect your employers any longer. You, you, you!

KRISTINE.   Are you coming to church with me, now? You could use a good sermon after your fine deed!

JEAN.   No, I'm not going to church today. You'll have to go alone and confess what you've been up to.

KRISTINE.   Yes, I'll do that, and I'll bring back enough forgiveness for you, too. The Savior suffered and died on the Cross for all our sins, and if we go to Him with faith and a penitent heart, He takes all our sins on Himself.

JEAN.   Even grocery sins?

JULIE.   And do you believe that, Kristine?

KRISTINE.   It's my living faith, as sure as I stand here. It's the faith I learned as a child, Miss Julie, and kept ever since. "Where sin abounded, grace did much more abound!"

JULIE.   Oh, if I only had your faith. If only…

KRISTINE.   Well, you see, we can't have it without God's special grace, and that isn't given to everyone—

JULIE.   Who is it given to then?

KRISTINE.   That's the great secret of the workings of grace, Miss Julie, and God is no respecter of persons, for the last shall be the first…

JULIE.   Then He does respect the last.

KRISTINE   (*continuing*).   …and it is easier for a camel to go through the eye of a needle, than for a rich man to enter the Kingdom of God. That's how it is, Miss Julie! Anyhow, I'm going now—alone, and on the way I'm going to tell the groom not to let any horses out, in case anyone wants to leave before the Count gets back!—Goodbye! (*Leaves.*)

JEAN.   What a witch!—And all this because of a greenfinch!—

JULIE (*dully*). Never mind the greenfinch!—Can you see any way out of this? Any end to it?

JEAN (*thinking*). No!

JULIE. What would you do in my place?

JEAN. In your place? Let's see—as a person of position, as a woman who had— fallen. I don't know—wait, now I know.

JULIE (*taking the razor and making a gesture*). You mean like this?

JEAN. Yes! But—understand—*I* wouldn't do it! That's the difference between us!

JULIE. Because you're a man and I'm a woman? What sort of difference is that?

JEAN. The usual difference—between a man and a woman.

JULIE (*with the razor in her hand*). I want to, but I can't!—My father couldn't either, the time he should have done it.

JEAN. No, he shouldn't have! He had to revenge himself first.

JULIE. And now my mother is revenged again, through me.

JEAN. Didn't you ever love your father, Miss Julie?

JULIE. Oh yes, deeply, but I've hated him, too. I must have done so without realizing it! It was he who brought me up to despise my own sex, making me half woman, half man. Whose fault is what's happened? My father's, my mother's, my own? My own? I don't have anything that's my own. I don't have a single thought that I didn't get from my father, not in emotion that I didn't get from my mother, and this last idea—that all people are equal—I got that from my fiancé.—That's why I called him a swine! How can it be my fault? Shall I let Jesus take on the blame, the way Kristine does?—No, I'm too proud to do that and too sensible—thanks to my father's teachings.—And as for someone rich not going to heaven, that's a lie. But Kristine won't get in—how will she explain the money she has in the savings bank? Whose fault is it?—What does it matter whose fault it is? I'm still the one who has to bear the blame, face the consequences...

JEAN. Yes, but...(*The bell rings sharply twice.* MISS JULIE *jumps up.* JEAN *changes his coat.*) The Count is back! Do you suppose Kristine—(*He goes to the speaking tube, taps the lid, and listens.*)

JULIE. He's been to his desk!

JEAN. It's Jean, sir! (*Listening; the audience cannot hear the Count's voice.*) Yes, sir! (*Listening.*) Yes, sir! Right away! (*Listening.*) At once, sir! (*Listening*) I see, in half an hour!

JULIE (*desperately frightened*). What did he say? Dear Lord, what did he say?

JEAN. He wants his boots and his coffee in half an hour.

JULIE. So, in half an hour! Oh, I'm so tired. I'm not able to do anything. I can't repent, can't run away, can't stay, can't live—can't die! Help me now! Order me, and I'll obey like a dog! Do me this last service, save my honor, save his name! You know what I *should* do, but don't have the will to...You will it, you order me to do it!

JEAN. I don't know why—but now I can't either—I don't understand.—It's as if this coat made it impossible for me to order you to do anything.—And now, since the Count spoke to me—I—I can't really explain it—but—ah, it's the damn lackey in me!—I think if the Count came down here now—and ordered me to cut my throat, I'd do it on the spot.

JULIE.   Then pretend you're he, and I'm you!—You gave such a good performance before when you knelt at my feet.—You were a real nobleman.—Or—have you ever seen a hypnotist in the theater? (JEAN *nods.*) He says to his subject. "Take the broom," and he takes it. He says: "Sweep," and he sweeps—

JEAN.   But the subject has to be asleep.

JULIE (*ecstatically*).   I'm already asleep.—The whole room is like smoke around me…and you look like an iron stove…shaped like a man in black, with a tall hat—and your eyes glow like coals when the fire is dying—and your face is a white patch, like ashes—(*The sunlight has reached the floor and now shines on Jean.*)—it's so warm and good—(*She rubs her hands as if warming them before a fire.*)—and bright—and so peaceful!

JEAN (*taking the razor and putting it in her hand*).   Here's the broom! Go now while it's bright—out to the barn—and…(*Whispers in her ear.*)

JULIE (*awake*).   Thank you. I'm going now to rest! But just tell me—that those who are first can also receive the gift of grace. Say it, even if you don't believe it.

JEAN.   The first? No, I can't—But wait—Miss Julie—now I know! You're no longer among the first—you're now among—the last!

JULIE.   That's true.—I'm among the very last. I'm the last one of all! Oh!—But now I can't go!—Tell me once more to go!

JEAN.   No, now I can't either! I can't!

JULIE.   And the first shall be the last!

JEAN.   Don't think, don't think! Your taking all my strength from me, making me a coward.—What was that? I thought the bell moved!—No! Shall we stuff paper in it?—To be so afraid of a bell!—But it isn't just a bell.—There's someone behind it—a hand sets it in motion—and something else sets the hand in motion.—Maybe if you cover your ears—cover your ears! But then it rings even louder! rings until someone answers.—And then it's too late! And then the police come—and—then—(*The bell rings twice loudly,* JEAN *flinches, then straightens up.*) It's horrible! But there's no other way!—Go! (MISS JULIE *walks firmly out through the door.*)

Translated by Harry G. Carlson

Journal Entry

What is your evaluation of Jean? To what extent do you empathize with him?

Textual Considerations

1. What does Jean mean when he tells Julie, "You've fallen down to my level and I'll lift you up again"?
2. What do Julie's and Jean's dreams reveal about their expectations as human beings? Explain.

3. What is Kristine's role? Characterize her relationship with Jean and Julie.
4. Do you view Julie as a tragic character? Explain.
5. Discuss the Count's boots, the riding whip, and the bell that Jean is afraid of at the end of the play.
6. What is the thematic significance of the fairy-tale elements in the play? Considering his realistic theme, why would Strindberg explore these elements?

Cultural Contexts

1. How does Strindberg's play illustrate the issue of "social climbing or falling, of higher and lower, better or worse, man or woman" in the Preface to *Miss Julie*?
2. Working with your group, identify the circumstances that lead Julie to commit suicide. Can you reach a consensus about a better solution?

WRITING TOPICS

1. Discuss the interplay of rationality and irrationality in "The Yellow Wallpaper" and/or *Medea*. Trace this theme in either text pointing out ironies and contradictions you observed.

2. In "Home Burial," the husband says "a man must partly give up being a man/With women folk." What does he mean? To what extent do you agree or disagree? How is his thesis relevant to the theme of identity in gender relationships?

3. Compare and contrast the portrayals of husbands by Chopin, Walker, Freeman, and/or Rifaat. To what extent does each find identity and fulfillment in his role? Cite evidence to support your view.

4. Woman as rebel is the focus of the texts by Freeman, Two Eagles, Behn, and Sexton. Analyze the causes and effects of their rebellion on the gender relations in each text.

5. Several authors representing diverse cultures focus on economics and gender. Compare and contrast the degree to which economics shapes gender relationships in *Medea, Miss Julie,* and/or "Another Evening at the Club."

6. Conflict plays a major role in "The Yellow Wallpaper" and "Roselily." Analyze the causes and effects of the protagonists' desires for personal autonomy versus the responsibility implicit in their roles as wives.

7. Meier and Woolf discuss professions and gender from different perspectives. Review both essays, and write an analysis of the extent to which audience gender influenced their choices of situation, examples, and vocabulary.

8. Apply to the characters of Medea and Miss Julie the concept that women's worst enemy is the enemy inside themselves or their inability to change their own ingrained psychological structures. Cite evidence from both plays to support your point of view.

9. Women's sexuality is explained from different vantage points in several poems. Compare and contrast the attitudes toward this issue in the poems by Greenberg, Behn, Sexton, and de la Cruz.

10. According to the French feminist Simon de Beauvoir, "The word love has by no means the same sense for both sexes, and this is one of the most serious misunderstandings that divide them." Apply this thesis to any three texts in Part Two.

11. In "The Storm" and "A Respectable Woman," Chopin challenges traditional views of romantic love and marital fidelity, suggesting that for both men and women marriage may involve compromise as well as subordination of personal identity. Using both texts, argue for or against Chopin's point of view on marriage.

PART ASSIGNMENTS

RESEARCH TOPICS

1. Several works in Part Two examine the history of women from different sociohistorical points of view. To understand what these texts portray in light of the women's liberation movement, investigate the history of one of the following: Mary Wollstonecraft's *A Vindication of the Rights of Women* (1790), Olympe de Gorges's *Declaration of the Rights of Women and Female Citizens* (1791), the suffragette movement in nineteenth-century England, the movement of the American feminists in the 1970s, or the black women's movement in America in the three last decades. Sources: Search under Women-History, Women-France, Feminism, Gender, American Women and Politics, African-American Women-History.
      You may also check:
   Krichmar, Albert. *The Women's Movement in the Seventies: An International English-Language Bibliography.*
   Sims, Janet. *The Progress of Afro-American Women: A Selected Bibliography and Resource Guide.*
   Williams, Ora. *American Black Women in the Arts and Social Sciences: A Bibliographic Survey,* revised and expanded edition.

2. To associate visual and verbal arts, look at how some world-famous paintings such as Adolf Rifino's *The Married Couple,* Mary Cassatt's paintings on maternity, and Picasso's *Portrait of Gertrude Stein* evoke specific images of women as wives, mothers, and intellectuals. Then investigate how women are represented in some of the literary portraits in this part. Consider also how these visual and literary texts reflect cultural revisions of women's images.

3. To examine how different societies have developed rigid codes of masculinity, write a documented paper on three literary texts of your choice that portray stereotypical images of men as tough, powerful, stoic, successful, and sexually aggressive. Consider also their effects on personal identity. You may also use primary texts such as "Another Evening at the Club," "Ragazza," "Home Burial," and "She Proves the Inconsistency...."

GROUP RESEARCH TOPIC

The films *The Crying Game, Dead Ringers, Psycho, Vertigo,* and *Zelig* have male protagonists with identity problems. Discuss one or two of these films in depth, identifying what you think the nature of the problem is in each case. In your opinion, is the source of the problem, as presented in the story, directly traceable to the character's personal history, or does it seem a product of social conventions or prohibitions?

PART THREE
War and Violence

Fiction

A Mystery of Heroism, Stephen Crane ◆ *The Sniper*, Liam O'Flaherty ◆ *Silence*, Tadeusz Borowski ◆ *The Hour of Truth*, Isabel Allende ◆ *Spoils of War*, Janice Mirikitani ◆ *The Curse*, Andre Dubus ◆ *Battle Royal*, Ralph Ellison

Essays

A Brother's Murder, Brent Staples ◆ *Vietnam: What I Remember*, David W. Powell

Poetry

The Man He Killed, Thomas Hardy ◆ *What Were They Like?*, Denise Levertov ◆ *Babiy Yar*, Yevgeny Yevtushenko ◆ *Prisons of Silence*, Janice Mirikitani ◆ *Disabled*, Wilfred Owen ◆ *The Dying Veteran*, Walt Whitman ◆ *First Practice*, Gary Gildner ◆ *Hope*, Ariel Dorfman ◆ *Quote from the Bureau of Information, from the* Argus, *August 27, 1986: "The Situation in Soweto Is Not Abnormal,"* Mavis Smallberg ◆ *Waking This Morning*, Muriel Rukeyser ◆ *The Artilleryman's Vision*, Walt Whitman ◆ *The Colonel*, Carolyn Forché ◆ *The Visitor*, Carolyn Forché ◆ *The Memory of Elena*, Carolyn Forché ◆ *As Children Together*, Carolyn Forché

Drama

Lysistrata, Aristophanes ◆ *Picnic on the Battlefield*, Fernando Arrabal

Why do nations go to war? What causes individuals to engage in violence? What is the relation between power and violence? Why do poets, artists, musicians, and filmmakers create images celebrating the glories of war? What causes so many people to prefer conflict and tension to stability and calm? According to German-American social philosopher Hannah Arendt (1906–1975), a major cause of war throughout human history is the conflict between freedom and tyranny. Ironically, even in the name of freedom, innocent people are tortured, strangled, exiled, and murdered.

In fact, ordinary people often bear a greater share of the human costs of war than do their leaders who initiate the conflicts. The writers of many texts in Part Three try to make sense of a world where violence is perpetrated not only by the horrors of war but also by the racial and ethnic conflicts erupting almost daily in cities throughout the United States and other countries of the world.

Why has the human imagination always been captivated by heroism and the horrors of war? And why do so few literary works celebrate the virtues and possibilities of peace? The texts in this part pose many questions about the nature and consequences of war and violence. Some, such as Walt Whitman's "The Dying Veteran," celebrate the glory and victory of war, whereas others, such as Wilfred Owen's "Disabled," portray the alienation and rejection experienced by returning veterans wounded physically and psychologically in the trench warfare of World War I.

Another series of texts here explores the arbitrariness of war by attacking the tradition of "the blind hatred of the enemy." Although Thomas Hardy and Denise Levertov belong to different historical moments, each poet, in "The Man He Killed" and "What Were They Like?" evokes war's irrationality by attempting to portray the enemy as a human being with a personal and cultural identity. "The Sniper," a story that dramatizes the suspense of an urban guerrilla episode during civil war in Ireland, brings the concern of the "myth of the enemy" even closer to home.

One of the most devastating aspects of World War II was Hitler's attempt to exterminate the Jewish people in the death camps of the Third Reich. In "Silence," by Tadeusz Borowski, you will enter the bizarre world of the concentration camp, a terrifying reminder of human depravity, and in Yevtushenko's "Babiy Yar," you will share the courageous attempts of the poet to identify with the "enemy"—the Jewish victims of Stalin's massacre.

Other contemporary selections in Part Three focus on Latin America, recreating conditions analogous to those of war: violence, torture, and dictatorship. In "Hope" for example, the Chilean poet Ariel Dorfman meditates on the "times," the "world," and the "land" that brutalized human beings through the use of torture, while Carolyn Forché, writing on her experiences in El Salvador, reminds us that the human spirit can sometimes transcend the tortured body.

To what extent can the violence of war abroad become also the catalyst for racial and sexual violence at home? Janice Mirikitani's "Spoils of War" and David W. Powell's "Vietnam: What I Remember" portray the effects of post-traumatic stress disorder on Vietnam veterans and civilian victims.

It is generally acknowledged that alienation and apathy often lead to violence, and we read daily about gratuitous acts of violence, the subject of Andre Dubus's "The Curse" and Brent Staples's "A Brother's Murder". Racial violence is also a daily reality whether in a small town in the South in "Battle Royal," or in Soweto, a Black township in South Africa.

As you explore the complexities of war and violence in these and other texts, you may find yourself reexamining your presuppositions about both and considering alternative solutions to conflict. As Arendt again reminds us, "The end of war…is peace or victory; but to the question *and what is the end of peace?* there is no answer. Peace is an absolute, even though in recorded history persons of warfare have nearly always outlasted persons of peace." Perhaps it is time, in John Lennon's words, to "give peace a chance."

Stephen Crane
1896

A Mystery of Heroism

The dark uniforms of the men were so coated with dust from the incessant wrestling of the two armies that the regiment almost seemed a part of the clay bank which shielded them from the shells. On the top of the hill a battery was arguing in tremendous roars with some other guns, and to the eye of the infantry, the artillerymen, the guns, the caissons, the horses, were distinctly outlined upon the blue sky. When a piece was fired, a red streak as round as a log flashed low in the heavens, like a monstrous bolt of lightning. The men of the battery wore white duck trousers, which somehow emphasized their legs; and when they ran and crowded in little groups at the bidding of the shouting officers, it was more impressive than usual to the infantry.

Fred Collins, of A Company, was saying: "Thunder! I wisht I had a drink. Ain't there any water round here?" Then somebody yelled, "There goes th' bugler!"

As the eyes of half the regiment swept in one machinelike movement there was an instant's picture of a horse in a great convulsive leap of a death wound and a rider leaning back with a crooked arm and spread fingers before his face. On the ground was the crimson terror of an exploding shell, with fibres of flame that seemed like lances. A glittering bugle swung clear of the rider's back as fell headlong the horse and the man. In the air was an odour as from a conflagration.

Sometimes they of the infantry looked down at a fair little meadow which spread at their feet. Its long, green grass was rippling gently in a breeze. Beyond it was the gray form of a house half torn to pieces by shells and by the busy axes of soldiers who had pursued firewood. The line of an old fence was now dimly marked by long weeds and by an occasional post. A shell had blown the well-house to fragments. Little lines of gray smoke ribboning upward from some embers indicated the place where had stood the barn.

From beyond a curtain of green woods there came the sound of some stupendous scuffle, as if two animals of the size of islands were fighting. At a distance there were occasional appearances of swift-moving men, horses, batteries, flags, and with the crashing of infantry volleys were heard, often, wild and frenzied cheers. In the midst of it all Smith and Ferguson, two privates of A Company, were engaged in a heated discussion, which involved the greatest questions of the national existence.

The battery on the hill presently engaged in a frightful duel. The white legs of the gunners scampered this way and that way, and the officers redoubled their shouts. The guns, with their demeanours of stolidity and courage, were typical of something infinitely self-possessed in this clamour of death that swirled around the hill.

One of a "swing" team was suddenly smitten quivering to the ground, and his maddened brethren dragged his torn body in their struggle to escape from this turmoil and danger. A young soldier astride one of the leaders swore and fumed in his saddle, and furiously jerked at the bridle. An officer screamed out an order so violently that his voice broke and ended the sentence in a falsetto shriek.

The leading company of the infantry regiment was somewhat exposed, and the colonel ordered it moved more fully under the shelter of the hill. There was the clank of steel against steel.

A lieutenant of the battery rode down and passed them, holding his right arm carefully in his left hand. And it was as if this arm was not at all a part of him, but belonged to another man. His sober and reflective charger went slowly. The officer's face was grimy and perspiring, and his uniform was tousled as if he had been in direct grapple with an enemy. He smiled grimly when the men stared at him. He turned his horse toward the meadow.

Collins, of A Company, said: "I wisht I had a drink. I bet there's water in that there ol' well yonder!"

"Yes; but how you goin' to git it?"

For the little meadow which intervened was now suffering a terrible onslaught of shells. Its green and beautiful calm had vanished utterly. Brown earth was being flung in monstrous handfuls. And there was a massacre of the young blades of grass. They were being torn, burned, obliterated. Some curious fortune of the battle had made this gentle little meadow the object of the red hate of the shells, and each one as it exploded seemed like an imprecation in the face of a maiden.

The wounded officer who was riding across this expanse said to himself, "Why, they couldn't shoot any harder if the whole army was massed here!"

A shell struck the gray ruins of the house, and as, after the roar, the shattered wall fell in fragments, there was a noise which resembled the flapping of shutters during a wild gale of winter. Indeed, the infantry paused in the shelter of the bank appeared as men standing upon a shore contemplating a madness of the sea. The angel of calamity had under its glance the battery upon the hill. Fewer white-legged men laboured about the guns. A shell had smitten one of the pieces, and after the flare, the smoke, the dust, the wrath of this blow were gone, it was possible to see white legs stretched horizontally on the ground. And at that interval to the rear, where it is the business of battery horses to stand with their noses to the fight awaiting the command to drag their guns out of the destruction or into it or wheresoever these incomprehensible humans demanded with whip and spur—in this line of passive and dumb spectators, whose fluttering hearts yet would not let them forget the iron laws of man's control of them—in this rank of brute-soldiers there had been relentless and hideous carnage. From the ruck of bleeding and prostrate horses, the men of the infantry could see one animal raising its stricken body with its fore legs, and turning its nose with mystic and profound eloquence toward the sky.

Some comrades joked Collins about his thirst. "Well, if yeh want a drink so bad, why don't yeh go git it!"

"Well, I will in a minnet, if yeh don't shut up!"

A lieutenant of artillery floundered his horse straight down the hill with as great concern as it were level ground. As he galloped past the colonel of the infantry, he threw up his hand in swift salute. "We've got to get out of that," he roared angrily. He was a black-bearded officer, and his eyes, which resembled beads, sparkled like those of an insane man. His jumping horse sped along the column of infantry.

The fat major, standing carelessly with his sword held horizontally behind him and with his legs far apart, looked after the receding horseman and laughed. "He wants to get back with orders pretty quick, or there'll be no batt'ry left," he observed.

The wise young captain of the second company hazarded to the lieutenant colonel that the enemy's infantry would probably soon attack the hill, and the lieutenant colonel snubbed him.

A private in one of the rear companies looked out over the meadow, and then turned to a companion and said, "Look there, Jim!" It was the wounded officer from the battery, who some time before had started to ride across the meadow, supporting his right arm carefully with his left hand. This man had encountered a shell apparently at a time when no one perceived him, and he could now be seen lying face downward with a stirruped foot stretched across the body of his dead horse. A leg of the charger extended slantingly upward precisely as stiff as a stake. Around this motionless pair the shells still howled.

There was a quarrel in A Company. Collins was shaking his fist in the faces of some laughing comrades. "Dern yeh! I ain't afraid t' go. If yeh say much, I will go!"

"Oh course, yeh will! You'll run through that there medder, won't yeh?"

Collins said, in a terrible voice, "You see now!" At this ominous threat his comrades broke into renewed jeers.

Collins gave them a dark scowl and went to find his captain. The latter was conversing with the colonel of the regiment.

"Captain," said Collins, saluting and standing at attention—in those days all trousers bagged at the knees—"captain, I want t' get permission to go git some water from that there well over yonder!"

The colonel and the captain swung about simultaneously and stared across the meadow. The captain laughed. "You must be pretty thirsty, Collins?"

"Yes sir, I am."

"Well—ah," said the captain. After a moment he asked, "Can't you wait?"

"No, sir."

The colonel was watching Collin's face. "Look here, my lad," he said, in a pious sort of voice—"look here, my lad"—Collins was not a lad—"don't you think that's taking pretty big risks for a little drink of water?"

"I dunno," said Collins uncomfortably. Some of the resentment toward his companions, which perhaps had forced him into this affair, was beginning to fade. "I dunno whether 'tis."

The colonel and the captain contemplated him for a time.

"Well," said the captain finally.

"Well," said the colonel, "if you want to go, why, go."

Collins saluted. "Much obliged t' yeh."

As he moved away the colonel called after him. "Take some of the other boys' canteens with you an' hurry back now."

"Yes, sir, I will."

The colonel and the captain looked at each other then, for it had suddenly occurred that they could not for the life of them tell whether Collins wanted to go or whether he did not.

They turned to regard Collins, and as they perceived him surrounded by gesticulating comrades, the colonel said: "Well, by thunder! I guess he's going."

Collins appeared as a man dreaming. In the midst of the questions, the advice, the warnings, all the excited talk of his company mates, he maintained a curious silence.

They were very busy in preparing him for his ordeal. When they inspected him carefully it was somewhat like the examination that grooms give a horse before a race; and they were amazed, staggered by the whole affair. Their astonishment found vent in strange repetitions.

"Are yeh sure a-goin'?" they demanded again and again.

"Certainly I am," cried Collins, at last furiously.

He strode sullenly away from them. He was swinging five or six canteens by their cords. It seemed that his cap would not remain firmly on his head, and often he reached up and pulled it down over his brow.

There was a general movement in the compact column. The long animal-like thing moved slightly. Its four hundred eyes were turned upon the figure of Collins.

"Well, sir, if that ain't th' dernest thing! I never thought Fred Collins had the blood in him for that kind of business."

"What's he goin' to do, anyhow?"

"He's goin' to that well there after water."

"We ain't dyin' of thirst, are we? That's foolishness."

"Well, somebody put him up to it, an' he's doin' it."

"Say, he must be a desperate cuss."

When Collins faced the meadow and walked away from the regiment, he was vaguely conscious that a chasm, the deep valley of all prides, was suddenly between him and his comrades. It was provisional, but the provision was that he return as a victor. He had blindly been led by quaint emotions, and laid himself under an obligation to walk squarely up to the face of death.

But he was not sure that he wished to make a retraction, even if he could do so without shame. As a matter of truth, he was sure of very little. He was mainly surprised.

It seemed to him supernaturally strange that he had allowed his mind to manoeuver his body into such a situation. He understood that it might be called dramatically great.

However, he had no full appreciation of anything, excepting that he was actually conscious of being dazed. He could feel his dulled mind grouping after the form and colour of this incident. He wondered why he did not feel some keen agony of fear cutting his sense like a knife. He wondered at this, because human expression had said loudly for centuries that men should feel afraid of certain things, and that all men who did not feel this fear were phenomena—heroes.

He was, then, a hero. He suffered that disappointment which we would all have if we discovered that we were ourselves capable of those deeds which we most admire in history and legend. This, then, was a hero. After all, heroes were not much.

No, it could not be true. He was not a hero. Heroes had no shames in their lives, and, as for him, he remembered borrowing fifteen dollars from a friend and promising to pay it back the next day, and then avoiding that friend for ten months. When at home his mother had aroused him for the early labour of his life on the farm, it had often been his fashion to be irritable, childish, diabolical; and his mother had died since he had come to the war.

He saw that, in this matter of the well, the canteens, the shells, he was an intruder in the land of fine deeds.

He was now about thirty paces from his comrades. The regiment had just turned its many faces toward him.

From the forest of terrific noises there suddenly emerged a little uneven line of men. They fired fiercely and rapidly at distant foliage on which appeared little puffs of white smoke. The spatter of skirmish firing was added to the thunder of the guns on the hill. The little line of men ran forward. A colour sergeant fell flat with his flag as if he had slipped on ice. There was a hoarse cheering from this distant field.

Collins suddenly felt that two demon fingers were pressed into his ears. He could see nothing but flying arrows, flaming red. He lurched from the shock of this explosion, but he made a mad rush for the house, which he viewed as a man submerged to the neck in a boiling surf might view the shore. In the air, little pieces of shell howled and the earthquake explosions drove him insane with the menace of their roar. As he ran the canteens knocked together with a rhythmical tinkling.

As he neared the house, each detail of the scene became vivid to him. He was aware of some bricks of the vanished chimney lying on the sod. There was a door which hung by one hinge.

Rifle bullets called forth by the insistent skirmishers came from the far-off bank of foliage. They mingled with the shells and the pieces of shells until the air was torn in all directions by hootings, yells, howls. The sky was full of fiends who directed all their wild rage at his head.

When he came to the well, he flung himself face downward and peered into its darkness. There were furtive silver glintings some feet from the surface. He grabbed one of the canteens and, unfastening its cap, swung it down by the cord. The water flowed slowly in with an indolent gurgle.

And now as he lay with his face turned away he was suddenly smitten with the terror. It came upon his heart like the grasp of claws. All the power faded from his muscles. For an instant he was no more than a dead man.

The canteen filled with maddening slowness, in the manner of all bottles. Presently he recovered his strength and addressed a screaming oath to it. He leaned over until it seemed as if he intended to try to push water into it with his hands.

His eyes as he gazed down into the well shone like two pieces of metal and in their expression was a great appeal and a great curse. The stupid water derided him.

There was the blaring thunder of a shell. Crimson light shone through the swift-boiling smoke and made a pink reflection on part of the wall of the well. Collins jerked out his arm and canteen with the same motion that a man would use in withdrawing his head from a furnace.

He scrambled erect and glared and hesitated. On the ground near him lay the old well bucket, with a length of rusty chain. He lowered it swiftly into the well. The bucket struck the water and then, turning lazily over, sank. When, with hand reaching tremblingly over hand, he hauled it out, it knocked often against the walls of the well and spilled some of its contents.

In running with a filled bucket, a man can adopt but one kind of gait. So through this terrible field over which screamed practical angels of death Collins ran in the manner of a farmer chased out of a dairy by a bull.

His face went staring white with anticipation—anticipation of a blow that would whirl him around and down. He would fall as he had seen other men fall, the life knocked out of them so suddenly that their knees were no more quick to touch the ground than their heads. He saw the long blue line of the regiment, but his comrades were standing looking at him from the edge of an impossible star. He was aware of some deep wheel ruts and hoofprints in the sod beneath his feet.

The artillery officer who had fallen in this meadow had been making groans in the teeth of the tempest of sound. These futile cries, wrenched from him by his agony, were heard only by shells, bullets. When wild-eyed Collins came running, this officer raised himself. His face contorted and blanched from pain, he was about to utter some great beseeching cry. But suddenly his face straightened and he called: "Say, young man, give me a drink of water, will you?"

Collins had no room amid his emotions for surprise. He was mad from the threats of destruction.

"I can't," he screamed, and in his reply was a full description of his quaking apprehension. His cap was gone and his hair was riotous. His clothes made it appear that he had been dragged over the ground by the heels. He ran on.

The officer's head sank down and one elbow crooked. His foot in its brass bound stirrup still stretched over the body of his horse and the other leg was under the steed.

But Collins turned. He came dashing back. His face had now turned gray and in his eyes was all terror. "Here it is! here it is!"

The officer was as a man gone in drink. His arm bent like a twig. His head drooped as if his neck were of willow. He was sinking to the ground, to lie face downward.

Collins grabbed him by the shoulder. "Here it is. Here's your drink. Turn over. Turn over, man, for God's sake!"

With Collins hauling at his shoulder, the officer twisted his body and fell with his face turned toward that region where lived the unspeakable noises of the swirling missiles. There was the faintest shadow of a smile on his lips as he looked at Collins. He gave a sigh, a little primitive breath like that from a child.

Collins tried to hold the bucket steady, but his shaking hands caused the water to splash all over the face of the dying man. Then he jerked it away and ran on.

The regiment gave him a welcoming roar. The grimed faces were wrinkled in laughter.

His captain waved the bucket away. "Give it to the men!"

The two genial, skylarking young lieutenants were the first to gain possession of it. They played over it in their fashion.

When one tried to drink the other teasingly knocked his elbow. "Don't, Billie! You'll make me spill it," said the one. The other laughed.

Suddenly there was an oath, the thud of wood on the ground, and a swift murmur of astonishment among the ranks. The two lieutenants glared at each other. The bucket lay on the ground empty.

Journal Entry

Speculate on the motives that trigger Collins's act of heroism.

Textual Considerations

1. In the opening paragraph, Crane contrasts the dark silhouettes on the hill of the artillerymen, the guns, the caissons, and the horses with the blue sky. He further contrasts the red streak from the fired ammunition with the white duck trousers of the battery men. At what other point in the story does Crane use color contrast to represent battle scenes? To what effect?
2. Irony is a key element in this text. Cite some particularly ironic actions in the narrative, and discuss their significance in relation to your understanding of the text's meaning and tone.
3. Reflect on the significance of the text's title. How does Crane define heroism—as an individual value or a social action dictated by circumstances? To what extent does Crane explain the "mystery"?

Cultural Contexts

1. Discuss the political and social significance associated with individual heroism and the war hero. How might you respond to the hardships of war under these circumstances?
2. Working with your group, construct a profile of Fred Collins. Chart the stages in his feelings about his fellow soldiers, as well as his thoughts about heroism. Does he consider himself heroic? Why does he stop to give water to the dying lieutenant? Is this a heroic act? Explain.

Liam O'Flaherty
1923

The Sniper

The long June twilight faded into night. Dublin lay enveloped in darkness but for the dim light of the moon that shone through fleecy clouds, casting a pale light as of approaching dawn over the streets and the dark waters of the Liffey. Around the beleaguered Four Courts the heavy guns roared. Here and there through the city, machine-guns and rifles broke the silence of the night, spasmodically, like dogs barking on lone farms. Republicans and Free Staters were waging civil war.

On a roof-top near O'Connell Bridge, a Republican sniper lay watching. Beside him lay his rifle and over his shoulders were slung a pair of field glasses. His face was the face of a student, thin and ascetic, but his eyes had the cold gleam of the fanatic. They were deep and thoughtful, the eyes of a man who is used to looking at death.

He was eating a sandwich hungrily. He had eaten nothing since morning. He had been too excited to eat. He finished the sandwich, and, taking a flask of whiskey from his pocket, he took a short draught. Then he returned the flask to his pocket. He paused for a moment, considering whether he should risk a smoke. It was dangerous. The flash might be seen in the darkness and there were enemies watching. He decided to take the risk.

Placing a cigarette between his lips, he struck a match. There was a flash and a bullet whizzed over his head. He dropped immediately. He had seen the flash. It came from the opposite side of the street.

He rolled over the roof to a chimney stack in the rear, and slowly drew himself up behind it, until his eyes were level with the top of the parapet. There was nothing to be seen—just the dim outline of the opposite housetop against the blue sky. His enemy was under cover.

Just then an armored car came across the bridge and advanced slowly up the street. It stopped on the opposite of the street, fifty yards ahead. The sniper could hear the dull panting of the motor. His heart beat faster. It was an enemy car. He wanted to fire, but he knew it was useless. His bullets would never pierce the steel that covered the gray monster.

Then round the corner of a side street came an old woman, her head covered by a tattered shawl. She began to talk to the man in the turret of the car. She was pointing to the roof where the sniper lay. An informer.

The turret opened. A man's head and shoulders appeared, looking toward the sniper. The sniper raised his rifle and fired. The head fell heavily on the turret wall. The woman darted toward the side street. The sniper fired again. The woman whirled round and fell with a shriek into the gutter.

Suddenly from the opposite roof a shot rang out and the sniper dropped his rifle with a curse. The rifle clattered to the roof. The sniper thought the noise would wake the dead. He stopped to pick the rifle up. He couldn't lift it. His forearm was dead.

"Christ," he muttered, "I'm hit."

Dropping flat onto the roof, he crawled back to the parapet. With his left hand he felt the injured right forearm. There was no pain—just a deadened sensation, as if the arm had been cut off.

Quickly he drew his knife from his pocket, opened it on the breast-work of the parapet, and ripped open the sleeve. There was a small hole where the bullet had entered. On the other side there was no hole. The bullet had lodged in the bone. It must have fractured it. He bent the arm below the wound. The arm bent back easily. He ground his teeth to overcome the pain.

Then taking out the field dressing, he ripped open the packet with his knife. He broke the neck of the iodine bottle and let the bitter fluid drip into the wound. A paroxysm of pain swept through him. He placed the cotton wadding over the wound and wrapped the dressing over it. He tied the ends with his teeth.

Then he lay against the parapet, and, closing his eyes, he made an effort of will to overcome the pain.

In the street beneath all was still. The armored car had retired speedily over the bridge, with the machine-gunner's head hanging lifelessly over the turret. The woman's corpse lay still in the gutter.

The sniper lay still for a long time nursing his wounded arm and planning escape. Morning must not find him wounded on the roof. The enemy on the opposite roof covered his escape. He must kill that enemy and he could not use his rifle. He had only a revolver to do it. Then he thought of a plan.

Taking off his cap, he placed it over the muzzle of his rifle. Then he pushed the rifle slowly over the parapet, until the cap was visible from the opposite side of the street. Almost immediately there was a report, and a bullet pierced the center of the cap. The sniper slanted the rifle forward. The cap slipped down into the street. Then catching the rifle in the middle, the sniper dropped his left hand over the roof and let it hang, lifelessly. After a few moments he let the rifle drop to the street. Then he sank to the roof, dragging his hand with him.

Crawling quickly to the left, he peered up at the corner of the roof. His ruse had succeeded. The other sniper, seeing the cap and rifle fall, thought he had killed his man. He was now standing before a row of chimney pots, looking across, with his head clearly silhouetted against the western sky.

The Republican sniper smiled and lifted his revolver above the edge of the parapet. The distance was about fifty yards—a hard shot in the dim light, and his right arm was paining him like a thousand devils. He took a steady aim. His hand trembled with eagerness. Pressing his lips together, he took a deep breath through his nostrils and fired. He was almost deafened with the report and his arm shook with the recoil.

Then when the smoke cleared he peered across and uttered a cry of joy. His enemy had been hit. He was reeling over the parapet in his death agony. He struggled to keep his feet, but he was slowly falling forward, as if in a dream. The rifle fell from his grasp, hit the parapet, fell over, bounded off the pole of a barber's shop beneath and then clattered on the pavement.

Then the dying man on the roof crumpled up and fell forward. The body turned over and over in space and hit the ground with a dull thud. Then it lay still.

The sniper looked at his enemy falling and he shuddered. The lust of battle died in him. He became bitten by remorse. The sweat stood out in beads on his forehead. Weakened by his wound and the long summer day of fasting and watching on the roof, he revolted from the sight of the shattered mass of his dead enemy. His teeth chattered, he began to gibber to himself, cursing the war, cursing himself, cursing everybody.

He looked at the smoking revolver in his hand, and with an oath he hurled it to the roof at his feet. The revolver went off with the concussion and the bullet whizzed past the sniper's head. He was frightened back to his senses by the shock. His nerves steadied. The cloud of fear scattered from his mind and he laughed.

Taking the whiskey flask from his pocket, he emptied it at a draught. He felt reckless under the influence of the spirit. He decided to leave the roof now and look for his company commander, to report. Everywhere around was quiet. There was not much danger in going through the streets. He picked up his revolver and put it in his pocket. Then he crawled down through the sky-light to the house underneath.

When the sniper reached the laneway on the street level, he felt a sudden curiosity as to the identity of the enemy sniper whom he had killed. He decided that he was a good shot, whoever he was. He wondered did he know him. Perhaps he had been in his own company before the split in the army. He decided to risk going over to have a look at him. He peered round the corner into O'Connell Street. In the upper part of the street there was heavy firing, but around here all was quiet.

The sniper darted across the street. A machine-gun tore up the ground around him with a hail of bullets, but he escaped. He threw himself face downward beside the corpse. The machine-gun stopped.

Then the sniper turned over the dead body and looked into his brother's face.

Journal Entry

To what extent does "The Sniper" present both brothers as victims of the "myth of the enemy"?

Textual Considerations

1. Observe O'Flaherty's frequent use of irony in "The Sniper," and analyze its effects on the poem's meaning, style, and tone.
2. Investigate the effects of the narrative point of view on the development of the story. To what extent does the narrator's stance affect your evaluation of the sniper?
3. Chart the stages in the sniper's responses to his situation, and evaluate their plausibility.

Cultural Contexts

1. To what extent do you share the sniper's commitment to a political cause? Under what circumstances can you imagine risking your life because of that commitment?
2. How does the violence of civil wars, like that in the war between the Republicans and the Free Staters in Ireland, compare to the violence that results from war among nations? Consider the extent to which family and religious ties continue to prevail in the midst of civil wars.

Tadeusz Borowski
1967

Silence

At last they seized him inside the German barracks, just as he was about to climb over the window ledge. In absolute silence they pulled him down to the floor and panting with hate dragged him into a dark alley. Here, closely surrounded by a silent mob, they began tearing at him with greedy hands.

Suddenly from the camp gate a whispered warning was passed from one mouth to another. A company of soldiers, their bodies leaning forward, their rifles on the ready, came running down the camp's main road, weaving between the clusters of men in stripes standing in the way. The crowd scattered and vanished inside the blocks. In the packed, noisy barracks the prisoners were cooking food pilfered during the night from neighbouring farmers. In the bunks and in the passageways between them, they were grinding grain in small flour-mills, slicing meat on heavy slabs of wood, peeling potatoes and throwing the peels on to the floor. They were playing cards for stolen cigars, stirring batter for pancakes, gulping down hot soup, and lazily killing fleas. A stifling odour of sweat hung in the air, mingled with the smell of food, with smoke and with steam that liquefied along the ceiling beams and fell on the men, the bunks and the food in large, heavy drops, like autumn rain.

There was a stir at the door. A young American officer with a tin helmet on his head entered the block and looked with curiosity at the bunks and the tables. He wore a freshly pressed uniform; his revolver was hanging down, strapped in an open holster that dangled against his thigh. He was assisted by the translator who wore a yellow band reading "interpreter" on the sleeve of his civilian coat, and by the chairman of the Prisoners' Committee, dressed in a white summer coat, a pair of tuxedo trousers and tennis shoes. The men in the barracks fell silent. Leaning out of their bunks and lifting their eyes from the kettles, bowls and cups, they gazed attentively into the officer's face.

"Gentlemen," said the officer with a friendly smile, taking off his helmet—and the interpreter proceeded at once to translate sentence after sentence—"I know, of course, that after what you have gone through and after what you have seen, you must feel a deep hate for your tormentors. But we, the soldiers of America, and you, the people of Europe, have fought so that law should prevail over lawlessness. We must show our respect for the law. I assure you that the guilty will be punished, in this camp as well as in all the others. You have already seen, for example, that the S.S. men were made to bury the dead."

"...right, we could use the lot at the back of the hospital. A few of them are still around," whispered one of the men in a bottom bunk.

"...or one of the pits," whispered another. He sat straddling the bunk, his fingers firmly clutching the blanket.

"Shut up! Can't you wait a little longer? Now listen to what the American has to say," a third man, stretched across the foot of the same bunk, spoke in an angry whisper. The American officer was now hidden from their view behind the thick crowd gathered at the other end of the block.

"Comrades, our new Kommandant gives you his word of honour that all the criminals of the S.S. as well as among the prisoners will be punished," said the translator. The men in the bunks broke into applause and shouts. In smiles and gestures they tried to convey their friendly approval of the young man from across the ocean.

"And so the Kommandant requests," went on the translator, his voice turning somewhat hoarse, "that you try to be patient and do not commit lawless deeds, which may only lead to trouble, and please pass the sons of bitches over to the camp guards. How about it, men?"

The block answered with a prolonged shout. The American thanked the translator and wished the prisoners a good rest and an early reunion with their dear ones. Accompanied by a friendly hum of voices, he left the block and proceeded to the next.

Not until after he had visited all the blocks and returned with the soldiers to his headquarters did we pull our man off the bunk—where covered with blankets and half-smothered with the weight of our bodies he lay gagged, his face buried in the straw mattress—and dragged him on to the cement floor under the stove, where the entire block, grunting and growling with hatred, trampled him to death.

Journal Entry

Respond to the setting of the concentration camp in "Silence." Imagine yourself in the place of the survivors.

Textual Considerations

1. Explore the thematic nuances of the story's title. Consider, for example, the effects of juxtaposing the silence of the concentration camp survivors with the speech of the young American officer through his interpreter.
2. Review the story carefully, and discuss how Borowski uses the physical appearance and language of the survivors to reinforce their psychic distance from the outside world.

3. How successful is "Silence" in portraying not only the narrator's realistic re-creation of a concentration camp but also his own disillusionment and horror of war?

Cultural Contexts

1. Working with your group, support or challenge the thesis that in killing one of their former oppressors, the inmates in "Silence" perpetuate the violence that victimized them.
2. Analyze what "Silence" conveys about the survivors' need for revenge. Consider, too, what the text implies about the ability of the young American officer and other non-inmates to judge the actions of the inmates.

Isabel Allende
1985

The Hour of Truth

Alba was curled up in the darkness. They had ripped the tape from her eyes and replaced it with a tight bandage. She was afraid. As she recalled her Uncle Nicolás's training, and his warning about the danger of being afraid of fear, she concentrated on trying to control the shaking of her body and shutting her ears to the terrifying sounds that reached her side. She tried to visualize her happiest moments with Miguel, groping for a means to outwit time and find the strength for what she knew lay ahead. She told herself that she had to endure a few hours without her nerves betraying her, until her grandfather was able to set in motion the heavy machinery of his power and influence to get her out of there. She searched her memory for a trip to the coast with Miguel, in autumn, long before the hurricane of events had turned the world upside down, when things were still called by familiar names and words had a single meaning; when people, freedom, and *compañero* were just that—people, freedom, and *compañero*—and had not yet become passwords. She tried to relive that moment—the damp red earth and the intense scent of the pine and eucalyptus forests in which a carpet of dry leaves lay steeping after the long hot summer and where the coppery sunlight filtered down through the treetops. She tried to recall the cold, the silence, and that precious feeling of owning the world, of being twenty years old and having her whole life ahead of her, of making love slowly and calmly, drunk with the scent of the forest and their love, without a past, without suspecting the future, with just the incredible richness of that present moment in which they stared at each other, smelled each other, kissed each other, and explored each other's bodies, wrapped in the whisper of the wind among the trees and the sound of the nearby waves breaking against the rocks at the foot of the cliff, exploding in a crash of pungent surf, and the two of them embracing underneath a single poncho like Siamese twins, laughing and swearing that this would last forever, that they were the only ones in the whole world who had discovered love.

Alba heard the screams, the long moans, and the radio playing full blast. The woods, Miguel, and love were lost in the deep well of her terror and she resigned herself to facing her fate without subterfuge.

She calculated that a whole night and the better part of the following day had passed when the door was finally opened and two men took her from her cell. With insults and threats they led her in to Colonel García, whom she could recognize blindfolded by his habitual cruelty, even before he opened his mouth. She felt his hands take her face, his thick fingers touch her ears and neck.

"Now you're going to tell me where your lover is," he told her. "That will save us both a lot of unpleasantness."

Alba breathed a sigh of relief. That meant they had not arrested Miguel!

"I want to go to the bathroom," Alba said in the strongest voice she could summon up.

"I see you're not planning to cooperate, Alba. That's too bad." García sighed. "The boys will have to do their job. I can't stand in their way."

There was a brief silence and she made a superhuman effort to remember the pine forest and Miguel's love, but her ideas got tangled up and she no longer knew if she was dreaming or where this stench of sweat, excrement, blood, and urine was coming from, or the radio announcer describing some Finnish goals that had nothing to do with her in the middle of other, nearer, more clearly audible shouts. A brutal slap knocked her to the floor. Violent hands lifted her to her feet. Ferocious fingers fastened themselves to her breasts, crushing her nipples. She was completely overcome by fear. Strange voices pressed in on her. She heard Miguel's name but did not know what they were asking her, and kept repeating a monumental *no* while they beat her, manhandled her, pulled off her blouse, and she could no longer think, could only say *no, no,* and *no* and calculate how much longer she could resist before her strength gave out, not knowing this was only the beginning, until she felt herself begin to faint and the men left her alone, lying on the floor, for what seemed to her a very short time.

She soon heard García's voice again and guessed it was his hands that were helping her to her feet, leading her toward a chair, straightening her clothes, and buttoning her blouse.

"My God!" he said. "Look what they've done to you! I warned you, Alba. Try to relax now, I'm going to give you a cup of coffee."

Alba began to cry. The warm liquid brought her back to life, but she could not taste it because when she swallowed it was mixed with blood. García held the cup, guiding it carefully toward her lips like a nurse.

"Do you want a cigarette?"

"I want to go to the bathroom," she said, pronouncing each syllable with difficulty with her swollen lips.

"Of course, Alba. They'll take you to the bathroom and then you can get some rest. I'm your friend. I understand your situation perfectly. You're in love, and that's why you want to protect him. I know you don't have anything to do with the guerrillas. But the boys don't believe me when I tell them. They won't be satisfied until you tell them where Miguel is. Actually they've already got him surrounded. They know exactly where he is. They'll catch him, but they want to be sure that you have nothing to do with the guerrillas. You understand? If you protect him and refuse to talk, they'll continue to suspect you. Tell them what they want to know and then I'll personally escort you home. You'll tell them, right?"

"I want to go to the bathroom," Alba repeated.

"I see you're just as stubborn as your grandfather. All right. You can go to the bathroom. I'm going to give you a chance to think things over," García said.

They took her to a toilet and she was forced to ignore the man who stood beside her, holding on to her arm. After that they returned her to her cell. In the tiny, solitary cube where she was being held, she tried to clarify her thoughts, but she was tortured by the pain of her beating, her thirst, the bandage pressing on her temples, the drone of the radio, the terror of approaching footsteps and her relief when they moved away, the shouts and the orders. She curled up like a fetus on the floor and surrendered to her pain. She remained in that position for hours, perhaps days. A man came twice to take her to the bathroom. He led her to a fetid lavatory where she was unable to wash because there was no water. He allowed her a minute, placing her on the toilet seat next to another person as silent and sluggish as herself. She could not tell if it was a woman or a man. At first she wept, wishing her Uncle Nicholás had given her a special course in how to withstand humiliation, which she found worse than pain, but she finally resigned herself to her own filth and stopped thinking about her unbearable need to wash. They gave her boiled corn, a small piece of chicken, and a bit of ice cream, which she identified by their taste, smell, and temperature, and which she wolfed down with her hands, astonished to be given such luxurious food, unexpected in a place like that....

The third time they took her in to Esteban García, Alba was more prepared, because through the walls of her cell she could hear what was going on in the next room, where they were interrogating other prisoners, and she had no illusions. She did not even try to evoke the woods where she had shared the joy of love.

"Well, Alba, I've given you time to think things over. Now the two of us are going to talk and you're going to tell me where Miguel is and we're going to get this over with quickly," García said.

"I want to go to the bathroom," Alba answered.

"I see you're making fun of me, Alba," he said. "I'm sorry, but we don't have any time to waste."

Alba made no response.

"Take off your clothes!" García ordered in another voice.

She did not obey. They stripped her violently, pulling off her slacks despite her kicking. The memory of her adolescence and Miguel's kiss in the garden gave her the strength of hatred. She struggled against him, until they got tired of beating her and gave her a short break, which she used to invoke the understanding spirits of her grandmother, so that they would help her die. But no one answered her call for help. Two hands lifted her up, and four laid her on a cold, hard metal cot with springs that hurt her back, and bound her wrists and ankles with leather thongs.

"For the last time, Alba. Where is Miguel?" García asked.

She shook her head in silence. They had tied her head down with another thong.

"When you're ready to talk, raise a finger," he said.

Alba heard another voice.

"I'll work the machine," it said.

Then she felt the atrocious pain that coursed through her body, filling it completely, and that she would never forget as long as she lived. She sank into darkness.

"Bastards! I told you to be careful with her!" she heard Esteban García say from far away. She felt them opening her eyelids, but all she saw was a misty brightness. Then she felt a prick in her arm and sank back into unconsciousness.

A century later Alba awoke wet and naked. She did not know if she was bathed with sweat, or water, or urine. She could not move, recalled nothing, and had no idea where she was or what had caused the intense pain that had reduced her to a heap of raw meat. She felt the thirst of the Sahara and called out for water.

"Wait, *compañera*," someone said beside her. "Wait until morning. If you drink water, you'll get convulsions, and you could die."

She opened her eyes. They were no longer bandaged. A vaguely familiar face was leaning over her, and hands were wrapping her in a blanket.

"Do you remember me? I'm Ana Díaz. We went to the university together. Don't you recognize me?"

Alba shook her head, closed her eyes, and surrendered to the sweet illusion of death. But she awakened a few hours later, and when she moved she realized that she ached to the last fiber of her body.

"You'll feel better soon," said a woman who was stroking her face and pushing away the locks of damp hair that hid her eyes. "Don't move, and try to relax. I'll be here next to you. You need to rest."

"What happened?" Alba whispered.

"They really roughed you up, *compañera*," the other woman said sadly.

"Who are you?" Alba asked.

"Ana Díaz. I've been here for a week. They also got my *compañero*, Andrés, but he's still alive. I see him once a day, when they take them to the bathroom."

"Ana Díaz?" Alba murmured.

"That's right. We weren't so close back then, but it's never too late to start. The truth is, you're the last person I expected to meet here, Countess," the woman said gently. "Don't talk now. Try to sleep. That way the time will go faster for you. Your memory will gradually come back. Don't worry. It's because of the electricity."

But Alba was unable to sleep, for the door of her cell opened and a man walked in.

"Put the bandage back on her!" he ordered Ana Díaz.

"Please...can't you see how weak she is? Let her rest a little while...."

"Do as I say!"

Ana bent over the cot and put the bandage over her eyes. Then she removed the blanket and tried to dress her, but the guard pulled her away, lifted the prisoner by her arms, and sat her up. Another man came in to help him, and between them they carried her out because she could not walk. Alba was sure that she was dying, if she was not already dead. She could tell they were walking down a hallway in which the sound of their footsteps echoed. She felt a hand on her face, lifting her head.

"You can give her water. Wash her and give her another shot. See if she can swallow some coffee and bring her back to me," García said.

"Do you want us to dress her?"

"No."

Alba was in García's hands a long time. After a few days, he realized she had recognized him, but he did not abandon his precaution of keeping her blindfolded, even when they were alone. Every day new prisoners arrived and others were led away. Alba heard the vehicles, the shouts, and the gate being closed. She tried to keep track of the number of prisoners, but it was almost impossible. Ana Díaz thought there were close to two hundred. García was very busy, but he never let a day go by without seeing Alba, alternating unbridled violence with the pretense that he was her good friend. At times he appeared to be genuinely moved, personally spooning soup into her mouth, but the day he plunged her head into a bucket full of excrement until she fainted from disgust, Alba understood that he was not trying to learn Miguel's true whereabouts but to avenge himself for injuries that had been inflicted on him from birth, and that nothing she could confess would have any effect on her fate as the private prisoner of Colonel García. This allowed her to venture slowly out of the private circle of her terror. Her fear began to ebb and she was able to feel compassion for the others, for those they hung by their arms, for the newcomers, for the man whose shackled legs were run over by a truck. They brought all the prisoners into the courtyard at dawn and forced them to watch, because this was also a personal matter between the colonel and his prisoner. It was the first time Alba had opened her eyes outside the darkness of her cell, and the gentle splendor of the morning and the frost shining on the stones, where puddles of rain had collected overnight, seemed unbearably radiant to her. They dragged the man, who offered no resistance, out into the courtyard. He could not stand, and they left him lying on the ground. The guards had covered their faces with handkerchiefs so no one would ever be able to identify them in the improbable event that circumstances changed. Alba closed her eyes when she heard the truck's engine, but she could not close her ears to the sound of his howl, which stayed in her memory forever....

One day Colonel García was surprised to find himself caressing Alba like a lover and talking to her of his childhood in the country, when he would see her walking hand in hand with her grandfather, dressed in her starched pinafores and with the green halo of her hair, while he, barefoot in the mud, swore that one day he would make her pay for her arrogance and avenge himself for his cursed bastard fate. Rigid and absent, naked and trembling with disgust and cold, Alba neither heard nor felt him, but that crack in his eagerness to torture her sounded an alarm in the colonel's mind. He ordered Alba to be thrown in the doghouse, and furiously prepared to forget that she existed.

The doghouse was a small, sealed cell like a dark, frozen, airless tomb. There were six of them altogether, constructed in an empty water tank especially for punishment. They were used for relatively short stretches of time, because no one could withstand them very long, at most a few days, before beginning to ramble—to lose the sense of things, the meaning of words, and the anxiety of passing time—or simply, beginning to die. At first, huddled in her sepulcher, unable either to stand up or sit down despite her small size, Alba managed to stave off madness. Now that she was alone, she realized how much she needed Ana Díaz. She thought she heard an imperceptible tapping in the distance, as if someone were sending her coded messages from another cell, but she soon stopped paying attention to it because she realized that all attempts at communication were completely hopeless. She gave up, deciding to end this torture once and for all. She stopped eating, and only when her feebleness became too much for her did she take a sip of water. She tried not to breathe or move, and began eagerly to await her death. She stayed like this for a long time.... Word went out that she was dying. The guards opened the hatch of the doghouse and lifted her effortlessly, because she was very light. They took her back to Colonel García, whose hatred had returned during these days, but she did not recognize him. She was beyond his power.

Translated by Magda Bogin

Journal Entry

Imagine yourself in Alba's situation, and write a journal entry on your possible reactions.

Textual Considerations

1. Create a profile of Colonel Garcia. What personal, social, and political factors account for his ambivalent reactions toward Alba?
2. Allende uses a variety of narrative techniques, including flashback, repetition, dialogue, and interior monologue to communicate Alba's thoughts and emotions. Select at least three examples that help you to empathize with her.
3. How does Allende's juxtaposition of fantasy and reality in the story affect the portrayal of Alba's character as well as her ability to endure torture?

Cultural Considerations

1. Dictatorships like the one Allende describes did not rule out the use of torture to combat the alleged Communist threat in Latin America. Quote from the story responses that show the kind of threat someone like Alba might pose to such a system.

Janice Mirikitani
1987

Spoils of War

Violet ran up the familiar path of Telman Park determined today to make five miles. She knew the exact spot of her destination, through the eucalyptus, past the emergency telephone box, up to the twin boulders where she would sit triumphantly and rest in the warm sun.

He watched her from his green volkswagen van. Her black hair bouncing at her shoulder blades, her sturdy thighs and sleek runner's calves. Her small breasts jousled with each step under the sweatshirt that read, "Lotus Blossom Doesn't Live Here."

> Spirit of the bayonet.
> red/march
> white/hup
> blue/eyes front
> square your piece
> left/right
> kill 'em
> thrust/jab
> jab
> jab/kill 'em,
> "hey mamasan,
> joto mate ichiban"
> poontang one/two
> poontang three/four
> when we're done
> we'll kill some more.

Of all the joggers he saw, this was the one he wanted. He would park and watch the several who, at the same time each day, would run the path up into the wooded hills of the park.

Violet started running after she had met Josh. In fact, she started doing a lot of things. All her life she had been introverted, studious, conscientious, shy. During her last graduate year, life revolted around her. There were so many demonstrations on campus against the Vietnam war, she didn't pay attention to the noises—the speeches, doomsday messages from wild-eyed street preachers and twitching panhandlers. So when the police stormed the gathered protestors, Violet did not move out of the way in time as the sweep of billyclubs and helmets picked her up like a wave. Violet hit the cement with her elbow, and curled up reflexively to protect her head from the stampede of legs and feet. Josh had stumbled over her and scrambling up, lifted her with him.

In the months of their new friendship, the world she had pulled around herself like a narrow corridor began to swell and pulse as they talked of civil rights, the war, military tycoonism, racism that had many faces. They saw and touched their common wounds.

Josh talked about his war. He who escaped the draft, his mother's endless work to help him through college, his father whose heart was crushed by the humiliation of worklessness. His father's death gave him life, the circumstance for exemption from the military, and the freedom to revolt, protest.

Violet talked about her war. The sheets of silence that covered history from the moment the gates slammed her parents into concentration camps in Arkansas. Her mother distant and forgetful. Her father demanding, critical. It didn't seem to matter what Violet achieved. They kept their silence like blades beneath their tongues.

Violet passed the old eucalyptus, branching high, its constant falling leaves and shedding bark making the air smell pungent. She noticed the green van, dismissed it in the glaring light of afternoon.

He crouched lower behind the wheel as she passed, seeing her closer, the dark sloping eyes, her olive skin browned by the sun, her delicate mouth and bones above her cheek. The beads of sweat popping around her brow.

> They all had Vietnamese women.
> None like mine.
> She was bamboo thin,
> her fingers clutching
> the hem of her sleeve
> like a child.
> I felt red flame
> licking the nape of my neck burning
> deeper than napalm.
> She was quiet,
> her eyes, darker than night
> helped me forget my My Lais.
> Her beautiful body
> curling around me,
> flesh cocooned me against the
> jungle where eyes were like rain,
> Her arms like ivory bracelets
> encircling my pain.

Flesh whole, sensual, shining
amidst the stench of rotting wounds
that fed the fat flies.
The insatiable flies of Vietnam.

Violet felt her anger draining with each step. The pounds shed, the tightening of her thighs, the new curves at her hips, and the thoughts of leaving home soon. Free as the wind in her face. Free from the jagged silences of her mother, the brooding disapproval of her father. Violet had informed them that she would be moving in with Josh. Perhaps they would live in Oregon where he was interviewing for a job at the University. She smiled, thinking of Josh's return, his sardonic grin when she told him of her parent's reaction. Josh who encouraged her to run, to strengthen herself, to speak her mind, to open her body, so long wrapped in years of suffocation. Her body that she had felt pitifully shapeless, small, powerless, burdened with blame and fault. If only he had not died. He was not due for another month. Her mother's face, pinched in pain as water and blood ran from her, rushed to the hospital. Her mother's body, wracked, gray, heaving and bellowing. The child tearing to exit too soon. She could still hear the screams from her mother's bones. The son, born dead. She remembered feeling alone. The weight of their grief, the sense of regret that she remained alive, on her small shoulders. All these years, the weight like boulders, the weight now shedding with each step.

The sun was a hot hand on her back as Violet ran through the threaded leaves, cracking beneath her steady feet.

He could feel the drugs wearing off. His skin twitching. He imagined the sores popping anew, the smell from jungle rot seeping from his pale flesh, tinted blue. He knew he would vomit.

She never withheld her warm thighs,
even when gorged with woman blood,
hot blood
sucking me deeper into her.
All the blood that would fill
a river.
Those jungles, villages like
a body split, slit, gouged.
Blood on me.
Swelling within her,
my blade, gleaming in the moonlight
exits flesh, flashes in her eyes.
She licks the blood from the shaft.
Deep, I thrust it past her teeth.
She took it all
her throat tightening on it
blood bubbling from the edges
of her lips.

Her arms circling my hips,
her hands moving in my groin
with grenade.
My blade cuts the arm away,
splits her womb
that spumes hot blood.

Violet noticed the day emptier, the sun hotter. No wind. She would reach her
boulders today. Her mouth opened slightly as she pushed her breath. The path
became clearer, the trees very still. Like entering a strange new place. She remembered her corridor where she withdrew, compressed by whispers of guilt, mother's
unhappiness, father's loneliness. Her narrow corridor, airless. Dark. Her flesh lined
the walls. Josh's hands touching, warming her surfaces, expanding. His long runner's body entering her corners. Breathing. She discovers sensation. Muscles moving, sinews of desire. Nerve endings alive.

Violet stood before her parents and shouted. Her mother threatened to kill
herself. Her father informed her she could never bring Josh into his house. It was
bad enough to marry outside her race, but to live in sin with someone especially
that color is endless disgrace. Violet's fury unleashed like exploding walls. She
would leave this week. Run free of them. Lift it all from her like the wind picking
up leaves and spinning them to the sky.

The son, blue and breathless, wrinkled like a raisin. Mother gave up back then,
switched off her eyes. Her dull face all these years never saw her daughter's pain.
Well, Violet didn't want to take it on anymore. Can't bring him back to life. Can't
trade places, can't be what they want, no matter what she did. Had he lived, he'd
be in college or a soldier drafted, maybe dead anyway in Southeast Asia.

Violet running faster. She'd live her own life. She could see the boulders now.

He, crouching behind the trees, watched her lengthening shadow climbing
the boulder where she lay down, stretched her bare arms and legs glistening with
sweat. Her body lifted by her panting breath.

He pulls her by both legs onto the ground. She is surprised, not knowing how
she fell. He pulls her to him, hand over her mouth and drags her into the trees. Her
legs are strong, digging into the soft earth, resisting, thrashing. He reveals the long
knife unsheathed, whispers that he will cut her throat if she screams. Violet retreats
into her corridor, breathing quietly through her nose. He leads her far from the
path, under brush and thicket of trees. He commands her to kneel in the leaves.
Violet, terror exploding, screams, her fists beating against his pressing body, suffocating, scarred, distorted flesh. He falls upon her like a rock. His fists beat her
again, brutally again, until she is unconscious. He pulls her shorts off, and gently.
Gently. Caressing, kisses her slightly open mouth, her neck, her still arms. Inserts
his blade in her womb and makes her bleed.

After, he carefully dresses himself. With a wide arched swing of his sharp knife,
he severs her arm above the elbow.

Wiping the blood from his blade, gently he wraps the arm in his flak jacket.
Carries it like a child to his van and leaves.

The wind is still, the sun falling, casting long shadows from the boulders, the trees. In the thicket, the faint hum of flies gathering.

> Spirit of the bayonet.
> red/march
> white/hup
> blue/eyes front
> Square your piece
> left/right
> kill 'em
> thrust/jab
> jab
> jab/kill 'em
> "hey mamasan
> joto mate ichiban"
> poontang one/two
> poontang three/four
> when we're done
> we'll kill some more.

Journal Entry

Record your responses to the rape and violence to which Violet is subjected.

Textual Considerations

1. Mirikitani uses irony throughout the story to reinforce the theme. Contrast, for example, the discrepancies between Violet's expectations for her jog through the park, expressed in the first paragraph, with the climactic events of the story's conclusion. Cite other examples of irony, and show how they contribute to the relation between war and sexual violence in the story.
2. What is the significance of the story's title? To how many characters does it apply? To how many wars? Explain.
3. The narrative structure of "Spoils of War" is complex. What do we learn of Violet's past and present? What resolution does she reach concerning her future? Review the poetic interjections. What do they reveal about the veteran's past? How do they affect your attitude toward him?

Cultural Contexts

1. Discuss with your group the extent to which both Violet and the veteran are victims of war. What does the story suggest about the political impact of the Vietnam War on American society approximately twenty-five years later?
2. To what extent do "Spoils of War" and "Vietnam: What I Remember" support or challenge the image of the Vietnam veteran as an antihero?

Andre Dubus
1988

The Curse

Mitchell Hayes was forty-nine years old, but when the cops left him in the bar with Bob, the manager, he felt much older. He did not know what it was like to be very old, a shrunken and wrinkled man, but he assumed it was like this: fatigue beyond relieving by rest, by sleep. He also was not a small man. His weight moved up and down in the 170s, and he was five feet, ten inches tall. But now his body seemed short and thin. Bob stood at one end of the bar; he was a large, black-haired man, and there was nothing in front of him but an ashtray he was using. He looked at Mitchell at the cash register and said, "Forget it. You heard what Smitty said."

Mitchell looked away, at the front door. He had put the chairs upside down on the tables. He looked from the door past Bob to the empty space of floor at the rear; sometimes people danced there, to the jukebox. Opposite Bob, on the wall behind the bar, was a telephone; Mitchell looked at it. He had told Smitty there were five guys, and when he moved to the phone, one of them stepped around the corner of the bar and shoved him, one hand against Mitchell's chest, and it pushed him backward; he nearly fell. That was when they were getting rough with her at the bar. When they took her to the floor, Mitchell looked once toward her sounds, then looked down at the duckboard he stood on, or at the belly or chest of a young man in front of him.

He knew they were not drunk. They had been drinking before they came to his place, a loud popping of motorcycles outside, then walking into the empty bar, young and sunburned and carrying helmets and wearing thick leather jackets in August. They stood in front of Mitchell and drank drafts. When he took their first order, he thought they were on drugs, and later, watching them, he was certain. They were not relaxed in the way of most drinkers near closing time. Their eyes were quick, alert as wary animals, and they spoke loudly, with passion, but their passion was strange and disturbing, because they were only chatting, bantering. Mitchell knew nothing of the effects of drugs, so could not guess what was in their blood. He feared and hated drugs because of his work and because he was the stepfather of teenagers: a boy and a girl. He gave last call and served them and leaned against the counter behind him.

Then the door opened and the girl walked in from the night, a girl he had never seen, and she crossed the floor toward Mitchell. He stepped forward to tell her she had missed last call; but before he spoke, she asked for change for the cigarette machine. She was young—he guessed nineteen to twenty-one—and deeply tanned and had dark hair. She was sober and wore jeans and a dark-blue T-shirt. He gave her the quarters, but she was standing between two of the men and she did not get to the machine.

When it was over and she lay crying on the cleared circle of floor, he left the bar and picked up the jeans and T-shirt beside her and crouched and handed them to her. She did not look at him. She laid the clothes across her breasts and what Mitchell thought of now as her wound. He left her and dialed 911, then Bob's number. He woke up Bob. Then he picked up her sneakers from the floor and placed them beside her and squatted near her face, her crying. He wanted to speak to her and touch her, hold a hand or press her brow, but he could not.

The cruiser was there quickly, the siren coming east from town, then slowing and deepening as the car stopped outside. He was glad Smitty was one of them; he had gone to high school with Smitty. The other was Dave, and Mitchell knew him because it was a small town. When they saw the girl, Dave went out to the cruiser to call for an ambulance; and when he came back, he said two other cruisers had those scumbags and were taking them in. The girl was still crying and could not talk to Smitty and Dave. She was crying when a man and a woman lifted her onto a stretcher and rolled her out the door and she vanished forever in a siren.

Bob came in while Smitty and Dave were sitting at the bar drinking coffee and Smitty was writing his report; Mitchell stood behind the bar. Bob sat next to Dave as Mitchell said, "I could have stopped them, Smitty."

"That's our job," Smitty said. "You want to be in the hospital now?"

Mitchell did not answer. When Smitty and Dave left, he got a glass of Coke from the cobra and had a cigarette with Bob. They did not talk. Then Mitchell washed his glass and Bob's cup and they left, turning off the lights. Outside, Mitchell locked the front door, feeling the sudden night air after almost ten hours of air conditioning. When he had come to work, the day had been very hot, and now he thought it would not have happened in winter. They had stopped for a beer on their way somewhere from the beach; he had heard them say that. But the beach was not the reason. He did not know the reason, but he knew it would not have happened in winter. The night was cool, and now he could smell trees. He turned and looked at the road in front of the bar. Bob stood beside him on the small porch.

"If the regulars had been here..." Bob said.

He turned and with his hand resting on the wooden rail, he walked down the ramp to the ground. At his car, he stopped and looked over its roof at Mitchell.

"You take it easy," he said.

Mitchell nodded. When Bob got into his car and left, he went down the ramp and drove home to his house on a street that he thought was neither good nor bad. The houses were small, and there were old large houses used now as apartments for families. Most of the people had work, most of the mothers cared for their children and most of the children were clean and looked like they lived in homes, not caves like some he saw in town. He worried about the older kids, one group of them, anyway. They were idle. When he was a boy in a town farther up the Merrimack River, he and his friends committed every mischievous act he could recall on afternoons and nights when they were idle. His stepchildren were not part of that group. They had friends from the high school, The front-porch light was on for him and one in the kitchen at the rear of the house. He went in the front door and switched off the porch light and walked through the living and dining rooms to the kitchen. He got a can of beer from the refrigerator, turned out the light, and sat at the table. When he could see, he took a cigarette from Susan's pack in front of him.

Down the hall, he heard Susan move on the bed, then get up, and he hoped it wasn't for the bathroom but for him. He had met her eight years ago, when he had given up on ever marrying and having kids; then, one night, she came into the bar with two of her girlfriends from work. She made six dollars an hour going to homes of invalids, mostly what she called her little old ladies, and bathing them. She got the house from her marriage, and child support the guy paid for a few months till he left town and went south. She came barefoot down the hall and stood in the kitchen doorway and said, "Are you all right?"

"No."

She sat across from him, and he told her. Very soon, she held his hand. She was good. He knew if he had fought all five of them and was lying in pieces in the hospital bed, she would tell him he had done the right thing, as she was telling him now. He liked her strong hand on his. It was a professional hand, and he wanted from her something he had never wanted before: to lie in bed while she bathed him. When they went to bed, he did not think he would be able to sleep, but she knelt beside him and massaged his shoulders and rubbed his temples and pressed her hands on his forehead. He woke to the voices of Marty and Joyce in the kitchen. They had summer jobs, and always when they woke him, he went back to sleep till noon, but now he got up and dressed and went to the kitchen door. Susan was at the stove, her back to him, and Marty and Joyce were talking and smoking. He said, "Good morning," and stepped into the room.

"What are you doing up?" Joyce said.

She was a pretty girl with her mother's wide cheekbones, and Marty was a tall, good-looking boy, and Mitchell felt as old as he had before he slept. Susan was watching him. Then she poured him a cup of coffee and put it at his place and he sat. Marty said, "You getting up for the day?"

"Something happened last night. At the bar." They tried to conceal their excitement, but he saw it in their eyes. "I should have stopped it. I think I *could* have stopped it. That's the point. There were these five guys. They were on motorcycles, but they weren't bikers. Just punks. They came in late, when everybody else had gone home. It was a slow night, anyway. Everybody was at the beach."

"They rob you?" Marty asked.

"No. A girl came in. Young. Nice-looking. You know: just a girl, minding her business."

They nodded, and their eyes were apprehensive.

"She wanted cigarette change; that's all. Those guys were on dope. Coke or something. You know: They were flying in place."

"Did they rape her?" Joyce said.

"Yes, honey."

"The *fuck*ers."

Susan opened her mouth, then closed it, and Joyce reached quickly for Susan's pack of cigarettes. Mitchell held his lighter for her and said, "When they started getting rough with her at the bar, I went for the phone. One of them stopped me. He shoved me; that's all. I should have hit him with a bottle."

Marty reached over the table with his big hand and held Mitchell's shoulder.

"No, Mitch. Five guys that mean. And coked up or whatever. No way. You wouldn't be here this morning."

"I don't know. There was always a guy with me. But just one guy, taking turns."

"Great," Joyce said. Marty's hand was on Mitchell's left shoulder; she put hers on his right hand.

"They took her to the hospital," he said. "The guys are in jail."

"They are?" Joyce said.

"I called the cops. When they left."

"You'll be a good witness," Joyce said.

He looked at her proud face.

"At the trial," she said.

The day was hot, but that night, most of the regulars came to the bar. Some of the younger ones came on motorcycles. They were a good crowd: They all worked, except the retired ones, and no one ever bothered the women, not even the young ones with their summer tans. Everyone talked about it: Some had read the newspaper story, some had heard the story in town, and they wanted to hear it from Mitchell. He told it as often as they asked, but he did not finish it, because he was working hard and could not stay with any group of customers long enough.

He watched their faces. Not one of them, even the women, looked at him as if he had not cared enough for the girl or was a coward. Many of them even appeared sympathetic, making him feel for moments that he was a survivor of something horrible; and when that feeling left him, he was ashamed. He felt tired and old, making drinks and change, talking and moving up and down the bar. At the stool at the far end, Bob drank coffee; and whenever Mitchell looked at him, he smiled or nodded and once raised his right fist, with the thumb up.

Reggie was drinking too much. He did that two or three times a month, and Mitchell had to shut him off, and Reggie always took it humbly. He was a big, gentle man with a long brown beard. But tonight, shutting off Reggie demanded from Mitchell an act of will, and when the eleven-o'clock news came on the television and Reggie ordered another shot and a draft, Mitchell pretended not to hear him. He served the customers at the other end of the bar, where Bob was. He could hear Reggie calling, "Hey, Mitch; shot and a draft, Mitch."

Mitchell was close to Bob now. Bob said softly, "He's had enough."

Mitchell nodded and went to Reggie, leaned closer to him, so he could speak quietly, and said, "Sorry, Reggie. Time for coffee. I don't want you dead out there."

Reggie blinked at him.

"OK, Mitch." He pulled some bills from his pocket and put them on the bar. Mitchell glanced at them and saw at least a ten-dollar tip. When he ran up Reggie's tab, the change was $16.50, and he dropped the coins and shoved the bills into the beer mug beside the cash register. The mug was full of bills, as it was on most nights, and he kept his hand in there, pressing Reggie's into the others, and saw the sunburned young men holding her down on the floor and one kneeling between her legs, spread and held, and he heard their cheering voices and her screaming and groaning and finally weeping and weeping and weeping, until she was the siren crying, then fading into the night. From the floor behind him, far across the room, he felt her pain and terror and grief, then her curse upon him. The curse moved into his back and spread down and up his spine, into his stomach and legs and arms and shoulders until he quivered with it. He wished he were alone so he could kneel to receive it.

Journal Entry

To what extent are the woman and Mitchell both victims of the rapists in "The Curse"?

Textual Considerations

1. Analyze the character of Mitchell. Do you agree with his family and friends that his intervention would have accomplished nothing? Why or why not?
2. Discuss how the author's use of omniscient narration affects the meaning and tone of the story.
3. Review the last paragraph. What does it reveal about Mitchell's psychological state? How does it add to the implications of the story's title?

Cultural Contexts

1. Discuss with your group the effects of being a witness to violence. To what extent should people get involved? Is action or inaction most likely to result in the psychological suffering of the witness? How might you have responded in Mitchell's situation?

Ralph Ellison
1947

Battle Royal

It goes a long way back, some twenty years. All my life I had been looking for something, and everywhere I turned someone tried to tell me what it was. I accepted their answers too, though they were often in contradiction and even self-contradictory. I was naive. I was looking for myself and asking everyone except myself questions which I, and only I, could answer. It took me a long time and much painful boomeranging of my expectations to achieve a realization everyone else appears to have been born with: That I am nobody but myself. But first I had to discover that I am an invisible man!

And yet I am no freak of nature, nor of history. I was in the cards, other things having been equal (or unequal) eighty-five years ago. I am not ashamed of my grandparents for having been slaves. I am only ashamed of myself for having at one time been ashamed. About eighty-five years ago they were told that they were free, united with others of our country in everything pertaining to the common good, and, in everything social, separate like the fingers of the hand. And they believed it. They exulted in it. They stayed in their place, worked hard, and brought up my father to do the same. But my grandfather is the one. He was an odd old guy, my grandfather, and I am told I take after him. It was he who caused the trouble. On his deathbed he called my father to him and said, "Son, after I'm gone I want you to keep up the good fight. I never told you, but our life is a war and I have been a traitor all my born days, a spy in the enemy's country ever since I give up my gun back in the Reconstruction. Live with your head in the lion's mouth. I want you to overcome 'em with yeses, undermine 'em with grins, agree 'em to death and destruction, let 'em swoller you till they vomit or bust wide open." They thought the old man had gone out of his mind. He had been the meekest of men. The younger children were rushed from the room, the shades drawn, and the flame of the lamp turned so low that it sputtered on the wick like the old man's breathing. "Learn it to the younguns," he whispered fiercely; then he died.

But my folks were more alarmed over his last words than over his dying. It was as though he had not died at all, his words caused so much anxiety. I was warned emphatically to forget what he had said and, indeed, this is the first time it has been mentioned outside the family circle. It had a tremendous effect upon me, however. I could never be sure of what he meant. Grandfather had been a quiet old man who never made any trouble, yet on his deathbed he had called himself a traitor and a spy, and he had spoken of his meekness as a dangerous activity. It became a constant puzzle which lay unanswered in the back of my mind. And whenever things went well for me I remembered my grandfather and felt guilty and uncomfortable. It was as though I was carrying out his advice in spite of myself. And to make it worse, everyone loved me for it. I was praised by the most lily-white men of the town. I was considered an example of desirable conduct—just as my grandfather had been. And what puzzled me was that the old man had defined it as *treachery*. When I was praised for my conduct I felt a guilt that in some way I was doing something that was really against the wishes of the white folks, that if they had understood they would have desired me to act just the opposite, that I should have been sulky and mean, and that that really would have been what they wanted, even though they were fooled and thought they wanted me to act as I did. It made me afraid that some day they would look upon me as a traitor and I would be lost. Still I was more afraid to act any other way because they didn't like that at all. The old man's words were like a curse. On my graduation day I delivered an oration in which I showed that humility was the secret, indeed, the very essence of progress. (Not that I believed this—how could I, remembering my grandfather?—I only believed that it worked.) It was a great success. Everyone praised me and I was invited to give the speech at a gathering of the town's leading white citizens. It was a triumph for our whole community.

It was in the main ballroom of the leading hotel. When I got there I discovered that it was on the occasion of a smoker, and I was told that since I was to be there anyway I might as well take part in the battle royal to be fought by some of my schoolmates as part of the entertainment. The battle royal came first.

All of the town's big shots were there in their tuxedoes, wolfing down the buffet foods, drinking beer and whiskey and smoking black cigars. It was a large room with a high ceiling. Chairs were arranged in neat rows around three sides of a portable boxing ring. The fourth side was clear, revealing a gleaming space of polished floor. I had some misgivings over the battle royal, by the way. Not from a distaste for fighting but because I didn't care too much for the other fellows who were to take part. They were tough guys who seemed to have no grandfather's curse worrying their minds. No one could mistake their toughness. And besides, I suspected that fighting a battle royal might detract from the dignity of my speech. In those pre-invisible days I visualized myself as a potential Booker T. Washington. But the other fellows didn't care too much for me either, and there were nine of them. I felt superior to them in my way, and I didn't like the manner in which we were all crowded together into the servants' elevator. Nor did they like my being there. In fact, as the warmly lighted floors flashed past the elevator we had words over the fact that I, by taking part in the fight, had knocked one of their friends out of a night's work.

We were led out of the elevator through a rococo hall into an anteroom and told to get into our fighting togs. Each of us was issued a pair of boxing gloves and ushered out into the big mirrored hall, which we entered looking cautiously about us and whispering, lest we might accidentally be heard above the noise of the room. It was foggy with cigar smoke. And already the whiskey was taking effect. I was shocked to see some of the most important men of the town quite tipsy. They were all there—bankers, lawyers, judges, doctors, fire chiefs, teachers, merchants. Even one of the more fashionable pastors. Something we could not see was going on up front. A clarinet was vibrating sensuously and the men were standing up and moving eagerly forward. We were a small tight group, clustered together, our bare upper bodies touching and shining with anticipatory sweat; while up front the big shots were becoming increasingly excited over something we still could not see. Suddenly I heard the school superintendent, who had told me to come, yell, "Bring up the shines, gentlemen! Bring up the little shines!"

We were rushed up to the front of the ballroom, where it smelled even more strongly of tobacco and whiskey. Then we were pushed into place. I almost wet my pants. A sea of faces, some hostile, some amused, ringed around us, and in the center, facing us, stood a magnificent blonde—stark naked. There was dead silence. I felt a blast of cold air chill me. I tried to back away, but they were behind me and around me. Some of the boys stood with lowered heads, trembling. I felt a wave of irrational guilt and fear. My teeth chattered, my skin turned to goose flesh, my knees knocked. Yet I was strongly attracted and looked in spite of myself. Had the price of looking been blindness, I would have looked. The hair was yellow like that of a circus kewpie doll, the face heavily powdered and rouged, as though to form an abstract mask, the eyes hollow and smeared a cool blue, the color of a baboon's butt. I felt a desire to spit upon her as my eyes brushed slowly over her body. Her breasts were firm and round as the domes of East Indian temples, and I stood so close as to see the fine skin texture and beads of pearly perspiration glistening like dew around the pink and erected buds of her nipples. I wanted at one and the same time to run from the room, to sink through the floor, or go to her and cover her from my eyes and the eyes of the others with my body; to feel the soft thighs, to caress her and destroy her, to love her and murder her, to hide from her, and yet to stroke where below, the small American flag tattooed upon her belly her thighs formed a capital V. I had a notion that of all in the room she saw only me with her impersonal eyes.

And then she began to dance, a slow sensuous movement, the smoke of a hundred cigars clinging to her like the thinnest of veils. She seemed like a fair bird-girl girdled in veils calling to me from the angry surface of some gray and threatening sea. I was transported. Then I became aware of the clarinet playing and the big shots yelling at us. Some threatened us if we looked and others, if we did not. On my right I saw one boy faint. And now a man grabbed a silver pitcher from a table and stepped close as he dashed ice water upon him and stood him up and forced two of us to support him as his head hung and moans issued from his thick bluish lips. Another boy began to plead to go home. He was the largest of the group, wearing dark red fighting trunks much too small to conceal the erection which projected from him as though in answer to the insinuating low-registered moaning of the clarinet. He tried to hide himself with his boxing gloves.

And all the while the blonde continued dancing, smiling faintly at the big shots who watched her with fascination, and faintly smiling at our fear. I noticed a certain merchant who followed her hungrily, his lips loose and drooling. He was a large man who wore diamond studs in a shirtfront which swelled with the ample paunch underneath, and each time the blonde swayed her undulating hips he ran his hand through the thin hair of his bald head and, with his arms upheld, his posture clumsy like that of an intoxicated panda, wound his belly in a slow and obscene grind. This creature was completely hypnotized. The music had quickened. As the dancer flung herself about with a detached expression on her face, the men began reaching out to touch her. I could see their beefy fingers sink into the soft flesh. Some of the others tried to stop them and she began to move around the floor in graceful circles, as they gave chase, slipping and sliding over the polished floor. It was mad. Chairs went crashing, drinks were spilt, as they ran laughing and howling after her. They caught her just as she reached a door, raised her from the floor, and tossed her as college boys are tossed at a hazing, and above her red, fixed-smiling lips I saw the terror and disgust in her eyes, almost like my own terror and that which I saw in some of the other boys. As I watched, they tossed her twice and her soft breasts seemed to flatten against the air, and her legs flung wildly as she spun. Some of the more sober ones helped her to escape. And I started off the floor, heading for the anteroom with the rest of the boys.

Some were still crying and in hysteria. But as we tried to leave we were stopped and ordered to get into the ring. There was nothing to do but what we were told. All ten of us climbed under the ropes and allowed ourselves to be blindfolded with broad bands of white cloth. One of the men seemed to feel a bit sympathetic and tried to cheer us up as we stood with our backs against the ropes. Some of us tried to grin. "See that boy over there?" one of the men said. "I want you to run across at the bell and give it to him right in the belly. If you don't get him, I'm going to get you. I don't like his looks." Each of us was told the same. The blindfolds were put on. Yet even then I had been going over my speech. In my mind each word was as bright as flame. I felt the cloth pressed into place, and frowned so that it would be loosened when I relaxed.

But now I felt a sudden fit of blind terror. I was unused to darkness. It was as though I had suddenly found myself in a dark room filled with poisonous cotton-mouths. I could hear the bleary voices yelling insistently for the battle royal to begin.

"Get going in there!"

"Let me at that big nigger!"

I strained to pick up the school superintendent's voice, as though to squeeze some security out of that slightly more familiar sound.

"Let me at those black sonsabitches!" someone yelled.

"No, Jackson, no!" another voice yelled. "Here, somebody, help me hold Jack."

"I want to get at that ginger-colored nigger. Tear him limb from limb," the first voice yelled.

I stood against the ropes trembling. For in those days I was what they called ginger-colored, and he sounded as though he might crunch me between his teeth like a crisp ginger cookie.

Quite a struggle was going on. Chairs were being kicked about and I could hear voices grunting as with a terrific effort. I wanted to see, to see more desperately than ever before. But the blindfold was tight as a thick skin-puckering scab and when I raised my gloved hands to push the layers of white aside a voice yelled, "Oh, no you don't, black bastard! Leave that alone!"

"Ring the bell before Jackson kills him a coon!" someone boomed in the sudden silence. And I heard the bell clang and the sound of the feet scuffling forward.

A glove smacked against my head. I pivoted, striking out stiffly as someone went past, and felt the jar ripple along the length of my arm to my shoulder. Then it seemed as though all nine of the boys had turned upon me at once. Blows pounded me from all sides while I struck out as best I could. So many blows landed upon me that I wondered if I were not the only blindfolded fighter in the ring or if the man called Jackson hadn't succeeded in getting me after all.

Blindfolded, I could no longer control my motions. I had no dignity. I stumbled about like a baby or a drunken man. The smoke had become thicker and with each new blow it seemed to sear and further restrict my lungs. My saliva became like hot bitter glue. A glove connected with my head, filling my mouth with warm blood. It was everywhere. I could not tell if the moisture I felt upon my body was sweat or blood. A blow landed hard against the nape of my neck. I felt myself going over, my head hitting the floor. Streaks of blue light filled the black world behind the blindfold. I lay prone, pretending that I was knocked out, but felt myself seized by hands and yanked to my feet. "Get going, black boy! Mix it up!" My arms were like lead, my head smarting from blows. I managed to feel my way to the ropes and held on, trying to catch my breath. A glove landed in my mid-section and I went over again, feeling as though the smoke had become a knife jabbed into my guts. Pushed this way and that by the legs milling around me, I finally pulled erect and discovered that I could see the black, sweat-washed forms weaving in the smoky-blue atmosphere like drunken dancers weaving to the rapid drum-like thuds of blows.

Everyone fought hysterically. It was complete anarchy. Everybody fought everybody else. No group fought together for long. Two, three, four, fought one, then turned to fight each other, were themselves attacked. Blows landed below the belt and in the kidney, with the gloves open as well as closed, and with my eye partly opened now there was not so much terror. I moved carefully, avoiding blows, although not too many to attract attention, fighting from group to group. The boys groped about like blind, cautious crabs crouching to protect their mid-sections, their heads pulled in short against their shoulders, their arms stretched nervously before them, with their fists testing the smoke-filled air like the knobbed feelers of hypersensitive snails. In one corner I glimpsed a boy violently punching the air and heard him scream in pain as he smashed his hand against a ring post. For a second I saw him bent over holding his hand, then going down as a blow caught his unprotected head. I played one group against the other, slipping in and throwing a punch then stepping out of range while pushing the others into the melee to take the blows blindly aimed at me. The smoke was agonizing and there were no rounds, no bells at three minute intervals to relieve our exhaustion. The room spun round me, a swirl of lights, smoke, sweating bodies surrounded by tense white faces. I bled from both nose and mouth, the blood spattering upon my chest.

The men kept yelling, "Slug him, black boy! Knock his guts out!"

"Uppercut him! Kill him! Kill that big boy!"

Taking a fake fall, I saw a boy going down heavily beside me as though we were felled by a single blow, saw a sneaker-clad foot shoot into his groin as the two who had knocked him down stumbled upon him. I rolled out of range, feeling a twinge of nausea.

The harder we fought the more threatening the men became. And yet, I had begun to worry about my speech again. How would it go? Would they recognize my ability? What would they give me?

I was fighting automatically when suddenly I noticed that one after another of the boys was leaving the ring. I was surprised, filled with panic, as though I had been left alone with an unknown danger. Then I understood. The boys had arranged it among themselves. It was the custom for the two men left in the ring to slug it out for the winner's prize. I discovered this too late. When the bell sounded two men in tuxedoes leaped into the ring and removed the blindfold. I found myself facing Tatlock, the biggest of the gang. I felt sick at my stomach. Hardly had the bell stopped ringing in my ears than it clanged again and I saw him moving swiftly toward me. Thinking of nothing else to do I hit him smash on the nose. He kept coming, bringing the rank sharp violence of stale sweat. His face was a black blank of a face, only his eyes alive—with hate of me and aglow with a feverish terror from what had happened to us all. I became anxious. I wanted to deliver my speech and he came at me as though he meant to beat it out of me. I smashed him again and again, taking his blows as they came. Then on a sudden impulse I struck him lightly and as we clinched, I whispered, "Fake like I knocked you out, you can have the prize."

"I'll break your behind," he whispered hoarsely.

"For *them?*"

"For *me,* sonofabitch!"

They were yelling for us to break it up and Tatlock spun me half around with a blow, and as a joggled camera sweeps in a reeling scene, I saw the howling red faces crouching tense beneath the cloud of blue-gray smoke. For a moment the world wavered, unraveled, flowed, then my head cleared and Tatlock bounced before me. That fluttering shadow before my eyes was his jabbing left hand. Then falling forward, my head against his damp shoulder, I whispered,

"I'll make it five dollars more."

"Go to hell!"

But his muscles relaxed a trifle beneath my pressure and I breathed, "Seven?"

"Give it to your ma," he said, ripping me beneath the heart.

And while I still held him I butted him and moved away. I felt myself bombarded with punches. I fought back with hopeless desperation. I wanted to deliver my speech more than anything else in the world, because I felt that only these men could judge truly my ability, and now this stupid clown was ruining my chances. I began fighting carefully now, moving in to punch him and out again with my greater speed. A lucky blow to his chin and I had him going too—until I heard a loud voice yell, "I got my money on the big boy."

Hearing this, I almost dropped my guard. I was confused: Should I try to win against the voice out there? Would not this go against my speech and was not this a moment for humility, for nonresistance? A blow to my head as I danced about sent my right eye popping like a jack-in-the-box and settled my dilemma. The room went red as I fell. It was a dream fall, my body languid and fastidious as to where to land, until the floor became impatient and smashed up to meet me. A moment later I came to. An hypnotic voice said FIVE emphatically. And I lay there, hazily watching a dark red spot of my own blood shaping itself into a butterfly, glistening and soaking into the soiled gray world of the canvas.

When the voice drawled TEN I was lifted up and dragged to a chair. I sat dazed. My eye pained and swelled with each throb of my pounding heart and I wondered if now I would be allowed to speak. I was wringing wet, my mouth still bleeding. We were grouped along the wall now. The other boys ignored me as they congratulated Tatlock and speculated as to how much they would be paid. One boy whimpered over his smashed hand. Looking up front, I saw attendants in white jackets rolling the portable ring away and placing a small square rug in the vacant space surrounded by chairs. Perhaps, I thought, I will stand on the rug to deliver my speech.

Then the M.C. called to us, "Come on up here boys and get your money."

We ran forward to where the men laughed and talked in their chairs, waiting. Everyone seemed friendly now.

"There it is on the rug," the man said. I saw the rug covered with coins of all dimensions and a few crumpled bills. But what excited me, scattered here and there, were the gold pieces.

"Boys, it's all yours," the man said. "You get all you grab."

"That's right, Sambo," a blond man said, winking at me confidentially.

I trembled with excitement, forgetting my pain. I would get the gold and the bills, I thought. I would use both hands. I would throw my body against the boys nearest me to block them from the gold.

"Get down around the rug now," the man commanded, "and don't anyone touch it until I give the signal."

"This ought to be good," I heard.

As told, we got around the square rug on our knees. Slowly the man raised his freckled hand as we followed it upward with our eyes.

I heard, "These niggers look like they're about to pray!"

Then, "Ready," the man said. "Go!"

I lunged for a yellow coin lying on the blue design of the carpet, touching it and sending a surprised shriek to join those rising around me. I tried frantically to remove my hand but could not let go. A hot, violent force tore through my body, shaking me like a wet rat. The rug was electrified. The hair bristled up on my head as I shook myself free. My muscles jumped, my nerves jangled, writhed. But I saw that this was not stopping the other boys. Laughing in fear and embarrassment, some were holding back and scooping up the coins knocked off by the painful contortions of the others. The men roared above us as we struggled.

"Pick it up, goddamnit, pick it up!" someone called like a bass-voiced parrot. "Go on, get it!"

I crawled rapidly around the floor, picking up the coins, trying to avoid the coppers and to get greenbacks and the gold. Ignoring the shock by laughing, as I brushed the coins off quickly, I discovered that I could contain the electricity—a contradiction, but it works. Then the men began to push us onto the rug. Laughing embarrassedly, we struggled out of their hands and kept after the coins. We were all wet and slippery and hard to hold. Suddenly I saw a boy lifted into the air, glistening with sweat like a circus seal, and dropped, his wet back landing flush upon the charged rug, heard him yell and saw him literally dance upon his back, his elbows beating a frenzied tattoo upon the floor, his muscles twitching like the flesh of a horse stung by many flies. When he finally rolled off, his face was gray and no one stopped him when he ran from the floor amid booming laughter.

"Get the money," the M.C. called. "That's good hard American cash!"

And we snatched and grabbed, snatched and grabbed. I was careful not to come too close to the rug now, and when I felt the hot whiskey breath descend upon me like a cloud of foul air I reached out and grabbed the leg of a chair. It was occupied and I held on desperately.

"Leggo, nigger! Leggo!"

The huge face wavered down to mine as he tried to push me free. But my body was slippery and he was too drunk. It was Mr. Colcord, who owned a chain of movie houses and "entertainment palaces." Each time he grabbed me I slipped out of his hands. It became a real struggle. I feared the rug more than I did the drunk, so I held on, surprising myself for a moment by trying to topple *him* upon the rug. It was such an enormous idea that I found myself actually carrying it out. I tried not to be obvious, yet when I grabbed his leg, trying to tumble him out of the chair, he raised up roaring with laughter, and, looking at me with soberness dead in the eye, kicked me viciously in the chest. The chair leg flew out of my hand and I felt myself going and rolled. It was as though I had rolled through a bed of hot coals. It seemed a whole century would pass before I would roll free, a century in which I was seared through the deepest levels of my body to the fearful breath within me and the breath seared and heated to the point of explosion. It'll all be over in a flash, I thought as I rolled clear. It'll all be over in a flash.

But not yet, the men on the other side were waiting, red faces swollen as though from apoplexy as they bent forward in their chairs. Seeing their fingers coming toward me I rolled away as a fumbled football rolls off the receiver's fingertips, back into the coals. That time I luckily sent the rug sliding out of place and heard the coins ringing against the floor and the boys scuffling to pick them up and the M.C. calling, "All right, boys, that's all. Go get dressed and get your money."

I was limp as a dish rag. My back felt as though it had been beaten with wires.

When we had dressed the M.C. came in and gave us each five dollars, except Tatlock, who got ten for being last in the ring. Then he told us to leave. I was not to get a chance to deliver my speech, I thought. I was going out into the dim alley in despair when I was stopped and told to go back. I returned to the ballroom, where the men were pushing back their chairs and gathering in groups to talk.

The M.C. knocked on a table for quiet. "Gentlemen," he said, "we almost forgot an important part of the program. A most serious part, gentlemen. This boy was brought here to deliver a speech which he made at his graduation yesterday..."

"Bravo!"

"I'm told that he is the smartest boy we've got out there in Greenwood. I'm told that he knows more big words than a pocket-sized dictionary."

Much applause and laughter.

"So now, gentlemen, I want you to give him your attention."

There was still laughter as I faced them, my mouth dry, my eye throbbing. I began slowly, but evidently my throat was tense, because they began shouting, "Louder! Louder!"

"We of the younger generation extol the wisdom of that great leader and educator," I shouted, "who first spoke these flaming words of wisdom: A ship lost at sea for many days suddenly sighted a friendly vessel. From the mast of the unfortunate vessel was seen a signal: "Water, water, we die of thirst!" The answer from the friendly vessel came back: "Cast down your bucket where you are." The captain of the distressed vessel, at last heeding the injunction, cast down his bucket, and it came up full of fresh sparkling water from the mouth of the Amazon River.' And like him I say, and in his words, 'To those of my race who depend upon bettering their condition in a foreign land, or who underestimate the importance of cultivating friendly relations with the Southern white man, who is his next-door neighbor, I would say: "Cast down your bucket where you are"—cast it down in making friends in every manly way of the people of all races by whom we are surrounded…'"

I spoke automatically and with such fervor that I did not realize that the men were still talking and laughing until my dry mouth, filling up with blood from the cut, almost strangled me. I coughed, wanting to stop and go to one of the tall brass, sand-filled spittoons to relieve myself, but a few of the men, especially the superintendent, were listening and I was afraid. So I gulped it down, blood, saliva and all, and continued. (What powers of endurance I had during those days! What enthusiasm! What a belief in the rightness of things!) I spoke even louder in spite of the pain. But still they talked and still they laughed, as though deaf with cotton in dirty ears. So I spoke with greater emotional emphasis. I closed my ears and swallowed blood until I was nauseated. The speech seemed a hundred times as long as before, but I could not leave out a single word. All had to be said, each memorized nuance considered, rendered. Nor was that all. Whenever I uttered a word of three or more syllables a group of voices would yell for me to repeat it. I used the phrase "social responsibility" and they yelled:

"What's that word you say, boy?"

"Social responsibility," I said.

"What?"

"Social…"

"Louder."

"…responsibility."

"More!"

"Respon—"

"Repeat!"

"—sibility."

The room filled with the uproar of laughter until, no doubt, distracted by having to gulp down my blood, I made a mistake and yelled a phrase I had often seen denounced in newspaper editorials, heard debated in private.

"Social…"

"What?" they yelled.

"…equality—"

The laughter hung smokelike in the sudden stillness. I opened my eyes, puzzled. Sounds of displeasure filled the room. The M.C. rushed forward. They shouted hostile phrases at me. But I did not understand.

A small dry mustached man in the front row blared out, "Say that slowly, son!"

"What, sir?"

"What you just said!"

"Social responsibility, sir," I said.

"You weren't being smart, were you, boy?" he said, not unkindly.

"No, sir!"

"You sure that about 'equality' was a mistake?"

"Oh, yes, sir," I said. "I was swallowing blood."

"Well, you had better speak more slowly so we can understand. We mean to do right by you, but you've got to know your place at all times. All right, now, go on with your speech."

I was afraid. I wanted to leave but I wanted also to speak and I was afraid they'd snatch me down.

"Thank you, sir," I said, beginning where I had left off, and having them ignore me as before.

Yet when I finished there was a thunderous applause. I was surprised to see the superintendent come forth with a package wrapped in white tissue paper, and, gesturing for quiet, address the men.

"Gentlemen, you see that I did not overpraise this boy. He makes a good speech and some day he'll lead his people in the proper paths. And I don't have to tell you that that is important in these days and times. This is a good, smart boy, and so to encourage him in the right direction, in the name of the Board of Education I wish to present him a prize in the form of this..."

He paused, removing the tissue paper and revealing a gleaming calfskin brief case.

"...in the form of this first-class article from Shad Whitmore's shop."

"Boy," he said, addressing me, "take this prize and keep it well. Consider it a badge of office. Prize it. Keep developing as you are and some day it will be filled with important papers that will help shape the destiny of your people."

I was so moved that I could hardly express my thanks. A rope of bloody saliva forming a shape like an undiscovered continent drooled upon the leather and I wiped it quickly away. I felt an importance that I had never dreamed.

"Open it and see what's inside," I was told.

My fingers a-tremble, I complied, smelling the fresh leather and finding an official-looking document inside. It was a scholarship to the state college for Negroes. My eyes filled with tears and I ran awkwardly off the floor.

I was overjoyed; I did not even mind when I discovered that the gold pieces I had scrambled for were brass pocket tokens advertising a certain make of automobile.

When I reached home everyone was excited. Next day the neighbors came to congratulate me. I even felt safe from grandfather, whose deathbed curse usually spoiled my triumphs. I stood beneath his photograph with my briefcase in hand and smiled triumphantly into his stolid black peasant's face. It was a face that fascinated me. The eyes seemed to follow everywhere I went.

That night I dreamed I was at a circus with him and that he refused to laugh at the clowns no matter what they did. Then later he told me to open my brief case and read what was inside and I did, finding an official envelope stamped with the state seal; and inside the envelope I found another and another, endlessly, and I thought I would fall of weariness. "Them's years," he said. "Now open that one." And I did and in it I found an engraved document containing a short message in letters of gold. "Read it," my grandfather said. "Out loud!"

"To Whom It May Concern," I intoned. "Keep This Nigger-Boy Running."

I awoke with the old man's laughter ringing in my ears.

Journal Entry

Review the story's first paragraph and explain why achieving identity is contingent upon accepting invisibility.

Textual Considerations

1. The narrator admits to being naive. Cite evidence from the story that supports this insight.
2. According to Ellison, the battle royal "is an initiation ritual to which all greenhorns are subjected." How do you respond to the boxing scenes? Why are the boxers blindfolded? How do the town's "leading White citizens" behave during the match and the wired money game?
3. What symbolic functions does the blonde serve? What is the significance of her tattoo? To what extent is she, like the boys, a puppet of the drunken group?
4. Review the narrator's speech. What ironies does it contain given the situation?
5. What is your interpretation of the narrator's dream? Is there a connection between "Keep This Nigger-Boy Running" and his dying grandfather's advice? Explain.

Cultural Contexts

1. Discuss with your group the connections between racial and sexual exploitation in the story and in American society.
2. What is the relation between sex and violence in "Battle Royal"? To what extent are the author's critiques still valid?

Brent Staples
1986

A Brother's Murder

It has been more than two years since my telephone rang with the news that my younger brother Blake—just 22 years old—had been murdered. The young man who killed him was only 24. Wearing a ski mask, he emerged from a car, fired six times at close range with a massive .44 Magnum, then fled. The two had once been inseparable friends. A senseless rivalry—beginning, I think, with an argument over a girlfriend—escalated from posturing, to threats, to violence, to murder. The way the two were living, death could have come to either of them from anywhere. In fact, the assailant had already survived multiple gunshot wounds from an incident much like the one in which my brother lost his life.

As I wept for Blake I felt wrenched backward into events and circumstances that had seemed light-years gone. Though a decade apart, we both were raised in Chester, Pennsylvania, an angry, heavily black, heavily poor, industrial city southwest of Philadelphia. There, in the 1960's, I was introduced to mortality, not by the old and failing, but by beautiful young men who lay wrecked after sudden explosions of violence. The first, I remember from my 14th year—Johnny, brash lover of fast cars, stabbed to death two doors from my house in a fight over a pool game. The next year, my teenage cousin, Wesley, whom I loved very much, was shot dead. The summers blur. Milton, an angry young neighbor, shot a crosstown rival, wounding him badly. William, another teen-age neighbor, took a shotgun blast to the shoulder in some urban drama and displayed his bandages proudly. His brother, Leonard, severely beaten, lost an eye and donned a black patch. It went on.

I recall not long before I left for college, two local Vietnam veterans—one from the Marines, one from the Army—arguing fiercely, nearly at blows about which outfit had done the most in the war. The most killing, they meant. Not much later, I read a magazine article that set that dispute in a context. In the story, a noncommissioned officer—a sergeant, I believe—said he would pass up any number of affluent, suburban-born recruits to get hard-core soldiers from the inner city. They jumped into the rice paddies with "their manhood on their sleeves," I believe he said. These two items—the veterans arguing and the sergeant's words—still characterize for me the circumstances under which black men in their teens and twenties kill one another with such frequency. With a touchy paranoia born of living battered lives, they are desperate to be real men. Killing is only *machismo* taken to the extreme. Incursions to be punished by death were many and minor, and they remain so: they include stepping on the wrong toe, literally; cheating in a drug deal; simply saying "I dare you" to someone holding a gun; crossing territorial lines in a gang dispute. My brother grew up to wear his manhood on his sleeve. And when he died, he was in that group—black, male and in its teens and early twenties—that is far and away the most likely to murder or be murdered.

I left the East Coast after college, spent the mid- and late-1970s in Chicago as a graduate student, taught for a time, then became a journalist. Within ten years of leaving my hometown, I was overeducated and "upwardly mobile," ensconced on a quiet, tree-lined street where voices raised in anger were scarcely ever heard. The telephone, like some grim umbilical, kept me connected to the old world with news of deaths, imprisonings and misfortune. I felt emotionally beaten up. Perhaps to protect myself, I added a psychological dimension to the physical distance I had achieved. I rarely visited my hometown. I shut it out.

As I fled the past, so Blake embraced it. On Christmas of 1983, I traveled from Chicago to a black section of Roanoke, Virginia, where he then lived. The desolate public housing projects, the hopeless, idle young men crashing against one another—these reminded me of the embittered town we'd grown up in. It was a place where once I would have been comfortable, or at least sure of myself. Now, hearing of my brother's forays into crime, his scrapes with police and street thugs, I was scared, unsteady on foreign terrain.

I saw that Blake's romance with the street life and the hustler image had flowered dangerously. One evening that late December, standing in some Roanoke dive among drug dealers and grim, hair-trigger losers, I told him I feared for his life. He had affected the image of the tough he wanted to be. But behind the dark glasses and the swagger, I glimpsed the baby-faced toddler I'd once watched over. I nearly wept. I wanted desperately for him to live. The young think themselves immortal, and a dangerous light shone in his eyes as he spoke laughingly of making fools of the policemen who had raided his apartment looking for drugs. He cried out as I took his right hand. A line of stitches lay between the thumb and index finger. Kickback from a shotgun, he explained, nothing serious. Gunplay had become part of his life.

I lacked the language simply to say: Thousands have lived this for you and died. I fought the urge to lift him bodily and shake him. This place and the way you are living smells of death to me, I said. Take some time away, I said. Let's go downtown tomorrow and buy a plane ticket anywhere, take a bus trip, anything to get away and cool things off. He took my alarm casually. We arranged to meet the following night—an appointment he would not keep. We embraced as though through glass. I drove away.

As I stood in my apartment in Chicago holding the receiver that evening in February 1984, I felt as though part of my soul had been cut away. I questioned myself then, and I still do. Did I not reach back soon enough or earnestly enough for him? For weeks I awoke crying from a recurrent dream in which I chased him, urgently trying to get him to read a document I had, as though reading it would protect him from what had happened in waking life. His eyes shining like black diamonds, he smiled and danced just beyond my grasp. When I reached for him, I caught only the space where he had been.

Journal Entry

Respond to Staples's statement that he "was introduced to mortality, not by the old and failing, but by beautiful young men who lay wrecked after sudden explosions of violence."

Textual Considerations

1. What do we learn about Blake's way of life from the essay's first paragraph?
2. How did the narrator escape the fate of the other young men in the ghetto? Does the fact that he did escape alter your opinion of those who didn't? Explain.
3. "As I fled the past, so Blake embraced it." How does this choice affect the brother's relationship?
4. Staples uses several flashbacks in the essay. Identify these examples, and discuss their impact on the essay's purpose.
5. Staples tries to maintain an objective tone. Are there points at which his tone becomes more personal? What examples can you cite? What is their effect?

Cultural Contexts

1. Discuss with your group Staples's reasons for including the argument between the Vietnam veterans. How does it add to your understanding of his thesis that "killing is only *machismo* taken to the extreme." To what extent do you agree with his point of view?

David W. Powell
1994

*Vietnam: What I Remember**

The following events come to my conscious memory uninvited. I not only remember them vividly, I reexperience them with all my senses:

Froze with fright, standing up, the first time I was under fire
Watched two marines try to break open the skull of a dead Viet Cong with a large rock
Observed a marine intentionally shoot a girl four or six years of age
Watched the girl's grandfather carry her into our line of fire, sobbing
Had a lieutenant who delighted in sneaking up on me when I was on watch at night

*From "Patriotism Revisited," a memoir.

Was offered a blood-soaked flak jacket and a helmet with a bullet hole through it as my first field equipment

Had my boots rot off during an operation in the field

Observed two captured nurses being beaten and raped by marines

Rifle-butted a girl of twelve in the face when she would not move away

Strangled a captured Viet Cong for refusing to talk to an interpreter

Discovered brain matter on barbed wire I was stretching out

Observed a marine laugh as he stepped on the chest of a dead Viet Cong and watched blood squirt out of the enemy's wounds

Awoke to find a buffalo leech on my leg

Was abandoned under fire when a rocket jammed in my launcher

Was abandoned under fire when I was shot

Hit head and fell in open field. Watched my fellow marines run by me to seek cover for themselves

Received letter from wife telling me how much fun she and a girlfriend had on Friday nights when they went out to bars to dance

Watched fellow marine shoot himself in the foot to get evacuated

Heard same man cry in his sleep when he was returned to the company

Found marine boot with foot in it in a hedgerow

Almost run over by retreating U.S. tank

Saw Lt. Spivey hit a head-high booby trap

Nearly murdered villager for stealing my laundry

Watched Prestridge test his new M-16 by shooting a woman getting water from a nearby well

Identified Haas's remains

Exchanged letters with Haas's mother

Had an artillery canister fall six inches in front of my head

Was about to put on fresh boots when I discovered lice swimming in them

Saw seven-foot python climbing in ceiling just above my head

Bullets sounding like bees digging up ground all around me

Nearly trapped in Da Nang village my last night in Vietnam

Robbed by marines while I slept in Okinawa after tour was over

Circled over El Toro air base for two hours so that President Johnson could land and be photographed greeting returning veterans

●

Since my return I have held eighteen different jobs and have been unemployed for several six-month periods. This is a direct result of my Post Traumatic Stress Disorder, specifically a disdain for being told to do tasks I do not want to do; an exaggerated startle response, which is terribly embarrassing to me; and a lack of control over emotional flooding.

I divorced my first wife two years after I got out of the service. I divorced my second wife in 1982. I separated from a four year relationship in 1987. I have not had a significant relationship with a woman since then. I have no significant male or female friendships. I am aloof from my immediate family, who live in Tucson, Arizona.

Journal Entry

Record your responses to "Vietnam: What I Remember."

Textual Considerations

1. How does Powell's cataloging the events that come to his "conscious memory uninvited" develop the poem's meaning?
2. Powell uses the verbs *observed* and *watched* several times. In these instance, what do these memories have in common?
3. What is the tone of the last two paragraphs? How do they differ thematically and stylistically from the rest of the memoir?

Cultural Contexts

1. Discuss with your group why Powell chose to name his memoir "Patriotism Revisited." Is it an appropriate title? Why or why not?

Hardy, Levertov, and Yevtushenko

Thomas Hardy
1902

The Man He Killed

"Had he and I but met
By some old ancient inn,
We should have sat us down to wet
Right many a nipperkin!

"But ranged as infantry,   5
And staring face to face,
I shot at him as he at me,
And killed him in his place.

"I shot him dead because—
Because he was my foe,   10
Just so: my foe of course he was;
That's clear enough; although

"He thought he'd 'list, perhaps,
Off-hand like—just as I—
Was out of work—had sold his traps—   15
No other reason why.

"Yes; quaint and curious war is!
You shoot a fellow down
You'd treat if met where any bar is,
Or help to half-a-crown."   20

Denise Levertov
1966

What Were They Like?

1) Did the people of Vietnam
   use lanterns of stone?
2) Did they hold ceremonies
   to reverence the opening of buds?
3) Were they inclined to quiet laughter?   5
4) Did they use bone and ivory,
   jade and silver, for ornament?
5) Had they an epic poem?
6) Did they distinguish between speech and singing?

1) Sir, their light hearts turned to stone.   10
   It is not remembered whether in gardens
   stone lanterns illumined pleasant ways.
2) Perhaps they gathered once to delight in blossom,
   but after the children were killed
   there were no more buds.   15
3) Sir, laughter is bitter to the burned mouth.
4) A dream ago, perhaps. Ornament is for joy.
   All the bones were charred.
5) It is not remembered. Remember,
   most were peasants; their life   20
   was in rice and bamboo.
   When peaceful clouds were reflected in the paddies
   and the water buffalo stepped surely along terraces,
   maybe fathers told their sons old tales.
   When bombs smashed those mirrors   25
   there was time only to scream.
6) There is no echo yet
   of their speech which was like a song.
   It was reported their singing resembled
   the flight of moths in moonlight.   30
   Who can say? It is silent now.

Yevgeny Yevtushenko
1962

Babiy Yar

Over Babiy Yar
there are no memorials.
The steep hillside like a rough inscription.
I am frightened.
Today I am as old as the Jewish race.   5
I seem to myself a Jew at this moment.
I, wandering in Egypt.
I, crucified. I perishing.
Even today the mark of the nails.
I think also of Dreyfus. I am he.   10
The Philistine my judge and my accuser.
Cut off by bars and cornered,
ringed round, spat at, lied about;
the screaming ladies with the Brussels lace
poke me in the face with parasols.   15
I am also a boy in Belostok,
the dropping blood spreads across the floor,
the public-bar heroes are rioting
in an equal stench of garlic and of drink.
I have no strength, go spinning from a boot,   20
shriek useless prayers that they don't listen to;
with a cackle of "Thrash the kikes and save Russia!"
the corn-chandler is beating up my mother.
I seem to myself like Anna Frank
to be transparent as an April twig   25
and am in love, I have no need for words,
I need for us to look at one another.
How little we have to see or to smell
separated from foliage and the sky,
how much, how much in the dark room   30
gently embracing each other.
They're coming. Don't be afraid.
The booming and banging of the spring.
It's coming this way. Come to me.
Quickly, give me your lips.   35
They're battering in the door. Roar of the ice.

Over Babiy Yar
rustle of the wild grass.

The trees look threatening, look like judges.
And everything is one silent cry.
Taking my hat off
I feel myself slowly going grey.
And I am one silent cry
over the many thousands of the buried;
am every old man killed here,
every child killed here.
O my Russian people, I know you.
Your nature is international.
Foul hands rattle your clean name.
I know the goodness of my country.
How horrible it is that pompous title
the anti-semites calmly call themselves,
Society of the Russian People.
No part of me can ever forget it.
When the last anti-semite on the earth
is buried for ever
let the International ring out.
No Jewish blood runs among my blood,
but I am as bitterly and hardly hated
by every anti-semite
as if I were a Jew. By this
I am a Russian.

◆

Journal Entry

On what aspects of war's destructiveness does each speaker focus?

Textual Considerations

1. How does the setting reinforce the theme in Hardy's and Yevtushenko's texts?
2. Consider how the sentence structure of "The Man He Killed" conveys the attitude of the speaker toward his so-called foe. What indications are there that the speaker is trying to clarify for himself his reasons for killing? Characterize your response to his situation.
3. What is the effect of Levertov's raising a series of questions followed by a series of answers? Who might the questioner be? Is his occupation important?
4. Who is answering? Does his nationality matter? Characterize the attitude of the person answering the questions, the questions themselves, the people of Vietnam, and the war.
5. Yevtushenko uses literary techniques such as flashbacks and first person narrator to reinforce the meanings of "Babiy Yar." Cite the examples you found most effective.
6. The poem is divided into two relatively long stanzas. What aspects of its thematic organization justify this division?

7. In the latter part of "Babiy Yar," Yevtushenko addresses the Russian people. Characterize his attitude toward them. Does it surprise you that Yevtushenko's poem was originally banned in Russia because he was regarded as a traitor? Explain.

Cultural Contexts

1. In "Babiy Yar," Yevtushenko refers to historical places and people. Review the poem and research the significance of his allusions to Dreyfus, Brussels, Belostok, and so on. Discuss with your group what these references have in common.
2. What kinds of responses do poems like "The Man He Killed," "What Were They Like?" and "Babiy Yar" elicit? To what extent, for example, do you agree with Hardy's speaker that war "quaint and curious is"? Explain.

Mirikitani and Owen

Janice Mirikitani
1987

Prisons of Silence

1.
The strongest prisons are built
with walls of silence.

2.
Morning light falls between us
like a wall.
We have laid beside each other   5
as we have for years.
Before the war, when life
would clamor through our windows,
we woke joyfully to the work.

I keep those moments   10
like a living silent seed.

After day's work, I would
smell the damp soil in his hands,
his hands that felt the outlines
of my body in the velvet   15
night of summers.

I hold his warm hands to this
cold wall of flesh
as I have for years.

3.

Jap! 20
Filthy Jap!

Who lives within me?

Abandoned homes, confiscated land,
loyalty oaths, barbed wire prisons
in a strange wasteland. 25

Go home, Jap!
Where is home?

A country of betrayal.
No one speaks to us.

We would not speak to each other. 30

We were accused.

Hands in our hair,
hands that spread our legs
and searched our thighs for secret weapons,
hands that knit barbed wire 35
to cripple our flight.

Giant hot hands flung me,
fluttering, speechless into
barbed wire, thorns in a broken wing.

The strongest prisons are built 40
with walls of silence.

4.

I watched him depart that day
from the tedious wall of wire,
the humps of barracks,
handsome in his uniform. 45

I would look each day for letters
from a wall of time,
waiting for approach of my deliverance
from a wall of dust.

I do not remember 50
reading about his death
only the wall of wind
that encased me, as I turned my head.

5.

U.S. Japs hailed as heroes!

I do not know the face of this country 55
it is inhabited by strangers
who call me obscene names.

Jap. Go home.
Where is home?

I am alone wandering   60
in this desert.

Where is home?
Who lives within me?

A stranger with a knife in her tongue
and broken wing,   65
mad from separations and losses cruel
as hunger.

Walls suffocate her as a tomb,
encasing history.

6.
I have kept myself contained   70
within these walls shaped to my body
and buried my rage.
I rebuilt my life
like a wall, unquestioning.
Obeyed their laws…their laws.   75

   7.
   All persons of Japanese ancestry
      filthy jap.
   Both alien and non-alien
      japs are enemy aliens.
   To be incarcerated   80
      for their own good
   A military necessity
      The army to handle only the japs
   Where is home?
   A country of betrayal.   85

8.
This wall of silence crumbles
from the bigness of their crimes.
This silent wall
crushed by living memory.

He awakens from the tomb   90
I have made for myself
and unearths my rage.

I must speak.

9.
He faces me in this small
room of myself.   95

I find the windows
where light escapes.

From this cell of history
this mute grave,
we birth our rage.   100

We heal our tongues.

We listen to ourselves

    Korematsu, Hirabayashi, Yasui.

We ignite the syllables of our names.

We give testimony.   105

We hear the bigness of our sounds freed
like many clapping hands,
thundering for reparations.

We give testimony.

Our noise is dangerous.   110

10.
We beat our hands
like wings healed.

We soar
from these walls of silence.

Wilfred Owen
1920

Disabled

He sat in a wheeled chair, waiting for dark,
And shivered in his ghastly suit of grey,
Legless, sewn short at elbow. Through the park
Voices of boys rang saddening like a hymn,
Voices of play and pleasure after day,   5
Till gathering sleep had mothered them from him.

           …

About this time Town used to swing so gay
When glow-lamps budded in the light blue trees,

And girls glanced lovelier as the air grew dim,—
In the old times, before he threw away his knees.   10
Now he will never feel again how slim
Girls' waists are, or how warm their subtle hands.
All of them touch him like some queer disease.

       …

There was an artist silly for his face,
For it was younger than his youth, last year.   15
Now, he is old; his back will never brace;
He's lost his colour very far from here,
Poured it down shell-holes till the veins ran dry,
And half his lifetime lapsed in the hot race
And leap of purple spurted from his thigh.   20

       …

One time he liked a blood-smear down his leg,
After the matches, carried shoulder-high.
It was after football, when he'd drunk a peg,
He thought he'd better join.—He wonders why.
Someone had said he'd look a god in kilts,   25
That's why; and maybe, too, to please his Meg,
Aye, that was it, to please the giddy jilts
He asked to join. He didn't have to beg;
Smiling they wrote his lie: aged nineteen years.
Germans he scarcely thought of; all their guilt,   30
And Austria's, did not move him. And no fears
Of Fear came yet. He thought of jewelled hilts
For daggers in plaid socks; of smart salutes;
And care of arms; and leave; and pay arrears;
Esprit de corps; and hints for young recruits.   35
And soon, he was drafted out with drums and cheers.

       …

Some cheered him home, but not as crowds cheer Goal.
Only a solemn man who brought him fruits
Thanked him; and then enquired about his soul.

       …

Now, he will spend a few sick years in institutes,   40
And do what things the rules consider wise,
And take whatever pity they may dole.
Tonight he noticed how the women's eyes
Passed from him to the strong men that were whole.
How cold and late it is! Why don't they come   45
And put him into bed? Why don't they come?

Journal Entry

Speculate on the physical and psychological effects of being wounded in war.

Textual Considerations

1. Review sections 3, 8, and 9 of "Prisons of Silence" and find examples from the poem to answer the following questions: What enables the victims to break through their silence? To what extent does their testimony make possible their transformation from victims to victors?
2. The narrator of "Prisons of Silence" frequently juxtaposes the discourses of silence and speech. Investigate the various relationships between silence and powerlessness and between speech and power in the poem.
3. Analyze the effects of Owen's juxtaposing images from the soldier's past and present life.
4. Characterize the tone of "Disabled." Is the speaker angry, bitter, resigned? How does tone reinforce theme?
5. How does society's attitude toward the soldier change after his injury? On what aspects of war and people's attitude toward war does the speaker comment?

Cultural Contexts

1. "Prisons of Silence" dramatizes the decision of the United States to relegate Americans of Japanese ancestry to prison camps after the Japanese attack on Pearl Harbor during World War II. Identify the images that most effectively chart the progression of their physical displacement and psychological alienation.
2. Examine the relationship between war and sex by analyzing the gender-related issues explored in lines 9–13, 25–28, and 43–44 of "Disabled." To what extent is the military uniform still considered a magnet of sexual attraction?

Whitman and Gildner

◆

Walt Whitman
1892

The Dying Veteran

(A Long Island incident—early part of the nineteenth century)

Amid these days of order, ease, prosperity,
Amid the current songs of beauty, peace, decorum,
I cast a reminiscence—(likely 'twill offend you,
I heard it in my boyhood;)—More than a generation since,
A queer old savage man, a fighter under Washington himself, 5
(Large, brave, cleanly, hot-blooded, no talker, rather spiritualistic,

Had fought in the ranks—fought well—had been all through the
    Revolutionary war,)
Lay dying—sons, daughters, church-deacons, lovingly tending him,
Sharping their sense, their ears, towards his murmuring, half-caught words:
"Let me return again to my war-days,   10
To the sights and scenes—to forming the line of battle,
To the scouts ahead reconnoitering,
To the cannons, the grim artillery,
To the galloping aids, carrying orders,
To the wounded, the fallen, the heat, the suspense,   15
The perfume strong, the smoke, the deafening noise;
Away with your life of peace!—your joys of peace!
Give me my old wild battle-life again!"

Gary Gildner
1969

First Practice

After the doctor checked to see
we weren't ruptured,
the man with the short cigar took us
under the grade school,
where we went in case of attack   5
or storm, and said
he was Clifford Hill, he was
a man who believed dogs
ate dogs, he had once killed
for his country, and if   10
there were any girls present
for them to leave now.
                No one
left. OK, he said, he said I take
that to mean you are hungry   15
men who hate to lose as much
as I do. OK. Then
he made two lines of us
facing each other,
and across the way, he said,   20
is the man you hate most
in the world,

and if we are to win
that title I want to see how.
But I don't want to see   25
any marks when you're dressed,
he said. He said, *Now.*

Journal Entry

What significance do you see in the speakers in "The Dying Veteran" and "First Practice" being war veterans?

Textual Considerations

1. Discuss the comparisons that Whitman's speaker makes between war and peace. To what extent do you agree with his perspective on peace?
2. "First Practice" does not express directly the effects of the forces put in motion by "the man with the short cigar." These effects, however, are the real subject of the poem. What are they?
3. Gildner's poem bristles with tense drama. Characterize some of the dramatic effects, and analyze how the poet achieves them. Consider, for example, the meaning of the command "But I don't want to see / any marks when you're dressed."

Cultural Contexts

1. Discuss with your group the concept of masculinity expressed in each poem. What does each poem suggest about the relation between war and violence?
2. Characterize Gildner's attitude toward the incident in "First Practice" and speculate on what the poem implies about sports and violence.

Dorfman and Smallberg

Ariel Dorfman
1988

Hope

My son has been
missing
since May 8
of last year.

They took him   5
just for a few hours
they said
just for some routine
questioning.

After the car left,   10
the car with no license plate,
we couldn't

    find out

anything else
about him.   15

But now things have changed.
We heard from a compañero
who just got out
that five months later
they were torturing him   20
in Villa Grimaldi,
at the end of September
they were questioning him
in the red house
that belonged to the Grimaldis.   25

    They say they recognized
    his voice his screams
    they say.

Somebody tell me frankly
what times are these   30
what kind of world
what country?
What I'm asking is
how can it be
that a father's   35
joy
a mother's
joy
is knowing
that they   40
that they are still
torturing
their son?
Which means
that he was alive   45
five months later

and our greatest
hope
will be to find out
next year   50
that they're still torturing him
eight months later

and he may   might   could
still be alive.

Mavis Smallberg
1988

Quote from the Bureau of Information, from the Argus, *August 27, 1986:* *"The Situation in Soweto Is Not Abnormal"*

Everything's normal in Soweto today.
We reasonably killed eleven.
They were making a fuss in the street
You know us,
We don't stand any fuss   5
Not us
So we typically killed eleven
And wounded an average sixty-two
And you?

Went on a regular patrol to a school.   10
Some children were breaking a rule.
They burned their identity cards.
White kids don't carry 'em
Don't need to, you know
Black kids don't carry 'em   15
Don't want to, you know
The whole thing was just about to erupt,
When we routinely went to beat them up.

Cornered a few of 'em and rained down the blows
Split one's head.   She's dead,   20
But nobody knows.
Naturally the children ran all around
So we just shot down those that we found.
Bullets, birdshot, buckshot,
What the hell? It's all run-of-the-mill!   25
Saw this "comrade" walking alone,
Shot him down before he got home.
Ja, he died.
You should've seen the ones that we fried.

What a fire!   What a blaze!   30
Children crying, people dying.
One woman got shot in the hip
That really shut up her lip!
Now she can't walk.   Mmm, there was some talk.
Ja, the situation in Soweto is not   35
Abnormal today.

What's abnormal, anyway?
What's monstrous, deviant, abhorrent,
weird about gassing a baby
Shooting a child, raping a mother   40
or crippling a father?
What's odd about killing the people we fear?
No, the situation in Soweto
is quite normal today.

Journal Entry

Discuss Dorfman's and Smallberg's texts as protest poems.

Textual Considerations

1. Compare and contrast the tone of both texts. How does tone contribute to meaning in each poem?
2. Evaluate the role of the authorities in each poem.
3. Analyze the various meanings of Dorfman's title.
4. Review the last section of Smallberg's poem, and discuss how the change in point of view affects the meaning.

Cultural Contexts

1. Discuss with your group the violence and suffering depicted in each poem. Consider what both poems express about the conflict between authorities and individuals, parents and children, the suspension of human rights, and humankind's capacity to inflict cruelty.

Rukeyser and Whitman

Muriel Rukeyser
1973

Waking This Morning

Waking this morning,
a violent woman in the violent day
Laughing.

       Past the line of memory
along the long body of your life,   5
in which move childhood, youth, your lifetime of touch,
eyes, lips, chest, belly, sex, legs, to the waves of the sheet.
I look past the little plant
on the city windowsill
to the tall towers bookshaped, crushed together in greed,   10
the river flashing flowing corroded,
the intricate harbor and the sea, the wars, the moon, the planets, all who
      people space
in the sun visible invisible.
African violets in the light
breathing, in a breathing universe.   I want strong peace, and delight,   15
the wild good.
I want to make my touch poems:
to find my morning, to find you entire
alive moving among the anti-touch people.

       I say across the waves of the air to you: 20
today once more
I will try to be non-violent
one more day
this morning, waking the world away
in the violent day.   25

Walt Whitman
1886

The Artilleryman's Vision *

While my wife at my side lies slumbering, and the wars are over long,
And my head on the pillow rests at home, and the vacant midnight passes,
And through the stillness, through the dark, I hear, just hear, the breath of my
 infant,
There in the room as I wake from sleep this vision presses upon me;
The engagement opens there and then in fantasy unreal,   5
The skirmishers begin, they crawl cautiously ahead, I hear the irregular snap!
 snap!
I hear the sounds of the different missiles, the short *t-h-t! t-h-t!* of the rifle-balls,
I see the shells exploding leaving small white clouds, I hear the great shells
 shrieking as they pass,
The grape like the hum and whirr of wind through the trees, (tumultuous now
 the contest rages,)
All the scenes at the batteries rise in detail before me again,   10
The crashing and smoking, the pride of the men in their pieces,
The chief-gunner ranges and sights his piece and selects a fuse of the right time,
After firing I see him lean aside and look eagerly off to note the effect;
Elsewhere I hear the cry of a regiment charging, (the young colonel leads
 himself this time with brandish'd sword,)
I see the gaps cut by the enemy's volleys, (quickly fill'd up, no delay,)   15
I breathe the suffocating smoke, then the flat clouds hover low concealing all;
Now a strange lull for a few seconds, not a shot fired on either side,
Then resumed the chaos louder than ever, with eager calls and orders of officers,
While from some distant part of the field the wind wafts to my ears a shout of
 applause, (some special success,)
And ever the sound of the cannon far or near, (rousing even in dreams a
 devilish exultation and all the old mad joy in the depths of my soul,)   20
And ever the hastening of infantry shifting positions, batteries, cavalry, moving
 hither and thither,
(The falling, dying, I heed not, the wounded dripping and red I heed not,
 some to the rear are hobbling,)
(Grime, heat, rush, aide-de-camps galloping by or on a full run,
With the patter of small arms, the warning *s-s-t* of the rifles, (these in my vision
 I hear or see,)
And bombs bursting in air, and at night the vari-color'd rockets.   25

---

*First published as "The Veteran's Vision" in the 1865 edition of *Leaves of Grass* and with this title
in the 1871 edition.

◆

Journal Entry

To what extent are "Waking This Morning" and "The Artilleryman's Vision" critical of war?

Textual Considerations

1. Discuss the effects on meaning of the speaker's juxtaposing images of past and present, violence and antiviolence, touch and antitouch in "Waking This Morning."
2. Evaluate Whitman's use of visual imagery. To what other senses does the poem appeal?
3. Explain the effects of the contrasting images of war and peace in Whitman's poem.

Cultural Contexts

1. Discuss with your group your responses to the veteran's "vision." To what extent has he "survived" the war?

Carolyn Forché ◆

Carolyn Forché
1978

The Colonel

What you have heard is true. I was in his house. His wife carried a tray of coffee and sugar. His daughter filed her nails, his son went out for the night. There were daily papers, pet dogs, a pistol on the cushion beside him. The moon swung bare on its black cord over the house. On the television was a cop show. It was in English. Broken bottles were embedded in the walls around the house to scoop the kneecaps from a man's legs or cut his hands to lace. On the windows there were gratings like those in liquor stores. We had dinner, rack of lamb, good wine, a gold bell was on the table for calling the maid. The maid brought green mangoes, salt, a type of bread. I was asked how I enjoyed the country. There was a brief commercial in Spanish. His wife took everything away. There was some talk then of how difficult it had become to govern. The parrot said hello on the terrace. The colonel told it to shut up, and pushed himself from the table. My friend said to me with his eyes: say nothing. The colonel returned with a sack used to bring groceries home. He spilled many human ears on the table. They were like dried peach halves. There is no other way to say this. He took one of them in his hands, shook it in our faces, dropped it into a water glass. It came alive there. I am tired of fooling around he said. As for the rights of anyone, tell your people they can go fuck themselves. He swept the ears to the floor with his arm and held the last of his wine in the air. Something for your poetry, no? he said. Some of the ears on the floor caught this scrap of his voice. Some of the ears on the floor were pressed to the ground.

Carolyn Forché
1979

The Visitor

In Spanish he whispers there is no time left.
It is the sound of scythes arcing in wheat,
the ache of some field song in Salvador.
The wind along the prison, cautious
as Francisco's hands on the inside, touching   5
the walls as he walks, it is his wife's breath
slipping into his cell each night while he
imagines his hand to be hers. It is a small country.

There is nothing one man will not do to another.

Carolyn Forché
1977

The Memory of Elena

We spend our morning
in the flower stalls counting
the dark tongues of bells
that hang from the ropes waiting
for the silence of an hour.   5
We find a table, ask for *paella,*
cold soup and wine, where a calm
light trembles years behind us.

In Buenos Aires only three
years ago, it was the last time his hand   10
slipped into her dress, with pearls
cooling her throat and bells like
these, chipping at the night—

As she talks, the hollow
clopping of a horse, the sound   15
of bones touches together.
The *paella* comes, a bed of rice
and *camarones,* fingers and shells,
the lips of those whose lips
have been removed, mussels   20
the soft blue of a leg socket.

The is not *paella,* this is what
has become of those who remained
in Buenos Aires. This is the ring
of a rifle report on the stones,   25
her hand over his mouth,
her husband falling against her.

These are the flowers we bought
this morning, the dahlias tossed
on his grave and bells   30
waiting with their tongues cut out
for this particular silence.

Carolyn Forché
1980

As Children Together

Under the sloped snow
pinned all winter with Christmas
lights, we waited for your father
to whittle his soap cakes
away, finish the whisky,   5
your mother to carry her coffee
from room to room closing lights
cubed in the snow at our feet.

Holding each other's
coat sleeves we slid down   10
the roads in our tight
black dresses, past
crystal swamps and the death
face of each dark house,
over the golden ice   15
of tobacco spit, the blue
quiet of ponds, with town
glowing behind the blind
white hills and a scant
snow ticking in the stars.   20
You hummed *blanche comme*
la neige and spoke of Montreal
where a québecoise could sing,
take any man's face
to her unfastened blouse   25
and wake to wine
on the bedside table.
I always believed this,
Victoria, that there might
be a way to get out.   30

You were ashamed of that house,
its round tins of surplus flour,
chipped beef and white beans,
relief checks and winter trips
that always ended in deer   35
tied stiff to the car rack,
the accordion breath of your uncles
down from the north, and what
you called the stupidity
of the Michigan French.   40

Your mirror grew ringed
with photos of servicemen
who had taken your breasts
in their hands, the buttons
of your blouses in their teeth,   45
who had given you the silk
tassles of their graduation,
jackets embroidered with dragons
from the Far East. You kept
the corks that had fired   50
from the bottles over their beds,
their letters with each city

blackened, envelopes of hair
from their shaved heads.

I am going to have it, you said.   55
Flowers wrapped in paper from carts
in Montreal, a plane lifting out
of Detroit, a satin bed, a table
cluttered with bottles of scent.

So standing in a platter of ice   60
outside a Catholic dance hall
you took their collars
in your fine chilled hands
and lied your age to adulthood.

I did not then have breasts of my own,   65
nor any letters from bootcamp
and when one of the men who had
gathered around you took my mouth
to his own there was nothing
other than the dance hall music   70
rising to the arms of iced trees.

I don't know where you are now, Victoria.
They say you have children, a trailer
in the snow near our town,
and the husband you found as a girl   75
returned from the Far East broken
cursing holy blood at the table
where nightly a pile of white shavings
is paid from the edge of his knife.

If you read this poem, write to me.   80
I have been to Paris since we parted.

◆

Journal Entry

Respond to Forché's conviction that "the twentieth-century human condition demands a poetry of witness."

Textual Considerations

1. Forché refers to "The Colonel" as a "documentary poem." What stylistic aspects of the text suggest journalistic prose?
2. What portrait of the Colonel emerges in the poem? How does Forché's ironic juxtaposition of domestic and violent images affect that portrayal? Cite three examples you find most effective.

3. Explain the meaning of the poem's last line.
4. The setting for "The Visitor" is the dark recesses of a Salvadoran prison. Cite images that best evoke the prisoner's unbearable solitude and sense of impending violence.
5. The speaker in "The Memory of Elena" addresses an imaginary listener to whom she shows several significant objects. What story emerges from the descriptions of the flowers and *paella*?
6. How does the juxtaposition of past and present in Elena's memories reinforce the horror of personal destruction caused by political dictatorships?
7. Forché's autobiographical poem "As Children Together" focuses on her own childhood and her friendship with Victoria. What portrait of Victoria emerges in the text? What economic realities contribute to Victoria's inability to fulfill her dream to go to Montreal?

Cultural Considerations

1. Forché went to El Salvador as a journalist, poet, and human rights observer (1979–1980). She is committed to the concept that poetry should link the political and the personal, and that one function of the poet is to inform the audience of the horrors of the twentieth-century atrocities. With your group, share your journal entries on Forchés poems as well as your response to her concept of the poet's responsibility.

Aristophanes
411 B.C.

Lysistrata

CHARACTERS[1]

LYSISTRATA
CALONICE } *Athenian women*
MYRRHINE
LAMPITO *a Spartan woman*
LEADER OF THE CHORUS OF OLD MEN
CHORUS OF OLD MEN
LEADER OF THE CHORUS OF OLD WOMEN
CHORUS OF OLD WOMEN
ATHENIAN MAGISTRATE
THREE ATHENIAN WOMEN
CINESIAS
an Athenian, husband of MYRRHINE
SPARTAN HERALD
SPARTAN AMBASSADORS
ATHENIAN AMBASSADORS
TWO ATHENIAN CITIZENS
CHORUS OF ATHENIANS
CHORUS OF SPARTANS

> SCENE. *In Athens, beneath the Acropolis. In the center of the stage is the Propylaea, or gateway to the Acropolis; to one side is a small grotto, sacred to Pan. The Orchestra represents a slope leading up to the gate-way. It is early in the morning.* LYSISTRATA *is pacing impatiently up and down.*

PROLOGUE[2]

LYS.   If they'd been summoned to worship the God of Wine, or Pan, or to visit the Queen of Love, why, you couldn't have pushed your way through the streets

---

[1] *characters:* "As is usual in ancient comedy, the leading characters have significant names. Lysistrata is 'She who disbands the armies'; Myrrhine's name is chosen to suggest *myrton*, a Greek word meaning *pudenda muliebria*; Lampito is a celebrated Spartan name; Cinesias, although a real name in Athens, is chosen to suggest a Greek verb *kinein, to move,* then *to make love, to have intercourse;* and the name of his deme, Paionidai, suggests the verb *paiein*, which has about the same significance." [Translator's note.]

for all the timbrels. But now there's not a single woman here—except my neighbor; here she comes. [*Enter* CALONICE.] Good day to you, Calonice.

CAL. And to you, Lysistrata. [*Noticing* LYSISTRATA'S *impatient air.*] But what ails you? Don't scowl, my dear; it's not becoming to you to knit your brows like that.

LYS. [*sadly*]. Ah, Calonice, my heart aches; I'm so annoyed at us women. For among men we have a reputation for sly trickery—

CAL. And rightly too, on my word!

LYS. —but when they were told to meet here to consider a matter of no small importance, they lie abed and don't come.

CAL. Oh, they'll come all right, my dear. It's not easy for a woman to get out, you know. One is working on her husband, another is getting up the maid, another has to put the baby to bed, or wash and feed it.

LYS. But after all, there are other matters more important than all that.

CAL. My dear Lysistrata, just what is this matter you've summoned us women to consider? What's up? Something big?

LYS. Very big.

CAL. [*interested*]. Is it stout, too?

LYS. [*smiling*]. Yes indeed—both big and stout.

CAL. What? And the women still haven't come?

LYS. It's not what you suppose; they'd come soon enough for *that*. But I've worked up something, and for many a sleepless night I've turned it this way and that.

CAL. [*in mock disappointment*]. Oh, I guess it's pretty fine and slender, if you've turned it this way and that.

LYS. So fine that the safety of the whole of Greece lies in us women.

CAL. In us women? It depends on a very slender reed then.

LYS. Our country's fortunes are in our hands; and whether the Spartans shall perish—

CAL. Good! Let them perish, by all means.

LYS. —and the Boeotians shall be completely annihilated.

CAL. Not completely! Please spare the eels.[3]

LYS. As for Athens, I won't use any such unpleasant words. But you understand what I mean. But if the women will meet here—the Spartans, the Boeotians, and we Athenians—then all together we will save Greece.

CAL. But what could women do that's clever or distinguished? We just sit around all dolled up in silk robes, looking pretty in our sheer gowns and evening slippers.

LYS. These are just the things I hope will save us: these silk robes, perfumes, evening slippers, rouge, and our chiffon blouses.

CAL. How so?

LYS. So never a man alive will lift a spear against the foe—

---

[2] *prologue:* the division of the text into its constituent parts—prologue, párodos, scenes, choral episodes, and éxodos—follows Dudley Fitts, *Aristophanes'* Lysistrata: *An English Version*, Harcourt Brace Jovanovich, Inc., 1954, 1962. [3] *eels:* Boeotia was noted for its seafood, especially its eels.

CAL. I'll get a silk gown at once.

LYS. —or take up his shield—

CAL. I'll put on my sheerest gown!

LYS. —or sword.

CAL. I'll buy a pair of evening slippers.

LYS. Well then, shouldn't the women have come?

CAL. Come? Why, they should have *flown* here.

LYS. Well, my dear, just watch: they'll act in true Athenian fashion—everything too late! And now there's not a woman here from the shore or from Salamis.

CAL. They're coming, I'm sure; at daybreak they were laying-to their oars to cross the straits.

LYS. And those I expected would be the first to come—the women of Acharnae—they haven't arrived.

CAL. Yet the wife of Theagenes means to come: she consulted Hecate about it. [*Seeing a group of women approaching.*] But look! Here come a few. And there are some more over here. Hurrah! Where do they come from?

LYS. From Anagyra.

CAL. Yes indeed! We've raised up quite a stink from Anagyra[4] anyway.

[*Enter* MYRRHINE *in haste, followed by several other women.*]

MYR. [*breathlessly*]. Have we come in time, Lysistrata? What do you say? Why so quiet?

LYS. I can't say much for you, Myrrhine, coming at this hour on such important business.

MYR. Why, I had trouble finding my girdle in the dark. But if it's so important, we're here now; tell us.

LYS. No. Let's wait a little for the women from Boeotia and the Peloponnesus.

MYR. That's a much better suggestion. Look! Here comes Lampito now.

[*Enter* LAMPITO *with two other women.*]

LYS. Greetings, my dear Spartan friend. How pretty you look, my dear. What a smooth complexion and well-developed figure. You could throttle an ox.

LAM. Faith, yes, I think I could. I take exercises and kick my heels against my bum. [*She demonstrates with a few steps of the Spartan "bottom-kicking" dance.*]

LYS. And what splendid breasts you have.

LAM. La! You handle me like a prize steer.

LYS. And who is this young lady with you?

LAM. Faith, she's an Ambassadress from Boeotia.

LYS. Oh yes, a Boeotian, and blooming like a garden too.

CAL. [*lifting up her skirt*]. My word! How neatly her garden's weeded![5]

---

[4] *stink from Anagyra:* a punning reference to a proverbial phrase. The deme or township of Anagyra took its name from an ill-smelling plant, to stir which meant, colloquially, to raise a stink.

[5] *weeded:* i.e., depilated.

LYS.   And who is the other girl?

LAM.   Oh, she's a Corinthian swell.

MYR.   [*after a rapid examination*]. Yes indeed. She swells very nicely [*pointing*] here and here.

LAM.   Who has gathered together this company of women?

LYS.   I have.

LAM.   Speak up, then. What do you want?

MYR.   Yes, my dear, do tell us what this important matter is.

LYS.   Very well, I'll tell you. But before I speak, let me ask you a little question.

MYR.   Anything you like.

LYS.   [*earnestly*]. Tell me: don't you yearn for the fathers of your children, who are away at the wars? I know you all have husbands abroad.

CAL.   Why, yes; mercy me! my husband's been away for five months in Thrace keeping guard on—Eucrates.[6]

MYR.   And mine for seven whole months in Pylus.

LAM.   And mine, as soon as ever he returns from the fray, readjusts his shield and flies out of the house again.

LYS.   And as for lovers, there's not even a ghost of one left. Since the Milesians revolted from us,[7] I've not even seen an eight-inch dingus to be a leather consolation for us widows. Are you willing, if I can find a way, to help me end the war?

MYR.   Goodness, yes! I'd do it, even if I had to pawn my dress and—get drunk on the spot!

CAL.   And I, even if I had to let myself be split in two like a flounder.

LAM.   I'd climb up Mt. Taygetus[8] if I could catch a glimpse of peace.

LYS.   I'll tell you, then, in plain and simple words. My friends, if we are going to force our men to make peace, we must do without—

MYR.   Without what? Tell us.

LYS.   Will you do it?

MYR.   We'll do it, if it kills us.

LYS.   Well then, we must do without sex altogether. [*General consternation.*] Why do you turn away? Where go you? Why turn so pale? Why those tears? Will you do it or not? What means this hesitation?

MYR.   I won't do it! Let the war go on.

CAL.   Nor I! Let the war go on.

LYS.   So, my little flounder? Didn't you say just now you'd split yourself in half?

CAL.   Anything else you like. I'm willing, even if I have to walk through fire. Anything rather than sex. There's nothing like it, my dear.

LYS.   [*to* MYRRHINE]. What about you?

MYR.   [*sullenly*]. I'm willing to walk through fire, too.

---

[6] *Eucrates:* an Athenian general who, according to unverified tradition, was mercenary and traitorous.   [7] *Milesians...us:* Milesia was recognized for its leather goods among which, apparently, were dildos, the lack of which Lysistrata here laments.   [8] *Mt. Taygetus:* a mountain range looming over Sparta.

LYS.   Oh vile and cursed breed! No wonder they make tragedies about us: we're naught but "love-affairs and bassinets."[9] But you, my dear Spartan friend, if you alone are with me, our enterprise might yet succeed. Will you vote with me?

LAM.   'Tis cruel hard, by my faith, for a woman to sleep alone without her nooky; but for all that, we certainly do need peace.

LYS.   O my dearest friend! You're the only real woman here.

CAL.   [*wavering*]. Well, if we do refrain from—[*shuddering*] what you say (God forbid!), would that bring peace?

LYS.   My goodness, yes! If we sit at home all rouged and powdered, dressed in our sheerest gowns, and neatly depilated, our men will get excited and want to take us; but if you don't come to them and keep away, they'll soon make a truce.

LAM.   Aye; Menelaus caught sight of Helen's naked breast and dropped his sword,[10] they say.

CAL.   What if the men give us up?

LYS.   "Flay a skinned dog," as Pherecrates[11] says.

CAL.   Rubbish! These make-shifts are no good. But suppose they grab us and drag us into the bedroom?

LYS.   Hold on to the door.

CAL.   And if they beat us?

LYS.   Give in with a bad grace. There's no pleasure in it for them when they have to use violence. And you must torment them in every possible way. They'll give up soon enough; a man gets no joy if he doesn't get along with his wife.

MYR.   If this is your opinion, we agree.

LAM.   As for our own men, we can persuade them to make a just and fair peace; but what about the Athenian rabble? Who will persuade them not to start any more monkeyshines?

LYS.   Don't worry. We guarantee to convince them.

LAM.   Not while their ships are rigged so well and they have that mighty treasure in the temple of Athene.

LYS.   We've taken good care for that too: we shall seize the Acropolis today. The older women have orders to do this, and while we are making our arrangements, they are to pretend to make a sacrifice and occupy the Acropolis.

LAM.   All will be well then. That's a very fine idea.

LYS.   Let's ratify this, Lampito, with the most solemn oath.

LAM.   Tell us what oath we shall swear.

---

9 *"love-affairs and bassinets:"* Lysistrata's point seems to be that although women have passionate and tender experiences, which are the material of tragedy, they lack character, resolution, fortitude. 10 *Menelaus...sword:* in Euripides' *Andromache,* "Menelaus, about to stab his faithless wife, is overcome by her beauty and drops his sword." [Fitts's note.]   11 *Pherecrates:* a comic writer none of whose work is extant. The quoted phrase seems tantamount to "absurd" or "impossible," but most translators assume that Aristophanes is twisting it ironically. One reads: "We'll have to take things into our own hands"; another: "We'd have to fall back on ourselves."

LYS. All right? Where's our Policewoman? [*To a Scythian slave.*] What are you gaping at? Set a shield upside-down here in front of me, and give me the sacred meats.

CAL. Lysistrata, what sort of an oath are we to take?

LYS. What oath? I'm going to slaughter a sheep over the shield, as they do in Aeschylus.[12]

CAL. Don't, Lysistrata! No oaths about peace over a shield.

LYS. What shall the oath be, then?

CAL. How about getting a white horse somewhere and cutting out its entrails for the sacrifice?

LYS. White horse indeed!

CAL. Well then, how shall we swear?

MYR. I'll tell you: let's place a large black bowl upside-down and then slaughter— a flask of Thasian wine. And then let's swear—not to pour in a single drop of water.

LAM. Lord! How I like that oath!

LYS. Someone bring out a bowl and a flask.

[*A slave brings the utensils for the sacrifice.*]

CAL. Look, my friends! What a big jar! Here's a cup that 'twould give me joy to handle. [*She picks up the bowl.*]

LYS. Set it down and put your hands on our victim. [*As* CALONICE *places her hands on the flask.*] O Lady of Persuasion and dear Loving Cup, graciously vouchsafe to receive this sacrifice from us women. [*She pours the wine into the bowl.*]

CAL. The blood has a good color and spurts out nicely.

LAM. Faith, it has a pleasant smell, too.

MYR. Oh, let me be the first to swear, ladies!

CAL. No, by my Lady! Not unless you're alloted the first turn.

LYS. Place all your hands on the cup, and one of you repeat on behalf of all what I say. Then all will swear and ratify the oath. *I will suffer no man, be he husband or lover,*

CAL. *I will suffer no man, be he husband or lover,*

LYS. *To approach me all hot and horny.* [*As* CALONICE *hesitates.*] Say it!

CAL. [*slowly and painfully*]. *To approach me all hot and horny.* O Lysistrata, I feel so weak in the knees!

LYS. *I will remain at home unmated,*

CAL. *I will remain at home unmated,*

LYS. *Wearing my sheerest gown and carefully adorned,*

CAL. *Wearing my sheerest gown and carefully adorned,*

LYS. *That my husband may burn with desire for me.*

CAL. *That my husband may burn with desire for me.*

LYS. *And if he takes me by force against my will,*

---

[12] *Aeschylus:* "In the *Seven against Thebes.*" [Translator's note.]

CAL.   *And if he takes me by force against my will,*

LYS.   *I shall do it badly and keep from moving.*

CAL.   *I shall do it badly and keep from moving.*

LYS.   *I will not stretch my slippers toward the ceiling,*

CAL.   *I will not stretch my slippers toward the ceiling,*

LYS.   *Nor will I take the posture of the lioness on the knife-handle.*[13]

CAL.   *Nor will I take the posture of the lioness on the knife-handle.*

LYS.   *If I keep this oath, may I be permitted to drink from this cup,*

CAL.   *If I keep this oath, may I be permitted to drink from this cup,*

LYS.   *But if I break it, may the cup be filled with water.*

CAL.   *But if I break it, may the cup be filled with water.*

LYS.   Do you all swear to this?

ALL.   I do, so help me!

LYS.   Come then, I'll just consummate this offering. [*She takes a long drink from the cup.*]

CAL.   [*snatching the cup away*]. Shares, my dear! Let's drink to our continued friendship.

        [*A shout is heard from offstage.*]

LAM.   What's that shouting?

LYS.   That's what I was telling you: the women have just seized the Acropolis. Now, Lampito, go home and arrange matters in Sparta; and leave these two ladies here as hostages. We'll enter the Acropolis to join our friends and help them lock the gates.

CAL.   Don't you suppose the men will come to attack us?

LYS.   Don't worry about them. Neither threats nor fire will suffice to open the gates, except on the terms we've stated.

CAL.   I should say not! Else we'd belie our reputation as unmanageable pests.

    [LAMPITO *leaves the stage, The other women retire and enter the Acropolis through the Propylaea.*]

[*Enter the* CHORUS OF OLD MEN, *carrying fire-pots and a load of heavy sticks.*]

PÁRODOS

LEADER OF MEN.   Onward, Draces, step by step, though your shoulder's aching.
    Cursèd logs of olive-wood, what a load you're making!

1ST SEMI-CHORUS OF OLD MEN [*singing*].
    Aye, many surprises await a man who lives to a ripe old age;
    For who could suppose, Strymodorus my lad, that the women we've nourished (alas!),
    Who sat at home to vex our days,
    Would seize the holy image here,
    And occupy this sacred shrine.

---

[13] *posture...knife-handle:* i.e., on all fours.

With bolts and bars, with fell design,
To lock the Propylaea?

LEADER.   Come with speed, Philourgus, come! to the temple hast'ning.
There we'll heap these logs about in a circle round them,
And whoever has conspired, raising this rebellion,
Shall be roasted, scorched, and burnt, all without exception,
Doomed by one unanimous vote—but first the wife of Lycon.[14]

2ND SEMI-CHORUS   [*singing*].
No, no! by Demeter, while I'm alive, no woman shall mock at me.
Not even the Spartan Cleomenes,[15] our citadel first to seize,
Got off unscathed; for all his pride
And haughty Spartan arrogance,
He left his arms and sneaked away,
Stripped to his shirt, unkempt, unshav'd,
With six years' filth still on him.

LEADER.   I besieged that hero bold, sleeping at my station,
Marshalled at these holy gates sixteen deep against him.
Shall I not these cursèd pests punish for their daring,
Burning these Euripides-and-God-detested women?
Aye! Or else may Marathon overturn my trophy.

1ST SEMI-CHORUS   [*singing*].
There remains of my road
Just this brow of the hill;
There I speed on my way.
Drag the logs up the hill, though we've got no ass to help.
(God! my shoulder's bruised and sore!)
Onward still must we go.
Blow the fire! Don't let it go out
Now we're near the end of our road.

ALL   [*blowing on the fire-pots*].   Whew! Whew! Drat the smoke!

2ND SEMI-CHORUS   [*singing*].
Lord, what smoke rushing forth
From the pot, like a dog
Running mad, bites my eyes!
This must be Lemnos-fire.[16] What a sharp and stinging smoke!
Rushing onward to the shrine
Aid the gods. Once for all
Show your mettle, Laches my boy!
To the rescue hastening all!

ALL   [*blowing on the fire-pots*]. Whew! Whew! Drat the smoke!

---

[14] *wife of Lycon:* Rhodia, the wife of the demagogue, much lampooned for the laxness of her morality.   [15] *Cleomenes:* a Spartan king who occupied the Acropolis for two days (not six years!) almost a hundred years before the incidents of the play. The men of the chorus would seem either extraordinarily old or invested with a communal but unreliable memory.   [16] *Lemnos-fire:* according to Fitts, a bad pun, the Greek words for Lemnos (an Island in the Aegean) and for sore eyes being similar.

[*The chorus has now reached the edge of the orchestra nearest the stage, in front of the Propylaea. They begin laying their logs and fire-pots on the ground.*]

LEADER.   Thank heaven, this fire is still alive. Now let's first put down these logs here and place our torches in the pots to catch; then let's make a rush for the gates with a battering-ram. If the women don't unbar the gate at our summons, we'll have to smoke them out.

Let me put down my load. Ouch! That hurts! [*To the audience.*] Would any of the generals in Samos[17] like to lend a hand with this log? [*Throwing down a log.*] Well, *that* won't break my back any more, at any rate. [*Turning to his fire-pot.*] Your job, my little pot, is to keep those coals alive and furnish me shortly with a red-hot torch.

O mistress Victory, be my ally and grant me to rout these audacious women in the Acropolis.

[*While the men are busy with their logs and fires, the* CHORUS OF OLD WOMEN *enters, carrying pitchers of water.*]

LEADER OF WOMEN.   What's this I see? Smoke and flames? Is that a fire ablazing? Let's rush upon them. Hurry up! They'll find us women ready.

1ST SEMI-CHORUS OF OLD WOMEN   [*singing*].
With wingèd foot onward I fly,
Ere the flames consume Neodice;
Lest Critylla be overwhelmed
By a lawless, accurst herd of old men.
I shudder with fear. Am I too late to aid them?
At break of the day filled we our jars with water
Fresh from the spring, pushing our way straight through the crowds. Oh, what a din!
Mid crockery crashing, jostled by slavegirls,
Sped we to save them, aiding our neighbors,
Bearing this water to put out the flames.

2ND SEMI-CHORUS OF OLD WOMEN   [*singing*].
Such news I've heard: doddering fools
Come with logs, like furnace-attendants,
Loaded down with three hundred pounds
Breathing many a vain, blustering threat,
That all these abhorred sluts will be burnt to charcoal.
O goddess, I pray never may they be kindled;
Grant them to save Greece and our men; madness and war help them to end.
With this as our purpose, golden-plumed Maiden,[18]
Guardian of Athens, seized we thy precinct.

---

[17] *Samos:* an island in the Aegean that was still allied to Athens.   [18] *golden-plumed Maiden:* Athene.

Be my ally, Warrior-maiden,
'Gainst these old men, bearing water with me.

> [*The women have now reached their position in the orchestra, and their* LEADER *advances toward the* LEADER OF THE MEN.]

L. WOM. Hold on there! What's this, you utter scoundrels? No decent, God-fearing citizens would act like this.

L. MEN. Oho! Here's something unexpected: a swarm of women have come out to attack us.

L. WOM. What, do we frighten you? Surely you don't think we're too many for you. And yet there are ten thousand times more of us whom you haven't even seen.

L. MEN. What say, Phaedria? Shall we let these women wag their tongues? Shan't we take our sticks and break them over their backs?

L. WOM. Let's set our pitchers on the ground; then if anyone lays a hand on us, they won't get in our way.

L. MEN. By God! If someone gave them two or three smacks on the jaw, like Bupalus,[19] they wouldn't talk so much!

L. WOM. Go on, hit me, somebody! Here's my jaw! But no other bitch will bite a piece out of you before me.

L. MEN. Silence! or I'll knock out your—senility!

L. WOM. Just lay one finger on Stratyllis, I dare you!

L. MEN. Suppose I dust you off with this fist? What will you do?

L. WOM. I'll tear the living guts out of you with my teeth.

L. MEN. No poet is more clever than Euripedes: "There is no beast so shameless as a woman."

L. WOM. Let's pick up our jars of water, Rhodippe.

L. MEN. Why have you come here with water, you detestable slut?

L. WOM. And why have you come with fire, you funeral vault? To cremate yourself?

L. MEN. To light a fire and singe your friends.

L. WOM. And I've brought water to put out your fire.

L. MEN. What? You'll put out my fire?

L. WOM. Just try and see!

L. MEN. I wonder: shall I scorch you with this torch of mine?

L. WOM. If you've got any soap, I'll give you a bath.

L. MEN. Give *me* a bath, you stinking hag?

L. WOM. Yes—a bridal bath!

L. MEN. Just listen to her! What crust!

L. WOM. Well, I'm a free citizen.

L. MEN. I'll put an end to your bawling. [*The men pick up their torches.*]

L. WOM. You'll never do jury duty again. [*The women pick up their pitchers.*]

L. MEN. Singe her hair for her!

---

[19] *Bupalus:* according to the poet Hipponax, Bupalus was the recipient, not the bestower, of smacks on the jaw.

L. WOM.   Do your duty, water! [*The women empty their pitchers on the men.*]

L. MEN.   Ow! Ow! For heaven's sake!

L. WOM.   Is it too hot?

L. MEN.   What do you mean "hot"? Stop! What are you doing?

L. WOM.   I'm watering you, so you'll be fresh and green.

L. MEN.   But I'm all withered up with shaking.

L. WOM.   Well, you've got a fire; why don't you dry yourself?

SCENE I

[*Enter an Athenian* MAGISTRATE, *accompanied by four Scythian policemen.*]

MAG.   Have these wanton women flared up again with their timbrels and their continual worship of Sabazius?[20] Is this another Adonisdirge upon the rooftops— which we heard not long ago in the Assembly? That confounded Demostratus was urging us to sail to Sicily, and the whirling women shouted, "Woe for Adonis!"[21] And then Demostratus said we'd best enroll the infantry from Zacynthus, and a tipsy woman on the roof shrieked, "Beat your breasts for Adonis!" And that vile and filthy lunatic forced his measure through. Such license do our women take.

L. MEN.   What if you heard of the insolence of these women here? Besides their other violent acts, they threw water all over us, and we have to shake out our clothes just as if we'd leaked in them.

MAG.   And rightly too, by God! For we ourselves lead the women astray and teach them to play the wanton; from these roots such notions blossom forth. A man goes into the jeweler's shop and says, "About that necklace you made for my wife, goldsmith: last night, while she was dancing, the fastening-bolt slipped out of the hole. I have to sail over to Salamis today; if you're free, do come around tonight and fit in a new bolt for her." Another goes to the shoemaker, a strapping young fellow with manly parts, and says, "See here, cobbler, the sandalstrap chafes my wife's little—toe; it's so tender. Come around during the siesta and stretch it a little, so she'll be more comfortable." Now we see the results of such treatment: here I'm a special Councillor and need money to procure oars for the galleys; and I'm locked out of the Treasury by these women.

But this is no time to stand around. Bring up crowbars there! I'll put an end to their insolence. [*To one of the policemen.*] What are you gaping at, you wretch? What are you staring at? Got an eye out for a tavern, eh? Set your crowbars here to the gates and force them open. [*Retiring to a safe distance.*] I'll help from over here.

---

[20] *Sabazius:* a Thracian and Phrygian deity whom the Greeks usually identified with Dionysus.

[21] *Demostratus…Adonis:* Demostratus took a leading part in selling the disastrous Sicilian expedition to the Athenian assembly. Plutarch records the women's dirge for Adonis as among the evil omens precedent to the expedition.

[*The gates are thrown open and* LYSISTRATA *comes out followed by several other women.*]

LYS.   Don't force the gates; I'm coming out of my own accord. We don't need crowbars here; what we need is good sound commonsense.

MAG.   Is that so, you strumpet? Where's my policeman? Officer, arrest her and tie her arms behind her back.

LYS.   By Artemis, if he lays a finger on me, he'll pay for it, even if he is a public servant.

[*The policeman retires in terror.*]

MAG.   You there, are you afraid? Seize her round the waist—and you, too. Tie her up, both of you!

1ST WOMAN   [*as the second policeman approaches* LYSISTRATA]. By Pandrosus,[22] if you but touch her with your hand, I'll kick the stuffings out of you.

[*The second policeman retires in terror.*]

MAG.   Just listen to that: "kick the stuffings out." Where's another policeman? Tie *her* up first, for her chatter.

2ND WOMAN.   By the Goddess of the Light,[23] if you lay the tip of your finger on her, you'll soon need a doctor.

[*The third policemen retires in terror.*]

MAG.   What's this? Where's my policeman? Seize *her* too. I'll soon stop your sallies.

3RD WOMAN.   By the Goddess of Tauros,[24] if you go near her, I'll tear out your hair until it shrieks with pain.

[*The fourth policeman retires in terror.*]

MAG.   Oh, damn it all! I've run out of policemen. But women must never defeat us. Officers, let's charge them all together. Close up your ranks!

[*The policemen rally for a mass attack.*]

LYS.   By heaven, you'll soon find out that we have four companies of warrior-women, all fully equipped within!

MAG.   [*advancing*]. Twist their arms off, men!

LYS.   [*shouting*]. To the rescue, my valiant women!
O sellers-of-barley-green-stuffs-and-eggs,
O sellers-of-garlic, ye keepers-of-taverns, and vendors-of-bread,
Grapple! Smite! Smash!
Won't you heap filth on them? Give them a tongue-lashing!

---

[22] *Pandrosus:* goddess of the dew. Parker wonders if *pandrosus (all-bedewing)* may not have been another epithet for Artemis, "classical antiquity's best-at-tested virgin, who is otherwise invoked here in three out of the four instances"—Aristophanes, *Lysistrata,* Douglass Parker, trans., The Complete Greek Comedy, William Arrowsmith, ed. (Ann Arbor: The University of Michigan Press, 1964).   [23] *Goddess of the Light:* Artemis.   [24] *Goddess of Tauros:* Artemis. Tauros is the Crimea.

[*The women beat off the policemen.*]

Halt! Withdraw! No looting on the field.

MAG. Damn it! My police-force has put up a very poor show.

LYS. What did you expect? Did you think you were attacking slaves? Didn't you
know that women are filled with passion?

MAG. Aye, passion enough—for a good strong drink!

L. MEN. O chief and leader of this land, why spend your words in vain?
Don't argue with these shameless beasts. You know not how we've fared:
A soapless bath they've given us; our clothes are soundly soaked.

L. WOM. Poor fool! You never should attack or strike a peaceful girl.
But if you do, your eyes must swell. For I am quite content
To sit unmoved, like modest maids, in peace and cause no pain;
But let a man stir up my hive, he'll find me like a wasp.

CHORUS OF MEN [*singing*].
O God, whatever shall we do with creatures like Womankind?
This can't be endured by any man alive. Question them!
Let us try to find out what this means.
To what end have they seized on this shrine,
This steep and rugged, high and holy,
Undefiled Acropolis?

L. MEN. Come, put your questions; don't give in, and probe her every statement.
For base and shameful it would be to leave this plot untested.

MAG. Well then, first of all I wish to ask her this: for what purpose have you
barred us from the Acropolis?

LYS. To keep the treasure safe, so you won't make war on account of it.

MAG. What? Do we make war on account of the treasure?

LYS. Yes, and you cause all our other troubles for it, too. Peisander[25] and those
greedy office-seekers keep things stirred up so they can find occasions to steal.
Now let them do what they like: they'll never again make off with any of this
money.

MAG. What will you do?

LYS. What a question! We'll administer it ourselves.

MAG. *You* will administer the treasure?

LYS. What's so strange in that? Don't we administer the household money for
you?

MAG. That's different.

LYS. How is it different?

MAG. We've got to make war with this money.

LYS. But that's the very first thing: you mustn't make war.

MAG. How else can we be saved?

LYS. We'll save you.

MAG. *You?*

---

[25] *Peisander:* "Engineer of the oligarchic revolt which overthrew the Athenian constitution in May 411
and set up the Council of Four Hundred." [Parker's note.]

LYS. Yes, we!

MAG. God forbid!

LYS. We'll save you, whether you want it or not.

MAG. Oh! This is terrible!

LYS. You don't like it, but we're going to do it none the less.

MAG. Good God! it's illegal!

LYS. We *will* save you, my little man!

MAG. Suppose I don't want you to?

LYS. That's all the more reason.

MAG. What business have you with war and peace?

LYS. I'll explain.

MAG. [*shaking his fist*]. Speak up, or you'll smart for it.

LYS. Just listen, and try to keep your hands still.

MAG. I can't. I'm so mad I can't stop them.

FIRST WOMAN. Then you'll be the one to smart for it.

MAG. Croak to yourself, old hag! [*To* LYSISTRATA.] Now then, speak up.

LYS. Very well. Formerly we endured the war for a good long time with our usual restraint, no matter what you men did. You wouldn't let us say "boo," although nothing you did suited us. But we watched you well, and though we stayed at home we'd often hear of some terribly stupid measure you'd proposed. Then, though grieving at heart, we'd smile sweetly and say, "What was passed in the Assembly today about writing on the treaty stone?" "What's that to you?" my husband would say. "Hold your tongue!" And I held my tongue.

1ST WOMAN. But I wouldn't have—not I!

MAG. You'd have been soundly smacked, if you hadn't kept still.

LYS. So I kept still at home. Then we'd hear of some plan still worse than the first; we'd say, "Husband, how could you pass such a stupid proposal?" He'd scowl at me and say, "If you don't mind your spinning, your head will be sore for weeks. *War shall be the concern of Men.*"[26]

MAG. And he was right, upon my word!

LYS. Why right, you confounded fool, when your proposals were so stupid and we weren't allowed to make suggestions?

"There's not a *man* left in the country," says one. "No, not one," says another. Therefore all we women have decided in council to make a common effort to save Greece. How long should we have waited? Now, if you're willing to listen to our excellent proposals and keep silence for us in your turn, we still may save you.

MAG. We men keep silence for you? That's terrible; I won't endure it!

LYS. Silence!

MAG. Silence for *you*, you wench, when you're wearing a snood?[27] I'd rather die!

LYS. Well, if that's all that bothers you—here! take my snood and tie it round your head. [*During the following words the women dress up the* MAGISTRATE *in*

[26] *War...Men:* Homer, *Iliad* vi. 492. (Translator's note.) [27] *snood:* the Greek word is variously translated *snood, fillet, wimple.* To the magistrate it signifies female inferiority.

women's garments.] And *now* keep quiet! Here, take this spinning basket, too, and card your wool with robes tucked up, munching on beans. *War shall be the concern of Women!*

L. Wom. Arise and leave your pitchers, girls; no time is this to falter.
  We too must aid our loyal friends; our turn has come for action.

Chorus of Women [*singing*].
  I'll never tire of aiding them with song and dance; never may
  Faintness keep my legs from moving to and fro endlessly.
  For I yearn to do all for my friends;
  They have charm, they have wit, they have grace,
  With courage, brains, and best of virtues—
  Patriotic sapience.

L. Wom. Come, child of manliest ancient dames, off spring of stinging nettles,
  Advance with rage unsoftened; for fair breezes speed you onward.

Lys. If only sweet Eros and the Cyprian Queen of Love[28] shed charm over our breasts and limbs and inspire our men with amorous longing and priapic spasms, I think we may soon be called Peacemakers among the Greeks.

Mag. What will you do?

Lys. First of all, we'll stop those fellows who run madly about the Marketplace in arms.

1st Wom. Indeed we shall, by the Queen of Paphos.[29]

Lys. For now they roam about the market, amid the pots and greenstuffs, armed to the teeth like Corybantes.

Mag. That's what manly fellows ought to do!

Lys. But it's so silly: a chap with a Gorgon-emblazoned shield buying pickled herring.

1st Wom. Why, just the other day I saw one of those long-haired dandies who command our cavalry ride up on horseback and pour into his bronze helmet the egg broth he'd bought from an old dame. And there was a Thracian slinger too, shaking his lance like Tereus; he'd scared the life out of the poor fig peddler and was gulping down all her ripest fruit.

Mag. How can you stop all the confusion in the various states and bring them together?

Lys. Very easily.

Mag. Tell me how.

Lys. Just like a ball of wool, when it's confused and snarled: we take it thus, and draw out a thread here and a thread there with our spindles; thus we'll unsnarl this war, if no one prevents us, and draw together the various states with embassies here and embassies there.

Mag. Do you suppose you can stop this dreadful business with balls of wool and spindles, you nitwits?

Lys. Why, if *you* had any wits, you'd manage all affairs of state like our woolworking.

---

[28] *Cyprion…Love:* Aphrodite. [29] *Queen of Paphos:* Aphrodite, who was believed to have risen from the sea near Paphos in western Cyprus.

MAG.   How so?

LYS.   First you ought to treat the city as we do when we wash the dirt out of a fleece: stretch it out and pluck and thrash out of the city all those prickly scoundrels; aye, and card out those who conspire and stick together to gain office, pulling off their heads. Then card the wool, all of it, into one fair basket of goodwill, mingling in the aliens residing here, any loyal foreigners, and anyone who's in debt to the Treasury; and consider that all our colonies lie scattered round about like remnants; from all of these collect the wool and gather it together here, wind up a great ball, and then weave a good stout cloak for the democracy.

MAG.   Dreadful! Talking about thrashing and winding balls of wool, when you haven't the slightest share in the war.

LYS.   Why, you dirty scoundrel, we bear more than twice as much as you. First, we bear children and send off our sons as soldiers.

MAG.   Hush! Let bygones be bygones!

LYS.   Then, when we ought to be happy and enjoy our youth, we sleep alone because of your expeditions abroad. But never mind us married women: I grieve most for the maids who grow old at home unwed.

MAG.   Don't men grow old, too?

LYS.   For heaven's sake! That's not the same thing. When a man comes home, no matter how grey he is, he soon finds a girl to marry. But woman's bloom is short and fleeting; if she doesn't grasp her chance, no man is willing to marry her and she sits at home a prey to every fortune-teller.

MAG.   [*coarsely*]. But if a man can still get it up—

LYS.   See here, you: what's the matter? Aren't you dead yet? There's plenty of room for you. Buy yourself a shroud and I'll bake you a honey-cake. [*Handing him a copper coin for his passage across the Styx.*] Here's your fare! Now get yourself a wreath.

> [*During the following dialogue the women dress up the* MAGISTRATE *as a corpse.*]

1ST WOM.   Here, take these fillets.

2ND WOM.   Here, take this wreath.

LYS.   What do you want? What's lacking? Get moving; off to the ferry! Charon is calling you; don't keep him from sailing.

MAG.   Am I to endure these insults? By God! I'm going straight to the magistrates to show them how I've been treated.

LYS.   Are you grumbling that you haven't been properly laid out? Well, the day after tomorrow we'll send around all the usual offerings early in the morning.

> [*The* MAGISTRATE *goes out still wearing his funeral decorations.* LYSISTRATA *and the women retire into the Acropolis.*]

CHORAL EPISODE

L. MEN.   Wake, ye sons of freedom, wake! 'Tis no time for sleeping.
Up and at them, like a man! Let us strip for action.

[*The* CHORUS OF MEN *remove their outer cloaks.*]

CHORUS OF MEN   [*singing*].
    Surely there is something here greater than meets the eye;
    For without a doubt I smell Hippias' tyranny.[30]
    Dreadful fear assails me lest certain bands of Spartan men,
    Meeting here with Cleisthenes,[31] have inspired through treachery
    All these god-detested women secretly to seize
    Athens' treasure in the temple, and to stop that pay
    Whence I live at my ease.[32]

L. MEN.   Now isn't it terrible for them to advise the state and chatter about
    shields, being mere women?
        And they think to reconcile us with the Spartans—men who hold nothing
    sacred any more than hungry wolves. Surely this is a web of deceit, my friends,
    to conceal an attempt at tyranny. But they'll never lord it over me; I'll be on
    my guard and from now on,
        "The blade I bear a myrtle spray shall wear." I'll occupy the market under
    arms and stand next to Aristogeiton.
        Thus I'll stand beside him. [*He strikes the pose of the famous statue of tyran-
    nicides, with one arm raised.*) And here's my chance to take this accurst old hag
    and—[*striking the* LEADER OF WOMEN] smack her on the jaw!

L. WOM.   You'll go home in such a state your Ma won't recognize you!
    Ladies all, upon the ground let us place these garments.

[*The* CHORUS OF WOMEN *remove their outer garments.*]

CHORUS OF WOM.   [*singing*]. Citizens of Athens, hear useful words for the state.
    Rightly; for it nurtured me in my youth royally.
    As a child of seven years carried I the sacred box;[33]
    Then I was a Miller-maid, grinding at Athene's shrine;
    Next I wore the saffron robe and played Brauronia's Bear;
    And I walked as Basket-bearer, wearing chains of figs,
    As a sweet maiden fair.

---

[30] *Hippias' tyranny:* Hippias, the last of the Tyrants of Athens, ruled 527–510 B.C.   [31] *Cleisthenes:* a notorious homosexual, also mentioned unmentionably [Fitts's phrasal at l. 8, p. 82.   [32] *stop...ease:* this phrase and l. 70, p. 69. ("You'll never do jury-duty again") make it reasonably clear that the basic source of income for the old men of the chorus is jury duty, for which they received three obols a day. The money, says Parker, "would naturally be stored inside the Citadel in the Treasury."   [33] *carried...box:* "Since this passage is frequently cited as primary evidence for the *cursus honorum* of a high-born young girl in fifth-century Athens, here are the steps set forth a bit more explic-itly: (1) *arréphoros* ('relic-bearer') to Athene, one of four little girls who carried the Goddess' sacred objects in Her semi-annual festival of the *Arréphoria;* (2) *aletris* ('mill-girl') to the Founding Mother (doubtless Athene), one of the girls who ground the meal to be made into sacrificial cakes; (3) *arktos* ('she-bear') at the *Brauronia,* a festival of Artemis held every fifth year at Brauron In Attika, centering on a myth which told of the killing of a tame bear sacred to that goddess; and (4) *kanéphoiros* ('basket-bearer'), the maiden who bore the sacrificial cake and led the procession at Athens' most important fes-tivals, such as the City Dionysia and the Great Panathenaia." [Parker's note.]

L. WOM.   Therefore, am I not bound to give good advice to the city?

Don't take it ill that I was born a woman, if I contribute something better than our present troubles. I pay my share; for I contribute MEN. But you miserable old fools contribute nothing, and after squandering our ancestral treasure, the fruit of the Persian Wars, you make no contribution in return. And now, all on account of you, we're facing ruin.

What, muttering, are you? If you annoy me, I'll take this hard, rough slipper and—[*striking the* LEADER OF MEN] smack you on the jaw!

CHORUS OF MEN   [*singing*].

This is outright insolence! Things go from bad to worse.
If you're men with any guts, prepare to meet the foe.
Let us strip our tunics off! We need the smell of male
Vigor. And we cannot fight all swaddled up in clothes.

[They strip off their tunics.]

Come then, my comrades, on to the battle, ye who once to Leipsydrion[34] came;
Then ye were MEN. Now call back your youthful vigor.
With light, wingèd footstep advance,
Shaking old age from your frame.

L. MEN.   If any of us give these wenches the slightest hold, they'll stop at nothing: such is their cunning.

They will even build ships and sail against us, like Artemisia.[35] Or if they turn to mounting, I count our Knights as done for: a woman's such a tricky jockey when she gets astraddle, with a good firm seat for trotting. Just look at those Amazons that Micon painted, fighting on horseback against men!

But we must throw them all in the pillory—[*seizing and choking the* LEADER OF WOMEN] grabbing hold of yonder neck!

CHORUS OF WOM.   [*singing*].

'Ware my anger! Like a boar 'twill rush upon you men.
Soon you'll bawl aloud for help, you'll be so soundly trimmed!
Come, my friends, let's strip with speed, and lay aside these robes;
Catch the scent of women's rage. Attack with tooth and nail!

[They strip off their tunics.]

Now then, come near me, you miserable man! you'll never eat garlic or black beans again.
And if you utter a single hard word, in rage I will "nurse" you as once
The beetle requited her foe.[36]

---

[34] *Leipsydrion:* a mountain slope north of Athens where, a century before the time of the play, the exiled Alkmaionids or Patriots for a time fought off the the forces of the tyrant Hippias.   [35] *Artemisia:* "Queen of Halikarnassos, who, as an ally of the Persian King Xerxes in his invasion of Greece, fought with particular distinction at the sea battle of Salamis in 480." (Parker's note.]   [36] *beetle...foe:* Aesop's fable (No. 223), *The Eagle and the Beetle* [translator's note]. Injured by the eagle, the beetle retaliated by breaking the eagle's eggs wherever they were laid—even in the bosom of Zeus.

L. WOM.   For you don't worry me; no, not so long as my Lampito lives and our Theban friend, the noble Ismenia.

You can't do anything, not even if you pass a dozen—decrees! You miserable fool, all our neighbors hate you. Why, just the other day when I was holding a festival for Hecate, I invited as a playmate from our neighbors the Boeotians a charming, well-bred Copaic—eel. But they refused to send me one on account of your decrees.

And you'll never stop passing decrees until I grab your foot and—[*tripping up the* LEADER OF MEN] toss you down and break your neck!

[*Here an interval of five days is supposed to elapse.*]

SCENE II

[LYSISTRATA *comes out from the Acropolis.*]

L. WOM.   [*dramatically*]. Empress of this great emprise and undertaking,
Why come you forth, I pray, with frowning brow?
LYS.   Ah, these cursèd women! Their deeds and female notions make me pace up and down in utter despair.
L. WOM.   Ah, what sayest thou?
LYS.   The truth, alas! the truth.
L. WOM.   What dreadful tale hast thou to tell thy friends?
LYS.   'Tis shame to speak, and not to speak is hard.
L. WOM.   Hide not from me whatever woes we suffer.
LYS.   Well then, to put it briefly, we want—laying!
L. WOM.   O Zeus, Zeus!
LYS.   Why call on Zeus? That's the way things are. I can no longer keep them away from the men, and they're all deserting. I caught one wriggling through a hole near the grotto of Pan, another sliding down a rope, another deserting her post; and yesterday I found one getting on a sparrow's back to fly off to Orsilochus,[37] and had to pull her back by the hair. They're digging up all sorts of excuses to get home. Look, here comes one of them now. [*A woman comes hastily out of the Acropolis.*] Here you! Where are you off to in such a hurry?
1ST WOM.   I want to go home. My very best wool is being devoured by moths.
LYS.   Moths? Nonsense! Go back inside.
1ST WOM.   I'll come back; I swear it. I just want to lay it out on the bed.
LYS.   Well, you won't lay it out, and you won't go home, either.
1ST WOM.   Shall I let my wool be ruined?
LYS.   If necessary, yes. [*Another woman comes out.*]
2ND WOM.   Oh dear! Oh dear! My precious flax! I left it at home all unpeeled.
LYS.   Here's another one, going home for her "flax." Come back here!
2ND WOM.   But I just want to work it up a little and then I'll be right back.
LYS.   No indeed! If you start this, all the other women will want to do the same.
[*A third woman comes out.*]

---

[37] *Orsilochus:* keeper of a brothel.

3RD WOM.   O Eilithyia, goddess of travail, stop my labor till I come to a lawful spot!

LYS.   What's this nonsense?

3RD WOM.   I'm going to have a baby—right now!

LYS.   But you weren't even pregnant yesterday.

3RD WOM.   Well, I am today. O Lysistrata, do send me home to see a midwife, right away.

LYS.   What are you talking about? [*Putting her hand on her stomach.*] What's this hard lump here?

3RD WOM.   A little boy.

LYS.   My goodness, what have you got there? It seems hollow; I'll just find out. [*Pulling aside her robe.*] Why, you silly goose, you've got Athene's sacred helmet there. And you said you were having a baby!

3RD WOM.   Well, I *am* having one, I swear!

LYS.   Then what's this helmet for?

3RD WOM.   If the baby starts coming while I'm still in the Acropolis, I'll creep into this like a pigeon and give birth to it there.

LYS.   Stuff and nonsense! It's plain enough what you're up to. You just wait here for the christening of this—helmet.

3RD WOM.   But I can't sleep in the Acropolis since I saw the sacred snake.

1ST WOM.   And I'm dying for lack of sleep: the hooting of the owls keeps me awake.

LYS.   Enough of these shams, you wretched creatures. You want your husbands, I suppose. Well, don't you think they want us? I'm sure they're spending miserable nights. Hold out, my friends, and endure for just a little while. There's an oracle that we shall conquer, if we don't split up. [*Producing a roll of paper.*] Here it is.

1ST WOM.   Tell us what it says.

LYS.   Listen.
  "When in the length of time the Swallows shall gather together,
  Fleeing the Hoopoe's amorous flight and the Cockatoo shunning,
  Then shall your woes be ended and Zeus who thunders in heaven
  Set what's below on top—"

1ST WOM.   What? Are we going to be on top?

LYS.   "But if the Swallows rebel and flutter away from the temple,
  Never a bird in the world shall seem more wanton and worthless."

1ST WOM.   That's clear enough, upon my word!

LYS.   By all that's holy, let's not give up the struggle now. Let's go back inside. It would be a shame, my dear friends, to disobey the oracle.

[*The women all retire to the Acropolis again.*]

CHORAL EPISODE

CHORUS OF MEN   [*singing*].   I have a tale to tell,
  Which I know full well.

It was told me
In the nursery.

Once there was a likely lad,
 Melanion they name him;
The thought of marriage made him mad,
 For which I cannot blame him.

So off he went to mountains fair;
 (No women to upbraid him!)
A mighty hunter of the hare,
 He had a dog to aid him.

He never came back home to see
 Detested women's faces.
He showed a shrewd mentality.
 With him I'd fain change places!

ONE OF THE MEN [*to one of the women*].
 Come here, old dame; give me a kiss.
WOM. You'll ne'er eat garlic, if you dare!
MAN. I want to kick you—just like this!
WOM. Oh, there's a leg with bushy hair!
MAN. Myronides and Phormio[38]
 Were hairy—and they thrashed the foe.
CHORUS OF WOMEN [*singing*]. I have another tale,
 With which to assail
  Your contention
  'Bout Melanion.

Once upon a time a man
 Named Timon left our city,
To live in some deserted land.
 (We thought him rather witty.)

He dwelt alone amidst the thorn;
 In solitude he brooded.
From some grim Fury he was born:
 Such hatred he exuded.

He cursed you men, as scoundrels through
 And through, till life he ended.
He couldn't stand the sight of YOU!
 But women he befriended.

WOM. [*to one of the men*]. I'll smash your face in, if you like.
MAN. Oh no, please don't! You frighten me.

---

[38] *Myronides and Phormio:* respectively a victorious Athenian general, admiral.

Wom.   I'll lift my foot—and thus I'll strike.
Man.   Aha! Look there! What's that I see?
Wom.   Whate'er you see, you cannot say
  That I'm not neatly trimmed today.

SCENE III

[Lysistrata *appears on the wall of the Acropolis.*]

Lys.   Hello! Hello! Girls, come here quick!

[*Several women appear beside her.*]

Wom.   What is it? Why are you calling?
Lys.   I see a man coming: he's in a dreadful state. He's mad with passion. O
  Queen of Cyprus, Cythera, and Paphos, just keep on this way!
Wom.   Where is the fellow?
Lys.   There, beside the shrine of Demeter.
Wom.   Oh yes, so he is. Who is he?
Lys.   Let's see. Do any of you know him?
Myr.   Yes indeed. That's my husband, Cinesias.
Lys.   It's up to you, now: roast him, rack him, fool him, love him—and leave him!
  Do everything, except what our oath forbids.
Myr.   Don't worry; I'll do it.
Lys.   I'll stay here to tease him and warm him up a bit. Off with you.

  [*The other women retire from the wall. Enter* Cinesias *followed by a slave
  carrying a baby.* Ciniesias *is obviously in great pain and distress.*]

Cin.   [*groaning*]. Oh-h! Oh-h-h! This is killing me! O God, what tortures I'm
  suffering!
Lys.   [*from the wall*]. Who's that within our lines?
Cin.   Me.
Lys.   A *man*?
Cin.   [*pointing*]. A *man*, indeed!
Lys.   Well, go away!
Cin.   Who are you to send me away?
Lys.   The captain of the guard.
Cin.   Oh, for heaven's sake, call out Myrrhine for me.
Lys.   Call Myrrhine? Nonsense! Who are you?
Cin.   Her husband, Cinesias of Paionidai.
Lys.   [*appearing much impressed*]. Oh, greetings, friend. Your name is not without
  honor here among us. Your wife is always talking about you, and whenever she
  takes an egg or an apple, she says, "Here's to my dear Cinesias!"
Cin.   [*quivering with excitement*]. Oh, ye gods in heaven!
Lys.   Indeed she does! And whenever our conversations turn to men, your wife
  immediately says, "All men are mere rubbish compared with Cinesias."
Cin.   [*groaning*]. Oh! Do call her for me.

LYS.   Why should I? What will you give me?

CIN.   Whatever you want. All I have is yours—and you see what I've got!

LYS.   Well then, I'll go down and call her. [*She descends.*]

CIN.   And hurry up! I've had no joy of life ever since she left home. When I go in the house, I feel awful: everything seems so empty and I can't enjoy my dinner. I'm in such a state all the time!

MYR.   [*from behind the wall*]. I *do* love him so. But he won't let me love him. No, no! Don't ask me to see him!

CIN.   O my darling, O Myrrhine honey, why do you do this to me? [MYRRHINE *appears on the wall.*] Come down here!

MYR.   No, I won't come down.

CIN.   Won't you come, Myrrhine, when *I* call you?

MYR.   No; you don't want me.

CIN.   *Don't want you?* I'm in agony!

MYR.   I'm going now.

CIN.   Please don't! At least, listen to your baby. [*To the baby.*] Here you, call your mamma! [*Pinching the baby.*]

BABY.   Ma-ma! Ma-ma! Ma-ma!

CIN.   [*to* MYRRHINE]. What's the matter with you? Have you no pity for your child, who hasn't been washed or fed for five whole days?

MYR.   Oh, poor child; your father pays no attention to you.

CIN.   Come down then, you heartless wretch, for the baby's sake.

MYR.   Oh, what it is to be a mother! I've got to come down, I suppose. [*She leaves the wall and shortly reappears at the gate.*]

CIN.   [*to himself*]. She seems much younger, and she has such a sweet look about her. Oh, the way she teases me! And her pretty, provoking ways make me burn with longing.

MYR.   [*coming out of the gate and taking the baby*]. O my sweet little angel. Naughty papa! Here, let Mummy kiss you, Mamma's little sweetheart! [*She fondles the baby lovingly.*]

CIN.   [*in despair*]. You heartless creature, why do you do this? Why follow these other women and make both of us suffer so? [*He tries to embrace her.*]

MYR.   Don't touch me!

CIN.   You're letting all our things at home go to wrack and ruin.

MYR.   I don't care.

CIN.   You don't care that your wool is being plucked to pieces by the chickens?

MYR.   Not in the least.

CIN.   And you haven't celebrated the rites of Aphrodite for ever so long. Won't you come home?

MYR.   Not on your life, unless you men make a truce and stop the war.

CIN.   Well then, if that pleases you, we'll do it.

MYR.   Well then, if that pleases *you*, I'll come home—afterwards! Right now I'm on oath not to.

CIN.   Then just lie down here with me for a moment.

MYR.   No—[*in a teasing voice*] and yet, I won't say I don't love you.

CIN.   You love me? Oh, do lie down here, Myrrhine dear!

MYR.   What, you silly fool! in front of the baby?

CIN.   [*hastily thrusting the baby at the slave*]. Of course not. Here—home! Take him, Manes! [*The slave goes off with the baby.*] See, the baby's out of the way. Now won't you lie down?

MYR.   But where, my dear?

CIN.   Where? The grotto of Pan's a lovely spot.

MYR.   How could I purify myself before returning to the shrine?

CIN.   Easily: just wash here in the Clepsydra.

MYR.   And then, shall I go back on my oath?

CIN.   On my head be it! Don't worry about the oath.

MYR.   All right, then. Just let me bring out a bed.

CIN.   No, don't. The ground's all right.

MYR.   Heavens, no! Bad as you are, I won't let you lie on the bare ground. [*She goes into the Acropolis.*]

CIN.   Why, she really loves me; it's plain to see.

MYR.   [*returning with a bed*]. There! Now hurry up and lie down. I'll just slip off this dress. But—let's see: oh yes, I must fetch a mattress.

CIN.   Nonsense! No mattress for me.

MYR.   Yes indeed! It's not nice on the bare springs.

CIN.   Give me a kiss.

MYR.   [*giving him a hasty kiss*]. There! [*She goes.*]

CIN.   [*in mingled distress and delight*]. Oh-h! Hurry back!

MYR.   [*returning with a mattress*]. Here's the mattress; lie down on it. I'm taking my things off now—but—let's see: you have no pillow.

CIN.   I don't *want* a pillow!

MYR.   But I do. [*She goes.*]

CIN.   Cheated again, just like Heracles and his dinner![39]

MYR.   [*returning with a pillow*]. Here lift your head. [*To herself, wondering how else to tease him.*] Is that all?

CIN.   Surely that's all! Do come here, precious!

MYR.   I'm taking off my girdle. But remember: don't go back on your promise about the truce.

CIN.   Hope to die, if I do.

MYR.   You don't have a blanket.

CIN.   [*shouting in exasperation*]. *I don't want one!* I WANT TO—

MYR.   Sh-h! There, there, I'll be back in a minute. [*She goes.*]

CIN.   She'll be the death of me with these bedclothes.

MYR.   [*returning with a blanket*]. Here, get up.

CIN.   I've got *this* up!

MYR.   Would you like some perfume?

CIN.   Good heavens, no! I won't have it!

---

[39] *Heracles...dinner:* "A stock comedy bit wherein the glutton hero, raving with hunger is systematically diddled of his dinner by his hosts." [Parker's note.]

MYR. Yes, you shall, whether you want it or not. [*She goes.*]

CIN. O lord! Confound all perfumes anyway!

MYR. [*returning with a flask*]. Stretch out your hand and put some on.

CIN. [*suspiciously*]. By God, I don't much like this perfume. It smacks of shilly-shallying, and has no scent of the marriage-bed.

MYR. Oh dear! This is Rhodian perfume I've brought.

CIN. It's quite all right, dear. Never mind.

MYR. Don't be silly! [*She goes out with the flask.*]

CIN. Damn the man who first concocted perfumes!

MYR. [*returning with another flask*]. Here, try this flask.

CIN. I've got another one all ready for you. Come, you wretch, lie down and stop bringing me things.

MYR. All right; I'm taking off my shoes. But, my dear, see that you vote for peace.

CIN. [*absently*]. I'll consider it. [MYRRHINE *runs away to the Acropolis.*] I'm ruined! The wench has skinned me and run away! [*Chanting, in tragic style.*] Alas! Alas! Deceived, deserted by this fairest of women, whom shall I—lay? Ah, my poor child, how shall I nurture thee? Where's Cynalopex?[40] I needs must hire a nurse!

L. MEN. [*chanting*]. Ah, wretched man, in dreadful wise beguiled, betrayed, thy soul is sore distressed. I pity thee, alas! alas! What soul, what loins, what liver could stand this strain? How firm and unyielding he stands, with naught to aid him of a morning.

CIN. O lord! O Zeus! What tortures I endure!

L. MEN. This is the way she's treated you, that vile and cursèd wanton.

L. WOM. Nay, not vile and cursèd, but sweet and dear.

L. MEN. Sweet, you say? Nay, hateful, hateful!

CIN. Hateful indeed! O Zeus, Zeus!

    Seize her and snatch her away,

    Like a handful of dust, in a mighty,

    Fiery tempest! Whirl her aloft, then let her drop

    Down to the earth, with a crash, as she falls—

    On the point of this waiting

    Thingummybob! [*He goes out.*]

SCENE IV

[*Enter a Spartan* HERALD *in an obvious state of excitement, which he is doing his best to conceal.*]

HER. Where can I find the Senate or the Prytanes?[41] I've got an important message. [*The Athenian* MAGISTRATE *enters.*]

MAG. Say there, are you a man or Priapus?

HER. [*in annoyance*]. I'm a herald, you lout! I've come from Sparta about the truce.

[40] *Cynalopex:* a pimp. The "poor little child" in the preceding line is Cinesias's phallus. [41] *Prytanes:* members of the executive committee of the Senate.

MAG.   Is that a spear you've got under your cloak?

HER.   No, of course not!

MAG.   Why do you twist and turn so? Why hold your cloak in front of you? Did you rupture yourself on the trip?

HER.   By gum, the fellow's an old fool.

MAG.   [*pointing*]. Why, you dirty rascal, you're all excited.

HER.   Not at all. Stop this tomfoolery.

MAG.   Well, what's that I see?

HER.   A Spartan message-staff.

MAG.   Oh, certainly! That's just the kind of message-staff I've got. But tell me the honest truth: how are things going in Sparta?

HER.   All the land of Sparta is up in arms—and our allies are up, too. We need Pellene.[42]

MAG.   What brought this trouble on you? A sudden Panic?

HER.   No, Lampito started it and then all the other women in Sparta with one accord chased their husbands out of their beds.

MAG.   How do you feel?

HER.   Terrible. We walk around the city bent over like men lighting matches in a wind. For our women won't let us touch them until we all agree and make peace throughout Greece.

MAG.   This is a general conspiracy of the women; I see it now. Well, hurry back and tell the Spartans to send ambassadors here with full powers to arrange a truce. And I'll go tell the Council to choose ambassadors from here; I've got a little something here that will persuade them!

HER.   I'll fly there; for you've made an excellent suggestion.

[*The* HERALD *and the* MAGISTRATE *depart on opposite sides of the stage.*]

CHORAL EPISODE

L. MEN.   No beast or fire is harder than womankind to tame,
　Nor is the spotted leopard so devoid of shame.

L. WOM.   Knowing this, you dare provoke us to attack?
　I'd be your steady friend, if you'd but take us back.

L. MEN.   I'll never cease my hatred keen of womankind.

L. WOM.   Just as you will. But now just let me help you find
　That cloak you threw aside. You look so silly there
　Without your clothes. Here, put it on and don't go bare.

L. MEN.   That's very kind, and shows you're not entirely bad.
　But I threw off my things when I was good and mad.

---

[42] *Pellene:* a petty state allied with Sparta. Commentators differ as to the point here. Perhaps it's that, after the string of double entendres, one expects yet another or the plain truth (they need women) and receives instead an answer merely military and, given the relative unimportance of Pellene, comically unsatisfactory.

L. WOM. At last you seem a man, and won't be mocked, my lad.
　　If you'd been nice to me, I'd take this little gnat
　　That's in your eye and pluck it out for you, like that.
L. MEN. So that's what's bothered me and bit my eye so long!
　　Please dig it out for me. I own that I've been wrong.
L. WOM. I'll do so, though you've been a most ill-natured brat.
　　Ye gods! See here! A huge and monstrous little gnat!
L. MEN. Oh, how that helps! For it was digging wells in me.
　　And now it's out, my tears are flowing fast and free.
L. WOM. Here, let me wipe them off, although you're such a knave,
　　And kiss me.
L. MEN. No!
L. WOM. Whate'er you say, a kiss I'll have. [*She kisses him.*]
L. MEN. Oh, confound these women! They've a coaxing way about them.
　　He was wise and never spoke a truer word, who said,
　　"We can't live with women, but we cannot live without them."
　　Now I'll make a truce with you. We'll fight no more; instead
　　I will not injure you if you do me no wrong.
　　And now let's join our ranks and then begin a song.
COMBINED CHORUS [*singing*]. Athenians, we're not prepared,
　　To say a single ugly word
　　About our fellow-citizens.
　　Quite the contrary: we desire but to say and to do
　　Naught but good. Quite enough are the ills now on hand.

　　Men and women, be advised:
　　　　If anyone requires
　　Money—minae two or three—,
　　　　We've got what he desires.

　　My purse is yours, on easy terms:
　　　　When Peace shall reappear,
　　Whate'er you've borrowed will be due.
　　　　So speak up without fear.

　　You needn't pay me back, you see,
　　If you can get a cent from me!

　　We're about to entertain
　　　　Some foreign gentlemen;
　　We've soup and tender, fresh-killed pork.
　　　　Come round to dine at ten.

　　Come early; wash and dress with care,
　　　　And bring the children, too.
　　Then step right in, no "by your leave."
　　　　We'll be expecting you.

Walk in as if you owned the place.
You'll find the door—shut in your face!

SCENE V

> [*Enter a group of Spartan* AMBASSADORS; *they are in the same desperate condition as the Herald in the previous scene.*)

LEADER OF CHORUS: Here come the envoys from Sparta, sprouting long beards and looking for all the world as if they were carrying pigpens in front of them. Greetings, gentlemen of Sparta. Tell me, in what state have you come?

SPARTAN.   Why waste words? You can plainly see what state we've come in!

L. CHO.   Wow! You're in a pretty high-strung condition, and it seems to be getting worse.

SPA.   It's indescribable. Won't someone please arrange a peace for us—in any way you like.

L. CHO.   Here come our own, native ambassadors, crouching like wrestlers and holding their clothes in front of them; this seems an athletic kind of malady.

> [*Enter several Athenian* AMBASSADORS.]

ATH.   Can anyone tell us where Lysistrata is? You see our condition.

L. CHO.   Here's another case of the same complaint. Tell me, are the attacks worse in the morning?

ATH.   No, we're always afflicted this way. If someone doesn't soon arrange a truce, you'd better not let me get my hands on—Cleisthenes![43]

L. CHO.   If you're smart, you'll arrange your cloaks so none of the fellows who smashed the Hermae[44] can see you.

ATH.   Right you are; a very good suggestion.

SPA.   Aye, by all means. Here, let's hitch up our clothes.

ATH.   Greetings, Spartan. We've suffered dreadful things.

SPA.   My dear fellow, we'd have suffered still worse if one of those fellows had seen us in this condition.

ATH.   Well, gentlemen, we must get down to business. What's your errand here?

SPA.   We're ambassadors about peace.

ATH.   Excellent; so are we. Only Lysistrata can arrange things for us; shall we summon her?

SPA.   Aye, and Lysistratus too, if you like.

L. CHO.   No need to summon her, it seems. She's coming out of her own accord.

> [*Enter* LYSISTRATA *accompanied by a statue of a nude female figure, which represents Reconciliation.*]

---

[43] *Cloisthenes:* cf. l, 9, p. 76, and note.   [44] *fellows...Hermae:* just before the sailing of the Sicilian expedition vandals smashed off the heads and phalluses of the statues of Hermes that served the Athenians as boundary markers and protectors of houses.

Hail, noblest of women; now must thou be
A judge shrewd and subtle, mild and severe,
Be sweet yet majestic: all manners employ.
The leaders of Hellas, caught by thy love-charms,
Have come to thy judgment, their charges submitting.

LYS.   This is no difficult task, if one catch them still in amorous passion, before they've resorted to each other. But I'll soon find out. Where's Reconciliation? Go, first bring the Spartans here, and don't seize them rudely and violently, as our tactless husbands used to do, but as befits a woman, like an old, familiar friend; if they won't give you their hands, take them however you can. Then go fetch these Athenians here, taking hold of whatever they offer you. Now then, men of Sparta, stand here beside me, and you Athenians on the other side, and listen to my words.

I am a woman, it is true, but I have a mind; I'm not badly off in native wit, and by listening to my father and my elders, I've had a decent schooling.

Now I intend to give you a scolding which you both deserve. With one common font you worship at the same altars, just like brothers, at Olympia, at Thermopylae, at Delphi—how many more might I name, if time permitted— and the Barbarians stand by waiting with their armies; yet you are destroying the men and towns of Greece.

ATH.   Oh, this tension is killing me!

LYS.   And now, men of Sparta—to turn to you—don't you remember how the Spartan Pericleidas came here once as a suppliant, and sitting at our altar, all pale with fear in his crimson cloak, begged us for an army? For all Messene had attacked you and the god sent an earthquake too? Then Cimon went forth with four thousand hoplites and saved all Lacedaemon. Such was the aid you received from Athens, and now you lay waste the country which once treated you so well.

ATH.   [*hotly*]. They're in the wrong, Lysistrata, upon my word, they are!

SPA.   [*absently, looking at the statue of Reconciliation*]. We're in the wrong. What hips! How lovely they are!

LYS.   Don't think I'm going to let you Athenians off. Don't you remember how the Spartans came in arms when you were wearing the rough, sheepskin cloak of slaves and slew the host of Thessalians, the comrades and allies of Hippias? Fighting with you on that day, alone of all the Greeks, they set you free and instead of a sheepskin gave your folk a handsome robe to wear.

SPA.   [*looking at* LYSISTRATA]. I've never seen a more distinguished woman.

ATH.   [*looking at Reconciliation*]. I've never seen a more voluptuous body!

LYS.   Why then, with these many noble deeds to think of, do you fight each other? Why don't you stop this villainy? Why not make peace? Tell me, what prevents it?

SPA.   [*waving vaguely at Reconciliation*]. We're willing, if you're willing to give up your position on yonder flank.

LYS.   What position, my good man?

SPA.   Pylus; we've been panting for it for ever so long.

ATH.   No, by God! You shan't have it!

LYS.   Let them have it, my friend.

ATH.   Then what shall we have to rouse things up with?

LYS.   Ask for another place in exchange.

ATH.   Well, let's see: first of all [*pointing to various parts of Reconciliation's anatomy*] give us Echinus here, this Maliac Inlet in back there, and these two Megarian legs.

SPA.   No, by heavens! You can't have *everything*, you crazy fool!

LYS.   Let it go. Don't fight over a pair of legs.

ATH.   [*taking off his cloak*]. I think I'll strip and do a little planting now.

SPA.   [*following suit*]. And I'll just do a little fertilizing, by gosh!

LYS.   Wait until the truce is concluded. Now if you've decided on this course, hold a conference and discuss the matter with your allies.

ATH.   Allies? Don't be ridiculous! They're in the same state we are. Won't all our allies want the same thing we do—to jump in bed with their women?

SPA.   Ours will, I know.

ATH.   Especially the Carystians, by God!

LYS.   Very well. Now purify yourselves, that your wives may feast and entertain you in the Acropolis; we've provisions by the basketful. Exchange your oaths and pledges there, and then each of you may take his wife and go home.

ATH.   Let's go at once.

SPA.   Come on, where you will.

ATH.   For God's sake, let's hurry!

[*They all go into the Acropolis.*]

CHO.   [*singing*]. Whate'er I have of coverlets
　　　　And robes of varied hue
　　And golden trinkets,—without stint
　　　　I offer them to you.

　　Take what you will and bear it home,
　　　　Your children to delight,
　　Or if your girl's a Basket-maid;
　　　　Just choose whate'er's in sight.

　　There's naught within so well secured
　　　　You cannot break the seal
　　And bear it off; just help yourselves;
　　　　No hesitation feel.

　　But you'll see nothing, though you try,
　　Unless you've sharper eyes than I!

　　If anyone needs bread to feed
　　　　A growing family,
　　I've lots of wheat and full-grown loaves;
　　　　So just apply to me.

Let every poor man who desires
   Come round and bring a sack
To fetch the grain; my slave is there
   To load it on his back.

But don't come near my door, I say:
   Beware the dog, and stay away!

ÉXODOS

[*An* ATHENIAN *enters carrying a torch; he knocks at the gate.*]

ATH.   Open the door! [*To the* CHORUS, *which is clustered around the gate.*] Make way, won't you! What are you hanging around for? Want me to singe you with this torch? [*To himself.*] No; it's a stale trick, I won't do it! [*To the audience.*] Still, if I've got to do it to please you, I suppose I'll have to take the trouble.

[*A* SECOND ATHENIAN *comes out of the gate.*]

2ND ATH.   And I'll help you.

1ST ATH.   [*waving his torch at the* CHORUS]. Get out! Go bawl your heads off! Move on there, so the Spartans can leave in peace when the banquet's over.

[*They brandish their torches until the* CHORUS *leaves the Orchestra.*]

2ND ATH.   I've never seen such a pleasant banquet: the Spartans are charming fellows, indeed they are! And we Athenians are very witty in our cups.

1ST ATH.   Naturally: for when we're sober we're never at our best. If the Athenians would listen to me, we'd always get a little tipsy on our embassies. As things are now, we go to Sparta when we're sober and look around to stir up trouble. And then we don't hear what they say—and as for what they *don't* say, we have all sorts of suspicions. And then we bring back varying reports about the mission. But this time everything is pleasant; even if a man should sing the Telamon song when he ought to sing "Cleitagoras," we'd praise him and swear it was excellent.[45]

[*The two* CHORUSES *return, as a* CHORUS OF ATHENIANS *and a* CHORUS OF SPARTANS.]

Here they come back again. Go to the devil, you scoundrels!

2ND ATH.   Get out, I say! They're coming out from the feast.

[*Enter the Spartan and Athenian envoys, followed by* LYSISTRATA *and all the women.*]

SPA.   [*to one of his fellow-envoys*]. My good fellow, take up your pipes; I want to do a fancy two-step and sing a jolly song for the Athenians.

ATH.   Yes, do take up your pipes, by all means. I'd love to see you dance.

---

[45] *swear...excellent:* the reference here is to a song-capping game, common at Athenian banquets, and to the gaffe of failing to follow one's cue.

SPA. [*singing and dancing with the* CHORUS OF SPARTANS].
 These youths inspire
To song and dance, O Memory;
Stir up my Muse, to tell how we
And Athens' men, in our galleys clashing
At Artemisium, 'gainst foemen dashing
 In godlike ire,
Conquered the Persian[46] and set Greece free.

 Leonidas
Led on his valiant warriors
Whetting their teeth like angry boars.
Abundant foam on their lips was flow'ring,
A stream of sweat from their limbs was show'ring.

 The Persian was
Numberless as the sand on the shores.

O Huntress[47] who slayest the beasts in the glade,
O Virgin divine, hither come to our truce,
Unite us in bonds which all time will not loose.
Grant us to find in this treaty, we pray,
An unfailing source of true friendship today,
And all of our days, helping us to refrain
From weaseling tricks which bring war in their train.
 Then hither, come hither! O huntress maid.

LYS. Come then, since all is fairly done, men of Sparta, lead away your wives, and you, Athenians, take yours. Let every man stand beside his wife, and every wife beside her man, and then, to celebrate our fortune, let's dance. And in the future, let's take care to avoid these misunderstandings.

CHORUS OF ATHENIANS [*singing and dancing*].
 Lead on the dances, your graces revealing.
Call Artemis hither, call Artemis' twin,
Leader of dances, Apollo the Healing,
Kindly God—hither! let's summon him in!

 Nysian[48] Bacchus call,
Who with his Maenads, his eyes flashing fire,
 Dances, and last of all
Zeus of the thunderbolt flaming, the Sire,
 And Hera in majesty,
 Queen of prosperity.

 Come, ye Powers who dwell above
Unforgetting, our witnesses be

---

[46] *Conquered the Persian:* Xerxes, at the battle of Salamis. [47] *Huntress:* Artemis. [48] *Nysian:* Nysa was the mountain on which Bacchus was said to have been reared.

Of Peace with bonds of harmonious love—
The Peace which Cypris[49] has wrought for me.
   Alleluia! Io Paean!
   Leap in joy—hurrah! hurrah!
   'Tis victory—hurrah! hurrah!
   Euoi! Euoi! Euai! Euai!

LYS. [*to the Spartans*]. Come now, sing a new song to cap ours.

CHORUS OF SPARTANS   [*singing and dancing*].
   Leaving Taygetus fair and renown'd,
   Muse of Laconia,[50] hither come:
   Amyclae's god in hymns resound,
   Athene of the Brazen Home,
   And Castor and Pollux, Tyndareus' sons,
   Who sport where Eurotas murmuring runs.

   On with the dance! Heia! Ho!
      All leaping along,
   Mantles a-swinging as we go!
      Of Sparta our song.
   There the holy chorus ever gladdens,
   There the beat of stamping feet,
   As our winsome fillies, lovely maidens,
   Dance, beside Eurotas' banks a-skipping,—
      Nimbly go to and fro
   Hast'ning, leaping feet in measures tripping,
   Like the Bacchae's revels, hair a-streaming.
   Leda's child, divine and mild,
   Leads the holy dance, her fair face beaming.
   On with the dance! as your hand
      Presses the hair
   Streaming away unconfined.
      Leap in the air
   Light as a deer; footsteps resound
   Aiding our dance, beating the ground.
   Praise Athene, Maid divine, unrivalled in her might,
   Dweller in the Brazen Home, unconquered in the fight.

      [*All go out singing and dancing.*]

                    Translated into English Prose and Verse by Charles T. Murphy

---

[49] *Cypris:* Aphrodite.   [50] *Laconia:* the country of which Sparta was the capital. In the following lines further references to Sparta appear. Amyclae was a town on the river Eurotas near to Sparta that had a famous sanctuary and throne of Apollo. The Brazen Home was a temple on the Spartan Acropolis. Tyndareus had been a king of Sparta. His sons, by Leda, were worshipped in Sparta as the tutelary gods of warlike youth.

Journal Entry

React to the statement that Lysistrata opposes war because "war's a man's affair" that brings with it the glorification of male competitiveness.

Textual Considerations

1. Analyze the function of the choruses in Aristophanes' play. To what extent do the male and female choruses in *Lysistrata* stimulate the comic action of the play? How do they reinforce the relationship between sex and war? In what manner do they provoke a confrontation between male and female values?
2. Examine characterization by analyzing the role that Lysistrata plays in Aristophanes' comedy. Don't overlook the fact that Lysistrata's name means "Dismisser of Armies." Consider how she reacts to the women who attempt to desert.
3. Investigate the issue of power relations in *Lysistrata*. Quote from the text to defend your position on who wins and who holds the real power in Lysistrata's society.

Cultural Contexts

1. Quote from the text to initiate a discussion on the way the women in *Lysistrata* use their bodies and their sexuality to undermine the traditional notions of masculinity.
2. To generate a debate about the battle of the sexes in *Lysistrata,* write some arguments in defense of both: Lysistrata's position as women's leader and a guardian of Athens' values, versus men's feelings about being deprived of sex and leadership. Which position do you support?
3. In Greek plays such as *Lysistrata,* as well as in Shakespeare's plays, female roles were played by males. What kinds of responses might the theatrical convention of an all-male cast evoke from a modern audience?

Fernando Arrabal
1967

Picnic on the Battlefield

CHARACTERS

ZAPO, *a soldier*
MONSIEUR TÉPAN, *the soldier's father*
MADAME TÉPAN, *the soldier's mother*
ZÉPO, *an enemy soldier*
First Stretcher Bearer
Second Stretcher Bearer

*A battlefield. The stage is covered with barbed wire and sandbags. The battle
is at its height. Rifle shots, exploding bombs and machine guns can be heard.*
ZAPO *is alone on the stage; flat on his stomach, hidden among the
sandbags. He is very frightened. The sound of the fighting stops. Silence.*
ZAPO *takes a ball of wool and some needles out of a canvas workbag
and starts knitting a pullover, which is already quite far advanced. The
field telephone, which is by his side, suddenly starts ringing.*

ZAPO.   Hallo, hallo…yes, Captain…yes, I'm the sentry of sector 47… Nothing
new, Captain…Excuse me, Captain, but when's the fighting going to start
again? And what am I supposed to do with the hand-grenades? Do I chuck
them in front of me or behind me?…Don't get me wrong. I didn't mean to
annoy you…Captain, I really feel terribly lonely, couldn't you send me someone to keep me company?…even if it's only a nanny-goat? [*The* CAPTAIN *is
obviously severely reprimanding him.*]   Whatever you say, Captain, whatever
you say. [ZAPO *hangs up. He mutters to himself. Silence. Enter* MONSIEUR *and*
MADAME TÉPAN *carrying baskets as if they were going on a picnic. They address
their son, who has his back turned and doesn't see them come in.*]

MONS. T.   [*ceremoniously*].   Stand up, my son, and kiss your mother on the
brow. [ZAPO, *surprised, gets up and kisses his mother very respectfully on the
forehead. He is about to speak, but his father doesn't give him a chance.*]   And
now, kiss *me*.

ZAPO.   But, dear Father and dear Mother, how did you dare to come all this way,
to such a dangerous place? You must leave at once.

MONS T.   So you think you've got something to teach your father about war and
danger, do you? All this is just a game to me. How many times—to take the
first example that comes to mind—have I got off an underground train while
it was still moving.

MME. T.   We thought you must be bored, so we came to pay you a little visit. This
war must be a bit tedious, after all.

ZAPO.   It all depends.

MONS. T.   I know exactly what happens. To start with you're attracted by the nov-
elty of it all. It's fun to kill people, and throw hand-grenades about, and wear
uniforms—you feel smart, but in the end you get bored stiff. You'd have found
it much more interesting in my day. Wars were much more lively, much more
highly colored. And then, the best thing was that there were horses, plenty of
horses. It was a real pleasure; if the Captain ordered us to attack, there we all
were immediately, on horseback, in our red uniforms. It was a sight to be seen.
And then there were the charges at the gallop, sword in hand, and suddenly
you found yourself face to face with the enemy, and he was equal to the occasion too—with his horses—there were always horses, lots of horses, with their
well-rounded rumps—in his highly-polished boots, and his green uniform.

MME. T.   No, no, the enemy uniform wasn't green. It was blue. I remember distinctly that it was blue.

MONS. T.   I tell you it was green.

MME. T.   When I was little, how many times did I go out to the balcony to watch the battle and say to the neighbour's little boy: 'I bet you a gum-drop the blues win.' And the blues were our enemies.

MONS. T.   Oh, well, you must be right, then.

MME. T.   I've always liked battles. As a child I always said that when I grew up I wanted to be a Colonel of dragoons. But my mother wouldn't hear of it, you know how she will stick to her principles at all costs.

MONS. T.   Your mother's just a half-wit.

ZAPO.   I'm sorry, but you really must go. You can't come into a war unless you're a soldier.

MONS. T.   I don't give a damn, we came here to have a picnic with you in the country and to enjoy our Sunday.

MME. T.   And I've prepared an excellent meal, too. Sausage, hard-boiled eggs— you know how you like them!—ham sandwiches, red wine, salad, and cakes.

ZAPO.   All right, let's have it your way. But if the Captain comes he'll be absolutely furious. Because he isn't at all keen on us having visits when we're at the front. He never stops telling us: 'Discipline and hand-grenades are what's wanted in war, not visits.'

MONS. T.   Don't worry, I'll have a few words to say to your Captain.

ZAPO.   And what if we have to start fighting again?

MONS. T.   You needn't think that'll frighten me, it won't be the first fighting I've seen. Now if only it was battles on horseback! Times have changed, you can't understand.   [*Pause.*]   We came by motor bike. No one said a word to us.

ZAPO.   They must have thought you were the referees.

MONS. T.   We had enough trouble getting through, though. What with all the tanks and jeeps.

MME. T.   And do you remember the bottle-neck that cannon caused, just when we got here?

MONS. T.   You mustn't be surprised at anything in wartime, everyone knows that.

MME. T.   Good, let's start our meal.

MONS. T.   You're quite right, I feel as hungry as a hunter. It's the smell of gunpowder.

MME. T.   We'll sit on the rug while we're eating.

ZAPO.   Can I bring my rifle with me?

MME. T.   You leave your rifle alone. It's not good manners to bring your rifle to table with you.   [*Pause.*]   But you're absolutely filthy, my boy. How on earth did you get into such a state? Let's have a look at your hands.

ZAPO   [*ashamed, holding out his hands*].   I had to crawl about on the ground during the manoeuvres.

MME. T.   And what about your ears?

ZAPO.   I washed them this morning.

MME. T.   Well that's all right, then. And your teeth?   [*He shows them.*]   Very good. Who's going to give her little boy a great big kiss for cleaning his teeth so nicely?   [*To her husband.*]   Well, go on, kiss your son for cleaning his teeth so nicely. [M. TÉPAN *kisses his son.*] Because, you know, there's one thing I *will* not have, and that's making fighting a war an excuse for not washing.

ZAPO. Yes, mother. [*They eat.*]

MONS. T. Well, my boy, did you make a good score?

ZAPO. When?

MONS. T. In the last few days, of course.

ZAPO. Where?

MONS. T. At the moment, since you're fighting a war.

ZAPO. No, nothing much. I didn't make a good score. Hardly ever scored a bull.

MONS. T. Which are you best at shooting, enemy horses or soldiers?

ZAPO. No, not horses, there aren't any horses any more.

MONS. T. Well, soldiers then?

ZAPO. Could be.

MONS. T. Could be? Aren't you sure?

ZAPO. Well you see...I shoot without taking aim, [*pause*] and at the same time I say a Pater Noster for the chap I've shot.

MONS. T. You must be braver than that. Like your father.

MME. T. I'm going to put a record on. [*She puts a record on the gramophone—a pasodoble. All three are sitting on the ground, listening.*]

MONS. T. That really *is* music. Yes indeed, ole! [*The music continues. Enter an enemy soldier: ZÉPO. He is dressed like ZAPO. The only difference is the colour of their uniforms. ZÉPO is in green and ZAPO is in grey. ZÉPO listens to the music openmouthed. He is behind the family so they can't see him. The record ends. As he gets up ZAPO discovers ZÉPO. Both put their hands up. M. and MME. TÉPAN look at them in surprise.*] What's going on? [*ZAPO reacts—he hesitates. Finally, looking as if he's made up his mind, he points his rifle at ZÉPO.*]

ZAPO. Hands up! [*ZÉPO puts his hands up even higher, looking even more terrified. ZAPO doesn't know what to do. Suddenly he goes over quickly to ZÉPO and touches him gently on the shoulder, like a child playing a game of 'tag'.*] Got you! [*To his father, very pleased.*] There we are! A prisoner!

MONS. T. Fine. And now what're you going to do with him?

ZAPO. I don't know, but, well, could be—they might make me a corporal.

MONS. T. In the meantime, you'd better tie him up.

ZAPO. Tie him up? Why?

MONS. T. Prisoners always get tied up!

ZAPO. How?

MONS. T. Tie up his hands.

MME. T. Yes, there's no doubt about it, you must tie up his hands, I've always seen them do that.

ZAPO. Right. [*To his prisoner.*] Put your hands together, if you please.

ZÉPO. Don't hurt me too much.

ZAPO. I won't.

ZÉPO. Ow! You're hurting me.

MONS. T. Now, now, don't maltreat your prisoner.

MME. T.   Is that the way I brought you up? How many times have I told you that we must be considerate of our fellow-men?

ZAPO.   I didn't do it on purpose.   [*To* ZÉPO.]   And like that, does it hurt?

ZÉPO.   No, it's all right like that.

MONS. T.   Tell him straight out, say what you mean, don't mind us.

ZÉPO.   It's all right like that.

MONS. T.   Now his feet.

ZAPO.   His feet as well, whatever next?

MONS. T.   Didn't they teach you the rules?

ZAPO.   Yes.

MONS. T.   Well then!

ZAPO   [*very politely, to* ZÉPO].   Would you be good enough to sit on the ground, please?

ZÉPO.   Yes, but don't hurt me.

MME. T.   You'll see, he'll take a dislike to you.

ZAPO.   No he won't, no he won't. I'm not hurting you, am I?

ZÉPO.   No, that's perfect.

ZAPO.   Papa, why don't you take a photo of the prisoner on the ground and me with my foot on his stomach?

MONS. T.   Oh, yes that'd look good.

ZÉPO.   Oh no, not that!

MME. T.   Say yes, don't be obstinate.

ZÉPO.   No, I said no, and no it is.

MME. T.   But just a little teeny weeny photo, what harm could that do you? And we could put it in the dining room, next to the life-saving certificate my husband won thirteen years ago.

ZÉPO.   No—you won't shift me.

ZAPO.   But why won't you let us?

ZÉPO.   I'm engaged. And if she sees the photo one day, she'll say I don't know how to fight a war properly.

ZAPO.   No she won't, all you'll need to say is that it isn't you, it's a panther.

MME. T.   Come on, do say yes.

ZÉPO.   All right then. But only to please you.

ZAPO.   Lie down flat.   [ZÉPO *lies down.* ZAPO *puts a foot on his stomach and grabs his rifle with a martial air.*]

MME. T.   Stick your chest out a bit further.

ZAPO.   Like this?

MME. T.   Yes like that, and don't breathe.

MONS. T.   Try to look like a hero.

ZAPO.   What d'you mean, like a hero?

MONS. T.   It's quite simple; try and look like the butcher does when he's boasting about his successes with the girls.

ZAPO.   Like this?

MONS. T.   Yes, like that.

MME. T.   The most important thing is to puff your chest out and not breathe.

ZÉPO.   Have you nearly finished?

MONS. T.   Just be patient a moment. One…two…three.

ZAPO.   I hope I'll come out well.

MME. T.   Yes, you looked very martial.

MONS. T.   You were fine.

MME. T.   It makes me want to have my photo taken with you.

MONS. T.   Now there's a good idea.

ZAPO.   Right. I'll take it if you like.

MME. T.   Give me your helmet to make me look like a soldier.

ZÉPO.   I don't want any more photos. Even one's far too many.

ZAPO.   Don't take it like that. After all, what harm can it do you?

ZÉPO.   It's my last word.

MONS. T.   [*to his wife*].   Don't press the point, prisoners are always very sensitive.
   If we go on he'll get cross and spoil our fun.

ZAPO.   Right, what're we going to do with him, then?

MME. T.   We could invite him to lunch. What do you say?

MONS. T.   I don't see why not.

ZAPO   [*to* ZÉPO].   Well, will you have lunch with us, then?

ZÉPO.   Er…

MONS. T.   We brought a good bottle with us.

ZÉPO.   Oh well, all right then.

MME. T.   Make yourself at home, don't be afraid to ask for anything you want.

ZÉPO.   All right.

MONS. T.   And what about you, did you make a good score?

ZÉPO.   When?

MONS. T.   In the last few days, of course.

ZÉPO.   Where?

MONS. T.   At the moment, since you're fighting a war.

ZÉPO.   No, nothing much. I didn't make a good score, hardly ever scored a bull.

MONS. T.   Which are you best at shooting? Enemy horses or soldiers?

ZÉPO.   No, not horses, they aren't any horses any more.

MONS. T.   Well, soldiers, then?

ZÉPO.   Could be.

MONS. T.   Could be? Aren't you sure?

ZÉPO.   Well you see…I shoot without taking aim,   [*pause*]   and at the same
   time I say an Ave Maria for the chap I've shot.

ZAPO.   An Ave Maria? I'd have thought you'd have said a Pater Noster.

ZÉPO.   No, always an Ave Maria.   [*Pause*]   It's shorter.

MONS. T.   Come come, my dear fellow, you must be brave.

MME. T.   [*to* ZÉPO].   We can untie you if you like.

ZÉPO.   No, don't bother, it doesn't matter.

MONS. T.   Don't start getting stand-offish with us now. If you'd like us to untie
   you, say so.

MME. T.   Make yourself comfortable.

ZÉPO.   Well, if that's how you feel, you can untie my feet, but it's only to please you.

MONS. T.   Zapo, untie him.   [ZAPO *unties him.*]

MME. T.   Well, do you feel better?

ZÉPO.   Yes, of course. I really am putting you to a lot of inconvenience.

MONS. T.   Not at all, just make yourself at home. And if you'd like us to untie your hands you only have to say so.

ZÉPO.   No, not my hands, I don't want to impose upon you.

MONS. T.   No no, my dear chap, no no. I tell you, it's no trouble at all.

ZÉPO.   Right…Well then, untie my hands too. But only for lunch, eh? I don't want you to think that you give me an inch and I take an ell.[1]

MONS. T.   Untie his hands, son.

MME. T.   Well, since our distinguished prisoner is so charming, we're going to have a marvelous day in the country.

ZÉPO.   Don't call me your distinguished prisoner; just call me your prisoner.

MME. T.   Won't that embarrass you?

ZÉPO.   No, no, not at all.

MONS. T.   Well, I must say you're modest.   [*Noise of aeroplanes.*]

ZAPO.   Aeroplanes. They're sure to be coming to bomb us. [ZAPO *and* ZÉPO *throw themselves on the sandbags and hide.*] [*To his parents.*] Take cover. The bombs will fall on you. [*The noise of the aeroplanes overpowers all the other noises. Bombs immediately start to fall. Shells explode very near the stage but not on it. A deafening noise.* ZAPO *and* ZÉPO *are cowering down between the sandbags.* M. TÉPAN *goes on talking calmly to his wife, and she answers in the same unruffled way. We can't hear what they are saying because of the bombing.* MME. TÉPAN *goes over to one of the baskets and takes an umbrella out of it. She opens it.* M. *and* MME. TÉPAN *shelter under it as if it were raining. They are standing up. They shift rhythmically from one foot to the other and talk about their personal affairs. The bombing continues. Finally the aeroplanes go away. Silence.* M. TÉPAN *stretches an arm outside the umbrella to make sure that nothing more is falling from the heavens.*]

MONS. T.   [*to his wife*].   You can shut your umbrella. [MME. TÉPAN *does so. They both go over to their son and tap him lightly on the behind with the umbrella.*] Come on, out you come. The bombing's over. [ZAPO *and* ZÉPO *come out of their hiding place.*]

ZAPO.   Didn't you get hit?

MONS. T.   What d'you think could happen to your father? [*Proudly.*] Little bombs like that! Don't make me laugh! [*Enter, left, two Red Cross Soldiers. They are carrying a stretcher.*]

1ST STRETCHER BEARER.   Any dead here?

ZAPO.   No, no one around these parts.

1ST STRETCHER BEARER.   Are you sure you've looked properly?

ZAPO.   Sure.

1ST STRETCHER BEARER.   And there isn't a single person dead?

ZAPO.   I've already told you there isn't.

---

[1] *ell:* A unit of measure equal to 45 inches.

1ST STRETCHER BEARER.   No one wounded, even?

ZAPO.   Not even that.

2ND STRETCHER BEARER   [*to the* 1ST S. B.].   Well, now we're in a mess!   [*To* ZAPO *persuasively.*]   Just look again, search everywhere, and see if you can't find us a stiff.

1ST STRETCHER BEARER.   Don't keep on about it, they've told you quite clearly there aren't any.

2ND STRETCHER BEARER.   What a lousy trick!

ZAPO.   I'm terribly sorry. I promise you I didn't do it on purpose.

2ND STRETCHER BEARER.   That's what they all say. That no one's dead and that they didn't do it on purpose.

1ST STRETCHER BEARER.   Oh, let the chap alone!

MONS. T.   [*obligingly*].   We should be only too pleased to help you. At your service.

2ND STRETCHER BEARER.   Well, really, if things go on like this I don't know what the Captain will say to us.

MONS. T.   But what's it all about?

2ND STRETCHER BEARER.   Quite simply that the others' wrists are aching with carting so many corpses and wounded men about, and that we haven't found any yet. And it's not because we haven't looked!

MONS. T.   Well, yes, that really is annoying.   [*To* ZAPO.]   Are you quite sure no one's dead?

ZAPO.   Obviously, Papa.

MONS. T.   Have you looked under all the sandbags?

ZAPO.   Yes, Papa.

MONS. T.   [*angrily*].   Well then, you might as well say straight out that you don't want to lift a finger to help these gentlemen, when they're so nice, too!

1ST STRETCHER BEARER.   Don't be angry with him. Let him be. We must just hope we'll have more luck in another trench and that all the lot'll be dead.

MONS. T.   I should be delighted.

MME. T.   Me too. There's nothing I like more than people who put their hearts into their work.

MONS. T.   [*indignantly, addressing his remarks to the wings*].   Then is no one going to do anything for these gentlemen?

ZAPO.   If it only rested with me, it'd already be done.

ZÉPO.   I can say the same.

MONS. T.   But look here, is neither of you even wounded?

ZAPO   [*ashamed*].   No, not me.

MONS. T.   [*to* ZÉPO].   What about you?

ZÉPO   [*ashamed*].   Me neither. I never have any luck.

MME. T.   [*pleased*].   Now I remember! This morning, when I was peeling the onions, I cut my finger. Will that do you?

MONS. T.   Of course it will!   [*Enthusiastically.*]   They'll take you off at once!

1ST STRETCHER BEARER.   No, that won't work. With ladies it doesn't work.

MONS. T.   We're no further advanced, then.

1ST STRETCHER BEARER.   Never mind.

2ND STRETCHER BEARER.   We may be able to make up for it in the other trenches.
[*They start to go off.*]

MONS. T.   Don't worry! If we find a dead man we'll keep him for you! No fear of
us giving him to anyone else!

2ND STRETCHER BEARER.   Thank you very much, sir.

MONS. T.   Quite all right, old chap, think nothing of it.   [*The two stretcher bearers
say goodbye. All four answer them. The stretcher bearers go out.*]

MME. T.   That's what's so pleasant about spending a Sunday in the country. You
always meet such nice people.

MONS. T.   [*pause*].   But why are you enemies?

MME. T.   Your father is the only one who's capable of thinking such ideas; don't
forget he's a former student of the Ecole Normale, *and* a philatelist.[2]

ZÉPO.   I don't know, I'm not very well educated.

MME. T.   Was it by birth, or did you become enemies afterwards?

ZÉPO.   I don't know, I don't know anything about it.

MONS. T.   Well then, how did you come to be in the war?

ZÉPO.   One day, at home, I was just mending my mother's iron, a man came and
asked me: 'Are you Zépo?' 'Yes.' 'Right, you must come to the war.' And so I
asked him: 'But what war?' and he said: 'Don't you read the papers then?
You're just a peasant!' I told him I did read the papers but not the war bits....

ZAPO.   Just how it was with me—exactly how it was with me.

MONS. T.   Yes, they came to fetch you too.

MME. T.   No, it wasn't quite the same; that day you weren't mending an iron, you
were mending the car.

MONS. T.   I was talking about the rest of it.   [*To* ZÉPO.]   Go on, what happened
then?

ZÉPO.   Then I told him I had a fiancée and that if I didn't take her to the pictures
on Sundays she wouldn't like it. He said that wasn't the least bit important.

ZAPO.   Just how it was with me—exactly how it was with me.

ZÉPO.   And then my father came down, and he said I couldn't go to the war
because I didn't have a horse.

ZAPO.   Just what my father said.

ZÉPO.   The man said you didn't need a horse any more, and I asked him if I could
take my fiancée with me. He said no. Then I asked whether I could take my
aunt with me so that she could make me one of her custards on Thursdays;
I'm very fond of them.

MME. T.   [*realizing that she'd forgotten it*].   Oh! The custard!

ZÉPO.   He said no again.

ZAPO.   Same as with me.

ZÉPO.   And ever since then I've been alone in the trench nearly all the time.

MME. T.   I think you and your distinguished prisoner might play together this
afternoon, as you're so close to each other and so bored.

---

[2] *Ecole Normale...philatelist:* Student of the Teacher's College and a stamp collector.

ZAPO.   Oh no, Mother, I'm too afraid, he's an enemy.

MONS. T.   Now now, you mustn't be afraid.

ZAPO.   If you only knew what the General was saying about the enemy!

MME. T.   What did he say?

ZAPO.   He said the enemy are very nasty people. When they take prisoners they put little stones in their shoes so that it hurts them to walk.

MME. T.   How awful! What barbarians!

MONS. T.   [*indignantly, to* ZÉPO].   And aren't you ashamed to belong to an army of criminals?

ZÉPO.   I haven't done anything. I don't do anybody any harm.

MME. T.   He was trying to take us in, pretending to be such a little saint!

MONS. T.   We oughtn't to have untied him. You never know, we only need to turn our backs and he'll be putting a stone in our shoes.

ZÉPO.   Don't be so nasty to me.

MONS. T.   What'd you think we *should* be, then? I'm indignant. I know what I'll do. I'll go and find the Captain and ask him to let me fight in the war.

ZAPO.   He won't let you, you're too old.

MONS. T.   Then I'll buy myself a horse and a sword and come and fight on my own account.

MME. T.   Bravo! If I were a man I'd do the same.

ZÉPO.   Don't be like that with me, Madame. Anyway I'll tell you something—our General told us the same thing about you.

MME. T.   How could he dare tell such a lie!

ZAPO.   No—but the same thing really?

ZÉPO.   Yes, the same thing.

MONS. T.   Perhaps it was the same man who talked to you both?

MME. T.   Well if it was the same man he might at least have said something different. That's a fine thing—saying the same thing to everyone!

MONS. T.   [*to* ZÉPO *in a different tone of voice*].   Another little drink?

MME. T.   I hope you liked our lunch?

MONS. T.   In any case, it was better than last Sunday.

ZÉPO.   What happened?

MONS. T.   Well, we went to the country and we put the food on the rug. While we'd got our backs turned a cow ate up all our lunch, and the napkins as well.

ZÉPO.   What a greedy cow!

MONS. T.   Yes, but afterwards, to get our own back, we ate the cow. [*They laugh.*]

ZAPO [*to* ZÉPO].   They couldn't have been very hungry after that!

MONS. T.   Cheers! [*They all drink.*]

MME. T.   [*to* ZÉPO].   And what do you do to amuse yourself in the trench?

ZÉPO.   I spend my time making flowers out of rags, to amuse myself. I get terribly bored.

MME. T.   And what do you do with the flowers?

ZÉPO.   At the beginning I used to send them to my fiancée, but one day she told me that the greenhouse and the cellar were already full of them and that she didn't know what to do with them any more, and she asked me, if I didn't mind, to send her something else.

MME. T.   And what did you do?

ZÉPO.   I go on making rag flowers to pass the time.

MME. T.   Do you throw them away afterwards, then?

ZÉPO.   No, I've found a way to use them now. I give one flower for each pal who dies. That way I know that even if I make an awful lot there'll never be enough.

MONS. T.   That's a good solution you've hit on.

ZÉPO   [*shyly*].   Yes.

ZAPO.   Well, what I do is knit, so as not to get bored.

MME. T.   But tell me, are all the soldiers as bored as you?

ZÉPO.   It all depends on what they do to amuse themselves.

ZAPO.   It's the same on our side.

MONS. T.   Then let's stop the war.

ZÉPO.   How?

MONS. T.   It's very simple.   [*To* ZAPO.]   You just tell your pals that the enemy soldiers don't want to fight a war, and you   [*to* ZÉPO]   say the same to your comrades. And then everyone goes home.

ZAPO.   Marvellous!

MME. T.   And then you'll be able to finish mending the iron.

ZAPO.   How is it that no one thought of such a good idea before?

MME. T.   Your father is the only one who's capable of thinking such ideas; don't forget he's a former student of the Ecole Normale, *and* a philatelist.

ZÉPO.   But what will the sergeant-majors and corporals do?

MONS. T.   We'll give them some guitars and castanets to keep them quiet!

ZÉPO.   Very good idea.

MONS. T.   You see how easy it is. Everything's fixed.

ZÉPO.   We shall have a tremendous success.

ZAPO.   My pals will be terribly pleased.

MME. T.   What d'you say to putting on the pasodoble we were playing just now, to celebrate?

ZÉPO.   Perfect.

ZAPO.   Yes, put the record on, Mother.   [MME. TÉPAN *puts a record on. She turns the handle. She waits. Nothing can be heard.*]

MONS. T.   I can't hear a thing.

MME. T.   Oh, how silly of me! Instead of putting a record on I put on a beret. [*She puts the record on. A gay pasodoble is heard.* ZAPO *dances with* ZÉPO *and* MME. TÉPAN *with her husband. They are all very gay. The field telephone rings. None of the four hears it. They go on dancing busily. The telephone rings again. The dance continues.*

The battle starts up again with a terrific din of bombs, shots and bursts of machine-gun fire. None of the four has seen anything and they go on dancing merrily. A burst of machine-gun fire mows them all down. They fall to the ground, stone dead. A shot must have grazed the gramophone; the record keeps repeating the same thing, like a scratched record. The music of the scratched record can be heard till the end of the play. The two STRETCHER BEARERS *enter left. They are carrying the empty stretcher.*]

SUDDEN CURTAIN

Journal Entry

What are the effects on meaning of juxtaposing *picnic* and *battlefield* in the play's title?

Textual Considerations

1. What attitudes about war does the playwright convey by having Zépo and Zapo double and mirror each other?
2. What role do the parents play in the drama? Contrast their views of war with those of Zépo and Zapo.
3. How do you respond to the play's ending? Does the author foreshadow it at an earlier point in the play? Cite evidence for your answer.

Cultural Contexts

1. Discuss with your group the statement that "*Picnic on the Battlefield* portrays war as a private, social, and political game devoid of moral purpose." Quote from the text to support your points of view. Compare and contrast your attitudes about war with those of Arrabal.

PART ASSIGNMENTS

WRITING TOPICS

1. In "A Brother's Murder," Staples cites many examples of the violence and dangers inherent in ghetto life. Write an essay discussing the impressions that his brother's experiences made on you, including any stereotypes you had to modify as a result of reading about them. Clarify your purpose and meaning. Think of a provocative statement to begin your essay, and end with an effective comparison.

2. Powell and Mirikitani focus on the aftermath of the Vietnam War. Write an essay applying the significance of the title "Spoils of War" to both texts. In Mirikitani's story, cite specific examples including the thoughts of Violet and the Vietnam veteran.

3. Consider the relationship of race and violence in "Spoils of War," "A Brother's Murder," and/or "Battle Royal." What does each text imply about racial stereotypes?

4. "The Sniper," "Silence," and "The Curse" make use of the literary convention of the surprise ending. Review the last paragraph of each story, and write an analysis of the meanings they introduce or the ironies they reinforce.

5. How is the theme of the mutilated body presented in "Disabled" relevant to the experiences of Vietnam War veterans in the films *Coming Home* or *Born on the Fourth of July.*

6. Explore the themes of physical and psychological violence in the stories by Dubus and Ellison.

7. Apply the notion of the "Myth of the Enemy" to "The Sniper," "The Man He Killed," and/or *Picnic on the Battlefield*. To what extent does each text reinforce the arbitrary nature of war? How does war also alter the normal order?

8. The relation between patriotism and heroism is the focus of the texts by Whitman (two poems), Powell, and Arrabal. With whose point of view are you most in agreement? Cite evidence you found most convincing.

9. Traditionally, antiwar dramas portray images of suffering and death. To what extent is *Lysistrata* an antiwar play?

10. Compare and contrast the use of humor in the dramas by Aristophanes and Arrabal. What examples did you find most effective in reinforcing the playwright's point of view?

RESEARCH TOPICS

1. War songs such as "Lili Marlene," "For Johnny," "When This Bleeding War Is Over," and "Hymn of Hate"—and many others that emphasize either the patriotic view of war or various forms of war protest—became an important part of the tradition of World Wars I and II. Research

some lyrics from World Wars I and II, the Vietnam War, and the Persian Gulf War, and write a documented paper analyzing their function as war poetry. Speculate on other functions they may have served.

2. Write a documented paper summarizing the history of women in World Wars I and II, the Vietnam War, and/or the Persian Gulf War. Starting with the domestic view of women as lovers, mothers, and peacemakers, and the image of women as the "stepdaughters" of war—nurses, doctors, ambulance drivers—move to the modern view of women actively engaged in war.

3. To investigate the relationship between race and war, write a documented paper on the history of African-American soldiers. Examine the contributions they made to American history from the time of the Civil War to the time of the Vietnam War. You may need to rely on testimonials of slaves, abolitionists, and veterans from the two world wars and the Vietnam War. Among other sources, you might check:

McPherson, James M. *The Negro's Civil War: How American Blacks Felt and Acted during the War for the Union.*
Wallace, Terry. *Bloods: An Oral History of the Vietnam War by Black Veterans.*

4. The films *The Pawnbroker* and *Sophie's Choice* are about characters whose experiences during World War II left lasting marks on their lives. Analyze these characters by observing the specific ways in which their behavior and personalities manifest their past experiences, and then consider what, if anything, might be done to help them reconcile their pasts.

GROUP RESEARCH TOPIC

Using Stanley Kubrick's film *Full Metal Jacket* as your primary source, analyze with your group the ways in which the director uses the Vietnam War to expose the violence, sexism, and racism inherent in American society. Consult at least three critical discussions of the film for your group report.

PART FOUR

Race and Difference

Fiction

The Lesson, Toni Cade Bambara ◆ *The Loudest Voice*, Grace Paley ◆ *I Stand Here Ironing*, Tillie Olsen ◆ *The Stolen Party*, Liliana Heker ◆ *Puertoricanness*, Aurora Levins Morales ◆ *Jasmine*, Bharati Mukherjee

Essays

Growing Up Asian in America, Kesaya E. Noda ◆ *Gay*, Anna Quindlen

Poetry

I Hear America Singing, Walt Whitman ◆ *Poet Power*, Denise Levertov ◆ *The Melting Pot*, Dudley Randall ◆ *Public School No. 18: Paterson, New Jersey*, Maria Mazziotti Gillan ◆ *My Blackness Is the Beauty of This Land*, Lance Jeffers ◆ *Telephone Conversation*, Wole Soyinka ◆ *On the Subway*, Sharon Olds ◆ *Richard Cory*, Edwin Arlington Robinson ◆ *Latero Story*, Tato Laviera ◆ *AIDS*, May Sarton ◆ *How to Watch Your Brother Die*, Michael Lassell ◆ *Cross Plains, Wisconsin*, Martín Espada ◆ *Jorge the Church Janitor Finally Quits*, Martín Espada ◆ *Federico's Ghost*, Martín Espada ◆ *Tony Went to the Bodega But He Didn't Buy Anything*, Martín Espada

Drama

Othello, the Moor of Venice, William Shakespeare ◆ *The Kiss of the Spider Woman*, Manuel Puig

"Ours is the only nation to have a dream and give its name to one—the American Dream," wrote the literary critic Lionel Trilling almost fifty years ago. Although the United States continues to be a nation of immigrants in search of that dream, many groups have felt excluded from the right to equality promised in the Declaration of Independence of 1776. These groups are challenging the ideal of the "melting pot," which was first expressed in Hector St. Jean de Crevecoeur's 1781 statement that "individuals of all nations are melted down in a new race of men" and which has shaped the collective consciousness of North Americans for almost two centuries.

In fact, in a 1991 interview, the Asian-American writer Bharati Mukherjee proposed that the metaphor of a "fusion chamber," in which elements interact but do not melt, has perhaps become a more appropriate metaphor to describe the new, multiracial democracy of the present time and that of the approaching twenty-first century. The African-American novelist Toni Morrison concurs: "We have to acknowledge that the thing we call 'literature' is pluralistic now, just as society ought to be. The melting pot never worked."

Much of the literature in Part Four portrays the irrationality of racism and the politics of exclusion and examines their effects on the marginalized groups that continue to challenge myths of assimilation and justice for all. Walt Whitman's poem "I Hear America Singing" (1867), for instance, celebrates the delight of diversity in what Whitman envisions as a truly democratic America. In a strong epic voice, Whitman communicates to all Americans, regardless of class and race, the idealized vision of democracy engraved in the Declaration of Independence (1776) and the Gettysburg Address (1863). However, in Lance Jeffers's poem "My Blackness Is the Beauty of This Land," written almost 150 years after Whitman's poem, we can see the failure of Whitman's idealistic dream in the images of blackness and whiteness that constitute the racial consciousness of the United States. And Dudley Randall's vivid image of the melting pot as one in which "*Johann* and *Jan* and *Jean* and *Juan, / Giovanni* and *Ivan /* step in and then step out again / all freshly christened *John,*" while Sam is repeatedly thrown out because of his "black stain," reinforces two of the myth's most fundamental failures: its inability to accommodate ethnic diversity and difference, and its historical exclusion of African Americans.

To what extent can we say that perceptions of race, ethnicity, and class have also shaped the identities of Chicanos, Asian Americans, Italian Americans, Native Americans, and Latinos, who live on the fringes of both worlds? Does ethnic identity preclude cultural assimilation in the United States? Several texts, including "Latero Story" and "Puertoricanness," record how bilingual and bicultural differences have determined their speakers' identities and contributed to a double consciousness with which they confront their feelings of linguistic, geographical, and emotional displacement. In "Public School No. 18: Paterson, New Jersey," the Italian-American speaker finally learns as an adult to find her own voice and an identity strong enough to confront and challenge the myth of Anglo-Saxon superiority reinforced by the educational institutions she attended.

That personal and social inequities resulting in emotional exclusion and entrapment are not confined to the United States is apparent in the South-African poet Wole Soyinka's "Telephone Conversation," set in London, and in the Argentinian writer Liliana Heker's "The Stolen Party," set in Argentina.

Cultural attitudes toward homosexuals and lesbians have also resulted in social and political exclusion. Some texts included here address the issue of AIDS and attempt to explore new definitions of and meanings for the concept of love. Two poems, "AIDS" and "How to Watch Your Brother Die," focus on the issue of sexual preference and the gay community's capacity for grief, rage, and desire for connection.

As you read these and other texts in this part, consider how factors such as ethnicity, gender, and class have contributed to or detracted from your own position of privilege in U.S. society. As you read Walt Whitman's poem, you might consider formulating a new definition of the American Dream appropriate to the more diverse and complex society of the approaching twenty-first century.

Toni Cade Bambara
1972

The Lesson

Back in the days when everyone was old and stupid or young and fool-ish and me and Sugar were the only ones just right, this lady moved on our block with nappy hair and proper speech and no makeup. And quite naturally we laughed at her, laughed the way we did at the junk man who went about his business like he was some big-time president and his sorry-ass horse his secretary. And we kinda hated her too, hated the way we did the winos who cluttered up our parks and pissed on our handball walls and stank up our hallways and stairs so you couldn't halfway play hide-and-seek without a goddamn gas mask. Miss Moore was her name. The only woman on the block with no first name. And she was black as hell, cept for her feet, which were fish-white and spooky. And she was always planning these boring-ass things for us to do, us being my cousin, mostly, who lived on the block cause we all moved North the same time and to the same apartment then spread out gradual to breathe. And our parents would yank our heads into some kinda shape and crisp up our clothes so we'd be presentable for travel with Miss Moore, who always looked like she was going to church, though she never did. Which is just one of the things the grownups talked about when they talked behind her back like a dog. But when she came calling with some sachet she'd sewed up or some gingerbread she'd made or some book, why then they'd all be too embar-rassed to turn her down and we'd get handed over all spruced up. She'd been to college and said it was only right that she should take responsibility for the young ones' education, and she not even related by marriage or blood. So they'd go for it. Specially Aunt Gretchen. She was the main gofer in the family. You got some ole dumb shit foolishness you want somebody to go for, you send for Aunt Gretchen. She been screwed into the go-along for so long, it's a blood-deep natural thing with her. Which is how she got saddled with me and Sugar and Junior in the first place while our mothers were in a la-de-da apartment up the block having a good ole time.

So this one day Miss Moore rounds us all up at the mailbox and it's puredee hot and she's knockin herself out about arithmetic. And school suppose to let up in summer I heard, but she don't never let up. And the starch in my pinafore scratching the shit outta me and I'm really hating this nappy-head bitch and her goddamn college degree. I'd much rather go to the pool or to the show where it's cool. So me and Sugar leaning on the mailbox being surly, which is a Miss Moore word. And Flyboy checking out what everybody brought for lunch. And Fat Butt already wasting his peanut-butter-and-jelly sandwich like the pig he is. And Junebug punchin on Q.T.'s arm for potato chips. And Rosie Giraffe shifting from one hip to the other waiting for somebody to step on her foot or ask her if she from Georgia so she can kick ass, preferably Mercedes'. And Miss Moore asking us do we know what money is, like we a bunch of retards. I mean real money, she say, like it's only poker chips or monopoly papers we lay on the grocer. So right away I'm tired of this and say so. And would much rather snatch Sugar and go to the Sunset and terrorize the West Indian kids and take their hair ribbons and their money too. And Miss Moore files that remark away for next week's lesson on brotherhood, I can tell. And finally I say we oughta get to the subway cause it's cooler and besides we might meet some cute boys. Sugar done swiped her mama's lipstick, so we ready.

So we heading down the street and she's boring us silly about what things cost and what our parents make and how much goes for rent and how money ain't divided up right in this country. And then she gets to the part about we all poor and live in the slums, which I don't feature. And I'm ready to speak on that, but she steps out in the street and hails two cabs just like that. Then she hustles half the crew in with her and hands me a five-dollar bill and tells me to calculate 10 percent tip for the driver. And we're off. Me and Sugar and Junebug and Flyboy hangin out the window and hollering to everybody, putting lipstick on each other cause Flyboy a faggot anyway, and making farts with our sweaty armpits. But I'm mostly trying to figure how to spend this money. But they all fascinated with the meter ticking and Junebug starts laying bets as to how much it'll read when Flyboy can't hold his breath no more. Then Sugar lays bets as to how much it'll be when we get there. So I'm stuck. Don't nobody want to go for my plan, which is to jump out at the next light and run off to the first bar-b-que we can find. Then the driver tells us to get the hell out cause we there already. And the meter reads eighty-five cents. And I'm stalling to figure out the tip and Sugar say give him a dime. And I decide he don't need it bad as I do, so later for him. But then he tries to take off with Junebug foot still in the door so we talk about his mama something ferocious. Then we check out that we on Fifth Avenue and everybody dressed up in stockings. One lady in a fur coat, hot as it is. White folks crazy.

"This is the place," Miss Moore say, presenting it to us in the voice she uses at the museum. "Let's look in the windows before we go in."

"Can we steal?" Sugar asks very serious like she's getting the ground rules squared away before she plays. "I beg your pardon," say Miss Moore, and we fall out. So she leads us around the windows of the toy store and me and Sugar screamin, "This is mine, that's mine, I gotta have that, that was made for me, I was born for that," till Big Butt drowns us out.

"Hey, I'm goin to buy that there."

"That there? You don't even know what it is, stupid."

"I do so," he say punchin on Rosie Giraffe. "It's a microscope."

"Whatcha gonna do with a microscope, fool?"

"Look at things."

"Like what, Ronald?" ask Miss Moore. And Big Butt ain't got the first notion. So here go Miss Moore gabbing about the thousands of bacteria in a drop of water and the somethinorother in a speck of blood and the million and one living things in the air around us is invisible to the naked eye. And what she say that for? Junebug go to town on that "naked" and we rolling. Then Miss Moore ask what it cost. So we all jam into the window smudgin it up and the price tag say $300. So then she ask how long'd take for Big Butt and Junebug to save up their allowances. "Too long," I say. "Yeh," adds Sugar, "outgrown it by that time." And Miss Moore say no, you never outgrow learning instruments. "Why, even medical students and interns and," blah, blah, blah. And we ready to choke Big Butt for bringing it up in the first damn place.

"This here costs four hundred eighty dollars," says Rosie Giraffe. So we pile up all over her to see what she pointin out. My eyes tell me it's a chunk of glass cracked with something heavy, and different-color inks dripped into the splits, then the whole thing put into a oven or something. But for $480 it don't make sense.

"That's a paperweight made of semi-precious stones fused together under tremendous pressure," she explains slowly, with her hands doing the mining and all the factory work.

"So what's a paperweight?" asks Rosie Giraffe.

"To weigh paper with, dumbbell," say Flyboy, the wise man from the East.

"Not exactly," say Miss Moore, which is what she say when you warm or way off too. "It's to weigh paper down so it won't scatter and make your desk untidy." So right away me and Sugar curtsy to each other and then to Mercedes who is more the tidy type.

"We don't keep paper on top of the desk in my class," say Junebug, figuring Miss Moore crazy or lyin one.

"At home, then," she say. "Don't you have a calendar and pencil case and a blotter and a letter-opener on your desk at home where you do your homework?" And she know damn well what our homes look like cause she nosys around in them every chance she gets.

"I don't even have a desk," say Junebug. "Do we?"

"No. And I don't get no homework neither," says Big Butt.

"And I don't even have a home," say Flyboy like he do at school to keep the white folks off his back and sorry for him. Send this poor kid to camp posters, is his specialty.

"I do," says Mercedes. "I have a box of stationery on my desk and a picture of my cat. My godmother bought the stationery and the desk. There's a big rose on each sheet and the envelopes smell like roses."

"Who wants to know about your smelly-ass stationery," say Rosie Giraffe fore I can get my two cents in.

"It's important to have a work area all your own so that..."

"Will you look at this sailboat, please," say Flyboy, cuttin her off and pointin to the thing like it was his. So once again we tumble all over each other to gaze at this magnificent thing in the toy store which is just big enough to maybe sail two kittens across the pond if you strap them to the posts tight. We all start reciting the price tag like we in assembly. "Handcrafted sailboat of fiberglass at one thousand one hundred ninety-five dollars."

"Unbelievable," I hear myself say and am really stunned. I read it again for myself just in case the group recitation put me in a trance. Same thing. For some reason this pisses me off. We look at Miss Moore and she lookin at us, waiting for I dunno what.

"Who'd pay all that when you can buy a sailboat set for a quarter at Pop's, a tube of glue for a dime, and a ball of string for eight cents? It must have a motor and a whole lot else besides," I say. "My sailboat cost me about fifty cents."

"But will it take water?" say Mercedes with her smart ass.

"Took mine to Alley Pond Park once," say Flyboy. "String broke. Lost it. Pity."

"Sailed mine in Central Park and it keeled over and sank. Had to ask my father for another dollar."

"And you got the strap," laugh Big Butt. "The jerk didn't even have a string on it. My old man wailed on his behind."

Little Q.T. was staring hard at the sailboat and you could see he wanted it bad. But he too little and somebody'd just take it from him. So what the hell. "This boat for kids, Miss Moore?"

"Parents silly to buy something like that just to get all broke up," say Rosie Giraffe.

"That much money it should last forever," I figure.

"My father'd buy it for me if I wanted it."

"Your father, my ass," say Rosie Giraffe getting a chance to finally push Mercedes.

"Must be rich people shop here," say Q.T.

"You are a very bright boy," say Flyboy. "What was your first clue?" And he rap him on the head with the back of his knuckles, since Q.T. the only one he could get away with. Though Q.T. liable to come up behind you years later and get his licks in when you half expect it.

"What I want to know is," I says to Miss Moore though I never talk to her, I wouldn't give the bitch that satisfaction, "is how much a real boat costs? I figure a thousand'd get you a yacht any day."

"Why don't you check that out," she says, "and report back to the group?" Which really pains my ass. If you gonna mess up a perfectly good swim day least you could do is have some answers. "Let's go in," she say like she got something up her sleeve. Only she don't lead the way. So me and Sugar turn the corner to where the entrance is, but when we get there I kinda hang back. Not that I'm scared, what's there to be afraid of, just a toy store. But I feel funny, shame. But what I got to be shamed about? Got as much right to go in as anybody. But somehow I can't seem to get hold of the door, so I step away for Sugar to lead. But she hangs back too. And I look at her and she looks at me and this is ridiculous. I mean, damn, I have never ever been shy about doing nothing or going nowhere. But then Mercedes steps up and then Rosie Giraffe and Big Butt crowd in behind and shove, and next thing we all stuffed into the doorway with only Mercedes squeezing past us, smoothing out her jumper and walking right down the aisle. Then the rest of us tumble in like a glued-together jigsaw done all wrong. And people lookin at us. And it's like the time me and Sugar crashed into the Catholic church on a dare. But once we got in there and everything so hushed and holy and the candles and the bowin and the handkerchiefs on all the drooping heads, I just couldn't go through with the plan. Which was for me to run up to the altar and do a tap dance while Sugar played the nose flute and messed around in the holy water. And Sugar kept givin me the elbow. Then later teased me so bad I tied her up in the shower and turned it on and locked her in. And she'd be there till this day if Aunt Gretchen hadn't finally figured I was lyin about the boarder takin a shower.

Same thing in the store. We all walkin on tiptoe and hardly touchin the games and puzzles and things. And I watched Miss Moore who is steady watchin us like she waitin for a sign. Like Mama Drewery watches the sky and sniffs the air and takes note of just how much slant is in the bird formation. Then me and Sugar bump smack into each other, so busy gazing at the toys, specially the sailboat. But we don't laugh and go into our fat-lady bump-stomach routine. We just stare at that price tag. Then Sugar run a finger over the whole boat. And I'm jealous and want to hit her. Maybe not her, but I sure want to punch somebody in the mouth.

"Watcha bring us here for, Miss Moore?"

"You sound angry, Sylvia. Are you mad about something?" Givin me one of them grins like she tellin a grown-up joke that never turns out to be funny. And she's lookin very closely at me like maybe she planning to do my portrait from memory. I'm mad, but I won't give her that satisfaction. So I slouch around the store bein very bored and say, "Let's go."

Me and Sugar at the back of the train watchin the tracks whizzin by large then small then getting gobbled up in the dark. I'm thinkin about this tricky toy I saw in the store. A clown that somersaults on a bar then does chin-ups just cause you yank lightly at his leg. Cost $35. I could see me askin my mother for a $35 birthday clown. "You wanna who that costs what?" she'd say, cocking her head to the side to get a better view of the hole in my head. Thirty-five dollars could buy new bunk beds for Junior and Gretchen's boy. Thirty-five dollars and the whole household could go visit Granddaddy Nelson in the country. Thirty-five dollars would pay for the rent and the piano bill too. Who are these people that spend that much for per-forming clowns and $1000 for toy sailboats? What kinda work they do and how they live and how come we ain't in on it? Where we are is who we are, Miss Moore always pointin out. But it don't necessarily have to be that way, she always adds then waits for somebody to say that poor people have to wake up and demand their share of the pie and don't none of us know what kind of pie she talking about in the first damn place. But she ain't so smart cause I still got her four dollars from the taxi and she sure ain't gettin it. Messin up my day with this shit. Sugar nudges me in my pocket and winks.

Miss Moore lines us up in front of the mailbox where we started from, seem like years ago, and I got a headache for thinkin so hard. And we lean all over each other so we can hold up under the draggy-ass lecture she always finishes us off with at the end before we thank her for borin us to tears. But she just looks at us like she readin tea leaves. Finally she say, "Well, what did you think of F. A. O. Schwarz?"

Rosie Giraffe mumbles, "White folks crazy."

"I'd like to go there again when I get my birthday money," says Mercedes, and we shove her out the pack so she has to lean on the mailbox by herself.

"I'd like a shower. Tiring day," say Flyboy.

Then Sugar surprises me by sayin, "You know, Miss Moore, I don't think all of us here put together eat in a year what that sailboat costs." And Miss Moore lights up like somebody goosed her. "And?" she say, urging Sugar on. Only I'm standin on her foot so she don't continue.

"Imagine for a minute what kind of society it is in which some people can spend on a toy what it would cost to feed a family of six or seven. What do you think?"

"I think," say Sugar pushing me off her feet like she never done before, cause I whip her ass in a minute, "that this is not much of a democracy if you ask me. Equal chance to pursue happiness means an equal crack at the dough, don't it?" Miss Moore is beside herself and I am disgusted with Sugar's treachery. So I stand on her foot one more time to see if she'll shove me. She shuts up, and Miss Moore looks at me, sorrowfully I'm thinkin. And somethin weird is goin on, I can feel it in my chest.

"Anybody else learn anything today?" lookin dead at me. I walk away and Sugar has to run to catch up and don't even seem to notice when I shrug her arm off my shoulder.

"Well, we got four dollars anyway," she says.

"Uh hunh."

"We could go to Hascombs and get half a chocolate layer and then go to the Sunset and still have plenty money for potato chips and ice cream sodas."

"Un hunh."

"Race you to Hascombs," she say.

We start down the block and she gets ahead which is O.K. by me cause I'm going to the West End and then over to the Drive to think this day through. She can run if she want to and even run faster. But ain't nobody gonna beat me at nuthin.

Journal Entry

How does Bambara use humor to enhance meaning in "The Lesson"?

Textual Considerations

1. What does Miss Moore hope to accomplish during the class outing? What lesson does she want to teach? Does it need teaching? Why? To what extent does Miss Moore's method of teaching succeed?
2. Although the reader knows that Sylvia is angry, she will not admit her feelings to Miss Moore. Why not? Does Sylvia know what has made her angry? Explain.
3. With which character in the story do you most empathize? Why?
4. How does your attitude toward the expensive toys compare to that of the children? How do you account for similarities and/or differences in your responses?

Cultural Considerations

1. "White folks crazy" appears twice in "The Lesson." What situations give rise to this conclusion? What emotions are the children expressing through these words? What is the significance of Sylvia's resolve that "ain't nobody gonna beat me at nuthin"?
2. Miss Moore, the mentor of the neighborhood children, teaches them about social inequities through their visit to F. A. O. Schwartz. To what extent do you agree with Sugar that the United States "is not much of a democracy.... Equal chance to pursue happiness means an equal crack at the dough, don't it?"

Grace Paley
1956

The Loudest Voice

There is a certain place where dumb-waiters[1] boom, doors slam, dishes crash; every window is a mother's mouth bidding the street shut up, go skate somewhere else, come home. My voice is the loudest.

There, my own mother is still as full of breathing as me and the grocer stands up to speak to her. "Mrs. Abramowitz," he says, "people should not be afraid of their children."

"Ah, Mr. Bialik," my mother replies, "if you say to her or her father 'Ssh,' they say, 'In the grave it will be quiet.'"

"From Coney Island to the cemetery," says my papa. "It's the same subway; it's the same fare."

I am right next to the pickle barrel. My pinky is making tiny whirlpools in the brine. I stop a moment to announce: "Campbell's Tomato Soup. Campbell's Vegetable Beef Soup. Campbell's S-c-otch Broth..."

"Be quiet," the grocer says, "the labels are coming off."

"Please, Shirley, be a little quiet," my mother begs me.

In that place the whole street groans: Be quiet! Be quiet! but steals from the happy chorus of my inside self not a tittle or a jot.

There, too, but just around the corner, is a red brick building that has been old for many years. Every morning the children stand before it in double lines which must be straight. They are not insulted. They are waiting anyway.

I am usually among them. I am, in fact, the first, since I begin with "A."

One cold morning the monitor tapped me on the shoulder. "Go to Room 409, Shirley Abramowitz," he said. I did as I was told. I went in a hurry up a down

---

[1]A small elevator for moving food, garbage, etc. between floors.

staircase to Room 409, which contained sixth-graders. I had to wait at the desk without wiggling until Mr. Hilton, their teacher, had time to speak.

After five minutes he said, "Shirley?"

"What?" I whispered.

He said, "My! My! Shirley Abramowitz! They told me you had a particularly loud, clear voice and read with lots of expression. Could that be true?"

"Oh yes," I whispered.

"In that case, don't be silly; I might very well be your teacher someday. Speak up, speak up."

"Yes," I shouted.

"More like it," he said. "Now, Shirley, can you put a ribbon in your hair or a bobby pin? It's too messy."

"Yes!" I bawled.

"Now, now, calm down." He turned to the class. "Children, not a sound. Open at page 39. Read till 52. When you finish, start again." He looked me over once more. "Now, Shirley, you know, I suppose, that Christmas is coming. We are preparing a beautiful play. Most of the parts have been given out. But I still need a child with a strong voice, lots of stamina. Do you know what stamina is? You do? Smart kid. You know, I heard you read 'The Lord is my shepherd'[2] in Assembly yesterday. I was very impressed. Wonderful delivery. Mrs. Jordan, your teacher, speaks highly of you. Now listen to me, Shirley Abramowitz, if you want to take the part and be in the play, repeat after me, 'I swear to work harder than I ever did before.'"

I looked to heaven and said at once, "Oh, I swear." I kissed my pinky and looked at God.

"That is an actor's life, my dear," he explained: "Like a soldier's, never tardy or disobedient to his general, the director. Everything," he said, "absolutely everything will depend on you."

That afternoon, all over the building, children scraped and scrubbed the turkeys and the sheaves of corn off the schoolroom windows. Goodbye Thanksgiving. The next morning a monitor brought red paper and green paper from the office. We made new shapes and hung them on the walls and glued them to the doors.

The teachers became happier and happier. Their heads were ringing like the bells of childhood. My best friend Evie was prone to evil, but she did not get a single demerit for whispering. We learned "Holy Night" without an error. "How wonderful!" said Miss Glacé, the student teacher. "To think that some of you don't even speak the language!" We learned "Deck the Halls" and "Hark! The Herald Angels." ...They weren't ashamed and we weren't embarrassed.

Oh, but when my mother heard about it all, she said to my father: "Misha, you don't know what's going on there. Cramer is the head of the Tickets Committee."

"Who?" asked my father. "Cramer? Oh yes, an active woman."

"Active? Active has to have a reason. Listen," she said sadly, "I'm surprised to see my neighbors making tra-la-la for Christmas."

---

[2] Psalm 23: A Psalm of David.

My father couldn't think of what to say to that. Then he decided: "You're in America! Clara, you wanted to come here. In Palestine the Arabs would be eating you alive. Europe you had pogroms.[3] Argentina is full of Indians. Here you got Christmas.... Some joke, ha?"

"Very funny, Misha. What is becoming of you? If we came to a new country a long time ago to run away from tyrants, and instead we fall into a creeping pogrom, that our children learn a lot of lies, so what's the joke? Ach, Misha, your idealism is going away."

"So is your sense of humor."

"That I never had, but idealism you had a lot of."

"I'm the same Misha Abramovitch, I didn't change an iota. Ask anyone."

"Only ask me," says my mama, may she rest in peace. "I got the answer."

Meanwhile the neighbors had to think of what to say too.

Marty's father said: "You know, he has a very important part, my boy."

"Mine also," said Mr. Sauerfeld.

"Not my boy!" said Mrs. Klieg. "I said to him no. The answer is no. When I say no! I mean no!"

The rabbi's wife said, "It's disgusting!" But no one listened to her. Under the narrow sky of God's great wisdom she wore a strawberry-blond wig.[4]

Everyday was noisy and full of experience. I was Right-hand Man. Mr. Hilton said: "How could I get along without you, Shirley?"

He said: "Your mother and father ought to get down on their knees every night and thank God for giving them a child like you."

He also said: "You're absolutely a pleasure to work with, my dear, dear child."

Sometimes he said: "For God's sakes, what did I do with the script? Shirley! Shirley! Find it."

Then I answered quietly: "Here it is, Mr. Hilton."

Once in a while, when he was very tired, he would cry out: "Shirley, I'm just tired of screaming at those kids. Will you tell Ira Pushkov not to come in till Lester points to that star the second time?"

Then I roared: "Ira Pushkov, what's the matter with you? Dope! Mr. Hilton told you five times already, don't come in till Lester points to that star the second time."

"Ach, Clara," my father asked, "what does she do there till six o'clock she can't even put the plates on the table?"

"Christmas," said my mother coldly.

"Ho! Ho!" my father said. "Christmas. What's the harm? After all, history teaches everyone. We learn from reading this is a holiday from pagan times also, candles, lights, even Chanukah.[5] So we learn it's not altogether Christian. So if they think it's a private holiday, they're only ignorant, not patriotic. What belongs to history, belongs to all men. You want to go back to the Middle Ages? Is it better to shave your head with a secondhand razor? Does it hurt Shirley to learn to speak

---

[3]An organized and often officially encouraged massacre or persecution of a minority group, especially one conducted against the Jews.   [4]Wigs are worn by orthodox Jewish women after they marry.   [5]An eight-day Jewish festival celebrated in December or late November, commemorating the Maccabees' victory over the Syrians in 165 B.C. and the rededication of the Temple at Jerusalem.

up? It does not. So maybe someday she won't live between the kitchen and the shop.[6] She's not a fool."

I thank you, Papa, for your kindness. It is true about me to this day. I am foolish but I am not a fool.

That night my father kissed me and said with great interest in my career, "Shirley, tomorrow's your big day. Congrats."

"Save it," my mother said. Then she shut all the windows in order to prevent tonsillitis.

In the morning it snowed. On the street corner a tree had been decorated for us by a kind city administration. In order to miss its chilly shadow our neighbors walked three blocks east to buy a loaf of bread. The butcher pulled down black window shades to keep the colored lights from shining on his chickens. Oh, not me. On the way to school, with both my hands I tossed it a kiss of tolerance. Poor thing, it was a stranger in Egypt.[7]

I walked straight into the auditorium past the staring children. "Go ahead. Shirley!" said the monitors. Four boys, big for their age, had already started work as propmen and stagehands.

Mr. Hilton was very nervous. He was not even happy. Whatever he started to say ended in a sideward look of sadness. He sat slumped in the middle of the first row and asked me to help Miss Glacé. I did this, although she thought my voice too resonant and said, "Show-off!"

Parents began to arrive long before we were ready. They wanted to make a good impression. From among the yards of drapes I peeked out at the audience. I saw my embarrassed mother.

Ira, Lester, and Meyer were pasted to their beards by Miss Glacé. She almost forgot to thread the star on its wire, but I reminded her. I coughed a few times to clear my throat. Miss Glacé looked around and saw that everyone was in costume and on line waiting to play his part. She whispered, "All right...." Then:

Jackie Sauerfeld, the prettiest boy in first grade, parted the curtains with his skinny elbow and in a high voice sang out:

"Parents dear
We are here
To make a Christmas play in time.
It we give
In narrative
And illustrate with pantomime."

He disappeared.

My voice burst immediately from the wings to the great shock of Ira, Lester, and Meyer, who were waiting for it but were surprised all the same.

"I remember, I remember, the house where I was born..."[8]

[6] Jewish immigrant women who worked in sweatshops.   [7] An allusion to Moses' sojourn in Egypt. See Exodus 2:2. As the persecuted Israelites were out of place in Egypt, so was the Christmas tree in an all-Jewish neighborhood.   [8] A sentimental poem by Thomas Hood (1789–1845).

Miss Glacé yanked the curtain open and there it was, the house—an old hay-loft, where Celia Kornbluh lay in the straw with Cindy Lou, her favorite doll. Ira, Lester, and Meyer moved slowly from the wings toward her, sometimes pointing to a moving star and sometimes ahead to Cindy Lou.

It was a long story and it was a sad story. I carefully pronounced all the words about my lonesome childhood, while little Eddie Braunstein wandered upstage and down with his shepherd's stick, looking for sheep. I brought up lonesomeness again, and not being understood at all except by some women everybody hated. Eddie was too small for that and Marty Graff took his place, wearing his father's prayer shawl. I announced twelve friends, and half the boys in the fourth grade gathered round Marty, who stood on an orange crate while my voice harangued. Sorrowful and loud, I declaimed about love and God and Man, but because of the terrible deceit of Abie Stock we came suddenly to a famous moment. Marty, whose remembering tongue I was, waited at the foot of the cross. He stared desperately at the audience. I groaned, "My God, my God, why hast thou forsaken me?"[9] The soldiers who were sheiks grabbed poor Marty to pin him up to die, but he wrenched free, turned again to the audience, and spread his arms aloft to show despair and the end. I murmured at the top of my voice, "The rest is silence,[10] but as everyone in this room, in this city—in this world—now knows, I shall have life eternal."

That night Mrs. Kornbluh visited our kitchen for a glass of tea.

"How's the virgin?"[11] asked my father with a look of concern.

"For a man with a daughter, you got a fresh mouth, Abramovitch."

"Here," said my father kindly, "have some lemon, it'll sweeten your disposition."

They debated a little in Yiddish, then fell in a puddle of Russian and Polish. What I understood next was my father, who said, "Still and all, it was certainly a beautiful affair, you have to admit, introducing us to the beliefs of a different culture."

"Well, yes," said Mrs. Kornbluh. "The only thing...you know Charlie Turner—that cute boy in Celia's class—a couple others? They got very small parts or no part at all. In very bad taste, it seemed to me. After all, it's their religion."

"Ach," explained my mother, "what could Mr. Hilton do? They got very small voices: after all, why should they holler? The English language they know from the beginning by heart. They're blond like angels. You think it's so important they should get in the play? Christmas...the whole piece of goods...they own it."

I listened and listened until I couldn't listen any more. Too sleepy, I climbed out of bed and kneeled. I made a little church of my hands and said, "Hear, O Israel[12]..." Then I called out in Yiddish, "Please, good night, good night. Ssh." My father said, "Ssh yourself," and slammed the kitchen door.

I was happy. I fell asleep at once. I had prayed for everybody: my talking family, cousins far away, passersby, and all the lonesome Christians. I expected to be heard. My voice was certainly the loudest.

---

[9] Psalm 22, A Psalm of David. Also the fourth of the seven last words of Christ on the cross.

[10] *Hamlet,* V, ii.   [11] The virgin Mary portrayed by Mrs. Kornbluh's daughter in the school play.

[12] "Hear, O Israel, the Lord Our God, the Lord is One." The most often recited Jewish prayer.

Journal Entry

What are the literal and symbolic meanings of the story's title?

Textual Considerations

1. Characterize Shirley's father. To what extent do you agree with him that "history teaches everyone" and that "what belongs to history, belongs to all"?
2. How does Shirley's mother view the relation between immigrants and the dominant culture? To what extent do you agree with her assessment?
3. Consider Mr. Hilton's role in the story. What qualities in Shirley does he encourage her to develop? What do you think Shirley learns from her encounters with Mr. Hilton?
4. How does Paley's use of humor and dialogue contribute to the meaning and characterizations?

Cultural Contexts

1. Discuss with your group the dilemmas that immigrant parents confront in trying to preserve their ethnic heritage for their children while wishing them to assimilate and succeed in their new land. Consider also the role of language in this situation.

Tillie Olsen
1956

I Stand Here Ironing

I stand here ironing, and what you asked me moves tormented back and forth with the iron.

"I wish you would manage the time to come in and talk with me about your daughter. I'm sure you can help me understand her. She's a youngster who needs help and whom I'm deeply interested in helping."

"Who needs help." Even if I came, what good would it do? You think because I am her mother I have a key, or that in some way you could use me as a key? She has lived for nineteen years. There is all that life that has happened outside of me, beyond me.

And when is there time to remember, to sift, to weigh, to estimate, to total? I will start and there will be an interruption and I will have to gather it all together again. Or I will become engulfed with all I did or did not do, with what should have been and what cannot be helped.

She was a beautiful baby. The first and only one of our five that was beautiful at birth. You do not guess how new and uneasy her tenancy in her now-loveliness. You did not know her all those years she was thought homely, or see her poring over her baby pictures, making me tell her over and over how beautiful she had been—and would be, I would tell her—and was now, to the seeing eye. But the seeing eyes were few or non-existent. Including mine.

I nursed her. They feel that's important nowadays. I nursed all the children, but with her, with all the fierce rigidity of first motherhood, I did like the books then said. Though her cries battered me to trembling and my breasts ached with swollenness, I waited till the clock decreed.

Why do I put that first? I do not even know if it matters, or if it explains anything.

She was a beautiful baby. She blew shining bubbles of sound. She loved motion, loved light, loved colour and music and textures. She would lie on the floor in her blue overalls patting the surface so hard in ecstasy her hands and feet would blur. She was a miracle to me, but when she was eight months old I had to leave her daytimes with the woman downstairs to whom she was no miracle at all, for I worked or looked for work and for Emily's father, who "could no longer endure" (he wrote in his good-bye note) "sharing want with us."

I was nineteen. It was the pre-relief, pre-WPA world of the depression. I would start running as soon as I got off the street-car, running up the stairs, the place smelling sour, and awake or asleep to startle awake, when she saw me she would break into a clogged weeping that could not be comforted, a weeping I can yet hear.

After a while I found a job hashing at night so I could be with her days, and it was better. But it came to where I had to bring her to his family and leave her.

It took a long time to raise the money for her fare back. Then she got chicken pox and I had to wait longer. When she finally came, I hardly knew her, walking quick and nervous like her father, looking like her father, thin, and dressed in a shoddy red that yellowed her skin and glared at the pock marks. All the baby love-liness gone.

She was two. Old enough for nursery school they said, and I did not know then what I know now—the fatigue of the long day, and the lacerations of group life in nurseries that are only parking places for children.

Except that it would have made no difference if I had known. It was the only place there was. It was the only way we could be together, the only way I could hold a job.

And even without knowing, I knew. I knew the teacher that was evil because all these years it has curdled into my memory, the little boy hunched in the corner, her rasp, "why aren't you outside, because Alvin hits you? that's no reason, go out, scaredy." I knew Emily hated it even if she did not clutch and implore "don't go Mommy" like the other children, mornings.

She always had a reason why we should stay home. Momma, you look sick, Momma. I feel sick. Momma, the teachers aren't there today, they're sick. Momma, we can't go, there was a fire there last night. Momma, it's a holiday today, no school, they told me.

But never a direct protest, never rebellion. I think of our others in their three-, four-year-oldness—the explosions, the tempers, the denunciations, the demands—and I feel suddenly ill. I put the iron down. What in me demanded that goodness in her? And what was the cost, the cost to her of such goodness?

The old man living in the back once said in his gentle way: "You should smile at Emily more when you look at her." What *was* in my face when I looked at her? I loved her. There were all the acts of love.

It was only with the others I remembered what he said, and it was the face of joy, and not of care or tightness or worry I turned to them—too late for Emily. She does not smile easily, let alone almost always as her brothers and sisters do. Her face is closed and sombre, but when she wants, how fluid. You must have seen it in her pantomimes, you spoke of her rare gift for comedy on the stage that rouses a laughter out of the audience so dear they applaud and applaud and do not want to let her go.

Where does it come from, that comedy? There was none of it in her when she came back to me that second time, after I had had to send her away again. She had a new daddy now to learn to love, and I think perhaps it was a better time. Except when we left her alone nights, telling ourselves she was old enough.

"Can't you go some other time, Mommy, like tomorrow?" she would ask. "Will it be just a little while you'll be gone? Do you promise?"

The time we came back, the front door open, the clock on the floor in the hall. She rigid awake. "It wasn't just a little while. I didn't cry. Three times I called you, just three times, and then I ran downstairs to open the door so you could come faster. The clock talked loud. I threw it away, it scared me what it talked."

She said the clock talked loud again that night I went to the hospital to have Susan. She was delirious with the fever that comes before red measles, but she was fully conscious all the week I was gone and the week after we were home when she could not come near the new baby or me.

She did not get well. She stayed skeleton thin, not wanting to eat, and night after night she had nightmares. She would call for me, and I would rouse from exhaustion to sleepily call back: "You're all right, darling, go to sleep, it's just a dream," and if she still called, in a sterner voice, "now go to sleep, Emily, there's nothing to hurt you." Twice, only twice, when I had to get up for Susan anyhow, I went in to sit with her.

Now when it is too late (as if she would let me hold and comfort her like I do the others) I get up and go to her at once at her moan or restless stirring. "Are you awake, Emily? Can I get you something, dear?" And the answer is always the same: "No, I'm all right, go back to sleep, Mother."

They persuaded me at the clinic to send her away to a convalescent home in the country where "she can have the kind of food and care you can't manage for her, and you'll be free to concentrate on the new baby." They still send children to that place. I see pictures on the society page of sleek young women planning affairs to raise money for it, or dancing at the affairs, or decorating Easter eggs or filling Christmas stockings for the children.

They never have a picture of the children so I do not know if the girls still wear those gigantic red bows and the ravaged looks on the every other Sunday when parents can come to visit "unless otherwise notified"—as we were notified the first six weeks.

Oh it is a handsome place, green lawns and tall trees and fluted flower beds. High up on the balconies of each cottage the children stand, the girls in their red bows and white dresses, the boys in white suits and giant red ties. The parents stand below shrieking up to be heard and the children shriek down to be heard, and between them the invisible wall "Not To Be Contaminated by Parental Germs or Physical Affection."

There was a tiny girl who always stood hand in hand with Emily. Her parents never came. One visit she was gone. "They moved her to Rose Cottage," Emily shouted in explanation. "They don't like you to love anybody here."

She wrote once a week, the laboured writing of a seven-year-old. "I am fine. How is the baby. If I write my letter nicely I will have a star. Love." There never was a star. We wrote every other day, letters she could never hold or keep but only hear read—once. "We simply do not have room for children to keep any personal possessions," they patiently explained when we pieced one Sunday's shrieking together to plead how much it would mean to Emily, who loved so to keep things, to be allowed to keep her letters and cards.

Each visit she looked frailer. "She isn't eating," they told us.

(They had runny eggs for breakfast or mush with lumps, Emily said later, I'd hold it in my mouth and not swallow. Nothing ever tasted good, just when they had chicken.)

It took us eight months to get her released home, and only the fact that she gained back so little of her seven lost pounds convinced the social worker.

I used to try to hold and love her after she came back, but her body would stay stiff, and after a while she'd push away. She ate little. Food sickened her, and I think much of life too. Oh she had physical lightness and brightness, twinkling by on skates, bouncing like a ball up and down up and down over the jump rope, skimming over the hill; but these were momentary.

She fretted about her appearance, thin and dark and foreign-looking at a time when every little girl was supposed to look or thought she should look like a chubby blonde replica of Shirley Temple. The door-bell sometimes rang for her, but no one seemed to come and play in the house or be a best friend. Maybe because we moved so much.

There was a boy she loved painfully through two school semesters. Months later she told me how she had taken pennies from my purse to buy him candy. "Liquorice was his favourite and I brought him some every day, but he still liked Jennifer better'n me. Why, Mommy?" The kind of question for which there is no answer.

School was a worry to her. She was not glib or quick in a world where glibness and quickness were easily confused with ability to learn. To her overworked and exasperated teachers she was an overconscientious "slow learner" who kept trying to catch up and was absent entirely too often.

I let her be absent, though sometimes the illness was imaginary. How different from my now-strictness about attendance with the others. I wasn't working. We had a new baby, I was home anyhow. Sometimes, after Susan grew old enough, I would keep her home from school, too, to have them all together.

Mostly Emily had asthma, and her breathing, harsh and laboured, would fill the house with a curiously tranquil sound. I would bring the two old dresser mirrors and her boxes of collections to her bed. She would select beads and single earrings, bottle tops and shells, dried flowers and pebbles, old postcards and scraps, all sorts of oddments; then she and Susan would play Kingdom, setting up landscapes and furniture, peopling them with action.

Those were the only times of peaceful companionship between her and Susan. I have edged away from it, that poisonous feeling between them, that terrible balancing of hurts and needs I had to do between the two, and did so badly, those earlier years.

Oh there are conflicts between the others too, each one human, needing, demanding, hurting, taking—but only between Emily and Susan, no, Emily toward Susan that corroding resentment. It seems so obvious on the surface, yet it is not obvious. Susan, the second child, Susan, golden- and curly-haired and chubby, quick and articulate and assured, everything in appearance and manner Emily was not; Susan, not able to resist Emily's precious things, losing or sometimes clumsily breaking them; Susan telling jokes and riddles to company for applause while Emily sat silent (to say to me later: that was *my* riddle, Mother, I told it to Susan); Susan, who for all the five years' difference in age was just a year behind Emily in developing physically.

I am glad for that slow physical development that widened the difference between her and her contemporaries, though she suffered over it. She was too vulnerable for that terrible world of youthful competition, of preening and parading, of constant measuring of yourself against every other, of envy, "If I had that copper hair," or "If I had that skin...." She tormented herself enough about not looking like the others, there was enough of the unsureness, the having to be conscious of words before you speak, the constant caring—what are they thinking of me? What kind of an impression am I making?—there was enough without having it all magnified by the merciless physical drives.

Ronnie is calling. He is wet and I change him. It is rare there is such a cry now. That time of motherhood is almost behind me when the ear is not one's own but must always be racked and listening for the child cry, the child call. We sit for a while and I hold him, looking out over the city spread in charcoal with its soft aisles of light. "*Shoogily*," he breathes and curls closer. I carry him back to bed, asleep. *Shoogily*. A funny word, a family word, inherited from Emily, invented by her to say: *comfort*.

In this and other ways she leaves her seal, I say aloud. And startle at my saying it. What do I mean? What did I start to gather together, to try and make coherent? I was at the terrible, growing years. War years. I do not remember them well. I was working, there were four smaller ones now, there was not time for her. She had to help be a mother, and housekeeper, and shopper. She had to set her seal. Mornings of crisis and near hysteria trying to get lunches packed, hair combed, coats and shoes found, everyone to school or Child Care on time, the baby ready for transportation. And always the paper scribbled on by a smaller one, the book looked at by Susan then mislaid, the homework not done. Running out to that huge school where she was one, she was lost, she was a drop; suffering over the unpreparedness, stammering and unsure in her classes.

There was so little time left at night after the kids were bedded down. She would struggle over books, always eating (it was in those years she developed her enormous appetite that is legendary in our family) and I would be ironing, or preparing food for the next day, or writing V-mail to Bill, or tending the baby. Sometimes, to make me laugh, or out of her despair, she would imitate happenings or types at school.

I think I said once: "Why don't you do something like this in the school amateur show?" One morning she phoned me at work, hardly understandable through the weeping: "Mother, I did it. I won, I won; they gave me first prize; they clapped and clapped and wouldn't let me go."

Now suddenly she was Somebody, and as imprisoned in her difference as she had been in anonymity.

She began to be asked to perform at other high schools, even in colleges, then at city and state-wide affairs. The first one we went to, I only recognized her that first moment when thin, shy, she almost drowned herself into the curtains. Then: Was this Emily? The control, the command, the convulsing and deadly clowning, the spell, then the roaring, stamping audience, unwilling to let this rare and precious laughter out of their lives.

Afterwards: You ought to do something about her with a gift like that—but without money or knowing how, what does one do? We have left it all to her, and the gift has as often eddied inside, clogged and clotted, as been used and growing.

She is coming. She runs up the stairs two at a time with her light graceful step, and I know she is happy tonight. Whatever it was that occasioned your call did not happen today.

"Aren't you ever going to finish the ironing, Mother? Whistler painted his mother in a rocker. I'd have to paint mine standing over an ironing-board." This is one of her communicative nights and she tells me everything and nothing as she fixes herself a plate of food out of the icebox.

She is so lovely. Why did you want me to come in at all? Why were you concerned? She will find her way.

She starts up the stairs to bed. "Don't get me up with the rest in the morning." "But I thought you were having midterms." "Oh, those," she comes back in, kisses me, and says quite lightly, "in a couple of years when we'll all be atom-dead they won't matter a bit."

She has said it before. She *believes* it. But because I have been dredging the past, and all that compounds a human being is so heavy and meaningful in me, I cannot endure it tonight.

I will never total it all. I will never come in to say: She was a child seldom smiled at. Her father left me before she was a year old. I had to work her first six years when there was work, or I sent her home and to his relatives. There were years she had care she hated. She was dark and thin and foreign-looking in a world where the prestige went to blondness and curly hair and dimples, she was slow where glibness was prized. She was a child of anxious, not proud, love. We were poor and could not afford for her the soil of easy growth. I was a young mother, I was a distracted mother. There were the other children pushing up, demanding. Her younger sister seemed all that she was not. There were years she did not want me to touch her. She kept too much in herself, her life was such she had to keep too much in herself. My wisdom came too late. She has much to her and probably nothing will come of it. She is a child of her age, of depression, of war, of fear.

Let her be. So all that is in her will not bloom—but in how many does it? There is still enough left to live by. Only help her to know—help make it so there is cause for her to know that she is more than this dress on the ironing-board, helpless before the iron.

Journal Entry

React to the narrator's idea that the poor can't afford "the soil of easy growth" for their children.

Textual Considerations

1. Relate the title of the story to the events that occur. To what extent is the iron the dominant symbol of the story? What does it symbolize? What other symbols can you identify?
2. Examine the bonds that tie mother and daughter in Olsen's text. How well does the mother succeed in building a good relationship with her daughter? What kind of resentment might Emily feel toward her mother?
3. How does point of view function in the story? To what extent might the narrative be considered an interior monologue? What does the narrator reveal about herself? About her understanding of Emily?

Cultural Contexts

1. Olsen's story is set partly during the Depression, when the child star Shirley Temple dominated American movies. Share with your group what you feel about the narrator's criticism of that time in expressions such as "She was dark and thin and foreign-looking in a world where the prestige went to blondness and curly hair and dimples" and "She is a child of her age, of depression, of war, of fear." To what extent do you consider Emily a victim of socioeconomic circumstances?
2. Emily's mother represents the plight of single parents in the 1930s. Debate with your group what can be done to help the young, distracted mothers of the 1990s who are trying to raise children by themselves. Consider also what these mothers might do to help themselves.

Liliana Heker
1986

The Stolen Party

As soon as she arrived she went straight to the kitchen to see if the monkey was there. It was: what a relief! She wouldn't have liked to admit that her mother had been right. *Monkeys at a birthday?* her mother had sneered. *Get away with you, believing any nonsense you're told!* She was cross, but not because of the monkey, the girl thought; it's just because of the party.

"I don't like you going," she told her. "It's a rich people's party."

"Rich people go to Heaven too," said the girl, who studied religion at school.

"Get away with Heaven," said the mother. "The problem with you, young lady, is that you like to fart higher than your ass."

The girl didn't approve of the way her mother spoke. She was barely nine, and one of the best in her class.

"I'm going because I've been invited," she said. "And I've been invited because Luciana is my friend. So there."

"Ah yes, your friend," her mother grumbled. She paused. "Listen, Rosaura," she said at last. "That one's not your friend. You know what you are to them? The maid's daughter, that's what."

Rosaura blinked hard: she wasn't going to cry. Then she yelled: "Shut up! You know nothing about being friends!"

Every afternoon she used to go to Luciana's house and they would both finish their homework while Rosaura's mother did the cleaning. They had their tea in the kitchen and they told each other secrets. Rosaura loved everything in the big house, and she also loved the people who lived there.

"I'm going because it will be the most lovely party in the whole world, Luciana told me it would. There will be a magician, and he will bring a monkey and everything."

The mother swung around to take a good look at her child, and pompously put her hands on her hips.

"Monkeys at a birthday?" she said. "Get away with you, believing any nonsense you're told!"

Rosaura was deeply offended. She thought it unfair of her mother to accuse other people of being liars simply because they were rich. Rosaura too wanted to be rich, of course. If one day she managed to live in a beautiful palace, would her mother stop loving her? She felt very sad. She wanted to go to that party more than anything else in the world.

"I'll die if I don't go," she whispered almost without moving her lips.

And she wasn't sure whether she had been heard, but on the morning of the party, she discovered that her mother had starched her Christmas dress. And in the afternoon, after washing her hair, her mother rinsed it in apple vinegar so that it would be all nice and shiny. Before going out, Rosaura admired herself in the mirror, with her white dress and glossy hair, and thought she looked terribly pretty.

Señora Ines also seemed to notice. As soon as she saw her, she said:

"How lovely you look today, Rosaura."

Rosaura gave her starched skirt a slight toss with her hands and walked into the party with a firm step. She said hello to Luciana and asked about the monkey. Luciana put on a secretive look and whispered into Rosaura's ear: "He's in the kitchen. But don't tell anyone, because it's a surprise."

Rosaura wanted to make sure. Carefully she entered the kitchen and there she saw it: deep in thought, inside its cage. It looked so funny that the girl stood there for a while, watching it, and later, every so often, she would slip out of the party unseen and go and admire it. Rosaura was the only one allowed into the kitchen. Señora Ines had said: "You yes, but not the others, they're much too boisterous, they might break something." Rosaura had never broken anything. She even managed the jug of orange juice, carrying it from the kitchen into the dining room. She held it carefully and didn't spill a single drop. And Señora Ines had said: "Are you sure you can manage a jug as big as that?" Of course she could manage. She wasn't a butterfingers, like the others. Like that blonde girl with the bow in her hair. As soon as she saw Rosaura, the girl with the bow had said:

"And you? Who are you?"

"I'm a friend of Luciana," said Rosaura.

"No," said the girl with the bow, "you are not a friend of Luciana because I'm her cousin and I know all her friends. And I don't know you."

"So what," said Rosaura. "I come here every afternoon with my mother and we do our homework together."

"You and your mother do your homework together?" asked the girl, laughing.

"I and Luciana do our homework together," said Rosaura, very seriously.

The girl with the bow shrugged her shoulders.

"That's not being friends," she said. "Do you go to school together?"

"No."

"So where do you know her from?" said the girl, getting impatient.

Rosaura remembered her mother's words perfectly. She took a deep breath.

"I'm the daughter of the employee," she said.

Her mother had said very clearly: "If someone asks, you say you're the daughter of the employee; that's all." She also told her to add: "And proud of it." But Rosaura thought that never in her life would she dare say something of the sort.

"What employee?" said the girl with the bow. "Employee in a shop?"

"No," said Rosaura angrily. "My mother doesn't sell anything in any shop, so there."

"So how come she's an employee?" said the girl with the bow.

Just then Señora Ines arrived saying *shh shh,* and asked Rosaura if she wouldn't mind helping serve out the hotdogs, as she knew the house so much better than the others.

"See?" said Rosaura to the girl with the bow, and when no one was looking she kicked her in the shin.

Apart from the girl with the bow, all the others were delightful. The one she liked best was Luciana, with her golden birthday crown; and then the boys. Rosaura won the sack race, and nobody managed to catch her when they played tag. When they split into two teams to play charades, all the boys wanted her for their side. Rosaura felt she had never been so happy in all her life.

But the best was still to come. The best came after Luciana blew out the candles. First the cake. Señora Ines had asked her to help pass the cake around, and Rosaura had enjoyed the task immensely, because everyone called out to her, shouting "Me, me!" Rosaura remembered a story in which there was a queen who had the power of life or death over her subjects. She had always loved that, having the power of life or death. To Luciana and the boys she gave the largest pieces, and to the girl with the bow she gave a slice so thin one could see through it.

After the cake came the magician, tall and bony, with a fine red cape. A true magician: he could untie handkerchiefs by blowing on them and make a chain with links that had no openings. He could guess what cards were pulled out from a pack, and the monkey was his assistant. He called the monkey "partner." "Let's see here, partner," he would say, "turn over a card." And, "Don't run away, partner: time to work now."

The final trick was wonderful. One of the children had to hold the monkey in his arms and the magician said he would make him disappear.

"What, the boy?" they all shouted.

"No, the monkey!" shouted back the magician.

Rosaura thought that this was truly the most amusing party in the whole world.

The magician asked a small fat boy to come and help, but the small fat boy got frightened almost at once and dropped the monkey on the floor. The magician picked him up carefully, whispered something in his ear, and the monkey nodded almost as if he understood.

"You mustn't be so unmanly, my friend," the magician said to the fat boy.

"What's unmanly?" said the fat boy.

The magician turned around as if to look for spies.

"A sissy," said the magician. "Go sit down."

Then he stared at all the faces, one by one. Rosaura felt her heart tremble.

"You, with the Spanish eyes," said the magician. And everyone saw that he was pointing at her.

She wasn't afraid. Neither holding the monkey, nor when the magician made him vanish; not even when, at the end, the magician flung his red cape over Rosaura's head and uttered a few magic words...and the monkey reappeared, chattering happily, in her arms. The children clapped furiously. And before Rosaura returned to her seat, the magician said:

"Thank you very much, my little countess."

She was so pleased with the compliment that a while later, when her mother came to fetch her, that was the first thing she told her.

"I helped the magician and he said to me, 'Thank you very much, my little countess.'"

It was strange because up to then Rosaura had thought that she was angry with her mother. All along Rosaura had imagined that she would say to her: "See that the monkey wasn't a lie?" But instead she was so thrilled that she told her mother all about the wonderful magician.

Her mother tapped her on the head and said: "So now we're a countess!"

But one could see that she was beaming.

And now they both stood in the entrance, because a moment ago Señora Ines, smiling, had said: "Please wait here a second."

Her mother suddenly seemed worried.

"What is it?" she asked Rosaura.

"What is what?" said Rosaura. "It's nothing; she just wants to get the presents for those who are leaving, see?"

She pointed at the fat boy and at a girl with pigtails who were also waiting there, next to their mothers. And she explained about the presents. She knew, because she had been watching those who left before her. When one of the girls was about to leave, Señora Ines would give her a bracelet. When a boy left, Señora Ines gave him a yo-yo. Rosaura preferred the yo-yo because it sparkled, but she didn't mention that to her mother. Her mother might have said: "So why don't you ask for one, you blockhead?" That's what her mother was like. Rosaura didn't feel like explaining that she'd be horribly ashamed to be the odd one out. Instead she said:

"I was the best-behaved at the party."

And she said no more because Señora Ines came out into the hall with two bags, one pink and one blue.

First she went up to the fat boy, gave him a yo-yo out of the blue bag, and the fat boy left with mother. Then she went up to the girl and gave her a bracelet out of the pink bag, and the girl with the pigtails left as well.

Finally she came up to Rosaura and her mother. She had a big smile on her face and Rosaura liked that. Señora Ines looked down at her, then looked up at her mother, and then said something that made Rosaura proud:

"What a marvelous daughter you have, Herminia."

For an instant, Rosaura thought that she'd give her two presents: the bracelet and the yo-yo. Señora Ines bent down as if about to look for something. Rosaura also leaned forward, stretching out her arm. But she never completed the movement.

Señora Ines didn't look in the pink bag. Nor did she look in the blue bag. Instead she rummaged in her purse. In her hand appeared two bills.

"You really and truly earned this," she said handing them over. "Thank you for all your help, my pet."

Rosaura felt her arms stiffen, stick close to her body, and then she noticed her mother's hand on her shoulder. Instinctively she pressed herself against her mother's body. That was all. Except her eyes. Rosaura's eyes had a cold, clear look that fixed itself on Señora Ines's face.

Señora Ines, motionless, stood there with her hand outstretched. As if she didn't dare draw it back. As if the slightest change might shatter an infinitely delicate balance.

Journal Entry

Analyze the significance of the story's title, "The Stolen Party."

Textual Considerations

1. Explore the mother–daughter relationship. How does it change during the course of the story? What lesson does each learn?
2. Examine the narrative structure of the story. Consider, for example, the author's use of flashback, as well as her plot construction of rising action, climax, and dénouement.
3. Explain the significance of the last paragraph. If the story were told from the point of view of Señora Ines, would we see that the problem was also hers and not only Rosaura's? Explain.

Cultural Contexts

1. React to the idea that people like Rosaura are judged not by their character but by their position in society. Debate whether this mode of differentiation by class is as unfair as differentiation by skin color.
2. Heker's story is set in Latin America. Could it have taken place in the United States instead? Why or why not?

Aurora Levins Morales
1986

Puertoricanness

It was Puerto Rico waking up inside her. Puerto Rico waking her up at 6:00 a.m., remembering the rooster that used to crow over on 59th Street and the neighbors all cursed "that damn rooster," but she loved him, waited to hear his harsh voice carving up the Oakland sky and eating it like chopped corn, so obliviously sure of himself, crowing all alone with miles of houses around him. She was like that rooster.

Often she could hear them in her dreams. Not the lone rooster of 59th Street (or some street nearby…she had never found the exact yard though she had tried), but the wild careening hysterical roosters of 3:00 a.m. in Bartolo, screaming at the night and screaming again at the day.

It was Puerto Rico waking up inside her, uncurling and showing open the door she had kept neatly shut for years and years. Maybe since the first time she was an immigrant, when she refused to speak Spanish in nursery school. Certainly since the last time, when at thirteen she found herself between languages, between countries, with no land feeling at all solid under her feet. The mulberry trees of Chicago, that first summer, had looked so utterly pitiful beside her memory of flamboyan and banana and.... No, not even the individual trees and bushes but the mass of them, the overwhelming profusion of green life that was the home of her comfort and nest of her dreams.

The door was opening. She could no longer keep her accent under lock and key. It seeped out, masquerading as dyslexia, stuttering, halting, unable to speak the word which will surely come out in the wrong language, wearing the wrong clothes. Doesn't that girl know how to dress? Doesn't she know how to date, what to say to a professor, how to behave at a dinner table laid with silver and crystal and too many forks?

Yesterday she answered her husband's request that she listen to the whole of his thoughts before commenting by screaming. "This is how we talk. I will not wait sedately for you to finish. Interrupt me back!" She drank pineapple juice three or four times a day. Not Lotus, just Co-op brand, but it was *piña*,[1] and it was sweet and yellow. And she was letting the clock slip away from her into a world of morning and afternoon and night, instead of "five-forty-one-and-twenty seconds—beep."

There were things she noticed about herself, the Puertoricanness of which she had kept hidden all these years, but which had persisted as habits, as idiosyncrasies of her nature. The way she left a pot of food on the stove all day, eating out of it whenever hunger struck her, liking to have something ready. The way she had lacked food to offer Elena in the old days and had stamped on the desire to do so because it *was* Puerto Rican: Come, mija...¿quieres café?[2] The way she was embarrassed and irritated by Ana's unannounced visits, just dropping by, keeping the country habits after a generation of city life. So unlike the cluttered datebooks of all her friends, making appointments to speak to each other on the phone days in advance. Now she yearned for that clocklessness, for the perpetual food pots of her childhood. Even in the poorest houses a plate of white rice and brown beans with calabaza[3] or green bananas and oil.

She had told Sally that Puerto Ricans lived as if they were all in a small town still, a small town of six million spread out over tens of thousands of square miles, and that the small town that was her country needed to include Manila Avenue in Oakland now, because she was moving back into it. She would not fight the waking early anymore, or the eating all day, or the desire to let time slip between her fingers and allow her work to shape it. Work, eating, sleep, lovemaking, play—to let them shape the day instead of letting the day shape them. Since she could not right now, in the endless bartering of a woman with two countries, bring herself to trade in one-half of her heart for the other, exchange this loneliness for another perhaps harsher one, she would live as a Puerto Rican lives en la isla,[4] right here in north

---

[1] Pineapple.   [2] "Eat, darling, you want some coffee?"   [3] Pumpkin.   [4] On the island.

Oakland, plant the bananales[5] and cafetales[6] of her heart around her bedroom door, sleep under the shadow of their bloom and the carving hoarseness of the roosters, wake to blue-rimmed white enamel cups of jugo de piña[7] and plates of guineo verde,[8] and heat pots of rice with bits of meat in them on the stove all day.

There was a woman in her who had never had the chance to move through this house the way she wanted to, a woman raised to be like those women of her childhood, hardworking and humorous and clear. That woman was yawning up out of sleep and into this cluttered daily routine of a Northern California writer living at the edges of Berkeley. She was taking over, putting doilies on the word processor, not bothering to make appointments, talking to the neighbors, riding miles on the bus to buy bacalao,[9] making her presence felt…and she was all Puerto Rican, every bit of her.

Journal Entry

Respond to the protagonist's desire to live again in a "clockless" world.

Textual Considerations

1. Discuss Morales's use of repetition to reinforce the story's theme. Cite examples of repetition that you found particularly effective.
2. Make a list of the protagonist's associations with Puertoricanness. Why had she felt compelled to hide her ethnicity?
3. Review the last paragraph of the story. What does it suggest about the cost of cultural displacement?

Cultural Contexts

1. Discuss with your group the speaker's point of view on whether ethnic identity and cultural assimilation are mutually exclusive. To what extent do you agree with her? Explain.

Bharati Mukherjee
1988

Jasmine

Jasmine came to Detroit from Port-of-Spain, Trinidad, by way of Canada. She crossed the border at Windsor in the back of a gray van loaded with mattresses and box springs. The plan was for her to hide in an empty mattress box if she heard the driver say, "All bad weather seems to come down from Canada,

---

[5] Banana plants. [6] Coffee trees. [7] Pineapple juice. [8] Green bananas, or Plantains. [9] Codfish.

doesn't it?" to the customs man. But she didn't have to crawl into a box and hold her breath. The customs man didn't ask to look in.

The driver let her off at a scary intersection on Woodward Avenue and gave her instructions on how to get to the Plantations Motel in Southfield. The trick was to keep changing vehicles, he said. That threw off the immigration guys real quick.

Jasmine took money for cab fare out of the pocket of the great big raincoat that the van driver had given her. The raincoat looked like something that nuns in Port-of-Spain sold in church bazaars. Jasmine was glad to have a coat with wool lining, though; and anyway, who would know in Detroit that she was Dr. Vassanji's daughter?

All the bills in her hand looked the same. She would have to be careful when she paid the cabdriver. Money in Detroit wasn't pretty the way it was back home, or even in Canada, but she liked this money better. Why should money be pretty, like a picture? Pretty money is only good for putting on your walls maybe. The dollar bills felt businesslike, serious. Back home at work, she used to count out thousands of Trinidad dollars every day and not even think of them as real. Real money was worn and green, American dollars. Holding the bills in her fist on a street corner meant she had made it in okay. She'd outsmarted the guys at the border. Now it was up to her to use her wits to do something with her life. As her Daddy kept saying, "Girl, is opportunity come only once." The girls she'd worked with at the bank in Port-of-Spain had gone green as bananas when she'd walked in with her ticket on Air Canada. Trinidad was too tiny. That was the trouble. Trinidad was an island stuck in the middle of nowhere. What kind of place was that for a girl with ambition?

The Plantations Motel was run by a family of Trinidad Indians who had come from the tuppenny-ha'penny country town, Chaguanas. The Daboos were nobodies back home. They were lucky, that's all. They'd gotten here before the rush and bought up a motel and an ice cream parlor. Jasmine felt very superior when she saw Mr. Daboo in the motel's reception area. He was a pumpkin-shaped man with very black skin and Elvis Presley sideburns turning white. They looked like earmuffs. Mrs. Daboo was a bumpkin, too; short, fat, flapping around in house slippers. The Daboo daughters seemed very American, though. They didn't seem to know that they were nobodies, and kept looking at her and giggling.

She knew she would be short of cash for a great long while. Besides, she wasn't sure she wanted to wear bright leather boots and leotards like Viola and Loretta. The smartest move she could make would be to put a down payment on a husband. Her Daddy had told her to talk to the Daboos first chance. The Daboos ran a service fixing up illegals with islanders who had made it in legally. Daddy had paid three thousand back in Trinidad, with the Daboos and the mattress man getting part of it. They should throw in a good-earning husband for that kind of money.

The Daboos asked her to keep books for them and to clean the rooms in the new wing, and she could stay in 16B as long as she liked. They showed her 16B. They said she could cook her own roti; Mr. Daboo would bring in a stove, two gas rings that you could fold up in a metal box. The room was quite grand, Jasmine thought. It had a double bed, a TV, a pink sink and matching bathtub. Mrs. Daboo said Jasmine wasn't the big-city Port-of-Spain type she'd expected. Mr. Daboo said that he wanted her to stay because it was nice to have a neat, cheerful person around. It wasn't a bad deal, better than stories she'd heard about Trinidad girls in the States.

All day every day except Sundays Jasmine worked. There wasn't just the book-keeping and the cleaning up. Mr. Daboo had her working on the match-up marriage service. Jasmine's job was to check up on social security cards, call clients' bosses for references, and make sure credit information wasn't false. Dermatologists and engineers living in Bloomfield Hills, store owners on Canfield and Woodward: she treated them all as potential liars. One of the first things she learned was that Ann Arbor was a magic word. A boy goes to Ann Arbor and gets an education, and all the barriers come crashing down. So Ann Arbor was the place to be.

She didn't mind the work. She was learning about Detroit, every side of it. Sunday mornings she helped unload packing crates of Caribbean spices in a shop on the next block. For the first time in her life, she was working for a black man, an African. So what if the boss was black? This was a new life, and she wanted to learn everything. Her Sunday boss, Mr. Anthony, was a courtly, Christian, church-going man, and paid her the only wages she had in her pocket. Viola and Loretta, for all their fancy American ways, wouldn't go out with blacks.

One Friday afternoon she was writing up the credit info on a Guyanese Muslim who worked in an assembly plant when Loretta said that enough was enough and there was no need for Jasmine to be her father's drudge.

"Is time to have fun," Viola said, "We're going to Ann Arbor."

Jasmine filed the sheet on the Guyanese man who probably now would never get a wife and got her raincoat. Loretta's boyfriend had a Cadillac parked out front. It was the longest car Jasmine had ever been in and louder than a country bus. Viola's boyfriend got out of the front seat. "Oh, oh, sweet things," he said to Jasmine. "Get in front." He was a talker. She'd learned that much from working on the matrimonial match-ups. She didn't believe him for a second when he said that there were dudes out there dying to ask her out.

Loretta's boyfriend said, "You have eyes I could leap into, girl."

Jasmine knew he was just talking. They sounded like Port-of-Spain boys of three years ago. It didn't surprise her that these Trinidad country boys in Detroit were still behind the times, even of Port-of-Spain. She sat very stiff between the two men, hands on her purse. The Daboo girls laughed in the back seat.

On the highway the girls told her about the reggae night in Ann Arbor. Kevin and the Krazee Islanders. Malcolm's Lovers. All the big reggae groups in the Midwest were converging for the West Indian Students Association fall bash. The ticket didn't come cheap but Jasmine wouldn't let the fellows pay. She wasn't that kind of girl.

The reggae and steel drums brought out the old Jasmine. The rum punch, the dancing, the dreadlocks, the whole combination. She hadn't heard real music since she got to Detroit, where music was supposed to be so famous. The Daboo girls kept turning on rock stuff in the motel lobby whenever their father left the area. She hadn't danced, really *danced,* since she'd left home. It felt so good to dance. She felt hot and sweaty and sexy. The boys at the dance were more than sweet talkers; they moved with assurance and spoke of their futures in America. The bartender gave her two free drinks and said, "Is ready when you are, girl." She ignored him but she felt all hot and good deep inside. She knew Ann Arbor was a special place.

When it was time to pile back into Loretta's boyfriend's Cadillac, she just couldn't face going back to the Plantations Motel and to the Daboos with their accounting books and messy files.

"I don't know what happen, girl," she said to Loretta. "I feel all crazy inside. Maybe is time for me to pursue higher studies in this town."

"This Ann Arbor, girl, they don't just take you off the street. It *cost* like hell."

She spent the night on a bashed-up sofa in the Student Union. She was a well-dressed, respectable girl, and she didn't expect anyone to question her right to sleep on the furniture. Many others were doing the same thing. In the morning, a boy in an army parka showed her the way to the Placement Office. He was a big, blond, clumsy boy, not bad-looking except for the blond eyelashes. He didn't scare her, as did most Americans. She let him buy her a Coke and a hotdog. That evening she had a job with the Moffitts.

Bill Moffitt taught molecular biology and Lara Hatch-Moffitt, his wife, was a performance artist. A performance artist, said Lara, was very different from being an actress, though Jasmine still didn't understand what the difference might be. The Moffitts had a little girl, Muffin, whom Jasmine was to look after, though for the first few months she might have to help out with the housework and the cooking because Lara said she was deep into performance rehearsals. That was all right with her, Jasmine said, maybe a little too quickly. She explained she came from a big family and was used to heavy-duty cooking and cleaning. This wasn't the time to say anything about Ram, the family servant. Americans like the Moffitts wouldn't understand about keeping servants. Ram and she weren't in similar situations. Here mother's helpers, which is what Lara had called her—Americans were good with words to cover their shame—seemed to be as good as anyone.

Ann Arbor was a huge small town. She couldn't imagine any kind of school the size of the University of Michigan. She meant to sign up for courses in the spring. Bill brought home a catalogue bigger than the phonebook for all of Trinidad. The university had courses in everything. It would be hard to choose; she'd have to get help from Bill. He wasn't like a professor, not the ones back home where even high school teachers called themselves professors and acted like little potentates. He wore blue jeans and thick sweaters with holes in the elbows and used phrases like "in vitro" as he watched her curry up fish. Dr. Parveen back home—he called himself "doctor" when everybody knew he didn't have even a Master's degree—was never seen without his cotton jacket which had gotten really ratty at the cuffs and lapel edges. She hadn't learned anything in the two years she'd put into college. She'd learned more from working in the bank for two months than she had at college. It was the assistant manager, Personal Loans Department, Mr. Singh, who had turned her on to the Daboos and to smooth, bargain-priced emigration.

Jasmine liked Lara. Lara was easygoing. She didn't spend the time she had between rehearsals telling Jasmine how to cook and clean American-style. Mrs.

Daboo did that in 16B. Mrs. Daboo would barge in with a plate of stale samosas and snoop around giving free advice on how mainstream Americans did things. As if she were dumb or something! As if she couldn't keep her own eyes open and make her mind up for herself. Sunday mornings she had to share the butcher-block workspace in the kitchen with Bill. He made the Sunday brunch from new recipes in *Gourmet* and *Cuisine*. Jasmine hadn't seen a man cook who didn't have to or wasn't getting paid to do it. Things were topsy-turvy in the Moffitt house. Lara went on two- and three-day road trips and Bill stayed home. But even her Daddy, who'd never poured himself a cup of tea, wouldn't put Bill down as a woman. The mornings Bill tried out something complicated, a Cajun shrimp, sausage, and beans dish, for instance, Jasmine skipped church services. The Moffitts didn't go to church, though they seemed to be good Christians. They just didn't talk church talk, which suited her fine.

Lara showed her the room she would have all to herself in the finished basement. There was a big, old TV, not in color like the motel's and a portable typewriter on a desk which Lara said she would find handy when it came time to turn in her term papers. Jasmine didn't say anything about not being a student. She was a student of life, wasn't she? There was a scary moment after they'd discussed what she could expect as salary, which was three times more than anything Mr. Daboo was supposed to pay her but hadn't. She thought Bill Moffitt was going to ask her about her visa or her green card[1] number and social security. But all Bill did was smile and smile at her—he had a wide, pink, baby face—and play with a button on his corduroy jacket. The button would need sewing back on, firmly.

Lara said, "I think I'm going to like you, Jasmine. You have a something about you. A something real special. I'll just bet you've acted, haven't you?" The idea amused her, but she merely smiled and accepted Lara's hug. The interview was over.

Then Bill opened a bottle of Soave and told stories about camping in northern Michigan. He'd been raised there. Jasmine didn't see the point in sleeping in tents; the woods sounded cold and wild and creepy. But she said, "Is exactly what I want to try out come summer, man. Campin and huntin."

Lara asked about Port-of-Spain. There was nothing to tell about her hometown that wouldn't shame her in front of nice white American folk like the Moffitts. The place was shabby, the people were grasping and cheating and lying and life was full of despair and drink and wanting. But by the time she finished, the island sounded romantic. Lara said, "It wouldn't surprise me one bit if you were a writer, Jasmine."

Two months passed. Jasmine knew she was lucky to have found a small, clean, friendly family like the Moffitts to build her new life around. "Man!" she'd exclaim as she vacuumed the wide-plank wood floors or ironed (Lara wore pure silk or pure cotton). "In this country Jesus givin out good luck only!" By this time they knew she wasn't a student, but they didn't care and said they wouldn't report her. They never asked if she was illegal on top of it.

---

[1] Work permit issued only to immigrants who have permanent resident status in the U.S.

To savor her new sense of being a happy, lucky person, she would put herself through a series of "what ifs": what if Mr. Singh in Port-of-Spain hadn't turned her on to the Daboos and loaned her two thousand! What if she'd been ugly like the Mintoo girl and the manager hadn't even offered! What if the customs man had unlocked the door of the van! Her Daddy liked to say, "You is a helluva girl, Jasmine."

"Thank you, Jesus," Jasmine said, as she carried on.

Christmas Day the Moffitts treated her just like family. They gave her a red cashmere sweater with a V neck so deep it made her blush. If Lara had worn it, her bosom wouldn't hang out like melons. For the holiday weekend Bill drove her to the Daboos in Detroit. "You work too hard," Bill said to her. "Learn to be more selfish. Come on, throw your weight around." She'd rather not have spent time with the Daboos, but that first afternoon of the interview she'd told Bill and Lara that Mr. Daboo was her mother's first cousin. She had thought it shameful in those days to have no papers, no family, no roots. Now Loretta and Viola in tight, bright pants seemed trashy like girls at Two-Johnny Bissoondath's Bar back home. She was stuck with the story of the Daboos being family. Village bumpkins, ha! She would break out. Soon.

Jasmine had Bill drop her off at the RenCen. The Plantations Motel, in fact, the whole Riverfront area, was too seamy. She'd managed to cut herself off mentally from anything too islandy. She loved her Daddy and Mummy, but she didn't think of them that often anymore. Mummy had expected her to be homesick and come flying right back home. "Is blowin sweat-of-brow money is what you doin, Pa," Mummy had scolded. She loved them, but she'd become her own person. That was something that Lara said: "I am my own person."

The Daboos acted thrilled to see her back. "What you drinkin, Jasmine girl?" Mr. Daboo kept asking. "You drinkin sherry or what?" Pouring her little glasses of sherry instead of rum was a sure sign he thought she had become whitefolk-fancy. The Daboo sisters were very friendly, but Jasmine considered them too wild. Both Loretta and Viola had changed boyfriends. Both were seeing black men they'd danced with in Ann Arbor. Each night at bedtime, Mr. Daboo cried. "In Trinidad we stayin we side, they stayin they side. Here, everything mixed up. Is helluva confusion, no?"

On New Year's Eve the Daboo girls and their black friends went to a dance. Mr. and Mrs. Daboo and Jasmine watched TV for a while. Then Mr. Daboo got out a brooch from his pocket and pinned it on Jasmine's red sweater. It was a Christmasy brooch, a miniature sleigh loaded down with snowed-on mistletoe. Before she could pull away, he kissed her on the lips. "Good luck for the New Year!" he said. She lifted her head and saw tears. "Is year for dreams comin true."

Jasmine started to cry, too. There was nothing wrong, but Mr. Daboo, Mrs. Daboo, she, everybody was crying.

What for? This is where she wanted to be. She'd spent some damned uncomfortable times with the assistant manager to get approval for her loan. She thought of Daddy. He would be playing poker and fanning himself with a magazine. Her married sisters would be rolling out the dough for stacks and stacks of roti, and

Mummy would be steamed purple from stirring the big pot of goat curry on the stove. She missed them. But. It felt strange to think of anyone celebrating New Year's Eve in summery clothes.

In March Lara and her performing group went on the road. Jasmine knew that the group didn't work from scripts. The group didn't use a stage, either; instead, it took over supermarkets, senior citizens' centers, and school halls, without notice. Jasmine didn't understand the performance world. But she was glad that Lara said, "I'm not going to lay a guilt trip on myself. Muffie's in super hands," before she left.

Muffie didn't need much looking after. She played Trivial Pursuit all day, usually pretending to be two persons, sometimes Jasmine, whose accent she could imitate. Since Jasmine didn't know any of the answers, she couldn't help. Muffie was a quiet, precocious child with see-through blue eyes like her dad's, and red braids. In the early evenings Jasmine cooked supper, something special she hadn't forgotten from her island days. After supper she and Muffie watched some TV, and Bill read. When Muffie went to bed, Bill and she sat together for a bit with their glasses of Soave. Bill, Muffie, and she were a family, almost.

Down in her basement room that late, dark winter, she had trouble sleeping. She wanted to stay awake and think of Bill. Even when she fell asleep it didn't feel like sleep because Bill came barging into her dreams in his funny, loose-jointed, clumsy way. It was mad to think of him all the time, and stupid and sinful; but she couldn't help it. Whenever she put back a book he'd taken off the shelf to read or whenever she put his clothes through the washer and dryer, she felt sick in a giddy, wonderful way. When Lara came back things would get back to normal. Meantime she wanted the performance group miles away.

Lara called in at least twice a week. She said things like, "We've finally obliterated the margin between realspace and performancespace." Jasmine filled her in on Muffie's doings and the mail. Bill always closed with, "I love you. We miss you, hon."

One night after Lara had called—she was in Lincoln, Nebraska—Bill said to Jasmine, "Let's dance."

She hadn't danced since the reggae night she'd had too many rum punches. Her toes began to throb and clench. She untied her apron and the fraying, knotted-up laces of her running shoes.

Bill went around the downstairs rooms turning down lights. "We need atmosphere," he said. He got a small, tidy fire going in the living room grate and pulled the Turkish scatter rug closer to it. Lara didn't like anybody walking on the Turkish rug, but Bill meant to have his way. The hissing logs, the plants in the dimmed light, the thick patterned rug: everything was changed. This wasn't the room she cleaned every day.

He stood close to her. She smoothed her skirt down with both hands.

"I want you to choose the record," he said.

"I don't know your music."

She brought her hand high to his face. His skin was baby smooth.

"I want *you* to pick," he said. "You are your own person now."

"You got island music?"

He laughed, "What do you think?" The stereo was in a cabinet with albums packed tight alphabetically into the bottom three shelves. "Calypso has not been a force in my life."

She couldn't help laughing. "Calypso? Oh, man." She pulled dust jackets out at random. Lara's records. The Flying Lizards. The Violent Femmes. There was so much still to pick up on!

"This one," she said, finally.

He took the record out of her hand. "God!" he laughed. "Lara must have found this in a garage sale!" He laid the old record on the turntable. It was "Music for Lovers," something the nuns had taught her to foxtrot to way back in Port-of-Spain.

They danced so close that she could feel his heart heaving and crashing against her head. She liked it, she liked it very much. She didn't care what happened.

"Come on," Bill whispered. "If it feels right, do it." He began to take her clothes off.

"Don't Bill," she pleaded.

"Come on, baby," he whispered again. "You're a blossom, a flower."

He took off his fisherman's knit pullover, the corduroy pants, the blue shorts. She kept pace. She'd never had such an effect on a man: He nearly flung his socks and Adidas into the fire. "You feel so good," he said. "You smell so good. You're really something, flower of Trinidad."

"Flower of Ann Arbor," she said, "not Trinidad."

She felt so good she was dizzy. She'd never felt this good on the island where men did this all the time, and girls went along with it always for favors. You couldn't feel really good in a nothing place. She was thinking this as they made love on the Turkish carpet in front of the fire: she was a bright, pretty girl with no visa, no papers, and no birth certificate. No nothing other than what she wanted to invent and tell. She was a girl rushing wildly into the future.

His hand moved up her throat and forced her lips apart and it felt so good, so right, that she forgot all the dreariness of her new life and gave herself up to it.

Journal Entry

What does the future hold for Jasmine? What do you imagine she would be doing in five years?

Textual Considerations

1. Jasmine is described as "a girl with ambition." What is she ambitious for? Does she accomplish her ambition? How? What are her other outstanding characteristics? Compare her experiences in Michigan with those in Trinidad.

2. Jasmine thinks that what she learned about "bargain-priced emigration" from the assistant bank manager in Trinidad was more important than anything she learned in two years of college. What does this tell us about Jasmine? What is the tone of the phrase "bargain-priced emigration"? How do you interpret the sentence "She'd

spent some damned uncomfortable times with the assistant manager to get approval for her loan"?

3. Stories develop mainly from conflict: between two or more characters, within a character as the result of some psychological force (guilt, jealousy), or between a character and some impersonal force such as poverty or disease. What is the main conflict in this story? Between what or whom? Is the struggle resolved?

Cultural Contexts

1. "In this country Jesus givin out good luck only!" Why did Jasmine think Ann Arbor was "the place to be"? To what extent was she captured by the promise of the American Dream? Was she lucky to work for the Moffitts? Why or why not?

2. Examine with your group the portrait of the American family as exemplified by the Moffitts. Consider their attitudes toward marriage, child raising, and careers. To what extent does your group share their values?

Kesaya E. Noda
1989

Growing Up Asian in America

Sometimes when I was growing up, my identity seemed to hurtle toward me and paste itself right to my face. I felt that way, encountering the stereotypes of my race perpetuated by non-Japanese people (primarily white) who may or may not have had contact with other Japanese in America. "You don't like cheese, do you?" someone would ask. "I know your people don't like cheese." Sometimes questions came making allusions to history. That was another aspect of the identity. Events that had happened quite apart from the me who stood silent in that moment connected my face with an incomprehensible past. "Your parents were in California? Were they in those camps during the war?" And sometimes there were phrases or nicknames: "Lotus Blossom." I was sometimes addressed or referred to as racially Japanese, sometimes as Japanese American, and sometimes as an Asian woman. Confusions and distortions abounded.

How is one to know and define oneself? From the inside—within a context that is self-defined, from a grounding in community and a connection with culture and history that are comfortably accepted? Or from the outside—in terms of messages received from the media and people who are often ignorant? Even as an adult I can still see two sides of my face and past. I can see from the inside out, in freedom. And I can see from the outside in, driven by the old voices of childhood and lost in anger and fear.

I Am Racially Japanese

A voice from my childhood says: "You are other. You are less than. You are unalterably alien." This voice has its own history. We have indeed been seen as other and alien since the early years of our arrival in the United States. The very first immigrants were welcomed and sought as laborers to replace the dwindling numbers of Chinese, whose influx had been cut off by the Chinese Exclusion Act of 1882. The Japanese fell natural heir to the same anti-Asian prejudice that had arisen against the Chinese. As soon as they began striking for better wages, they were no longer welcomed.

I can see myself today as a person historically defined by law and custom as being forever alien. Being neither "free white," nor "African," our people in California were deemed "aliens, ineligible for citizenship," no matter how long they intended to stay here. Aliens ineligible for citizenship were prohibited from owning, buying, or leasing land. They did not and could not belong here. The voice in me remembers that I am always a *Japanese* American in the eyes of many. A third-generation German American is an American. A third-generation Japanese

623

American is a Japanese American. Being Japanese means being a danger to the country during the war and knowing how to use chopsticks. I wear this history on my face.

I move to the other side. I see a different light and claim a different context. My race is a line that stretches across ocean and time to link me to the shrine where my grandmother was raised. Two high, white banners lift in the wind at the top of the stone steps leading to the shrine. It is time for the summer festival. Black characters are written against the sky as boldly as the clouds, as lightly as kites, as sharply as the big black crows I used to see above the fields in New Hampshire. At festival time there is liquor and food, ritual, discipline, and abandonment. There is music and drunkenness and invocation. There is hope. Another season has come. Another season has gone.

I am racially Japanese. I have a certain claim to this crazy place where the prayers intoned by a neighboring Shinto priest (standing in for my grandmother's nephew who is sick) are drowned out by the rehearsals for the pop singing contest in which most of the villagers will compete later that night. The village elders, the priest, and I stand respectfully upon the immaculate, shining wooden floor of the outer shrine, bowing our heads before the hidden powers. During the patchy intervals when I can hear him, I notice the priest has a stutter. His voice flutters up to my ears only occasionally because two men and a women are singing gustily into a microphone in the compound, testing the sound system. A prerecorded tape of guitars, samisens, and drums accompanies them. Rock music and Shinto prayers. That night, to loud applause and cheers, a young man is given the award for the most *netsuretsu*—passionate, burning—rendition of a song. We roar our approval of the reward. Never mind that his voice had wandered and slid, now slightly above, now slightly below the given line of the melody. Netsuretsu. Netsuretsu.

In the morning, my grandmother's sister kneels at the foot of the stone stairs to offer her morning prayers. She is too crippled to climb the stairs, so each morning she kneels here upon the path. She shuts her eyes for a few seconds, her motions as matter of fact as when she washes rice. I linger longer than she does, so reluctant to leave, savoring the connection I feel with my grandmother in America, the past, and the power that lives and shines in the morning sun.

Our family has served this shrine for generations. The family's need to protect this claim to identity and place outweighs any individual claim to any individual hope. I am Japanese.

I Am a Japanese American

"Weak." I hear the voice from my childhood years. "Passive," I hear. Our parents and grandparents were the ones who were put into those camps. They went without resistance; they offered cooperation as proof of loyalty to America. "Victim," I hear. And, "Silent."

Our parents are painted as hard workers who were socially uncomfortable and had difficulty expressing even the smallest opinion. Clean, quiet, motivated, and determined to match the American way; that is us, and that is the story of our time here.

"Why did you go into those camps?" I raged at my parents, frightened by my own inner silence and timidity. "Why didn't you do anything to resist? Why didn't you name it the injustice it was?" Couldn't our parents even think? Couldn't they? Why were we so passive?

I shift my vision and my stance. I am in California. My uncle is in the midst of the sweet potato harvest. He is pressed, trying to get the harvesting crews onto the field as quickly as possible, worried about the flow of equipment and people. His big pickup is pulled off to the side, motor running, door ajar. I see two tractors in the yard in front of an old shed; the flatbed harvesting platform on which the work-ers will stand has already been brought over from the other field. It's early morn-ing. The workers stand loosely grouped and at ease, but my uncle looks as harried and tense as a police officer trying to unsnarl a New York City traffic jam. Driving toward the shed, I pull my car off the road to make way for an approaching tractor. The front wheels of the car sink luxuriously into the soft, white sand by the road-side and the car slides to a dreamy halt, tail still on the road. I try to move forward. I try to move back. The front bites contentedly into the sand, the back lifts itself at a jaunty angle. My uncle sees me and storms down the road, running. He is shout-ing before he is even near me.

"What's the matter with you?" he screams. "What the hell are you doing?" In his frenzy, he grabs his hat off his head and slashes it through the air across his knee. He is beside himself. "Don't you know how to drive in sand? What's the mat-ter with you? You've blocked the whole roadway. How am I supposed to get my tractors out of here? Can't you use your head? You've cut off the whole roadway, and we've got to get out of here."

I stand on the road before him helplessly thinking, "No, I don't know how to drive in sand. I've never driven in sand."

"I'm sorry, uncle," I say, burying a smile beneath a look of sincere apology. I notice my deep amusement and my affection for him with great curiosity. I am usu-ally devastated by anger. Not this time.

During the several years that follow I learn about the people and the place, and much more about what has happened in this California village where my parents grew up. The issei, our grandparents, made this settlement in the desert. Their first crops were eaten by rabbits and ravaged by insects. The land was so barren that men walking from house to house sometimes got lost. Women came here too. They bore children in 114-degree heat, then carried the babies with them into the fields to nurse when they reached the end of each row of grapes or other truck-farm crops.

I had had no idea what it meant to buy this kind of land and make it grow green. Or how, when the war came, there was no space at all for the subtlety of being who we were—Japanese Americans. Either/or was the way. I hadn't under-stood that people were literally afraid for their lives then, that their money had been frozen in banks; that there was a five-mile travel limit; that when the early evening curfew came and they were inside their houses, some of them watched helplessly as people they knew went into their barns to steal their belongings. The police were patrolling the road, interested only in violators of curfew. There was no help for them in the face of thievery. I had not been able to imagine before what it must have felt like to be an American—to know absolutely that one is an American—and yet to have almost everyone else deny it. Not only deny it, but challenge that identity with machine guns and troops of white American soldiers. In those circumstances it was difficult to say, "I'm a Japanese American." "American" had to do.

But now I can say that I am a Japanese American. It means I have a place here in this country, too. I have a place here on the East Coast, where our neighbor is so much a part of our family that my mother never passes her house at night without glancing at the lights to see if she is home and safe; where my parents have hauled hundreds of pounds of rocks from fields and arduously planted Christmas trees and blueberries, lilacs, asparagus, and crab apples; where my father still dreams of angling a stream to a new bed so that he can dig a pond in the field and fill it with water and fish. "The neighbors already came for their Christmas tree?" he asks in December. "Did they like it? Did they like it?"

I have a place on the West Coast where my relatives still farm, where I heard the stories of feuds and backbiting, and where I saw that people survived and flourished because fundamentally they trusted and relied upon one another. A death in the family is not just a death in a family; it is a death in the community. I saw people help each other with money, materials, labor, attention, and time. I saw men gather once a year, without fail, to clean the grounds of a ninety-year-old woman who had helped the community before, during, and after the war. I saw her remembering them with birthday cards sent to each of their children.

I come from a people with a long memory and a distinctive grace. We live our thanks. And we are Americans. Japanese Americans.

I Am a Japanese-American Woman

Woman. The last piece of my identity. It has been easier by far for me to know myself in Japan and to see my place in America than it has been to accept my line of connection with my own mother. She was my dark self, a figure in whom I thought I saw all that I feared most in myself. Growing into womanhood and looking for some model of strength. I turned away from her. Of course, I could not find what I sought. I was looking for a black feminist or a white feminist. My mother is neither white nor black.

My mother is a woman who speaks with her life as much as with her tongue. I think of her with her own mother. Grandmother had Parkinson's disease and it had frozen her gait and set her fingers, tongue, and feet jerking and trembling in a terrible dance. My aunts and uncles wanted her to be able to live in her own home. They fed her, bathed her, dressed her, awoke at midnight to take her for one last trip to the bathroom. My aunts (her daughters-in-law) did most of the care, but my mother went from New Hampshire to California each summer to spend a month living with Grandmother, because she wanted to and because she wanted to give my aunts at least a small rest. During those hot summer days, mother lay on the couch watching the television or reading, cooking foods that Grandmother liked, and speaking little. Grandmother thrived under her care.

The time finally came when it was too dangerous for Grandmother to live alone. My relatives kept finding her on the floor beside her bed when they went to wake her in the mornings. My mother flew to California to help clean the house and make arrangements for Grandmother to enter a local nursing home. On her last day at home, while Grandmother was sitting in her big, overstuffed armchair, hair combed and wearing a green summer dress, my mother went to her and knelt at her feet. "Here, Mamma," she said. "I've polished your shoes." She lifted Grandmother's legs and helped her into the shiny black shoes. My Grandmother looked down and smiled slightly. She left her house walking, supported by her children, carrying her pocket book, and wearing her polished black shoes. "Look, Mamma," my mom had said, kneeling. "I've polished your shoes."

Just the other day, my mother came to Boston to visit. She had recently lost a lot of weight and was pleased with her new shape and her feeling of good health. "Look at me, Kes," she exclaimed, turning toward me, front and back, as naked as the day she was born. I saw her small breasts and the wide, brown scar, belly button to pubic hair, that marked her because my brother and I were both born by Caesarean section. Her hips were small. I was not a large baby, but there was so little room for me in her that when she was carrying me she could not even begin to bend over toward the floor. She hated it, she said.

"Don't I look good? Don't you think I look good?"

I looked at my mother, smiling and as happy as she, thinking of all the times I have seen her naked. I have seen both my parents naked throughout my life, as they have seen me. From childhood through adulthood we've had our naked moments, sharing baths, idle conversations picked up as we moved between showers and closets, hurried moments at the beginning of days, quiet moments at the end of days.

I know this to be Japanese, this ease with the physical, and it makes me think of an old Japanese folk song. A young nursemaid, a fifteen-year-old girl, is singing a lullaby to a baby who is strapped to her back. The nursemaid has been sent as a servant to a place far from her own home. "We're the beggars," she says, "and they are the nice people. Nice people wear fine sashes. Nice clothes."

> *If I should drop dead,*
> *bury me by the roadside!*
> *I'll give a flower*
> *to everyone who passes.*
> *What kind of flower?*
> *The cam-cam-camellia [tsun-tsun-tsubaki]*
> *watered by Heaven:*
> *alms water.*

The nursemaid is the intersection of heaven and earth, the intersection of the human, the natural world, the body, and the soul. In this song, with clear eyes, she looks steadily at life, which is sometimes so very terrible and sad. I think of her while looking at my mother, who is standing on the red and purple carpet before me, laughing, without any clothes.

I am my mother's daughter. And I am myself
I am a Japanese-American woman.

Epilogue

I recently heard a man from West Africa share some memories of his childhood. He was raised Muslim, but when he was a young man, he found himself deeply drawn to Christianity. He struggled against his inner impulse for years, trying to avoid the church yet feeling pushed to return to it again and again. "I would have done *anything* to avoid the change," he said. At last, he became Christian. Afterwards he was afraid to go home, fearing that he would not be accepted. The fear was groundless, he discovered, when at last he retuned—he had separated himself, but his family and friends (all Muslim) had not separated themselves from him.

The man, who is now a professor of religion, said that in the Africa he knew as a child and a young man, pluralism was embraced rather than feared. There was "a kind of tolerance that did not deny your particularity," he said. He alluded to zestful, spontaneous debates that would sometimes loudly erupt between Muslims and Christians in the village's public spaces. His memories of an atheist who harangued the villagers when he came to visit them once a week moved me deeply. Perhaps the man was an agricultural advisor or inspector. He harassed the women. He would say: "Don't go to the fields! Don't even bother to go to the fields. Let God take care of you. He'll send you the food. If you believe in God, why do you need to work? You don't need to work! Let God put the seeds in the ground. Stay home."

The professor said, "The women laughed, you know? They just laughed. Their attitude was, 'Here is a child of God. When will he come home?'"

The storyteller, the professor of religion, smiled a most fantastic tender smile as he told this story, "In my country, there is a deep affirmation of the oneness of God," he said. "The atheist and the women were having quite different experiences in their encounter, though the atheist did not know this. He saw himself as quite separate from the women. But the women did not see themselves as being separate from him. 'Here is a child of God,' they said. 'When will he come home?'"

Journal Entry

Respond to Noda's question "How is one to know and define oneself?"

Textual Considerations

1. Noda hears a voice from her childhood say: "You are other. You are less than. You are unalterably alien." What evidence does she cite in this section of her essay which addresses the issue of being "historically defined"?
2. What factors are involved in being a Japanese American according to Noda? Which images are most effective? Is there a recurring motif? Cite evidence.
3. What stages does Noda go through, particularly with her mother, as she shapes her identity as a Japanese-American woman?
4. Do you agree with the sentiments of the Epilogue about the unity of all things? Why or why not?

Cultural Contexts

1. Discuss with your group whether it is possible in the United States to embrace rather than fear pluralism. What is involved in fostering a tolerance that does not deny the particularity of the individual?
2. Discuss the link between perception of race and presentation of the self in the struggle to achieve ethnic identify.

Anna Quindlen
1987

Gay

When he went home last year he realized for the first time that he would be buried there, in the small, gritty industrial town he had loathed for as long as he could remember. He looked out the window of his bedroom and saw the siding on the house next door and knew that he was trapped, as surely as if he had never left for the city. Late one night, before he was to go back to his own apartment, his father tried to have a conversation with him, halting and slow, about drug use and the damage it could do to your body. At that moment he understood that it would be more soothing to his parents to think that he was a heroin addict than that he was a homosexual.

This is part of the story of a friend of a friend of mine. She went to his funeral not too long ago. The funeral home forced the family to pay extra to embalm him. Luckily, the local paper did not need to print the cause of death. His parents' friends did not ask what killed him, and his parents didn't talk about it. He had AIDS. His parents had figured out at the same time that he was dying and that he slept with men. He tried to talk to them about his illness; he didn't want to discuss his homosexuality. That would have been too hard for them all.

Never have the lines between sex and death been so close, the chasm between parent and child so wide. His parents hoped almost until the end that some nice girl would "cure" him. They even hinted broadly that my friend might be that nice girl. After the funeral, as she helped with the dishes in their small kitchen with the window onto the backyard, she lost her temper at the subterfuge and said to his mother: "He was gay. Why is that more terrible than that he is dead?" The mother did not speak, but raised her hands from the soapy water and held them up as though to ward off the words.

I suppose this is true of many parents. For some it is simply that they think homosexuality is against God, against nature, condemns their sons to hell. For others it is something else, more difficult to put into words. It makes their children too different from them. We do not want our children to be too different—so different that they face social disapprobation and ostracism, so different that they die before we do. His parents did not know any homosexuals, or at least they did not believe they did. His parents did not know what homosexuals were like.

They are like us. They are us. Isn't that true? And yet, there is a difference. Perhaps mothers sometimes have an easier time accepting this. After all, they must accept early on that there are profound sexual differences between them and their sons. Fathers think their boys will be basically like them. Sometimes they are. And sometimes, in a way that comes to mean so much, they are not.

I have thought of this a fair amount because I am the mother of sons. I have managed to convince myself that I love my children so much that nothing they could do would turn me against them, or away from them, that nothing would make me take their pictures off the bureau and hide them in a drawer. A friend says I am fooling myself, that I would at least be disappointed and perhaps distressed if, like his, my sons' sexual orientation was not hetero. Maybe he's right. There are some obvious reasons to feel that way. If the incidence of AIDS remains higher among homosexuals than among heterosexuals, it would be one less thing they could die of. If societal prejudices remain constant, it would be one less thing they could be ostracized for.

But this I think I know: I think I could live with having a son who was homosexual. But it would break my heart if he was homosexual and felt that he could not tell me so, felt that I was not the kind of mother who could hear that particular truth. That is a kind of death, too, and it kills both your life with your child and all you have left after the funeral: the relationship that can live on inside you, if you have nurtured it.

In the days following his death, the mother of my friend's friend mourned the fact that she had known little of his life, had not wanted to know. "I spent too much time worrying about what he was," she said. Not who. What. And it turned out that there was not enough time, not with almost daily obituaries of people barely three decades old, dead of a disease she had never heard of when she first wondered about the kind of friends her boy had and why he didn't date more.

It reminded me that often we take our sweet time dealing with the things that we do not like about our children: the marriage we could not accept, the profession we disapproved of, the sexual orientation we may hate and fear. Sometimes we vow that we will never, never accept those things. The stories my friend told me about the illness, the death, the funeral and, especially, about the parents reminded me that sometimes we do not have all the time we think to make our peace with who our children are. It reminded me that "never" can last a long, long time, perhaps much longer than we intended, deep in our hearts, when we first invoked its terrible endless power.

Journal Entry

Imagine yourself as the young gay man, and write a letter to your parents explaining your sexual preference.

Textual Considerations

1. To what extent do you agree with Quindlen that parents are reluctant to accept children who are too different from them?
2. Respond to the statement "never have the lines between sex and death been so close, the chasm between parent and child so wide."
3. What is Quindlen's supposition about being the mother of a homosexual? Do you agree with her? Why or why not?

Cultural Contexts

1. What societal stereotypes might account for the gay man's parents to prefer "to think that he was a heroin addict than that he was a homosexual?"? What is your response to their preference?

Whitman, Levertov, and Randall

Walt Whitman
1865

I Hear America Singing

I hear America singing, the varied carols I hear,
Those of mechanics, each one singing his as it should be blithe and strong,
The carpenter singing his as he measures his plank or beam,
The mason singing his as he makes ready for work, or leaves off work,
The boatman singing what belongs to him on his boat, the deck-hand singing
    on the steamboat deck,   5
The shoemaker singing as he sits on his bench, the hatter singing as he stands,
The wood-cutter's song, the ploughboy's on his way in the morning, or at noon
    intermission or at sundown,
The delicious singing of the mother, or of the young wife at work, or of the girl
    sewing or washing,
Each singing what belongs to him or her and to none else,
The day what belongs to the day—at night the party of young fellows,
    robust, friendly,   10
Singing with open mouths their strong melodious songs.

Denise Levertov
1987

Poet Power

Riding by taxi, Brooklyn to Queens,
a grey spring day. The Hispanic driver,
when I ask, 'Es usted Mexicano?' tells me
No, he's an exile from Uruguay. And I say,
'The only other Uraguayan I've met   5
was a writer—maybe
you know his name?—
        Mario Benedetti?

And he takes both hands
off the wheel and swings round,   10
glittering with joy: '*Benedetti!*
Mario Benedetti!!'
            There are
hallelujahs in his voice—
we execute a perfect   15
figure 8 on the shining highway,
and rise aloft, high above traffic, flying
all the rest of the way in the blue sky, azul, azul!

Dudley Randall
1968

The Melting Pot

There is a magic melting pot
where any girl or man
can step in Czech or Greek or Scot,
step out American.

Johann and *Jan* and *Jean* and *Juan,*   5
Giovanni and *Ivan*
step in and then step out again
all freshly christened *John.*

Sam, watching, said, "Why, I was here
even before they came,"   10
and stepped in too, but was tossed out
before he passed the brim.

And every time Sam tried that pot
they threw him out again.

"Keep out. This is our private pot   15
We don't want your black stain."

At last, thrown out a thousand times,
Sam said, "I don't give a damn.
Shove your old pot. You can like it or not,
but I'll be just what I am."   20

Journal Entry

Analyze the thematic significance of the title of each poem.

Textual Considerations

1. Discuss the effectiveness of the metaphor of song to reinforce the meaning in Whitman's poem.
2. What images in Levertov's text best express the joy of the taxi driver?
3. Analyze Randall's use of irony in "The Melting Pot." Which examples are most effective?

Cultural Contexts

1. Contrast the speakers' views on cultural diversity and equality in the three poems. In "The Melting Pot," to what extent is Sam's rage justified? Why has he triumphed in spite of being rejected? Is "The Melting Pot" a viable or even desirable reality in contemporary U.S. society? Explain.

Gillan and Jeffers

Maria Mazziotti Gillan
1984

Public School No. 18: Paterson, New Jersey

Miss Wilson's eyes, opaque
as blue glass, fix on me:
"We must speak English.
We're in America now."
I want to say, "I am American,"   5
but the evidence is stacked against me.

My mother scrubs my scalp raw, wraps
my shining hair in white rags
to make it curl; Miss Wilson

drags me to the window, checks my hair   10
for lice. My face wants to hide.

At home, my words smooth in my mouth,
I chatter and am proud. In school,
I am silent; I grope for the right English
words, fear the Italian word will sprout   15
from my mouth like a rose.

I fear the progression of teachers
in their sprigged dresses,
their Anglo-Saxon faces.

Without words, they tell me   20
to be ashamed.
I am.
I deny that booted country
even from myself,
want to be still   25
and untouchable
as these women
who teach me to hate myself.

Years later, in a white
Kansas City house,   30
the psychology professor tells me
I remind him of the Mafia leader
on the cover of *Time* magazine.
My anger spits
venomous from my mouth: 35

I am proud of my mother,
dressed all in black,
proud of my father
with his broken tongue,
proud of the laughter   40
and noise of our house.

Remember me, ladies,
the silent one?
I have found my voice
and my rage will blow   45
your house down.

Lance Jeffers
1969

My Blackness Is the Beauty of This Land

My blackness is the beauty of this land,
my blackness,
tender and strong, wounded and wise,
my blackness:
I, drawing black grandmother, smile muscular and sweet,   5
unstraightened white hair soon to grow in earth,
work thickened hand thoughtful and gentle on grandson's
    head,
my heart is bloody-razored by a million memories' thrall:

    remembering the crook-necked cracker who spat   10
      on my naked body,
    remembering the splintering of my son's spirit
      because he remembered to be proud
    remembering the tragic eyes in my daughter's
      dark face when she learned her color's   15
      meaning,

and my own dark rage a rusty knife with teeth to gnaw
    my bowels,
my agony ripped loose by anguished shouts in Sunday's
    humble church,   20
my agony rainbowed to ecstasy when my feet oversoared
    Montgomery's slime,
ah, this hurt, this hate, this ecstasy before I die,
and all my love a strong cathedral!
My blackness is the beauty of this land!   25

Lay this against my whiteness, this land!
Lay me, young Brutus stamping hard on the cat's tail,
gutting the Indian, gouging the nigger,
booting Little Rock's Minniejean Brown in the buttocks and
    boast,   30
    my sharp white teeth derision-bared as I the
      conqueror crush!

Skyscraper-I, white hands burying God's human clouds
    beneath
                the dust!   35
Skyscraper-I, slim blond young Empire
            thrusting up my loveless bayonet to rape the
                sky,
then shrink all my long body with filth and in the gutter lie
as lie I will to perfume this armpit garbage,   40

While I here standing black beside
wrench tears from which the lies would suck the salt
to make me more American than America…
But yet my love and yet my hate shall civilize this land,
this land's salvation.   45

Journal Entry

Respond to the critique of American values expressed in both poems.

Textual Considerations

1. Identify images of power and powerlessness in each poem, and analyze their causes and effects.
2. Compare and contrast the functions of skin color in both poems, and assess the degree to which awareness of color affects the speakers' sense of exclusion.
3. Comment on Jeffers's imagery of the cathedral and the skyscraper. Why are these images appropriate for the meaning?

Cultural Contexts

1. Compare and contrast both poets' concepts of their "country" or "land." Explain the paradoxes in the last stanza of Jeffers's poem and the rage in the concluding stanzas of Gillan's poem. With which speaker do you most identify? Why?

Soyinka and Olds

Wole Soyinka
1960

Telephone Conversation

The price seemed reasonable, location
Indifferent. The landlady swore she lived
Off premises. Nothing remained
But self-confession. "Madam," I warned,
"I hate a wasted journey—I am African."   5
Silence. Silenced transmission of
Pressurized good-breeding. Voice, when it came,
Lipstick coated, long gold-rolled
Cigarette-holder pipped. Caught I was, foully.
"HOW DARK?"... I had not misheard..."ARE YOU LIGHT   10
OR VERY DARK?" Button B. Button A. Stench
Of rancid breath of public hide-and-speak.
Red booth. Red pillar-box. Red double-tiered
Omnibus squelching tar. It *was* real! Shamed
By ill-mannered silence, surrender   15
Pushed dumbfoundment to beg simplification.
Considerate she was, varying the emphasis—
"ARE YOU DARK? OR VERY LIGHT?" Revelation came.
"You mean—like plain or milk chocolate?"
Her assent was clinical, crushing in its light   20
Impersonality. Rapidly, wave-length adjusted,
I chose. "West African sepia"—and as afterthought,
"Down in my passport." Silence for spectroscopic
 Flight of fancy, till truthfulness clanged her accent
Hard on the mouthpiece. "WHAT'S THAT?" conceding   25
"DON'T KNOW WHAT THAT IS." "Like brunette."
"THAT'S DARK, ISN'T IT?" "Not altogether.
Facially, I am brunette, but madam, you should see
The rest of me. Palm of my hand, soles of my feet
Are a peroxide blonde. Friction, caused—   30
Foolishly madam—by sitting down, has turned
My bottom raven black—One moment madam!"—sensing
Her receiver rearing on the thunderclap
About my ears—"Madam," I pleaded, "wouldn't you rather
See for yourself?"   35

Sharon Olds
1987

On the Subway

The boy and I face each other.
His feet are huge, in black sneakers
laced with white in a complex pattern like a
set of intentional scars. We are stuck on
opposite sides of the car, a couple of   5
molecules stuck in a rod of light
rapidly moving through darkness. He has the
casual cold look of a mugger,
alert under hooded lids. He is wearing
red, like the inside of the body   10
exposed. I am wearing dark fur, the
whole skin of an animal taken and
used. I look at his raw face,
he looks at my fur coat, and I don't
know if I am in his power—   15
he could take my coat so easily, my
briefcase, my life—
or if he is in my power, the way I am
living off his life, eating the steak
he does not eat, as if I am taking   20
the food from his mouth. And he is black
and I am white, and without meaning or
trying to I must profit from his darkness,
the way he absorbs the murderous beams of the
nation's heart, as black cotton   25
absorbs the heat of the sun and holds it. There is
no way to know how easy this
white skin makes my life, this
life he could take so easily and
break across his knee like a stick the way his   30
own back is being broken, the
rod of his soul that at birth was dark and
fluid and rich as the heart of a seedling
ready to thrust up into any available light.

Journal Entry

How does each poet use setting to enhance the theme?

Textual Considerations

1. Create a profile of the landlady in "Telephone Conversation." How does the speaker use visual and sensory imagery to communicate her attitude toward skin color. Cite examples.
2. What profile of the speaker emerges in the poem? How do you interpret the last four lines of the text?
3. How does Olds use color to heighten differences in race and social class in "On the Subway"?
4. Explain lines 20–25. To what extent do you agree with the speaker that exploitation on the basis of race continues today as it did in the days of slavery?
5. Define the conflict in the poem. Is it between the speaker and the boy? An internal conflict within the speaker herself? Explain.

Cultural Contexts

1. Discuss with your group the thematic significance of the titles of both poems. To what extent are both texts concerned with the interplay of power and powerlessness? Explain.

Robinson and Laviera

Edwin Arlington Robinson
1896

Richard Cory

Whenever Richard Cory went down town,
We people on the pavement looked at him:
He was a gentleman from sole to crown,
Clean favored, and imperially slim.

And he was always quietly arrayed,
And he was always human when he talked;
But still he fluttered pulses when he said,
"Good-morning," and he glittered when he walked.

5

And he was rich—yes, richer than a king—
And admirably schooled in every grace: 10
In fine, we thought that he was everything
To make us wish that we were in his place.

So on we worked, and waited for the light,
And went without the meat, and cursed the bread;
And Richard Cory, one calm summer night,   15
Went home and put a bullet through his head.

Tato Laviera
1988

Latero¹ Story

i am a twentieth-century welfare recipient
moonlighting in the sun as a latero
a job invented by national state laws
designed to re-cycle aluminum cans
returned to consumer's acid laden   5
gastric inflammation pituitary glands
coca diet rites low cal godsons
of artificially flavored malignant
indigestions somewhere down the line
of a cancerous cell   10

i collect garbage cans in outdoor facilities
congested with putrid residues
my hands shelving themselves
opening plastic bags never knowing
what they'll encounter   15

several times a day i touch evil rituals
cut throats of chickens
tongues of poisoned rats
salivating my index finger
smells of month old rotten foods   20
next to pamper's diarrhea
        dry blood infectious diseases
hypodermic needles tissued with
heroin water drops pilfered in
slimy greases hazardous waste materials   25

but i cannot use rubber gloves
they undermine my daily profits

i am twentieth-century welfare recipient
moonlighting in the day as a latero
that is the only opportunity i have   30
to make it big in america
some day i might become experienced enough
to offer technical assistance
to other lateros
i am thinking of publishing   35
my own guide to latero's collection
and a latero's union offering
medical dental benefits

i am a twentieth-century welfare recipient
moonlighting in the night as a latero   40
i am considered some kind of expert
at collecting cans during fifth avenue parades
i can now hire workers at twenty
five cents an hour guaranteed salary
and fifty per cent two and one half cents   45
profit on each can collected

i am a twentieth-century welfare recipient
moonlighting in midnight as a latero
i am becoming an entrepreneur
an american success story   50
i have hired bag ladies to keep peddlers
from my territories
i have read in some guide to success
that in order to get rich
to make it big   55
i have to sacrifice myself
moonlighting until dawn by digging
deeper into the extra can
margin of profit
i am on my way up the opportunistic   60
ladder of success
in ten years i will quit welfare
to become a legitimate businessman
i'll soon become a latero executive
with corporate conglomerate intents   65
god bless america

---

[1] From Spanish *lata:* can. A man who picks up cans from garbage containers and the streets.

Journal Entry

React to the issue of social class as both poems convey it.

Textual Considerations

1. Cite words or phrases associating Richard Cory with wealth or royalty, and discuss how these affect your response to him.
2. Comment on Robinson's use of irony.
3. Characterize the tone of Laviera's poem, and comment on its appropriateness to his theme.
4. Much of Laviera's poetry belongs to the oral tradition. What does that suggest about his purpose and audience? How do you respond to his style?

Cultural Contexts

1. Discuss with your group the treatment of success in both poems. Why did Richard Cory commit suicide, despite his wealth and social status? What kind of success does the Latero envisage for himself? To what extent does your concept of success resemble his?

Sarton and Lassell ◆

May Sarton
1988

AIDS

We are stretched to meet a new dimension
Of love, a more demanding range
Where despair and hope must intertwine.
How grow to meet it? Intention
Here can neither move nor change   5
The raw truth. Death is on the line.
It comes to separate and estrange
Lover from lover in some reckless design.
Where do we go from here?

Fear.   Fear.   Fear.   Fear.   10

Our world has never been more stark
Or more in peril.

It is very lonely now in the dark.
Lonely and sterile.

And yet in the simple turn of a head   15
Mercy lives. I heard it when someone said
"I must go now to a dying friend.
Every night at nine I tuck him into bed,
And give him a shot of morphine,"
And added, "I go where I have never been."   20
I saw he meant into a new discipline
He had not imagined before, and a new grace.

Every day now we meet face to face.
Every day now devotion is the test.
Through the long hours, the hard, caring nights   25
We are forging a new union. We are blest.
As closed hands open to each other
Closed lives open to strange tenderness.
We are learning the hard way how to mother.
Who says it is easy? But we have the power.   30
I watch the faces deepen all around me.
It is the time of change, the saving hour.
The word is not fear, the word we live,
But an old word suddenly made new,
As we learn it again, as we bring it alive: 35

Love.   Love.   Love.   Love.

Michael Lassell
1985

How to Watch Your Brother Die

When the call comes, be calm
Say to your wife, "My brother is dying. I have
to fly to California."
Try not to be shocked that he already looks like a cadaver.
Say to the young man sitting by your brother's side,   5
"I'm his brother."

Try not to be shocked when the young man says,
"I'm his lover. Thanks for coming."

Listen to the doctor with a steel face on.
Sign the necessary forms.   10
Tell the doctor you will take care of everything.
Wonder why doctors are so remote.

Watch the lover's eyes as they stare into
your brother's eyes as they stare into
space.   15
Wonder what they see there.
Remember the time he was jealous and
opened your eyebrows with a sharp stick.
Forgive him out loud
even if he can't understand you.   20
Realize the scar will be
all that's left of him.

Over coffee in the hospital cafeteria
say to the lover, "You're an extremely good-looking
young man."   25
Hear him say,
"I never thought I was good enough looking to
deserve your brother."
Watch the tears well up in his eyes. Say,
"I'm sorry. I don't know what it means to be   30
the lover of another man."
Hear him say,
"It's just like a wife, only the commitment is
deeper because the odds against you are so much
greater."   35
Say nothing, but
take his hand like a brother's.

Drive to Mexico for unproven drugs that might
help him live longer.
Explain what they are to the border guard.   40
Fill with rage when he informs you,
"You can't bring those across."
Begin to grow loud.
Feel the lover's hand on your arm,
restraining you. See in the guard's eye   45
how much a man can hate another man.
Say to the lover, "How can you stand it?"
Hear him say, "You get used to it."

Think of one of your children getting used to
another man's hatred.   50

Call your wife on the telephone. Tell her
"He hasn't much time.
I'll be home soon." Before you hang up, say,
"How could anyone's commitment be deeper than
a husband and wife?" Hear her say,   55
"Please, I don't want to know all the details."

When he slips into an irrevocable coma
hold his lover in your arms while he sobs,
no longer strong. Wonder how much longer
you will be able to be strong.   60
Feel how it feels to hold a man in your arms
whose arms are used to holding men.
Offer God anything to bring your brother back.
Know you have nothing God could possibly want.
Curse God, but do not   65
abandon Him.

Stare at the face of the funeral director
when he tells you he will not
embalm the body for fear of
contamination. Let him see in your eyes   70
how much a man can hate a man.

Stand beside a casket covered in flowers,
white flowers. Say,
"Thank you for coming" to each of several hundred men
who file past in tears, some of them   75
holding hands. Know that your brother's life
was not what you imagined. Overhear two mourners say,
"I wonder who'll be next."

Arrange to take an early flight home.
His lover will drive you to the airport.   80
When your flight is announced say,
awkwardly, "If I can do anything, please
let me know." Do not flinch when he says,
"Forgive yourself for not wanting to know him
after he told you. He did."   85
Stop and let it soak in. Say,
"He forgave me, or he knew himself?"
"Both," the lover will say, not knowing what else
to do. Hold him like a brother while he
kisses you on the cheek. Think that   90

you haven't been kissed by a man since
your father died. Think,
"This is no moment not to be strong." Fly
first class and drink scotch. Stroke
your split eyebrow with a finger   95
and think of your brother alive. Smile
at the memory and think
how your children will feel in your arms,
warm and friendly and without challenge.

Journal Entry

Respond to the mood evoked by each poet. How would you characterize their attitudes toward death?

Textural Considerations

1. To what extent do you agree with the speaker in "AIDS" that "our world has never been more stark/Or more in peril"?
2. How do you respond to the idea that words like "fear," "mercy," and "love" evoke new meanings in the context of AIDS?
3. Lassell uses contrasting images of love and hate in "How to Watch Your Brother Die." Cite examples of each.
4. Analyze the functions of dialogue in Lassell's poem. Consider, for example, what the speaker's "conversations" reveal about himself, his wife, his relationship to his brother, and to his brother's lover.
5. Explain the last two words of the poem.

Cultural Contexts

1. Review with your group your responses to question 4. What do the various conversations suggest about the relationship of the gay community to the larger society? Make a list of the images that you associate with gays and lesbians. To what extent do you agree that people should be free to express their sexual preferences?

Espada

Martín Espada
1990

Cross Plains, Wisconsin

Blue bandanna
across the forehead,
beard bristling
like a straw broom,
sleeveless T-shirt   5
of the Puerto Rican flag
with Puerto Rico stamped
across the chest,
a foreign name on the license,
evidence enough   10
for the cop to announce
that the choice is cash or jail,
that today
the fine for speeding
is exactly   15
sixty-seven dollars,
and his car
will follow my car
out of town

Martín Espada
1990

Jorge the Church Janitor
Finally Quits

No one asks
where I am from,
I must be
from the country of janitors,

I have always mopped this floor.   5
Honduras, you are a squatter's camp
outside the city
of their understanding.

No one can speak
my name,   10
I host the fiesta
of the bathroom,
stirring the toilet
like a punchbowl.
The Spanish music of my name   15
is lost
when the guests complain
about toilet paper.

What they say
must be true: 20
I am smart,
but I have a bad attitude.

No one knows
that I quit tonight,
maybe the mop   25
will push on without me,
sniffing along the floor
like a crazy squid
with stringy gray tentacles.
They will call it Jorge.   30

Martín Espada
1990

Federico's Ghost

The story is
that whole families of fruitpickers
still crept between the furrows
of the field at dusk,
when for reasons of whiskey or whatever   5
the cropduster plane sprayed anyway,

floating a pesticide drizzle
over the pickers
who thrashed like dark birds
in a glistening white net,   10
except for Federico,
a skinny boy who stood apart
in his own green row,
and, knowing the pilot
would not understand in Spanish   15
that he was the son of a whore,
instead jerked his arm
and thrust an obscene finger.

The pilot understood.
He circled the plane and sprayed again,   20
watching a fine gauze of poison
drift over the brown bodies
that cowered and scurried on the ground,
and aiming for Federico,
leaving the skin beneath his shirt   25
wet and blistered,
but still pumping his finger at the sky.

After Federico died,
rumors at the labor camp
told of tomatoes picked and smashed at night,   30
growers muttering of vandal children
or communists in camp,
first threatening to call Immigration,
then promising every Sunday off
if only the smashing of tomatoes would stop.   35

Still tomatoes were picked and squashed
in the dark,
and the old women in camp
said it was Federico,
laboring after sundown   40
to cool the burns on his arms,
flinging tomatoes
at the cropduster
that hummed like a mosquito
lost in his ear,   45
and kept his soul awake.

Martín Espada
1987

Tony Went to the Bodega[1] But He Didn't Buy Anything
para Angel Guadalupe

Tony's father left the family
and the Long Island city projects,
leaving a mongrel-skinny puertorriqueño boy
nine years old
who had to find work.   5

Makengo the Cuban
let him work at the bodega.
In grocery aisles
he learned the steps of the dry-mop mambo,
banging the cash register   10
like piano percussion
in the spotlight of Machito's orchestra,
polite with the abuelas[2] who bought on credit,
practicing the grin on customers
he'd seen Makengo grin   15
with his bad yellow teeth.

Tony left the projects too,
with a scholarship for law school.
But he cursed the cold primavera[3]
in Boston;   20
the cooking of his neighbors
left no smell in the hallway,
and no one spoke Spanish
(not even the radio).

So Tony walked without a map   25
through the city,
a landscape of hostile condominiums
and the darkness of white faces,
sidewalk-searcher lost
till he discovered the projects.   30

Tony went to the bodega
but he didn't buy anything:

he sat by the doorway satisfied
to watch la gente[4] (people
island-brown as him)   35
crowd in and out,
hablando español,[5]
thought: this is beautiful,
and grinned
his bodega grin.   40

This is a rice and beans
success story:
Today Tony lives on Tremont Street,
above the bodega.

[1]Bodega   grocery and liquor store; in the dedication, after the title, *para* means "for."

[2]grandmothers

[3]spring season

[4]the people

[5]speaking Spanish

Journal Entry

Respond to Espada's philosophy that "any oppressive social condition, before it can be changed, must be named and condemned in words that pervade by stirring the emotions, awakening the senses." How does it apply to his own poetry?

Textual Considerations

1. Analyze the effects of withholding the use of the personal pronoun until the end of "Cross Plains, Wisconsin."
2. What factors contributed to the fine imposed by the policeman?
3. Characterize Jorge. How does the congregation affect his sense of identity? Why does he quit?
4. What is the tone of the poem? Serious? Humorous? Objective? Ironic?
5. Why does Federico act as he did? What is your response to his actions?
6. How do the growers modify their first reactions to the migrant workers? Why?
7. Explain the significance of the final simile.
8. Characterize Tony. Why does he return to his roots? How do you respond to that decision?
9. Why does Espada mention Tony's father in the first part of the poem?

Cultural Contexts

1. Espada's poems document racism, dehumanizing labor, and personal and political resistance. Discuss with your group your responses to these poems of the political imagination. To what extent do you agree or disagree that the poet should protest social injustices?

DRAMA

William Shakespeare
1604

Othello, the Moor of Venice

THE NAMES OF THE ACTORS

OTHELLO, *the Moor*
BRABANTIO, *a senator, father to* DESDEMONA
CASSIO, *an honourable lieutenant to* OTHELLO
IAGO, OTHELLO*'s ancient, a villain.*
RODERIGO, *a gulled gentleman.*
DUKE OF VENICE
SENATORS *of Venice.*
MONTANO, *governor of Cyprus.*
LODOVICO *and* GRATIANO, *kinsmen to* BRABANTIO, *two noble Venetians*
Sailors
Clown
DESDEMONA, *daughter to* BRABANTIO *and wife to* OTHELLO
EMILIA, *wife to* IAGO
BIANCA, *a courtesan and mistress to* CASSIO
Messenger, Herald, Officers, Gentlemen, Musicians, *and* Attendants

[SCENE. *Venice: a sea-port in Cyprus*]

ACT I

SCENE I.   *Venice. A street.*

[*Enter* RODERIGO *and* IAGO.]

ROD.   Tush! never tell me; I take it much unkindly
  That thou, Iago, who hast had my purse
  As if the strings were thine, shouldst know of this.
IAGO.   'Sblood,[1] but you'll not hear me:
  If ever I did dream of such a matter,
  Abhor me.
ROD.   Thou told'st me thou didst hold him in thy hate.
IAGO.   Despise me, if I do not. Three great ones of the city,[2]
  In personal suit to make me his lieutenant,
  Off-capp'd to him:[3] and, by the faith of man,   10

[1] *'Sblood* an oath, "by God's blood"   [2] *great ones of the city* Iago means to indicate his importance in the community; this is suggested also by his use of the word *worth* in line 11   [3] *him* Othello

I know my price, I am worth no worse a place:
But he, as loving his own pride and purposes,
Evades them, with a bombast circumstance
Horribly stuff'd with epithets of war;
And, in conclusion,
Nonsuits[4] my mediators; for, "Certes," says he,
"I have already chose my officer."
And what was he?
Forsooth, a great arithmetician,[5]
One Michael Cassio, a Florentine,   20
A fellow almost damn'd in a fair wife;[6]
That never set a squadron in the field,
Nor the division[7] of a battle knows
More than a spinster; unless the bookish theoric,[8]
Wherein the toged[9] consuls can propose[10]
As masterly as he: mere prattle, without practice,
Is all his soldiership. But he, sir, had th' election:
And I, of whom his eyes had seen the proof
At Rhodes, at Cyprus[11] and on other grounds
Christian and heathen, must be be-lee'd and calm'd   30
By debitor and creditor: this counter-caster,[12]
He, in good time,[13] must his lieutenant be,
And I—God bless the mark![14]—his Moorship's ancient.[15]
ROD.   By heaven, I rather would have been his hangman.
IAGO.   Why, there's no remedy; 'tis the curse of service,
Preferment goes by letter and affection,
And not by old gradation,[16] where each second
Stood heir to th' first. Now, sir, be judge yourself,
Whether I in any just term am affin'd[17]
To love the Moor.
ROD.   I would not follow then.   40
IAGO.   O, sir, content you;
I follow him to serve my turn upon him:
We cannot all be masters, nor all masters
Cannot be truly follow'd. You shall mark
Many a duteous and knee-crooking knave,

---

[4] *Nonsuits* rejects   [5] *arithmetician* a man whose military knowledge was merely theoretical, based on books of tactics   [6] *A...wife* Cassio does not seem to be married, but his counterpart in Shakespeare's source did have a wife   [7] *division* disposition of a battle line   [8] *theoric* theory   [9] *toged* wearing the toga   [10] *propose* discuss   [11] *Rhodes, Cyprus* islands in the Mediterranean south of Asia Minor, long subject to contention between the Venetians and the Turks   [12] *counter-caster* a sort of bookkeeper; contemptuous term   [13] *in good time* forsooth   [14] *God bless the mark* anciently, a pious interjection to avert evil omens   [15] *ancient* standardbearer, ensign   [16] *old gradation* seniority; Iago here expresses a characteristic prejudice of professional soldiers   [17] *affin'd* bound

That, doting on his own obsequious bondage,
Wears out his time, much like his master's ass,
For nought but provender, and when he's old, cashier'd:
Whip me such honest knaves. Others there are
Who, trimm'd in forms and visages of duty,   50
Keep yet their hearts attending on themselves,
And, throwing but shows of service on their lords,
Do well thrive by them and when they have lin'd their coats
Do themselves homage: these fellows have some soul;
And such a one do I profess myself. For, sir,
It is as sure as you are Roderigo,
Were I the Moor, I would not be Iago:[18]
In following him, I follow but myself;
Heaven is my judge, nor I for love and duty,
But seeming so, for my peculiar end: 60
For when my outward action doth demonstrate
The native act and figure of my heart
In compliment extern,[19] 'tis not long after
But I will wear my heart upon my sleeve
For daws to peck at: I am not what I am.
ROD.   What a full fortune does the thick-lips[20] owe,
  If he can carry 't thus!
IAGO.   Call up her father,
  Rouse him: make after him, poison his delight,
  Proclaim him in the streets; incense her kinsmen,
  And, though he in a fertile climate dwell,   70
  Plague him with flies: though that his joy be joy,
  Yet throw such changes of vexation on 't,
  As it may lose some colour.
ROD.   Here is her father's house; I'll call aloud.
IAGO.   Do, with like timorous[21] accent and dire yell
  As when, by night and negligence, the fire
  Is spied in populous cities.
ROD.   What, ho, Brabantio! Signior Brabantio, ho!
IAGO.   Awake! what, ho, Brabantio! thieves! thieves! thieves!
  Look to your house, your daughter and your bags!   80
  Thieves! thieves!

[BRABANTIO *appears above at a window.*]

BRA.   What is the reason of this terrible summons?
  What is the matter there?

---

[18] *Were…Iago* Were I in the position of the Moor, I should not feel as Iago feels [19] *compliment extern* outward civility [20] *thick-lips* Elizabethans often applied the term *Moor* to Negroes [21] *timorous* frightening

ROD.   Signior, is all your family within?

IAGO.   Are your doors lock'd?

BRA.   Why, wherefore ask you this?

IAGO.   'Zounds, sir, y' are robb'd; for shame, put on your gown;

   Your heart is burst, you have lost half your soul;

   Even now, now, very now, an old black ram

   Is tupping your white ewe. Arise, arise:

   Awake the snorting[22] citizens with the bell,   90

   Or else the devil will make a grandsire of you:

   Arise, I say.

BRA.   What, have you lost your wits?

ROD.   Most reverend signior, do you know my voice?

BRA.   Not I: what are you?

ROD.   My name is Roderigo.

BRA.   The worser welcome:

   I have charg'd thee not to haunt about my doors:

   In honest plainness thou has heard me say

   My daughter is not for thee; and now, in madness,

   Being full of supper and distemp'ring draughts,

   Upon malicious bravery,[23] doest thou come   100

   To start[24] my quiet.

ROD.   Sir, sir, sir,—

BRA.   But thou must needs be sure

   My spirit and my place have in them power

   To make this bitter to thee.

ROD.   Patience, good sir.

BRA.   What tell'st thou me of robbing? this is Venice;

   My house is not a grange.[25]

ROD.   Most grave Brabantio,

   In simple and pure soul I come to you.

IAGO.   'Zounds, sir, you are one of those that will not serve God, if the devil bid
   you. Because we come to do you service and you think we are ruffians, you'll
   have your daughter covered with a Barbary horse, you'll have your nephews[26]   110
   neigh to you; you'll have coursers for cousins and gennets[27] for germans.[28]

BRA.   What profane wretch art thou?

IAGO.   I am one, sir, that comes to tell you your daughter and the Moor are now
   making the beast with two backs.

BRA.   Thou art a villain.

IAGO.   You are—a senator.

BRA.   This thou shalt answer; I know thee, Roderigo.

ROD.   Sir, I will answer any thing. But, I beseech you,

   If 't be your pleasure and most wise consent,

---

[22] *snorting* snoring   [23] *bravery* defiance, bravado   [24] *start* disrupt   [25] *grange* isolated
farmhouse   [26] *nephews* grandsons   [27] *gennets* small Spanish horses   [28] *germans* near relatives

As partly I find it is, that your fair daughter,
At this odd-even[29] and dull watch o' th' night,   120
Transported, with no worse nor better guard
But with a knave of common hire, a gondolier,
To the gross clasps of a lascivious Moor,—
If this be known to you and your allowance,[30]
We then have done you bold and saucy wrongs;
But if you know not this, my manners tell me
We have your wrong rebuke. Do not believe
That, from[31] the sense of all civility,
I thus would play and trifle with your reverence:
Your daughter, if you have not given her leave,   130
I say again, hath made a gross revolt;
Tying her duty, beauty, wit and fortunes
In an extravagant[32] and wheeling[33] stranger
Of here and every where. Straight satisfy yourself:
If she be in her chamber or your house,
Let loose on me the justice of the state
For thus deluding you.
BRA.   Strike on the tinder,[34] ho!
Give me a taper! call up my people!
This accident[35] is not unlike my dream:
Belief of it oppresses me already.   140
Light, I say! light?   [*Exit above.*]
IAGO.   Farewell; for I must leave you:
If seems not meet, nor wholesome to my place,
To be produc'd—as, if I stay, I shall—
Against the Moor: for I do know the state,
However this may gall him with some check,[36]
Cannot with safety cast[37] him, for he's embark'd
With such loud reason to the Cyprus wars,
Which even now stand in act,[38] that, for their souls,
Another of his fathom[39] they have none,
To lead their business: in which regard,   150
Though I do hate him as I do hell-pains,
Yet, for necessity of present life,
I must show out a flag and sign of love,
Which is indeed but sign. That you shall surely find him,
Lead to the Sagittary[40] the raised search:
And there will I be with him. So, farewell.   [*Exit.*]

---

[29] *odd-even* between night and morning   [30] *allowance* permission   [31] *from* contrary to
[32] *extravagant* wandering   [33] *wheeling* vagabond   [34] *tinder* charred linen kept in a metal box,
and ignited by a spark from flint and steel   [35] *accident* occurrence, event   [36] *check* rebuke
[37] *cast* dismiss   [38] *stand in act* are going on   [39] *fathom* ability   [40] *Sagittary* probably an inn

[*Enter below* BRABANTIO *with* SERVANTS *and torches.*]

BRA. It is too true an evil; gone she is;
   And what's to come of my despised time
   Is nought but bitterness. Now, Roderigo,
   Where didst thou see her? O unhappy girl!   160
   With the Moor, say'st thou? Who would be a father!
   How didst thou know 'twas she? O, she deceives me
   Past thought! What said she to you? Get moe[41] tapers:
   Raise all my kindred. Are they married, think you?
ROD. Truly, I think they are.
BRA. O heaven! How got she out? O treason of the blood!
   Fathers, from hence trust not your daughters' minds
   By what you see them act. Is[42] there not charms
   By which the property[43] of youth and maidhood
   May be abus'd? Have you not read, Roderigo,   170
   Of some such thing?
ROD.   Yes, sir, I have indeed.
BRA. Call up my brother. O, would you[44] had had her!
   Some one way, some another. Do you know
   Where we may apprehend her and the Moor?
ROD. I think I can discover him, if you please
   To get good guard and go along with me.
BRA. Pray you, lead on. At every house I'll call;
   I may command at most. Get weapons, ho!
   And raise some special officers of night.[45]
   On, good Roderigo: I will deserve your pains. [*Exeunt.*]   180

SCENE II. *Another street.*

[*Enter* OTHELLO, IAGO, ATTENDANTS *with torches.*]

IAGO. Though in the trade of war I have slain men,
   Yet do I hold it very stuff o' th' conscience
   To do no contriv'd murder: I lack iniquity
   Sometime to do me service: nine or ten times
   I had thought t' have yerk'd[46] him here under the ribs.
OTH. 'Tis better as it is.
IAGO.   Nay, but he prated,
   And spoke such scurvy and provoking terms
   Against your honour
   That, with the little godliness I have,
   I did full hard forbear him. But, I pray you, sir,   10
   Are you fast married? Be assur'd of this,

---

[41] *moe* more [42] *Is* are [43] *property* special quality [44] *you* Roderigo [45] *officers of night* police
[46] *yerk'd* stabbed

That the magnifico[47] is much belov'd,
And hath in his effect[48] a voice potential[49]
As double[50] as the duke's: he will divorce you;
Or put upon you what restraint and grievance
The law, with all his might to enforce it on,
Will give him cable.

OTH.   Let him do his spite;
My services, which I have done the signiory[51]
Shall out-tongue his complaints. 'Tis yet to know—
Which, when I know that boasting is an honour,   20
I shall promulgate—I fetch my life and being
From men of royal siege,[52] and my demerits[53]
May speak unbonneted[54] to as proud a fortune
As this that I have reach'd: for know, Iago,
But that I love the gentle Desdemona,
I would not my unhoused free condition
Put into circumscription and confine
For the sea's worth. But, look! what lights come yond?

IAGO.   Those are the raised father and his friends:
You were best go in.

OTH.   Not I; I must be found: 30
My parts, my title and my perfect soul[55]
Shall manifest me rightly. Is it they?

IAGO.   By Janus, I think no.

> [*Enter* CASSIO *and certain* OFFICERS *with torches.*]

OTH.   The servants of the duke, and my lieutenant.
The goodness of the night upon you, friends!
What is the news?

CAS.   The duke does greet you, general,
And he requires your haste-post-haste appearance,
Even on the instant.

OTH.   What is the matter, think you?

CAS.   Something from Cyprus, as I may divine:
It is a business of some heat: the galleys   40
Have sent a dozen sequent[56] messengers
This very night at one another's heels,
And many of the consuls,[57] rais'd and met,
Are at the duke's already: you have been hotly call'd for;
When, being not at your lodging to be found,

---

[47] *magnifico* Venetian grandee (i.e., Brabantio)   [48] *effect* influence   [49] *potential* powerful
[50] *double* twice as influential as most men's   [51] *signiory* Venetian government   [52] *siege* rank
[53] *demerits* deserts   [54] *unbonneted* on equal terms   [55] *perfect soul* unflawed conscience
[56] *sequent* successive   [57] *consuls* senators

The senate hath sent about three several[58] quests
To search you out.
OTH.   'Tis well I am found by you.
I will but spend a word here in the house.
And go with you.   [*Exit.*]
CAS.   Ancient, what makes he here?
IAGO.   'Faith, he to-night hath boarded a land carack:[59]   50
If it prove lawful prize, he's made for ever.
CAS.   I do not understand.
IAGO.   He's married.
CAS.   To who?

[*Enter* OTHELLO.]

IAGO.   Marry, to—Come, captain, will you go?
OTH.   Have with you.
CAS.   Here comes another troop to seek for you.

[*Enter* BRABANTIO, RODERIGO, *with* OFFICERS *and torches.*]

IAGO.   It is Brabantio. General, be advis'd;
He comes to bad intent.
OTH.   Holla! stand there!
ROD.   Signior, it is the Moor.
BRA.   Down with him, thief!   [*They draw on both sides.*]
IAGO.   You, Roderigo! come, sir, I am for you.
OTH.   Keep up your bright swords, for the dew will rust them.
Good Signior, you shall more command with years   60
Than with your weapons.
BRA.   O thou foul thief, where hast thou stow'd my daughter?
Damn'd as thou art, thou has enchanted her;
For I'll refer me to all things of sense,[60]
If she in chains of magic were not bound,
Whether a maid so tender, fair and happy,
So opposite to marriage that she shunn'd
The wealthy curled darlings of our nation,
Would ever have, t' incur a general mock
Run from her guardage[61] to the sooty bosom   70
Of such a thing as thou, to fear, not to delight
Judge me the world, if 'tis not gross in sense[62]
That thou has practis'd on her with foul charms,
Abus'd her delicate youth with drugs or minerals[63]

---

[58] *several* separate   [59] *carack* large merchant ship   [60] *things of sense* commonsense understandings of the natural order   [61] *guardage* guardianship   [62] *gross in sense* easily discernible in apprehension or perception   [63] *minerals* medicine, poison

That weaken motion:[64] I'll have't disputed on;[65]
'Tis probable and palpable to thinking.
I therefore apprehend and do attach thee
For an abuser of the world,[66] a practiser
Of arts inhibited[67] and out of warrant.
Lay hold upon him: if he do resist,   80
Subdue him at his peril.
OTH.   Hold your hands,
Both you of my inclining,[68] and the rest:
Were it my cue to fight, I should have known it
Without a prompter. Wither will you that I go
To answer this charge?
BRA.   To prison, till fit time
Of law and course of direct session[69]
Call thee to answer.
OTH.   What if I do obey?
How may the duke be therewith satisfied,
Whose messengers are here about my side,
Upon some present business of the state   90
To bring me to him?
FIRST OFF.   'Tis true, most worthy signior;
The duke's in council, and your noble self,
I am sure, is sent for.
BRA.   How! the duke in council!
In this time of night! Bring him away:
Mine's not an idle cause: the duke himself,
Or any of my brothers of the state
Cannot but feel this wrong as 'twere their own;
For if such actions may have passage free,
Bond-slaves and pagans[70] shall our statesmen be.   [*Exeunt.*]

SCENE III.   *A council-chamber.*

[*Enter* DUKE, SENATORS *and* OFFICERS *set at a table, with lights and* ATTENDANTS.]

DUKE.   There is no composition in these news
That gives them credit.
FIRST SEN.   Indeed, they are disproportion'd;[71]
My letters say a hundred and seven galleys.
DUKE.   And mine, a hundred forty.
SEC. SEN.   And mine, two hundred:
But though they jump[72] not on a just account,—

---

[64] *motion* thought, reason   [65] *disputed on* argued in court by professional counsel   [66] *abuser of the world* corrupter of society   [67] *inhibited* prohibited   [68] *inclining* following, party   [69] *course of direct session* regular legal proceedings   [70] *Bond-slaves and pagans* contemptuous reference to Othello's past history   [71] *disproportion'd* inconsistent   [72] *jump* agree

As in these cases, where the aim[73] reports,
'Tis oft with difference—yet do they all confirm
A Turkish fleet, and bearing up to Cyprus.
DUKE.   Nay, it is possible enough to judgment:
   I do not so secure me[74] in the error,   10
   But the main article[75] I do approve
   In fearful sense.
SAILOR   [*Within*].   What, ho! what, ho! what, ho!
FIRST OFF.   A messenger from the galleys.

[Enter SAILOR.]

DUKE.   Now, what's the business?
SAIL.   The Turkish preparation makes for Rhodes;
   So was I bid report here to the state
   By Signior Angelo.
DUKE.   How say you by this change?
FIRST SEN.   This cannot be,
   By no assay[76] of reason: 'tis a pageant,
   To keep us in false gaze. When we consider
   Th' importancy of Cyprus to the Turk,   20
   And let ourselves again but understand,
   That as it more concerns the Turk than Rhodes,
   So may he with more facile question[77] bear it,
   For that it stands not in such warlike brace,[78]
   But altogether lacks th' abilities
   That Rhodes is dress'd in: if we make thought of this,
   We must not think the Turk is so unskilful
   To leave that latest which concerns him first,
   Neglecting an attempt of ease and gain,
   To wake and wage a danger profitless.   30
DUKE.   Nay, in all confidence, he's not for Rhodes.
FIRST OFF.   Here is more news.

[Enter a MESSENGER.]

MESS.   The Ottomites, reverend and gracious,
   Steering with due course toward the isle of Rhodes,
   Have there injointed them with an after fleet.
FIRST SEN.   Ay, so I thought. How many, as you guess?
MESS.   Of thirty sail: and now they do re-stem[79]
   Their backward course, bearing with frank appearance
   Their purposes toward Cyprus. Signior Montano,

---

[73] *aim* conjecture   [74] *secure me* feel myself secure   [75] *main article* i.e., that the Turkish fleet is threatening   [76] *assay* test   [77] *more facile question* greater facility of effort   [78] *brace* state of defense   [79] *re-stem* steer again

Your trusty and most valiant servitor, 40
With his free duty recommends you thus,
And prays you to believe him.
DUKE.   'Tis certain, then, for Cyprus.
Marcus Luccicos, is not he in town?
FIRST SEN.   He's now in Florence.
DUKE.   Write from us to him; post-posthaste dispatch.
FIRST SEN.   Here comes Brabantio and the valiant Moor.

[*Enter* BRABANTIO, OTHELLO, CASSIO, IAGO, RODERIGO, *and* OFFICERS.]

DUKE.   Valiant, Othello, we must straight employ you
Against the general enemy Ottoman.
[*To* BRABANTIO]   I did not see you; welcome, gentle signior; 50
We lack'd your counsel and your help to-night.
BRA.   So did I yours. Good your grace, pardon me;
Neither my place nor aught I heard of business
Hath rais'd me from my bed, nor does the general care
Take hold on me, for my particular grief
Is of so flood-gate and o'erbearing nature
That it engluts[80] and swallows other sorrows
And it is still itself.
DUKE.   Why, what's the matter?
BRA.   My daughter! O, my daughter!
DUKE *and* SEN.   Dead?
BRA.   Ay, to me;
She is abus'd, stol'n from me, and corrupted 60
By spells and medicines bought of mountebanks;
For nature so preposterously to err,
Being not deficient, blind, or lame of sense,
Sans witchcraft could not.
DUKE.   Whoe'er he be that in this foul proceeding
Hath thus beguil'd your daughter of herself
And you of her, the bloody book of law
You shall yourself read in the bitter letter
After your own sense, yea, though our proper son
Stood in your action.[81]
BRA.   Humbly I thank your grace. 70
Here is the man, this Moor, whom now, it seems,
Your special mandate for the state-affairs
Hath hither brought.
DUKE *and* SEN.   We are very sorry for 't.
DUKE   [*To* OTHELLO].   What, in your own part, can you say to this?
BRA.   Nothing, but this is so.

---

[80] *engluts* engulfs   [81] *Stood…action* was under your accusation

OTH.   Most potent, grave, and reverend signiors,
My very noble and approv'd good masters,
That I have ta'en away this old man's daughter,
It is most true; true, I have married her:
The very head and front of my offending   80
Hath this extent, no more. Rude am I in my speech,
And little bless'd with the soft phrase of peace;
For since these arms of mine had seven years' pith,[82]
Till now some nine moons wasted, they have us'd
Their dearest action in the tented field,
And little of this great world can I speak,
More than pertains to feats of broil and battle,
And therefore little shall I grace my cause
In speaking for myself. Yet, by your gracious patience,[83]
I will a round unvarnish'd tale deliver   90
Of my whole course of love; what drugs, what charms,
What conjuration and what mighty magic,
For such proceeding I am charg'd withal,
I won his daughter.
BRA.   A maiden never bold;
Of spirit so still and quiet, that her motion
Blush'd at herself;[84] and she, in spite of nature,
Of years, of country, credit, every thing,
To fall in love with what she fear'd to look on!
It is a judgement maim'd and most imperfect
That will confess perfection so could err   100
Against all rules of nature, and must be driven
To find our practices of cunning hell,
Why this should be. I therefore vouch[85] again
That with some mixtures pow'rful o'er the blood,
Or with some dram conjur'd to this effect,
He wrought upon her.
DUKE.   To vouch this, is no proof,
Without more wider and more overt test
Than these thin habits and poor likelihoods
Of modern seeming do prefer against him.
FIRST SEN.   But, Othello, speak: 110
Did you by indirect and forced courses
Subdue and poison this young maid's affections?
Or came it by request and such fair question
As soul to soul affordeth?

---

[82] *pith* strength, vigor   [83] *patience* suffering, permission   [84] *motion...herself* inward impulses blushed at themselves   [85] *vouch* assert

OTH.   I do beseech you,
   Send for the lady to the Sagittary,
   And let her speak of me before her father:
   If you do find me foul in her report,
   The trust, the office I do hold of you,
   Not only take away, but let your sentence
   Even fall upon my life.
DUKE.   Fetch Desdemona hither.   120
OTH.   Ancient, conduct them; you best know the place.   [*Exeunt* IAGO *and*
   ATTENDANTS.]
   And, till she come, as truly as to heaven
   I do confess the vices of my blood,
   So justly to your grave ear I'll present
   How I did thrive in this fair lady's love,
   And she in mine.
DUKE.   Say it, Othello.
OTH.   Her father lov'd me; oft invited me;
   Still question'd me the story of my life,
   From year to year, the battles, sieges, fortunes,   130
   That I have pass'd.
   I ran it through, even from my boyish days,
   To th' very moment that he bade me tell it;
   Wherein I spake of most disastrous chances,
   Of moving accidents by flood and field,
   Of hair-breadth scapes i' th' imminent[86] deadly breach,
   Of being taken by the insolent foe
   And sold to slavery, of my redemption thence
   And portance[87] in my travels' history:
   Wherein of antres[88] vast and deserts idle,[89]   140
   Rough quarries, rocks and hills whose heads touch heaven,
   It was my hint[90] to speak,—such was the process;
   And of the Cannibals that each other eat,[91]
   The Anthropophagi[92] and men whose heads
   Do grow beneath their shoulders. This to hear
   Would Desdemona seriously incline:
   But still the house-affairs would draw her thence:
   Which ever as she could with haste dispatch,
   She 'ld come again, and with a greedy ear
   Devour up my discourse: which I observing,   150
   Took once a pliant hour, and found good means
   To draw from her a prayer of earnest heart

---

[86] *imminent* i.e., impending parts when a gap has been made in a fortification
[87] *portance* conduct   [88] *antres* caverns   [89] *idle* barren, unprofitable   [90] *hint* occasion   [91] *eat* ate
[92] *Anthropophagi* man-eaters

That I would all my pilgrimage dilate,[93]
Whereof by parcels she had something heard,
But not intentively;[94] I did consent,
And often did beguile her of her tears,
When I did speak some distressful stroke
That my youth suffer'd. My story being done,
She gave me for my pains a world of sighs:
She swore, in faith, 'twas strange, 'twas passing strange,   160
'Twas pitiful, 'twas wondrous pitiful:
She wish'd she had not heard it, yet she wish'd
That heaven had made her such a man: she thank'd me,
And bade me, if I had a friend that lov'd her,
I should but teach him how to tell my story,
And that would woo her. Upon this hint I spake:
She lov'd me for the dangers I had pass'd,
And I lov'd her that she did pity them.
This only is the witchcraft I have us'd:
Here comes the lady; let her witness it.   170

[*Enter* DESDEMONA, IAGO *and* ATTENDANTS.]

DUKE.   I think this tale would win my daughter too.
    Good Brabantio,
    Take up this mangled matter at the best:
    Men do their broken weapons rather use
    Than their bare hands.
BRA.   I pray you, hear her speak:
    If she confess that she was half the wooer,
    Destruction on my head, if my bad blame
    Light on the man! Come hither, gentle mistress:
    Do you perceive in all this noble company
    Where most you owe obedience?
DES.   My noble father,   180
    I do perceive here a divided duty:[95]
    To you I am bound for life and education;
    My life and education both do learn me
    How to respect you; you are the lord of duty;
    I am hitherto your daughter: but here's my husband,
    And so much duty as my mother show'd
    To you, preferring you before her father,
    So much I challenge that I may profess
    Due to the Moor my lord.

---

[93] *dilate* relate in detail   [94] *intentively* with full attention   [95] *divided duty* Desdemona recognizes that she still owes a duty to her father even after marriage

BRA.   God be with you! I have done.
   Please it your grace, on to[96] the state-affairs: 190
   I had rather to adopt a child than get[97] it.
   Come hither, Moor:
   I here do give thee that with all my heart
   Which, but thou hast already, with all my heart
   I would keep from thee. For your sake,[98] jewel,
   I am glad at soul I have no other child;
   For thy escape would teach me tyranny,
   To hang clogs on them. I have done, my lord.
DUKE.   Let me speak like yourself,[99] and lay a sentence,[100]
   Which, as a grise[101] or step, may help these lovers   200
   Into your favour.
   When remedies are past, the griefs are ended
   By seeing the worst, which late on hopes depended.
   To mourn a mischief that is past and gone
   Is the next[102] way to draw new mischief on.
   Which cannot be preserv'd when fortune takes,
   Patience her injury a mock'ry makes.
   The robb'd that smiles steals something from the thief;
   He robs himself that spends a bootless grief.
BRA.   So let the Turk of Cyprus us beguile;   210
   We lost it now, so long as we can smile.
   He bears the sentence well that nothing bears
   But the free comfort[103] which from thence he hears,
   But he bears both the sentence and the sorrow
   That, to pay grief, must of poor patience borrow.
   These sentences, to sugar, or to gall,
   Being strong on both sides, are equivocal:
   But words are words; I never yet did hear
   That the bruis'd heart was pierced through the ear.
   I humbly beseech you, proceed to th' affairs of state.   220
DUKE.   The Turk with a most mighty preparation makes for Cyprus. Othello, the
   fortitude[104] of the place is best known to you; and though we have there a sub-
   stitute of most allowed[105] sufficiency, yet opinion, a sovereign mistress of effects,
   throws a more safer voice on you:[106] you must therefore be content to slubber[107]
   the gloss of your new fortunes with this more stubborn and boistrous expedition.
OTH.   The tyrant custom, most grave senators,
   Hath made the flinty and steel couch of war

---

[96] *on to* i.e., proceed with   [97] *get* beget   [98] *For your sake* on your account   [99] *like yourself* i.e., as you
would, in your proper temper   [100] *sentence* maxim   [101] *grise* step   [102] *next* nearest   [103] *comfort* i.e., the
consolation that it may be borne with patience   [104] *fortitude* strength   [105] *allowed* acknowledged
[106] *opinion…on you* public opinion, an important determiner of affairs, chooses you as the best man
[107] *slubber* soil, sully

My thrice-driven[108] bed of down: I do agnize[109]
A natural and prompt alacrity 230
I find in hardness[110] and do undertake
These present wars against the Ottomites.
Most humbly therefore bending to your state,
I crave fit disposition for my wife,
Due reference of place and exhibition,[111]
With such accommodation and besort[112]
As levels with her breeding.
DUKE.   If you please,
  Be 't at her father's.
BRA.   I'll not have it so.
OTH. Nor I.
DES.   Nor I; I would not there reside,
  To put my father in impatient thoughts 240
  By being in his eye. Most gracious duke,
  To my unfolding lend your prosperous[113] ear
  And let me find a charter[114] in your voice,
  T' assist my simpleness.[115]
DUKE. What would you, Desdemona?
DES. That I did love the Moor to live with him,
  My downright violence and storm of fortunes
  May trumpet to the world: my heart's subdu'd
  Even to the very quality of my lord:
  I saw Othello's visage in his mind, 250
  And to his honours and his valiant parts
  Did I my soul and fortunes consecrate.
  So that, dear lords, if I be left behind,
  A moth of peace, and he go to the war,
  The rites for why I love him are bereft me,
  And I a heavy interim shall support
  By his dear absence. Let me go with him.
OTH. Let her have your voices.
  Vouch with me, heaven, I therefore beg it not,
  To please the palate of my appetite, 260
  Nor to comply with heat—the young affects[116]
  In me defunct—and proper satisfaction,
  But to be free and bounteous to her mind:
  And heaven defend your good souls, that you think
  I will your serious and great business scant
  When she is with me: no, when light-wing'd toys

---

[108] *thrive-driven* thrice sifted   [109] *agnize* know in myself   [110] *hardness* hardship
[111] *exhibition* allowance   [112] *besort* suitable company   [113] *prosperous* propitious
[114] *charter* privilege   [115] *simpleness* simplicity   [116] *affects* inclinations, desires

Of feather'd Cupid seel[117] with wanton dullness
My speculative and offic'd instruments,[118]
That[119] my disports[120] corrupt and taint[121] my business,
Let housewives make a skillet of my helm,   270
And all indign[122] and base adversities
Make head against my estimation![123]
DUKE.   Be it as you shall privately determine,
   Either for her stay or going: th' affair cries haste,
   And speed must answer for it.
FIRST SEN.   You must away to-night.
OTH.   With all my heart.
DUKE.   At nine i' th' morning here we'll meet again.
   Othello, leave some officer behind,
   And he shall our commission bring to you;
   With such things else of quality and respect   280
   As doth import[124] you.
OTH.   So please your grace, my ancient;
   A man he is of honesty and trust:
   To his conveyance I assign my wife,
   With what else needful your good grace shall think
   To be sent after me.
DUKE.   Let it be so.
   Good night to every one.   [*To* BRA.]   And, noble signior,
   If virtue no delighted[125] beauty lack,
   Your son-in-law is far more fair than black.
FIRST SEN.   Adieu, brave Moor; use Desdemona well.
BRA.   Look to her, Moor, if thou hast eyes to see;
   She has deceiv'd her father, and may thee.   [*Exeunt* DUKE, SENATORS,   290
      OFFICERS, &*c.*]
OTH.   My life upon her faith! Honest Iago,[126]
   My Desdemona must I leave to thee:
   I prithee, let thy wife attend on her;
   And bring them after in the best advantage.
   Come, Desdemona; I have but an hour
   Of love, of worldly matters and direction,
   To spend with thee: we must obey the time.   [*Exit with* DESDEMONA.]
ROD.   Iago—
IAGO.   What say'st thou, noble heart?   300
ROD.   What will I do, thinkest thou?

---

[117] *seel* in falconry, to make blind by sewing up the eyes of the hawk in training
[118] *speculative...instruments* ability to see and reason clearly   [119] *That* so that
[120] *disports* pastimes   [121] *taint* impair   [122] *indign* unworthy, shameful
[123] *estimation* reputation   [124] *import* concern   [125] *delighted* delightful   [126] *Honest Iago* an evidence of
Iago's carefully built reputation

IAGO.   Why, go to bed, and sleep.

ROD.   I will incontinently[127] drown myself.

IAGO.   If thou dost, I shall never love thee after. Why, thou silly gentleman!

ROD.   It is silliness to live when to live is torment; and then have we a prescription
to die when death is our physician.

IAGO.   O villanous! I have looked upon the world for four times seven years; and
since I could distinguish betwixt a benefit and an injury, I never found man
that knew how to love himself. Ere I would say, I would drown myself for the
love of a guinea-hen, I would change my humanity with a baboon.   310

ROD.   What should I do? I confess it is my shame to be so fond; but it is not in my
virtue[128] to amend it.

IAGO.   Virtue! a fig! 'tis in ourselves that we are thus or thus. Our bodies are our
gardens, to the which our wills are gardeners; so that if we will plant nettles,
or sow lettuce, set hyssop[129] and weed up thyme, supply it with one gender[130]
of herbs, or distract it with many, either to have it sterile with idleness,[131] or
manured with industry, why, the power and corrigible authority[132] of this lies
in our wills. If the balance of our lives had not one scale of reason to poise
another of sensuality, the blood and baseness of our natures would conduct us
to most preposterous conclusions:[133] but we have reason to cool our raging   320
motions,[134] our carnal stings, our unbitted[135] lusts, whereof I take this that
you call love to be a sect[136] or scion.

ROD.   It cannot be.

IAGO.   It is merely a lust of the blood and a permission of the will. Come, be a
man. Drown thyself! drown cats and blind puppies. I have professed me thy
friend and I confess me knit to thy deserving with cables of perdurable[137]
toughness; I could never better stead thee than now. Put money in thy purse;
follow thou the wars; defeat the favour[138] with an usurped beard; I say, put
money in thy purse. It cannot be that Desdemona should long continue her
love to the Moor,—put money in thy purse,—nor he his to her: it was a violent   330
commencement in her, and thou shalt see an answerable sequestration:[139]—
put but money in thy purse. These Moors are changeable in their wills:—fill
thy purse with money:—the food that to him now is as luscious as locusts,[140]
shall be to him shortly as bitter as coloquintida.[141] She must change for youth:
when she is sated with his body, she will find the error of her choice: she must
have change, she must: therefore put money in thy purse. If thou wilt needs
damn thyself, do it a more delicate way than drowning. Make all the money

---

[127] *incontinently* immediately   [128] *virtue* strength   [129] *hyssop* an herb of the mint family   [130] *gender* kind
[131] *idleness* want of cultivation   [132] *corrigible authority* the power to correct   [133] *reason…motions* Iago
understands the warfare between reason and sensuality, but his ethics are totally inverted; reason works
in him not good, as it should according to natural law, but evil, which he has chosen for his
good   [134] *motions* appetites   [135] *unbitted* uncontrolled   [136] *sect* cutting   [137] *perdurable* very
durable   [138] *defeat thy favour* disguise and disfigure thy face   [139] *answerable sequestration* a separation
corresponding   [140] *locusts* of doubtful meaning; defined as fruit of the carob tree, as honeysuckle, and
as lollipops or sugar sticks   [141] *coloquintida* colocynth, or bitter apple, a purgative

thou canst: if sanctimony and a frail vow betwixt an erring[142] barbarian and a super-subtle Venetian be too hard for my wits and all the tribe of hell, thou shalt enjoy her; therefore make money. A pox of drowning thyself! it is clean out of the way: seek thou rather to be hanged in compassing thy joy than to be drowned and go without her. 340

ROD.   Wilt thou be fast to my hopes, if I depend on the issue?

IAGO.   Thou art sure of me:—go, make money:—I have told thee often, and I re-tell thee again and again, I hate the Moor: my cause is hearted;[143] thine hath no less reason. Let us be conjunctive[144] in our revenge against him; if thou canst cuckold him, thou dost thyself a pleasure, me a sport. There are many events in the womb of time which will be delivered. Traverse![145] go, provide thy money. We shall have more of this to-morrow. Adieu.

ROD.   Where shall we meet i' the morning? 350

IAGO.   At my lodging.

ROD.   I'll be with thee betimes.

IAGO.   Go to; farewell. Do you hear, Roderigo?

ROD.   What say you?

IAGO.   No more of drowning, do you hear?

ROD.   I am changed: I'll go sell all my land.   [*Exit*]

IAGO.   Thus do I ever make my fool my purse;
　For I mine own gain'd knowledge should profane,
　If I would time expend with such a snipe,[146]
　But for my sport and profit. I hate the Moor; 360
　And it is thought abroad, that 'twixt my sheets
　H' as done my office: I know not if 't be true;
　But I, for mere suspicion in that kind,
　Will do as if for surety. He holds me well;
　The better shall my purpose work on him.
　Cassio's a proper man: let me see now:
　To get his place and to plume up[147] my will
　In double knavery—How, how?—Let's see:—
　After some time, to abuse Othello's ears
　That he[148] is too familiar with his wife. 370
　He hath a person and a smooth dispose[149]
　To be suspected, fram'd to make women false.
　The Moor is of a free[150] and open nature,
　That thinks men honest that but seem to be so,
　And will as tenderly be led by th' nose
　As asses are.
　I have 't. It is engend'red. Hell and night
　Must bring this monstrous birth to the world's light.   [*Exit.*]

---

[142] *erring* wandering　[143] *hearted* fixed in the heart　[144] *conjunctive* united　[145] *Traverse* go (military term)　[146] *snipe* gull, fool　[147] *plume up* glorify, gratify　[148] *he* i.e., Cassio　[149] *dispose* external manner　[150] *free* frank

ACT II

SCENE I.   *A Sea-port in Cyprus. An open place near the quay.*

[*Enter* MONTANO *and two* GENTLEMEN.]

MON.   What from the cape can you discern at sea?
FIRST GENT.   Nothing at all: it is a high-wrought flood;
    I cannot, 'twixt the heaven and the main,
    Descry a sail.
MON.   Methinks the wind hath spoke aloud at land;
    A fuller blast ne'er shook our battlements:
    If it hath ruffian'd[1] so upon the sea,
    What ribs of oak, what mountains melt on them,
    Can hold the mortise?[2] What shall we hear of this?
SEC. GENT.   A segregation[3] of the Turkish fleet: 10
    For do but stand upon the foaming shore,
    The chidden billow seems to pelt the clouds:
    The wind-shak'd surge, with high and monstrous mane,
    Seems to cast water on the burning bear,[4]
    And quench the guards[5] of th' ever-fixed pole:
    I never did like molestation view
    On the enchafed[6] flood.
MON.   If that the Turkish fleet
    Be not enshelter'd and embay'd, they are drown'd;
    It is impossible they bear it out.

[*Enter a third* GENTLEMAN.]

THIRD GENT.   News, lads! our wars are done   20
    The desperate tempest hath so bang'd the Turks,
    That their designment[7] halts: a noble ship of Venice
    Hath seen a grievous wrack and sufferance[8]
    On most part of their fleet.
MON.   How! is this true?
THIRD GENT.   The ship is here put in,
    A Veronesa; Michael Cassio,
    Lieutenant to the warlike Moor Othello,
    Is come on shore: the Moor himself at sea,
    And is in full commission here for Cyprus.
MON.   I am glad on 't; 'tis a worthy governor.   30
THIRD GENT.   But this same Cassio, though he speak of comfort
    Touching the Turkish loss, yet he looks sadly,

ACT II   [1]*ruffian'd* raged   [2]*mortise* the socket hollowed out in fitting timbers   [3]*segregation* dispersion   [4]*bear* a constellation   [5]*quench the guards* overwhelm the stars near the polestar   [6]*enchafed* angry   [7]*designment* enterprise   [8]*sufferance* disaster

And prays the Moor be safe; for they were parted
With foul and violent tempest.
MON.   Pray heavens he be;
  For I have serv'd him, and the man commands
  Like a full[9] soldier. Let's to the seaside, ho!
  As well to see the vessel that's come in
  As to throw out our eyes for brave Othello,
  Even till we make the main and th' aerial blue
  And indistinct regard.[10]
THIRD GENT.   Come, let's do so;   40
  For every minute is expectancy
  Of more arrivance.[11]

[*Enter* CASSIO.]

CAS. Thanks, you the valiant of this warlike isle,
  That so approve the Moor! O, let the heavens
  Give him defence against the elements,
  For I have lost him on a dangerous sea.
MON. Is he well shipp'd?
CAS. His bark is stoutly timber'd, and his pilot
  Of very expert and approv'd allowance;[12]
  Therefore my hopes, not surfeited to death,   50
  Stand in bold cure. [*A cry within.*] "A sail, a sail, a sail!"

[*Enter a fourth* GENTLEMAN.]

CAS. What noise?
FOURTH GENT. The town is empty; on the brow o' th' sea
  Stand ranks of people, and they cry "A sail!"
CAS. My hopes do shape him for the governor. [*Guns heard.*]
SEC. GENT. They do discharge their shot of courtesy:
  Our friends at least.
CAS.   I pray you, sir, go forth,
  And give us truth who 'tis that is arriv'd.
SEC. GENT. I shall. [*Exit.*]
MON. But, good lieutenant, is your general wiv'd?   60
CAS. Most fortunately: he hath achiev'd a maid
  That paragons[13] description and wild fame;
  One that excels the quirks[14] of blazoning[15] pens,
  And in th' essential vesture of creation[16]
  Does tire the ingener.[17]

---

[9] *full* perfect [10] *make...regard* cause the blue of the sea and the air to grow indistinguishable in
our view [11] *arrivance* arrival [12] *allowance* reputation [13] *paragons* surpasses [14] *quirks* witty conceits
[15] *blazoning* setting forth honorably in words [16] *vesture of creation* the real qualities with which
creation has invested her [17] *ingener* inventor, praiser

[*Enter second* GENTLEMAN.]

How now! who has put in?

SEC. GENT.   'Tis one Iago, ancient to the general.

CAS.   Has had most favourable and happy speed:
Tempests themselves, high seas and howling winds,
The gutter'd[18] rocks and congregated sands,—
Traitors ensteep'd[19] to clog the guiltless keel,—   70
As having sense of beauty, do omit
Their mortal[20] natures, letting go safely by
The divine Desdemona.

MON.   What is she?

CAS.   She that I spake of, our great captain's captain,
Left in the conduct of the bold Iago,
Whose footing here anticipates our thoughts
A se'nnight's[21] speed. Great Jove, Othello guard,
And swell his sail with thine own powr'ful breath,
That he may bless this bay with his tall ship,
Make love's quick pants in Desdemona's arms,   80
Give renew'd fire to our extinced spirits,
And bring all Cyprus comfort!

[*Enter* DESDEMONA, IAGO, RODERIGO, *and* EMILIA *with* ATTENDANTS.]

O, behold!
The riches of the ship is come on shore!
You men of Cyprus, let her have your knees.
Hail to thee, lady! and the grace of heaven,
Before, behind thee and on every hand,
Enwheel thou round!

DES.   I thank you, valiant Cassio.
What tidings can you tell me of my lord?

CAS.   He is not yet arriv'd: nor know I aught
But that he's well and will be shortly here.   90

DES.   O, but I fear—How lost you company?

CAS.   The great contention of the sea and skies
Parted our fellowship—But, hark! a sail.

[*Within*]   "A sail, a sail!"   [*Guns heard.*]

SEC. GENT.   They give their greeting to the citadel:
This likewise is a friend.

CAS.   See for the news.   [*Exit* GENTLEMAN.]
Good ancient, you are welcome.   [*To* EMILIA]   Welcome, mistress:
Let is not gall your patience, good Iago,

---

[18]*gutter'd* jagged, trenched   [19]*ensteep'd* lying under water   [20]*mortal* deadly   [21]*se'nnight's* week's

That I extend my manners; 'tis my breeding
That gives me this bold show of courtesy. [*Kissing her.*]   100

IAGO.   Sir, would she give you so much of her lips
  As of her tongue she oft bestows on me,
  You would have enough.

DES.   Alas, she has no speech.

IAGO.   In faith, too much;
  I find it still, when I have list to sleep:
  Marry, before your ladyship, I grant,
  She puts her tongue a little in her heart,
  And chides with thinking.

EMIL.   You have little cause to say so.

IAGO.   Come on, come on; you are pictures out of doors,   110
  Bells in your parlours, wild-cats in your kitchens,
  Saints in your injuries, devils being offended,
  Players in your housewifery, and housewives[22] in your beds.

DES.   O, fie upon thee, slanderer!

IAGO.   Nay, it is true, or else I am a Turk:
  You rise to play and go to bed to work.

EMIL.   You shall not write my praise.

IAGO.   No, let me not.

DES.   What wouldst thou write of me, if thou shouldst praise me?

IAGO.   O gentle lady, do not put me to 't;
  For I am nothing, if not critical.[23]   120

DES.   Come on, assay. There's one gone to the harbour?

IAGO.   Ay, madam.

DES.   I am not merry; but I do beguile
  The thing I am, by seeming otherwise.
  Come, how wouldst thou praise me?

IAGO.   I am about it; but indeed my invention
  Comes from my pate as birdlime[24] does from frieze;[25]
  It plucks out brains and all: but my Muse labours,
  And thus she is deliver'd.
  If she be fair and wise, fairness and wit,   130
  The one's for use, the other useth it.

DES.   Well praised! How if she be black and witty?

IAGO.   If she be black, and thereto have a wit,
  She'll find a white[26] that shall her blackness fit.

DES.   Worse and worse.

EMIL.   How if fair and foolish?

IAGO.   She never yet was foolish that was fair;
  For even her folly help'd her to an heir.

---

[22] *housewives* hussies   [23] *critical* censorious   [24] *birdlime* sticky substance smeared on twigs to catch small birds   [25] *frieze* coarse woolen cloth   [26] *white* a fair person, with a wordplay on *wight*

DES. These are old fond[27] paradoxes to make fools laugh i' the alehouse.
    What miserable praise hast thou for her that's foul and foolish? 140
IAGO. There's none so foul and foolish thereunto,
    But does foul pranks which fair and wise ones do.
DES. O heavy ignorance! thou praisest the worst best. But what praise couldst
    thou bestow on a deserving woman indeed, one that, in the authority of her
    merit, did justly put on the vouch[28] of her malice itself?
IAGO. She that was ever fair and never proud,
    Had tongue at will and yet was never loud,
    Never lack'd gold and yet went never gay,
    Fled from her wish and yet said "Now I may,"
    She that being ang'rd, her revenge being nigh, 150
    Bade her wrong stay and her displeasure fly,
    She that in wisdom never was so frail
    To change the cod's head for the salmon's tail,[29]
    She that could think and ne'er disclose her mind,
    See suitors following and not look behind,
    She was a wight, if ever such wight were,—
DES. To do what?
IAGO. To suckle fools and chronicle small beer.[30]
DES. O most lame and impotent conclusion! Do not learn of him, Emilia, though
    he be thy husband. How say you, Cassio? is he not a most profane and liberal[31] 160
    counsellor?
CAS. He speaks home,[32] madam: you may relish him more in the soldier than in
    the scholar.
IAGO. [*Aside*]. He takes her by the palm: ay, well said, whisper: with as little a
    web as this will I ensnare as great a fly as Cassio. Ay, smile upon her, do; I will
    gyve[33] thee in thine own courtship.[34] You say true; 'tis so, indeed: if such
    tricks as these strip you out of your lieutenantry, it had been better you had
    not kissed your three fingers[35] so oft, which now again you are most apt to
    play the sir[36] in. Very good; well kissed! an excellent courtesy! 'tis so, indeed.
    Yet again your fingers to your lips? would they were clyster-pipes[37] for your 170
    sake. [*Trumpet within.*] The Moor! I know his trumpet.
CAS. 'Tis truly so.
DES. Let's meet him and receive him.
CAS. Lo, where he comes!

              [*Enter* OTHELLO *and* ATTENDANTS.]

OTH. O my fair warrior!
DES.   My dear Othello!

---

[27] *fond* foolish   [28] *put on the vouch* compel the approval   [29] *To change...tail* to exchange a delicacy for mere refuse   [30] *chronicle small beer* keep petty household accounts   [31] *liberal* licentious [32] *speaks home* i.e., without reserve   [33] *gyve* fetter, shackle   [34] *courship* courtesy   [35] *kissed your three fingers* he kisses his own hand as a token of reverence   [36] *the sir* i.e., the fine gentleman [37] *clyster-pipes* tubes used for enemas

OTH.   It gives me wonder great as my content
      To see you here before me. O my soul's joy!
      If after every tempest come such calms,
      May the winds blow till they have waken'd death!
      And let the labouring bark climb hills of seas   180
      Olympus-high and duck again as low
      As hell 's from heaven! If it were now to die,
      'Twere now to be most happy; for, I fear,
      My soul hath her content so absolute
      That not another comfort like to this
      Succeeds in unknown fate.
DES.   The heavens forbid
      But that our loves and comforts should increase,
      Even as our days grow!
OTH.   Amen to that, sweet powers!
      I cannot speak enough of this content;
      It stops me here; it is too much of joy;   190
      And this, and this, the greatest discords be   [*Kissing her*]
      That e'er our hearts shall make!
IAGO   [*Aside*].   O, you are well tun'd now!
      But I'll set down the pegs[38] that make this music,
      As honest as I am.
OTH.   Come, let us to the castle.
      News, friends, our wars are done, the Turks are drowned.
      How does my old acquaintance of this isle?
      Honey, you shall be well desir'd in Cyprus;
      I have found greatest love amongst them. O my sweet,
      I prattle out of fashion, and I dote
      In mine own comforts. I prithee, good Iago,   200
      Go to the bay and disembark my coffers:
      Bring thou the master to the citadel;
      He is a good one, and his worthiness
      Does challenge much respect. Come, Desdemona,
      Once more, well met at Cyprus.   [*Exeunt* OTHELLO *and* DESDEMONA *and all but*
         IAGO *and* RODERIGO.]
IAGO [*to an* ATTENDANT].   Do thou meet me presently at the harbour. [*To*
      ROD.]   Come hither. If thou be'st valiant,—as, they say, base men being in
      love have then a nobility in their natures more than is native to them,—list me.
      The lieutenant tonight watches on the court of guard.[39]—First, I must tell
      thee this—Desdemona is directly in love with him.   210
ROD.   With him! why 'tis not possible.

---

[38] *set down the pegs* lower the pitch of the strings, i.e., disturb the harmony   [39] *court of guard* guardhouse

IAGO.   Lay thy finger thus, and let thy soul be instructed. Mark me with what violence she first loved the Moor, but for bragging and telling her fantastical lies: and will she love him still for prating? let not thy discreet heart think it. Her eye must be fed; and what delight shall she have to look on the devil? When the blood is made dull with the act of sport, there should be, again to inflame it and to give satiety a fresh appetite, loveliness in favour, sympathy in years, manners and beauties; all which the Moor is defective in: now, for want of these required conveniences, her delicate tenderness will find itself abused, begin to heave the gorge, disrelish and abhor the Moor; very nature will instruct her in it and compel her to some second choice. Now, sir, this 220 granted,—as it is a most pregnant and unforced position—who stands so eminent in the degree of this fortune as Cassio does? a knave very voluble; no further conscionable[40] than in putting on the mere form of civil and humane seeming, for the better compassing of his salt[41] and most hidden loose affection? why, none; why, none: a slipper[42] and subtle knave, a finder of occasions, that has an eye can stamp and counterfeit advantages, though true advantage never present itself; a devilish knave. Besides, the knave is handsome, young, and hath all those requisites in him that folly and green minds look after: a pes- 230 tilent complete knave; and the woman hath found him already.

ROD.   I cannot believe that in her; she's full of most blessed condition.

IAGO.   Blessed fig's-end! the wine she drinks is made of grapes: if she had been blessed, she would never have loved the Moor. Blessed pudding! Didst thou not see her paddle with the palm of his hand? didst not mark that?

ROD.   Yes, that I did; but that was but courtesy.

IAGO.   Lechery, by this hand; an index and obscure prologue to the history of lust and foul thoughts. They met so near with their lips that their breaths embraced together. Villainous thoughts, Roderigo! when these mutualities so marshall the way, hard at hand comes the master and main exercise, the incorporate conclusion. Pish! But, sir, be you ruled by me: I have brought you from Venice. Watch you to-night; for the command, I'll lay't upon you. Cassio 240 knows you not. I'll not be far from you: do you find some occasion to anger Cassio, either by speaking too loud, or tainting[43] his discipline; or from what other course you please, which the time shall more favourably minister.

ROD.   Well.

IAGO.   Sir, he is rash and very sudden in choler, and haply may strike at you: provoke him, that he may; for even out of that will I cause these of Cyprus to mutiny; whose qualification[44] shall come into no true taste again but by the displanting of Cassio. So shall you have a shorter journey to your desires by the means I shall then have to prefer them; and the impediment most profitably removed, without the which there were no expectation of our prosperity. 250

ROD.   I will do this if I can bring it to any opportunity.

---

[40] *conscionable* conscientious   [41] *salt* licentious   [42] *slipper* slippery   [43] *tainting* disparaging
[44] *qualification* appeasement

IAGO. I warrant thee. Meet me by and by[45] at the citadel: I must fetch his necessaries ashore. Farewell.

ROD. Adieu. [*Exit*]

IAGO. That Cassio loves her, I do well believe 't;
That she loves him, 'tis apt[46] and of great credit:[47]
The Moor, howbeit that I endure him not,
Is of a constant, loving, noble nature,
And I dare think he'll prove to Desdemona   260
A most dear husband. Now I do love her too;
Not out of absolute lust, though peradventure
I stand accountant for as great a sin,
But partly led to diet my revenge,
For that I do suspect the lusty Moor
Hath leap'd into my seat; the thought whereof
Doth, like a poisonous mineral, gnaw my inwards;
And nothing can or shall content my soul
Till I am even'd with him, wife for wife,
Or failing so, yet that I put the Moor   270
At least into a jealousy so strong
That judgement cannot cure. Which thing to do,
If this poor trash[48] of Venice, whom I trash[49]
For his quick hunting, stand the putting on,[50]
I'll have Michael Cassio on the hip,[51]
Abuse him to the Moor in the rank garb—
For I fear Cassio with my night-cap too—
Make the Moor thank me, love me and reward me,
For making him egregiously an ass
And practicing upon his peace and quiet   280
Even to madness. 'Tis here, but yet confus'd:
Knavery's plain face is never seen till us'd. [*Exit.*]

SCENE II. *A street.*

[*Enter Othello's* HERALD *with a proclamation.*]

HER. It is Othello's pleasure, our noble and valiant general, that, upon certain
tidings now arrived, importing the mere perdition[52] of the Turkish fleet, every
man put himself into triumph; some to dance, some to make bonfires, each
man to what sport and revels his addiction leads him: for, besides these bene-
ficial news, it is the celebration of his nuptial. So much was his pleasure should
be proclaimed. All offices[53] are open, and there is full liberty of feasting from
this present hour of five till the bell have told eleven. Heaven bless the isle of
Cyprus and our general Othello! [*Exit.*]

---

[45] *by and by* immediately   [46] *apt* probable   [47] *credit* credibility   [48] *trash* worthless thing (Roderigo)
[49] *trash* hold in check   [50] *putting on* incitement to quarrel   [51] *on the hip* at my mercy (wrestling term)
[52] *mere perdition* complete destruction   [53] *offices* rooms where food and drink were kept

Scene III. *A hall in the castle.*

[*Enter* Othello, Desdemona, Cassio, *and* Attendants.]

Oth.   Good Michael, look you to the guard to-night:
  Let's teach ourselves that honourable stop,[54]
  Not to outsport discretion.
Cas.   Iago hath direction what to do;
  But, notwithstanding, with my personal eye
  Will I look to 't.
Oth.   Iago is most honest.
  Michael, goodnight: to-morrow with your earliest
  Let me have speech with you.   [*To* Desdemona]   Come, my dear love,
  The purchase made, the fruits to ensue;
  That profit's yet to come 'tween me and you.   10
  Good night.   [*Exit* Othello, *with* Desdemona *and* Attendants.]

[*Enter* Iago.]

Cas.   Welcome, Iago; we must to the watch.
Iago.   Not this hour, lieutenant; 'tis not yet ten o' the clock. Our general cast[55] us thus early for the love of his Desdemona; who let us not therefore blame: he hath not yet made wanton the night with her; and she is sport for Jove.
Cas.   She's a most exquisite lady.
Iago.   And, I'll warrant her, full of game.
Cas.   Indeed, she's a most fresh and delicate creature.
Iago.   What an eye she has! methinks it sounds a parley of provocation.
Cas.   An inviting eye; and yet methinks right modest.   20
Iago.   And when she speaks, is it not an alarum to love?
Cas.   She is indeed perfection.
Iago.   Well, happiness to their sheets! Come, lieutenant, I have a stoup[56] of wine; and here without are a brace of Cyprus gallants that would fain have a measure to the health of black Othello.
Cas.   Not to-night, good Iago: I have very poor and unhappy brains for drinking: I could well wish courtesy would invent some other custom of entertainment.
Iago.   O, they are our friends; but one cup: I'll drink for you.
Cas.   I have drunk but one cup to-night, and that was craftily qualified[57] too, and, behold, what innovation[58] it makes here:[59] I am unfortunate in the infirmity,   30 and dare not task my weakness with any more.
Iago.   What, man! 'tis a night of revels: the gallants desire it.
Cas.   Where are they?
Iago.   Here at the door; I pray you, call them in.
Cas.   I'll do 't; but it dislikes me.   [*Exit.*]

---

[54] *stop* restraint   [55] *cast* dismissed   [56] *stoup* measure of liquor, two quarts
[57] *qualified* diluted   [58] *innovation* disturbance   [59] *here* i.e., in Cassio's head

IAGO.   If I can fasten but one cup upon him,
　With that which he hath drunk to-night already,
　He'll be as full of quarrel and offence
　As my young mistress' dog. Now, my sick fool Roderigo,
　Whom love hath turn'd almost the wrong side out,　　　　　　　40
　To Desdemona hath to-night carous'd
　Potations pottle-deep;[60] and he's to watch:
　Three lads of Cyprus, noble swelling spirits,
　That hold their honours in a wary distance,[61]
　The very elements[62] of this warlike isle,
　Have I to-night fluster'd with flowing cups,
　And they watch[63] too. Now, 'mongst this flock of drunkards,
　Am I to put our Cassio in some action
　That may offend the isle.—But here they come:

　　[*Enter* CASSIO, MONTANO, *and* GENTLEMEN; SERVANTS *following with wine.*]

　If consequence do but approve[64] my dream,　　　　　　　　　50
　My boat sails freely, both with wind and stream.
CAS.　'Fore God, they have given me a rouse[65] already.
MON.　Good faith, a little one; not past a pint, as I am a soldier.
IAGO.　Some wine, ho!
　[*Sings*]   And let me the canakin[66] clink, clink;
　　　　　And let me the canakin clink:
　　　　　　A soldier's a man;
　　　　　　A life's but a span;
　　　　　Why, then, let a soldier drink.
Some wine, boys!　　　　　　　　　　　　　　　　　　　　　60
CAS.　'Fore God, an excellent song.
IAGO.　I learned it in England, where, indeed, they are most potent in potting:
　your Dane, your German, and your swag-bellied Hollander—Drink, ho!—are
　nothing to your English.
CAS.　Is your Englishman so expert in his drinking?
IAGO.　Why, he drinks you, with facility, your Dane dead drunk; he sweats not to
　overthrow your Almain;[67] he gives your Hollander a vomit, ere the next pottle
　can be filled.
CAS.　To the health of our general!
MON.　I am for it, lieutenant; and I'll do you justice.[68]　　　　　70
IAGO.　O sweet England!　[*Sings.*]
　King Stephen was a worthy peer,
　　His breeches cost him but a crown;

---

[60] *pottle-deep* to the bottom of the tankard　[61] *bold...distance* i.e., are extremely sensitive of their honor
[62] *very elements* true representatives　[63] *watch* are members of the guard　[64] *approve* confirm　[65] *rouse*
full draft of liquor　[66] *canakin* small drinking vessel　[67] *Almain* German　[68] *I'll...justice* i.e., drink as
much as you

He held them sixpence all too dear,
  With that he call'd the tailor lown.[69]

He was a wight of high renown,
  And thou art but of low degree:
'Tis pride that pulls the country down;
  Then take thine auld cloak about thee.
  Some wine, ho!   80

CAS. Why, this is a more exquisite song than the other.

IAGO. Will you hear't again?

CAS. No; for I hold him to be unworthy of his place that does those things. Well, God's above all; and there be souls must be saved, and there be souls must not be saved.

IAGO. It's true, good lieutenant.

CAS. For mine own part,—no offence to the general, nor any man of quality,—I hope to be saved.

IAGO. And so do I too, lieutenant.

CAS. Ay, but, by your leave, not before me; the lieutenant is to be saved before the   90
ancient. Let's have no more of this; let 's to our affairs.—God forgive us our sins!—Gentlemen, let's look to our business. Do not think, gentlemen, I am drunk: this is my ancient; this is my right hand, and this is my left: I am not drunk now; I can stand well enough, and speak well enough.

ALL. Excellent well.

CAS. Why, very well then; you must not think then that I am drunk.   [*Exit*]

MON. To th' platform, masters; come, let's set the watch.

IAGO. You see this fellow that is gone before;
  He's soldier fit to stand by Caesar
  And give direction: and do but see his vice;   100
  'Tis to his virtue a just equinox,[70]
  The one as long as th' other: 'tis pity of him.
  I fear the trust Othello puts him in,
  On some odd time of his infirmity,
  Will shake this island.

MON.   But is he often thus?

IAGO. 'Tis evermore the prologue to his sleep:
  He'll watch the horologe[71] a double set,[72]
  If drink rock not his cradle.

MON.   It were well
  The general were put in mind of it.
  Perhaps he sees it not; or his good nature   110
  Prizes the virtue that appears in Cassio,
  And looks not on his evils: is not this true?

---

[69] *lown* lout, loon   [70] *equinox* equal length of days and nights; used figuratively to mean "counterpart"
[71] *horologe* clock   [72] *double set* twice around

[*Enter* RODERIGO.]

IAGO. [*Aside to him*]. How now, Roderigo!
   I pray you, after the lieutenant; go. [*Exit* RODERIGO.]
MON. And 'tis great pity that the noble Moor
   Should hazard such a place as his own second
   With one of an ingraft[73] infirmity:
   It were an honest action to say
   So to the Moor.
IAGO.   Not I, for this fair island:
   I do love Cassio well; and would do much   120
   To cure him of this evil—But, hark! what noise? [*Cry within:* "Help! help!"]

[*Enter* CASSIO, *pursuing* RODERIGO.]

CAS. 'Zounds, you rogue! you rascal!
MON.   What's the matter, lieutenant?
CAS. A knave teach me my duty!
   I'll beat the knave into a twiggen[74] bottle.
ROD. Beat me!
CAS.   Dost thou prate, rogue? [*Striking* RODERIGO.]
MON.   Nay, good lieutenant; [*Staying him.*]
   I pray you, sir, hold your hand.
CAS.   Let me go, sir,
   Or I'll knock you o'er the mazzard.[75]
MON.   Come, come, you're drunk.
CAS. Drunk! [*They fight.*]
IAGO. [*aside to* RODERIGO]. Away, I say; go out, and cry a mutiny.
   [*Exit* RODERIGO.]
   Nay, good lieutenant,—God's will, gentlemen;—   130
   Help, ho!—Lieutenant,—sir,—Montano,—sir,—
   Help, masters!—Here's a goodly watch indeed! [*Bell rings.*]
   Who's that which rings the bell?—Diablo,[76] ho!
   The town will rise:[77] God's will, lieutenant, hold!
   You'll be asham'd for ever.

[*Enter* OTHELLO *and* ATTENDANTS.]

OTH.   What is the matter here?
MON. 'Zounds, I bleed still; I am hurt to th' death
   He dies! [*Thrusts at* CASSIO.]
OTH. Hold, for your lives!
IAGO. Hold, ho! Lieutenant,—sir,—Montano,—gentlemen,—
   Have your forgot all sense of place and duty?   140
   Hold! the general speaks to you; hold, for shame!

[73] *ingraft* ingrafted, inveterate   [74] *twiggen* covered with woven twigs   [75] *mazzard* head   [76] *Diablo* the
devil   [77] *rise* grow riotous

OTH.   Why, how now, ho! from whence ariseth this?
  Are we turn'd Turks[78] and to ourselves do that
  Which heaven hath forbid the Ottomites?
  For Christian shame, put by this barbarous brawl:
  He that stirs next to carve for[79] his own rage
  Holds his soul light; he dies upon his motion.
  Silence that dreadful bell: it frights the isle
  From her propriety.[80] What is the matter, masters?
  Honest Iago, that looks dead with grieving,   150
  Speak, who began this? on thy love, I charge thee.
IAGO.   I do not know: friends all but now, even now,
  In quarter,[81] and in terms like bride and groom
  Devesting them for bed; and then, but now—
  As if some planet had unwitted men—
  Swords out, and tilting one at other's breast,
  In opposition bloody. I cannot speak
  Any beginning to this peevish odds;[82]
  And would in action glorious I had lost
  Those legs that brought me to a part of it!   160
OTH.   How comes it, Michael, you are thus forgot?
CAS.   I pray you, pardon me; I cannot speak.
OTH.   Worthy Montano, you were wont be civil;
  The gravity and stillness of your youth
  The world hath noted, and your name is great
  In mouths of wisest censure:[83] what's the matter,
  That you unlace[84] your reputation thus
  And spend your rich opinion for the name
  Of a night-brawler? give me answer to it.   170
MON.   Worthy Othello, I am hurt to danger:
  Your officer, Iago, can inform you,—
  While I spare speech, which something now offends me,—
  Of all that I do know: nor know I aught
  By me that's said or done amiss this night;
  Unless self-charity be sometimes a vice,
  And to defend ourselves it be a sin
  When violence assails us.
OTH.   Now, by heaven,
  My blood begins my safer guides to rule;
  And passion, having my best judgement collied,[85]
  Assays to lead the way: if I once stir,   180
  Or do but lift this arm, the best of you

---

[78] *turn'd Turks* changed completely for the worse; proverbial   [79] *carve for* indulge   [80] *propriety* proper
state or condition   [81] *In quarter* on terms   [82] *peevish odds* childish quarrel   [83] *censure* judgment
[84] *unlace* degrade   [85] *collied* darkened

Shall sink in my rebuke. Give me to know
How this foul rout began, who set it on;
And he that is approv'd in[86] this offence,
Though he had twinn'd with me, both at birth,
Shall lose me. What! in a town of war,
Yet wild, the people's hearts brimful of fear,
To manage private and domestic quarrel,
In night, and on the court and guard[87] of safety!
'Tis monstrous. Iago, who began 't?   190
MON.   If partially affin'd,[88] or leagu'd in office,
Thou dost deliver more or less than truth,
Thou art no soldier.
IAGO.   Touch me not so near:
I had rather have this tongue cut from my mouth
Than it should do offence to Michael Cassio;
Yet, I persuade myself, to speak the truth,
Shall nothing wrong him. Thus it is, general.
Montano and myself being in speech,
There comes a fellow crying out for help;
And Cassio following him with determin'd sword,   200
To execute[89] upon him. Sir, this gentleman
Steps in to Cassio, and entreats his pause:
Myself the crying fellow did pursue,
Lest by his clamour—as it so fell out—
The town might fall in fright: he, swift of foot,
Outran my purpose; and I return'd the rather
For that I heard the clink and fall of swords,
And Cassio high in oath; which till to-night
I ne'er might say before. When I came back—
For this was brief—I found them close together,   210
At blow and thrust; even as again they were
When you yourself did part them.
More of this matter cannot I report:
But men are men; the best sometimes forget:
Though Cassio did some little wrong to him,
As men in rage strike those that wish them best,
Yet surely, Cassio, I believe, receive'd
From him that fled some strange indignity,
Which patience could not pass.
OTH.   I know, Iago,
Thy honesty and love doth mince this matter,   220

---

[86] *approv'd in* found guilty of   [87] *court and guard* spot and guarding place, i.e., the main guardhouse
[88] *affin'd* bound by a tie   [89] *execute* give effect to (his anger)

Making it light to Cassio. Cassio, I love thee;
But never more be officer of mine.

[*Enter* DESDEMONA, *attended.*]

Look, if my gentle love be not rais'd up!
I'll make thee an example.
DES.   What's the matter?
OTH.   All's well now, sweeting; come away to bed.
Sir, for your hurts, myself will be your surgeon:
Lead him off.   [*To* MONTANO, *who is led off.*]
Iago, look with care about the town,
And silence those whom this vile brawl distracted.
Come, Desdemona: 'tis the soldier's life   230
To have their balmy slumbers wak'd with strife.   [*Exit with all but* IAGO *and*
    CASSIO.]
IAGO.   What, are you hurt, lieutenant?
CAS.   Ay, past all surgery.
IAGO.   Marry, God forbid!
CAS.   Reputation, reputation, reputation! O, I have lost my reputation! I have lost
    the immortal part of myself, and what remains is bestial. My reputation, Iago,
    my reputation!
IAGO.   As I am an honest man, I thought you had received some bodily wound;
    there is more sense in that than in reputation. Reputation is an idle and most
    false imposition; oft got without merit, and lost without deserving: you have   240
    lost no reputation at all, unless you repute yourself such a loser. What, man!
    there are ways to recover the general again: you are but now cast in his mood,
    a punishment more in policy than in malice; even so as one would beat his
    offenceless dog to affright an imperious lion: sue to him again, and he 's yours.
CAS.   I will rather sue to be despised than to deceive so good a commander with
    so slight, so drunken, and so indiscreet an officer. Drunk? and speak parrot?[90]
    and squabble? swagger? swear? and discourse fustian[91] with one's own
    shadow? O thou invisible spirit of wine, if thou has no name to be known by,
    let us call thee devil!
IAGO.   What was he that you followed with your sword? What had he done to you?   250
CAS.   I know not.
IAGO.   Is't possible?
CAS.   I remember a mass of things, but nothing distinctly; a quarrel, but nothing
    wherefore. O God, that men should put an enemy in their mouths to steal
    away their brains! that we should, with joy, pleasance, revel and applause,
    transform ourselves into beasts!
IAGO.   Why, but you are now well enough: how came you thus recovered?
CAS.   It hath pleased the devil drunkenness to give place to the devil wrath: one
    unperfectness[92] shows me another, to make me frankly despise myself.

[90]*speak parrot* talk nonsense   [91]*discourse fustian* talked nonsense   [92]*unperfectness* imperfection

IAGO.   Come, you are too severe a moraler: as the time, the place, and the condi-   260
tion of this country stands, I could heartily wish this had not befallen; but,
since it is as it is, mend it for your own good.

CAS.   I will ask him for my place again; he shall tell me I am a drunkard! Had I as
many mouths as Hydra,[93] such an answer would stop them all. To be now a
sensible man, by and by a fool, and presently a beast! O strange! Every inordi-
nate cup is unblessed and the ingredient is a devil.

IAGO.   Come, come, good wine is a good familiar creature, if it be well used:
exclaim no more against it. And, good lieutenant, I think you think I love you.

CAS.   I have well approved[94] it, sir. I drunk!

IAGO.   You or any man living may be a drunk at a time, man. I'll tell you what you   270
shall do. Our general's wife is now the general: I may say so in this respect, for
that he hath devoted and given up himself to the contemplation, mark, and
denotement[95] of her parts and graces: confess yourself freely to her; importune her help to put you in your place again: she is of so free, so kind, so apt,
so blessed a dispositon, she holds it a vice in her goodness not to do more than
she is requested: this broken joint between you and her husband entreat her
to splinter;[96] and, my fortunes against any lay[97] worth naming, this crack of
your love shall grow stronger than it was before.

CAS.   You advise me well.

IAGO.   I protest, in the sincerity of love and honest kindness.   280

CAS.   I think it freely; and betimes in the morning I will beseech the virtuous Desdemona to undertake for me: I am desperate of my fortunes if they check[98] me
here.

IAGO.   You are in the right. Good night, lieutenant; I must to the watch.

CAS.   Good night, honest Iago.   [*Exit* CASSIO.]

IAGO.   And what 's he then that says I play the villain?
When this advice is free I give the honest,
Probal[99] to thinking and indeed the course
To win the Moor again? For 'tis most easy
Th' inclining[100] Desdemona to subdue[101]   290
In any honest suit: she 's fram'd as fruitful
As the free elements. And then for her
To win the Moor—were 't to renounce his baptism,
All seals and symbols of redeemed sin,
His soul is so enfetter'd to her love,
That she may make, unmake, do what she list,
Even as her appetite shall play the god
With his weak function. How am I then a villain
To counsel Cassio to this parallel[102] course,

---

[93] *Hydra* a monster with many heads, slain by Hercules as the second of his twelve labors
[94] *approved* proved   [95] *denotement* observation   [96] *splinter* bind with splints   [97] *lay* stake, wager
[98] *check* repulse   [99] *Probal* probable   [100] *inclining* favorably disposed   [101] *subdue* persuade
[102] *parallel* probably, corresponding to his best interest

Directly to his good? Divinity of hell!   300
When devils will the blackest sins put on,[103]
They do suggest[104] at first with heavenly shows,
As I do now; for whiles this honest fool
Plies Desdemona to repair his fortunes
And she for him pleads strongly to the Moor,
I'll pour this pestilence into his ear,
That she repeals him[105] for her body's lust;
And by how much she strives to do him good,
She shall under her credit with the Moor,
So will I turn her virtue into pitch,   310
And out of her own goodness make the net
That shall enmesh them all.

[Enter RODERIGO.]

How now, Roderigo!

ROD.   I do not follow here in the chase, not like a hound that hunts, but one that
fills up the cry.[106] My money is almost spent; I have been tonight exceedingly
well cudgelléd; and I think the issue will be, I shall have so much experience
for my pains, and so, with no money at all and a little more wit, return again
to Venice.

IAGO.   How poor are they that have not patience!
What wound did ever heal but by degrees?
Thou know'st we work by wit, and not by witchcraft;   320
And wit depends on dilatory time.
Does 't not go well? Cassio hath beaten thee,
And thou, by that small hurt, hast cashier'd[107] Cassio:
Though other things grow fair against the sun,
Yet fruits that blossom first will first be ripe:
Content thyself awhile. By th' mass, 'tis morning;
Pleasure and action make the hours seem short.
Retire thee; go where thou art billeted:
Away, I say; thou shalt know more hereafter:
Nay, get thee gone.   [Exit RODERIGO.]
Two things are to be done: 330
My wife must move for Cassio to her mistress;
I'll set her on;
Myself the while to draw the Moor apart,
And bring him jump[108] when he may Cassio find
Soliciting his wife: ay, that's the way:
Dull not device by coldness and delay.   [Exit.]

---

[103] *put on* further   [104] *suggest* tempt   [105] *repeals him* i.e., attempts to get him restored   [106] *cry* pack
[107] *cashier'd* dismissed from service   [108] *jump* precisely

ACT III

SCENE I.   *Before the castle.*

[*Enter* CASSIO *and* MUSICIANS.]

CAS.   Masters, play here; I will content[1] your pains;
  Something that's brief; and bid "Good morrow, general."   [*They play.*]

[*Enter* CLOWN.]

CLO.   Why, masters, have your instruments been in Naples, that they speak i' the
  nose[2] thus?
FIRST MUS.   How, sir, how!
CLO.   Are these, I pray you, wind-instruments?
FIRST MUS.   Ay, marry, are they, sir.
CLO.   O, thereby hangs a tail.
FIRST MUS.   Whereby hangs a tale,[3] sir?
CLO.   Marry, sir, by many a wind-instrument that I know. But, masters, here 's   10
  money for you: and the general so likes your music, that he desires you, for
  love's sake, to make no more noise with it.
FIRST MUS.   Well, sir, we will not.
CLO.   If you have any music that may not be heard, to 't again: but, as they say, to
  hear music the general does not greatly care.
FIRST MUS.   We have none such, sir.
CLO.   Then put up your pipes in your bag, for I'll away: go; vanish into air;
  away!   [*Exeunt* MUSICIANS.]
CAS.   Dost thou hear, my honest friend?
CLO.   No, I hear not your honest friend; I hear you.   20
CAS.   Prithee, keep up thy quillets. There's a poor piece of gold for thee: if the
  gentlewoman that attends the general's wife be stirring, tell her there 's one
  Cassio entreats her a little favour of speech: wilt thou do this?
CLO.   She is stirring, sir: if she will stir hither, I shall seem to notify unto her.
CAS.   Do, good my friend.   [*Exit* CLOWN.]

[*Enter* IAGO.]

  In happy time, Iago.
IAGO.   You have not been a-bed, then?
CAS.   Why, no; the day had broke
  Before we parted. I have made bold, Iago,
  To send in to your wife: my suit to her

ACT III [1] *content* reward   [2] *speak i' the nose* i.e., like Neapolitans, who spoke a nasal dialect (with a joke
on syphillis, which attacks the nose)   [3] *tale* pun on *tail,* a wind instrument of sorts

Is, that she will to virtuous Desdemona
  Procure me some access.   30
IAGO.   I'll send her to you presently;
  And I'll devise a means to draw the Moor
  Out of the way, that your converse and business
  May be more free.
CAS.   I humbly thank you for 't.   [*Exit* IAGO.]
                               I never knew
  A Florentine more kind and honest.

[*Enter* EMILIA.]

EMIL.   Good morrow, good lieutenant: I am sorry
  For your displeasure; but all will sure be well.
  The general and his wife are talking of it;
  And she speaks for you stoutly: the Moor replies,   40
  That he you hurt is of great fame in Cyprus
  And great affinity[4] and that in wholesome wisdom
  He might not but refuse you, but he protests he loves you
  And needs no other suitor but his likings
  To take the safest occasion by the front[5]
  To bring you in again.
CAS.   Yet, I beseech you,
  If you think fit, or that it may be done,
  Give me advantage of some brief discourse
  With Desdemona alone.
EMIL.   Pray you, come in:
  I will bestow you where you shall have time   50
  To speak your bosom freely.
CAS.   I am much bound to you.   [*Exeunt.*]

SCENE II.   *A room in the castle.*

[*Enter* OTHELLO, IAGO, *and* GENTLEMEN.]

OTH.   These letters give, Iago, to the pilot;
  And by him do my duties to the senate:
  That done, I will be walking on the works:[6]
  Repair there to me.
IAGO.   Well, my good lord, I'll do 't.
OTH.   This fortification, gentlemen, shall we see 't?
GENT.   We'll wait upon your lordship.   [*Exeunt.*]

---

[4] *affinity* kindred, family connection   [5] *by the front* i.e., by the forelock   [6] *works* earthworks, fortifications

SCENE III.   *The garden of the castle.*

[*Enter* DESDEMONA, CASSIO, *and* EMILIA.]

DES.   Be thou assur'd, good Cassio, I will do
　　All my abilities in thy behalf.
EMIL.   Good madam, do: I warrant it grieves my husband,
　　As if the case were his.
DES.   O, that 's an honest fellow. Do not doubt, Cassio,
　　But I will have my lord and you again
　　As friendly as you were.
CAS.　　　　　　　　Bounteous madam,
　　Whatever shall become of Michael Cassio,
　　He's never any thing but your true servant.
DES.   I know 't; I thank you. You do love my lord:　　　　　　10
　　You have known him long; and be you well assur'd
　　He shall in strangeness[7] stand no farther off
　　Than in a politic distance.
CAS.　　　　　　　　Ay, but lady,
　　That policy may either last so long
　　Or feed upon such nice and waterish diet,
　　Or breed itself so out of circumstance,[8]
　　That, I being absent and my place supplied,
　　My general will forget my love and service.
DES.   Do not doubt[9] that; before Emilia here
　　I give thee warrant of thy place: assure thee,　　　　　　20
　　If I do vow a friendship, I'll perform it
　　To the last article: my lord shall never rest;
　　I'll watch him tame[10] and talk him out of patience;
　　His bed shall seem a school, his board a shrift;[11]
　　I'll intermingle every thing he does
　　With Cassio's suit: therefore be merry, Cassio;
　　For thy solicitor shall rather die
　　Than give thy cause away.[12]

[*Enter* OTHELLO *and* IAGO *at a distance.*]

EMIL.   Madam, here comes my lord.
CAS.   Madam, I'll take my leave.　　　　　　30
DES.   Why, stay, and hear me speak.
CAS.   Madam, not now: I am very ill at ease,
　　Unfit for mine own purposes.
DES.   Well, do your discretion.   [*Exit* CASSIO.]

---

[7] *strangeness* distant behavior　[8] *breed...circumstance* increase itself so on account of accidents
[9] *doubt* fear　[10] *watch him tame* tame him by keeping him from sleeping (a term from falconry)
[11] *shrift* confessional　[12] *away* up

IAGO.   Ha! I like not that.
OTH.   What dost thou say?
IAGO.   Nothing, my lord: or if—I know not what.
OTH.   Was not that Cassio parted from my wife?
IAGO.   Cassio, my lord! No, sure, I cannot think it,
    That he would steal away so guilty-like,
    Seeing you coming.
OTH.   I do believe 'twas he.   40
DES.   How now, my lord!
    I have been talking with a suitor here,
    A man that languishes in your displeasure.
OTH.   Who is 't you mean?
DES.   Why, your lieutenant, Cassio. Good my lord,
    If I have any grace or power to move you,
    His present reconciliation take;
    For if he be not one that truly loves you,
    That errs in ignorance and not in cunning,
    I have no judgement in an honest face: 50
    I prithee, call him back.
OTH.   Went he hence now?
DES.   Ay, sooth; so humbled
    That he hath left part of his grief with me,
    To suffer with him. Good love, call him back.
OTH.   Not now, sweet Desdemona; some other time.
DES.   But shall 't be shortly?
OTH.   The sooner, sweet, for you.
DES.   Shall 't be to-night at supper?
OTH.   No, not to-night.
DES.   To-morrow dinner, then?
OTH.   I shall not dine at home;
    I meet the captains at the citadel.
DES.   Why, then, to-morrow night; or Tuesday morn;   60
    On Tuesday noon, or night; on Wednesday morn:
    I prithee, name the time, but let it not
    Exceed three days: in faith, he's penitent;
    And yet his trespass, in our common reason[13]—
    Save that, they say, the wars must make examples
    Out of their best—is not almost a fault
    T' incur a private check. When shall he come?
    Tell me, Othello: I wonder in my soul,
    What you would ask me, that I should deny,
    Or stand so mamm'ring on.[14] What! Michael Cassio,   70
    That came a-wooing with you, and so many a time,

---

[13] *common reason* everyday judgments   [14] *mamm'ring on* wavering

When I have spoke of you dispraisingly,
Hath ta'en your part; to have so much to do
To bring him in! Trust me, I could do much,—
OTH.   Prithee, no more: let him come when he will;
  I will deny thee nothing.
DES.   Why, this is not a boon;
  'Tis as I should entreat you wear your gloves,
  Or feed on nourishing dishes, or keep you warm,
  Or sue to you to do a peculiar profit
  To your own person: nay, when I have a suit   80
  Wherein I mean to touch your love indeed,
  It shall be full of poise[15] and difficult weight
  And fearful to be granted.
OTH.   I will deny thee nothing:
  Whereon, I do beseech thee, grant me this,
  To leave me but a little to myself.
DES.   Shall I deny you? no: farewell, my lord.
OTH.   Farewell, my Desdemona: I'll come to thee straight.
DES.   Emilia, come. Be as your fancies teach you;
  Whate'er you be, I am obedient.   [*Exit with* EMILIA.]
OTH.   Excellent wretch![16] Perdition catch my soul,   90
  But I do love thee! and when I love thee not,
  Chaos is come again.
IAGO.   My noble lord,—
OTH.   What dost thou say, Iago?
IAGO.   Did Michael Cassio, when you woo'd my lady,
  Know of your love?
OTH.   He did, from first to last: why dost thou ask?
IAGO.   But for a satisfaction of my thought;
  No further harm.
OTH.   Why of thy thought, Iago?
IAGO.   I did not think he had been acquainted with her.
OTH.   O, yes; and went between us very oft.   100
IAGO.   Indeed!
OTH.   Indeed! ay, indeed: discern'st thou aught in that?
  Is he not honest?
IAGO.   Honest, my lord!
OTH.   Honest! ay, honest.
IAGO.   My lord, for aught I know.
OTH.   What dost thou think?
IAGO.   Think, my lord!
OTH.   Think, my lord!
  By heaven, he echoes me,

---

[15] *poise* weight, heaviness   [16] *wretch* term of affectionate endearment with a connotation of pity

As if there were some monster in his thought
Too hideous to be shown. Thou dost mean something:
I heard thee say even now, thou lik'st not that,
When Cassio left my wife: what didst not like?   110
And when I told thee he was of my counsel
In my whole course of wooing, thou criedst "Indeed!"
And didst contract and purse thy brow together,
As if thou then hadst shut up in thy brain
Some horrible conceit: if thou dost love me,
Show me thy thought.

IAGO.   My lord, you know I love you.

OTH.   I think thou dost;
And, for I know thou 'rt full of love and honesty,
And weigh'st thy words before thou giv'st them breath,
Therefore these stops of thine fright me more: 120
For such things in a false disloyal knave
Are tricks of custom, but in a man that's just
They 're close delations,[17] working from the heart
That passion cannot rule.

IAGO.   For Michael Cassio,
I dare be sworn I think that he is honest.

OTH.   I think so too.

IAGO.   Men should be what they seem;
Or those that be not, would they might seem none!

OTH.   Certain, men should be what they seem.

IAGO.   Why, then, I think Cassio 's an honest man.

OTH.   Nay, yet there 's more in this: 130
I prithee, speak to me as to thy thinkings,
As thou dost ruminate, and give thy worst of thoughts
The worst of words.

IAGO.   Good my lord, pardon me:
Though I am bound to every act of duty,
I am not bound to that all slaves are free to.
Utter my thoughts? Why, say they are vile and false:
As where 's that palace whereinto foul things
Sometimes intrude not? who has a breast so pure,
But some uncleanly apprehensions
Keep leets[18] and law-days[19] and in sessions sit   140
With meditations lawful?

OTH.   Thou dost conspire against thy friend, Iago,
If thou but think'st him wrong'd and mak'st his ear
A stranger to thy thoughts.

---

[17] *close delations* secret or involuntary accusations   [18] *Keep leets* hold courts   [19] *law-days* court days

IAGO.   I do beseech you—
   Though I perchance am vicious[20] in my guess,
   As, I confess, it is my nature's plague
   To spy into abuses, and oft my jealousy[21]
   Shapes faults that are not—that your wisdom yet,
   From one that so imperfectly conceits,[22]
   Would take no notice, nor build yourself a trouble   150
   Out of his scattering and unsure observance.
   It were not for your quiet nor your good,
   Nor for my manhood, honesty, or wisdom,
   To let you know my thoughts.
OTH.   What dost thou mean?
IAGO.   Good name in man and woman, dear my lord,
   Is the immediate jewel of their souls:
   Who steals my purse steals trash: 'tis something, nothing;
   'Twas mine, 'tis his, and has been slave to thousands;
   But he that filches from me my good name
   Robs me of that which not enriches him   160
   And makes me poor indeed.
OTH.   By heaven, I'll know thy thoughts.
IAGO.   You cannot, if my heart were in your hand;
   Nor shall not, whilst 'tis in my custody.
OTH.   Ha!
IAGO.   Oh, beware, my lord, of jealousy;
   It is the green-ey'd monster which doth mock
   The meat it feeds on: that cuckhold lives in bliss
   Who certain of his fate, loves not his wronger;
   But, O, what damned minutes tells her o'er
   Who dotes, yet doubts, suspects, yet strongly loves!   170
OTH.   O misery!
IAGO.   Poor and content is rich and rich enough,
   But riches fineless[23] is as poor as winter
   To him that ever fears he shall be poor.
   Good God, the souls of all my tribe defend
   From jealousy!
OTH.   Why, why is this?
   Think'st thou I'd make a life of jealousy,
   To follow still the changes of the moon
   With fresh suspicions? No; to be once in doubt
   Is once to be resolv'd: exchange me for a goat,   180
   When I shall turn the business of my soul
   To such exsufflicate and blown[24] surmises,

---

[20] *vicious* wrong   [21] *jealousy* suspicion of evil   [22] *conceits* judges   [23] *fineless* boundless
[24] *exsufflicate and blown* unsubstantial and inflated, flyblown

Matching thy inference. 'Tis not to make me jealous
To say my wife is fair, feeds well, loves company,
Is free of speech, sings, plays and dances well;
Where virtue is, these are more virtuous;
Nor from mine own weak merits will I draw
The smallest fear or doubt of her revolt:
For she had eyes, and chose me. No, Iago;
I'll see before I doubt; when I doubt, prove;   190
And on the proof, there is no more but this,—
Away at once with love or jealousy!

IAGO.   I am glad of this; for now I shall have reason
To show the love and duty that I bear you
With franker spirit: therefore, as I am bound,
Receive it from me. I speak not yet of proof.
Look to your wife; observe her well with Cassio;
Wear your eye thus, not jealous nor secure.[25]
I would not have your free and noble nature,
Out of self-bounty,[26] be abus'd; look to 't: 200
I know our country disposition well;
In Venice they do let heaven see the pranks
They dare not show their husbands; their best conscience
Is not to leave 't undone, but keep 't unknown.

OTH.   Dost thou say so?

IAGO.   She did deceive her father, marrying you;
And when she seem'd to shake and fear your looks,
She lov'd them most.

OTH.   And so she did.

IAGO.   Why, go to then;
She that, so young, could give out such a seeming,[27]
To seel[28] her father's eyes up close as oak—   210
He thought 'twas witchcraft—but I am much to blame;
I humbly do beseech you of your pardon
For too much loving you.

OTH.   I am bound to thee for ever.

IAGO.   I see this hath a little dash'd your spirits.

OTH.   Not a jot, not a jot.

IAGO.   I' faith, I fear it has.
I hope you will consider what is spoke
Comes from my love. But I do see y' are mov'd:
I am to pray you not to strain my speech
To grosser issues nor to larger reach[29]
Than to suspicion.   220

---

[25] *secure* free from uneasiness   [26] *self-bounty* inherent or natural goodness   [27] *seeming* false appearance
[28] *seel* blind (a term from falconry)   [29] *reach* meaning

OTH.   I will not.

IAGO.   Should you do so, my lord,
My speech would fall into such vile success
As my thoughts aim not at. Cassio 's my worthy friend—
My lord, I see y' are mov'd.

OTH.   No, not much mov'd:
I do not think but Desdemona's honest.

IAGO.   Long live she so! and long live you to think so!

OTH.   And yet, how nature erring from itself,—

IAGO.   Ay, there's the point: as—to be bold with you—
Not to affect many proposed matches
Of her own clime, complexion, and degree,   230
Whereto we see in all things nature tends—
Foh! one may smell in such a will[30] most rank,
Foul disproportion,[31] thoughts unnatural.
But pardon me; I do not in position[32]
Distinctly speak of her; though I may fear
Her will, recoiling to[33] her better judgment,
May fall to match you with her country forms[34]
And happily repent.[35]

OTH.   Farewell, farewell:
If more thou dost perceive, let me know more;
Set on they wife to observe: leave me, Iago.   240

IAGO   [*going*].   My lord take my leave.

OTH.   Why did I marry? This honest creature doubtless
Sees and knows more, much more, than he unfolds.

IAGO   [*returning*].   My Lord, I would I might entreat your honour
To scan this thing no farther; leave it to time:
Although 'tis fit that Cassio have his place,
For, sure, he fills it up with great ability,
Yet, if you please to hold him off awhile,
You shall by that perceive him and his means:
Note, if your lady strain his entertainment[36]   250
With any strong or vehement importunity;
Much will be seen in that. In the mean time,
Let me be thought too busy in my fears—
As worthy cause I have to fear I am—
And hold her free,[37] I do beseech your honour.

OTH.   Fear not my government.[38]

IAGO.   I once more take my leave.   [*Exit.*]

---

[30] *will* sensuality   [31] *disproportion* abnormality   [32] *position* general argument   [33] *recoiling to* falling back upon, or recoiling against   [34] *fall…forms* happen to compare you with Venetian norms of handsomeness   [35] *repent* i.e., of her marriage   [36] *strain his entertainment* urge his reinstatement   [37] *hold her free* regard her as innocent   [38] *government* self-control

OTH. This fellow 's of exceeding honesty,
And knows all qualities, with a learned spirit,
Of human dealings. If I do prove her haggard,[39]   260
Though that her jesses[40] were my dear heartstrings,
I 'ld whistle her off and let her down the wind,
To prey at fortune.[41] Haply, for I am black
And have not those soft parts of conversation
That chamberers[42] have, or for I am declin'd
Into the vale of years,—yet that 's not much—
She 's gone. I am abus'd: and my relief
Must be to loathe her. O curse of marriage,
That we can call these delicate creatures ours,
And not their appetites! I had rather be a toad,   270
And live upon the vapour of a dungeon,
Than keep a corner in the thing I love
For others' uses. Yet, 'tis the plague of great ones;
Prerogativ'd[43] are they less than the base;
'Tis destiny unshunnable, like death:
Even then this forked[44] plague is fated to us
When we do quicken.[45] Look where she comes:

[*Enter* DESDEMONA *and* EMILIA.]

If she be false, O, then heaven mocks itself!
I'll not believe 't.
DES.   How now, my dear Othello!
Your dinner, and the generous[46] islanders   280
By you invited, do attend your presence.
OTH. I am to blame.
DES.   Why do you speak so faintly?
Are you not well?
OTH. I have a pain upon my forehead here.
DES. 'Faith, that 's with watching;[47] 'twill away again:
Let me but bind it hard, within this hour
It will be well.
OTH.   Your napkin is too little: [*He puts the handkerchief from him;
and it drops.*]
Let it alone. Come, I'll go in with you.
DES. I am very sorry that you are not well. [*Exit with* OTHELLO.]
EMIL. I am glad I have found this napkin: 290
This was her first remembrance from the Moor:
My wayward husband hath a hundred times

---

[39] *haggard* a wild female duck   [40] *jesses* straps fastened around the legs of a trained hawk
[41] *at fortune* at random   [42] *chamberers* gallants   [43] *Prerogativ'd* privileged   [44] *forked* an allusion to the
horns of the cuckold   [45] *quicken* receive life   [46] *generous* noble   [47] *watching* working late

Woo'd me to steal it; but she so loves the token,
For he conjur'd her she should ever keep it,
That she reserves it evermore about her
To kiss and talk to. I'll have the work ta'en out,[48]
And give 't Iago: what he will do with it
Heaven knows, not I;
I nothing but to please his fantasy.

[*Enter* IAGO.]

IAGO.   How now! what do you here alone?   300
EMIL.   Do not you chide; I have a thing for you.
IAGO.   A thing for me? it is a common thing[49]—
EMIL.   Ha!
IAGO.   To have a foolish wife.
EMIL.   O, is that all? What will you give me now
   For that same handkerchief?
IAGO.   What handkerchief?
EMIL.   What handkerchief!
   Why, that the Moor first gave Desdemona;
   That which so often you did bid me steal.
IAGO.   Hast stol'n it from her?   310
EMIL.   No, 'faith; she let it drop by negligence,
   And, to th' advantage, I, being here, took 't up.
   Look, here it is.
IAGO.   A good wench; give it to me.
EMIL.   What will you do with 't, that you have been so earnest
   To have me filch it?
IAGO.   [*Snatching it*]   Why, what is that to you?
EMIL.   If it be not for some purpose of import,
   Give 't me again: poor lady, she'll run mad
   When she shall lack it.
IAGO.   Be not acknown on 't;[50] I have use for it.
   Go, leave me.   [*Exit* EMILIA.]   320
   I will in Cassio's lodging lose this napkin,
   And let him find it. Trifles light as air
   Are to the jealous confirmations strong
   As proofs of holy writ: this may do something.
   The Moor already changes with my poison:
   Dangerous conceits are, in their natures, poisons,
   Which at the first are scarce found to distaste,
   But with a little act[51] upon the blood,
   Burn like the mines of sulphur. I did say so:

---

[48] *work ta'en out* design copied   [49] *common thing common* suggests coarseness and availability to all, and *thing* is slang for female sexual organs   [50] *Be...on't* do not confess knowledge of it   [51] *act* action, working

[*Enter* OTHELLO.]

Look, where he comes! Not poppy, nor mandragora,   330
Nor all the drowsy syrups of the world,
Shall ever medicine thee to that sweet sleep
Which thou owedst yesterday.
OTH.   Ha! ha! false to me?
IAGO.   Why, how now, general! no more of that.
OTH.   Avaunt! be gone! thou has set me on the rack;
  I swear 'tis better to be much abus'd
  Than but to know 't a little.
IAGO.   How now, my lord!
OTH.   What sense had I of her stol'n hours of lust?
  I saw 't not, thought it not, it harm'd not me:
  I slept the next night well, fed well, was free and merry;   340
  I found not Cassio's kisses on her lips:
  He that is robb'd, not wanting what is stol'n,
  Let him not know 't, and he 's not robb'd at all.
IAGO.   I am sorry to hear this.
OTH.   I had been happy, if the general camp,
  Pioners[52] and all, had tasted her sweet body,
  So I had nothing known. O, now, for ever
  Farewell the tranquil mind! farewell content!
  Farewell the plumed troop, and the big wars,
  That make ambition virtue! O, farewell!   350
  Farewell the neighing steed, and the shrill trump,
  The spirit-stirring drum, th' ear-piercing fife,
  The royal banner, and all quality,
  Pride, pomp and circumstance[53] of glorious war!
  And, O you mortal engines,[54] whose rude throats
  Th' immortal Jove's dread clamours counterfeit,
  Farewell! Othello's occupation 's gone!
IAGO.   Is 't possible, my lord?
OTH.   Villain, be sure thou prove my love a whore,
  Be sure of it; give me the ocular proof;   360
  Or, by the worth of mine eternal soul,
  Thou hadst been better have been born a dog
  Than answer my wak'd wrath!
IAGO.   Is 't come to this?
OTH.   Make me to see 't; or, at the least, so prove it,
  That the probation bear no hinge nor loop
  To hang a doubt on; or woe upon thy life!

---

[52] *Pioners* sappers, a low grade of soldiers   [53] *circumstance* attendant fact; here, formal display
[54] *mortal engines* i.e., cannon

IAGO.   My noble lord,—

OTH.   If thou dost slander her and torture me,
Never pray more; abandon all remorse;
On horror's head horrors[55] accumulate;   370
Do deeds to make heaven weep, all earth amaz'd;
For nothing canst thou to damnation add
Greater than that.

IAGO.   O grace! O heaven forgive me!
Are you a man? have you a soul or sense?
God be wi' you; take mine office. O wretched fool,
That liv'st to make thine honesty a vice!
O monstrous world! Take note, take note, O world,
To be direct and honest is not safe.
I thank you for this profit; and from hence
I'll love no friend, sith love breeds such offence.   380

OTH.   Nay, stay: thou shouldst be honest.

IAGO.   I should be wise, for honesty 's a fool
and loses that it works for.

OTH.   By the world,
I think my wife be honest and think she is not;
I think thou are just and think thou are not.
I'll have some proof. Her name, that was as fresh
As Dian's visage, is now begrim'd and black
As mine own face. If there be cords, or knives,
Poison, or fire, or suffocating streams,
I'll not endure it. Would I were satisfied!   390

IAGO.   I see, sir, you are eaten up with passion:
I do repent me that I put it to you.
You would be satisfied!

OTH.   Would! nay, I will.

IAGO.   And may: but, how? how satisfied, my lord?
Would you, the supervisor, grossly gape on—
Behold her topp'd?

OTH.   Death and damnation! O!

IAGO.   It were a tedious difficulty, I think,
To bring them to that prospect: damn them then,
If ever mortal eyes do see them bolster[56]
More than their own! What then? how then?   400
What shall I say? Where 's satisfaction?
It is impossible you should see this,
Were they as prime as goats, as hot as monkeys,
As salt[57] as wolves in pride, and fools as gross

---

[55] *horrors* object of *accumulate*   [56] *bolster* lie together   [57] *salt* wanton, sexual

As ignorance made drunk. But yet, I say,
If imputation[58] and strong circumstances,
Which lead directly to the door of truth,
Will give you satisfaction, you may have 't.
OTH.   Give me a living reason she 's disloyal.
IAGO.   I do not like the office: 410
But, sith I am ent'red in this cause so far,
Prick'd to 't by foolish honesty and love,
I will go on. I lay with Cassio lately;
And, being troubled with a raging tooth,
I could not sleep.
There are a kind of men so loose of soul,
That in their sleeps will mutter their affairs:
One of this kind is Cassio:
In sleep I heard him say "Sweet Desdemona,
Let us be wary, let us hide our loves";   420
And then, sir, would he grip and wring my hand,
Cry, "O sweet creature!" and then kiss me hard,
As if he pluck'd up kisses by the roots
That grew upon my lips: then laid his leg
Over my thigh, and sigh'd, and kiss'd; and then
Cried "Cursed fate that gave thee to the Moor!"
OTH.   O monstrous! monstrous!
IAGO.   Nay, this was but his dream.
OTH.   But this denoted a foregone conclusion:[59]
'Tis a shrewd doubt, though it be but a dream.
IAGO.   And this may help to thicken other proofs   430
That do demonstrate thinly.
OTH.   I'll tear her all to pieces.
IAGO.   Nay, but be wise; yet we see nothing done;
She may be honest yet. Tell me but this,
Have you not sometimes seen a handkerchief
Spotted with strawberries in your wife's hand?
OTH.   I gave her such a one; 'twas my first gift.
IAGO.   I know not that: but such a handkerchief—
I am sure it was your wife's—did I to-day
See Cassio wipe his beard with.
OTH.   If it be that,—
IAGO.   If it be that, or any that was hers,   440
It speaks against her with the other proofs.
OTH.   O, that the slave had forty thousand lives!

---

[58] *imputation* i.e., opinion founded on strong circumstantial evidence   [59] *foregone conclusion* previous
trial or experience (not used in our sense)

One is too poor, too weak for my revenge.
Now do I see 'tis true. Look here, Iago;
All my fond love thus do I blow to heaven.
'Tis gone.
Arise, black vengeance, from the hollow hell!
Yield up, O love, thy crown and hearted[60] throne
To tyrannous hate! Swell, bosom, with thy fraught,[61]
For 'tis of apsics'[62] tongues!

IAGO.   Yet be content   450

OTH.   O, blood, blood, blood!

IAGO.   Patience, I say; your mind perhaps may change.

OTH.   Never, Iago. Like to the Pontic sea,
Whose icy current and compulsive course
Ne'er feels retiring ebb, but keeps due on
To the Propontic and the Hellespont,
Even so my bloody thoughts, with violent pace,
Shall ne'er look back, ne'er ebb to humble love,
Till that a capable and wide revenge
Swallow them up. Now, by yond marble[63] heaven,   460
[*Kneels*]   In the due reverence of a sacred vow
I here engage my words.

IAGO.   Do not rise yet.
[*Kneels*]   Witness, you ever-burning lights above,
You elements that clip us round about,
Witness that here Iago doth give up
The execution[64] of his wit, hands, heart,
To wrong'd Othello's service! Let him command,
And to obey shall be in me remorse,[65]
What bloody business ever.   [*They rise.*]

OTH.   I greet thy love,
Not with vain thanks, but with acceptance bounteous,   470
And will upon the instant put thee to 't:
Within these three days let me hear thee say
That Cassio 's not alive.

IAGO.   My friend is dead; 'tis done at your request:
But let her live.

OTH.   Damn her, lewd minx! O, damn her! damn her!
Come, go with me apart; I will withdraw,
To furnish me with some swift means of death
For the fair devil. Now art thou my lieutenant.

IAGO.   I am your own for ever.   [*Exeunt.*]   480

---

[60]*hearted* fixed in the heart   [61]*fraught* freight, burden   [62]*aspics'* venemous serpents'
[63]*marble* i.e., gleaming like marble   [64]*execution* exercise   [65]*remorse* pity for Othello's wrongs

SCENE IV.   *Before the castle.*

[*Enter* DESDEMONA, EMILIA, *and* CLOWN.]

DES.   Do you know, sirrah, where Lieutenant Cassio lies?
CLO.   I dare not say he lies any where.
DES.   Why, man?
CLO.   He's a soldier, and for one to say a soldier lies, is stabbing.
DES.   Go to; where lodges he?
CLO.   To tell you where he lodges, is to tell you where I lie.
DES.   Can any thing be made of this?
CLO.   I know not where he lodges, and for me to devise a lodging and say he lies here or he lies there, were to lie in mine own throat.
DES.   Can you inquire him out, and be edified by report?   10
CLO.   I will catechize the world for him, that is, make questions, and by them answer.
DES.   Seek him, bid him come hither: tell him I have moved my lord on his behalf, and hope all will be well.
CLO.   To do this is within the compass of man's wit; and therefore I will attempt the doing it.   [*Exit* Clown.]
DES.   Where should I lose that handkerchief, Emilia?
EMIL.   I know not, madam.
DES.   Believe me, I had rather lost my purse
Full of crusadoes:[66] and, but my noble Moor   20
Is true of mind and made of no such baseness
As jealous creatures are, it were enough
To put him to ill thinking.
EMIL.   Is he not jealous?
DES.   Who, he? I think the sun where he was born
Drew all such humours from him.
EMIL.   Look, where he comes.

[*Enter* OTHELLO.]

DES.   I will not leave him now till Cassio
Be call'd to him.—How is 't with you, my lord?
OTH.   Well, my good lady.   [*Aside*]   O, hardness, to dissemble!—
How do you do, Desdemona?
DES.   Well, my good lord.
OTH.   Give me your hand: this hand is moist, my lady.   30
DES.   It yet hath felt no age nor known no sorrow.
OTH.   This argues fruitfulness and liberal heart:
Hot, hot, and moist: this hand of yours requires
A sequester[67] from liberty, fasting and prayer,

---

[66] *crusadoes* Portugese gold coins   [67] *sequester* separation, sequestration

Much castigation, exercise devout;
For here 's a young and sweating devil here,
That commonly rebels. 'Tis a good hand,
A frank one.
DES.   You may, indeed, say so:
For 'twas that hand that gave away my heart.
OTH.   A liberal hand: the hearts of old gave hands;   40
But our new heraldry is hands, not hearts.[68]
DES.   I cannot speak of this. Come now, your promise.
OTH.   What promise, chuck?
DES.   I have sent to bid Cassio come speak with you.
OTH.   I have a salt and sorry rheum[69] offends me;
Lend my thy handkerchief.
DES.   Here, my lord.
OTH.   That which I gave you.
DES.   I have it not about me.
OTH.   Not?
DES.   No, indeed, my lord.
OTH.   That 's a fault.
That handkerchief
Did an Egyptian[70] to my mother give;   50
She was a charmer, and could almost read
The thoughts of people: she told her, while she kept it,
'Twould make her amiable and subdue my father
Entirely to her love, but if she lost it
Or made a gift of it, my father's eye
Should hold her loathed and his spirits should hunt
After new fancies: she, dying, gave it me;
And bid me, when my fate would have me wive,
To give it her. I did so: and take heed on 't;
Make it a darling like your precious eye;   60
To lose 't or give 't away were such perdition
As nothing else could match.
DES.   Is 't possible?
OTH.   'Tis true: there 's magic in the web of it:
A sibyl, that had numb'red in the world
The sun to course two hundred compasses,
In her prophetic fury sew'd the work;
The worms were hallow'd that did breed the silk;
And it was dy'd in mummy[71] which the skilful
Conserv'd of[72] maidens' hearts.

---

[68] *new...hearts* a current expression referring to marriages in which there is a joining of hands without the giving of hearts [69] *sorry rheum* distressful head cold [70] *Egyptian* gypsy [71] *mummy* medicinal or magical preparation drained from the flesh of mummified bodies [72] *Conserv'd of* preserved out of

Des.   Indeed! is 't true?

Oth.   Most veritable; therefore look 't well.   70

Des.   Then would to God that I had never seen 't!

Oth.   Ha! wherefore?

Des.   Why do you speak so startingly and rash?

Oth.   Is 't lost? is 't gone? speak, is it out o' the' way?

Des.   Heaven bless us!

Oth.   Say you?

Des.   It is not lost; but what if it were?

Oth.   How!

Des.   I say, it is not lost.

Oth.   Fetch 't, let me see 't.

Des.   Why, so I can sir, but I will not now.   80
   This is a trick to put me from my suit:
   Pray you, let Cassio be receiv'd again.

Oth.   Fetch me the handkerchief: my mind misgives.

Des.   Come, come:
   You'll never meet a more sufficient man.

Oth.   The handkerchief!

Des.   I pray, talk me of Cassio.

Oth.   The handkerchief!   90

Des.   A man that all his time
   Hath founded his good fortunes on your love,
   Shar'd dangers with you,—

Oth.   The handkerchief!

Des.   In sooth, you are to blame.

Oth.   Away!   [*Exit* Othello.]

Emil.   Is not this man jealous?

Des.   I ne'er saw this before.
   Sure, there 's some wonder in this handkerchief:
   I am most unhappy in the loss of it.

Emil.   'Tis not a year or two shows us a man:
   They are all but stomachs, and we all but food;
   They eat us hungerly, and when they are full,
   They belch us.

[*Enter* Iago *and* Cassio.]

                              Look you, Cassio and my husband!   100

Iago.   There is no other way; 'tis she must do 't:
   And, lo, the happiness! go, and importune her.

Des.   How now, good Cassio! what 's the news with you?

Cas.   Madam, my former suit: I do beseech you
   That by your virtuous means I may again
   Exist, and be a member of his love
   Whom I with all the office of my heart

Entirely honour: I would not be delay'd.
If my offence be of such mortal kind
That nor my service past, nor present sorrows,   110
Nor purpos'd merit in futurity,
Can ransom me into his love again,
But to know so much be my benefit;[73]
So shall I clothe me in a forc'd content,
And shut myself up in some other course,
To fortune's alms.

DES.   Alas, thrice-gentle Cassio!
My advocation[74] is not now in tune;
My lord is not my lord; nor should I know him,
Were he in favour as in humour alter'd.
So help me every spirit sanctified   120
As I have spoken for you all my best
And stood within the blank[75] of his displeasure
For my free speech! You must awhile be patient:
What I can do I will; and more I will
Than for myself I dare: let that suffice you.

IAGO.   Is my lord angry?

EMIL.   He went hence but now,
And certainly in strange unquietness.

IAGO.   Can he be angry? I have seen the cannon,
When it hath blown his ranks into the air,
And, like the devil, from his very arm   130
Puff'd his own brother:—and can he be angry?
Something of moment then: I will go meet him:
There 's matter in 't indeed, if he be angry.

DES.   I prithee, do so.   [*Exit* IAGO.]
                  Something, sure, of state,
Either from Venice, or some unhatch'd practice
Made demonstrable here in Cyprus to him,
Hath puddled[76] his clear spirit; and in such cases
Men's natures wrangle with inferior things,
Though great ones are their object. 'Tis even so;
For let our finger ache, and it indues[77]   140
Our other healthful members even to a sense
Of pain: nay, we must think men are not gods,
Nor of them look for such observancy
As fits the bridal. Beshrew me much, Emilia,
I was, unhandsome[78] warrior as I am,

---

[73] *to know…benefit* to know that my case is hopeless will end my vain endeavor   [74] *advocation* advocacy
[75] *blank* white spot in the center of a target; here, range   [76] *puddled* sullied the purity of
[77] *indues* brings to the same condition   [78] *unhandsome* unfair

Arraigning his unkindness with my soul;
But now I find I had suborn'd the witness,
And he 's indicted falsely.

EMIL. Pray heaven it be state-matters, as you think,
And no conception[79] nor no jealous toy   150
Concerning you.

DES. Alas the day! I never gave him cause.

EMIL. But jealous souls will not be answer'd so;
They are not ever jealous for the cause,
But jealous for they are jealous: 'tis a monster
Begot upon itself, born on itself.

DES. Heaven keep that monster from Othello's mind!

EMIL. Lady, amen.

DES. I will go seek him. Cassio, walk here about:
If I do find him fit, I'll move your suit   160
And seek to effect it to my uttermost.

CAS. I humbly thank your ladyship. [*Exit* DESDEMONA *with* EMILIA.]

[*Enter* BIANCA.]

BIAN. Save you, friend Cassio!

CAS.   What make you from home?
How is 't with you, my most fair Bianca?
I' faith, sweet love, I was coming to your house.

BIAN. And I was going to your lodging, Cassio.
What, keep a week away? seven days and nights?
Eight score eight hours? and lovers' absent hours,
More tedious than the dial eight score times?
O weary reck'ning!

CAS.   Pardon me, Bianca.   170
I have this while with leaden thoughts been press'd;
But I shall, in a more continuate[80] time,
Strike off this score of absence. Sweet Bianca, [*Giving her* DESDEMONA'*s*
    handkerchief.]
Take me this work out.[81]

BIAN.   O Cassio, whence came this?
This is some token from a newer friend:
To the felt absence now I feel a cause:
Is 't come to this? Well, well.

CAS.   Go to, woman!
Throw your vile guesses in the devil's teeth,
From whence you have them. You are jealous now
That this is from some mistress, some remembrance: 180
No, in good troth, Bianca.

---

[79] *conception* mere fancy [80] *continuate* uninterrupted [81] *Take…out* i.e., copy this embroidery for me

BIAN. Why, whose is it?

CAS. I know not, sweet: I found it in my chamber.
  I like the work well: ere it be demanded—
  As like enough it will—I would have it copied:
  Take it, and do 't; and leave me for this time.

BIAN. Leave you! wherefore?

CAS. I do attend here on the general;
  And think it no addition, nor my wish,
  To have him see me woman'd.

BIAN. Why, I pray you?

CAS. Not that I love you not.

BIAN. But that you do not love me.   190
  I pray you, bring me on the way a little,
  And say if I shall see you soon at night.

CAS. 'Tis but a little way that I can bring you;
  For I attend here: but I'll see you soon.

BIAN. 'Tis very good; I must be circumstance'd.[82]   [*Exeunt omnes.*]

ACT IV

SCENE I.   *Cyprus. Before the castle.*

[*Enter* OTHELLO *and* IAGO.]

IAGO. Will you think so?

OTH. Think so, Iago!

IAGO. What,
  To kiss in private?

OTH. An unauthoriz'd kiss.

IAGO. Or to be naked with her friend in bed
  An hour or more, not meaning any harm?

OTH. Naked in bed, Iago, and not mean harm!
  It is hypocrisy against the devil:
  They that mean virtuously, and yet do so,
  The devil their virtue tempts, and they tempt heaven.

IAGO. So[1] they do nothing, 'tis a venial slip:
  But if I give my wife a handkerchief,—   10

OTH. What then?

IAGO. Why, then, 'tis hers, my lord: and, being hers,
  She may, I think, bestow 't on any man.

OTH. She is protectress of her honour too:
  May she give that?

IAGO. Her honour is an essence that 's not seen;
  They have it very oft that have it not:
  But, for the handkerchief,—

---

[82] *circumstance'd* governed by circumstances   ACT IV   [1] *So* as long as

OTH.　By heaven, I would most gladly have forgot it.
　　Thou said'st—O, it comes o'er my memory,　　　　　　　　　　20
　　As doth the raven o'er the infected house,[2]
　　Boding to all—he had my handkerchief.
IAGO.　Ay, what of that?
OTH.　　　　　　　　　　That's not so good now.
IAGO.　　　　　　　　　　　　　　　　　　What,
　　If I had said I had seen him do you wrong?
　　Or hear him say,—as knaves be such abroad,
　　Who having, by their own importunate suit,
　　Or voluntary dotage of some mistress,
　　Convinced or supplied[3] them, cannot choose
　　But they must blab—
OTH.　　　　　　　　　Hath he said anything?
IAGO.　He hath, my lord; but be you well assur'd,　　　　　　　30
　　No more than he'll unswear.
OTH.　　　　　　　　　　What hath he said?
IAGO.　'Faith, that he did—I know not what he did.
OTH.　What? What?
IAGO.　Lie—
OTH.　　　　With her?
IAGO.　　　　　　　　With her, on her; what you will.
OTH.　Lie with her! lie on her! We say lie on her, when they belie her. Lie with her!
　　that's fulsome.—Handkerchief—confessions—handkerchief!—To confess, and
　　be hanged for his labour;—first, to be hanged, and then to confess.—I tremble
　　at it. Nature would not invest herself in such shadowing passion without some
　　instruction.[4] It is not words that shake me thus. Pish! Noses, ears, and lips.—
　　Is 't possible?—Confess—handkerchief—O devil!　[*Falls in a trance.*]　　40
IAGO.　Work on,
　　My medicine, work! Thus credulous fools are caught;
　　And many worthy and chaste dames even thus,
　　All guiltless, meet reproach. What, ho! my lord!
　　My lord, I say! Othello!

[*Enter* CASSIO.]

How now, Cassio!
CAS.　What 's the matter?
IAGO.　My lord is fall'n into an epilepsy:
　　This is his second fit; he had one yesterday.
CAS.　Rub him about the temples.

---

[2] *raven…house* allusion to the belief that the raven hovered over a house of sickness or infection
[3] *Convinced or supplied* i.e., mistresses gained by importunity and those who doted voluntarily
[4] *Nature…instruction* i.e., my jealousy cannot be merely the result of natural imagination, but must
have some foundation in fact

IAGO.   No, forbear;
  The lethargy[5] must have his quiet course: 50
  If not, he foams at mouth and by and by
  Breaks out to savage madness. Look, he stirs:
  Do you withdraw yourself a little while,
  He will recover straight: when he is gone,
  I would on great occasion speak with you.   [*Exit* CASSIO.]
  How is it, general? have you not hurt your head?
OTH.   Dost thou mock me?
IAGO.   I mock you! no, by heaven.
  Would you would bear your fortune like a man!
OTH.   A horned man 's a monster and a beast.
IAGO.   There 's many a beast then in a populous city,
  And many a civil[6] monster.   60
OTH.   Did he confess it?
IAGO.   Good sir, be a man;
  Think every bearded fellow that 's but yok'd
  May draw with you:[7] there 's millions now alive
  That nightly lie in those unproper[8] beds
  Which they dare swear peculiar:[9] your case is better.
  O, 'tis the spite of hell, the fiend's arch-mock,
  To lip a wanton in a secure couch,
  And to suppose her chaste! No, let me know;
  And knowing what I am, I know what she shall be.   70
OTH.   O, thou art wise; 'tis certain.
IAGO.   Stand you awhile apart;
  Confine yourself but in a patient list.[10]
  Whilst you were here o'erwhelmed with your grief—
  A passion most unsuiting such a man—
  Cassio came hither: I shifted him away,
  And laid good 'scuse upon your ecstasy,
  Bade him anon return and here speak with me;
  The which he promis'd. Do but encave[11] yourself,
  And mark the fleers,[12] the gibes, and notable scorns,
  That dwell in every region of his face;   80
  For I will make him tell the tale anew,
  Where, how, how oft, how long ago, and when
  He hath, and is again to cope your wife:
  I say, but mark his gesture. Marry, patience;
  Or I shall say y' are all in all in spleen,
  And nothing of a man.

---

[5] *lethargy* unconscious condition   [6] *civil* i.e., in civilized society   [7] *draw with you* i.e., share your fate
as cuckold   [8] *unproper* not belonging exclusively to an individual   [9] *peculiar* private, one's own
[10] *patient list* within the bounds of patience   [11] *encave* conceal   [12] *fleers* sneers

OTH.   Dost thou hear, Iago?
 I will be found most cunning in my patience;
 But—dost thou hear?—most bloody.
IAGO.   That 's not amiss;
 But yet keep time[13] in all. Will you withdraw? [OTHELLO *retires.*]
 Now will I question Cassio of Bianca,   90
 A housewife that by selling her desires
 Buys herself bread and clothes: it is a creature
 That dotes on Cassio; as 'tis the strumpet's plague
 To beguile many and be beguil'd by one:
 He, when he hears of her, cannot refrain
 From the excess of laughter. Here he comes:

       [*Enter* CASSIO.]

 As he shall smile, Othello shall go mad;
 And his unbookish[14] jealousy must conster[15]
 Poor Cassio's smiles, gestures and light behaviour,
 Quite in the wrong. How do you know, lieutenant?   100
CAS. The worser that you give me the addition[16]
 Whose want even kills me.
IAGO. Ply Desdemona well, and you are sure on 't
 [*Speaking lower*] Now, if this suit lay in Bianca's power,
 How quickly should you speed!
CAS.   Alas, poor caitiff!
OTH. Look, how he laughs already!
IAGO. I never knew woman love man so.
CAS. Alas, poor rogue! I think, i' faith, she loves me.
OTH. Now he denies it faintly, and laughs it out.
IAGO. Do you hear, Cassio?
OTH.   Now he importunes him   110
 To tell o'er: go to; well said, well said.
IAGO. She gives it out that you shall marry her:
 Do you intend it?
CAS. Ha, ha, ha!
OTH. Do you triumph, Roman?[17] do you triumph?
CAS. I marry her! what? a customer![18] Prithee, bear some charity to my wit; do
  not think it so unwholesome. Ha, ha, ha!
OTH. So, so, so, so: they laugh that win.
IAGO. 'Faith, the cry goes that you shall marry her.
CAS. Prithee, say true.   120
IAGO. I am a very villain else.

---

[13] *keep time* use judgment and order [14] *unbookish* uninstructed [15] *conster* construe [16] *addition* title
[17] *Roman* epithet arising from the association of the Romans with the idea of triumph
[18] *customer* prostitute

OTH.   Have you scored me?[19] Well.

CAS.   This is the monkey's own giving out: she is persuaded I will marry her, out of her own love and flattery, not out of my promise.

OTH.   Iago beckons me; now he begins the story.

CAS.   She was here even now; she haunts me in every place. I was the other day talking on the seabank with certain Venetians; and thither comes the bauble,[20] and, by this hand, she falls me thus about my neck—

OTH.   Crying, 'O dear Cassio!' as it were: his gesture imports it.

CAS.   So hangs, and lolls, and weeps upon me; so shakes, and pulls me: ha, ha, ha!   130

OTH.   Now he tells how she plucked him to my chamber. O, I see that nose of yours, but not that dog I shall throw it to.

CAS.   Well, I must leave her company.

IAGO.   Before me![21] look, where she comes.

[*Enter* BIANCA.]

CAS.   'Tis such another fitchew![22] marry, a perfumed one.—What do you mean by this haunting of me?

BIAN.   Let the devil and his dam haunt you! What did you mean by that same handkerchief you gave me even now? I was a fine fool to take it. I must take out the work?—A likely piece of work, that you should find it in your cham-ber, and not know who left it there! This is some minx's token, and I must   140
take out the work? There; give it your hobby-horse:[23] wheresoever you had it, I'll take out no work on 't.

CAS.   How now, my sweet Bianca! how now! how now!

OTH.   By heaven, that should be my handkerchief!

BIAN.   An you'll come to supper to-night, you may; an you will not, come when you are next prepared for.   [*Exit.*]

IAGO.   After her, after her.

CAS.   'Faith, I must; she'll rail in the street else.

IAGO.   Will you sup there?

CAS.   Yes, I intend so.   150

IAGO.   Well, I may chance to see you; for I would very fain speak with you.

CAS.   Prithee, come; will you?

IAGO.   Go to; say no more.   [*Exit* CASSIO.]

OTH [*advancing*].   How shall I murder him, Iago?

IAGO.   Did you perceive how he laughed at his vice?

OTH.   O Iago!

IAGO.   And did you see the handkerchief?

OTH.   Was that mine?

IAGO.   Yours, by this hand: and to see how he prizes the foolish woman your wife! She gave it him, and he hath given it his whore.   160

---

[19] *scored me* made up my reckoning, or branded me   [20] *bauble* plaything   [21] *Before me!* On my soul!
[22] *fitchew* polecat (because of her strong perfume; also, slang word for a prostitute)
[23] *hobby-horse* harlot

OTH.   I would have him nine years a-killing. A fine woman! a fair woman! a sweet
woman!

IAGO.   Nay, you must forget that.

OTH.   Ay, let her rot, and perish, and be damned to-night; for she shall not live:
no, my heart is turned to stone; I strike it, and it hurts my hand. O, the world
hath not a sweeter creature: she might lie by an emperor's side and command
him tasks.

IAGO.   Nay, that 's not your way.[24]

OTH.   Hang her! I do but say what she is: so delicate with her needle: an admirable
musician: O! she will sing the savageness out of a bear: of so high and plente-   170
ous wit and invention:—

IAGO.   She 's the worse for all this.

OTH.   O, a thousand thousand times: and then, of so gentle a condition!

IAGO.   Ay, too gentle.

OTH.   Nay, that 's certain: but yet the pity of it, Iago! O Iago, the pity of it, Iago!

IAGO.   If you are so fond over her iniquity, give her patent[25] to offend; for, if it
touch not you, it comes near nobody.

OTH.   I will chop her into messes;[26] cuckold me!

IAGO.   O, 'tis foul in her

OTH.   With mine officer!   180

IAGO.   That 's fouler.

OTH.   Get me some poison, Iago; this night: I'll not expostulate with her, lest her
body and beauty unprovide[27] my mind again: this night, Iago.

IAGO.   Do it not with poison, strangle her in her bed, even the bed she hath
contaminated.

OTH.   Good, good: the justice of it pleases: very good.

IAGO.   And for Cassio, let me be his undertaker:[28] you shall hear more by midnight.

OTH.   Excellent good.   [*A trumpet within.*]   What trumpet is that same?

IAGO.   I warrant something from Venice.

[*Enter* LODOVICO, DESDEMONA, *and* ATTENDANTS.]

'Tis Lodovico.

This comes from the duke: and, see, your wife's with him.   190

LOD.   God save you, worthy general!

OTH.   With all my heart, sir.

LOD.   The duke and the senators of Venice greet you.   [*Gives him a letter.*]

OTH.   I kiss the instrument of their pleasures.   [*Opens the letter, and reads.*]

DES.   And what 's the news, good cousin Lodovico?

IAGO.   I am very glad to see you, signior;
Welcome to Cyprus.

LOD.   I thank you. How does Lieutenant Cassio?

---

[24] *your way* i.e., the way you should think of her   [25] *patent* license   [26] *messes* dishes of food
[27] *unprovide* weaken, unfit   [28] *let…undertaker* i.e., let me settle with him

IAGO. Lives, sir.

DES. Cousin, there 's fall'n between him and my lord
An unkind breach: but you shall make all well.   200

OTH. Are you sure of that?

DES. My lord?

OTH. [*reads*]. "This fail you not to do, as you will—"

LOD. He did not call; he 's busy in the paper.
Is there division 'twixt my lord and Cassio?

DES. A most unhappy one: I would do much
T' atone them, for the love I bear to Cassio.

OTH. Fire and brimstone!

DES.   My lord?

OTH.   Are you wise?

DES. What, is he angry?

LOD.   May be the letter mov'd him:
For, as I think, they do command him home,
Deputing Cassio in his government.[29]   210

DES. Trust me, I am glad on 't.

OTH.   Indeed!

DES.   My lord?

OTH. I am glad to see you mad.

DES.   Why, sweet Othello,—

OTH [*striking her*]. Devil!

DES. I have not deserv'd this.

LOD. My lord, this would not be believ'd in Venice,
Though I should swear I saw 't; 'tis very much:
Make her amends; she weeps.

OTH.   O devil, devil!
If that the earth could teem with woman's tears,
Each drop she falls would prove a crocodile.[30]
Out of my sight!

DES.   I will not stay to offend you. [*Going.*]   220

LOD. Truly, an obedient lady:
I do beseech your lordship, call her back.

OTH. Mistress!

DES.   My lord?

OTH.   What would you with her, sir?

LOD. Who, I, my lord?

OTH. Ay; you did wish that I would make her turn:
Sir, she can turn, and turn, and yet go on,
And turn again; and she can weep, sir, weep;
And she 's obedient, as you say, obedient,

---

[29] *government* office   [30] *prove a crocodile* i.e., by weeping crocodile tears; it was believed the crocodile shed tears over the body of the person it was eating

Very obedient. Proceed you in your tears.
Concerning this, sir,—O well-painted passion,[31]!— 230
I am commanded home. Get you away;
I'll send for you anon. Sir, I obey the mandate,
And will return to Venice. Hence, avaunt!   [*Exit* DESDEMONA.]
Cassio shall have my place. And, sir, to-night,
I do entreat that we may sup together:
You are welcome, sir, to Cyprus.—Goats and monkeys!   [*Exit.*]
LOD.   Is this the noble Moor whom our full senate
Call all in all sufficient? Is this the nature
Whom passion could not shake? whose solid virtue
The shot of accident, nor dart of chance, 240
Could neither graze nor pierce?
IAGO.   He is much chang'd.
LOD.   Are his wits safe? is he not light of brain?
IAGO.   He 's that he is: I may not breathe my censure
What he might be: if what he might he is not,
I would to heaven he were!
LOD.   What, strike his wife!
IAGO.   'Faith, that was not so well; yet would I knew
That stroke would prove the worst!
LOD.   Is it his use?
Or did the letters work upon his blood,
And new-create this fault?
IAGO.   Alas, alas!
It is not honesty in me to speak 250
What I have seen and known. You shall observe him,
And his own courses will denote him so
That I may save my speech: do but go after,
And mark how he continues.
LOD.   I am sorry that I am deceiv'd in him.   [*Exeunt.*]

SCENE II.   *A room in the castle.*

[*Enter* OTHELLO *and* EMILIA.]

OTH.   You have seen nothing then?
EMIL.   Nor ever heard, nor ever did suspect.
OTH.   Yes, you have seen Cassio and she together.
EMIL.   But then I saw no harm, and then I heard
Each syllable that breath made up between them.
OTH.   What, did they never whisper?
EMIL.   Never, my lord.
OTH.   Nor send you out 'o th' way?

___

[31] *well-painted passion* well-simulated emotion

EMIL. Never.

OTH. To fetch her fan, her gloves, her mask, nor nothing?

EMIL. Never, my lord. 10

OTH. That 's strange.

EMIL. I durst, my lord, to wager she is honest,
Lay down my soul at stake: if you think other,
Remove your thought: it doth abuse your bosom.
If any wretch have put this in your head,
Let heaven requite it with the serpent's curse!
For, if she be not honest, chaste, and true,
There 's no man happy; the purest of their wives
Is foul as slander.

OTH. Bid her come hither: go. [*Exit* EMILIA.]
She says enough; yet she 's a simple bawd 20
That cannot say as much. This is a subtle whore,
A closet lock and key[32] of villanous secrets:
And yet she'll kneel and pray; I have seen her do 't.

[*Enter* DESDEMONA *and* EMILIA.]

DES. My lord, what is your will?

OTH. Pray, chuck, come hither.

DES. What is your pleasure?

OTH. Let me see your eyes;
Look in my face.

DES. What horrible fancy 's this?

OTH [*to* EMILIA]. Some of your function,[33] mistress;
Leave procreants[34] alone and shut the door;
Cough, or cry "hem," if any body come:
Your mystery, your mystery:[35] nay, dispatch. [*Exit* EMILIA.] 30

DES. Upon my knees, what doth your speech import?
I understand a fury in your words,
But not the words.

OTH. Why, what art thou?

DES. Your wife, my lord; your true
And loyal wife.

OTH. Come, swear it, damn thyself;
Lest, being like one of heaven, the devils themselves
Should fear to seize thee: therefore be double damn'd:
Swear thou are honest.

DES. Heaven doth truly know it.

OTH. Heaven truly knows that thou art false as hell.

DES. To whom, my lord? with whom? how am I false? 40

---

[32] *closet lock and key* complete storeroom [33] *Some...function* i.e., set to work in your chosen profession, that of bawd [34] *procreants* mating couples [35] *mystery* trade, occupation

OTH.   O Desdemona! away! away! away!

DES.   Alas the heavy day! Why do you weep?
   Am I the motive of these tears, my lord?
   If haply you my father do suspect
   An instrument of this your calling back,
   Lay not your blame on me: if you have lost him,
   Why, I have lost him too.

OTH.   Had it pleas'd heaven
   To try me with affliction; had they[36] rain'd
   All kinds of sores and shames on my bare head,
   Steep'd me in poverty to the very lips,   50
   Given to captivity me and my utmost hopes,
   I should have found in some place of my soul
   A drop of patience: but, alas, to make me
   A fixed figure for the time of scorn
   To point his slow unmoving finger at![37]
   Yet could I bear that too; well, very well:
   But there, where I have garner'd up my heart,
   Where either I must live, or bear no life;
   The fountain from the which my current runs,
   Or else dries up; to be discarded thence!   60
   Or keep it as a cistern for foul toads
   To knot and gender[38] in! Turn thy complexion[39] there,
   Patience, thou young and rose-lipp'd cherubin,—
   Ay, there, look grim as hell!

DES.   I hope my noble lord esteems me honest.

OTH.   O, ay; as summer flies are in the shambles,[40]
   That quicken[41] even with blowing. O thou weed,
   Who are so lovely fair and smell'st so sweet
   That the sense aches at thee, would thou hads't ne'er been born!

DES.   Alas, what ignorant sin have I committed?   70

OTH.   Was this fair paper, this most goodly book,
   Made to write "whore" upon? What committed!
   Committed! O thou public commoner![42]
   I should make very forges of my cheeks,
   That would to cinders burn up modesty,
   Did I but speak they deeds. What committed!
   Heaven stops the nose at it and the moon winks,
   The bawdy wind that kisses all it meets
   Is hush'd within the hollow mine of earth,

---

[36] *they* heavenly powers [37] *A...at* Othello possibly thinks of himself as a man set in a pillory at whom the scornful world points in mockery. There seems to be a comparison with the sundial, whose gnomon, or indicator, becomes the finger of scornful time [38] *gender* engender [39] *Turn thy complexion* grow pale [40] *shambles* slaughterhouse [41] *quicken* come to life [42] *commoner* prostitute

And will not hear it. What committed! 80
Impudent strumpet!

DES. By heaven, you do me wrong.

OTH. Are not you a strumpet?

DES. No, as I am a Christian:
If to preserve this vessel[43] for my lord
From any other foul unlawful touch
Be not to be a strumpet, I am none.

OTH. What, not a whore?

DES. No, as I shall be sav'd.

OTH. Is 't possible?

DES. O, heaven forgive us!

OTH. I cry you mercy, then:
I took you for the cunning whore of Venice
That married with Othello. [*Raising his voice.*] You, mistress, 90
That have the office opposite to Saint Peter,
And keep the gate of hell!

[*Enter* EMILIA.]

You, you, ay, you!
We have done our course; there 's money for your pains:
I pray you, turn the key and keep our counsel. [*Exit.*]

EMIL. Alas, what does this gentleman conceive?
How do you, madam? how do you, my good lady?

DES. 'Faith, half asleep.

EMIL. Good madam, what 's the matter with my lord?

DES. With who?

EMIL. Why, with my lord, madam. 100

DES. Who is thy lord?

EMIL. He that is yours, sweet lady.

DES. I have none: do not talk to me, Emilia;
I cannot weep; nor answers have I none,
But what should go by water.[44] Prithee, tonight
Lay on my bed my wedding sheets: remember;
And call thy husband hither.

EMIL. Here 's a change indeed! [*Exit.*]

DES. 'Tis meet I should be us'd so, very meet.
How have I been behav'd, that he might stick
The small'st opinion on my least misuse?[45]

[*Enter* IAGO *and* EMILIA.]

IAGO. What is your pleasure, madam? How is 't with you? 110

---

[43] *vessel* body [44] *go by water* be expressed by tears [45] *misuse* evil conduct

DES.   I cannot tell. Those that do teach young babes
   Do it with gentle means and easy tasks:
   He might have chid me so; for, in good faith,
   I am a child to chiding.
IAGO.   What is the matter, lady?
EMIL.   Alas, Iago, my lord hath so bewhor'd her,
   Thrown such despite[46] and heavy terms upon her,
   As true hearts cannot bear.
DES.   Am I that name, Iago?
IAGO.   What name, fair lady?
DES.   Such as she said my lord did say I was.
EMIL.   He call'd her whore: a beggar in his drink   120
   Could not have laid such terms upon his callet.[47]
IAGO.   Why did he so?
DES.   I do not know; I am sure I am none such.
IAGO.   Do not weep, do not weep. Alas the day!
EMIL.   Hath she forsook so many noble matches,
   Her father and her country and her friends,
   To be call'd whore? would it not make one weep?
DES.   It is my wretched fortune.
IAGO.   Beshrew him for 't!
   How comes this trick upon him?
DES.   Nay, heaven doth know.
EMIL.   I will be hang'd, if some eternal villain,   130
   Some busy and insinuating rogue,
   Some cogging,[48] cozening slave, to get some office,
   Have not devis'd this slander; I will be hang'd else.
IAGO.   Fie, there is no such man; it is impossible.
DES.   If any such there be, heaven pardon him!
EMIL.   A halter pardon him! and hell gnaw his bones!
   Why should he call her whore? who keeps her company?
   What place? what time? what form? what likelihood?
   The Moor's abus'd by some most villainous knave,
   Some base notorious knave, some scurvy fellow.   140
   O heaven, that such companions thou 'ldst unfold,
   And put in every honest hand a whip
   To lash the rascals naked through the world
   Even from the east to th' west!
IAGO.   Speak within door.[49]
EMIL.   O, fie upon them! Some such squire he was
   That turn'd your wit the seamy side without,
   And made you to suspect me with the Moor.

---

[46] *despite* contempt, scorn   [47] *callet* lewd woman   [48] *coggin* cheating   [49] *Speak…door* i.e., not so loud

IAGO.   You are a fool; go to.

DES.   Alas, Iago.

  What shall I do to win my lord again?

  Good friend, go to him; for, by this light of heaven,   150

  I know not how I lost him. Here I kneel:

  If e'er by will did trespass 'gainst his love,

  Either in discourse of thought or actual deed,

  Or that mine eyes, mine ears, or any sense,

  Delighted them in any other form;

  Or that I do not yet, and ever did,

  And ever will—though he do shake me off

  To beggarly divorcement—love him dearly,

  Comfort forswear me! Unkindness may do much;

  And his unkindness may defeat my life,   160

  But never taint my lord. I cannot say "whore":

  It doth abhor me now I speak the word;

  To do the act that might the addition[50] earn

  Not the world's mass of vanity could make me.

IAGO.   I pray you, be content; 'tis but his humour:

  The business of the state does him offence,

  And he does chide with you.

DES.   If 'twere no other,—

IAGO.   'Tis but so, I warrant.   [*Trumpets within.*]

  Hark, how these instruments summon to supper!

  The messengers of Venice stay the meat;[51]   170

  Go in, and weep not; all things shall be well.   [*Exeunt* DESDEMONA *and* EMILIA.]

[*Enter* RODERIGO.]

  How now, Roderigo!

ROD.   I do not find that thou dealest justly with me.

IAGO.   What in the contrary?

ROD.   Everyday thou daffest me[52] with some device, Iago; and rather, as it seems
    to me now, keepest from me all conveniency[53] than suppliest me with the least
    advantage of hope. I will indeed no longer endure it, nor am I yet persuaded
    to put up[54] in peace what already I have foolishly suffered.

IAGO.   Will you hear me, Roderigo?

ROD.   'Faith, I have heard too much, for your words and performances are no kin 180
    together.

IAGO.   You charge me most unjustly.

ROD.   With nought but truth. I have wasted myself out of my means. The jewels
    you have had from me to deliver to Desdemona would half have corrupted a

---

[50] *addition* title   [51] *stay the meat* are waiting for supper   [52] *daffest me* puts me off with an excuse
[53] *conveniency* advantage, opportunity   [54] *put up* submit to

votarist:[55] you have told me she hath received them and returned me expectations and comforts of sudden respect and acquaintance, but I find none.

IAGO.   Well; go to; very well.

ROD.   Very well! go to! I cannot go to, man; nor 'tis not very well: nay, I think it is scurvy, and begin to find myself fopped[56] in it.

IAGO.   Very well.   190

ROD.   I tell you 'tis not very well. I will make myself known to Desdemona: if she will return me my jewels, I will give over my suit and repent my unlawful solicitation; if not, assure yourself I will seek satisfaction of you.

IAGO.   You have said now.[57]

ROD.   Ay, and said nothing but what I protest intendment[58] of doing.

IAGO.   Why, now I see there 's mettle in thee, and even from this instant do build on thee a better opinion than ever before. Give my thy hand, Roderigo: thou hast taken against me a most just exception; but yet, I protest, I have dealt most directly in thy affair.

ROD.   It hath not appeared.   200

IAGO.   I grant indeed it had not appeared, and your suspicion is not without wit and judgement. But, Roderigo, if thou hast that in thee indeed, which I have greater reason to believe now than ever, I mean purpose, courage and valour, this night show it: if thou the next night following enjoy not Desdemona, take me from this world with treachery and devise engines for[59] my life.

ROD.   Well, what is it? is it within reason and compass?

IAGO.   Sir, there is especial commission come from Venice to depute Cassio in Othello's place.

ROD.   Is that true? why, then Othello and Desdemona return again to Venice.

IAGO.   O, no; he goes into Mauritania[60] and takes away with him the fair Desde-   210
mona, unless his abode be lingered here by some accident: wherein none can be so determinate[61] as the removing of Cassio.

ROD.   How do you mean, removing of him?

IAGO.   Why, by making him uncapable of Othello's place; knocking out his brains.

ROD.   And that you would have me to do?

IAGO.   Ay, if you dare do yourself a profit and a right. He sups to-night with a harlotry,[62] and thither will I go to him: he knows not yet of his honourable fortune. If you will watch his going thence, which I will fashion to fall out between twelve and one, you may take him at your pleasure: I will be near to second your attempt, and he shall fall between us. Come, stand not amazed at   220
it, but go along with me; I will show you such a necessity in his death that you shall think yourself bound to put it to him. It is now high[63] supper-time, and the night grows to waste: about it.

ROD.   I will hear further reason for this.

IAGO.   And you shall be satisfied.   [*Exeunt.*]

---

[55] *votarist* nun   [56] *fopped* fooled   [57] *You...now* well said, quite right   [58] *intendment* purpose, intention
[59] *engines for* plots against   [60] *Mauritania* Roman name of northwest Africa, supposed land of the
Moors   [61] *determinate* decisive   [62] *harlotry* courtesan   [63] *high* quite

SCENE III.   *Another room in the castle.*

[*Enter* OTHELLO, LODOVICO, DESDEMONA, EMILIA, *and* ATTENDANTS.]

LOD.   I do beseech you, sir, trouble yourself no further.
OTH.   O, pardon me; 'twill do me good to walk.
LOD.   Madam, good night; I humbly thank your ladyship.
DES.   Your honour is most welcome.
OTH.   Will you walk, sir?
  O,—Desdemona,—
DES.   My lord?
OTH.   Get you to bed on th' instant; I will be returned forthwith: dismiss your
  attendant there: look 't be done.
DES.   I will, my lord.   [*Exit* OTHELLLO, *with* LODOVICO *and* ATTENDANTS.]
EMIL.   How goes it now? he looks gentler than he did.   10
DES.   He says he will return incontinent:[64]
  He hath commanded me to go to bed,
  And bade me to dismiss you.
EMIL.   Dismiss me!
DES.   It was his bidding; therefore, good Emilia,
  Give me my nightly wearing, and adieu:
  We must not now displease him.
EMIL.   I would you had never seen him!
DES.   So would not I: my love doth so approve him,
  That even his stubbornness,[65] his checks,[66] his frowns,—
  Prithee, unpin me,—have grace and favour in them.   20
EMIL.   I have laid those sheets you bade me on the bed.
DES.   All 's one. Good faith, how foolish are our minds!
  If I do die before thee, prithee, shroud me
  In one of those same sheets.
EMIL.   Come, come, you talk.
DES.   My mother had a maid call'd Barbary:
  She was in love, and he she lov'd prov'd mad
  And did forsake her: she had a song of 'willow';
  An old thing 'twas, but it express'd her fortune,
  And she died singing it: that song to-night
  Will not go from my mind; I have much to do,   30
  But to[67] go hang my head all at one side,
  And sing it like poor Barbary. Prithee, dispatch.
EMIL.   Shall I go fetch your night-gown?[68]
DES.   No, unpin me here.
  This Lodovico is a proper man.
EMIL.   A very handsome man.

---

[64] *incontinent* immediately   [65] *stubbornness* harshness   [66] *checks* rebukes   [67] *But to* not to
[68] *night-gown* dressing gown

DES.   He speaks well.

EMIL.   I know a lady in Venice would have walked barefoot to Palestine for a touch of his nether lip.

DES   [*Singing*].   The poor soul sat sighing by a sycamore tree,
    Sing all a green willow;   40
  Her hand on her bosom, her head on her knee,
    Sing willow, willow, willow:
  The fresh streams ran by her, and murmur'd her moans;
    Sing willow, willow, willow;
  Her salt tears fell from her, and soft'ned the stones;—
  Lay by these:—
  [*Singing*]   Sing willow, willow, willow;
  Prithee, hie thee; he'll come anon:—
  [*Singing*]   Sing all a green willow must be my garland.
    Let nobody blame him; his scorn I approve,—   50
  Nay, that 's not next.—Hark! who is 't that knocks?

EMIL.   It 's the wind.

DES   [*Singing*].   I call'd my love false love; but what said he then?
     Sing willow, willow, willow:
    If I court moe women, you'll couch with moe men.—
  So, get thee gone; good night. Mine eyes do itch;
  Doth that bode weeping?

EMIL.   'Tis neither here nor there.

DES.   I have heard it said so. O, these men, these men!
  Dost thou in conscience think,—tell me, Emilia,—
  That there be women do abuse their husbands   60
  In such gross kind?

EMIL.   There be some such, no question.

DES.   Wouldst thou do such a deed for all the world?

EMIL.   Why, would not you?

DES.   No, by this heavenly light!

EMIL.   Nor I neither by this heavenly light; I might do't as well i' the dark.

DES.   Wouldst thou do such a deed for all the world?

EMIL.   The world 's a huge thing: it is a great price
  For a small vice.

DES.   In troth, I think thou wouldst not.

EMIL.   In troth, I think I should; and undo 't when I had done. Marry, I would not do such a thing for a joint-ring,[69] nor for measures of lawn, nor for gowns, 70 petticoats, nor caps, nor any petty exhibition;[70] but, for all the whole world,— why, who would not make her husband a cuckold to make him a monarch? I should venture purgatory for 't.

DES.   Beshrew me, if I would do such a wrong
  For the whole world.

---

[69] *joint-ring* a ring made in separable halves as a lover's token   [70] *exhibition* gift, present

EMIL. Why, the wrong is but a wrong i' the world; and having the world for your
labour, 'tis a wrong in your own world, and you might quickly make it right.

DES. I do not think there is any such woman.

EMIL. Yes, a dozen; and as many to the vantage[71] as would store the world they
played for. 80

But I do think it is their husband's faults
If wives do fall: say that they slack their duties,
And pour our treasures into foreign laps,[72]
Or else break out in peevish jealousies,
Throwing restraint upon us; or say they strike us,
Or scant our former having in despite;[73]
Why, we have galls,[74] and though we have some grace,
Yet have we some revenge. Let husbands know
Their wives have sense like them: they see and smell
And have their palates both for sweet and sour, 90
As husbands have. What is it that they do
When they change us for others? Is it sport?
I think it is: and doth affection breed it?
I think it doth: is 't frailty that thus errs?
It is so too: and have not we affections,
Desires for sport, and frailty, as men have?
Then let them use us well: else let them know,
The ills we do, their ills instruct us so.

DES. Good night, good night: heaven me such uses send,
Not to pick bad from bad, but by bad mend! [*Exeunt.*] 100

ACT V

SCENE I. *Cyprus. A street.*

[*Enter* IAGO *and* RODERIGO.]

IAGO. Here stand behind this bulk;[1] straight will he come:
Wear thy good rapier bare, and put it home:
Quick, quick; fear nothing; I'll be at they elbow:
It makes us, or it mars us; think on that,
And fix most firm thy resolution.

ROD. Be near at hand; I may miscarry in 't.

IAGO. Here, at thy hand: be bold, and take thy stand. [*Retires.*]

ROD. I have no great devotion to the deed;
And yet he hath given me satisfying reasons:
'Tis but a man gone. Forth, my sword: he dies.

---

[71] *to the vantage* in addition [72] *pour...laps* i.e., are unfaithful [73] *scant...despite* reduce our allowance
to spite us [74] *have galls* are capable of resenting injury and insult ACT V [1] *bulk* framework projecting
from the front of a shop

IAGO.   I have rubb'd this young quat[2] almost to the sense,[3]   10
   And he grows angry. Now, whether he kill Cassio,
   Or Cassio him, or each do kill the other,
   Every way makes my gain: live Roderigo,
   He calls me to a restitution large
   Of gold and jewels that I bobb'd[4] from him,
   As gifts to Desdemona;
   It must not be: if Cassio do remain,
   He hath a daily beauty in his life
   That makes me ugly; and, besides, the Moor   20
   May unfold me to him; there stand I in much peril:
   No, he must die. But so: I hear him coming.

[*Enter* CASSIO.]

ROD.   I know his gait, 'tis he.—Villain, thou diest!   [*Makes a pass at* CASSIO.]
CAS.   That thrust had been mine enemy indeed,
   But that my coat[5] is better than thou know'st:
   I will make proof of thine.   [*Draws, and wounds* RODERIGO.]
ROD.   O, I am slain!

[IAGO *from behind wounds* CASSIO *in the leg, and exits.*]

CAS.   I am maim'd for ever. Help, ho! murder! murder!   [*Falls.*]

[*Enter* OTHELLO.]

OTH.   The voice of Cassio: Iago keeps his word.
ROD.   O, villain that I am!
OTH.   It is even so.
CAS.   O, help, ho! light! a surgeon!   30
OTH.   'Tis he:—O brave Iago, honest and just,
   That hast such noble sense of they friends's wrong!
   Thou teachest me. Minion, your dear lies dead,
   And your unblest fate hies: strumpet, I come.
   Forth of my heart those charms, thine eyes, are blotted;
   Thy bed, lust-stain'd, shall with lust's blood be spotted.   [*Exit* OTHELLO.]

[*Enter* LODOVICO *and* GRATIANO.]

CAS.   What, ho! no watch? no passage?[6] murder! murder!
GRA.   'Tis some mischance; the cry is very direful.
CAS.   O, help!
LOD.   Hark!
ROD.   O wretched villain!

---

[2] *quat* pimple, pustule; used contemptuously   [3] *to the sense* to the quick   [4] *bobb'd* filched cunningly
[5] *coat* coat of mail   [6] *passage* people passing

LOD.   Two or three groan: it is a heavy[7] night;
  These may be counterfeits: let 's think 't unsafe
  To come in to the cry without more help.
ROD.   Nobody come? then shall I bleed to death.
LOD.   Hark!   40

[Enter IAGO *with a light.]*

GRA.   Here 's one comes in his shirt, with light and weapons.
IAGO.   Who 's there? whose noise is this that cries on[8] murder?
LOD.   We do not know.
IAGO.   Did not you hear a cry?
CAS.   Here, here! for heaven's sake, help me!
IAGO.   What's the matter?   50
GRA.   This is Othello's ancient, as I take it.
LOD.   The same indeed; a very valiant fellow.
IAGO.   What are you here that cry so grievously?
CAS.   Iago? O, I am spoil'd, undone by villains!
  Give me some help.
IAGO.   O me, lieutenant! what villains have done this?
CAS.   I think that one of them is hereabout,
  And cannot make away.
IAGO.   O treacherous villains!
  What are you there? come in, and give some help. *[To* LODOVICO *and*
    GRATIANO.*]*
ROD.   O, help me here!   60
CAS.   That 's one of them.
IAGO.   O murd'rous slave! O villain! *[Stabs* RODERIGO.*]*
ROD.   O damn'd Iago! O inhuman dog!
IAGO.   Kill men i' th' dark!—Where be these bloody thieves?—
  How silent in this town!—Ho! murder! murder!—
  What[9] may you be? are you of good or evil?
LOD.   As you shall prove us, praise us.
IAGO.   Signior Lodovico?
LOD.   He, sir.
IAGO.   I cry you mercy. Here 's Cassio hurt by villains.
GRA.   Cassio!   70
IAGO.   How is 't, brother!
CAS.   My leg is cut in two.
IAGO.   Marry, heaven forbid!
  Light, gentlemen: I'll bind it with my shirt.

[Enter BIANCA.*]*

[7] *heavy* thick, cloudy   [8] *cries on* cries out   [9] *What* who

BIAN.   What is the matter, ho? who is 't that cried?

IAGO.   Who is 't that cried?

BIAN.   O my dear Cassio! my sweet Cassio!
  O Cassio, Cassio, Cassio!

IAGO.   O notable strumpet! Cassio, may you suspect
  Who they should be that have thus mangled you?

CAS.   No.   80

GRA.   I am sorry to find you thus: I have been to seek you.

IAGO.   Lend me a garter. So. O, for a chair,[10]
  To bear him easily hence!

BIAN.   Alas, he faints! O Cassio, Cassio, Cassio!

IAGO.   Gentlemen all, I do suspect this trash[11]
  To be a party in this injury.
  Patience awhile, good Cassio. Come, come;
  Lend me a light. Know we this face or no?
  Alas, my friend and my dear countryman
  Roderigo! no:—yes, sure:—O heaven! Roderigo.   90

GRA.   What, of Venice?

IAGO.   Even he, sir: did you know him?

GRA.   Know him! ay.

IAGO.   Signior Gratiano? I cry your gentle pardon;
  These bloody accidents must excuse my manners,
  That so neglected you.

GRA.   I am so glad to see you.

IAGO.   How do you, Cassio? O, a chair, a chair!

GRA.   Roderigo!

IAGO.   He, he, 'tis he. [*A chair brought in.*]   O, that's well said; the chair.
  Some good man bear him carefully from hence;
  I'll fetch the general's surgeon.   [*To* BIANCA]   For you, mistress,   100
  Save you your labour. He that lies slain here, Cassio,
  Was my dear friend: what malice was between you?

CAS.   None in the world; nor do I know the man.

IAGO [*To* BIAN.].   What, look you pale? O, bear him out o' th' air.

[CASSIO *and* RODERIGO *are borne off.*]

  Stay you, good gentlemen. Look you pale, mistress?
  Do you perceive the gastness[12] of her eye?
  Nay, if you stare, we shall hear more anon.
  Behold her well; I pray you, look upon her:
  Do you see, gentlemen? nay, guiltiness will speak,
  Though tongues were out of use.   110

[*Enter* EMILIA.]

---

[10] *chair* sedan chair   [11] *trash* worthless thing, i.e., Bianca   [12] *gastness* terror, ghastliness

EMIL.   'Las, what 's the matter? what 's the matter, husband?

IAGO.   Cassio hath here been set on in the dark
  By Roderigo and fellows that are scap'd:
  He 's almost slain, and Roderigo dead.

EMIL.   Alas, good gentlemen! alas, good Cassio!

IAGO.   This is the fruit of whoring. Prithee, Emilia.
  Go know of Cassio where he supp'd to-night.
  [*To* BIANCA]   What, do you shake at that?

BIAN.   He supp'd at my house; but I therefore shake not.

IAGO.   O, did he so? I charge you, go with me.   120

EMIL.   Fie, fie upon thee, strumpet!

BIAN.   I am no strumpet; but of life as honest
  As you that thus abuse me.

EMIL.   As I! foh! fie upon thee!

IAGO.   Kind gentlemen, let 's go see poor Cassio dress'd.
  Come, mistress, you must tell 's another tale.
  Emilia, run you to the citadel,
  And tell my lord and lady what hath happ'd.
  Will you go on afore?   [*Aside*]   This is the night
  That either makes me or fordoes[13] me quite.   [*Exeunt.*]

SCENE II.   *A bedchamber in the castle.*

[*Enter* OTHELLO *with a light;* DESDEMONA *in her bed.*]

OTH.   It is the cause, it is the cause,[14] my soul,—
  Let me not name it to you, you chaste stars!—
  It is the cause. Yet I'll not shed her blood;
  Nor scar that whiter skin of hers than snow,
  And smooth as monumental alabaster.
  Yet she must die, else she'll betray more men.
  Put out the light, and then put out the light:
  If I quench thee, thou flaming minister,
  I can again thy former light restore,
  Should I repent me: but once put out thy light,   10
  Thou cunning'st pattern of excelling nature,
  I know not where is that Promethean heat[15]
  That can thy light relume.[16] When I have pluck'd the rose,
  I cannot give it vital growth again,
  It needs must wither: I'll smell thee on the tree.   [*Kissing her.*]
  O balmy breath, that dost almost persuade
  Justice to break her sword! One more, one more.

---

[13] *fordoes* undoes, ruins   [14] *It is the cause* i.e., the cause of justice on which Othello must act, Desdemona's deed, which is too unmentionable to be named to the chaste stars   [15] *Promethean heat* divine fire; allusion to the theft of fire from heaven by Prometheus   [16] *relume* rekindle

Be thus when thou art dead, and I will kill thee,
And love thee after. One more, and that 's the last:
So sweet was ne'er so fatal. I must weep,   20
But they are cruel tears: this sorrow 's heavenly;[17]
It strikes where it doth love. She wakes.

DES.   Who 's there? Othello?

OTH.   Ay, Desdemona.

DES.   Will you come to bed, my lord?

OTH.   Have you pray'd to-night, Desdemona?

DES.   Ay, my lord.

OTH.   If you bethink yourself of any crime
Unreconcil'd as yet to heaven and grace,
Solicit for it straight.

DES.   Alack, my lord, what may you mean by that?

OTH.   Well, do it, and be brief; I will walk by: 30
I would not kill thy unprepared spirit;
No; heaven forfend! I would not kill thy soul.

DES.   Talk you of killing?

OTH.   Ay, I do.

DES.   Then heaven
Have mercy on me!

OTH.   Amen, with all my heart!

DES.   If you say so, I hope you will not kill me.

OTH.   Hum!

DES.   And yet I fear you; for you 're fatal then
When your eyes roll so: why I should fear I know not,
Since guiltiness I know not; but yet I feel I fear.

OTH.   Think on thy sins.

DES.   They are loves I bear to you.   40

OTH.   Ay, and for that thou diest.

DES.   That death 's unnatural that kills for loving.
Alas, why gnaw you so your nether lip?
Some bloody passion shakes your very frame:
These are portents; but yet I hope, I hope,
They do not point on me.

OTH.   Peace, and be still!

DES.   I will so. What 's the matter?

OTH.   That handkerchief which I so lov'd and gave thee
Thou gav'st to Cassio.

DES.   No, by my life and soul!
Send for the man, and ask him.

---

[17] *this…heavenly* this tenderness, with which I lament the punishment which justice compels me to inflict, is a holy passion

OTH.   Sweet soul, take heed,   50
  Take heed of perjury; thou are on thy deathbed.

DES.   Ay, but not yet to die.

OTH.   Yes, presently:
  Therefore confess thee freely of thy sin;
  For to deny each article with oath
  Cannot remove nor choke the strong conception[18]
  That I do groan withal. Thou art to die.

DES.   Then Lord have mercy on me!

OTH.   I say, amen.

DES.   And have you mercy too! I never did
  Offend you in my life; never lov'd Cassio
  But with such general warranty of heaven   60
  As I might love; I never gave him token.

OTH.   By heaven, I saw my handkerchief in 's hand.
  O perjur'd woman! thou dost stone[19] my heart,
  And makest me call what I intend to do
  A murder, which I thought a sacrifice:
  I saw the handkerchief.

DES.   He found it then;
  I never gave it him: send for him hither;
  Let him confess a truth.

OTH.   He hath confess'd.

DES.   What, my Lord?

OTH.   That he hath us'd thee.

DES.   How? unlawfully?

OTH.   Ay.   70

DES.   He will not say so.

OTH.   No, his mouth is stopp'd;
  Honest Iago hath ta'en order[20] for 't.

DES.   O! my fear interprets: what, is he dead?

OTH.   Had all his hairs been lives, my great revenge
  Had stomach for them all.

DES.   Alas! he is betray'd and I undone.

OTH.   Out, strumpet! weep'st thou for him to my face?

DES.   O, banish me, my lord, but kill me not!

OTH.   Down, strumpet!

DES.   Kill me to-morrow: let me live to-night!   80

OTH.   Nay, if you strive,—

DES.   But half an hour!

OTH.   Being done, there is no pause.[21]

---

[18] *conception* plan, intention   [19] *stone* turn to stone, harden; Othello means that he will be tempted to kill her in sheer anger because of her perjury   [20] *ta'en order* taken measures   [21] *Being...pause* i.e., when the execution of the deed has once begun, there is no stopping

DES.   But while I say one prayer!

OTH.   It is too late.   [*Smothers her.*]

EMIL   [*at the door*].   My lord, my lord! what, ho! my lord, my lord!

OTH.   What noise is this? Not dead? not yet quite dead?
  I that am cruel am yet merciful;
  I would not have thee linger in thy pain:
  So, so.

EMIL   [*within*].   What, ho! my lord, my lord!

OTH.   Who's there?

EMIL   [*within*].   O, good my lord, I would speak a word with you!   90

OTH.   Yes: 'tis Emilia. By and by. She 's dead.
  'Tis like she comes to speak of Cassio's death.—
  The noise was here. Ha! no more moving?
  Still as the grave. Shall she come in? were 't good?—
  I think she stirs again:—no. What 's best to do?
  If she come in, she'll sure speak to my wife:
  My wife! my wife! what wife? I have no wife.
  O, insupportable! O heavy hour!
  Methinks it should be now a huge eclipse
  Of sun and moon, and that th' affrighted globe   100
  Should yawn[22] at alteration.[23]

EMIL.   [*Within*]   I do beseech you
  That I may speak with you, O, good my lord!

OTH.   I had forgot thee: O, come in, Emilia:
  Soft; by and by. Let me the curtains draw.
  Where art thou?   [*Closes bed-curtains and opens door.*]

[*Enter* EMILIA.]

     What 's the matter with thee now?

EMIL.   O, my good lord, yonder's foul murders done!

OTH.   What, now?

EMIL.   But now, my lord.

OTH.   It is the very error[24] of the moon;
  She comes more nearer earth than she was wont,   110
  And makes men mad.

EMIL.   Cassio, my lord, hath kill'd a young Venetian
  Call'd Roderigo.

OTH.   Roderigo kill'd!
  And Cassio kill'd!

EMIL.   No, Cassio is not kill'd.

OTH.   Not Cassio kill'd! then murder 's out of tune,
  And sweet revenge grows harsh.

---

[22] *yawn* gape in amazement   [23] *at alteration* at the change   [24] *error* irregularity

DES.   O, falsely, falsely murder'd!

EMIL.   Alas, what cry is that?

OTH.   That! what!

EMIL.   Out, and alas! that was my lady's voice.
   Help, help, ho! help. O lady, speak again!   120
   Sweet Desdemona! O sweet mistress, speak!

DES.   A guiltless death I die.

EMIL.   O, who hath done this deed?

DES.   Nobody; I myself. Farewell:
   Commend me to my kind lord: O, farewell!   [*Dies*]

OTH.   Why, how should she be murd'red?

EMIL.   Alas, who knows?

OTH.   You heard her say herself, it was not I.

EMIL.   She said so: I must needs report the truth.

OTH.   She's, like a liar, gone to burning hell:
   'Twas I that kill'd her.

EMIL.   O, the more angel she,   130
   And you the blacker devil!

OTH.   She turn'd to folly,[25] and she was a whore.

EMIL.   Thou dost belie her, and thou art a devil.

OTH.   She was false as water.

EMIL.   Thou art rash as fire, to say
   That she was false: O, she was heavenly true!

OTH.   Cassio did top her; ask thy husband else.
   O, I were damned beneath all depth in hell,
   But that I did proceed upon just grounds
   To this extremity. Thy husband knew it all.

EMIL.   My husband!   140

OTH.   Thy husband.

EMIL.   That she was false to wedlock?

OTH.   Ay, with Cassio. Nay, had she been true,
   If heaven would make me such another world
   Of one entire and perfect chrysolite,[26]
   I'ld not have sold her for it.

EMIL.   My husband!

OTH.   Ay, 'twas he that told me first:
   An honest man he is, and hates the slime
   That sticks on filthy deeds.

EMIL.   My husband!

OTH.   What needs this iterance,[27] woman? I say thy husband.   150

EMIL.   O mistress, villainy hath made mocks with[28] love!
   My husband say that she was false!

---

[25] *folly* unchastity   [26] *chrysolite* the golden stone; a name given to various precious stones of green color
[27] *iterance* iteration, repetition   [28] *made mocks with* derided, made sport of

OTH.   He, woman;
   I say thy husband: dost understand the word?
   My friend, thy husband, honest, honest Iago.
EMIL.   If he say so, may his pernicious soul
   Rot half a grain a day! he lies to th' heart:
   She was too fond of her most filthy bargain.
OTH.   Ha!
EMIL.   Do thy worst:
   This deed of thine is no more worthy heaven   160
   Than thou wast worthy her.
OTH.   Peace, you were best.
EMIL.   Thou hast not half that power to do me harm
   As I have to be hurt.[29] O gull! O dolt!
   As ignorant as dirt! thou hast done a deed—
   I care not for thy sword; I'll make thee known,
   Though I lost twenty lives.—Help! help, ho! help!
   The Moor hath kill'd my mistress! Murder! murder!

        [*Enter* MONTANO, GRATIANO, *and* IAGO *with others.*]

MON.   What is the matter! How now, general!
EMIL.   O, are you come, Iago? you have done well,
   That men must lay their murders on your neck.   170
GRA.   What is the matter?
EMIL.   Disprove this villain, if thou be'st a man:
   He says thou told'st him that his wife was false:
   I know thou didst not, thou 'rt not such a villain:
   Speak, for my heart is full.
IAGO.   I told him what I thought, and told no more
   Than what he found himself was apt[30] and true.
EMIL.   But did you ever tell him she was false?
IAGO.   I did.
EMIL.   You told a lie; an odious, damned lie;   180
   Upon my soul, a lie, a wicked lie.
   She false with Cassio!—did you say with Cassio?
IAGO.   With Cassio, mistress. Go to, charm[31] your tongue.
EMIL.   I will not charm my tongue; I am bound to speak:
   My mistress here lies murdered in her bed,—
ALL.   O heavens forfend!
EMIL.   And your reports have set the murder on.
OTH.   Nay, stare not, masters: it is true, indeed.
GRA.   'Tis a strange truth.
MON.   O monstrous act!

---

[29] *to be hurt* i.e., to endure hurting   [30] *apt* natural, likely   [31] *charm* keep silent

EMIL.   Villainy, villainy, villainy!   190
   I think upon 't, I think: I smell 't: O villainy—
   I thought so then:[32] I'll kill myself for grief:—
   O villainy, villainy!
IAGO.   What, are you mad? I charge you, get you home.
EMIL.   Good gentlemen, let me have leave to speak:
   'Tis proper I obey him, but not now.
   Perchance, Iago, I will ne'er go home.
OTH.   O! O! O! [*He falls on the bed.*]
EMIL.   Nay, lay thee down and roar;
   For thou hast kill'd the sweetest innocent
   That e'er did lift up eye.
OTH.   [*Rising*] O, she was foul!   200
   I scarce did know you, uncle: there lies your niece,
   Whose breath, indeed, these hands have newly stopp'd:
   I know this act shows horrible and grim.
GRA.   Poor Desdemona! I am glad thy father's dead:
   Thy match was mortal to him, and pure grief
   Shore[33] his old thread in twain: did he live now,
   This sight would make him do a desperate turn,
   Yea, curse his better angel from his side,
   And fall to reprobation.[34]
OTH.   'Tis pitiful; but yet Iago knows   210
   That she with Cassio hath the act of shame
   A thousand times committed; Cassio confess'd it:
   And she did gratify his amorous works
   With that recognizance[35] and pledge of love
   Which I first gave her; I saw it in his hand:
   It was a handkerchief, an antique token
   My father gave my mother.
EMIL.   O heaven! O heavenly pow'rs!
IAGO.   Come, hold your peace.
EMIL.   'Twill out, 'twill out: I peace!
   No, I will speak as liberal as the north:[36]   220
   Let heaven and men and devils, let them all,
   All, all, cry shame against me, yet I'll speak.
IAGO.   Be wise, and get you home.
EMIL.   I will not! [IAGO *Offers to stab* EMILIA.]
GRA.   Fie!
   Your sword upon a woman?

---

[32] *then* i.e., at some earlier time, probably IV, ii, when she suspected the machinations of *some eternal villain;* she did not, however, know that villain to be Iago until this moment   [33] *Shore* cut   [34] *reprobation* damnation, rejection by God   [35] *recognizance* token   [36] *liberal as the north* freely as the north wind

EMIL.   O thou dull Moor! that handkerchief thou speak'st of
   I found by fortune[37] and did give my husband;
   For often, with solemn earnestness,
   More than indeed belong'd to such a trifle,
   He begg'd me to steal it.
IAGO.   Villainous whore!
EMIL.   She give it Cassio! no, alas! I found it,   230
   And I did give 't my husband.
IAGO.   Filth, thou liest!
EMIL.   By heaven, I do not, I do not, gentlemen.
   O murd'rous coxcomb![38] what should such a fool
   Do with so good a wife!
OTH.   Are there no stones in heaven[39]
   But what serves for the thunder?—Precious villain!   [*He runs at* IAGO: IAGO,
    from behind, stabs EMILIA, *and exits.*]
GRA.   The woman falls; sure, he hath kill'd his wife.
EMIL.   Ay, ay: O, lay me by my mistress' side.
GRA.   He 's gone, but his wife 's kill'd.
MON.   'Tis a notorious villain. Take you this weapon,
   Which I have here recover'd from the Moor: 240
   Come, guard the door without; let him not pass,
   But kill him rather. I'll after that same villain,
   For 'tis a damned slave.   [*Exit with all but* OTHELLO *and* EMILIA.]
OTH.   I am not valiant neither,
   But every puny whipster[40] gets my sword:
   But why should honour outlive honesty?[41]
   Let it go all.
EMIL.   What did thy song bode, lady?
   Hark, canst thou hear me? I will play the swan,
   And die in music.   [*Singing*]   Willow, willow, willow.—
   Moor, she was chaste; she lov'd thee, cruel Moor;
   So come my soul to bliss, as I speak true;   250
   So speaking as I think, I die, I die.   [*Dies.*]
OTH.   I have another weapon in this chamber;
   It is a sword of Spain, the ice-brook's temper[42]:—
   O, here it is. Uncle, I must come forth.
GRA   [*within*].   If thou attempt it, it will cost thee dear:
   Thou hast no weapon, and perforce must suffer.
OTH.   Look in upon me then and speak with me,
   Or, naked[43] as I am, I will assault thee.

---

[37] *fortune* chance   [38] *coxcomb* fool; addressed to Othello   [39] *stones in heaven* thunderbolts. It was supposed that real stones fell with the thunder and caused the damage   [40] *whipster* contemptible fellow
[41] *honour outlive honesty* Othello realizes that he has done a shameful deed; he asks why his reputation for valor should endure   [42] *ice-brook's temper* usually defined as "tempered in ice-cold water"
[43] *naked* unarmed

[*Enter* GRATIANO.]

GRA. What is the matter?

OTH. Behold, I have a weapon;
A better never did itself sustain   260
Upon a soldier's thigh: I have seen the day,
That, with this little arm and this good sword,
I have made my way through more impediments
Than twenty times your stop:[44] but, O vain boast!
Who can control his fate? 'tis not so now.
Be not afraid, though you do see me weapon'd;
Here is my journey's end, here is my butt,[45]
And very sea-mark[46] of my utmost sail.
Do you go back dismay'd? 'tis a lost fear;
Man[47] but a rush[48] against Othello's breast,   270
And he retires. Where should Othello go?
Now, how dost thou look now? O ill-starr'd wench!
Pale as thy smock! when we shall meet at compt,[49]
This look of thine will hurl my soul from heaven,
And fiends will snatch at it. Cold, cold, my girl!
Even like thy chastity. O cursed, cursed slave!
Whip me, ye devils,
From the possession of this heavenly sight!
Blow me about in winds! roast me in sulphur!
Wash me in steep-down gulfs of liquid fire!   280
O Desdemona! Dead Desdemona! dead!
Oh! Oh!

[*Enter* LODOVICO, CASSIO, *carried in a chair,* MONTANO, *and* IAGO, *prisoner,*
With OFFICERS.]

LOD. Where is this rash and most unfortunate man?

OTH. That 's he that was Othello: here I am.

LOD. Where is that viper? bring the villian forth.

OTH. I look down towards his feet;[50] but that 's a fable.
If that thou be'st a devil, I cannot kill thee.   [*Wounds* IAGO.]

LOD. Wrench his sword from him.

IAGO. I bleed sir; but not kill'd.

OTH. I am not sorry neither: I 'ld have thee live;
For, in my sense, 'tis happiness to die.   290

LOD. O thou Othello, that wert once so good,
Fall'n in the practice of a damned slave,
What shall be said to thee?

---

[44] *stop* power   [45] *butt* mark for archery, goal, limit   [46] *sea-mark* beacon (marking his destination or
limit)   [47] *Man* provide, as in manning a gun   [48] *rush* reed   [49] *compt* account, judgment day   [50] *towards
his feet* i.e., to see if they were cloven like a devil's

OTH.   Why, any thing:
   An honourable murder, if you will;
   For nought I did in hate, but all in honour.
LOD.   This wretch hath part confess'd his villainy:
   Did you and he consent in Cassio's death?
OTH.   Ay.
CAS.   Dear general, I never gave you cause.
OTH.   I do believe it, and I ask your pardon.   300
   Will you, I pray, demand that demi-devil
   Why he hath thus ensnar'd my soul and body?
IAGO.   Demand me nothing: what you know, you know:
   From this time forth I never will speak word.
LOD.   What, not to pray?
GRA.   Torments will ope your lips.
OTH.   Well, thou dost best.
LOD.   Sir, you shall understand what hath befall'n,
   Which, as I think, you know not. Here is a letter
   Found in the pocket of the slain Roderigo;
And here another: the one of them imports   ·   310
   The death of Cassio to be undertook
   By Roderigo
OTH.   O villain!
CAS.   Most heathenish and most gross!
LOD.   Now here 's another discontented[51] paper,
   Found in his pocket too; and this, it seems,
   Roderigo meant t' have sent this damned villain;
   But that belike Iago in the interim
   Came in and satisfied him.
OTH.   O thou pernicious caitiff[52]!—
   How came you, Cassio, by that handkerchief
   That was my wife's?
CAS.   I found it in my chamber: 320
   And he himself confess'd but even now
   That there he dropp'd it for a special purpose
   Which wrought to his desire.
OTH.   O fool! O fool! fool!
CAS.   There is besides in Roderigo's letter,
   How he upbraids Iago, that he made him
   Brave[53] me upon the watch; whereon it came
   That I was cast:[54] and even but now he spake,
   After long seeming dead, Iago hurt him,
   Iago set him on.

---

[51] *discontented* expressing   dissatisfaction   [52] *caitiff* wretch   [53] *Brave* defy   [54] *cast* dismissed

LOD.　　You must forsake this room, and go with us:　　　　　　　　　330
　　　Your power and your command is taken off,[55]
　　　And Cassio rules in Cyprus. For this slave,
　　　If there be any cunning cruelty
　　　That can torment him much and hold him long,
　　　It shall be his. You shall close prisoner rest,
　　　Till that the nature of your fault be known
　　　To the Venetian state. Come, bring him away.
OTH.　　Soft you; a word or two before you go.
　　　I have done the state some service, and they know 't.
　　　No more of that. I pray you, in your letters,　　　　　　　　　340
　　　When you shall these unlucky deeds relate,
　　　Speak of me as I am; nothing extenuate,[56]
　　　Nor set down aught in malice: then must you speak
　　　Of one that lov'd not wisely but too well;
　　　Of one not easily jealous, but being wrought,
　　　Perplex'd[57] in the extreme; of one whose hand,
　　　Like the base Judean,[58] threw a pearl away
　　　Richer than all his tribe; of one whose subdu'd eyes,
　　　Albeit unused to the melting mood,
　　　Drop tears as fast as the Arabian trees　　　　　　　　　　350
　　　Their medicinal gum. Set you down this;
　　　And say besides, that in Aleppo[59] once,
　　　Where a malignant and a turban'd Turk
　　　Beat a Venetian and traduc'd the state,
　　　I took by th' throat the circumcised dog,
　　　And smote him, thus. 　[*Stabs himself.*]
LOD.　　O bloody period![60]
GRA.　　　　　　　　　　All that is spoke is marr'd.
OTH.　　I kiss'd thee ere I kill'd thee: no way but this;
　　　Killing myself, to die upon a kiss.

　　　　　　　　[*Falls on the bed, and dies.*]

CAS.　　This did I fear, but thought he had no weapon;　　　　　　360
　　　For he was great of heart.
LOD.　　　　　　　　　[*To* IAGO]　　O Spartan dog,[61]
　　　More fell than anguish, hunger, or the sea!
　　　Look on the tragic loading of this bed;
　　　This is thy work: the object poisons sight;

---

[55] *taken off* taken away　[56] *extenuate* diminish, depreciate; the idea is contrasted with the thought of *malice* in the following line　[57] *Perplex'd* confounded, distracted　[58] *Judean* infidel or disbeliever　[59] *Aleppo* a Turkish city where the Venetians had special trading privileges. It is stated that it was immediate death for a Christian to strike a Turk in Aleppo; Othello risked his life for the honor of Venice　[60] *period* termination, conclusion　[61] *Spartan dog* Spartan dogs were noted for their savagery

Let it be hid, Gratiano, keep the house,
And seize upon the fortunes of the Moor,
For they succeed on you. To you, lord governor,
Remains the censure of this hellish villain;
The time, the place, the torture: O, enforce it!
Myself will straight abroad; and to the state   370
This heavy act with heavy heart relate.   [*Exeunt.*]

Journal Entry

How effective is Shakespeare's play in portraying the presence of a black moor in a
white society? Consider Brabantio's, the Duke's, Iago's, and Othello's various attitudes
toward the issue of race relations.

Textual Considerations

1. To analyze the structural development of *Othello,* consider Othello's autobiographical speeches in act 1, scene 3. Explain how Othello's portrait of himself and his cultural background might have contributed to his manipulation by Iago.
2. Analyze the images of women in *Othello* from the viewpoint of social class and the
   position women occupied in Venetian society. Don't overlook Cassio's treatment of
   Desdemona and Bianca, as well as the various images of women with which Iago
   entertains his audience in act 2, scene 1.
3. Consider the extent to which the settings of the play suggest a symbolic contrast
   between the social and political order of Venice and Cyprus. To what extent do these
   symbolic settings reflect psychological changes in Othello?
4. What kinds of responses do Iago's soliloquies and asides evoke from the audience?
   Consider the audience's feelings of comfort, discomfort, fear, sympathy, repulsion,
   expectation, and suspense.
5. Analyze the images of women that Desdemona uses in act 1, scene 3, lines 185–88,
   and in act 4, scene 3, lines 25–32. To what extent do these images help Desdemona
   justify her actions and communicate her feelings and emotions? How effective is
   Desdemona's use of language in both passages?

Cultural Contexts

1. The explanations behind Iago's motives for destroying Othello have ranged from
   Iago's dissatisfaction with Othello's poor distribution of power within the ranks of
   his army, to Iago's pleasure and excitement in manipulating people, to Iago's
   "motiveless malignity." What other motives can you and your classmates attribute to
   Iago? How effective are these motives in view of the closure Iago imposes on this
   issue at the end of the play: "what you know, you know: / From this time forth I
   will never speak a word" (act 5, scene 2, ll. 304–305)?
2. Some of the lines in *Othello,* such as "Were I the Moor, I would not be Iago" (act 1,
   scene 1, l. 57), suggest Iago's dissatisfaction with his sense of self. Identify other
   lines and speeches that support the viewpoint that Iago needs to fashion a new identity for himself.

Manual Puig
1981

The Kiss of the Spider Woman *

Act One

SCENE I.

(*Scene: A small cell in the Villa Devoto prison in Buenos Aires. The stage is in total darkness. Suddenly two overhead white spots light up the heads of the two men. They are sitting down, looking in opposite directions.*)

MOLINA.   You can see there's something special about her, that she's not any ordinary woman. Quite young…and her face more round than oval, with a little pointy chin like a cat's.

VALENTIN.   And her eyes?

MOLINA.   Most probably green. She looks up at the model, the black panther lying down in its cage in the zoo. But she scratches her pencil against the sketch pad and the panther sees her.

VALENTIN.   How come it didn't smell her before?

MOLINA (*deliberately not answering*).   But, who's that behind her? Someone trying to light a cigarette, but the wind blows out the match.

VALENTIN.   Who is it?

MOLINA.   Hold on. She flusters. He's no matinée idol but he's nice-looking, in a hat with a low brim. He touches the brim like he's saluting and says the drawing is terrific. She fiddles with the curls of her fringe.

VALENTIN.   Go on.

MOLINA.   He can tell she's a foreigner by her accent. She tells him that she came to New York when the war broke out. He asks her if she's homesick. And then it's like a cloud passes across her eyes and she tells him she comes from the mountains, someplace not far from Transylvania.

VALENTIN.   Where Dracula comes from.

MOLINA.   The next day he's in his office with some colleagues—he's an architect—and this girl, another architect he works with—and when the clock strikes three he just wants to drop everything and go to the zoo. It's right across the street. And the architect girl asks him why he's so happy. Deep down, she's really in love with him, no use her pretending otherwise.

VALENTIN.   Is she a dog?

MOLINA.   No, nothing out of this world: chestnut hair, but pleasant enough. But the other one, the one at the zoo, Irene—no, Irina—has disappeared. As time

---

*A play based on his novel of the same title.

goes by he just can't get her out of his mind until one day he's walking down this fashionable avenue and he notices something in the window of an art gallery. They're pictures by an artist who only paints…panthers. The guy goes in and there's Irina being congratulated by all the guests. And I don't remember what comes next.

VALENTIN.   Try to remember…

MOLINA.   Hold on a sec…Okay,…then the architect goes up and congratulates her too. She drops the critics and walks off with him. He tells her that he just happened to be passing by, really he was on his way to buy a present.

VALENTIN.   For the girl architect.

MOLINA.   Now he's wondering if he's got enough money with him to buy two presents. And he stops outside a shop and she gets a funny feeling when she sees what kind of shop it is. There are all different kinds of birds in little cages sipping fresh water from their bowls.

VALENTIN.   Excuse me…is there any water in the bottle?

MOLINA.   Yes, I filled it up when they let us out to the toilet.

> (*The white light which up till now has lit just their heads widens to fully light both actors: we see the cell for the first time.*)

VALENTIN.   That's okay then.

MOLINA.   Do you want some? It's nice and cool.

VALENTIN.   No or we won't have enough for tea in the morning. Go on.

MOLINA.   Don't exaggerate. We've got enough to last all day.

VALENTIN.   Don't spoil me. I forgot to fetch some when they let us out to shower. If it wasn't for you we wouldn't have any.

MOLINA.   Look, there's plenty…Anyway, when they go inside that shop it's like— I don't know what—it's like the devil just came in. The birds, blind with fear, fly into the wire mesh and hurt their wings. She grabs his hand and drags him outside. Straight away the birds calm down. She asks him to let her go home. When he comes back into the shop the birds are chirruping and singing just like normal and he buys one for the other girl's birthday. And then…it's no good, I can't remember what happens next, I'm pooped.

VALENTIN.   Just a little more.

MOLINA.   When I'm sleepy my memory goes. I'll carry on with the morning tea.

VALENTIN.   No, it's better at night. During the day I don't want to bother with this trivia. There are more important things…(*Molina shrugs.*) If I'm not reading and I'm keeping quiet it's because I'm thinking. But don't take it wrong.

MOLINA (*upset by Valentin's remark. With almost concealed irony*).   I shan't bother you. You can count on that!

VALENTIN.   I see you understand. See you in the morning. (*He settles down to sleep.*)

MOLINA.   Till tomorrow. Pleasant dreams of Irina. (*Molina settles down too, but he is troubled by something.*)

VALENTIN.   I prefer the architect girl.

MOLINA.   I'd already guessed that.

SCENE II.

(*Scene: Molina and Valentin are sitting in different positions. They do not look at one another. Only their heads are lit: seconds later the night light comes on.*)

MOLINA.   So they go on seeing each other and they fall in love. She pampers him, cuddles up in his arms, but when he wants to hold her tight and kiss her she slips away from him. She asks him not to kiss her but to let her kiss him with her full lips, but she keeps her mouth shut tight.   (*Valentin is about to interrupt but Molina forges ahead.*)   So, on their next date they go to this quaint restaurant. He tells her she's prettier than ever in her shimmering black blouse. But she's lost her appetite, she can't manage a thing, and they leave. It's snowing gently. The noise of the city is muffled but far away you can just hear the growling of wild animals. The zoo's close, that's why. Barely in a whisper she says she's afraid to return to her house and spend the night alone. He hails a taxi and they go to his house. It's a huge place, all *fin de siècle;* it used to be his mother's.

VALENTIN.   And what does he do?

MOLINA.   Nothing. He lights up his pipe and looks over at her. You always guessed he had a kind heart.

VALENTIN.   I'd like to ask you something: how do you picture his mother?

MOLINA.   So you can make fun of her?

VALENTIN.   I swear I won't.

MOLINA.   I don't know…someone really charming. She made her husband happy and her children too. She's always well groomed.

VALENTIN.   And do you picture her scrubbing floors?

MOLINA.   No, she's always impeccable. The high-necked dress hides the wrinkles round her throat.

VALENTIN.   Always impeccable. With servants. People with no other choice than to fetch and carry for her. And, of course, she was happy with her husband who also exploited her in his turn, kept her locked up in the house like a slave, waiting for him…

MOLINA.   …Listen…

VALENTIN.   …waiting for him to come home every night from his chambers or his surgery. And she condoned the system, fed all this crap to her son and now he trips over the panther woman. Serves him right.

MOLINA   (*irritated*).   Why did you have to bring up all that?…I'd forgotten all about this dump while I was telling you the movie.

VALENTIN.   I'd forgotten about it too.

MOLINA.   Well, then…Why d'you have to go and break the spell?

VALENTIN.   Let me explain.…

MOLINA.   Fine, but not now, tomorrow.… Why did I get lumbered with you and not the panther woman's boyfriend?

VALENTIN.   That's another story and one that doesn't interest me.

MOLINA.   Are you frightened to talk about it?

VALENTIN.   It bores me. I know all about it—even though you've never said a word.

MOLINA.   Fine. I told you I got done for corruption of minors. There's nothing else to add. So don't come the psychologist with me.

VALENTIN   (*shielding himself behind humor*).   Admit that you like him because he smokes a pipe.

MOLINA.   No, it's not that. It's because he's gentle and understanding.

VALENTIN.   His mother castrated him, that's all.

MOLINA.   I like him and that's that. And you like the architect girl—what's so Bolshy about her?

VALENTIN.   I prefer her to the panther woman, that's for sure. But the guy with the pipe won't suit you.

MOLINA.   Why not?

VALENTIN.   Your intentions aren't exactly chaste, are they?

MOLINA.   Of course not.

VALENTIN.   Exactly. He likes Irina because she's frigid and he doesn't have to pounce on her and that's why he takes her to the house where his mother is still present even if she is dead.

MOLINA   (*getting angrier and angrier*).   Continue.

VALENTIN.   If he's still kept all his mother's things it's because he wants to remain a child. He doesn't bring home a woman but a child to play with.

MOLINA.   That's all in your head. I don't even know if the place is his mother's— I said that because I liked the place and since I saw antiques there I told you it belonged to his mother. For all I know he rents it furnished.

VALENTIN.   So you're making up half the movie?

MOLINA.   I'm not, I swear. But—you know—there are some things I add to fill it out for you. The house, for example. And, in any case, don't forget I'm a window dresser and that's almost like being an interior designer.... Well, she begins to tell him her story but I don't remember all the details.... I remember that in her village, a long time ago, there used to be panther-women. And these tales frightened her a lot when she was a little girl.

VALENTIN.   And the birds?...Why were they afraid of her?

MOLINA.   That's what the architect asks her. And what does she say? She doesn't say anything! And the scene ends with him in pyjamas and a dressing gown, good quality, no pattern, something serviceable—and he looks at her sleeping on the sofa from his bedroom door and he lights up his pipe and stands there...thoughtful.

VALENTIN.   Do you know what I like about it? That it's like an allegory of women's fear of submitting to the male, because when it comes to sex, the animal part takes over. You see?

MOLINA   (*he doesn't approve of Valentin's comments*).   Irina wakes up, it's morning already.

VALENTIN.   She wakes up because of the cold, like us.

MOLINA (*irritated*).   I knew you were going to say that.... She's woken up by the canary, singing in its cage. At first she's afraid to go near it, but the little bird is chirpy so she dares to move a little closer. She heaves a big sigh of relief because the bird isn't frightened of her. And then she makes breakfast...toast and cereals and pancakes...

VALENTIN.   Don't mention food.

MOLINA.   ...and pancakes...

VALENTIN.   I'm serious. Neither food nor women.

MOLINA.   She wakes him up and he's all happy to see her settling in and so he asks her to stay there forever and marry him. And she says, yes, from the bottom of her heart and she looks around and the curtains look so beautiful to her, they're made of thick dark velvet.

(*Aggressively.*)   And now you can fully appreciate the *fin de siècle* decor. Then Irina asks him if he truly wants her to be his wife to give her just a little more time, just long enough for her to get over her fears.

VALENTIN.   You can see what's going on with her, can't you?

MOLINA.   Hold on. He agrees and they get married. And on their wedding night she sleeps in the bed and he sleeps on the couch.

VALENTIN.   Looking at his mother's ornaments. Admit it, it's your ideal home, isn't it?

MOLINA.   Of course it is! Now I've got to put up with you telling me the same thing they all say.

VALENTIN.   What d'you mean? What do they all say?

MOLINA.   They're all the same, they all tell me the same thing.

VALENTIN.   What?

MOLINA.   That I was fussed over as a kid and that's why I'm like I am now, that I was clinging to my mother's skirts, but it's never too late to straighten out and all I need is a good woman because there's nothing better than a good woman.

VALENTIN.   And that's what they all tell you?

MOLINA.   And this is what I tell them.... You're dead right!...and since there's nothing better than a woman...I want to be one! So spare me the advice please, because I know what I feel like and it's all as clear as day to me.

VALENTIN.   I don't see it as clear—at least, not the way you've just put it.

MOLINA.   I don't need you telling me what's what—if you want I'll go on with the picture, if not, ciao.... I'll just whisper it to myself, and *arrivederci,* Sparafucile!

VALENTIN.   Who's Sparafucile?

MOLINA.   You don't have a clue about opera. He's the hatchet man in *Rigoletto*.... Where were we?

VALENTIN.   The wedding night. He hasn't laid a finger on her.

MOLINA.   And I forgot to tell you that they'd agreed she'd go and see a psycho-analyst.

VALENTIN.   Excuse me again...don't get upset.

MOLINA.   What is it?

VALENTIN   (*less communicative than ever, somber*).   I can't keep my mind on the story.

MOLINA.   Is it boring you?

VALENTIN.   No, it's not that. It's…My head is in a state.   (*He talks more to himself than to Molina.*)   I just want to be quiet for a while. I don't know if this has ever happened to you, that you're just about to understand something, you've got the end of the thread and if you don't yank it now…you'll lose it.

MOLINA.   Why do you like the architect girl?

VALENTIN.   It has to come out some way or other….   (*Self-contemptuous.*) Weakness, I mean…

MOLINA.   Ttt…it's not weakness.

VALENTIN   (*bitter, impersonally*).   Funny how you just can't avoid getting attached to something. It's…it's as if the mind just oozed sentiment constantly.

MOLINA.   Is that what you believe?

VALENTIN.   Like a leaky tap. Drips falling over anything.

MOLINA.   Anything?

VALENTIN.   You can't stop the drips.

MOLINA.   And you don't want to be reminded of your girlfriend, is that it?

VALENTIN   (*mistrustful*).   How do you know whether I have a girlfriend?

MOLINA.   It's only natural.

VALENTIN.   I can't help it…. I get attached to anything that reminds me of her. Anyway, I'd do better to get my mind on what I ought to, right?

MOLINA.   Yank the thread.

VALENTIN.   Exactly.

MOLINA.   And if you get it all in a tangle, Missy Valentina, you'll flunk needle-work.

VALENTIN.   Don't worry on my account.

MOLINA.   Okay, I won't say another word.

VALENTIN.   And don't call me Valentina. I'm not a woman.

MOLINA.   How should I know?

VALENTIN.   I'm sorry, Molina, but I don't give demonstrations.

MOLINA.   I wasn't asking for one.

SCENE III.

(*Scene: Night. The prison light is on. Molina and Valentin are sitting on the floor, eating.*)

VALENTIN   (*speaking as soon as he finishes his last mouthful*).   You're a good cook.

MOLINA.   Thank you, Valentin.

VALENTIN.   It could cause problems later on. I'm getting spoiled.

MOLINA.   You're crazy. Live for today!

VALENTIN.   I don't believe in that live for today crap. We haven't earned that par-adise yet.

MOLINA.   Do you believe in Heaven and Hell?

VALENTIN.   Hold on a minute. If we're going to have a discussion then we need a framework. Otherwise you'll just ramble on.

MOLINA.   I'm not going to ramble.

VALENTIN.   Okay. I'll state an opening proposition. Let me put it to you like this.

MOLINA.   Put it any way you like.

VALENTIN.   I can't live just for today. All I do is determined by the ongoing political struggle. D'you get me? Everything that I endure here, which is bad enough…is nothing if you compare it to torture…but you don't know what that's like.

MOLINA.   I can imagine.

VALENTIN.   No, Molina, you can't imagine what it's like.… Well, anyway, I can put up with all this because there's a blueprint. The essential thing is the social revolution and the pleasures of the senses come second. The greatest pleasure, well, it's knowing that I'm part of the most noble cause…my ideas, for instance… (*The prison lights go out. The BLUE nighttime light stays on.*) It's eight…

MOLINA.   What do you mean "your ideas"?

VALENTIN.   My ideals. Marxism. And that good feeling is one I can experience anywhere, even here in this cell, and even in torture. And that's my strength.

MOLINA.   And what about your girlfriend?

VALENTIN.   That has to be second too. And I'm second for her. Because she also knows what's most important. (*Molina remains silent.*) You don't look convinced.

MOLINA.   Don't mind me. I'm going to turn in soon.

VALENTIN.   You're mad! What about the panther-woman?

MOLINA.   Tomorrow.

VALENTIN.   What's up?

MOLINA.   Look, Valentin, that's me. I get hurt easy. I cooked that food for you, with my supplies, and worse still I give you half my avocado—which is my favorite and could have eaten tomorrow…Result? You throw it in my face that I'm spoiling you.…

VALENTIN.   Don't be so soft! It's just like a…

MOLINA.   Say it!

VALENTIN.   Say what?

MOLINA.   I know what you were going to say, Valentin.

VALENTIN.   Cut it out.

MOLINA.   "It's just like a woman." That's what you were going to say.

VALENTIN.   Yes.

MOLINA.   And what's wrong with being soft like a woman? Why can't a man—or whatever—a dog, or a fairy—why can't he be sensitive if he feels like it?

VALENTIN.   In excess, it can get in a man's way.

MOLINA.   In the way of what? Of torturing someone?

VALENTIN.   No, of getting rid of the torturers.

MOLINA.   But if all men were like women then there'd be no torturers.

VALENTIN.   And what would you do without men?

MOLINA.   You're right. They're brutes, but I need them.

VALENTIN.   Molina…you just said that if all men were like women there'd be no torturers. You've got a point there; kind of weird, but a point at least.

MOLINA.   The way you say things. (*Imitating Valentin.*) "A point at least."

VALENTIN.   I'm sorry I upset you.

MOLINA.   I'm not upset.

VALENTIN.   Well, cheer up, don't reproach me.

MOLINA.   Do you want me to go on with the picture?

VALENTIN.   Yeah, man, of course.

MOLINA.   Man? What man? Tell me so he won't get away.

VALENTIN   (*trying to hide that he finds this funny*).   Start.

MOLINA.   Irina goes along to the psychoanalyst who's a ladykiller, real handsome.

VALENTIN.   Tell me what you mean by real handsome. I'd like to know.

MOLINA.   Well, let's get this straight, he isn't my type at all.

VALENTIN.   Who's the actor?

MOLINA.   I don't remember. Too skinny for my taste. With a pencil moustache. But there's something about him, so full of himself, he just puts you off. And he puts off Irina. She skips the next appointment, she lies to her husband and instead of going to the doctor's she puts on that black fleecy coat and goes to the zoo, to look at the panther. The keeper comes along, opens the cage, throws in the meat and closes the door again. But he's absent-minded and leaves the key in the lock. Irina sneaks up to the door and puts her hand on the key. And she just stands there, musing, rapt in her thoughts.

VALENTIN.   What does she do then?

MOLINA.   That's all for tonight. I'll continue tomorrow.

VALENTIN.   At least, let me ask you something.

MOLINA.   What?

VALENTIN.   Who do you identify with? Irina or the architect girl?

MOLINA.   With Irina—who do you think? *Moi*—always with the leading lady.

VALENTIN.   Continue.

MOLINA.   What about you? I guess you're stuck because the guy is such a wimp.

VALENTIN.   Don't laugh—with the psychoanalyst. But I didn't say anything about your choice, so don't mock mine.... You know something? I'm finding it hard to keep my mind on it.

MOLINA.   What's the problem?

VALENTIN.   Nothing.

MOLINA.   Come on, open up a little.

VALENTIN.   When you said the girl was there in front of the cage, I imagined it was my girl who was in danger.

MOLINA.   I understand.

VALENTIN.   I shouldn't be telling you this, Molina. But I guess you've figured it all out for yourself anyhow. My girl is in the organization too.

MOLINA.   So what.

VALENTIN.   It's only that I don't want to burden you with information it's better you don't know.

MOLINA.   With me, it's not a woman, a girlfriend I mean. It's my mother. She's got blood pressure and a weak heart.

VALENTIN.   People can live for years with that.

MOLINA.   Sure, but they don't need more aggravation, Valentin. Imagine the shame of having a son inside—and why.

VALENTIN. Look, the worst has already happened, hasn't it?

MOLINA. Yes, but the risk is ever-present inside her. It's that dodgy heart.

VALENTIN. She's waiting for you. Eight years'll fly by, what with remission and all that....

MOLINA (*a little contrived*). Tell me about your girlfriend if you like....

VALENTIN. I'd give anything to hold her in my arms right now.

MOLINA. It won't be long. You're not in for life.

VALENTIN. Something might happen to her.

MOLINA. Write to her, tell her not to take chances, that you need her.

VALENTIN. Never. Impossible. If you think like that you'll never change anything in the world.

MOLINA (*not realizing he's mocking Valentin*). And you think you're going to change the world?

VALENTIN. Yes, and I don't care that you laugh. It makes people laugh to hear this, but what I have to do before anything is to change the world.

MOLINA. Sure, but you can't do it just like that, *and* on your own.

VALENTIN. But I'm not on my own—that's it! I'm with her and all those other people who think like we do. That's the end of the thread that slips through my fingers...I'm not apart from my comrades—I'm with them, right now!... It doesn't matter whether I can see them or not.

MOLINA (*with a slight drawl, skeptically*). If that makes you feel good, terrific!

VALENTIN. Christ, what a moron!

MOLINA. Sticks and stones...

VALENTIN. Don't provoke me then. I'm not some loudmouth who just spouts off about politics in a bar. The proof is that I'm in here.

MOLINA. I'm sorry.

VALENTIN. It's okay...

MOLINA (*pretending not to pry*). You were going to tell me something...about your girlfriend.

VALENTIN. We'd better drop that.

MOLINA. As you like...

VALENTIN. Why it gets me so upset, I can't fathom.

MOLINA. Better not, then, if it upsets you...

VALENTIN. The one thing I shouldn't tell you is her name.

MOLINA. What sort of girl is she?

VALENTIN. She's twenty-four, two years younger than me.

MOLINA. Thirteen years younger than me.... No, I tell a lie, sixteen.

VALENTIN. She was always politically conscious. First it was...well, I needn't be shy with you, at first it was because of the sexual revolution.

MOLINA (*bracing himself for some saucy tidbit*). That I wouldn't miss.

VALENTIN. She comes from a bourgeois family, not really wealthy, but comfortably off. But as a kid and all through her adolescence she had to watch her parents destroy each other. Her father was cheating her mother, you know what I mean?

MOLINA. No, I don't.

VALENTIN.   Cheating her by not telling her he needed other relationships. I don't hold with monogamy.

MOLINA.   But it's beautiful when a couple love each other for ever and ever.

VALENTIN.   Is that what you'd like?

MOLINA.   It's my dream.

VALENTIN.   Why do you like men then?

MOLINA.   What's that got to do with it? I want to marry a man—to love and to cherish, for ever and ever.

VALENTIN.   So, basically, you're just a bourgeois man?

MOLINA.   A bourgeois lady, please.

VALENTIN.   If you were a woman you'd think otherwise.

MOLINA.   The only thing I want is to live forever with a wonderful man.

VALENTIN.   And that's impossible because…well, if he's a man, he wants a woman …you'll always be living in a fool's paradise.

MOLINA.   Go on about your girlfriend. I don't want to talk about me.

VALENTIN.   She was brought up to be the lady of the house. Piano lessons, French, drawing…. I'll tell you the rest tomorrow, Molina…I want to think about something I was studying today.

MOLINA.   Now you're getting your own back.

VALENTIN.   No, silly. I'm tired, too.

MOLINA.   I'm not sleepy at all.

SCENE IV.

(*Scene: Night. The prison lights are on. Valentin is engrossed in a book. Molina, restless, is flicking through a magazine he already knows backwards.*)

VALENTIN (*lifting his head from the book*).   Why are they late with dinner? Next door had it ages ago.

MOLINA   (*ironic*).   Is *that* all you're studying tonight? I'm not hungry, thank goodness.

VALENTIN.   That's unusual. Don't you feel well?

MOLINA.   No, just nerves.

VALENTIN.   Listen…I think they're coming.

MOLINA.   Hide the magazines or they'll pinch them.

VALENTIN.   I'm famished.

MOLINA.   Please Valentin, don't make a scene with the guards.

VALENTIN.   No.

(*Through the grille in the door come two plates of porridge—one visibly more loaded than the other. Molina looks at Valentin.*)

VALENTIN.   Porridge.

MOLINA.   Yes. (*Molina looks at the two plates which Valentin has collected from the hatch. Exchanging an enigmatic glance with the invisible guard*).   Thank you.

VALENTIN (*to guard*). What about this one? Why's it got less? (*To Molina.*) I didn't say anything for your sake. Otherwise I'd have thrown it in his face, this bloody glue.

MOLINA. What's the use of complaining?

VALENTIN. One plate's only got half as much as the other. That bastard guard, he's out of his fucking mind.

MOLINA. It's okay, Valentin, I'll take the small portion.

VALENTIN (*serving Molina the large one*). No, you like porridge, you always lap it up.

MOLINA. Skip the chivalry. You have it.

VALENTIN. I told you no.

MOLINA. Why should I have the big one?

VALENTIN. Because I know you like porridge.

MOLINA. But I'm not hungry.

VALENTIN. Eat it, it'll do you good. (*Valentin starts eating from the small plate.*)

MOLINA. No.

VALENTIN. It's not too bad today.

MOLINA. I don't want it.

VALENTIN. Afraid of putting on weight?

MOLINA. No.

VALENTIN. Get stuck in then. This porridge à la glue isn't so bad today. This small plate is plenty for me.

MOLINA (*starts eating, overcoming his resistance; his voice nostalgic now*). Thursday. Ladies day. The cinema in my neighborhood used to show a romantic triple feature on Thursdays. Years ago now.

VALENTIN. Is that where you saw the panther-woman?

MOLINA. No, that was in a smart little cinema in that German neighborhood where all those posh houses with gardens are. My house was near there, but in the rundown part. Every Monday they'd show a German-language feature. Even during the war. They still do.

VALENTIN. Nazi propaganda films.

MOLINA. But the musical numbers were fabulous!

VALENTIN. You're touched. (*He finishes his dinner.*) They'll be turning off the lights soon, that's it for studying today. (*Unconsciously authoritarian.*) You can go on with the film now—Irina's hand was on the key in the lock.

MOLINA (*picking at his porridge*). She takes the key out of the lock and gives it back to the keeper. The old follow thanks her and she goes back home to wait for her husband. She's all out to kiss him, on the mouth this time.

VALENTIN (*absorbed*). Mmmm…

MOLINA. Irina calls him up at his office, it's getting late, and the girl architect answers. Irina hangs up. She's eaten up with jealousy. She paces up and down the apartment like a caged beast, and when she walks by the bird cage she notices that the bird's wings are flapping frenetically. She can't control herself and she opens the little door and puts her hand right inside the cage. The little bird drops stone dead before she even touches it. Irina panics and flees from the house looking for her husband, but, of course, she has to go past the bar on the corner and she sees them both inside. And she just wants to tear the other woman to shreds. Irina only wears black clothes but she's never again worn that blouse he liked so much, the one in the restaurant scene, with all the rhinestones.

VALENTIN.   What are they?

MOLINA   (*shocked*).   Rhinestones! I don't believe this! You don't know...?

VALENTIN.   I haven't the faintest.

MOLINA.   They're like diamonds only worthless; little pieces of glass that shine.

(*At this moment the cell light goes out.*)

VALENTIN.   I'm going to turn in early tonight. I've had enough of all this drivel.

MOLINA   (*overreacting, but deeply hurt*).   Thank goodness there's no light so I don't have to see your face. Don't ever speak another word to me!

(*Note: The production must establish that when the blue light is on— meaning nighttime—THEY CANNOT SEE EACH OTHER, and so are free to express themselves as they like in gestures and body language.*)

VALENTIN.   I'm sorry...(*Molina stays silent.*) Really, I'm sorry, I didn't think you'd get so upset.

MOLINA.   You upset me because it's one of my favorite movies, you can't know... (*He starts to cry.*)   ...you didn't see it.

VALENTIN.   Are you crazy? It's nothing to cry about.

MOLINA.   I'll...I'll cry if I feel like it.

VALENTIN.   Suit yourself.... I'm very sorry.

MOLINA.   And don't get the idea you've made me cry. It's because today's my mother's birthday and I'm dying to be with her.... And not with you. (*Pause.*)   Ay!... Ay!... I don't feel well.

VALENTIN.   What's wrong?

MOLINA.   Ay!... Ay!

VALENTIN.   What is it? What's the matter?

MOLINA.   The girl's fucked!

VALENTIN.   Which girl?

MOLINA.   Me, dummy. It's my stomach.

VALENTIN.   Do you want to throw up?

MOLINA.   The pain's lower down. It's in my guts.

VALENTIN.   I'll call the guard, okay?

MOLINA.   No, it'll pass, Valentin.

VALENTIN.   The food didn't do anything to me.

MOLINA.   I bet it's my nerves. I've been on edge all day. I think it's letting up now.

VALENTIN.   Try to relax. Relax your arms and legs, let them go loose.

MOLINA.   Yes, that's better. I think it's going.

VALENTIN.   Do you want to go to sleep?

MOLINA.   I don't know…Ugh! it's awful…

VALENTIN.   Maybe it'd be better if you talk, it'll take your mind off the pain.

MOLINA.   You mean the movie?

VALENTIN.   Where had we got to?

MOLINA.   Afraid I'm going to croak before we get to the end?

VALENTIN.   This is for your benefit. We broke off when they were in the bar on the corner.

MOLINA.   Okay…the two of them get up together to leave and Irina takes cover behind a tree. The architect girl decides to take the shortcut home through the park. He told her everything while they were in the bar, that Irina doesn't make love to him, that she has nightmares about panther-women and all. The other girl, who'd just got used to the idea that she'd lost him, now begins to think maybe she has a chance again. So she's walking along and then you hear heels clicking behind her. She turns round and sees the silhouette of a woman. And then the clicking gets faster and now, right, the girl begins to get frightened, because you know what it's like when you've been talking about scary things…. But she's right in the middle of the park and if she starts to run she'll be in even worse trouble…and, then, suddenly, you can't hear the human footsteps anymore…. Ay!…Ay!… it's still hurting me.

SCENE V.

(*Scene: Day. Valentin is lying down, doubled up with stomach pains. Molina stands looking on at him.*)

VALENTIN.   You can't imagine how much it hurts. Like a stabbing pain.

MOLINA.   Just what I had two days ago.

VALENTIN.   And each time it gets worse, Molina.

MOLINA.   You should go to the clinic.

VALENTIN.   Don't be thick, I already told you I don't want to go.

MOLINA.   They'll only give you a little seconol. It can't harm you.

VALENTIN.   Of course it can; you can get hooked on it. You don't have a clue.

MOLINA.   About what?

VALENTIN.   Nothing.

MOLINA.   Go on, tell me. Don't be like that.

VALENTIN.   It happened to one of my comrades once. They got him hooked, his will power just went. A political prisoner can't afford to end up in a prison hospital. You follow me? Never. Once you're in there they come along and interrogate you and you have no resistance…. Ay!…Ay!…It feels like my guts are splitting open. Aaargh!

MOLINA.   I told you not to gobble down your food like that.

VALENTIN   (*raising himself with difficulty*).   You were right. I'm ready to burst.

MOLINA.   Stretch out a little.

VALENTIN.   No, I don't want to sleep, I had nightmares all last night and this morning.

MOLINA (*relenting, like a middle-class housewife*). I swore I wouldn't tell you another film. I'll probably go to hell for breaking my word.

VALENTIN. Ay!... Oh, fucking hell... (*Molina hesitates.*) You carry on. Pay no attention if I groan.

MOLINA. I'll tell you another movie, one for tummy ache. Now, you seemed keen on those German movies, am I right?

VALENTIN. In their propaganda machine...but, listen, go, on with the panther-woman. We left off where the architect girl stopped hearing the human foot-steps behind her in the park.

MOLINA. Well...she's shaking with fear, she won't dare turn around in case she sees the panther. She stops for a second to see if she still can't hear the woman's footsteps, but there's nothing, absolute silence, and then suddenly she begins to notice this rustling noise coming from the bushes being stirred by the wind...or maybe by something else.... (*Molina imitates the actions he describes.*) And she turns round with a start.

VALENTIN. I think I want to go to the toilet again.

MOLINA. Shall I call them to open up?

VALENTIN. They'll catch on that I'm ill.

MOLINA. They're not going to whip you into hospital for a dose of the runs.

VALENTIN. It'll go away, carry on with the story.

MOLINA. Okay... (*Repeating the same actions.*) ...she turns around with a start...

VALENTIN. Ay!...ay! the pain...

MOLINA (*suddenly*). Tell me something: you never told me why your mother doesn't bring you any food.

VALENTIN. She's a...a difficult woman. That's why I don't talk about her. She could never stand my ideas—she believes she's entitled to everything she's got, her family's got a certain position to keep up.

MOLINA. The family name.

VALENTIN. Only second league, but a name all the same.

MOLINA. Let her know that she can bring you a week's supplies at a time. You're only spiting yourself.

VALENTIN. If I'm in here it's because I brought it on myself, it's got nothing to do with her.

MOLINA. My mother didn't visit lately 'cos she's ill, did I tell you?

VALENTIN. You never mentioned it.

MOLINA. She thinks she's going to recover from one minute to the next. She won't let anyone but her bring me food, so I'm in a pickle.

VALENTIN. If you could get out of this hole she'd improve, right?

MOLINA. You're a mind reader.... Okay, let's get on with it. (*Repeating the same action as before.*) She turns round with a start.

VALENTIN. Ay!... Ay!... What have I gone and done? I'm sorry.

MOLINA. No, no...hold still, don't clean yourself with the sheet, wait a second.

VALENTIN. No, not your shirt...

MOLINA. Here, take it, wipe yourself with it. You'll need the sheet to keep warm.

VALENTIN. No, you haven't got a change of shirt.

MOLINA.   Wait…get up, that way it won't go through…like this…mind it doesn't soil the sheet.

VALENTIN.   Did it go through?

MOLINA.   Your underpants held it in. Here, take them off…

VALENTIN.   I'm embarrassed…

MOLINA.   Didn't you say you have to be a man…? So what's all this about being embarrassed?

VALENTIN.   Wrap my underpants up well, Molina, so they don't smell.

MOLINA.   I know how to handle this. You see…all wrapped up in the shirt. It'll be easier to wash than the sheet. Take the toilet paper.

VALENTIN.   No, not yours. You'll have none left.

MOLINA.   You never had any. So cut it out.

VALENTIN.   Thank you. (*He takes the tissue and wipes himself and hands the roll back to Molina.*)

MOLINA.   You're welcome. Relax a little, you're shaking.

VALENTIN.   It's with rage. I could cry…I'm furious for letting myself get caught.

MOLINA.   Calm down. Pull yourself together. (*Valentin watches Molina wrap the shirt and soiled tissue in a newspaper.*)

VALENTIN.   Good idea…so it won't smell, eh?

MOLINA.   Clever, isn't it?

VALENTIN.   I'm freezing.

MOLINA   (*Meanwhile lighting the stove and putting water on to boil*).   I'm just making some tea. We're down to the last little bag. It's camomile, good for the nerves.

VALENTIN.   No, leave it, it'll go away now.

MOLINA.   Don't be silly.

VALENTIN.   You're crazy—you're using up all your supplies.

MOLINA.   I'll be getting more soon.

VALENTIN.   But your mother's sick and can't come.

MOLINA.   I'll continue. (*With irony. Repeating the same gestures as before but without the same élan.*)   She turns round with a start. The rustling noise gets nearer and she lets rip with a desperate scream, when…whack! the door of the bus opens in front of her. The driver saw her standing there and stopped for her.… The tea's almost ready. (*Molina pours the hot water.*)

VALENTIN.   Thanks. I mean that sincerely. And I want to apologize.… sometimes I get too rough and hurt people without thinking.

MOLINA.   Don't talk nonsense.

VALENTIN.   Instead of a film, I want to tell you something real. About me. I lied when I told you about my girlfriend. I was talking about another one, someone I loved very much. I didn't tell you the truth about my real girlfriend, you'd like her a lot, she's just a sweet and simple kid, but really courageous.

MOLINA.   Please don't tell me anything about her. I don't want to know anything about your political business.

VALENTIN.   Don't be dumb. Who's going to question you about me?

MOLINA.   They might interrogate me.

VALENTIN (*finishing his tea; much improved*).   You trust me, don't you?

MOLINA.   Yes...

VALENTIN.   Well, then...Inside here it's got to be share and share alike.

MOLINA.   It's not that...

VALENTIN (*he lies down on the pillow, relaxing*).   There's nothing worse than feeling bad about having hurt someone. And I hurt her, I forced her to join the organization when she wasn't ready for it, she's very...unsophisticated.

MOLINA.   But don't tell me anymore now. I'm doing the telling for the moment. Where were we? Where did we stop?...   (*Hearing no response, Molina looks at Valentin who has fallen asleep.*)   How did it continue? What comes next? (*Molina feels proud of having helped his fellow cellmate.*)

SCENE VI.

(*Scene. Daylight. Both Molina and Valentin are stretched out on their beds, lost in a private sorrow. In the distance we hear a bolero tune.*)

MOLINA (*singing softly*).   "My love, I write to you again
The night brings an urge to inquire
If you, too, dear, recall the tender pain
And the sad dreams our love would inspire."

VALENTIN.   What's that you're singing?'

MOLINA.   A bolero. "My letter."

VALENTIN.   Only you would go for that stuff.

MOLINA.   What's wrong with it?

VALENTIN.   It's romantic eyewash, that's what. You're daft.

MOLINA.   I'm sorry. I think I've put my foot in it.

VALENTIN.   In what?

MOLINA.   Well, after you got that letter you were really down in the dumps and here I am singing about sad love letters.

VALENTIN.   It was some bad news. You can read it if you like.

MOLINA.   Better not.

VALENTIN.   Don't start all that again; no one's going to ask you anything. Besides, they read it through before I did. (*He unfolds the letter and reads it as he talks.*)

MOLINA.   The handwriting's like hen's tracks.

VALENTIN.   She didn't have much education.... One of the comrades was killed, and now she's leader of the group. It's all written in CODE.

MOLINA.   Ah...

VALENTIN.   And she writes that she's having relations with another of the lads, just like I told her.

MOLINA.   What relations?

VALENTIN.   She was missing me too much. In the organization we take an oath not to get too involved with someone because it can paralyze you when you go into action.

MOLINA.   Into action?

VALENTIN.   Direct action. Risking your life.... We can't afford to worry about someone who wants us to go on living because it makes you scared of dying. Well, maybe not scared exactly, but you hate the suffering it'll cause others. And that's why she's having a relationship with another comrade.

MOLINA.   You said that your girlfriend wasn't really the one you told me about.

VALENTIN.   Damn, staring at this letter has made me dizzy again.

MOLINA.   You're still weak.

VALENTIN.   I'm shivering and I feel queasy.   (*He covers himself with the sheet.*)

MOLINA.   I told you not to start taking food again.

VALENTIN.   But I was famished.   (*Molina helps Valentin wrap up well.*)

MOLINA.   You were getting better yesterday and then you went and ate and got sick again. And today it's the same story. Promise me you won't touch a thing tomorrow.

VALENTIN.   The girl I told you about, the bourgeois one, she joined the organization with me but she dropped out and tried to persuade me to split with her.

MOLINA.   Why?

VALENTIN.   She loved life too much and she was happy just to be with me, that's all she wanted. So we had to break up.

MOLINA.   Because you loved each other too much.

VALENTIN.   You make it sound like one of your boleros.

MOLINA.   The truth is you mock those songs because they're too close to home. You laugh to keep from crying. As a tango says.

VALENTIN.   I was lying low for a while in that guy's flat, the one they killed. With his wife and kid. I even used to change the kid's nappies.... And do you want to know what the worst of it is? I can't write to a single one of them without blowing them to the police.

MOLINA.   Not even to your girlfriend?

VALENTIN   (*straggling to hold back his tears*).   Oh, God!... what a mess!... it's all so sad!

MOLINA.   There's nothing you can do.

VALENTIN.   Help me get my arm from under...the blanket.

MOLINA.   What for?

VALENTIN.   Give me your hand, Molina. Squeeze hard...

MOLINA.   Hold it tight.

VALENTIN.   There's something else. It's wrecking me. It's shameful, awful...

MOLINA.   Tell me, get it off your chest.

VALENTIN.   It's...the girl I want to hear from, the one I want to have next to me right now and hug and kiss...it's not the one in the movement, but the other one...Marta, that's her name...

MOLINA.   If that's what you feel deep down...Oh, I forgot, if your stomach feels real empty, there's a few digestives I'd forgotten all about. (*Without taking his hand from Valentin's he reaches for the packet of digestives.*)

VALENTIN.   For all I shoot my mouth off about progress...when it comes to women, what I really like is a woman with class and I'm just like all the reactionary sons-of-bitches that killed my comrade.... The same, exactly the same...

MOLINA. That's not true...

VALENTIN. And sometimes I think maybe I don't even love Marta because of who she is but because she's got...class...I'm just like all the other class-conscious sons-of-bitches...in the world.

GUARD'S VOICE. Luis Alberto Molina! To the visiting room!

(*Valentin and Molina let go of each other's hand as if caught in a shameful act. The cell door opens and Molina exits, but not before he's managed to slip the biscuits under Valentin's blanket. Hereafter, the dialogue is on prerecorded tape. Meanwhile, Valentin remains on stage and takes the biscuits from under his covers, manages to find just three at the bottom of the large packet and begins to eat them, one at a time, savoring each one.*)

WARDEN'S VOICE. Stop shaking, man, no one's going to do anything to you.

MOLINA'S VOICE. I had a bad stomach ache before, sir, but I'm fine now.

WARDEN'S VOICE. You've got nothing to be afraid of. We've made it look like you've had a visitor. The other one won't suspect a thing.

MOLINA'S VOICE. No, he won't suspect anything.

WARDEN'S VOICE. At home last night I had dinner with your protector and he had some good news for you. Your mother is on the road to recovery...it seems the chance of your pardon is doing her good...

MOLINA'S VOICE. Are you sure?

WARDEN'S VOICE. What's the matter with you? Why are you trembling?...You should be jubilant.... Well, have you got any news for me yet? Has he told you anything? Is he opening up to you?

MOLINA'S VOICE. No, sir, not so far. You have to take these things a step at a time.

WARDEN'S VOICE. Didn't it help at all when we weakened him physically?

MOLINA'S VOICE. I had to eat the first plate of fixed food myself.

WARDEN'S VOICE. You shouldn't have done that.

MOLINA'S VOICE. The truth is he doesn't like porridge and since one portion was bigger than the other...he insisted I eat it. If I'd refused he might have got suspicious. You told me, sir, that the doctored food would be on the newest plate but they made a mistake piling it high like that.

WARDEN'S VOICE. Ah, well, in that case, I'm obliged to you, Molina. I'm sorry about the mistake.

MOLINA'S VOICE. Now you should let him get some of his strength back.

WARDEN'S VOICE (*irritated*). That's for us to decide. We know what we're doing. And when you get back to your cell say you had a visit from your mother. That'll explain why you're so excited.

MOLINA'S VOICE. No, I couldn't say that, she always brings me a food parcel.

WARDEN'S VOICE. Okay, we'll send out for some groceries. Think of it as a reward for the trouble with the porridge. Poor Molina!

MOLINA'S VOICE. Thank you, Warden.

WARDEN'S VOICE. Reel off a list of what she usually brings. (*Pause.*) Now!

MOLINA'S VOICE. To you?

WARDEN'S VOICE.   Yes, and be quick about it, I've got work to catch up with.

MOLINA'S VOICE (*as the curtain falls*).   A tin of treacle, a can of peaches...two roast chickens...a big bag of sugar...two packs of tea, one breakfast, one camomile...powdered milk, a bar of soap, bathsize...oh, let me think a second, my mind's a complete blank...

Act II

SCENE VII.

(*Scene: Lighting as in previous scene. The cell door opens and Molina enters with a shopping bag.*)

MOLINA.   Look what I've got!!!

VALENTIN.   No! Your mother?

MOLINA.   Yes!!

VALENTIN.   So she's better now?

MOLINA.   A little better.... And look what she brought me. Ooops! Sorry, brought us!

VALENTIN (*secretly flattered*).   No, it's for you. Cut the nonsense.

MOLINA.   Shut it, you're the invalid. The chickens are for you, they'll get you back on your feet.

VALENTIN.   No, I won't let you do this.

MOLINA.   It's no sacrifice. I can go without the chicken if it means I don't have to put up with your pong... No, listen, I'm being serious now, you've got to stop eating this pig swill they serve in here. At least for a day or two.

VALENTIN.   You think so?

MOLINA.   And then when you're better...Close your eyes. (*Valentin closes his eyes and Molina places a large tin in one of his hands.*)   Three guesses...

VALENTIN.   Ahem...er...er... (*Enjoying the game. Molina places an identical one in Valentin's other hand.*)

MOLINA.   The weight ought to help you...

VALENTIN.   Heavy all right...I give up.

MOLINA.   Open your eyes.

VALENTIN.   Treacle!

MOLINA.   But you can't have it yet, not until you're better. And this is for both of us.

VALENTIN.   Marvellous.

MOLINA.   First...we'll have a cup of camomile tea because my nerves are shot and you can have a drumstick, no, better not, it's only five.... Anyway, we can have tea and some biscuits, they're even lighter than those digestives.

VALENTIN.   Please, can't I have one right away?

MOLINA.   Why not! But no treacle on it—just marmalade!... Luckily, everything she brought is easy to get down so it won't give you any trouble. Except the treacle for the time being.

VALENTIN.   Oh, Molina, I'm wilting with hunger. Why won't you let me have that chicken leg now?

MOLINA   (*he hesitates a moment*).   Here...

VALENTIN (*wolfing down the chicken*).   Honest, I really was beginning to feel bad....   (*He devours the chicken.*)   Thanks...

MOLINA.   You're welcome.

VALENTIN (*his mouth full*).   But there's just one thing missing to round off the picnic.

MOLINA.   Tut, and I thought I was supposed to be the pervert here.

VALENTIN.   Stop fooling around! What we need is a movie...

MOLINA.   Ah!... Well, now there's a scene where Irina has a completely new hair-style.

VALENTIN.   Oh, I'm sorry, I don't feel too good, it's that dizziness again.

MOLINA.   Are you positive?

VALENTIN.   Yes, it's been threatening all night.

MOLINA.   But it can't be the chicken. Maybe you're imagining it.

VALENTIN.   I felt full up all of a sudden.

MOLINA.   That's because you wolfed it down without even chewing.

VALENTIN.   And this itching is driving me wild. I don't know when I last had a bath.

MOLINA.   Don't even think about that. That freezing water in your present state! (*Pause.*)   Anyway, she looks stunning here, you can see her reflection in a window-pane, it's drizzling and all the drops are running down the glass. She's got raven black hair and it's all scooped up in a bun. Let me describe it to you....

VALENTIN.   It's all scooped up, okay, never mind the silly details....

MOLINA.   Silly, my foot! And she's got a rhinestone flower in her hair.

VALENTIN (*very agitated now because of his itch*).   I know what rhinestones are so you can save your breath!

MOLINA.   My, you are touchy today!

VALENTIN.   Do you mind if I say something?

MOLINA.   Go ahead.

VALENTIN.   I feel all screwed up—and confused. If it's not too much trouble I'd like to dictate a letter to her. Would you mind taking it down?... I get dizzy if I try to focus my eyes too hard.

MOLINA.   Let me get a pencil.

VALENTIN.   You're very kind to me.

MOLINA.   We'll do a rough draft first on a bit of paper.

VALENTIN.   Here, take my pen-case.

MOLINA.   Wait till I sharpen this pencil.

VALENTIN (*short-tempered*).   I told you! Use one of mine!

MOLINA.   Okay, don't blow your top!

VALENTIN.   I'm sorry, it's just that everything is going black.

MOLINA.   Okay, ready, shoot...

VALENTIN (*very sad*).   Dear Marta...you don't expect this letter.... In your case, it won't endanger you.... I'm feeling...lonely, I need you, I want to be...near you...I want you to give me...a word of encouragement.

MOLINA.   ..."of encouragement"...

VALENTIN.   ...in this moment I couldn't face my comrades, I'd be ashamed of being so weak.... I have sores all over inside, I need somebody to pour some honey...over my wounds.... And only you could understand...because you too were brought up in a nice clean house to enjoy life to the full,...I can't accept becoming a martyr, it makes me angry to be one...or, it isn't that, I see it clearer now...I'm afraid because I'm sick, horribly afraid of dying...that it may just end here, that my life has amounted to nothing more than this, I never exploited anyone...and ever since I had any sense I've been struggling against the exploitation of my fellow man...

MOLINA. Go on.

VALENTIN. Where was I?

MOLINA. "My fellow man"...

VALENTIN. ...because I want to go out into the street one day and not die. And sometimes I get this idea that never ever again will I be able to touch a woman, and I can't accept it, and when I think of women I only see you, and what a relief it would be to believe that right until I finish writing this letter you'll be thinking of me...and that you'll be running your hands over your body I so well remember...

MOLINA. Hold on, don't go so fast.

VALENTIN. over your body I so well remember, and you'll be thinking that it's my hand...it would be as if I were touching you, darling...because there's still something of me inside you, isn't that so? Just as your own scent has stayed in my nose...beneath my fingertips lies a sort of memory of your skin, do you understand me? Although it's not a matter of understanding...it's a matter of believing, and sometimes I'm convinced that I took something of you with me...and that I haven't lost it, and then sometimes not, I feel there's just me all alone in this cell... (*Pause.*)

MOLINA. Yes, "all alone in this cell"...Go on.

VALENTIN. ...because nothing leaves any trace, and my luck in having had such happiness with you, of spending those nights and afternoons and mornings of sheer enjoyment, none of this is any use now, just the opposite, it all turns against me, because I miss you madly, and all I can feel is the torture of my loneliness, and in my nose there is only the stench of this cell, and of myself...and I can't have a wash because I'm ill, really weak, and the cold water would give me pneumonia and beneath my fingertips what I feel is the chill of my fear of death, I can feel it in my joints...what a terrible thing to lose hope and that's what's happened to me...

MOLINA. I'm sorry for butting in...

VALENTIN. What is it?

MOLINA. When you finish dictating the letter there's something I want to say.

VALENTIN (*wound up*). What?

MOLINA. Because if you take one of those freezing showers it'll kill you.

VALENTIN (*almost hysterical*). And?... So what? Tell me, for Christ's sake.

MOLINA. I could help you to get cleaned up. You see, we've got the hot water we were going to use to boil the potatoes and we've got two towels, so we lather one of them and you do your front and I'll do the back and then you can dry yourself with the other towel.

VALENTIN.   And then I'd stop itching?

MOLINA.   Sure. And we'd clean a bit at a time so you won't catch cold.

VALENTIN.   And you'll help me?

MOLINA.   Of course I will.

VALENTIN.   When?

MOLINA.   Now, if you like. The water's boiling, we can mix it with a little cold water. (*Molina starts to do this.*)

VALENTIN (*who can't believe in such happiness*).   And I'd be able to get to sleep without scratching?

MOLINA.   Take your shirt off. I'll put some more water on.   (*He mixes the hot and cold water.*)

VALENTIN.   Give me the letter, Molina.

MOLINA.   What for?

VALENTIN.   Just hand it over.

MOLINA.   Here. (*Valentin tears it up.*) What are you doing???

VALENTIN.   This. (*He tears it into quarters.*)   Let's not mention it again.

MOLINA.   As you like…

VALENTIN.   It's wrong to get carried away like that by despair.

MOLINA.   But it's good to get it into the open. You said so yourself.

VALENTIN.   But it's bad for me. I have to learn to restrain myself. (*Pause.*) Listen, I mean it, one day I'll thank you properly for all this. (*Molina puts more water on the stove.*)   Are you going to waste all that water?

MOLINA.   Yes…and don't be daft, there's no need to thank me. (*Molina signals to Valentin to turn around.*)

VALENTIN.   Tell me, how does the movie end, just the last scene.

MOLINA (*scrubbing Valentin's back*).   It's either all or nothing.

VALENTIN.   Why?

MOLINA.   Because of the details. Her hairdo is important, it's the style that women wear, or used to wear, when they wanted to show that this was a crucial moment in their lives, because the hair all scooped up in a bun which left the neck bare, gave the woman's face a certain nobility. (*Valentin, despite the tensions and turmoil of the difficult day, changes his expression and smiles.*) Why have you got that mocking little grin on your face? I don't see anything to laugh at.

VALENTIN.   Because my back doesn't itch anymore!

Scene VIII.

(*Scene. Day. Molina is tidying up his belongings with extreme care so as not to wake Valentin. Valentin, nevertheless, wakes up. Both of them are charged with renewed energy and the dialogue begins at its normal pace but accelerates rapidly into tenseness.*)

VALENTIN.   Good morning.

MOLINA.   Good morning.

VALENTIN.   What's the time?

MOLINA. Ten past ten. I call my mother "ten past ten," the poor dear, because of the way her feet stick out when she walks.

VALENTIN. It's late.

MOLINA. When they brought the tea round you just turned over and carried on sleeping.

VALENTIN. What were you saying about your old lady?

MOLINA. Look who's still sleeping. Nothing. Sleep well?

VALENTIN. I feel a lot better.

MOLINA. You don't feel dizzy?

VALENTIN. Lying in bed, no.

MOLINA. Great—why don't you try to walk a little?

VALENTIN. No—you'll laugh.

MOLINA. At what?

VALENTIN. Something that happens to a normal healthy man when he wakes up in the morning with too much energy.

MOLINA. You've got a hard-on? Well, God bless…

VALENTIN. But look away, please. I get embarrassed. (*He gets up to wash his face with water from the jug.*)

MOLINA (*he puts his hand over his eyes and looks away*). My eyes are shut tight.

VALENTIN. It's all thanks to your food. My legs are a bit shaky still, but I don't feel queasy. You can look now. (*He gets back into bed.*) I'll lie down a bit more.

MOLINA (*overprotective and smothering*). I'll put the water on for tea.

VALENTIN. No, just reheat the crap they brought us this morning.

MOLINA. I threw it out when I went to the loo. You must look after yourself properly if you want to get better.

VALENTIN. It embarrasses me to use up your things. I'm better now.

MOLINA. Button it.

VALENTIN. No, listen…

MOLINA. Listen nothing. My mother's bringing stuff again.

VALENTIN. Okay, thanks, but just for today. (*He collects his books together.*)

MOLINA. And no reading. Rest!… I'll start another film while I'm making the tea.

VALENTIN. I'd better try and study, if I can, now that I'm on form. (*He starts to read.*)

MOLINA. Won't it be too tiring?

VALENTIN. I'll give it a go.

MOLINA. You're a real fanatic.

VALENTIN (*throwing the book to the ground as his tenseness increases*). I can't…the words are jumping around.

MOLINA. I told you so. Are you feeling dizzy?

VALENTIN. Only when I try to read.

MOLINA. You know what it is? It's probably just a temporary weakness—if you have a ham sandwich you'll be right as rain.

VALENTIN. Do you think so?

MOLINA. Sure, and then later, after you've had lunch and another little snooze you'll feel up to studying again.

VALENTIN.   I feel lazy as hell. I'll just lie down.

MOLINA   (*schoolmistressy*).   No, lying in bed only weakens the constitution, you'd be better standing or at least sitting up.   (*Molina hands him the tea.*)

VALENTIN.   This is the last day I'm taking any more of this.

MOLINA   (*mistress of the situation*).   Ha! Ha! I already told the guard not to bring you any more tea in the morning.

VALENTIN.   Listen, you decide what you want for yourself, but I want them to bring me the tea even if it is horse's piss.

MOLINA.   You don't know the first thing about a healthy diet.

VALENTIN   (*trying to control himself*).   I'm not joking Molina, I don't like other people controlling my life.

MOLINA   (*counting on his fingers*).   Today is Wednesday...everything will hang on what happens on Monday. That's what my lawyer says. I don't believe in appeals and all that but if there's someone who can pull a few strings, maybe there's a chance.

VALENTIN.   I hope so.

MOLINA   (*with concealed cunning, as he makes more tea*).   If they let me out...who knows who you'll get as a cellmate.

VALENTIN.   Haven't you had breakfast yet?

MOLINA.   I didn't want to disturb you. You were sleeping.   (*He takes Valentin's cup to refill it.*)   Will you join me in another cup?

VALENTIN.   No, thanks.

MOLINA   (*opening a new packet, not letting Valentin see*).   Tell me, what are you going to study later on?

VALENTIN.   What are you doing?

MOLINA.   A surprise. Tell me what you're reading.

VALENTIN.   Nothing...

MOLINA.   Cat got your tongue?... And now...we untie the mystery parcel... which I had hidden about my person...and, what have we got here?... Something that goes a treat with tea...a cherry madeira!

VALENTIN.   No, thanks.

MOLINA.   What d'you mean "no"?...the kettle's on...Oh, I know why not—you want to go to the loo. Ask them to open up and then fly back here.

VALENTIN.   For Christ's sake, don't tell me what to do!

MOLINA   (*he squeezes Valentin's chin*).   Oh, come on, let me pamper you a little.

VALENTIN.   That's enough...you prick!

MOLINA.   Are you crazy?... What's the matter with you?

VALENTIN   (*he hurls the teacup and the cake against the wall*).   Shut your fucking trap!

MOLINA.   The cake... (*Valentin is silent.*)   Look what you've done...if the stove's broke, we're done for.... (*Pause.*)   ...and the saucer... (*Pause.*)   ...and the tea...

VALENTIN.   I'm sorry...(*Molina is silent now.*)   I lost control...I'm really sorry. (*Molina remains silent.*)   The stove is okay; but the paraffin spilled. (*Molina still doesn't answer.*)   ... I'm sorry I got carried away, forgive me....

MOLINA (*deeply wounded*). There's nothing to forgive.

VALENTIN. There is. A lot.

MOLINA. Forget it. Nothing happened.

VALENTIN. It did, I'm dying with shame. (*Molina says nothing.*) ... I behaved like an animal.... Look, I'll call the guard and fill up the bottle while I'm at it. We're almost out of water.... Molina, please, look at me. Raise your head. (*Molina remains silent.*)

GUARD'S VOICE. Luis Alberto Molina. To the visiting room!

> (*The door opens and Molina exits. The recorded dialogue begins as soon as Molina moves toward the door. Molina returns with the provisions to find Valentin picking up the things he has just thrown on the floor. Molina starts to unpack the shopping bag. The recorded dialogue is heard while the action takes place on stage.*)

WARDEN'S VOICE. Today's Monday, Molina, what have you got for me?

MOLINA'S VOICE. Nothing, I'm afraid, sir.

WARDEN'S VOICE. Indeed.

MOLINA'S VOICE. But he's taking me more into his confidence.

WARDEN'S VOICE. The problem is they're putting pressure on me, Molina. From the top: from the President's private office. You understand what I'm saying to you, Molina? They want to try interrogation again. Less carrot, more stick.

MOLINA'S VOICE. Not that sir. It'd be even worse if you lost him in interrogation.

WARDEN'S VOICE. That's what I tell them, but they won't listen.

MOLINA'S VOICE. Just one more week, sir. Please. I have an idea...

WARDEN'S VOICE. What?

MOLINA'S VOICE. He's a hard nut but he has an emotional side.

WARDEN'S VOICE. So?

MOLINA'S VOICE. Well, if the guard were to come and say they're moving me to another block in a week's time because of the appeal, that might really soften him up.

WARDEN'S VOICE. What are you driving at?

MOLINA'S VOICE. Nothing, I swear. It's just a hunch. If he thinks I'm leaving soon he'll feel like opening up even more with me. Prisoners are like that, sir...when one of their pals is leaving they feel more defenseless than ever.

> (*At this moment Molina is back in the cell and he takes out the food as the Warden's Voice mentions each item. Valentin looks at Molina.*)

WARDEN'S VOICE. Guard, take this down: two roast chickens, four baked apples, one carton of coleslaw, one pound of bacon, one pound of cooked ham, four French loaves, four pieces of crystallized fruit (*the recorded voice begins to fade out*) ...a carton of orange juice, two cherry madeiras...

MOLINA (*very calm and very sad; still upset by Valentin's remarks*). This is the bacon and this one's the ham. I'm going to make a sandwich while the bread's fresh. You fix yourself whatever you want.

VALENTIN   (*deeply ashamed*).   Thank you.

MOLINA   (*reserved, calm*).   I'm going to cut this roll in half and spread it with butter and have a ham sandwich. And a baked apple.

VALENTIN.   Sounds delicious.

MOLINA.   If you'd like some of the chicken while it's still warm, go ahead. Feel free.

VALENTIN.   Thank you, Molina.

MOLINA.   We'll each fend for ourselves. Then I won't get on your nerves.

VALENTIN.   If that's what you prefer.

MOLINA.   There's some crystallized fruit, too. All I ask is you leave me the pumpkin. Otherwise, take what you want.

VALENTIN   (*finding it hard to apologize*).   I'm still embarrassed…because of that tantrum.

MOLINA.   Don't be silly.

VALENTIN.   If I got annoyed with you…it was because you were kind to me…and I didn't want…to treat you the same way.

MOLINA.   Look, I've been thinking too and I remembered something you once said, right?…that when you're involved in a struggle like that, well, it's not too convenient to get fond of someone. Well, fond is maybe going too far.… Or, why not? Fond as a friend.

VALENTIN.   That's a very noble way of looking at it.

MOLINA.   You see, sometimes I do understand what you tell me.

VALENTIN.   But are we so fettered by the world outside that we can't act like human beings just for a minute…? Is the enemy out there that powerful?

MOLINA.   I don't follow.

VALENTIN.   Our persecutors are on the outside, not inside this cell.… The problem is I'm so brainwashed that it freaks me out when someone is nice to me without asking anything in return.

MOLINA.   I don't know about that…

VALENTIN.   About what?

MOLINA.   Don't get me wrong, but if I'm nice to you, well, it's because I want you to be my friend…and why not admit it?… I want your affection. Just like I treat my mother well because she's a good person and I want her to love me. And you're a good person too, and unselfish because you're risking your life for an ideal…that I don't understand but, all the same, it's not just for yourself.… Don't look away like that, are you embarrassed?

VALENTIN.   A bit. (*He looks Molina in the face.*)

MOLINA.   And that's why I respect you and have warm feelings toward you…and why I want you to like me…because, you see, my mother's love is the only good thing I've felt in my life, because she likes me…just the way I am.

VALENTIN   (*pointing to the loaf Molina put aside*).   Can I cut the loaf for you?

MOLINA.   Of course…

VALENTIN   (*cutting the loaf*).   And did you never have good friends that meant a lot to you?

MOLINA.   My friends were all…screaming queens, like me, we never really count on each other because…how can I express it?—because we know we're so easily frightened off. We're always looking, you know, for friendship, or whatever, with somebody more serious, with a man, you see? And that just doesn't happen, right? Because what a man wants is a woman.

VALENTIN   (*taking a slice of ham for Molina's sandwich*).   And are all homosexuals like that?

MOLINA.   Oh no, there are some who fall in love with each other. But me and my friends we're women. One hundred percent. We don't go in for those little games. We're normal women; *we* only go to bed with men.

VALENTIN   (*too absorbed to see the funny side of this*).   Butter?

MOLINA.   Yes, thanks. There's something I have to tell you.

VALENTIN.   Of course, the movie…

MOLINA   (*with cunning, but nervous all the same*).   My lawyer said things were looking up.

VALENTIN.   What a creep I am! I didn't ask you.

MOLINA.   And when there's an appeal pending, the prisoner gets moved to another block in the prison. They'll probably shift me within a week or so.

VALENTIN   (*upset by this but dissimulating*).   That's terrific…you ought to be pleased.

MOLINA.   I don't want to dwell on it too much, build my hopes…. Have some coleslaw.

VALENTIN.   Should I?

MOLINA.   It's very good.

VALENTIN.   Your news made me lose my appetite.   (*He gets up.*)

MOLINA.   Pretend I didn't say anything, nothing's settled yet.

VALENTIN.   No, it all looks good for you, we should be happy.

MOLINA.   Have some salad.

VALENTIN.   I don't know what's wrong, but all of a sudden I don't feel too good.

MOLINA.   Is your stomach hurting?

VALENTIN.   No…it's my head. I'm all confused.

MOLINA.   About what?

VALENTIN.   Let me rest for a while.

> (*Valentin sits down again, resting his head in his palms. The light changes to indicate a shift to a different time—the two characters stay where they are: there is a special tension, a hypersensitivity in the air.*)

MOLINA.   The guy is all muddled up, he doesn't know how to handle this freaky wife of his. She comes in, sees that he's dead serious and goes to the bathroom to put away her shoes, all dirty with mud. He says he went to the doctor's to look for her and found out that she didn't go anymore. Then she breaks into tears and tells him that she's just what she always feared, a mad woman with hallucinations or even worse, a panther-woman. Then he gives in and takes her in his arms and you were right, she's really just a little girl for him, because when he sees her so defenseless and lost, he feels again he loves her with all his heart and tells her that everything will sort itself out.... (*Molina sighs deeply.*) Ahhh...!

VALENTIN.   What a sigh!

MOLINA.   Life is so difficult....

VALENTIN.   What's the matter?

MOLINA.   I don't know, I'm afraid of building up my hopes of getting out of here...and that I'll get put in some other cell and spend my life there with God knows what sort of creep.

VALENTIN.   Don't lose sight of this. Your mother's health is the most precious thing to you, right?

MOLINA.   Yes...

VALENTIN.   Think about her recovery. Period!

MOLINA   (*he laughs involuntarily in his distress*).   I don't want to think about it.

VALENTIN.   What's wrong?

MOLINA.   Nothing!

VALENTIN.   Don't bury your head in the pillow.... Are you keeping something from me?

MOLINA.   It's...

VALENTIN.   It's what?... Look, when you get out of here you're going to be a free man. You can join a political organization if you like.

MOLINA.   You're crazy! They won't trust a fag.

VALENTIN.   But I can tell you who to speak to....

MOLINA   (*suddenly forceful, raising his head from the pillow*).   Promise me on whatever you hold most dear, never, never, you understand, never tell me anything about your comrades.

VALENTIN.   But who would ever think you're seeing them?

MOLINA.   They could interrogate me, whatever, but if I know nothing, I say nothing.

VALENTIN.   In any case, there are all kinds of groups, of political action; there are even some who just sit and talk. When you get out things'll be different.

MOLINA.   Things *won't* be different. That's the worst of it.

VALENTIN.   How many times have I seen you cry? Come on, you annoy me with your sniveling.

MOLINA.   It's just that I can't take any more.... I've had nothing but bad luck...always. (*The prison light goes out.*)

VALENTIN.   Lights out already?... In the first place you must join a group, avoid being alone.

MOLINA.   I don't understand any of that...(*Suddenly grave.*)... *and I don't believe in it much either.*

VALENTIN   (*tough*).   Then like it or lump it.

MOLINA   (*still crying a little*).   Let's...skip it.

VALENTIN   (*conciliatory*).   Come on, don't be like that.... (*He pats Molina on the back affectionately.*)

MOLINA.   I'm asking you...please don't touch me.

VALENTIN.   Can't a friend pat you on the back?

MOLINA.   It makes it worse....

VALENTIN.   Why?... Tell me what's troubling you....

MOLINA   (*with deep, deep feeling*).   I'm so tired, Valentin.... I'm tired of suffering. I hurt all over inside.

VALENTIN.   Where does it hurt you?

MOLINA.   Inside my chest and my throat.... Why does sadness always get you
there? It's choking me, like a knot....

VALENTIN.   It's true, that's where people always feel it.   (*Molina is quiet.*)   Is it
hurting you a lot, this knot?

MOLINA.   Yes.

VALENTIN.   Is it here?

MOLINA.   Yes.

VALENTIN.   Want me to stroke it...here?

MOLINA.   Yes.

VALENTIN   (*after a short pause*).   This is relaxing....

MOLINA.   Why relaxing, Valentin?

VALENTIN.   Not to think about myself for a while. Thinking about you, that you
need me, and I can be of some use to you.

MOLINA.   You're always looking for explanations.... You're crazy.

VALENTIN.   I don't want events to get the better of me. I want to know why they
happen.

MOLINA.   Can I touch you?

VALENTIN.   Yes...

MOLINA.   I want to touch that mole—the little round one over your eye.   (*Pause.
Molina touches the mole.*)   You're very kind.

VALENTIN.   No, you're the one who's kind.

MOLINA.   If you like you can do what you want with me...because I want it too....
If it won't disgust you...

VALENTIN.   Don't say that—let's not say anything.   (*Valentin goes under Molina's
top sheet.*)   Shift a bit closer to the wall.....   (*Pause.*)   You can't see a thing
it's so dark.

MOLINA.   Gently...   (*Pause.*)   No, it hurts too much like that. (*Pause.*) Slowly
please...   (*Pause.*)   That's it...   (*Pause.*)   ...thanks...

VALENTIN.   Thank you, too. Are you feeling better?

MOLINA.   Yes. And what about you, Valentin?

VALENTIN.   Don't ask me....I don't know anything anymore....

MOLINA.   Oh,...it's beautiful...

VALENTIN.   Don't say anything...not for now...

MOLINA.   It's just that I feel...such strange things.... Without thinking, I just
lifted my hand to my eye, looking for that mole.

VALENTIN.   What mole?... *I'm* the one with the mole, not you.

MOLINA.   I know, but I just lifted up my hand...to touch the mole...I don't have.

VALENTIN.   Ssh, try and keep quiet for a while....

MOLINA.   And do you know what else I felt, but only for a minute, no longer...

VALENTIN.   Tell me, but keep still, like that....

MOLINA.   For just a minute, it felt like I wasn't here...not in here, nor anywhere else... (*Pause.*) It felt like I wasn't here, there was just you.... Or that I wasn't me anymore. As if I was...you.

SCENE IX.

(*Scene. Day. Molina and Valentin are in their beds.*)

VALENTIN.   Good morning. (*He is reinvigorated, happy.*)

MOLINA   (*also highly charged*).   Good morning, Valentin.

VALENTIN.   Did you sleep well?

MOLINA.   Yes. (*Calmly, not insisting.*)   Would you like tea or coffee?

VALENTIN.   Coffee. To wake me up well—and study. Try to get back into the swing of things.... What about you? Is the gloom over? Or not?

MOLINA.   Yes it is, but I feel groggy. I can't think...my mind's a blank.

VALENTIN.   I don't want to think about anything either, so I'm going to read. That'll keep my mind off things.

MOLINA.   Off what? Feeling guilty about what happened?

VALENTIN.   I'm more and more convinced that sex is innocence itself.

MOLINA.   Can I ask you a favor?... Let's not discuss anything, just for today.

VALENTIN.   Whatever you like.

MOLINA.   I feel...fine and I don't want anything to rob me of that feeling. I haven't felt so good since I was a kid. Since my mother bought me some toy.

VALENTIN.   Do you remember what toy you liked most?

MOLINA.   A doll.

VALENTIN.   Ay!! (*He starts to laugh.*)

MOLINA.   What's funny about that?

VALENTIN.   As a psychologist I would starve.

MOLINA.   Why?

VALENTIN.   Nothing...I was just wondering if there was any link between your favorite toy and...me.

MOLINA   (*playing along*).   It was your own fault for asking.

VALENTIN.   Are you sure it wasn't a boy doll?

MOLINA.   Absolutely. She had blond braids and a little Tyrolese folk dress. (*They laugh together, unselfconsciously.*)

VALENTIN.   One question.... Physically, you're as much a man as I am.

MOLINA.   Ummm...

VALENTIN.   Why then don't you behave like a man.... I don't mean with women if you're not attracted to them, but with another man?

MOLINA.   It's not me. I only enjoy myself like that.

VALENTIN.   Well, if you like being a woman...you shouldn't feel diminished because of that. (*Molina doesn't answer.*)   I mean you shouldn't feel you owe anyone, or feel obliged to them because that's what you happen to like.... You shouldn't yield...

MOLINA.   But if a man is…my husband, he has to be boss to feel good. That's only natural.

VALENTIN.   No, the man and the woman should be equal partners inside the home. Otherwise, it's exploitation. Don't you see?

MOLINA.   But there's no thrill in that.

VALENTIN.   What?

MOLINA.   Since you want to know about it…. The thrill is that when a man embraces you, you're a bit afraid.

VALENTIN.   Who put that idea into your head? That's all crap.

MOLINA.   But it's what I feel.

VALENTIN.   It's not what you feel—it's what you were taught to feel. Being a woman doesn't make you…how should I say?…a martyr. And if I didn't think it would hurt like hell I'd ask you to do it to me, to show you that all this business about being macho doesn't give anyone rights over another person.

MOLINA.   (*now disturbed*).   This is getting us nowhere.

VALENTIN.   On the contrary, I want to talk about it.

MOLINA.   Well, I don't, so that's it. I'm begging you, no more please.

GUARD'S VOICE.   Prisoner Luis Alberto Molina! To the visiting room!

(*The door opens and Molina exits. Valentin, contented, sorts through his books, lays out his pencil and paper and begins to read. Meanwhile, we hear the Warden's Voice.*)

WARDEN'S VOICE.   Put me through to your boss, please…. How's it going? Nothing this end. Yes, that's why I called. He's on his way here now…. Yes, they need the information, I'm aware of that…. And if Molina still hasn't found out anything, what should I do with him?… Are you sure?… Let him out today?… But why today?… Yes, of course, there's no time to lose. Quite, and if the other one gives him a message Molina will lead us straight to the group…. I've got it, yes, we'll give him just enough time for the other to pass on the message…. The tricky thing will be if Molina catches on that he's under surveillance…. It's hard to anticipate the reactions of someone like Molina: a pervert after all.

(*The cell door opens and Molina comes back in, totally deflated.*)

MOLINA.   Poor Valentin, you're looking at my hands.

VALENTIN.   I didn't mean to.

MOLINA.   Your eyes give you away, poor love….

VALENTIN.   Such language…

MOLINA.   I didn't get a parcel. You'll have to forgive me…. Ay! Valentin…

VALENTIN.   What's wrong?

MOLINA.   Ay, you can't imagine…

VALENTIN.   What's up? Tell me!

MOLINA.   I'm going.

VALENTIN.   To another cell…. What a nuisance!

MOLINA.　No, they're releasing me.

VALENTIN.　No.

MOLINA.　I'm out on parole.

VALENTIN (*exploding with unexpected happiness*).　But that's incredible!

MOLINA　(*confused by the way Valentin's taking this*).　You're very kind to be so pleased for me.

VALENTIN.　I'm happy for you too, of course…but, it's terrific! And I guarantee there's not the slightest risk.

MOLINA.　What are you saying?

VALENTIN.　Listen,…I had to get urgent information out to my people and I was dying with frustration because I couldn't do anything about it. I was racking my brains trying to find a way…. And you come and serve it to me on a plate.

MOLINA　(*as if he'd just had an electric shock*).　I can't do that, you're out of your head.

VALENTIN.　You'll memorize it in a minute. That's how easy it is. All you have to do is tell them that Number Three Command has been knocked out and they have to go to Corrientes for new orders.

MOLINA.　No, I'm on parole, they can lock me up again for anything.

VALENTIN.　I give you my word there's no risk.

MOLINA.　I'm pleading with you. I don't want to hear another word. Not who they are or where they are. Nothing.

VALENTIN.　Don't you want me to get out one day too?

MOLINA.　Of here?

VALENTIN.　Yes, to be free.

MOLINA.　There's nothing I want more. But listen to me, I'm telling you for your own good…. I'm not good at this sort of thing, if they catch me, I'll spill everything.

VALENTIN.　I'll answer for my comrades. You just have to wait a few days and then call from a public telephone, and make an appointment with someone in some bogus place.

MOLINA.　What do you mean "a bogus place"?

VALENTIN.　You just give them a name in code, let's say the Ritz cinema, and that means a certain bench in a particular square.

MOLINA.　I'm frightened.

VALENTIN.　You won't be when I explain the procedure to you.

MOLINA.　But if the phone's tapped I'll get in trouble.

VALENTIN.　Not from a public callbox and if you disguise your voice. It's the easiest thing in the world, I'll show you how to do it. There are millions of ways— a sweet in your mouth, or a toothpick under your tongue…

MOLINA.　No.

VALENTIN.　We'll discuss it later.

MOLINA.　No!!!

VALENTIN.　Whatever you say. (*Molina flops on the bed, all done in, and buries his face in the pillow.*) Look at me please.

MOLINA (*not looking at Valentin*). I made a promise, I don't know who to, maybe God, even though I don't much believe in that.

VALENTIN. Yes...

MOLINA. I swore that I'd sacrifice anything if I could only get out of here and look after my mother. And my wish has come true.

VALENTIN. It was very generous of you to put someone else first.

MOLINA. But where's the justice in it? I always get left with nothing...

VALENTIN. You have your mother and she needs you. You have to assume that responsibility.

MOLINA. Listen, my mother's already had her life, she's lived, been married, had a child...she's old now, and her life is almost finished....

VALENTIN. But she's still alive....

MOLINA. And so am I...But when is my life going to begin?... When is it my turn for something good to happen? To have something for myself?

VALENTIN. You can start a new life outside....

MOLINA. All I want is to stay with you.... (*Valentin doesn't say anything.*) Does that embarrass you?

VALENTIN. No,...er, well, yes...

MOLINA. Yes what?

VALENTIN. That...it makes me a little embarrassed.

MOLINA. If I can relay the information will you get out sooner?

VALENTIN. It's a way of helping the cause.

MOLINA. But you won't get out quickly? You just think it'll bring the revolution a bit closer.

VALENTIN. Yes, Molinita.... Don't dwell on it, we'll discuss it later.

MOLINA. There's no time left to discuss.

VALENTIN. Besides, we have to finish the panther movie.

MOLINA. It's a sad ending.

VALENTIN. How?

MOLINA. She's a flawed woman. (*With his usual irony.*) All of us flawed women come to a sad ending.

VALENTIN (*laughing*). And the psychoanalyst? Does he get her in the end?

MOLINA. She gets him! And good! No, it's not so terrible, she just tears him to pieces.

VALENTIN. Does she kill him?

MOLINA. In the movie, yes. In real life, no.

VALENTIN. Tell me.

MOLINA. Let's see. Irina goes from bad to worse, she's insanely jealous of the other girl and tries to kill her. But the other one's lucky like hell and she gets away. Then one day the husband, who's at his wits' end now, arranges to meet the psychoanalyst at their house while she's out. But things get all muddled up and when the psychoanalyst arrives she's there on her own. He tries to take advantage of the situation and throws himself at her and kisses her. And right there she turns into a panther. By the time the husband he gets home the guy's bled to death. Meanwhile, Irina has made it to the zoo and she sidles up to the panther's cage. She's all alone, in the night. That afternoon she got the key when the keeper left it in the lock. It's like Irina's in another world. The husband is on his way with the cops at top speed. Irina opens the panther's cage and it pounces on her and mortally wounds her with the first blow. The animal is scared away by the police siren, it dashes out into the street, a car runs over it and kills it.

VALENTIN.   I'm going to miss you, Molinita.

MOLINA.   The movies, at least.

VALENTIN.   At least.

MOLINA.   I want to ask you for a going away present. Something that we never did, although we got up to worse.

VALENTIN.   What?

MOLINA.   A kiss.

VALENTIN.   It's true. We never did.

MOLINA.   But right at the end, just as I'm leaving.

VALENTIN.   Okay.

MOLINA.   I'm curious.... Did the idea of kissing me disgust you?

VALENTIN.   Ummm... Maybe I was afraid you'd turn into a panther.

MOLINA.   I'm not the panther-woman.

VALENTIN.   I know.

MOLINA.   It's not fun to be a panther-woman, no one can kiss you. Or anything else.

VALENTIN.   You're the spider-woman who traps men in her web.

MOLINA   (*flattered*).   How sweet! I like that!

VALENTIN.   And now it's your turn to promise me something: that you'll make people respect you, that you won't let anybody take advantage of you.... Promise me you won't let anybody degrade you.

GUARD'S VOICE.   Prisoner Luis Alberto Molina, be ready with your belongings!

MOLINA.   Valentin...

VALENTIN.   What?

MOLINA.   Nothing, it doesn't matter....   (*Pause.*)   Valentin...

VALENTIN.   What is it?

MOLINA.   Rubbish, skip it.

VALENTIN.   Do you want...?

MOLINA.   What?

VALENTIN.   The kiss.

MOLINA.   No, it was something else.

VALENTIN.   Don't you want your kiss now?

MOLINA.   Yes, if it won't disgust you.

VALENTIN.   Don't get me mad.   (*He walks over to Molina and timidly gives him a kiss on the mouth.*)

MOLINA.   Thank you.

VALENTIN.   Thank you.

MOLINA   (*after a long pause*).   And now give me the number of your comrades.

VALENTIN. If you want.

MOLINA. I'll get the message to them.

VALENTIN. Okay...Is that what you wanted to ask?

MOLINA. Yes.

VALENTIN (*he kisses Molina one more time*). You don't know how happy you've made me. It's 323-1025.

> (*Bolero music starts playing: it chokes Valentin's voice as he gives his instructions. Molina and Valentin separate slowly. Molina puts all his belongings into a duffel bag. They are now openly brokenhearted; Molina can hardly keep his mind on what he's doing. Valentin looks at him in total helplessness. Their taped voices are heard as all this action takes place on stage.*)

MOLINA'S VOICE. What happened to me, Valentin, when I got out of here?

VALENTIN'S VOICE. The police kept you under constant surveillance, listened in on your phone, everything. The first call you got was from an uncle, your godfather: he told you not to dally with minors again. You told him what he deserved, that he should go to hell, because in jail you'd learned what dignity was. Your friends telephoned and you called each other Greta and Marlene and Marilyn and the police thought maybe it was a secret code. You got a job as a window dresser and then finally one day you called my comrades. You took your mother to the movies and bought her some fashion magazines. And one day you went to meet my friends but the police were shadowing you and they arrested you. My friends opened fire and killed you from their getaway car as you'd asked them to if the police caught you. And that was all.... And what about me, Molina, what happened to me?

MOLINA'S VOICE. They tortured you a lot...and then your wounds turned septic. A nurse took pity on you and secretly he gave you some morphine and you had a dream.

VALENTIN'S VOICE. About what?

MOLINA'S VOICE. You dreamed that inside you, in your chest, you were carrying Marta and that you'd never ever be apart from one another. And she asked you if you regretted what had happened to me, my death, which she said was your fault.

VALENTIN'S VOICE. And what did I answer her?

MOLINA'S VOICE. You replied that I had died for a noble and selfless ideal. And she said that wasn't true, she said that I had sacrificed myself just so I could die like the heroine in a movie. And you said that only I knew the answer. And you dreamed you were very hungry when you escaped from prison and that you ended up on a savage island and in the middle of the jungle you met a spider woman who gave you food to eat. And she was so lonely there in the jungle but you had to carry on with your struggle and go back to join your comrades, and your strength was restored by the food the spider woman gave you.

VALENTIN'S VOICE. And, at the end, did I get away from the police or did they catch up with me?

MOLINA'S VOICE.   No, at the end you left the island, you were glad to be reunited with your comrades in the struggle, because it was a short dream, but a pleasant one....

> (*The door opens. Molina and Valentin embrace one another with infinite sadness. Molina exits. The door closes behind him. Curtain.*)

Translated by Allan J. Baker

Journal Entry

Record your responses to scene VIII of the play.

Textual Considerations

1. Characterize Molina. What has his life been like? Why does he feel so deeply about the story he narrates? How and why does Valentin affect him?
2. Characterize Valentin. What has his life been like? What are his values? What political changes does he want to effect? How does he respond to Molina's story of the panther-woman? How and why does Molina affect him?
3. How does Puig use setting to enhance the theme? Consider, for example, the physical restrictions to which the characters are subjected. How do they respond to being confined? How might you respond in a similar situation?
4. Although Molina is gay and Valentin is heterosexual, to what extent are their views about male–female relations stereotypical? Explain.
5. In what ways have Molina and Valentin changed by the end of the play? How has your attitude toward them changed? Explain.
6. What is the symbolic significance of the play's title?

Cultural Contexts

1. The play dramatizes the brutality of contemporary Latin-American military regimes and their imprisonment of homosexuals and political dissidents, as well as the extent to which surveillance and torture affect political, sexual, and human identity. What kind of political change does Puig advocate through the friendship that Molina and Valentin form? Is Puig's drama mostly concerned with homosexuality? Why or why not?

PART ASSIGNMENTS

WRITING TOPICS

1. Identify and analyze the sources of racial hostility in "The Melting Pot," "Telephone Conversation," and "On the Subway." To what extent do the poems reinforce or negate the concept that people can modify ingrained assumptions about race?

2. Compare and contrast the portrayals of the immigrant experience in the United States as portrayed in "Jasmine" and "The Loudest Voice." Consider the chronology and cultural background of each text, and discuss the extent to which the ideal of "The Melting Pot" applies to either story.

3. Compare and contrast the portrayal of the themes of ethnic identification and cultural assimilation in the stories by Paley, Morales, and Mukherjee. With which protagonist do you most empathize? Cite reasons.

4. Compare and contrast the portrayals of the American Dream in the texts by King, Morales, Laviera, Randall, and/or Jeffers. What factors might account for differences in their point of view?

5. Personal and cultural alienation is a recurring motif in the poems by Espada. Analyze the causes and effects of the various speakers' sense of exclusion. To what extent are anger and rebellion part of their response? To what effect?

6. Write an essay on the issue of race in *Othello*. Identify the racists in the play, and discuss their effect on Othello. Pay particular attention to Iago's determination to undermine Othello's self-confidence by focusing not only on his being black but also an outsider in Venetian society.

7. Economic inequity in the United States is the focus of the texts by Bambara, Laviera, and Espada. Compare and contrast the speakers' responses to their situations. How does tone affect the meaning in each text?

8. Discuss the issue of gender relations in *Othello*. Consider, for example, how social class and the patriarchal tradition have shaped the personal identities of Iago, Emilia, and Desdemona.

9. "To be an American means something more than to belong to a specific group of Americans. To be an American is to acknowledge a collective identity that simultaneously transcends and encompasses our disparate identities and communities" (Elizabeth Fox-Genovese). Examine any two texts from Part Four that contradict or affirm this point of view.

10. In *The Kiss of the Spider Woman*, setting functions as the third character. Analyze the effects of the play's setting on the relationship of Molina and Valentin, as well as on the dual themes of sexual preference and political oppression.

PART ASSIGNMENTS

RESEARCH TOPICS

1. In a documented paper, analyze Walt Whitman's concept of the expansive self and his democratic vision of humanity in his poem *Song of Myself*. To what extent is Whitman considered naive in believing that American ideals of freedom and brotherhood are possible?
2. To understand better the cultural background for the chronology and setting of Grace Paley's "The Loudest Voice," view the film *Ellis Island* or *Hester Street* and/or read *A Bintel Brief: A Bundle of Letters to the Jewish Daily Forward* (New York: Ballantine, 1971). Write an essay on what you learned about the Jewish immigrant experience, including the conflict between first- and second-generation immigrants.
3. To explore further themes of African-American drama performed in the 1950s, read either William Branch's *Medal for Willie* (1951) or *In Splendid Error* (1955), Alice Childress's *Trouble in Mind* (1955), or Lorraine Hansberry's *A Raisin in the Sun* (1959). Write a paper on what you learned about the effects of racism on the dreams of many African Americans, about marginalization as a result of segregation, and about the role of the civil rights movement of the 1950s, including the Montgomery bus boycott and the civil disobedience of Rosa Parks (1955).

GROUP RESEARCH TOPIC

The literature of AIDS has flourished in the last decade, providing readers with new voices and perspectives with which to view the epidemic and its inherent sense of loss. Working with your group examine at least three works—poems, short stories, or plays—that explore the AIDS issue. Investigate the premises these texts advance in relation to the epidemic, the discourse of AIDS, and the emotional outlets that help people deal with the presence and absence of AIDS victims.

Sources you might consult include:

Gross, Gregory D. "Coming Up for Air: Three AIDS Plays." *Journal of American Culture 15* (Summer 1992): 63–67.

Klein Michael, ed. *Poets for Life: Seventy-six Poets Respond to AIDS*. New York: Crown, 1989.

Lily, Mark, ed. *Lesbian and Gay Writing*. Philadelphia: Temple Univ. Press, 1990.

Mars-Jones, Adam. "Remission." In *The Darker Proof: Stories from a Crisis*. Eds. Edmund White and Adam Mars-Jones. New York: New American Library, 1988.

Morse, Carl, and Joan Larkin, eds. "Gay and Lesbian Poetry." *In Our Time: An Anthology.* New York: St. Martin's Press, 1988.

Osborn, M. Elizabeth, ed. *The Way We Live Now: American Plays and the AIDS Crisis.* New York: Theater Communications Group, 1990.

Preston, John, ed. *Personal Dispatches: Writers Confront AIDS.* New York: St. Martin's Press, 1991.

PART FIVE

Individualism and Community

Fiction

The Metamorphosis, Franz Kafka ◆ *Hands*, Sherwood Anderson ◆ *Eveline*, James Joyce ◆ *A Red Sweater*, Fae Myenne Ng ◆ *A Rose for Emily*, William Faulkner ◆ *The Guest*, Albert Camus ◆ *Dead Men's Path*, Chinua Achebe

Essays

The Rewards of Living a Solitary Life, May Sarton ◆ *I Have a Dream*, Martin Luther King, Jr.

Poetry

Disillusionment of Ten O'Clock, Wallace Stevens ◆ *The Unknown Citizen*, W. H. Auden ◆ *Port Authority Terminal: 9 A.M. Monday*, Chad Walsh ◆ *People*, Yevgeny Yevtushenko ◆ *Street Kid*, Duane Niatum ◆ *Black Jackets*, Thom Gunn ◆ *Mending Wall*, Robert Frost ◆ *Summer Solstice, New York City*, Sharon Olds ◆ *What the Gossips Saw*, Leo Romero ◆ *History*, Gary Soto ◆ *To My Father*, Diane di Prima ◆ *Constantly Risking Absurdity*, Lawrence Ferlinghetti ◆ *The Writer*, Richard Wilbur ◆ *Volcanoes Be in Sicily*, Emily Dickinson ◆ *The Soul Selects Her Own Society—*, Emily Dickinson ◆ *Much Madness Is Divinest Sense—*, Emily Dickinson ◆ *Tell All the Truth But Tell It Slant—*, Emily Dickinson

Drama

Antigone, Sophocles ◆ *Trifles*, Susan Glaspell

"Postmodern life will place a premium on relationships, not individualism," predicts a contemporary psychologist as he looks ahead to the next century. Cross-cultural studies show marked variations in social relationships, but one theme remains constant: we are social beings. Not many of us could or would want to live a life of isolation. Many questions haunt us, however, about the relation between our private and communal selves. How can we reconcile our individual quests for identity with the sometimes conflicting demands of social responsibility? To what extent should we rebel against social conformity? What kind of threats, if any, do individuals pose to the community? Are individual rights and social responsibility irreconcilable? What are the necessary preconditions for individual participation in any society?

Culture, according to anthropologist Bronislaw Malinowski, is the "artificial, secondary environment" that human beings superimpose on nature. We human beings, then, are in both nature and culture, and both influence our choices. A diversity of cultures, which the following selections illustrate, creates many opportunities for choices and sometimes leads to great difficulty in actually choosing. While nature is passively selecting the fittest organisms for survival, we humans are actively, sometimes painfully, making a variety of choices—personal, ethical, political, economic—for a number of reasons both rational and emotional. Many of these choices concern other people and our relations with them; others involve coming to terms with our cultural or institutional pasts. Are cultural and historical factors limitations on freedom of choice, or do they allow more opportunity for individual action and imagination? Do we increase our individual choices to the degree that we free ourselves from history and culture?

Several texts in Part Five will engage you also in the various debates raised by the voices of individuals and of the community in different historical and cross-cultural contexts. These voices speak out personally and politically through the conversations they re-create among racially and socially diverse groups. The stories "Eveline" and "A Red Sweater," for example, explore the degree to which the individual identities of the Irish and Chinese-American female protagonists have been shaped by their social and cultural environments. The way in which communities deal with threats against their autonomy is the subject of "The Guest," "Hands," and "Dead Men's Path." These stories also evaluate various forces that lead cross-cultural communities of the American Midwest, Africa, and Algeria to defend themselves against the external threats imposed on them by nature, political authority, and their own fellow beings.

Poems such as "People," "Street Kid," and "Black Jackets" extend the discussion of individualism and community through the claim they place on the uniqueness of human beings, despite their obscure or alienated condition. Others such as "History" and "To My Father" explore the complex role of the family as a mediating element between individuals and their collective worlds. And "Mending Wall" and "Summer Solstice" focus on the concept of boundaries in relationships, addressing our desires for both solitude and solidarity, personal space and social interaction.

The dramas in Part Five are concerned with civil disobedience, a subject debated by artists and philosophers throughout human history. Although Sophocles, in his Greek tragedy *Antigone,* presents conflicts such as between male and female, youth and age, and religious and secular beliefs, his main concern is the decision of Antigone, who insists on obeying her conscience even if it means violating the laws of the state. Susan Glaspell's play *Trifles,* set on an isolated midwestern farm in the late nineteenth century, also addresses conflicts between men and women, but her primary focus is on the two female protagonists' decision to choose in favor of their own concept of justice, even if that choice involves disobeying the law.

As you read these and other texts in this part, you too will be asked to make judgments about issues such as personal freedom and social responsibility, rebellion and conformity, the right of an individual to participate in acts of civil disobedience, the conflicting demands of individual preference and familial obligation, and the extent to which personal identity is shaped by external social forces.

 **FICTION**

Franz Kafka
1915

The Metamorphosis

I

As Gregor Samsa awoke one morning from uneasy dreams he found himself transformed in his bed into a gigantic insect. He was lying on his hard, as it were armor-plated, back and when he lifted his head a little he could see his dome-like brown belly divided into stiff arched segments on top of which the bed quilt could hardly keep in position and was about to slide off completely. His numerous legs, which were pitifully thin compared to the rest of his bulk, waved helplessly before his eyes.

What has happened to me? he thought. It was no dream. His room, a regular human bedroom, only rather too small, lay quiet between the four familiar walls. Above the table on which a collection of cloth samples was unpacked and spread out—Samsa was a commercial traveler—hung the picture which he had recently cut out of an illustrated magazine and put into a pretty gilt frame. It showed a lady, with a fur cap on and a fur stole, sitting upright and holding out to the spectator a huge fur muff into which the whole of her forearm had vanished!

Gregor's eyes turned next to the window, and the overcast sky—one could hear rain drops beating on the window gutter—made him quite melancholy. What about sleeping a little longer and forgetting all this nonsense, he thought, but it could not be done, for he was accustomed to sleep on his right side and in his present condition he could not turn himself over. However violently he forced himself towards his right side he always rolled on to his back again. He tried it at least a hundred times, shutting his eyes to keep from seeing his struggling legs, and only desisted when he began to feel in his side a faint dull ache he had never experienced before.

Oh God, he thought, what an exhausting job I've picked on! Traveling about day in, day out. It's much more irritating work than doing the actual business in the office, and on top of that there's the trouble of constant traveling, of worrying about train connections, the bed and irregular meals, casual acquaintances that are always new and never become intimate friends. The devil take it all! He felt a slight itching up on his belly; slowly pushed himself on his back nearer to the top of the bed so that he could lift his head more easily; identified the itching place which was surrounded by many small white spots the nature of which he could not understand and made to touch it with a leg, but drew the leg back immediately, for the contact made a cold shiver run through him.

He slid down again into his former position. This getting up early, he thought, makes one quite stupid. A man needs his sleep. Other commercials live like harem women. For instance, when I come back to the hotel of a morning to write up the orders I've got, these others are only sitting down to breakfast. Let me just try that with my chief; I'd be sacked on the spot. Anyhow, that might be quite a good thing for me, who can tell? If I didn't have to hold my hand because of my parents I'd have given notice long ago. I'd have gone to the chief and told him exactly what I think of him. That would knock him endways from his desk! It's a queer way of doing, too, this sitting on high at a desk and talking down to employees, especially when they have to come quite near because the chief is hard of hearing. Well, there's still hope; once I've saved enough money to pay back my parents' debts to him—that should take another five or six years—I'll do it without fail. I'll cut myself completely loose then. For the moment, though, I'd better get up, since my train goes at five.

He looked at the alarm clock ticking on the chest. Heavenly Father! he thought. It was half-past six o'clock and the hands were quietly moving on, it was even past the half-hour, it was getting on toward a quarter to seven. Had the alarm clock not gone off? From the bed one could see that it had been properly set for four o'clock; of course it must have gone off. Yes, but was it possible to sleep quietly through that ear-splitting noise? Well, he had not slept quietly, yet apparently all the more soundly for that. But what was he to do now? The next train went at seven o'clock; to catch that he would need to hurry like mad and his samples weren't even packed up, and he himself wasn't feeling particularly fresh and active. And even if he did catch the train he wouldn't avoid a row with the chief, since the firm's porter would have been waiting for the five o'clock train and would long since have reported his failure to turn up. The porter was a creature of the chief's, spineless and stupid. Well, supposing he were to say he was sick? But that would be most unpleasant and would look suspicious, since during his five years' employment he had not been ill once. The chief himself would be sure to come with the sick-insurance doctor, would reproach his parents with their son's laziness and would cut all excuses short by referring to the insurance doctor, who of course regarded all mankind as perfectly healthy malingerers. And would he be so far wrong on this occasion? Gregor really felt quite well, apart from a drowsiness that was utterly superfluous after such a long sleep, and he was even unusually hungry.

As all this was running through his mind at top speed without his being able to decide to leave his bed—the alarm clock had just struck a quarter to seven— there came a cautious tap at the door behind the head of his bed. "Gregor," said a voice—it was his mother's—"it's a quarter to seven. Hadn't you a train to catch?" That gentle voice! Gregor had a shock as he heard his own voice answering hers, unmistakably his own voice, it was true, but with a persistent horrible twittering squeak behind it like an undertone, that left the words in their clear shape only for the first moment and then rose up reverberating round them to destroy their sense, so that one could not be sure one had heard them rightly. Gregor wanted to answer at length and explain everything, but in the circumstances he confined himself to saying: "Yes, yes, thank you, Mother, I'm getting up now." The wooden door between them must have kept the change in his voice from being noticeable outside, for his mother contented herself with this statement and shuffled away. Yet this brief exchange of words had made the other members of the family aware that Gregor was still in the house, as they had not expected, and at one of the side doors his father was already knocking, gently, yet with his fist. "Gregor, Gregor," he called, "what's the matter with you?" And after a little while he called again in a deeper voice: "Gregor! Gregor!" At the other side door his sister was saying in a low, plaintive tone: "Gregor? Aren't you well? Are you needing anything?" He answered them both at once: "I'm just ready," and did his best to make his voice sound as normal as possible by enunciating the words very clearly and leaving long pauses between them. So his father went back to his breakfast, but his sister whispered: "Gregor, open the door, do." However, he was not thinking of opening the door, and felt thankful for the prudent habit he had acquired in traveling of locking all doors during the night, even at home.

His immediate attention was to get up quietly without being disturbed, to put on his clothes and above all eat his breakfast, and only then to consider what else was to be done, since in bed, he was well aware, his meditations would come to no sensible conclusion. He remembered that often enough in bed he had felt small aches and pains, probably caused by awkward postures, which had proved purely imaginary once he got up, and he looked forward eagerly to seeing this morning's delusions gradually fall away. That the change in his voice was nothing but the precursor of a severe chill, a standing ailment of commercial travelers, he had not the least possible doubt.

To get rid of the quilt was quite easy; he had only to inflate himself a little and it fell off by itself. But the next move was difficult, especially because he was so uncommonly broad. He would have needed arms and hands to hoist himself up; instead he had only the numerous little legs which never stopped waving in all directions and which he could not control in the least. When he tried to bend one of them it was the first to stretch itself straight; and did he succeed at last in making it do what he wanted, all the other legs meanwhile waved the more wildly in a high degree of unpleasant agitation. "But what's the use of lying idle in bed," said Gregor to himself.

He thought that he might get out of bed with the lower part of his body first, but this lower part, which he had not yet seen and of which he could form no clear conception, proved too difficult to move; it shifted so slowly, and when finally, almost wild with annoyance, he gathered his forces together and thrust out recklessly, he had miscalculated the direction and bumped heavily against the lower end of the bed, and the stinging pain he felt informed him that precisely this lower part of his body was at the moment probably the most sensitive.

So he tried to get the top part of himself out first, and cautiously moved his head towards the edge of the bed. That proved easy enough, and despite its breadth and mass the bulk of his body at last slowly followed the movement of his head. Still, when he finally got his head free over the edge of the bed he felt too scared to go on advancing, for after all if he let himself fall in this way it would take a miracle to keep his head from being injured. And at all costs he must not lose consciousness now, precisely now; he would rather stay in bed.

But when after a repetition of the same efforts he lay in his former position again, sighing, and watched his little legs struggling against each other more wildly than ever, if that were possible, and saw no way of bringing any order into this arbitrary confusion, he told himself again that it was impossible to stay in bed and that the most sensible course was to risk everything for the smallest hope of getting away from it. At the same time he did not forget meanwhile to remind himself that cool reflection, the coolest possible, was much better than desperate resolves. In such moments he focused his eyes as sharply as possible on the window, but, unfortunately, the prospect of the morning fog, which muffled even the other side of the narrow street, brought him little encouragement and comfort. "Seven o'clock already," he said to himself when the alarm clock chimed again, "seven o'clock already and still such a thick fog." And for a little while he lay quiet, breathing lightly, as if perhaps expecting such complete repose to restore all things to their real and normal condition.

But then he said to himself: "Before it strikes a quarter past seven I must be quite out of this bed, without fail. Anyhow, by that time someone will have come from the office to ask for me, since it opens before seven." And he set himself to rocking his whole body at once in a regular rhythm, with the idea of swinging it out of the bed. If he tipped himself out in that way he could keep his head from injury by lifting it at an acute angle when he fell. His back seemed to be hard and was not likely to suffer from a fall on the carpet. His biggest worry was the loud crash he would not be able to help making, which would probably cause anxiety, if not terror, behind all the doors. Still, he must take the risk.

When he was already half out of the bed—the new method was more a game than an effort, for he needed only to hitch himself across by rocking to and fro—it struck him how simple it would be if he could get help. Two strong people—he thought of his father and the servant girl—would be amply sufficient; they would only have to thrust their arms under his convex back, lever him out of the bed, bend down with their burden and then be patient enough to let him turn himself right over on to the floor, where it was to be hoped his legs would then find their proper function. Well, ignoring the fact that the doors were all locked, ought he really to call for help? In spite of his misery he could not suppress a smile at the very idea of it.

He had got so far that he could barely keep his equilibrium when he rocked himself strongly, and he would have to nerve himself very soon for the final decision since in five minutes' time it would be a quarter past seven—when the front door bell rang. "That's someone from the office," he said to himself, and grew almost rigid, while his little legs jigged about all the faster. For a moment everything stayed quiet. "They're not going to open the door," said Gregor to himself, catching at some kind of irrational hope. But then of course the servant girl went as usual to the door with her heavy tread and opened it. Gregor needed only to hear the first good morning of the visitor to know immediately who it was—the chief clerk himself. What a fate, to be condemned to work for a firm where the smallest omission at once gave rise to the gravest suspicion! Were all employees in a body nothing but scoundrels, was there not among them one single loyal devoted man who, had he wasted only an hour or so of the firm's time in a morning, was so tormented by conscience as to be driven out of his mind and actually incapable of leaving his bed? Wouldn't it really have been sufficient to send an apprentice to inquire—if any inquiry were necessary at all—did the chief clerk himself have to come and thus indicate to the entire family, an innocent family, that this suspicious circumstance could be investigated by no one less versed in affairs than himself? And more through the agitation caused by these reflections than through any act of will Gregor swung himself out of bed with all his strength. There was a loud thump, but it was not really a crash. His fall was broken to some extent by the carpet, his back, too, was less stiff than he thought, and so there was merely a dull thud, not so very startling. Only he had not lifted his head carefully enough and had hit it; he turned it and rubbed it on the carpet in pain and irritation.

"That was something falling down in there," said the chief clerk in the next room to the left. Gregor tried to suppose to himself that something like what had happened to him today might some day happen to the chief clerk; one really could not deny that it was possible. But as if in brusque reply to this supposition the chief clerk took a couple of firm steps in the next-door room and his patent leather boots creaked. From the right-hand room his sister was whispering to inform him of the situation: "Gregor, the chief clerk's here." "I know," muttered Gregor to himself; but he didn't dare to make his voice loud enough for his sister to hear it.

"Gregor," said his father now from the left-hand room, "the chief clerk has come and wants to know why you didn't catch the early train. We don't know what to say to him. Besides, he wants to talk to you in person. So open the door, please. He will be good enough to excuse the untidiness of your room." "Good morning, Mr. Samsa," the chief clerk was calling amiably meanwhile. "He's not well," said his mother to the visitor, while his father was still speaking through the door, "he's not well, sir, believe me. What else would make him miss a train! The boy thinks about nothing but his work. It makes me almost cross the way he never goes out in the evenings; he's been here the last eight days and has stayed at home every single evening. He just sits there quietly at the table reading a newspaper or looking through railway timetables. The only amusement he gets is doing fretwork. For instance, he spent two or three evenings cutting out a little picture frame; you would be surprised to see how pretty it is; it's hanging in his room; you'll see it in a minute when Gregor opens the door. I must say I'm glad you've come, sir; we should never have got him to unlock the door by ourselves; he's so obstinate; and I'm sure he's unwell, though he wouldn't have it to be so this morning." "I'm just coming," said Gregor slowly and carefully, not moving an inch for fear of losing one word of the conversation. "I can't think of any other explanation, madam," said the chief clerk, "I hope it's nothing serious. Although on the other hand I must say that we men of business—fortunately or unfortunately—very often simply have to ignore any slight indisposition, since business must be attended to." "Well, can the chief clerk come in now?" asked Gregor's father impatiently, again knocking on the door. "No," said Gregor. In the left-hand room a painful silence followed this refusal, in the right-hand room his sister began to sob.

Why didn't his sister join the others? She was probably newly out of bed and hadn't even begun to put on her clothes yet. Well, why was she crying? Because he wouldn't get up and let the chief clerk come in, because he was in danger of losing his job, and because the chief would begin dunning his parents again for the old debts? Surely these were things one didn't need to worry about for the present. Gregor was still at home and not in the least thinking of deserting the family. At the moment, true, he was lying on the carpet and no one who knew the condition he was in could seriously expect him to admit the chief clerk. But for such a small discourtesy, which could plausibly be explained away somehow later on, Gregor could hardly be dismissed on the spot. And it seemed to Gregor that it would be much more sensible to leave him in peace for the present than to trouble him with tears and entreaties. Still, of course, their uncertainty bewildered them all and excused their behavior.

"Mr. Samsa," the chief clerk called now in a louder voice, "what's the matter with you? Here you are, barricading yourself in your room, giving only 'yes' and 'no' for answers, causing your parents a lot of unnecessary trouble and neglecting—I mention this only in passing—neglecting your business duties in an incredible fashion. I am speaking here in the name of your parents and of your chief, and I beg you quite seriously to give me an immediate and precise explanation. You amaze me, you amaze me. I thought you were a quiet, dependable person, and now all at once you seem bent on making a disgraceful exhibition of yourself. The chief did hint to me early this morning a possible explanation for your disappearance—with reference to the cash payments that were entrusted to you recently—but I almost pledged my solemn word of honor that this could not be so. But now that I see how incredibly obstinate you are, I no longer have the slightest desire to take your part at all. And your position in the firm is not so unassailable. I came with the intention of telling you all this in private, but since you are wasting my time so needlessly I don't see why your parents shouldn't hear it too. For some time past your work has been most unsatisfactory; this is not the season of the year for a business boom, of course, we admit that, but a season of the year for doing no business at all, that does not exist, Mr. Samsa, must not exist."

"But sir," cried Gregor, beside himself and in his agitation forgetting everything else, "I'm just going to open the door this very minute. A slight illness, an attack of giddiness, has kept me from getting up. I'm still lying in bed. But I feel all right again. I'm getting out of bed now. Just give me a moment or two longer! I'm not quite so well as I thought. But I'm all right, really. How a thing like that can suddenly strike one down! Only last night I was quite well, my parents can tell you, or rather I did have a slight presentiment. I must have showed some sign of it. Why didn't I report it at the office! But one always thinks that an indisposition can be got over without staying in the house. Oh sir, do spare my parents! All that you're reproaching me with now has no foundation; no one has ever said a word to me about it. Perhaps you haven't looked at the last orders I sent in. Anyhow, I can still catch the eight o'clock train, I'm much the better for my few hours' rest.

Don't let me detain you here, sir; I'll be attending to business very soon, and do be good enough to tell the chief so and to make my excuses to him!"

And while all this was tumbling out pell-mell and Gregor hardly knew what he was saying, he had reached the chest quite easily, perhaps because of the practice he had had in bed, and was now trying to lever himself upright by means of it. He meant actually to open the door, actually to show himself and speak to the chief clerk; he was eager to find out what the others, after all their insistence, would say at the sight of him. If they were horrified then the responsibility was no longer his and he could stay quiet. But if they took it calmly, then he had no reason either to be upset, and could really get to the station for the eight o'clock train if he hurried. At first he slipped down a few times from the polished surface of the chest, but at length with a last heave he stood upright; he paid no more attention to the pains in the lower part of his body, however they smarted. Then he let himself fall against the back of a near-by chair, and clung with his little legs to the edges of it. That brought him into control of himself again and he stopped speaking, for now he could listen to what the chief clerk was saying.

"Did you understand a word of it?" the chief clerk was asking; "surely he can't be trying to make fools of us?" "Oh dear," cried his mother, in tears, "perhaps he's terribly ill and we're tormenting him. Grete! Grete!" she called out then. "Yes Mother?" called his sister from the other side. They were calling to each other across Gregor's room. "You must go this minute for the doctor. Gregor is ill. Go for the doctor, quick. Did you hear how he was speaking?" "That was no human voice," said the chief clerk in a voice noticeably low beside the shrillness of the mother's. "Anna! Anna!" his father was calling through the hall to the kitchen, clapping his hands, "get a locksmith at once!" And the two girls were already running through the hall with a swish of skirts—how could his sister have got dressed so quickly?—and were tearing the front door open. There was no sound of its closing again; they had evidently left it open, as one does in houses where some great misfortune has happened.

But Gregor was now much calmer. The words he uttered were no longer understandable, apparently, although they seemed clear enough to him, even clearer than before, perhaps because his ear had grown accustomed to the sound of them. Yet at any rate people now believed that something was wrong with him, and were ready to help him. The positive certainty with which these first measures had been taken comforted him. He felt himself drawn once more into the human circle and hoped for great and remarkable results from both the doctor and the locksmith, without really distinguishing precisely between them. To make his voice as clear as possible for the decisive conversation that was now imminent he coughed a little, as quietly as he could, of course, since this noise too might not sound like a human cough for all he was able to judge. In the next room meanwhile there was complete silence. Perhaps his parents were sitting at the table with the chief clerk, whispering, perhaps they were all leaning against the door and listening.

Slowly Gregor pushed the chair towards the door, then let go of it, caught hold of the door for support—the soles at the end of his little legs were somewhat sticky—and rested against it for a moment after his efforts. Then he set himself to turning the key in the lock with his mouth. It seemed, unhappily, that he hadn't really any teeth—what could he grip the key with?—but on the other hand his jaws were certainly very strong; with their help he did manage to set the key in motion, heedless of the fact that he was undoubtedly damaging them somewhere, since a brown fluid issued from his mouth, flowed over the key and dripped on the floor. "Just listen to that," said the chief clerk next door; "he's turning the key." That was a great encouragement to Gregor; but they should all have shouted encouragement to him, his father and mother too: "Go on, Gregor," they should have called out, "keep going, hold on to that key!" And in the belief that they were all following his efforts intensely, he clenched his jaws recklessly on the key with all the force at his command. As the turning of the key progressed he circled round the lock, holding on now only with his mouth, pushing on the key, as required, or pulling it down again with all the weight of his body. The louder click of the finally yielding lock literally quickened Gregor. With a deep breath of relief he said to himself: "So I didn't need the locksmith," and laid his head on the handle to open the door wide.

Since he had to pull the door towards him, he was still invisible when it was really wide open. He had to edge himself slowly round the near half of the double door, and to do it very carefully if he was not to fall plump upon his back just on the threshold. He was still carrying out this difficult manoeuvre, with no time to observe anything else, when he heard the chief clerk utter a loud "Oh!"—it sounded like a gust of wind—and now he could see the man, standing as he was nearest to the door, clapping one hand before his open mouth and slowly backing away as if driven by some invisible steady pressure. His mother—in spite of the chief clerk's being there her hair was still undone and sticking up in all directions—first clasped her hands and looked at his father, then took two steps towards Gregor and fell on the floor among her outspread skirts, her face quite hidden on her breast. His father knotted his fist with a fierce expression on his face as if he meant to knock Gregor back into his room, then looked uncertainly round the living room, covered his eyes with his hands and wept till his great chest heaved.

Gregor did not go now into the living room, but leaned against the inside of the firmly shut wing of the door, so that only half his body was visible and his head above it bending sideways to look at the others. The light had meanwhile strengthened; on the other side of the street one could see clearly a section of the endlessly long, dark gray building opposite—it was a hospital—abruptly punctuated by its row of regular windows; the rain was still falling, but only in large singly discernible and literally singly splashing drops. The breakfast dishes were set out on the table lavishly, for breakfast was the most important meal of the day to Gregor's father, who lingered it out for hours over various newspapers. Right opposite Gregor on the wall hung a photograph of himself on military service, as a lieutenant, hand on sword, a carefree smile on his face, inviting one to respect his uniform and military bearing. The door leading to the hall was open, and one could see that the front door stood open too, showing the landing beyond and the beginning of the stairs going down.

"Well," said Gregor, knowing perfectly that he was the only one who had retained any composure, "I'll put my clothes on at once, pack up my samples and start off. Will you only let me go? You see, sir, I'm not obstinate, and I'm willing to work; traveling is a hard life, but I couldn't live without it. Where are you going, sir? To the office? Yes? Will you give a true account of all this? One can be temporarily incapacitated, but that's just the moment for remembering former services and bearing in mind that later on, when the incapacity has been got over, one will certainly work with all the more industry and concentration. I'm loyally bound to serve the chief, you know that very well. Besides, I have to provide for my parents and my sister. I'm in great difficulties, but I'll get out of them again. Don't make things any worse for me than they are. Stand up for me in the firm. Travelers are not popular there, I know. People think they earn sacks of money and just have a good time. A prejudice there's no particular reason for revising. But you, sir, have a more comprehensive view of affairs than the rest of the staff, yes, let me tell you in confidence, a more comprehensive view than the chief himself, who, being the owner, lets his judgment easily be swayed against one of his employees. And you know very well that the traveler, who is never seen in the office almost the whole year round, can so easily fall a victim to gossip and ill luck and unfounded complaints, which he mostly knows nothing about, except when he comes back exhausted from his rounds, and only then suffers in person from their evil consequences, which he can no longer trace back to the original causes. Sir, sir, don't go away without a word to me to show that you think me in the right at least to some extent!"

But at Gregor's very first words the chief clerk had already backed away and only stared at him with parted lips over one twitching shoulder. And while Gregor was speaking he did not stand still one moment but stole away towards the door, without taking his eyes off Gregor, yet only an inch at a time, as if obeying some secret injunction to leave the room. He was already at the hall, and the suddenness with which he took his last step out of the living room would have made one believe he had burned the sole of his foot. Once in the hall he stretched his right arm before him towards the staircase, as if some supernatural power were waiting there to deliver him.

Gregor perceived that the chief clerk must on no account be allowed to go away in this frame of mind if his position in the firm were not to be endangered to the utmost. His parents did not understand this so well; they had convinced themselves in the course of years that Gregor was settled for life in this firm, and besides they were so occupied with their immediate troubles that all foresight had forsaken them. Yet Gregor had this foresight. The chief clerk must be detained, soothed, persuaded and finally won over; the whole future of Gregor and his family depended on it! If only his sister had been there! She was intelligent; she had begun to cry while Gregor was still lying on his back. And no doubt the chief clerk, so partial to ladies, would have been guided by her; she would have shut the door of the flat and in the hall talked him out of his horror. But she was not there, and Gregor would have to handle the situation himself. And without remembering that he was still unaware what powers of movement he possessed, without even remembering that his words in all possibility, indeed in all likelihood, would again be unintelligible, he let go of the wing of the door, pushed himself through the opening, started to walk towards the chief clerk, who was already ridiculously clinging with both hands to the railing on the landing; but immediately, as he was feeling for a support, he fell down with a little cry upon all his numerous legs. Hardly was he down when he experienced for the first time a sense of physical comfort; his legs had firm ground under them; they were completely obedient, as he noted with joy; they even strove to carry him forward in whatever direction he chose; and he was inclined to believe that a final relief from all his sufferings was at hand. But in the same moment as he found himself on the floor, rocking with suppressed eagerness to move, not far from his mother, indeed just in front of her, she, who had seemed so completely crushed, sprang all at once to her feet, her arms and fingers outspread, cried: "Help, for God's sake, help!" bent her head down as if to see Gregor better, yet on the contrary kept backing senselessly away; had quite forgotten that the laden table stood behind her; sat upon it hastily, as if in absence of mind, when she bumped into it; and seemed altogether unaware that the big coffee pot beside her was upset and pouring coffee in a flood over the carpet.

"Mother, Mother," said Gregor in a low voice, and looked up at her. The chief clerk, for the moment, had quite slipped from his mind; instead, he could not resist snapping his jaws together at the sight of the streaming coffee. That made his mother scream again, she fled from the table and fell into the arms of his father, who hastened to catch her. But Gregor had now no time to spare for his parents; the chief clerk was already on the stairs; with his chin on the banisters he was taking one last backward look. Gregor made a spring, to be as sure as possible of overtaking him; the chief clerk must have divined his intention, for he leaped down several steps and vanished; he was still yelling "Ugh!" and it echoed through the whole staircase.

Unfortunately, the flight of the chief clerk seemed completely to upset Gregor's father, who had remained relatively calm until now, for instead of running after the man himself, or at least not hindering Gregor in his pursuit, he seized in his right hand the walking stick which the chief clerk had left behind on a chair, together with a hat and greatcoat, snatched in his left hand a large newspaper from the table and began stamping his feet and flourishing the stick and the newspaper to drive Gregor back into his room. No entreaty of Gregor's availed, indeed no entreaty was even understood, however humbly he bent his head his father only stamped on the floor the more loudly. Behind his father his mother had torn open a window, despite the cold weather, and was leaning far out of it with her face in her hands. A strong draught set in from the street to the staircase, the window curtains blew in, the newspapers on the table fluttered, stray pages whisked over the floor. Pitilessly Gregor's father drove him back, hissing and crying "Shoo!" like a savage. But Gregor was quite unpracticed in walking backwards, it really was a slow business. If he only had a chance to turn round he could get back to his room at once, but he was afraid of exasperating his father by the slowness of such a rotation and at any moment the stick in his father's hand might hit him a fatal blow on the back or on the head. In the end, however, nothing else was left for him to do since to his horror he observed that in moving backwards he could not even control the direction he took; and so, keeping an anxious eye on his father all the time over his shoulder, he began to turn round as quickly as he could, which was in reality very slowly. Perhaps his father noted his good intentions, for he did not interfere except every now and then to help him in the manoeuvre from a distance with the point of the stick. If only he would have stopped making that unbearable hissing noise! It made Gregor quite lose his head. He had turned almost completely round when the hissing noise so distracted him that he even turned a little the wrong way again. But when at last his head was fortunately right in front of the doorway, it appeared that his body was too broad simply to get through the opening. His father, of course, in his present mood was far from thinking of such a thing as opening the other half of the door, to let Gregor have enough space. He had merely the fixed idea of driving Gregor back into his room as quickly as possible. He would never have suffered Gregor to make the circumstantial preparations for standing up on end and perhaps slipping his way through the door. Maybe he was now making more noise than ever to urge Gregor forward, as if no obstacle impeded him; to Gregor, anyhow, the noise in his rear sounded no longer like the voice of one single father; this was really no joke, and Gregor thrust himself—come what might—into the doorway. One side of his body rose up, he was tilted at an angle in the doorway, his flank was quite bruised, horrid blotches stained the white door, soon he was stuck fast and, left to himself, could not have moved at all, his legs on one side fluttered trembling in the air, those on the other were crushed painfully to the floor—when from behind his father gave him a strong push which was literally a deliverance and he flew far into the room, bleeding freely. The door was slammed behind him with the stick, and then at last there was silence.

II

Not until it was twilight did Gregor awake out of a deep sleep, more like a swoon than a sleep. He would certainly have waked up of his own accord not much later, for he felt himself sufficiently rested and well-slept, but it seemed to him as if a fleeting step and a cautious shutting of the door leading into the hall had aroused him. The electric lights in the street cast a pale sheen here and there on the ceiling and the upper surfaces of the furniture, but down below, where he lay, it was dark. Slowly, awkwardly trying out his feelers, which he now first learned to appreciate, he pushed his way to the door to see what had been happening there. His left side felt like one single long, unpleasantly tense scar, and he had actually to limp on his two rows of legs. One little leg, moreover, had been severely damaged in the course of that morning's events—it was almost a miracle that only one had been damaged—and trailed uselessly behind him.

He had reached the door before he discovered what had really drawn him to it: the smell of food. For there stood a basin filled with fresh milk in which floated little sops of white bread. He could almost have laughed with joy, since he was now still hungrier than in the morning, and he dipped his head almost over the eyes straight into the milk. But soon in disappointment he withdrew it again; not only did he find it difficult to feed because of his tender left side—and he could only feed with the palpitating collaboration of his whole body—he did not like the milk either, although milk had been his favorite drink and that was certainly why his sister had set it there for him, indeed it was almost with repulsion that he turned away from the basin and crawled back to the middle of the room.

He could see through the crack of the door that the gas was turned on in the living room, but while usually at this time his father made a habit of reading the afternoon newspaper in a loud voice to his mother and occasionally to his sister as well, not a sound was now to be heard. Well, perhaps his father had recently given up this habit of reading aloud, which his sister had mentioned so often in conversation and in her letters. But there was the same silence all around, although the flat was certainly not empty of occupants. "What a quiet life our family has been leading," said Gregor to himself, and as he sat there motionless staring into the darkness he felt great pride in the fact that he had been able to provide such a life for his parents and sister in such a fine flat. But what if all the quiet, the comfort, the contentment were now to end in horror? To keep himself from being lost in such thoughts Gregor took refuge in movement and crawled up and down the room.

Once during the long evening one of the side doors was opened a little and quickly shut again, later the other side door too; someone had apparently wanted to come in and then thought better of it. Gregor now stationed himself immediately before the living room door, determined to persuade any hesitating visitor to come in or at least to discover who it might be; but the door was not opened again and he waited in vain. In the early morning, when the doors were locked, they had all wanted to come in, now that he had opened one door and the other had apparently been opened during the day, no one came in and even the keys were on the other side of the doors.

It was late at night before the gas went out in the living room, and Gregor could easily tell that his parents and his sister had all stayed awake until then, for he could clearly hear the three of them stealing away on tiptoe. No one was likely to visit him, not until the morning, that was certain; so he had plenty of time to meditate at his leisure on how he was to arrange his life afresh. But the lofty, empty room in which he had to lie flat on the floor filled him with an apprehension he could not account for, since it had been his very own room for the past five years— and with a half-unconscious action, not without a slight feeling of shame, he scuttled under the sofa, where he felt comfortable at once, although his back was a little cramped and he could not lift his head up, and his only regret was that his body was too broad to get the whole of it under the sofa.

He stayed there all night, spending his time partly in a light slumber, from which his hunger kept waking him up with a start, and partly in worrying and sketching vague hopes, which all led to the same conclusion, that he must lie low for the present and, by exercising patience and the utmost consideration, help the family to bear the inconvenience he was bound to cause them in his present condition.

Very early in the morning, it was still almost night, Gregor had the chance to test the strength of his new resolutions, for his sister, nearly fully dressed, opened the door from the hall and peered in. She did not see him at once, yet when she caught sight of him under the sofa—well, he had to be somewhere, he couldn't have flown away, could he?—she was so startled that without being able to help it she slammed the door shut again. But as if regretting her behavior she opened the door again immediately and came in on tiptoe, as if she were visiting an invalid or even a stranger. Gregor had pushed his head forward to the very edge of the sofa and watched her. Would she notice that he had left the milk standing, and not for lack of hunger, and would she bring in some other kind of food more to his taste? If she did not do it of her own accord, he would rather starve than draw her attention to the fact, although he felt a wild impulse to dart out from under the sofa, throw himself at her feet and beg her for something to eat. But his sister at once noticed, with surprise, that the basin was still full, except for a little milk that had been spilt all around it, she lifted it immediately, not with her bare hands, true, but with a cloth and carried it away. Gregor was wildly curious to know what she would bring instead, and made various speculations about it. Yet what she actually did next, in the goodness of her heart, he could never have guessed at. To find out what he liked she brought him a whole selection of food, all set out on an old newspaper. There were old, half-decayed vegetables, bones from last night's supper covered with a white sauce that had thickened; some raisins and almonds; a piece of cheese that Gregor would have called uneatable two days ago; a dry roll of bread, a buttered roll, and a roll both buttered and salted. Besides all that, she set down again the same basin, into which she had poured some water, and which was apparently to be reserved for his exclusive use. And with fine tact, knowing that Gregor would not eat in her presence, she withdrew quickly and even turned the key, to let him understand that he could take his ease as much as he liked. Gregor's legs all whizzed towards the food. His wounds must have healed completely, moreover, for he felt no disability, which amazed him and made him reflect how more than a month ago he had cut one finger a little with a knife and had still suffered pain from the wound only the day before yesterday. Am I less sensitive now? he thought, and sucked greedily at the cheese, which above all the other edibles attracted him at once and strongly. One after another and with tears of satisfaction in his eyes he quickly devoured the cheese, the vegetables and the sauce; the fresh food, on the other hand, had no charms for him, he could not even stand the smell of it and actually dragged away to some little distance the things he could eat. He had long finished his meal and was only lying lazily on the same spot when his sister turned the key slowly as a sign for him to retreat. That roused him at once, although he was nearly asleep, and he hurried under the sofa again. But it took considerable self-control for him to stay under the sofa, even for the short time his sister was in the room, since the large meal had swollen his body somewhat and he was so cramped he could hardly breathe. Slight attacks of breathlessness afflicted him and his eyes were starting a little out of his head as he watched his unsuspecting sister sweeping together with a broom not only the remains of what he had eaten but even the things he had not touched, as if these were now of no use to anyone, and hastily shoveling it all into a bucket, which she covered with a wooden lid and carried away. Hardly had she turned her back when Gregor came from under the sofa and stretched and puffed himself out.

In this manner Gregor was fed, once in the early morning while his parents and the servant girl were still asleep, and a second time after they had all had their midday dinner, for then his parents took a short nap and the servant girl could be sent out on some errand or other by his sister. Not that they would have wanted him to starve, of course, but perhaps they could not have borne to know more about his feeding than from hearsay, perhaps too his sister wanted to spare them such little anxieties wherever possible, since they had quite enough to bear as it was.

Under what pretext the doctor and the locksmith had been got rid of on that first morning Gregor could not discover, for since what he said was not understood by the others it never struck any of them, not even his sister, that he could understand what they said, and so whenever his sister came into his room he had to content himself with hearing her utter only a sigh now and then and an occasional appeal to the saints. Later on, when she had got a little used to the situation—of course she could never get completely used to it—she sometimes threw out a remark which was kindly meant or could be so interpreted. "Well, he liked his dinner today," she would say when Gregor had made a good clearance of his food; and when he had not eaten, which gradually happened more and more often, she would say almost sadly: "Everything's been left standing again."

But although Gregor could get no news directly, he overheard a lot from the neighboring rooms, and as soon as voices were audible, he would run to the door of the room concerned and press his whole body against it. In the first few days especially there was no conversation that did not refer to him somehow, even if only indirectly. For two whole days there were family consultations at every mealtime about what should be done; but also between meals the same subject was discussed, for there were always at least two members of the family at home, since no one wanted to be alone in the flat and to leave it quite empty was unthinkable. And on the very first of these days the household cook—it was not quite clear what and how much she knew of the situation—went down on her knees to his mother and begged leave to go, and when she departed, a quarter of an hour later, gave thanks for her dismissal with tears in her eyes as if for the greatest benefit that could have been conferred on her, and without any prompting swore a solemn oath that she would never say a single word to anyone about what had happened.

Now Gregor's sister had to cook too, helping her mother; true, the cooking did not amount to much, for they ate scarcely anything. Gregor was always hearing one of the family vainly urging another to eat and getting no answer but: "Thanks, I've had all I want," or something similar. Perhaps they drank nothing either. Time and again his sister kept asking his father if he wouldn't like some beer and offered kindly to go and fetch it herself, and when he made no answer suggested that she could ask the concierge to fetch it, so that he need feel no sense of obligation, but then a round "No" came from his father and no more was said about it.

In the course of that very first day Gregor's father explained the family's financial position and prospects to both his mother and his sister. Now and then he rose from the table to get some voucher or memorandum out of the small safe he had rescued from the collapse of his business five years earlier. One could hear him opening the complicated lock and rustling papers out and shutting it again. This statement made by his father was the first cheerful information Gregor had heard since his imprisonment. He had been of the opinion that nothing at all was left over from his father's business, at least his father had never said anything to the contrary, and of course he had not asked him directly. At that time Gregor's sole desire was to do his utmost to help the family to forget as soon as possible the catastrophe which had overwhelmed the business and thrown them all into a state of complete despair. And so he had set to work with unusual ardor and almost overnight had become a commercial traveler instead of a little clerk, with of course much greater chances of earning money, and his success was immediately translated into good round coin which he could lay on the table for his amazed and happy family. These had been fine times, and they had never recurred, at least not with the same sense of glory, although later on Gregor had earned so much money that he was able to meet the expenses of the whole household and did so. They had simply got used to it, both the family and Gregor; the money was gratefully accepted and gladly given, but there was no special uprush of warm feeling. With his sister alone had he remained intimate, and it was a secret plan of his that she, who loved music, unlike himself, and could play movingly on the violin, should be sent next year to study at the Conservatorium, despite the great expense that would entail, which must be made up in some other way. During his brief visits home the Conservatorium was often mentioned in the talks he had with his sister, but always merely as a beautiful dream which could never come true, and his parents discouraged even those innocent references to it; yet Gregor had made up his mind firmly about it and meant to announce the fact with due solemnity on Christmas Day.

Such were the thoughts, completely futile in his present condition, that went through his head as he stood clinging upright to the door and listening. Sometimes out of sheer weariness he had to give up listening and let his head fall negligently against the door, but he always had to pull himself together again at once, for even the slight sound his head made was audible next door and brought all conversation to a stop. "What can he be doing now?" his father would say after a while, obviously turning towards the door, and only then would the interrupted conversation gradually be set going again.

Gregor was now informed as amply as he could wish—for his father tended to repeat himself in his explanations, partly because it was a long time since he had handled such matters and partly because his mother could not always grasp things at once—that a certain amount of investments, a very small amount it was true, had survived the wreck of their fortunes and had even increased a little because the dividends had not been touched meanwhile. And besides that, the money Gregor brought home every month—he had kept only a few dollars for himself—had never been quite used up and now amounted to a small capital sum. Behind the door Gregor nodded his head eagerly, rejoiced at this evidence of unexpected thrift and foresight. True, he could really have paid off some more of his father's debts to the chief with his extra money, and so brought much nearer the day on which he could quit his job, but doubtless it was better the way his father had arranged it.

Yet this capital was by no means sufficient to let the family live on the interest of it; for one year, perhaps, or at the most two, they could live on the principal, that was all. It was simply a sum that ought not to be touched and should be kept for a rainy day; money for living expenses would have to be earned. Now his father was still hale enough but an old man, and he had done no work for the past five years and could not be expected to do much; during these five years, the first years of leisure in his laborious though unsuccessful life, he had grown rather fat and become sluggish. And Gregor's old mother, how was she to earn a living with her asthma, which troubled her even when she walked through the flat and kept her lying on a sofa every other day panting for breath beside an open window? And was his sister to earn her bread, she who was still a child of seventeen and whose life hitherto had been so pleasant, consisting as it did in dressing herself nicely, sleeping long, helping in the housekeeping, going out to a few modest entertainments and above all playing the violin? At first whenever the need for earning money was mentioned Gregor let go his hold on the door and threw himself down on the cool leather sofa beside it, he felt so hot with shame and grief.

Often he just lay there the long nights through without sleeping at all, scrabbling for long hours on the leather. Or he nerved himself to the great effort of pushing an armchair to the window, then crawled up over the window sill and, braced against the chair, leaned against the window panes, obviously in some recollection of the sense of freedom that looking out of a window always used to give him. For in reality day by day things that were even a little way off were growing dimmer to his sight; the hospital across the street, which he used to execrate for being all too often before his eyes, was now quite beyond his range of vision, and if he had not known that he lived in Charlotte Street, a quiet street but still a city street, he might have believed that his window gave on a desert waste where gray sky and gray land blended indistinguishably into each other. His quick-witted sister only needed to observe twice that the armchair stood by the window; after that whenever she had tidied the room she always pushed the chair back to the same place at the window and even left the inner casements open.

If he could have spoken to her and thanked her for all she had to do for him, he could have borne her ministrations better; as it was, they oppressed him. She certainly tried to make as light as possible of whatever was disagreeable in her task, and as time went on she succeeded, of course, more and more, but time brought more enlightenment to Gregor too. The very way she came in distressed him. Hardly was she in the room when she rushed to the window, without even taking time to shut the door, careful as she was usually to shield the sight of Gregor's room from the others, and as if she were almost suffocating tore the casements open with hasty fingers, standing then in the open draught for a while even in the bitterest cold and drawing deep breaths. This noisy scurry of hers upset Gregor twice a day; he would crouch trembling under the sofa all the time, knowing quite well that she would certainly have spared him such a disturbance had she found it at all possible to stay in his presence without opening the window.

On one occasion, about a month after Gregor's metamorphosis, when there was surely no reason for her to be still startled at his appearance, she came a little earlier than usual and found him gazing out the window, quite motionless, and thus well placed to look like a bogey. Gregor would not have been surprised had she not come in at all, for she could not immediately open the window while he was there, but not only did she retreat, she jumped back as if in alarm and banged the door shut; a stranger might well have thought that he had been lying in wait for her there meaning to bite her. Of course he hid himself under the sofa at once, but he had to wait until midday before she came again, and seemed more ill at ease than usual. This made him realize how repulsive the sight of him still was to her, and that it was bound to go on being repulsive, and what an effort it must cost her not to run away even from the sight of the small portion of his body that stuck out from under the sofa. In order to spare her that, therefore, one day he carried a sheet on his back to the sofa—it cost him four hours' labor—and arranged it there in such a way as to hide him completely, so that even if she were to bend down she could not see him. Had she considered the sheet unnecessary, she would certainly have stripped it off the sofa again, for it was clear enough that this curtaining and confining of himself was not likely to conduce Gregor's comfort, but she left it where it was, and Gregor even fancied that he caught a thankful glance from her eye when he lifted the sheet carefully a very little with his head to see how she was taking the new arrangement.

For the first fortnight his parents could not bring themselves to the point of entering his room, and he often heard them expressing their appreciation of his sister's activities, whereas formerly they had frequently scolded her for being as they thought a somewhat useless daughter. But now, both of them often waited outside the door, his father and his mother, while his sister tidied his room, and as soon as she came out she had to tell them exactly how things were in the room, what Gregor had eaten, how he had conducted himself this time and whether there was not perhaps some slight improvement in his condition. His mother, moreover, began relatively soon to want to visit him, but his father and sister dissuaded her at first with arguments which Gregor listened to very attentively and altogether approved. Later, however, she had to be held back by main force, and when she cried out: "Do let me in to Gregor, he is my unfortunate son! Can't you understand that I must go in to him?" Gregor thought that it might be well to have her come in, not every day, of course, but perhaps once a week; she understood things, after all, much better than his sister, who was only a child despite the efforts she was making and had perhaps taken on so difficult a task merely out of childish thoughtlessness.

Gregor's desire to see his mother was soon fulfilled. During the daytime he did not want to show himself at the window, out of consideration for his parents, but he could not crawl very far around the few square yards of floor space he had, nor could he bear lying quietly at rest all during the night, while he was fast losing any interest he had ever taken in food, so that for mere recreation he had formed the habit of crawling crisscross over the walls and ceiling. He especially enjoyed hanging suspended from the ceiling; it was much better than lying on the floor; one could breathe more freely; one's body swung and rocked lightly; and in the almost blissful absorption induced by this suspension it could happen to his own surprise that he let go and fell plump on the floor. Yet he now had his body much better under control than formerly, and even such a big fall did him no harm. His sister at once remarked the new distraction Gregor had found for himself—he left traces behind him of the sticky stuff on his soles wherever he crawled—and she got the idea in her head of giving him as wide a field as possible to crawl in and of removing the pieces of furniture that hindered him, above all the chest of drawers and the writing desk. But that was more than she could manage all by herself; she did not dare ask her father to help her; and as for the servant girl, a young creature of sixteen who had had the courage to stay on after the cook's departure, she could not be asked to help, for she had begged as an especial favor that she might keep the kitchen door locked and open it only on a definite summons; so there was nothing left but to apply to her mother at an hour when her father was out. And the old lady did come, with exclamations of joyful eagerness, which, however, died away at the door of Gregor's room. Gregor's sister, of course, went in first, to see that everything was in order before letting his mother enter. In great haste Gregor pulled the sheet lower and rucked it more in folds so that it really looked as if it had been thrown accidentally over the sofa. And this time he did not peer out from under it; he renounced the pleasure of seeing his mother on this occasion and was only glad that she had come at all. "Come in, he's out of sight," said his sister, obviously leading her mother in by the hand. Gregor could now hear the two women struggling to shift the heavy old chest from its place, and his sister claiming the greater part of the labor for herself, without listening to the admonitions of her mother who feared she might overstrain herself. It took a long time. After at least a quarter of an hour's tugging his mother objected that the chest had better be left where it was, for in the first place it was too heavy and could never be got out before his father came home, and standing in the middle of the room like that it would only hamper Gregor's movements, while in the second place it was not at all certain that removing the furniture would be doing a service to Gregor. She was inclined to think to the contrary; the sight of the naked walls made her own heart heavy, and why shouldn't Gregor have the same feeling, considering that he had been used to his furniture for so long and might feel forlorn without it. "And doesn't it look," she concluded in a low voice—in fact she had been almost whispering all the time as if to avoid letting Gregor, whose exact whereabouts she did not know, hear even the tones of her voice, for she was convinced that he could not understand her words—"doesn't it look as if we were showing him, by taking away his furniture, that we have given up hope of his ever getting better and are just leaving him coldly to himself? I think it would be best to keep his room exactly as it has always been, so that when he comes back to us he will find everything unchanged and be able all the more easily to forget what has happened in between."

On hearing these words from his mother Gregor realized that the lack of all direct human speech for the past two months together with the monotony of family life must have confused his mind, otherwise he could not account for the fact that he had quite earnestly looked forward to having his room emptied of furnishing. Did he really want his warm room, so comfortably fitted with old family furniture, to be turned into a naked den in which he would certainly be able to crawl unhampered in all directions but at the price of shedding simultaneously all recollection of his human background? He had indeed been so near the brink of forgetfulness that only the voice of his mother, which he had not heard for so long, had drawn him back from it. Nothing should be taken out of his room; everything must stay as it was; he could not dispense with the good influence of the furniture on his state of mind; and even if the furniture did hamper him in his senseless crawling round and round, that was no drawback but a great advantage.

Unfortunately his sister was of the contrary opinion; she had grown accustomed, and not without reason, to consider herself an expert in Gregor's affairs as against her parents, and so her mother's advice was now enough to make her determined on the removal not only of the chest and the writing desk, which had been her first intention, but of all the furniture except the indispensable sofa. This determination was not, of course, merely the outcome of childish recalcitrance and of the self-confidence she had recently developed so unexpectedly and at such cost; she had in fact perceived that Gregor needed a lot of space to crawl about in, while on the other hand he never used the furniture at all, so far as could be seen. Another factor might have been also the enthusiastic temperament of an adolescent girl, which seeks to indulge itself on every opportunity and which now tempted Grete to exaggerate the horror of her brother's circumstances in order that she might do all the more for him. In a room where Gregor lorded it all alone over empty walls no one save herself was likely ever to set foot.

And so she was not to be moved from her resolve by her mother who seemed moreover to be ill at ease in Gregor's room and therefore unsure of herself, was soon reduced to silence and helped her daughter as best she could to push the chest outside. Now, Gregor could do without the chest, if need be, but the writing desk he must retain. As soon as the two women had got the chest out of his room, groaning as they pushed it, Gregor stuck his head out from under the sofa to see how he might intervene as kindly and cautiously as possible. But as bad luck would have it, his mother was the first to return, leaving Grete clasping the chest in the room next door where she was trying to shift it all by herself, without of course moving it from the spot. His mother however was not accustomed to the sight of him, it might sicken her and so in alarm Gregor backed quickly to the other end of the sofa, yet could not prevent the sheet from swaying a little in front. That was enough to put her on the alert. She paused, stood still for a moment and then went back to Grete.

Although Gregor kept reassuring himself that nothing out of the way was happening, but only a few bits of furniture were being changed around, he soon had to admit that all this trotting to and fro of the two women, their little ejaculations and the scraping of furniture along the floor affected him like a vast disturbance coming from all sides at once, and however much he tucked in his head and legs and cowered to the very floor he was bound to confess that he would not be able to stand it for long. They were clearing his room out; taking away everything he loved; the chest in which he kept his fret saw and other tools was already dragged off; they were now loosening the writing desk which had almost sunk into the floor, the desk at which he had done all his homework when he was at the commercial academy, at the grammar school before that, and, yes, even at the primary school—he had no more time to waste in weighing the good intentions of the two women, whose existence he had by now forgotten, for they were so exhausted that they were laboring in silence and nothing could be heard but the heavy scuffling of their feet.

And so he rushed out—the women were just leaning against the writing desk in the next room to give themselves a breather—and four times changed his direction, since he really did not know what to rescue first, then on the wall opposite, which was already otherwise cleared, he was struck by the picture of the lady muffled in so much fur and quickly crawled up to it and pressed himself to the glass, which was a good surface to hold on to and comforted his hot belly. This picture at least, which was entirely hidden beneath him, was going to be removed by nobody. He turned his head towards the door of the living room so as to observe the women when they came back.

They had not allowed themselves much of a rest and were already coming; Grete had twined her arm round her mother and was almost supporting her. "Well, what shall we take now?" said Grete, looking round. Her eyes met Gregor's from the wall. She kept her composure, presumably because of her mother, bent her head down to her mother, to keep her from looking up, and said, although in a fluttering, unpremeditated voice: "Come, hadn't we better go back to the living room for a moment?" Her intentions were clear enough to Gregor, she wanted to bestow her mother in safety and then chase him down from the wall. Well, just let her try it! He clung to his picture and would not give it up. He would rather fly in Grete's face.

But Grete's words had succeeded in disquieting her mother, who took a step to one side, caught sight of the huge brown mass on the flowered wallpaper, and before she was really conscious that what she saw was Gregor screamed in a loud, hoarse voice: "Oh God, oh God!" fell with outspread arms over the sofa as if giving up and did not move. "Gregor!" cried his sister, shaking her fist and glaring at him. This was the first time she had directly addressed him since his metamorphosis. She ran into the next room for some aromatic essence with which to rouse her mother from her fainting fit. Gregor wanted to help too—there was still time to rescue the picture—but he was stuck fast to the glass and had to tear himself loose; he then ran after his sister into the next room as if he could advise her, as he used to do; but then had to stand helplessly behind her; she meanwhile searched among various small bottles and when she turned round started in alarm at the sight of him; one bottle fell on the floor and broke; a splinter of glass cut Gregor's face and some kind of corrosive medicine splashed him; without pausing a moment longer Grete gathered up all the bottles she could carry and ran to her mother with them; she banged the door shut with her foot. Gregor was now cut off from his mother, who was perhaps nearly dying because of him; he dared not open the door for fear of frightening away his sister, who had to stay with her mother; there was nothing he could do but wait; and harassed by self-reproach and worry he began now to crawl to and fro, over everything, walls, furniture, and ceiling, and finally in his despair, when the noble room seemed to be reeling round him, fell down on to the middle of the big table.

A little while elapsed. Gregor was still lying there feebly and all around was quiet, perhaps that was a good omen. Then the doorbell rang. The servant girl was of course locked in her kitchen, and Grete would have to open the door. It was his father. "What's been happening?" were his first words; Grete's face must have told him everything. Grete answered in a muffled voice, apparently hiding her head on his breast: "Mother has been fainting, but she's better now. Gregor's broken loose." "Just what I expected," said his father, "just what I've been telling you, but you women would never listen." It was clear to Gregor that his father had taken the worst interpretation of Grete's all too brief statement and was assuming that Gregor had been guilty of some violent act. Therefore Gregor must now try to propitiate his father, since he had neither time nor means for an explanation. And so he fled to the door of his own room and crouched against it, to let his father see as soon as he came in from the hall that his son had the good intention of getting back into his room immediately and that it was not necessary to drive him there, but that if only the door were opened he would disappear at once.

Yet his father was not in the mood to perceive such fine distinctions. "Ah!" he cried as soon as he appeared, in a tone which sounded at once angry and exultant. Gregor drew his head back from the door and lifted it to look at his father. Truly, this was not the father he had imagined to himself; admittedly he had been too absorbed of late in his new recreation of crawling over the ceiling to take the same interest as before in what was happening elsewhere in the flat, and he ought really to be prepared for some changes. And yet, and yet, could that be his father? The man who used to lie wearily sunk in bed whenever Gregor set out on a business journey; who welcomed him back of an evening lying in a long chair in a dressing gown; who could not really rise to his feet but only lifted his arms in greeting, and on the rare occasions when he did go out with his family, on one or two Sundays a year and on high holidays, walked between Gregor and his mother, who were slow walkers anyhow, even more slowly than they did, muffled in his old greatcoat, shuffling laboriously forward with the help of his crook-handled stick which he set down most cautiously at every step and, whenever he wanted to say anything, nearly always came to a full stop and gathered his escort around him? Now he was standing there in fine shape; dressed in a smart blue uniform with gold buttons, such as bank messengers wear; his strong double chin bulged over the stiff high collar of his jacket; from under his bushy eyebrows his black eyes darted fresh and penetrating glances; his onetime tangled white hair had been combed flat on either side of a shining and carefully exact parting. He pitched his cap, which bore a gold monogram, probably the badge of some bank, in a wide sweep across the whole room on to a sofa and with the tail-ends of his jacket thrown back, his hands in his trouser pockets, advanced with a grim visage towards Gregor. Likely enough he did not himself know what he meant to do; at any rate he lifted his feet uncommonly high, and Gregor was dumbfounded at the enormous size of his shoe soles. But Gregor could not risk standing up to him, aware as he had been from the very first day of his new life that his father believed only the severest measures suitable for dealing with him. And so he ran before his father, stopping when he stopped and scuttling forward again when his father made any kind of move. In this way they circled the room several times without anything decisive happening; indeed the whole operation did not even look like a pursuit because it was carried out so slowly. And so Gregor did not leave the floor, for he feared that his father might take as a piece of peculiar wickedness any excursion of his over the walls or the ceiling. All the same, he could not stay this course much longer, for while his father took one step he had to carry out a whole series of movements. He was already beginning to feel breathless, just as in his former life his lungs had not been very dependable. As he was staggering along, trying to concentrate his energy on running, hardly keeping his eyes open; in his dazed state never even thinking of any other escape than simply going forward; and having almost forgotten that the walls were free to him, which in this room were well provided with finely carved pieces of furniture full of knobs and crevices—suddenly something lightly flung landed close behind him and rolled before him. It was an apple; a second apple followed immediately; Gregor came to a stop in alarm; there was no point in running on, for his father was determined to bombard him. He had filled his pockets with fruit from the dish on the sideboard and was now shying apple after apple, without taking particularly good aim for the moment. The small red apples rolled about the floor as if magnetized and cannoned into each other. An apple thrown without much force grazed Gregor's back and glanced off harmlessly. But another following immediately landed right on his back and sank in; Gregor wanted to drag himself forward, as if this startling, incredible pain could be left behind him; but he felt as if nailed to the spot and flattened himself out in a complete derangement of all his senses. With his last conscious look he saw the door of his room being torn open and his mother rushing out ahead of his screaming sister, in her underbodice, for her daughter had loosened her clothing to let her breathe more freely and recover from her swoon, he saw his mother rushing toward his father, leaving one after another behind her on the floor her loosened petticoats, stumbling over her petticoats straight to his father and embracing him, in complete union with him— but here Gregor's sight began to fail—with her hands clasped round his father's neck as she begged for her son's life.

III

The serious injury done to Gregor, which disabled him for more than a month— the apple went on sticking in his body as a visible reminder, since no one bothered to remove it—seemed to have made even his father recollect that Gregor was a member of the family, despite his present unfortunate and repulsive shape, and ought not to be treated as an enemy, that, on the contrary, family duty required the suppression of disgust and the exercise of patience, nothing but patience.

And although his injury had impaired, probably for ever, his power of movement, and for the time being it took him long, long minutes to creep across his room like an old invalid—there was no question now of crawling up the wall—yet in his own opinion he was sufficiently compensated for this worsening of his condition by the fact that towards evening the living-room door, which he used to watch intently for an hour or two beforehand, was always thrown open, so that lying in the darkness of his room, invisible to the family, he could see them all at the lamp-lit table and listen to their talk, by general consent as it were, very different from his earlier eavesdropping.

True, their intercourse lacked the lively character of former times, which he had always called to mind with a certain wistfulness in the small hotel bedrooms where he had been wont to throw himself down, tired out, on damp bedding. They were now mostly very silent. Soon after supper his father would fall asleep in his armchair; his mother and sister would admonish each other to be silent; his mother, bending low over the lamp, stitched at fine sewing for an underwear firm; his sister, who had taken a job as a salesgirl, was learning shorthand and French in the evenings on the chance of bettering herself. Sometimes his father woke up, and as if quite unaware that he had been sleeping said to his mother: "What a lot of sewing you're doing today!" and at once fell asleep again, while the two women exchanged a tired smile.

With a kind of mulishness his father persisted in keeping his uniform on even in the house; his dressing gown hung uselessly on its peg and he slept fully dressed where he sat, as if he were ready for service at any moment and even here only at the beck and call of his superior. As a result, his uniform, which was not brand-new to start with, began to look dirty, despite all the loving care of the mother and sister to keep it clean, and Gregor often spent whole evenings gazing at the many greasy spots on the garment, gleaming with gold buttons always in a high state of polish, in which the old man sat sleeping in extreme discomfort and yet quite peacefully.

As soon as the clock struck ten his mother tried to rouse his father with gentle words and to persuade him after that to get into bed, for sitting there he could not have a proper sleep and that was what he needed most, since he had to go to duty at six. But with the mulishness that had obsessed him since he became a bank messenger he always insisted on staying longer at the table, although he regularly fell asleep again and in the end only with the greatest trouble could be got out of his armchair and into his bed. However insistently Gregor's mother and sister kept urging him with gentle reminders, he would go on slowly shaking his head for a quarter of an hour, keeping his eyes shut, and refuse to get to his feet. The mother plucked at his sleeve, whispering endearments in his ear, the sister left her lessons to come to her mother's help, but Gregor's father was not to be caught. He would only sink down deeper in his chair. Not until the two women hoisted him up by the armpits did he open his eyes and look at them both, one after the other, usually with the remark: "This is a life. This is the peace and quiet of my old age." And leaning on the two of them he would heave himself up, with difficulty, as if he were a great burden to himself, suffer them to lead him as far as the door and then wave them off and go on alone, while the mother abandoned her needlework and the sister her pen in order to run after him and help him farther.

Who could find time, in this overworked and tired-out family, to bother about Gregor more than was absolutely needful? The household was reduced more and more; the servant girl was turned off; a gigantic bony charwoman with white hair flying round her head came in morning and evening to do the rough work; everything else was done by Gregor's mother, as well as great piles of sewing. Even various family ornaments, which his mother and sister used to wear with pride at parties and celebrations, had to be sold, as Gregor discovered of an evening from hearing them all discuss the prices obtained. But what they lamented most was the fact that they could not leave the flat which was much too big for their present circumstances, because they could not think of any way to shift Gregor. Yet Gregor saw well enough that consideration for him was not the main difficulty preventing the removal, for they could have easily shifted him in some suitable box with a few air holes in it; what really kept them from moving into another flat was rather their own complete hopelessness and the belief that they had been singled out for a misfortune such as had never happened to any of their relations or acquaintances. They fulfilled to the uttermost all that the world demands of poor people, the father fetched breakfast for the small clerks in the bank, the mother devoted her energy to making underwear for strangers, the sister trotted to and fro behind the counter at the behest of customers, but more than this they had not the strength to do. And the wound in Gregor's back began to nag at him afresh when his mother and sister, after getting his father into bed, came back again, left their work lying, drew close to each other and sat cheek by cheek; when his mother, pointing towards his room, said: "Shut that door now, Grete," and he was left again in darkness, while next door the women mingled their tears or perhaps sat dry-eyed staring at the table.

Gregor hardly slept at all by night or by day. He was often haunted by the idea that next time the door opened he would take the family's affairs in hand again just as he used to do; once more, after this long interval, there appeared in his thoughts the figures of the chief and the chief clerk, the commercial travelers and the apprentices, the porter who was so dull-witted, two or three friends in other firms, a chambermaid in one of the rural hotels, a sweet and fleeting memory, a cashier in a milliner's shop, whom he had wooed earnestly but too slowly—they all appeared, together with strangers or people he had quite forgotten, but instead of helping him and his family they were one and all unapproachable and he was glad when they vanished. At other times he would not be in the mood to bother about his family, he was only filled with rage at the way they were neglecting him, and although he had no clear idea of what he might care to eat he would make plans for getting into the larder to take the food that was after all his due, even if he were not hungry. His sister no longer took thought to bring him what might especially please him, but in the morning and at noon before she went to business hurriedly pushed into his room with her foot any food that was available, and in the evening cleared it out again with one sweep of the broom, heedless of whether it had been merely tasted, or—as most frequently happened—left untouched. The cleaning of his room, which she now always did in the evenings, could not have been more hastily done. Streaks of dirt stretched along the walls, here and there lay balls of dust and filth. At first Gregor used to station himself in some particularly filthy corner when his sister arrived, in order to reproach her with it, so to speak. But he could have sat there for weeks without getting her to make any improvements; she could see the dirt as well as he did, but she had simply made up her mind to leave it alone. And yet, with a touchiness that was new to her, which seemed anyhow to have infected the whole family, she jealously guarded her claim to be the sole caretaker of Gregor's room. His mother once subjected his room to a thorough cleaning, which was achieved only by means of several buckets of water—all this dampness of course upset Gregor too and he lay widespread, sulky and motionless on the sofa—but she was well punished for it. Hardly had his sister noticed the changed aspect of his room that evening than she rushed in high dudgeon into the living room and, despite the imploringly raised hands of her mother, burst into a storm of weeping, while her parents—her father had of course been startled out of his chair—looked on at first in helpless amazement; then they too began to go into action; the father reproached the mother on his right for not having left the cleaning of Gregor's room to his sister; shrieked at the sister on his left that never again was she allowed to clean Gregor's room; while the mother tried to pull the father into his bedroom, since he was beyond himself with agitation; the sister, shaken with sobs, then beat upon the table with her small fists; and Gregor hissed loudly with rage because not one of them thought of shutting the door to spare him such a spectacle and so much noise.

Still, even if the sister, exhausted by her daily work, had grown tired of looking after Gregor as she did formerly, there was no need for his mother's intervention or for Gregor's being neglected at all. The charwoman was there. This old widow, whose strong bony frame had enabled her to survive the worst a long life could offer, by no means recoiled from Gregor. Without being in the least curious she had once by chance opened the door of his room and at the sight of Gregor, who, taken by surprise, began to rush to and fro although no one was chasing him, merely stood there with her arms folded. From that time she never failed to open his door a little for a moment, morning and evening, to have a look at him. At first she even used to call him to her, with words which apparently she took to be friendly, such as: "Come along, then, you old dung beetle!" or "Look at the old dung beetle, then!" To such allocutions Gregor made no answer, but stayed motionless where he was, as if the door had never been opened. Instead of being allowed to disturb him so senselessly whenever the whim took her, she should rather have been ordered to clean out his room daily, that charwoman! Once, early in the morning—heavy rain was lashing on the windowpanes, perhaps a sign that spring was on the way—Gregor was so exasperated when she began addressing him again that he ran at her, as if to attack her, although slowly and feebly enough. But the charwoman instead of showing fright merely lifted high a chair that happened to be beside the door, and as she stood there with her mouth wide open it was clear that she meant to shut it only when she brought the chair down on Gregor's back. "So you're not coming any nearer?" she asked, as Gregor turned away again, and quietly put the chair back into the corner.

Gregor was now eating hardly anything. Only when he happened to pass the food laid out for him did he take a bit of something in his mouth as a pastime, kept it there for an hour at a time and usually spat it out again. At first he thought it was chagrin over the state of his room that prevented him from eating, yet he soon got used to the various changes in his room. It had become a habit in the family to push into his room things there was no room for elsewhere, and there were plenty of these now, since one of the rooms had been let to three lodgers. Three serious gentlemen—all three of them with full beards, as Gregor once observed through a crack in the door—had a passion for order, not only in their own room but, since they were now members of the household, in all its arrangements, especially in the kitchen. Superfluous, not to say dirty, objects they could not bear. Besides, they had brought with them most of the furnishings they needed. For this reason many things could be dispensed with that it was no use trying to sell but that should not be thrown away either. All of them found their way into Gregor's room. The ash can likewise and the kitchen garbage can. Anything that was not needed for the moment was simply flung into Gregor's room by the charwoman, who did everything in a hurry; fortunately Gregor usually saw only the object, whatever it was, and the hand that held it. Perhaps she intended to take the things away again as time and opportunity offered, or to collect them until she could throw them all out in a heap, but in fact they just lay wherever she happened to throw them, except when Gregor pushed his way through the junk heap and shifted it somewhat, at first out of necessity, because he had not room enough to crawl, but later with increasing enjoyment, although after such excursions, being sad and weary to death, he would lie motionless for hours. And since the lodgers often ate their supper at home in the common living room, the living-room door stayed shut many an evening, yet Gregor reconciled himself quite easily to the shutting of the door, for often enough on evenings when it was opened he had disregarded it entirely and lain in the darkest corner of his room, quite unnoticed by the family. But on one occasion the charwoman left the door open a little and it stayed ajar even when the lodgers came in for supper and the lamp was lit. They set themselves at the top end of the table where formerly Gregor and his father and mother had eaten their meals, unfolded their napkins and took knife and fork in hand. At once his mother appeared in the other doorway with a dish of meat and close behind her his sister with a dish of potatoes piled high. The food steamed with a thick vapor. The lodgers bent over the food set before them as if to scrutinize it before eating, in fact the man in the middle, who seemed to pass for an authority with the other two, cut a piece of meat as it lay on the dish, obviously to discover if it were tender or should be sent back to the kitchen. He showed satisfaction, and Gregor's mother and sister, who had been watching anxiously, breathed freely and began to smile.

The family itself took its meals in the kitchen. None the less, Gregor's father came into the living room before going into the kitchen and with one prolonged bow, cap in hand, made a round of the table. The lodgers all stood up and murmured something in their beards. When they were alone again they ate their food in almost complete silence. It seemed remarkable to Gregor that among the various noises coming from the table he could always distinguish the sound of their masticating teeth, as if this were a sign to Gregor that one needed teeth in order to eat, and that with toothless jaws even of the finest make one could do nothing. "I'm hungry enough," said Gregor sadly to himself, "but not for that kind of food. How these lodgers are stuffing themselves, and here am I dying of starvation!"

On that very evening—during the whole of his time there Gregor could not remember ever having heard the violin—the sound of violin-playing came from the kitchen. The lodgers had already finished their supper, the one in the middle had brought out a newspaper and given the other two a page apiece, and now they were leaning back at ease reading and smoking. When the violin began to play they pricked up their ears, got to their feet, and went on tiptoe to the hall door where they stood huddled together. Their movements must have been heard in the kitchen, for Gregor's father called out: "Is the violin-playing disturbing you, gentlemen? It can be stopped at once." "On the contrary," said the middle lodger, "could not Fräulein Samsa come and play in this room, beside us, where it is much more convenient and comfortable?" "Oh certainly," cried Gregor's father, as if he were the violin-player. The lodgers came back into the living room and waited. Presently Gregor's father arrived with the music stand, his mother carrying the music and his sister with the violin. His sister quietly made everything ready to start playing; his parents, who had never let rooms before and so had an exaggerated idea of the courtesy due to lodgers, did not venture to sit down on their own chairs; his father leaned against the door, the right hand thrust between two buttons of his livery coat, which was formally buttoned up; but his mother was offered a chair by one of the lodgers and, since she left the chair just where he had happened to put it, sat down in a corner to one side.

Gregor's sister began to play; the father and mother, from either side, intently watched the movements of her hands. Gregor, attracted by the playing, ventured to move forward a little until his head was actually inside the living room. He felt hardly any surprise at his growing lack of consideration for the others; there had been a time when he prided himself on being considerate. And yet just on this occasion he had more reason than ever to hide himself, since owing to the amount of dust which lay thick in his room and rose into the air at the slightest movement, he too was covered with dust; fluff and hair and remnants of food trailed with him, caught on his back and along his sides; his indifference to everything was much too great for him to turn on his back and scrape himself clean on the carpet, as once he had several times a day. And in spite of his condition, no shame deterred him from advancing a little over the spotless floor of the living room.

To be sure, no one was aware of him. The family was entirely absorbed in the violin-playing; the lodgers, however, who first of all had stationed themselves, hands in pockets, much too close behind the music stand so that they could all have read the music, which must have bothered his sister, had soon retreated to the window, half-whispering with downbent heads, and stayed there while his father turned an anxious eye on them. Indeed, they were making it more than obvious that they had been disappointed in their expectation of hearing good or enjoyable violin-playing, that they had had more than enough of the performance and only out of courtesy suffered a continued disturbance of their peace. From the way they all kept blowing the smoke of their cigars high in the air through nose and mouth one could divine their irritation. And yet Gregor's sister was playing so beautifully. Her face leaned sideways, intently and sadly her eyes followed the notes of music. Gregor crawled a little farther forward and lowered his head to the ground so that it might be possible for his eyes to meet hers. Was he an animal, that music had such an effect upon him? He felt as if the way were opening before him to the unknown nourishment he craved. He was determined to push forward till he reached his sister, to pull at her skirt and so let her know that she was to come into his room with her violin, for no one here appreciated her playing as he would appreciate it. He would never let her out of his room, at least, not so long as he lived; his frightful appearance would become, for the first time, useful to him; he would watch all the doors of his room at night and spit at intruders; but his sister should need no constraint, she should stay with him of her own free will; she should sit beside him on the sofa, bend down her ear to him and hear him confide that he had had the firm intention of sending her to the Conservatorium, and that, but for his mishap, last Christmas—surely Christmas was long past?—he would have announced it to everybody without allowing a single objection. After this confession his sister would be so touched that she would burst into tears, and Gregor would then raise himself to her shoulder and kiss her on the neck, which, now that she went to business, she kept free of any ribbon or collar.

"Mr. Samsa!" cried the middle lodger, to Gregor's father, and pointed, without wasting any more words, at Gregor, now working himself slowly forwards. The violin fell silent, the middle lodger first smiled to his friends with a shake of the head and then looked at Gregor again. Instead of driving Gregor out, his father seemed to think it more needful to begin by soothing the lodgers, although they were not at all agitated and apparently found Gregor more entertaining than the violin-playing. He hurried towards them and, spreading out his arms, tried to urge them back into their own room and at the same time to block their view of Gregor. They now began to be really a little angry, one could not tell whether because of the old man's behavior or because it had just dawned on them that all unwittingly they had such a neighbor as Gregor next door. They demanded explanations of his father, they waved their arms like him, tugged uneasily at their beards, and only with reluctance backed towards their room. Meanwhile Gregor's sister, who stood there as if lost when her playing was so abruptly broken off, came to life again, pulled herself together all at once after standing for a while holding violin and bow in nervelessly hanging hands and staring at her music, pushed her violin into the lap of her mother, who was still sitting in her chair fighting asthmatically for breath, and ran into the lodgers' room to which they were now being shepherded by her father more quickly than before. One could see the pillows and blankets on the beds flying under her accustomed fingers and being laid in order. Before the lodgers had actually reached their room she had finished making the beds and slipped out.

The old man seemed once more to be so possessed by his mulish self-assertiveness that he was forgetting all the respect he should show to his lodgers. He kept driving them on and driving them on until in the very door of the bedroom the middle lodger stamped his foot loudly on the floor and so brought him to a halt. "I beg to announce," said the lodger, lifting one hand and looking also at Gregor's mother and sister, "that because of the disgusting conditions prevailing in this household and family"—here he spat on the floor with emphatic brevity—"I give you notice on the spot. Naturally I won't pay you a penny for the days I have lived here, on the contrary I shall consider bringing an action for damages against you, based on claims—believe me—that will be easily susceptible of proof." He ceased and stared straight in front of him, as if he expected something. In fact his two friends at once rushed into the breach with these words: "And we too give notice on the spot." On that he seized the door-handle and shut the door with a slam.

Gregor's father, groping with his hands, staggered forward and fell from his chair; it looked as if he were stretching himself there for his ordinary evening nap, but the marked jerkings of his head, which was as if uncontrollable, showed that he was far from asleep. Gregor had simply stayed quietly all the time on the spot where the lodgers had espied him. Disappointment at the failure of his plan, perhaps also the weakness arising from extreme hunger, made it impossible for him to move. He feared, with a fair degree of certainty, that at any moment the general tension would discharge itself in a combined attack upon him, and he lay waiting. He did not react even to the noise made by the violin as it fell off his mother's lap from under her trembling fingers and gave out a resonant note.

"My dear parents," said his sister, slapping her hand on the table by way of introduction, "things can't go on like this. Perhaps you don't realize that, but I do. I won't utter my brother's name in the presence of this creature, and so all I say is: we must try to get rid of it. We've tried to look after it and to put up with it as far as is humanly possible, and I don't think anyone could reproach us in the slightest."

"She is more than right," said Gregor's father to himself. His mother, who was still choking for lack of breath, began to cough hollowly into her hand with a wild look in her eyes.

His sister rushed over to her and held her forehead. His father's thoughts seemed to have lost their vagueness at Grete's words, he sat more upright, fingering his service cap that lay among the plates still lying on the table from the lodgers' supper, and from time to time looked at the still form of Gregor.

"We must try to get rid of it," his sister now said explicitly to her father, since her mother was coughing too much to hear a word, "it will be the death of both of you, I can see that coming. When one has to work as hard as we do, all of us, one can't stand this continual torment at home on top of it. At least I can't stand it any longer." And she burst into such a passion of sobbing that her tears dropped on her mother's face, where she wiped them off mechanically.

"My dear," said the old man sympathetically, and with evident understanding, "but what can we do?"

Gregor's sister merely shrugged her shoulders to indicate the feeling of helplessness that had now overmastered her during her weeping fit, in contrast to her former confidence.

"If he could understand us," said her father, half questioningly; Grete, still sobbing, vehemently waved a hand to show how unthinkable that was.

"If he could understand us," repeated the old man, shutting his eyes to consider his daughter's conviction that understanding was impossible, "then perhaps we might come to some agreement with him. But as it is—"

"He must go," cried Gregor's sister, "that's the only solution, Father. You must just try to get rid of the idea that this is Gregor. The fact that we've believed it for so long is the root of all our trouble. But how can it be Gregor? If this were Gregor, he would have realized long ago that human beings can't live with such a creature, and he'd have gone away on his own accord. Then we wouldn't have any brother, but we'd be able to go on living and keep his memory in honor. As it is, this creature persecutes us, drives away our lodgers, obviously wants the whole apartment to himself and would have us all sleep in the gutter. Just look, Father," she shrieked all at once, "he's at it again!" And in an access of panic that was quite incomprehensible to Gregor she even quitted her mother, literally thrusting the chair from her as if she would rather sacrifice her mother than stay so near to Gregor, and rushed behind her father, who also rose up, being simply upset by her agitation, and half-spread his arms out as if to protect her.

Yet Gregor had not the slightest intention of frightening anyone, far less his sister. He had only begun to turn round in order to crawl back to his room, but it was certainly a startling operation to watch, since because of his disabled condition he could not execute the difficult turning movements except by lifting his head and then bracing it against the floor over and over again. He paused and looked round. His good intentions seemed to have been recognized; the alarm had been only momentary. Now they were all watching him in melancholy silence. His mother lay in her chair, her legs stiffly outstretched and pressed together, her eyes almost closing for sheer weariness; his father and his sister were sitting beside each other, his sister's arm around the old man's neck.

Perhaps I can go on turning round now, thought Gregor, and began his labors again. He could not stop himself from panting with the effort, and had to pause now and then to take breath. Nor did anyone harass him, he was left entirely to himself. When he had completed the turn-round he began at once to crawl straight back. He was amazed at the distance separating him from his room and could not understand how in his weak state he had managed to accomplish the same journey so recently, almost without remarking it. Intent on crawling as fast as possible, he barely noticed that not a single word, not an ejaculation from his family, interfered with his progress. Only when he was already in the doorway did he turn his head round, not completely, for his neck muscles were getting stiff, but enough to see that nothing had changed behind him except that his sister had risen to her feet. His last glance fell on his mother, who was now quite overcome by sleep.

Hardly was he well inside his room when the door was hastily pushed shut, bolted and locked. The sudden noise in his rear startled him so much that his little legs gave beneath him. It was his sister who had shown such haste. She had been standing ready waiting and had made a light spring forward, Gregor had not even heard her coming, and she cried "At last!" to her parents as she turned the key in the lock.

"And what now?" said Gregor to himself, looking round in the darkness. Soon he made the discovery that he was unable to stir a limb. This did not surprise him, rather it seemed unnatural that he should ever actually have been able to move on these feeble little legs. Otherwise he felt relatively comfortable. True, his whole body was aching, but it seemed that the pain was gradually growing less and would finally pass away. The rotting apple in his back and the inflamed area around it, all covered with soft dust, already hardly troubled him. He thought of his family with tenderness and love. The decision that he must disappear was one that he held to even more strongly than his sister, if that were possible. In this state of vacant and peaceful meditation he remained until the tower clock struck three in the morning. The first broadening of light in the world outside the window entered his consciousness once more. Then his head sank to the floor of its own accord and from his nostrils came the last faint flicker of his breath.

When the charwoman arrived early in the morning—what between her strength and her impatience she slammed all the doors so loudly, never mind how often she had been begged not to do so, that no one in the whole apartment could enjoy any quiet sleep after her arrival—she noticed nothing unusual as she took her customary peep into Gregor's room. She thought he was lying motionless on purpose, pretending to be in the sulks; she credited him with every kind of intelligence. Since she happened to have the long-handled broom in her hand she tried to tickle him up with it from the doorway. When that too produced no reaction she felt provoked and poked at him a little harder, and only when she had pushed him along the floor without meeting any resistance was her attention aroused. It did not take her long to establish the truth of the matter, and her eyes widened, she let out a whistle, yet did not waste much time over it but tore open the door of the Samsas' bedroom and yelled into the darkness at the top of her voice: "Just look at this, it's dead; it's lying here dead and done for!"

Mr. and Mrs. Samsa started up in their double bed and before they realized the nature of the charwoman's announcement had some difficulty in overcoming the shock of it. But then they got out of bed quickly, one on either side, Mr. Samsa throwing a blanket over his shoulders, Mrs. Samsa in nothing but her nightgown; in this array they entered Gregor's room. Meanwhile the door of the living room opened, too, where Grete had been sleeping since the advent of the lodgers; she was completely dressed as if she had not been to bed, which seemed to be confirmed also by the paleness of her face. "Dead?" said Mrs. Samsa, looking questioningly at the charwoman, although she could have investigated for herself, and the fact was obvious enough without investigation. "I should say so," said the charwoman, proving her words by pushing Gregor's corpse a long way to one side with her broomstick. Mrs. Samsa made a movement as if to stop her, but checked it. "Well," said Mr. Samsa, "now thanks be to God." He crossed himself, and the three women followed his example. Grete, whose eyes never left the corpse, said: "Just see how thin he was. It's such a long time since he's eaten anything. The food came out again just as it went in." Indeed, Gregor's body was completely flat and dry, as could only now be seen when it was no longer supported by the legs and nothing prevented one from looking closely at it.

"Come in beside us, Grete, for a little while," said Mrs. Samsa with a tremulous smile, and Grete, not without looking back at the corpse, followed her parents into their bedroom. The charwoman shut the door and opened the window wide. Although it was so early in the morning a certain softness was perceptible in the fresh air. After all, it was already the end of March.

The three lodgers emerged from their room and were surprised to see no breakfast; they had been forgotten. "Where's our breakfast?" said the middle lodger peevishly to the charwoman. But she put her finger to her lips and hastily, without a word, indicated by gestures that they should go into Gregor's room. They did so and stood, their hands in the pockets of their somewhat shabby coats, around Gregor's corpse in the room where it was now fully light.

At that the door of the Samsas' bedroom opened and Mr. Samsa appeared in his uniform, his wife on one arm, his daughter on the other. They all looked a little as if they had been crying; from time to time Grete hid her face on her father's arm.

"Leave my house at once!" said Mr. Samsa, and pointed to the door without disengaging himself from the women. "What do you mean by that?" said the middle lodger, taken somewhat aback, with a feeble smile. The two others put their hands behind them and kept rubbing them together, as if in gleeful expectation of a fine set-to in which they were bound to come off the winners. "I mean just what I say," answered Mr. Samsa, and advanced in a straight line with his two companions towards the lodger. He stood his ground at first quietly, looking at the floor as if his thoughts were taking a new pattern in his head. "Then let us go, by all means," he said, and looked up at Mr. Samsa as if in a sudden access of humility he were expecting some renewed sanction for this decision. Mr. Samsa merely nodded briefly once or twice with meaning eyes. Upon that the lodger really did go with long strides into the hall, his two friends had been listening and had quite stopped rubbing their hands for some moments and now went scuttling after him as if afraid that Mr. Samsa might get into the hall before them and cut them off from their leader. In the hall they all three took their hats from the rack, their sticks from the umbrella stand, bowed in silence and quitted the apartment. With a suspiciousness which proved quite unfounded Mr. Samsa and the two women followed them out to the landing; leaning over the banister they watched the three figures slowly but surely going down the long stairs, vanishing from sight at a certain turn of the staircase on every floor and coming into view again after a moment or so; the more they dwindled, the more the Samsa family's interest in them dwindled, and when a butcher's boy met them and passed them on the stairs coming up proudly with a tray on his head, Mr. Samsa and the two women soon left the landing and as if a burden had been lifted from them went back into their apartment.

They decided to spend this day in resting and going for a stroll; they had not only deserved such a respite from work, but absolutely needed it. And so they sat down at the table and wrote three notes of excuse, Mr. Samsa to his board of management, Mrs. Samsa to her employer and Grete to the head of her firm. While they were writing, the charwoman came in to say that she was going now, since her morning's work was finished. At first they only nodded without looking up, but as she kept hovering there they eyed her irritably. "Well?" said Mr. Samsa. The charwoman stood grinning in the doorway as if she had good news to impart to the family but meant not to say a word unless properly questioned. The small ostrich feather standing upright on her hat, which had annoyed Mr. Samsa ever since she was engaged, was waving gaily in all directions. "Well, what is it, then?" asked Mrs. Samsa, who obtained more respect from the charwoman than the others. "Oh," said the charwoman, giggling so amiably that she could not at once continue, "just this, you don't need to bother about how to get rid of the thing next door. It's been seen to already." Mrs. Samsa and Grete bent over their letters again, as if preoccupied; Mr. Samsa, who perceived that she was eager to begin describing it all in detail, stopped her with a decisive hand. But since she was not allowed to tell her story, she remembered the great hurry she was in, being obviously deeply huffed: "Bye, everybody," she said, whirling off violently, and departed with a frightful slamming of doors.

"She'll be given notice tonight," said Mr. Samsa, but neither from his wife nor his daughter did he get any answer, for the charwoman seemed to have shattered again the composure they had barely achieved. They rose, went to the window and stayed there, clasping each other tight. Mr. Samsa turned in his chair to look at them and quietly observed them for a little. Then he called out: "Come along, now, do. Let bygones be bygones. And you might have some consideration for me." The two of them complied at once, hastened to him, caressed him and quickly finished their letters.

Then they all three left the apartment together, which was more than they had done for months, and went by tram into the open country outside the town. The tram, in which they were the only passengers, was filled with warm sunshine. Leaning comfortably back in their seats they canvassed their prospects for the future, and it appeared on closer inspection that these were not at all bad, for the jobs they had got, which so far they had never really discussed with each other, were all three admirable and likely to lead to better things later on. The greatest immediate improvement in their condition would of course arise from moving to another house; they wanted to take a smaller and cheaper but also better situated and more easily run apartment than the one they had, which Gregor had selected. While they were thus conversing, it struck both Mr. and Mrs. Samsa, almost at the same moment, as they became aware of their daughter's increasing vivacity, that in spite of all the sorrow of recent times, which had made her cheeks pale, she had bloomed into a pretty girl with a good figure. They grew quieter and half unconsciously exchanged glances of complete agreement, having come to the conclusion that it would soon be time to find a good husband for her. And it was like a confirmation of their new dreams and excellent intentions that at the end of their journey their daughter sprang to her feet first and stretched her young body.

Translated by Will and Edwin Muir.

Journal Entry

Record your responses to the first sentence of "The Metamorphosis." Characterize the narrator's tone.

Textual Considerations

1. Characterize the narrator's attitude toward Gregor. What does he reveal about Gregor's job and relationship with his boss?
2. Analyze Gregor's relationship with his sister. How does her treatment of him change as the story continues? To what extent is her final betrayal inevitable?
3. Food plays an important role in the story. Analyze its effects on theme.
4. Characterize Gregor's father. To what extent has he exploited Gregor? Why is it ironic that as Gregor's situation deteriorates that of his family improves?
5. Consider the roles of the three lodgers and the charwoman. How are their attitudes toward Gregor similar to or different from those of his family?
6. Compare and contrast Kafka's treatment of time in parts one and two. How is it reflective of Gregor's psychological state?
7. How many "metamorphoses" occur in the story? Consider, for example, the final scene. How does it differ stylistically from the rest of the story?

Cultural Contexts

1. Discuss with your group the extent to which Gregor is responsible for his sense of alienation. Does he deserve his fate? Of what is he guilty? Is he a victim of the self-ishness or manipulation of others? What might Kafka be implying about one's relationship to oneself versus responsibility to family and community?
2. Many critics attribute Kafka's thematic preoccupation with exile and alienation to his biographical circumstances. Kafka was a Jew raised in a Gentile world, he suffered from tuberculosis, was terrified of his domineering and judgmental father, and was a sensitive artist in a typical middle-class society. Debate with your group the degree to which Gregor's sense of isolation may be explained solely by these circumstances.

Sherwood Anderson
1919

Hands

Upon the half decayed veranda of a small frame house that stood near the edge of a ravine near the town of Winesburg, Ohio, a fat little old man walked nervously up and down. Across a long field that had been seeded for clover but that had produced only a dense crop of yellow mustard weeds, he could see the public highway along which went a wagon filled with berry pickers returning from the fields. The berry pickers, youths and maidens, laughed and shouted boisterously. A boy clad in a blue shirt leaped from the wagon and attempted to drag after him one of the maidens, who screamed and protested shrilly. The feet of the boy in the road kicked up a cloud of dust that floated across the face of the departing sun. Over the long field came a thin girlish voice. "Oh, you Wing Biddlebaum, comb your hair, it's falling into your eyes," commanded the voice to the man, who was bald and whose nervous little hands fiddled about the bare white forehead as though arranging a mass of tangled locks.

Wing Biddlebaum, forever frightened and beset by a ghostly band of doubts, did not think of himself as in any way a part of the life of the town where he had lived for twenty years. Among all the people of Winesburg but one had come close to him. With George Willard, son of Tom Willard, the proprietor of the New Willard House, he had formed something like a friendship. George Willard was the reporter on the *Winesburg Eagle* and sometimes in the evenings he walked out along the highway to Wing Biddlebaum's house. Now as the old man walked up and down on the veranda, his hands moving nervously about, he was hoping that George Willard would come and spend the evening with him. After the wagon containing the berry pickers had passed, he went across the field through the tall mustard weeds and climbing a rail fence peered anxiously along the road to the town. For a moment he stood thus, rubbing his hands together and looking up and down the road, and then, fear overcoming him, ran back to walk again upon the porch on his own house.

In the presence of George Willard, Wing Biddlebaum, who for twenty years had been the town mystery, lost something of his timidity, and his shadowy personality, submerged in a sea of doubts, came forth to look at the world. With the young reporter at his side, he ventured in the light of day into Main Street or strode up and down on the rickety front porch of his own house, talking excitedly. The voice that had been low and trembling became shrill and loud. The bent figure straightened. With a kind of wriggle, like a fish returned to the brook by the fisherman, Biddlebaum the silent began to talk, striving to put into words the ideas that had been accumulated by his mind during long years of silence.

Wing Biddlebaum talked much with his hands. The slender expressive fingers, forever active, forever striving to conceal themselves in his pockets or behind his back, came forth and became the piston rods of his machinery of expression.

The story of Wing Biddlebaum is a story of hands. Their restless activity, like unto the beating of the wings of an imprisoned bird, had given him his name. Some obscure poet of the town had thought of it. The hands alarmed their owner. He wanted to keep them hidden away and looked with amazement at the quiet inexpressive hands of other men who worked beside him in the fields, or passed, driving sleepy teams on country roads.

When he talked to George Willard, Wing Biddlebaum closed his fists and beat with them upon a table or on the walls of his house. The action made him more comfortable. If the desire to talk came to him when the two were walking in the fields, he sought out a stump or the top board of a fence and with his hands pounding busily talked with renewed ease.

The story of Wing Biddlebaum's hands is worth a book in itself. Sympathetically set forth it would tap many strange, beautiful qualities in obscure men. It is a job for a poet. In Winesburg the hands had attracted attention merely because of their activity. With them Wing Biddlebaum had picked as high as a hundred and forty quarts of strawberries in a day. They became his distinguishing feature, the source of his fame. Also they made more grotesque an already grotesque and elusive individuality. Winesburg was proud of the hands of Wing Biddlebaum in the same spirit in which it was proud of Banker White's new stone house and Wesley Moyer's bay stallion, Tony Tip, that had won the two-fifteen trot at the fall races in Cleveland.

As for George Willard, he had many times wanted to ask about the hands. At times an almost overwhelming curiosity had taken hold of him. He felt that there must be a reason for their strange activity and their inclination to keep hidden away and only a growing respect for Wing Biddlebaum kept him from blurting out the questions that were often in his mind.

Once he had been on the point of asking. The two were walking in the fields on a summer afternoon and had stopped to sit upon a grassy bank. All afternoon Wing Biddlebaum had talked as one inspired. By a fence he had stopped and beating like a giant woodpecker upon the top board had shouted at George Willard, condemning his tendency to be too much influenced by the people about him. "You are destroying yourself," he cried. "You have the inclination to be alone and to dream and you are afraid of dreams. You want to be like others in town here. You hear them talk and you try to imitate them."

On the grassy bank Wing Biddlebaum had tried again to drive his point home. His voice became soft and reminiscent, and with a sigh of contentment he launched into a long rambling talk, speaking as one lost in a dream.

Out of the dream Wing Biddlebaum made a picture for George Willard. In the picture men lived again in a kind of pastoral golden age. Across a green open country came clean-limbed young men, some afoot, some mounted upon horses. In crowds the young men came to gather about the feet of an old man who sat beneath a tree in a tiny garden and who talked to them.

Wing Biddlebaum became wholly inspired. For once he forgot the hands. Slowly they stole forth and lay upon George Willard's shoulders. Something new and bold came into the voice that talked. "You must try to forget all you have learned," said the old man. "You must begin to dream. From this time on you must shut your ears to the roaring of the voices."

Pausing in his speech, Wing Biddlebaum looked long and earnestly at George Willard. His eyes glowed. Again he raised the hands to caress the boy and then a look of horror swept over his face.

With a convulsive movement of his body, Wing Biddlebaum sprang to his feet and thrust his hands deep into his trousers pockets. Tears came to his eyes. "I must be getting along home. I can talk no more with you," he said nervously.

Without looking back, the old man had hurried down the hillside and across a meadow, leaving George Willard perplexed and frightened upon the grassy slope. With a shiver of dread the boy arose and went along the road toward town. "I'll not ask him about his hands," he thought, touched by the memory of the terror he had seen in the man's eyes. "There's something wrong, but I don't want to know what it is. His hands have something to do with his fear of me and of everyone."

And George Willard was right. Let us look briefly into the story of the hands. Perhaps our talking of them will arouse the poet who will tell the hidden wonder story of the influence for which the hands were but fluttering pennants of promise.

In his youth Wing Biddlebaum had been a school teacher in a town in Pennsylvania. He was not then known as Wing Biddlebaum, but went by the less euphonic name of Adolph Myers. As Adolph Myers he was much loved by the boys of his school.

Adolph Myers was meant by nature to be a teacher of youth. He was one of those rare, little-understood men who rule by a power so gentle that it passes as a lovable weakness. In their feeling for the boys under their charge such men are not unlike the finer sort of women in their love of men.

And yet that is but crudely stated. It needs the poet there. With the boys of his school, Adolph Myers had walked in the evening or had sat talking until dusk upon the schoolhouse steps lost in a kind of dream. Here and there went his hands, caressing the shoulders of the boys, playing about the tousled heads. As he talked his voice became soft and musical. There was a caress in that also. In a way the voice and the hands, the stroking of the shoulders and the touching of the hair were a part of the schoolmaster's effort to carry a dream into the young minds. By the caress that was in his fingers he expressed himself. He was one of those men in whom the force that creates life is diffused, not centralized. Under the caress of his hands doubt and disbelief went out of the minds of the boys and they began also to dream.

And then the tragedy. A half-witted boy of the school became enamored of the young master. In his bed at night he imagined unspeakable things and in the morning went forth to tell his dreams as facts. Strange, hideous accusations fell from his loose-hung lips. Through the Pennsylvania town went a shiver. Hidden, shadowy doubts that had been in men's minds concerning Adolph Myers were galvanized into beliefs.

The tragedy did not linger. Trembling lads were jerked out of bed and questioned. "He put his arms about me," said one. "His fingers were always playing in my hair," said another.

One afternoon a man of the town, Henry Bradford, who kept a saloon, came to the schoolhouse door. Calling Adolph Myers into the school yard he began to beat him with his fists. As his hard knuckles beat down into the frightened face of the schoolmaster, his wrath, became more and more terrible. Screaming with dismay, the children ran here and there like disturbed insects. "I'll teach you to put your hands on my boy, you beast," roared the saloon keeper, who tired of beating the master, had begun to kick him about the yard.

Adolph Myers was driven from the Pennsylvania town in the night. With lanterns in their hands a dozen men came to the door of the house where he lived alone and commanded that he dress and come forth. It was raining and one of the men had a rope in his hands. They had intended to hang the schoolmaster, but something in his figure, so small, white, and pitiful, touched their hearts and they let him escape. As he ran away into the darkness they repented of their weakness and ran after him, swearing and throwing sticks and great balls of soft mud at the figure that screamed and ran faster and faster into the darkness.

For twenty years Adolph Myers had lived alone in Winesburg. He was but forty but looked sixty-five. The name of Biddlebaum he got from a box of goods seen at a freight station as he hurried through an eastern Ohio town. He had an aunt in Winesburg, a black-toothed old woman who raised chickens, and with her he lived until she died. He had been ill for a year after the experience in Pennsylvania, and after his recovery worked as a day laborer in the fields, going timidly about and striving to conceal his hands. Although he did not understand what had happened he felt that the hands must be to blame. Again and again the fathers of the boys talked of the hands. "Keep your hands to yourself," the saloon keeper had roared, dancing with fury in the schoolhouse yard.

Upon the veranda of his house by the ravine, Wing Biddlebaum continued to walk up and down until the sun had disappeared and the road beyond the field was lost in the grey shadows. Going into his house he cut slices of bread and spread honey upon them. When the rumble of the evening train that took away the express cars loaded with the day's harvest of berries had passed and restored the silence of the summer night, he went again to walk upon the veranda. In the darkness he could not see the hands and they became quiet. Although he still hungered for the presence of the boy, who was the medium through which he expressed his love of man, the hunger became again a part of his loneliness and his waiting. Lighting a lamp, Wing Biddlebaum washed the few dishes soiled by his simple meal and, setting up a folding cot by the screen door that led to the porch, prepared to undress for the night. A few stray white bread crumbs lay on the cleanly washed floor by the table; putting the lamp upon a low stool he began to pick up the crumbs, carrying them to his mouth one by one with unbelievable rapidity. In the dense blotch of light beneath the table, the kneeling figure looked like a priest engaged in some service of his church. The nervous expressive fingers, flashing in and out of the light, might well have been mistaken for the fingers of the devotee going swiftly through decade after decade of his rosary.

Journal Entry

Respond to the Pennsylvania community's treatment of Wing Biddlebaum.

Textual Considerations

1. How does "Hands" allow readers to see the reality of Biddlebaum's identity for themselves, whereas Biddlebaum himself "did not understand what had happened [and] he felt that the hands must be to blame"? Focus on the role that the narrator plays in Anderson's story.
2. Anderson juxtaposes Biddlebaum, a fat little old man, with the community of "youths and maidens, [who] laughed and shouted boisterously." Analyze the encounter of these opposing characters in terms of the relationship between the individual and the community.
3. Consider whether the issue of power fits into the overall development of the plot in "Hands." Investigate this issue in relation to the two communities in "Hands," as well as to Biddlebaum himself, whom the narrator describes as "one of those rare, little-understood men who rule by a power so gentle that it passes as a lovable weakness."
4. Respond to the religious imagery at the end of the story by analyzing what it suggests in terms of Biddlebaum's value as an individual.

Cultural Contexts

1. Some psychologists now see humankind as fundamentally divided beings who are split biologically, sexually, linguistically, and socially. Discuss with your group whether one can apply the concept of the split individual to Wing Biddlebaum in "Hands."
2. "Hands" offers a dynamic investigation into the way a community reacts to an individual's potential threat. Can your group reach a consensus on whether there is any foundation for this threat? How would you characterize it?

James Joyce
1916

Eveline

She sat at the window watching the evening invade the avenue. Her head was leaned against the window curtains and in her nostrils was the odor of dusty cretonne. She was tired.

Few people passed. The man out of the last house passed on his way home; she heard his footsteps clicking along the concrete pavement and afterwards crunching on the cinder path before the new red houses. One time there used to be a field there in which they used to play every evening with other people's children. Then a man from Belfast bought the field and built houses in it—not like their little brown houses but bright brick houses with shining roofs. The children of the avenue used to play together in that field—the Devines, the Waters, the Dunns, little Keogh the cripple, she and her brothers and sisters. Ernest, however, never played: he was too grown up. Her father used often to hunt them in out of the field with his blackthorn stick; but usually little Keogh used to keep *nix* and call out when he saw her father coming. Still they seemed to have been rather happy then. Her father was not so bad then; and besides, her mother was alive. That was a long time ago; she and her brothers and sisters were all grown up; her mother was dead. Tizzie Dunn was dead, too, and the Waters had gone back to England. Everything changes. Now she was going to go away like the others, to leave her home.

Home! She looked round the room, reviewing all its familiar objects which she had dusted once a week for so many years, wondering where on earth all the dust came from. Perhaps she would never see again those familiar objects from which she had never dreamed of being divided. And yet during all those years she had never found out the name of the priest whose yellowing photograph hung on the wall above the broken harmonium beside the colored print of the promises made to Blessed Margaret Mary Alacoque. He had been a school friend of her father. Whenever he showed the photograph to a visitor her father used to pass it with a casual word:

—He is in Melbourne now.

She had consented to go away, to leave her home. Was that wise? She tried to weigh each side of the question. In her home anyway she had shelter and food; she had those whom she had known all her life about her. Of course she had to work hard both in the house and at business. What would they say of her in the Stores when they found out that she had run away with a fellow? Say she was a fool, perhaps; and her place would be filled up by advertisement. Miss Gavan would be glad. She had always had an edge on her, especially whenever there were people listening.

—Miss Hill, don't you see these ladies are waiting?

—Look lively, Miss Hill, please.

She would not cry many tears at leaving the Stores.

But in her new home, in a distant unknown country, it would not be like that. Then she would be married—she, Eveline. People would treat her with respect then. She would not be treated as her mother had been. Even now, though she was over nineteen, she sometimes felt herself in danger of her father's violence. She knew it was that that had given her the palpitations. When they were growing up he had never gone for her, like he used to go for Harry and Ernest, because she was a girl; but latterly he had begun to threaten her and say what he would do to her only for her dead mother's sake. And now she had nobody to protect her. Ernest was dead and Harry, who was in the church decorating business, was nearly always down somewhere in the country. Besides, the invariable squabble for money on Saturday nights had begun to weary her unspeakably. She always gave her entire wages—seven shillings—and Harry always sent up what he could but the trouble was to get any money from her father. He said she used to squander the money, that she had no head, that he wasn't going to give her his hard-earned money to throw about the streets, and much more, for he was usually fairly bad of a Saturday night. In the end he would give her the money and ask her had she any intention of buying Sunday's dinner. Then she had to rush out as quickly as she could and do her marketing, holding her black leather purse tightly in her hand as she elbowed her way through the crowds and returning home late under her load of provisions. She had hard work to keep the house together and to see that the two young children who had been left to her charge went to school regularly and got their meals regularly. It was hard work—a hard life—but now that she was about to leave it she did not find it a wholly undesirable life.

She was about to explore another life with Frank. Frank was very kind, manly, open-hearted. She was to go away with him by the night-boat to be his wife and to live with him in Buenos Ayres where he had a home waiting for her. How well she remembered the first time she had seen him; he was lodging in a house on the main road where she used to visit. It seemed a few weeks ago. He was standing at the gate, his peaked cap pushed back on his head and his hair tumbled forward over a face of bronze. Then they had come to know each other. He used to meet her outside the Stores every evening and see her home. He took her to see *The Bohemian Girl* and she felt elated as she sat in an unaccustomed part of the theatre with him. He was awfully fond of music and sang a little. People knew that they were courting and, when he sang about the lass that loves a sailor, she always felt pleasantly confused. He used to call her Poppens out of fun. First of all it had been an excitement for her to have a fellow and then she had begun to like him. He had tales of distant countries. He had started as a deck boy at a pound a month on a ship of the Allan Line going out to Canada. He told her the names of the ships he had been on and the names of the different services. He had sailed through the Straits of Magellan and he told her stories of the terrible Patagonians. He had fallen on his feet in Buenos Ayres, he said, and had come over to the old country just for a holiday. Of course, her father had found out the affair and had forbidden her to have anything to say to him.

—I know these sailor chaps, he said.

One day he had quarrelled with Frank and after that she had to meet her lover secretly.

The evening deepened in the avenue. The white of two letters in her lap grew indistinct. One was to Harry; the other was to her father. Ernest had been her favorite but she liked Harry too. Her father was becoming old lately, she noticed; he would miss her. Sometimes he could be very nice. Not long before, when she had been laid up for a day, he had read her out a ghost story and made toast for her at the fire. Another day, when their mother was alive, they had all gone for a picnic to the Hill of Howth. She remembered her father putting on her mother's bonnet to make the children laugh.

Her time was running out but she continued to sit by the window, leaning her head against the window curtain, inhaling the odor of dusty cretonne. Down far in the avenue she could hear a street organ playing. She knew the air. Strange that it should come that very night to remind her of the promise to her mother, her promise to keep the home together as long as she could. She remembered the last night of her mother's illness; she was again in the close dark room at the other side of the hall and outside she heard a melancholy air of Italy. The organ-player had been ordered to go away and given sixpence. She remembered her father strutting back into the sickroom saying:

—Damned Italians! coming over here!

As she mused, the pitiful vision of her mother's life laid its spell on the very quick of her being—that life of commonplace sacrifices closing in final craziness. She trembled as she heard again her mother's voice saying constantly with foolish insistence:

—Derevaun Seraun! Derevaun Seraun!

She stood up in a sudden impulse of terror. Escape! She must escape! Frank would save her. He would give her life, perhaps love, too. But she wanted to live. Why should she be unhappy? She had a right to happiness. Frank would take her in his arms, fold her in his arms. He would save her.

She stood among the swaying crowd in the station at the North Wall. He held her hand and she knew that he was speaking to her, saying something about the passage over and over again. The station was full of soldiers with brown baggages. Through the wide doors of the sheds she caught a glimpse of the black mass of the boat, lying in beside the quay wall, with illumined portholes. She answered nothing. She felt her cheek pale and cold and, out of a maze of distress, she prayed to God to direct her, to show her what was her duty. The boat blew a long mournful whistle into the mist. If she went, tomorrow she would be on the sea with Frank, steaming towards Buenos Ayres. Their passage had been booked. Could she still draw back after all he had done for her? Her distress awoke a nausea in her body and she kept moving her lips in silent fervent prayer.

A bell clanged upon her heart. She felt him seize her hand:

—Come!

All the seas of the world tumbled about her heart. He was drawing her into them: he would drown her. She gripped with both hands at the iron railing.

—Come!

No! No! No! It was impossible. Her hands clutched the iron in frenzy. Amid the seas she sent a cry of anguish!

—Eveline! Evvy!

He rushed beyond the barrier and called to her to follow. He was shouted at to go on but he still called to her. She set her white face to him, passive, like a helpless animal. Her eyes gave him no sign of love or farewell or recognition.

Journal Entry

Imagine yourself in Eveline's position. How might your choice be similar to or different from hers?

Textual Considerations

1. Characterize Frank. To what extent is he a romantic figure? Why is he unable to persuade Eveline to choose her own happiness?
2. Consider the role of religion in "Eveline." How does it contribute to Eveline's sense of paralysis? What other factors might also be cited?
3. To what extent is Eveline's inability to choose her own happiness attributable to her role as daughter and as a single woman in an Irish Catholic environment at the turn of the century? What other factors might have contributed to her sense of paralysis?
4. Discuss the appropriateness of dust as the dominant symbol in the story. Can you find other symbols in the text?

Cultural Contexts

1. Initiate a group discussion on "Eveline" by locating the forces of tradition and change that shape Joyce's story.
2. Discuss Joyce's story as a social document that reflects or criticizes the values of the Irish community.

Fae Myenne Ng
1987

A Red Sweater

I chose red for my sister. Fierce, dark red. Made in Hong Kong. Hand Wash Only because it's got that skin of fuzz. She'll look happy. That's good. Everything's perfect, for a minute. That seems enough.

Red. For Good Luck. Of course. This fire-red sweater is swollen with good cheer. Wear it, I will tell her. You'll look lucky.

We're a family of three girls. By Chinese standards, that's not lucky. "Too bad," outsiders whisper, "...nothing but daughters. A failed family."

First, Middle, and End girl. Our order of birth marked us. That came to tell more than our given names.

My eldest sister, Lisa, lives at home. She quit San Francisco State, one semester short of a psychology degree. One day she said, "Forget about it, I'm tired." She's working full time at Pacific Bell now. Nine hundred a month with benefits. Mah and Deh think it's a great deal. They tell everybody, "Yes, our Number One makes good pay, but that's not even counting the discount. If we call Hong Kong, China even, there's forty percent off!" As if anyone in their part of China had a telephone.

Number Two, the in-between, jumped off the "M" floor three years ago. Not true! What happened? Why? Too sad! All we say about that is, "It was her choice."

We sent Mah to Hong Kong. When she left Hong Kong thirty years ago, she was the envy of all: "Lucky girl! You'll never have to work." To marry a sojourner was to have a future. Thirty years in the land of gold and good fortune, and then she returned to tell the story: three daughters, one dead, one unmarried, another who-cares-where, the thirty years in sweatshops, and the prince of the Golden Mountain turned into a toad. I'm glad I didn't have to go with her. I felt her shame and regret. To return, seeking solace and comfort, instead of offering banquets and stories of the good life.

I'm the youngest. I started flying with American the year Mah returned to Hong Kong, so I got her a good discount. She thought I was good for something then. But when she returned, I was pregnant.

"Get an abortion," she said. "Drop the baby," she screamed.

"No."

"Then get married."

"No. I don't want to."

I was going to get an abortion all along. I just didn't like the way they talked about the whole thing. They made me feel like dirt, that I was a disgrace. Now I can see how I used it as an opportunity. Sometimes I wonder if there wasn't another way. Everything about those years was so steamy and angry. There didn't seem to be any answers.

"I have no eyes for you," Mah said.

"Don't call us," Deh said.

They wouldn't talk to me. They ranted idioms to each other for days. The apartment was filled with images and curses I couldn't perceive. I got the general idea: I was a rotten, no-good, dead thing. I would die in a gutter without rice in my belly. My spirit—if I had one—wouldn't be fed. I wouldn't see good days in this life or the next.

My parents always had a special way of saying things.

Now I'm based in Honolulu. When our middle sister jumped, she kind of closed the world. The family just sort of fell apart. I left. Now, I try to make up for it; the folks still won't see me, but I try to keep in touch with them through Lisa.

Flying cuts up your life, hits hardest during the holidays. I'm always sensitive then. I feel like I'm missing something, that people are doing something really important while I'm up in the sky, flying through time zones.

So I like to see Lisa around the beginning of the year. January, New Year's, and February, New Year's again, double luckiness with our birthdays in between. With so much going on, there's always something to talk about.

"You pick the place this year," I tell her.

"Around here?"

"No," I say. "Around here" means the food is good and the living hard. You eat a steaming rice plate, and then you feel like rushing home to sew garments or assemble radio parts or something. We eat together only once a year, so I feel we should splurge. Besides, at the Chinatown places, you have nothing to talk about except the bare issues. In American restaurants, the atmosphere helps you along. I want nice light and a view and handsome waiters.

"Let's go somewhere with a view," I say.

We decide to go to Following Sea, a new place on the Pier 39 track. We're early, the restaurant isn't crowded. It's been clear all day, so I think the sunset will be nice. I ask for a window table. I turn to talk to my sister, but she's already talking to a waiter. He's got that dark island tone that she likes. He's looking her up and down. My sister does not blink at it. She holds his look and orders two Johnny Walkers. I pick up a fork, turn it around in my hand. I seldom use chopsticks now. At home, I eat my rice in a plate, with a fork. The only chopsticks I own, I wear in my hair. For a moment, I feel strange sitting here at this unfamiliar table. I don't know this tablecloth, this linen, these candles. Everything seems foreign. It feels like we should be different people. But each time I look up, she's the same. I know this person. She's my sister. We sat together with chopsticks, mismatched bowls, braids, and braces, across the formica tabletop.

"I like three-pronged forks," I say, pressing my thumb against the sharp points.

My sister rolls her eyes. She lights a cigarette.

I ask for one.

I finally say, "So, what's new?"

"Not much." Her voice is sullen. She doesn't look at me. Once a year, I come in, asking questions. She's got the answers, but she hates them. For me, I think she's got the peace of heart, knowing that she's done her share for Mah and Deh. She thinks I have the peace, not caring. Her life is full of questions, too, but I have no answers.

I look around the restaurant. The sunset is not spectacular, and we don't comment on it. The waiters are lighting candles. Ours is bringing the drinks. He stops very close to my sister, seems to breathe her in. She raises her face toward him. "Ready?" he asks. My sister orders for us. The waiter struts off.

"Tight ass," I say.

"The best," she says.

My scotch tastes good. It reminds me of Deh. Johnny Walker or Seagrams 7, that's what they served at Chinese banquets. Nine courses and a bottle. No ice. We learned to drink it Chinese style, in teacups. Deh drank from his rice bowl, sipping it like hot soup. By the end of the meal, he took it like cool tea, in bold mouthfuls. We sat watching, our teacups in our laps, his three giggly girls.

Relaxed, I'm thinking there's a connection. Johnny Walker then and Johnny Walker now. I ask for another cigarette and this one I enjoy. Now my Johnny Walker pops with ice. I twirl the glass to make the ice tinkle.

We clink glasses. Three times for good luck. She giggles. I feel better.

"Nice sweater," I say.

"Michael Owyang," she says. She laughs. The light from the candle makes her eyes shimmer. She's got Mah's eyes. Eyes that make you want to talk. Lisa is reed-thin and tall. She's got a body that clothes look good on. My sister slips something on, and it wraps her like skin. Fabric has pulse on her.

"Happy birthday, soon," I say.

"Thanks, and to yours too, just as soon."

"Here's to Johnny Walker in shark's fin soup," I say.

"And squab dinners."

"'I Love Lucy,'" I say.

We laugh. It makes us feel like children again. We remember how to be sisters. I raise my glass, "To 'I Love Lucy,' squab dinners, and brown bags."

"To bones," she says.

"Bones," I repeat. This is a funny story that gets sad, and knowing it, I keep laughing. I am surprised how much memory there is in one word. Pigeons. Only recently did I learn they're called squab. Our word for them was pigeon—on a plate or flying over Portsmouth Square. A good meal at forty cents a bird. In line by dawn, we waited at the butcher's listening for the slow churning motor of the trucks. We watched the live fish flushing out of the tanks into the garbage pails. We smelled the honey-crushed cha sui bows baking. When the white laundry truck turned into Wentworth, there was a puffing trail of feathers following it. A stench filled the alley. The crowd squeezed in around the truck. Old ladies reached into the crates, squeezing and tugging for the plumpest pigeons.

My sister and I picked the white ones, those with the most expressive eyes. Dove birds, we called them. We fed them leftover rice in water, and as long as they stayed plump, they were our pets, our baby dove birds. And then one day we'd come home from school and find them cooked. They were a special, nutritious treat. Mah let us fill our bowls high with little pigeon parts: legs, breasts, and wings, and take them out to the front room to watch "I Love Lucy." We took brown bags for the bones. We balanced our bowls on our laps and laughed at Lucy. We leaned forward, our chopsticks crossed in mid-air, and called out, "Mah! Mah! Come watch! Watch Lucy cry!"

But she always sat alone in the kitchen sucking out the sweetness of the lesser parts: necks, backs, and the head. "Bones are sweeter than you know," she always said. She came out to check the bags. "Clean bones," she said, shaking the bags. "No waste," she said.

Our dinners come with a warning. "Plate's hot. Don't touch." My sister orders a carafe of house white. "Enjoy," he says, smiling at my sister. She doesn't look up.

I can't remember how to say scallops in Chinese. I ask my sister, she doesn't know either. The food isn't great. Or maybe we just don't have the taste buds in us to go crazy over it. Sometimes I get very hungry for Chinese flavors: black beans, garlic and ginger, shrimp paste and sesame oil. These are tastes we grew up with, still dream about. Crave. Run around town after. Duck liver sausage, bean curd, jook, salted fish, and fried dace with black beans. Western flavors don't stand out, the surroundings do. Three pronged forks. Pink tablecloths. Fresh flowers. Cute waiters. An odd difference.

"Maybe we should have gone to Sun Hung Heung. At least the vegetables are real," I say.

"Hung toh-yee-foo-won-tun!" she says.

"Yeah, yum!" I say.

I remember Deh teaching us how to pick bok choy, his favorite vegetable. "Stick your fingernail into the stem. Juicy and firm, good. Limp and tough, no good." The three of us followed Deh, punching our thumbnails into every stem of bok choy we saw.

"Deh still eating bok choy?"

"Breakfast, lunch and dinner." My sister throws her head back, and laughs. It is Deh's motion. She recites in a mimic tone. "Your Deh, all he needs is a good hot bowl of rice and a plate full of greens. A good monk."

There was always bok choy. Even though it was nonstop for Mah—rushing to the sweatshop in the morning, out to shop on break, and then home to cook by evening—she did this for him. A plate of bok choy, steaming with the taste of ginger and garlic. He said she made good rice. Timed full-fire until the first boil, medium until the grains formed a crust along the sides of the pot, and then low-flamed to let the rice steam. Firm, that's how Deh liked his rice.

The waiter brings the wine, asks if everything is all right.

"Everything," my sister says.

There's something else about this meeting. I can hear it in the edge of her voice. She doesn't say anything and I don't ask. Her lips make a contorting line; her face looks sour. She lets out a breath. It sounds like she's been holding it in too long.

"Another fight. The bank line," she says. "He waited four times in the bank line. Mah ran around outside shopping. He was doing her a favor. She was doing him a favor. Mah wouldn't stop yelling. 'Get out and go die! Useless Thing! Stinking Corpse!'"

I know he answered. His voice must have had that fortune teller's tone to it. You listened because you knew it was a warning.

He always threatened to disappear, jump off the Golden Gate. His thousand-year-old threat. I've heard it all before. "I will go. Even when dead, I won't be far enough away. Curse the good will that blinded me into taking you as wife!"

I give Lisa some of my scallops. "Eat," I tell her.

She keeps talking. "Of course, you know how Mah thinks, that nobody should complain because she's been the one working all these years."

I nod. I start eating, hoping she'll follow.

One bite and she's talking again. "You know what shopping with Mah is like, either you stand outside with the bags like a servant, or inside like a marker, holding a place in line. You know how she gets into being frugal—saving time because it's the one free thing in her life. Well, they're at the bank and she had him hold her place in line while she runs up and down Stockton doing her quick shopping maneuvers. So he's in line, and it's his turn, but she's not back. So he has to start all over at the back again. Then it's his turn but she's still not back. When she finally comes in, she's got bags in both hands, and he's going through the line for the fourth time. Of course she doesn't say sorry or anything."

I interrupt. "How do you know all this?" I tell myself not to come back next year. I tell myself to apply for another transfer, to the East Coast.

"She told me. Word for word." Lisa spears a scallop, puts it in her mouth. I know it's cold by now. "Word for word," she repeats. She cuts a piece of chicken. "Try," she says.

I think about how we're sisters. We eat slowly, chewing carefully like old people. A way to make things last, to fool the stomach.

Mah and Deh both worked too hard; it's as if their marriage was a marriage of toil—of toiling together. The idea is that the next generation can marry for love.

In the old country, matches were made, strangers were wedded, and that was fate. Those days, sojourners like Deh were considered princes. To become the wife to such a man was to be saved from the war-torn villages.

Saved to work. After dinner, with the rice still in between her teeth, Mah sat down at her Singer. When we pulled out the wall-bed, she was still there, sewing. The street noises stopped long before she did. The hot lamp made all the stitches blur together. And in the mornings, long before any of us awoke, she was already there, sewing again.

His work was hard, too. He ran a laundry on Polk Street. He sailed with the American President Lines. Things started to look up when he owned the take-out place in Vallejo, and then his partner ran off. So he went to Alaska and worked the canneries.

She was good to him, too. We remember. How else would we have known him all those years he worked in Guam, in the Fiji Islands, in Alaska? Mah always gave him majestic welcomes home. It was her excitement that made us remember him.

I look around. The restaurant is full. The waiters move quickly.

I know Deh. His words are ugly. I've heard him. I've listened. And I've always wished for the street noises, as if in the traffic of sound, I believe I can escape. I know the hard color of his eyes and the tightness of his jaw. I can almost hear his teeth grind. I know this. Years of it.

Their lives weren't easy. So is their discontent without reason?

What about the first one? You didn't even think to come to the hospital. The first one, I say! Son or daughter, dead or alive, you didn't even come!

What about living or dying? Which did you want for me that time you pushed me back to work before my back brace was off?

Money! Money! Money to eat with, to buy clothes with, to pass this life with!

Don't start that again! Everything I make at that dead place I hand...

How come...
What about...
So...

It was obvious. The stories themselves mean little. It was how hot and furious they could become.

Is there no end to it? What makes their ugliness so alive, so thick and impossible to let go of?

"I don't want to think about it anymore." The way she says it surprises me. This time I listen. I imagine what it would be like to take her place. It will be my turn one day.

"Ron," she says, wiggling her fingers above the candle. "A fun thing."

The opal flickers above the flame. I tell her that I want to get her something special for her birthday, "...next trip I get abroad." She looks up at me, smiles.

For a minute, my sister seems happy. But she won't be able to hold onto it. She grabs at things out of despair, out of fear. Gifts grow old for her. Emotions never ripen, they sour. Everything slips away from her. Nothing sustains her. Her beauty has made her fragile.

We should have eaten in Chinatown. We could have gone for coffee in North Beach, then for jook at Sam Wo's.

"No work, it's been like that for months, just odd jobs," she says.

I'm thinking, it's not like I haven't done my share. I was a kid once, I did things because I felt I should. I helped fill out forms at the Chinatown employment agencies. I went with him to the Seaman's Union. I waited too, listening and hoping for those calls: "Busboy! Presser! Prep Man!" His bags were packed, he was always ready to go. "On standby," he said.

Every week. All the same. Quitting and looking to start all over again. In the end, it was like never having gone anywhere. It was like the bank line, waiting for nothing.

How many times did my sister and I have to hold them apart? The flat *ting!* sound as the blade slapped onto the linoleum floor, the wooden handle of the knife slamming into the corner. Was it she or I who screamed, repeating all of their ugliest words? Who shook them? Who made them stop?

The waiter comes to take the plates. He stands by my sister for a moment. I raise my glass to the waiter.

"You two Chinese?" he asks.

"No," I say, finishing off my wine. I roll my eyes. I wish I had another Johnny Walker. Suddenly I don't care.

"We're two sisters," I say. I laugh. I ask for the check, leave a good tip. I see him slip my sister a box of matches.

Outside, the air is cool and brisk. My sister links her arm into mine. We walk up Bay onto Chestnut. We pass Galileo High School and then turn down Van Ness to head toward the pier. The bay is black. The foghorns sound far away. We walk the whole length of the pier without talking.

The water is white where it slaps against the wooden stakes.

For a long time Lisa's wanted out. She can stay at that point of endurance forever. Desire that becomes old feels too good, it's seductive. I know how hard it is to go.

The heart never travels. You have to be heartless. My sister holds that heart, too close and for too long. This is her weakness, and I like to think, used to be mine. Lisa endures too much.

We're lucky, not like the bondmaids growing up in service, or the newborn daughters whose mouths were stuffed with ashes. Courtesans with the three-inch feet, beardless, soft-shouldered eunuchs, and the frightened child-brides, they're all stories to us. We're the lucky generation. Our parents forced themselves to live through the humiliation in this country so that we could have it better. We know so little of the old country. We repeat names of Grandfathers and Uncles, but they will always be strangers to us. Family exists only because somebody has a story, and knowing the story connects us to a history. To us, the deformed man is oddly compelling, the forgotten man is a good story. A beautiful woman suffers.

I want her beauty to buy her out.

The sweater cost two weeks pay. Like the forty-cent birds that are now a delicacy, this is a special treat. The money doesn't mean anything. It is, if anything, time. Time is what I would like to give her.

A red sweater. One hundred percent angora. The skin of fuzz will be a fierce rouge on her naked breasts.

Red. Lucky. Wear it. Find that man. The new one. Wrap yourself around him. Feel the pulsing between you. Fuck him and think about it. One hundred percent. Hand Wash Only. Worn Once.

Journal Entry

Respond to the following: "We're a family of three girls. By Chinese standards, that's not lucky. "Too bad," outsiders whisper, "…nothing but daughters. A failed family."

Textual Considerations

1. The author uses irony to reinforce the meaning in "A Red Sweater." One example is the discrepancy between Mah's and the community's expectations when she left Hong Kong and the disappointing reality of her situation on her return thirty years later. Cite at least two other examples of irony and show how they enhance the theme.
2. Analyze the role of the parents. How has their relationship affected each of them? How has it influenced the narrator and Lisa?

3. The red sweater is the dominant symbol in the story. What conscious and unconscious meanings does it acquire?

Cultural Contexts

1. React to the protagonist's statement that "I am surprised how much memory there is in one word." How do her memories contribute to her sense of self? How are they related to the advice she gives Lisa at the end of the story?
2. "We're the lucky generation. Our parents forced themselves to live through the humiliation in this country so we could have it better." Are they, in fact, the lucky ones? Explain. Consider, for example, if the narrator and her sister have a sense of their extended family and if they have experienced a feeling of community in the United States.

William Faulkner
1930

A Rose for Emily

I

When Miss Emily Grierson died, our whole town went to her funeral: the men through a sort of respectful affection for a fallen monument, the women mostly out of curiosity to see the inside of her house, which no one save an old manservant—a combined gardener and cook—had seen in at least ten years.

It was a big, squarish frame house that had once been white, decorated with cupolas and spires and scrolled balconies in the heavily lightsome style of the seventies, set on what had once been our most select street. But garages and cotton gins had encroached and obliterated even the august names of that neighborhood; only Miss Emily's house was left, lifting its stubborn and coquettish decay above the cotton wagons and the gasoline pumps—an eyesore among eyesores. And now Miss Emily had gone to join the representatives of those august names where they lay in the cedar-bemused cemetery among the ranked and anonymous graves of Union and Confederate soldiers who fell at the battle of Jefferson.

Alive, Miss Emily had been a tradition, a duty, and a care; a sort of hereditary obligation upon the town, dating from that day in 1894 when Colonel Sartoris,[1] the mayor—he who fathered the edict that no Negro woman should appear on the

---

[1] A major figure among Faulkner's fictional inhabitants of Yoknapatawpha County.

streets without an apron—remitted her taxes, the dispensation dating from the death of her father on into perpetuity. Not that Miss Emily would have accepted charity. Colonel Sartoris invented an involved tale to the effect that Miss Emily's father had loaned money to the town, which the town, as a matter of business, preferred this way of repaying. Only a man of Colonel Sartoris' generation and thought could have invented it, and only a woman could have believed it.

When the next generation, with its more modern ideas, became mayors and aldermen, this arrangement created some little dissatisfaction. On the first of the year they mailed her a tax notice. February came, and there was no reply. They wrote her a formal letter, asking her to call at the sheriff's office at her convenience. A week later the mayor wrote her himself, offering to call or to send his car for her, and received in reply a note on paper of an archaic shape, in a thin, flowing calligraphy in faded ink, to the effect that she no longer went out at all. The tax notice was also enclosed, without comment.

They called a special meeting of the Board of Aldermen. A deputation waited upon her, knocked at the door through which no visitor had passed since she ceased giving china-painting lessons eight or ten years earlier. They were admitted by the old Negro into a dim hall from which a stairway mounted into still more shadow. It smelled of dust and disuse—a close, dank smell. The Negro led them into the parlor. It was furnished in heavy, leather-covered furniture. When the Negro opened the blinds of one window, a faint dust rose sluggishly about their thighs, spinning with slow motes in the single, sun-ray. On a tarnished gilt easel before the fireplace stood a crayon portrait of Miss Emily's father.

They rose when she entered—a small, fat woman in black, with a thin gold chain descending to her waist and vanishing into her belt, leaning on an ebony cane with a tarnished gold head. Her skeleton was small and spare; perhaps that was why what would have been merely plumpness in another, was obesity in her. She looked bloated, like a body long submerged in motionless water, and of that pallid hue. Her eyes, lost in the fatty ridges of her face, looked like two small pieces of coal pressed into a lump of dough as they moved from one face to another while the visitors stated their errand.

She did not ask them to sit. She just stood in the door and listened quietly until the spokesman came to a stumbling halt. Then they could hear the invisible watch ticking at the end of the gold chain.

Her voice was dry and cold. "I have no taxes in Jefferson. Colonel Sartoris explained it to me. Perhaps one of you can gain access to the city records and satisfy yourselves."

"But we have. We are the city authorities, Miss Emily. Didn't you get a notice from the sheriff, signed by him?"

"I received a paper, yes," Miss Emily said. "Perhaps he considers himself the sheriff.... I have no taxes in Jefferson."

"But there is nothing on the books to show that, you see. We must go by the—"

"See Colonel Sartoris. I have no taxes in Jefferson."

"But, Miss Emily—"

"See Colonel Sartoris." (Colonel Sartoris had been dead almost ten years.) "I have no taxes in Jefferson. Tobe!" The Negro appeared. "Show these gentlemen out."

II

So she vanquished them, horse and foot, just as she had vanquished their fathers thirty years before about the smell. That was two years after her father's death and a short time after her sweetheart—the one we believed would marry her—had deserted her. After her father's death she went out very little; after her sweetheart went away, people hardly saw her at all. A few of the ladies had the temerity to call, but were not received, and the only sign of life about the place was the Negro man—a young man then—going in and out with a market basket.

"Just as if a man—any man—could keep a kitchen properly," the ladies said; so they were not surprised when the smell developed. It was another link between the gross, teeming world and the high and mighty Griersons.

A neighbor, a woman, complained to the mayor, Judge Stevens, eighty years old.

"But what will you have me do about it, madam?" he said.

"Why, send her word to stop it," the woman said. "Isn't there a law?"

"I'm sure that won't be necessary," Judge Stevens said. "It's probably just a snake or a rat that nigger of hers killed in the yard. I'll speak to him about it."

The next day he received two more complaints, one from a man who came in diffident deprecation. "We really must do something about it, Judge. I'd be the last one in the world to bother Miss Emily, but we've got to do something." That night the Board of Aldermen met—three gray-beards and one younger man, a member of the rising generation.

"It's simple enough," he said. "Send her word to have her place cleaned up. Give her a certain time to do it in, and if she don't…"

"Dammit, sir," Judge Stevens said, "will you accuse a lady to her face of smelling bad?"

So the next night, after midnight, four men crossed Miss Emily's lawn and slunk about the house like burglars, sniffing along the base of the brickwork and at the cellar openings while one of them performed a regular sowing motion with his hand out of a sack slung from his shoulder. They broke open the cellar door and sprinkled lime there, and in all the outbuildings. As they recrossed the lawn, a window that had been dark was lighted and Miss Emily sat in it, the light behind her, and her upright torso motionless as that of an idol. They crept quietly across the lawn and into the shadow of the locusts that lined the street. After a week or two the smell went away.

That was when people had begun to feel really sorry for her. People in our town, remembering how old lady Wyatt, her great-aunt, had gone completely crazy at last, believed that the Griersons held themselves a little too high for what they really were. None of the young men were quite good enough for Miss Emily and such. We had long thought of them as a tableau; Miss Emily a slender figure in white in the background, her father a spraddled silhouette in the foreground, his back to her and clutching a horsewhip,[2] the two of them framed by the back-flung front door. So when she got to be thirty and was still single, we were not pleased exactly, but vindicated; even with insanity in the family she wouldn't have turned down all of her chances if they had really materialized.

When her father died, it got about that the house was all that was left to her; and in a way, people were glad. At last they could pity Miss Emily. Being left alone, and a pauper, she had become humanized. Now she too would know the old thrill and the old despair of a penny more or less.

The day after his death all the ladies prepared to call at the house and offer condolence and aid, as is our custom. Miss Emily met them at the door, dressed as usual and with no trace of grief on her face. She told them that her father was not dead. She did that for three days, with the ministers calling on her, and the doctors, trying to persuade her to let them dispose of the body. Just as they were about to resort to law and force, she broke down, and they buried her father quickly.

We did not say she was crazy then. We believed she had to do that. We remembered all the young men her father had driven away, and we knew that with nothing left, she would have to cling to that which had robbed her, as people will.

III

She was sick for a long time. When we saw her again, her hair was cut short, making her look like a girl, with a vague resemblance to those angels in colored church windows—sort of tragic and serene.

The town had just let the contracts for paving the sidewalks, and in the summer after her father's death they began to work. The construction company came with niggers and mules and machinery, and a foreman named Homer Barron, a Yankee—a big, dark, ready man, with a big voice and eyes lighter than his face. The little boys would follow in groups to hear him cuss the niggers, and the niggers singing in time to the rise and fall of picks. Pretty soon he knew everybody in town. Whenever you heard a lot of laughing anywhere about the square, Homer Barron would be in the center of the group. Presently we began to see him and Miss Emily on Sunday afternoons driving in the yellow-wheeled buggy and the matched team of bays from the livery stable.

At first we were glad that Miss Emily would have an interest, because the ladies all said, "Of course a Grierson would not think seriously of a Northerner, a day laborer." But there were still others, older people, who said that even grief could not cause a real lady to forget *noblesse oblige*[3]—without calling it *noblesse oblige*. They just said, "Poor Emily. Her kinsfolk should come to her." She had some kin in Alabama; but years ago her father had fallen out with them over the estate of old lady Wyatt, the crazy woman, and there was no communication between the two families. They had not even been represented at the funeral.

---

[2] The horsewhip was the legendary weapon used by American fathers to protect their daughters from unwelcome suitors.

[3] The obligations of the upper class.

And as soon as the old people said, "Poor Emily," the whispering began. "Do you suppose it's really so?" they said to one another. "Of course it is. What else could…" This behind their hands; rustling of craned silk and satin behind jalousies closed upon the sun of Sunday afternoon as the thin, swift clop-clop-clop of the matched team passed: "Poor Emily."

She carried her head high enough—even when we believed that she was fallen. It was as if she demanded more than ever the recognition of her dignity as the last Grierson; as if it had wanted that touch of earthiness to reaffirm her imperviousness. Like when she bought the rat poison, the arsenic. That was over a year after they had begun to say "Poor Emily," and while the two female cousins were visiting her.

"I want some poison," she said to the druggist. She was over thirty then, still a slight woman, though thinner than usual, with cold, haughty black eyes in a face the flesh of which was strained across the temples and about the eyesockets as you imagine a lighthouse-keeper's face ought to look. "I want some poison," she said.

"Yes, Miss Emily. What kind? For rats and such? I'd recom—"

"I want the best you have. I don't care what kind."

The druggist named several. "They'll kill anything up to an elephant. But what you want is—"

"Arsenic," Miss Emily, said. "Is that a good one?"

"Is…arsenic? Yes ma'am. But what you want—"

"I want arsenic."

The druggist looked down at her. She looked back at him, erect, her face like a strained flag. "Why, of course," the druggist said. "If that's what you want. But the law requires you to tell what you are going to use it for."

Miss Emily just stared at him, her head tilted back in order to look him eye for eye, until he looked away and went and got the arsenic and wrapped it up. The Negro delivery boy brought her the package; the druggist didn't come back. When she opened the package at home there was written on the box, under the skull and bones: "For rats."

IV

So the next day we all said, "She will kill herself"; and we said it would be the best thing. When she had first begun to be seen with Homer Barron, we had said, "She will marry him." Then we said, "She will persuade him yet," because Homer himself had remarked—he liked men, and it was known that he drank with the younger men in the Elk's Club—that he was not a marrying man. Later we said, "Poor Emily," behind the jalousies as they passed on Sunday afternoon in the glittering buggy, Miss Emily with her head high and Homer Barron with his hat cocked and a cigar in his teeth, reins and whip in a yellow glove.

Then some of the ladies began to say that it was a disgrace to the town and a bad example to the young people. The men did not want to interfere, but at last the ladies forced the Baptist minister—Miss Emily's people were Episcopal—to call upon her. He would never divulge what happened during that interview, but he refused to go back again. The next Sunday they again drove about the streets, and the following day the minister's wife wrote to Miss Emily's relations in Alabama.

So she had blood-kin under her roof again and we sat back to watch developments. At first nothing happened. Then we were sure that they were to be married. We learned that Miss Emily had been to the jeweler's and ordered a man's toilet set in silver, with the letters H. B. on each piece. Two days later we learned that she had bought a complete outfit of men's clothing, including a nightshirt, and we said, "They are married." We were really glad. We were glad because the two female cousins were even more Grierson than Miss Emily had ever been.

So we were not surprised when Homer Barron—the streets had been finished some time since—was gone. We were a little disappointed that there was not a public blowing-off, but we believed that he had gone on to prepare for Miss Emily's coming, or to give her a chance to get rid of the cousins. (By that time it was a cabal, and we were all Miss Emily's allies to help circumvent the cousins.) Sure enough, after another week they departed. And, as we had expected all along, within three days Homer Barron was back in town. A neighbor saw the Negro man admit him at the kitchen door at dusk one evening.

And that was the last we saw of Homer Barron. And of Miss Emily for some time. The Negro man went in and out with the market basket, but the front door remained closed. Now and then we would see her at a window for a moment, as the men did that night when they sprinkled the lime, but for almost six months she did not appear on the streets. Then we knew that this was to be expected too; as if that quality of her father which had thwarted her woman's life so many times had been too virulent and too furious to die.

When we next saw Miss Emily, she had grown fat and her hair was turning gray. During the next few years it grew grayer and grayer until it attained an even pepper-and-salt iron-gray, when it ceased turning. Up to the day of her death at seventy-four it was still that vigorous iron-gray, like the hair of an active man.

From that time on her front door remained closed, save for a period of six or seven years, when she was about forty, during which she gave lessons in china-painting. She fitted up a studio in one of the downstairs rooms, where the daughters and granddaughters of Colonel Sartoris' contemporaries were sent to her with the same regularity and in the same spirit that they were sent on Sundays with a twenty-five cent piece for the collection plate. Meanwhile her taxes had been remitted.

Then the newer generation became the backbone and the spirit of the town, and the painting pupils grew up and fell away and did not send their children to her with boxes of color and tedious brushes and pictures cut from the ladies' magazines. The front door closed upon the last one and remained closed for good. When the town got free postal delivery Miss Emily alone refused to let them fasten the metal numbers above her door and attach a mailbox to it. She would not listen to them.

Daily, monthly, yearly we watched the Negro grow grayer and more stooped, going in and out with the market basket. Each December we sent her a tax notice, which would be returned by the post office a week later, unclaimed. Now and then we would see her in one of the downstairs windows—she had evidently shut up the top floor of the house—like the carven torso of an idol in a niche, looking or not looking at us, we could never tell which. Thus she passed from generation to generation—dear, inescapable, impervious, tranquil, and perverse.

And so she died. Fell ill in the house filled with dust and shadows, with only a doddering Negro man to wait on her. We did not even know she was sick; we had long since given up trying to get any information from the Negro. He talked to no one, probably not even to her, for his voice had grown harsh and rusty, as if from disuse.

She died in one of the downstairs rooms, in a heavy walnut bed with a curtain, her gray head propped on a pillow yellow and moldy with age and lack of sunlight.

V

The Negro met the first of the ladies at the front door and let them in, with their hushed, sibilant voices and their quick, curious glances, and then he disappeared. He walked right through the house and out the back and was not seen again.

The two female cousins came at once. They held the funeral on the second day, with the town coming to look at Miss Emily beneath a mass of bought flowers, with the crayon face of her father musing profoundly above the bier and the ladies sibilant and macabre; and the very old men—some in their brushed Confederate uniforms—on the porch and the lawn, talking of Miss Emily as if she had been a contemporary of theirs, believing that they had danced with her and courted her perhaps, confusing time with its mathematical progression, as the old do, to whom all the past is not a diminishing road, but, instead, a huge meadow which no winter ever quite touches, divided from them now by the narrow bottleneck, of the most recent decade of years.

Already we knew that there was one room in that region above stairs which no one had seen in forty years, and which would have to be forced. They waited until Miss Emily was decently in the ground before they opened it.

The violence of breaking down the door seemed to fill this room with pervading dust. A thin, acrid pall as of the tomb seemed to lie everywhere upon this room decked and furnished as for a bridal: upon the valance curtains of faded rose color, upon the rose-shaded lights, upon the dressing table, upon the delicate array of crystal and the man's toilet things backed with tarnished silver, silver so tarnished that the monogram was obscured. Among them lay a collar and tie, as if they had just been removed, which, lifted, left upon the surface a pale crescent in the dust. Upon a chair hung the suit, carefully folded; beneath it the two mute shoes and the discarded socks.

The man himself lay in the bed.

For a long while we just stood there, looking down at the profound and flesh-less grin. The body had apparently once lain in the attitude of an embrace, but now the long sleep that outlasts love, that conquers even the grimace of love, had cuck-olded him. What was left of him, rotted beneath what was left of the nightshirt, had become inextricable from the bed in which he lay; and upon him and upon the pillow beside him lay that even coating of the patient and biding dust.

Then we noticed that in the second pillow was the indentation of a head. One of us lifted something from it, and leaning forward, that faint and invisible dust dry and acrid in the nostrils, we saw a long strand of iron-gray hair.

Journal Entry

What is meant by the title "A Rose for Emily"?

Textual Considerations

1. Several characters influence Miss Emily's actions. Analyze her father's affect on her life. What kind of person is Homer? What is his role in the story? Why does Miss Emily's servant stay with her so faithfully during her life and leave so abruptly after her death?
2. Symbols of decay abound in the story. Identify at least three. How far has Emily Grierson, the "fallen monument," actually fallen? What does the last line mean?
3. This story is a series of character glimpses that when put together create a montage of the life of Emily Grierson. How does the author move from one scene to another? What effect is achieved by his disjointed chronology? What, for instance, would have happened had he begun at the beginning and moved in chronological sequence to the end? Recreate the actual sequence of events.

Cultural Contexts

1. Characterize the narrator and the townspeople. How do they regard the Grierson family? What is Miss Emily's attitude toward them? Why does Faulkner tell the story through the eyes of an anonymous townsperson?
2. Discuss with your group Faulkner's purpose in writing this story. Is there a philosophical, social, or moral theme? How important to the theme is the setting of the story? Miss Emily's position in the town? The passage of time?

Albert Camus
1957

The Guest

The schoolmaster was watching the two men climb toward him. One was on horseback, the other on foot. They had not yet tackled the abrupt rise leading to the schoolhouse built on the hillside. They were toiling onward, making slow progress in the snow, among the stones, on the vast expanse of the high, deserted plateau. From time to time the horse stumbled. Without hearing anything yet, he could see the breath issuing from the horse's nostrils. One of the men, at least, knew the region. They were following the trail although it had disappeared days ago under a layer of dirty white snow. The schoolmaster calculated that it would take them half an hour to get onto the hill. It was cold; he went back into the school to get a sweater.

He crossed the empty, frigid classroom. On the blackboard the four rivers of France, drawn with four different colored chalks, had been flowing toward their estuaries for the past three days. Snow had suddenly fallen in mid-October after eight months of drought without the transition of rain, and the twenty pupils, more or less, who lived in the villages scattered over the plateau had stopped coming. With fair weather they would return. Daru now heated only the single room that was his lodging, adjoining the classroom and giving also onto the plateau to the east. Like the class windows, his window looked to the south too. On that side the school was a few kilometers from the point where the plateau began to slope toward the south. In clear weather could be seen the purple mass of the mountain range where the gap opened onto the desert.

Somewhat warmed, Daru returned to the window from which he had first seen the two men. They were no longer visible. Hence they must have tackled the rise. The sky was not so dark, for the snow had stopped falling during the night. The morning had opened with a dirty light which had scarcely become brighter as the ceiling of clouds lifted. At two in the afternoon it seemed as if the day were merely beginning. But still this was better than those three days when the thick snow was falling amidst unbroken darkness with little gusts of wind that rattled the double door of the classroom. Then Daru had spent long hours in his room, leaving it only to go to the shed and feed the chickens or get some coal. Fortunately the delivery truck from Tadjid, the nearest village to the north, had brought his supplies two days before the blizzard. It would return in forty-eight hours.

Besides, he had enough to resist a siege, for the little room was cluttered with bags of wheat that the administration left as a stock to distribute to those of his pupils whose families had suffered from the drought. Actually they had all been victims because they were all poor. Every day Daru would distribute a ration to the children. They had missed it, he knew, during these bad days. Possibly one of the fathers or big brothers would come this afternoon and he could supply them with grain. It was just a matter of carrying them over to the next harvest. Now shiploads of wheat were arriving from France and the worst was over. But it would be hard to forget that poverty, that army of ragged ghosts wandering in the sunlight, the plateaus burned to a cinder month after month, the earth shriveled up little by little, literally scorched, every stone bursting into dust under one's foot. The sheep had died then by thousands and even a few men, here and there, sometimes without anyone's knowing.

In contrast with such poverty, he who lived almost like a monk in his remote schoolhouse, nonetheless satisfied with the little he had and with the rough life, had felt like a lord with his white-washed walls, his narrow couch, his unpainted shelves, his well, and his provision of water and food. And suddenly this snow, without warning, without the foretaste of rain. This is the way the region was, cruel to live in, even without men—who didn't help matters either. But Daru had been born here. Everywhere else, he felt exiled.

He stepped out onto the terrace in front of the schoolhouse. The two men were now halfway up the slope. He recognized the horseman as Balducci, the old gendarme he had known for a long time. Balducci was holding on the end of a rope an Arab who was walking behind him with hands bound and head lowered. The gendarme waved a greeting to which Daru did not reply, lost as he was in contemplation of the Arab dressed in a faded blue jellaba, his feet in sandals but covered with socks of heavy raw wool, his head surmounted by a narrow, short *chèche*. They were approaching. Balducci was holding back his horse in order not to hurt the Arab and the group was advancing slowly.

Within earshot, Balducci shouted: "One hour to do the three kilometers from El Ameur!" Daru did not answer. Short and square in his thick sweater, he watched them climb. Not once had the Arab raised his head. "Hello," said Daru when they got up onto the terrace. "Come in and warm up." Balducci painfully got down from his horse without letting go the rope. From under his bristling mustache he smiled at the schoolmaster. His little dark eyes, deep-set under a tanned forehead, and his mouth surrounded with wrinkles made him look attentive and studious. Daru took the bridle, led the horse to the shed, and came back to the two men, who were now waiting for him in the school. He led them into his room. "I am going to heat up the classroom," he said. "We'll be more comfortable there." When he entered the room again, Balducci was on the couch. He had undone the rope tying him to the Arab, who had squatted near the stove. His hands still bound, the *chèche* pushed back on his head, he was looking toward the window. At first Daru noticed only his huge lips, fat, smooth, almost Negroid; yet his nose was straight, his eyes were dark and full of fever. The *chèche* revealed an obstinate forehead and, under the weathered skin now rather discolored by the cold, the whole face had a restless and rebellious look that struck Daru when the Arab, turning his face toward him, looked him straight in the eyes. "Go into the other room," said the schoolmaster, "and I'll make you some mint tea." "Thanks," Balducci said. "What a chore! How I long for retirement." And addressing his prisoner in Arabic: "Come on, you." The Arab got up and, slowly, holding his bound wrists in front of him, went into the classroom.

With the tea, Daru brought a chair. But Balducci was already enthroned on the nearest pupil's desk and the Arab had squatted against the teacher's platform facing the stove, which stood between the desk and the window. When he held out the glass of tea to the prisoner, Daru hesitated at the sight of his bound hands. "He might perhaps be untied." "Sure," said Balducci. "That was for the trip." He started to get to his feet. But Daru, setting the glass on the floor, had knelt beside the Arab. Without saying anything, the Arab watched him with his feverish eyes. Once his hands were free, he rubbed his swollen wrists against each other, took the glass of tea, and sucked up the burning liquid in swift little sips.

"Good," said Daru. "And where are you headed?"

Balducci withdrew his mustache from the tea. "Here, son."

"Odd pupils! And you're spending the night?"

"No. I'm going back to El Ameur. And you will deliver this fellow to Tinguit. He is expected at police headquarters."

Balducci was looking at Daru with a friendly little smile.

"What's this story?" asked the schoolmaster. "Are you pulling my leg?"

"No, son. Those are the orders."

"The orders? I'm not…" Daru hesitated, not wanting to hurt the old Corsican. "I mean, that's not my job."

"What! What's the meaning of that? In wartime people do all kinds of jobs."

"Then I'll wait for the declaration of war!"

Balducci nodded.

"O.K. But the orders exist and they concern you too. Things are brewing, it appears. There is talk of a forthcoming revolt. We are mobilized, in a way."

Daru still had his obstinate look.

"Listen, son," Balducci said. "I like you and you must understand. There's only a dozen of us at El Ameur to patrol throughout the whole territory of a small department and I must get back in a hurry. I was told to hand this guy over to you and return without delay. He couldn't be kept there. His village was beginning to stir; they wanted to take him back. You must take him to Tanguit tomorrow before the day is over. Twenty kilometers shouldn't faze a husky fellow like you. After that, all will be over. You'll come back to your pupils and your comfortable life."

Behind the wall the horse could be heard snorting and pawing the earth. Daru was looking out the window. Decidedly, the weather was clearing and the light was increasing over the snowy plateau. When all the snow was melted, the sun would take over again and once more would burn the fields of stone. For days, still, the unchanging sky would shed its dry light on the solitary expanse where nothing had any connection with man.

"After all," he said, turning around toward Balducci, "what did he do?" And, before the gendarme had opened his mouth, he asked: "Does he speak French?"

"No, not a word. We had been looking for him for a month, but they were hiding him. He killed his cousin."

"Is he against us?"

"I don't think so. But you can never be sure."

"Why did he kill?"

"A family squabble, I think. One owed the other grain, it seems. It's not at all clear. In short, he killed his cousin with a billhook. You know, like a sheep, *kreezk!*"

Balducci made the gesture of drawing a blade across his throat and the Arab, his attention attracted, watched him with a sort of anxiety. Daru felt a sudden wrath against the man, against all men with their rotten spite, their tireless hates, their blood lust.

But the kettle was singing on the stove. He served Balducci more tea, hesitated, then served the Arab again, who, a second time, drank avidly. His raised arms made the jellaba fall open and the schoolmaster saw his thin, muscular chest.

"Thanks, kid," Balducci said. "And now, I'm off."

He got up and went toward the Arab, taking a small rope from his pocket.

"What are you doing?" Daru asked dryly.

Balducci, disconcerted, showed him the rope.

"Don't bother."

The old gendarme hesitated. "It's up to you. Of course, you are armed?"

"I have my shotgun."

"Where?"

"In the trunk."

"You ought to have it near your bed."

"Why? I have nothing to fear."

"You're crazy, son. If there's an uprising, no one is safe, we're all in the same boat."

"I'll defend myself. I'll have time to see them coming."

Balducci began to laugh, then suddenly the mustache covered the white teeth.

"You'll have time? O.K. That's just what I was saying. You have always been a little cracked. That's why I like you, my son was like that."

At the same time he took out his revolver and put it on the desk.

"Keep it; I don't need two weapons from here to El Ameur."

The revolver shone against the black paint of the table. When the gendarme turned toward him, the schoolmaster caught the smell of leather and horseflesh.

"Listen, Balducci," Daru said suddenly, "every bit of this disgusts me, and first of all your fellow here. But I won't hand him over. Fight, yes, if I have to. But not that."

The old gendarme stood in front of him and looked at him severely.

"You're being a fool," he said slowly. "I don't like it either. You don't get used to putting a rope on a man even after years of it, and you're even ashamed—yes, ashamed. But you can't let them have their way."

"I won't hand him over," Daru said again.

"It's an order, son, and I repeat it."

"That's right. Repeat to them what I've said to you: I won't hand him over."

Balducci made a visible effort to reflect. He looked at the Arab and at Daru. At last he decided.

"No, I won't tell them anything. If you want to drop us, go ahead; I'll not denounce you. I have an order to deliver the prisoner and I'm doing so. And now you'll just sign this paper for me."

"There's no need. I'll not deny that you left him with me."

"Don't be mean with me. I know you'll tell the truth. You're from hereabouts and you are a man. But you must sign, that's the rule."

Daru opened his drawer, took out a little square bottle of purple ink, the red wooden penholder with the "sergeant-major" pen he used for making models of penmanship, and signed. The gendarme carefully folded the paper and put it into his wallet. Then he moved toward the door.

"I'll see you off," Daru said.

"No," said Balducci. "There's no use being polite. You insulted me."

He looked at the Arab, motionless in the same spot, sniffed peevishly, and turned away toward the door. "Good-by, son," he said. The door shut behind him. Balducci appeared suddenly outside the window and then disappeared. His footsteps were muffled by the snow. The house stirred on the other side of the wall and several chickens fluttered in fright. A moment later Balducci reappeared outside the window leading the horse by the bridle. He walked toward the little rise without turning around and disappeared from sight with the horse following him. A big stone could be heard bouncing down. Daru walked back toward the prisoner, who, without stirring, never took his eyes off him. "Wait," the schoolmaster said in Arabic and went toward the bedroom. As he was going through the door, he had a second thought, went to the desk, took the revolver, and stuck it in his pocket. Then, without looking back, he went into his room.

For some time he lay on his couch watching the sky gradually close over, listening to the silence. It was this silence that had seemed painful to him during the first days here, after the war. He had requested a post in the little town at the base of the foothills separating the upper plateaus from the desert. There, rocky walls, green and black to the north, pink and lavender to the south, marked the frontier of eternal summer. He had been named to a post farther north, on the plateau itself. In the beginning, the solitude and the silence had been hard for him on those wastelands peopled only by stones. Occasionally, furrows suggested cultivation, but they had been dug to uncover a certain kind of stone good for building. The only plowing here was to harvest rocks. Elsewhere a thin layer of soil accumulated in the hollows would be scraped out to enrich paltry village gardens. This is the way it was: bare rock covered three quarters of the region. Towns sprang up, flourished, then disappeared; men came by, loved one another or fought bitterly, then died. No one in this desert, neither he nor his guest, mattered. And yet, outside this desert neither of them, Daru knew, could have really lived.

When he got up, no noise came from the classroom. He was amazed at the unmixed joy he derived from the mere thought that the Arab might have fled and that he would be alone with no decision to make. But the prisoner was there. He had merely stretched out between the stove and the desk. With eyes open, he was staring at the ceiling. In that position, his thick lips were particularly noticeable, giving him a pouting look. "Come," said Daru. The Arab got up and followed him. In the bedroom, the schoolmaster pointed to a chair near the table under the window. The Arab sat down without taking his eyes off Daru.

"Are you hungry?"

"Yes," the prisoner said.

Daru set the table for two. He took flour and oil, shaped a cake in a frying-pan, and lighted the little stove that functioned on bottled gas. While the cake was cooking, he went out to the shed to get cheese, eggs, dates, and condensed milk. When the cake was done he set it on the window sill to cool, heated some condensed milk diluted with water, and beat up the eggs into an omelette. In one of his motions he knocked against the revolver stuck in his right pocket. He set the bowl down, went into the classroom, and put the revolver in his desk drawer. When he came back to the room, night was falling. He put on the light and served the Arab. "Eat," he said. The Arab took a piece of the cake, lifted it eagerly to his mouth, and stopped short.

"And you?" he asked.

"After you. I'll eat too."

The thick lips opened slightly. The Arab hesitated, then bit into the cake determinedly.

The meal over, the Arab looked at the schoolmaster. "Are you the judge?"

"No, I'm simply keeping you until tomorrow."

"Why do you eat with me?"

"I'm hungry."

The Arab fell silent. Daru got up and went out. He brought back a folding bed from the shed, set it up between the table and the stove, perpendicular to his own bed. From a large suitcase which, upright in a corner, served as a shelf for papers, he took two blankets and arranged them on the camp bed. Then he stopped, felt useless, and sat down on his bed. There was nothing more to do or to get ready. He had to look at this man. He looked at him, therefore, trying to imagine his face bursting with rage. He couldn't do so. He could see nothing but the dark yet shining eyes and the animal mouth.

"Why did you kill him?" he asked in a voice whose hostile tone surprised him.

The Arab looked away.

"He ran away. I ran after him."

He raised his eyes to Daru again and they were full of a sort of woeful interrogation. "Now what will they do to me?"

"Are you afraid?"

He stiffened, turning his eyes away.

"Are you sorry?"

The Arab stared at him openmouthed. Obviously he did not understand. Daru's annoyance was growing. At the same time he felt awkward and self-conscious with his big body wedged between the two beds.

"Lie down there," he said impatiently. "That's your bed."

The Arab didn't move. He called to Daru:

"Tell me!"

The schoolmaster looked at him.

"Is the gendarme coming back tomorrow?"

"I don't know."

"Are you coming with us?"

"I don't know. Why?"

The prisoner got up and stretched out on top of the blankets, his feet toward the window. The light from the electric bulb shone straight into his eyes and he closed them at once.

"Why?" Daru repeated, standing beside the bed,

The Arab opened his eyes under the blinding light and looked at him, trying not to blink.

"Come with us," he said.

In the middle of the night, Daru was still not asleep. He had gone to bed after undressing completely; he generally slept naked. But when he suddenly realized that he had nothing on, he hesitated. He felt vulnerable and the temptation came to him to put his clothes back on. Then he shrugged his shoulders; after all, he wasn't a child and, if need be, he could break his adversary in two. From his bed he could observe him, lying on his back, still motionless with his eyes closed under the harsh light. When Daru turned out the light, the darkness seemed to coagulate all of a sudden. Little by little, the night came back to life in the window where the starless sky was stirring gently. The schoolmaster soon made out the body lying at his feet. The Arab still did not move, but his eyes seemed open. A faint wind was prowling around the schoolhouse. Perhaps it would drive away the clouds and the sun would reappear.

During the night the wind increased. The hens fluttered a little and then were silent. The Arab turned over on his side with his back to Daru, who thought he heard him moan. Then he listened for his guest's breathing; it became heavier and more regular. He listened to that breath so close to him and mused without being able to go to sleep. In this room where he had been sleeping alone for a year, this presence bothered him. But it bothered him also by imposing on him a sort of brotherhood he knew well but refused to accept in the present circumstances. Men who share the same rooms, soldiers or prisoners, develop a strange alliance as if, having cast off their armor with their clothing, they fraternized every evening, over and above their differences, in the ancient community of dream and fatigue. But Daru shook himself; he didn't like such musings, and it was essential to sleep.

A little later, however, when the Arab stirred slightly, the schoolmaster was still not asleep. When the prisoner made a second move, he stiffened, on the alert. The Arab was lifting himself slowly on his arms with almost the motion of a sleepwalker. Seated upright in bed, he waited motionless without turning his head toward Daru, as if he were listening attentively. Daru did not stir; it had just occurred to him that the revolver was still in the drawer of his desk. It was better to act at once. Yet he continued to observe the prisoner, who, with the same slithery motion, put his feet on the ground, waited again, then began to stand up slowly. Daru was about to call out to him when the Arab began to walk, in a quite natural but extraordinarily silent way. He was heading toward the door at the end of the room that opened into the shed. He lifted the latch with precaution and went out, pushing the door behind him but without shutting it. Daru had not stirred. "He is running away," he merely thought. "Good riddance!" Yet he listened attentively. The hens were not fluttering; the guest must be on the plateau. A faint sound of water reached him, and he didn't know what it was until the Arab again stood framed in the doorway, closed the door carefully, and came back to bed without a sound. Then Daru turned his back on him and fell asleep. Still later he seemed, from the depths of his sleep, to hear furtive steps around the schoolhouse. "I'm dreaming! I'm dreaming!" he repeated to himself. And he went on sleeping. When he awoke, the sky was clear; the loose window let in a cold, pure air. The Arab was asleep, hunched up under the blankets now, his mouth open, utterly relaxed. But when Daru shook him, he started dreadfully, staring at Daru with wild eyes as if he had never seen him and such a frightened expression that the schoolmaster stepped back. "Don't be afraid. It's me. You must eat." The Arab nodded his head and said yes. Calm had returned to his face, but his expression was vacant and listless.

The coffee was ready. They drank it together on the folding bed as they munched their pieces of the cake. Then Daru led the Arab under the shed and showed him the faucet where he washed. He went back into the room, folded the blankets and the bed, made his own bed and put the room in order. Then he went through the classroom and out onto the terrace. The sun was already rising in the blue sky; a soft, bright light was bathing the deserted plateau. On the ridge the snow was melting in spots. The stones were about to reappear. Crouched on the edge of the plateau, the schoolmaster looked at the deserted expanse. He thought of Balducci. He had hurt him, for he had sent him off in a way as if he didn't want to be associated with him. He could still hear the gendarme's farewell and, without knowing why, he felt strangely empty and vulnerable. At that moment, from the other side of the schoolhouse, the prisoner coughed. Daru listened to him almost despite himself and then, furious, threw a pebble that whistled through the air before sinking in the snow. That man's stupid crime revolted him, but to hand him over was contrary to honor. Merely thinking of it made him smart with humiliation. And he cursed at one and the same time his own people who had sent him this Arab and the Arab too who had dared to kill and not managed to get away. Daru got up, walked in a circle on the terrace, waited motionless, and then went back into the schoolhouse.

The Arab, leaning over the cement floor of the shed, was washing his teeth with two fingers. Daru looked at him and said: "Come." He went back into the room ahead of the prisoner. He slipped a hunting-jacket on over his sweater and put on walking-shoes. Standing, he waited until the Arab had put on his *chèche* and sandals. They went into the classroom and the schoolmaster pointed to the exit, saying: "Go head." The fellow didn't budge. "I'm coming," said Daru. The Arab went out. Daru went back into the room and made a package of pieces of rusk, dates, and sugar. In the classroom, before going out, he hesitated a second in front of his desk, then crossed the threshold and locked the door. "That's the way," he said. He started toward the east, followed by the prisoner. But, a short distance from the schoolhouse, he thought he heard a slight sound behind them. He retraced his steps and examined the surroundings of the house; there was no one there. The Arab watched him without seeming to understand. "Come on," said Daru.

They walked for an hour and rested beside a sharp peak of limestone. The snow was melting faster and faster and the sun was drinking up the puddles at once, rapidly cleaning the plateau, which gradually dried and vibrated like the air itself. When they resumed walking, the ground rang under their feet. From time to time a bird rent the space in front of them with a joyful cry. Daru breathed in deeply the fresh morning light. He felt a sort of rapture before the vast familiar expanse, now almost entirely yellow under its dome of blue sky. They walked an hour more, descending toward the south. They reached a level height made up of crumbly rocks. From there on, the plateau sloped down, eastward, toward a low plain where there were a few spindly trees and, to the south, toward outcroppings of rock that gave the landscape a chaotic look.

Daru surveyed the two directions. There was nothing but the sky on the horizon. Not a man could be seen. He turned toward the Arab, who was looking at him blankly. Daru held out the package to him. "Take it," he said. "There are dates, bread, and sugar. You can hold out for two days. Here are a thousand francs too." The Arab took the package and the money but kept his full hands at chest level as if he didn't know what to do with what was being given him. "Now look," the schoolmaster said as he pointed in the direction of the east, "there's the way to Tinguit. You have a two-hour walk. At Tinguit you'll find the administration and the police. They are expecting you." The Arab looked toward the east, still holding the package and the money against his chest. Daru took his elbow and turned him rather roughly toward the south. At the foot of the height on which they stood could be seen a faint path. "That's the trail across the plateau. In a day's walk from here you'll find pasturelands and the first nomads. They'll take you in and shelter you according to their law." The Arab had now turned toward Daru and a sort of panic was visible in his expression. "Listen," he said. Daru shook his head: "No, be quiet. Now I'm leaving you." He turned his back on him, took two long steps in the direction of the school, looked hesitantly at the motionless Arab, and started off again. For a few minutes he heard nothing but his own step resounding on the cold ground and did not turn his head. A moment later, however, he turned around. The Arab was still there on the edge of the hill, his arms hanging now, and he was looking at the schoolmaster. Daru felt something rise in his throat. But he swore with impatience, waved vaguely, and started off again. He had already gone some distance when he again stopped and looked. There was no longer anyone on the hill.

Daru hesitated. The sun was now rather high in the sky and was beginning to beat down on his head. The schoolmaster retraced his steps, at first somewhat uncertainly, then with decision. When he reached the little hill, he was bathed in sweat. He climbed it as fast as he could and stopped, out of breath, at the top. The rock-fields to the south stood out sharply against the blue sky, but on the plain to the east a steamy heat was already rising. And in that slight haze, Daru, with heavy heart, made out the Arab walking slowly on the road to prison.

A little later, standing before the window of the classroom, the schoolmaster was watching the clear light bathing the whole surface of the plateau, but he hardly saw it. Behind him on the blackboard, among the winding French rivers, sprawled the clumsily chalked-up words he had just read: "You handed over our brother. You will pay for this." Daru looked at the sky, the plateau, and, beyond, the invisible lands stretching all the way to the sea. In this vast landscape he had loved so much, he was alone.

Translated by Justin O'Brien

Journal Entry

Respond to Daru's choice to live apart from society.

Textual Considerations

1. The narrator describes this part of Algeria as "cruel to live in." What details reinforce this description? Why doesn't Daru leave? Where in the story does he indicate his attitude toward the land?
2. What does Daru think of humanity? What connection is there between his attitude toward people and his profession?
3. Describe the relationship between Balducci and Daru. To what extent are they foils to each other?

4. Daru, the French Algerian, must play host to an Arab. How does he behave toward his guest? How does the guest respond to the host?
5. To what extent do we see the action through Daru's eyes? Do we enter the mind of any character other than Daru? Could the story have been written in the first person? What different effect would a first-person narration create?

Cultural Contexts

1. "That stupid man's crime revolted him, but to hand him over was contrary to honor." Why does Daru's philosophy make it dishonorable to turn in a murderer? What is your response to such a philosophy?
2. Why does Daru give the Arab a choice, rather than setting him on the path to freedom? Why does Daru observe the Arab's choice with "heavy heart"? What is your response? What irony is implicit in the last paragraph?

Chinua Achebe
1972

Dead Men's Path

Michael Obi's hopes were fulfilled much earlier than he had expected. He was appointed headmaster of Ndume Central School in January 1949. It had always been an unprogressive school, so the Mission authorities decided to send a young and energetic man to run it. Obi accepted this responsibility with enthusiasm. He had many wonderful ideas and this was an opportunity to put them into practice. He had had sound secondary school education which designated him a "pivotal teacher" in the official records and set him apart from the other headmasters in the mission field. He was outspoken in his condemnation of the narrow views of these older and often less-educated ones.

"We shall make a good job of it, shan't we?" he asked his young wife when they first heard the joyful news of his promotion.

"We shall do our best," she replied. "We shall have such beautiful gardens and everything will be just *modern* and delightful..." In their two years of married life she had become completely infected by his passion for "modern methods" and his denigration of "these old and superannuated people in the teaching field who would be better employed as traders in the Onitsha market." She began to see herself already as the admired wife of the young headmaster, the queen of the school.

The wives of the other teachers would envy her position. She would set the fashion in everything...Then, suddenly, it occurred to her that there might not be other wives. Wavering between hope and fear, she asked her husband, looking anxiously at him.

"All our colleagues are young and unmarried," he said with enthusiasm which for once she did not share. "Which is a good thing," he continued.

"Why?"

"Why? They will give all their time and energy to the school."

Nancy was downcast. For a few minutes she became skeptical about the new school; but it was only for a few minutes. Her little personal misfortune could not blind her to her husband's happy prospects. She looked at him as he sat folded up in a chair. He was stoop-shouldered and looked frail. But he sometimes surprised people with sudden bursts of physical energy. In his present posture, however, all his bodily strength seemed to have retired behind his deep-set eyes, giving them an extraordinary power of penetration. He was only twenty-six, but looked thirty or more. On the whole, he was not unhandsome.

"A penny for your thoughts, Mike," said Nancy after a while, imitating the woman's magazine she read.

"I was thinking what a grand opportunity we've got at last to show these people how a school should be run."

Ndume School was backward in every sense of the word. Mr. Obi put his whole life into the work, and his wife hers too. He had two aims. A high standard of teaching was insisted upon, and the school compound was to be turned into a place of beauty. Nancy's dream-gardens came to life with the coming of the rains, and blossomed. Beautiful hibiscus and allamanda hedges in brilliant red and yellow marked out the carefully tended school compound from the rank neighbourhood bushes.

One evening as Obi was admiring his work he was scandalized to see an old woman from the village hobble right across the compound, through a marigold flower-bed and the hedges. On going up there he found faint signs of an almost disused path from the village across the school compound to the bush on the other side.

"It amazes me," said Obi to one of his teachers who had been three years in the school, "that you people allowed the villagers to make use of this footpath. It is simply incredible." He shook his head.

"The path," said the teacher apologetically, "appears to be very important to them. Although it is hardly used, it connects the village shrine with their place of burial."

"And what has that got to do with the school?" asked the headmaster.

"Well, I don't know," replied the other with a shrug of the shoulders. "But I remember there was a big row some time ago when we attempted to close it."

"That was some time ago. But it will not be used now," said Obi as he walked away. "What will the Government Education Officer think of this when he comes to inspect the school next week? The villagers might, for all I know, decide to use the schoolroom for a pagan ritual during the inspection."

Heavy sticks were planted closely across the path at the two places where it entered and left the school premises. These were further strengthened with barbed wire.

Three days later the village priest of *Ani* called on the headmaster. He was an old man and walked with a slight stoop. He carried a stout walking-stick which he usually tapped on the floor, by way of emphasis, each time he made a new point in his argument.

"I have heard," he said after the usual exchange of cordialities, "that our ancestral footpath has recently been closed..."

"Yes," replied Mr. Obi. "We cannot allow people to make a highway of our school compound."

"Look here, my son," said the priest bringing down his walking-stick, "this path was here before you were born and before your father was born. The whole life of this village depends on it. Our dead relatives depart by it and our ancestors visit us by it. But most important, it is the path of children coming in to be born..."

Mr. Obi listened with a satisfied smile on his face.

"The whole purpose of our school," he said finally, "is to eradicate just such beliefs as that. Dead men do not require footpaths. The whole idea is just fantastic. Our duty is to teach your children to laugh at such ideas."

"What you say may be true," replied the priest, "but we follow the practices of our fathers. If you re-open the path we shall have nothing to quarrel about. What I always say is: let the hawk perch and let the eagle perch." He rose to go.

"I am sorry," said the young headmaster. "But the school compound cannot be a thoroughfare. It is against our regulations. I would suggest your constructing another path, skirting our premises. We can even get our boys to help in building it. I don't suppose the ancestors will find the little detour too burdensome."

"I have no more words to say," said the old priest, already outside.

Two days later a young woman in the village died in childbed. A diviner was immediately consulted and he prescribed heavy sacrifices to propitiate ancestors insulted by the fence.

Obi woke up next morning among the ruins of his work. The beautiful hedges were torn up not just near the path but right round the school, the flowers trampled to death and one of the school buildings pulled down...That day, the white Supervisor came to inspect the school and wrote a nasty report on the state of the premises but more seriously about the "tribal-war situation developing between the school and the village, arising in part from the misguided zeal of the new headmaster."

Journal Entry

React to Obi's reverence for modern things.

Textual Considerations

1. Characterize Obi's attitude toward the teachers and the people in the community.
2. Speculate on the implications of the story's title. To what extent do you agree with Obi's reasons for closing the path?
3. Explain what the supervisor means by "misguided zeal." Does Obi's race play a role in the supervisor's evaluation? Did Obi deserve his censure? Why or why not?

Cultural Considerations

1. Consider with your group why Obi and the village priest are unable to negotiate a compromise. Explain the implications of the priest's plea to "let the hawk perch and let the eagle perch."
2. The conflict between individual aspirations and communal rites is central to this story. With whom do you empathize—Obi, who insisted on "civilizing the pagans," or the villagers, who used the path that "connects the village shrine with their place of burial"?

May Sarton
1990

The Rewards of Living a Solitary Life

The other day an acquaintance of mine, a gregarious and charming man, told me he had found himself unexpectedly alone in New York for an hour or two between appointments. He went to the Whitney and spent the "empty" time looking at things in solitary bliss. For him it proved to be a shock nearly as great as falling in love to discover that he could enjoy himself so much alone.

What had he been afraid of, I asked myself? That, suddenly alone, he would discover that he bored himself, or that there was, quite simply, no self there to meet? But having taken the plunge, he is now on the brink of adventure; he is about to be launched into his own inner space, space as immense, unexplored, and sometimes frightening as outer space to the astronaut. His every perception will come to him with a new freshness and, for a time, seem startlingly original. For anyone who can see things for himself with a naked eye becomes, for a moment or two, something of a genius. With another human being present vision becomes double vision, inevitably. We are busy wondering, what does my companion see or think of this, and what do I think of it? The original impact gets lost, or diffused.

"Music I heard with you was more than music."[1] Exactly. And therefore music *itself* can only be heard alone. Solitude is the salt of personhood. It brings out the authentic flavor of every experience.

"Alone one is never lonely: the spirit adventures, walking/In a quiet garden, in a cool house, abiding single there."

Loneliness is most acutely felt with other people, for with others, even with a lover sometimes, we suffer from our differences of taste, temperament, mood. Human intercourse often demands that we soften the edge of perception, or withdraw at the very instant of personal truth for fear of hurting, or of being inappropriately present, which is to say naked, in a social situation. Alone we can afford to be wholly whatever we are, and to feel whatever we feel absolutely. That is a great luxury!

For me the most interesting thing about a solitary life, and mine has been that for the last twenty years, is that it becomes increasingly rewarding. When I can wake up and watch the sun rise over the ocean, as I do most days, and know that I have an entire day ahead, uninterrupted, in which to write a few pages, take a walk with my dog, lie down in the afternoon for a long think (why does one think better in a horizontal position?), read and listen to music, I am flooded with happiness.

---

[1] **"Music...music":** A line from Conrad Aiken's *Bread and Music* (1914).

I am lonely only when I am overtired, when I have worked too long without a break, when for the time being I feel empty and need filling up. And I am lonely sometimes when I come back home after a lecture trip, when I have seen a lot of people and talked a lot, and am full to the brim with experience that needs to be sorted out.

Then for a little while the house feels huge and empty, and I wonder where my self is hiding. It has to be recaptured slowly by watering the plants, perhaps, and looking again at each one as though it were a person, by feeding the two cats, by cooking a meal.

It takes a while, as I watch the surf blowing up in fountains at the end of the field, but the moment comes when the world falls away, and the self emerges again from the deep unconscious; bringing back all I have recently experienced to be explored and slowly understood, when I can converse again with my hidden powers, and so grow, and so be renewed, till death do us part.

Journal Entry

Respond to Sarton's metaphor that "solitude is the salt of personhood."

Textual Considerations

1. Explain the statement that "anyone who can see things for himself with a naked eye becomes, for a moment or two, something of a genius."
2. What evidence is there to support Sarton's thesis that solitude is rewarding?
3. How does Sarton's conclusion connect with her introduction?
4. Is Sarton seeking to inform or persuade her audience? To what extent does she persuade you?

Cultural Contexts

1. Discuss with your group the differences between being *alone* and *lonely.* Is it possible to feel alone in a room full of people? Why or why not?

Martin Luther King, Jr.
1963

I Have a Dream

I am happy to join with you today in what will go down in history as the greatest demonstration for freedom in the history of our nation.

Five score years ago, a great American in whose symbolic shadow we stand today, signed the Emancipation Proclamation. This momentous decree came as a great beacon light of hope to millions of Negro slaves who had been seared in the flames of withering injustice. It came as a joyous daybreak to end the long night of their captivity. But one hundred years later, the Negro still is not free. One hundred years later, the life of the Negro is still sadly crippled by the manacles of segregation and the chains of discrimination. One hundred years later, the Negro lives on a lonely island of poverty in the midst of a vast ocean of material prosperity. One hundred years later, the Negro, is still anguished in the corners of American society and finds himself in exile in his own land. And so we have come here today to dramatize a shameful condition.

In a sense we have come to our nation's capital to cash a check. When the architects of our republic wrote the magnificent words of the Constitution and the Declaration of Independence, they were signing a promissory note to which every American was to fall heir. This note was the promise that all men—yes, Black men as well as white men—would be guaranteed the inalienable rights of life, liberty, and the pursuit of happiness.

It is obvious today that America has defaulted on this promissory note insofar as her citizens of color are concerned. Instead of honoring this sacred obligation, America has given the Negro people a bad check, a check which has come back marked "insufficient funds." But we refuse to believe that the bank of justice is bankrupt. We refuse to believe that there are insufficient funds in the great vaults of opportunity of this nation; and so we have come to cash this check, a check that will give us upon demand the riches of freedom and the security of justice.

We have also come to this hallowed spot to remind America of the fierce urgency of *now*. This is no time to engage in the luxury of cooling off or to take the tranquilizing drug of gradualism. *Now* is the time to make real the promises of democracy. *Now* is the time to rise from the dark and desolate valley of segregation to the sunlit path of racial justice. *Now* is the time to lift our nation from the quicksands of racial injustice to the solid rock of brotherhood. *Now* is the time to make justice a reality for all of God's children.

It would be fatal for the nation to overlook the urgency of the moment. This sweltering summer of the Negro's legitimate discontent will not pass until there is an invigorating autumn of freedom and equality. Nineteen Sixty-three is not an end, but a beginning. And those who hope that the Negro needed to blow off steam and will now be content will have a rude awakening if the nation returns to business as usual. There will be neither rest nor tranquility in America until the Negro is granted his citizenship rights. The whirlwinds of revolt will continue to shake the foundations of our nation until the bright day of justice emerges.

But there is something that I must say to my people who stand on the warm threshold which leads into the palace of justice. In the process of gaining our rightful place, we must not be guilty of wrongful deeds. Let us not seek to satisfy our thirst for freedom by drinking from the cup of bitterness and hatred. We must forever conduct our struggle on the high plane of dignity and discipline. We must not allow our creative protest to degenerate into physical violence. Again and again we must rise to the majestic heights of meeting physical force with soul force. And the marvelous new militancy which has engulfed the Negro community must not lead us to a distrust of all white people; for many of our white brothers, as evidenced by their presence here today, have come to realize that their destiny is tied up with our destiny, and they have come to realize that their freedom is inextricably bound to our freedom.

We cannot walk alone. And as we walk we must make the pledge that we shall always march ahead. We cannot turn back. There are those who are asking the devotees of civil rights, "When will you be satisfied?" We can never be satisfied as long as the Negro is the victim of the unspeakable horrors of police brutality. We can never be satisfied as long as our bodies, heavy with the fatigue of travel, cannot gain lodging in the motels of the highways and the hotels of the cities. We cannot be satisfied as long as the Negro's basic mobility is from a smaller ghetto to a larger one. We can never be satisfied as long as our children are stripped of their selfhood and robbed of their dignity by signs stating "For Whites Only." We cannot be satisfied as long as the Negro in Mississippi cannot vote and a Negro in New York believes he has nothing for which to vote. No, no, we are not satisfied, and we will not be satisfied until justice rolls down like waters and righteousness like a mighty stream.

I am not unmindful that some of you have come here out of great trials and tribulations. Some of you have come fresh from narrow jail cells. Some of you have come from areas where your quest for freedom left you battered by the storms of persecution and staggered by the winds of police brutality. You have been the veterans of creative suffering. Continue to work with the faith that unearned suffering is redemptive.

Go back to Mississippi, and go back to Alabama. Go back to South Carolina. Go back to Georgia. Go back to Louisiana. Go back to the slums and ghettos of our Northern cities, knowing that somehow this situation can and will be changed. Let us not wallow in the valley of despair.

I say to you today, my friends, even though we face the difficulties of today and tomorrow, I still have a dream. It is a dream deeply rooted in the American dream. I have a dream that one day this nation will rise up and live out the true meaning of its creed: "We hold these truths to be self-evident, that all men are created equal." I have a dream that one day, on the red hills of Georgia, sons of former slaves and the sons of former slave owners will be able to sit down together at the table of brotherhood. I have a dream that one day even the state of Mississippi, a state sweltering with the heat of injustice, sweltering with the heat of oppression, will be transformed into an oasis of freedom and justice. I have a dream that my four children will one day live in a nation where they will not be judged by the color of their skin, but by the content of their character.

I have a dream today. I have a dream that one day down in Alabama—with its vicious racists, with its governor's lips dripping with the words of interposition and nullification—one day right there in Alabama, little Black boys and Black girls will be able to join hands with little white boys and white girls as sisters and brothers.

I have a dream today. I have a dream that one day every valley shall be exalted and every hill and mountain shall be made low, the rough places will be made plain and the crooked places will be made straight, and the glory of the Lord shall be revealed, and all flesh shall see it together.

This is our hope. This is the faith that I go back to the South with. And with this faith we will be able to hew out of the mountain of despair a stone of hope. With this faith we will be able to transform the jangling discords of our nation into a beautiful symphony of brotherhood. With this faith we will be able to work together, to play together, to struggle together, to go to jail together, to stand up for freedom together, knowing that we will be free one day.

And this will be the day—this will be the day when all God's children will be able to sing with new meaning:.

> My country, 'tis of thee,
>   Sweet land of liberty;
>   Of thee I sing;
>   Land where my fathers died,
>   Land of the Pilgrims' pride,
>   From every Mountainside
>   Let freedom ring.

And if America is to be a great nation, this must become true.

And so let freedom ring from the prodigious hilltops of New Hampshire. Let freedom ring from the mighty mountains of New York. Let freedom ring from the heightening Alleghenies of Pennsylvania. Let freedom ring from the snowcapped Rockies of Colorado. Let freedom ring from the curvaceous slopes of California.

But not only that. Let freedom ring from Stone Mountain of Georgia. Let freedom ring from Lookout Mountain of Tennessee. Let freedom ring from every hill and molehill of Mississippi. "From every Mountainside let freedom ring."

And when this happens—when we allow freedom to ring, when we let it ring from every village and every hamlet, from every state and every city—we will be able to speed up that day when all of God's children, Black men and white men, Jews and Gentiles, Protestants and Catholics, will be able to join hands and sing in the words of the old Negro spiritual: "Free at last! Free at last! Thank God Almighty. We are free at last!"

Journal Entry

King uses the word *freedom* several times in his speech. What do you think he means by it? Consider the different possible meanings of freedom to the various members of his audience. What does it mean to you?

Textual Considerations

1. Why is the phrase *five score years ago* more appropriate than a hundred years ago or in 1863? Why does he later repeat the phrase *one hundred years later* so often?
2. When King speaks of "cash[ing] a check" or "insufficient funds," is he talking about money? Explain.
3. What evidence is there that King is writing for an audience that included whites?
4. "You have been the veterans of creative suffering." Can suffering be creative? How?

5. One characteristic of persuasion is that it uses connotative diction and figurative language to appeal to the reader's emotions. What words or expressions do you find that make you react emotionally?

6. Characterize the tone of the speech. Is it objective, angry, neutral? Explain your answer.

Cultural Contexts

1. King says his dream is "rooted in the American dream." What is that? King's quotation connects it with the Declaration of Independence. Is the American Dream more than the hopes and rights expressed in that document? If so, in what way?

2. What events in Mississippi in the early 1960s might have caused King to single out that state? Why would he specifically mention Georgia? Why Alabama?

Wallace Stevens
1928

Disillusionment of Ten O'Clock

The houses are haunted
By white night-gowns.
None are green,
Or purple with green rings,
Or green with yellow rings,   5
Or yellow with blue rings.
None of them are strange,
With socks of lace
And beaded ceintures.
People are not going   10
To dream of baboons and periwinkles.
Only, here and there, an old sailor,
Drunk and asleep in his boots,
Catches tigers
In red weather.   15

W. H. Auden
1939

The Unknown Citizen
(To JS/07/M/378
This Marble Monument
Is Erected by the State)

He was found by the Bureau of Statistics to be
One against whom there was no official complaint,
And all the reports on his conduct agree
That, in the modern sense of an old-fashioned word, he was a saint,

For in everything he did he served the Greater Community.   5
Except for the War till the day he retired
He worked in a factory and never got fired,
But satisfied his employers, Fudge Motors Inc.
Yet he wasn't a scab or odd in his views,
For his Union reports that he paid his dues,   10
(Our report on his Union shows it was sound)
And our Social Psychology workers found
That he was popular with his mates and liked a drink.
The Press are convinced that he bought a paper every day
And that his reactions to advertisements were normal in every way.   15
Policies taken out in his name prove that he was fully insured,
And his Health-card shows he was once in hospital but left it cured,
Both Producers Research and High-Grade Living declare
He was fully sensible to the advantages of the Installment Plan
And had everything necessary to the Modern Man,   20
A phonograph, a radio, a car and a frigidaire.
Our researchers into Public Opinion are content
That he held the proper opinions for the time of year;
When there was peace, he was for peace; when there was war, he went.
He was married and added five children to the population,   25
Which our Eugenist says was the right number for a parent of his generation,
And our teachers report that he never interfered with their education.
Was he free? Was he happy? The question is absurd:
Had anything been wrong, we should certainly have heard.

Chad Walsh
1969

Port Authority Terminal:
9 A.M. Monday

From buses beached like an invasion fleet
They fill the waiting room with striding feet.

Their faces, white, and void of hate or pity,
Move on tall bodies toward the conquered city.

Among the lesser breeds of black and brown   5
They board their taxis with an absent frown,

Each to his concrete citadel,
To rule the city and to buy and sell.

At five o'clock they ride the buses back,
Leaving their Irish to guard the brown and black.   10

At six a drink, at seven dinner's served.
At ten or twelve, depressed, undressed, unnerved,

They mount their wives, dismount, they doze and dream
Apocalyptic Negroes in a stream

Of moving torches, marching from the slums,   15
Beating a band of garbage pails for drums,

Marching, with school-age children in their arms,
Advancing on the suburbs and the farms,

To integrate the schools and burn the houses…
The normal morning comes, the clock arouses   20

Junior and senior executive alike.
Back on the bus, and down the usual pike.

From buses beached like an invasion fleet
They fill the waiting room with striding feet.

◆

Journal Entry

Discuss the irony implicit in the titles of the three poems.

Textual Considerations

1. How does Stevens use color to convey his concepts of individuality and conformity?
2. What function does the old sailor have in the poem?
3. Analyze the argumentative development of Stevens's poem in relation to what the poem suggests about illusions and disillusionment.
4. According to Auden, what are the conditions for sainthood in the modern world?
5. List the ways in which "The Unknown Citizen" conformed to his role in society. What is your response to the way he lived his life?
6. Comment on Walsh's image of commuters as soldiers and New York City as a battlefield.
7. What is implied in the speaker's description of the commuters' faces as "void of hate or pity" and as containing "an absent frown"?

Cultural Contexts

1. Discuss with your group what all three poems suggest about the relationship between the individual and society. Identify the images that most effectively characterize this relationship.

2. Discuss the relationships of the various ethnic groups described in Walsh's poem. To what extent is this poem, written in the late 1960s, still relevant? Comment on the speaker's description of the home lives of the commuters.

Yevtushenko, Niatum, and Gunn

Yevgeny Yevtushenko
1962

People

No people are uninteresting.
Their fate is like the chronicle of planets.

Nothing in them is not particular,
and planet is dissimilar from planet.

And if a man lived in obscurity   5
making his friends in that obscurity
obscurity is not uninteresting.

To each his world is private,
and in that world one excellent minute.

And in that world one tragic minute.   10
These are private.

In any man who dies there dies with him
his first snow and kiss and fight.
It goes with him.

They are left books and bridges   15
and painted canvas and machinery.

Whose fate is to survive.
But what has gone is also not nothing:

by the rule of the game something has gone.
Not people die but worlds die in them.   20

Whom we knew as faulty, the earth's creatures.
Of whom, essentially, what did we know?

Brother of a brother? Friend of friends?
Lover of lover?

We who knew our fathers   25
in everything, in nothing.

They perish. They cannot be brought back.
The secret worlds are not regenerated.

And every time again and again
I make my lament against destruction.   30

Duane Niatum
1978

Street Kid

I stand before the window that opens
to a field of sagebrush—
California country northeast of San Francisco.
Holding to the earth and its shield of silence,
The sun burns my thirteen years into the hill.   5
The white breath of twilight
Whirrs with insects crawling down the glass
Between the bars. But it is the meadowlark
Warbling at the end of the fence
That sets me apart from the rest of the boys,   10
The cool toughs playing ping pong
And cards before lock-up.
When this new home stops calling on memory,
As well as my nickname, Injun Joe,
Given to me by the brothers,   15
The Blacks, the Chicanos, the others growing
Lean as this solitude, I step
From the window into the darkness
Reach my soul building a nest against the wall.

Thom Gunn
1973

Black Jackets

In the silence that prolongs the span
Rawly of music when the record ends,
    The red-haired boy who drove a van
In weekday overalls but, like his friends,

    Wore cycle boots and jacket here   5
To suit the Sunday hangout he was in,
    Heard, as he stretched back from his beer,
Leather creak softly round his neck and chin.

    Before him, on a coal-black sleeve
Remote exertion had lined, scratched, and burned   10
    Insignia that could not revive
The heroic fall or climb where they were earned.

    On the other drinkers bent together,
Concocting selves for their impervious kit,
    He saw it as no more than leather   15
Which, taut across the shoulders grown to it,

    Sent through the dimness of a bar
As sudden and anonymous hints of light
    As those that shipping give, that are
Now flickers in the Bay, now lost in night.   20

    He stretched out like a cat, and rolled
The bitterish taste of beer upon his tongue,
    And listened to a joke being told:
The present was the things he stayed among.

    If it was only loss he wore,   25
He wore it to assert, with fierce devotion,
    Complicity and nothing more.
He recollected his initiation,

    And one especially of the rites.
For on his shoulders they had put tattoos: 30
    The group's name on the left, The Knights,
And on the right the slogan Born To Lose.

Journal Entry

Reflect on Yevtushenko's idea that "obscurity is not uninteresting" as you examine the theme of private versus communal selves in the three poems.

Textual Considerations

1. Analyze Yevtushenko's use of symbolism in "People." To what events might the "excellent minute" and the "tragic minute" refer? What other examples reinforce the poem's meanings about individual uniqueness, mortality, and our ability to know another person?
2. Comment on the effectiveness of Niatum's use of nature imagery to suggest his protagonist's emotional state. How does his identification with the meadowlark, for example, help us to understand better his protagonist?
3. How does Gunn use setting to enhance meaning in "Black Jackets"? Discuss also the implications of the tattoos in the poem's last stanza.
4. Quote from each poem to support your opinion as to whether the poetic voices they raise verge entirely on disillusionment, loss, violence, and marginalized identities, or whether they also raise voices of protest and hope against despondency.

Cultural Contexts

1. The protagonists of "Black Jackets" and "Street Kid" are struggling to find their individual and collective identities in cultures from which they feel essentially alienated. To what extent do they succeed? Use quotes from the poems to support your position. With which protagonist do you most empathize? Why?
2. Use "Black Jackets" and "Street Kid" to debate the extent to which these poems challenge traditional concepts of success and individual fulfillment.

Frost, Olds, and Romero

Robert Frost
1914

Mending Wall

Something there is that doesn't love a wall,
That sends the frozen-ground-swell under it
And spills the upper boulders in the sun,
And makes gaps even two can pass abreast.
The work of hunters is another thing:
I have come after them and made repair
Where they have left not one stone on a stone,

5

But they would have the rabbit out of hiding,
To please the yelping dogs. The gaps I mean,
No one has seen them made or heard them made,   10
But at spring mending-time we find them there.
I let my neighbor know beyond the hill;
And on a day we meet to walk the line
And set the wall between us once again.
We keep the wall between us as we go.   15
To each the boulders that have fallen to each.
And some are loaves and some so nearly balls
We have to use a spell to make them balance:
'Stay where you are until our backs are turned!'
We wear our fingers rough with handling them.   20
Oh, just another kind of outdoor game,
One on a side. It comes to little more:
There where it is we do not need the wall:
He is all pine and I am apple orchard.
My apple trees will never get across   25
And eat the cones under his pines, I tell him.
He only says, 'Good fences make good neighbors.'
Spring is the mischief in me, and I wonder
If I could put a notion in his head:
'*Why* do they make good neighbors? Isn't it   30
Where there are cows? But here there are no cows.
Before I built a wall I'd ask to know
What I was walling in or walling out,
And to whom I was like to give offense.
Something there is that doesn't love a wall,   35
That wants it down.' I could say 'Elves' to him,
But it's not elves exactly, and I'd rather
He said it for himself. I see him there,
Bringing a stone grasped firmly by the top
In each hand, like an old-stone savage armed.   40
He moves in darkness as it seems to me,
Not of woods only and the shade of trees.
He will not go behind his father's saying,
And he likes having thought of it so well
He says again, 'Good fences make good neighbors.'   45

Sharon Olds
1987

Summer Solstice, New York City

By the end of the longest day of the year he could not stand it,
he went up the iron stairs through the roof of the building
and over the soft, tarry surface
to the edge, put one leg over the complex green tin cornice
and said if they came a step closer that was it.   5
Then the huge machinery of the earth began to work for his life,
the cops came in their suits blue-gray as the sky on a cloudy evening,
and one put on a bulletproof vest, a
black shell around his own life,
life of his children's father, in case   10
the man was armed, and one, slung with a
rope like the sign of his bounden duty,
came up out of a hole in the top of the neighboring building,
like the gold hole they say is in the top of the head,
and began to lurk toward the man who wanted to die.   15
The tallest cop approached him directly,
softly, slowly, talking to him, talking, talking,
while the man's leg hung over the lip of the next world,
and the crowd gathered in the street, silent, and the
dark hairy net with its implacable grid was   20
unfolded near the curb and spread out and
stretched as the sheet is prepared to receive at a birth.
Then they all came a little closer
where he squatted next to his death, his shirt
glowing its milky glow like something   25
growing in a dish at night in the dark in a lab, and then
everything stopped
as his body jerked and he
stepped down from the parapet and went toward them
and they closed on him, I thought they were going to   30
beat him up, as a mother whose child has been
lost will scream at the child when it's found, they
took him by the arms and held him up and
leaned him against the wall of the chimney and the
tall cop lit a cigarette   35
in his own mouth, and gave it to him, and
then they all lit cigarettes, and the
red glowing ends burned like the
tiny campfires we lit at night
back at the beginning of the world.   40

Leo Romero
1981

What the Gossips Saw

Everyone pitied Escolastica, her leg
had swollen like a watermelon in the summer
It had practically happened over night
She was seventeen, beautiful and soon
to be married to Guillermo who was working   5
in the mines at Terreros, eighty miles away
far up in the mountains, in the wilderness
Poor Escolastica, the old women would say
on seeing her hobble to the well with a bucket
carrying her leg as if it were the weight   10
of the devil, surely it was a curse from heaven
for some misdeed, the young women who were
jealous would murmur, yet they were grieved too
having heard that the doctor might cut
her leg, one of a pair of the most perfect legs   15
in the valley, and it was a topic of great
interest and conjecture among the villagers
whether Guillermo would still marry her
if she were crippled, a one-legged woman—
as if life weren't hard enough for a woman   20
with two legs—how could she manage

Guillermo returned and married Escolastica
even though she had but one leg, the sound
of her wooden leg pounding down the wooden aisle
stayed in everyone's memory for as long   25
as they lived, women cried at the sight
of her beauty, black hair so dark
that the night could get lost in it, a face
more alluring than a full moon

Escolastica went to the dances with her husband   30
and watched and laughed but never danced
though once she had been the best dancer
and could wear holes in a pair of shoes
in a matter of a night, and her waist had been
as light to the touch as a hummingbird's flight   35
And Escolastica bore five children, only half
what most women bore, yet they were healthy
In Escolastica's presence, no one would mention
the absence of her leg, though she walked heavily

And it was not long before the gossips   40
spread their poison, that she must be in cohorts
with the devil, had given him her leg
for the power to bewitch Guillermo's heart
and cloud his eyes so that he could not see
what was so clear to them all   45

♦

Journal Entry

Compare and contrast the concepts of community in each poem.

Textual Considerations

1. Frost's, Olds's, and Romero's poetic styles are rich in simple, direct language. Choose examples of natural speech patterns from each poem and analyze the way in which these poets' conversational styles invite comparison with one another.
2. Analyze Frost's use of the word *fences,* Old's use of the phrase *machinery of the earth,* and Romero's use of the term *a one-legged woman.* Explain what each suggests about the relationship of the individual to society.
3. Consider the importance of the word *saw* in the title "What the Gossips Saw." What other allusions to sight can you find in Romero's poem? Analyze what this poem both articulates and implies about communal opinion.
4. Frost and Olds address the issues of boundaries or fences in relationships: our often conflicting needs for solitude and solidarity, identity and community, and personal space and relatedness. What new meanings about relationships can you draw from these poems?

Cultural Contexts

1. Take a position about the role the community plays in molding people's identity and destiny. What issues seem of greatest concern to the community in "What the Gossips Saw"? Chart the progress of the community's reaction to Escolastica and Guillermo.
2. Working with your group, reconstruct the circumstances under which each of you would risk your life to save another's. Can you imagine yourself in the place of the cops in Olds's poem? How does the poem address the conflict between individual rights and the claims of communal obligation? Were the cops only doing their jobs? Explain.

Gary Soto
1977

History

Grandma lit the stove.
Morning sunlight
Lengthened in spears
Across the linoleum floor.
Wrapped in a shawl,   5
Her eyes small
With sleep.
She sliced papas,[1]
Pounded chiles
With a stone   10
Brought from Guadalajara.[2]
                         After
Grandpa left for work,
She hosed down
The walk her sons paved   15
And in the shade
Of a chinaberry,
Unearthed her
Secret cigar box
Of bright coins   20
And bills, counted them
In English,
Then in Spanish,
And buried them elsewhere.
Later, back   25
From the market,
Where no one saw her,
She pulled out
Pepper and beet, spines
Of asparagus   30
From her blouse,
Tiny chocolates
From under a paisley bandana,
And smiled.

That was the '50s,   35
And Grandma in her '50s.
A face streaked
From cutting grapes
And boxing plums.
I remember her insides   40
Were washed of tapeworm.
Her arms swelled into knobs
Of small growths—
Her second son
Dropped from a ladder   45
And was dust.
And yet I do not know
The sorrows
That sent her praying
In the dark of a closet,   50
The tear that fell
At night
When she touched
Loose skin
Of belly and breasts.   55
I do not know why
Her face shines
Or what goes beyond this shine,
Only the stories
That pulled her   60
From Taxco[3] to San Joaquin,
Delano to Westside,[4]
The places
In which we all begin.

[1] Potatoes.

[2] A city in Mexico.

[3] A city in Mexico.

[4] Places in California.

Diane di Prima
1979

To My Father

In my dreams you stand among roses.
You are still the fine gardener you were.
You worry about mother.
You are still the fierce wind, the intolerable force
that almost broke me.   5
Who forced my young body into awkward and proper clothes
Who spoke of his standing in the community.
And men's touch is still a little absurd to me
because you trembled when you touched me.
What external law were you expounding?   10
How can I take your name like prayer?
My youngest son has your eyes.
Why are you knocking at the doors of my brain?
You kept all their rules and more.
What were you promised that you cannot rest?   15
What fierce, angry honesty in the darkness?
What can you hope who had preferred my death
to the birth of my oldest daughter?
O fierce hummer of tunes
Forget, eat the black seedcake.   20
In my dreams you stand at the door of your house
and weep for your wife, my mother.

Journal Entry

Analyze the function of memory in the portrayals of family relationships in each poem.

Textual Considerations

1. To what extent are the speakers in these poems emotionally involved or detached? Examine their narrative strategies. To whom are the poems addressed, and do the speakers talk directly or indirectly about the intensity of their emotions? Discuss the significance of the differences in their methods of address.
2. Characterize Soto's grandmother, and explain how his relationship with her has affected his self-concept.
3. Di Prima addressed a series of questions to her dead father. How do they contribute to your understanding of their relationship? To what extent does gender affect her memories of him?

Cultural Contexts

1. Discuss how the family context of support, rejection, or solidarity affects the making of the individual self in "History" and "To My Father." Expand your discussion by evaluating the role of the family as a mediating element between the individual and his or her collective world.
2. Working with your group, list the various images of family members in these poems. Then discuss the reasons for the paradoxical relationship between solitude and solidarity that pervades each poem.

Ferlinghetti and Wilbur

Lawrence Ferlinghetti
1958

Constantly Risking Absurdity

Constantly risking absurdity
                    and death
        whenever he performs
                    above the heads
                                of his audience   5
        the poet like an acrobat
                        climbs on rime
                                to a high wire of his own making
        and balancing on eyebeams
                            above a sea of faces   10
                paces his way
                        to the other side of day
        performing entrechats
                        and sleight-of-foot tricks
        and other high theatrics   15
                        and all without mistaking
                any thing
                        for what it may not be

        For he's the super realist
                        who must perforce perceive   20
                taut truth
                            before the taking of each stance or step
        in his supposed advance

                              toward that still higher perch
where Beauty stands and waits   25
                    with gravity
                              to start her death-defying leap
And he
          a little charleychaplin man
                              who may or may not catch   30
              her fair eternal form
                          spreadeagled in the empty air
              of existence

Richard Wilbur
1971

The Writer

In her room at the prow of the house
Where light breaks, and the windows are tossed with linden,
My daughter is writing a story.

I pause in the stairwell, hearing
From her shut door a commotion of typewriter-keys   5
Like a chain hauled over a gunwale.

Young as she is, the stuff
Of her life is a great cargo, and some of it heavy:
I wish her a lucky passage.

But now it is she who pauses,   10
As if to reject my thought and its easy figure.
A stillness greatens, in which

The whole house seems to be thinking,
And then she is at it again with a bunched clamor
Of strokes, and again is silent.   15

I remember the dazed starling
Which was trapped in that very room, two years ago;
How we stole in, lifted a sash

And retreated, not to affright it;
And how for a helpless hour, through the crack of the door,   20
We watched the sleek, wild, dark

And iridescent creature
Batter against the brilliance, drop like a glove
To the hard floor, or the desk-top,

And wait then, humped and bloody,   25
For the wits to try it again; and how our spirits
Rose when, suddenly sure,

It lifted off from a chair-back,
Beating a smooth course for the right window
And clearing the sill of the world.   30

It is always a matter, my darling,
Of life or death, as I had forgotten. I wish
What I wished you before, but harder.

◆

Journal Entry

Explain the allusions to death in both poems.

Textual Considerations

1. Ferlinghetti's poem is based on the simile of the poet as acrobat. Why is it an appropriate comparison for the poem's subject?
2. How does the structure of Ferlinghetti's poem contribute to its meaning?
3. Respond to the concept of the poet as "the super realist." Why does the poet sometimes "not catch" Beauty?
4. The beginning of "The Writer" draws an elaborate comparison between the daughter's writing and a sea voyage. Review the poem, and explain each of the sea images.
5. What is the similarity between the daughter's efforts to write and the starling's effort to escape? What does the speaker learn from the example of the starlings?
6. Who is "The Writer"?

Cultural Contexts

1. Discuss the artist's relationship to audience in both poems. What attitude toward himself is the speaker expressing in calling himself "a little charleychaplin man"? Why is he constantly risking absurdity? What is "always a matter of life and death" in "The Writer"? What do both poems suggest about the creative process? Explain the role of community in both texts.

Emily Dickinson
c. 1914

Volcanoes Be in Sicily

Volcanoes be in Sicily
And South America
I judge from my Geography—
Volcanos nearer here
A Lava step at any time   5
Am I inclined to climb—
A Crater I may contemplate
Vesuvius at Home.

Emily Dickinson
c. 1862

The Soul Selects Her Own Society—

The Soul selects her own Society—
Then—shuts the Door—
To her divine Majority—
Present no more—

Unmoved—she notes the Chariots—pausing—   5
At her low Gate—
Unmoved—an Emperor be kneeling
Upon her Mat—

I've known her—from an ample nation—
Choose One—   10
Then—close the Valves of her attention—
Like Stone—

Emily Dickinson
c. 1862

Much Madness Is Divinest Sense—

Much Madness is divinest Sense—
To a discerning Eye—
Much Sense—the starkest Madness—
'Tis the Majority
In this, as All, prevail—   5
Assent—and you are sane—
Demur—you're straightway dangerous—
And handled with a Chain—

Emily Dickinson
c. 1868

Tell All the Truth But Tell It Slant—

Tell all the Truth but tell it slant—
Success in Circuit lies
Too bright for our infirm Delight
To Truth's superb surprise
As Lightning to the Children eased   5
With explanation kind
The Truth must dazzle gradually
Or every man be blind—

Journal Entry

Create a profile of the speaker in each poem.

Textual Considerations

1. Explain the paradox in the first four lines of "Volcanoes Be in Sicily."
2. Analyze the literal and symbolic significance of volcanoes in the poem.
3. Explain how Dickinson's use of door imagery contributes to the unity and meaning of "The Soul Selects Her Own Society—."

4. Analyze Dickinson's use of paradox to enhance the meaning in "Much Madness Is Divinest Sense—."
5. To what extent do you agree with the speaker in "Tell All the Truth But Tell It Slant—"?
6. How do you respond to her descriptions of truth? Explain the last two lines of the text.

Cultural Contexts

1. In 1991, the late May Sarton, a contemporary American poet, described the function of poetry as follows:

> For poetry exists to break through
> to below the level of reason
> where the angels and monsters
> that the amenities keep in the cellar
> may come out to dance,
> to rove and roar,
> growling and singing,
> to bring life back to the enclosed rooms
> where too often we are only
> living and partly living.

What might Sarton mean by juxtaposing "angels" and "monsters"? What does her choice of verbs suggest about the function of poetry? Why are the rooms "enclosed"? Explain the last two lines. To what extent does Sarton's concept of poetry apply to Dickinson's texts? What is your response to Sarton's description of the role of poetry in people's lives?

Sophocles
441 BC

Antigone

PERSONS REPRESENTED

ANTIGONE
ISMENE
EURYDICE
CREON
HAIMON
TEIRESIAS
A Sentry
A Messenger
Chorus

SCENE: *Before the palace of* CREON, *King of Thebes. A central double door, and two lateral doors. A platform extends the length of the façade, and from this platform three steps lead down into the "orchestra," or chorus-ground.* TIME: *dawn of the day after the repulse of the Argive army from the assault on Thebes.*

PROLOGUE

[ANTIGONE *and* ISMENE *enter from the central door of the Palace.*]

ANTIGONE.   Ismenê, dear sister,
  You would think that we had already suffered enough
  For the curse on Oedipus:
  I cannot imagine any grief
  That you and I have not gone through. And now—
  Have they told you of the new decree of our King Creon?
ISMENE.   I have heard nothing: I know
  That two sisters lost two brothers, a double death
  In a single hour; and I know that the Argive army
  Fled in the night; but beyond this, nothing.
ANTIGONE.   I thought so. And that is why I wanted you
  To come out here with me. There is something we must do.
ISMENE.   Why do you speak so strangely?
ANTIGONE.   Listen, Ismenê:
  Creon buried our brother Eteoclês
  With military honors, gave him a soldier's funeral,

And it was right that he should; but Polyneicês,
Who fought as bravely and died as miserably,—
They say that Creon has sworn
No one shall bury him, no one mourn for him,
But his body must lie in the fields, a sweet treasure
For carrion birds to find as they search for food.
That is what they say, and our good Creon is coming here
To announce it publicly; and the penalty—
Stoning to death in the public square!

                                  There it is,
And now you can prove what you are:
A true sister, or a traitor to your family.

ISMENE.   Antigonê, you are mad! What could I possibly do?

ANTIGONE.   You must decide whether you will help me or not.

ISMENE.   I do not understand you. Help you in what?

ANTIGONE.   Ismenê, I am going to bury him. Will you come?

ISMENE.   Bury him! You have just said the new law forbids it.

ANTIGONE.   He is my brother. And he is your brother, too.

ISMENE.   But think of the danger! Think what Creon will do!

ANTIGONE.   Creon is not strong enough to stand in my way.

ISMENE.   Ah sister!
Oedipus died, everyone hating him
For what his own search brought to light, his eyes
Ripped out by his own hand; and Iocastê died,
His mother and wife at once: she twisted the cords
That strangled her life; and our two brothers died,
Each killed by the other's sword. And we are left:
But oh, Antigonê!
Think how much more terrible than these
Our own death would be if we should go against Creon
And do what he has forbidden! We are only women,
We cannot fight with men, Antigonê!
The law is strong, we must give in to the law
In this thing, and in worse. I beg the Dead
To forgive me, but I am helpless: I must yield
To those in authority. And I think it is dangerous business
To be always meddling.

ANTIGONE.   If that is what you think,
I should not want you, even if you asked to come.
You have made your choice, you can be what you want to be.
But I will bury him; and if I must die,
I say that this crime is holy: I shall lie down
With him in death, and I shall be as dear
To him as he to me.

                    It is the dead,

Not the living, who make the longest demands:
We die for ever...
                              You may do as you like,
Since apparently the laws of the gods mean nothing to you.
ISMENE.   They mean a great deal to me; but I have no strength
To break laws that were made for the public good.
ANTIGONE.   That must be your excuse, I suppose. But as for me,
I will bury the brother I love.
ISMENE.   Antigonê,
I am so afraid for you!
ANTIGONE.   You need not be:
You have yourself to consider, after all.
ISMENE.   But no one must hear of this, you must tell no one!
I will keep it a secret, I promise!
ANTIGONE.   Oh tell it! Tell everyone!
Think how they'll hate you when it all comes out
If they learn that you knew about it all the time!
ISMENE.   So fiery! You should be cold with fear.
ANTIGONE.   Perhaps. But I am only doing what I must.
ISMENE.   But can you do it? I say that you cannot.
ANTIGONE.   Very well: when my strength gives out, I shall do no more.
ISMENE.   Impossible things should not be tried at all.
ANTIGONE.   Go away, Ismenê:
I shall be hating you soon, and the dead will too,
For your words are hateful. Leave me my foolish plan:
I am not afraid of the danger; if it means death,
It will not be the worst of deaths—death without honor.
ISMENE.   Go then, if you feel that you must.
You are unwise,
But a loyal friend indeed to those who love you.   [*Exit into the Palace.*
     ANTIGONE *goes off, L. Enter the* CHORUS.]

PÁRODOS

CHORUS.   Now the long blade of the sun, lying   [STROPHE 1]
Level east to west, touches with glory
Thebes of the Seven Gates. Open, unlidded
Eye of golden day! O marching light
Across the eddy and rush of Dircê's stream,
Striking the white shields of the enemy
Thrown headlong backward from the blaze of morning!
CHORAGOS.   Polyneicês their commander
Roused them with windy phrases,
He the wild eagle screaming
Insults above our land,

His wings their shields of snow,
His crest their marshalled helms.

CHORUS.   Against our seven gates in a yawning ring   [ANTISTROPHE 1]
The famished spears came onward in the night;
But before his jaws were sated with our blood,
Or pinefire took the garland of our towers,
He was thrown back; and as he turned, great Thebes—
No tender victim for his noisy power—
Rose like a dragon behind him, shouting war.

CHORAGOS.   For God hates utterly
The bray of bragging tongues;
And when he beheld their smiling,
Their swagger of golden helms,
The frown of his thunder blasted
Their first man from our walls.

CHORUS.   We heard his shout of triumph high in the air   [STROPHE 2]
Turn to a scream; far out in a flaming arc
He fell with his windy torch, and the earth struck him.
And others storming in fury no less than his
Found shock of death in the dusty joy of battle.

CHORAGOS.   Seven captains at seven gates
Yielded their clanging arms to the god
That bends the battle-line and breaks it.
These two only, brothers in blood,
Face to face in matchless rage,
Mirroring each the other's death,
Clashed in long combat.

CHORUS.   But now in the beautiful morning of victory   [ANTISTROPHE 2]
Let Thebes of the many chariots sing for joy!
With hearts for dancing we'll take leave of war:
Our temples shall be sweet with hymns of praise,
And the long night shall echo with our chorus.

SCENE I

CHORAGOS.   But now at last our new King is coming:
Creon of Thebes, Menoikeus' son.
In this auspicious dawn of his reign
What are the new complexities
That shifting Fate has woven for him?
What is his counsel? Why has he summoned
The old men to hear him?

[*Enter* CREON *from the Palace, C. He addresses the* CHORUS *from the top step.*]

CREON.   Gentlemen: I have the honor to inform you that our Ship of State, which
recent storms have threatened to destroy, has come safely to harbor at last,

guided by the merciful wisdom of Heaven. I have summoned you here this morning because I know that I can depend upon you: your devotion to King Laïos was absolute; you never hesitated in your duty to our late ruler Oedipus; and when Oedipus died, your loyalty was transferred to his children. Unfortunately, as you know, his two sons, the princes Eteoclês and Polyneicês, have killed each other in battle; and I, as the next in blood, have succeeded to the full power of the throne.

I am aware, of course, that no Ruler can expect complete loyalty from his subjects until he has been tested in office. Nevertheless, I say to you at the very outset that I have nothing but contempt for the kind of Governor who is afraid, for whatever reason, to follow the course that he knows is best for the State; and as for the man who sets private friendship above the public welfare,—I have no use for him, either. I call God to witness that if I saw my country headed for ruin, I should not be afraid to speak out plainly; and I need hardly remind you that I would never have any dealings with an enemy of the people. No one values friendship more highly than I; but we must remember that friends made at the risk of wrecking our Ship are not real friends at all.

These are my principles, at any rate, and that is why I have made the following decision concerning the sons of Oedipus: Eteoclês, who died as a man should die, fighting for his country, is to be buried with full military honors, with all the ceremony that is usual when the greatest heroes die; but his brother Polyneicês, who broke his exile to come back with fire and sword against his native city and the shrines of his fathers' gods, whose one idea was to spill the blood of his blood and sell his own people into slavery—Polyneicês, I say, is to have no burial: no man is to touch him or say the least prayer for him; he shall lie on the plain, unburied; and the birds and the scavenging dogs can do with him whatever they like.

This is my command, and you can see the wisdom behind it. As long as I am King, no traitor is going to be honored with the loyal man. But whoever shows by word and deed that he is on the side of the State,—he shall have my respect while he is living, and my reverence when he is dead.

CHORAGOS.   If that is your will, Creon son of Menoikeus,
    You have the right to enforce it: we are yours.
CREON.   That is my will. Take care that you do your part.
CHORAGOS.   We are old men: let the younger ones carry it out.
CREON.   I do not mean that: the sentries have been appointed.
CHORAGOS.   Then what is it that you would have us do?
CREON.   You will give no support to whoever breaks this law.
CHORAGOS.   Only a crazy man is in love with death!
CREON.   And death it is; yet money talks, and the wisest
    Have sometimes been known to count a few coins too many.   [*Enter* SENTRY
    from L.]
SENTRY.   I'll not say that I'm out of breath from running, King, because every
    time I stopped to think about what I have to tell you, I felt like going back.
    And all the time a voice kept saying, "You fool, don't you know you're walk-

ing straight into trouble?"; and then another voice: "Yes, but if you let somebody else get the news to Creon first, it will be even worse than that for you!"
But good sense won out, at least I hope it was good sense, and here I am with
a story that makes no sense at all; but I'll tell it anyhow, because, as they say,
what's going to happen's going to happen, and—

CREON.   Come to the point. What have you to say?

SENTRY.   I did not do it. I did not see who did it. You must not punish me for what
someone else has done.

CREON.   A comprehensive defense! More effective, perhaps,
   If I knew its purpose. Come: what is it?

SENTRY.   A dreadful thing...I don't know how to put it—

CREON.   Out with it!

SENTRY.   Well, then;
   The dead man—

                         Polyneicês—

[*Pause. The* SENTRY *is overcome, fumbles for words.* CREON *waits impassively.*]

                                   out there—

                                              someone,—

New dust on the slimy flesh!

                         [*Pause. No sign from* CREON]

Someone has given it burial that way, and
Gone...

                         [*Long pause.* CREON *finally speaks with deadly control:*]

CREON.   And the man who dared do this?

SENTRY.   I swear I
   Do not know! You must believe me!
                                   Listen:
   The ground was dry, not a sign of digging, no,
   Not a wheeltrack in the dust, no trace of anyone.
   It was when they relieved us this morning: and one of them,
   The corporal, pointed to it.
                         There it was,
   The strangest—
               Look:
   The body, just mounded over with light dust: you see?
   Not buried really, but as if they'd covered it
   Just enough for the ghost's peace. And no sign
   Of dogs or any wild animal that had been there.

   And then what a scene there was! Every man of us
   Accusing the other: we all proved the other man did it,
   We all had proof that we could not have done it.

We were ready to take hot iron in our hands,
Walk through fire, swear by all the gods,
It was not I!
I do not know who it was, but it was not I!

[CREON's *rage has been mounting steadily, but the* SENTRY *is too intent upon
his story to notice it*]

And then, when this came to nothing, someone said
A thing that silenced us and made us stare
Down at the ground: you had to be told the news,
And one of us had to do it! We threw the dice,
And the bad luck fell to me. So here I am,
No happier to be here than you are to have me:
Nobody likes the man who brings bad news.
CHORAGOS.   I have been wondering, King: can it be that the gods have done this?
CREON.   [*Furiously*]   Stop!
    Must you doddering wrecks
Go out of your heads entirely? "The gods!"
Intolerable!
The gods favor this corpse? Why? How had he served them?
Tried to loot their temples, burn their images,
Yes, and the whole State, and its laws with it!
Is it your senile opinion that the gods love to honor bad men?
A pious thought!—

                    No, from the very beginning
There have been those who have whispered together,
Stiff-necked anarchists, putting their heads together,
Scheming against me in alleys. These are the men,
And they have bribed my own guard to do this thing.

Money!   [*Sententiously*]
There's nothing in the world so demoralizing as money.
Down go your cities,
Homes gone, men gone, honest hearts corrupted,
Crookedness of all kinds, and all for money!   [*To* SENTRY]
                    But you—!
I swear by God and by the throne of God,
The man who has done this thing shall pay for it!
Find that man, bring him here to me, or your death
Will be the least of your problems: I'll string you up
Alive, and there will be certain ways to make you
Discover your employer before you die;
And the process may teach you a lesson you seem to have missed:
The dearest profit is sometimes all too dear:

That depends on the source. Do you understand me?
A fortune won is often misfortune.
SENTRY. King, may I speak?
CREON.   Your very voice distresses me.
SENTRY. Are you sure that it is my voice, and not your conscience?
CREON. By God, he wants to analyze me now!
SENTRY. It is not what I say, but what has been done, that hurts you.
CREON. You talk too much.
SENTRY.   Maybe; but I've done nothing.
CREON. Sold your soul for some silver: that's all you've done.
SENTRY. How dreadful it is when the right judge judges wrong!
CREON. Your figures of speech
    May entertain you now; but unless you bring me the man,
    You will get little profit from them in the end.   [*Exit* CREON *into the Palace.*]
SENTRY. "Bring me the man"—!
    I'd like nothing better than bringing him the man!
    But bring him or not, you have seen the last of me here.
    At any rate, I am safe!   [*Exit* SENTRY]

ODE I

CHORUS.   [STROPHE 1]
    Numberless are the world's wonders, but none
    More wonderful than man; the stormgray sea
    Yields to his prows, the huge crests bear him high;
    Earth, holy and inexhaustible, is graven
    With shining furrows where his plows have gone
    Year after year, the timeless labor of stallions.

    The lightboned birds and beasts that cling to cover,   [ANTISTOPHE 1]
    The lithe fish lighting their reaches of dim water,
    All are taken, tamed in the net of his mind;
    The lion on the hill, the wild horse windy-maned,
    Resign to him; and his blunt yoke has broken
    The sultry shoulders of the mountain bull.

    Words also, and thought as rapid as air,   [STROPHE 2]
    He fashions to his good use; statecraft is his,
    And his the skill that deflects the arrows of snow,
    The spears of winter rain: from every wind
    He has made himself secure—from all but one:
    In the late wind of death he cannot stand.

    O clear intelligence, force beyond all measure!   [ANTISTROPHE 2]
    O fate of man, working both good and evil!

When the laws are kept, how proudly his city stands!
When the laws are broken, what of his city then?
Never may the anárchic man find rest at my hearth,
Never be it said that my thoughts are his thoughts.

SCENE II

[*Re-enter* SENTRY *leading* ANTIGONE.]

CHORAGOS.   What does this mean? Surely this captive woman
  Is the Princess, Antigonê. Why should she be taken?
SENTRY.   Here is the one who did it! We caught her
  In the very act of burying him.—Where is Creon?
CHORAGOS.   Just coming from the house.

[*Enter* CREON, *C.*]

CREON.   What has happened?
  Why have you come back so soon?
SENTRY.   [*Expansively*]   O King,
  A man should never be too sure of anything:
  I would have sworn
  That you'd not see me here again: your anger
  Frightened me so, and the things you threatened me with;
  But how could I tell then
  That I'd be able to solve the case so soon?

  No dice-throwing this time: I was only too glad to come!

  Here is this woman. She is the guilty one:
  We found her trying to bury him.
  Take her, then; question her; judge her as you will.
  I am through with the whole thing now, and glád óf it.
CREON.   But this is Antigonê! Why have you brought her here?
SENTRY.   She was burying him, I tell you!
CREON.   [*Severely*]   Is this the truth?
SENTRY.   I saw her with my own eyes. Can I say more?
CREON.   The details: come, tell me quickly!
SENTRY.   It was like this:
  After those terrible threats of yours, King,
  We went back and brushed the dust away from the body.
  The flesh was soft by now, and stinking,
  So we sat on a hill to windward and kept guard.
  No napping this time! We kept each other awake.
  But nothing happened until the white round sun
  Whirled in the center of the round sky over us:
  Then, suddenly,

A storm of dust roared up from the earth, and the sky
Went out, the plain vanished with all its trees
In the stinging dark. We closed our eyes and endured it.
The whirlwind lasted a long time, but it passed;
And then we looked, and there was Antigonê!
I have seen
A mother bird come back to a stripped nest, heard
Her crying bitterly a broken note or two
For the young ones stolen. Just so, when this girl
Found the bare corpse, and all her love's work wasted,
She wept, and cried on heaven to damn the hands
That had done this thing.
              And then she brought more dust
And sprinkled wine three times for her brother's ghost.

We ran and took her at once. She was not afraid,
Not even when we charged her with what she had done.
She denied nothing.
           And this was a comfort to me,
And some uneasiness: for it is a good thing
To escape from death, but it is no great pleasure
To bring death to a friend.
           Yet I always say
There is nothing so comfortable as your own safe skin!
CREON.　[*Slowly, dangerously*]　And you, Antigonê,
  You with your head hanging,—do you confess this thing?
ANTIGONE.　I do. I deny nothing.
CREON.　　　　　[*To* SENTRY:]　You may go.　[*Exit* SENTRY]

[*To* ANTIGONE:]

Tell me, tell me briefly:
  Had you heard my proclamation touching this matter?
ANTIGONE.　It was public. Could I help hearing it?
CREON.　And yet you dared defy the law.
ANTIGONE.　　　　　　　　　　　　　　I dared.
  It was not God's proclamation. That final Justice
  That rules the world below makes no such laws.

Your edict, King, was strong,
But all your strength is weakness itself against
The immortal unrecorded laws of God.
They are not merely now: they were, and shall be,
Operative for ever, beyond man utterly.

I knew I must die, even without your decree:
I am only mortal. And if I must die
Now, before it is my time to die,
Surely this is no hardship: can anyone
Living, as I live, with evil all about me,
Think Death less than a friend? This death of mine
Is of no importance; but if I had left my brother
Lying in death unburied, I should have suffered.
Now I do not.
                    You smile at me. Ah Creon,
Think me a fool, if you like; but it may well be
That a fool convicts me of folly.

CHORAGOS. Like father, like daughter: both headstrong, deaf to reason!
    She has never learned to yield.

CREON.   She has much to learn.
    The inflexible heart breaks first, the toughest iron
    Cracks first, and the wildest horses bend their necks
    At the pull of the smallest curb.
                              Pride? In a slave?
    This girl is guilty of double insolence,
    Breaking the given laws and boasting of it.
    Who is the man here,
    She or I, if this crime goes unpunished?
    Sister's child, or more than sister's child,
    Or closer yet in blood—she and her sister
    Win bitter death for this!

[*To* SERVANTS:]

                Go, some of you,
    Arrest Ismenê. I accuse her equally.
    Bring her: you will find her sniffling in the house there.

    Her mind's a traitor: crimes kept in the dark
    Cry for light, and the guardian brain shudders;
    But how much worse than this
    Is brazen boasting of barefaced anarchy!

ANTIGONE. Creon, what more do you want than my death?

CREON.   Nothing.
    That gives me everything.

ANTIGONE.   Then I beg you: kill me.
    This talking is a great weariness: your words
    Are distasteful to me, and I am sure that mine
    Seem so to you. And yet they should not seem so:
    I should have praise and honor for what I have done.
    All these men here would praise me

Were their lips not frozen shut with fear of you. [*Bitterly*]
Ah the good fortune of kings,
Licensed to say and do whatever they please!

CREON. You are alone here in that opinion.

ANTIGONE. No, they are with me. But they keep their tongues in leash.

CREON. Maybe. But you are guilty, and they are not.

ANTIGONE. There is no guilt in reverence for the dead.

CREON. But Eteoclês—was he not your brother too?

ANTIGONE. My brother too.

CREON.   And you insult his memory?

ANTIGONE. [*Softly*] The dead man would not say that I insult it.

CREON. He would: for you honor a traitor as much as him.

ANTIGONE. His own brother, traitor or not, and equal in blood.

CREON. He made war on his country. Eteoclês defended it.

ANTIGONE. Nevertheless, there are honors due all the dead.

CREON. But not the same for the wicked as for the just.

ANTIGONE. Ah Creon, Creon,
Which of us can say what the gods hold wicked?

CREON. An enemy is an enemy, even dead.

ANTIGONE. It is my nature to join in love, not hate.

CREON. [*Finally losing patience*] Go join him, then; if you must have your love,
Find it in hell!

CHORAGOS. But see, Ismenê comes:

[*Enter* ISMENE, *guarded*]

Those tears are sisterly, the cloud
That shadows her eyes rains down gentle sorrow.

CREON. You, too, Ismenê,
Snake in my ordered house, sucking my blood
Stealthily—and all the time I never knew
That these two sisters were aiming at my throne!

                                                   Ismenê,
Do you confess your share in this crime, or deny it?
Answer me.

ISMENE. Yes, if she will let me say so. I am guilty.

ANTIGONE. [*Coldly*] No, Ismenê. You have no right to say so.
You would not help me, and I will not have you help me.

ISMENE. But now I know what you meant; and I am here
To join you, to take my share of punishment.

ANTIGONE. The dead man and the gods who rule the dead
Know whose act this was. Words are not friends.

ISMENE. Do you refuse me, Antigonê? I want to die with you:
I too have a duty that I must discharge to the dead.

ANTIGONE. You shall not lessen my death by sharing it.

ISMENE. What do I care for life when you are dead?

ANTIGONE.   Ask Creon. You're always hanging on his opinions.

ISMENE.   You are laughing at me. Why, Antigonê?

ANTIGONE.   It's a joyless laughter, Ismenê.

ISMENE.   But can I do nothing?

ANTIGONE.   Yes. Save yourself. I shall not envy you.
  There are others who will praise you; I shall have honor, too.

ISMENE.   But we are equally guilty!

ANTIGONE.   No more, Ismenê.
  You are alive, but I belong to Death.

CREON.   [*To the* CHORUS:]   Gentlemen, I beg you to observe these girls:
  One has just now lost her mind; the other,
  It seems, has never had a mind at all.

ISMENE.   Grief teaches the steadiest minds to waver, King.

CREON.   Yours certainly did, when you assumed guilt with the guilty!

ISMENE.   But how could I go on living without her?

CREON.   You are.
  She is already dead.

ISMENE.   But your own son's bride!

CREON.   There are places enough for him to push his plow.
  I want no wicked women for my sons!

ISMENE.   O dearest Haimon, how your father wrongs you!

CREON.   I've had enough of your childish talk of marriage!

CHORAGOS.   Do you really intend to steal this girl from your son?

CREON.   No; Death will do that for me.

CHORAGOS.   Then she must die?

CREON.   [*Ironically*]   You dazzle me.
                        —But enough of this talk!

[*To* GUARDS:]

You, there, take them away and guard them well:
For they are but women, and even brave men run
When they see Death coming.   [*Exeunt* ISMENE, ANTIGONE, *and* GUARDS]

ODE II

CHORUS.   Fortunate is the man who has never tasted God's vengeance! [STROPHE 1]
  Where once the anger of heaven has struck, that house is shaken
  For ever: damnation rises behind each child
  Like a wave cresting out of the black northeast,
  When the long darkness under sea roars up
  And bursts drumming death upon the whirlwhipped sand.

  I have seen this gathering sorrow from time long past   [ANTISTROPHE 1]
  Loom upon Oedipus' children: generation from generation
  Takes the compulsive rage of the enemy god.

So lately this last flower of Oedipus' line
Drank the sunlight! but now a passionate word
And a handful of dust have closed up all its beauty.

What mortal arrogance   [STROPHE 2]
    Transcends the wrath of Zeus?
Sleep cannot lull him, nor the effortless long months
Of the timeless gods: but he is young for ever,
And his house is the shining day of high Olympos.
    All that is and shall be,
    And all the past, is his.
No pride on earth is free of the curse of heaven.

The straying dreams of men   [ANTISTROPHE 2]
    May bring them ghosts of joy:
But as they drowse, the waking embers burn them;
Or they walk with fixed éyes, as blind men walk.
But the ancient wisdom speaks for our own time:
    Fate works most for woe
    With Folly's fairest show.
Man's little pleasure is the spring of sorrow.

SCENE III

CHORAGOS.   But here is Haimon, King, the last of all your sons.
    Is it grief for Antigonê that brings him here,
    And bitterness at being robbed of his bride?

[*Enter* HAIMON]

CREON.   We shall soon see, and no need of diviners.

                                                        —Son,
    You have heard my final judgment on that girl:
    Have you come here hating me, or have you come
    With deference and with love, whatever I do?
HAIMON.   I am your son, father. You are my guide.
    You make things clear for me, and I obey you.
    No marriage means more to me than your continuing wisdom.
CREON.   Good. That is the way to behave: subordinate
    Everything else, my son, to your father's will.
    This is what a man prays for, that he may get
    Sons attentive and dutiful in his house,
    Each hating his father's enemies,
    Honoring his father's friends. But if his sons
    Fail him, if they turn out unprofitably,
    What has he fathered but trouble for himself
    And amusement for the malicious?

                                        So you are right
Not to lose your head over this woman.
Your pleasure with her would soon grow cold, Haimon,
And then you'd have a hellcat in bed and elsewhere.
Let her find her husband in Hell!
Of all the people in this city, only she
Has had contempt for my law and broken it.

Do you want me to show myself weak before the people?
Or to break my sworn word? No, and I will not.
The woman dies.
I suppose she'll plead "family ties." Well, let her.
If I permit my own family to rebel,
How shall I earn the world's obedience?
Show me the man who keeps his house in hand,
He's fit for public authority.
                              I'll have no dealings
With law-breakers, critics of the government:
Whoever is chosen to govern should be obeyed—
Must be obeyed, in all things, great and small,
Just and unjust! O Haimon,
The man who knows how to obey, and that man only,
Knows how to give commands when the time comes.
You can depend on him, no matter how fast
The spears come: he's a good soldier, he'll stick it out.

Anarchy, anarchy! Show me a greater evil!
This is why cities tumble and the great houses rain down,
This is what scatters armies!

No, no: good lives are made so by discipline.
We keep the laws then, and the lawmakers,
And no woman shall seduce us. If we must lose,
Let's lose to a man, at least! Is a woman stronger than we?
CHORAGOS.   Unless time has rusted my wits,
    What you say, King, is said with point and dignity.
HAIMON. [*Boyishly earnest*] Father:
    Reason is God's crowning gift to man, and you are right
    To warn me against losing mine. I cannot say—
    I hope that I shall never want to say!—that you
    Have reasoned badly. Yet there are other men
    Who can reason too; and their opinions might be helpful.
    You are not in a position to know everything
    That people say or do, or what they feel:
    Your temper terrifies them—everyone

Will tell you only what you like to hear.
But I, at any rate, can listen; and I have heard them
Muttering and whispering in the dark about this girl.
They say no woman has ever, so unreasonably,
Died so shameful a death for a generous act:
"She covered her brother's body. Is this indecent?
She kept him from dogs and vultures. Is this a crime?
Death?—She should have all the honor that we can give her!"

This is the way they talk out there in the city.

You must believe me:
Nothing is closer to me than your happiness.
What could be closer? Must not any son
Value his father's fortune as his father does his?
I beg you, do not be unchangeable:
Do not believe that you alone can be right.
The man who thinks that,
The man who maintains that only he has the power
To reason correctly, the gift to speak, the soul—
A man like that, when you know him, turns out empty.

It is not reason never to yield to reason!

In flood time you can see how some trees bend,
And because they bend, even their twigs are safe,
While stubborn trees are torn up, roots and all.
And the same thing happens in sailing:
Make your sheet fast, never slacken,—and over you go,
Head over heels and under: and there's your voyage.

Forget you are angry! Let yourself be moved!
I know I am young; but please let me say this:
The ideal condition
Would be, I admit, that men should be right by instinct;
But since we are all too likely to go astray,
The reasonable thing is to learn from those who can teach.
CHORAGOS.   You will do well to listen to him, King,
  If what he says is sensible. And you, Haimon,
  Must listen to your father.—Both speak well.
CREON.   You consider it right for a man of my years and experience
  To go to school to a boy?
HAIMON.   It is not right
  If I am wrong. But if I am young, and right,
  What does my age matter?

CREON.   You think it right to stand up for an anarchist?

HAIMON.   Not at all. I pay no respect to criminals.

CREON.   Then she is not a criminal?

HAIMON.   The City would deny it, to a man.

CREON.   And the City proposes to teach me how to rule?

HAIMON.   Ah. Who is it that's talking like a boy now?

CREON.   My voice is the one voice giving orders in this City!

HAIMON.   It is no City if it takes orders from one voice.

CREON.   The State is the King!

HAIMON.   Yes, if the State is a desert.   [*Pause*]

CREON.   This boy, it seems, has sold out to a woman.

HAIMON.   If you are a woman: my concern is only for you.

CREON.   So? Your "concern"! In a public brawl with your father!

HAIMON.   How about you, in a public brawl with justice?

CREON.   With justice, when all that I do is within my rights?

HAIMON.   You have no right to trample on God's right.

CREON.   [*Completely out of control*]   Fool, adolescent fool! Taken in by a woman!

HAIMON.   You'll never see me taken in by anything vile.

CREON.   Every word you say is for her!

HAIMON.   [*Quietly darkly*]   And for you.

And for me. And for the gods under the earth.

CREON.   You'll never marry her while she lives.

HAIMON.   Then she must die.—But her death will cause another.

CREON.   Another?

Have you lost your senses? Is this an open threat?

HAIMON.   There is no threat in speaking to emptiness.

CREON.   I swear you'll regret this superior tone of yours!

You are the empty one!

HAIMON.   If you were not my father,

I'd say you were perverse.

CREON.   You girlstruck fool, don't play at words with me!

HAIMON.   I am sorry. You prefer silence.

CREON.   Now, by God—!

I swear, by all the gods in heaven above us,

You'll watch it, I swear you shall!

[*To the* SERVANTS:]

Bring her out!

Bring the woman out! Let her die before his eyes!

Here, this instant, with her bridegroom beside her!

HAIMON.   Not here, no; she will not die here, King.

And you will never see my face again.

Go on raving as long as you've a friend to endure you.   [*Exit* HAIMON]

CHORAGOS.   Gone, gone.

Creon, a young man in a rage is dangerous!

CREON.   Let him do, or dream to do, more than a man can.
   He shall not save these girls from death.
CHORAGOS.   These girls?
   You have sentenced them both?
CREON.   No, you are right.
   I will not kill the one whose hands are clean.
CHORAGOS.   But Antigonê?
CREON.   [*Somberly*]   I will carry her far away
   Out there in the wilderness, and lock her
   Living in a vault of stone. She shall have food,
   As the custom is, to absolve the State of her death.
   And there let her pray to the gods of hell:
   They are her only gods:
   Perhaps they will show her an escape from death
   Or she may learn,
                  though late,
   That piety shown the dead is pity in vain.   [*Exit* CREON]

ODE III

CHORUS.   Love, unconquerable   [STROPHE]
   Waster of rich men, keeper
   Of warm lights and all-night vigil
   In the soft face of a girl:
   Sea-wanderer, forest-visitor!
   Even the pure Immortals cannot escape you,
   And mortal man, in his one day's dusk,
   Trembles before your glory.

   Surely you swerve upon ruin   [ANTISTROPHE]
   The just man's consenting heart,
   As here you have made bright anger
   Strike between father and son—
   And none has conquered but Love!
   A girl's glánce wórking the will of heaven:
   Pleasure to her alone who mocks us,
   Merciless Aphroditê.

SCENE IV

CHORAGOS.   [*As* ANTIGONE *enters guarded*]   But I can no longer stand in awe of
   this,
   Nor, seeing what I see, keep back my tears.
   Here is Antigonê, passing to that chamber
   Where we all find sleep at last.
ANTIGONE.   Look upon me, friends, and pity me   [STROPHE 1]
   Turning back at the night's edge to say
   Good-by to the sun that shines for me no longer;

Now sleepy Death
Summons me down to Acheron, that cold shore:
There is no bridesong there, nor any music.
CHORUS. Yet not unpraised, not without a kind of honor,
You walk at last into the underworld;
Untouched by sickness, broken by no sword.
What woman has ever found your way to death?
ANTIGONE. How often I have heard the story of Niobê,   [ANTISTROPHE 1]
Tantalos' wretched daughter, how the stone
Clung fast about her, ivy-close: and they say
The rain falls endlessly
And sifting soft snow; her tears are never done.
I feel the loneliness of her death in mine.
CHORUS. But she was born of heaven, and you
Are woman, woman-born. If her death is yours,
A mortal woman's, is this not for you
Glory in our world and in the world beyond?
ANTIGONE. You laugh at me. Ah, friends, friends,   [STROPHE 2]
Can you not wait until I am dead? O Thebes,
O men many-charioted, in love with Fortune,
Dear springs of Dircê, sacred Theban grove,
Be witnesses for me, denied all pity,
Unjustly judged! and think a word of love
For her whose path turns
Under dark earth, where there are no more tears.
CHORUS. You have passed beyond human daring and come at last
Into a place of stone where Justice sits.
I cannot tell
What shape of your father's guilt appears in this.
ANTIGONE. You have touched it at last: that bridal bed   [ANTISTROPHE 2]
Unspeakable, horror of son and mother mingling:
Their crime, infection of all our family!
O Oedipus, father and brother!
Your marriage strikes from the grave to murder mine.
I have been a stranger here in my own land:
All my life
The blasphemy of my birth has followed me.
CHORUS. Reverence is a virtue, but strength
Lives in established law: that must prevail.
You have made your choice,
Your death is the doing of your conscious hand.
ANTIGONE. Then let me go, since all your words are bitter,   [EPODE]
And the very light of the sun is cold to me.
Lead me to my vigil, where I must have
Neither love nor lamentation; no song, but silence.

[CREON *interrupts impatiently*]

CREON.   If dirges and planned lamentations could put off death,
Men would be singing for ever.

[*To the* SERVANTS:]

Take her, go!
You know your orders: take her to the vault
And leave her alone there. And if she lives or dies,
That's her affair, not ours: our hands are clean.
ANTIGONE.   O tomb, vaulted bride-bed in eternal rock,
Soon I shall be with my own again
Where Persephonê welcomes the thin ghosts underground:
And I shall see my father again, and you, mother,
And dearest Polyneicês—

dearest indeed
To me, since it was my hand
That washed him clean and poured the ritual wine:
And my reward is death before my time!

And yet, as men's hearts know, I have done no wrong,
I have not sinned before God. Or if I have,
I shall know the truth in death. But if the guilt
Lies upon Creon who judged me, then, I pray,
May his punishment equal my own.
CHORAGOS.   O passionate heart,
Unyielding, tormented still by the same winds!
CREON.   Her guards shall have good cause to regret their delaying.
ANTIGONE.   Ah! That voice is like the voice of death!
CREON.   I can give you no reason to think you are mistaken.
ANTIGONE.   Thebes, and you my fathers' gods,
And rulers of Thebes, you see me now, the last
Unhappy daughter of a line of kings,
Your kings, led away to death. You will remember
What things I suffer, and at what men's hands,
Because I would not transgress the laws of heaven.

[*To the* GUARDS, *simply:*]

Come: let us wait no longer.   [*Exit* ANTIGONE, *L., guarded*]

ODE IV

CHORUS.   All Danaê's beauty was locked away   [STROPHE 1]
In a brazen cell where the sunlight could not come:
A small room, still as any grave, enclosed her.
Yet she was a princess too,

And Zeus in a rain of gold poured love upon her.
O child, child,
No power in wealth or war
Or tough sea-blackened ships
Can prevail against untiring Destiny!

And Dryas' son also, that furious king,   [ANTISTROPHE 1]
Bore the god's prisoning anger for his pride:
Sealed up by Dionysos in deaf stone,
His madness died among echoes.
So at the last he learned what dreadful power
His tongue had mocked:
For he had profaned the revels,
And fired the wrath of the nine
Implacable Sisters that love the sound of the flute.

And old men tell a half-remembered tale   [STROPHE 2]
Of horror done where a dark ledge splits the sea
And a double surf beats on the gráy shóres:
How a king's new woman, sick
With hatred for the queen he had imprisoned,
Ripped out his two sons' eyes with her bloody hands
While grinning Arês watched the shuttle plunge
Four times: four blind wounds crying for revenge,

Crying, tears and blood mingled.—Piteously born,   [ANTISTROPHE 2]
Those sons whose mother was of heavenly birth!
Her father was the god of the North Wind
And she was cradled by gales,
She raced with young colts on the glittering hills
And walked untrammeled in the open light:
But in her marriage deathless Fate found means
To build a tomb like yours for all her joy.

SCENE V

[Enter blind TEIRESIAS, *led by a boy. The opening speeches of* TEIRESIAS *should be in singsong contrast to the realistic lines of* CREON.*]*

TEIRESIAS.   This is the way the blind man comes, Princes, Princes,
  Lock-step, two heads lit by the eyes of one.
CREON.   What new thing have you to tell us, old Teiresias?
TEIRESIAS.   I have much to tell you: listen to the prophet, Creon.
CREON.   I am not aware that I have ever failed to listen.
TEIRESIAS.   Then you have done wisely, King, and ruled well.

CREON. I admit my debt to you. But what have you to say?

TEIRESIAS. This, Creon: you stand once more on the edge of fate.

CREON. What do you mean? Your words are a kind of dread.

TEIRESIAS. Listen, Creon:

I was sitting in my chair of augury, at the place
Where the birds gather about me. They were all a-chatter,
As is their habit, when suddenly I heard
A strange note in their jangling, a scream, a
Whirring fury; I knew that they were fighting,
Tearing each other, dying
In a whirlwind of wings clashing. And I was afraid.
I began the rites of burnt-offering at the altar,
But Hephaistos failed me: instead of bright flame,
There was only the sputtering slime of the fat thigh-flesh
Melting: the entrails dissolved in gray smoke,
The bare bone burst from the welter. And no blaze!

This was a sign from heaven. My boy described it,
Seeing for me as I see for others.

I tell you, Creon, you yourself have brought
This new calamity upon us. Our hearths and altars
Are stained with the corruption of dogs and carrion birds
That glut themselves on the corpse of Oedipus' son.
The gods are deaf when we pray to them, their fire
Recoils from our offering, their birds of omen
Have no cry of comfort, for they are gorged
With the thick blood of the dead.
                              O my son,
These are no trifles! Think: all men make mistakes,
But a good man yields when he knows his course is wrong,
And repairs the evil. The only crime is pride.

Give in to the dead man, then: do not fight with a corpse—
What glory is it to kill a man who is dead?
Think, I beg you:
It is for your own good that I speak as I do.
You should be able to yield for your own good.

CREON. It seems that prophets have made me their especial province.
All my life long
I have been a kind of butt for the dull arrows
Of doddering fortune-tellers!
                              No, Teiresias:
If your birds—if the great eagles of God himself
Should carry him stinking bit by bit to heaven,

I would not yield. I am not afraid of pollution:
No man can defile the gods.
                              Do what you will,
Go into business, make money, speculate
In India gold or that synthetic gold from Sardis,
Get rich otherwise than by my consent to bury him.
Teiresias, it is a sorry thing when a wise man
Sells his wisdom, lets out his words for hire!

TEIRESIAS.   Ah Creon! Is there no man left in the world—
CREON.   To do what?—Come, let's have the aphorism!
TEIRESIAS.   No man who knows that wisdom outweighs any wealth?
CREON.   As surely as bribes are baser than any baseness.
TEIRESIAS.   You are sick, Creon! You are deathly sick!
CREON.   As you say: it is not my place to challenge a prophet.
TEIRESIAS.   Yet you have said my prophecy is for sale.
CREON.   The generation of prophets has always loved gold.
TEIRESIAS.   The generation of kings has always loved brass.
CREON.   You forget yourself! You are speaking to your King.
TEIRESIAS.   I know it. You are a king because of me.
CREON.   You have a certain skill; but you have sold out.
TEIRESIAS.   King, you will drive me to words that—
CREON.   Say them, say them!
Only remember: I will not pay you for them.
TEIRESIAS.   No, you will find them too costly.
CREON.   No doubt. Speak:
Whatever you say, you will not change my will.
TEIRESIAS.   Then take this, and take it to heart!
The time is not far off when you shall pay back
Corpse for corpse, flesh of your own flesh.
You have thrust the child of this world into living night,
You have kept from the gods below the child that is theirs:
The one in a grave before her death, the other,
Dead, denied the grave. This is your crime:
And the Furies and the dark gods of Hell
Are swift with terrible punishment for you.

Do you want to buy me now, Creon?

                              Not many days,
And your house will be full of men and women weeping,
And curses will be hurled at you from far
Cities grieving for sons unburied, left to rot
Before the walls of Thebes.

These are my arrows, Creon: they are all for you.

But come, child: lead me home.   [*To* BOY:]
Let him waste his fine anger upon younger men.
Maybe he will learn at last
To control a wiser tongue in a better head.   [*Exit* TEIRESIAS]
CHORAGOS.   The old man has gone, King, but his words
Remain to plague us. I am old, too,
But I cannot remember that he was ever false.
CREON.   That is true.... It troubles me.
Oh it is hard to give in! but it is worse
To risk everything for stubborn pride.
CHORAGOS.   Creon: take my advice.
CREON.   What shall I do?
CHORAGOS.   Go quickly: free Antigonê from her vault
And build a tomb for the body of Polyneicês.
CREON.   You would have me do this?
CHORAGOS.   Creon, yes!
And it must be done at once: God moves
Swiftly to cancel the folly of stubborn men.
CREON.   It is hard to deny the heart! But I
Will do it: I will not fight with destiny.
CHORAGOS.   You must go yourself, you cannot leave it to others.
CREON.   I will go.
               —Bring axes, servants:
Come with me to the tomb. I buried her, I
Will set her free.
               Oh quickly!
My mind misgives—
The laws of the gods are mighty, and a man must serve them
To the last day of his life!   [*Exit* CREON]

PÆAN

CHORAGOS.   God of many names   [STROPHE 1]
CHORUS.   O Iacchos
                                    son
of Kadmeian Sémelê
                          O born of the Thunder!
Guardian of the West
                          Regent
of Eleusis' plain
                          O Prince of maenad Thebes
and the Dragon Field by rippling Ismenos:
CHORAGOS.   God of many names   [ANTISTROPHE 1]
CHORUS.   the flame of torches
flares on our hills

the nymphs of Iacchos
dance at the spring of Castalia:

from the vine-close mountain
come ah come in ivy:
Evohé evohé! sings through the streets of Thebes

CHORAGOS.   God of many names   [STROPHE 2]
CHORUS.   Iacchos of Thebes
heavenly Child
of Sémelê bride of the Thunderer!
The shadow of plague is upon us:
come
with clement feet
oh come from Parnasos
down the long slopes
across the lamenting water

CHORAGOS.   Iô Fire! Chorister of the throbbing stars!   [ANTISTROPHE 2]
O purest among the voices of the night!
Thou son of God, blaze for us!

CHORUS.   Come with choric rapture of circling Maenads
Who cry *Iô Iacche!*
God of many names!

ÉXODOS

[*Enter* MESSENGER, *L.*]

MESSENGER.   Men of the line of Kadmos, you who live
Near Amphion's citadel:
I cannot say
Of any condition of human life "This is fixed,
This is clearly good, or bad." Fate raises up,
And Fate casts down the happy and unhappy alike:
No man can foretell his Fate.
Take the case of Creon:
Creon was happy once, as I count happiness:
Victorious in battle, sole governor of the land,
Fortunate father of children nobly born.
And now it has all gone from him! Who can say
That a man is still alive when his life's joy fails?
He is a walking dead man. Grant him rich,
Let him live like a king in his great house:
If his pleasure is gone, I would not give
So much as the shadow of smoke for all he owns.

CHORAGOS.   Your words hint at sorrow: what is your news for us?

MESSENGER.   They are dead. The living are guilty of their death.

CHORAGOS.   Who is guilty? Who is dead? Speak!

MESSENGER.   Haimon.
  Haimon is dead; and the hand that killed him
  Is his own hand.
CHORAGOS.   His father's? or his own?
MESSENGER. His own, driven mad by the murder his father had done.
CHORAGOS. Teiresias, Teiresias, how clearly you saw it all!
MESSENGER. This is my news: you must draw what conclusions you can from it.
CHORAGOS. But look: Eurydicê, our Queen:
  Has she overheard us?

[Enter EURYDICE *from the Palace, C.]*

EURYDICE. I have heard something, friends:
  As I was unlocking the gate of Pallas' shrine,
  For I needed her help today, I heard a voice
  Telling of some new sorrow. And I fainted
  There at the temple with all my maidens about me.
  But speak again: whatever it is, I can bear it:
  Grief and I are no strangers.
MESSENGER.   Dearest Lady,
  I will tell you plainly all that I have seen.
  I shall not try to comfort you: what is the use,
  Since comfort could lie only in what is not true?
  The truth is always best.
                      I went with Creon
  To the outer plain where Polyneicês was lying,
  No friend to pity him, his body shredded by dogs.
  We made our prayers in that place to Hecatê
  And Pluto, that they would be merciful. And we bathed
  The corpse with holy water, and we brought
  Fresh-broken branches to burn what was left of it,
  And upon the urn we heaped up a towering barrow
  Of the earth of his own land.
                    When we were done, we ran
  To the vault where Antigonê lay on her couch of stone.
  One of the servants had gone ahead,
  And while he was yet far off he heard a voice
  Grieving within the chamber, and he came back
  And told Creon. And as the King went closer,
  The air was full of wailing, the words lost,
  And he begged us to make all haste. "Am I a prophet?"
  He said, weeping, "And must I walk this road,
  The saddest of all that I have gone before?
  My son's voice calls me on. Oh quickly, quickly!
  Look through the crevice there, and tell me
  If it is Haimon, or some deception of the gods!"

We obeyed; and in the cavern's farthest corner
We saw her lying:
She had made a noose of her fine linen veil
And hanged herself. Haimon lay beside her,
His arms about her waist, lamenting her,
His love lost under ground, crying out
That his father had stolen her away from him.

When Creon saw him the tears rushed to his eyes
And he called to him: "What have you done, child? Speak to me.
What are you thinking that makes your eyes so strange?
O my son, my son, I come to you on my knees!"
But Haimon spat in his face. He said not a word,
Staring—
        And suddenly drew his sword
And lunged. Creon shrank back, the blade missed; and the boy,
Desperate against himself, drove it half its length
Into his own side, and fell. And as he died
He gathered Antigonê close in his arms again,
Choking, his blood bright red on her white cheek.
And now he lies dead with the dead, and she is his
At last, his bride in the houses of the dead. [*Exit* EURYDICE *into the Palace*]

CHORAGOS.   She has left us without a word. What can this mean?

MESSENGER.   It troubles me, too; yet she knows what is best,
Her grief is too great for public lamentation,
And doubtless she has gone to her chamber to weep
For her dead son, leading her maidens in his dirge.

CHORAGOS.   It may be so: but I fear this deep silence. [*Pause*]

MESSENGER.   I will see what she is doing. I will go in. [*Exit* MESSENGER *into the Palace*]

[*Enter* CREON *with attendants, bearing* HAIMON'*s body*]

CHORAGOS.   But here is the King himself: oh look at him,
Bearing his own damnation in his arms.

CREON.   Nothing you say can touch me any more.
My own blind heart has brought me
From darkness to final darkness. Here you see
The father murdering, the murdered son—
And all my civic wisdom!

Haimon my son, so young, so young to die,
I was the fool, not you; and you died for me.

CHORAGOS.   That is the truth; but you were late in learning it.

CREON.   This truth is hard to bear. Surely a god
Has crushed me beneath the hugest weight of heaven,

And driven me headlong a barbaric way
To trample out the thing I held most dear.

The pains that men will take to come to pain!

[*Enter* MESSENGER *from the Palace*]

MESSENGER.   The burden you carry in your hands is heavy,
But it is not all: you will find more in your house.
CREON.   What burden worse than this shall I find there?
MESSENGER.   The Queen is dead.
CREON.   O port of death, deaf world,
Is there no pity for me? And you, Angel of evil,
I was dead, and your words are death again.
Is it true, boy? Can it be true?
Is my wife dead? Has death bred death?
MESSENGER.   You can see for yourself.

[*The doors are opened, and the body of* EURYDICE *is disclosed within.*]

CREON.   Oh pity!
All true, all true, and more than I can bear!
O my wife, my son!
MESSENGER.   She stood before the altar, and her heart
Welcomed the knife her own hand guided,
And a great cry burst from her lips for Megareus dead,
And for Haimon dead, her sons; and her last breath
Was a curse for their father, the murderer of her sons.
And she fell, and the dark flowed in through her closing eyes.
CREON.   O god, I am sick with fear.
Are there no swords here? Has no one a blow for me?
MESSENGER.   Her curse is upon you for the deaths of both.
CREON.   It is right that it should be. I alone am guilty.
I know it, and I say it. Lead me in,
Quickly, friends.
I have neither life nor substance. Lead me in.
CHORAGOS.   You are right, if there can be right in so much wrong.
The briefest way is best in a world of sorrow.
CREON.   Let it come,
Let death come quickly, and be kind to me.
I would not ever see the sun again.
CHORAGOS.   All that will come when it will; but we, meanwhile,
Have much to do. Leave the future to itself.
CREON.   All my heart was in that prayer!
CHORAGOS.   Then do not pray any more: the sky is deaf.
CREON.   Lead me away. I have been rash and foolish.
I have killed my son and my wife.

I look for comfort; my comfort lies here dead.
Whatever my hands have touched has come to nothing.
Fate has brought all my pride to a thought of dust.

[*As* CREON *is being led into the house, the* CHORAGOS *advances and speaks
directly to the audience*]

CHORAGOS.   There is no happiness where there is no wisdom;
No wisdom but in submission to the gods.
Big words are always punished,
And proud men in old age learn to be wise.

English version by Dudley Fitts and Robert Fitzgerald

Journal Entry

To what extent is Ismene a foil for Antigone? What is your evaluation of Ismene's point
of view that individuals must obey the law?

Textual Considerations

1. What are Creon's reasons for denying the rite of burial to Polyneices, and why does
   he decide to punish those who break that law?
2. What is Teiresias's function in the drama? Define the nature of the conflict between
   him and Creon.
3. Conflict is a major element of plot in *Antigone*. In addition to the conflict of gender,
   in what other conflicts are Creon and Antigone involved?
4. Comment on the role of the Chorus in the drama. Does it provide any insights into
   the situation confronting Creon and Antigone? Explain.
5. To what extent are Antigone and Creon responsible for their individual tragedies,
   and to what extent are they victims of fate?

Cultural Contexts

1. Discuss with your group the political implications of the debate between Creon and
   Haimon. Split your group into two, and debate the merits and fallacies of Haimon's
   and Creon's political points of view on the role of the people.
2. Debate also whether, according to Sophocles, Antigone and Creon might represent
   equal dangers to the state.

Susan Glaspell
1916

Trifles

CHARACTERS

GEORGE HENDERSON, *County attorney*
HENRY PETERS, *Sheriff*
LEWIS HALE, *A neighboring farmer*
MRS. PETERS
MRS. HALE

SCENE. *The kitchen in the now abandoned farmhouse of* JOHN WRIGHT, *a gloomy kitchen, and left without having been put in order—unwashed pans under the sink, a loaf of bread outside the breadbox, a dish towel on the table—other signs of incompleted work. At the rear the outer door opens and the* SHERIFF *comes in followed by the* COUNTY ATTORNEY *and* HALE. *The* SHERIFF *and* HALE *are men in middle life, the* COUNTY ATTORNEY *is a young man; all are much bundled up and go at once to the stove. They are followed by two women—the* SHERIFF'S *wife first; she is a slight wiry woman, a thin nervous face.* MRS. HALE *is larger and would ordinarily be called more comfortable looking, but she is disturbed now and looks fearfully about as she enters. The women have come in slowly, and stand close together near the door.*

COUNTY ATTORNEY. [*Rubbing his hands.*] This feels good. Come up to the fire, ladies.

MRS. PETERS. [*After taking a step forward.*] I'm not—cold.

SHERIFF. [*Unbuttoning his overcoat and stepping away from the stove as if to mark the beginning of official business.*] Now, Mr. Hale, before you move things about, you explain to Mr. Henderson just what you saw when you came here yesterday morning.

COUNTY ATTORNEY. By the way, has anything been moved? Are things just as you left them yesterday?

SHERIFF. [*Looking about.*] It's just the same. When it dropped below zero last night I thought I'd better send Frank out this morning to make a fire for us— no use getting pneumonia with a big case on, but I told him not to touch anything except the stove—and you know Frank.

COUNTY ATTORNEY. Somebody should have been left here yesterday.

SHERIFF. Oh—yesterday. When I had to send Frank to Morris Center for that man who went crazy—I want you to know I had my hands full yesterday, I knew you could get back from Omaha by today and as long as I went over everything here myself—

COUNTY ATTORNEY. Well, Mr Hale, tell just what happened when you came here yesterday morning.

HALE. Harry and I had started to town with a load of potatoes. We came along the road from my place and as I got here I said, "I'm going to see if I can't get John Wright to go in with me on a party telephone." I spoke to Wright about it once before and he put me off, saying folks talked too much anyway, and all he asked was peace and quiet—I guess you know how much he talked himself; but I thought maybe if I went to the house and talked about it before his wife, though I said to Harry I didn't know as what his wife wanted made much difference to John—

COUNTY ATTORNEY. Let's talk about that later, Mr. Hale. I do want to talk about that, but tell now just what happened when you got to the house.

HALE. I didn't hear or see anything; I knocked at the door, and still it was all quiet inside. I knew they must be up, it was past eight o'clock. So I knocked again, and I thought I heard somebody say, "Come in." I wasn't sure, I'm not sure yet, but I opened the door—this door [*Indicating the door by which the two women are still standing.*] and there in that rocker— [*Pointing to it.*] sat Mrs. Wright.

[*They all look at the rocker.*]

COUNTY ATTORNEY. What—was she doing?

HALE. She was rockin' back and forth. She had her apron in her hand and was kind of—pleating it.

COUNTY ATTORNEY. And how did she—look?

HALE. Well, she looked queer.

COUNTY ATTORNEY. How do you mean—queer?

HALE. Well, as if she didn't know what she was going to do next. And kind of done up.

COUNTY ATTORNEY. How did she seem to feel about your coming?

HALE. Why, I don't think she minded—one way or other. She didn't pay much attention. I said, "How do, Mrs. Wright, it's cold, ain't it?" And she said, "Is it?"—and went on kind of pleating at her apron. Well, I was surprised; she didn't ask me to come up to the stove or to set down, but just sat there, not even looking at me, so I said, "I want to see John." And then she—laughed. I guess you would call it a laugh. I thought of Harry and the team outside, so I said a little sharply "Can't I see John?" "No," she says, kind o' dull like. "Ain't he home?" says I. "Yes," says she, "he's home." "Then why can't I see him?" I asked her, out of patience. "'Cause he's dead," says she. "*Dead?*" says I. She just nodded her head, not getting a bit excited, but rockin' back and forth. "Why—where is he?" says I, not knowing what to say. She just pointed upstairs—like that [*Himself pointing to the room above*]. I got up, with the idea of going up there. I walked from there to here—then I says, "Why, what did he die of?" "He died of a rope round his neck," says she, and just went on pleating at her apron. Well, I went out and called Harry. I thought I might—need help. We went upstairs and there he was lyin'—

COUNTY ATTORNEY. I think I'd rather have you go into that upstairs, where you can point it all out. Just go on now with the rest of the story.

HALE. Well, my first thought was to get that rope off. It looked...[*Stops, his face twitches.*]...but Harry, he went up to him, and he said, "No, he's dead all right, and we'd better not touch anything." So we went back down stairs. She was still sitting that same way. "Has anybody been notified?" I asked. "No," she says, unconcerned. "Who did this, Mrs. Wright?" said Harry. He said it businesslike—and she stopped pleatin' of her apron. "I don't know," she says. "You don't *know?*" says Harry. "No," says she. "Weren't you sleepin in the bed with him?" says Harry. "Yes," says she, "but I was on the inside." "Somebody slipped a rope around his neck and strangled him and you didn't wake up?" says Harry. "I didn't wake up," she said after him. We must 'a looked as if we didn't see how that could be, for after a minute she said, "I sleep sound." Harry was going to ask her more questions but I said maybe we ought to let her tell her story first to the coroner, or the sheriff, so Harry went fast as he could to Rivers' place, where there's a telephone.

COUNTY ATTORNEY. And what did Mrs. Wright do when she knew that you had gone for the coroner?

HALE. She moved from that chair to this one over here [*Pointing to small chair in the corner.*] and just sat there with her hands together and looking down. I got a feeling that I ought to make some conversation, so I said I had come in to see if John wanted to put in a telephone, and at that she started to laugh, and then she stopped and looked at me—scared. [*The* COUNTY ATTORNEY, *who has had his notebook out, makes a note.*] I dunno, maybe it wasn't scared. I wouldn't like to say it was. Soon Harry got back, and then Dr. Lloyd came, and you, Mr. Peters, and so I guess that's all I know that you don't.

COUNTY ATTORNEY. [*Looking around.*] I guess we'll go upstairs first—and then out to the barn and around there. [*To the* SHERIFF] You're convinced that there was nothing important here—nothing that would point to any motive.

SHERIFF. Nothing here but kitchen things.

[*The* COUNTY ATTORNEY, *after again looking around the kitchen, opens the door of a cupboard closet. He gets up on a chair and looks on a shelf. Pulls his hand away, sticky.*]

COUNTY ATTORNEY. Here's a nice mess.

[*The women draw nearer.*]

MRS. PETERS [*To the other woman.*]. Oh, her fruit, it did freeze. [*To the* COUNTY ATTORNEY] She worried about that when it turned so cold. She said the fire'd go out and her jars would break.

SHERIFF. Well, can you beat the women! Held for murder and worryin' about her preserves.

COUNTY ATTORNEY. I guess before we're through she may have something more serious than preserves to worry about.

HALE. Well, women are used to worrying over trifles.

[*The two women move a little closer together.*]

COUNTY ATTORNEY. [*With the gallantry of a young politician.*] And yet, for all their worries, what would we do without the ladies? [*The women do not unbend. He goes to the sink, takes a dipperful of water from the pail and pouring it into a basin, washes his hands. Starts to wipe them on the roller towel, turns it for a cleaner place.*] Dirty towels! [*Kicks his foot against the pans under the sink.*] Not much of a housekeeper, would you say, ladies?

MRS. HALE. [*Stiffly.*] There's a great deal of work to be done on a farm.

COUNTY ATTORNEY. To be sure. And yet [*With a little bow to her*] I know there are some Dickson county farmhouses which do not have such roller towels.

[*He gives it a pull to expose its full length again.*]

MRS. HALE. Those towels get dirty awful quick. Men's hands aren't always as clean as they might be.

COUNTY ATTORNEY. Ah, loyal to your sex, I see. But you and Mrs. Wright were neighbors. I suppose you were friends, too.

MRS. HALE. [*Shaking her head.*] I've not seen much of her of late years. I've not been in this house—it's more than a year.

COUNTY ATTORNEY. And why was that? You didn't like her?

MRS. HALE. I liked her all well enough. Farmers's wives have their hands full, Mr. Henderson. And then—

COUNTY ATTORNEY. Yes—?

MRS. HALE. [*Looking about.*] It never seemed a cheerful place.

COUNTY ATTORNEY. No—it's not cheerful. I shouldn't say she had the homemaking instinct.

MRS. HALE. Well, I don't know as Wright had, either.

COUNTY ATTORNEY. You mean that they didn't get on very well?

MRS. HALE. No, I don't mean anything. But I don't think a place'd be any cheerfuller for John Wright's being in it.

COUNTY ATTORNEY. I'd like to talk more of that a little later. I want to get the lay of things upstairs now.

[*He goes to the left, where three steps lead to a door.*]

SHERIFF. I suppose anything Mrs. Peters does'll be all right. She was to take in some clothes for her, you know, and a few little things. We left in such a hurry yesterday.

COUNTY ATTORNEY. Yes, but I would like to see what you take, Mrs. Peters, and keep an eye out for anything that might be of use to us.

MRS. PETERS. Yes, Mr. Henderson.

[*The women listen to the men's steps on the stairs, then look about the kitchen.*]

MRS. HALE. I'd hate to have men coming into my kitchen, snooping around and criticising.

[*She arranges the pans under the sink which the* County Attorney *had shoved out of place.*]

MRS. PETERS. Of course it's no more than their duty.

MRS. HALE. Duty's all right, but I guess that deputy sheriff that came out to make the fire might have got a little of this on. [*Gives the roller towel a pull.*] Wish I'd thought of that sooner. Seems mean to talk about her for not having things slicked up when she had to come away in such a hurry.

MRS. PETERS. [*Who has gone to a small table in the left rear corner of the room and lifted one end of a towel that covers a pan.*] She had bread set.

[*Stands still.*]

MRS. HALE. [*Eyes fixed on a loaf of bread beside the breadbox, which is on a low shelf at the other side of the room. Moves slowly toward it.*] She was going to put this in there. [*Picks up loaf, then abruptly drops it. In a manner of returning to familiar things.*] It's a shame about her fruit. I wonder if it's all gone. [*Gets up on the chair and looks.*] I think there's some here that's all right, Mrs. Peters. Yes—here; [*Holding it toward the window.*] this is cherries, too. [*Looking again.*] I declare I believe that's the only one. [*Gets down, bottle in her hand. Goes to the sink and wipes it off on the outside.*] She'll feel awful after all her hard work in the hot weather. I remember the afternoon I put up my cherries last summer. [*She puts the bottle on the big kitchen table, center of the room. With a sigh, is about to sit down in the rocking-chair. Before she is seated realizes what chair it is; with a slow look at it, steps back. The chair which she has touched rocks back and forth.*]

MRS. PETERS. Well, I must get those things from the front room closet. [*She goes to the door at the right, but after looking into the other room, steps back.*] You coming with me, Mrs. Hale? You could help me carry them.

[*They go in the other room; reappear,* MRS. PETERS *carrying a dress and skirt,* MRS. HALE *following with a pair of shoes.*]

MRS. PETERS. My, it's cold in there.

[*She puts the clothes on the big table, and hurries to the stove.*]

MRS. HALE. [*Examining her skirt.*] Wright was close. I think maybe that's why she kept so much to herself. She didn't even belong to the Ladies Aid. I suppose she felt she couldn't do her part, and then you don't enjoy things when you feel shabby. She used to wear pretty clothes and be lively, when she was Minnie Foster, one of the town girls singing in the choir. But that—oh, that was thirty years ago. This all you was to take in?

MRS. PETERS. She said she wanted an apron. Funny thing to want, for there isn't much to get you dirty in jail, goodness knows. But I suppose just to make her feel more natural. She said they was in the top drawer in this cupboard. Yes, here. And then her little shawl that always hung behind the door. [*Opens stair door and looks.*] Yes, here it is.

[*Quickly shuts door leading upstairs.*]

MRS. HALE. [*Abruptly moving toward her.*] Mrs. Peters?

MRS. PETERS. Yes, Mrs. Hale?

MRS. HALE. Do you think she did it?

MRS. PETERS. [*In a frightened voice.*] Oh, I don't know.

MRS. HALE. Well, I don't think she did. Asking for an apron and her little shawl. Worrying about her fruit.

MRS. PETERS. [*Starts to speak, glances up, where footsteps are heard in the room above. In a low voice*]. Mr. Peters says it looks bad for her. Mr. Henderson is awful sarcastic in a speech and he'll make fun of her sayin' she didn't wake up.

MRS. HALE. Well, I guess John Wright didn't wake when they was slipping that rope under his neck.

MRS. PETERS. No, it's strange. It must have been done awful crafty and still. They say it was such a—funny way to kill a man, rigging it all up like that.

MRS. HALE. That's just what Mr. Hale said. There was a gun in the house. He says that's what he can't understand.

MRS. PETERS. Mr. Henderson said coming out that what was needed for the case was a motive; something to show anger, or—sudden feeling.

MRS. HALE. [*Who is standing by the table.*] Well, I don't see any signs of anger around here. [*She puts her hand on the dish towel which lies on the table, stands looking down at table, one half of which is clean, the other half messy.*] It's wiped to here. [*Makes a move as if to finish work, then turns and looks at loaf of bread outside the breadbox. Drops towel. In that voice of coming back to familiar things.*] Wonder how they are finding things upstairs. I hope she had it a little more red-up up there. You know, it seems kind of *sneaking*. Locking her up in town and then coming out here and trying to get her own house to turn against her!

MRS. PETERS. But Mrs. Hale, the law is the law.

MRS. HALE. I s'pose 'tis. [*Unbuttoning her coat.*] Better loosen up your things, Mrs. Peters. You won't feel them when you go out.

[MRS. PETERS *takes off her fur tippet, goes to hang it on hook at back of room, stands looking at the under part of the small corner table.*]

MRS. PETERS. She was piecing a quilt.

[*She brings the large sewing basket and they look at the bright pieces.*]

MRS. HALE. It's log cabin pattern. Pretty, isn't it? I wonder if she was goin' to quilt it or just knot it?

[*Footsteps have been heard coming down the stairs. The* SHERIFF *enters followed by* HALE *and the* COUNTY ATTORNEY.]

SHERIFF. They wonder if she was going to quilt it or just knot it!

[*The men laugh; the women look abashed.*]

COUNTY ATTORNEY. [*Rubbing his hands over the stove.*] Frank's fire didn't do too much up there, did it? Well, let's go out to the barn and get that cleared up.

[*The men go outside.*]

MRS. HALE. [*Resentfully.*] I don't know as there's anything so strange, our takin' up our time with little things while we're waiting for them to get the evidence. [*She sits down at the big table smoothing out a block with decision.*] I don't see as it's anything to laugh about.

MRS. PETERS. [*Apologetically.*] Of course they've got awful important things on their minds.

[*Pulls up a chair and joins* MRS. HALE *at the table.*]

MRS. HALE. [*Examining another block.*] Mrs. Peters, look at this one. Here, this is the one she was working on, and look at the sewing. All the rest of it has been so nice and even. And look at this! It's all over the place. Why, it looks as if she didn't know what she was about!

[*After she has said this they look at each other, then start to glance back at the door. After an instant* MRS. HALE *has pulled at a knot and ripped the sewing.*]

MRS. PETERS. Oh, what are you doing, Mrs. Hale?

MRS. HALE. [*Mildly.*] Just pulling out a stitch or two that's not sewed very good. [*Threading a needle.*] Bad sewing always makes me fidgety.

MRS. PETERS. [*Nervously.*] I don't think we ought to touch things.

MRS. HALE. I'll just finish up this end. [*Suddenly stopping and leaning forward.*] Mrs. Peters?

MRS. PETERS. Yes, Mrs. Hale?

MRS. HALE. What do you suppose she was so nervous about?

MRS. PETERS. Oh—I don't know. I don't know as she was nervous. I sometimes sew awful queer when I'm just tired. [MRS. HALE *starts to say something, looks at* MRS. PETERS, *then goes on sewing.*] Well, I must get these things wrapped up. They may be through sooner than we think. [*Putting apron and other things together.*] I wonder where I can find a piece of paper, and string.

MRS. HALE. In that cupboard, maybe.

MRS. PETERS. [*Looking in cupboard.*] Why, here's a birdcage. [*Holds it up.*] Did she have a bird, Mrs. Hale?

MRS. HALE. Why, I don't know whether she did or not—I've not been here for so long. There was a man around last year selling canaries cheap, but I don't know as she took one; maybe she did. She used to sing real pretty herself.

MRS. PETERS [*Glancing around.*]. Seems funny to think of a bird here. But she must have had one, or why would she have a cage? I wonder what happened to it.

MRS. HALE. I s'pose maybe the cat got it.

MRS. PETERS.   No, she didn't have a cat. She's got that feeling some people have about cats—afraid of them. My cat got in her room and she was real upset and asked me to take it out.

MRS. HALE.   My sister Bessie was like that. Queer, ain't it?

MRS. PETERS.   [*Examining the cage.*]   Why, look at this door. It's broke. One hinge is pulled apart.

MRS. HALE.   [*Looking too.*]   Looks as if someone must have been rough with it.

MRS. PETERS.   Why, yes.

[*She brings the cage forward and puts it on the table.*]

MRS. HALE.   I wish if they're going to find any evidence they'd be about it. I don't like this place.

MRS. PETERS.   But I'm awful glad you came with me, Mrs. Hale. It would be lonesome for me sitting here alone.

MRS. HALE.   It would, wouldn't it?   [*Dropping her sewing.*]   But I tell you what I do wish, Mrs. Peters. I wish I had come over sometimes when *she* was here. I—   [*Looking around the room.*]   —wish I had.

MRS. PETERS.   But of course you were awfully busy, Mrs. Hale—your house and your children.

MRS. HALE.   I could've come. I stayed away because it weren't cheerful—and that's why I ought to have come. I—I've never liked this place. Maybe because it's down in a hollow and you don't see the road. I dunno what it is but it's a lonesome place and always was. I wish I had come over to see Minnie Foster sometimes. I can see now—

[*Shakes her head.*]

MRS. PETERS.   Well, you musn't reproach yourself, Mrs. Hale. Somehow we just don't see how it is with other folks until—something comes up.

MRS. HALE.   Not having children makes less work—but it makes a quiet house, and Wright out to work all day, and no company when he did come in. Did you know John Wright, Mrs. Peters?

MRS. PETERS.   Not to know him; I've seen him in town. They say he was a good man.

MRS. HALE.   Yes—good; he didn't drink, and kept his word as well as most, I guess, and paid his debts. But he was a hard man, Mrs. Peters. Just to pass the time of day with him—   [*Shivers.*]   Like a raw wind that gets to the bone. [*Pauses, her eye falling on the cage.*]   I should think she would 'a wanted a bird. But what do you suppose went with it?

MRS. PETERS.   I don't know, unless it got sick and died.

[*She reaches over and swings the broken door, swings it again. Both women watch it.*]

MRS. HALE.   You weren't raised round here, were you?   [MRS. PETERS *shakes her head.*]   You didn't know—her?

MRS. PETERS.   Not till they brought her yesterday.

MRS. HALE. She—come to think of it, she was kind of like a bird herself—real sweet and pretty, but kind of timid and—fluttery. How—she—did—change. [*Silence; then as if struck by a happy thought and relieved to get back to every day things.*] Tell you what, Mrs. Peters, why don't you take the quilt in with you? It might take up her mind.

MRS. PETERS. Why, I think that's a real nice idea, Mrs. Hale. There couldn't possibly be any objection to it, could there? Now, just what would I take? I wonder if her patches are in here—and her things. [*They look in the sewing basket.*]

MRS. HALE. Here's some red. I expect this has got sewing things in it. [*Brings out a fancy box.*] What a pretty box. Looks like something somebody would give you. Maybe her scissors are in here. [*Opens box. Suddenly puts her hand to her nose.*] Why— [MRS. PETERS *bends nearer, then turns her face away.*] There's something wrapped up in this piece of silk.

MRS. PETERS. Why, this isn't her scissors.

MRS. HALE. [*Lifting the silk.*] Oh, Mrs. Peters—its—

[MRS. PETERS *bends closer.*]

MRS. PETERS. It's the bird.

MRS. HALE. [*Jumping up.*] But, Mrs. Peters—look at it! Its neck! Look at its neck. It's all—other side *to.*

MRS. PETERS. Somebody—wrung—its—neck.

[*Their eyes meet. A look of growing comprehension, of horror. Steps are heard outside.* MRS. HALE *slips box under quilt pieces, and sinks into her chair. Enter* SHERIFF *and* COUNTY ATTORNEY. MRS. PETERS *rises.*]

COUNTY ATTORNEY. [*As one turning from serious things to little pleasantries.*] Well, ladies, have you decided whether she was going to quilt it or knot it?

MRS. PETERS. We think she was going to—knot it.

COUNTY ATTORNEY. Well, that's interesting, I'm sure. [*Seeing the bird cage.*] Has the bird flown?

MRS. HALE. [*Putting more quilt pieces over the box.*] We think the—cat got it.

COUNTY ATTORNEY. [*Preoccupied.*] Is there a cat?

[MRS. HALE *glances in a quick covert way at* MRS. PETERS.]

MRS. PETERS. Well, not *now.* They're superstitious, you know. They leave.

COUNTY ATTORNEY. [*To* SHERIFF PETERS, *continuing an interrupted conversation.*] No sign at all of anyone having come from the outside. Their own rope. Now let's go up again and go over it piece by piece. [*They start upstairs.*] It would have to have been someone who knew just the—

[MRS. PETERS *sits down. The two women sit there not looking at one another, but as if peering into something and at the same time holding back. When they talk now it is in the manner of feeling their way over strange ground, as if afraid of what they are saying, but as if they can not help saying it.*]

MRS. HALE.   She liked the bird. She was going to bury it in that pretty box.

MRS. PETERS.   [*In a whisper.*]   When I was a girl—my kitten—there was a boy took a hatchet, and before my eyes—and before I could get there—   [*Covers her face an instant.*]   If they hadn't held me back I would have—   [*Catches herself, looks upstairs where steps are heard, falters weakly.*]   —hurt him.

MRS. HALE.   [*With a slow look around her.*]   I wonder how it would seem never to have had any children around.   [*Pause.*]   No, Wright wouldn't like the bird—a thing that sang. She used to sing. He killed that, too.

MRS. PETERS.   [*Moving uneasily.*]   We don't know who killed the bird.

MRS. HALE.   I knew John Wright.

MRS. PETERS.   It was an awful thing was done in this house that night, Mrs. Hale. Killing a man while he slept, slipping a rope around his neck that choked the life out of him.

MRS. HALE.   His neck. Choked the life out of him.

[*Her hand goes out and rests on the birdcage.*]

MRS. PETERS.   [*With rising voice.*]   We don't know who killed him. We don't *know.*

MRS. HALE.   [*Her own feeling not interrupted.*]   If there'd been years and years of nothing, then a bird to sing to you, it would be awful—still, after the bird was still.

MRS. PETERS.   [*Something within her speaking.*]   I know what stillness is. When we homesteaded in Dakota, and my first baby died—after he was two years old, and me with no other then—

MRS. HALE.   [*Moving.*]   How soon do you suppose they'll be through, looking for the evidence?

MRS. PETERS.   I know what stillness is.   [*Pulling herself back.*]   The law has got to punish crime, Mrs. Hale.

MRS. HALE.   [*Not as if answering that.*]   I wish you'd seen Minnie Foster when she wore a white dress and blue ribbons and stood up there in the choir and sang.   [*A look around the room.*]   Oh, I *wish* I'd come over here once in awhile! That was a crime! That was a crime! Who's going to punish that?

MRS. PETERS.   [*Looking upstairs.*]   We mustn't—take on.

MRS. HALE.   I might have known she needed help! I know how things can be—for women. I tell you, it's queer, Mrs. Peters. We live close together and we live far apart. We all go through the same things—it's all just a different kind of the same thing.   [*Brushes her eyes; noticing the bottle of fruit, reaches out for it.*]   If I was you I wouldn't tell her her fruit was gone. Tell her it *ain't.* Tell her it's all right. Take this in to prove it to her. She—she may never know whether it was broke or not.

MRS. PETERS.   [*Takes the bottle, looks about for something to wrap it in; takes petticoat from the clothes brought from the other room, very nervously begins winding this around the bottle. In a false voice.*]   My, it's a good thing the men couldn't hear us. Wouldn't they just laugh! Getting all stirred up over a little thing like a—dead canary. As if that could have anything to do with—with—wouldn't they *laugh!*

[*The men are heard coming down stairs.*]

MRS. HALE. [*Under her breath.*]   Maybe they would—maybe they wouldn't.
COUNTY ATTORNEY.   No, Peters, it's all perfectly clear except a reason for doing it. But you know juries when it comes to women. If there was some definite thing. Something to show—something to make a story about—a thing that would connect up with this strange way of doing it—

[*The women's eyes meet for an instant. Enter* HALE *from outer door.*]

HALE.   Well, I've got the team around. Pretty cold out there.
COUNTY ATTORNEY.   I'm going to stay here a while by myself. [*To the* SHERIFF] You can send Frank out for me, can't you? I want to go over everything. I'm not satisfied we can't do better.
SHERIFF.   Do you want to see what Mrs. Peters is going to take in?

[*The* COUNTY ATTORNEY *goes to the table, picks up the apron, laughs.*]

COUNTY ATTORNEY.   Oh, I guess they're not very dangerous things the ladies have picked out. [*Moves a few things about, disturbing the quilt pieces which cover the box. Steps back.*]   No, Mrs. Peters doesn't need supervising. For that matter, a sheriff's wife is married to the law. Ever think of it that way, Mrs. Peters?
MRS. PETERS.   Not—just that way.
SHERIFF.   [*Chuckling.*]   Married to the law. [*Moves toward the other room.*]   I just want you to come here a minute, George. We ought to take a look at these windows.
COUNTY ATTORNEY.   [*Scoffingly.*]   Oh, windows!
SHERIFF.   We'll be right out, Mr. Hale.

[HALE *goes outside. The* SHERIFF *follows the* COUNTY ATTORNEY *into the other room. Then* MRS. HALE *rises, hands tight together, looking intensely at* MRS. PETERS, *whose eyes make a slow turn, finally meeting* MRS. HALE*'s. A moment* MRS. HALE *holds her, then her own eyes point to where the box is concealed. Suddenly* MRS. PETERS *throws back quilt pieces and tries to put the box in the bag she is wearing. It is too big. She opens box, starts to take bird out, cannot touch it, goes to pieces, stands there helpless. Sound of a knob turning in the other room.* MRS. HALE *snatches the box and puts it in the pocket of her big coat. Enter* COUNTY ATTORNEY *and* SHERIFF.]

COUNTY ATTORNEY.   [*Facetiously.*]   Well, Henry, at least we found out that she was not going to quilt it. She was going to—what is it you call it, ladies?
MRS. HALE.   [*Her hand against her pocket.*]   We call it—knot it, Mr. Henderson.

CURTAIN

Journal Entry

Discuss the interaction of the individual and the community in *Trifles*.

Textual Considerations

1. Why do you suppose Glaspell chooses not to have either of the Wrights appear on stage?
2. Discuss the significance of the bird cage and the quilt as dominant symbols in the play, and explain their relationship to the theme.
3. What is the meaning of the play's title?

Cultural Contexts

1. Discuss with your group the portrayal of male characters in *Trifles*. Is Glaspell being unfair? What does the play reveal about gender roles in marriage? What is your concept of the Wright's relationship?
2. Discuss the moral and legal questions raised in the play. Consider, for example, how many crimes have been committed and what kind of punishment seems appropriate for Mrs. Wright's crime. Evaluate also the decision of Mrs. Hale and Mrs. Peters to withhold evidence.

PART ASSIGNMENTS

WRITING TOPICS

1. Many of the texts in Part Five make statements for or against conformity to accepted norms. Using "The Guest" and "A Rose for Emily," analyze the degree to which nonconformity influenced the choices of Daru and Miss Emily. Use evidence from both stories to support your point of view.

2. Compare and contrast the role of the family in "The Metamorphosis," "Eveline," "A Red Sweater," and/or "A Rose for Emily." To what extent do the members of the family contribute to the autonomy of the protagonists in any two stories?

3. Analyze the functions of setting in "Eveline" and "A Rose for Emily." What role did the setting play in shaping the choices of both protagonists?

4. Compare and contrast the portrayals of the community in "Hands" and "Dead Men's Path." What causes the members of both communities to behave as they do? Are they seeking to decrease or even to destroy the rights of the individual protagonists? Explain.

5. Would it be fair to describe Antigone or Daru in "The Guest" as rebels? Write an analysis of the causes and effects of their rebellion, including your attitude toward it.

6. Analyze the role of the forces of authority in the selections by Faulkner, Camus, Sophocles, or Glaspell. What positions do they take? How do they enhance or impede the dialogue between our private and communal selves? What did you learn about the relationship between the individual and the law?

7. Kafka described "The Metamorphosis" as a story in which "the dream reveals the reality." What does this comment suggest about the underlying psychological significance of Gregor's physical transformation?

8. In "I Have a Dream," King imagines that "one day, on the red hills of Georgia, the sons of former slaves and the sons of former slave owners will be able to sit down together at the table of brotherhood." To what extent has this dream been realized?

9. The role of the artist is the focal point of the poems by Dickinson, Ferlinghetti, and Wilbur. How does each envision the relationship between artist and audience? Compare and contrast their concepts of community.

10. To what extent are Creon and Antigone equally autocratic individuals who ignore the point of view of the community as expressed by Ismene, Haimon, and the Chorus? Is Sophocles suggesting that both protagonists are threats to the stability of the state because of their failure to negotiate? Cite evidence to support your point of view.

11. Analyze the relationship between the individual and society as portrayed in "Mending Wall" and "Summer Solstice, New York City." To

what extent does each speaker reconcile the concepts of personal space and social interaction?

12. The limitations of conformity are explored in the poems by Stevens, Dickinson, Auden, and Walsh. Choose images from all four texts that express the speakers' attitudes toward the constraints of predictability and respectability. To what extent do you agree or disagree with their points of view?

RESEARCH TOPICS

1. To examine racism and the sociopolitical conditions produced by apartheid in South Africa, write a documented paper discussing how literary texts, such as Alan Paton's *Cry, the Beloved County* and Donald Woods's *Biko,* assumed an active role in awakening South African consciousness. Consult bibliographic sources in your library and see this book's "Researching Literary Sources" appendix for the uses of secondary sources and the Modern Language Association (MLA) style of documentation.

2. In a documented paper, explore the relationship between the individual and the community in any three short stories from James Joyce's *Dubliners* or from Sherwood Anderson's *Winesburg, Ohio.*

3. Using two or three sources on ancient Greek culture, write a research paper on Greek religion, with particular references to burial customs and belief in the afterlife.

4. Write a documented paper on the relationship between the individual and society in any four poems by one of the following poets: Dickinson, Frost, Gunn, Olds, or Romero.

GROUP RESEARCH TOPIC

Several texts in this part, including *Antigone* and *Trifles,* address civil disobedience and the historic right of the individual to engage in social protest. Working with your group, write a documented essay on this issue, consulting at least two of the following sources: Plato's *Crito,* Henry David Thoreau's *On Civil Disobedience,* Martin Luther King, Jr.'s "Letter from a Birmingham Jail," Thomas Jefferson's "The Declaration of Independence," and/or Elizabeth Cady Stanton's "Declaration of Sentiments and Resolutions." Given a choice between a society in which individual rights come first and one in which community needs have priority, which would you choose?

An Introduction to the Elements of Fiction, Poetry, and Drama

FICTION

What do we mean by *fiction?* For the novelist Toni Morrison, "fiction, by definition, is distinct from fact. Presumably it's the product of imagination—invention—and it claims the freedom to dispense with 'what really happened' or where it really happened, or when it really happened, and nothing in it needs to be publicly verifiable, although much of it can be verified." Morrison goes on to say, however, that as a storyteller she is less interested in the distinction between fiction and fact than in that between fact and truth, "because facts can exist without human intelligence, but truth cannot." Fiction, then, is concerned with what the novelist William Faulkner calls "the verities and truths of the heart."

Tales, fables, parables, epic poems, and romances, and even the fairy tales you heard as a child, rank among the most ancient modes of fiction, kept alive by the power of the human voice to narrate and transmit the excitement and authenticity of imaginary actions and events. Short stories, however, belong to a more contemporary mode of narrative fiction and gained in recognition through the works of nineteenth-century American and European writers, including Edgar Allan Poe, Mary E. Wilkins Freeman, Anton Chekhov, and Guy de Maupassant.

This appendix introduces several technical terms, such as *character, plot, setting, theme, narrator,* and *style and tone,* that are used to describe the formal elements of a short story. Getting acquainted with these terms will help you to understand how short stories are put together and make it easier for you both to read them and to write about them.

Character

A *character* is a fictional person in a story, and readers' first reactions to him or her are usually based on their subjective capacity to empathize with the character's experiences. A character is often revealed through his or her actions, which provide readers with clues about the character's personality, motives, and expectations. Many stories present a conflict between the protagonist (the story's central character) and the antagonist (the opposing character or force); the conflict is revealed through the author's use of dialogue and narrative. In Alifa Rifaat's story "Another Evening at the Club" (p. 369) for instance, the main character or protagonist, Samia, is in conflict with her husband, the antagonist, because of her inability to liberate herself from his dominating behavior.

Fictional characters are sometimes referred to as *round* or *flat, static* or *dynamic*. A round character is usually more fully developed, challenging readers to analyze the character's motives and evaluate his or her actions. Round characters change, grow, and possess a credible personality, like the mother in Mary E. Wilkins Freeman's short story "The Revolt of 'Mother'" (p. 330). Flat characters, in contrast, usually play a minor role in a story, act predictably, and are often presented as stereotypes. The minister in Freeman's story, for example, is presented as an unimaginative and inflexible individual. In fact, he is in many ways a foil to Mrs. Penn, because he has a totally opposite personality.

Plot

Plot is the arrangement of the events in a story according to a pattern devised by the writer and inferred by the reader. Often the plot develops when characters and situations oppose each other, creating conflicts that grow and eventually reach a climax, the point of highest intensity of the story. After this climatic turning point, the action of the story finally declines, moving toward a resolution of the conflict.

Although the time frame in a story may vary from recapturing an intense, momentary experience to narrating an event that covers a much longer period, the storyteller must focus on what Poe terms the "single effect" as the action of the story moves toward a resolution of the conflict.

"Another Evening at the Club" provides an example of a plot centered on a conflict between Samia and her husband. The action starts to rise in dramatic intensity (*the rising action*) when Samia's loss of her emerald ring destabilizes her relationship with her husband. After this initial exposition, or narrative introduction of characters and situation, the action reaches its crisis (the *climax* of the action) when Samia's husband refuses to exonerate the maid, even though he knows she is innocent. Notice that this external conflict also parallels the internal conflict of the protagonist when she recognizes the degree of the husband's control over her and her inability to oppose him. The action of the story moves toward the resolution of its conflict (*the falling action*) when Samia yields to her husband's authority.

While many writers continue to follow this traditional model of plot development, some contemporary authors deviate from it. Liam O'Flaherty, in "The

Sniper" (p. 479), for example, and Stephen Crane, in "A Mystery of Heroism" (p. 472), prefer the surprise ending, while James Joyce in "Araby" (p. 131), ends his story without a resolution of the protagonist's inner conflict.

Although the typical fictional plot has a beginning, a middle, and an end, authors may also vary their patterns of narration. In "The Sniper," the story's events unfold in the order in which they took place, following a *chronological* development. In "Another Evening at the Club," Rifaat uses *flashbacks,* selecting a few episodes to build a plot that moves backward and forward in time: the action begins in the present with Samia's anguish at her husband's decision to blame the maid for the theft of the ring; then, through the use of flashbacks, the author reports past events that illustrate the position that women like Samia occupy in a patriarchal culture. Rifaat also uses *suspense* or uncertainty, creating a sense of anticipation and curiosity about what the protagonist will do next. Will she defend the servant accused of stealing the ring? How will her husband react when he finds out that the ring was not stolen? Many stories also use *foreshadowing,* providing details and hints about what will happen next. In William Shakespeare's play (p. 221), the title "The Tragedy of Hamlet" functions as a foreshadowing, anticipating the outcome of the story.

Fictional devices such as flashback and foreshadowing do not operate in isolation but rather work together with characterization, setting, point of view, style, and tone to create a unified effect.

Setting

The time, place, and social context of a story constitute its *setting.* In Nathaniel Hawthorne's "Young Goodman Brown" (p. 121), the somber atmosphere that pervades the whole story, including the protagonist's moral despondency, emerges from Hawthorne's representation of a supernatural setting. By situating Young Goodman Brown's mysterious journey in a gloomy, dreamlike forest, Hawthorne prepares the reader for Brown's brutal confrontation with "the great power of blackness." Other stories reconstruct historical moments with great precision. The setting of "The Sky Is Gray" (p. 100) transports readers to the American South in the 1940s, and the mythical narrative of "A Power Struggle" (p. 92) describes primeval times. Still others tell of events that could have taken place anywhere and at any time.

As you read a short story, watch for details related to time, place, and social context that reveal the motivation of the protagonist and establish the story's credibility. Pay particular attention to the writer's use of visual imagery aimed at helping you to create mental pictures of the setting and assessing its effects on the characters' actions.

Theme

Theme may be defined as the central or dominant idea of the story reinforced by the interaction of fictional devices such as character, plot, setting, and point of view. The theme is the overall generalization we can make about the story's meaning and significance. Sometimes the theme can be stated in a short phrase. For instance, "the rights of the community versus those of an individual" is one theme that emerges in Achebe's short story "Dead Men's Path" (p. 850). The theme of "The Sky Is Gray" (p. 100) is complex, because the story is concerned not only with the relationship between the narrator and his mother but also with the complexity of race relationships in the American South in the 1940s.

To define the theme of a story, look for clues provided by the author such as the title, imagery, symbolism, and dialogue between the characters. A story may evoke a range of meanings. And readers—because of their diverse interests, cultural backgrounds, and expectations—will react individually and produce varied meanings. Meanings should be supported by evidence from the story, however.

Narrator

The voice that narrates a story is not necessarily the writer's; while the author writes the story, the narrator tells it. The *narrator* is a technique that writers use to create a particular point of view from which they will tell the story, present the actions, and shape the readers' responses. Narrators can report external and internal events, but most important, they express the narrative angle that writers use to tell the story.

Narrators are *omniscient* when they know everything or almost everything that happens in the story, including what goes on inside the minds of the characters. They are presumed to be *reliable*. In "The Storm" (p. 345) by Kate Chopin, the narrator penetrates several minds: Calixta's, the wife who faces the storm at home; Bobinot's, the absent husband, who is especially concerned about his wife's safety; Alcée, Calixta's seducer, and Clarisse, Alcée's wife. By exposing the effect of the storm upon these characters, the omniscient narrator provides glimpses of their different views of life and marriage. By exposing their interior thoughts, the omniscient narrator provides glimpses of a dramatic dialogue between two opposing points of view. Omniscient narrators tend to be objective, emotionally removed from the action, and to use the third-person *he, she, it,* and *they* to create a *third-person* point of view.

Narrators are *first person* when they report the events from the point of view of the *I*, or first person. A first-person narrator differs from an omniscient narrator because the *I* both participates in the action and communicates a single point of view. This type of narrator usually creates a greater degree of intimacy with the reader, as in "A Red Sweater" (p. 825). The writer's choice of a narrator is important because it determines the *point of view* (or the voice and angle from which the narrator tells the story) and thereby affects the story's tone and meaning.

Narrators are *unreliable* when they do not possess a full understanding of the events they narrate and when the reader can see more than they do. In "The Sky Is Gray," the reader encounters implications of issues related to race and class that escape the young African-American narrator. The narrator's lack of awareness is evident in the dentist's office scene when a college student disagrees with an older preacher about the existence of God and racial injustices.

Style and Tone

Style refers to the way writers express themselves. Style depends on *diction* (the writer's choice of vocabulary), *syntax* (grammar and sentence structure), as well as *voice* and *rhythm*. Style reveals the writer's linguistic choices or preferences and therefore is as private and unique as their personalities and identities. Note the sharp contrast, for example, between Kate Chopin's dramatic use of words and images to infuse them with symbolic significance in "The Storm" (p. 345) and Fae Myenne Ng's straight, concise style, created to evoke the rhythm of a colloquial conversation in "A Red Sweater" (p. 825). To make their language unique and particular, writers also use devices such as the following:

Irony is the discrepancy between what is expected and what actually happens. The title of Franz Kafka's story "The Metamorphosis" (p. 784) is ironic because it reverses the reader's expectations of a positive change from an inferior to a superior transformation. Verbal irony is the descrepancy between what the words convey and what they actually mean, as in the title of Stephen Crane's "A Mystery of Heroism." (p. 472).

A *symbol* is something—a word or an object—that stands for an idea beyond a literal meaning. In "A Red Sweater," the red sweater may function as a symbol that evokes ideas about female identity and sexuality.

A *metaphor* is a figure of speech that compares two dissimilar elements without using *like* or *as:* "The rain was coming down in sheets" ("The Storm," p. 346). A *simile* is a comparison using *like* or *as:* "Her lips were as red and moist as pomegranate seed" ("The Storm," p. 346).

Tone is the manner, mood, pervading attitude, or tone of voice that writers establish in relation to the characters, situations, and readers. You may think of tone as the various tones of voice that fiction writers establish through style. Authors use a variety of different tones, including intimate or distant, ironic or direct, hostile or sympathetic, formal or casual, humorous or serious, and emotional or objective.

In "First Confession" (p. 86), for example, Frank O'Connor uses humor to communicate his young protagonist's terror, reinforced by his sister's threats of punishment, as he faces his first religious confession. In "Jasmine" (p. 614), Bharati Mukherjee uses irony to portray her protagonist's experiences as an illegal alien in the United States.

That successful creators of short fiction must be involved with the intricacies of their craft is clear, but remember also that their primary purpose is to use language to communicate to you. As the novelist William Faulkner reminds us, in his 1950 Nobel prize acceptance speech, writers like to tell and retell stories about "love and honor and pity and pride and compassion and sacrifice"—in other words, stories about the lives and experiences of all human beings.

POETRY

What is poetry? The nineteenth-century poet William Wordsworth defines it as "an overflow of powerful feelings;" for the contemporary poet Adrienne Rich, "poems are like dreams; in them you put what you don't know you know." Many other contemporary poets extend the power of poetry to a cultural context. Javier Heraud, for example, speaks of "the songs of oppressed peoples, / the new songs of liberated peoples."

Poets, like other artists, regardless of their historical moment, write for a variety of different reasons, but they share an imaginative view of language and a belief in the power of words. Compare, for example, Emily Dickinson's thoughts on words expressed in her poem number 1212:

A word is dead
When it is said,
Some say.
I say it just
Begins to live
That day.

with those of Anne Sexton in her poem "Words," written a century later:

Words and eggs must be handled with care,
Once broken they are impossible
things to repair.

Both poets focus on the possibilities and power of words, emphasizing the ability of language to shape and express human experiences. Despite the contradictory claims and concerns with which different generations define poetry, there is some consensus that poetry combines emotional expression, meanings, and experiences through rhythm, images, structural form, and, above all, words.

Voice and Tone

The voice that communicates the feelings, emotions, and meanings of the poem is called the speaker. The speaker's voice is not the voice of the poet but a created voice, or *persona*. Shakespeare, in his love sonnets, often uses the persona of a lover to express his views on love. Robert Browning, in "My Last Duchess" (p. 397), assumes the persona of a Renaissance duke to communicate a portrait of his former wife. The speaker's voice, like that of a real person, may change and express different tones throughout the poem as his or her attitudes vary toward the subject, him- or herself, and the reader. In "Those Winter Sundays," by Robert Hayden (p. 175), the speaker's tone is at first meditative, but in the last lines ("What did I know / of love's austere and lonely offices?") his tone becomes more remorseful.

The Poetic Elements: Images, Simile, Metaphor, Symbol, Personification, Paradox

Notice that the language of poetry is especially rich in creating images that evoke the senses of sight, smell, taste, and touch. To achieve their purposes, writers use not only language that communicates images literally but also figurative language that compares objects, describes emotions, and appeals to the reader's imagination through figures of speech such as simile, metaphor, symbol, personification, and paradox. To become an effective reader of poetry, you should learn to recognize how these elements reinforce poetic meaning.

Images are words and phrases that communicate sensory experiences and convey moods and emotions. Notice how in "Fern Hill" (p. 162), for example, Dylan Thomas uses visual images such as "All the sun long," "All the moon long," and "the lamb white days" to capture a vision of childhood embedded in the idyllic bright, white colors of joy and innocence.

A *simile* is a direct comparison between two explicit terms, usually introduced by "like" or "as." In "For My Lover, Returning to His Wife" (p. 405), the ironic speaker of Anne Sexton's poem compares her lover's wife to a "cast-iron pot" and his children to "delicate balloons." Through these similes, the speaker comes to terms with the solid presence of the wife and the vulnerable existence of the children in her lover's life as opposed to the fragility of her own claim on him.

A *metaphor* is an implicit comparison that omits *like* or *as*. "For My Lover, Returning to His Wife" also ends with the metaphor "I am a watercolor. / I wash off." Much of the meaning of this poem depends on the contrast that the speaker, the lover of a married man, establishes between the wife's permanent position in her husband's life and her own transient presence.

A *symbol* is a sign that points to meanings beyond its literal significance. The cross, for instance, is an archetype universally accepted as a symbol of Christianity. In John Keats's "Bright Star" (p. 407), the "bright star" points beyond the literal meaning the word suggests to function as a symbol that affirms and negates the idealized view of love.

Personification is the attribution of human qualities to animals, ideas, or inanimate things. It is used in these lines from Henry Wadsworth Longfellow's "The Jewish Cemetery at Newport" (p. 160):

Pride and humiliation hand in hand
Walked with them through the world wherever they went.

A *paradox* is a statement that appears to be contradictory and absurd but displays an element of truth. In Yevgeny Yevtushenko's poem "People" (p. 863), the paradox "We who knew our fathers / in everything, in nothing" suggests our inability to know or understand fully another human being, even a parent.

Types of Poetry—Lyric, Dramatic, and Narrative

A *lyric poem* is usually a short composition depicting the speaker's deepest emotions and feelings. Lyric poems are especially effective in arousing personal participation of readers and in stirring their sensations, feelings, and emotions. Songs, elegies, odes, and sonnets fall into this category.

A *dramatic poem* uses dramatic monologue or dialogue and assumes the presence of another character besides the speaker of the poem. In Robert Browning's "My Last Dutchess" (p. 397), and also in his poem "Porphyrias's Lover" (p. 399), for instance, the speakers seem to assume the presence of an audience.

A *narrative poem* usually emphasizes action or the plot. "The Young Warrior" (p. 404), by Gayle Two Eagles, may be considered a short narrative poem in which the speaker narrates through brief biographical data the elements that constitute her identity as a young Lakota warrior.

The Forms of Poetry

Some poems in this anthology use structural forms long established by literary history and tradition. In fact, for many poets a vision of poetic completion revolves around an idea of poetic structure or the formal beauty of a poetic pattern. Thus, to read a poem effectively and establish a dialogue with its poetic voice, you should be able to recognize some of the elements related to poetic form.

Meter is the recurrent pattern of stressed and unstressed syllables in a poetic line. Together with elements such as rhyme and pause, meter determines the rhythm of the poem. One way to identify the metrical pattern of a poem is to mark the accented and unaccented syllables of the poetic line, as in the example below from a sonnet by Shakespeare:

My mistress' eyes are nothing like the sun

Next, divide the line into feet, the basic unit of measurement, according to patterns of accented and unaccented syllables. These are the five most common types of poetic feet.

iambic	(˘ `)	forget
trochee	(` ˘)	morning
anapest	(˘ ˘ `)	at a house
dactyl	(` ˘ ˘)	separate
spondee	(` `)	come, now

Shakespeare's line thus marked becomes five feet of iambs:

My mis/ tress' eyes/ are no/ thing like/ the sun/
    1   2   3   4   5

Notice that the length of the poetic lines depends on the number of poetic feet they possess, and they are defined by the following terms:

one foot = monometer
two feet = dimeter
three feet = trimeter
four feet = tetrameter
five feet = pentameter
six feet = hexameter

Shakespeare's line "My mistress' eyes are nothing like the sun," is a good example of iambic pentameter, one of the most common patterns in English poetry.

Two other terms you should recognize in relation to meter are *caesura,* a pause or pauses within the poetic line, and *enjambment,* a poetic line that carries its meaning and sound to the next line. The lines below, from the poem "The Faithful Wife," by Barbara L. Greenberg (p. 382), provide us with a good example of a caesura followed by an enjambment:

> But if I *were* to have a lover, it would be someone
> who could take nothing from you.

Notice that the caesura occurs after the first phrase "But if I *were* to have a lover," and the enjambment occurs when the following sentence spills over into the next line. If the poet had broken the first line after the comma, the second line as it now stands would have lost its emphasis.

A *stanza* is a group of two or more poetic lines forming the same metrical pattern or a closely similar pattern that is repeated throughout the poem. Most stanzas combine a fixed pattern of poetic lines with a fixed *rhyme scheme.* Thomas Hardy's poem "The Man He Killed" (p. 516) follows the traditional pattern of the *ballad stanza:* a quatrain (four-line stanza) with alternating tetrameter (four-feet line) and trimeter (three-feet line).

> Had he and I but met
> By some old ancient inn,
> We should have sat us down to wet
> Right many a nipperkin!

Notice, however, that Hardy varies the typical rhyme scheme of the ballad stanza, in which only the second and fourth lines rhyme (which is called an *abcb* scheme), by also rhyming his first and third lines, for an *abab* scheme.

Conventionally, the English *sonnet* is a poem of fourteen iambic pentameter lines. Immortalized by the fourteenth-century Italian poet Petrarch, the sonnet spread throughout Europe, becoming a major cultural form with which sonneteers represented and explored the terms of their inward self and public life. Shakespeare and many other English poets used the *abab cdcd efef gg* rhyme scheme, which marks the division of a sonnet into three quatrains (four lines) and a couplet (two rhyming lines). John Keats also uses this Shakespearean sonnet pattern in "Bright Star" (p. 407).

Blank verse is unrhymed iambic pentameter. Because it is very close to human speech, blank verse became an ideal dramatic medium and was used by Shakespeare in many of his plays.

Free verse is poetry that does not follow a fixed pattern of rhythm, rhyme, and stanzaic arrangements. Like Walt Whitman, many poets have abandoned any kind of poetic structure for free verse, relying instead on a pattern based largely on repetition and parallel grammatical structure. The primary focus of free verse is not the external poetic form but the presence of an internal voice of address. One example is Whitman's "Song of Myself."

> I celebrate myself, and sing myself,
> And what I assume you shall assume,
> For every atom belonging to me as good belongs to you.

Most contemporary poets either use free verse or combine traditional and new patterns.

Poetry as Performance: The Sounds of Poetry

Reading a poem aloud is more than encountering actions and situations that the poet's creative imagination reshaped as meanings, rhythms, and emotions; it is an act of oral delivery conveying to the poetic discourse a special kind of situation and point of view comparable to the performance of a play. In fact, in most ancient cultures, and in some contemporary ones, poetry had strong ties to the oral tradition, and it was often meant to be sung and accompanied by musical instruments like the lyre. Although the oral delivery of poetry has been widely replaced by silent reading, reading a poem aloud will allow you to recover the emotional and phonic potential through which poetry expresses its relation to music and to life's dramatic possibilities. You will encounter the poetic voice—the voice that speaks the poem—in the act of expressing the poem's full potentiality.

To form layers of poetic meaning, poets throughout the centuries have explored several phonic devices such as alliteration, repetition, onomatopoeia, assonance, as well as effects of orchestration, the clash of consonants. Here are some of the most common poetic devices.

Alliteration is the repetition of the initial sounds of the words in a poetic line. In "Moving Away [1]" (p. 158), Gary Soto combines alliteration (repetition of the plosive sound {k}) and *assonance* (repetition of vowel sounds) along three poetic lines.

> From a <u>c</u>oldness I
> <u>C</u>ould not understand
> And <u>c</u>upped the crucifix beneath the <u>c</u>overs.

Repetition refers to the repetition of a single word or phrase; the repetition of a refrain or a specific line or lines in a poem; or the repetition of a slightly changed version of a poetic line.

Onomatopoeia is the use of words that evoke or imitate the sounds they describe such as *slam, murmur,* and *splash.*

DRAMA

Unlike fiction and most poetry, plays are intended to be performed before an audience, making drama primarily a communal art form in which the playwright collaborates with actors, director, set, lighting, and costume designers to produce an aural, visual, and social experience. If you are unable to see a performance of the plays included in this book, try to view a video production of *Antigone, Medea, Hamlet,* or *Miss Julie.*

What is the function of drama? Although its purpose and functions have evolved from ancient Greece to the present, according to contemporary playwright Arthur Miller, "all plays we call great, let alone those we call serious, are ultimately involved with some aspects of a single problem. It is this. How may man make of the outside world a home?" Unlike Greek playwrights or Shakespeare, many modern dramatists, like Miller, are most concerned with presenting social issues onstage. In the last decade, for example, several dramas have focused on the suffering and death caused by two contemporary forms of plague, cancer and AIDS, demonstrating the playwright's commitment to exploring the relation between the individual and society and to urging the audience to consider its personal and social commitment.

The Basic Elements of Drama

Characterization. *Dramatis personae* are the characters in a play. Usually the names of the persons who appear in a play, the dramatic characters, are listed at the beginning, often with a brief description. Read this list carefully to understand who the characters are.

As you read the play, pay attention not only to the dialogue of the characters but also to what the *stage directions* say about their entrances and exits, clothing, tone of voice, facial expressions, gestures, and movements.

As in fiction, the *protagonist,* or main character, of a play opposes the *antagonist,* or the character or other elements that defy his or her stability. In some plays there is a fairly simple contrast, as between Medea and Jason and between Medea and Athenian law, whereas in others, as in *Antigone,* there is a more complex or involved contrast—not just between Antigone and Creon but also between Antigone and Ismene and Creon and Haimon and between religious and civil law. Often, if you recognize different sides of the conflict between a protagonist and an antagonist, you will be able to identify the core of the dramatic action of the play.

It is also important to notice that characters and dramatic action are intrinsically connected with each other. In Susan Glaspell's *Trifles,* for instance, dramatic action emerges from the inner motivation and goals, which account for the inability of the characters—the female protagonists and male antagonists—to abide by the same set of gender-related assumptions.

Plot. *Plot* may be defined as the arrangement of the dramatic action of a play. A typical plot structure follows a pattern of rising and falling action along five major steps: the exposition (or presentation of the dramatic situation), the rising action, the climax, the falling action, and the conclusion. The arrangement of the dramatic action in *Hamlet* may be illustrated by the so-called pyramid pattern, which is not always as symmetrical as the diagram below suggests.

To understand how the plot develops, consider the dramatic crisis that follows the major conflict, as well as *subplots,* or secondary lines of action connected with

Exposition	Rising action	Climax	Falling action	Conclusion
Death of old Hamlet	Appearance of ghost	From the play within the play to the killing of Polonius	Ophelia's death Hamlet's return	Hamlet's death
Accession of Claudius	Hamlet's promise of revenge			
Marriage of Claudius				

the main plot. In *Miss Julie,* for instance, the crisis involving Christine, the cook, reflects and comments on the major conflicts centered on Julie and Jean.

One can look at the plot arrangement of Greek plays such as *Antigone* and *Medea* from the point of view of the conventions of *time, place,* and *action*. According to these conventions, traditionally attributed to Aristotle and the later dramatic theorists of the Renaissance (although Shakespeare did not observe them), the action of a play should not exceed a period of twenty-four hours (unity of time). Its locale should always remain the same (unity of place), and its actions and incidents should all contribute to the resolution of the plot (unity of action). An analysis of *Antigone* and *Medea* from the viewpoint of these conventions will reveal the dramatic freedom taken in the film versions of these classical plays.

Theme.   *Theme* is the central idea or ideas dramatized in a play. Although you can look for a play's theme in the title, conflict, characters, or scenery, the ideas and the meanings you identify will depend on your own set of beliefs, assumptions, and experiences. The play *The Kiss of the Spider Woman,* for instance, explores what happens when two male characters, a revolutionary and a homosexual, liberate themselves from the oppressive constrictions of their own psyches.

Types of Plays: Tragedy and Comedy

According to Aristotle, whose *Poetics* provides an analysis of the nature of classical drama, *tragedy* is the highest form of literary art. It deals with protagonists who are better than we are because of their engagement in honorable or dignified actions and their capacity to maintain their human dignity when withstanding adversity and suffering. Tragic protagonists are often also somehow connected with the religious and political destiny of their country. *Antigone,* for example, asks deeply religious questions about an individual's responsibility to the laws of God and the laws of the state. Greek and Shakespearean tragedies such as *Antigone, Medea,* and *Hamlet* are centered on the struggle that the protagonists, the *tragic heroes* and *heroines,* conduct against antagonistic forces.

The major event in a tragedy is the downfall that the protagonist suffers as a result of external causes (fate, coincidence), internal causes (ambition, excessive pride or hubris), or some error or frailty for which he or she is at least partially responsible. According to Aristotle, the spectators are purged of the emotions of "pity and fear" as they watch the hero or the heroine fall from greatness and as they witness the self-knowledge that the tragic protagonist gains in the process. The term *catharsis* refers to the emotional process that spectators undergo when they view a tragedy.

For modern playwrights, the protagonists of tragedies are no longer extraordinary beings but ordinary human beings caught in the struggle to shape their identities amid the crude realities of external and internal circumstances. In *The Kiss of the Spider Woman*, for instance, Manuel Puig explores the causes and effects of political and sexual violence on Valentin and Molina. In the modern tragedy, the audience is urged to confront the corresponding social issues. Sometimes, in contemporary plays, the audience is also asked to participate in the actual performance of the play, or to construct meanings that determine the conclusion of the play.

In its ancient origins, *comedy* was a type of drama, designed to celebrate the renewal of life. Classical comedies usually dealt with the lives of ordinary people caught in personal and social conflicts, which they attempted to overcome through wit and humor. Unlike classical tragedies, which focus on heroes and heroines who are greater than ordinary human beings, classical comedies explore the lives of ordinary people facing the realities of love, sex, and class. Tragedies usually lead to a sense of wasted human potential in the death of the protagonist, whereas comedies tend to promote a happy ending through the reestablishment of social norms. Most contemporary plays, however, combine the hilarious ingredients of comedy with the dramatic overtones of tragedy, as seen in *Picnic on the Battlefield*, Fernando Arrabal's humorous portrayal of the irrationality of war.

Kinds of Theater

Greek theater developed in Athens in connection with religious celebrations in honor of Dionysus, the god of wine and revelry. Athenian drama festivals also gained social and political meaning, becoming an intrinsic part of Athenian cultural life.

Plays such as *Medea* and *Antigone* were performed in large, semicircular amphitheaters like the Theater of Dionysus at Athens, which could hold about seventeen thousand spectators. To cope with the physical conditions of such huge amphitheaters, actors had to look larger than life by wearing masks, padded costumes, elevated shoes, and mouthpieces that amplified their voices. Women's roles were performed by male actors because in Greek culture, as in many other early cultures, performances by women were taboo.

Greek plays such as *Antigone* usually alternate dramatic episodes with choral odes, following a five-part dramatic structure:

Prologue	Parados	Episodia/Stasimon	Exodos
Background information	Chorus, Evaluation of situation	Debates followed by choral odes	Last scene

The *chorus* consisted of a group of about twelve actors (often led by a leader, or *choragos*) who sang and danced in the *orchestra*, an area at the foot of the amphitheater. The chorus served several other functions as well: it represented the voice of the community, commented on the events of the play, provided background

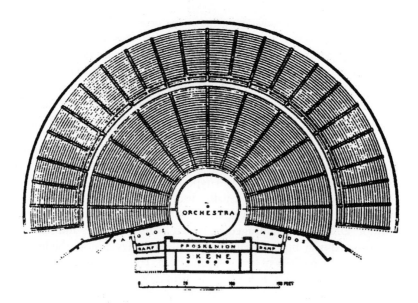

Illustration of a Greek Amphitheater at Epidaurus

information about the story, and sometimes participated in the dramatic action. As part of its choreography, the chorus moved from right to left across the orchestra, the "dancing place" of the stage, as they sang the *strophe*, or the choral lyric, of the ode, and from left to right as they sang the *antistrophe*.

When reading a Greek play, keep in mind the following theatrical conventions:

Comic relief is provided by comic speeches or scenes that occur in a serious play. Consider, for example, the relief from dramatic action that the character of the sentry provides in *Antigone*.

Dramatic irony is a double meaning that occurs when the audience possesses foreknowledge of the situation and is therefore better informed than the characters. An effective example of dramatic irony occurs when Creon says after Haimon's death that nothing else could hurt him. However, he speaks this moments before he finds out about his wife's death, of which the audience is already aware.

Elizabethan theater, including Shakespearean theater, refers to plays written during the reign of Queen Elizabeth I of England, (1558–1603). Compared to the huge Greek amphitheaters, the Elizabethan playhouse was small, seating a maximum of three thousand spectators. Its stage, as the illustration on page 937 shows, protruded into the orchestra so that the audience and actors could enjoy a more intimate theatrical atmosphere. Since Elizabethan theater used little setting, it was the power of Shakespeare's poetic language that stimulated the spectators to exercise their imagination and visualize places like the platform of the watch at the royal castle at Elsinore in *Hamlet*.

Although the text of *Hamlet* shows a series of structural divisions into acts and scenes, in Shakespeare's day *Hamlet* and the other Shakespearean plays were per-

Illustration of a Shakespearean Playhouse

formed without any intermission. In Elizabethan theater, as in Greek theater, female roles were performed by male actors. The first actresses appeared on the English stage only after the Restoration of Charles II in 1660.

Shakespearean plays employ the theatrical conventions of soliloquy and aside:

A *soliloquy* is a speech delivered by a character who is alone on the stage. Through these speeches, such as Hamlet's famous soliloquy "O, what a rogue and peasant slave am I!" (2.2.475), actors reveal their thoughts, feelings, inner struggles, and psychological complexity, securing their ties with the audience. The critic Ralph Berry believes that soliloquies permit the actors to establish a special kind of relationship with the audience. It is in his sequence of soliloquies, Berry argues, that Hamlet manages to seduce the audience.

An *aside* is a short speech that a character delivers in an undertone directly to the audience and that is not heard by the other actors onstage. For instance, Hamlet's aside "A little more than kin, and less than kind!" (1.2.65) invites the audience to share the state of mind he has adopted against Claudius.

Realistic Theater dates from nineteenth-century Europe. One of its purposes was to set the daily reality of middle-class life against antagonistic social conventions. The physical conditions of the picture-frame stage, with its proscenium arch, favored the exhibiting of realistic, lifelike pictures of everyday life. *Miss Julie*, by August Strindberg, is a good example of a play that relies on the conditions of a specific, realistic setting: Julie's kitchen conveys to the audience the degree to which her life is influenced and dominated by the social theme of broken barriers.

Theater of the absurd, which has developed in the second half of the twentieth century, portrays human beings as antiheroes caught in a world that is basically irrational, unpredictable, and illogical. Playwright Eugene Ionesco (b. 1912) defined theater of the absurd as "that which has no purpose or goal or objective." Two major techniques of absurdist drama include the lack of logically connected events and the presence of characters whose fragmented language, personalities, and nihilistic attitudes undermine their ability to control their own destiny. *Picnic on the Battlefield,* Fernando Arrabal's absurdist play, provides a good example of a drama whose challenges to a rational view of life verge on the absurd. Instead of constructing a classical plot or creating characters with developed personalities, Arrabal presents one dramatic episode in which the characters Zapo and Zepo are so similar that they are practically interchangeable. Although absurdist theater can be performed on any kind of stage, twentieth-century dramatists prefer a stage with only a few props that are suggestive of a realistic setting or symbolic of the play's meaning.

FICTION, POETRY, AND DRAMA
AS CULTURAL PRODUCTIONS

As part of your reading experience, *Literature Across Cultures* asks you not only to analyze the formal aspects of literature but also to integrate your study of the literary genres with a cultural focus that attempts to discover connections among literature, film, culture, and society. Such interactions will enable you not only to consider the interpretation of the literary text but to understand also its historical and cultural significance.

In addition to the Cultural Contexts questions after each reading selection in this anthology, the following list of topics will help you to initiate a culturally oriented discussion of literature and film.

1. To examine the relation between the text and its social reality, consider the relation between writers and the cultural and historical issues of their times. Your focus here should be the literary text and its cultural (philosophical, religious, sociohistorical, and political) perspectives.

2. Focus on the physical and social aspects of the setting, attempting to define the tensions and relations between the setting and the speaker.

3. Notice how many plots, especially in fiction, tend to challenge or reinforce the conventional focus concerning the quest for individual identity and the sometimes competing values of the community.

4. When you study characterization, explore private and public attitudes toward race, class, gender, law, economics, and justice.

5. Think about the extent to which social and psychological forces such as heredity, environment, or fate control the action of individuals. Are indi-

viduals presented as victims of society? What kinds of responses do they develop to counteract the influence of society?

<small>YOU MAY ALSO CONSIDER THE FOLLOWING TOPICS:</small>

6. The interplay of gender and power.

7. Gender differences.

8. Male gender construction.

9. The male patriarchal psyche and its definition of masculinity.

10. Sex role stereotypes supporting traditional notions of masculine aggression and feminine passivity.

11. The conflict between the individual and the social self.

12. Individuality and community as the core of American character.

13. Individual aspirations and community responsibility.

14. The psychological drama of the individual self.

15. The presence of the self in social, sexual, and cultural contexts.

16. The relation between war and violence.

17. Issues of cultural identity, gender, politics, and class. Their effects on individual and social identity.

18. Individuality and identity as products of a fixed historical era.

19. The forces of tradition and change and their effects on individual and communal lives.

20. The politics of domestic life; the organization of the family; the separation of private and public responsibility.

21. Changing concepts of the role of the family.

22. The politics of domestic life as affected by gender and class.

23. The significance of single-parent households.

24. The nature of mother–daughter, father–daughter, father–son, mother–son relations.

25. The role of the family in validating or manipulating one's sense of self.

26. The ethnic structure of the family and its effects on gender identity and communal relationships.

27. The literary text as a protest against racism or sexism.

28. The relation between war and sexual violence.

29. Immigration and its influence on contemporary culture.

30. The dominant ideology of the text: who has power, who benefits from portrayal of power.

31. The dynamics of male–female relations both within and outside of conventional social roles.

32. Women as creators and shapers of culture and history.

33. Evolving images and representations of women and men.

34. The causes and effects of sexism and domestic violence.

35. The sexual division of labor and its effects on gender relations.

36. Class distinction and class mobility within society; the causes of exclusion from the mainstream.

37. The interplay of class, race, and economics.

38. The causes and effects of segregation and integration.

39. Racial stereotypes, racial differences, and racial dominance; their effects on individuals and group identity.

40. Causes and effects of racial, sexual, and economic oppression.

41. Stereotypes of sexuality and race; the function of color in literary and social contexts.

42. The relation among racism, sexism, and violence; attitudes toward sexual preferences and sexual differences.

43. Concepts of the melting pot versus ethnic identity.

44. The notion of tragedy, moving away from Aristotelian stress on character and tragic flaw toward a concern for the sociopolitical roles of men and women.

45. Causes and effects of sociopolitical order and disorder.

46. AIDS; the discrimination imposed on AIDS victims; the effects of AIDS on the family and on gender relationships.

47. The attempt to understand our individualism and participate in it.

48. How writers situate their work in relation to the collective past.

49. The role that movies have assumed as powerful cultural agents in rewriting the past.

50. Films as articulators of gender roles; films, in which male–female relationships are central to the story, as a reflection of traditional and/or social perspectives on gender roles.

51. Gender, race, sex, violence, and identity as prominent cultural issues in films.

52. How a film that you believe addresses an important issue in contemporary society either endorses the standard criteria of values or questions how standards of behavior are created and applied.

53. Portrayals of World War II and the Vietnam war in film.

54. Literature and film as articulators of male and female experiences of war.

55. Consider a popular film genre (e.g., western, melodrama, war, science fiction) as a reflection of certain accepted norms of behavior and traditional values of American society.

Researching Literary Sources

WHAT IS A RESEARCH PAPER?

A research paper is a writing assignment in which the writer poses a specific question or problem and then investigates, analyzes, and evaluates that issue, documenting the sources used.

If your instructor does not assign a specific topic for your literary research paper, browse through a few articles or books in which your author and his or her works are discussed.

SOME AREAS TO EXPLORE IN FICTION: characters, plot, setting, the role of the narrator, style, tone, and symbolism

SOME AREAS TO EXPLORE IN POETRY: voice, tone, sound, symbolism, poetic elements such as images, similes, metaphors, symbols, paradoxes, diction, and irony

SOME AREAS TO EXPLORE IN DRAMA: plot, structure, characterization, theme, theatrical conventions such as comic relief, dramatic irony, soliloquy, the dramatic genres (tragedy, comedy), and different kinds of theater staging

SOME CULTURAL AREAS TO EXPLORE: topics related to issues, such as race, class, gender, construction of the self, power relations, the politics of inclusion and exclusion, attitudes toward authority

Notice that comparison-and-contrast topics, involving characters in the same work or in different works, as well as topics related to plot, setting, dramatic structure, voice, tone, and cultural issues, are usually very effective. See pages 938–941 for a list of cultural issues.

942

WHAT ARE PRIMARY AND SECONDARY SOURCES?

The poem, short story, or play you are discussing is considered a primary source; the books, articles, and any other material you consult at the library during the investigation of your thesis are known as secondary sources. If you are writing a research paper on *Hamlet,* the text of Shakespeare's play is considered your primary source; the current scholarship on *Hamlet* that you will consult at the library will be your secondary sources.

Secondary Sources: Using the Library

Your goal in using the library for literary research may be

1. simply to get a better idea of what a poem, short story, or play is about.

2. to research an author's life.

3. to write an in-depth paper on what you have read.

In any of these cases you can obtain help from books and articles in the library.

Where to Start.   The library's card catalog, which lists all the books the library owns, is the place to begin. Many libraries now have their catalog in computer form rather than on cards. In either case, the library's catalog should be your first stop.

How to Locate a Book.   Locate a book by looking under one of three categories in the catalog: subject, author, or title.

1. **Subject.**   If you do not know the name of a specific book, look up a subject:

   American Literature, 20th Century
   Puerto Rican Authors
   Women in Literature

   Help with the exact wording of subject headings can be found in the *Library of Congress Subject Headings* list, a set of books usually kept near the catalog or the reference desk. The author may also be the subject of a book and can be found by consulting the subject file. Along with biographical information, there will be critical and analytical works concerning the author and his or her writings.

2. **Author.**   Under the author's name you will find all the books he or she has written. Look up the author's last name first—for example, Hayden, Robert. If a last name begins with *Mc,* it is interfiled with authors whose names begin with *Mac.*

3. **Title.**   If you know the title of a book, look for the first word of the title—for *Tell Me a Riddle,* look for *Tell.* Disregard initial articles such as *A, An,* or *The*—for *A Doll's House,* look for *Doll's.*

You will rarely find a poem or short story listed in the catalog under its name. Refer to the list of author's books and look for the individual poem or short story in the index or contents pages.

To find information on the author, consult general and specialized encyclopedias. An example of the latter is *Contemporary Authors,* a multivolume set that presents biographical information about thousands of twentieth-century writers representing a variety of nationalities. Each entry includes personal and career details about the author, a short critical comment, bibliographies of his or her works, and sources of additional information.

For authors prior to the twentieth century, consult works such as

American Authors, 1600–1900
British Authors Before 1800
British Authors of the 19th Century
European Authors, 1000–1900
The Reader's Encyclopedia

Other specialized biographical information can be found in

Mexican-American Biographies: A Historical Dictionary, 1836–1987
Asian-American Literature: An Annotated Bibliography
Black American Writers Past and Present
American Women Writers: Bibliographical Essays

Five important sources of criticism of poems, short stories, and plays are the following multivolume sets:

Humanities Index
MLA International Bibliography of Books and Articles
Essay and General Literature Index
Contemporary Literary Criticism
Twentieth-Century Literary Criticism

Humanities Index is a cumulative index to articles in English language periodicals on literature as well as history, linguistics, language, and philology. Because of its wide range of subject matter, it is less comprehensive than others in this category. The entries are listed by author and subject and arranged in one alphabet.

MLA (Modern Language Association) *International Bibliography of Books and Articles* is the most comprehensive index (published since 1921) to scholarly discussions of literary works. Volumes are arranged by country and then by century and author. Genres, themes, and other topics are also included.

Essay and General Literature Index provides a means of finding essays in anthologies. Its coverage extends back to 1900 and continues to the present.

Contemporary Literary Criticism contains excerpts from criticism of works by living authors of poems, short stories, novels and plays. Critical evaluations are taken from scholarly journals, general magazines, book review periodicals and books spanning periods from a writer's first works to the present. Because an author may be represented in more than one volume, use the master index.

Twentieth-Century Literary Criticism presents significant passages from criticism of the works of poets, short-story writers, novelists, and playwrights who died between 1900 and 1960.

Two excellent sources of detailed descriptions of reference books that can aid in literary investigations are *A Reference Guide for English Studies* and *Literary Research Guide*.

HOW TO FIND YOUR SOURCES

A discussion of the poem "My Last Duchess," by Robert Browning, may be included in a collection of essays on poetry in general or in a book about all of Browning's works. How do you find it?

One way is to use *Essay and General Literature Index,* which is designed to help you find a specific subject in chapters or parts of books (see previous discussion). Under Browning, Robert, you will find studies of his works under the subdivision "About Individual Works."

Reference books that may help you find sources of poetry criticism are

> *Poetry Explication: A Checklist of Interpretations Since 1925 of British and American Poems Past and Present*
> *Crowell's Handbook of Contemporary American Poetry*
> *American and British Poetry: A Guide to the Criticism 1925–1978*
> *Explicator Cyclopedia*
> *Magill's Critical Survey of Poetry*

Sherwood Anderson's short story "Hands" can be looked up in *Essay and General Literature Index* in the same manner as Browning's poem. *Twentieth-Century Short Story Explication* is another source of criticism on short stories.

For further help, see also

> *American Short Fiction Criticism and Scholarship*
> *Explicator Cyclopedia, Prose*
> *Magill's Critical Survey of Short Fiction*

Sophocles' play *Antigone* can be researched in a manner similar to a poem or short story. Additional drama sources include

> *Drama Criticism Index*
> *Drama Criticism*
> *Modern Drama*
> *European Drama Criticism*
> *American Drama Criticism: Interpretations 1890–1977*
> *The Major Shakespearean Tragedies*

Keep in mind these general guidelines as you research literary sources:

1. Be aware of whether a reference book contains the critique itself or offers only a list of places to find criticism.

2. Don't judge a book by its title. Investigate what information can be found in the book by reading the preface or introduction. "Recent" or "Modern" in the title may be misleading.

3. Find out what time period, countries, and genres are included in each reference book.

4. Use more than one book as a source of information.

5. Copy complete information (title, author, publisher and year of publication) as you use the book.

Ask the librarian for help if you can't find information on your own!

Electronic Research Sources

Many students now have access to computers and other electronic sources on their campuses, either in a library, a dormitory room, or at home. If you are at home or in a dorm, library hours will not keep you from doing basic research.

The previous instructions for print sources also apply to electronic sources with some modifications. For instance, you can search for information by author, title, subject, key word, or call number.

Indexes to periodicals such as the *Humanities Index, Reader's Guide to Periodical Literature,* and *MLA Bibliography* may be available on CD-ROMS (Compact Disc-Read Only Memory). In place of multi-volume print sets arranged year-by-year, a disc interfiles many years and saves the searcher valuable time. Public libraries often use this means of providing research sources.

In universities and colleges, this information may be provided on a computer that also functions as an online catalog and/or offers other available information.

A typical menu on a college library computer may resemble CUNY+PLUS, provided by the City University of New York.

Select a database by entering one of the following codes.

DPAC	CUNY Online Catalog
	Newspaper and Periodical Indexes
DNEW	Newspaper Index
DPER	Magazine and Journal Index
	Index to Medical Periodicals
MEDL	Medline

Select a database label.
Database Selection: *Student types here.*
If you type in DPAC, the next screen will read,

Use the following command	To search by
A=	Author
T=	Title
S=	Subject
K=	Keyword
C=	Call Number

If you type in DPER, the following screen appears:

DPER contains citations from four periodical indexes produced by the H. W. Wilson Company. These four indexes cover over 800 journals. DPER covers sciences, the humanities, the social sciences, and general periodicals.

SEARCH OPTIONS:	ENTER:
SUBJECT HEADING	s=military finance
AUTHOR	a=sagan
TITLE	t=journey to the stars
KEYWORD	k=defense spending

Internet.   If you live on a college campus, you may have access to the Internet in your dormitory or library. If your college does not provide access, there are a few alternatives. You may have a computer and modem at home to connect to the Internet. Some public libraries give free time, but they may limit you to a half hour or less. Some communities have Freenets, that is, computer systems available to the public. They may require a one-time registration fee, but generally offer the service without charge and time is usually restricted.

Instructions for finding literary sources on the Internet vary with the provider. It would be difficult to duplicate the multitude of ways to access information, so look to your provider for up-to-date directions.

Be warned that the information found on the Internet is sometimes unreliable. Always ask a librarian or your instructor to help evaluate sources. The same rules of plagiarism apply for computer sources as for print sources (see p. 948). You must document electronic information just as you do books, periodicals, and so on. Study the examples following "Taking Notes" to give proper credit to your sources.

BOOKS ABOUT INTERNET

Campbell, Dave and Mary. *The Student's Guide to Doing Research on the Internet.* Reading: Addison-Wesley, 1995.

Harmon, Charles, ed. *Using the Internet Online Services and CD-ROMS for Writing Research and Term Papers.* New York: Neal-Schuman, 1996.

Levine, John R. and Carol Baroudi. *The Internet for Dummies.* San Mateo: IDG Books Worldwide, 1993.

Maloy, Timothy. *The Internet Research Guide.* New York: Allworth, 1996.

HOW TO DOCUMENT A RESEARCH PAPER

Plagiarism

The act of using another person's work word-for-word and not giving that person credit is called plagiarism. A student can be expelled or suspended for not providing documentation. Plagiarism also includes using another's thoughts in a paraphrase and not attributing them to the source. However, common knowledge such as the fact that Shakespeare wrote comedies and tragedies or the date of a war need not be credited. To document your sources efficiently, learn to take notes on all the information you may need later.

Taking Notes

To record information about your sources, use 4″ × 6″ note cards and write the following bibliographical details:

- ◆ name of author, editor, or translator (if any)
- ◆ title of the work and subtitle
- ◆ editions (if not the first)
- ◆ place of publication
- ◆ publishing company
- ◆ date

If working with periodicals, you must also write down volume and page numbers. You will need this information when you write the list of Works Cited, which will appear at the end of your paper.

Write each quotation that interests you on a separate card. Read it a few times, and then try to write it in your own words as if you were explaining it to someone.

If you do copy word for word from the source and use the passage in your paper, put quotation marks around it.

Quoting

Use an introductory phrase before citing sources in the body of your essay:

> As Sigmund Freud has noted, "..."
> In the words of Toni Morrison, "..."
> In the late 1940s, Simone de Beauvoir offered the argument that "..."
> "...," suggests Stephen J. Greenblatt.

Verbs such as the following may help you to communicate a fact, advance an idea, refute an argument, make suggestions, and draw conclusions:

agree	confirm	insist	report
argue	deny	note	suggest
claim	emphasize	refute	think
communicate	endorse	reject	write

Short Quotations. Quotations from other sources need not always be complete sentences. You can integrate phrases or parts of a sentence into your own text:

> Among many other things, Barbara Christian suggests the impor-
> tance of "practical slave culture without which black people
> as an abused race would not have been able to survive" (72).

In the example above, (72) refers to the page number. A reader of your paper can refer to your list of Works Cited to find out that this quotation came from:

> Christian, Barbara. <u>Black Women Novelists: The Development of
> a Tradition, 1892-1976</u>. Westport: Greenwood, 1980.

Use ellipsis marks (three spaced periods) to indicate that something has been omitted from the text:

> Among many other things, Barbara Christian suggests the impor-
> tance of "practical slave culture without which black
> people...would not have been able to survive" (72).

The format for parenthetical citation used above follows the guidelines that the Modern Language Association of America (MLA) established for research papers on literary subjects. See also the *MLA Handbook for Writers of Research Papers* (fourth edition) published by the Modern Language Association.

Long Quotations. A long quotation of more than three lines should be indented ten spaces. Since the indented format indicates that the words are taken from a secondary source, a long quotation does not need quotation marks.

Randall Jarrell demonstrates his enthusiasm for Robert Frost's
poetry when he asserts in *Poetry and the Age:*

> Frost's virtues are extraordinary. No other living
> poet has written so well about the actions of ordi-
> nary men; his wonderful dramatic monologues or dra-
> matic scenes come out of a knowledge of people that
> few poets have had, and they are written in a verse
> that uses, sometimes with absolute mastery, the
> rhythms of actual speech. (28)

In MLA style, used here, the parenthetical citation comes two spaces after the
period that ends the long quotation.

Quoting from a Poem. When quoting from poetry, use slash marks to designate
the end of a line, and duplicate the capitalization and punctuation of the poem:

Yevgeny Yevtushenko creates images that stimulate our imagination when he writes, "Here I plod through ancient Egypt / Here
I perish crucified, on the cross."

If quoting more than a few lines of poetry, indent but do not use quotation
marks.

In the example below, Martin Espada uses alliteration to
paint a vivid picture of his protagonist:

> Blue bandanna
> across the forehead,
> beard bristling
> like a straw broom
> sleeveless T-shirt
> of the Puerto Rican flag

Quoting from a Play. When quoting from a play, always give act, scene, and lines
in Arabic (not Roman) numerals:

Hamlet observes Claudius and says, "Now might I do it pat, now
he is praying, / And now I'll do it" (3.3.73-74).

OR

Hamlet hesitates as he observes Claudius:

> Now might I do it pat, now he is praying,
> And now I'll do it. And so he goes to Heaven,

```
And so I am revenged.  That would be scanned:
A villain kill my father, and for that
I, his sole son, do this same villain send
To Heaven.  (3.3.73-78)
```

When quoting from plays that are not divided into acts, such as *Antigone*, give the scenes and line numbers:

```
You have heard my final judgment on that girl:
Have you come here hating me, or have you come
With difference and with love, whatever I do? (3.5-8)
```

Also indicate the speakers if you are quoting dialogue or a passage in which more than two characters speak:

```
Hamlet. Ha, ha! Are you honest?
Ophelia. My lord?
Hamlet. Are you fair?
Ophelia. What means your lordship?
Hamlet. That if you be honest and fair, your honesty should
    admit not discourse to your beauty?  (3.1.103-107)
```

Paraphrasing

When you do not quote exactly from a source, you can paraphrase or report the information in your own words, using roughly the same number of words you found in the source.

The following quote by R. W. B. Lewis

```
            A certain Melvillian grandeur went into the config-
            uration of her tragically conceived hero. Despite
            her early disclaimers, the spirit of Nathaniel Haw-
            thorne pervades the New England landscape of the
            novella.... The role of the inquisitive city-born
            narrator is deployed with a good deal of cunning and
            artistry of Henry James.  (309)
```

could be paraphrased in your paper in the following form:

```
R. W. B. Lewis notes the influence of Herman Melville,
Nathaniel Hawthorne, and Henry James on Edith Wharton's novel
Ethan Frome.  The nobility of the hero derives from the epic
characters of Melville's style with the added urban outlook of
the Jamesian protagonist.  The atmosphere is similar to that
found in Hawthorne's depiction of New England.  (309)
```

The source would be listed at the end of the paper as

    Lewis, R. W. B. <u>Edith Wharton: A Biography</u>. New York: Harper,
        1975.

Works Cited

The list of Works Cited, containing the names of the authors and works you referred to or cited in your paper, should be arranged alphabetically and typed on a separate page at the end of your essay.

Sample Entries

BOOK BY ONE AUTHOR

    Meier, Matt S. <u>Mexican American Bibliography: A Historical
        Dictionary, 1836-1987</u>. Westport: Greenwood, 1988.

BOOK BY TWO OR THREE AUTHORS

    Gilbert, Sandra M., and Susan Gubar. <u>The Madwoman in the Attic:
        The Woman Writer and the Nineteenth-Century Literary Imag-
        ination</u>. New Haven: Yale UP, 1979.

BOOK BY FOUR OR MORE AUTHORS

    Gatto, Joseph, et al. <u>Exploring Visual Design</u>. 2nd ed.
        Worcester: Davis, 1987.

BOOK WITH AN EDITOR

    Stetson, Erlene, ed. <u>Black Sister: Poetry by Black American
        Women, 1746-1980</u>. Bloomington: Indiana UP, 1981.

TWO OR MORE BOOKS BY THE SAME AUTHOR

    Frye, Northrup. <u>Anatomy of Criticism: Four Essays</u>. Prince-
        ton: Princeton UP, 1957.

    ---. <u>The Myth of Deliverance: Reflections on Shakespeare's
        Problem Comedies</u>. Toronto: U of Toronto P, 1983.

WORK IN AN ANTHOLOGY OR COLLECTION

    Berghahn, Marion. "Images of Africa in the Writings of James
        Baldwin." <u>James Baldwin</u>. Ed. Harold Bloom. New York:
        Chelsea, 1986.

MULTIVOLUME WORK

Wimsatt, William K., and Cleanth Brooks. <u>Literary Criticism:</u>
<u>A Short History</u>. 2 vols. Chicago: U Chicago P, 1979.

ARTICLE IN A JOURNAL THAT PAGES EACH ISSUE SEPARATELY

Giles, Ronald K. "Archetype and Irony in <u>The Natural</u>." <u>English</u>
<u>Journal</u> 75.4 (1986): 49-54.

**ARTICLE IN A JOURNAL THAT USES CONTINUOUS PAGE NUMBERS FROM JANUARY
TO DECEMBER**

Conboy, Sheila C. "Exhibition and Inhibition: The Body Scene
in <u>Dubliners</u>." <u>Twentieth-Century Literature</u> 37 (1991):
405-414.

ARTICLE IN A NEWSPAPER

McDowell, Edwin. "Black Writers Gain Audiences and Visibility
in Publishing." <u>New York Times</u> 12 Feb. 1991: C11.

BOOK REVIEW

Gonzalez, Ray. Rev. of <u>City of Coughing and Dead Radiators,</u> by
Martín Espada. <u>The Nation</u> 30 Jan. 1994: 131-3.

FILM

<u>Hamlet</u> Dir. Franco Zefferelli. With Mel Gibson and Glenn
Close. Columbia, 1990.

AUDIOTAPE

<u>The Metamorphosis.</u> Read by James Mason. Audiocassette. Caed-
mon/Harper, 1962.

COMPUTER

Alston, Robin. "The Battle of the Books." <u>Humanist</u> 7.0176
(10 Sept. 1993): 10 pp. Online. Internet. 10 Oct. 1993.

(This is an article from a magazine that was read on the Internet.)
See the *MLA Handbook for Writers of Research Papers* for more information.

TWO SAMPLE RESEARCH PAPERS: MLA STYLE

DeAngeli 1

Patricia DeAngeli

Professor Shaw

English 102

April 8, 1994

Wall, Cracked or Broken: Female Roles

in "The Yellow Wallpaper"

A wall, however cracked or broken, can appear as smooth and flawless or as ripped and
torn as the paper upon it. Only by peeling
away the paper can we see what truly lurks beneath. In Charlotte Perkins Gilman's "The Yellow Wallpaper," the wallpaper covers the wall
beneath as the expectations of the protagonist's husband cover her true self. The very
pattern of the wallpaper is representative of
the contradictory and erratic restrictions society places upon the protagonist and women in
general: "when you follow the lame, uncertain
curves for a little distance they suddenly commit suicide--plunge off at outrageous angles,
destroy themselves in unheard of
contradictions" (395).

Society usually demands that women accept
their assigned roles and not deviate from them.
Yet to some, like the protagonist of "The Yellow Wallpaper," such roles are unfulfilling or
meaningless. Her husband in "The Yellow Wallpaper" has thrust on her the roles of wife,
mother, and housekeeper. However, those roles
are empty: the baby has a nanny, her sister-in-

Last name:
1/2 inch from
the top of
each page

Heading:
double-spaced
1 inch from
the top

Title:
centered
double-spaced

Short citation:
– quotation
   marks
– page
   numbers
– the period at
   the end

DeAngeli 2

law keeps the house, and her husband treats her like a child, not a wife. The one role she wants and needs--that of writer--is denied her.

Besides the traditional roles assigned to the protagonist, her husband, discounting her fears about her health, acts as if she were an invalid by giving her "a schedule prescription for each hour in the day" (394). As the protagonist acknowledges, "he takes all care from me" (394). The room he chooses for her, the nursery, merely reinforces her dependent status. He expects her to do as she is told and, in effect, to behave as an invalid or a child. When she tries to discuss her worries about her illness with him, he lovingly patronizes her: "Bless her little heart, she shall be as sick as she pleases!" (400).

The protagonist struggles to break free of the role into which society has cast her and to express herself creatively. However, as she is forbidden to write, to create stories, and to occupy her mind in any meaningful way, she starts to occupy herself with the wallpaper. As Haney-Peritz suggests, "Ironically, it is precisely because the narrator is patient enough to follow some of the doctor's orders [her husband's] that she finds it necessary to deal with the yellow wallpaper" (115).

The way that the protagonist sees the paper, by sight and scent, may be taken as a re-

Short citation

Short citation

Short citation introduced by a phrase

Brackets indicate that words are not in the original text

DeAngeli 3

flection of the oppressive roles society imposed on women in Gilman's time. The patriarchal structure in "The Yellow Wallpaper" shows
the limited use women were allowed to make of
themselves in a male-dominated society. Like
the smell the protagonist is obsessed with, wom-
en's limitations were also encountered everywhere, permeating every aspect of a woman's life:

> . . . the smell is here. It creeps
> all over the house. I find it hover-
> ing in the dining-room, skulking in
> the parlor, hiding in the hall, lying
> in wait for me on the stairs. . . .
> It is not bad--at first, and very gen-
> tle, but quite the subtlest, most en-
> during odor I have ever met. (402)

At first the wallpaper pattern merely irri-
tates the protagonist, but, as she begins to
study it, she concludes that there is something
beneath the design: "I didn't realize for a
long time what the thing was that showed behind, that dim sub-pattern, but now I am quite
sure it is a woman" (401). She is now fascinated by the paper, and the woman behind it.
In Bader's words, "[T]he narrative pauses to
suggest that an external reality hitherto objec-
tively perceived and transparently visible can
blur and dissolve, that the firm, knowable texture of a familiar world can be shaken and
lost" (176).

Long citation:
– no quotation
  marks
– indented ten
  spaces
– followed by
  the period
  and page
  numbers in
  parentheses

DeAngeli 4

She starts to identify with the woman behind the paper because the wallpaper and its in-
habitant parallel her own situation. Both are
trapped by bars and must creep in order to do
what they desire. Both are also trying to free
themselves. The tragedy of one woman mirrors
and reflects the tragedy of the other: "And she
is all the time trying to climb through. But nobody could climb through that pattern--it strangles so" (402).

The protagonist can't reconcile her husband's kind and gentle treatment of her with
the jailer of her imagination. Once she has escaped from the paper, she seems proud that she
has finally escaped from her roles and outwit-
ted her husband. Yet she is mistrustful and
fearful of being returned to the prison of social expectations: "I've got out at last . . .
in spite of you and Jane. And I've pulled off
most of the paper, so you can't put me
back!" (405).

Short citation

Short citation

DeAngeli 5

Works Cited

Bader, J. "The Dissolving Vision: Realism in
     Jewett, Freeman and Gilman." <u>American Re-
     alism: New Essays</u>. Ed. Eric J. Sandquist.
     Baltimore: Johns Hopkins UP, 1982.

Gilman, Charlotte Perkins. "The Yellow Wallpa-
     per." <u>Literature Across Cultures</u>. Ed.
     Sheena Gillespie, Terezinha Fonseca, and
     Carol Sanger. Boston: Allyn, 1994: 393–
     405.

Haney-Peritz, Janice. "Monumental Feminism and
     Literature's Ancestral House: Another Look
     at 'The Yellow Wallpaper.'" <u>Women's Stud-
     ies</u> 12 (1986): 113–28.

List of Works Cited:
– typed on a separate page
– double-spaced
– heading is centered and typed 1 inch from the top of the page
– in alphabetical order
– after first line, all lines indented five spaces

Isabel Pipolo

Professor Robson

Introduction to Literature

January 17, 1995

Antigone: the Woman, the Heroine, the Role Model

     The character of Antigone in Sophocles'
play has many different facets. She represents
something as a woman, as a heroine, and as a
role model. However, on closer examination,
can we say that all these facets come together
to form a unique character and personality? Or
can we say that if taken separately, any one
of these individual personal traits would be
enough to describe her?

     As a Greek woman, Antigone is very differ-
ent even within Sophocles' play. She especially contrasts with the law-abiding Ismene.
As Ismene is overwhelmed by Creon's power, she
expects Antigone to behave as a typical woman
and submit to men: "we must be sensible. Remember we are women, / we're not born to contend
with men. Then too, / we're underlings, ruled
by much stronger hands, / so we must submit in
this, and things still worse" (2.74-77). Antigone, however, is independent and believes
that she has a right to her own opinions.
Moreover, she is willing to defend them at all
costs even if it means forsaking the roles--tra-
ditionally assigned to women--of marriage and
children.

Pipolo 2

Thus, while Ismene views her womanhood in traditional ways, Antigone discovers strength in her female nature and uses it to her own advantage. Unlike Ismene, Antigone is not afraid to defy her king. As the passage below shows, she values marriage and children, but she is willing to give them up for the honor of burying her brother:

> And now he leads me off, a captive
> in his hands, with no part in the bri-
> dal-song, the bridal-bed, denied all
> joy of marriage, raising children--
> deserted so by loved ones, struck by
> fate, I descend alive to the caverns
> of the dead. (2.1008-12)

Unlike Creon's, Antigone's values seem to be deeply rooted in her duties to the dead members of her family. She values her emotional ties to brother Polyneices over her ties to country and king.

As a woman, too, Antigone resents the way Creon sexualizes the power hierarchy in Thebes. As Segal writes in his essay "Sophocles' Praise of Man and the Conflicts of the *Antigone*," "Antigone's struggle is the woman's emotional resistance to the ordered male reason of the state" (66). However, the conflict between Antigone and Creon can go beyond the debate between a woman and a man. It can be further defined, as Segal mentions, as Creon's inabil-

Pipolo 3

ity to grasp the reasons, the motives, and the
nature of the "woman's resistance." In such a
debate, Antigone comes out as more typically
"female" or at least as representing the emotional side of human nature.

Antigone's display of her female nature in
such a rash and unrelenting way can be better
understood when we realize that Antigone is
still a very young, impetuous woman. Bowra remarks in his book <u>Sophoclean Tragedy</u> that Antigone "is young, a girl on the verge of
womanhood, not yet married, with a girl's di-
rectness and refusal to compromise" (90). Because of her age, Antigone expresses her love
for her brother in a less "rational" way than
we might expect.

Antigone can also be considered a heroine,
not only in the context of the play but also
in a more universal sense. Even though she is
oppressed and stifled by Creon and his laws,
which she considers unjust, she shows a heroic
kind of resilience, courage, and determination
to fight him to death to defend her own principles. If we see Creon representing the "state"
in a more general sense, then Antigone symbolizes the heroic moral claims of individual conscience.

In the play, Creon is often portrayed as
the blind, stubborn leader who is drunk on his
own power: "The city is the king's--that's the

law!" (1.825). As Rebecca Bushnell writes in
her book Prophesying Tragedy, "Creon is tyrannical in his belief in the power of his own
voice and his separation of himself from the
claims of humanity" (54). He also raises the
power of the city and his rule above the religious traditions of the people. According to
the critic Gerald Else, this empowerment of the
state defied what the Greeks considered the
natural order: "Creon [exalts] the city above
the gods and their laws, thus subverting the hi-
erarchical order" (12).

Antigone is also portrayed in the play as
an oppressed member of society who envisions
power and glory as the outcome of her heroic
struggle against impossible odds:

> Give me glory! What greater glory
> could I win then to give my own
> brother decent burial? These citi-
> zens here would all agree, they would
> praise me too if their lips weren't
> locked in fear. (2.562-65)

Antigone is a representative of the common people who are unable to voice their opinions because of the threat of political dictatorship.
As she rises as a heroic figure, she becomes
an ideal for those who are not strong enough
to stand up on their own and fight. Because
of her strength, obstinate personality, and
moral convictions, she also becomes a role

Pipolo 5

model for her sister Ismene and for those who believe she is right.

Even though Antigone has some influence over Ismene, this is not enough to convince her sister to defy Creon, his patriarchal system, and his public policy. By the end of the play, however, after Ismene has been convinced of the heroic purpose of Antigone's madness and is willing to die with her, Antigone will not let her. She feels that Ismene would be sharing the glory for a courageous act in which she had no part: "Never share my dying, / don't lay claim to what you never touched. / My death will be enough" (2.615–17).

Antigone also becomes a role model for Haimon, her cousin and husband-to-be. In spite of his initial assurance of his loyalty to his father, Haimon proves that he and the people of Thebes support Antigone. He tries to lend his support to her by discussing the situation with his father, but he fails to convince Creon of his error. As Ruth Scodel writes in her book *Sophocles,* "Haemon can join [Antigone] only by joining in her death" (50). Haimon's suicide, in fact, may be seen as his final act in support of Antigone.

What is most remarkable about Antigone's influence over Haimon is that her actions motivate him to challenge his father's private and public authority. It is to Antigone that Hai-

Pipolo 6

mon owes his loyalty. Not only does Haimon betray his father to someone else, but he also
betrays him for a woman, which is exactly what
Creon seems to fear throughout. As Segal remarks in his essay,

> [Creon] sees in Antigone a challenge
> to his whole way of living and his ba-
> sic attitudes toward the world. And
> of course he is right, for Antigone's
> full acceptance of her womanly na-
> ture, her absolute valuation of the
> bonds of blood and affection, is a to-
> tal denial of Creon's obsessively mas-
> culine rationality. (70)

In betraying his father, therefore, and
siding with Antigone, Haimon not only breaks
his bonds of loyalty to father and family, but
breaks them in conjunction with his affirmation
of female power. His attitude especially an-
tagonizes his father. The fact that Haimon
takes such action against Creon's powerful
voice may be considered a sign that Antigone
functioned as a role model to him.

The individual traits that make up Antigone's character, portraying her as a woman,
a heroine, and a role model, are all important
factors in understanding her motivations and
what she symbolizes as a whole. None of them
on their own, however, is enough to completely
explain her, since she has so many different

Pipolo 7

sides. Bowra describes her character as a complex one that can be seen from different perspectives at different times:

> She is a human being, moved by
> deep affection and capable of true
> love. . . . She is no embodiment of
> abstract devotion to duty, no martyr
> for martyrdom's sake, but a girl of
> strong character and strong feelings.
> Her motives are fundamentally simple,
> but are displayed now in one light,
> now in another, as her circumstances
> or her needs vary. (90)

However, together with each one of her individual facets, Antigone also shows a dark and complex side to her personality. It is this darkness and complexity, in fact, that makes her so interesting. She is also guided by what we might consider some self-centered, negative drives.

She is inspired by her loyalty to her family and to the gods, but what really drives her and what enables her to stand resolute against Creon's decree is her tragic inability to negotiate, compromise, or see any kind of virtue in somebody else's argument. Such personality traits make Antigone inflexible and unable to relate well to others. Eventually they lead her to death. However, they also are what really makes Antigone different and notice-

Pipolo 8

able in this play. She is fighting for what she believes in, and even though she is far from perfect, she is carrying out her fight her own way.

Therefore, as a whole, we could say that what Antigone really represents is a complete human being. She means well when she defends her individual conscience against Creon's public policy. However, she is undone by her own frailties and cannot overcome them. She becomes a heroine because she is able to fight for what she believes in, and in this process, she shows much strength as a woman. She also becomes a role model for several of the characters in the play. However, as she cannot and does not try to meet anyone's expectations of her, eventually her inability to compromise causes her undoing.

Pipolo 9

Works Cited

Bowra, C. M. <u>Sophoclean Tragedy</u>. Oxford:
Oxford UP, 1944.

Bushnell, Rebecca W. <u>Prophesying Tragedy</u>.
Ithaca: Cornell UP, 1988.

Else, Gerald. <u>The Madness of Antigone</u>. Heidel-
berg: Carl Winter, 1976.

Scodel, Ruth. <u>Sophocles</u>. Boston: Twayne, 1984.

Segal, Charles Paul. "Sophocles' Praise of Man
and the Conflicts of the <u>Antigone</u>." <u>Sopho-
cles</u>. Ed. Thomas Woodard. Englewood
Cliffs: Prentice, 1966.

Sophocles. <u>Antigone. The Three Theban Plays</u>.
Trans. Robert Fagles. Middlesex, Eng.:
Penguin, 1984.

Critical Approaches: A Case Study of Hamlet

You have probably noticed that at times your response to a literary text may differ greatly from that of your classmates. Sometimes as you listen to these various voices in your literature class, you may even wonder whether you have all read the same text. Diverse factors such as your personalities, lifestyles, social environments, and experiences may lead you to adopt various kinds of value judgments, and to react differently to the stories, poems, and plays that you read. Like you, literary critics also come up with different responses to and diverse interpretations of the same literary work. Often they also adopt reading strategies that reflect a personal affiliation to various critical theories, such as formalism, psychoanalytic criticism, reader-response criticism, feminist criticism, and the New Historicism.

The selections following highlight five different ways that literary critics have chosen to interpret Shakespeare's *Hamlet.* As you read them, you will discover how each can illuminate your reading of *Hamlet,* making you aware of new ways to reach its literary complexity. Sigmund Freud once said that the poets and artists of the past had anticipated most of his findings about the unconscious. Freud's thesis may also be applied to *Hamlet,* the literary complexity of which seems to have anticipated the possibilities of various critical interpretations.

Notice that while none of the interpretations in this appendix claims to express an ideal evaluation of *Hamlet,* each will help you to uncover the rich complexity, ambiguity, and suggestiveness of Shakespeare's play.

PSYCHOANALYTIC CRITICISM

What Is the Focus of Psychoanalytic Criticism?

Psychoanalytic criticism takes the methods used to analyze the behavior of people in real-life situations and applies them to the dramatized patterns of human behavior in literature. Overall, it explores some basic assumptions devised by the pioneer of psychoanalysis, Sigmund Freud (1856–1939). Most important among these are Freud's fundamental ideas about the structure of the human psyche, his theory of repression, and the Oedipus complex model that Freud applied to his reading of *Hamlet.*

Freud's Theory of Repression.   Freud viewed one part of the human psyche, the **id** or unconscious, as the site of our instincts, or the unconscious part of ourselves that is biologically rooted and is always pressing for some kind of satisfaction. For Freud, the id basically fulfilled the principle of life he called the "pleasure principle." The **ego** or the "**I**," on the other hand, forms the rational part of the psyche. The ego opposes the id, as well as the **superego** or conscience. In a simplified view, the superego is that part of ourselves that regulates our moral judgment, telling us what is right or wrong. Based on this structural model, Freud developed his theory of **repression.** In his theory, the id becomes the repository of repressed material such as pain, sexual desires, wishes, and fears that the ego and superego tend to censor because of social mores, taboos, and other factors. As Freud viewed it, such repressed forces might eventually be reactivated to emerge either through our creative activities or through our fantasies, dreams, language, slips of the tongue, neuroses, repressed fears, and other sorts of mental conflicts.

The Oedipus Complex.   The name "Oedipus" takes us back to the Greek hero Oedipus who unwittingly kills his father and marries his mother. By **Oedipus complex** Freud meant to define one of the major repressed wishes of a boy's childhood: his desire to identify with the father and replace him in the affection of the mother. Psychoanalysts who came after Freud constructed a feminine version of the Oedipus complex, called the Electra complex. Named after a Greek legend in which the heroine Electra kills her mother to avenge the death of her father, the Electra complex describes a girl's unconscious wish to take the mother's place in the affection of the father.

A Psychoanalytic Reading of *Hamlet*

In his analysis of *Hamlet,* which was later amplified by his disciple and biographer Ernest Jones, Freud used his theory of repression and his overall assessment of the Oedipus complex to raise the issue of how Hamlet's strong repressed desire for his mother prevents him from fulfilling the task assigned to him by his father's ghost.

Sigmund Freud

"The Interpretation of Dreams"

Another of the great creations of tragic poetry, Shakespeare's *Hamlet,* has its roots in the same soil as *Oedipus Rex.* But the changed treatment of the same material reveals the whole difference in the mental life of these two widely separated epochs of civilization: the secular advance of repression in the emotional life of mankind. In the *Oedipus* the child's wishful phantasy that underlies it is brought into the open and realized as it would be in a dream. In *Hamlet* it remains repressed; and—just as in the case of a neurosis—we only learn of its existence from its inhibiting consequences. Strangely enough, the overwhelming effect produced by the more modern tragedy has turned out to be compatible with the fact that people have remained completely in the dark as to the hero's character. The play is built up on Hamlet's hesitations over fulfilling the task of revenge that is assigned to him; but its text offers no reasons or motives for these hesitations and an immense variety of attempts at interpreting them have failed to produce a result. According to the view which was originated by Goethe and is still the prevailing one to-day, Hamlet represents the type of man whose power of direct action is paralysed by an excessive development of his intellect. (He is "sicklied o'er with the pale cast of thought.") According to another view, the dramatist has tried to portray a pathologically irresolute character which might be classed as neurasthenic. The plot of the drama shows us, however, that Hamlet is far from being represented as a person incapable of taking any action. We see him doing so on two occasions: first in a sudden outburst of temper, when he runs his sword through the eavesdropper behind the arras, and secondly in a premeditated and even crafty fashion, when, with all the callousness of a Renaissance prince, he sends the two courtiers to the death that had been planned for himself. What is it, then, that inhibits him in fulfilling the task set him by his father's ghost? The answer, once again, is that it is the peculiar nature of the task. Hamlet is able to do anything—except take vengeance on the man who did away with his father and took that father's place with his mother, the man who shows him the repressed wishes of his own childhood realized. Thus the loathing which should drive him on to revenge is replaced in him by self-reproaches, by scruples of conscience, which remind him that he himself is literally no better than the sinner whom he is to punish.

Freud's psychoanalytic theories have been complemented, disputed, and revised by many of his followers. For instance, Carl Gustav Jung (1875–1961), Freud's student and later opponent, replaced Freud's main focus on "sex" with a theory of the **collective unconscious.** Unlike Freud, who highlights the individual history of repressed wishes, Jung emphasizes the importance of the collective unconscious, also known as racial memory, or the collective desires of the human race. The French psychoanalyst Jacques Lacan (1901–1981) shifted Freud's view from mental processes to argue that the unconscious is structured like a language.

A Psychosocial Reading of *Hamlet*

Recent psychoanalytic thought, as well as some post-Freudian development in psychoanalysis, has opened up the criticism of *Hamlet* to different approaches. One such approach is known as the psychosocial. Without ignoring the psychosexual implications of the play, a psychosocial approach to *Hamlet,* such as the one David Leverenz adopts in his article "The Women in *Hamlet:* An Interpersonal View," emphasizes the role that culture plays in shaping Hamlet's identity. On the basis of such a rationale, Leverenz argues that the real tragedy of *Hamlet* is that Hamlet finally does act. He assumes the aggressive masculine role that the patriarchal structure of power imposes on him, even though he views it as quite meaningless.

David Leverenz

"The Women in Hamlet: *An Interpersonal View"*

Hamlet's tragedy is the forced triumph of filial duty over sensitivity to his own heart. To fulfil various fathers' commands, he has to deny his self-awareness, just as Gertrude and Ophelia have done. That denial is equivalent to suicide, as the language of the last act shows. His puritanical cries about whoredom in himself and others, his hysterical outbursts to Ophelia about nunneries and painted women, are the outer shell of a horror at what the nurtured, loving, and well-loved soul has been corrupted to. From a more modern perspective than the play allows, we can sense that the destruction of good mothering is the real issue, at least from Hamlet's point of view.

Freudians, too many of whom have their own paternal answers to "Who's there," see Hamlet as an unconscious Claudius-Oedipus, or as a man baffled by pre-Oedipal ambivalences about his weak-willed, passionate, fickle mother. While acknowledging Hamlet's parricidal and matricidal impulses, we should see these inchoate feelings as responses, not innate drives. Interpersonal expectations, more than self-contained desires, are what divide Hamlet from himself and conscript him to false social purposes. In this perspective, taken from Harry Stack Sullivan, R. D. Laing, and D. W. Winnicott, Hamlet's supposed delay is a natural reaction to overwhelming interpersonal confusion. His self-preoccupation is paradoxically grounded not so much in himself as in the extraordinary and unremitting array of "mixed signals" that separate role from self, reason from feeling, duty from love.

Hamlet has no way of unambiguously understanding what anyone says to him. The girl who supposedly loves him inexplicably refuses his attentions. His grieving mother suddenly marries. His dead father, suddenly alive, twice tells him to deny his anger at his mother's shocking change of heart. Two of his best friends 'make love to this employment' of snooping against him (V.ii.57). Polonius, Claudius, and the Ghost all manifest themselves as loving fathers, yet expect the worst from their sons and spy on their children, either directly or through messengers. Who is this "uncle-father" and "aunt-mother" (II.ii.366), or this courtier-father, who preach the unity of being true to oneself and others yet are false to everyone, who can "smile, smile, and be a villain" (I.v.108)? Gertrude's inconstancy not only brings on disgust and incestuous feelings, it is also the sign of diseased doubleness in everyone who has accommodated to his or her social role. Usurping Claudius is the symbol of all those "pretenders," who are now trying to bring Hamlet into line. No wonder Hamlet weeps at the sight of a genuine actor—the irony reveals the problem—playing Hecuba's grief. The male expressing a woman's constancy once again mirrors Hamlet's need. And the role, though feigned, at least is openly played. The actor's tears are the play's one unambigious reflection of the grief Hamlet thought his mother shared with him before the onset of so many multitudinous double-dealings.

To kill or not to kill cannot be entertained when one is not even sure of existing with any integrity. Being, not desiring or revenging, is the question. Freudians assume that everyone has strong desires blocked by stronger repressions, but contemporary work with schizophrenics reveals the tragic variety of people whose voices are only amalgams of other people's voices, with caustic self-observation or a still more terrifying vacuum as their incessant inward reality. This is Hamlet to a degree, as it is Ophelia completely. As Laing says of her in *The Divided Self,* "in her madness, there is no one there. She is not a person. There is no integral selfhood expressed through her actions or utterances. Incomprehensible statements are said by nothing. She has already died. There is now only a vacuum where there was once a person." Laing misrepresents her state only because there are many voices in Ophelia's madness speaking through her, all making sense, and none of them her own. She becomes the mirror for a madness-inducing world. Hamlet resists these pressures at the cost of a terrifying isolation. Once he thinks his mother has abandoned him, there is nothing and no one to "mirror" his feelings, as Winnicott puts it. Hamlet is utterly alone, beyond the loving semi-understanding of reasonable Horatio or obedient Ophelia.

A world of fathers and sons, ambition and lust, considers grief "unmanly," as Claudius preaches (I.ii.94). Hamlet seems to agree, at least to himself, citing his "whorish" doubts as the cause of his inability to take manly filial action. This female imagery, which reflects the play's male-centered world view, represents a covert homosexual fantasy, according to Freudian interpretation. Certainly Hamlet's idealisations of his father and of Horatio's friendship show a hunger for male closeness. Poisoning in the ear may unconsciously evoke anal intercourse. And the climactic swordplay with Laertes does lead to a brotherly understanding. But these instances of covert homosexual desire are responses to a lack. Poisoning in the ear evokes conscious and unconscious perversity to intimate the perversion of communication, especially between men. The woman in Hamlet is the source of his most acute perceptions about the diseased, disordered patriarchal society that tries to "play upon this pipe" of Hamlet's soul (III.ii.336), even as a ghost returning from the dead.

Reading Contexts

FREUD'S TEXT

1. Why, according to Freud, have Shakespeare's readers and critics remained completely in the dark in their attempts to interpret Hamlet's character?

2. Freud mentions that the Hamlet theory developed by the German poet Goethe (1749–1832) still prevailed in his time. Describe Goethe's theory, and summarize the arguments that Freud developed to refute Goethe's romantic interpretation of Hamlet's character. How does Freud's psychoanalytic interpretation differ from Goethe's romantic one?

LEVERENZ'S TEXT

1. Explain the distinction between Freud's psychosexual interpretation and Leverenz's psychosocial interpretation of *Hamlet,* which highlights the idea that we are creatures of culture.

2. Leverenz argues that "interpersonal expectations, more than self-contained desires, are what divide Hamlet from himself and conscript him to false social purposes." In your opinion, is Leverenz's argument complex enough to explain the Hamlet problem?

3. One of the major arguments running through Leverenz's article supports the idea that Hamlet is manipulated and ultimately controlled by the male roles that patriarchal society imposes on him. Do you agree or disagree with Leverenz?

Psychoanalytic Criticism: Reading References. The reading references in this section include a series of works that, although not directly connected with *Hamlet,* highlight some of the critical ideas that inform the modern reading of *Hamlet.*

Erlich, Avi. *Hamlet's Absent Father.* Princeton: Princeton UP, 1977.

Freud, Sigmund. "The Interpretation of Dreams." *The Standard Edition of the Complete Psychological Works.* Ed. James Strachey. London: Hogarth, 1953–1974.

Kurtzweil, Edith, and William Philips, eds. *Literature and Psychoanalysis.* New York: Columbia UP, 1983.

Lacan, Jacques. "Desire and the Interpretation of Desire in *Hamlet.*" *Literature and Psychoanalysis: The Question of Reading: Otherwise.* Ed. Shoshana Felman. Baltimore: Johns Hopkins UP, 1982.

Leverenz, David. "The Women in *Hamlet:* An Interpersonal View." *Hamlet: Contemporary Critical Essays.* Ed. Martin Coyle. New York: St. Martin's, 1992.

Skura, Meredith. *The Literary Use of the Psychoanalytic Process.* New Haven: Yale UP, 1981.

Wright, Elizabeth. *Psychoanalytic Criticism.* London: Methuen, 1984.

FORMALISM/NEW CRITICISM

What Is the Major Focus of Formalism?

Formalism seeks to emphasize the importance of the formal elements of literature or the formal qualities related to the language, form, and content of a literary text. It directly opposes any extrinsic kind of criticism that views the literary text as a product of the author's intentions or as a reflection of ethical and sociocultural forces. In modern formalist criticism, especially in the works of formalist critics known as New Critics, literature is alienated and isolated from the actual world, seeking to fulfill the purposes of revealing deeper truths and embodying a unified vision of life in the shaped structure of a work of art.

Formalism flourished from the 1940s to the 1960s. To some extent, the close reading it advocates has remained a major goal not only for formalists but for all readers who rely on formal devices, such as imagery, irony, paradox, symbols, diction, plot, characterization, and narrative techniques, to understand the meanings of a literary text. A formalist reading of poetry can show, for instance, how a poem can integrate an ideal order of form and content by relating its phonic devices (aspects related to sounds, rhythm, and meter) to its images, symbols, and overall mode of poetic construction.

A New Critical Reading of *Hamlet*

Since a major focus of the New Critical method or formalism is the construction of literary craft, formalist critics have explored Shakespeare's use of character, language, and staging to validate the dramatic world of *Hamlet*. In "Hamlet and His Problems," T. S. Eliot applies formalist strategies to argue that feelings and emotions can be viewed as an objective mode of construction and be formally channeled in art. Shakespeare fails in *Hamlet,* Eliot argues, because he is unable to find "an objective correlative" or "a set of objects, a situation, a chain of events which shall be the formula of that *particular* emotion." Thus, as Eliot sees it, emotions and feelings in *Hamlet* exceed the literary form of Shakespeare's tragedy and cannot be expressed in art—they are "in excess of the facts." As to Gertrude, Eliot remarks that she "arouses in Hamlet the feeling which she is incapable of representing."

T. S. Eliot

"Hamlet and His Problems"

The only way of expressing emotion in the form of art is by finding an "objective correlative": in other words, a set of objects, a situation, a chain of events which shall be the formula of that *particular* emotion; such that when the external facts, which must terminate in sensory experience, are given, the emotion

is immediately evoked. If you examine any of Shakespeare's more successful tragedies, you will find this exact equivalence; you will find that the state of mind of
Lady Macbeth walking in her sleep has been communicated to you by a skilful
accumulation of imagined sensory impressions; the words of Macbeth on hearing
of his wife's death strike us as if, given the sequence of events, these words were
automatically released by the last event in the series. The artistic "inevitability" lies
in this complete adequacy of the external to the emotion; and this is precisely what
is deficient in *Hamlet*. Hamlet (the man) is dominated by an emotion which is
inexpressible, because it is in *excess* of the facts as they appear. And the supposed
identity of Hamlet with his author is genuine to this point: that Hamlet's bafflement at the absence of objective equivalent to his feelings is a prolongation of the
bafflement of his creator in the face of his artistic problem. Hamlet is up against the
difficulty that his disgust is occasioned by his mother, but that his mother is not an
adequate equivalent for it; his disgust envelops and exceeds her. It is thus a feeling
which he cannot understand; he cannot objectify it, and it therefore remains to poison life and obstruct action. None of the possible actions can satisfy it; and nothing
that Shakespeare can do with the plot can express Hamlet for him. And it must be
noticed the the very nature of the *données* of the problem precludes objective
equivalence. To have heightened the criminality of Gertrude would have been to
provide the formula for a totally different emotion in Hamlet; it is just *because* her
character is so negative and insignificant that she arouses in Hamlet the feeling
which she is incapable of representing.

Reading Contexts

1. New Criticism or formalism attempts to present a unified vision of a work of art
   in which every element, such as a word, an image, or a situation, contributes to
   a formal view of unity. With this in mind, analyze the use that Eliot makes of
   words like *deficient, excess, not adequate,* and *negative* to support his reading of
   Hamlet.

2. According to Hazard Adams, what Eliot really meant by the "objective correlative" is not very clear. Examine Eliot's definition of this concept in the beginning of the first paragraph of Eliot's essay, and then decide whether you agree
   or disagree with Adams.

Formalism/New Criticism: Reading References

Brooks, Cleanth, and Robert Penn Warren. *Understanding Poetry.* New York:
  Henry Holt, 1938.
Crane, Ronald Salmon. *The Languages of Criticism and the Structure of Poetry.*
  Toronto: U of Toronto P, 1953.
Eliot, T. S. "Hamlet and His Problems." *Selected Essays.* New York: Harcourt,
  1960.
Warren, Austin. *Rage for Order: Essays in Criticism.* Ann Arbor: U of Michigan
  P, 1948.

READER-RESPONSE CRITICISM

What Is the Focus of Reader-Response Criticism?

Reader-response criticism places much emphasis on the literary experience of individual readers not only as interpreters of texts but as producers of meanings. One of its basic assumptions is that each reading of a text by a single reader will be different because the dynamic and subjective scope of the reader's responses makes each reader react in different ways. Thus, the major focus of reader-response criticism is the diversity and plurality of the reader's interpretive experiences. As individual readers are apt to be influenced by social, communal, cultural, and political values, reader-response criticism also focuses on how women, individuals, and groups, in different social settings and in different time periods, read texts. Some studies show, for instance, how readers can interact with the texts' gaps, ambiguities, and pluralities or use the reading process itself to revise and build up their own expectations as readers.

A Reader-Response Analysis of *Hamlet*

Reader-response criticism can make us understand why we encounter such diverse interpretive responses to our study of *Hamlet*. The critic Norman N. Holland, for instance, explains how three different readers can respond to *Hamlet* and construct the meaning of this play according to their emotional and psychological reactions to the concept of authority. For Holland, as for most reader-response critics, whenever a text threatens the identity of its readers, the readers question, rewrite, and project their feelings on it.

In the following passage, another reader-response critic, Stephen Booth, analyzes *Hamlet* in terms of the audience's response to the play. For Booth, the audience not only is involved in constructing the meaning of *Hamlet* but is also affected when its character and experience are altered and revised by the reading process itself. Thus, at times *Hamlet*'s audience is invited to settle its mind, to get information, to develop double and contrary responses to Claudius, while at other times it gets frustrated, finding its focus shifted and its understanding threatened. At least once the audience is taken to the brink of intellectual terror. Most important, according to Booth, the audience never knows what it would have done in Hamlet's situation. Notice how Booth focuses on the position that the audience occupies in shaping the literary experience of act 2 of *Hamlet*.

Stephen Booth

"On the Value of Hamlet*"*

The audience sets out into Act II knowing what Hamlet knows, knowing Hamlet's plans, and secure in its superiority to the characters who do not. (Usually an audience is superior to the central characters: it knows that Desdemona is innocent, Othello does not; it knows what it would do when Lear foolishly divides his kingdom; it knows how Birnam Wood came to come to Dunsinane. In *Hamlet,* however, the audience never knows what it would have done in Hamlet's situation; in fact, since the King's successful plot in the duel with Laertes changes Hamlet's situation so that he becomes as much the avenger of his own death as of his father's, the audience never knows what Hamlet would have done. Except for brief periods near the end of the play, the audience never has insight or knowledge superior to Hamlet's or, indeed, different from Hamlet's. Instead of having superiority *to* Hamlet, the audience goes into the second act to share the superiority *of* Hamlet.) The audience knows that Hamlet will play mad, and its expectations are quickly confirmed. Just seventy-five lines into Act II, Ophelia comes in and describes a kind of behavior in Hamlet that sounds like the behavior of a young man of limited theatrical ability who is pretending to be mad (II.i.77–84). Our confidence that this behavior so puzzling to others is well within our grasp is strengthened by the reminder of the ghost, the immediate cause of the promised pretense, in Ophelia's comparison of Hamlet to a creature "loosed out of hell / To speak of horrors."

Before Ophelia's entrance, II.ii has presented an example of the baseness and foolishness of Polonius, the character upon whom both the audience and Hamlet exercise their superiority throughout Act II. Polonius seems base because he is arranging to spy on Laertes. He instructs his spy in ways to use the "bait of falsehood"—to find out directions by indirections (II.i.74). He is so sure that he knows everything, and so sure that his petty scheme is not only foolproof but brilliant, that he is as contemptible mentally as he is morally. The audience laughs at him because he loses his train of thought in pompous byways, so that, eventually, he forgets what he set out to say: "What was I about to say?…I was about to say something! Where did I leave?" (II.i.50–51). When Ophelia reports Hamlet's behavior, Polonius takes what is apparently Hamlet's bait: "Mad for thy love?" (II.i.85). He also thinks of (and then spends the rest of the act finding evidence for) a specific cause for Hamlet's madness: he is mad for love of Ophelia. The audience knows (1) Hamlet will pretend madness, (2) Polonius is a fool, and (3) what is actually bothering Hamlet. Through the rest of the act, the audience laughs at Polonius for being fooled by Hamlet. It continues to laugh at Polonius' inability to keep his mind on a track (II.ii.85–130); it also laughs at him for the opposite fault—he has a one-track mind and sees anything and everything as evidence that Hamlet is mad for love (II.ii.173–212; 394–402). Hamlet, whom the audience knows and understands, spends a good part of the rest of the scene making Polonius demonstrate his foolishness.

Reading Contexts

1. What kind of argument is Booth trying to make when he mentions that the audience in *Hamlet* "never knows what it would have done in Hamlet's situation"? Notice that while the formalist or New Critical approach to *Hamlet* privileges character analysis, Booth's overall assumptions privilege the position of the audience.

2. How would you characterize Booth's portrayal of the audience in *Hamlet?* To what extent does the audience in *Hamlet* function as a reflection and a mirror of Hamlet's own frustrations and contradictions? Where do you stand in relation to this reader-response reading of *Hamlet?*

Reader-Response Criticism: Reference Readings

Booth, Stephen. "On the Value of *Hamlet.*" *Reinterpretations of Elizabethan Drama.* Ed. Norman Rabkin. New York: Columbia UP, 1969.

Eco, Umberto. *The Role of the Reader.* Bloomington: Indiana UP, 1979.

Iser, Wolfgang. *The Implied Reader: Patterns of Communication in Prose Fiction from Bunyan to Beckett.* Baltimore: Johns Hopkins UP, 1974.

Suleiman, Susan R., and Inge Crossman, eds. *The Reader in the Text: Essays on Audience and Interpretation.* Princeton: Princeton UP, 1980.

Tompkins, Jane P. "An Introduction to Reader-Response Criticism." *Reader-Response Criticism: From Formalism to Post-Structuralism.* Ed. Jane P. Tompkins. Baltimore: Johns Hopkins UP, 1980.

FEMINIST CRITICISM

What Is the Focus of Feminist Criticism?

Modern feminist criticism emerged in the late 1960s and early 1970s out of a sociopolitical movement aimed at the defense of women's rights. It addressed the need women felt to reinterpret literature, to rewrite history, and to change the power structure that has traditionally defined male and female relationships in patriarchal societies. Like Marxist, African-American, and the New Historical Criticism, the socially oriented perspective of feminist criticism has spread its voice in many directions. Among other things, it has promoted a reevaluation of the Freudian theory of sexual differences, a reassessment of female and male writing, a revision of the role of gender in literature, and a critique of the oppressive rationale of patriarchal ideology.

In her essay "This Sex Which Is Not One," the feminist critic Luce Irigaray has revised Freud's theory of sex difference, protesting against the view of woman as a biological version of the male model. In following the assumptions of Jacques Lacan, French feminists have also criticized, among other things, the logic of language that associates positive qualities such as those related to creativity, light, logic, and power with masculinity. Many feminists like Hélène Cixous, who tend to draw a relationship between women's writing and women's bodies, have also attempted to create a language or a specific kind of women's writing (*écriture feminine*) that refuses participation in masculine discourse.

Other feminists have promoted a feminist critique of masculine ideology, protesting against the political marginalization women have suffered as blacks, chicanos, Asian Americans, and lesbians. For the feminist critic Catharine R. Stimpson, the defiance of sexual difference, the celebration of sexual difference, and the recognition of differences constitute the three major principles of feminist criticism.

Many of the critical efforts of feminists have also been aimed at the study of women's history and the role of women in literary tradition.

A Feminist Reading of *Hamlet*

One of the major contributions that feminist literary criticism has made to our reading of *Hamlet* has been its revisionist affirmation that female characters such as Gertrude and Ophelia possess a narrative of their own or a form of feminine discourse.

Notice in the following passage that Diane Elizabeth Dreher's feminist analysis of *Hamlet* opens new possibilities for an evaluation of Ophelia. By analyzing the forces that shaped Ophelia's identity as a "dominated daughter," Dreher liberates Ophelia from the rigid stereotypes that traditional criticism has ascribed to her. According to Dreher, because of the "fearful domination" that Polonius, Laertes, and Hamlet exercised on Ophelia, which cast her in the role of the "other," Ophelia is unable to grasp the full complexity of her self and resolve the crisis of her identity. As Dreher sees it, Ophelia is defined as a simpleminded creature only when evaluated from a male-oriented viewpoint.

Diane Elizabeth Dreher

"Dominated Daughters"

A feminist analysis of Ophelia's behavior demonstrates that she is not the simpleminded creature she seems. Traditional readings of her character have been as superficial as nineteenth-century productions, which portrayed her as a simple, pretty girl of flowers whose mad scenes were artfully sung and danced. As Helena Faucit realized and dared to play her to a stunned audience in 1844–45, Ophelia actually does go mad. There is pain and struggle beneath that sweet surface. Her misfortune merits not only our pity but our censure of traditional mores that make women repress themselves and behave like automatons.

Contrary to prevailing opinion, Ophelia is more than a simple girl, living in "a world of dumb ideas and feelings." The pity of it is that Ophelia *does* think and feel. A careful examination of the text in I.iii reveals that she loves Hamlet and thinks for herself, but is forced to repress all this at her father's command, conforming to the stifling patriarchal concept of female behavior that subordinates women to their "honor," their procreative function in male society.

Torn between what she feels and what she is told to be, Ophelia is tormented by the crisis of identity. As one critic pointed out long ago, "she is not aware of the nature of her own feelings; they are prematurely developed in their full force before she has strength to bear them." Caught in adolescent uncertainty between childhood and adulthood, she cannot enter the stage of intimacy and adult commitment because she does not yet know who she is. Carol Gilligan has pointed to the difficulties young women have in individuation. Raised with an emphasis on empathy rather than autonomy, girls tend to subordinate their own needs to those of others. Ophelia experiences severe role confusion in which her personal feelings are suppressed in favor of external expectations....

Ophelia has been condemned for letting her father dominate her, for failing to "observe the fundamental responsibilities that hold together an existence." But let us consider the situation from her point of view. As a young woman, she is, first of all, more inclined to defer to the wishes of others than follow her own feelings. Ophelia errs in trusting her father, but she is not the only person in the play who has taken a parent at face value. Hamlet failed to recognize his mother's moral weakness until her marriage to Claudius. Furthermore, reverence for one's parents was expected of Renaissance youth. As Harley Granville-Barker emphasized, "we may call her docility a fault, when, as she is bid, she shuts herself away from Hamlet; but how not to trust to her brother's care for her and her father's wisdom?" Like Othello, Ophelia errs in trusting the wrong moral guide: in his case a friend who had shared dangers on the battlefield, in hers a father to whom convention bound her duty and obedience. Polonius' warning, seconded by her brother's, gains greater credibility. But most significant, her moral guides have not only told her how to behave; they have redefined her entire universe, inculcating in Ophelia a view of human sexuality as nasty and brutish as that which infects Othello. Ophelia sees herself in a world in which sexuality transforms human beings into beasts, with men the predators and women their prey.

Reading Contexts

1. Describe the traditional critical assumptions about Ophelia, and then contrast them with Dreher's. Explain how Dreher collapses the traditional view of Ophelia, offering insights into a new representation of this character.

2. To what extent does Dreher's argument about the rival claims of individuation and external expectations help to explain Ophelia's identity crisis? Where do you stand in relation to this argument?

Feminist Literary Criticism: Reading References

Abel, Elizabeth, ed. *Writing and Sexual Difference.* Chicago: U of Chicago P, 1982.

Carby, Hazel V. *Reconstructing Womanhood: The Emergence of the Afro-American Woman Novelist.* New York: Oxford UP, 1987.

de Beauvoir, Simone. *The Second Sex.* Trans. and ed. H. M. Parshley. New York: Knopf, 1953.

Dreher, Diane Elizabeth. *Dominance and Defiance: Fathers and Daughters in Shakespeare.* Kentucky: U of Kentucky P, 1986.

Showalter, Elaine. "Representing Ophelia: Women, Madness and the Responsibilities of Feminist Criticism." *Shakespeare and the Question of Theory* Ed. Patricia Parker and Geoffrey Hartman. London: Methuen, 1985.

THE NEW HISTORICISM

What Is the Focus of the New Historicism?

The New Historicism, or cultural poetics, may be defined as a form of political criticism closely related to Marxist criticism. One of its main goals is to focus on the critical study of power relations, politics, and ideology. For the New Historicist critics, such as Stephen Greenblatt, who coined the term "New Historical" in the early 1980s, this criticism displaces the traditional view of history as a discipline committed to an altruistic search for truth and to a faithful reconstruction of the dates and events of the past. Instead, the New Historicist perspective advocates a focus on a historical dynamic or a view of history in action. Its aim is to erase the boundaries among disciplines such as literature, history, and the social sciences. The ideas of the French philosopher and historian Michel Foucault (1926–1984) seem to inform much of the rationale that New Historicism established for the complex relation among language, power, and knowledge.

New Historical critics tend to view Shakespeare's plays as political acts reflecting and shaping the collective codes and beliefs of Shakespeare's times. New Historicists also affirm the reciprocity between the text and the world, which they attempt to rewrite by showing how sociopolitical practices and institutions such as the theater can shape and transform cultural meanings. When considering the relation between text and reader, the New Historicists advocate the reciprocity between these two elements, viewing them as dynamic forces interacting with and responding to each other.

A New Historical Reading of *Hamlet*

Leonard Tennenhouse's reading of *Hamlet* shows Shakespeare's play as a critique of power relations centered on a struggle for power between Hamlet and Claudius. According to Tennenhouse, the political struggle in *Hamlet* emerges from the clash between two different claims to the throne of Denmark: Hamlet's, which is based on blood and popular support, and Claudius's, which is based on his marriage to Gertrude and his use of force.

By approaching Shakespeare's tragedy through the critical lens traditionally applied in the criticism of history plays such as *Richard III, Richard II,* and *Henry IV,* Tennenhouse has erased the boundaries that traditional and formalist criticism insisted on establishing between Shakespeare's tragedies and his history plays. In his critique of the play-within-the-play in *Hamlet,* Tennenhouse also shifts the focus from Hamlet's goal of "catch[ing] the conscience of the King" to Hamlet's crime against the state. Tennenhouse also argues that in the play-within-the-play Hamlet fails because the political force he generates amounts to a mere symbolic gesture.

Leonard Tennenhouse

"Power in Hamlet *"*

Hamlet rehearses [the] dilemma of a state torn between two competitors, neither of whom can embody the mystical power of blood and land associated with the natural body. Hamlet's claim to power derives from his position as son in a patrilinear system as well as from "popular support." It is this support which Claudius consistently lacks and which, at the same time, prevents him from moving openly against Hamlet. Following the murder of Polonius, for example, Claudius says of Hamlet, "Yet must not we put the strong law on him. / He's lov'd of the distracted multitude..." (IV.iii.3–4). But this alone does not guarantee authority. Hamlet is not by nature capable of exercising force. To signal this lack, Shakespeare has given him the speech of Stoical writing, which shifts all action onto a mental plane where any show of force becomes self-inflicted aggression. We find this identification of force with self-assault made explicit in Hamlet's speeches on suicide as well as those in which he berates himself for his inability to act.

In contrast with Hamlet, Claudius's authority comes by way of his marriage to Gertrude. Where he would be second to Hamlet and Hamlet's line in a patrilineal system, the queen's husband and uncle of the king's son occupies the privileged male position in a matrilineal system. Like one of the successful figures from a history play, Claudius overthrew the reigning patriarch. Like one of the successful courtiers in a romantic comedy, he married into the aristocratic community. What is perhaps more important, he has taken the position through the effective use of force. Thus Shakespeare sets in opposition the two claims to authority—the exercise of force and the magic of blood—by means of these two members of the royal family. Because each has a claim, neither Hamlet nor Claudius achieves legitimate control over Denmark. Each one consequently assaults the aristocratic body in attempting to acquire the crown. It is to be expected that Claudius could not legally possess the crown, the matrilinear succession having the weaker claim on British political thinking. Thus the tragedy resides not in his failure but in the impossibility of Hamlet's rising according to Elizabethan strategies of state. This calls the relationship between the metaphysics of patriarchy and the force of law into question.

Reading Contexts

1. Find the sentences that best describe the two rival claims to power that Tennenhouse discusses in his text. Analyze the way these images of power reflect Tennenhouse's political views of *Hamlet*.

2. What conclusions can you draw from Tennenhouse's reading of this scene? Decide whether or not you agree or disagree with Tennenhouse's interpretation of *Hamlet*.

The New Historicism: Reading References

Greenblatt, Stephen J. *Renaissance Self-Fashioning: From More to Shakespeare.* Chicago: U of Chicago P, 1980.
———, ed. *Representing the English Renaissance.* Berkeley: U of California P, 1988.
Hunt, Lynn, ed. *The New Cultural History.* Berkeley: U of California P, 1989.
Lindenberger, Herbert. "Toward a New History in Literature Studies." *Profession: Selected Articles from the Bulletin of the Association of Departments of English and the Association of Departments of Foreign Languages.* New York: MLA, 1984.
Tennenhouse, Leonard. "Power in *Hamlet*." *Hamlet.* Ed. Martin Coyle. New York: St. Martin's, 1992.
Veeser, H. Aram, ed. *The New Historicism.* New York: Routledge, 1989.

FILM VERSIONS OF *HAMLET*

Some Celebrated Film Versions of *Hamlet*

Many versions of Shakespeare's *Hamlet* have been produced. In the early days of film history, it was fashionable to film famous stage actors in their famous roles so that movie audiences, primarily composed of working- and middle-class people who might never see a live performance, would be exposed to what was once thought an experience available only to the elite. Thus, producers filmed selective parts or abridged versions of Sarah Bernhardt's or John Barrymore's Hamlet. Of course, before sound this made the experience a bit pointless, since the essence of the play—Shakespeare's language—was not heard coming from the actors' mouths but was abbreviated and provided in the form of intertitles.

In the sound era, at least five film versions of the play have appeared, one of them a moody Russian film of 1964. The four best-known English language films are Laurence Olivier's 1948 version, which the actor also produced and directed and which won the Academy Award as best picture of that year; a British film of 1969 starring Nicol Williamson as Hamlet; in 1990 the Franco Zeffirelli production with Mel Gibson; and the 1996 version of *Hamlet,* directed by Kenneth Branagh. A teleplay of the Richard Burton version, directed by the great English actor John Gielgud in 1964, is also available.

There are as many variations in approach and interpretation among the films as there have been among the many stage productions.

The Olivier Version of *Hamlet*. Olivier's is undoubtedly the most respected version, but because it is so celebrated one tends to forget that it is still a specific reading of the play, and not necessarily the only legitimate one. His is very much a Freudian Hamlet: key scenes and speeches are composed and delivered in ways that make the Oedipal conflict central to the action and the primary cause of Hamlet's delay in avenging his father's murder. Olivier is also a more sensitive prince than either Williamson or Gibson. His affinity with the arts and culture and the best of human instincts is completely credible, making the vengeful task before him seem even more intolerable.

The Zeffirelli Version of *Hamlet*. The Zeffirelli film does not provide an interpretation that embraces the contradictions within the character. It evades the problem by deleting many of the richest and most complex lines in Hamlet's speeches, substituting whirling action scenes that attempt to depict a man of rugged determination. In the clinch, however, Zeffirelli still seems unable to escape the Oedipal implications, and in what is perhaps the boldest and most tasteless moment in the film, he has Hamlet kiss his mother passionately on the mouth in close-up at the very moment the father's ghost enters the bedchamber. We might wonder how this version accords with the character as perceived in Shakespeare's play.

The Branagh Version of *Hamlet*. Branagh's majestic seventy-millimeter, postmodern production of *Hamlet* emphasizes performance, action, showmanship, special effects, color, and ornate sets. In a dashing free version that uses the ornate gilt chambers of Blenheim Palace as the setting of Elsinore, Branagh casts Shakespearean actors Derek Jacobi (Claudius), Kate Winslet (Ophelia), John Gielgud (Priam), and Judy Dench (Hecuba), as well as international movie stars Jack Lemmon, Charlton Heston, Billy Crystal, Gerard Depardieu, and Robin Williams in small roles. In addition, Branagh boldly plays the full Shakespearean text in a nearly four-hour film.

Branagh's production of *Hamlet* also obliterates the pretense of a sophisticated, critical approach to the play and makes the play accessible to a movie audience more concerned with the dynamic energy, the dramatic purpose, and the literal meanings of Shakespeare's tragedy. In Branagh's own words, "Sex, violence, sword fights, the ghost of a dead father, a journey into madness, the politics of a country, and family at war—a quite extraordinary story."

A Note About Film and Videos

Throughout the history of film—which celebrated its centennial in 1995—movies have served a number of purposes and assumed a number of roles in the development of twentieth-century culture. No history of this century, no serious consideration of the forces that have helped to shape it, could conceivably ignore the impact of movies.

From the birth of film, movies have documented events, personalities, and places, providing not only invaluable sources of information to scholars but a sense of how things looked and felt. The French brothers August and Louis Lumiere were among the very first in the late 1890s to film the world around them, and the often spectacular results of their efforts still exist for anyone to behold. We can walk into virtually any film museum in the world and see "living" testimony of what New York or Paris or San Francisco looked like at the time of our grandparents or great-grandparents; we can see how people dressed and in what vehicles they traveled. We can view actual footage of immigrants aboard ships taking them to the United States at the turn of the century. If we are celebrity conscious, we can gaze at Czar Nicholas of Russia long before the Russian Revolution, or at writers Leo Tolstoy and George Bernard Shaw walking through their gardens.

Also from the first, movies have played tricks on our imaginations. In the films of George Melies, a contemporary of the Lumiere brothers, things disappear, illusory composites of people and objects are created before our eyes, feats that would be the envy of any stage magician are performed.

In a different application of imagination, photographers with an artistic inclination saw new possibilities to re-create the world, rather than merely record it, by finding abstract and lyrical designs in nature. In none of these examples did stories or narratives play major roles, although they often provided a minimal structure to anecdotal and incidental sketches.

The most popular line of development for movies, however, was certainly the one that made storytelling the primary goal. Narrative films emerged so quickly and became so commonplace that most people don't realize they were not the first kind of movies made and are not necessarily superior to the others.

FILM AND LITERATURE

Narrative films occupy an appropriate place in a literature anthology because they share with dramatic and prose literature many common features, such as theme, plot, characterization, the use of imagery, narrative point of view, and a number of rhetorical devices that have film and literary equivalents, such as metaphors and symbols.

Films have always looked to literature—to novels, plays, short stories, even poems—for sources and subject matter. Some filmmakers believed that the primary goal of movies was to introduce larger audiences to classic plays and performances they would otherwise never have a chance to see. While filmmakers continue to adapt works of literature to the screen (Stanley Kubrick's *Full Metal Jacket,* for example, is based on Gustav Hasford's novel of Vietnam, *The Short-timers*), many films do not rely on preexisting literary texts.

Films have been inspired by literature in ways other than that of direct adaptation. Many films, like works of literature, are rereadings or reimaginings of famous myths and tales. Steven Spielberg's *Hook,* for example, presumes the audience's familiarity with the Peter Pan story, but creates an entirely new contemporary allegory inspired by the original tale's themes of growing up and maturity.

Whatever their origins, however, most films must be tailored so as to be accessible to many people and to observe a relatively clear narrative structure. A film cannot be taken in at our leisure, or mulled over, or put aside as one might a novel. We are a captive audience when we watch a movie for the first time—at least if this occurs in a theater. We are bound to the pacing and flow of information, which have been preset by the filmmaker. If our attention lapses, or if we chat with the person next to us, we may—and invariably do—miss something crucial. Of course, in the age of the VCR we can view and review movies dozens of times to get to know them better, but this luxury was unavailable throughout most of film history.

Furthermore, ideas can be more fully explained in a novel or in a play, and characters often more fully developed. One has only to think of most film versions of Shakespeare's plays to realize this. This does not mean that narrative films are more shallow than literary works; it means that most great works of literature are great precisely because they can accomplish things that other art forms cannot. Hence, a great novel or play will rarely be made into a great film. But the obverse is also true. Great films could never be translated into literature since they have undoubtedly utilized the visual and audio powers of the film medium to achieve their impact. Alfred Hitchcock, one of film history's greatest directors, remarked that he never attempted to film a serious work of literature because to the degree that it was great literature it would be impossible to translate it into film terms.

Instead, he took a French potboiler and a horror novel and made the classic films *Vertigo* and *Psycho,* respectively.

This leads us to a consideration of how best to approach a study of film. To ensure a clarity of structure for the viewer to find his or her way, Hollywood developed genres that have proved to be more durable and elastic than one might have thought.

GENRE

By definition, *genre* movies follow certain formulaic conventions such as conforming to certain patterns of structuring stories and creating heroes, heroines, and villains. Horror films, westerns, musicals, science fiction, crime and detective stories, and melodramas are all examples of the most readily recognized movie genres. But the concept of genre is hardly limited to these more popular examples. American and European filmmakers have also been attracted to historical epics and biographical dramas for half a century. Much as the word *genre* may not instantly form on our lips when we think of films such as *Lawrence of Arabia, Gandhi, Hoffa,* or *Malcolm X,* all of these films are examples of the biographical drama, a genre that has as long a history as any other and as many conventions and formulas. One of its conventions is that we must see how the central figure was singled out and marked for greatness, even if we question the morality of that figure's actions. Specific thresholds and moments of crisis and transformation are normally a part of the life being chronicled because they help to crystallize the important stages of the character's evolution and therefore justify the narrative development toward the specific goal. The biographical genre "explains" a life by giving it a familiar shape, structure, and purpose.

The question of genre is both unavoidable and productive because it allows us to recognize ways in which a particular film resembles or differs from others. A consideration of a film's place within a genre tradition highlights the ways in which it conforms to familiar—and therefore safe—patterns, as well as the ways in which it may be unique. Genre study also reveals the expectations that audiences bring to the movies, as well as their capacity and willingness to accept revisions of cherished formulas. *Full Metal Jacket* and *Thelma and Louise* are two films that are unconventional in their relation to their generic bases, but their most striking and important features are best seen in the context of the conventions of their respective genres. In that way we can appreciate how these films point toward new and enlightened ways of perceiving characters, situations, and reality.

PSYCHOLOGY AND CHARACTER

In addition to relying on words and dialogue and other traditional literary methods of perceiving characterization, films can convey or reinforce certain behavioral traits through nonliterary means. One of these is the undeniable influence of actors and actresses. Audiences form relationships with film performers and expect certain traits of character regardless of the specific role a performer is playing. We have, presumably, moved away from such restrictions, but they have not entirely disappeared.

A good case in point is Clint Eastwood, who has been engaged in genre movies—particularly westerns and crime thrillers—for his entire career, and has a clearly established persona and mode of interaction with which his considerable international audience is familiar. While he was never a conventional hero of morally unimpeachable character, he has in recent years often broken entirely with the concept of the hero, challenging his audience's preconceived notions of those genres in which heroes play so crucial a part.

In *Unforgiven,* for example, Eastwood demythicizes the concept of the hero and, by disrupting the conventions of the western genre, creates a disturbing allegory of modern times. In this film the law is represented by a sadistic and self-righteous sheriff. When the Eastwood character with a shady past takes revenge on the sheriff for beating his friend to death, the audience may feel some satisfaction. But the avenger's angry and bloodthirsty behavior is hardly the stuff of heroism. We are left with an unpleasant taste in our mouths and the conviction that violence simply begets more violence, that justice has not really been accomplished.

Studying a film from the perspective of its relationship to genre conventions is revealing in terms of character psychology as well. A typical western or war film, for example, often relies on character *types* rather than fully rounded human beings. We can predict the behavior of a character *type,* but not always that of a more complex character. When a genre film shows us characters behaving in unfamiliar ways, it is revising a concept of genre and character.

POINT OF VIEW

In literature, *point of view* refers to the perspective through which an action, an event, or an entire story is seen and/or told. While it is often carelessly applied or overlooked in film analysis, point of view can be a key to understanding the entire structure and look of a film. Most films employ a combination of a kind of omniscient third person with intermittent moments or passages in which a particular character may govern the perspective on an action. This is because a first-person point of view is more difficult to sustain in a movie than in literature, where the dominating voice is constantly reinforced by the simple use of pronouns such as *I* or *we.* In films, however, unless a character is constantly narrating on the soundtrack, we tend to accept what we see as objective given reality, rather than as the exclusive or restrictive view of a particular character.

Nevertheless, there *are* cinematic ways of conveying and reinforcing a first-person narrative point of view in a film. For example, if we seem to be following and watching the actions and behavior of one character more than another, this *may* indicate that we are supposed to experience the film's events from this character's perspective. Generally, we need more evidence before we can say that this was the intention of the filmmaker.

Often camera angles, camera movements, and editing have a great deal to do with establishing a point of view and allowing the spectator to share the experience with a character, or in some cases, a group of characters. In the film *E.T.*, for example, there is a tendency to frame images at a camera angle consistent with the height of E.T. and the children who adopt the creature. Frontal shots of male adults are also consciously avoided in the film. Together, these techniques tend to privilege the child's perspective as the dominant fictional point of view in the film.

If we find that the way a character looks at other characters and things becomes the way *we* look at them, it is usually a sign that the character's point of view is being represented. If the camera often sides with a character instead of showing us things the character cannot witness, then we can assume that the camera's eye at such times is identified with the character's eyes and mind. If the character is excluded from a specific action and remains ignorant, the audience is also excluded and remains ignorant.

LANGUAGE

Language is naturally a significant part of a film's composition. As in literature, it reflects the cultural and social circumstances of characters as well as their abilities or limitations in dealing with the world. There was a time when most characters spoke a uniform literary English in American and British films, no matter what their backgrounds were. As films became more committed to reflecting social reality, this rule gave way to a more heterogeneous representation of linguistic differences.

Contemporary films are especially vital sources of the impact and variety of language experiences, since they cover such a range of worldly experience and give us views of cultures, subcultures, alien cultures, and foreign cultures that would normally be completely beyond the average filmgoer's life experience.

The way in which language affects or even constructs certain realities can also be especially dramatically and compellingly demonstrated in films. Language, for example, plays an important part in creating the claustrophobic militaristic atmosphere in *Full Metal Jacket*. During the basic training of the marines, the sergeant berates and humiliates them with a constant barrage of sexist and scatological imagery, reinforcing the artificial machismo and conformist thinking that is the focus of the film's bitter critique. The onslaught lets the viewer *feel* the relentless brainwashing at work.

The language in recent films by young African-American filmmakers about various African-American experiences—*Boyz 'n the Hood, New Jack City,* and *Juice,* to name a few—is a significant part of those experiences. Not only does it provide non-African-American viewers with a clear sense of black culture, but it allows African-American viewers to have a more authentic connection to the stories, characters, and experiences in films—something African-American audiences were sorely deprived of for the better part of film history.

GENDER

The issue of gender has become prominent in cultural studies in general, and has been an active part of literary and film scholarship for the past dozen years. As the issue enters more and more into the nonacademic, social sphere, it naturally affects the kinds of movies that are made. Some films raise the subject directly, placing in the foreground some aspect of the theme of the relations between the sexes. This might be the exposing of sexist behavior or attitudes in various contexts such as the workplace (e.g., *Working Girl*), or it might be the reversing of assumptions of a genre by having women behave and play roles normally associated with men.

For example, *Thelma and Louise* is a road movie set in the majestic West, the genre and turf that traditionally belonged to the rugged western hero, yet its protagonists are female. *Alien* and *Aliens* upturned the conventions of science-fiction/ horror films by killing off the male characters, leaving a bold, courageous woman the lone survivor who must fight the monster to the death.

Some films, however, go beyond a mere revising of genre expectations to probe the deeper psychological underpinnings of sexist behavior. Such a work is *Full Metal Jacket,* a staggering revision of the war film in that its climactic sequence depicts a company of hard-core marines being attacked by and then tracking down and killing an enemy sniper who turns out to be a young Vietnamese woman.

IMAGERY AND TECHNIQUE

Last but not least, any serious consideration of how narrative movies do their work must note the simple fact that they are primarily *visual* and *audio* experiences. Everything—settings, costumes, actors, camera angles, lighting, the use of color, and the way shots are framed, composed, and edited—has a powerful visual impact on the viewer. Dialogue, music, and sound effects have similarly powerful effects. In both cases, these important dimensions of the film experience are often unconsciously absorbed or entirely ignored by spectators. Too many media reviewers discuss or review films as if they were nothing but illustrations of preexisting literary texts with good or bad performances.

Most good movies and certainly all great ones are so not because they have great plots or themes and memorable lines. They leave their mark because they have effectively used the elements of the medium. Just as any great poem or play must convey its important ideas through great and imaginative language, the single most important element of literature, any great film must convey its ideas and its emotional and psychological force through the elements unique to film.

When Stanley Kubrick repeatedly frames the shots inside of the marine barracks in *Full Metal Jacket* with perfectly symmetrical compositions—the recruits lined up on either side of the screen as the bullying sergeant walks between them in screen center telling them what they must do to make the grade—we witness a visual metaphor that captures the idea and the feelings associated with rigid conformity.

When the protagonists of *Thelma and Louise* drive through Monument Valley, it is hardly a mere backdrop to the action, for the connotative dimensions of this setting are steeped in the conventions of what was once a privileged male genre. Thus, the atmosphere, the mood, and the meaning of the film are all affected by the way the setting and its reference to film history are used.

Francis Ford Coppola concludes *The Godfather* by juxtaposing the scene in church in which Michael Corleone witnesses the baptism of his sister's child with various scenes in different places in which men are being killed on his orders. We are forced to note that a parallel is being drawn, particularly when similar gestures are made by the priest and the killers and that the irony of such parallels exposes the hypocrisy of the character's life. This is almost entirely conveyed through the power of editing.

ON USING VIDEO

The study of film has been transformed by the advent and proliferation of video. Undoubtedly, many students, along with the general population, see more movies in the video format than on a theater screen. This is a mixed blessing. On the one hand, many visual and compositional aspects of films are lost or significantly altered on video, and the reduction of the size of the image alone makes it less compelling. In addition, watching movies at home is nevertheless subject to many distractions that unquestionably affect the unique and exclusive experience of a film. However, videos make movies as accessible as books so that students can check and recheck the facts about a film through repeated viewings just as easily as they might re-read a poem or a short story in preparation for a paper or an exam. Videos have also extended the life of many films and allowed them to become a part of the available culture—like literature and musical recordings—that students can remain in touch with and quote from as freely as they might cite a phrase from a book or a lyric from a song. Consequently, the opportunity to see and re-see a movie on video makes it possible to examine more closely and thoroughly the plot, narrative structure, characterization, theme, and genre elements.

Biographical Endnotes

Achebe, Chinua (b. 1930)

Born in Nigeria, Achebe is considered one of Africa's most accomplished writers. He was educated at the University College of Ibadan and London University, and then took up a career in radio broadcasting. Dismayed with European writers' depiction of African life, he decided that Africans should tell their own stories and proceeded to write his first novel, *Things Fall Apart* (1958). This book has been translated into forty-five languages; has been adapted for stage, television, and radio; has won awards for its author; and is considered a classic in English. The novel's theme reflects Achebe's belief that outside influences eradicate traditional culture and values. When military forces took over Nigeria's government, Achebe left for the United States, taught at the University of Massachusetts, and lectured around the country. "Dead Men's Path" takes up his themes of loss of respect for tradition, and the past versus the present. His latest work includes *The Trouble with Nigeria* (1984), *Anthills of the Savannah* (1988), *Arrow of God* (1989), *A Man of the People* (1989), *Hopes and Impediments: Selected Essays* (1990), and *Girls at War: And Other Stories* (1991).

Agee, James (1909–1955)

Author, playwright and critic, Agee, was born and raised in the Cumberland mountain region of Tennessee, the setting for his two novels *The Morning Watch* (1954) and *Death in the Family* ("Knoxville: Summer 1915," the selection in this anthology, is taken from that book.) The latter work is a sensitive portrayal of a family whose life is shattered by the father's untimely death. The novel was published posthumously in 1957 and received a Pulitzer Prize. Agee also wrote for *Time, The Nation* and *Fortune* magazines. An article about Alabama sharecroppers commissioned by *Fortune* became the bitter but moving book, *Let Us Now Praise Famous Men* (1941). Agee also wrote screenplays (*The African Queen, The Red Badge of Courage,* and *The Night of the Hunter*) and was a film critic. Two volumes of his reviews are collected in *Agee on Film* (1958, 1960).

Allende, Isabel (b. 1942)

Born in Chile, Allende fled to Venezuela when her uncle, President Salvador Allende, was assassinated. She was detained and tortured by Augusto Pinochet's government. The chapter included in this anthology is from her first novel, *The House of Spirits* (1982). It recounts the lives of four generations of a Latin American family who are oppressed by rich landowners and a military dictatorship. Allende now lives in California. She has also authored *Of Love and Shadows* (1988), *The Stories of Eva Luna* (1991), and *Paula* (1994).

Anderson, Sherwood (1876–1941)

Born in Camden, Ohio, Anderson was a self-educated man who, at the age of thirty-six, left his wife and business to resettle in Chicago and become a writer. His masterpiece, a collection of short stories titled *Winesburg, Ohio,* portrays life in a typical small midwestern town where many inhabitants are frustrated creatively and emotionally. "Hands" is the first story in that collection.

Aristophanes (445–380 B.C.)

Born in Greece, Aristophanes became a comic playwright at the age of eighteen. Of the more than forty plays he wrote, only eleven remain. The targets of his humor were people from all walks of life: philosophers, politicians, poets, warriors, the young and old, the rich and poor. *Lysistrata* was written during the twenty-seven-year war between Athens and Sparta.

Arrabal, Fernando (b. 1932)

Arrabal, born in Spanish Morocco, lived his early years in Madrid. At the age of twenty-three, finding life in Spain intolerable because of parental problems and the atmosphere of political oppression, he moved to Paris, where he still resides. Tuberculosis sapped his strength and his early works mirror the despair he experienced because of his illness. He regained his health after an operation in 1957, and his plays were soon produced in Paris theaters. He refers to his work as "panic theater" in the tradition of the theater of the absurd. *Picnic on the Battlefield* was written when he was fourteen and is the most frequently performed of his plays. Arrabal's concerns are the horrors of civil war, betrayal, torture, tyranny, and human helplessness in an alien universe.

Auden, W. H. (1907–1973)

Born in England and educated at Oxford, Wystan Hugh Auden's father was a medical officer with wide general and literary interests. When the family moved to the industrial city of Birmingham, Auden's firsthand observation of economic depression led to his early Marxist sympathies. Engineering and technological subjects initially interested him, but, at a friend's suggestion, in his early teens he started writing poetry. At Oxford he further cultivated his creative talents and formed friendships with other future poets such as Stephen Spender and Cecil Day Lewis. His first volume of poems, *Poems,* was published in 1930. His experiences in the Spanish Civil War reinforced his Marxist tendencies, and his poems address England's social problems. A few months before World War II, Auden moved to the United States and later became a citizen. The move to America roughly coincides with his conversion to Christianity and his rejection of his Marxist ideology that lead him to revise some of his earlier works to reflect his religiosity. Between 1941 and 1948, Auden produced four long poems—*New Year Letter, The Sea and the Mirror, For the Time Being,* and *The Age of Anxiety.* He won the Pulitzer Prize for the latter poem; the title reflects the atmosphere of the 1930's. His later poems include *Nones* (1951), *Homage to Clio* (1960), and *City Without Walls* (1969). *The Dyer's Hand* (1962) and *The Enchafed Flood* (1950) are distinguished collections of critical essays. A revised edition of his *Selected Poems* appeared in 1979 after his death.

Bambara, Toni Cade (1939–1995)

Bambara grew up in New York City, deeply conscious of the inequities of race and class. A graduate of Queens College and City College of New York, she became a social worker, educator, and filmmaker. Her short story collections such as *Gorilla, My Love* (1972), *The Sea Birds Are Still Alive* (1977), and *The Salt Eaters* (1980) deal particularly with the problems of women in urban environments. With humor and candor, she skillfully portrays the politics and culture of community life.

Behn, Afra (1640?–1689)

The early details of Behn's life have not been conclusively established, but most historians agree that she and her family probably sailed from England to Surinam in South America in 1663. Her father was to become lieutenant governor but died during the trip. Although she lived in Surinam less than a year, Behn had such vivid impressions of the country that she later incorporated them in a novel, *Oroonoko: or, The Royal Slave* (1688). On her return to England in 1664, she married a wealthy London merchant and became popular at the court of Charles II. Unfortunately, her husband died in 1666, and for reasons unknown she was left an impoverished widow. For a short time she became a spy for Charles II but was not remunerated for her work. In desperation, she turned to writing, an unheard of female occupation. Her first play *The Forced Marriage; or The Jealous Bridegroom* proved successful and she continued writing plays, featuring sexual promiscuity and amorous intrigues in the mode of the day. Her poems are less coarse than many of her contemporaries, but she freely discusses female sexual desires and issues concerning gender roles. Critics charged her with indecency, but she fought back claiming that she was singled out because of her gender. Never possessing much wealth, she lived in less than healthy conditions, which led to an early death. Behn was honored by burial in Westminster Abbey and has won the admiration of many feminists, including Virginia Woolf.

Borowski, Tadeusz (1922–1951)

Born of Polish parents in the Soviet Ukraine, Borowski lived a life of poverty and oppression. When he was four, his father was sent to an Arctic labor camp. Four years later, his mother was sent to Siberia. The family was reunited in Warsaw before World War II. Borowski wrote poetry and managed to take classes, despite the ban on education for Jews. He was eventually arrested by the Gestapo and sent to the concentration camp at Auschwitz. There he observed the horror and brutality perpetrated on the victims. He also witnessed prisoners betraying each other in order to survive. Borowski became a hospital orderly to escape extermination. The American forces freed him and his fellow prisoners in 1945. Borowski returned to Warsaw where he wrote short stories based on his experiences. His work has been criticized because he portrays some of the victims who resorted to betrayal and other criminal acts. Ironically, Borowski committed suicide using gas when he was twenty-nine.

Browning, Robert (1812–1889)

Born in England, Browning was a relatively unrecognized poet until his middle age. In fact, for a time he was better known for his dramatic rescue of Elizabeth Barrett from her tyrannical father. The couple had carried on a love affair through poetry and letters until they eloped and escaped to Italy, where they lived until her death in 1861. During his life in Italy, Browning developed his dramatic monologues, in which a person reveals his or her motives and thoughts through speech. Browning researched many subjects of the Italian Renaissance. His most famous work is *The Ring and the Book* (1868–1869), one of the longest poems in English literature.

Camus, Albert (1913–1960)

An Algerian-born French writer of novels, essays and plays, Camus is identified with the concept of absurdity, the problem of man's desire for a rational universe as compared with the reality of its incoherence. Camus was only ten-months-old when his father was killed in World War I. Brought up in poverty by his illiterate mother, he fortunately encountered a teacher who encouraged his studies. Subsequently, he earned a scholarship to a lycée (secondary school) where he studied philosophy and read widely. In 1930 he had the first of many attacks of tuberculosis, and in the late 1930's he commenced his lifelong journals and completed his first novel, *A Happy Death*. During World War II, he lived in Paris and was editor of the French Resistance's newspaper *Combat*. Throughout his life, he struggled to find a positive solution to the dilemma of the absurd. At the age of 44, he was awarded the Nobel Prize for literature in recognition of his profound humanism.

Some of his most famous works include *The Stranger* (1942, tr. 1946), *The Myth of Sisyphus* (1942, tr. 1955), *The Plague* (1947, tr. 1948), *The Outsider* (1942, tr. 1946), *The Rebel* (1951, tr. 1953), and *The Fall* (1956, tr. 1957). His final novel, *The First Man,* was published posthumously in 1995. Camus died in an automobile crash in 1960.

Cervantes, Lorna Dee (b. 1954)

Cervantes, born in San Francisco, is a descendant of an old Californian Mexican family. With the breakup of her parents' marriage, she and her mother and brother moved to San Jose. Unhappy experiences in the public schools led her to seek an outlet in poetry when she was eight. In her teens she became active in the Chicano movement and the American Indian movement. In 1980, her poems were published under the title *Emplumada*. She continues to express the conflicts experienced by those of Chicano heritage who try to coexist with the white majority.

Chopin, Kate (1851–1904)

Chopin was born in St. Louis, and moved to New Orleans when she married a Louisiana Creole. Her short stories and novels usually take place in that locale. Her last novel, *The Awakening* (1899), found a new audience during the women's movement of the 1960s, not only because it examined a woman's search for personal identity but also for its interest in financial and sexual autonomy.

Crane, Stephen (1871–1900)

Born in Newark, New Jersey, Crane was a journalist, short-story writer, novelist, and poet. He is best known for *The Red Badge of Courage* (1895), a realistic study of the mind of a soldier in the Civil War. This classic is remarkable for its accuracy because Crane had not experienced war when he wrote it. Later, as a war correspondent, he covered the Spanish-American War and the Greco-Turkish War. He died of tuberculosis at twenty-eight in self-imposed exile. His war stories reflected his wish to shatter the beliefs of those who saw war as a romantic and idealized experience. Among the best known of his many short stories are "The Open Boat," "The Blue Hotel," and "The Bride Comes to Yellow Sky."

Cruz, Sor (Sister) Juana Inés de la (1651?–1695)

Born in Nepantla, Mexico, to a Spanish father and a Creole mother, Cruz was one of the earliest authors in the Americas. At the age of three, she followed her sister to school and learned to read and write. With the guidance of her learned grandfather, she became educated far beyond any of her contemporaries. Cruz attracted the attention of the royal court in Mexico City, where she became a lady-in-waiting to the viceroy's wife. During those two years, she started writing poetry. Abruptly, at nineteen, she entered a convent. She continued to study and write, but her superiors demanded that she devote herself to church duties. When she refused to comply, and argued that women should not have to submit to men's orders, she was accused of heresy. Sor Juana yielded and gave up her intellectual pursuits. While nursing her sister nuns during a plague in 1695, she contracted the disease and died.

Dickinson, Emily (1830–1886)

Born in Amherst, Massachusetts, Dickinson was educated at schools for females, and then retired to her home. She rarely left it, and saw only family and a few friends during her lifetime. Although she wrote almost two thousand poems, only two were published while she lived. Many of her poems reflect her interest in the dialectic of private and public selves.

di Prima, Diane (b. 1934)

Di Prima, born in Brooklyn, New York, now lives in San Francisco and is a member of the faculty at New College of California. She was educated at Swarthmore College but left before graduation to settle in Greenwich Village and take up a bohemian lifestyle. There she became part of the countercultural community that included poets of the Beat Generation such as Allen Ginsberg and Jack Kerouac. She and Amiri Baraka edited a monthly literary journal, the *Floating Bear,* in which avant-garde and nontraditional work found an audience. In subsequent years, her poetry reflected her interests in the Vietnam War protests, Buddhism, Hinduism, Zen, and the women's movement. She has also explored the influence of her Italian-American heritage on her personal experience as a woman and as an artist. Di Prima has written twenty-one books of prose and poetry, among them *Pieces of a Song: Selected Poems* (1989), *Memoirs of a Beatnik* (1989), and *ZipCode: Selected Plays* (1992).

Dorfman, Ariel (b. 1942)

Born in Argentina, Dorfman relocated to Chile, became a citizen, and worked as a teacher, journalist, and author. When Salvador Allende, the elected president of Chile, was assassinated in 1973, Augusto Pinochet became the military dictator. Because of Dorfman's repeated denunciations of the government and its methods of ruling, he was exiled. He eventually settled in the United States, and travels to Europe, where he lectures and writes. His play *Death and the Maiden* (1992) takes place in a South American dictatorship. He has also authored *Last Waltz in Santiago* (1988), *My House Is on Fire: Short Stories* (1991), *Some Write to the Future: Essays on Contemporary Latin American Fiction* (1991), and *Konfidenz* (1995).

Doro, Sue (b. 1937)

Born in Berlin, Wisconsin, Doro was writing by the age of twelve. She was a machinist for thirteen years and is the mother of five children. Her poems and prose have been published in the *Village Voice, Chicano Tribune,* and various women's and union magazines as well as working-class anthologies such as *Paper Work* (1992) and *If I Had a Hammer* (1992). She is also the author of three books of poetry and prose on the subject of her blue-collar work experience and its relationship to family and personal life: *Of Birds and Factories* (1982), *Heart, Home and Hard-Hats* (1986), and *Blue Collar Goodbyes* (1993).

Dorris, Michael A. (1945–1997)

In his writings Dorris, a mixed-blood Modoc, dispels the stereotypes attached to Native Americans. He was educated at Georgetown and Yale Universities—the first person in his family to earn a college degree. As a professor at Dartmouth College, he established the Native American Studies Program. At Dartmouth he met and married the author Louise Erdrich, who is a mixed-blood Chippewa. The setting of Dorris' first book, *A Yellow Raft in Blue Water*, is an Indian reservation in Montana and presents the views of three characters on their restricted lives. Before his marriage, Dorris adopted a three-year-old Sioux boy. This experience led him to research Fetal Alcohol Syndrome (FAS) because the child had many physical and mental problems. *The Broken Cord: A Father's Story* (1989) relates the events leading up to the adoption and Dorris's realization that all the love in the world could not counteract the child's irreversible physical and mental problems. Some of his works include: *Morning Girl* (1992), *Working Men* (1993), *Rooms in the House* (1993), *Guests* (1994), *Sees Behind Trees* (1996), and *Cloud Chamber* (1997). Together, he and Louise Erdrich wrote *Route Two and Back* (1991) and *The Crown of Columbus* (1991).

Dubus, Andre (b. 1936)

Born in Lake Charles, Louisiana, and educated in his home state, Dubus became an officer in the United States Marine Corps at age twenty-two. After five years, he resigned, resumed his education, and became a teacher of fiction and creative writing at Bradford College in Massachusetts. In 1970, one of his stories was chosen for the annual volume of *Best American Short Stories*. Dubus has written eight short-story collections, including *The Times Are Never So Bad* (1983), *The Last Worthless Evening* (1986), *Collected Stories* (1988), and *Dancing After Hours* (1996). "The Curse" was written while he was convalescing from the loss of his leg in a highway accident. The themes of frailty and fallibility can be noted in Dubus's works.

Ellison, Ralph (Waldo) (1914–1994)

His childhood was spent in his birthplace, Oklahoma City, Oklahoma where his widowed mother supported the family as a domestic servant. She brought home discarded books and phonograph records from places she worked. Ellison's first love was music, and he played the trumpet. In 1933 he was awarded a scholarship to Tuskegee Institute in Alabama to study the trumpet and symphonic composition, but he eventually had to drop out due to lack of funds. After a move to New York City and a variety of jobs, he met the authors Langston Hughes and Richard Wright, both of whom encouraged him to write. Supported by the WPA Federal Writer's Project, he was able to support himself, and a number of his short stories were published. In 1952 his novel *Invisible Man* was acclaimed as the definitive exposition of the black man's plight in America. "Battle Royal," written as a short story, was included in the first chapter of the novel. *Invisible Man* won the National Book Award in 1953. The rest of his life was spent writing essays (collected in 1964 in *Shadow and Act*), short stories, and a novel that he left unfinished at his death in 1994. He was a professor of Contemporary Literature and Culture at New York University until his retirement. Many manuscripts have been found since he died, and some stories have been published (e.g., "Boy on a Train," and "I Did Not Learn Their Names" in *New Yorker* magazine, April 29 & May 6, 1996 respectively).

Emanuel, James A. (b. 1921)

Born in Alliance, Nebraska, Emanuel was educated at Howard, Northwestern, and Columbia universities, and is professor emeritus at City College of the City University of New York. Poet, biographer, and critic, he has published several volumes of poetry, including *The Treehouse and Other Poems* (1961), *Panther Man* (1970), and *The Broken Bowl: New and Uncollected Poems* (1983). In the last decade, he has written most of his poetry and prose in Europe.

Espada, Martín (b. 1957)

Born in Brooklyn, New York, Espada is considered one of the leading poets of Latino heritage. Educated at the University of Wisconsin and Northeastern University, his work experience encompasses a variety of jobs from bouncer to radio journalist in Nicaragua. At present he is a tenant lawyer in Boston. The themes of his poetry include immigrants, hard work, and poverty. His published works include *The Immigrant's Iceboy's Bolero* (1982), *Trumpets from the Islands of Their Eviction* (1987), *Rebellion Is the Circle of a Lover's Hands* (1990), *City of Coughing and Dead Radiators* (1993), and *Imagine the Angels of Bread* (1996).

Euripides (480–406 B.C.)

Born on the Greek island of Salamis, Euripides was a writer of tragedies. Today he is considered as great a dramatist as Sophocles and Aeschylus, although during his lifetime he was not popular. His themes reflected a pessimistic view of life, and his criticism of social matters was not viewed approvingly. He attacked the inequalities of women's status in *Medea*, the emphasis on the glories of war in *The Trojan Women*, and the unjust treatment of illegitimate children in *Hippolytus*. Only nineteen of his eighty or ninety plays exist today, among them *Alcestis*, *Electra*, and *Ion*.

Faulkner, William (1897–1962)

Born in New Albany, Mississippi, Faulkner was raised in the nearby town of Oxford. He attended the University of Mississippi briefly before joining the Canadian Air Force in 1918. In the early 1920s he traveled to New York City, New

Orleans, and Europe. *The Marble Faun* (1924), a book of poems, was his first published work. In his third novel, *Sartoris* (1929), he invented the fictional county of Yoknapatawpha (similar to the setting of his Mississippi boyhood) that became the scene for many of his future works. Two recurring themes include the relationship of the past to the present and the disintegration of traditional Southern society. Among his distinguished works are *The Sound and the Fury* (1939), *As I Lay Dying* (1930), *Light In August* (1932), *Sanctuary* (1931) and *Absalom Absalom!* (1938). His distinguished writing earned him Pulitzer Prizes for *A Fable* (1954) and *The Reivers* (1962), and a Nobel Prize for literature in 1949.

Ferlinghetti, Lawrence (b. 1919)

Poet, playwright, and editor, Ferlinghetti is co-owner of City Lights Books in San Francisco and founder and editor of City Lights Publishing House. He was an important figure in the Beat movement of the 1950s, whose adherents were primarily concerned with rebelling against society and taking strong stands on political issues. Ferlinghetti writes in the language and speech rhythms of ordinary people rather than in formal poetic language and structures. In his poem "Constantly Risking Absurdity" (1958), he speculates on the poet's responsibility to society. His latest collection is *These Are My Rivers: New & Selected Poems, 1955–1993* (1993).

Forché, Carolyn (b. 1950)

Born in Detroit, Michigan, and educated at Michigan State University, Forché is a poet, journalist, and educator. While a journalist in El Salvador from 1978 to 1980, she reported on human rights conditions for Amnesty International. This experience greatly affected her poetry, and she also lectured extensively on the subject when she returned to the United States. Her poetry collections include *Gathering the Tribes* (1976), *The Country Between Us* (1981) and *The Angel of History* (1994). She is the editor of *Against Forgetting: Twentieth Century Poetry of Witness* (1993).

Freeman, Mary E. Wilkins (1852–1930)

Freeman, born in Randolph, Maine, is one of the few women of her time who earned her living through writing. When she was fifty years old, she married Dr. Charles Freeman and moved with him to New Jersey, but their marriage failed because of his alcoholism. She specialized in stories of people in remote New England villages, and her characters were often determined individualists, particularly the women who endured despite lack of possibilities and economic security. Her work, which was popular during her lifetime, lost favor after her death but has been revived in the last twenty years. Her best known works are: *A Humble Romance and Other Stories* (1887) and *A New England Nun and Other Stories* (1891).

Frost, Robert (1874–1963)

Born in San Francisco, Frost moved east with his family when he was a child, and his poems reflect New England life and people. He attended Dartmouth and Harvard for short periods, held a variety of jobs, and tried farming in New Hampshire. During these years, he wrote poetry but was rejected by publishers. Finally, he went to England where his poems were published. On his return to the United States, he met with more success. During his long life, he received four Pulitzer prizes and many other awards. At President John F. Kennedy's inauguration in 1961, he read his poem "The Gift Outright." In many of his poems, Frost uses nature as the backdrop for his reflections on human behavior. In 1994, the Library of America published the most comprehensive collection of his works in a single volume—*Collected Poems, Prose & Plays* consists of 1,036 pages.

Gaines, Ernest J. (b. 1933)

Born in Louisiana, Gaines spent his childhood working in the fields. When he moved to California, he attended San Francisco College and Stanford University. His work recounts the everyday lives of poor people whose experiences reflect the violence and deprivation of slavery and segregation. "The Sky Is Gray" is from his short-story collection *Bloodline* (1968). His many novels include *A Gathering of Old Men* (1983) and *A Lesson before Dying* (1993). Gaines's novel, *The Autobiography of Miss Jane Pittman* (1971) was made into a movie.

Gildner, Gary (b. 1938)

A teacher of creative writing at the University of Iowa, Gildner has published a number of works, among them *First Practice* (1970) and *Digging for Indians* (1972). His latest novel, *The Warsaw Sparks* (1990), was written after teaching American literature in Poland on a Fulbright scholarship.

Gillan, Maria Mazziotti

Born in New Jersey, Gillan has taught in a number of colleges. She is presently the director of the Poetry Center of Passaic County Community College in Paterson, New Jersey and editor of *Footwork: The Paterson Literary Review*. In addition to the many anthologies in which her work appears, she has written six books of poetry, including *Flowers from the Tree of Night* (1981) and *Where I Come From* (1995). With her daughter Jennifer, she has edited *Unsettling America: An Anthology of Contemporary Multicultural Poetry* (1994).

Gilman, Charlotte Perkins (1860–1935)

Born in Hartford, Connecticut, and educated at the Rhode Island School of Design, Gilman was a social critic and feminist who wrote prolifically about the necessity of social and sexual equality, particularly about women's need for economic independence. Following a nervous breakdown after the birth of her daughter, Gilman divorced her husband and devoted her time to lecturing and writing about feminist issues. Her nonfiction includes *Women and Economics* (1898) and *The Man-Made World* (1911). Her novels include *Herland* (1915) and *With Her in Ourland* (1916). "The Yellow Wallpaper" (1899) is a fictionalized account of Gilman's own postpartum depression.

Gilyard, Keith (b. 1952)

Gilyard has been a lifelong resident of New York City. Poet, prose writer, and educator, he has read and taught before various audiences for over twenty years. Since 1994 he has served on the faculty of Syracuse University, where he is a professor of English. Gilyard, who holds graduate degrees from Columbia University and New York University, is on the editorial board of the National Council of Teachers of English, and is serving a four-year term on the executive committee of the Conference on English Education.

His writings have appeared in *Before Columbus Review, Black American Literature Forum, College English, Community Review, Emerge, Essence, Johari II, Transition Press, The Treehouse: An Introduction to Literature,* and *White Paper, Black Poem.* He received a 1992 American Book Award for his educational memoir, *Voices of the Self: A Study of Language Competence.* His latest work is *Let's Flip the Script* (1996).

Glaspell, Susan (1882?–1948)

Born in Davenport, Iowa, Glaspell began her writing career as a reporter in Des Moines. Soon she was writing novels and plays. With her husband, George Cram Cook, she founded the Provincetown Players in 1915 as an alternative to the commercialism of Broadway. This group encouraged and produced drama by Eugene O'Neill and other American writers. In 1931, Glaspell was awarded the Pulitzer prize in Drama for *Alison's House,* based on the life of the poet Emily Dickinson. Much of her art, like that of Sherwood Anderson, is concerned with the effect of confining environments on personal autonomy.

Greenberg, Barbara L. (b. 1932)

Greenberg was born in Boston and received a bachelor's degree from Wellesley College and a master's degree from Simmons College. Living in Massachusetts with her husband and two children, she finds the themes for her short stories, plays, and poems in women's experiences of everyday life. Her published books include *The Spoils of August* (1974), *Fire Drills: Stories* (1982), and *The Never-Not Sonnets* (1989).

Gunn, Thom (b. 1929)

Born in England, Gunn was schooled in many different locations because of his father's journalistic profession and the wartime bombings. He served two years in the army, went to Paris to write, and finally returned to England, where he entered Cambridge University. With the publication of his book *Fighting Terms,* in 1954, he was considered one of the most promising young English poets. In the same year he was awarded a fellowship at Stanford University and has resided in California since then. His many collections include *Jack Straw's Castle* (1976), *Selected Poems 1950–1975* (1979), *The Passages of Joy* (1982), and *The Man with Night Sweats: Poems* (1992). Many of his poems portray the often-thwarted attempts of marginalized adolescents to find personal identity.

Hardy, Thomas (1860–1928)

Born in Dorset, England, Hardy became an architect but started writing in 1867. The success of one of his novels, *Far from the Madding Crowd* (1874), enabled him to give up architecture for a literary career. After two more successful novels, *Tess of the D'Urbervilles* (1891) and *Jude the Obscure* (1896), he gave up fiction for poetry. A reliance on language close to that of speech, and the subjects of fate, character, and environment (which characterized his novels), continued to permeate his poetry.

Hawthorne, Nathaniel (1804–1864)

A novelist and short-story writer, Hawthorne was born in Salem, Massachusetts and traced his roots to the Puritans. His ancestors were prominent in the 17th-century witch trials and in Quaker persecutions. Hawthorne incorporated his sense of guilt into his writing. After graduating from Bowdoin College, he devoted himself to writing for twelve years. He wrote sketches and stories for annuals and newspapers, and in 1837 his first collection of short stories *Twice-Told Tales* was published. This collection, along with the works of Edgar Allen Poe, helped establish the American short story as a legitimate literary form. Nine years later, he produced his second series, *Mosses from an Old Manse* (1846). Between the publishing of these two works, it became necessary for Hawthorne to better support his family, and he became a surveyor in the Boston Customs House. He and his wife lived on Brook Farm, an experiment in community living, for a short time but the lifestyle was not to his liking, and he moved to Concord, Massachusetts. There his neighbors included Ralph Waldo Emerson and Henry David Thoreau, the leading Transcendentalists of the nineteenth-century. Another move took him back to his birthplace in Salem. Again he served as a surveyor in a customs house, but after his political party was removed from power, he lost his job. His career as a novelist commenced with *The Scarlet Letter* (1850). Financial independence finally allowed him to spend all his time writing, and he wrote *The House of the Seven Gables* (1851) and *The Blithdale Romance* (1852). When his friend Franklin Pierce became the fourteenth president, Hawthorne was appointed U.S. Consul in Liverpool, England (1853–1857). His last published novel was *The Marble Faun* (1860). In the last years of his life, he wrote infrequently. Four unpublished novels were found among his notes after his death. His use of symbol and allegory influenced Herman Melville, author of *Moby Dick,* and later William Faulkner and Henry James.

Hayden, Robert (1913–1980)

Born and reared in a Detroit ghetto, Hayden not only suffered from the indignities of poverty but was ridiculed because of his poor eyesight. He immersed himself in books and attended Detroit City College and the University of Michigan, where he studied with the poet W. H. Auden. His poetry was not widely appreciated until the 1960s. He was the first African-American writer to serve as poetry consultant to the Library of Congress, and was a member of the American Academy and Institute of Arts and Letters. Among his important works are *Heart-Shape in the Dust* (1940), *Angle of Ascent* (1975), and *American Journal* (1979), in which he celebrates the triumphs of his people despite their years of slavery in the American South.

Head, Bessie (1937–1986)

Head, born in Natal, South Africa, to a white mother and a black father, was ostracized for her mixed parentage. Her mother was condemned to an insane asylum by her family and subsequently committed suicide. Head's childhood was unhappy in the care of foster parents and missionaries. She was educated and became a teacher, then a journalist. In the 1960s, when apartheid was the rule in South Africa, and violence and oppression reigned, Head attempted to obtain a passport to travel internationally. The permit was denied, and she accepted a teaching position in neighboring Botswana in 1964. Head and her son lived there but were refused citizenship until 1979. She wrote *When Rain Clouds Gather* (1968), *Maru* (1971), *A Question of Power* (1973), and many short stories. In her position as public historian, she grew increasingly interested in the traditions and background of her adopted country. It led her to interview the inhabitants of a village, about which she wrote *Serowe: Village of the Rain Wind* (1981). Her fervent belief was that everyone—white and black—must abandon power struggles. She died suddenly of hepatitis in 1986.

Heker, Liliana (b. 1943)

Born in Argentina, Heker has been a successful writer in her native country since she was a teenager. Although her country has been oppressed by military governments that brought death and strife, she urged her colleagues not to flee for safety. She has stayed to edit the literary magazine *El Ornitorrinco (The Platypus)*. Her works include *Those Who Beheld the Burning Bush* and *Zona de Clivage* (1989). The latter novel won the Buenos Aires Municipal Prize.

Hogan, Linda (b. 1947)

Hogan was born in Denver of Chickasaw heritage and earned a bachelor's degree from the University of Colorado. Her honors include the Five Civilized Tribes Playwriting Award in 1980 for *A Piece of Moon* and the 1986 Before Columbus Foundation's American Book Award for *Seeing Through the Sun*. Presently, Hogan is an associate professor of American Indian studies at the University of Minnesota. Her poems reflect her interest in preserving the Chickasaw culture. She works as a volunteer with environmental and wildlife groups. Her published works include *Eclipse* (1983), *Savings* (1988), *Mean Spirit* (1990), and *Solar Storms* (1995).

Jeffers, Lance (1919–1985)

Jeffers was born in Nebraska and received his bachelor's and master's degrees from Columbia University. He taught college English in many U.S. universities and ultimately became chairman of the English Department at Bowie State College in Maryland. His poetry was published in numerous journals and anthologies. Among his collected works are *When I Knew the Power of My Black Hand* (1975), *O Africa, Where I Baked My Black Bread* (1977), and *Grandsire* (1979).

Joyce, James (1882–1941)

Born in Dublin, Ireland, the eldest in a family of ten children, Joyce knew a life of poverty and efforts to maintain respectability. He was educated in Jesuit schools, where he was trained in Catholicism and the classics. However, he rebelled against his religion, his country, and his family, and at twenty he left Dublin for a life in Europe as an exile. By teaching languages and doing clerical work, he eked out a living for his common-law wife and their two children. His novel *Ulysses,* written in an innovative style, took seven years to complete. *Finnegans Wake,* his most experimental work, is written in a language he created. He also wrote poems, short stories, and one play. Despite his years of exile, all of his fiction is set in his native Dublin and portrays his attempt to free himself of religious and geographic restrictions.

Kafka, Franz (1883–1924)

Born in Prague, Czechoslovakia, Kafka spent an unhappy life as a victim of anti-Semitism and in a job he detested in an insurance company. His stories, such as "The Metamorphosis," (1915), and his three novels, *The Trial* (1925), *The Castle* (1926), and *Amerika* (1927), reflect his feelings of alienation from the community. When he died of tuberculosis at forty-one, he left his unpublished manuscripts to a friend with instructions that they be destroyed. Instead, the friend edited and published them, thereby establishing the obscure clerk as a world-renowned author.

Keats, John (1795–1821)

Born in London, Keats studied to be a doctor but he never practiced medicine. His early interest in literature and his friendship with poets inspired him to write poetry. Along with Lord Byron and Percy Bysshe Shelley, he established romantic poetry, with its emphasis on emotion and the imagination over reason and intelligence. Idealized love was the subject of many of his poems. At twenty-six, he died of tuberculosis.

Kenny, Maurice (b. 1929)

Born near the St. Lawrence River, the ancestral home of the Mohawk Indians, Kenny lived in New Jersey and in Watertown, New York, as a child. After high school he worked at a variety of jobs and lived in Mexico, Puerto Rico, and Chicago. Finally, he settled in Brooklyn and continued writing poetry until he experienced a near-fatal heart attack in 1974. Thereafter, he focused on his Native-American roots as subjects for his poetry, and is now considered one of the leading Native-American poets. As editor of a magazine and a publishing company, Kenny encourages other Native-American writers. In 1984, he received the Before Columbus Foundation's American Book Award for *The Mama Poems*. He has taught writing in Oklahoma and is now a professor at North Country Community College in Saranac Lake, New York. Some of his two dozen books include *Between Two Rivers: Selected Poems* (1987), *Greyhounding This America* (1987), *Rain and Other Fictions* (1990), and *On Second Thought: A Compilation* (1995).

King, Martin Luther, Jr. (1929–1968)

Born in Georgia, King was the son and grandson of Baptist ministers. He was educated at Morehouse College, Crozier Theological Seminary, and Boston University. He was pastor of a Baptist church in Montgomery, Alabama when Rosa Parks refused to relinquish her seat on a bus to a white person. King, influenced by the teachings of Mahatma Gandhi, led a non-violent bus boycott in 1955 that attracted national attention. This incident led to the U.S. Supreme Court's ruling that Alabama's bus segregation was unconstitutional. King wrote of the experience in *Stride Toward Freedom* (1958).

The message of passive resistance spread, and King and his followers organized many protests against segregation and injustice in the South. Although he was arrested, jailed, his home was bombed, and he was stabbed, King continued to preach his philosophy and gained respect and admiration all over the world. In 1963, his *Letter from the Birmingham Jail* replied to those who criticized his methods and beliefs. King organized the March on Washington in 1963 and delivered his memorable "I Have a Dream" speech. He was awarded the Noble Peace Prize in 1964—at 35, he was the youngest recipient. King continued to lead protests and coupled his message about segregation with opposition to the Vietnam War. While preparing to march with striking workers in Memphis, Tennessee in 1968, he was assassinated by James Earl Ray. His killer was sentenced to 99 years in prison.

Lassell, Michael (b. 1947)

Born in New York City, Lassell has earned degrees from Colgate University, California Institute of the Arts, and the Yale School of Drama. Now living in Los Angeles, he is managing editor of *LA Style* magazine and has worked as a critic, photographer, teacher, and writer. His book *Poems for Lost and Un-Lost Boys* won the Amelia Chapbook Award in 1986. *Decade Dance* (1990) is his latest published collection.

Laviera, Tato (b. 1951)

Laviera, born in Puerto Rico, has lived in New York City since 1960. He has taught creative writing at several northeastern universities, including Rutgers. His poetry and drama celebrate the ethnic diversity of New York City, and he often writes in English and Spanish as well as in "Spanglish," a mixture of the two languages used by several bilingual poets. He is deeply committed to preserving the oral traditions of Puerto Rico and the Caribbean, and, although his poetry is published in written form, it is meant to be sung and celebrated by the community. He has written *AmeRican* (1985), *Mainstream Ethics=Etica Corriente* (1988), and *La Carreta Made a U-Turn* (1992).

Levertov, Denise (b. 1923)

Born in England of Welsh and Jewish parents, Levertov was a nurse in World War II. She married an American writer and moved to the United States in 1948. Her poetic style was influenced by her affiliation with the Black Mountain poets of North Carolina, who advocated verse form that duplicates everyday speech patterns. Some of her poems focus on human relationships; many others express her commitment to social and environmental issues. Among her numerous collections of poetry are: *Light Up the Cave* (1981), *A Door in the Hive* (1989), *Evening Train* (1992), and a memoir, *Tesserae: Memories and Suppositions* (1995).

Longfellow, Henry Wadsworth (1807–1882)

Longfellow was born in Portland, Maine, graduated from Bowdoin College, and studied languages in Europe. On his return, he taught at Bowdoin and at Harvard University until he resigned to devote his life to writing poetry. He is best known for his narrative poems dramatizing U.S. history and legend in a simple and sentimental style. Longfellow was responsible for making poetry popular in this country through poems such as "Evangeline" (1847), "Song of Hiawatha" (1885), "The Courtship of Miles Standish" (1858), and "Paul Revere's Ride" (1863).

Lorde, Audre (1934–1992)

Born in New York City, Lorde was educated at Hunter College of the City University of New York and at Columbia University. She taught at various branches of the City University. Her publications include nine volumes of poetry, among them *Between Ourselves* (1976), *Chosen Poems* (1982), and *Our Dead Behind Us* (1987). In her autobiography, *Zami: A New Spelling of My Name* (1982), Lorde compares her expectations as an African American with those of her African-Caribbean immigrant parents. In 1991, she was named the official state poet of New York.

Lum, Wing Tek (b. 1946)

Born in Honolulu, Hawaii, Lum attended Brown University and Union Theological Seminary. Although primarily a businessman, Lum continues to write poetry as an avocation, treating familial and domestic experiences as well as sociopolitical issues. He received the Poetry Center's Discovery Award in 1970, the Creative Literature Award from the Association for Asian American Studies in 1988, and the Before Columbus Foundation Book Award in 1989. In his most recent work, he has moved on to a more complex understanding of pluralism, evoking Chinese pride, American patriotism and Hawaiian sensibilities.

McKay, Claude (1890–1948)

Born on the island of Jamaica to peasant farmers, McKay heard African folk tales when he was a child and came to appreciate his racial heritage. He was encouraged in his literary ambitions by an Englishman through whose efforts two of his poetry collections were published in England. In 1912, he came to the United States to study agriculture. After a few years of school, he left for New York City to become a writer. Although he had experienced discrimination in Jamaica, he was unprepared for the extreme racism he encountered in the United States. McKay channeled his anger into a collection of poetry, *Harlem Shadows* (1922), which heralded the Harlem Renaissance (a period of unprecedented creativity by black writers centered in Harlem). His poetry reflects his concern over the treatment of African Americans in U.S. society. His other works include *Home to Harlem* (1928), *Banjo* (1929), *Songs of Jamaica* (1911), *Constab Ballads* (1912), and *Spring in New Hampshire and Other Poems* (1920).

Marvell, Andrew (1621–1678)

Son of an Anglican clergyman, Marvell entered Cambridge and received his bachelor's degree in 1638. When his father died in 1640, he spent his inheritance on a four-year tour of the Continent. On his return, he tutored the daughter of a Lord General and wrote poems on gardens and country life. For most of his life, Marvell took an active interest in politics and wrote many satirical pamphlets about the controversies of the times. A friend of John Milton, Marvell was influential in saving the poet from prison after the Restoration. During the last twenty years of his life, he was a representative in Parliament. His poetical works were virtually ignored until 1921. T. S. Eliot wrote an essay commemorating Marvell's birth, and interest in his lyric poetry flourished. Other poems include "The Garden," "The Definition of Love," and "A Dialogue between Body and Soul."

Meier, Daniel (b. 1959)

A graduate of Wesleyan University and Harvard Graduate School of Education, Meier now teaches in an elementary school in Boston. His previous published work deals with the art of teaching and other educational issues.

Millay, Edna St. Vincent (1892–1950)

Born in Rockland, Maine, Millay began to write poetry at an early age. Her first poem, "Renascence," was published during her senior year in college. During the

1920s, she lived a bohemian life in Greenwich Village, where she acted in plays and continued to write poetry. Her love sonnets, which advocated sexual and emotional freedom for women, were particularly popular. In 1923, she won the Pulitzer prize in Poetry for *The Harp-Weaver and Other Poems*. She wrote infrequently during the last years of her life, and she died in relative obscurity.

Mirikitani, Janice (b. 1942)

A third-generation Japanese American, Mirikitani is program director and president of the Corporation at Glide Church/Urban Center, a community organization in California. Her poetry illuminates contemporary urban life and also focuses on the injustices experienced by Japanese Americans who were interned in U.S. camps during World War II. Her published books include *Awake in the River* and *Shedding Silence: Poetry and Prose* (1987).

Mora, Pat (b. 1942)

Born in El Paso, Texas, Mora now lives in Cincinnati. She received a bachelor's degree from Texas Western College and a master's degree from the University of Texas at El Paso. Her poetry reflects her Hispanic perspective, and she writes frequently on gender and political issues. Her work has been collected in *Chants* (1984), *Borders* (1986), *Communion* (1991), and *Aqua Santa–Holy Water* (1995).

Morales, Aurora Levins (b. 1954)

Born in Indiera Baja, Puerto Rico, to a Jewish father and a Puerto Rican mother, Morales began writing poetry at seven. Her parents' love of literature and commitment to social justice have influenced her poetry, fiction, and nonfiction. Morales's work has been included in many anthologies, journals, and magazines. *Getting Home Alive* (1986) was written in collaboration with her mother, Rosario Morales. She now resides in California.

Mukherjee, Bharati (b. 1940)

Born in Calcutta, India, Mukherjee has lived in Canada but is now a permanent resident of the United States. She received her doctorate from the University of Iowa and has taught at several academic institutions, including Skidmore College and Columbia University. Her novels include *The Tiger's Daughter* (1972), *The Wire* (1975), *The Middleman and Other Stories* (1988), and *Jasmine* (1989), an expansion of the story appearing in this anthology. Her themes often deal with immigrants adjusting to life in a new society. Her latest novel, *The Holder of the World* was published in 1993.

Ng, Fae Myenne (b. 1967)

Born in San Francisco, Ng as a child helped her mother in a sweatshop, noting that "one of my duties was to write the little code number of my mother's sewing machine onto the laundering tabs." She studied English at the University of California at Berkeley and received an M.F.A. from Columbia University; she now resides in Brooklyn. Her prose has been published in numerous anthologies and periodicals including *Harper's, The American Voice,* and *The City Lights Review.* Her novel *Bone* (1993) is an account of the attempts of an Asian-American family in San Francisco's Chinatown to cope with the suicide of the second of three daughters. Ng says of her novel "The whole ritual of sending the bones back to China was fascinating to me," a reference to the desire of many early Asian immigrants to be buried in their homeland. "Bone is what lasts, and I wanted to honor the quality of endurance in the human spirit."

Niatum, Duane (b. 1938)

Born in Seattle, this Native-American poet was educated at the University of Washington and Johns Hopkins University. Niatum has worked as an editor, librarian, and teacher. The Pacific Northwest Writers Conference has awarded him first prize in poetry twice. His books include *Ascending Red Cedar Moon* (1969), *Songs for the Harvester of Dreams* (1982), and *Pieces* (1981). His poems express the disappointments and dreams of his people as they attempt to reconcile their private and communal selves.

Noda, Kesaya F. (b. 1950)

Although born in California, Noda was raised in rural New Hampshire. After highschool graduation, she learned Japanese while studying in Japan. Following college, she researched and wrote *The Yamato Colony* (1981), a history of the California community where her grandparents settled and her parents were raised. Noda earned a master's degree from Harvard Divinity School, and now teaches at Lesley College in Cambridge, Massachusetts.

O'Connor, Frank (1903–1966)

O'Connor was born in Cork, Ireland. His real name was Michael O'Donovan. During his imprisonment in Ireland's 1923 civil war, he educated himself by reading Irish literature. He became a director of the Abbey Theatre in Dublin during the Irish Renaissance, a period in the 1920s when the Irish people awakened to the realization of the richness and value of their own culture. Subsequently, he moved to the United States, but his themes remained the Irish-English troubles and a realistic picture of contemporary life in Ireland. Two of his short-story collections are *Guests of the Nation* (1931) and *Dutch Interior* (1940). His autobiographical works include *An Only Child* (1960) and *My Father's Son* (1968).

O'Flaherty, Liam (1896–1984)

Born in the Aran Islands off the west coast of Ireland, O'Flaherty was educated for the priesthood but abandoned it and joined the Irish Guard before World War I. He was wounded and discharged in 1918. After completing his education, he traveled for several years, returning to Ireland in 1921 to fight with the Republicans against the Free Staters in the Irish civil war. He was exiled soon after, and while living in England he published his first short story "The Sniper." His best-known novel, *The Informer* (1925), became an Academy Award–winning film. However, *Famine* (1937), a novel based on the potato famine that claimed more than one million lives in Ireland during the 1840s, is considered his greatest work. Ireland's poor people were often the main characters in his stories.

Olds, Sharon (b. 1942)

Born in San Francisco, Olds, who now resides in New York City, graduated from Stanford University and received a doctorate from Columbia University. She has authored *Satan Says* (1980); *The Dead and the Living* (1984), for which she was awarded a National Book Critics Circle Award in poetry; and *The Gold Cell* (1987). Much of her work expresses her involvement with contemporary social issues and their effects on private and public selves. Her latest works include *The Father* (1992) and *The Wellspring* (1996).

Olsen, Tillie (b. 1913)

Olsen, born in Omaha, Nebraska, was determined to be a writer although she worked at many jobs and raised four children. She began working on her novel *Yonnondio* in the 1920s and finished it in the 1970s. The subjects of her short stories and novels are people who have been denied their chance at creativity because of their sex, race, or class. Olsen's work is often anthologized. *Tell Me a Riddle* (1961) and *Silences* (1978) are among her published works.

Owen, Wilfred (1893–1918)

Born in Shropshire, England, Owen is considered the most famous of the English poets of World War I. He expressed his hatred of war in descriptions of brutality and horror that he experienced on the battlefield. Owen died in action a week before the Armistice. "Above all this book is not concerned with Poetry, the subject of it is War, and the pity of War. The Poetry is in the pity. All a poet can do is warn," he wrote.

Paley, Grace (b. 1922)

Born in New York City, Paley attended Hunter College and New York University. As a child of Russian-Jewish immigrants, she grew up influenced by Russian literature and social activism. Her three short-story collections, *The Little Disturbances of Man* (1953), *Enormous Changes at the Last Minute* (1974), and *Later the Same Day* (1985), reflect her interest in the lives of working people in New York City. Critics have commented on her ability to record the cadences of New York speech as well as her humor and compassion for her characters. She remains actively involved in feminist and pacifist issues. Among the many honors she has received the latest is the 1993 Rea Award for the short story.

Powell, David W.

Powell served as a marine in Vietnam from 1965 to 1967. "Vietnam: What I Remember" is excerpted from Powell's memoir, "Patriotism Revisited," that he submitted to a creative writing class at the University of Arizona in Tucson.

Puig, Manuel (1932–1990)

As a young boy in Argentina, Puig constantly attended North American and European films. He was so obsessed with movies that he wanted to become either a director or a screenwriter. Neither career suited him, and he turned to fiction. His work, however, is saturated with references to films and popular culture. Puig's autobiographical novel, *Betrayed by Rita Hayworth*, was completed in 1965 but wasn't published until three years later. It was translated into English in 1971 and found an appreciative audience in the United States. Life in Argentina became increasingly uncomfortable for Puig when Juan Peron returned to power in 1971. The writer left the country and lived in Mexico, Brazil, and New York.

His subsequent novels, *Heartbreak Tango* (1973), *The Buenos Aires Affair: A Detective Novel* (1976) were not as popular, but his next novel, *The Kiss of the Spider Woman* (1979), gained instant success and was subsequently made into a movie and a Broadway musical. It was recognized as an attack on the political and cultural corruption of Argentina. His novels and plays continue to attract attention from readers and critics alike. He died from a heart attack in 1990.

Quindlen, Anna (b. 1953)

Quindlen started her career as a journalist immediately after graduating from Barnard College in New York City. The *New York Times* promoted her from general assignments to various columns, culminating in her highly-esteemed column, "Public and Private." In 1992, she won a Pulitzer prize for her commentaries in that column. In 1994, Quindlen left the *New York Times* to devote herself to writing novels. Her books to date include two compilations of her columns. *Living Out Loud* (1988) and *Thinking Out Loud* (1993): two novels, *Object Lessons* (1991) and *One True Thing* (1994); and a children's book, *The Tree That Came To Stay* (1993). Her work addresses universal concerns, treating them in a personal and intimate manner.

Randall, Dudley (b. 1914)

Randall, born in Washington, D.C., was encouraged by his parents to follow intellectual pursuits and earned degrees at Wayne State University and the University of Michigan. He became a librarian but maintained his lifelong interest in poetry. In the 1960s, Randall started the publishing company Broadside Press, which introduced hundreds of unknown black poets to the world. Gwendolyn Brooks, Margaret Walker, Amiri Baraka, Robert Hayden, Nikki Giovanni, Don Lee, and Audre Lorde are a few of the distinguished poets for whom Randall provided a forum. Many of these authors remained loyal to Broadside Press after their reputations were established, even though more lucrative contracts were offered by other publishing companies. *For Malcolm: Poems on the Life and Death of Malcolm X* remains one of Randall's most successful editorial accomplishments. His own poetry often points out the irony of the American Dream for black Americans and calls for survival through individuality.

Rifaat, Alifa (b. 1930)

Born in Cairo, Egypt, Rifaat still resides there. She wrote a short story when she was nine, but was punished for doing so. Although opposition to her writing continued in her Muslim family, her first short stories were published in 1955. Obstacles prevented her from writing for fifteen years during her marriage, but she resumed work in 1975 and has published hundreds of stories and a few novels. Themes related to the sexual and emotional problems encountered by married women in the Middle East dominate her fiction. Her collection *Distant View of a Minaret and Other Stories* was published in 1985.

Robinson, Edwin Arlington (1869–1935)

Born in Gardiner, Maine, Robinson wrote poetry at an early age. He studied at Harvard University but had to drop out when his family's fortunes declined. Moving to New York City, he worked at a number of unrewarding jobs but continued to write. President Theodore Roosevelt praised one of his books and secured him a post at the New York custom house. Poems like "Richard Cory" were written during his early years of creativity, when his themes focused on the isolation and loneliness of characters in small towns.

Romero, Leo (b. 1950)

Born in New Mexico, Romero uses his home state as the setting for many of his poems. Educated at the University of New Mexico and New Mexico State University, he is a leading writer of Chicano poetry. His works include *During the Growing Season* (1978), *Celso* (1985), *Desert Nights* (1989), *Going Home Away Indian* (1990), and *Rita and Los Angeles* (1995).

Rukeyser, Muriel (1913–1980)

Born in New York City, Rukeyser was educated at Vassar College and Columbia University. A journalist as well as a poet, she reported from Spain on the Spanish civil war and was one of the journalists arrested at the Scottsboro Trial in 1931, an important moment in the history of civil rights in the United States. Her poems, published over a period of forty years, reflect her commitment to her Jewish heritage, civil rights, and the antiwar movement. Since her death, two works have been published—*Out of Silence* (1992), and *A Muriel Rukeyser Reader* (1996).

Sarton, May (1912–1995)

Born in Belgium, Sarton was brought to the United States at the outbreak of World War I. Her early enthusiasms were poetry and acting. She joined Eva Le Gallienne's repertory theater in New York and later directed her own company. In the 1930s, she began to write poetry while supporting herself with teaching jobs, lecturing, and book reviewing. Sarton's main theme is the effect that love, in all its forms, has on personal relationships. Some of her works are *Encounter in April* (1937), *A Grain of Mustard Seed* (1971), *Collected Poems 1930–1973* (1974), *Halfway to Silence* (1980), and *The Silence Now: New and Uncollected Earlier Poems* (1988).

Throughout her life she kept journals in which she recorded the events of everyday life. They have been published in *Journal of Solitude* (1973), *At Seventy* (1984), and *Encore: A Journal of the Eightieth Year* (1993).

Chief Seattle (1788–1866)

Chief Seattle was born near the city that now bears his name, and was chief of the Squamish and allied Indian tribes in the 1800s. He saw the influx of settlers that poured into the Pacific Northwest region and, fearing that conflicts could cause wars between them and his tribes, encouraged friendships and trading relations with the newcomers. Seattle managed to maintain peace until 1854, when the governor of the Washington Territories proposed buying two million acres of tribal land. The selection included here is the chief's reply and it reflects his fears about the future. In the following year, treaty agreements were breached and Seattle chose not to fight in the Yakima War. Instead he consented to relocating his tribes to a reservation. When the city of Seattle was named for him, he objected, believing that after death, his spirit would be troubled each time his name was spoken.

Sexton, Anne (1928–1974)

Born in Newton, Massachusetts, Sexton was one of a group of successful modern "confessional" poets. After one of her nervous breakdowns, a psychiatrist suggested that she try writing as therapy. Her work is highly personal and reflects her preoccupation with suicide. She wrote several poems about her daughters and explored gender relationships in many of her works. In 1966, she received the Pulitzer prize for *Live or Die*. *The Death Notebooks* (1974) was her last published volume before she took her life at age forty-five.

Shakespeare, William (1564–1616)

Born in Stratford-on-Avon, England, Shakespeare was a poet and dramatist of the Elizabethan Age. Relatively little is known about his personal life. He received a grammar school education and in 1594 was a member of the Lord Chamberlain's company of actors. By 1597, Shakespeare had written at least a dozen plays, including comedies, histories, and one tragedy. His greatest plays include the tragedies *Julius Caesar* (1600), *Hamlet* (1601), *Othello* (1604), *King Lear* (1605), and *Macbeth* (1606). He also composed a series of 154 sonnets between 1593 and 1601.

Shoaib, Mahwash (b. 1973)

A native of Pakistan, Shoaib is a graduate of the University of Punjab and is currently a graduate student of English Literature at Queens College in New York

City. She is a poet, a writer, and a translator of poetry from her native Urdu to English. Keenly interested in philosophy as a way of life, she devotes her time between the study of language and literature, writing, and bibliophilia. Her aim is to realize her creative potential in both fiction and poetry.

Smallberg, Mavis (b. 1945)

A poet and a teacher, Smallberg lives in South Africa. Her works, which have appeared in underground journals, were banned in her country.

Song, Cathy (b. 1955)

Song was born in Honolulu. She attended the University of Hawaii, received a bachelor's degree from Wellesley College, and earned a master's degree at Boston University. Her first book, *Picture Bride* (1983), won the Yale Series of Younger Poets Award and was nominated for a National Book Critics Circle Award. Her poems reflect a deep awareness of her Asian heritage and the struggles of her people to find their own voices in contemporary culture. She has also written *Frameless Windows, Squares of Light* (1988), and *School Figures* (1994).

Sophocles (496–406 B.C.)

Born near Athens, Greece, Sophocles was the most popular playwright of his day. He also held posts in the military and political life of Athens. Of the more than one hundred plays that he wrote, only seven survive, among them three about Oedipus and his children, *Oedipus the King, Oedipus at Colonus,* and *Antigone.* Using mythology as the backdrop for his complex exploration of our private and public selves, Sophocles expressed the continuity of human experience.

Soto, Gary (b. 1952)

Soto was born in California's San Joaquin Valley to a family of migrant workers who toiled in the fruit and vegetable fields. Often the theme of his fiction, poetry, and nonfiction is the plight of the poor, especially Mexican Americans who have endured despite social inequities. He now teaches at the University of California. *Living Up the Street* received the 1985 Before Columbus Foundation's American Book Award. Among his other works are *The Elements of San Joaquin* (1977), *Father Is a Pillow Tied to a Broom* (1980), *Small Faces* (1986), *Who Will Know Us?* (1990), *Home Course in Religion* (1991), and *New and Selected Poems* (1995).

Soyinka, Wole (b. 1934)

Born in Nigeria, Soyinka, a poet, playwright, novelist, and essayist, was educated in his homeland and in England. Through his efforts, the theater in Nigeria has flourished. For his role in the political life of his country, he was imprisoned. Although denied the chance to write while in jail, he used scraps of cigarette and toilet papers to compose a collection of poems, which was smuggled out and published as *Poems from Prison* (1969). In 1986, he was awarded the Nobel prize in Literature. His themes, social injustice and the preservation of individual freedom, are developed with humor and satire. *The Open Sore of a Continent: A Personal Narrative of the Nigerian Crisis* was published in 1996.

Staples, Brent (b. 1951)

Staples is from Chester, Pennsylvania and has a Ph.D. in psychology from the University of Chicago. He is currently on the editorial board of the *New York Times,* where he writes on culture and politics. His autobiography, *Parallel Time: Growing Up in Black and White,* was published in 1994.

Stevens, Wallace (1879–1955)

Born in Pennsylvania and educated at Harvard, Stevens became a lawyer and for forty years worked for the Hartford (Connecticut) Accident and Indemnity Company. In his spare time he wrote poetry, but he was not recognized as a major poet until the latter part of his life. Many of his poems explore the issues of individuality and conformity. His *Collected Poems* (1954) won a Pulitzer prize. Among his poems are "The Emperor of Ice Cream," "Sunday Morning," and "Peter Quince at the Clavier."

Strindberg, (Johan) August (1849–1912)

Strindberg, considered one of Sweden's greatest writers, was born into poverty and had an unhappy childhood. Overly sensitive, he was unhappy at home and at school where his humble origins were ridiculed. In secondary school, he developed an interest in science that he maintained all of his life. Leaving the university without a degree, he held a variety of jobs—teacher, tutor, actor, journalist, landscape painter, medical student, librarian, and chemist. He suffered from alcoholism. During his failed career as an actor, he began writing plays. At age 23, he produced his great prose drama, *Master Olaf,* dealing with the clash between idealism and reality.

Strindberg founded theaters featuring experimental plays in Copenhagen and Stockholm. He experienced limited success in Sweden, but his plays were appreciated abroad, particularly in Germany. The theme of many of his sixty-five plays, several novels, and autobiographical works centers on the cruelty and hardships of life and the love/hate relationships between men and women. His best known works include: *The Dance of Death* (1901), *A Dream Play* (1902), *The Ghost Sonata* (1907), and *To Damascus* (Pt. 1, 1898; Pt. 2, 1904). English-speaking countries know him best for his plays *The Father* (1887) and *Miss Julie* (1888), examples of his naturalistic period.

Tapahonso, Luci (b. 1951)

Luci Tapahonso is a Navajo who lives in Albuquerque, New Mexico. Her latest work is *Sáanii Dahataal, the Women Are Singing: Poems and Stories* (1993).

Thomas, Dylan (1914–1953)

Thomas, born in Swansea, Wales, avoided formal education but began to write poems at an early age. By the age of twenty, he was a published poet. His voice impressed audiences who heard him read his works in lecture halls, on radio, and through recordings. His pastoral poems frequently reflect his joy in the frightening but beautiful processes of nature. "Do Not Go Gentle into That Good Night," "And death shall have no dominion," "A Refusal to Mourn Death, by Fire of a Child in London," and "Fern Hill" are among his best-known poems. *Portrait of the Artist As a Young Dog* (1940) recalls his childhood and youth in Wales. *Under Milk Wood* (1954) is an inventive radio play for voices.

Tolstoy, Count Leo (1828–1910)

A Russian novelist, social critic, religious reformer, philosopher, and champion of nonviolent protest, Tolstoy was born to a family of wealthy landowners. Although orphaned at the age of nine, his aunts became responsible for his upbringing, and he later wrote of his happy childhood. At school he did not apply himself to his studies and was expelled from the university after one year. When he inherited his family's estate, he led a dissolute life and eventually became bored with country living. In 1851 he joined the army, served in various theaters of war and was decorated for bravery. During this time he wrote a semi-autobiographical work, *Childhood* (1852), a book hailed as a major achievement. A few years later his *Sevastapool Sketches* (1855) was recognized as an unadorned account of the realities of war. In the 1860s, he married and returned to his estate where he improved the conditions of the peasants. During this period, he wrote his two greatest novels, *War and Peace* and *Anna Karenina*. In the 1870s, he experienced a deep depression that culminated in his conversion to a self-created form of Christianity. From 1878 to 1882, he devoted himself to works that expressed his views on religion and social issues, advocating pacifism and social justice for the lower classes. "The Death of Ivan Ilych," published in 1886, recounts the thoughts of a dying man and mirrors Tolstoy's own contemplations during his spiritual crisis. His later works include *The Kreutzer Sonata* (1890), *Master and Man* (1895), and *What Is Art?* (1898).

Two Eagles, Gayle

Two Eagles is a Lakota Indian living in South Dakota. She is the mother of two adopted children, is finishing her college degree, and writes of feminist concerns from a Native American perspective.

Vigil-Piñón, Evangelina (b. 1952)

Vigil-Piñón, a Latina, produced a volume of poetry, *Thirty an' Seen a Lot* (1982), that reflects her explanations of the relation between past and present as it pertains to the preservation of family, myth, culture, and history. The role of the woman as

1018 ◆ *Biographical Endnotes*

lifegiver, literally as well as metaphorically, is central to her poetic vision. In addition to *The Computer Is Down* (1987), she has contributed to and edited two anthologies: *Woman of Her Word: Hispanic Women Writers* (1983) and *Decade II: An Anniversary Anthology* (1993).

Wagner, Maryfrances Cusumano (b. 1947)

Born in Kansas City, Missouri, Wagner teaches high school English. Like many second-generation Italian Americans, she learned the Italian language during her adult life. Her poetry reflects her interest in traditional and present-day attitudes toward her ethnic heritage. She has written *Bandaged Watermelon and Other Rusty Ducks* (1976) and *Tonight Cicadas Sing* (1981).

Walker, Alice (b. 1944)

Born in Georgia to a family of sharecroppers, Walker was encouraged to excel in school and attended college in Atlanta and New York. Her first volume of poetry was published in 1968. In addition, she has written novels, short stories, and a book of essays. The *Color Purple* (1982) won a Pulitzer Prize and became a successful film. Her fiction examines the role of black women in a world dominated by sexism and racial oppression. Walker was active in the civil rights movement in Mississippi. In addition to *The Color Purple,* her novels include *The Third Life of Grange Copeland* (1973), *Meridian* (1976), and *The Temple of My Familiar* (1989). Her short-story collection includes *In Love and Trouble: Stories of Black Women* (1973) and *You Can't Keep a Good Woman Down* (1981). Her collected poetry appears in *Good Night, Willie Lee, I'll See You in the Morning* (1979); *Horses Make a Landscape More Beautiful* (1984); and *Possessing the Secret of Joy* (1992). An autobiography, *The Same River Twice: Honoring the Difficult: A Meditation of Life, Spirit, and the Making of the Film, The Color Purple, Ten Years Later* was published in 1996.

In 1994, the California State Board of Education removed two of Walker's short stories from one of its programs. "Roselily" was one of those banned because it concerned a teenage, unwed mother. *Alice Walker Banned* (1996) relates the controversy and includes newspaper articles, letters, and an assessment by Patricia Holt.

Walsh, Chad (1914–1991)

Born in South Boston and educated at the University of Virginia and the University of Michigan, Walsh was an ordained Episcopal priest. He taught English for many years at Beloit College. He published several volumes of poetry, including *The Unknown Dance* (1964) and *Hand Me Up My Begging Bowl* (1981) and received many literary awards. In an interview, he stated that his purpose in writing was to speak to his readers: "I assume that they and I have our ordinary humanity in common, and that what interests me ought to interest them."

Wharton, Edith (1862–1937)

Wharton, born in New York City to wealthy and socially prominent parents, married a Boston banker in 1885. However, resenting the restrictions of a society matron, she pursued her own intellectual interests. She wrote novels such as *The House of Mirth* (1902) and *The Custom of the Country* (1913), which probed the emptiness of life in aristocratic New York society. A favorite theme was the rigid code of manners and conventions that denied personal happiness to both men and women. In 1907, she moved permanently to Europe but continued to write books with American settings and themes of the ironies and tragedies of life. *The Age of Innocence* (1920) won a Pulitzer prize. The Cross of the Legion of Honor was awarded to her for relief work in World War I.

Whitman, Walt (1819–1892)

Born near Huntington, Long Island, in New York, Whitman held a variety of jobs, including office boy, carpenter, printer, schoolteacher, journalist, and editor. In 1855, he published a volume of poems entitled *Leaves of Grass,* but it was unfavorably reviewed because of its radical form and content. During the next thirty-five years, he revised and added to it in nine editions. When his brother was wounded in the Civil War, Whitman went to Virginia to nurse him. He stayed on in Washington, D.C., as a nurse in army hospitals. After the war, he was a clerk in a government office but was fired because *Leaves of Grass* was considered an immoral book. His verse was appreciated in Europe, however, and eventually he received recognition in his own country. "When Lilacs Last in the Dooryard Bloom'd" and "O Captain! My Captain!" commemorated the death of Abraham Lincoln. His war impressions appear in *Drum Taps and Specimen Days.* Some of his war poems reflect a nostalgic or romantic vision of war.

Wiesel, Elie (b. 1928)

Born in Rumania, Wiesel is a survivor of the Nazi concentration camps at Auschwitz and Buchenwald, where his parents and sister were killed. François Mauriac, the French novelist and essayist, urged Wiesel to write of the horrors of the war, and Wiesel produced *Night* in 1956. This memoir-novel recounts his family's death-camp sufferings and his own guilt at surviving. Since then, he has completed twenty-five books on Holocaust themes. Man's inhumanity to man, survival, and injustice are his subjects. In 1986, he was awarded the Nobel Peace Prize. *All Rivers Run to the Sea* (1995) contains his latest reflections on the Holocaust.

Wilbur, Richard (Purdy) (b. 1921)

A native of New York City, Wilbur earned his B.A. from Amherst College, an M.A. from Harvard, and served in the U.S. Army in World War II. He has taught

English at many Ivy League colleges. His poetry collections include *The Beautiful Changes* (1947), *Ceremony* (1950), *Things of This World* (Pulitzer and National Book Award, [1956]), *The Beastiary* (1955), *Advice to a Prophet* (1961), *The Poems of Richard Wilbur* (1963), *Walking to Sleep* (1960), and *The Mind Reader* (1971). He has also translated many of Molière's plays into English.

Woolf, Virginia (1882–1941)

Born in London, Woolf was reared in an upper-middle class family dominated by her father, Sir Leslie Stephen, a noted scholar. Because of her delicate health and her father's views on the proper place of women, she was tutored at home and had free access to his extensive library. After her father's death, she and her sister Vanessa hosted gatherings at their home in the Bloomsbury section of London, attracting literary and intellectual figures of the day. Woolf kept diaries from an early age and soon began writing novels and short stories. At first conventional in form, she later wrote in an innovative and distinguished manner in such novels as *Jacob's Room* (1922), *To the Lighthouse* (1927), and *Orlando* (1928). She used stream of consciousness, a form of interior dialogue similar to the technique of her contemporary James Joyce. An absence of conventional plot and action characterized her distinctive style. She and her husband Leonard Woolf, a writer on politics and economics, started the Hogarth Press, and the success of their first ventures in publishing led to a series of works by the best and most original young authors such as T. S. Eliot and E. M. Forster. The first English edition of the works of Sigmund Freud, the originator of psychoanalysis, highlighted their endeavors. A strong advocate of women's rights, Woolf's views are expressed in a group of essays, *A Room of One's Own* (1929) and *Three Guineas* (1938). The essay "Professions for Women" was originally a talk delivered in 1931 to The Women's Service League. During her life, she suffered numerous nervous breakdowns, and in 1941, fearing the onset of another attack and the subsequent treatments, she committed suicide.

Yevtushenko, Yevgeny (b. 1933)

Yevtushenko was born in Zima, Siberia, and had his first volume of poetry published when he was nineteen. He became prominent as the leader of the Soviet younger generation in its criticism of his country's policies. "Babiy Yar," his poem condemning the Nazi's murder of ninety-six thousand Jews in the Ukraine, caused consternation because it implied complicity on the part of the Soviet leadership. During the cold-war thaw in the late 1950s, he was allowed to travel to the United States to give poetry readings that attracted large audiences. In recent years, he again gained prominence for his support of Soviet president Mikhail Gorbachev's policy of *glasnost*. Some of his poems celebrate the everyday life of ordinary people. His works include *The Poetry of Yevgeny Yevtushenko* (1981), *Wild Berries* (1989), *Fatal Half Measures: The Cultures of Democracy in the Soviet Union* (1991), and *Don't Die Before You're Dead* (1995).

Glossary of Literary and Cultural Terms

Alienation   Emotional or intellectual separation from peer groups and/or society.

Allegory   A narrative that has a second meaning in addition to the obvious one. The meaning may be religious, moral, or political.

Alliteration   Repetition of the same consonant sounds usually at the beginning of words on the same line or in close proximity—"Stole with soft step its shining archway through", for example.

Allusion   A reference to a familiar mythical, historical, or literary person, place, or thing.

Ambiguity   Uncertainty or lack of clarity about meaning, where more than one meaning is possible, usually intended by the author.

Ambivalence   The existence of mutually conflicting attitudes or feelings.

Anachronism   Wrongful assignment of an event, person, or scene to a time when it did not exist.

Anecdote   Brief, unadorned narrative of an event or happening. It differs from a short story in that it is shorter, is a single episode, and has a simple plot.

Antagonist   The character in a drama, poem, or other fiction who opposes or rivals the protagonist.

Anticlimax   A trivial event immediately following significant events. The reader expects something greater or more serious to occur but finds a lesser happening.

Antihero   A protagonist who is deficient in attributes usually attributed to a hero.

Anti-semitism   Hostility toward Jews as a religious or racial minority group, often accompanied by social, economic, and/or political discrimination.

Apostrophe   A poetic figure of speech in which some abstract quality or personification is addressed, for example, "O ye Fountains, Meadows, Hills and Groves…"

Archetype   A universal theme, image, or narrative that occurs often in literature.

Assonance   In a line, sentence, or stanza, the repetition of similar vowel sounds although the consonants differ, for example, *penitent* and *reticence*.

Atmosphere   The overall mood of a literary work, often created by the setting or land-scape.

Ballad   A narrative poem in which the second and fourth lines rhyme. It often contains a refrain that is the repetition of the last line of each stanza.

Blank verse   A form of verse consisting of unrhymed lines of iambic pentameter.

Burlesque   A form of comedy characterized by ridiculous and exaggerated actions.

Canon   A criterion or standard of measurement; the generally accepted list of great works of literature or accepted list of an author's work.

Canto   A division or section of a long poem.

Catharsis   The effect of tragedy in relieving or purging the emotions of an audience. Aristotle explains the theory in his *Poetics.*

Chorus   In Greek drama, a group who comment on the actions or characters in the play.

Classical tragedy   Refers to the tragedy of the ancient Greeks and Romans. The rules of tragic composition are derived from Aristotle and Horace.

Climax   The point at which the action builds to its highest point, and the reader experiences his greatest emotional response.

Collective unconscious   A Jungian term arguing that racially inherited images and ideas persist in individual consciousness, and unconscious motivations are therefore collectively shared as well as personal.

Comedy   A play of a light and humorous nature with a happy ending.

Complication   The part of the plot in which the conflict of opposing forces is developed.

Conceit   A comparison between two very different objects.

Conflict   The struggle between opposing characters that causes tension or suspense.

Connotation   The implication(s) and overtones, qualities, feelings, and ideas a word suggests. Connotation goes beyond literal meaning or dictionary definition.

Consensus   General agreement and/or collective opinion of a group.

Controlling image   An image or metaphor that recurs in a literary work and symbolizes the theme such as the wallpaper in Charlotte Perkins Gilman's "The Yellow Wallpaper."

Convention   Any device, style, or subject matter that has become, through its recurring use, an accepted element of technique.

Couplet   Two successive lines of verse that rhyme.

Culture   The total pattern of human (learned) behavior embodied in thought, speech, action, and artifacts. It is dependent on the human capacity for learning and transmitting knowledge to succeeding generations through the use of tools, language, and systems of abstract thought.

Denotation   The literal meaning of a word as defined in a dictionary. It is the opposite of *connotation.*

Denouement   The dramatic climax to the main conflict in a literary work.

Diction   The writer's choice of words. Proper diction uses words appropriate to the author's ideas; poor diction stems from words that do not convey the author's intended meaning.

Discourse   Sets of statements that hold together around languages; any statements across culture that organize a mechanism, discipline, or sexuality; the social use of language.

Ego   The rational and conscious part of the psyche that opposes the id as well as the super-ego.

Elegy   A poem expressing sadness, often a lament for the dead.

Elizabethan Age   The English literary period named after Queen Elizabeth, lasting from 1558 until 1642, the year of the closing of the theaters. Notable names of the period include Shakespeare, Sidney, Spenser, and Marlowe.

Epic   A long narrative poem, dignified in theme and style with a hero who, through experiences of great adventure, accomplishes important deeds.

Epigram   A witty or clever saying, concisely expressed.

Epigraph   A quotation at the beginning of a work that is related to the theme.

Epilogue   A concluding statement, sometimes in verse, summarizing the themes of the work.

Epiphany   A moment of insight for a character, often resulting in a turning point.

Episode   An incident in the course of a series of events.

Erotic   Tending to excite sexual pleasure or desire.

Ethnicity   Ethnic quality or affiliation; physical or cultural characteristics that identify an individual with a particular race or religion.

Ethnocentrism   The tendency to judge other cultures by the standards of one's own.

Exclusion   The act of deliberately not including someone or something, or preventing entry into a place or activity.

Existentialism   A twentieth-century philosophy that denies the existence of a transcendent meaning to life and places the burden of justifying existence on individuals.

Exposition   A mode or form of discourse that conveys information, gives directions, or explains an idea that is difficult to understand.

Fable   A simple tale, either in prose or verse, told to illustrate a moral. The subject matter may be drawn from folklore.

Fantasy   An imaginative or fanciful work concerning supernatural or unnatural events or characters.

Farce   A dramatic piece intended to generate laughter through exaggerated or improbable situations.

Feminist criticism   A mode of analysis, a method of approaching life and politics, rather than a set of political conclusions about the oppression of women; examines representations of the feminine in all literature and often focuses on works written by women.

Figurative language   Words used to express meaning beyond the literal.

Flashback   A device by which the chronology of events is interrupted by relating events from the past.

Foil   A term for any character who, through extreme contrast, intensifies the character of another.

Foreshadowing   Subtle clues early in the narrative indicating what will happen later in the plot.

Free verse   Poetry that has irregular rhythm or none at all.

Gender   Characteristics and roles assigned to preferred patterns of behavior based on sex; sets of social attributions, characteristics, behavior, appearance, dress, expectations, roles, and so on made to individuals according to their gender assignment at birth.

Genre   The division of literature into difference categories, each distinguishable from the other, such as play, short story, poem, novel.

Hero/Heroine   (see TRAGIC HERO/HEROINE).

Heterocentrism   The tendency to judge or treat as invisible any sexual/affectional relationship that does not conform to the dominant heterosexual/marriage standard.

Heterosexism   The dominant ideology that maintains that heterosexuality is "natural" and superior to any other form of social/sexual relationship.

Hubris   The excessive arrogance or pride that results in the downfall of the protagonist.

Hyperbole   Obvious exaggeration, an extravagant statement, intentionally designed to give the reader a memorable image. A fisherman who brags that the one that got away was "big as a whale" almost certainly is speaking hyperbolically.

Id The driving force of the unconscious mind that is endowed with energy and is capable of motivating our actions.

Identity The set of behavioral or personal characteristics by which an individual is recognizable as a member of a group.

Ideology A system of beliefs used overtly or covertly to justify or legitimize preferred patterns of behavior.

Imagery The formation of pictures drawn with words, a reproduction of persons, objects, or sensations that are perceived through sight, sound, touch, taste, or smell.

Imperialism The imposition of the power of one state over the territories of another, normally by military means, in order to exploit subjugated populations to extract economic and political advantages.

Institution That which is established or constituted in society; an established way of behaving; an established procedure characteristic of group activity—schools, for example.

Internal rhyme Rhyming words that appear within a line of poetry.

Irony The undermining or contradicting of someone's expectations. Irony may be either verbal or dramatic. Verbal irony arises from a discrepancy, sometimes intentional and sometimes not, between what is said and what is meant, as when a dog jumps forward to bite you, and you say, "What a friendly dog!" Dramatic irony arises from a discrepancy between what someone expects to happen and what does happen, for example, if the dog that seemed so unfriendly to you saved your life.

Jargon The vocabulary or phrases peculiar to a particular profession or group. It may also mean a language or word incomprehensible or garbled to others.

Journal A daily written record of ideas, memories, experiences, or dreams. A journal can be used for prewriting and as a source for formal writing.

Literal The ordinary or primary meaning of a word or expression. Strict language without imagination or embellishment.

Lyric A brief, subjective poem with a songlike quality expressing emotion.

Marginalized Not fully explored or realized.

Melodrama A play written in a sensational manner pitting a stereotypical hero and villain against one another in violent, suspenseful, and emotional scenes.

Metaphor An implied comparison between unlike things such as "The road is a ribbon of moonlight."

Meter The measurement used in establishing the rhythm of a line of poetry. The unit within the line is a foot, each being a set relationship between accented and unaccented syllables. The most frequently used are iamb, trochee, anapest, and dactyl. For example, a line of five iambs is called iambic pentameter. See a specialized dictionary for an explanation of meter in detail.

Metonymy The substitution of the name of one object or concept for that of another to which it is related, for example, *the bottle* for *strong drink* or *The White House* for *the President.*

Misogyny Women-hating; the belief that women are inferior to men mentally, emotionally, and physically.

Mixed metaphor An implied comparison between two things that are inconsistent and incongruous.

Modernism A movement of the early twentieth century against the conventions of romantic literary representation. The modernists rejected the flowery and artificial language of Victorian literature and began using techniques such as stream of consciousness in fiction and free verse in poetry.

Monoculturalism   Pertaining to one culture to the exclusion of all other cultures.

Motif   A recurring character, theme, or situation that appears in many types of literature.

Motive   Whatever prompts a person to act in a particular way.

Multiculturalism   Assimilation of several cultures while allowing each culture to retain its separate identity.

Myth   A traditional or legendary story with roots in folk beliefs.

Narrative   The art, technique, or process of telling a story.

Naturalism   A school of writing that tries to show that human fate is controlled by environment and heredity, both of which humans do not understand.

Neurosis   Emotional disturbance due to unresolved unconscious conflicts and typically involving anxiety and depression.

New Criticism   An approach to criticism of literature that concentrates on textual criticism without referring to biographical or historical study.

Ode   A lyric poem that expresses exalted or enthusiastic emotion and often commemorates a person or event.

Oedipus complex   Repressed wishes of childhood to identify with the parent of one's own sex and to take his place in the affections of the parent of the opposite sex.

Onomatopoeia   A word whose pronunciation suggests its meaning such as, hiss, buzz, or bang.

Oppression   The conditions and experience of subordination and injustice. Oppression is the condition of being overwhelmed by the exercise of wrongful authority or power in a burdensome, wrongful manner, for example, the unjust or cruel treatment of subjects or inferiors; the imposition of unreasonable or unjust burdens.

Oxymoron   A figure of speech that produces an effect of seeming contradiction, for example, "Make haste slowly."

Parable   A short allegorical story designed to convey a truth or a moral lesson.

Paradox   A seemingly contradictory statement that, upon examination, contains a truth, for example, "damn with faint praise."

Pastoral   Any literary work that celebrates the simple rural life or those who live close to nature.

Pathos   The power of literature to evoke feelings of pity or compassion from the reader.

Patriarchy   A system in which men have all or most of the power and importance in a society or group. The patriarchal system is preserved through marriage and the family; it is rooted in biology rather than in economics or history.

Pentameter   A line of poetry that contains five metrical feet.

Persona   The mask or voice that the author creates to tell a story.

Personification   An abstract concept or inanimate object that is represented as having human qualities or characteristics. To write that "death rides a pale horse," for example, is to personify death.

Plagiarism   Using the words or ideas of another writer and representing them as one's original work.

Poetic justice   The ideal judgment that rewards virtue and punishes evil.

Point of view   The vantage point from which an author writes. In expository writing, an author may adopt a first-person or a third-person point of view.

Postmodernism   Literary and artistic philosophy that rejects all formal constraints. The postmodern artist tends to accept the world as fragmented and incoherent and to represent those characteristics in art, typically in a comic and self-reflexive style.

Projection   The unconscious process of attributing one's own feelings and/or attitudes to others, especially as defense against guilt or feelings of inferiority.

Protagonist The main character in a play or story, also called the hero or heroine.

Psyche The aggregate of the mental components of an individual, including both conscious and unconscious states and often regarded as an entity functioning apart from or independently of the body.

Pun A play on words based on the similarity of sound between two words differing in meaning. For example, "Ask for me tomorrow and you will find me a *grave* man."

Realism A literary movement that lasted from approximately the mid-nineteenth century to the early twentieth century in America, England, and France. Realism is characterized by the attempt to truthfully depict the lives of ordinary people through the accurate description of details and psychologically realistic characters.

Refrain A phrase or verse consisting of one or more lines repeated at intervals in a poem, usually at the end of a stanza.

Repression The exclusion from consciousness of painful, unpleasant, or unacceptable memories, desires, and impulses.

Rhetorical question A question not requiring a response. The answer is obvious and is intended to produce an effect.

Romanticism An artistic revolt of the late-eighteenth and early-nineteenth centuries against the traditional, formal, and orderly neoclassicism. The writers of this time dropped conventional poetic diction and forms in favor of freer forms and bolder language, and explored the grotesque, nature, mysticism, and emotional psychology in their art.

Satire A literary work in poetry or prose in which a subject or person is held up to scorn, derision, or ridicule with the intent of bringing about an improvement in a situation.

Scene An episode that relates one part of a play's story. Acts are usually composed of more than one scene. It may also refer to the setting of a work.

Setting The geographical location, historical era, physical and/or spiritual background against which the action takes place.

Sex The anatomical and physiological characteristics that distinguish males from females.

Simile A direct, explicit comparison between two things using *like* or *as* such as he ate *like* a pig; her heart felt light *as* a feather.

Social class Those having similar shares of power or wealth can be grouped together in a class, thus forming a stratum in the hierarchy of possessions.

Social structure The organized patterns of human behavior in a society.

Soliloquy A speech by one character in a play or other composition to disclose the speaker's innermost thoughts.

Sonnet A fourteen-line poem with a set rhyme scheme. There are two forms: the Italian (Petrarchan) and the English (Shakespearean). The Italian is divided into an eight-line stanza (octave) and a six line stanza (sestet). The rhyme scheme in the octave is *abba, abba* and the sestet is either *cde, cde* or *cdc, dcd*. The English form has four divisions: three quatrains and rhymed couplet, *abab, cdcd, efef* and *gg*.

Stream of consciousness A technique of writing in which a character's thoughts are presented as they occur in random sequence.

Subjectivity The personal element in writing. The more subjective a piece of writing, the more likely it is to be focused on the writer's opinions and feelings.

Superego The part of the unconscious that regulates our moral judgment.

Suspense Uncertainty or excitement resulting from the reader's anxiety in awaiting a decision or outcome.

Symbol   Any word, image, or description, any name, character or action that has a range of meanings and associations beyond it literal meaning. An eagle is a conventional symbol of the United States. It may also suggest freedom, power, or solitude.

Textual criticism   A form of scholarship that attempts to establish an authentic text in the exact form the author wrote it.

Theater of the absurd   Drama that points to the absurdity of the human condition, frequently employing unrealistic, untraditional dramatic devices.

Theme   The main idea of a literary work.

Theory   A way of making sense of or explaining some social phenomenon.

Tone   An author's attitude toward his or her subject. It may be angry, resigned, humorous, serious, sentimental, mocking, ironic, sarcastic, satirical, reasoning, emotional, or philosophic. One tone may predominate or many tones may be heard in a work.

Tragic hero/heroine   In classical Greek drama, a noble character who possesses a tragic flaw that leads to his or her destruction.

Understatement   An obvious downplaying or underrating. It is the opposite of hyperbole, though either may create a memorable image or an ironic effect. To say that "after they ate the apple, Adam and Even found life a bit tougher," is to understate their condition.

Verisimilitude   The appearance or semblance of truth.

Credits

PART TWO Gender and Identity

PART FIVE Individualism and Community

APPENDIX

Index of Authors and Titles

Index of First Lines

Index of First Lines

Index of Terms